AF816901

The Attorney's Handbook

on

Consumer Bankruptcy

and

Chapter 13

Argyle Publishing Company

Glenwood Springs, Colorado

Other books published by Argyle Publishing Company:

The Bankruptcy Issues Handbook (Provides in-depth coverage on Consumer Bankruptcy and Chapter 13 issues)

The Attorney's Handbook on Small Business Reorganization Under Chapter 11

Handbook on The Law of Small Business Enterprises

The Wills, Trusts and Estate Planning Handbook

See www.argylepub.com for more information

Forty-Sixth Edition, 2024

ISBN 13: 978-1-880730-73-7
Published and Distributed by

ARGYLE PUBLISHING COMPANY

P.O. Box 925
Glenwood Springs, Colorado 81602
Email: info@argylepub.com
Website: www.argylepub.com

Printed in the United States of America

Contents

Exhibits for Chapter Two

CHAPTER THREE - Adjustment of Debts under Chapter 13

Exhibits for Chapter Three

APPENDICES

Introduction

The Attorney's Handbook on Consumer Bankruptcy and Chapter 13 is designed to serve as a ready reference for attorneys and other legal professionals in the handling of chapter 7 and chapter 13 bankruptcy cases filed by consumer debtors. The handbook contains all resource materials needed to handle typical cases of this sort except the local rules, copies of which may be obtained from the local bankruptcy court or its website. The text and supplemental materials contained in this edition of the handbook incorporate all changes in the Bankruptcy Code and the Federal Rules of Bankruptcy Procedure through January 1, 2024

The supplemental materials contained in the handbook include the following:

1. Bankruptcy Worksheets designed for use in gathering data for the filing of a bankruptcy case. The worksheets may be photocopied from this book or downloaded from our Bankruptcy Forms for personal use, if desired.
2. Completed samples of official bankruptcy petitions, schedules, and statements.
3. Samples of motions, documents and pleadings frequently used in consumer bankruptcy cases.
4. The text of all relevant chapters of the Bankruptcy Code, current through January 1, 2024
5. The complete text of the Federal Rules of Bankruptcy Procedure, current through January 1, 2024.
6. The text of the relevant provisions of the Interim Rules of Bankruptcy Procedure.
7. Complete lists of property exempt under the laws of each state, under federal bankruptcy law, and under federal nonbankruptcy law. Each list is current through January 1, 2024.

Chapter one of the handbook contains a brief discussion on advising financially troubled consumer debtors. Included here are discussions of the relative appropriateness of nonbankruptcy remedies, a chapter 7 case, and a chapter 13 case for consumer debtors.

Chapters two and three deal, respectively, with the handling of chapter 7 and chapter 13 cases. Part A of each chapter contains a series of questions and answers designed to explain chapter 7 and chapter 13 to persons (including debtor-clients) who are not familiar with bankruptcy law or proceedings. These questions and answers may be photocopied from this book or downloaded from our Bankruptcy Forms, if desired. Part B of each chapter deals with the preparation of chapter 7 and chapter 13 cases and Part C of each chapter deals with the filing and handling of such cases.

In using this handbook, the reader is encouraged to use the subject indexes appearing on the last six pages of the handbook. Separate subject indexes are provided for chapter 7 and chapter 13 matters. The subject index refers the reader to the appropriate page of text, and the paragraph notes appearing on each page of text refer the reader to the location of the desired subject in the text.

This handbook is designed to serve as a ready reference in the day-to-day representation of debtors in chapter 7 and chapter 13 cases. It is not necessarily designed for in-depth legal research associated with such functions as brief writing. However, the author has attempted to support each significant legal proposition with a citation of authority that should lead the reader to more extensive authority on the subject. For more extensive reading on many of the issues discussed in this handbook, see **The Bankruptcy Issues Handbook**, Seventh Edition, 2015-2016, which complements this handbook by providing in-depth commentary and analysis on the issues that most often arise in chapter 7 and chapter 13 cases filed by consumer debtors.

And finally, always verify the source statute to confirm your understanding of the law.

CHAPTER ONE

Advising a Consumer Debtor

1.01 Analyzing a Debtor's Financial Problem

Before an attorney can advise a debtor on how best to resolve his or her financial difficulties, the debtor must truthfully and fully disclose his or her financial situation to the attorney. Unaided, most consumer debtors are unable or unwilling to recite every relevant detail of their financial situation to an attorney. It is the attorney's task, then, to ask the appropriate questions necessary to obtain the information from the debtor. The preliminary information needed to intelligently analyze a typical debtor's financial problem includes the following:

(1) The number of debts owed by the debtor.

(2) The approximate total dollar amount of all debts owed by the debtor.

(3) A brief description of each significant debt sufficient to determine whether it is dischargeable, whether it is secured, and whether there are codebtors.

(4) The debtor's attitude toward each significant debt (i.e., whether the debtor wishes to repay it, discharge it, etc.).

(5) A brief description of the debtor's significant assets and the extent to which each constitutes security for a debt.

(6) Whether foreclosures, repossessions, garnishments, attachments, or other actions that may require immediate bankruptcy relief have been initiated or threatened against the debtor or the debtor's property, and if so, by whom.

(7) The debtor's periodic income from all sources.

(8) Whether the debtor is currently in the military service. Although not covered in this handbook, the practitioner should be aware of The Servicemembers' Civil Relief Act (50 U.S.C. App. §§ 501—597b). This law provides for the temporary suspension of certain judicial proceedings or other transactions that may adversely affect an individual currently serving in the U.S. military. If a debtor is a current military servicemember, the use of Bankruptcy Form 2020, "Statement of Military Service" should be consulted.

In most cases the above information should enable the attorney to propose an appropriate remedy for a typical consumer debtor. The remedies available to most consumer debtors include: (1) determining the debtor's liability for a significant debt, (2) an out-of-court agreement with the debtor's creditors, (3) filing a proceeding under chapter 7 of the Bankruptcy Code, and (4) filing a proceeding under chapter 13 of the Bankruptcy Code.

For some consumer debtors, refinancing may also be an alternative. However, for most consumer debtors who have reached the point of consulting an attorney regarding their financial problem, refinancing is not a viable alternative.

1.02 The Nonbankruptcy Alternatives

For most financially-troubled consumer debtors the only nonbankruptcy alternatives are: (1) determining the extent of the debtor's liability for one or more significant debts, and (2) a formal or informal out-of-court agreement with creditors for the repayment of all or a significant portion of the debtor's debts. Determining the extent of the debtor's liability for a significant debt may be necessary if the debtor's financial crisis is caused by one or two large debts, such as a substantial child support obligation, an unliquidated claim for personal injury or breach of contract, or a large medical bill. In such instances the debtor is likely to need independent representation or advisement on the claim giving rise to the debt, rather than debt relief in general.

For a debtor who needs general debt relief, an out-of-court agreement with creditors offers the advantage of avoiding the stigma of bankruptcy. If such an agreement is simple and easy to negotiate, it may also be less expensive to the debtor than a bankruptcy proceeding. The principal disadvantage of such an agreement is that dissenting creditors cannot be bound thereunder and a single hostile creditor can often scuttle an otherwise workable agreement. Also, if the creditors are too numerous or geographically widespread, it may be logistically difficult to consummate an agreement. Finally, there is no way to prevent adverse creditor action while such an agreement is being negotiated.

An agreement with creditors is most likely to be feasible when there are only a few creditors, when most major creditors are unsecured and located in the same geographical area, when the debtor has sufficient income or assets with which to make realistic payments to creditors, and when the debtor does not need the emergency relief provided by the automatic stay that is provided in bankruptcy proceedings.

The best method of notifying creditors of a debtor's desire to negotiate an out-of-court agreement is by telephone. If the creditors are so numerous that telephoning is not practicable, an agreement with creditors is probably not practicable either. The agreement should be negotiated quickly because it is usually necessary to disclose the debtor's nonexempt assets to creditors, and delays may give hostile or aggressive creditors an opportunity or excuse to proceed against the assets.

When negotiating with creditors it is important to understand that it is not legally necessary to treat all creditors alike. Even creditors with identical claims can be treated differently. Some creditors may prefer to take substantially less than 100 cents on the dollar in return for early payment, while others may prefer to collect all or most of their claims over an extended period. However, the agreement will disclose each creditor's terms, and large discrepancies in creditor treatment may cause negotiation difficulties. A useful negotiating device is to compute the chapter 7 liquidation value of the debtor's estate and prorate it among the creditors so that each unsecured creditor will know what it would receive should the debtor file under chapter 7.

An agreement with creditors may be drafted so that the debtor makes payments directly to each creditor, or so that the debtor makes payments to a disbursing agent, who, in turn, makes the disbursements to creditors. Much depends upon the number of creditors and the preferences of the parties. If a disbursing agent is appointed, it is a better practice to appoint someone other than the debtor's attorney to perform this task: a major creditor or a bank are likely candidates. A sample Agreement With Creditors is set forth in Exhibit 1-A at the end of this chapter.

1.03 Chapter 7 vs. Chapter 13

If nonbankruptcy alternatives are not feasible, most consumer debtors must choose between a liquidation proceeding under chapter 7 of the Bankruptcy Code and a debt adjustment proceeding under chapter 13 of the Bankruptcy Code. A brief description of a chapter 7 case is set forth in section 2.01, infra, and a brief description of a chapter 13 case is set forth in section 3.01, infra. These sections should be consulted if the reader is unfamiliar with such proceedings.

The following factors should be considered in determining whether chapter 7 or chapter 13 is more appropriate for a consumer debtor:

(1) The dischargeability of debts. There are 18 classes of debts that are not dischargeable under chapter 7 (see section 2.17, infra, for a list). Some types of debts that are nondischargeable under chapter 7 may be dischargeable under chapter 13 (see section 3.18, infra, for a list of debts that are not dischargeable under chapter 13). If a person has substantial debts that are dischargeable under chapter 13 but not under chapter 7, chapter 13 may be preferable to chapter 7 for that person. The eligibility of a person for a discharge may also be a factor to consider. A person who has received a bankruptcy discharge in the last 8 years is not eligible for a chapter 7 discharge, but may be eligible for a chapter 13 discharge, so chapter 13 may be preferable for that person.

(2) Retaining secured property. A person who is in default on an important secured obligation, such as a home mortgage or an automobile loan, is usually permitted to cure the default within a reasonable period under chapter 13 and thereby retain the secured property. The curing of defaults in secured obligations is not usually feasible in a chapter 7 case. However, in a chapter 7 case the debtor is permitted to redeem or set aside liens against certain exempt personal property (see section 2.12, infra).

(3) Retaining nonexempt assets. In a chapter 7 case a debtor must turn all nonexempt property (or its cash equivalent) over to the trustee. In a chapter 13 case a debtor is usually permitted to retain his or her nonexempt property, provided that meaningful payments are made to unsecured creditors. Therefore, if a person has a large equity in his or her home or other important nonexempt assets, chapter 13 may be preferable.

(4) Income. In order to qualify under chapter 13, a debtor must have "regular income", which is defined as income sufficiently stable and regular to enable a debtor to make payments under a chapter 13 plan. If a person is unemployed or otherwise devoid of regular income, a chapter 13 case may not be feasible. On the other hand, chapter 7 may not be feasible for someone with disposable income of more than $151.25 a month and the ability to repay at least 25% of unsecured debt over the course of a 60-month period, because the chapter 7 case of such a person is likely to be dismissed by the court as an abuse of chapter 7 (see section 2.04, infra).

(5) Attitude toward debts. If a person has a sincere and realistic desire to repay all or most of his or her unsecured debts, chapter 13 may be preferable. If a person desires to repay only one or two debts, the best practice may be to file under chapter 7, if he or she qualifies under means testing, and later reaffirm the debts that the person wishes to repay. Finally, chapter 7 is usually preferable for the qualified person who simply wishes to obtain a fresh financial start by discharging his or her debts as quickly and inexpensively as possible.

(6) Time and expense. Chapter 13 cases normally last from three to five years, with a discharge granted at the close of the case. Chapter 7 cases of typical consumer debtors last about six months, and a discharge is normally granted about four months after the case is filed. In chapter 13 cases, the attorney's fees and administration expenses tend to be considerably more than in chapter 7 cases. If a person is not able or willing to make meaningful payments and otherwise comply with a chapter 13 plan during the entire duration of the plan and to bear the additional expenses involved, chapter 13 is probably not advisable for that person. Also, if anything is likely to occur during the duration of the case that would diminish or eliminate the person's ability to make payments under a plan, then a chapter 13 case may not be advisable.

Exhibit 1A - Agreement for Payment of Debts

WHEREAS, ________________________________, the debtor, is indebted to ____________ ____,
the creditors, for the debts shown on Schedule A attached hereto; and

WHEREAS, the debtor is unable to pay the debts described in Schedule A as they become due and is eligible for relief under the Bankruptcy Code; and

WHEREAS, the parties desire to provide for the payment of the debts shown in Schedule A upon the terms and within the periods set forth in Schedule A for each debt without the filing of an action under any chapter of the Bankruptcy Code.

THEREFORE, the parties agree as follows:

1. The debtor agrees to pay the sum of $ ___________ on the _________________ day(s) of every month as provided in paragraph 2 of this Agreement, commencing on ___________________________ and continuing until all sums required to pay the debts described in Schedule A upon the terms set forth in Schedule A have been paid.

2. The debtor shall transmit the payments described in paragraph 1 of this Agreement to __________ ____, the disbursing agent. The disbursing agent shall promptly forward the funds paid by the debtor under this Agreement to the creditors described in Schedule A in the following manner: The funds shall be prorated among the creditors in accordance with the ratio that the amount owed by the debtor to each creditor under the terms of this Agreement bears to the total amount owed to all creditors under the terms of this Agreement, except that if the amount owed to a creditor is or becomes less than $20.00, the balance of the amount owed to that creditor shall be paid in full. If no disbursing agent is provided for in this Agreement, or if the disbursing agent shall fail or refuse to perform the duties described in this paragraph, the debtor shall make payments directly to the creditors in the manner set forth in this paragraph.

3. The creditors agree to forbear from the filing or enforcement of any actions, liens, or security devices on the account of any debt covered in this Agreement, and further agree to take no action to collect any portion of any debt covered in this Agreement from the debtor or from any other person, for so long as the obligations required of the debtor hereunder are fulfilled, either by the debtor or the guarantor.

4. This Agreement shall become null and void in the event that the obligations required of the debtor hereunder are not fulfilled, or in the event that a proceeding under the Bankruptcy Code is lawfully commenced by or against the debtor. In either event, the parties shall not be deemed to have waived or forfeited any rights that would have existed had this Agreement not been entered into.

5. The debtor's obligations under this Agreement are guaranteed (or secured) by __________________ ____.

6. The terms of this Agreement shall be binding upon the parties, their legal representatives, successors, and assigns.

Dated: ________________________________

____________________ Debtor	____________________ Creditor
____________________ Disbursing Agent	____________________ Creditor
____________________ Guarantor	____________________ Creditor

CHAPTER TWO

Liquidation Under Chapter 7

Part A - Questions and Answers Regarding Chapter 7 Bankruptcy[1]

1. What is a chapter 7 bankruptcy case and how does it work?

A chapter 7 bankruptcy case is a proceeding under federal law in which the debtor seeks relief under chapter 7 of the Bankruptcy Code. Chapter 7 is that part (or chapter) of the Bankruptcy Code that deals with liquidation. The Bankruptcy Code is a federal law that deals with bankruptcy. A person who files a chapter 7 case is called a debtor. In a chapter 7 case, the debtor must turn his or her nonexempt property, if any exists, over to a trustee, who then converts the property to cash and pays the debtor's creditors. In return, the debtor receives a chapter 7 discharge, if he or she pays the filing fee, is eligible for the discharge, and obeys the orders and rules of the bankruptcy court.

2. What is a chapter 7 discharge?

It is a court order releasing a debtor from all of his or her dischargeable debts and ordering the creditors not to attempt to collect them from the debtor. A debt that is discharged is a debt that the debtor is released from and does not have to pay.

3. How does a person obtain a chapter 7 discharge?

A chapter 7 discharge is obtained by filing and maintaining a chapter 7 bankruptcy case and being eligible for a chapter 7 discharge. However, not all debts are discharged by a chapter 7 discharge. Certain types of debts are by law not dischargeable under chapter 7 and debts of this type will not be discharged even if the debtor receives a chapter 7 discharge.

4. Who is permitted to file and maintain a chapter 7 case?

Any person who resides in, does business in, or has property in the United States is permitted to file a chapter 7 bankruptcy case except a person who has intentionally dismissed a prior bankruptcy case within the last 180 days. To be permitted to maintain a chapter 7 bankruptcy case a person must qualify for chapter 7 relief under a process called means testing.

5. What is means testing?

Means testing is a method of determining a person's eligibility to maintain a chapter 7 case. Under means testing a person whose current monthly income from all sources multiplied by 12 exceeds the median annual income, as reported by the U.S. Census Bureau, for the person's state and family size, must show that he or she has a disposable monthly income of less than $151.25*. If disposable monthly income is greater than $252.50*, there is a presumption of abuse in filing a chapter 7 case. If monthly disposable income is between those two numbers, then you must determine whether the debtor could repay at least 25% of unsecured debt over the course of a 60-month period. If a debtor is deemed to be able to pay, their case will be dismissed or converted to chapter 13 unless special circumstances exist.

* Subject to adjustment on April 1, 2025.

---

1 *These questions and answers may be reproduced for use in your law practice.*

6. How is means testing carried out?

Every person who files a chapter 7 case must file a Chapter 7 Statement of Your Current Monthly Income (Official Form 122A-1) and a Chapter 7 Means Test Calculation (Official Form 122A-2). These forms, when completed and filed, show the person's current monthly income and the current monthly expenses that the person is allowed to claim. The person may also be questioned about his or her income and expenses at the meeting of creditors. From these sources a person's current monthly disposable income is calculated. This figure is then used to determine the amount of the monthly payment that the person can afford to make to his or her unsecured creditors. If the person's monthly disposable income is greater than $252.50*, the person will almost always be disqualified from maintaining a chapter 7 case and the case will be dismissed or, with the person's consent, converted to chapter 13.

* Subject to adjustment on April 1, 2025.

7. How is it decided whether a person is ineligible for chapter 7 under means testing?

The Chapter 7 Statement of Your Current Monthly Income (Official Form 122A-1) and a Chapter 7 Means Test Calculation (Official Form 122A-2) filed by the person will initially show whether the person is able to make monthly payments to unsecured creditors in the amount required for ineligibility. If so, the clerk of the bankruptcy court will send a notice to all creditors that a presumption of abuse has arisen in the case. The United States trustee then has until 10 days after the meeting of creditors to file a statement as to whether a presumption of abuse exists in the case. Then the United States trustee or any creditor can move to dismiss the case. The bankruptcy judge will ultimately decide whether the case should be dismissed.

8. What is a presumption of abuse and how does it affect the case?

When a chapter 7 case is filed by an ineligible person, under bankruptcy terminology that person is said to have abused the chapter 7 laws. When a person whose current monthly disposable income is such that he or she can afford to make monthly payments to unsecured creditors in the required amount, a presumption of abuse is said to arise in the case. If a presumption of abuse arises in a case, the case will be dismissed or converted to chapter 13 unless the person filing the case can prove the existence of special circumstances, such as a serious medical condition.

9. Who is eligible for a chapter 7 discharge?

Any person who is qualified to file and maintain a chapter 7 case is eligible for a chapter 7 discharge except the following (see 11 U.S.C. § 727):

(1) A person who has been granted a discharge in a chapter 7 case that was filed within the last 8 years.

(2) A person who has been granted a discharge in a chapter 13 case that was filed within the last 6 years, unless 70 percent or more of the debtor's unsecured claims were paid off in the chapter 13 case.

(3) A person who files and obtains court approval of a written waiver of discharge in the chapter 7 case.

(4) A person who conceals, transfers, or destroys his or her property with the intent to defraud his or her creditors or the trustee in the chapter 7 case.

(5) A person who conceals, destroys, or falsifies records of his or her financial condition or business transactions.

(6) A person who makes false statements or claims in the chapter 7 case, or who withholds recorded information from the trustee.

(7) A person who fails to satisfactorily explain any loss or deficiency of his or her assets.

(8) A person who refuses to answer questions or obey orders of the bankruptcy court, either in his or her bankruptcy case or in the bankruptcy case of a relative, business associate, or corporation with which he or she is associated.

(9) A person who, after filing the case, fails to complete an instructional course on personal financial management.

(10) A person who has been convicted of bankruptcy fraud or who owes a debt arising from a securities law violation.

10. What types of debts are not dischargeable in a chapter 7 case?

All debts of any type or amount, including out-of-state debts, are dischargeable in a chapter 7 case except for the types of debts that are by law nondischargeable in a chapter 7 case. The following is a list of the most common types of debts that are not dischargeable in a chapter 7 case:

(1) Most tax debts and debts that were incurred to pay nondischargeable federal tax debts.

(2) Debts for obtaining money, property, services, or credit by means of false pretenses, fraud, or a false financial statement, if the creditor files a complaint in the bankruptcy case.

(3) Debts not listed on the debtor's chapter 7 forms, unless the creditor knew of the bankruptcy case in time to file a claim.

(4) Debts for fraud, embezzlement, or larceny, if the creditor files a complaint in the bankruptcy case.

(5) Debts for domestic support obligations, which include debts for alimony, maintenance, or support, and certain other divorce-related debts, including property settlement debts.

(6) Debts for intentional or malicious injury to the person or property of another, if the creditor files a complaint in the bankruptcy case.

(7) Debts for certain fines or penalties.

(8) Debts for most educational benefits and student loans, unless a court finds that not discharging the debt would impose an undue hardship on the debtor and his or her dependents.

(9) Debts for personal injury or death caused by the debtor's operation of a motor vehicle, vessel or aircraft while intoxicated.

(10) Debts that were or could have been listed in a previous bankruptcy case of the debtor in which the debtor did not receive a discharge.

11. Who should not file a Chapter 7 case?

A person who is not eligible for a chapter 7 discharge should not file a chapter 7 case. Also, in most instances a person who has substantial debts that are not dischargeable under chapter 7 should not file a chapter 7 case. In addition, it is not usually advisable for a person with disposable income sufficient to make the required minimum payments to unsecured creditors to file a chapter 7 case, because a presumption of abuse will arise and the case will probably be dismissed or converted to chapter 13.

12. Is there anything that a person must do before a chapter 7 case can be filed?

Yes. A person is not permitted to file a chapter 7 case unless he or she has, during the 180 day period prior to filing, received from an approved nonprofit budget and credit counseling agency an individual or group briefing that outlined the opportunities for available credit counseling and assisted the person in performing a budget analysis. This briefing may be conducted by telephone or on the internet, if desired, and must be paid for by the person. When the chapter 7 case is filed, a certificate from the agency describing the services provided to the person must be filed with the court. A copy of any debt repayment plan prepared for the person by the agency must also be filed with the court. In emergency situations, the required credit counseling may be conducted after the case is filed.

13. How much is the filing fee in a chapter 7 case and when must it be paid?

The filing fee is $338.00 for either a single or a joint (husband and wife) case. The filing fee is payable when the case is filed. However, if the person filing can show that his or her income is less than 150 percent of the official poverty line and that he or she is unable to pay the filing fee, the court can waive payment of the filing fee. If the person filing is unable to pay the entire filing fee when the case is filed, it may be paid in up to four installments, with the final installment due within 120 days (use Official Form 103A). The period for payment may later be extended to 180 days by the court, if there is a valid reason for doing so. Unless payment is waived by the court, the entire filing fee must ultimately be paid or the case will be dismissed and no debts will be discharged.

14. Where should a chapter 7 case be filed?

A chapter 7 case is filed in the office of the clerk of the bankruptcy court in the district where the debtor has resided or maintained a principal place of business for the greater portion of the last 180 days. The bankruptcy court is a federal court and is a unit of the United States district court.

15. May a husband and wife file jointly under chapter 7?

Yes. A husband and wife may file a joint case under chapter 7. If a joint chapter 7 case is filed, only one set of bankruptcy forms is needed and only one filing fee is charged. However, both husband and wife must receive the required credit counseling before the case is filed and both must complete the required financial management course after the case is filed.

16. Under what circumstances should a joint chapter 7 case be filed?

A husband and wife should file a joint chapter 7 case if both of them are liable for one or more significant dischargeable debts. If both spouses are liable for a substantial debt and only one spouse files under chapter 7, the creditor may later attempt to collect the debt from the nonfiling spouse, even if he or she has no income or assets. In community property states it may not be necessary for both spouses to file if all substantial dischargeable debts are community debts. The community property states are Arizona, California, Idaho, Louisiana, Nevada, New Mexico, Texas, Washington, and Wisconsin (and Puerto Rico) (with Alaska being an opt-in community property state).

17. When is the best time to file a chapter 7 case?

The answer depends on the status of the person's dischargeable debts, the nature and status of the person's nonexempt assets, and the actions taken or threatened to be taken by creditors. The following rules should be followed:

(1) Don't file the case until all anticipated debts have been incurred, because only debts that have been incurred when the case is filed are dischargeable and it will be another eight years before the person is again eligible for a chapter 7 discharge. For example, a person who has incurred substantial medical expenses should not file a chapter 7 case until the illness or injury has been either cured or covered by insurance, as it will do little good to discharge, say, $100,000 of medical debts now and then incur another $100,000 in medical debts after the case has been filed.

(2) Don't file the case until the person filing has received all nonexempt assets to which he or she may be entitled. If the person is entitled to receive an income tax refund or a similar nonexempt asset in the near future, the case should not be filed until after the refund or asset has been received and disposed of. Otherwise, the refund or asset will have to be turned over to the trustee.

(3) Don't file the case if the person filing expects to acquire nonexempt property through inheritance, life insurance or divorce in the next 180 days, because the property may have to be turned over to the trustee.

(4) If an aggressive creditor has threatened to attach or garnishee a person's assets or income, the case should be filed immediately to take advantage of the automatic stay that accompanies the filing of a chapter 7 case (see Question 18, below). If a creditor has threatened to attach or garnishee the person's wages or if a foreclosure action has been filed against his or her home, it may be necessary to file the case immediately in order to protect the person's interest in the property.

18. How does the filing of a chapter 7 case by a person affect collection and other legal proceedings that have been filed against that person in other courts?

The filing of a chapter 7 case by a person automatically suspends virtually all collection and other legal proceedings pending against that person. A few days after a chapter 7 case is filed, the court will mail a notice to all creditors ordering them to refrain from any further action against the person. This court-ordered suspension of creditor activity against the person filing is called the automatic stay. If necessary, notice of the automatic stay may be served on a creditor earlier by the person or the person's attorney. Any creditor who intentionally violates the automatic stay may be held in contempt of court and may be liable in damages to the person filing. Criminal proceedings and actions to collect domestic support obligations from exempt property or property acquired by the person after the chapter 7 case was filed are not affected by the automatic stay. The automatic stay also does not protect cosigners and guarantors of the person filing, and a creditor may continue to collect debts from those persons after the case is filed. Persons who have had a prior bankruptcy case dismissed within the past year may be denied the protection of the automatic stay.

19. How does filing a chapter 7 case affect a person's credit rating?

It will usually worsen it, if that is possible. However, some financial institutions openly solicit business from persons who have recently filed under chapter 7, apparently because it will be at least 8 years before they can file another chapter 7 case. If there are compelling reasons for filing a chapter 7 case that are not within the person's control (such as an illness or an injury), some credit rating agencies may take that into account in rating the person's credit after filing.

20. Are the names of persons who file chapter 7 cases published?

When a chapter 7 case is filed, it becomes a public record and the names of the persons filing may be published by some credit-reporting agencies. However, newspapers do not usually report or publish the names of consumers who file chapter 7 cases.

21. Are employers notified of chapter 7 cases?

Employers are not usually notified when a chapter 7 case is filed. However, the trustee in a chapter 7 case often contacts an employer seeking information as to the status of the person's wages or salary at the time the case was filed or to verify a person's current monthly income. If there are compelling reasons for not informing an employer in a particular case, the trustee should be so informed and he or she may be willing to make other arrangements to obtain the necessary information.

22. Does a person lose any legal or civil rights by filing a chapter 7 case?

No. A chapter 7 case is not a criminal proceeding and a person does not lose any civil or constitutional rights.

23. May employers or governmental agencies discriminate against persons who file chapter 7 cases?

No. It is illegal for either private or governmental employers to discriminate against a person as to employment because that person has filed a chapter 7 case. It is also illegal for local, state, or federal governmental agencies to discriminate against a person as to the granting of licenses (including a driver's license), permits, student loans, and similar grants because that person has filed a chapter 7 case.

24. Will a person lose all of his or her property if he or she files a chapter 7 case?

Usually not. Certain property is exempt and may not be taken by creditors unless it is encumbered by a valid mortgage or lien. A person is usually allowed to retain his or her unencumbered exempt property in a chapter 7 case. A person may also be allowed to retain certain encumbered exempt property (see Question 34, below). Encumbered property is property against which a creditor has a valid lien, mortgage or other security interest.

25. What is exempt property?

Exempt property is property that is protected by law from the claims of creditors. However, if exempt property has been pledged to secure a debt or is otherwise encumbered by a valid lien or mortgage, the lien or mortgage holder may claim the exempt property by foreclosing upon or otherwise enforcing the creditor's lien or mortgage. In bankruptcy cases property may be exempt under either state or federal law. Exempt property typically includes all or a portion of a person's unpaid wages, home equity, household furniture, and personal effects. Your attorney can inform you as to the property that is exempt in your case.

26. When must a person appear in court in a chapter 7 case and what happens there?

The first court appearance is for a hearing called the "meeting of creditors," which is usually held about a month after the case is filed. The person filing the case must bring photo identification, his or her social security card, his or her most recent pay stub and all of his or her bank and investment account statements to this hearing. At this hearing the person is put under oath and questioned about his or her debts, assets, income and expenses by the hearing officer or trustee. In most chapter 7 consumer cases no creditors appear in court; but any creditor that does appear is usually allowed to question the person. For most persons this will be the only court appearance, but if the bankruptcy court decides not to grant the person a discharge or if the person wishes to reaffirm a debt, there may be another hearing about three months later which the person will have to attend.

27. What happens after the meeting of creditors?

After the meeting of creditors, the trustee may contact the person filing regarding his or her property and the court may issue certain orders to the person. These orders are sent by mail and may require the person to turn certain property over to the trustee, or provide the trustee with certain information. If the person fails to comply with these orders, the case may be dismissed, in which case his or her debts will not be discharged. The person must also attend and complete an instructional course on personal financial management and file a statement with the court showing completion of the course.

28. What is a trustee in a chapter 7 case, and what does he or she do?

The trustee is a person appointed by the United States trustee to examine the person who filed the case, collect the person's nonexempt property, and pay the expenses of the estate and the claims of creditors. In addition, the trustee has certain administrative duties in a chapter 7 case and is responsible for seeing to it that the person filing performs the required duties in the case. A trustee is appointed in a chapter 7 case, even if the person filing has no nonexempt property.

29. What are the responsibilities to the trustee of the person filing the case?

The law requires the person filing to cooperate with the trustee in the administration of a chapter 7 case, including the collection by the trustee of the person's nonexempt property. If the person does not cooperate with the trustee, the chapter 7 case may be dismissed and the person's debts will not be discharged. At least 7 days before the meeting of creditors the person filing must give the trustee and any requesting creditors copies of his or her most recent Federal income tax returns.

30. What happens to property that is turned over to the trustee?

It is usually converted to cash, which is used to pay the fees and expenses of the trustee, to pay the claims of priority creditors, and, if there is any left, to pay the claims of unsecured creditors.

31. What if a person has no nonexempt property for the trustee to collect?

If, from the bankruptcy forms filed, it appears that the person filing has no nonexempt property, a notice will be sent to the creditors advising them that there appears to be no assets from which to pay creditors, that it is unnecessary for them to file claims, and that if assets are later discovered they will then be given an opportunity to file claims. This type of case is referred to as a no-asset case. Most chapter 7 cases that are filed by consumers are no-asset cases.

32. How are secured creditors dealt with in a chapter 7 case?

Secured creditors are creditors with valid mortgages or liens against property of the person filing. Property that is encumbered by a valid mortgage or lien is called secured property. A secured creditor is usually permitted to repossess or foreclose on its secured property, unless the value of the secured property greatly exceeds the amount owed to the creditor. The claim of a secured creditor is called a secured claim and secured claims are collected from or enforced against encumbered property. Secured claims are not paid by the trustee. A secured creditor must prove the validity of its mortgage or lien and must usually obtain a court order before repossessing or foreclosing on encumbered property. Encumbered property should not be turned over to a secured creditor until a court order to do so has been obtained, unless the property is encumbered only to finance its purchase. The debtor may be permitted to retain certain types of encumbered personal property (see Question 34, below).

33. How are unsecured creditors dealt with in a chapter 7 case?

An unsecured creditor is a creditor without a valid lien or mortgage against property of the person filing. If the person filing has nonexempt assets, unsecured creditors may file claims with the court within 90 days after the first date set for the meeting of creditors. The trustee will examine these claims and file objections to those deemed improper. When the trustee has collected all of the person's nonexempt property and converted it to cash, and when the court has ruled on the trustee's objections to improper claims, the trustee will distribute the funds in the form of dividends to the unsecured creditors according to the priorities set forth in the Bankruptcy Code. Domestic support obligations, administrative expenses, claims for wages, salaries, and contributions to employee benefit plans, claims for the refund of certain deposits and tax claims, are given priority, in that order, in the payment of dividends by the trustee. If there are funds remaining after the payment of these priority claims, they are distributed pro rata to the remaining unsecured creditors. In chapter 7 cases filed by consumers, unsecured creditors usually get nothing.

34. What encumbered property may a person retain in a chapter 7 case?

A person may retain (or redeem) certain encumbered personal and household property, such as household furniture, appliances and goods, wearing apparel, and tools of trade, without payment to the secured creditor, if the property is exempt and if the mortgage or lien against the property was not incurred to finance the purchase of the property. A person may also retain without payment to the secured creditor any encumbered property that is both exempt and subject only to a judgment lien that is not divorce-related. Finally, a person may retain certain encumbered exempt personal, family, or household property by paying to the secured creditor an amount equal to the replacement value of the property, regardless of how much is owed to the creditor.

35. How may a person minimize the amount of money or property that must be turned over to the trustee in a chapter 7 case?

In a chapter 7 case the person filing is required to turn over to the trustee only the nonexempt money or property that he or she possessed at the time the case was filed. Many nonexempt assets are liquid in nature and tend to vary in size or amount from day to day. It is wise, therefore, to engage in some estate planning so as to minimize the value or amount of these liquid assets on the day and hour that the chapter 7 case is filed. The most common nonexempt liquid assets, and the assets that the trustee will be most likely to look for, include the following:

(1) cash,
(2) bank accounts,
(3) prepaid rent,
(4) landlord and utility deposits,
(5) accrued earnings and benefits,
(6) tax refunds, and
(7) sporting goods.

It is usually advantageous to take steps to ensure that the value of each of these assets is as low as possible on the day and hour that the chapter 7 case is filed. By doing this the person will not be cheating or acting illegally; he or she will simply be using the law to his or her advantage, much the same as a person who takes advantage of the tax laws by selling property at the appropriate time.

Cash. If possible, the person filing should have no cash on hand when the chapter 7 case is filed. Further, if he or she has received cash or the equivalent of cash in the form of a paycheck or the closing of a bank account shortly before the filing of the case, the funds should be disposed of for valid purposes and receipts should be obtained when disposing of the funds in order to prove to the trustee and the court that the funds were validly disposed of prior to the filing of the case. Money possessed or obtained shortly before the filing of a chapter 7 case may be spent on such items as food and groceries, the chapter 7 filing fee, the attorney's fee in the chapter 7 case, and the payment to creditors whose claims the person intends to reaffirm and continue paying after the filing of the chapter 7 case. Payments should not be made as gifts or loans to friends or relatives, however, as the trustee may later recover these payments.

Bank Accounts. The best practice is to close out all bank accounts before filing a chapter 7 case. If a bank account is not closed, the balance of the account should be as close to zero as the bank will allow and all outstanding checks must clear the account before the case is filed. If the person filing has written a check to someone for, say, $50 and if the check has not cleared the account when the case is filed, the $50 in the account to cover the outstanding check will be deemed an asset and will have to be paid to the trustee.

Prepaid Rent. If a person's rent is paid on the first day of the month and if the person's chapter 7 case is filed on the tenth day of the month, the portion of the rent covering the last 20 days of the month, if not exempt, will be deemed an asset and will later have to be paid to the trustee. If possible, the person should make arrangements with the landlord to pay rent only through the date that the case is to be filed and to pay the balance of the rent from funds acquired after the case is filed. If this is not possible, the case should be filed near the end of the rent period.

Landlord and Utility Deposits. Unless they are exempt, the person filing should attempt to obtain the refund of all landlord and utility deposits before filing a chapter 7 case. Otherwise, the deposits, or their cash equivalents, will have to be paid to the trustee, unless the deposits are exempt.

Accrued Earnings and Benefits. In most states, and under the federal law, only a certain percentage (usually 75% or thirty-five times the federal minimum hourly wage, whichever is larger) of a person's earnings are exempt. Therefore, the trustee may be allowed to take the nonexempt portion (usually 25%) of any accrued and unpaid wages, salary, commissions, vacation pay, sick leave pay, and other accrued and nonexempt employee benefits. Normally, then, the best time to file a chapter 7 case is the morning after payday. Even then, if the pay period does not end on payday, the person may have accrued earnings unless special arrangements are made with the employer. If annual leave or vacation pay is convertible to cash, it should be collected before the chapter 7 case is filed, as should any other nonexempt employee benefits that are convertible to cash.

Tax Refunds. In most states, a tax refund is not exempt and becomes the property of the trustee if it has not been received by the person prior to the filing of a chapter 7 case. Therefore, if a tax refund is expected, a chapter 7 case should not be filed until after the refund has been received and validly disposed of. Even if the case is filed before the end of the tax year, if the person filing later receives a refund, the trustee may be entitled to the portion of the refund earned prior to the filing of the case. The best practice, then, is to either file the chapter 7 case early in the tax year (but after the refund from the previous year has been received) or make arrangements to ensure that there will be no tax refund for that year.

Sporting Goods. If the person filing owns guns, fishing gear, skis, cameras, or similar items of value that are not exempt, he or she will later have to turn them, or their cash equivalent, over to the trustee. Such items should be disposed of prior to the filing of the case, especially if they are of considerable value.

36. May a utility company refuse to provide service to a person if the company's utility bill is discharged under chapter 7?

If, within 20 days after a chapter 7 case is filed, the person filing furnishes a utility company with a deposit or other security to ensure the payment of future utility services, it is illegal for a utility company to refuse to provide utility service to the person after the case is filed, or to otherwise discriminate against the person, if its bill for past utility services is discharged in the person's chapter 7 case.

37. What should a person do if he or she moves before the chapter 7 case is completed?

The person should immediately notify the bankruptcy court in writing of the new address. Because most communications between the person filing and the bankruptcy court are by mail, it is important that the bankruptcy court always have the person's current address. Otherwise, the person may fail to receive important notices and the chapter 7 case may be dismissed. Many courts have change-of-address forms for persons to use when they move, and one of these forms should be obtained if a move is planned.

38. How is a person notified when his or her discharge has been granted?

The person is usually notified by mail. Most courts send a form called "Discharge of Debtor" to the person filing and to all creditors. This form is a copy of the court order discharging the person from his or her dischargeable debts, and it serves as notice that the discharge has been granted and that creditors are forbidden from attempting to collect discharged debts. It is usually mailed about four months after a chapter 7 case is filed.

39. What if a person wishes to repay a dischargeable debt?

A person may repay as many dischargeable debts as desired after filing a chapter 7 case. By repaying one debt, a person does not become legally obligated to repay any other debts. The only dischargeable debt that a person is legally obligated to repay is one for which the person and the creditor have signed what is called a "reaffirmation agreement." If the person was not represented by an attorney in negotiating the reaffirmation agreement with the creditor, the reaffirmation agreement must be approved by the court to be valid. If the person was represented by an attorney in negotiating the reaffirmation agreement, the attorney must file the agreement and other required documents with the court in order for the agreement to be valid. If a dischargeable debt is not covered by a reaffirmation agreement, the person filing is not legally obligated to repay the debt, even if the person has made a payment on the debt since filing the chapter 7 case, has agreed in writing to repay the debt, or has waived the discharge of the debt in a waiver that was not approved by the bankruptcy court.

40. How long does a chapter 7 case last?

A successful chapter 7 case begins with the filing of the bankruptcy forms and ends with the closing of the case by the court. If there are no nonexempt assets for the trustee to collect, the case will most likely be closed shortly after the person filing receives his or her discharge, which is usually about four months after the case is filed. If there are nonexempt assets for the trustee to collect, the length of the case will depend on how long it takes the trustee to collect the assets and perform his or her other duties in the case. Most chapter 7 consumer cases with assets last about six months, but some last considerably longer.

41. What should a person do if a creditor later attempts to collect a debt that was discharged in his or her chapter 7 case?

When a chapter 7 discharge is granted, the court enters an order prohibiting creditors from later attempting to collect any discharged debt from the person filing. Any creditor who violates this court order may be held in contempt of court and may be liable to the person for damages. If a creditor later attempts to collect a discharged debt from the person, the person should give the creditor a copy of his or her chapter 7 discharge and inform the creditor in writing that the debt was discharged in the chapter 7 case. If the creditor persists, the person should contact an attorney. If a creditor files a lawsuit on a discharged debt, it is important to inform the court in which the lawsuit is filed that the debt was discharged in bankruptcy. The lawsuit should not be ignored because even though a judgment entered on a discharged debt can later be voided, voiding the judgment may require the services of an attorney, which could be costly.

42. How does a chapter 7 discharge affect the liability of cosigners and other parties who may be liable to a creditor on a discharged debt?

A chapter 7 discharge releases only the person or persons who filed the chapter 7 case. The liability of any other party on a debt is not affected by a chapter 7 discharge. Therefore, a person who has cosigned or guaranteed a debt for the person filing is still liable for the debt even if the person filing receives a chapter 7 discharge with respect to the debt. The only exception to this rule is in community property states where the spouse of the person filing is released from certain community debts by the chapter 7 discharge.

43. What is the role of the attorney for the person filing a chapter 7 case?

The attorney for the person filing performs the following functions in a typical chapter 7 consumer case:

(1) Analyze the amount and nature of the debts owed by the person filing and determine the best remedy for the person's financial problems.

(2) Advise the person filing of the relief available under chapter 7 and the other chapters of the Bankruptcy Code, and of the advisability of proceeding under each chapter.

(3) Assist the person in obtaining the required prebankruptcy budget and credit counseling briefing.

(4) Assemble the information and data necessary to prepare the chapter 7 forms for filing.

(5) Prepare the petitions, schedules, statements and other chapter 7 forms for filing with the bankruptcy court.

(6) Assist the person filing in arranging his or her assets so as to enable the person to retain as many of the assets as possible after the chapter 7 case.

(7) Filing the chapter 7 petitions, schedules, statements and other forms with the bankruptcy court, and, if necessary, notifying certain creditors of the commencement of the case.

(8) If necessary, assisting the person filing in reaffirming certain debts, redeeming personal property, setting aside mortgages or liens against exempt property, and otherwise carrying out the matters set forth in the statement of intention.

(9) Attending the meeting of creditors with the person and appearing with the person at any other hearings that may be held in the case.

(10) Assist the debtor in attending and completing the required instructional course on personal financial management.

(11) If necessary, preparing and filing amended schedules, statements, and other documents with the bankruptcy court in order to protect the rights of the person.

(12) If necessary, assisting the person in overcoming obstacles that may arise to the granting of a chapter 7 discharge.

The fee paid, or agreed to be paid, to an attorney representing the person filing in a chapter 7 case must be disclosed to and approved by the bankruptcy court. The court will allow the attorney to charge and collect only a reasonable fee. Most attorneys collect all or most of their fee before the case is filed.

CHAPTER TWO

Part B - Preparing a Chapter 7 Case

2.01 Chapter 7 - A General Description

Original jurisdiction for a chapter 7 case lies in the federal district court. In most districts, however, all voluntary petitions are referred by the district court to the bankruptcy court, which is a unit of the federal district court. Therefore, in most districts a voluntary chapter 7 case for a consumer debtor is initiated by the filing of a voluntary petition seeking relief under chapter 7 of the Bankruptcy Code with the clerk of the bankruptcy court in the district. The debtor must also prepare and file, usually with the petition, statements and schedules showing the debtor's assets and liabilities, current income and expenditures, and financial affairs at the time of filing. Unless the requirement is not in effect in the local district, the debtor must also file with the petition a certificate from an approved credit counseling agency stating, among other things, that the debtor has received credit counseling within the last 180 days. If a debt repayment plan was created for the debtor, a copy of the plan must also be filed with the petition. In addition, the debtor must file copies of records showing all payments received from his or her employer during the 60 day period prior to the filing of the bankruptcy case, records showing any interest that the debtor has in educational IRAs or qualified state tuition programs, a statement of current monthly income and means test calculation, a statement of intention, and copies of the debtor's most recent federal income tax returns.

filing of chapter 7 case, general aspects

chapter 7 case, documents to be filed

Most chapter 7 debtors whose current monthly income multiplied by 12 is above the median income for the debtor's state and family size are now subject to means testing as a prerequisite for chapter 7 eligibility. Basically, if means testing shows that the debtor has a monthly disposable income of $136.25 or more for 60 months, then the debtor's chapter 7 case may be deemed to be an abuse of the chapter 7 provisions and may either be dismissed or, with the consent of the debtor, converted to a case under chapter 13. The criteria for determining the debtor's ability to pay is the debtor's current monthly income less permitted deductions therefrom for certain living and other expenses. See section 2.07, infra, for further reading on means testing.

means testing, general aspects

The filing of a voluntary petition constitutes an order for relief under chapter 7, and an interim trustee is appointed by the United States trustee to examine the debtor, collect the debtor's nonexempt property and assets, and administer the debtor's bankruptcy estate. In chapter 7 consumer cases, the interim trustee normally serves throughout the case. While the debtor's interest in his or her nonexempt property must be turned over to the trustee, the debtor may retain his or her interest in any unencumbered property that is exempt under applicable state or federal law. Mortgaged or secured property of the debtor, the debt for which the debtor does not wish to reaffirm, must be turned over to the secured creditor, unless the property is exempt and the debtor wishes to redeem the property or challenge the validity of the creditor's lien. If the debtor has equity in secured property, the debtor's equity in the property is treated as unsecured property and the equity may be retained by the debtor if the property is exempt but must be turned over to the trustee if the property is not exempt.

chapter 7 case, effect of on debtor's property

If the debtor pays (or is excused from paying) the filing fee in the chapter 7 case, completes a course in personal financial management, and otherwise qualifies for a chapter 7 discharge, the debtor will be discharged from all dischargeable debts. See section 2.17, infra, for further reading on the chapter 7 discharge. In addition, in most cases the filing of a chapter 7 petition automatically stays all actions and proceedings against the debtor and his or her property, except criminal proceedings, certain governmental proceedings, and certain actions for the collection of alimony, maintenance or support. However, if the debtor has had one or more prior bankruptcy cases pending or dismissed within the last year, the automatic stay either may not go into effect or may terminate after 30 days. See section 2.10, infra, for further reading on the automatic stay.

chapter 7 discharge, requirements

automatic stay, general aspects

chapter 7 discharge, when not granted

The trustee or a creditor may file an objection to the granting of the debtor's chapter 7 discharge within the time set by the court. The most common grounds for denying a chapter 7 discharge are the failure of the debtor to pay (or be excused from paying) the filing fee in the chapter 7 case, the failure of the debtor to obey an order of the bankruptcy court, and where it is shown that the debtor received a discharge in another bankruptcy case filed within the last eight years. Also, in order to obtain (and retain) a chapter 7 discharge, the debtor must cooperate with the trustee in the administration of the case, including the collection of the debtor's nonexempt property.

chapter 7 case, debts not dischargeable

Certain types of debts are not dischargeable in a chapter 7 case, even if the debtor receives a discharge. The most common types of nondischargeable debts are most tax debts, most divorce-related debts, and most student loan debts. Other types of debts, including fraud debts, debts for malicious injury and debts for obtaining property money or through the use of false financial statements, are nondischargeable only if the creditor files a complaint to determine their dischargeability within the required time and proves their nondischargeability. See section 2.17, infra, for further reading on the dischargeability of debts.

chapter 7 case, rights of creditors

Unsecured creditors must file their claims within 90 days after the first date set for the meeting of creditors, unless it appears that the debtor has no nonexempt assets, in which case creditors are notified not to file claims. Except for certain personal property that the debtor may redeem or set aside liens against, secured creditors may reclaim or repossess the property upon which they have valid liens, after obtaining relief from the automatic stay and establishing the validity of their liens and claims.

chapter 7 case, court appearances

The debtor must appear in court for a hearing called the meeting of creditors, which is normally held about a month after the case is filed. The debtor's chapter 7 discharge is usually granted three or four months after the case is filed. If the debtor's chapter 7 discharge is not granted or if the debtor wishes to reaffirm a dischargeable debt and was not represented by an attorney when negotiating the reaffirmation agreement with the creditor, he or she will have to appear in court for another hearing. A chapter 7 case of a typical consumer debtor is closed about six months after the case is filed, or earlier if the debtor has no nonexempt assets.

title 11 cases, procedure and jurisdiction

core proceedings, what constitutes

As indicated above, the bankruptcy court is a unit of the federal district court. Each district court may provide that any or all title 11 cases and any or all proceedings arising under title 11 or in title 11 cases shall be referred to the bankruptcy judges in the district. See 28 U.S.C. § 157(a). In most districts, all voluntary chapter 7 cases are referred to the bankruptcy judges by the district court. Thereafter, the bankruptcy judges may hear and determine the referred title 11 cases and all core proceedings arising in such cases, and may enter final judgments and orders in such matters. See 28 U.S.C. § 157(b)(1). Core proceedings are those proceedings necessarily involved in the administration of a title 11 case, and include practically all matters arising in a typical chapter 7 consumer case. See 28 U.S.C. § 157(b)(2) for a list of proceedings included as core proceedings. It is left to the bankruptcy judge to determine, either on its own motion or on the motion of a party, whether a proceeding is core or non-core. Unless the parties agree otherwise, only the district court may issue a final order or judgment in a non-core proceeding. See 28 U.S.C. § 157(b)(3). The district court may, for cause, withdraw any case or proceeding previously referred to the bankruptcy court. See 28 U.S.C. § 157(d). The provisions of 28 U.S.C. § 157 are set forth in Appendix I of this handbook.

non-attorney bankruptcy petition preparers, duties and liabilities of

It should be noted that the Bankruptcy Code contains a section (Section 110) dealing with non-attorney bankruptcy petition preparers. See 11 U.S.C. § 110. This section establishes obligations and liabilities for non-attorney bankruptcy petition preparers, but does not apply to attorneys or to employees of attorneys. Section 110 is set forth in its entirety in Appendix I, infra. It should be noted that a corresponding criminal statute establishes the crime of "knowing disregard of bankruptcy law or rule," which is applicable only to non-attorney bankruptcy petition preparers. See 18 U.S.C. § 156. In addition, a non-attorney bankruptcy petition preparer must file a declaration with the United States trustee within 14 days after the filing of the case describing the fees and services provided to the debtor. See Bankruptcy Rule 2016(c). It should also be noted that a non-attorney bankruptcy petition preparer is a "debt relief agency" and must comply with the requirements of debt relief agencies set forth in sections 526, 527 and 528 of the Bankruptcy Code. See 11 U.S.C. § 101(12A). See section 2.03, infra, for further reading on the requirements imposed by the Bankruptcy Code on debt relief agencies.

2.02 The Local Bankruptcy Rules and Forms and the Interim Rules and Forms

Bankruptcy Rule 9029(a) permits a local district to adopt rules governing the practice and procedure in bankruptcy cases, provided that the rules are consistent with the Bankruptcy Code and the Federal Rules of Bankruptcy Procedure and do not prohibit or limit the use of the Official Bankruptcy Forms. The Federal Rules of Bankruptcy Procedure leave many administrative and procedural aspects of chapter 7 cases to the discretion of the local districts, and most districts have adopted local rules governing certain aspects of bankruptcy practice and procedure. Some districts have only limited local rules, and few, if any, local forms. Other districts have adopted extensive local rules and forms dealing with many aspects of chapter 7 cases, including the initial filing requirements. Many bankruptcy courts have adopted local rules and general orders dealing with electronic case management and the electronic filing of cases and documents. It is important to obtain a copy of the local rules prior to the commencement of a chapter 7 case. The clerk's office will usually provide copies of the local rules and forms upon request, or they may be available on line from the local bankruptcy court's website.

local rules, requirements and functions of

It should be noted here that if a particular matter is not governed by the Bankruptcy Code, the Federal Rules of Bankruptcy Procedure, or the local rules of the district, a bankruptcy judge may regulate the matter in any manner consistent with federal law, the Federal Rules of Bankruptcy Procedure, the Official Bankruptcy Forms and the local rules of the district. However, no sanction or other disadvantage may be imposed for noncompliance with any such judge-imposed requirement unless the alleged violator has been furnished in the particular case with actual notice of the requirement. See Bankruptcy Rule 9029(b).

procedure when there is no controlling law or rule

2.03 The Duties and Liabilities of the Debtor's Attorney

The Bankruptcy Reform Act of 2005 created an entity known as a "debt relief agency," which is defined as any person who provides bankruptcy assistance to an assisted person in return for the payment of money or other valuable consideration. See 11 U.S.C. § 101(12A). An "assisted person" is defined as any person whose debts consist primarily of consumer debts and whose nonexempt property is valued at less than $204,425*. See 11 U.S.C. § 101(3). An attorney who represents a consumer debtor in a chapter 7 bankruptcy proceeding is a debt relief agency.[1] The debtor's attorney will have to comply with the restrictions, disclosures and requirements imposed on debt relief agencies by the Bankruptcy Code. See 11 U.S.C. § 526, 527, 528.

* Subject to adjustment on April 1, 2019.

debt relief agency, debtor's attorney as

The restrictions imposed on debt relief agencies by section 526 of the Bankruptcy Code with respect to assisted persons are as follows:

debt relief agency, restrictions on

(1) It must perform every service that it informed an assisted person it would provide in connection with the bankruptcy case. See 11 U.S.C. § 526(a)(1).

(2) It must not make any statement, or counsel or advise any assisted person or prospective assisted person to make a statement in a document filed in a bankruptcy case, that is untrue or misleading, or that upon the exercise of reasonable care, should have been known by the agency to be untrue or misleading. See 11 U.S.C. § 526(a)(2).

(3) It must not misrepresent to any assisted person or prospective assisted person, directly or indirectly, affirmatively or by material omission, either the services that the agency will provide to the person or the benefits and risks that may result if the person becomes a debtor in a bankruptcy case. See 11 U.S.C. § 526(a)(3).

---

1 *See Milavetz v. United States,* 130 S. Ct. 1324, 1331 (2010).

(4) It must not advise an assisted person or prospective assisted person to incur more debt for an invalid purpose either in contemplation of filing a bankruptcy case or to pay an attorney fee in a bankruptcy case. See 11 U.S.C. § 526(a)(4) and Milavetz v. United States, 130 S. Ct 1324 (2010).

waiver of rights by assisted person, effect of

Any waiver by an assisted person of any protection or right provided by section 526 of the Bankruptcy Code is not enforceable against the debtor in any state or federal court but may be enforced against a debt relief agency. See 11 U.S.C. § 526(b). Further, any contract for bankruptcy assistance that does not comply with the material requirements of sections 526, 527 and 528 of the Bankruptcy Code is void and unenforceable against the assisted person, but may be enforced by the assisted person. See 11 U.S.C. § 526(c)(1).

debt relief agency, liability of to assisted perso

A debt relief agency is liable to an assisted person for the fees paid to the agency plus actual damages and a reasonable attorney's fee if the agency (1) intentionally or negligently fails to comply with any provision in sections 526, 527 or 528 of the Bankruptcy Code with respect to a bankruptcy case for the assisted person, (2) provided bankruptcy assistance to an assisted person in a bankruptcy case that is dismissed or converted to another chapter because of the agency's intentional or negligent failure to file any required document, or (3) intentionally or negligently disregarded the material requirements of the Bankruptcy Code or the Federal Rules of Bankruptcy Procedure that are applicable to the agency. See 11 U.S.C. § 526(c)(2).

debt relief agency, sanctions and penalties against

In addition to the civil liabilities of a debt relief agency described in the preceding paragraph, state officials who have reason to believe that section 526 of the Bankruptcy Code is being violated may bring actions in state or federal court to enjoin the violation and may bring an action on behalf of its residents to recover the actual damages incurred by assisted persons as a result of the violation, including costs and reasonable attorneys' fees. See 11 U.S.C. § 526(c)(3), (4). In addition, if the bankruptcy court, on its own motion or on the motion of the United States trustee or the debtor, finds that a person intentionally violated section 526 or engaged in a clear and consistent pattern or practice of violating section 526, it may enjoin the violation or impose an appropriate civil penalty against the violator. See 11 U.S.C. § 526(c)(5).

debt relief agency, disclosure requirements

The disclosures required to be made to an assisted person by a debt relief agency under section 527 of the Bankruptcy Code are as follows:

(1) It must provide the assisted person with a written copy of the notice required by section 342(b)(1) of the Bankruptcy Code, which is a brief description of chapters 7, 11, 12 and 13 of the Bankruptcy Code and the general purpose, benefits and costs of proceeding under each chapter and the types of services available from credit counseling agencies. See 11 U.S.C. § 527(a)(1). A form of this notice can be found in the Argyle Publishing Company Bankruptcy Forms.

(2) To the extent not covered in the notice described in the preceding paragraph, it must, within 3 business days after first offering to provide bankruptcy assistance to an assisted person, provide a clear and conspicuous written notice advising the assisted person –

(a) that all information provided by the assisted person for the petition and thereafter during the bankruptcy case must be complete, accurate, and truthful;

(b) that all of the assisted person's assets and all liabilities must be completely and accurately disclosed in the documents filed to commence the case and the replacement value of each asset must be stated in those documents and that reasonable inquiry to establish their value must be made;

(c) that the assisted person's current monthly income, the monthly expenses allowed under Code section 707(b)(2), and, in a case under chapter 13 of this title, disposable income (determined in accordance with Code section 707(b)(2)), must be stated after reasonable inquiry; and

(d) that the information an assisted person provides during the case may be audited and that a failure to provide such information may result in dismissal of the bankruptcy case or other sanction, including a criminal sanction. See 11 U.S.C. § 527(a)(2).

(3) The following statement (or one that is substantially similar), to the extent applicable, in a clear and conspicuous manner on a single document that is separate from all other documents and notices:

"IMPORTANT INFORMATION ABOUT BANKRUPTCY ASSISTANCE SERVICES FROM AN ATTORNEY OR BANKRUPTCY PETITION PREPARER.

If you decide to seek bankruptcy relief, you can represent yourself, you can hire an attorney to represent you, or you can get help in some localities from a bankruptcy petition preparer who is not an attorney. THE LAW REQUIRES AN ATTORNEY OR BANKRUPTCY PETITION PREPARER TO GIVE YOU A WRITTEN CONTRACT SPECIFYING WHAT THE ATTORNEY OR BANKRUPTCY PETITION PREPARER WILL DO FOR YOU AND HOW MUCH IT WILL COST. Ask to see the contract before you hire anyone.

debt relief agency, disclosure requirements

The following information helps you understand what must be done in a routine bankruptcy case to help you evaluate how much service you need. Although bankruptcy can be complex, many cases are routine.

Before filing a bankruptcy case, either you or your attorney should analyze your eligibility for different forms of debt relief available under the Bankruptcy Code and which form of relief is most likely to be beneficial for you. Be sure you understand the relief you can obtain and its limitations. To file a bankruptcy case, documents called a Petition, Schedules and Statement of Financial Affairs, and in some cases a Statement of Intention need to be prepared correctly and filed with the bankruptcy court. You will have to pay a filing fee to the bankruptcy court. Once your case starts, you will have to attend the required first meeting of creditors where you may be questioned by a court official called a "trustee" and by creditors.

debt relief agency, required notice to assisted person

If you choose to file a chapter 7 case, you may be asked by a creditor to reaffirm a debt. You may want help deciding whether to do so. A creditor is not permitted to coerce you into reaffirming your debts.

If you choose to file a chapter 13 case in which you repay your creditors what you can afford over 3 to 5 years, you may also want help with preparing your chapter 13 plan and with the confirmation hearing on your plan which will be before a bankruptcy judge.

If you select another type of relief under the Bankruptcy Code other than chapter 7 or chapter 13, you will want to find out what should be done from someone familiar with that type of relief.

Your bankruptcy case may also involve litigation. You are generally permitted to represent yourself in litigation in bankruptcy court, but only attorneys, not bankruptcy petition preparers, can give you legal advice." See 11 U.S.C. § 527(b).

(4) Except to the extent that the debt relief agency itself provides or obtains the information, it must provide the assisted person with reasonably sufficient information in a clear and conspicuous writing on how to obtain the information that the assisted person is required to provide in fulfilling his or her duties in the bankruptcy case, including –

(a) how to value assets at replacement value, determine current monthly income, the monthly expenses that are allowed under Code section 707(b)(2) and, in a chapter 13 case, how to determine disposable income in accordance with Code section 707(b)(2) and related calculations;

(b) how to complete the list of creditors, including how to determine what amount is owed and what address should be shown for the creditor; and

(c) how to determine what property is exempt and how to value exempt property at replacement value as defined in Code section 506. See 11 U.S.C. § 527(c).

debt relief agency, required information to assisted person

debt relief agency, required notices, when given

required notices and disclosures, sample of

The disclosure notices described in paragraphs (1), (3) and (4) above must be given to the assisted person by the debt relief agency prior to the commencement of the bankruptcy case and at the same time. See 11 U.S.C. § 342(b), 527(b), (c). The disclosure notice described in paragraph (2) above must be given within the period described in that paragraph. A debt relief agency must maintain copies of the disclosure notices described in paragraphs (1) and (2) above for 2 years after the date on which the notice was given to the assisted person. See 11 U.S.C. § 527(d). A complete set of the notices and disclosures required to be given to assisted persons by a debt relief agency under section 527 of the Bankruptcy Code is set forth in Exhibit 2-B at the end of this chapter.

debt relief agency, advertising requirements

In addition to the restrictions and disclosure requirements described above, a debt relief agency is subject to the following requirements under section 528 of the Bankruptcy Code:

(1) Within 5 business days after the first date that it provides bankruptcy assistance services to the assisted person and prior to the filing of the bankruptcy case, the agency must sign a written contract with the assisted person that clearly and conspicuously explains the services that the agency will provide to the assisted person and the fees or charges for the services and the terms of payment. See 11 U.S.C. § 528(a)(1).

(2) The agency must provide the assisted person with a copy of the fully executed and completed contract. See 11 U.S.C. § 528(a)(2).

debt relief agency, advertising, requirements

(3) The agency must clearly and conspicuously disclose in any advertisement of bankruptcy assistance services or the benefits of bankruptcy that are directed to the general public (whether in general media advertisements, seminars, or specific mailings, telephonic or electronic messages, or otherwise) that the services or benefits are with respect to title 11 bankruptcy relief. See 11 U.S.C. § 528(a)(3).

(4) The agency must clearly and conspicuously use the following statement in any of the advertisements described in paragraph (3) above. "We are a debt relief agency. We help people file for bankruptcy relief under the Bankruptcy Code." or a substantially similar statement. See 11 U.S.C. § 528(a)(4).

debt relief agency, advertising requirements

For purposes of the Code section 528 requirements listed above, advertisements directed to the general public by debt relief agencies of bankruptcy assistance services or the benefits of bankruptcy include (1) descriptions of bankruptcy assistance in connection with a chapter 13 plan, whether or not chapter 13 is specifically mentioned in the advertisement, and (2) statements such as "federally supervised repayment plan" or "federal debt restructuring help" or similar statements that could lead a reasonable consumer to believe that debt counseling was being offered when in fact the agency's services are directed toward providing bankruptcy assistance with a chapter 13 plan or other form of title 11 bankruptcy relief. See 11 U.S.C. § 528(b)(1).

debt relief agency, advertising requirements

Finally, advertisements by debt relief agencies directed to the general public indicating that the debt relief agency provides assistance with respect to credit defaults, mortgage foreclosures, eviction proceedings, excessive debt, debt collection pressure, or inability to pay a consumer debt must: (1) clearly and conspicuously disclose in the advertisement that the assistance may involve title 11 bankruptcy relief, and (2) include the following statement: "We are a debt relief agency. We help people file for bankruptcy relief under the Bankruptcy Code." or a substantially similar statement. See 11 U.S.C. § 528(b)(2).

debtor's attorney, personal liability of

In addition to the above-described requirements and restrictions imposed on debt relief agencies, the Bankruptcy Code also imposes personal liabilities on debtor's attorneys who violate Bankruptcy Rule 9011 in the filing or handling of a chapter 7 case. For example, the bankruptcy court, on its own initiative or on the motion of a party in interest, in accordance with the procedures set forth in Bankruptcy Rule 9011, may order the debtor's attorney to reimburse the trustee for all reasonable costs in prosecuting a motion to dismiss or convert a chapter 7 case for abuse under Code section 707(b), including reasonable attorneys' fees, if the trustee files the motion to dismiss or convert and the motion is granted by the court and the court finds that the action of the debtor's attorney violated Bankruptcy Rule 9011. See 11 U.S.C. § 707(b)(4)(A). In addition, if the court finds that the debtor's attorney violated Bankruptcy Rule 9011, the court, on its own initiative or on the motion of a party in interest, in accordance with procedures set forth in Bankruptcy Rule 9011, may order the assessment of an appropriate civil penalty against the debtor's attorney to be paid to the case trustee, the United States trustee, or the bankruptcy administrator (if one exists). See 11 U.S.C. § 707(b)(4)(B).Bankruptcy Rule 9011(b) provides as follows:

"(b) REPRESENTATIONS TO THE COURT. By presenting to the court (whether by signing, filing, submitting, or later advocating) a petition, pleading, written motion, or other paper, an attorney or unrepresented party is certifying that to the best of the person's knowledge, information, and belief, formed after an inquiry reasonable under the circumstances,- Bankruptcy Rule 9011(b), text of

(1) it is not being presented for any improper purpose, such as to harass or to cause unnecessary delay or needless increase in the cost of litigation;

(2) the claims, defenses, and other legal contentions therein are warranted by existing law or by a nonfrivolous argument for the extension, modification, or reversal of existing law or the establishment of new law;

(3) the allegations and other factual contentions have evidentiary support or, if specifically so identified, are likely to have evidentiary support after a reasonable opportunity for further investigation or discovery; and

(4) the denials of factual contentions are warranted on the evidence or, if specifically so identified, are reasonably based on a lack of information or belief."

With respect to the filing of a chapter 7 bankruptcy case, Bankruptcy Rule 9011(b) provides, in essence, that the debtor's attorney certifies by filing the case that to the best of his or her knowledge, information, and belief, formed after an inquiry that is reasonable under the circumstances, the case is not being filed for an improper purpose, the legal contentions set forth in the bankruptcy documents are warranted in law, and the facts set forth in the documents are supported by evidence. Bankruptcy Rule 9011(b), essence of

Two related questions arise. One is whether, or the extent to which, the filing by the debtor's attorney of a chapter 7 case that is later found to be an abuse of chapter 7 violates Bankruptcy Rule 9011 and thereby subjects the debtor's attorney to personal liability and sanctions under Code section 707(b)(4). The other is whether, or the extent to which, inaccuracies in the debtor's schedules can constitute a violation of Bankruptcy Rule 9011 by the debtor's attorney and thereby subject the attorney to personal liability and sanctions under Code section 707(b)(14). Bankruptcy Rule 9011(b), questions arising from

Bankruptcy Rule 9011(b) is likely to be construed in light of the provisions of sections 707(b)(4)(C) and (D) of the Bankruptcy Code. Section 707(b)(4)(C) provides that the signature of an attorney on a petition, pleading, or written motion constitutes a certification by the attorney that he or she has performed a reasonable investigation into the circumstances that gave rise to the document and has determined that the document is well grounded in fact, is warranted in law, and does not constitute an abuse under section 707(b)(1) of the Bankruptcy Code. In addition, Code section 707(b)(4)(D) explicitly provides that the signature of an attorney on a bankruptcy petition constitutes a certification that the attorney has no knowledge, after an inquiry, that the information in the schedules filed with the petition is incorrect. Bankruptcy Rule 9011(b), construction of

While only future bankruptcy litigation will determine the actual extent or scope of personal liability of debtors' attorneys' under Code section 707(b)(4) and Bankruptcy Rule 9011, it would appear that attorneys who represent debtors in chapter 7 cases would do well to abide by the following rules: debtor's attorneys, rules to follow

(1) All attorneys who file schedules and statements on a debtor's behalf make a certification regarding the representations contained therein. Although the certification is not an absolute guaranty of accuracy, it must be based upon the attorney's best knowledge, information and belief, "formed after an inquiry reasonable under the circumstances." In re Withrow, 405 B.R. 505, 512 (Bankr. App. 1st Cir. 2009). As such, attorneys should conduct at least the following five steps of due diligence: (1) educate the debtor to a reasonable degree; (2) review all documents for accuracy; (3) verify all statements with outside sources; (4) ensure the analysis is consistent; and (5) correct all mistakes promptly once they become known.

(2) To avoid personal liability and sanctions for filing a chapter 7 case that constitutes an abuse of chapter 7, the debtor's attorney should be certain that a presumption of abuse under section 707(b)(2) of the Bankruptcy Code does not arise under the facts of the case. To do this the attorney should insure that the information contained in the Statement of Current Monthly Income and Means Test Calculation is

debtor's attorneys, rules to follow

correct and accurate and under means testing does not indicate a presumption of abuse. In this regard, the attorney should make reasonable inquiry as to the correctness of the income and expense information provided by the debtor and should be knowledgeable as to the means testing requirements that are set forth in Code section 707(b)(2). The use of a third party investigative service or credit reporting service may be an avenue for an attorney to utilize to insure compliance with section 707(b)(2) when the client's information contained in the Statement of Current Monthly Income and Means Test Calculation is suspicious.

(2) To avoid personal liability and sanctions for filing a chapter 7 case that constitutes an abuse of chapter 7 in the absence of a presumption of abuse, the debtor's attorney should insure that the case is not being filed by the debtor in bad faith and that the totality of the debtor's financial situation does not demonstrate abuse. See 11 U.S.C. § 707(b)(3). In this regard, the attorney should perform reasonable investigation into matters such as the debtor's real motive for filing the case at this time, whether the debtor has filed previous bankruptcy cases in recent months or years, and the existence of omitted creditors or undisclosed assets. See 11 U.S.C. § 707(b)(4)(C)(i).

(3) To avoid personal liability and sanctions for filing bankruptcy schedules and documents that contain inaccurate or false information, the debtor's attorney should make an inquiry as to the correctness of the information that is reasonable under the circumstances. See Bankruptcy Rule 9011(b).

reasonable inquiry, what constitutes

The ultimate question, of course, is what constitutes the performance of a reasonable investigation or an inquiry that is reasonable under the circumstances. In this regard, it should be noted that it is generally held that Bankruptcy Rule 9011 requires that the attorney's actions comply with the objective standard of lawyerly performance and not the subjective standard of good faith. See In re Sullivan, 843 F. 2d 596 (1st Cir., 1988). It would appear, then, that reasonable inquiry is the degree of inquiry that a reasonably prudent lawyer would make under similar circumstances and not necessarily the degree of inquiry that the attorney in good faith thought was reasonable at the time. In this regard it is a good practice to independently verify as much of the information given by a debtor as is reasonably possible.

attorney's fee, review of by court and U.S. trustee

The fees charged by the debtor's attorney in a chapter 7 case, whether paid or agreed to be paid before or after the filing of the case, are subject to the review and approval of the bankruptcy court. See 11 U.S.C. § 329 and Bankruptcy Rule 2017. On the motion of a party in interest or on its own initiative, the court, after notice and a hearing, may determine whether any direct or indirect payment of money or transfer of property by the debtor to an attorney for services rendered or to be rendered in contemplation of the filing of a chapter 7 case by the debtor is excessive. See Bankruptcy Rule 2017(a). Attorneys for consumer debtors should be aware of the Civil Enforcement Initiative adopted by the United States Trustee Program for the purpose of protecting consumer debtors and others who are victimized by bankruptcy attorneys and petition preparers. The fees charged and the quality of services performed by bankruptcy attorneys are closely monitored by the United States trustee in most districts. As indicated above in this section, the fee agreement between the debtor and his or her attorney must be in writing and a copy of the agreement must be given to the debtor. See 11 U.S.C. § 528(a)(1), (2).

attorney's fee, excessive amount disposition of

On the motion of the debtor or the United States trustee, or on the court's own initiative, the court may, after notice and a hearing, determine whether any direct or indirect payment of money or transfer of property, or any agreement therefor, by the debtor to an attorney after the order for relief is excessive, if the payment or transfer, or agreement therefor, is for services in any way related to the case. See Bankruptcy Rule 2017(b). If the attorney's compensation is found by the court to exceed the reasonable value of any such services, the court may cancel the fee agreement or order that any payments received by the attorney, to the extent excessive, be returned to the entity that made the payments, or, if the funds or property would have been property of the debtor's estate, turned over to the trustee. See 11 U.S.C. § 329(b).

attorney's disclosure statement, form and contents

In practice, the debtor's attorney is required to file with the court (and transmit to the United States trustee) within 14 days after the order for relief, or as otherwise directed by the court, a statement disclosing the compensation paid or agreed to be paid to the attorney in the case. See Bankruptcy Rule 2016(b) and 11 U.S.C. § 329(a). While the form of this statement may be dealt with by local rule, it must substantially conform to Director's Form 2030, which is entitled Disclosure of Compensation of Attorney for Debtor. A sample of this form is set forth in Exhibit 2-A, at the end of this chapter.

In the disclosure statement, the attorney must disclose his or her entire compensation arrangement with the debtor and indicate the amount paid and the amount to be paid. It should be noted that an attorney's compensation includes not only the direct payment of money, but any direct or indirect payment of money or transfer of property, or agreement therefor, as long as the payment, transfer, or agreement is for services in any way related to the chapter 7 case. See Bankruptcy Rule 2017(b). Any agreement to share fees with other persons or attorneys, except members or regular associates of the attorney's law firm, must also be disclosed. See Bankruptcy Rule 2016(b). If a local form is not provided, Exhibit 2-A (Director's Form 2030) may be used.

attorney's compensation, what constitutes

The amount of compensation approved by bankruptcy courts for attorneys representing consumer debtors in chapter 7 cases varies considerably from district to district and from case to case. Generally, the amount ranges from $1,080 to $1,200 for representing a single debtor in a typical no-asset case through the discharge and reaffirmation hearing, although much depends upon the complexity of the particular case. Fees ranging from $1,200 to $2,500 are considered ordinary for representation of both debtors in a joint case.

attorney's compensation, amount of

A potential fee problem for attorneys representing consumer debtors in chapter 7 cases in some districts is the prepetition collection of fees for postpetition legal services. A few United States Trustees apparently believe that fees for postpetition legal services (such as representing the debtor at the meeting of creditors) that are paid to an attorney by the debtor prior to filing are property of the estate and must be turned over. At least two courts, however, have ruled to the contrary. See In re Jones, 236 B.R. 38 (D. Colo. 1999); In re Hodges, 289 B.R. 5 (Bankr. D. Kan., 2003); In re Wagers, 514 F.3d 1021 (10th Cir. 2007).

fees for postpetition legal services paid prior to filing, states of

It is usually in the interest of the debtor's attorney in a chapter 7 case to collect all, or as much as possible, of his or her compensation prior to the filing of the case because the attorney's claim for the balance of his or her compensation may be a dischargeable debt in the case. The Bankruptcy Code is not clear on the issue of the dischargeability of the fees of the debtor's attorney in a chapter 7 case. In re Hines, 147 F. 3d 1185 (9th Cir., 1998), unpaid legal fees owed to the debtor's attorney for legal services rendered prior to the filing of the bankruptcy case pursuant to a prepetition employment agreement were held dischargeable as a prepetition obligation of the debtor. The court further held that the attorney was precluded by the automatic stay from attempting to collect such fees from the debtor after the filing of the case. However, the court also held that the attorney had a claim in quantum meruit for reasonable compensation for legal services rendered by the attorney after the filing of the bankruptcy case which were not subject to discharge and the collection of which was not precluded by the automatic stay. If all or a portion of the attorney's compensation is unpaid when the case is filed, the safest practice is to have the compensation agreement guaranteed or secured by a nonfiling third party. Otherwise, the attorney should collect sufficient fees prior to the filing of the case to cover all prepetition legal services rendered by the attorney. A reaffirmation agreement reaffirming the balance of the attorney's compensation should not be used because of the obvious conflict of interest that such an agreement would present to the attorney. See In re Hines, supra, at 1190, and In re Jastrem, 224 B.R. 125 (Bank. E. D. Cal., 1998).

attorney's fee, when paid

unpaid fees of debtor's attorney, dischargeability and collection of

It should be noted that under Bankruptcy Rule 1006(b), a debtor's attorney is not precluded from collecting all or a portion of his or her fee from the debtor if the debtor seeks to pay the filing fee in installments. However, the fee should be collected from the debtor prior to the filing of the case because if the court grants leave to pay the filing fee in installments, the debtor is precluded from making further payments to his or her attorney until the filing fee is paid in full. See Bankruptcy Rule 1006(b)(3). There is nothing in 28 U.S.C. § 1930(f) or Bankruptcy Rule 1006(c) that prevents the collection of an attorney's fee from a debtor who seeks a waiver of the filing fee. However, the fees paid to an attorney must be disclosed in the debtor's application for waiver of the filing fee and the advance payment of a significant attorney's fee is likely to lessen the debtor's chances of getting the application approved by the court.

attorney's fee collection of when filing fee is paid in installments or waived

The services and functions typically performed by an attorney representing a consumer debtor in a chapter 7 case are summarized in the answer to Question 43 in Part A of this chapter, supra.

functions of debtor's attorney in chapter 7 case

2.04 Interviewing the Debtor - Matters to Cover

accurate filing data, how to obtain

It is important that the information collected from the debtor be both accurate and complete. Otherwise, the chapter 7 forms cannot be properly completed and the interests of the debtor will not be adequately served, and the debtor's attorney could later be found to be in violation of 11 U.S.C. § 526 and Bankruptcy Rule 9011. (See section 2.03, supra.) To this end, it is usually better to interview both the debtor and his or her spouse, if one exists, even if only one of them is contemplating filing. Many times it becomes evident during the interview that both spouses are liable for several of the debts and that a joint petition should be filed. If the local state has community property laws, it is especially important to confer with both spouses because of the liability of the spouses' community property for the debts of either spouse and because of the effect of the discharge of one spouse on the community creditors of the nonfiling spouse (see section 2.17, infra). Also, it often happens that the nonfiling spouse is more familiar with the family financial situation than the filing spouse. It is a good practice to independently verify as much of the information given by the debtor as possible, especially in cases where abuse is likely to be found.

bankruptcy work sheets, use of

The only proven method of gathering all of the needed information without repeated interviews and telephone calls is to use work sheets, or similar documents, that call for all of the required information without repetition and leave nothing to memory or chance. Some attorneys use an extra copy of the chapter 7 forms for this purpose; others have devised work sheets of their own. The attorney without work sheets will find the Bankruptcy Work Sheets appearing in Exhibit 2-C at the end of this chapter useful. Simply photocopy these work sheets and follow the instructions contained in them and all of the required information will have been assembled in the order appearing on the chapter 7 forms except for Statement of Current Income and Means Test Calculation. However, much of the information needed to complete this statement will appear in schedules I and J. It may be helpful to give a copy of the work sheets to the debtor prior to the interview. Once assembled, the information can easily be transferred from the work sheets to the appropriate schedules and statements, using the completed forms found in the exhibits at the end of this chapter as guides.

When interviewing the debtor (or debtors), the following matters should be addressed:

§527 disclosures and notices to debtor, when given

(1) Giving the debtor the disclosures and notices required under Code section 527. This Code section deals with debt relief agencies (which may presumably include debtors' attorneys) and the disclosures and notices required to be given by attorneys to debtors in chapter 7 cases. These disclosures and notices are listed and discussed in section 2.03, supra. Any required disclosures and notices that have not already been given should be given to the debtor at the beginning of the interview.

342(b)(1) notice to debtor, importance of giving

(2) Informing the debtor of the matters required under Code section 342(b)(1) and the potential of an audit under Code section 603. Code section 342(b)(1) requires each individual consumer debtor to be given written notice containing a brief description of chapters 7, 11, 12 and 13 of the Bankruptcy Code and the general purpose, benefits, and costs of proceeding under each of those chapters and the types of services that are available from credit counseling agencies. See 11 U.S.C. § 342(b), which requires the clerk to give this notice to each individual consumer debtor. 11 U.S.C. § 527(a)(1) requires the debtor's attorney to give the same notice to the debtor. This can be most easily accomplished by giving the debtor a copy of the Notice to Individual Consumer Debtor(s), a sample of which appears in Exhibit 2-U at the end of this chapter. This notice contains the information required to be given under 11 U.S.C. § 342(b)(1). It is important that this written notice be given to the debtor because the debtor's attorney must sign a declaration to this effect on Exhibit B on page 2 of the voluntary petition and the debtor must sign a similar declaration on page 3 of the voluntary petition, a sample of which appears in Exhibit 2-F at the end of this chapter.

§603 audits - potential of

The BAPCPA, at Section 603, established procedures for independent audits of debtors' petitions, schedules, and other information filed in cases on or after October 20, 2006. The debtor should be made aware of the potential of an audit and the ramifications of a finding of fraud.

(3) Determining whether a joint case should be filed. An individual and his or her spouse may file a joint petition under chapter 7. See 11 U.S.C. § 302(a). Only a husband and wife may file a joint petition under chapter 7, however, and an unmarried couple may not file a joint petition even if they are jointly liable for all or most of the debts, own property together, and live as husband and wife in every respect other than being lawfully married. The filing fee for a joint petition is the same as for a single petition, and normally only one set of statements and schedules need be prepared and filed in a joint case. In most instances, the cases of both parties in a joint petition will be consolidated and administered jointly under Bankruptcy Rule 1015(b), which means that the parties will have their court appearances scheduled for the same time and the same trustee will be appointed for both estates. If both spouses are liable for one or more significant dischargeable debts, they should normally file a joint petition. In instances where it is difficult to determine whether one or both spouses are liable for a significant dischargeable debt, the best practice is to file a joint petition if there is any chance that both spouses may be liable for the debt. However, if it is clear that only one spouse is liable for all significant dischargeable debts, a joint petition is not usually advisable. In community property states, if all of the debts of one spouse are community debts, a joint filing may not be necessary (see section 2.17, infra). In some cases it may not be advisable to file a joint petition because of an exemption-claiming hardship that may be imposed on one of the spouses. See section 2.08 for further reading on this issue.

joint petition, filing fee

joint case, how administered

joint petition, when advisable

joint petition, community property

joint petition, exemption laws

(4) Determining the debtor's eligibility to file a chapter 7 case. Of primary concern here for consumer debtors is whether the debtor has had a prior bankruptcy case dismissed within the last 180 days. If the debtor has been a debtor in a prior bankruptcy case that was dismissed within the last 180 days, the debtor is not eligible to file under any chapter of the Bankruptcy Code if the prior case was dismissed (1) because the debtor willfully failed to either abide by an order of the court or to appear before the court, or (2) because the debtor requested the dismissal after a creditor filed a request for relief from the automatic stay. See 11 U.S.C. § 109(g). The purpose of this statute is to prevent serial filings by debtors who seek to abuse the automatic stay and the other debtor relief provisions in the Bankruptcy Code. For an in-depth discussion of the issue of when a person is precluded from filing a bankruptcy case because he or she has been a debtor in another bankruptcy case within the preceding 180 days, see Williamson, The Bankruptcy Issues Handbook, 7th Ed., 2016 (Argyle Pub.) Art. 1.01. In addition, if the debtor has had one or more prior Bankruptcy cases dismissed within the past year, he or she may be denied some or all of the protection normally accorded by the automatic stay. See section 2.10, infra, for further reading on the effect of previous bankruptcy filings or dismissals on the automatic stay.

dismissal of previous bankruptcy case, eligibility of debtor

(5) Introducing the debtor to means testing and ascertaining the debtor's current monthly income and expenses. When the case is filed the debtor will have to complete and file a document called "Statement of Current Monthly Income and Means Test Calculation." The information on this document will be used for means testing purposes to determine the debtor's chapter 7 eligibility. Means testing is a process provided for in the Bankruptcy Code whereby it is determined whether the debtor has sufficient disposable income to repay a significant portion of his or her unsecured nonpriority debts. Under this process if it is shown that the debtor's current monthly income exceeds his or her permitted monthly expenses by a specified amount, which can be as little as $136.25 per month, a presumption of abuse will arise and the debtor's chapter 7 case will almost certainly be either dismissed or converted to chapter 13. It is important, therefore, that the required information be quickly and accurately obtained. The required information is listed and discussed in section 2.07, infra. If it appears that the debtor will not qualify for chapter 7 under the means testing criteria, the debtor should be so advised.

current monthly income, importance of

abuse of chapter 7, dismissal of case for

(6) Determining the debtor's eligibility for a chapter 7 discharge. The circumstances under which a chapter 7 discharge will not be granted are listed in section 2.17, infra. The debtor should be questioned as to each applicable circumstance to insure that he or she is eligible for a chapter 7 discharge. Having received a discharge in a chapter 7 case filed within the last 8 years is the most common cause of debtor ineligibility. If the debtor is not eligible for a chapter 7 discharge, his or her eligibility for a chapter 13 discharge should be investigated (see section 3.18, infra).

debtor's eligibility for chapter 7 discharge, importance of checking dischargeability of debts, necessity of checking

(7) Determining the dischargeability of the debtor's debts under chapter 7. Even if a debtor is eligible for chapter 7 and a chapter 7 discharge, the debtor may have debts that are nondischargeable under chapter 7. The types of debts that are not dischargeable under chapter 7 are listed in section 2.17, infra, and the debtor's debts should be checked against this list. In consumer cases, the most common types of nondischargeable debts are divorce-related debts, tax debts, debts for student loans, and debts for "luxury goods or services" or cash advances made within 90 days prior to the filing of the case. It is also important to ascertain whether any of the debtor's debts have been dealt with in a previous bankruptcy case. If so, it is important to determine how the prior case was concluded and the status of the debts in the prior case. If the debts were nondischargeable in the prior case, they may or may not be dischargeable in a later case depending on the reasons for their nondischargeability in the prior case. See section 2.17, infra, for further reading on the dischargeability of debts in chapter 7 cases.

names of all creditors, necessity of obtaining

(8) Obtaining the names and addresses of all potential creditors. In any bankruptcy case it is obviously important to obtain the names and correct addresses of all of the debtor's creditors, because the claims of unlisted or incorrectly listed creditors are likely not to be discharged in the case. See 11 U.S.C. § 523(a)(3) and section 2.17 infra. If a claim is unliquidated, if the debtor does not feel morally or legally obligated to a particular creditor, or if the debtor intends to repay a certain creditor (usually a friend, relative, or important business creditor), the debtor will often fail to identify or list that party as a creditor. The debtor should be questioned carefully to ascertain the existence of such creditors. It is also important to discover and list all nondischargeable claims. This is especially true of claims for domestic support obligations and tax claims, because if the debtor has nonexempt assets such claims are priority claims and may be paid, in part at least, by the trustee thereby relieving the debtor of a post-bankruptcy obligation.

retirement funds & IRAs, protection of in bankruptcy

negative estate planning, importance of

(9) Ascertaining whether the debtor will lose significant property by filing at this time. A list of the debtor's significant assets should be obtained and it should be determined whether the debtor is likely to lose any of these assets by filing under chapter 7. The availability of exemptions for these assets should be explored (see section 2.08, infra). If the debtor's domicile has changed within the last 730 days, the possibility of qualifying for more favorable exemption laws in another state under the domicile provisions of 11 U.S.C. § 522(b)(3)(A) should be examined (see paragraph (15) below). The debtor should be introduced to the concept of negative estate (or exemption) planning. The purpose of such planning is to reduce the amount of liquid assets that the debtor will possess at the time of filing. It may be necessary for the debtor to take steps prior to the filing of the chapter 7 case in order to avoid the subsequent loss of these assets or their cash equivalent. The manipulation of property by a debtor so as to maximize exemptions does not constitute grounds for dismissal. See In re Latimer, 82 B.R. 354 (Bankr. E. D. Pa. 1988); C.f. In re Padilla, 222 F.3d 1184 (9th Cir. 1999). The concept of negative estate planning is discussed in the answer to Question 35 in Part A of this chapter, supra.

chapter 7 process, necessity of informing debtor

(10) Informing the debtor of the chapter 7 process and of the rights and duties of debtors in chapter 7 cases. A chapter 7 case will proceed more smoothly if the debtor understands the chapter 7 process and the rights, duties and responsibilities of debtors in chapter 7 cases. Otherwise, if the debtor later becomes dissatisfied with the case, he or she will be likely to blame the attorney for any shortcomings. It is suggested that the debtor's attorney reproduce the questions and answers set forth in Part A of this chapter, supra, and give a copy of them to the debtor prior to the filing of the case. The questions and answers contained in Part A, supra, will answer many of the questions raised by consumer debtors. The duties and rights of debtors in chapter 7 cases are discussed in sections 2.11 and 2.12, infra.

payment of fees and costs, making arrangements for

(11) Making arrangements for the payment of the filing fee and the attorney's fee. The debtor should be advised that unless the debtor qualifies for a waiver of the filing fee, the entire filing fee must be paid, either when the case is filed or within the period set by the court (see section 2.09, infra), or the case will be dismissed and a discharge will not be granted. For the protection of both the attorney and the debtor, there should be no misunderstanding as to either the amount or the terms of the fee to be charged by the attorney for handling the case. The entire fee arrangement between the debtor and the attorney is required to be in writing and signed by all parties. See 11 U.S.C. § 528(a)(1), (2). A copy of the agreement must be given to the debtor. See section 2.03, supra, for further reading on the requirements of fee agreements in bankruptcy cases.

(12) Ascertaining the debtor's need for immediate bankruptcy relief. Consumer debtors frequently delay consulting with an attorney until one or more creditors have taken steps to repossess, foreclose upon, or garnish the debtor's property or earnings. If creditor action of this nature has been taken, or if such action is imminent, immediate steps to invoke the relief provided by the automatic stay should be taken. The relief provided by the automatic stay may be obtained by filing the bankruptcy petition and serving notice of such filing and of the automatic stay upon the appropriate creditors and other responsible parties (see section 2.09 and 2.10, infra). The need for immediate bankruptcy relief often depends upon the status of threatened creditor action under local law. For example, if under local law a debtor can redeem repossessed property until such time as the property has been lawfully sold by the creditor, it may be necessary to file a chapter 7 case and obtain the benefit of the automatic stay before the repossessed property is sold by the creditor. If a foreclosure action has been commenced against property in which the debtor has equity, it may be necessary to implement the relief provided by the automatic stay before the debtor's right to cure the default or redeem the property under local law has expired. In any event, it is important to ascertain the exact status of any actual or threatened creditor action against the debtor or the debtor's property. If the debtor is in need of immediate bankruptcy relief, he or she should request credit counseling at once because in order to file a case without having received the required prebankruptcy counseling it must be shown that the debtor was unable to obtain the required counseling within 7 days after making the request. See section 2.05, infra, for further reading on this issue.

immediate bankruptcy relief, necessity of

immediate bankruptcy relief, handling counseling requirement

(13) Discovering preferential or fraudulent transfers that may be avoidable in bankruptcy. Because the trustee is empowered to recover avoidable preferential or fraudulent transfers made by the debtor, it is important to ascertain whether the debtor has made such transfers. Preferential and fraudulent transfers are defined and discussed in section 2.16, infra. If the debtor has made significant transfers of property or funds to family members, friends, or business associates within the last 24 months that may be recoverable by the trustee, filing under chapter 7 may not be advisable, at least at this time. The existence and avoidability of such transfers should be checked. It should be noted here that most transfers of money or property by the debtor to a self-settled trust within 10 years of bankruptcy are avoidable by the trustee. See 11 U.S.C. § 548(e)(1). For an in-depth discussion on the most common types of prefiling transfers that may be avoidable in consumer bankruptcy cases, see Williamson, The Bankruptcy Issues Handbook, supra, Art. 1.14.

secured debts, determining debtor's intentions with respect to

transfers to self-settled trusts, avoidability of

(14) Ascertaining the debtor's intentions as to the handling of secured debts. If the debtor has debts that are secured by his or her property, it will be necessary to file a statement of the debtor's intentions as to the handling of these debts. Therefore, it should be ascertained whether the debtor has debts of this type. If the debtor has debts of this type, it should be ascertained with respect to each debt whether the debtor wishes to reaffirm the debt, redeem the secured property under Section 722 by paying the creditor the amount of the creditor's secured claim, avoid the lien on the property under Section 522(f), claim the property as exempt, or surrender the property to the creditor. Redeeming property under Section 722 and avoiding liens under Section 522(f) are discussed in section 2.12, infra, and the reaffirmation of debts is discussed in section 2.18, infra. Statements of intention are discussed in section 2.11, infra. The handling of these debts is an important function in many chapter 7 cases and the debtor's wishes and needs in this regard should be ascertained during the interview.

avoidable transfers, necessity of discovering

(15) Determining the debtor's state of domicile for exemption purposes. The debtor's place of domicile for the previous 730 days is important for exemption claiming purposes and should be ascertained. If the debtor has not been domiciled in a single state for the entire 730 day period, his or her place of domicile for the 180 day period just prior to the 730 day period should be carefully ascertained. See section 2.08, infra, for further reading on this matter. In a joint case the place of domicile of each debtor during those periods should be ascertained.

debtor's domicile, importance of

(16) Informing the debtor of the credit counseling and financial management course requirements. It is important that the debtor be made aware of these requirements early in the case. The debtor must attend a budget and credit counseling briefing prior to filing and must complete an instructional course in financial management as a condition of receiving a discharge. Arrangements should also be made for the payment of any fees required of the debtor for attending these briefings or courses. See section 2.05, infra, for further reading on these requirements.

credit counseling, importance of

2.05 The Credit Counseling and Financial Management Course Requirements

credit counseling by debtor, when required

credit counseling by debtor, filing requirements

Section 109(h) of the Bankruptcy Code provides that an individual may not file a petition under any chapter of the Bankruptcy Code unless he or she has, within 180 days prior to the date of filing, received from an approved nonprofit budget and credit counseling agency an individual or group briefing that outlined the opportunities for available credit counseling and assisted the individual in performing a related budget analysis. The briefing may be conducted in person, by telephone, or via the internet. See 11 U.S.C. § 109(h)(1). Unless excused, a debtor must file with the bankruptcy petition a certificate from an approved budget and credit counseling agency describing the services provided to the debtor together with any debt repayment plan prepared for the debtor by the agency. See 11 U.S.C. § 521(b) and Bankruptcy Rule 1007(b)(3).

credit counseling, when not required

The budget and credit counseling requirement described above is not applicable in districts where the United States trustee has determined that the approved nonprofit budget and credit counseling agencies for the district are not reasonably able to provide adequate services for those who need the services for bankruptcy purposes. See 11 U.S.C. § 109(h)(2)(A) and Bankruptcy Rule 1007(b)(3).

credit counseling after filing, when permitted

A debtor in need of immediate bankruptcy relief may file a bankruptcy petition without first receiving budget and credit counseling if the debtor files with the bankruptcy petition a certification that is satisfactory to the court describing exigent (i.e., requiring immediate aid or action) circumstances that merit a waiver of the budget and credit counseling requirement and states that he or she requested the counseling services from an approved agency but was unable to obtain the requested services within 7 days of making the request. See 11 U.S.C. § 109(h)(3)(A) and Bankruptcy Rule 1007(b)(3). However, such a debtor must obtain the required budget and credit counseling within 30 days after the date of filing of the bankruptcy petition. See 11 U.S.C. § 109(h)(3)(B).

credit counseling, when not required

The budget and credit counseling requirement does not apply to debtors who are unable to complete the requirement because of incapacity, disability, or active military duty in a military combat zone. To obtain a waiver of credit counseling on this ground a request for determination must be filed with the petition and the request must be approved by the court after notice and a hearing. See 11 U.S.C. § 109(h)(4) and Bankruptcy Rule 1007(b)(3), (c). For purposes of this waiver, "incapacity" means that the debtor is impaired by reason of mental illness or mental deficiency to the extent that he or she is incapable of realizing and making rational decisions with respect to his or her financial responsibilities. "Disability" means that the debtor is physically impaired to the extent that he or she is unable, after reasonable effort, to participate in an in-person, telephone or internet credit counseling briefing. See 11 U.S.C. § 109(h)(4).

financial management course, completion and filing requirements

In addition to the budget and credit counseling requirement described above, to receive a chapter 7 discharge, a debtor must complete an instructional course on personal financial management after the filing of the case. See 11 U.S.C. § 727(a)(11). The debtor is required to file a statement regarding completion of a course in personal financial management prepared on Official Form 423 within 60 days after the meeting of creditors. See Bankruptcy Rule 1007(b)(7), (c). A sample of this form is set forth in Exhibit 2-Z(2) at the end of this chapter.

financial management course, when not required

The instructional financial management course requirement described above does not apply to debtors who reside in districts where the United States trustee has determined that the approved instructional courses are not adequate to service individuals who need the course for bankruptcy purposes. See 11 U.S.C. § 727(a)(11). The financial management instructional course requirement also does not apply to debtors who are unable to complete the requirement because of incapacity, disability, or active military duty in a military combat zone. See 11 U.S.C. § 727(a)(11), 109(h)(4), and the discussion of this matter two paragraphs above.

credit counseling agencies, requirements of

credit counseling agencies, list of

The United States trustee is required to investigate and certify (or decertify) nonprofit budget and credit counseling agencies and instructional course providers in the area. See 11 U.S.C 111(b), (c), (d). One of the requirements of certification is that an instructional course provider must charge only a reasonable fee and must provide services without regard to ability to pay. See 11 U.S.C. § 111(d)(1)(E). The clerk of the bankruptcy court is required to maintain publicly available lists of approved budget and credit counseling agencies and instructional course providers. See 11 U.S.C. § 111(a). These lists may be posted on the website of the local bankruptcy court.

2.06 The Chapter 7 Bankruptcy Forms

Bankruptcy Rule 1001 provides that the Bankruptcy Rules and Official Forms shall govern the procedure in bankruptcy cases. Bankruptcy Rule 9009 provides that the Official Forms may be used with such alterations as may be appropriate and that the Official Forms may be combined and their contents rearranged to permit economies in their use. Bankruptcy Rule 9029 provides that the local bankruptcy rules may not prohibit or limit the use of the Official Forms.

official bankruptcy forms, use of

11 U.S.C. § 521(a)(1) requires a chapter 7 debtor to file a list of creditors, and, unless the court orders otherwise, a schedule of assets and liabilities, a schedule of current income and current expenditures, a statement of the debtor's financial affairs, a certificate by the debtor's attorney that he has delivered to the debtor the notice required by 11 U.S.C. § 342(b), copies of all pay advices or other evidences of payment received by the debtor from any employer within 60 days prior to the date of filing, a statement of the amount of monthly net income, itemized to show how it was calculated, and a statement disclosing any reasonably anticipated increase in income or expenditures during the next 12 months. A list of creditors is contained in the debtor's schedules of liabilities and need not be filed separately unless the schedules of liabilities are not filed with the petition. If the debtor is being evicted and wishes to preserve the automatic stay against the lessor, the certification required under 11 U.S.C. § 362(l) must be filed with the petition and served on the lessor. See the last page of section 2.10, infra.

statutory chapter 7 filing requirements

evicted debtor, filing requirements

Bankruptcy Rule 1007(b)(1) requires the debtor to file schedules of assets and liabilities, a schedule of current income and expenditures, a schedule of executory contracts and unexpired leases, a statement of financial affairs, copies of all payment advices or other evidence of payment, if any, (with all but the last four digits of the debtor's social security number edited out), received by the debtor from an employer within 60 days prior to filing, a record of any interest that the debtor has in an education IRA or qualified state tuition program, each prepared as prescribed by the appropriate Official Form if one exists. Bankruptcy Rules 1007(b)(2)-(4) requires an individual debtor in a chapter 7 case to file a statement of intention as required by 11 U.S.C. § 521(a) prepared as prescribed by the appropriate Official Form, and, unless the United States trustee has determined that the credit counseling requirement does not apply in the district, a certificate of credit counseling and any debt repayment plan prepared for the debtor, together with a statement of current income prepared on an official form and, if the debtor has current monthly income greater than the applicable median family income for the applicable state and household size, the means test calculations required by 11 U.S.C. § 707(b) prepared on the appropriate official form.

schedules and statements, filing requirements

The following forms may be necessary at the time of filing in a typical chapter 7 consumer case:

forms needed, typical case

- Voluntary Petition for Individuals Filing for Bankruptcy (Official Form 101)
- Chapter 7 Statement of Your Current Monthly Income and Means-Test Calculation (Official Form 122A–1)
- Statement of Exemption from Presumption of Abuse Under § 707(b)(2) (Official Form 122A–1Supp)
- Chapter 7 Means Test Calculation (Official Form 122A–2)
- Statement of Anticipated Increase in Income or Expenses (a local form, if needed)
- Your Statement About Your Social Security Numbers (Official Form 121)
- Certificate as to Credit Counseling (a local form)
- Debt Repayment Plan from credit counseling agency, if one exists
- Schedules A through J (Official Forms 106--Smmary, 106A/B, 106C, 106D, 106E/F, 106G, 106H, 106I, 106J, and 106J-2)
- Statement of Financial Affairs (Official Form 107)
- Application for Individuals to Pay the Filing Fee in Installments (Official Form 103A, if needed)
- Application to have the Chapter 7 Filing Fee Waived (Official Form 103B, if needed)
- Disclosure of Compensation of Attorney for Debtor (Director's Form 2030 or a local form)
- Statement of Intention for Individuals Filing under Chapter 7 (Official Form 108)
- Notice Required by 11 U.S.C. § 342(b) for Individuals Filing for Bankruptcy (Director's Form 2010)
- Copies of pay advices for last 60 days
- Statement of Interest in Education IRA or Qualified State Tuition Program (a local form, if needed)
- List of Names and Addresses of Persons to Receive Bankruptcy Notices. This is commonly referred to as the creditor matrix.
- Declaration Regarding Electronic Filing (a local form that is needed for electronically filed cases)

chapter 7 forms, where to find

Some districts may require additional local forms to be completed and filed in chapter 7 cases, and the local rules should be checked for such requirements. The required local forms are usually supplied by the clerk of the bankruptcy court or may be downloaded from the local bankruptcy court's website. The local rules often contain copies of these forms. The official forms are included on the Argyle Publishing Company Bankruptcy Forms.

electronic filing, necessity of forms

If the case is being filed electronically, paper bankruptcy forms may not be needed because the required information can be transmitted via the internet directly from the debtor's attorney's computer to the electronic files in the clerk's office. If the case is not being filed electronically, care should be taken to ensure that the filed forms can be electronically scanned. This means that the forms should not be stapled together or contain notes or unwieldy attachments. In most districts the scanning is done by personnel in the clerk's office, but in some districts the filer must do the scanning. In many districts electronic filing is now required.

2.07 Preparing Chapter 7 Bankruptcy Forms for Filing

preparation of forms, use of work sheets

When the proper forms have been obtained and the necessary information assembled, the next task is that of preparing the chapter 7 bankruptcy forms for filing. The forms will be similar to those appearing in the exhibits at the end of this chapter, and it is suggested that the exhibits be used as guides in preparing the forms for filing. If the Bankruptcy Worksheets appearing in Exhibit 2-C at the end of this chapter were used to assemble the information, the assembled data will be in the order required in the Statement of Your Current Monthly Income and Means-Test Calculation, Schedules A through J, and the Statement of Financial Affairs.

verification of forms, when required

It is important that the chapter 7 bankruptcy forms be properly and completely prepared, both substantively and technically. If the forms are technically incomplete or incorrect, the clerk is likely to refuse to process them and return them to the debtor's attorney for corrections. It should be noted here that Bankruptcy Rule 1008 requires that all petitions, lists, schedules, statements, and amendments thereto be verified or contain an unsworn declaration as provided in 28 U.S.C. § 1746. This rule applies only to the original copy of each document. Other documents need not contain an unsworn declaration or be verified unless specifically required by a particular Bankruptcy Rule. See Bankruptcy Rule 9011(e), (f).

signature of attorney, effect of

If the debtor is represented by an attorney, every petition, pleading, motion, and other paper filed in the case, other than a list, schedule, statement, or amendments thereto, must be signed by at least one attorney of record in the attorney's individual name, with the attorney's office address and telephone number stated. See Bankruptcy Rule 9011(a). An unrepresented debtor must personally sign each paper that requires a signature. An unsigned document will be stricken unless it is promptly signed. See Bankruptcy Rule 9011(a). Bankruptcy Rule 9011(b) and 11 U.S.C. § 707(b)(4) impose certification requirements on attorneys who sign bankruptcy petitions and document and liabilities for faulty certifications. For example, 11 U.S.C. § 707(b)(4)(D) provides that the signature of an attorney on the petition constitutes a certification that the attorney has no knowledge after an inquiry that the information in the schedules filed with the petition is incorrect. See section 2.03, supra, for further reading on the duties and liabilities of debtors' attorneys in bankruptcy cases.

filing of document by attorney, effect of, sanctions for violation

signature requirements electronically filed documents

In most districts there are local rules or general orders that deal with the signature requirements of electronically-filed documents. Generally, documents, such as bankruptcy petitions, which must contain original signatures or which require verification under Bankruptcy Rule 1008 or an unsworn declaration under 28 U.S.C. § 1746, may be filed electronically using a facsimile imaged or electronic signature (e.g., "/s/John Doe"). The original signed document must be retained by the attorney of record or the party originating the document for the locally-required retention period. Upon request, the original document must be provided to other parties or to the court for review. In most districts the local rules or general orders provide that the use of an attorney's password to file a document electronically constitutes the signature of that attorney for purposes of Bankruptcy Rule 9011. The local rules and general orders should be checked in this regard. They are usually available on the website of the local bankruptcy court.

chapter 7 forms, consistency of

Not only should the information on the forms be accurate and complete, but the forms should be consistent with one another. For example, if Schedule 106E/F shows a recent automobile repair bill, the automobile should appear in Schedule 106A/B, or its transfer reflected in the Statement of Financial Affairs. If a large debt for furniture appears in Schedule 106E/F, the furniture should appear in Schedule 106A/B.

If a debtor's chapter 7 forms are incomplete or incorrect, the debtor may be deprived of rights or property to which he or she would otherwise be entitled, or the debtor's attorney may later be sanctioned or find it necessary to file motions or prepare amended schedules and statements. Also, a fee may be charged for filing amended schedules. It obviously makes sense, both professionally and economically, to prepare the forms correctly. chapter 7 forms, amendment fee

The preparation of each document normally required in a chapter 7 case for a typical consumer debtor is discussed separately on the pages that follow.

Current Monthly Income and Means Test Calculation.

means testing, required form

Official Forms 122A-1 and 122A-2 are used to determine whether the debtor's income and expenses create a presumption of abuse that may prevent the debtor from obtaining relief under Chapter 7. Chapter 7 relief, of course, may be denied to a person who has primarily consumer debts if the Court finds that the person has enough income to repay creditors an amount that, under the Bankruptcy Code, would be a signification portion of their claims.

Form 122A-1: Statement of Your Current Monthly Income

Official Form 122A-1 is used for means testing purposes and serves two related functions. First, it is used to determine whether the debtor is exempt from means testing under 11 U.S.C. § 707(b)(7) and then, if the debtor is not exempt, whether a presumption of abuse under 11 U.S.C. § 707(b)(2) arises when the debtor's current monthly income and deductions are calculated. It is usually a good practice to complete this form first because if this document shows that a presumption of abuse arises for the debtor, in most cases it will be unwise for the debtor to file under chapter 7, at least at this time. This form must be completed by every individual chapter 7 debtor whose debts are primarily consumer debts. However, joint debtors need only complete a single form. This form will be used by the United States trustee to determine whether a presumption of abuse has arisen in the case under 11 U.S.C. § 707(b). See section 2.20, infra. for the rules and procedures governing the arising of a presumption of abuse. A completed sample of this form is set forth in Exhibit 2-E(1) at the end of this chapter. It may be used as a guide in preparing this form

Form 122A-1, purposes.

If the debtor is unmarried or married but living apart or legally separated from his or her spouse, then only the debtor's current income need be listed in Part 1 of Form 122A-1. If the debtor is legally separated or living apart from his or her spouse (for nonbankruptcy purposes) he or she must affirm under penalty of perjury that they are living apart for reasons that do not evade the means test requirement. If the debtor and his or her spouse are filing a joint petition or if the debtor files a single petition and is neither living apart nor legally separated from his or her spouse, then the current income of both spouses must be listed in Part 1 of the form.

income of debtor's spouse, handling of

As a matter of clarification, it should be noted that for purposes of determining whether the debtor is exempt from means testing, the income of a married debtor's spouse must be counted, even if the case is not a joint case, unless the spouses are either legally separated or living apart. See 11 U.S.C. § 707(b)(7)(A), (B). However, for purposes of determining whether a presumption of abuse arises for a nonexempt debtor under Code section 707(b)(2), the income of the debtor's spouse is only counted in a joint case. See 11 U.S.C. § 101(10A).

income of debtor's spouse, when counted

The income to be listed in Part 1 of Form 122A-1 is the average monthly income from all sources received by the debtor (and the debtor's spouse, if applicable) during the 6 month period ending on the last day of the calendar month immediately preceding the date on which the bankruptcy case was filed. For example, if the case was filed on May 10th, the 6 month period would end on April 30th. However, if the Schedule of Current Income is not filed with the petition, the 6 month period ends on the date on which the debtor's current income is determined by the court. See 11 U.S.C. § 101(10A)(A). If the debtor received different monthly amounts of income from a particular source during the 6 month period, the amount entered on the form should be the total amount received from that source during the 6 month divided by 6. Both taxable and non-taxable income is counted, as are amounts contributed by entities other than the debtor (or the debtor's spouse in a joint case) on a regular basis to the household expenses of the debtor, the debtor's dependents, and (in a joint case) the debtor's spouse if he or she is not otherwise a dependent. However, social security income and payments received by victims of crime or

current monthly income for §707(b)(7) purposes, how to determine terrorism are not counted. See 11 U.S.C 101(10A).

current monthly income, included amounts

The various lines in this part of the form (lines 2-9) call for all of the common types of income (including a line for regular contributions of support) and then include a "catch-all" line (line 10) for all other types of income. Unemployment compensation is given special treatment. Because the federal government provides funding for state unemployment compensation under the Social Security Act, it can be argued that unemployment compensation is a "benefit received under the Social Security Act" under 11 U.S.C. § 101(10A) and is therefore excludable from current monthly income. Line 8 of the form permits the debtor to list the amount, if any, of his or her unemployment compensation that is deemed to be a benefit under the Social Security Act and therefore not includable as current monthly income in line 8. The local state unemployment office may be able to provide this information. Although Form 122A-1 includes boxes for itemizing any unemployment compensation deemed to be a benefit under the Social Security Act, the practitioner should be aware that the U.S. Trustee Program issued a position statement in 2010 in which it specifically opposed any unemployment compensation being deemed a benefit under the Social Security Act. The revised Official Forms reflect this position.

means testing, debtors exempt from

Part 2 deals with the Code section 707(b)(7) exclusion from means testing (i.e., determining whether the debtor is subject to means testing). This form contains the calculation necessary to determine whether Code section 707(b)(2) is applicable to the debtor. Code section 707(b)(7) provides that if the debtor's current monthly income multiplied by 12 is equal to or less than the median family income for a similarly-sized family (as determined for the most recent year by the Bureau of Census) in the state where the debtor resides, then no one has standing to seek dismissal of the case under the presumption of abuse provisions of Code section 707(b)(2). This means that the debtor is exempt from and not subject to means testing. See 11 U.S.C. § 707(b)(7)(A).

median family income, how to obtain, importance of

The median family income for the debtor's state and household size may be obtained from Appendix V in the back of this book. If the applicable median income from the Bureau of Census tables (line 13 on Form 122A-1) is equal to or greater than the debtor's annualized current monthly income (i.e., current monthly income multiplied by 12) appearing in line 13 of the form, then a presumption of abuse cannot arise because the debtor is not subject to means testing and the rest of the form does not have to be completed. If the debtor's annualized current monthly income is greater than the applicable median income shown in line 13 of the form, then Form 122A-2 must be completed to ascertain whether a presumption of abuse arises under Code section 707(b)(2).

Stmt. of Exemption from Presumption of Abuse Under § 707(b)(2) (Form 122A-1Supp)

disabled veterans and active duty debtors, exemption of from means testing

Before discussing Form 122A-2, note that if the debtor is a disabled veteran whose indebtedness occurred primarily during a period when he or she was on active duty or while performing a homeland defense activity, the debtor is exempt from means testing and it will not be necessary to complete this form (other than checking the Veteran's Declaration box in Part I of the form) and a presumption of abuse will be deemed not to arise regardless of the amount of the debtor's current monthly income. See 11 U.S.C. § 707(b)(2)(D). Similarly, PL110-438 (2008), as amended by the National Guard and Reservist Debt Relief Extension Act of 2011, waives means testing for members of the National Guard or a reserve component of the Armed Forces who are or have been called to active duty or a homeland defense activity for more 90 days since September 11, 2001. The exemption from means testing under PL 110-438 is applicable during active duty or a homeland defense activity and extends for 540 days thereafter. See 11 U.S.C. § 707(b)(2)(D). To elect exclusion from means testing for such a debtor, the debtor's attorney must complete Part 2 of Official Form 122A-1Supp and complete the information pertaining to the debtor's service contained in that section.

Chapter 7 Means Test Calculation (Official Form 122A-2)

current monthly income for §707(b)(2) purposes, how to determine

Form 122A-2 is used to determine the debtor's current monthly income for purposes of determining whether a presumption of abuse under Code section 707(b)(2) arises in the case. In a joint case, the combined current monthly income from both spouses must appear in the form. If the case is not a joint case the current monthly income of the debtor's spouse is not includable unless the spouses are separated and the other spouse, though separated, contributes regularly to the support of the debtor and his or her dependents.

Calculating deductions

The next function is to determine and calculate the amount of the monthly deductions that the debtor is permitted to subtract from his or her current monthly income for means testing purposes. This function, which is usually the most difficult, is handled in Part 2 of the form.

For means testing purposes there are two types of deductions: deductions under the Internal Revenue Service (IRS) standards and deductions for actual expenses. The IRS has both National Standards and Local Standards for living, transportation and other standard expenses. The amounts of these standard expenses may be obtained from the Argyle Publishing Company Bankruptcy Forms. Most of the deductions from the debtor's current monthly income that are permitted for means testing purposes are listed in 11 U.S.C. § 707(b)(2)(A)(ii).

means testing, use of IRS standards

Lines 6–23 of the form deal with the deductions that are allowed under the IRS National and Local Standards. These deductions, it should be understood, are standard deductions and are not related to the debtor's actual expenses. They are determined by the debtor's place of residence, income, and family size. The amount to be listed on the form for the deductions allowed under the IRS standards may be obtained from the Argyle Publishing Company Bankruptcy Forms.

IRS standards, how determined, where found

11 U.S.C. § 707(b)(2)(A)(ii)(I) provides that the debtor's standard monthly expenses shall not include any payments for debts. Because of this requirement adjustments may have to be made to the IRS Local Standard deductions appearing in lines 8, 9, 11, 12, and 13 of the form if the debtor is making home mortgage or automobile loan payments.

IRS standards, exclusion from of debt payment

The IRS National Standards provide a single exemption allowance for food, clothing, household supplies, personal care, and miscellany, depending on income and household size. The form contains a single entry line (line 6) for the applicable allowance, which may be obtained from the website shown on this line of the form.

IRS National Standards, amount of

The IRS Local Standards provide separate deductions for housing and utilities and for transportation, with different amounts for different areas of the country, depending on family size and number of vehicles owned or leased. Each of the amounts specified by the IRS in the Local Standards are treated by the IRS as a cap on actual expenses, but because Code section 707(b)(2)(A)(ii) provides for the deductions to be in the amounts specified under the Local Standards, the form treats these amounts as allowed deductions. The IRS Local Standards for housing and utilities separate this expense category into a non-mortgage expense component and a mortgage/rental expense component. The utilities/maintenance expense is a simple allowance. However, for homeowners with mortgages, the mortgage/rental expense involves debt payment. Accordingly, the form requires debtors to deduct from the allowance for mortgage/rental expense the average monthly mortgage payment (principal and interest), up to the full amount of the IRS mortgage/rental expense. This average payment amount is the amount shown on the separate line 9b of the form as a deduction for debt payment and it should be deducted from the IRS Local Standard amount. See 11 U.S.C. § 707(b)(2)(A)(iii).

IRS Local Standards, housing & utilities

The IRS Local Standards for transportation separate this expense category into a vehicle operation/public transportation component and a component for ownership/lease expense. The amount of the vehicle operation/public transportation allowance depends on the number of vehicles the debtor operates (or for which the debtor pays the operating expenses), with debtors who do not operate vehicles being given a public transportation expense. As the instruction for this line item on the form makes clear, every debtor is entitled to transportation expense allowance of some amount. No debt payment is involved in the operation/public transportation component allowance. However, for debtors with debt secured by the vehicles that they operate, the ownership/lease expense component does involve debt payment. Accordingly, the form requires debtors to deduct from the allowance for ownership/lease expense the average monthly loan payment amount (principal and interest), up to the full amount of the IRS ownership/lease expense amount. This average payment amount should be the same amount that is listed as a deduction for payment of this debt in lines 33–38 of the form.

IRS Local Standards, transportation expenses, how to determine & list

There is also a National Standard for out-of-pocket health care expenses, which provides two different per-person allowances, depending on the individual's age. Each applicable National Standard is established by multiplying the number of household members in that age group, and then adding the two subtotals to obtain the total allowance, which is entered on line 7. The Supreme Court has ruled that a debtor who does not make any loan or lease payments on an automobile may not take the standard car-ownership deduction. See Ransom v. FIA Card Services, N.A. 131 S. Ct. 716 (2011).

IRS National Standards, out-of-pocket health care expenses, how to determine & list other necessary expenses, how to determine & list

The IRS does not set out allowances for "Other Necessary Expenses." Rather, it sets out a number of categories for such expenses, and describes the nature of the expenses that may be deducted in each of these categories. 11 U.S.C. § 707(b)(2)(A)(ii) permits a deduction for the debtor's actual expenses in these specified categories, subject to the requirement that payment of debt not be included. Several of the IRS categories deal with debt repayment and so are not included in the form. Several other categories deal with business expenses, and the form combines these categories into a single line entry. The remaining IRS categories are set out as individual line entries on the form (lines 16–23). Instructions on the individual entry lines reflect the limitations imposed by the IRS and the need to avoid inclusion of items deducted elsewhere on the form.

special expense deductions, how to list

In addition to the IRS expense deductions, 11 U.S.C. § 707(b)(2)(A)(ii) lists six special expense deductions. Each of these additional expense items is set out on a separate line entry in lines 25–31. Any expense that has already been included in the IRS deductions should not be included here. Contributions to tax-exempt charities that the debtor intends to continue are another permitted expense deduction. See 11 U.S.C. § 707(b)(1). They should be listed in line 31 of the form. Lines 33–36 require the debtor to list deductions for the payment of secured and priority debt.

current monthly expenses, total of

The total of all of the permitted monthly deductions from current monthly income should be listed on line 38 of the form. This is the amount that will be subtracted from the debtor's current monthly income to determine his or her monthly disposable income.

presumption of abuse, basic rule

In determining whether a presumption of abuse arises under Code section 707(b)(2), the basic rule is that a presumption of abuse is deemed to arise if the debtor's monthly disposable income multiplied by 60 is equal or greater than the lesser of $15,150* or 25 percent of the debtor's nonpriority unsecured debt, or $9,075* if that is less than the 25 percent figure. See 11 U.S.C. § 707(b)(2)(A)(i). For further reading on presumption of abuse and proceedings thereunder, see section 2.20, infra.

initial presumption of abuse, arising of, how to determine

Part 3 of the form is used to determine whether a presumption of abuse under Code section 707(b)(2) arises for the debtor in the case. In general, the total amount of the debtor's permitted monthly expenses (from line 38) are subtracted from the debtor's current monthly income for Code section 707(b)(2) purposes (from line 4) to obtain the debtor's monthly disposable income. This amount is then multiplied by 60 to obtain the debtor's 60 month disposable income. If the amount of the debtor's 60 month disposable income is less than $9,075* an initial presumption of abuse does not arise in the case. If the amount of the debtor's 60 month disposable income is more than $15,150* an initial presumption of abuse is deemed to arise in the case. Stated in terms of monthly disposable income, if the debtor's disposable monthly income is less than $151.25*, no presumption of abuse will arise. If disposable monthly income is above $252.50*, a presumption will always arise. If disposable monthly income is between the two, the debtor's unsecured debt must be considered. In either event, the appropriate box on the top of page 1 of the form should be checked.

initial presumption of abuse, arising of, how to determine

If the amount of the debtor's 60 month disposable income is more than $9,075* but less than $15,150*, the debtor must complete line 41 of Form 122A-2. In these lines the debtor's 60 month disposable income amount is compared to 25% of the total amount of the debtor's unsecured nonpriority debt (the amount of which should appear on Schedule E/F). If the amount of the debtor's 60 month disposable income is less than 25 percent of his or her unsecured nonpriority debt, then an initial presumption of abuse does not arise in the case. If the amount of the debtor's 60 month disposable income exceeds 25 percent of his or her unsecured nonpriority debt, then an initial presumption of abuse is deemed to arise in the case.

other necessary expenses listing of

If the debtor incurs any other monthly or periodic expenses that are required or necessary for the health and welfare of the debtor and his or her family that are not otherwise accounted for on Form 122A-2, these expenses should be listed in Part 4 of the form. The apparent reason for the listing of these expenses is that because 11 U.S.C. § 707(b)(2)(A)(ii)(I) does not expressly prohibit the inclusion of necessary expenses other than those listed in the statute, the court has the discretionary power to include these expenses as "other necessary expenses" in determining the debtor's monthly disposable income. Part 5 of the form is the verification, which must completed and signed by the debtor.

Statement About Your Social Security Numbers (Official Form 121)

Bankruptcy Rule 1007(f) provides that an individual debtor shall submit a verified statement that sets out the debtor's social security number or states that the debtor does not have a social security number. In a voluntary case Bankruptcy Rule 1007(f) requires the statement to be filed with the petition. The statement provides the information needed to include the debtor's full social security number in the notice of meeting of creditors as required by Bankruptcy Rule 2002(a)(1). The creditors, the trustee, and the United States Trustee will receive the debtor's full social security number, while the copy of the notice of meeting of creditors that goes into the court's file will show only the last four digits of the number. A completed sample of this form is set forth in Exhibit 2-D at the end of this chapter. The form is self explanatory and simple to complete.

statement of social security number, requirements and preparation of

Voluntary Petition for Individuals Filing for Bankruptcy (Official Form 101)

The 8 page voluntary petition, which is Official Form 101, is self-explanatory and easy to complete. A completed sample of this petition appears in Exhibit 2-F at the end of this chapter. It may be used as a guide in preparing this document. If a joint petition is not being filed the word "none" should appear in the spaces on page 1 of the petition that pertain to the joint debtor. Only the last 4 digits of the debtor's social security number should be shown on the petition. Each appropriate box should be checked on page 1 of the petition. The "Chapter 7" box should be checked on page 3 of the petition. If the filing fee will be paid when the case is filed, select the appropriate box in section 8 of the petition. Otherwise select the appropriate response. In section 9 of the petition it is important that any prior or pending bankruptcy case of the debtor that was filed within the last 8 years be identified in the appropriate spaces. In Section 16a, check yes (if debts are primarily consumer debts).

voluntary petition, preparation of

On page 7 of the petition should be signed by the debtor's attorney, who, by so signing declares that the attorney has informed the debtor that he or she may file under chapters 7, 11, 12, or 13 of the Bankruptcy Code and of the relief available under each chapter and that the attorney has delivered to the debtor the notice required by 11 U.S.C. § 342(b) and, in a case in which § 707(b)(4)(D) applies, certify that I have no knowledge after an inquiry that the information in the schedules filed with the petition is incorrect. See section 2.04, supra, for a description of this notice. The appropriate box in Part 4 should be checked and if the debtor owns or possesses property that may pose a threat to public safety, and the appropriate information should be filled out if so. The appropriate venue question should be answered (Question 6) and if the debtor is renting residential property and is being (or has been) evicted the appropriate box in Question 11 should be checked and you should fill out and file the Initial Statement About an Eviction Judgment Against You (Official Form 101A) with the bankruptcy petition.

§ 342(b) notice by attorney

Part 7 of the petition is the signature page and should be completed and signed by both the attorney and the debtor (or by both debtors in a joint case). It is important to note that by signing the petition a consumer debtor declares that he or she is aware of chapters 7, 11, 12 and 13 of the Bankruptcy Code, understands the relief available under each chapter, and chooses to proceed under chapter 7.

voluntary petition, signature requirements

Part 5 to the voluntary petition is entitled, "Individual Debtor's Statement of Compliance With Credit Counseling Requirement". This must be completed by all debtors with the voluntary petition. Part 5 ensures that debtors realize the significance of the pre-petition debt counseling requirement and the potentially fatal consequences to a debtor's case if he or she fails to meet the requirement. Each spouse to a joint case must complete Part 5. The form contains separate statements that the debtor may choose from concerning his or her particular situation vis-à-vis pre-petition credit counseling. If the debtor has received the required counseling prior to filing the voluntary petition, box 1 should be checked and a copy of the certificate received from the credit counseling agency must be attached to the petition. If no certificate is available, box 2 should be checked and the debtor must obtain and file a copy of the certificate within fourteen days after the case is filed. If the debtor requested counseling, but was unable to receive it during the seven days after the request was made, box 3 should be checked. The debtor must obtain credit counseling within thirty days of filing the case. The final boxes pertain to various reasons the debtor may be exempted from the pre-petition credit counseling requirement.

voluntary petition, Credit Counseling

Schedules.

In addition to the documents described above, a chapter 7 debtor must file separate schedules (Schedules A through J (Official Forms 106--Smmary, 106A/B, 106C, 106D, 106E/F, 106G, 106H, 106I, 106J, and 106J-2)), a Statement of Financial Affairs (Official Form 107), and in most cases a Statement of Intention for Individuals Filing under Chapter 7 (Official Form 108). Schedules A through J must be filed in all chapter 7 cases. Schedules A/B, C, D, and E/F are the debtor's schedules of assets and liabilities. Schedule G is a list of the debtor's executory contracts and unexpired leases. Schedule H is a list of codebtors (i.e., those liable with the debtor on one or more debts). Schedules I, J, and J-2 are schedules of the debtor's current income and current expenditures and must be filed even though they contain much of the information as is contained in the Statement of Current Monthly Income and Means Test Calculation.

chapter 7 debtor, required schedules and statements

The schedules should be filed in alphabetical order and should be preceded by a Summary of Your Assets and Liabilities and Certain Statistical Information (Official Form 106Sum) and followed by a Declaration About an Individual Debtor's Schedules (Official Form 106Dec). The order of the schedules (i.e., A through J alphabetically) corresponds to the customary pattern by which trustees review such documents and to the standard format of the accounting profession for balance sheets. The individual schedules need only contain the debtor's name and the case number, if one exists. The Summary of Schedules must necessarily be prepared last because it contains information from the other schedules.

official Forms 106, general requirements

Schedule A/B - Property (Official Form 106A/B)

Use Exhibit 2-G at the end of this chapter as a guide in preparing Schedule A/B: Property, which is Official Form 106A/B. All property in which the debtor has a legal, equitable or future interest should be listed in Schedule

A/B. Schedule A/B combines the old Schedules A and B into one schedule for all property types, real and personal. The new form uses seven categories likely to be more familiar to non-lawyers: real estate, vehicles, personal household items, financial assets, business-related property, farm- and commercial fishing-related property, and a catch-all category for property that was not listed elsewhere in the form. See 106 (Official Form 106) (Committee Note) (12/15). The instructions indicate the debtor should list items only once on the form; do not list them in more than one category.

Part 1 shows all real property owned by the debtor. This includes all real property owned as a cotenant or under community property laws, and real property in which the debtor has a life estate or a right or power excisable for the debtor's own benefit. However, real property interests resulting solely from executory contracts or unexpired leases should be listed in Schedule G and not on Schedule A/B. If the debtor owns no interest in any real property, then place a check next to the word "no" in Question 1. If a joint petition is being filed or if the debtor is married, indicate by the appropriate checked box whether the property is owned by the husband, wife, jointly or, in community property states, as community property. The value of the property should be the estimated current market value of the property without regard to any encumbrances or exemptions. Property you own includes property you have purchased, even if you owe money on it, such as a home with a mortgage or an automobile with a lien. The value of the portion that you own should be the value minus any portions owned by others (as co-tenants, for example). Any secured claim should not be deducted from the value. Instead, this information will be included in Schedule D: Creditors Who Have Claims Secured by Property.

real property

All interests of the debtor in personal property should be listed on Schedule A/B, as well, except interests resulting solely from executory contracts or unexpired leases, which should be listed on Schedule G. When completing Schedule A/B, the debtor should be informed that an intentional failure to disclose assets in a bankruptcy case is grounds for the denial or revocation of a chapter 7 discharge and is a federal criminal offense (making a false statement, concealing property, or obtaining money or property by fraud in connection with a bankruptcy case) and can result in fines up to $250,000, or imprisonment for up to 20 years, or both. 18 U.S.C. §§ 152, 1341, 1519, and 3571.

Schedule A/B, property listed on

bankruptcy crime, what constitutes

Schedule A/B should reflect the personal property of the debtor as of the time (i.e., the day and hour) that the case is filed, not necessarily as of the time of the debtor's interview with the attorney. If at all possible, the debtor should have no nonexempt cash, bank deposits, household or sporting goods, prepaid rent, accrued earnings, or tax refunds at the time of filing, because such items, or their cash equivalent, will be deemed property of the estate and must later be turned over to the trustee. The results of any negative estate planning required to reduce or eliminate nonexempt liquid assets of this type should be reflected in this schedule. Negative estate planning is discussed in the answer to Question 35 in Part A of this chapter, supra.

negative estate planning

In completing Schedule A/B, something should be checked for each question. The Instructions indicate that where there are similar items of minimal value (such as clothing), a total value may be reported. However, the debtor should separately describe and list individual items worth more than $500.

If additional space is needed to list or describe a particular category of property appearing on the schedule, a separate sheet should be used. The sheet should be identified with the case name, case number (if known), and the schedule and category number and attached to the last page of the Schedule A/B. If a joint petition is being filed or if the debtor is married, you may indicate whether the personal property is owned by the husband, wife, jointly, or, in community property states, as community property.

preparation requirements

attachments to

On Schedule A/B the debtor must report the current value of the property. The Instructions indicate that current value is fair market value as of the date of the filing of the petition. To make the process easier, the value should be the estimated current replacement value of the property as of the date of filing without deduction for costs of sale or marketing and without regards to any encumbrances or exemptions. See 11 U.S.C. §§ 506(a)(2), which provides that the replacement value of property acquired for personal, family or household purposes is the price a retail merchant would charge for the property, considering its age and condition. The value of such items as annuities or life insurance policies is normally the refund or cash surrender value of the policy or contract. It may be necessary to contact the debtor's insurance agent or company to determine the exact refund or cash surrender

personal property, valuation of

value of a policy or contract.

If the debtor has an interest in an educational IRA or under a qualified State tuition program, that interest should be shown in the response to item 24 in Schedule A/B. The debtor is required under 11 U.S.C. § 521(c) to file a record of these interests, if any exist, with the court. The debtor's response to item 24 should satisfy that requirement.

educational IRA state tuition program, interests in

Schedule C - The Property You Claim as Exempt (Official Form 106C)

Use Exhibit 2-H at the end of this chapter as a guide in preparing Schedule C. The debtor must elect the exemptions to which he or she is entitled (i.e., 11 U.S.C. § 522(b)(2), which designates the federal bankruptcy exemptions, or 11 U.S.C. § 522(b)(3), which designates the applicable state and federal nonbankruptcy exemptions) by checking the appropriate box at the top of the schedule. In a joint case, both debtors must make the same election. See section 2.08, infra, for further reading on the claiming of exemptions.

schedule C, election of exemptions

In completing Schedule C, each item of property claimed as exempt should be described sufficiently to insure the applicability of the exemption law to the property. If the property claimed as exempt is described in Schedule A/B, you may indicate which line it is in on Schedule A/B rather than duplicating the description. If a joint petition is being filed, the exemptions claimed by each debtor should be listed separately (see Exhibit 2-H).

schedule C, description of property

Complete lists of all property exempt under the federal bankruptcy exemptions (11 U.S.C. § 522(d)), under federal nonbankruptcy law, and under the law of each state are set forth in Appendix III in the back of this book. The property of the debtor as set forth in Schedule A/B should be checked against the applicable lists of exempt property to determine the debtor's exempt property. The value of the exemption claimed in the third column on Schedule C should be the amount allowed by the applicable exemption law or the current market value of the debtor's interest in the property, whichever is less. For example, if the debtor's equity in an automobile is $1,000 (e.g., a $4,000 vehicle that is subject to a $3,000 lien) and if the applicable exemption law permits a $1,500 motor vehicle exemption, the claimed exemption should be $1,000. For exempt personal property the value shown in the second column of Schedule C should be the estimated replacement value of the debtor's interest or equity in the property at the time of filing (i.e., the estimated replacement value of the property regardless of the exemption, but less any valid encumbrances against the property). See 11 U.S.C. § 522(a)(2).

schedule C, valuation of property, amount of exemption

Schedule D - Creditors Who Have Claims Secured by Property (Official Form 106D)

Use Exhibit 2-I at the end of this chapter as a guide in preparing Schedule D. All of the debtor's secured or partially-secured creditors should be listed on this schedule, including those whose claims may result from an executory contract or unexpired lease. Included here should be creditors holding mortgages, deeds of trust, statutory or judicial liens, garnishments and other lawful forms of security interests in real or personal property of the debtor. In community property states, secured community creditors should be included if the debtor is married, whether or not a joint petition is being filed. See section 2.17, infra, for a list of community property states. If the debtor has no secured debts, the box appearing near the top of Schedule D should be checked.

schedule D, creditors to be listed on

In completing Schedule D, the creditors should be listed in alphabetical order. The last four digits of the debtor's account number with each creditor should be listed. If a minor child is a creditor, do not list the child's name. See 11 U.S.C. § 112. Instead list, "a minor child" as the creditor and give the child's correct mailing address. If a party other than a spouse in a joint case is or may be liable with the debtor for the payment of a secured claim, an "X" should be typed in the appropriate location in the column marked "Codebtor". If a joint petition is being filed, indicate whether the husband, wife, both of them jointly, or, in community property states, their community property is liable for the claim by typing the appropriate letter in the column marked "Husband, Wife, Joint, or Community". If a claim is contingent, unliquidated, or disputed, the appropriate box(es) should be checked. The Instructions provide the following:

schedule D, preparation requirements

> "A claim is contingent if you are not obligated to pay it unless a particular event occurs after you file for bankruptcy. For example, if you cosigned someone else's note, you may not have to pay unless that other person later fails to repay the loan.

A claim is unliquidated if the amount of the debt cannot be readily determined, such as by referring to an agreement or by a simple computation. An unliquidated claim is one for which there may be a definite liability but where the value has not been set. For instance, if you were involved in a car accident, the victim may have an unliquidated claim against you because the amount of damages has not been determined.

A claim is disputed if you disagree about whether you owe the debt. For instance, if a bill collector demands payment for a bill you believe you already fully paid, you may describe the claim as disputed."

If a claim is only partially secured (i.e., if the amount of the claim exceeds the estimated value of the collateral), the estimated amount of the unsecured portion of the claim should appear in the column marked "Unsecured Portion, If Any".

Schedule E/F: Creditors Who Have Unsecured Claims (Official Form 106E/F)

Use Exhibit 2-J at the end of this chapter as a guide in preparing Schedule E/F. Schedule E/F consolidates information about priority and nonpriority unsecured claims into a single form. It replaces old forms 6E and 6F.

In Part 1, list all unsecured claims that are or may be entitled to priority of payment. Claims for domestic support obligations and tax claims are the most common types of unsecured priority claims. See 11 U.S.C. § 507(a) and section 2.19, infra, for a list of the types of priority claims in bankruptcy cases. The appropriate boxes should be checked to indicate the types of priority claims that are listed on the schedule. The claims must be listed separately by type of priority, and the types of priority claims listed on the schedule must be indicated by checking the appropriate boxes. Part 1 should be completed in substantially the same manner as that described above for Schedule D, except that the amount of the claim entitled to priority should be shown in the specified column. The type of priority for each claim should be checked. If the debtor has no unsecured priority debts of any type, the box at the beginning of Part 1 should be checked. It is especially important to list all qualifying tax claims and claims for domestic support obligations on Schedule E/F because these claims are also nondischargeable and it will be to the debtor's advantage if these claims are properly listed so that they can be paid, in part at least, by the trustee if there are funds in the estate.

Schedule E/F, preparation requirements

claims for domestic support obligations and taxes, importance of listing

In Part 2, list all general unsecured claims, including unsecured nonpriority claims resulting solely from executory contracts or unexpired leases (which should also be listed on Schedule G) and unsecured claims of codebtors and persons who have cosigned or guaranteed debts of the debtor. However, claims listed on Schedule D or Part 1 of Schedule E/F that are partially unsecured or partially without priority should not be repeated or duplicated on Part 2 of Schedule E/F. Accordingly, the unsecured portion of the claim of a partially-secured creditor should not be listed on Schedule E/F if the claim is listed on Schedule D.

Schedule E/F, creditors to be listed on

The creditors on Schedule E/F, Parts 1 and 2, should be listed alphabetically by surname or firm name to the extent feasible, with the name, mailing address and zip code shown. The last four digits of the debtor's account number, if any, with each creditor should also be listed. If the claim has been assigned, the name and address of the assignee should also be listed (see Exhibit 2-J). If a person other than a spouse in a joint case is or may also be liable for a particular debt, the appropriate box should be checked under the question "who incurred the debt?". If a particular claim is contingent, unliquidated, or disputed, the appropriate box should be checked (see information above for Schedule D for a definition of these types of claims). Only genuine or real disputes should be indicated, however, because a disputed claim may necessitate an additional court appearance for the debtor. If the debtor has no unsecured nonpriority debts, the box near the top of Part 2 should be checked.

Schedule E/F, preparation requirements

Part 2 asks you to indicate whether the debt is a nonpriority unsecured claim resulting from student loans, obligations arising out of a separation agreement or divorce that you did not report as priority claims, debts to pension or profit-sharing plans, and other similar debts, or other. You should fill out this information as some of these debts may be nondischargeable under 11 U.S.C. § 523(a)(8), (15) or (18) (i.e., student loan debts, property settlement debts, or debts for loans from retirement plans).

You should fill out and submit Part 3 if there are others to be notified about the bankruptcy, for a debt that was already listed in Parts 1 or 2; such as a collection agency trying to collect a debt you owe to someone else or if there are any additional creditors for any of the debts that listed in Parts 1 or 2. Part 4 asks for a total of all claims listed in Parts 1 and 2.

schedule F, amount of claim

The exact amount of each creditor's claim should be shown, if possible, so as to avoid the necessity of later responding to the trustee's inquiry should the creditor file a claim for a substantially different amount. It may be necessary to contact certain creditors to ascertain the exact amount of their claims. If the exact amount cannot be ascertained and an estimated amount is shown, an appropriate notation should be made on the schedule. In showing when the claim was incurred, the month and year is normally sufficient. If the claim has been assigned, the name and address of the assignee should be listed, unless a local rule provides otherwise.

assigned claim, how to list

unlisted or incorrectly listed creditor, dischargeability of debt owed to

For consumer debtors Schedule E/F is an especially important document because it contains most of the debts that the debtor wishes to discharge. It is important, therefore, that all unsecured creditors, including unsecured community creditors in community property states, be listed on this schedule and that their addresses be complete and accurate. Except in a "no asset" case, the claim of a creditor whose name is omitted from the schedule will not be discharged unless the creditor had notice or actual knowledge of the case in time to file a claim or, if necessary, a complaint to determine the dischargeability of the debt. See 11 U.S.C. § 523(a)(3). The debtor is required to make a good faith attempt to obtain the correct address of all creditors, and if a good-faith attempt is not made the claim of any incorrectly-listed creditor who fails to receive notice of the proceeding in time to file a claim may not be discharged. See In re Stone, 10 F. 3d 285 (5th Cir. 1999); In re Erb, 2012 WL 4682233 (Bank. N. D. Miss. 2012). However, if a debt is duly scheduled and the proper address of the creditor given, the creditor will be deemed to have received notice of the case and its claim will be discharged, even if the creditor failed to receive actual notice of the case. See, e.g., In re Alton, 837 F.2d 457, 460 (11th Cir. 1988); In re Rayborn, 307 B.R. 710 (Bankr. S.D. Ala. 2002). If an important creditor cannot be located, the feasibility of serving notice by publication under Bankruptcy Rule 2002(l) should be considered. For further reading on the dischargeability of debts owed to unlisted or improperly listed creditors, see Williamson, The Bankruptcy Issues Handbook, supra, Art. 1.12.

Schedule G - Executory Contracts and Unexpired Leases (Official Form 106G)

schedule G, parties to be listed on

Use Exhibit 2-K at the end of this chapter as a guide in preparing Schedule G. All executory contracts and unexpired leases of real or personal property to which the debtor is a party, including residential leases and timeshare interests, should be listed on this schedule, regardless of whether the debtor intends to continue performing his or her obligations under the contract or lease after the case is filed. If a minor child is a party to a listed contract or lease, the name of the child should not be listed and the phrase "a minor child" should be used instead. This form simply requires the debtor to identify the name and address of the other party to the contract or lease, and to state what the contract or lease deals with (it is a simplified version of the old Schedule D).

parties to contracts, listing of as creditors

If the debtor is or will upon rejection of the contract or lease become obligated to a party to an executory contract or unexpired lease, it is important that the party be listed as a creditor on the appropriate schedule (D, E/F depending on the status of the creditor under the contract or lease), because otherwise the creditor may not receive notice of the case and the debt might not be discharged. In the case of a lease, the type of property subject to the lease should be specified because leases of personal property or nonresidential real property must be assumed by the trustee within 60 days after the order for relief or the lease will be deemed rejected. See 11 U.S.C. § 365(d)(1).

executory contract, definition of

If the debtor has no executory contracts or unexpired leases, the appropriate box near the top of Schedule G should be checked. In determining whether the debtor is a party to an executory contract, it is important to understand the definition of an executory contract. An executory contract is a contract under which the obligations of both parties to the contract are unperformed to the extent that a failure of either party to complete its obligations under the contract would constitute a breach of contract sufficient to excuse performance by the other party. See In re Penn Traffic, 524 F.3d 373 (2nd Cir. 2008); In re Dean, 317 B.R. 482 (W. D. Pa. 2004). In other words, an executory contract is a contract under which performance remains due by both parties. Some examples of executory contracts and unexpired leases that will appear on Schedule G are: Residential leases (for example, a rental agreement for a place where you live or vacation, even if it is only a verbal or month-to-month arrangement); Service provider agreements (for example, contracts for cell phones and personal electronic devices); Internet and cable contracts; Vehicle leases; Supplier or service contracts (for example, contracts for lawn care or home alarm or security systems); Timeshare contracts or leases; Rent-to-own contracts; Employment contracts; Real estate listing agreements; Contracts to sell a residence, building, land, or other real property; Equipment leases; Leases for business or investment property; Supplier and service contracts for your business; Copyright and patent license agreements; and Development contracts. See Instructions on Bankruptcy Forms for Individuals.

Schedule H - Your Codebtors (Official Form 106H)

Use Exhibit 2-L at the end of this chapter as a guide in preparing Schedule H. Listed on this schedule should be the name and address of every person or entity, other than a spouse in a joint case, that is or may be liable with the debtor on any debt listed by the debtor in Schedules D, E/F, or G, including all guarantors or cosigners. In community property states, a married debtor filing a single petition should include the name and address of the nondebtor spouse on this schedule (all names used by the nondebtor spouse during the last six years should be listed). If there are no codebtors, the appropriate box should be checked.

schedule H, preparation requirements

Schedule I - Your Income (Official Form 106I)

Use Exhibit 2-M at the end of this chapter as a guide in preparing Schedule I. Much of the information listed on this schedule will have been gathered for purposes of completing the Statement of Current Income and Means Test Calculation (see above in this section) and the amounts appearing in both documents should be consistent. The column labeled "Spouse" should be completed if a joint petition is being filed and by a married debtor filing a single petition unless the spouses are separated. If the debtor has regular income from a business, profession or farm, a detailed statement describing the income should be attached to Schedule I. Again, the name of a minor child should not be stated.

schedule I, preparation requirements

Schedule J: Your Expenses (Official Forms 106J and 106J-2)

Use Exhibit 2-N at the end of this chapter as a guide in preparing Schedule J. As in Schedule I, much of the information needed for this schedule will have been gathered for purposes of completing the Statement of Current Income and Means Test Calculation (see Exhibit 2-C, infra, for Bankruptcy Worksheet) and amounts appearing in both documents should be consistent. If a joint petition is being filed and if the spouses maintain separate households, Debtor 2 must complete and include Schedule J-2: Expenses for Separate Household of Debtor 2 (Official Form 106J-2). If the debtor has regular expenses from the operation of a business, profession or farm, a separate statement describing such expenses should be prepared and attached to Schedule J.

schedule J, preparation requirements

Declaration About an Individual Debtor's Schedules (Official Form 106Dec)

Use Exhibit 2-O at the end of this chapter as a guide in preparing this document. The declaration is simple to complete and must be signed by the debtor or by both debtors if a joint petition is being filed. The form, which is to be signed by the debtor(s) and filed with the schedules, deletes the Declaration and Signature of Bankruptcy Petition Preparer (BPP).

Declaration to schedules, signatures required

Summary of Your Assets and Liabilities and Certain Statistical Info. (Off. Form 106Sum)

This document appears as Exhibit 2-P at the end of this chapter. There used to be two documents to complete, statistical information and a summary of schedules. This information is now all condensed to one document. The information required in the body of the document is self-explanatory and should be obtained from the appropriate schedules. Even though this document is completed last, it should appear as the first sheet of the schedules when filed with the court. Additionally, the clerk of the Bankruptcy Court is required to collect statistics regarding certain nondischargeable debts of consumer debtors. See 28 U.S.C. § 159. To aid the clerk in this function, individual consumer debtors are required in most districts to file a statistical summary sheet. Parts 1 through 3 have the debtor answer questions regarding assets, liabilities, income, and expenses. Part 4 collects certain statistical information for the courts.

summary of schedules

statistical summary

Statement of Financial Affairs for Individuals Filing for Bankruptcy (Official Form 107)

Use Exhibit 2-Q at the end of this chapter as a guide in preparing the statement of financial affairs. Unless the court orders otherwise, every chapter 7 debtor must file a statement of his or her financial affairs. See Bankruptcy Rule 1007(b)(1). In a joint case, both husband and wife should execute the statement of financial affairs. There are spaces on the new form for the information related to Debtor 1 and Debtor 2.

statement of financial affairs, filing requirements

Official Form 107 replaces the old Official Form 7, and is specifically for individuals filing for bankruptcy. The questions appearing in the statement of financial affairs are generally self-explanatory and each question should be answered completely. Each question should be answered by checking at least one of the boxes below the question. Most questions have yes/no answers, requiring additional details for a "yes" answer. If additional space is needed to fully answer a question, a separate sheet should be used. The separate sheet should be attached to the statement and identified with the name of the debtor, the case number (if one exists), and the number of the question being answered.

statement of financial affairs, preparation requirements

The debtor, or both debtors in a joint case, must sign the declaration on the last page of the statement of financial affairs. Debtors should be aware that making a false statement, concealing property, or obtaining money or property by fraud in connection with a bankruptcy case can result in fines up to $250,000, or imprisonment for up to 20 years, or both. 18 U.S.C. §§ 152, 1341, 1519, and 3571..

statement of financial affairs, signature requirements

Application for Individuals to Pay the Filing Fee in Installments (Official Form 103A)

Use Exhibit 2-R at the end of this chapter as a guide in preparing this document. Official Form 103A should be used for this document. Both the application and the order are simple and easy to complete. In completing the application, it should be remembered that the filing fee may be paid in up to four installments with the final installment payable not later than 120 days after the date of filing. See Bankruptcy Rule 1006(b)(2). For cause shown, the court may extend the time for any installment, provided that the last installment must be paid within 180 days after the date of filing. It should be noted that if the filing fee is being paid in installments, no further payments to the debtor's attorney may be made until the filing fee is paid in full. See Bankruptcy Rule 1006(b)(3).

application to pay filing fee in installments, preparation of

Application to Have the Chapter 7 Filing Fee Waived (Official Form 103B)

This application, which is Official Form 103B, must be completed and signed if the debtor is unable to pay the filing fee in installments and his or her total combined monthly income is less than 150% of the official poverty guideline last published by the U.S. Department of Health and Human Services (DHHS) applicable to the debtor's family size. See 28 U.S.C. § 1930(f)(1). Detailed information regarding the debtor's income, expenses, property, and payments to attorneys is required on this form. Use Exhibit 2-S at the end of this chapter as a guide in preparing this application.

application for waiver of filing fee, preparation of

Disclosure of Compensation of Attorney for Debtor (Director's Form 2030)

If a local form is not provided for this statement, use Director's Form 2030, a completed copy of which is set forth in Exhibit 2-A at the end of this chapter. See section 2.03, supra, for the preparation requirements of this statement. Unless otherwise directed by the court, this statement must be filed within 14 days after the date of filing in a voluntary case. See Bankruptcy Rule 2016(b). To avoid oversight, however, it is a good practice to file the statement with the petition when the case is filed. A copy of the attorney's disclosure statement should be retained by the attorney.

attorney's disclosure statement, preparation and filing requirements

Statement of Intention for Individuals Filing Under Chapter 7 (Official Form 108)

Use Exhibit 2-T at the end of this chapter as a guide in preparing this statement. Official Form 108 should be used for this statement. This statement is required by 11 U.S.C. § 521(a) and Bankruptcy Rule 1007(b)(2). A copy of the statement must be served on each creditor and lessor listed in the statement and on the trustee. A certificate of service should be filed with the statement. The statement of intention must be filed by the earlier of 30 days after the date of the filing of the petition or the date of the meeting of creditors, but it is often more convenient to file the statement with the petition. If two married people are filing together in a joint case, both are equally responsible for supplying correct information and both debtors must sign and date the form. If more space is needed, a separate sheet may be attached containing the debtor's name and case number (if known). See section 2.11, infra, for further reading on the preparation, service, and filing requirements of this statement.

statement of intention, preparation, service, and filing requirements

Notice Required by 11 U.S.C. § 342(b) (Director's Form 2010)

See Exhibit 2-U at the end of this chapter for a copy of the Notice Required by 11 U.S.C. § 342(b) for Individuals Filing for Bankruptcy (Director's Form 2010). Prior to the commencement of a chapter 7 case by an individual whose debts are primarily consumer debts, the clerk is required to give written notice to the individual indicating each chapter of title 11 under which the individual may file. See 11 U.S.C. § 342(b). This form is used to fulfill the clerk's statutory function. A local version of this form may be required, and the local rules should be checked in this regard.

clerk's notice to consumer debtor, requirement of

Declaration Regarding Electronic Filing.

This is a local form that must be filed in most districts if either the case or documents in the case are being filed electronically. The local form will be identical or similar to Exhibit 2-V at the end of this chapter. Use Exhibit 2-V at the end of this chapter as a guide in preparing this form. This form will not be needed if the case is not being filed electronically. See section 2.09, infra, for further reading on the need for and use of this document.

electronic filing declaration, preparation of

List of Names and Addresses of Persons to Receive Notices.

This list is required, usually in an electronic format to enable the Bankruptcy Noticing Center and the court to send the required notices in the case. This list should contain the names and addresses of all creditors, the debtor, the debtor's attorney, and all other parties entitled to receive notices in the case. Instructions on how to format the diskette or compact disk can often be found on the website of the local bankruptcy court. The local rules should be checked for additional requirements related to this list. The local rules should also be checked for additional documents or forms required to be filed in chapter 7 cases.

creditor matrix, preparation of

Certificate as to Credit Counseling.

This certificate is required by 11 U.S.C. § 109(h) and 521(b)(1). It must be completed by the debtor's budget and credit counseling agency and attached to the voluntary petition. See section 2.05, supra, for further reading on the credit counseling requirements in chapter 7 cases. A local form should be available for this certificate and the credit counseling agencies should have them.

credit counseling certificate, preparation of

2.08 Claiming Exemptions

federal bankruptcy exemptions, when applicable

A debtor may claim his or her exemptions from either of the following sources: (1) the property specified in 11 U.S.C. § 522(d) (i.e., the federal bankruptcy exemptions), unless precluded from doing so by state law, or (2) property that is exempt under federal law other than Section 522(d) or under applicable state or local law, and interests in property held by the debtor as a tenant by the entirety or as a joint tenant, to the extent exempt under nonbankruptcy law. See 11 U.S.C. § 522(b)(1). Thus, if state law precludes a debtor from using the federal bankruptcy exemptions, as is now the case in most states, then the debtor is limited to the exemptions described in (2) above. Lists of property that is exempt under the laws of each state, under the federal bankruptcy exemptions, and under federal nonbankruptcy law are set forth in Appendix III, in the back of this book.

state of domicile for exemption purposes, how to determine

If the debtor will be claiming his or her exemptions under state law, it is important to ascertain the debtor's state of domicile for exemption-claiming purposes. The debtor's state of domicile for exemption-claiming purposes is the state in which the debtor's domicile has been located for the 730 day period immediately preceding the date on which the bankruptcy case was filed. If the debtor's domicile has not been located in a single state for the entire 730 day period, the debtor's state of domicile for exemption-claiming purposes is the state in which the debtor's domicile was located for the 180 days immediately preceding the start of the 730 day period or for a longer portion of that 180 day period than in any other state. If the effect of these domiciliary requirements is to render the debtor ineligible for any exemption, the debtor may use the federal bankruptcy exemptions. See 11 U.S.C. § 522(b)(3)(A). If the debtor has not lived in the local state for the entire period of the previous 730 days, it is important to ascertain the debtor's whereabouts during the 180 day period described above so that the applicable exemption laws can be ascertained.

federal bankruptcy exemption, when applicable

The domicile rules described in the previous paragraph may also be applicable in determining whether the federal bankruptcy exemptions may be used by the debtor. For example, if the local state has opted out and does not permit its residents to use the federal bankruptcy exemption, if the debtor has not been domiciled in the local state for the entire 730 day period prior to filing, and if the laws of the state wherein the debtor was domiciled for the 180 day period prior to the 730 day period permit the use of the federal bankruptcy exemption, it appears that the debtor can use the federal bankruptcy exemptions, if desired. See 11 U.S.C. § 522(b)(2).

federal bankruptcy exemptions, use of in joint cases

If state law permits (i.e., does not preclude) the use of the federal bankruptcy exemptions, then the debtor may use either the federal bankruptcy exemptions or the nonbankruptcy federal and state exemptions, whichever are more favorable. The debtor must choose between the federal bankruptcy exemptions and the other exemptions, however, and may not use parts of each. If state law permits the use of the federal bankruptcy exemptions, the exemptions may be applied separately to each debtor in a joint case. See 11 U.S.C. § 522(m). In deciding whether to use the federal bankruptcy exemptions or the state exemption laws, it should be noted that the federal bankruptcy exemptions apply to any debtor and are not limited, as some state exemption laws are, to certain classes of debtors (such as heads of households).

joint case, choice of exemptions, procedure

In joint cases and in individual cases filed by debtors whose estates are administered jointly, both debtors must elect to exempt property either under the federal bankruptcy exemptions or under the state and nonbankruptcy federal exemption laws. The debtors must be given a reasonable period within which to choose the exemption laws to be used, but if they fail to choose the same laws, the federal bankruptcy exemptions will be applied to both debtors. See 11 U.S.C. § 522(b)(1), Bankruptcy Rule 1015(b), and section 2.05, supra.

schedule C, filing requirements, effect of failure to file

A debtor is required to list all property claimed as exempt in Schedule C. If a debtor fails to file a Schedule C or otherwise claim exemptions within the required period, a dependent of the debtor may file a list of exempt property within 30 days thereafter. See Bankruptcy Rule 4003(a) and 11 U.S.C. § 522(l), and see section 2.09, infra, for the Schedule C filing requirements. Because any exemptions not timely claimed by the debtor or dependent of the debtor may be deemed waived, it is important to list all exempt property on the Schedule C.

It is important to note that a debtor's tax-qualified retirement funds and IRAs are now exempt, regardless of whether the debtor claims his or her exemptions under the federal bankruptcy exemptions or under state law. Debtors who claim their exemptions under state law, whether by choice or because state law requires them to do so, may exempt retirement funds and IRAs that are qualified (i.e., tax-deferred) under the Internal Revenue Code regardless of whether these funds are exempt under state law. See 11 U.S.C. § 522(b)(4). Tax-qualified retirement funds and IRAs are also exempt under the federal bankruptcy exemptions. See 11 U.S.C. § 522(d)(12). However, there is a $1,362,800* exemption limit for most IRAs that is applicable to both statutes. See 11 U.S.C. § 522(n). To qualify for this exemption under either statute it will usually be necessary to show that the debtor's retirement funds or IRAs are in substantial compliance with the requirements of the Internal Revenue Code or that the failure to comply is not the fault of the debtor. See 11 U.S.C. § 522(b)(4)(B). It should also be noted that funds placed by the debtor in a qualified educational IRA or used to purchase tuition credits or certificates under a qualified state tuition program, while not exempt, are, within certain limitations, not includable in the debtor's bankruptcy estate. See 11 U.S.C. § 541(b). For in-depth reading on the treatment of retirement funds and IRAs in bankruptcy, see Williamson, The Bankruptcy Issues Handbook, supra, Art. 1.13.

retirement funds & IRAs, exemption of

If an exemption is allowed for "household goods", "tools of trade," or other vaguely defined term, most courts permit a broad construction of the term so as to encourage the debtor's rehabilitation. For example, the term "household goods" has been construed to include such items as furniture, stereo equipment, cameras, personal computers, and handguns (if used for personal protection). See In re Crawford, 226 B.R. 484 (Bankr. N.D. Ga. 1998); In re Mason, 254 B.R. 764 (Bankr. D. Idaho 2000); In re French, 177 B.R. 568 (Bankr. E. D. Tenn. 1995); but see In re Patterson, 825 F.2d 1140 (7th 1987) (applying narrow construction). The Bankruptcy Code contains a definition of the term "household goods," but the definition applies only to lien avoidance proceeding under section 522(f). See 11 U.S.C. § 522(f)(4). The term "tools of trade" includes items directly related to a business of the debtor, and has been construed to include the trucks, loader and fax machine of a home builder, but not to include the motor vehicle of a salesman, the breeding cattle of a farmer, or the tractor and trailer of truck driver. See In re Cordova, 394 B.R. 389 (Bankr. E. D. Va. 2008); In re Clifford, 222 B.R. 8 (Bankr. D. Conn. 1998); In re Gaydos, 441 B.R. 102 (N.D. Ohio 2010).

household goods, what constitutes

tools of trade, what constitutes

If a homestead or similar exemption is being claimed under state law, and if the law requires the exemption to be filed or recorded to be valid, the filing or recording requirements should be complied with before the chapter 7 petition is filed. The recorded or filed declaration of homestead, or other evidence of exemption, should be properly identified (by recording number and date) on Schedule C. The local rules should be checked for additional filing requirements, especially in connection with the claiming of homestead exemptions.

homestead exemption, recording requirements

If joint debtors must claim under a state homestead exemption law, if the homestead is owned jointly by the debtors, if their combined equity in the homestead exceeds the amount of the allowed exemption, and if local law permits the exemption to be claimed but once in joint case, it may be advantageous for only one spouse to file under chapter 7. Depending on the language of the state exemption statute, such a procedure may enable the filing spouse to report only one-half of the equity in the homestead as an asset in the case and still claim the full homestead exemption. It may then be possible for the other spouse to file under chapter 7 a few months later and again claim the full homestead exemption. The allowability of such a procedure under local law should be thoroughly checked before proceeding, however.

homestead exemption, jointly owned property

For debtors who claim their homestead exemption under state law there is a $189,050* cap on any increase in value of the exemption during the 1215 day period prior to filing if the debtor's domicile has changed during the 730 day period prior to filing. See 11 U.S.C. § 522(p)(1). There is also a fraud reduction imposed on the homestead exemption of debtors who claim their exemptions under state law and whose exemption was increased by reason of the disposition of nonexempt assets. See 11 U.S.C. § 522(o).

homestead exemption, limitations on

* Subject to increase on April 1, 2025.

waiver of exemptions, when not enforceable

It is common for a debtor to have waived one or more exemptions during the course of his or her financial transactions. Any waiver of exemptions should be checked, however, because many of these waivers are unenforceable in bankruptcy cases. A waiver of exemptions executed in favor of an unsecured creditor is unenforceable in a bankruptcy case with respect to the creditor's claim against exempt property. See 11 U.S.C. § 522(e). The debtor's right to set aside judicial liens and certain other security interests against exempt property under 11 U.S.C. § 522(f) is not affected by a waiver of exemptions (see section 2.12, infra). A waiver by the debtor of the right to set aside transfers of exempt property under 11 U.S.C. § 522(h) is unenforceable in a bankruptcy case. See 11 U.S.C. § 522(e).

transferred property, claiming exemptions on

A debtor may claim exemptions against previously transferred property that is recovered by the trustee, to the extent that the debtor could have exempted the property had it not been transferred, if the transfer of the property by the debtor was not voluntary and the debtor did not conceal the property, or if the debtor could have avoided the transfer under 11 U.S.C. § 522(f). See 11 U.S.C. § 522(g). If the trustee fails to act to recover property that the debtor could claim as exempt, the debtor may act to recover it and avoid liens against it. See 11 U.S.C. § 522(h),(i).

recovering involuntary transfers of exempt property under section 522(h), rules for

The debtor's right to recover or avoid liens against exempt property under Section 522(h) is an important right for many chapter 7 debtors. Exempt property (or an interest therein) lost by the debtor through wage garnishments, attachments, repossessions, homestead foreclosures and the filing of statutory or judgment liens may be recovered by the debtor under this Section. To be recoverable under Section 522(h), the transfer in question must have been involuntary or nonconsensual by the debtor, the existence of the transferred property must have been disclosed by the debtor, the transfer in question must be avoidable by the trustee, and the trustee must not have attempted to avoid the transfer. For an in-depth discussion on the extent to which a debtor may avoid involuntary transfers of exempt property under Section 522(h) of the Bankruptcy Code, see Williamson, The Bankruptcy Issues Handbook, supra, Art. 1.18.

after-acquired property, claiming exemptions on

The debtor is entitled to file a supplemental schedule claiming exemptions against property acquired within 180 days after the commencement of the case that is includible in the bankruptcy estate. See Bankruptcy Rule 1007(h), and section 2.11, infra. Finally, it should be noted that if a debtor intends to redeem exempt property under Section 722, the intention must be disclosed in the debtor's Statement of Intention. See section 2.11, infra, for further reading on statements of intention.

list of exempt property, filing objections to

Property claimed by the debtor as exempt is deemed exempt unless a timely objection is filed. See 11 U.S.C. § 522(l). A party in interest may file an objection to the debtor's list of exempt property, but the objection must be filed within 30 days after the conclusion of the meeting of creditors or within 30 days after the filing of any amendments to the list, whichever is later, except that an objection based on 11 U.S.C. § 522(q) may be filed at any time before the case is closed. The court may, for cause, extend the time for filing objections if, before the time to object expires, a party in interest files a request for an extension of time. See Bankruptcy Rule 4003(b)(1), (2). The Supreme Court has ruled that the 30 day period for filing objections to the debtor's list of exempt property is mandatory and that the exemptions claimed by the debtor must be granted if an objection or a request for an extension of time is not filed during that period, even if the claimed exemptions are clearly improper. See Taylor v. Freeland & Kronz, 503 U.S. 638, 112 S. Ct. 1644 (1992).

objections, value vs. item

In listing exemptions on Schedule C and asset values on Schedule A/B, the practitioner should be aware of the effect of the Supreme Court's ruling in Schwab v. Reilly, 130 S.Ct. 2652 (2010). In Schwab, the Court distinguished between claiming an exemption in an asset itself, and claiming an exemption in a dollar value of the asset. The Court ruled that under certain circumstances, a trustee need not object to a claimed exemption in order to preserve a claim to an asset, and may thereafter move to sell the asset and retain any excess proceeds where the asset is listed as exempt within specific statutory dollar limits, but in fact has a higher fair market value. If the client desires to retain the claimed asset itself, the true value of the asset should be listed in Schedule A/B, and exemption terms such as "100%", "unknown" or "to be determined" should be used on Schedule C. Using such terms places the trustee on notice that a timely objection must be filed, or the asset will be removed from the bankruptcy estate.

exemptions, types

After Schwab, there are now two different types of exemptions, with different obligations on a trustee or other interested party to object. If the governing statute allows an exemption the item itself (such as unmatured life insurance proceeds or social security benefits), the trustee need only object if the item claimed as exempt is not the same as the item allowed to be exempted. Alternatively, if the exemption is one defined by a specific dollar amount (such as a tools of the trade exemption), the trustee must object in a timely manner if the amount claimed as exempt exceeds the statutory monetary limit or if the debtor has demonstrated an intent to claim the entire value by claiming "100%", "unknown", or "to be determined". If the claimed exemption only enumerates a specific dollar amount, and the asset has a fair market value greater than the amount claimed as exempt, under Schwab v. Reilly the trustee need not object in order to preserve a claim to the asset for the estate and thereafter move to sell the asset.

objections to list of exempt property, procedure

Copies of the objection to the list of exempt property must be mailed to the trustee and to the person claiming the exemption (usually the debtor) and to the person's attorney. See Bankruptcy Rule 4003(b)(3). A notice of the time for filing objections to the debtor's list of exempt property is often contained in the notice of commencement of case. The objecting party has the burden of proving that the exemptions were not properly claimed, and the court, after a hearing on notice, must determine the issues presented by the objections. See Bankruptcy Rule 4003(c).

exempt property, liability of for debts after case

Unless the case is dismissed, the property claimed as exempt by the debtor is not liable, either during or after the case, for any debt of the debtor that arose, or is treated as having arisen, before the commencement of the case, except nondischargeable debts for taxes or domestic support obligations, debts secured by valid tax liens, debts secured by valid liens that are not avoided during the bankruptcy case, certain debts owed to a federal depository institutions regulatory agency, and debts for fraud in obtaining financial assistance from an institution of higher education. It should be noted that the debtor's exempt property is liable for domestic support obligations of the debtor after the bankruptcy case regardless of any provision of any nonbankruptcy law to the contrary. See 11 U.S.C. § 522(c).

CHAPTER TWO

PART C - FILING AND HANDLING A CHAPTER 7 CASE

2.09 FILING A CHAPTER 7 CASE – ELECTRONIC FILING

A chapter 7 case should be filed in a district in which the domicile, residence, principal place of business, or principal assets of the debtor have been located for 180 days immediately preceding the commencement of the case, or for a longer portion of such 180 day period than the domicile, residence, principal place of business, or principal assets were located in any other district. See 28 U.S.C. § 1408. Thus, a debtor who has resided in two districts during the 180 day period prior to the date of filing must have resided (or had a principal place of business or principal assets) in the local district for at least 91 days during that period in order to satisfy the venue requirements for filing in the local district.

venue requirements, chapter 7 case

If a chapter 7 case is commenced in an improper district, on the timely motion of a party in interest and after a hearing on notice to the debtor and other entities as directed by the court, the case may be dismissed or, if the court determines such to be in the interest of justice or for the convenience of the parties, transferred to another district. See 28 U.S.C. § 1406, 1412, and Bankruptcy Rule 1014(a)(2). If a chapter 7 case is filed in a proper district, the court may nevertheless order the case transferred to another district upon a finding that such a transfer is in the interest of justice or for the convenience of the parties. See 28 U.S.C. § 1412, and Bankruptcy Rule 1014(a)(1). If a timely motion is not filed, the right to object to venue may be deemed waived, as venue is not jurisdictional in bankruptcy cases. See In Re Potts, 724 F. 2d 47 (6th 1984); Advisory Committee's Notes to Bankruptcy Rule 1014. Motions relating to venue are core proceedings and may be heard and determined by a bankruptcy judge. See, e.g., In re Bavelis, 453 B.R. 832 (Bankr. S. D. Ohio 2011).

procedures when case filed in wrong district

If two or more cases by or against the same debtor are filed in different districts, the court in which the earlier case was commenced shall, upon the timely filing of a motion and after a hearing on notice, determine which case or cases shall proceed. Unless otherwise ordered by the court in which the earlier case was commenced, the proceedings in the other courts are stayed until the determination is made. See Bankruptcy Rule 1014(b).

two or more cases, same debtor, procedures

Unless otherwise provided in the local rules, only one copy of any petition, schedule, statement, list or other document that is either filed electronically or converted to an electronic format upon filing (i.e., scanned) need be filed. The local rules should be checked in this regard. If the local court has adopted the electronic case file and management system, only one copy of each bankruptcy form need be filed, even if the case is not filed electronically.

chapter 7 forms, number of copies

The total required filing fee in a chapter 7 case is $338 for either a single or a joint case. The $338 total filing fee consists of a $245 statutory filing fee, plus a $75 administrative fee and a $18 trustee surcharge. See 28 U.S.C. § 1930. The filing fee may be paid in full at the time of filing, may be paid in installments, or payment of the filing fee may be waived. The court may waive payment of the filing fee of an individual chapter 7 debtor if the court determines that the debtor is unable to pay the filing fee in installments and that the debtor's income is less than 150 percent of the official poverty line applicable to the debtor's family size. See 28 U.S.C. § 1930(f)(1). If the debtor does not qualify for waiver of the filing fee and cannot afford to pay the entire filing fee at the time of filing, the filing fee may be paid in up to four installments within the time limits set forth in Bankruptcy Rule 1006(b)(2) (120 days extendable to 180). It should be noted that if a chapter 7 case is filed electronically, the filing fee must be paid by charging a previously approved credit card of debtor's attorney, unless the filing fee is to be waived or paid in installments, in which case the appropriate application must be filed. See section 2.07, supra, for further reading on the preparation of these applications.

filing fee, amount, of

filing fee, waiver of

filing fee, method of payment in e-filed case

A voluntary chapter 7 case is commenced by filing a voluntary petition with the clerk of the bankruptcy court in the proper district and division. If a bankruptcy clerk has not been appointed in the district, the petition should

voluntary petition, where filed

be filed with the clerk of the district court. If the case is not being filed on an emergency basis, the schedules, statements, and other documents described in section 2.07, supra, should be filed with the petition.

emergency filing, procedure

If the debtor is in need of immediate bankruptcy relief and the case must be commenced before the schedules, statements, and other documents can be prepared, the case may be commenced by filing the petition accompanied by a list containing the names and addresses of all of the debtor's creditors. See Bankruptcy Rule 1007(a)(1). If the filing fee is not paid in full when the petition is filed, either an Application for Waiver of the Chapter 7 Filing Fee or an Application to Pay Filing Fee in Installments must also be prepared and filed with the petition. A certification under 11 U.S.C. § 109(h)(3) for a temporary exemption from the prefiling credit counseling requirement must also be prepared and filed. See Bankruptcy Rule 1007(b)(3). See section 2.05, supra, for further reading on this requirement.

schedules and statements, when filed

If not filed with the petition, the schedules and statements, other than the statement of intention and the certificate as to credit counseling and any debt repayment plans, must be filed within 14 days after the petition is filed. Any extension of the time for filing the schedules and statements may be granted by the court only on motion for cause shown and on notice to the United States trustee, the trustee, or other party as the court may direct. See Bankruptcy Rule 1007(c). A failure to file the schedules and statements within the required time constitutes grounds for dismissal of the case. See 11 U.S.C. § 707(a)(3). The filing requirements for the statement of intention are set forth in sections 2.07, supra, and 2.11, infra. See section 2.05, supra, for filing requirements of the certificate as to credit counseling and debt repayment plans.

notice of commencement of case

If it is important to deliver notice of the commencement of the case and of the automatic stay to certain creditors in advance of the mailing of the notice of commencement of case by the Bankruptcy Noticing Center, either a certified copy of the filed petition or a Certificate of Commencement of Case (Director's Form 2060) signed by the clerk may be used for this purpose. A letter or other written notice from the debtor's attorney containing the bankruptcy case number and the date and time of filing will also suffice in most cases.

Electronic Case Filing.

electronic case file and management system, general aspects

electronic case file system, requirements for use of

The Administrative Office of the United States Courts has established an electronic case file and management system for the U.S. Bankruptcy Courts. Under this system case files are maintained in an electronic format rather than in a paper format. This means that all court documents (with only limited exceptions for items such as bulky exhibits) must be either filed electronically or converted to an electronic format immediately upon filing via the electronic scanning of filed paper documents. To implement this system the bankruptcy court in each district has established a website through which bankruptcy documents may be filed electronically over the internet. This electronic case file and management system may be used by attorneys who have been given a password that will enable them to access the system. To obtain a password an attorney must complete a training session to acquaint the attorney (and staff members, if desired) with the electronic case file and management system.

electronic case file system, how to use

Upon the completion of training and the receipt of a password, an attorney may prepare bankruptcy forms and documents on the word processing program of his or her computer, convert or save them in a Portable Document Format (PDF) and file them via the internet with the court through its website. Scanned paper documents may also be saved in PDF and filed electronically in the same manner. The attorney may also access court files in this manner. Under this electronic system documents may be filed and court files accessed at any time of any day. To file a bankruptcy case electronically, an attorney must have an approved credit card on file in the clerk's office and the filing fees for all cases filed electronically by the attorney will be charged against the attorney's credit card.

electronic case file system, rules and requirements

Most bankruptcy courts have adopted rules and procedures governing electronic case filing and have posted them on its website. It is important to become aware of these requirements, both procedural and technical, because electronic case filing will soon become mandatory in most districts. The technical requirements for electronic case filing are the computer hardware, software and internet requirements. These requirements are usually posted on the local bankruptcy court's website. The attorney's computer and internet access systems must meet these requirements in order to participate in electronic case filing.

In most districts when a bankruptcy case is filed electronically, the debtor's attorney must file a written declaration with the court stating that the case has been filed electronically. This declaration must normally be filed within 5 days after the date of the electronic filing. The declaration must be signed by the debtor and by the debtor's attorney. This declaration is normally a local form and may be obtained either from the clerk's office or from the local bankruptcy court's website. A sample of such a declaration is set forth in Exhibit 2-V at the end of this chapter. The original copies of electronically filed documents must be retained by the filing attorney for a specified period. The length of this retention period varies from district to district and can usually be found on the local bankruptcy court's website or in the local rules. The retention period is usually a period that is not less than the maximum allowable time in which an appeal in the case may be completed.

electronic case filing, declaration requirements

electronic case filing, retention of original documents, time period

2.10 The Automatic Stay

Under 11 U.S.C. § 362(a) the filing of a bankruptcy petition by a consumer debtor operates as a stay, applicable to all entities, of the following acts or proceedings:

automatic stay, proceedings affected by

(1) the commencement or continuation, including the issuance or employment of process, of a judicial, administrative, or other proceeding against the debtor that was or could have been commenced before the filing of the petition, or to recover a claim against the debtor that arose before the commencement of the case;

(2) the enforcement against the debtor or the debtor's property of a judgment obtained before the commencement of the case;

(3) any act to obtain possession of property of or from the debtor's bankruptcy estate, or to exercise control over property of the estate;

(4) any act to create, perfect, or enforce any lien against property of the debtor's bankruptcy estate;

(5) any act to create, perfect, or enforce against property of the debtor, any lien to the extent that such lien secures a claim that arose before the commencement of the case;

(6) any act to collect, assess, or recover a claim against the debtor that arose before the commencement of the case;

(7) the setoff of any debt owing to the debtor that arose before the commencement of the case against any claim against the debtor; and

(8) the commencement or continuation of a U.S. Tax Court proceeding concerning the debtor for tax periods ending prior to the filing of the case.

Under 11 U.S.C. § 362(b) the filing of a bankruptcy petition by a typical consumer debtor does not stay the following acts or proceedings:

automatic stay, proceedings not affected by

(1) criminal proceedings against the debtor;

(2) the commencement or continuation of civil actions or proceedings to establish paternity, to establish or modify an order for domestic support obligations, concerning child custody or visitation, for the dissolution of a marriage (except for the division of estate property), or regarding domestic violence;

(3) the collection of a domestic support obligation from non-estate property;

(4) the withholding of income for payment of a domestic support obligation;

(5) the withholding, suspension or restriction of a driver's license or a professional or recreational license;

(6) the reporting of overdue child support to a consumer reporting agency;

(7) the interception of a tax refund;

(8) the enforcement of a medical obligation;

(9) acts taken to perfect interests in property to the extent that the trustee's rights and powers are subject to such perfection;

(10) the commencement or continuation of actions or proceedings of governmental units to enforce police or regulatory powers;

(11) certain acts by government units with respect to taxes (see 11 U.S.C. § 362(b)(9), (18));

(12) any act by a lessor under an expired lease of nonresidential real property to obtain possession of such property from the debtor;

(13) the presentment of a negotiable instrument and the giving of notice of and protesting dishonor of such an instrument;

(14) the withholding and collection of income from a debtor's wages for purposes of funding the debtor's qualified retirement plan;

(15) the enforcement of certain liens and security interests against real property of debtors who have filed prior bankruptcy cases [see 11 U.S.C. § 362(b)(20), (21)];

(16) eviction or unlawful detainer actions against the debtor where the lessor had obtained a prebankruptcy judgment of possession or where the debtor is endangering the property (see 11 U.S.C. § 362(b)(22), (23));

(17) transfers that are not avoidable under Code sections 544 and 549 (i.e., transfers that are not avoidable under state law and postpetition transfers); and

(18) the setoff of income tax refunds from prebankruptcy tax periods by governmental units.

automatic stay, duration of

Unless earlier terminated by the court, the automatic stay in a chapter 7 case continues as against property of the debtor's bankruptcy estate as long as the property remains in the estate. See 11 U.S.C. § 362(c)(1). Unless earlier terminated by the court, the stay of all other acts continues until the case is dismissed or closed, or until a discharge is granted or denied, whichever occurs first. See 11 U.S.C. § 362(c)(2). It should be noted that if a discharge is granted, it operates as an injunction against the commission of certain acts against the debtor and the debtor's property. See 11 U.S.C. § 524(a), and section 2.17, infra.

repeat filers, when automatic stay not effective

It is important to note that individual debtors who have been involved in recent bankruptcy cases are likely to be denied all or part of the protection normally given by the automatic stay. For example, the automatic stay will terminate 30 days after the date of filing of the present case if the debtor has had a prior chapter 7, 11 or 13 case pending or dismissed within one year prior to the date of filing of the present case, unless the prior case was dismissed and the present case filed as a result of 11 U.S.C. § 707(b). See 11 U.S.C. § 362(c)(3)(A). However, the debtor or other party in interest may keep the stay in effect by showing that the present case was filed in good faith. See 11 U.S.C. § 362(c)(3)(B). The automatic stay does not go into effect at all in the present case if the debtor has had two or more prior bankruptcy cases pending within the previous year that were dismissed. See 11 U.S.C. § 362(c)(4)(A). Again, a case that was refiled under 11 U.S.C. § 707(b) does not count as a prior case. The debtor or other party in interest may cause the stay in the present case to go into effect by showing that the present case was filed in good faith. See 11 U.S.C. § 362(c)(4)(B).

automatic stay, relief from

stay of order granting relief

Relief from the automatic stay may be granted by the court for cause upon the motion of an aggrieved party, after notice and a hearing. See 11 U.S.C. § 362(d), Bankruptcy Rule 4001(a)(1). Motions for relief from the stay filed by secured creditors seeking to reclaim or foreclose on their collateral is the most common type of relief from the stay sought in chapter 7 consumer cases. Ex parte relief from the automatic stay may also be granted upon a showing of immediate and irreparable damage to the moving party. See Bankruptcy Rule 4001(a)(2) and 11 U.S.C. § 362(f). It should be noted, however, that an order granting relief from the automatic stay (other than an order granting ex parte relief) is stayed for 14 days after the entry of the order, unless the court orders otherwise. See Bankruptcy Rule 4001(a)(3). For further reading on the handling of motions for relief from the automatic stay, see Williamson, The Attorney's Handbook on Small Business Reorganization Under Chapter 11, 9th Ed., 2013, section 4.01.

relief from stay, right of debtor to obtain, filing fee

In chapter 7 consumer cases, secured creditors often seek to reclaim or foreclose on their collateral. To do this, they must file a motion for relief from the automatic stay under Bankruptcy Rules 4001(a) and 9014 and pay a filing fee. If the secured property is exempt or abandoned property which the debtor has a right to redeem under 11 U.S.C. § § 722, exempt property against which the debtor may set aside a lien or security interest under 11 U.S.C. § 522(f), or exempt property in which the creditor's security interest has not been perfected, the debtor should oppose the motion for relief from stay. See section 2.12, infra, for further reading on the Section 722 and Section 522(f) rights of the debtor. If the secured property has little market value but is useful or of value to the debtor, it may be possible to negotiate a cash settlement in lieu of possession with a creditor with a valid security interest.

secured property, duties of debtor

If the debtor has an interest or equity in property that is sought to be reclaimed or foreclosed on by the creditor, notice of the motion for relief from the stay must be served on the debtor and the debtor's attorney. See Bankruptcy Rule 9014. However, if the property sought to be reclaimed is nonexempt property and has not been abandoned by the trustee, the motion for relief will normally involve the debtor only to the extent that the debtor must be advised of the outcome of the motion so as to know whether to turn the property over to the trustee or the creditor. Secured property should not be turned over to a creditor unless and until an order to that effect has been issued.

personal property, termination of stay as to

The automatic stay terminates with respect to personal property of the estate or of the debtor that is subject to a valid purchase money security interest if the debtor fails to either reaffirm the debt or redeem the property under Code section 722 within 45 days after the first meeting of creditors. If the debtor fails to act within this 45 day period, the property is no longer property of the estate and the creditor may take whatever action as to the property as is permitted under nonbankruptcy law, unless the court determines on the motion of the trustee filed before the expiration of such 45 day period, and after notice and a hearing, that the property is of consequential value or benefit to the estate, orders appropriate adequate protection of the creditor's interest, and orders the debtor to deliver any collateral in the debtor's possession to the trustee. See 11 U.S.C. § 521(a)(6).

eviction of debtor for nonpayment of rent, effect of stay on

The automatic stay does not stay the continuation of an eviction, unlawful detainer, or similar action for nonpayment of rent against the debtor by a lessor of residential property in which the debtor resides as a tenant under a lease or rental agreement if the lessor had obtained a judgment of possession against the debtor prior to the filing of the bankruptcy case. See 11 U.S.C. § 362(b)(22). However, the debtor can keep the stay in effect for 30 days by filing with the bankruptcy petition and serving on the lessor a sworn certification that under nonbankruptcy law the debtor is permitted to cure the monetary default that gave rise to the judgment of possession and by depositing with the clerk of the bankruptcy court an amount equal to any rent that would become due during the 30 day period after the filing of the bankruptcy case. See 11 U.S.C. § 362(l)(1). If the debtor, during the 30 day period, files with the court and serves on the lessor a further sworn certification that the debtor has cured the entire default, the stay will be permanently reinstated against the lessor unless the lessor files an objection to the certification, in which case the court must hold a hearing on the matter within 10 days. See 11 U.S.C. § 362(l)(2)(3). See 11 U.S.C. § 362(l)(4), (5) for a full description of the proceedings after the hearing.

eviction of debtor for property endangerment or drug use, effect of stay on

The automatic stay also does not stay an eviction proceeding against the debtor by a lessor of residential property where the eviction action is based on endangerment of the property or the illegal use of controlled substances on the property, if the lessor files with the court and serves on the debtor a sworn certification stating either that an eviction action has been filed by the lessor or that the debtor has, during the 30 day period prior to the bankruptcy filing, either endangered the property or illegally allowed the use of a controlled substance on the property. See 11 U.S.C. § 362(b)(23). The stay then terminates against the lessor 15 days after the filing of the certification unless the debtor files an objection to the certification , in which case the court must hold a hearing on the matter within 10 days. See 11 U.S.C. § 362(m)(1), (2). See 11 U.S.C. § 362(m)(2), (3) for a full description of the proceedings after the hearing.

violation of automatic stay, damages for

Creditor action in violation of the automatic stay is voidable at the request of the trustee or the debtor. See Matter of Lee, 35 B.R. 452. An individual debtor injured by a willful violation of the automatic stay may recover actual damages, including costs and attorney's fees, from the party violating the stay. Punitive damages may also be recovered when appropriate. See 11 U.S.C. § 362(h). Damages may be recovered under Section 362(h) if the creditor knew of the stay and its actions in violating the stay were intentionally performed. It need not be shown that the creditor actually intended to violate the stay. For further reading on the recovery of damages for violations of the automatic stay, see Williamson, The Bankruptcy Issues Handbook, supra, Art. 1.15.

automatic stay, effect on codebtors

It should be understood that in a chapter 7 case the automatic stay applies only to acts against the debtor and the debtor's property. It does not protect cosigners, guarantors or other codebtors. Consequently, the automatic stay in a chapter 7 case does not prevent a creditor from collecting a dischargeable debt from a guarantor or other codebtor of the debtor. See Browning Seed, Inc. v. Bayles, 812 F. 2d 999 (5th Cir., 1987). It also does not prevent a creditor from proceeding against property in which the debtor has no title or interest, even if the property secures a dischargeable debt of the debtor. See In Re Fairfield Group Partnership, 69 B.R. 318 (Bank. E. D. Tenn. 1987). However, if unusual circumstances exist wherein liability may be imposed on the debtor as a result of threatened action against another person, such as a person to whom the debtor is a guarantor, the stay may be extended by the court to proceedings against that person. See In Re Family Health Services, Inc., 105 B.R. 937 (Bankr. C. D. Cal. 1989);Hittle v. City of Stockton, 2012 WL 38886099 (Dist. E. D. Cal. Sep. 6, 2012).

2.11 Duties of the Debtor

duties of debtor in chapter 7 case

The duties of the debtor in a typical chapter 7 case include the following:

(1) Within 180 days prior to the filing of the bankruptcy case, the debtor must receive from an approved nonprofit budget and credit counseling agency an individual or group briefing and must file with the bankruptcy petition a certificate from the agency describing the services provided. A copy of any debt repayment plan prepared for the debtor by the agency must also be filed with the bankruptcy petition. See 11 U.S.C. § 109(h), 521(b), Bankruptcy Rule 1007(b)(3), and section 2.05, supra.

(2) The debtor must file an itemized statement of monthly net income and, unless exempt therefrom, submit to means testing to determine the debtor's eligibility for relief under chapter 7. See 11 U.S.C. § 521(a)(1)(B)(v) and section 2.07, supra.

(3) Unless the court orders otherwise, the debtor must file schedules of assets and liabilities, a schedule of current income and current expenditures, a schedule of executory contracts and unexpired leases, a statement of financial affairs, copies of all payment advices or other evidence of payment from the debtor's employer received within 60 days prior to the date of filing, a certificate from the debtor's attorney indicating that the debtor has been given the notice required under 11 U.S.C. § 342(b), and a statement disclosing any reasonably anticipated increase in income or expenditures over the 12 month period after the date of filing of the bankruptcy case. See Bankruptcy Rule 1007(b) and 11 U.S.C. § 521(a)(1)(A), (B). These documents are usually filed with the petition in consumer cases. If not, they must be filed within the times prescribed by Bankruptcy Rule 1007(c). See section 2.07, supra, for further reading.

(4) At least 7 days prior to the first date set for the meeting of creditors the debtor must give the trustee and any creditor, who so requests, a copy of the debtor's most recent Federal income tax return or a transcript thereof or a written statement that such documentation either does not exist or is not in the debtor's possession. See 11 U.S.C. § 521(e)(2)(A), Bankruptcy Rule 4002(b)(3), (4), and section 2.13, infra. The case is subject to dismissal if this duty is not timely performed. See 11 U.S.C. § 521(e)(2)(B) and section 2.20, infra.

(5) If the debtor has debts secured by property of the bankruptcy estate, the debtor must file within the required period a statement of the debtor's intention with respect to such property and carry out the specified intentions within the required period. See 11 U.S.C. § 521(a)(2) and Bankruptcy Rule 1007(b)(2). The Statement of Intention is discussed below in this section.

duties of debtor, list of

(6) The debtor must attend the meeting of creditors and submit to an examination and must bring to the meeting a picture identification issued by a governmental unit or other personal identifying information, evidence of his or her social security number (or a written statement that such documentation does not exist), evidence of the debtor's present income (such as his or her most recent pay stub), statements of each of the debtor's depository and investment accounts (unless the trustee or United States trustee instructs otherwise), and documentation of the debtor's monthly expenses listed in the Statement of Current Monthly Income and Means Test Calculation previously filed by the debtor in the case. See 11 U.S.C. § 343, Bankruptcy Rule 4002(a)(1), (b)(1), (2) and section 2.13, infra.

(7) The debtor must file with the court a record of any interest that the debtor has in an educational IRA or under a qualified State tuition program. See 11 U.S.C. § 521(c) and Bankruptcy Rule 1007(b)(1)(F). These interests are listed in Schedule B. See section 2.07, supra.

(8) The debtor must attend the hearing on any complaint filed objecting to the debtor's discharge and must testify if called as a witness. See Bankruptcy Rule 4002(a)(2) and section 2.17, infra.

(9) If a schedule of property has not been filed, the debtor must immediately inform the trustee in writing of the location of any real property in which the debtor has an interest and of the name and address of every person holding money or property subject to the debtor's withdrawal or order. See Bankruptcy Rule 4002(a)(3).

(10) The debtor must surrender to the trustee all property of the bankruptcy estate and any recorded information, including books, documents, records, and papers, relating to such property. See 11 U.S.C. § 521(a)(4).

(11) The debtor must relinquish possession of any personal property that constitutes valid security for the purchase price thereof, unless the debtor, within 45 days after the first meeting of creditors, either reaffirms the debt or redeems the property under Code section 722. See 11 U.S.C. § 521(a)(6) and section 2.10, supra.

duties of debtor, list of

(12) The debtor must cooperate with the trustee to the extent necessary to enable the trustee to perform his or her duties. See 11 U.S.C. § 521(a)(3) and Bankruptcy Rule 4002(a)(4).

(13) After the filing of the case and prior to receiving a discharge, the debtor must attend and complete an instructional course on personal financial management and file with the court a statement regarding completion of the course. See 11 U.S.C. § 727(a)(11), Bankruptcy Rule 1007(b)(7), and section 2.05, supra.

(14) The debtor must appear at the discharge hearing, if one is held, and at the reaffirmation hearing, if one is held, and present the required statement at the hearing. See 11 U.S.C. § 521(a)(5), 524(d), Bankruptcy Rule 4008, and section 2.18, infra.

(15) Within 14 days of acquiring knowledge thereof, the debtor must file a supplemental schedule with respect to any property that the debtor acquires or becomes entitled to acquire, within 180 days after the filing of the petition, by bequest, devise or inheritance, as a result of a divorce or property settlement agreement with the debtor's spouse, or as a beneficiary of a life insurance policy or death benefit plan. This duty continues even if the case is closed. See Bankruptcy Rule 1007(h), 11 U.S.C. § 541(a)(5), and section 2.15, infra.

(16) Unless payment of the filing fee was waived by the court, the debtor must pay the balance of the filing fee, if any, that was not paid when the petition was filed. See 28 U.S.C. § 1930(a) and Bankruptcy Rule 1017(b). Otherwise the case will be dismissed. See 11 U.S.C. § 707(a) and section 2.20, infra.

(17) If so requested by the court, the United States trustee or a party in interest, the debtor must file with the court copies of all Federal income tax returns that become due while the case is pending, including any delinquent returns and amendments to prior returns. This duty is discussed below in this section. See 11 U.S.C. § 521(f).

(18) The debtor must file with the appropriate taxing authority all tax returns that become due after the commencement of the case or obtain an extension of the due date for the filing thereof. Otherwise the case may be dismissed. See 11 U.S.C. § 521(j) and section 2.20, infra.

(19) The debtor must file a statement with the court showing any change of the debtor's address. See Bankruptcy Rule 4002(a)(5).

(20) The debtor must comply with all lawful orders of the bankruptcy court. See 11 U.S.C. § 727(a)(6),(d)(3).

The debtor should be advised of these duties, which, of course, do not end with the filing of the statements and schedules, nor with the meeting of creditors, nor even with the issuance of a chapter 7 discharge. A failure of the debtor to perform the required duties may result in the dismissal of the case or a denial or revocation of the debtor's discharge. See sections 2.17 and 2.20, infra. While a failure to keep the court advised of the debtor's current mailing address may not in itself constitute sufficient grounds for dismissal of the case or a denial or revocation of the debtor's discharge, it may result in the failure of the debtor to obey a court order or cooperate with the trustee, because communications with the debtor are normally carried out by mail. The local rules may contain additional duties for a chapter 7 debtor, and they should be checked in this regard.

duties of debtor, effect of failure to perform

incorrect address of debtor, effect of

If the debtor's schedules of assets and liabilities include debts secured by property of the bankruptcy estate, the debtor must file with the clerk a written statement of the debtor's intention with respect to the retention or surrender of the secured property, specifying whether the debtor intends to redeem the property from the lien, reaffirm the debt secured by the property, claim the property as exempt, or surrender the property. See 11 U.S.C. § 521(a)(2). Property of the bankruptcy estate is generally nonexempt unsecured property owned by the debtor prior

statement of intention, when required

to the case. See 11 U.S.C. § 541(a) and section 2.15, infra, for further reading on property of the estate.

statement of intention, filing and service requirements

The debtor must file a statement of intention using Official Form 108 within 30 days after the date of filing of the chapter 7 petition or by the date of the meeting of creditors, whichever is earlier, unless the court, for cause and within such period, grants additional time within which to file the statement. See 11 U.S.C. § 521(a)(2). A copy of the statement of intention must be served on the trustee and on the creditors named in the statement on or before the filing of the statement. See Bankruptcy Rule 1007(b)(2). Unless the local rules provided otherwise, the statement of intention may be served on the trustee and creditors by mail, in which event an appropriate certificate of service by mail should be filed with the statement. A sample Statement of Intention is set forth in Exhibit 2-T, at the end of this chapter.

performance of intentions, time requirements

The debtor is required to perform the intentions with respect to secured property as specified in the statement of intention within 30 days after the first date set for the meeting of creditors, unless the court, for cause and within the 30 day period, grants additional time. See 11 U.S.C. § 521(a)(2). Amendments to the statement of intention are governed by Bankruptcy Rule 1009(b), which provides that the statement may be amended by the debtor at any time before the expiration of the time for performing the intentions and that notice of any amendment must be given to the trustee and any entity affected thereby.

statement of intention, effect of failure to file or carry out

For debtors with debts secured by property of the bankruptcy estate, the filing of a statement of intention, as well as the carrying out of such intentions, constitutes an important aspect of a chapter 7 case. If the statement of intention is not timely and properly filed or if the debtor's intentions as set forth in the statement are not timely and properly carried out by the debtor, the debtor may lose property that he or she would otherwise be entitled to retain because the automatic stay is terminated with respect to secured personal property of the estate or of the debtor and such property is no longer property of the estate if the debtor fails to (1) file the statement of intention within the required period, (2) adequately indicate in the statement what the debtor's intentions are with respect to the secured property, or (3) take the action specified in the statement within the required period. See 11 U.S.C. § 362(h)(1). If the debtor fails to perform any of these three functions with respect to property that is subject to the statement of intention, the secured creditor will be free to repossess the property or otherwise exercise its nonbankruptcy rights regarding the property without the necessity of seeking relief from the automatic stay.

Federal income tax returns, filing of with court

At the request of the court, the United States Trustee, or a party in interest in a case under chapter 7, 11 or 13, an individual debtor must, at the same time filed with the taxing authority, file with the court copies or transcripts of the following Federal income tax documents: (1) each return required under applicable law for each tax year of the debtor that ends while the case is pending, (2) each return required under applicable law that had not been filed as of the date of the commencement of the case and that was subsequently filed for any tax year of the debtor that ended within 3 years prior to the commencement of the case, and (3) each amendment to any of these returns. See 11 U.S.C. § 521(f)(1)-(3). It should be noted that these filing requirements are in addition to the requirements under 11 U.S.C. § 521(e)(2)(A) and Bankruptcy Rule 4002(b)(3), (4), which are described in paragraph (4) on the first page of this section and discussed in section 2.20, infra.

contempt proceedings, bankruptcy judge

The debtor's conduct should be appropriate during any court appearance, as bankruptcy judges have contempt powers. Contempt committed in the presence of a bankruptcy judge may be determined summarily by the bankruptcy judge, and the order of contempt must recite the facts, be signed by the bankruptcy judge, and be entered of record. See Bankruptcy Rule 9020(a). Other contempt committed in the case may be determined by the bankruptcy judge only after a hearing on notice. See Bankruptcy Rule 9020(b). An order of contempt entered by a bankruptcy judge is effective 14 days after a copy thereof is served on the person named in the order unless an objection is filed, in which case the order must be reviewed by the district court under Bankruptcy Rule 9033. See Bankruptcy Rule 9020(c).

2.12 Rights of the Debtor

The rights of a debtor in a chapter 7 case include the following: rights of debtor in chapter 7 case

(1) The right to redeem certain exempt or abandoned property from liens. See 11 U.S.C. § 722 and 11 U.S.C. § 506(d). This right is discussed below in this section.

(2) The right to avoid or set aside (a) judicial liens against exempt property, (b) nonpossessory, nonpurchase money security interests against certain exempt personal property, and (c) unsecured liens. See 11 U.S.C. § 522(f) and 11 U.S.C. § 506(d). This right is discussed below in this section.

(3) The right to continued service from a utility company if a debt owed by the debtor to the utility for service rendered before the commencement of a chapter 7 case is not paid when due (i.e., is discharged). To retain this right, however, the debtor must, within 20 days after the date of the filing of the case, furnish adequate assurance of payment for future services in the form of a deposit or other security, the amount of which may be modified by the court if so requested. See 11 U.S.C. § 366. For an in-depth discussion on the extent to which a debtor's right to utility service is protected by 11 U.S.C. § 366, see Williamson, The Bankruptcy Issues Handbook, supra, Art. 1.04. utility service, debtors rights to

(4) The right to protection against discriminatory treatment as to employment by both private employers and governmental units, and as to the granting of licenses, permits, student loans, and certain other grants or acts by governmental units, solely on account of the filing of a chapter 7 case and certain matters related thereto. See 11 U.S.C. § 525. This right is discussed below in this section.

(5) The right to the protection provided by the automatic stay, unless the stay is terminated or does not go into effect with respect to the debtor or relief from the stay is granted by the court. See 11 U.S.C. § 362, Bankruptcy Rule 4001, and section 2.10, supra.

(6) The right to exclude from the bankruptcy estate property claimed as exempt under the applicable exemption laws, unless the exemption is lawfully waived. See 11 U.S.C. § 522(b), Bankruptcy Rule 4003, and section 2.08, supra.

(7) The right to a chapter 7 discharge, unless that right is lawfully waived or is denied or revoked by the court. See 11 U.S.C. § 727, Bankruptcy Rule 4004, and section 2.17, infra.

(8) The right to the discharge of certain debts unless a complaint to determine their dischargeability is timely filed. See 11 U.S.C. § 523(c), Bankruptcy Rule 4007(c), and section 2.17, infra.

(9) The right to file a complaint to determine the dischargeability of any debt at any time, even after the case has been closed. See Bankruptcy Rule 4007(b) and section 2.17, infra.

(10) The right to certain advisements by the debtor's attorney, the court, and the trustee regarding the reaffirmation of dischargeable debts. See 11 U.S.C. § 341(d), 524(d), and section 2.18, infra.

(11) The right to a written contract and certain notices and disclosures from the debtor's attorney. See 11 U.S.C. § 526, 527 and section 2.03, supra.

11 U.S.C. § 525 protects debtors from three types of discrimination: (1) discrimination by governmental units with respect to employment and with respect to the granting of licenses, permits, franchises and similar grants; (2) discrimination by private employers with respect to employment; and (3) discrimination with respect to the making or insuring of student loans. It has been held that the suspension of a debtor's driver's license by the state solely because of the nonpayment of a dischargeable debt is a violation of Section 525. See In Re Taylor, 27 B.R. 83. Section 525 also prohibits private employers from discriminating against debtors with respect to promotions and advancements as well as termination. For an in-depth discussion on the extent to which a debtor is protected from discrimination by Section 525 of the Bankruptcy Code and of the debtor's remedies for violations of Section 525, see Williamson, The Bankruptcy Issues Handbook, supra, Art. 1.03. discriminatory treatment, debtor's protection from

redemption of personal property under section 722

Under 11 U.S.C. § 722 the debtor may redeem tangible personal property intended primarily for personal, family, or household use from liens securing dischargeable consumer debts, if such property is exempt to the debtor or has been abandoned by the trustee, by paying to the lien holder the amount of the allowed secured claim secured by such lien. Further, any waiver by the debtor of this redemption right is void. A consumer debt is defined as a debt incurred by an individual primarily for a personal, family, or household purpose. See 11 U.S.C. § 101(8). A claim is deemed secured only to the extent of the value of the claimant's interest in the secured property (the amount of which cannot exceed the value of the property), and the balance of the claim, if any, is deemed unsecured. See 11 U.S.C. § 506(a). In most cases, therefore, the debtor may redeem exempt or abandoned personal property by paying to the creditor an amount equal to the value of the secured property as agreed upon by the parties or determined by the court, regardless of the amount of the underlying debt.

consumer debt, definition of

section 722 redemption, necessity of filing statement of intention

In order to redeem property under Section 722, the debtor must, within the required period, file and serve on the appropriate parties a statement of intention stating that the debtor intends to redeem the specified property under Section 722. Otherwise, the debtor may be precluded from redeeming the property. Further, it will be necessary for the debtor to carry out the redemption within 30 days after the first date set for the meeting of creditors, unless the court grants additional time. See 11 U.S.C. § 521(2). See sections 2.07 and 2.11, supra, for further reading on the preparation and filing requirements of the statement of intention.

section 722 redemption, when useful

Section 722 may be useful to the debtor in situations where the amount of the indebtedness greatly exceeds the market value of the secured property or if the property in question is of considerable value to the debtor but has little market value. The redemption of the debtor's furniture, appliances, and automobile can often be implemented under Section 722, frequently at a fraction of the outstanding indebtedness. The redemption of property under Section 722 may, at times, be achieved through negotiations with the creditor, often pursuant to an agreement by the debtor to reaffirm a portion of the debt. If court approval is required to enforce a Section 722 redemption, a lump sum payment by the debtor will be required because installment payments are not permitted under Section 722.

section 722 redemption, method of payment

section 722 redemption, motions, procedure

If a negotiated redemption is not feasible, a motion to redeem tangible personal property under Section 722 must be filed pursuant to Bankruptcy Rule 6008. The motion should request the court to authorize the redemption of the property and, if not previously determined, to determine the value of the creditor's allowed secured claim secured by such property. A sample of such a motion is set forth in Exhibit 2-W at the end of this chapter. At a hearing on a Rule 6008 motion, the debtor, as the owner of the property, is normally permitted to testify as to the value of the property. See Rule 701 of the Federal Rules of Evidence and the cases cited thereunder. In order to lend credibility to the debtor's testimony, he or she should be prepared to state the price paid for the property, its present condition, and when and from whom it was purchased or otherwise acquired. Recent photographs of the property may also be helpful.

proof of claim, when to object

If, prior to the hearing, the creditor files a proof of claim alleging an excessive value for the secured property, it may be necessary to file an objection to the allowance of the claim in order to preserve the debtor's right to dispute the amount of the claim. See 11 U.S.C. § 502(a) and Bankruptcy Rules 3001(f) and 3007. An objection to the allowance of the claim may be incorporated in the Rule 6008 motion, unless the local rules provide otherwise. In any event, the local rules should be checked for additional procedural requirements applicable to motions under Bankruptcy Rule 6008.

section 722 redemption, abandoned property

It should be remembered that property does not necessarily have to be exempt to be redeemable under Section 722. Qualifying property may also be redeemed if it has been abandoned by the trustee. If the property has little market value but is of value to the debtor, the trustee may be persuaded to abandon it by the payment of a token amount. If the trustee unreasonably refuses to abandon such property, a motion to compel its abandonment may be filed under Bankruptcy Rule 6007(b). See 11 U.S.C. § 554(b). A fee is charged for filing such a motion. For an in-depth discussion on the extent of a debtor's right to redeem property under Section 722 of the Bankruptcy Code, see Williamson, The Bankruptcy Issues Handbook, supra, Art. 2.03.

11 U.S.C. § 522(f)(1) provides that notwithstanding any waiver of exemptions, the debtor may avoid the fixing of a lien on an interest of the debtor in property, to the extent that the lien impairs an exemption to which the debtor would have been entitled, if the lien is a judicial lien (other than a judicial lien that secures a domestic support obligation) or a nonpossessory, nonpurchase-money security interest in any of the following property: (1) household furnishings, household goods, wearing apparel, appliances, books, animals, crops, musical instruments, or jewelry, held primarily for the personal, family, or household use of the debtor or a dependent of the debtor, (2) implements, professional books, or tools of the trade of the debtor or a dependent of the debtor, or (3) professionally prescribed health aids of the debtor or a dependent of the debtor. Thus, under section 522(f) the debtor may set aside most judicial liens against exempt real or personal property of any type and nonpurchase-money liens against the three classes of property described above if the property is exempt and not in the possession of the secured creditor.

avoiding liens under section 522(f), general aspects

As indicated above, under section 522(f) the debtor may not avoid a lien that secures a domestic support obligation. See 11 U.S.C. § 101(14A) for the definition of a domestic support obligation. Under this definition, the general rule is that while judicial liens securing domestic support obligations that have been assigned to or are owned or recoverable by governmental units or that have been voluntarily assigned to a nongovernmental entity for the purpose of collection may not be avoided under section 522(f), judicial liens securing domestic support obligations that have been involuntarily assigned to a nongovernmental entity or voluntarily assigned to a nongovernmental entity for a purpose other than collection may be avoided under section 522(f).

judicial liens for domestic support obligations, avoidability of under section 522(f)

For purposes of Section 522(f), a lien is deemed to impair a debtor's exemption to the extent that the sum of the lien in question plus the sum of all other valid liens against the property (voidable liens are not counted) plus the amount of the exemption that the debtor could claim if there were no liens against the property exceeds the value of the debtor's interest in the property if there were no liens. See 11 U.S.C. § 522(f)(2)(A). This statute, it should be noted, does not apply to mortgage foreclosure liens. See 11 U.S.C. § 522(f)(2)(C). See 11 U.S.C. § 522(f)(4) for an expansive definition of the term "household goods" for purposes of section 522(f).

impairment of exemption, what constitutes

household goods, definition of

11 U.S.C. § 522(f)(3) contains a limited exception to a debtor's ability to avoid nonpossessory, nonpurchase-money security interests in implements, professional books, or tools of the trade, farm animals, or crops of the debtor or a dependent of the debtor. This exception applies only in cases where the debtor claims his or her exemptions under state law, either voluntarily or because state law does not permit the use of the federal bankruptcy exemptions. This exception provides that if state law either provides for an exemption that is unlimited in amount or prohibits the avoidance of a consensual lien on property that could otherwise be claimed as exempt, then the debtor may not avoid a security interest in the types of property described above in this paragraph to the extent that the value of the property exceeds $6,825. See 11 U.S.C. § 522(f)(3). For an in-depth discussion on the extent to which a debtor can avoid liens on exempt property under Section 522(f), see Williamson, The Bankruptcy Issues Handbook, supra, Art. 1.05.

avoidance of security interest under section 522(f), limitation

A principal duty of the attorney for a consumer debtor in a chapter 7 case is to investigate the possibility or necessity of avoiding liens under Section 522(f). If the debtor has property subject to liens that are avoidable under Section 522(f), it may be possible to resolve the matter by agreement with the creditor. If not, it will be necessary to file a motion to avoid the lien under Bankruptcy Rule 4003(d). A sample of such a motion may be found in Exhibit 2-X at the end of this chapter. Proceedings under such motions are governed by Bankruptcy Rule 9014, which requires reasonable notice and a hearing. Some courts have local rules governing motions of this type, and they should be checked in this regard.

avoiding liens under section 522(f), procedure

avoiding liens, necessity of filing statement of intention

If the lien being avoided secures a consumer debt, as it usually does, the debtor must also file and serve on the appropriate parties a statement of intention in order to preserve his or her rights against the property in question. See sections 2.07 and 2.11, supra, for further reading on the preparation and filing requirements of a statement of intention.

avoiding liens under section 506(d), limitations

Most liens securing disallowed claims may be avoided under Section 506(d) of the Bankruptcy Code. See 11 U.S.C. § 506(d). To be voidable under Section 506(d), however, the lien must secure a claim that has been disallowed under Section 502. See In re Warner, 146 B.R. 253 (Bankr. N. D. Cal. 1992). The Supreme Court has held that the lien of a partially-secured creditor may not be bifurcated into secured and unsecured portions for purposes of avoiding the unsecured portion of the lien under Section 506(d). The court held that the lien of a partially-secured creditor may not be partially avoided or "stripped down" to the value of the secured property under Section 506(d). See Dewsnup v. Timm, 502 U.S. 410, 112 S.Ct. 773 (1992). Therefore, even if the otherwise valid lien of a partially-secured creditor is so junior that it is completely unsecured (i.e., the value of the creditor's secured claim is zero), the lien may not be avoided under Section 506(d). See Wachovia Mortgage v. Smoot, 2012 WL 4344599 (Bankr. E. D. N.Y. 2012). To avoid a lien under Section 506(d), it is usually necessary to file an adversary proceeding. See Bankruptcy Rule 7001(2). For an in-depth discussion of the extent to which a debtor may avoid liens under Section 506(d) of the Bankruptcy Code, see Williamson, The Bankruptcy Issues Handbook, supra, Art. 1.17.

unavoided lien, postbankruptcy effect of

avoiding lien, reopening case for

It is important to avoid as many liens as possible in a chapter 7 case because a valid, unavoided lien survives the bankruptcy case regardless of whether a proof of claim was filed by or on behalf of the creditor in the case. See 11 U.S.C. § 522(c). An unavoided lien of a creditor may be enforced after the bankruptcy case against the property securing the lien to the extent permitted under local law. See Johnson v. Home State Bank, 501 U.S. 78, 111 S.Ct. 2150 (1991). If the existence of a voidable lien is discovered after a case has been closed, the case may, in the court's discretion, be reopened for the purpose of avoiding the lien. See In re Ricks, 62 B.R. 681 (Bankr. S. D. Cal. 1986); In re Tarkington, 301 B.R. 502 (Bankr. E. D. Tenn. 2003)..

2.13 The Meeting of Creditors

The United States trustee must call a meeting of creditors to be held not less than 21 nor more than 40 days after the filing of a voluntary chapter 7 case. The meeting may be held at a regular place for holding court or at any other convenient place within the district designated by the United States trustee. If the place designated for the meeting is not regularly staffed by the United States trustee, the meeting may be held not more than 60 days after the filing of the case. See Bankruptcy Rule 2003(a).

Meeting of creditors, when and where held

A central Bankruptcy Noticing Center (BNC) has been established in Reston, Virginia by the Administrative Office of the United States Courts. This center now sends most routine notices in bankruptcy cases, including the notice of commencement of case. The BNC processes about 300,000 bankruptcy notices per day. The BNC also provides a free Electronic Bankruptcy Noticing service (EBN) to attorneys who elect to participate in the service. In lieu of paper notices, an electing attorney may choose to receive bankruptcy notices:

Bankruptcy Noticing Center, functions of

(1) By E-mail.
(2) By EDI. This is for high volume recipients.

For more information on EBN and how to sign up for it, see the EBN website at ebn.uscourts.gov or call the EBN toll free help line at 877-837-3424. Those who do not elect to sign up for EBN will continue to receive notices by mail from the BNC.

In practice, a few days after the commencement of a chapter 7 case, a document entitled "Notice of Chapter 7 Bankruptcy Case, Meeting of Creditors, and Deadlines" is sent by the BNC to the debtor and all creditors and other parties in interest. This document will be referred to as the notice of commencement of case. The exact content of the notice varies based on whether the proof of claim deadline is set (i.e. whether property appears to be available to pay creditors). If the debtor is an individual or joint debtor and the proof of claim deadline is not set (i.e. no property appears to be available to pay creditors), Official Form 309A is sent. If the proof of claim deadline is set (i.e. assets are available), Official Form 309B is sent. If the debtor is a corporation or partnership, Official Form 309C is sent if the proof of claim deadline is not set and Official Form 309D is sent if the proof of claim deadline is set.

notice of commencement of case, types of

In a voluntary case commenced by an individual debtor whose debts are primarily consumer debts, the clerk, or some other person as the court may direct (normally the BNC), must give the trustee and all creditors notice by mail of the order for relief not more than 21 days after the date of the order. See Bankruptcy Rule 2002(o). The clerk, or such other person as the court may direct, must also give the debtor, the trustee, and all creditors not less than 21 days notice of the meeting of creditors. See Bankruptcy Rule 2002(a). The meeting of creditors is often referred to as the Section 341(a) meeting.

order for relief and meeting of creditors, notice requirements

In the chapter 7 case of an individual with primarily consumer debts in which a presumption of abuse has arisen under 11 U.S.C. § 707(b), the clerk is required to give creditors notice of the presumption within 10 days after the filing of the case. If the debtor has not filed a statement indicating whether a presumption of abuse has arisen, the clerk must give notice to creditors within 10 days after the filing of the case that the debtor has not filed the required statement and that further notice will be given if a later filed statement indicates that a presumption of abuse has arisen. See Bankruptcy Rule 5008 and 11 U.S.C. § 342(d).

presumption of abuse, notice of

It should be noted that any notice that is required to be given by the debtor to any creditor must contain the name, address and the last 4 digits of taxpayer identification (social security) number of the debtor. However, if the notice concerns an amendment that adds a creditor to the schedules of assets and liabilities, the debtor shall include the full taxpayer identification number in the notice sent to that creditor, but the debtor shall include only the last 4 digits of the taxpayer identification number in the copy of the notice filed with the court. See 11 U.S.C. § 342(c)(1).

debtor's notice to creditor, identification requirements

meeting of creditors, who may examine the debtor

The United States trustee or a designee thereof must preside at the meeting of creditors. In consumer cases the business of the meeting normally consists of an examination of the debtor under oath by the trustee or by any creditor or representative thereof that may appear at the meeting. In this regard it should be noted that a creditor holding a consumer debt or any representative of the creditor (which may include an entity or an employee of an entity and may be a representative for more than 1 creditor) shall be permitted to appear at and participate in the meeting of creditors in a chapter 7 case, either alone or in conjunction with an attorney for the creditor. However, a creditor is not required to be represented by an attorney at the meeting of creditors. See 11 U.S.C. § 341(c).

meeting of creditors, general requirements

The presiding officer at the meeting of creditors must have the authority to administer oaths. See Bankruptcy Rule 2003(b)(1). The examination of the debtor may relate only to the acts, conduct, or property of the debtor, to the liabilities and financial condition of the debtor, or to matters which may affect the administration of the debtor's estate or the debtor's right to a discharge. See Bankruptcy Rule 2004(b). The court may neither preside at nor attend the meeting of creditors. See 11 U.S.C. § 341(c). It should be noted that trustees and creditors' committees are seldom elected in consumer cases, and the interim trustee appointed when the case is filed usually serves throughout the case.

meeting of creditors, advisement duties of trustee

Prior to the conclusion of the meeting of creditors, the trustee is required to orally examine the debtor to insure that the debtor is aware of (1) the potential consequences of seeking a bankruptcy discharge, including its effect on the debtor's credit history, (2) the debtor's ability to file a petition under another chapter of title 11, (3) the effect of receiving a bankruptcy discharge, and (4) the effect of reaffirming a debt, including the debtor's knowledge of the reaffirmation agreement requirements of 11 U.S.C. § 524(d). See 11 U.S.C. § 341(d). If this information is given in the form of a written document, the trustee must orally inquire as to whether the debtor is aware of the information.

meeting of creditors, examination and recording requirements

Any examination under oath at the meeting of creditors must be recorded verbatim by the United States trustee using electronic sound recording equipment or other means of recording. Such record must be preserved by the United States trustee and made available for public access for two years thereafter. Upon request, the United States trustee must provide a certified copy or transcript of the recording at the expense of the person making the request. See Bankruptcy Rule 2003(c). The meeting of creditors may be adjourned from time to time by announcement at the meeting of the adjourned date and time, without further written notice. See Bankruptcy Rule 2003(e). If not previously filed, the debtor's statement of intention must be filed at the meeting of creditors. See 11 U.S.C. § 521(a)(2), and section 2.11, supra. It should also be remembered that the debtor must have provided the trustee with the debtor's most recent income tax return at least 7 days prior to the meeting of creditors or the case is subject to dismissal under 11 U.S.C. § 521(e)(2)(B).

The debtor is required under Bankruptcy Rule 4002(b) to bring the following items and documents to the meeting of creditors and make them available to the trustee or provide a written statement that the document or item does not exist or, in the case of financial information, is not in the debtor's possession:

meeting of creditors, items required of debtors

(1) a picture identification issued by a governmental unit, or other personal identifying information that establishes the debtor's identity;

(2) evidence of the debtor's social security number;

(3) evidence of the debtor's income at the present time, such as the debtor's most recent pay stub;

(4) unless the trustee or the United States trustee instructs otherwise, statements for each of the debtor's depository and investment accounts (including checking accounts, savings accounts, money market accounts, mutual fund accounts and brokerage accounts) for the time period that includes the date of filing of the bankruptcy case; and

(5) documentation of the actual monthly expenses claimed on the Statement of Current Monthly Income and Means Test Calculation filed by the debtor in the case, to the extent required under 11 U.S.C. § 707(b)(2)(A) or (B).

In many districts written instructions are sent to the debtor, and often to the debtor's attorney, usually with the notice of commencement of case. These instructions may require the debtor to bring certain documents to the meeting. The debtor should, of course, bring the required documents to the meeting, otherwise the meeting may be postponed to a later date, and necessitate another court appearance. Even if they are not called for in the instructions issued by the court or United States trustee, the case is likely to proceed more smoothly if the debtor is instructed to bring certain important documents to the meeting of creditors. These documents may include the following:

meeting of creditors, documents required

(1) Deeds or other instruments of title to any real estate in which the debtor has an interest.

(2) The recorded evidence of the debtor's homestead exemption, if recording is required under state law to perfect the exemption.

(3) If necessary in the case, receipts showing how and where the debtor spent any money received just prior to the filing of the petition (see section 2.07, supra).

In most chapter 7 consumer cases, the meeting of creditors lasts only a few minutes and is quite informal, although the actual amount of time spent at the hearing will often depend on when a particular case is called, because several consumer cases are often scheduled for the same time. After the meeting of creditors, the matters remaining for the debtor's attorney in a typical consumer case may include filing amended schedules or statements, opposing objections to the debtor's discharge, reaffirming dischargeable debts, and carrying out the intentions specified in the statement of intention, including the redemption of personal property under Section 722 and the avoidance of liens against exempt property under Section 522(f).

meeting of creditors, length of hearing, matters remaining after

2.14 Filing Amended Schedules and Statements

If any of the schedules or statements filed in the case are incomplete or in an improper form, the clerk may refuse to process the case until amendments or corrected documents are filed curing the defects. A failure to comply with the requirements of the local rules is another common reason for the rejection of filed chapter 7 documents. When filed documents are rejected by the clerk, a notice or form letter is often sent to the debtor's attorney indicating the corrections that must be made before the case can be processed. A failure to file the required amended or corrected documents within the time stated in the notice or set forth in the local rules may result in the dismissal of the case. See 11 U.S.C. § 707(a).

amended documents, when required

Once the schedules and statements have been accepted by the clerk, the need to file amendments will not arise again in a typical consumer case until the meeting of creditors. If the addresses listed on the schedules for any of the creditors were incorrect, the notices mailed to those creditors by the clerk will have been returned to the court by the Postal Service by the time of the meeting of creditors, in which event the hearing officer may advise the debtor's attorney of their return. However, because there is a possibility that the claims of creditors who do not receive notice of the case may not be discharged (see section 2.07, supra), it is important that the court file be checked for returned notices, and the debtor's attorney should specifically inquire or personally check the file in this regard. It should be noted that unless otherwise ordered by the court in a case, the papers filed in a chapter 7 case and the dockets of the bankruptcy court are public records, open to examination by any entity at reasonable times without charge. See 11 U.S.C. § 107.

incorrect address of creditor, effect of

bankruptcy court file, public record

If a notice sent to a creditor has been returned because of an incorrect address or if it is discovered that a creditor has been omitted from the schedules, whether an amendment to the appropriate schedule should be filed depends on whether the case is a "no asset" case and whether the debt owed to the creditor is of a kind specified in 11 U.S.C. § 523(a)(3)(A) (i.e., is of a kind that requires the creditor to request a determination of dischargeability). The general rule is that debts owed to unlisted or improperly listed creditors in "no asset" cases are dischargeable even if the creditor does not receive notice of the case, provided that the omission was inadvertent and the debt is not of a type that requires a creditor to file a complaint to determine dischargeability. The reasoning behind this rule is that in "no asset" cases creditors are instructed not to file claims and the creditor is therefore not prejudiced by failing to receive notice of the case. See In re Stone, 10 F.3d 285 (5th Cir., 1994). Therefore, the appropriate schedule should be promptly amended if the case is not a "no asset" case or if the debt is of a kind specified in 11 U.S.C. § 523(a)(3)(B). In any event, written notice of the case should be sent to any omitted or incorrectly-listed creditor at the correct address. If the effect of the amendment is to add a creditor to the schedules, the debtor's full social security or other taxpayer identification number should appear on the notice sent to the creditor, but only the last four digits of the number should appear on the copy of the notice filed with the court. See 11 U.S.C. § 342(c)(1). See Williamson, The Bankruptcy Issues Handbook, supra, Art. 1.12 for further reading on the dischargeability of debts owed to unlisted or improperly listed creditors.

omitted or incorrectly listed creditor, necessity of amending schedule

It occasionally happens that the testimony of the debtor at the meeting of creditors reveals an obvious error or omission in either the schedules or the statement of financial affairs. Also, the need to file an amended Schedule C, showing revised or additional exemptions is not uncommon. Leave of court to file amendments is not required because Bankruptcy Rule 1009(a) provides that a voluntary petition, list, schedule, or statement may be amended by the debtor as a matter of course at any time before the case is closed. However, notice of the amendment must be given to the trustee and any entity affected thereby. It should be noted that the statement of intention may be amended by the debtor at any time before the expiration of the period in which the intentions are to be performed and that the debtor must give notice of the amendment to the trustee and any entity affected thereby. See Bankruptcy Rule 1009(b).

amended documents, right of debtor to file

When preparing amendments to schedules or statements, only the corrected information need be shown, and it is not necessary to repeat the unamended information contained in the original document unless the local rules provide otherwise. Use Exhibit 2-Y at the end of this chapter as a guide in preparing amended documents. The amended documents must be verified and filed in the same number of copies as required of the original documents and a copy of the amendment should be given to the trustee and any entity affected thereby. See Bankruptcy Rules 1008 and 1009(a). The fee for amending a list or schedule of creditors is $30, provided that the court may, for good cause, waive the charge. See Public Law 103-21, §406(a), 107 Stat. 1165 (also in notes to 28 U.S.C. § 1930). There is no fee for amending the other schedules or statements.

amended documents, preparation and filing requirements, fees

2.15 The Debtor's Bankruptcy Estate

Under 11 U.S.C. § 541(a), the commencement of a chapter 7 case creates an estate (i.e., the debtor's bankruptcy estate) comprised of the following property, wherever located:

debtor's bankruptcy estate, property included

(1) All legal or equitable interests of the debtor in property as of the commencement of the case, except powers that the debtor may exercise only for the benefit of another and otherwise-enforceable restrictions on the transfer of a beneficial interest of the debtor in a trust.

(2) All interests of the debtor and the debtor's spouse in community property as of the commencement of the case that is either under the sole, equal, or joint management and control of the debtor or is liable for an allowable claim against the debtor or the debtor and the debtor's spouse, to the extent that such interest is so liable.

(3) Any interest in property that the trustee recovers or preserves by avoiding transfers or otherwise.

(4) An interest in property that would have been property of the estate if such interest had been an interest of the debtor on the date the petition was filed, if the debtor acquires or becomes entitled to acquire the property within 180 days after such date - (a) by bequest, devise, or inheritance, (b) as a result of a property settlement agreement with the debtor's spouse or an interlocutory or final divorce decree, or (c) as a beneficiary of a life insurance policy or death benefit plan.

(5) Proceeds, product, offspring, rents, and profits of or from property of the estate, except earnings from services performed by an individual debtor after the commencement of the case.

(6) Any interest in property that the estate acquires after the commencement of the case.

Under 11 U.S.C. § 541(b), the following property is not included in the debtor's bankruptcy estate:

debtor's bankruptcy estate, property not included in

(1) any power that the debtor may exercise solely for the benefit of another entity;

(2) interests of the debtor as a lessee under expired leases of nonresidential real property;

(3) funds placed in education IRAs within 365 days prior to the filing of the bankruptcy case, with certain limitations (see 11 U.S.C. § 541(b)(5) for the specific limitations);

(4) funds used to purchase tuition credits under a qualified state tuition program with certain limitations (see 11 U.S.C. § 541(b)(6) for the specific limitations);

(5) amounts withheld by an employer from the debtor's wages as contributions to qualified retirement or employee benefit plans;

(6) tangible personal property that is being held as collateral for a loan or advance of money by a person licensed to do so where the property is in the possession of the pledgee and the debtor has no obligation to repay the money; and

(7) proceeds from the sale of certain money orders.

It should be noted that the above list of property that is not included in the debtor's bankruptcy estate contains only the property that is likely to exist in consumer bankruptcy cases. For a complete list of such property, see 11 U.S.C. § 541(b).

11 U.S.C. § 541(c)(2) provides that a restriction on the transfer of a beneficial interest of the debtor in a trust that is enforceable under applicable nonbankruptcy law is enforceable in a bankruptcy case. This provision has been construed by the Supreme Court to exclude from the bankruptcy estate the debtor's interest in an ERISA-qualified retirement plan. See Patterson v. Shumate, 504 U.S. 753, 112 S. Ct. 2242 (1992). However, an interest of the debtor in property becomes property of the estate notwithstanding any provisions that restrict or condition the transfer of the property by the debtor or that create an option to forfeit, modify, or terminate the debtor's interest in property upon the debtor's insolvency or on the filing of a bankruptcy case. See 11 U.S.C. § 541(c)(1). Property in which the debtor holds only legal title and not an equitable interest becomes property of the bankruptcy estate

debtor's interest in retirement plan, excludability from bankruptcy estate only to the extent of the debtor's legal title to the property. See 11 U.S.C. § 541(d).

after-acquired property, reporting requirements

Of special concern to consumer debtors is the provision in 11 U.S.C. § 541(a) above dealing with after-acquired property. Within 14 days after the information comes to the debtor's knowledge, or within such further time as the court may allow, the debtor is required to file a supplemental schedule with respect to any property that the debtor acquires, or becomes entitled to acquire, within 180 days after the date of filing of the petition - (1) by bequest, devise, or inheritance, (2) as a result of a property settlement agreement with the debtor's spouse or a divorce decree, or (3) as a beneficiary of a life insurance policy or death benefit plan. See Bankruptcy Rule 1007(h). The duty to file such a schedule continues notwithstanding the closing of the case before the schedule is or can be filed. However, if any of the property so acquired by the debtor is exempt, the debtor may claim the exemptions on the supplemental schedule. See Bankruptcy Rule 1007(h) and section 2.08, supra. A failure to file such a supplemental schedule may result in the denial or revocation of the debtor's chapter 7 discharge. See 11 U.S.C. § 727(a)(2)(B),(d)(2) and section 2.17, infra.

2.16 Duties and Powers of the United States Trustee and the Bankruptcy Trustee

United States trustee, appointment of

The Attorney General is required to appoint a United States trustee for each region and one or more assistant United States trustees in regions where the public interest so requires. See 28 U.S.C. § 581(a), 582. There are 21 such regions in the United States, each of which is composed of two or more districts. Generally, a United States trustee is responsible for appointing (or serving as) trustees in bankruptcy cases, monitoring the administration of bankruptcy cases, and generally relieving bankruptcy judges of administrative responsibilities and of the burden of appointing persons who may later litigate before them. See 28 U.S.C. § 586. In the states where the bankruptcy system is administered by a Bankruptcy Administrator instead of a United States trustee, the Bankruptcy Administrator has the authority to preside at the meeting of creditors and examine the debtor.

bankruptcy administrator, powers of

United States trustee, duties of in chapter 7 case

The duties and responsibilities of the United States trustee in chapter 7 cases are set forth in 28 U.S.C. § 586 and 11 U.S.C. § 111, 307, 341, 343, 701(a), and 704(b). In chapter 7 consumer cases, the duties and responsibilities of the United States trustee include the following:

(1) Appointing, from the panel of private trustees, a disinterested person to serve as interim trustee in the chapter 7 case, or serving as interim trustee in the case if no member of the panel is willing to serve.

(2) Convening and presiding at the meeting of creditors.

(3) Taking appropriate action to insure that all reports, schedules, and fees are promptly filed and paid.

(4) Monitoring the progress of the case and taking appropriate action to prevent undue delay.

(5) Raising and being heard on any issue in the case.

(6) Notifying the United States Attorney of matters relating to acts that may constitute a federal crime and assisting in the prosecution of such crimes.

(7) Review all materials filed by the debtor and, within 10 days after the date of the first meeting of creditors, file with the court a statement as to whether a presumption of abuse would arise in the debtor's case and within 30 days thereafter either file a motion to dismiss or convert the case or file a statement stating the reasons why such a motion is not appropriate.

(8) Investigate and approve or disapprove nonprofit budget and credit counseling agencies and instructional courses on personal financial management in the district and, if necessary, file a determination with the court that the credit counseling and/or financial management course requirements are not applicable in the district.

To enable the United States trustee to carry out its duty of monitoring bankruptcy cases, the clerk of the bankruptcy court is required to transmit to the United States trustee copies of all petitions, schedules, statements, and amendments thereto filed in the case. See Bankruptcy Rules 1002(b), 1007(l), 1009(c), and 5005(b). The clerk is also required to transmit to the United States trustee most notices that are issued in bankruptcy cases. See Bankruptcy Rule 2002(k). In addition, any person or party who files a pleading, motion, objection or similar paper relating to the approval of a compromise or settlement, the dismissal or conversion of a case, the employment of a professional person, an objection to or waiver or revocation of a discharge, or certain other enumerated matters must transmit a copy thereof to the United States trustee. See Bankruptcy Rule 9034.

United States trustee, documents transmitted to

interim trustee, appointment of

Promptly after the order for relief in a chapter 7 case, the United States trustee must appoint an interim trustee to serve in the case. The trustee must be a disinterested person who is a member of the panel of private trustees created under 28 U.S.C. § 586(a)(1), or who was serving as trustee in the case before it was converted to chapter 7. See 11 U.S.C. § 701(a). The interim trustee serves as trustee in a chapter 7 case unless the creditors elect a trustee, an event that seldom happens in chapter 7 consumer cases. See 11 U.S.C. § 702(d).

bankruptcy trustee, duties of in chapter 7 case

The duties of a bankruptcy trustee are set forth in 11 U.S.C. § 341(d), 704, Bankruptcy Rule 2015, and Part VI of the Bankruptcy Rules. The trustee's duties in a chapter 7 consumer case include the following:

duties of trustee, list of

(1) Examining the debtor at the meeting of creditors to insure that the debtor is aware of (a) the potential consequences of a bankruptcy discharge including its effect on the debtor's credit history, (b) the debtor's ability to file under a different chapter, (c) the effect of a bankruptcy discharge, and (d) the effect of reaffirming a debt including the debtor's knowledge of the reaffirmation agreement requirements of 11 U.S.C. § 524(d).

(2) Collecting and liquidating the property of the debtor's bankruptcy estate, and closing the estate as expeditiously as is compatible with the best interests of the parties in interest.

(3) Accounting for all property received and keeping a record of the receipt and disposition of all property and money received.

(4) Insuring that the debtor timely performs the intentions specified in the statement of intention.

(5) Investigating the financial affairs of the debtor.

(6) Examining proofs of claim and objecting to the allowance of any claim that is improper, if a purpose would be served.

(7) Opposing the discharge of the debtor, if advisable.

(8) Furnishing such information concerning the estate and its administration as is requested by the parties in interest, unless the court orders otherwise.

(9) Filing and transmitting to the United States trustee an inventory of the debtor's property, if such an inventory was not previously filed in the case.

(10) Giving notice of the case to every person known to be holding money or property subject to the withdrawal or order of the debtor.

(11) If there is a claim against the debtor for a domestic support obligation, provide the notices set forth in 11 U.S.C. § 704(c)(1) to the holder of the claim and to the state child support enforcement agency.

(12) Giving notice of any proposed abandonment of property of the estate.

(13) Making a final report and filing a final account of the administration of the estate with the court.

joint case, appointment of trustee

If a joint petition is filed, the debtors' estates are usually consolidated and administered jointly by a single trustee. See 11 U.S.C. § 302(b) and Bankruptcy Rules 1015(b) and 2009(c)(1). The trustee must attend the meetin of creditors and examine the debtor (or debtors in a joint case) as to his or her assets. Unless there is an applicable exemption, the trustee is likely to question the debtor closely as to any liquid assets possessed by the debtor at the time of filing. If it is determined at the hearing that the debtor possessed nonexempt assets at the time of filing, the trustee may request that the assets, or their cash equivalent, be turned over to the trustee by a specified date. After the hearing, the trustee may correspond with the debtor's employer to determine the status of the debtor's earnings at the time of filing. If nonexempt property is subsequently located, the trustee normally advises the debtor as to when and where to turn the property over. If the debtor disputes either the existence or the amount or value of any alleged nonexempt property claimed by the trustee, the request to turn over the property should be contested and the matter either negotiated with the trustee or litigated under Bankruptcy Rule 9014 or otherwise.

trustee, collection of nonexempt assets, procedure

purchase of trustee's interest in nonexempt property

The trustee may not always insist that nonexempt assets be turned over. It is often possible for the debtor to purchase the trustee's interest in such assets at a negotiated price. In such cases the trustee may permit the debtor to pay the agreed price in reasonable installments. Such a procedure may be convenient for a debtor whose homestead or other exemption doesn't quite cover the equity in the debtor's home or other property, and for a debtor with nonexempt personal property that is of value to the debtor but which has little market value. If the debtor has accounts receivable that are property of the estate, it may be possible to purchase them from the trustee at a negotiated price. The trustee may also sell the estate's equity or interest in secured property to a creditor with a security interest in the property.

sale of exempt property by trustee, procedure

If the trustee has a substantial interest in property, a portion of which is exempt, and if the debtor is unable to purchase the trustee's interest in the property, the trustee may sell the property and reimburse the debtor for the exempt portion of the property from the proceeds of the sale. If the estate's interest in otherwise exempt property is nominal, the trustee may abandon the property upon proper notice. See Bankruptcy Rule 6007(a). A trustee who unreasonably refuses to abandon the estate's interest in property may be compelled to do so by the filing of a motion under Bankruptcy Rule 6007(b). See 11 U.S.C. § 554(b).

trustee's fee, sources of

The noncontingent portion of the trustee's fee in a chapter 7 case is paid from the debtor's filing fee. In addition, if allowed by the court, the trustee's fee may include a percentage of all monies disbursed by the trustee in the case. The percentage portion of the trustee's fee may not exceed 25 percent of the first $5,000, 10 percent of the next $45,000, and five percent of the balance of all monies up to $1,000,000 that are disbursed to creditors. See 11 U.S.C. § 326(a), 330(b).

Insofar as they pertain to typical consumer cases, the powers of the trustee to set aside liens and transfers of property may be summarized as follows:

trustee's avoidance powers under local law

charitable contributions, avoidability of transfers for

(1) Under 11 U.S.C. § 544, the so-called "strong arm clause" of the Bankruptcy Code, the trustee has the power to avoid liens and other transfers that could be avoided by creditors under state law. Under Section 544(a) the trustee may avoid (i.e., invalidate or set aside) any lien, transfer of property or obligation incurred by the debtor that could be avoided under local law by - (a) a creditor that extends credit to the debtor at the time the bankruptcy case is commenced and obtains, with respect to such credit, a judicial lien against the debtor's property, (b) a creditor that extends credit to the debtor at the time the bankruptcy case is commenced and obtains, with respect to such credit, an execution that is returned unsatisfied or (c) a bona fide purchaser of real property from the debtor at the time the case was commenced who is permitted under local law to perfect the transfer. Section 544(a) gives the trustee the avoidance powers of a judgment creditor or bona fide purchaser of real estate under local law, whether or not such a creditor or purchaser actually exists. The specific powers of the trustee under this section depend largely on the law of the local state. Section 544(b)(1) permits the trustee to avoid transfers that are avoidable by unsecured creditors under local law, such as transfers made by the debtor in violation of state fraudulent conveyance or bulk sales laws. Section 544(b)(2) excepts transfers in the form of charitable contributions of less than 15 percent of the debtor's gross annual income from the trustee's avoidance powers under Section 544.

(2) Under 11 U.S.C 545, the trustee may avoid statutory liens on property of the debtor to the extent that the lien (1) became effective upon the filing of the case, the appointment of a custodian, or other acts of insolvency by the debtor, (2) was not perfected or enforceable when the case was commenced, or (3) is for rent or a lien of distress for rent. A statutory lien is a lien created solely by statute and not by agreement of the parties. Mechanics liens and tax liens are examples of statutory liens. A judicial or judgment lien is not a statutory lien.

statutory liens, avoidance of by trustee

(3) Under 11 U.S.C. § 547(b), the trustee may avoid as a preference any transfer of an interest in property of the debtor to or for the benefit of a creditor that - (a) was made for or on account of an antecedent debt owed by the debtor before the transfer, (b) was made while the debtor was insolvent, (c) was made on or within 90 days before the date of the filing of the petition or within one year before the date of filing if the creditor was an insider who had reasonable cause to believe that the debtor was insolvent at the time of the transfer, and (d) that enabled the creditor to receive more than it would have received as a creditor in the case if the transfer had not occurred. There are nine types of transfers, however, that may not be avoided as a preference. See 11 U.S.C. § 547(c). Included here are contemporaneous transfers for new value given to the debtor, most transfers made in the ordinary course of business, transfers that are bona fide payments of domestic support obligations, in the case of an individual debtor whose debts are primarily consumer debts, transfers of less than $600, and in the case of a debtor whose debts are not primarily consumer debts, transfers of less than $6,825. See 11 U.S.C. § 547(c).

preferential transfers, avoidance of by trustee

(4) Under 11 U.S.C. § 548(a)(1), the trustee may avoid as fraudulent any transfer of an interest of the debtor in property, or any obligation incurred by the debtor, that was made or incurred within two years prior to the date of the filing of the petition, if the debtor - (a) made the transfer or incurred the obligation with actual intent to hinder, delay, or defraud any entity to which the debtor was or became indebted, or (b) received less than a reasonably equivalent value in exchange for the transfer or obligation and was insolvent at the time or became insolvent, undercapitalized, or unable to pay his or her debts as a result of the transaction, or made the transfer or incurred the obligation for the benefit of an insider under an employment contract and not in the ordinary course of business. Transfers in the form of charitable contributions made by the debtor of less than 15 percent of the debtor's gross annual income are not avoidable, however. See 11 U.S.C. § 548(a)(2). See 11 U.S.C. § 548(d)(3) for the definition of "charitable contribution." Under 11 U.S.C. § 548(e)(1), the trustee may avoid any transfer made by the debtor within 10 years of bankruptcy to a self-settled trust if the debtor is a beneficiary of the trust and if the transfer was made with actual intent to hinder, delay or defraud any entity to which the debtor was or became indebted.

fraudulent transfers, avoidance of by trustee

charitable contributions, avoidability of transfers for

transfers to self-settled trusts, avoidability of

(5) Under 11 U.S.C. § 549(a), the trustee may avoid any unauthorized transfer of property of the bankruptcy estate that occurs after the commencement of the case, except - (a) a transfer to a good faith purchaser without knowledge of the commencement of the case and for present fair equivalent value, and (b) a transfer to a purchaser at a judicial sale of real property located in a county other than the county in which the case is commenced, unless a copy of the petition was recorded in such county prior to the transfer.

unauthorized transfers, avoidance of by trustee

For further reading on the types of prefiling transfers that may be avoidable in bankruptcy, see Williamson, The Bankruptcy Issues Handbook, supra, Art. 1.14.

avoidable transfers, reading on

The limitations on the trustee's avoiding powers are set forth in 11 U.S.C. § 546. These limitations include a requirement that an action to avoid under sections 544, 545, 547, 548 or 553 must be commenced within two years after the filing of the case and before the case is closed. The avoiding powers of the trustee are also subject to the rights of a creditor under the Uniform Commercial Code to maintain its secured position during the case by filing continuation or financing statements and the common law or statutory right of a creditor to reclaim goods delivered to the debtor provided that the goods are reclaimed within 45 days of receipt by the debtor or within 20 days after the commencement of the bankruptcy case if the 45 day period expires after the commencement of the case.

avoiding powers of trustee, limitations on

creditor's right to reclaim goods

It should be noted that the trustee is also subject to certain venue restrictions in commencing actions to recover money or property. See 28 U.S.C. § 1409. Of interest in consumer cases is the provision stating that the trustee may commence a proceeding to recover money or property worth less than $1,525 or a consumer debt of less than $22,700 or a debt against an non-insider of less than $27,750 only in the district in which the defendant resides. See 28 U.S.C. § 1409(b).*

actions by trustee, venue restrictions

* Dollar figures subject to change on April 1, 2025.

executory contracts, assumption or rejection by trustee

The trustee has extensive powers to assume or reject executory contracts and unexpired leases of the debtor. Generally, the trustee, with the approval of the court, may assume or reject any executory contract or unexpired lease of the debtor. See 11 U.S.C. § 365(a). However, if there has been a default in an executory contract or unexpired lease of the debtor, the trustee may not assume such contract or lease unless, at the time of the assumption, the trustee - (1) cures, or provides adequate assurance that he or she will promptly cure, such default, (2) provides compensation to the injured party, other than the debtor, for any actual losses resulting from the default, and (3) provides adequate assurance of future performance under the contract or lease. See 11 U.S.C. § 365(b). A proceeding to assume, reject, or assign an executory contract or unexpired lease is governed by Bankruptcy Rule 9014, which requires a motion, with notice and a hearing. See Bankruptcy Rule 6006(a). The powers and duties of the trustee with respect to executory contracts and unexpired leases are set forth in 11 U.S.C. § 365 and Bankruptcy Rule 6006. See section 2.07, supra, for a definition of the term "executory contract".

prohibition of ex parte contacts with bankruptcy judge

The trustee and any other party in interest, including the United States trustee, and any attorney, accountant, or employee of a party in interest, may not conduct or take part in ex parte contacts, meetings, or communications with a bankruptcy judge concerning matters affecting a particular case or proceeding. See Bankruptcy Rule 9003.

2.17 The Chapter 7 Discharge

chapter 7 discharge, eligibility requirements

In a chapter 7 case, the court must grant the debtor a discharge unless:

(1) the debtor is not an individual;

(2) the debtor, with intent to hinder, delay, or defraud a creditor or the trustee, has transferred, removed, destroyed, mutilated, or concealed - (a) property of the debtor, within one year before the date of filing, or (b) property of the bankruptcy estate, after the date of filing;

(3) the debtor has, without justification, concealed, destroyed, mutilated, falsified, or failed to keep or preserve recorded information from which the debtor's financial condition or business transactions may be ascertained;

(4) the debtor knowingly and fraudulently and in connection with the case - (a) made a false oath or account, (b) presented or used a false claim, (c) gave, offered, received, or attempted to obtain money, property, or advantage, or a promise of same, for acting or forbearing to act, or (d) withheld from the trustee recorded information relating to the debtor's property or financial affairs;

(5) the debtor has failed to satisfactorily explain, prior to the determination of the denial of discharge, any loss or deficiency of assets;

(6) the debtor has refused in the case - (a) to obey a lawful order of the court, other than an order to respond to a material question or to testify, (b) on the ground of privilege against self-incrimination, to respond to a material question approved by the court or to testify, after having been granted immunity with respect to same, or (c) on a ground other than privilege against self-incrimination, to respond to a material question or to testify;

(7)the debtor has committed any act specified in (2) through (6) above, within one year before the date of filing, or during the case, in connection with another bankruptcy case concerning an insider (i.e., a relative, partner, partnership, or corporation of the debtor);

(8) the debtor has been granted a discharge in a chapter 7 or chapter 11 case that was commenced within 8 years before the date of filing of the present case;

(9) the debtor has been granted a discharge in a chapter 12 or chapter 13 case that was commenced within six years before the date of filing of the present case, unless payments under the plan in the prior case totaled at least - (a) 100 percent of the allowed unsecured claims in such case, or (b) 70 percent of such claims and the plan was proposed by the debtor in good faith and was the debtor's best effort;

(10) the court approves a written waiver of discharge executed by the debtor after the order for relief under chapter 7. See 11 U.S.C. § 727(a);

(11) after filing the case, the debtor failed to complete an instructional course on personal financial management, unless the United States trustee has determined that this requirement does not apply in the district; or

(12) the court determines that there is reasonable cause to believe (1) that the debtor has been convicted of bankruptcy fraud under circumstances that demonstrate that the filing of the bankruptcy case was an abuse of title 11, or (2) that the debtor owes a debt arising from a securities law violation, or that a proceeding involving either of these matters is pending.

chapter 7 discharge, when granted

In a chapter 7 case filed by an individual debtor, the court must forthwith grant the debtor a discharge upon the expiration of the time fixed for the filing of complaints objecting to the discharge of the debtor and the 60 day period for filing motions to dismiss the case as a substantial abuse of chapter 7, unless (1) either a complaint objecting to the discharge of the debtor or a motion to extend the time for the filing thereof is pending, (2) a motion to dismiss the case under Section 707 is pending, (3) a motion to extend the time for filing a motion to dismiss the case for abuse under Bankruptcy Rule 1017(e) is pending, (4) the filing fee has not been paid, unless the court has waived the payment thereof, (5) the debtor has filed a waiver of discharge or requested that the granting of the discharge be delayed, (6) the debtor has not filed with the court a statement showing completion of a course in personal financial management (unless the United States trustee has determined that this requirement is not applicable in the district), (7) a motion to delay or postpone the discharge is pending, or (8) a presumption that a reaffirmation agreement is an undue hardship has arisen under 11 U.S.C. § 524(m). See Bankruptcy Rule 4004(c)(1).

personal finance course, requirement of

In order to be granted a discharge the debtor must take and complete an instructional course on personal financial management. The clerk's office should have a list of approved instructional course providers. The debtor must file a certificate of completion of this course with the court using Official Form 423 (Certification About a Financial Management Course). A sample of this certificate is set forth in Exhibit 2-Z(2) at the end of this chapter. See section 2.05, supra, for further reading on this requirement.

complaints objecting to discharge, motions to dismiss, filing deadlines

Complaints objecting to the discharge of the debtor under 11 U.S.C. § 727(a) and motions to dismiss for abuse under Section 707(b) and Bankruptcy Rule 1017(e) must be filed not later than 60 days following the first date set for the meeting of creditors, unless, on the request of a proper party filed within the 60 day period and after a hearing on notice, the court, for cause, extends the time for filing. See Bankruptcy Rule 1017(e) and Bankruptcy Rule 4004(a),(b). Not less than 28 days notice of the time for the filing of complaints objecting to the discharge of the debtor must be given to the United States trustee, all creditors, and the trustee. See Bankruptcy Rule 4004(a). This notice is usually contained in the notice of commencement of case (see Exhibit 2-T).

complaints objecting to discharge, procedure under

The trustee, a creditor, or the United States trustee may file complaints objecting to the discharge of the debtor. See 11 U.S.C. § 727(c)(1). At the request of a party in interest, the court may order the trustee to examine the acts and conduct of the debtor to determine whether grounds exist for a denial of discharge. See 11 U.S.C. § 727(c)(2). If a complaint objecting to the discharge of the debtor is filed, the proceeding commenced by the complaint is an adversary proceeding governed by Part VII of the Bankruptcy Rules. See Bankruptcy Rule 4004(d). That such a proceeding is a core proceeding, see 28 U.S.C. § 157(b)(2)(J). At the trial on such a complaint, the party filing the complaint has the burden of proving the objection. See Bankruptcy Rule 4005. The applicability of any local rules to such proceedings should also be checked.

granting of discharge, motion to defer

Notwithstanding the duty of the court to forthwith grant the debtor a chapter 7 discharge upon the expiration of the time for filing complaints or motions, on the motion of the debtor the court may defer the granting of the discharge for a period of 30 days and, on motion within such 30 day period, may defer the granting thereof to a date certain. See Bankruptcy Rule 4004(c)(2) and any applicable local rules. This provision is useful if the debtor is attempting to negotiate a reaffirmation agreement with a creditor, because such agreements must be made prior to the granting of the discharge to be enforceable. See 11 U.S.C. § 524(c), and section 2.18, infra.

discharge and reaffirmation hearing, when held

Not more than 30 days following the entry of an order granting or denying a discharge, and on not less than 10 days notice to the debtor and the trustee, the court may hold a discharge and reaffirmation hearing, which, if held, the debtor must attend. See 11 U.S.C. § 524(d) and Bankruptcy Rule 4008. Such a hearing need only be held if the debtor's discharge has been denied, if the debtor is not represented by an attorney and wishes to enter into a reaffirmation agreement with a creditor under 11 U.S.C. § 524(c), or if a presumption of undue hardship has arisen in connection with the reaffirmation agreement. See Bankruptcy Rule 4008. See section 2.18, infra, for further reading on reaffirmation agreements.

waiver of discharge

The debtor may waive the right to a chapter 7 discharge by filing and obtaining court approval of a written waiver of discharge executed by the debtor after the order for relief under chapter 7. See 11 U.S.C. § 727(a)(10), Bankruptcy Rule 4004(c)(1)(C), and any applicable local rules.

order of discharge, requirements, notice

The order of discharge must conform to the appropriate Official Form. See Bankruptcy Rule 4004(e). The clerk is required to promptly mail a copy of the final order of discharge to all creditors, the United States trustee, and the trustee. See Bankruptcy Rule 4004(g). If so desired, a final order of discharge may be registered in another district by filing a certified copy of the order with the clerk of the bankruptcy court in the other district. When so registered, the order of discharge has the same effect as an order of the court of the district where it is registered. See Bankruptcy Rule 4004(f). If an order is entered denying or revoking a discharge, if a waiver of discharge is filed and approved by the court, or if the case is closed without the entry of an order of discharge, the clerk must promptly give notice thereof to all parties in interest. See Bankruptcy Rule 4006.

On the request of the trustee, a creditor, or the United States trustee, and after notice and a hearing, the court, under 11 U.S.C. § 727(d), may revoke the chapter 7 discharge of a debtor if:

revocation of discharge, grounds for

(1) the discharge was obtained through the fraud of the debtor, and the requesting party did not know of such fraud until after the granting of the discharge;

(2) the debtor acquired property that is property of the bankruptcy estate, or became entitled to acquire property that would be property of the estate, and knowingly and fraudulently failed to deliver or report such property to the trustee;

(3) the debtor refused in the case - (a) to obey a lawful order of the court, other than an order to respond to a material question or to testify, (b) on the ground of privilege against self-incrimination, to respond to a material question approved by the court or to testify, after having been granted immunity with respect to the matter for which the privilege was invoked, or (c) on a ground other than privilege against self-incrimination, to respond to a material question approved by the court or to testify; or

(4) the debtor has failed to explain satisfactorily either a material misstatement in an audit referred to in 28 U.S.C. § 586(f) or a failure to make available for inspection all of the necessary items belonging to the debtor that were requested for the audit.

revocation of discharge, procedure

A proceeding to revoke a chapter 7 discharge is an adversary proceeding governed by Part VII of the Bankruptcy Rules, and the party seeking revocation of must file a complaint. See Bankruptcy Rule 7001. Complaints seeking the revocation of a discharge on the grounds stated in subparagraph (1) above must be filed within one year after the granting of the discharge. Complaints seeking revocation on the grounds stated in subparagraphs (2) and (3) above must be filed within one year after the granting of the discharge or before the closing of the case, whichever is later. See 11 U.S.C. § 727(e). The local rules should also be checked for requirements dealing with revocation proceedings.

chapter 7 discharge, debts not discharged by

A chapter 7 discharge in a voluntary case discharges an individual debtor from all debts that arose (or are deemed to have arisen) prior to the filing of the petition except debts that are nondischargeable under 11 U.S.C. § 523. See 11 U.S.C. § 727(b). Under 11 U.S.C. § 523(a), a chapter 7 discharge does not discharge an individual debtor from the following debts:

(1) Debts for the following taxes and customs duties -

dischargeability of tax debts

(a) income taxes and gross receipts taxes - (i) for tax years ending on or before the date of filing of the case for which returns, if required, were last due within three years before such date, (ii) assessed within 240 days before the date of filing of the case, plus additional periods if offers to compromise such taxes were made, or (iii) not assessed before, but assessable after the commencement of the case, excluding the taxes specified in (b) and (c) of this subparagraph;

(b) taxes with respect to which a return, or equivalent report or notice, if required, was either not filed or was filed late but within two years before the date of filing of the bankruptcy case;

(c) taxes with respect to which the debtor made a fraudulent return or taxes which the debtor willfully attempted to evade or defeat. The dischargeability of tax debts can be complex and complicated. For further reading on the dischargeability of tax debts, see Williamson, The Bankruptcy Issues Handbook, supra, Art.1.10.

(2) If the court so rules under a complaint to determine dischargeability, debts for obtaining money, property, services, or an extension, renewal, or refinance of credit by - (a) false pretenses, false representation, or actual fraud, other than a statement with respect to the debtor's financial condition or that of an insider (included here are debts of $725 or more for "luxury goods or services" or cash advances, which are discussed below), or (b) the use of a written statement with respect to the financial condition of the debtor or an insider that is materially false, on which the creditor reasonably relied, and that the debtor caused to be made or published with intent to deceive. For further reading on the dischargeability of debts obtained by fraud, false pretenses, or false financial statements, see Williamson, The Bankruptcy Issues Handbook, supra, Art. 1.11.

dischargeability of debts procured by fraud or false financial statements

(3) Debts that were neither listed nor scheduled in the case with the name of the creditor, if known, in time to permit the timely filing of a proof of claim, or, with respect to the debts described in subparagraphs (2), (4), or (6) of this paragraph, the timely filing of a complaint to determine dischargeability, unless the creditor had notice or actual knowledge of the case in time for such filing. For further reading on the dischargeability of debts owed to unlisted or improperly listed creditors, see Williamson, The Bankruptcy Issues Handbook, supra, Art. 1.12.

dischargeability of unlisted debts

(4) If the court so rules under a complaint to determine dischargeability, debts for embezzlement, larceny, or fraud or defalcation while acting in a fiduciary capacity.

dischargeability of debts for larceny or embezzlement

(5) Debts for a domestic support obligation. The dischargeability of these debts is discussed below in this section.

dischargeability of debts for a domestic support obligation

(6) If the court so rules under a complaint to determine dischargeability, debts for willful and malicious injury by the debtor to another entity or to the property of another entity. For further reading on the dischargeability of debts for willful and malicious injury, see Williamson, The Bankruptcy Issues Handbook, supra, Art. 1.08.

dischargeability of debts for willful or malicious injury

(7) Debts for fines, penalties, or forfeitures payable to and for the benefit of a governmental unit, except tax penalties related to a tax of a kind not specified in (1) above or imposed with respect to transactions or events that occurred more than three years before the date of filing of the petition. For further reading on the dischargeability of debts for tax penalties, see Williamson, The Bankruptcy Issues Handbook, supra, Art. 1.10.

dischargeability of debts for fines or penalties

(8) Unless excepting the debt from discharge would impose an undue hardship on the debtor or the debtor's dependents, debts for an education benefit overpayment or loan made, insured, or guaranteed by a governmental unit or made under a program funded in whole or in part by a governmental unit or nonprofit institution, or for an obligation to repay funds received as an educational benefit, scholarship or stipend, or any other qualified educational loan. The dischargeability of debts for student loans or educational obligations is discussed below in this section.

dischargeability of debts for student loans

(9) Debts for death or personal injury caused by the debtor's operation of a motor vehicle, vessel, or aircraft if such operation was unlawful because the debtor was intoxicated from using alcohol, a drug, or another substance. For further reading on the dischargeability of debts caused by drunk driving, see Williamson, The Bankruptcy Issues Handbook, supra, Art. 1.09.

dischargeability of debts caused by drunk driving

(10) Debts that were or could have been scheduled by the debtor in a prior bankruptcy case in which the debtor waived or was denied a discharge on any grounds other than having been granted a discharge in a prior bankruptcy case filed within the previous six years. The dischargeability of debts listed in a prior bankruptcy case is discussed below in this section.

dischargeability of debts listed in prior bankruptcy case

(11) Certain debts owed to a Federal depository institutions regulatory agency (see 11 U.S.C. § 523(a)(11), (12) for the particulars).

dischargeability of debts incurred to pay taxes

(12) debts for the payment of restitution in a Federal criminal case.

(13) Debts incurred to pay a nondischargeable Federal, State or Local tax, or to pay a fine or penalty imposed under a Federal election law.

dischargeability of property settlement debts

(14) Debts other than domestic support obligations that were incurred in the course of or in connection with a divorce or separation. Property settlement debts incurred in a divorce are likely to be nondischargeable under this exception. The dischargeability of these debts is discussed below in this section.

dischargeability of home ownership fees

(15) Debts for condominium, cooperative housing, or homeowners association lot fees or assessments that become due and payable after the filing of the case, for as long as the debtor has an interest therein.

court costs, dischargeability

(16) Debts for fees, costs and expenses imposed on a prisoner by a court in connection with the filing of a case, motion, complaint or appeal regardless of an assertion of poverty or prisoner status by the debtor.

loans from retirement plans, dischargeability of

(17) Debts for permitted loans owed to a pension, profit-sharing, stock bonus, or other plans that are qualified under the Internal Revenue Code.

debts for securities fraud, dischargeability

(18) Debts for violations of federal or state securities laws, or for common law fraud, deceit or manipulation in connection with the purchase or sale of securities, that result from a judgment, consent decree, or settlement agreement, or from a restitutionary or punitive court or administrative order (see 11 U.S.C. § 523(a)(19) for the specific provisions).

dischargeability in present case of debts not discharged in prior case

Notwithstanding the provisions of 11 U.S.C. § 523(a)(10), which are summarized in subparagraph (10) above, a debt that was excepted from discharge in a prior bankruptcy case of the debtor under subparagraphs (1), (3), or (8) above, is dischargeable in a later case, unless the debt is otherwise nondischargeable in the later case. See 11 U.S.C. § 523(b). Also, unless the court, for cause, ordered otherwise in the prior case, the dismissal of a prior bankruptcy case does not bar the discharge in a later case of the debts listed in the prior case if the debts were dischargeable in the prior case. See 11 U.S.C. § 349(a). For further reading on the dischargeability in a subsequent case of debts that were listed in a prior bankruptcy case, see Williamson, The Bankruptcy Issues Handbook, supra, Art. 1.02.

nondischargeable debts, dischargeability of related fees and costs

debts for attorneys fees, dischargeability of

In applying the above-listed exceptions to discharge, the general rule is that when a debt is determined to be nondischargeable, the attendant attorney fees, interest, and costs associated with the debt are also nondischargeable. See In Re Fitzgerald, 109 B.R. 893 (Bankr. N. D. Ind. 1989). Thus, attorney fees awarded in a divorce decree wherein alimony, maintenance, or support was awarded are generally held to be in the nature of alimony, maintenance or support and therefore nondischargeable. See In Re Williams, 703 F. 2d 1055 (8th Cir. 1983); But see In re Lowther, 321 F.3d 946 (10th Cir. 2002). However, if an obligation for attorneys fees incurred in connection with a nondischargeable debt is either not provided for in the order or debt instrument or is not directly attendant to the nondischargeable debt, then the attorney-fee obligation is likely to be dischargeable. Debts for attorney fees that are incurred in connection with dischargeable debts are clearly dischargeable.

divorce-related debts, dischargeability of

The dischargeability of divorce-related debts is an issue that arises in many consumer bankruptcy cases. Divorce-related debts that qualify as a domestic support obligation are nondischargeable under 11 U.S.C. § 523(a)(5). See 11 U.S.C. § 101(14A) for the definition of "domestic support obligation." Divorce-related debts of a property-settlement nature, while not nondischargeable under 11 U.S.C. § 523(a)(5), are nondischargeable under 11 U.S.C. § 523(a)(15). It should be noted that nondischargeability under Code sections 523(a)(5) and 523(a)(15) is self-executing, which means that the creditor is not required to take action in the bankruptcy case in order to establish the nondischargeability of the debt. For further reading on the dischargeability of divorce-related debts, see Williamson, The Bankruptcy Issues Handbook, supra, Art. 1.07.

Debts for obtaining money, property, services or credit by actual fraud, if proven by a creditor filing a complaint to determine dischargeability, are nondischargeable under 11 U.S.C. § 523(a)(2) (i.e., subparagraph (2)(a) above). Under this section, a mere failure of a debtor to fulfill a promise to pay for goods or services is not fraudulent. However, if a debtor purchases or obtains goods, services or money on credit with no intention of paying the debt or with knowledge that it will be financially impossible to pay the debt, the debt may be deemed fraudulent and nondischargeable under Section 523(a)(2). See In Re Schmidt, 70 B.R. 634 (Bankr. N. D. Ind. 1984). Credit purchases made by a debtor on the eve of bankruptcy are likely to be deemed fraudulent under this section, especially if the financial condition of the debtor at the time was such that repayment was virtually impossible. See In Re Schrader, 55 B.R. 608 (Bankr. W. D. Va. 1985); In re Abercrombie, 148 B.R. 964 (Bankr. M. D. Fla. 1992). The standard of proof required of a creditor seeking to establish the nondischargeability of a debt under 11 U.S.C. § 523(a) is that of a "preponderance of the evidence". "Clear and convincing evidence" is not required to establish any of the exceptions to discharge, including fraud. See Grogan v. Garner, 498 U.S. 279, 111 S. Ct. 654 (1991).

debts procured by fraud, dischargeability, burden of proof

non-dischargeability of debt, degree of proof required

It should be noted that the following debts of an individual debtor are presumed to be nondischargeable: (1) consumer debts aggregating $725 or more owed to a single creditor for "luxury goods or services" incurred on or within 90 days before the order for relief, and (2) cash advances aggregating more than $1,000 that are extensions of consumer credit under an open end credit plan obtained on or within 70 days before the order for relief. See 11 U.S.C. § 523(a)(2)(C). "Luxury goods or services" do not include goods or services reasonably acquired for the support or maintenance of the debtor or a dependent of the debtor, and "extensions of consumer credit under an open end credit plan" means cash advances under a plan wherein the creditor reasonably contemplates repeated transactions, which prescribes the terms of such transactions, and which provides for a finance charge on the unpaid balance. See 11 U.S.C. § 523(a)(2)(C) and 15 U.S.C. § 1602(i). The issue of whether particular goods purchased by the debtor constitute "luxury goods" must be determined in light of the debtor's personal circumstances. See In re George, 381 B.R. 911 (Bankr. M. D. Fla. 2007); In re Chase, 372 B.R. 133 (Bankr. S. D. N.Y. 2007).

debts for luxury goods or services or cash advances, dischargeablility

luxury goods or services, what constitutes

The statutory presumption of nondischargeability has the effect of imposing on the debtor the burden of coming forward with evidence sufficient to rebut the presumption. If such evidence is produced, however, the burden of establishing the nondischargeability of the debt reverts to the creditor. See In re Ritter, 404 B.R. 811 (Bankr. E. D. Pa. 2009); In re Green, 296 B.R. 173 (Bankr. C. D. Ill. 2003). For further reading on the dischargeability of consumer debts for luxury goods or services and cash advances, see Williamson, The Bankruptcy Issues Handbook, supra, Art. 1.11.

luxury goods, effect of presumption

The issue of the nondischargeability of debts for student loans or educational obligations under 11 U.S.C. § 523(a)(8) frequently arises in chapter 7 consumer cases. It should be noted initially that the nondischargeability of debts for qualifying student loans or educational obligations is self executing, which means that it is not necessary for the creditor to file an objection or complaint, or even to appear in the chapter 7 case, in order for the debt to be nondischargeable. Accordingly, a post-discharge attempt to collect a qualifying student loan does not violate the discharge injunction issued by the bankruptcy court. See In Re Barth, 86 B.R. 146 (Bankr. W. D. Wis. 1988); In re Hamblin, 277 B.R. 676 (Bankr. S. D. Miss. 2002). Further, the nondischargeability of a student loan debt in a chapter 7 case can be determined in a state court, because the issue is not within the exclusive jurisdiction of the bankruptcy court. See In Re Craig, 56 B.R. 479 (Bankr. W. D. Mo. 1985).

debts for student loans, nondischargeablity of

Unless excepting the debt from discharge would impose an undue hardship on the debtor and his or her dependents, the following education-related debts are nondischargeable under 11 U.S.C. § 523(a)(8):

(1) an educational benefit overpayment or loan made, insured or guaranteed by a governmental unit, or made under a program funded in whole or in part by a governmental unit or nonprofit institution;

(2) an obligation to repay funds received as an educational benefit, scholarship or stipend; or

(3) any other educational loan incurred by an individual debtor that is a "qualified education loan" (as defined in 26 U.S.C. § 221(d)(1)).

Under the above definitions, not only are educational loans and benefits received from or guaranteed or funded by governmental units and nonprofit institutions nondischargeable, but so are educational loans and benefits received by the debtor from profit-making and other nongovernmental entities. The only educational loans and obligations that are dischargeable are those owed to family members or to entities owned or controlled by the debtor and those that

debts for student loans, undue hardship, what constitutes

qualify under the "undue hardship" exception listed above. It should be noted that educational loans and obligations incurred on behalf of the debtor or a spouse or dependent of the debtor are equally nondischargeable under paragraph (3) above.

As stated above, a debtor may establish that a qualifying student loan or educational obligation is dischargeable by proving that the nondischarge of the loan or obligation will impose an undue hardship on the debtor and his or her dependents. Undue hardship may be proven by showing that, based on the debtor's current income and expenses, the debtor and his or her dependents cannot maintain a minimal standard of living if forced to repay the loan, that such circumstances are likely to continue for a significant portion of the repayment period, and that the debtor has made a good faith effort to repay the loan. See Brunner v. New York State Higher Educational Services Corp., 831 F. 2d 395 (2d Cir. 1987) (establishing the three prong "Brunner" test). A minority of Circuits apply a "totality of circumstances" test. See, e.g., Brandsdon v. Educational Credit Mgt. Corp., 435 B.R. 791 (BAP 1 2010). For further reading on the dischargeability of debts for educational loans and benefits, see Williamson, The Bankruptcy Issues Handbook, supra, Art. 1.06.

complaint to determine dischargeability of debt, when required

same, when debtor may recover costs and attorney's fees

The debtor is discharged from the debts specified in paragraphs (2), (4), and (6) three pages above unless the creditor to whom the debt is owed timely files a complaint to determine the dischargeability of the debt and the court, after a hearing on notice, determines that the debt shall not be discharged. See 11 U.S.C. § 523(c) and Bankruptcy Rule 4007(c). It should be noted that if a creditor files a complaint to determine the dischargeability of a consumer debt under paragraph (2) above, and if the debt is found by the court to be dischargeable, the court may enter judgment against the creditor and in favor of the debtor in the amount of the debtor's costs plus a reasonable attorney's fee for the proceeding if the court finds that the position of the creditor was not substantially justified, except that such costs and fees shall not be awarded if special circumstances would make such an award unjust. See 11 U.S.C. § 523(d). For further reading on the issue of when a debtor may recover costs and attorney's fees from a creditor who unsuccessfully files a complaint to determine the dischargeability of a debt, see Williamson, The Bankruptcy Issues Handbook, supra, Art 1.16.

same, filing and notice requirements

Complaints to determine the dischargeability of debts under 11 U.S.C. § 523(c) must be filed not later than 60 days after the first date set for the meeting of creditors, whether or not the meeting is actually held on that date. Creditors must be given at least 30 days notice of the time for the filing of such complaints, which notice is customarily contained in the notice of commencement of case (Exhibit 2-T). Upon motion filed before the time for filing has expired, the court may, for cause and after a hearing on notice, extend the time for the filing of such complaints. See Bankruptcy Rule 4007(c).

same, procedure under

A proceeding commenced by the filing of a complaint to determine the dischargeability of a debt is an adversary proceeding governed by Part VII of the Bankruptcy Rules. See Bankruptcy Rule 4007(e). However, the court need not determine the issues raised by such a complaint until after it has ruled on any complaints filed objecting to the discharge of the debtor under 11 U.S.C. § 727(a). See Advisory Committee's Notes to Bankruptcy Rule 4007. Some districts have local rules governing the procedures under complaints to determine the dischargeability of debts under 11 U.S.C. § 523(c).

complaint to determine the dischargeability of any debt, filing requirements and fee

It is important to understand that complaints may be filed to determine the dischargeability of any debt, not just those that are discharged if a complaint is not filed. A complaint to determine the dischargeability of a debt other than the debts described in the third paragraph above may be filed by the debtor or a creditor at any time, either during the case or after the case has been closed. See Bankruptcy Rule 4007(a),(b). This is a useful procedure for determining the status of debts whose dischargeability is questionable. There is a filing fee for such a complaint, except that a child support creditor may appear and intervene without charge if a form describing the child support debt is filed.

chapter 7 discharge, effect of on discharged debts

A chapter 7 discharge discharges the debtor from all dischargeable debts that arose before the date the petition was filed or that are deemed to have arisen before such date, regardless of whether a proof of claim is filed or allowed. See 11 U.S.C. § 727(b). Except with respect to certain community debts and property (see below, this section), the discharge of a debt does not affect the liability of any other entity for the discharged debt and does not affect the liability of the property of any other entity for the discharged debt. See 11 U.S.C. § 524(e).

An order of discharge in a chapter 7 case has the following effect on the discharged debts and liabilities of a chapter 7 debtor:

order of discharge, effect of

(1) It voids any judgment at any time obtained, to the extent that such judgment is a determination of the personal liability of the debtor with respect to a discharged debt, whether or not discharge of the debt is waived.

(2) It operates as an injunction against the commencement or continuation of an action, the employment of process, or any act, to collect, recover, or offset a discharged debt as a personal liability of the debtor, whether or not discharge of the debt is waived.

(3) It operates as an injunction against the commencement or continuation of an action, the employment of process, or an act, to collect or recover from, or offset against, certain community property of the debtor acquired after the commencement of the case, on account of an allowable community claim, except such claims that are not dischargeable against the debtor or that would not be dischargeable against the debtor's spouse in a similar case concerning the spouse, whether or not discharge of the debt based on the community claim is waived. See 11 U.S.C. § 524(a).

chapter 7 discharge, effect of in community property states

community property states, list of

In community property states, all of the community property of the debtor and the debtor's spouse, with some minor exceptions, becomes property of the debtor's bankruptcy estate, whether or not the debtor's spouse files under chapter 7. See 11 U.S.C. § 541(a)(2). The community creditors of the debtor and the debtor's spouse are permitted to share in the distribution of the community property. See 11 U.S.C. § 726(c). The community creditors of the nonfiling spouse, with only limited exceptions, are then enjoined and precluded from later moving against community property of the nonfiling spouse acquired after the commencement of the debtor's case. See 11 U.S.C. § 524(a)(3). Thus, in community property states the nonfiling spouse of the debtor may receive a discharge of community debts without filing under chapter 7. The states with community property laws include Arizona, California, Idaho, Louisiana, Nevada, New Mexico, Texas, and Washington.

attempt to collect discharged debt, debtor's obligation

Occasionally a creditor will seek to collect a claim against the debtor that was discharged in a chapter 7 case. If the debtor does not wish to pay the claim, the creditor should be advised, preferably in writing, that the debt has been discharged and of the injunctive effect of the order of discharge. A copy of the debtor's order of discharge, which sets forth the injunctive relief granted by the court in connection with the discharge, will provide the creditor with the required notice. It should be noted that except for debts covered by enforceable reaffirmation agreements (see section 2.18, infra), the debtor is not legally obligated to pay any portion of a discharged debt under any circumstances, even if the debtor has voluntarily repaid a portion of the debt after the discharge. Further, a creditor may not offset any portion of a discharged debt against a post-petition obligation owed by the creditor to the debtor. See 11 U.S.C. § 524(a). A creditor in any postbankruptcy litigation has the burden of proving that the debt in question was nondischargeable. See, e.g., In re Jones, 296 B.R. 447 (Bankr. M. D. Tenn. 2003).

attempt to collect discharged debt, creditor's liability

If a creditor pursues a discharged claim against the debtor, the creditor may be held in contempt of court and may be liable to the debtor for damages. See In Re Bock, 297 B.R. 22 (Bankr. W. D. N.C. 2002); In re Nibbelink, 403 B.R. 113 (M. D. Fla. 2009). If a dispute later arises as to whether a debt was discharged in the chapter 7 case, the case may be reopened without the payment of an additional filing fee for the purpose of filing a complaint to determine the dischargeability of the debt. See 11 U.S.C. § 350(b); Bankruptcy Rule 4007(b).

chapter 7 discharge, effect of on codebtors and liens

avoiding unsecured liens, necessity of

It should be understood that a chapter 7 discharge relates only to the personal liability of the debtor for the discharged debts. The liability of codebtors, sureties and guarantors of the debtor is not affected by the discharge, and creditors with valid liens that were not avoided during the case may proceed against property of the debtor that is subject to such liens, including exempt property. See 11 U.S.C. § 522 (c)(2); Johnson v. Home State Bank, 501 U.S. 78, 111 S.Ct. 2150 (1991). Because the unchallenged lien of a creditor who does not file a proof of claim survives the bankruptcy case (see In Re Tarnow, 749 F.2d 464 (7th Cir. 1984); In re Hamlett, 322 F.3d 342 (4th Cir. 2003)), the debtor's attorney should insure that the liens of all such creditors are avoided during the case. General liens of judgment and tax creditors and mortgage liens of creditors with little or no security (i.e., second or third mortgage holders) are often not asserted by the creditor during the case. It is important that such liens be avoided, if possible, during the case so that they will not survive the case and encumber the debtor's postbankruptcy property. If a lien is avoided by the bankruptcy court, a written order avoiding the lien should be obtained so that it can be recorded, if necessary, or otherwise used to avoid the lien of record.

avoiding liens, general aspects

Judgment liens that encumber exempt property of the debtor may be avoided under 11 U.S.C. § 522(f) and most liens securing disallowed claims may be avoided under 11 U.S.C. § 506(d). For a lien to be avoidable under Section 506(d), however, the creditor's underlying claim must be disallowed under 11 U.S.C. § 502. See In re Warner, 146 B.R. 253 (Bankr. N. D. Cal. 1992). The claim of a partially-secured creditor may not be bifurcated into secured and unsecured portions for the purpose of avoiding the lien securing the unsecured portion of the claim under Section 506(d). The reason for this is that the Supreme Court has ruled that the lien of a partially-secured creditor may not be "stripped down" under Section 506(d) to the value of the creditor's allowed secured claim. See Dewsnup v. Timm, 502 U.S. 410 , 112 S.Ct. 773 (1992). This means that the lien of a partially-secured creditor survives the bankruptcy case in its entirety and may be enforced after the case to the full extent permitted under local law. See section 2.12, supra, for further reading on the avoidance of liens under Sections 522(f) and 506(d). For further reading on the extent to which a debtor may avoid liens under Section 506(d) of the Bankruptcy Code, see Williamson, The Bankruptcy Issues Handbook, supra, Art. 1.17.

discharge of debt as income to debtor, rule

It should be understood that even though the discharge of a debt in a bankruptcy case relieves the debtor of an obligation, it does not constitute "income" to the debtor for federal income tax purposes. While the release or discharge of an enforceable obligation to pay money may constitute income to the obligor in some situations, 26 U.S.C. § 108(a) clearly provides that gross income does not include amounts the obligations for which are discharged in a title 11 case.

2.18 Reaffirming Dischargeable Debts

Under 11 U.S.C. § 524(c), an agreement between a holder of a claim and the debtor, the consideration for which is wholly or partially based on a dischargeable debt, is enforceable, to the extent that it is otherwise enforceable under nonbankruptcy law and whether or not discharge of the debt is waived, only if:

enforceable reaffirmation agreement, requirements of

(1) the agreement was made before the granting of the chapter 7 discharge;

(2) the debtor files a statement in support of the agreement and receives the disclosures required under 11 U.S.C. § 524(k) at or before the time at which the debtor signed the agreement. The statement and disclosures are discussed below in this section;

(3) the agreement, with the appropriate cover sheet as required by Bankruptcy Rule 4008(a), is filed with the court, accompanied by a declaration or certification by the attorney that represented the debtor in negotiating the agreement with the creditor stating that the agreement represents a fully informed and voluntary agreement by the debtor and does not impose an undue hardship on the debtor or a dependent of the debtor and that the attorney has fully advised the debtor of the legal effect and consequences of the agreement and of a default thereunder by the debtor;

(4) the debtor does not rescind the agreement at any time prior to discharge or within 60 days after the agreement has been filed with the court, whichever occurs later, by giving notice of rescission to the holder of the claim;

(5) the court, at the discharge and reaffirmation hearing, informs the debtor that he or she is not legally required to enter into the agreement, and of the legal effects and consequences of the agreement and of a default thereunder; and

(6) if the debtor was not represented by an attorney in negotiating the agreement and if the debt is not a consumer debt secured by real property, the court approves the agreement as not imposing an undue hardship on the debtor or a dependent of the debtor and as being in the best interest of the debtor.

The disclosures required under 11 U.S.C. § 524(k) consist of a disclosure statement meeting the requirements of 11 U.S.C. § 524(k)(3), a reaffirmation agreement meeting the requirements of 11 U.S.C. § 524(k)(4), a declaration of the debtor's attorney meeting the requirements of 11 U.S.C. § 524(k)(5), and a statement of the debtor in support of the reaffirmation agreement meeting the requirements of 11 U.S.C. § 524(k)(6). See 11 U.S.C. § 524(k)(2) for a description of the general drafting requirements for these documents. The required disclosure statement must contain the provisions set forth in 11 U.S.C. § 524(k)(3), which are specific and lengthy. The general form of the reaffirmation agreement is set forth in 11 U.S.C. § 524(k)(4) and must be followed. The language required in the attorney's declaration (or certification) is set forth in 11 U.S.C. § 524(k)(5). The required language of the Debtor's Statement in Support of Reaffirmation Agreement is set forth in 11 U.S.C. § 524(k)(6). Among other things, this document must set forth the debtor's monthly income and monthly expenses. However, if the debtor is represented by an attorney and if the debt being reaffirmed is owed to a credit union, only the simple 3-line statement set forth in 11 U.S.C. § 524(k)(6)(B) is required. If the debtor is not represented by an attorney in connection with the reaffirmation agreement, the motion and order set forth in 11 U.S.C. § 524(k)(7) and (8) must be prepared and submitted to the court. A form for each of these documents is contained in Bankruptcy Form 2400A and 427, a sample of which is set forth in Exhibit 2-Z(1) at the end of this chapter.

reaffirmation agreement, required documents

As indicated above, if the debtor was represented by an attorney in connection with the reaffirmation agreement and if a presumption of undue hardship (see below) does not exist, court approval of the agreement is not required and a hearing on the agreement is not required. See 11 U.S.C. § 524(d). Also, whether or not the debtor was represented by an attorney during the negotiations, if the consideration for the reaffirmation agreement is based in whole or in part on a consumer debt secured by real property (such as a home mortgage), court approval of the agreement is not required. See 11 U.S.C. § 524(c)(6)(B). It is, of course, important that the attorney fully advise the debtor as to the legal effect of the reaffirmation agreement and of the consequences of a default under the agreement by the debtor because the attorney's declaration contains a statement to this effect.

reaffirmation agreement, when court approval not required

If the debtor's Statement in Support of Reaffirmation Agreement shows that the debtor's net monthly income (i.e., monthly income less monthly expenses) is insufficient to make the payments called for in the reaffirmation agreement, a presumption of undue hardship on the debtor is created, in which case court approval of the reaffirmation agreement must be obtained and the attorney's certification must state that in the opinion of the attorney, the debtor is able to make the payments. See 11 U.S.C. § 524(k)(5)(B). The presumption of undue hardship continues for 60 days after the reaffirmation agreement is filed with the court, unless the 60 day period is extended for cause (after notice and a hearing) prior to its expiration. The presumption of undue hardship must be reviewed by the court and may be rebutted in writing by the debtor by showing other sources of funds with which to make the payments called for in the reaffirmation agreement. If the presumption is not rebutted to the satisfaction of the court, the court, after notice and a hearing held prior to the entry of the debtor's discharge, may disapprove the reaffirmation agreement, unless the creditor is a credit union, in which case a presumption of undue hardship cannot arise. See 11 U.S.C. § 524(m)(2). It should be noted that the debtor may not receive a discharge as long as a presumption of undue hardship exists. See Bankruptcy Rule 4004(c)(1)(J).

reaffirmation agreement, presumption of undue hardship, procedure

If the debtor was represented by an attorney in connection with the reaffirmation agreement and an undue hardship does not exist, court approval of a reaffirmation agreement is not required and it will only be necessary for the debtor's attorney to file the reaffirmation agreement and the other required documents with the court. Bankruptcy Forms 2400A and 427 should be used in preparing the reaffirmation documents. In addition to the reaffirmation agreement, Bankruptcy Form 2400A contains the required disclosures, instructions and notices to the debtor, an attorney's certification, the debtor's statement in support of reaffirmation agreement, a motion for court approval of the agreement, and a proposed order approving the agreement. The motion and order are needed only if the debtor is not represented by an attorney. Completed samples of the Bankruptcy Form 2400A and 427 documents, other than the motion and order, are set forth in Exhibit 2-Z(1) at the end of this chapter. The agreement portion of Form 2400A is designed for simple reaffirmation agreements, however, and should not be relied upon if the debtor's arrangement with the creditor is complicated. If the agreement with the creditor is not a simple one, a separate reaffirmation agreement should be drafted and incorporated by reference into the agreement portion of Form 2400A. If the debt being reaffirmed is a consumer debt secured by property of the bankruptcy estate (as is often the case), it will also be necessary to file a statement of intention and serve it upon the appropriate parties within the required period. See section 2.11, supra, for further reading on the statement of intention.

reaffirmation documents, preparation requirements

statement of intention, necessity of filing

unrepresented debtor, when reaffirmation hearing required

If the debtor wishes to enter into a reaffirmation agreement and is not represented by an attorney in connection with the agreement, the court is required to hold a reaffirmation hearing for the purpose of advising the debtor concerning the agreement and determining whether the agreement imposes an undue hardship on the debtor and is in the best interest of the debtor. See 11 U.S.C. § 524(d). If the debtor does not wish to enter into a reaffirmation agreement or was represented by an attorney during the course of negotiating the reaffirmation agreement, a reaffirmation hearing is not required. If the debtor wishes to enter into a reaffirmation agreement and was not represented by an attorney in negotiating the agreement, Bankruptcy Forms 2400A and 2400B, which contain information needed by the court to determine whether a hearing is required, should be filed early in the case so that a reaffirmation hearing can be scheduled by the court. It is important to note that a reaffirmation hearing is required whenever the debtor was not represented by an attorney in connection with the reaffirmation agreement, even if court approval of the agreement is not required because the debt being reaffirmed is a consumer debt secured by real property. See 11 U.S.C. § 524(d)(2).

reaffirmation agreement, necessity of filing

It is important to understand that even if an undue hardship does not exist and the debtor was represented by an attorney in connection with the reaffirmation agreement and a reaffirmation hearing is not required, it is still necessary to file the reaffirmation agreement and other required documents with the court in order for the reaffirmation agreement to be valid. See 11 U.S.C. § 524(c)(3).

order of discharge, necessity of deferring

It should be noted that Bankruptcy Rule 4004(c)(2) permits the court, upon the motion of the debtor, to defer the entry of an order granting a discharge for 30 days, and, upon a further motion made within such 30 day period, to a date certain. This provision may be useful when negotiating a reaffirmation agreement because of the requirement that such agreements be made prior to the granting of the discharge.

court approval of reaffirmation agreement, procedure

If court approval of a reaffirmation agreement is required, either because the debtor is not represented by an attorney or because a presumption of undue hardship exists, the debtor's motion for approval of the reaffirmation agreement must be filed with the court prior to or at the discharge and reaffirmation hearing, which must be held within 30 days after the order granting or denying the debtor's discharge. See Bankruptcy Rule 4008 and Form 2400B. The Debtor's Statement in Support of Reaffirmation Agreement must be accompanied by a statement of the total income and total expense amounts appearing on schedules I and J. Any difference between the amounts appearing on schedules I and J and on the Debtor's Statement in Support of Reaffirmation Agreement must be explained in the accompanying statement. See Bankruptcy Rule 4008. Many districts have local rules governing procedures for obtaining court approval of reaffirmation agreements, and they should be checked in this regard.

voluntary repayment of debt, debtor's rights

It should be understood that nothing contained in 11 U.S.C. § 524(c) or (d) prevents a debtor from voluntarily paying a discharged or dischargeable debt. See 11 U.S.C. § 524(f). The debtor should be advised, however, that he or she is not legally obligated to pay (or continue paying) a creditor with whom he or she does not have an valid reaffirmation agreement, even if the debtor has waived the discharge of the debt in writing, agreed in writing to repay the debt, or made one or more payments on the debt after the commencement of the chapter 7 case. See 11 U.S.C. § 524(a), 727(b). Further, any judgment entered against the debtor based on a discharged debt is voidable at the request of the debtor. See In re Cruz, 254 B.R. 801 (Bankr. S. D. N.Y. 2000) .

2.19 Creditors - Claims, Setoffs, and Dividends

An unsecured creditor must file a proof of claim with the clerk of the bankruptcy court within 70 days after the first date set for the meeting of creditors for the claim to be allowed, unless the claim is filed on the creditor's behalf by the trustee, the debtor or a codebtor, or a guarantor. See Bankruptcy Rule 3002(a),(b),(c). There are six exceptions to the 70 day requirement for filing proofs of unsecured claims. The exceptions deal with claims by governmental units (who under 11 U.S.C. § 502(b)(9) have 180 days to file a claim), claims for infants or incompetents, claims which become allowable as a result of judgments, claims arising from the rejection of executory contracts or unexpired leases, and claims in chapter 7 no-asset cases where a notice of no dividend is given and nonexempt assets are later discovered. See Bankruptcy Rule 3002(c). The clerk, or some other person as the court may direct, must give each creditor notice of the time allowed for the filing of claims. See Bankruptcy Rule 2002(f). This notice is normally contained in the notice of commencement of case.

proof of claim, time for filing, notice of

If notice of insufficient assets to pay a dividend (i.e., a notice of no dividend) is given in the notice of commencement of case, and if the trustee subsequently notifies the court that payment of a dividend appears possible, the clerk must notify the creditors of that fact and that proofs of claim may be filed within 90 days after the mailing of the notice. See Bankruptcy Rule 3002(c)(5). It should be noted that a creditor is entitled to be notified in a bankruptcy case at the address specified in 11 U.S.C. § 342(c)(2). Also, a creditor may file a notice of address with the court under 11 U.S.C. § 342(e) or (f).

notice of no dividend

address of creditor, notice of

Secured creditors are not specifically dealt with in the Rules of Bankruptcy Procedure, although it is clear that they may file claims. Many districts have adopted local rules dealing with the filing of claims and evidences of security interests by secured creditors. In some districts they are required to file proofs of claim within a certain period if they are claiming a security interest in property of the estate. In other districts they are required to file evidences of their lien or security interest with the trustee within a certain period. The local rules should be checked in this regard.

secured claims, filing requirements

If a security interest in property of the debtor is claimed, a proof of claim must be accompanied by evidence that the security interest has been perfected. See Bankruptcy Rule 3001(d). In most consumer cases secured creditors proceed against their security instead of filing a claim, unless the local rules require such a filing. However, if the debtor or another entity contests the creditor's right to proceed against the secured property, the creditor may have to file a claim in order to assert or prove its standing as the holder of an allowed secured claim. In any event, before proceeding against its security, a secured creditor must file a motion for relief from the automatic stay under Bankruptcy Rule 4001 and any applicable local rules. It should be noted, however, that the automatic stay terminates with respect to personal property of the estate or of the debtor that is subject to a valid purchase money security interest if the debtor fails to either reaffirm the debt or redeem the property under Code section 722 within 45 days after the first meeting of creditors. The creditor may then exercise its nonbankruptcy remedies against the property, unless the trustee moves to extend the stay. See 11 U.S.C. § 521(a)(6) and section 2.10, supra. The debtor's rights and duties with respect to proceedings against his or her property are discussed in section 2.10, supra.

secured claims, procedure for reclaiming security

personal property, termination of stay with respect to

An allowed secured claim of a creditor that is secured by a lien on property of the bankruptcy estate, or that is subject to a setoff, is a secured claim only to the extent of the value of the creditor's interest in the property, or to the extent of the amount subject to setoff, as the case may be. See 11 U.S.C. § 506(a). The balance of the claim is deemed unsecured. The value of a partially-secured creditor's interest in the property is determined in light of the purpose of the valuation and of any proposed disposition or use of the property. The valuation may be made in conjunction with any hearing on the disposition of the property or on the motion of any party in interest. See 11 U.S.C. § 506(a)(1) and Bankruptcy Rule 3012. However, if the debtor is an individual in a case under chapter 7 or 13, value with respect to personal property securing an allowed claim is determined based on the replacement value of such property as of the date of the filing of the petition without deduction for costs of sale or marketing. With respect to property acquired for personal, family, or household purposes, replacement value means the price a retail merchant would charge for property of that kind considering the age and condition of the property at the time value is determined. See 11 U.S.C. § 506(a)(2).

secured claim, extent of allowance

under-secured creditor, survival of lien

Under 11 U.S.C. § 506(d), the lien of a partially-secured creditor who files a proof of claim is deemed void to the extent that it does not secure an allowed secured claim. However, if such a creditor does not file a proof of claim, the creditor's lien survives the bankruptcy proceeding unless it is challenged by the debtor. See In Re Tarnow, 749 F.2d 464 (7th Cir. 1984); In re Hamlett, 322 F.3d 342 (4th Cir. 2003). Therefore, a creditor with little security may be well advised not to file a proof of claim on the chance that the debtor will not avoid the lien and thereby permit it to survive the case.

secured claim, inclusion of costs and fees

If the value of the secured property exceeds the amount of the allowed secured claim (i.e., if the creditor is over secured), the creditor may also be allowed to collect interest on the claim and any reasonable fees, costs, and charges provided for in the agreement under which the claim arose. See 11 U.S.C. § 506(b). In addition, the trustee may recover the expenses of preserving or disposing of the property. See 11 U.S.C. § 506(c).

proof of claim, general requirements

A proof of claim, including a claim for wages, salary, or commissions, must conform to Official Form 410. See Bankruptcy Rule 3001(a). In some districts a proof of claim form is contained on the reverse side of the notice of commencement of case. A proof of claim must be executed by the creditor or the creditor's authorized agent, except for claims filed on the creditor's behalf by the trustee, the debtor, a codebtor, or a person who has secured the creditor. See Bankruptcy Rules 3001(b), 3004, and 3005. When a claim, or an interest in property of the debtor securing the claim, is based on a writing, the original or a duplicate of the writing must be filed with the proof of claim. If the writing has been lost or destroyed, a statement of the circumstances of its loss or destruction must be filed with the claim. See Bankruptcy Rule 3001(c). A sample proof of claim is set forth in Exhibit 3-G, at the end of chapter three, infra.

proof of claim, information required

Bankruptcy Rule 3001(c)(2) requires additional information to be filed with the proof of claim in consumer debtor cases. This additional information includes: (1) an itemization of interest, fees, expenses, and other charges included in the claim which were incurred before the petition was filed; (2) a statement of the amount necessary to cure any prepetition default on a claim secured by a security interest in the debtor's property; and, (3) if a claim is secured by a security interest in the debtor's principal residence, an escrow account statement as of the petition date, if an escrow account has been established. Sanctions may be imposed on a creditor who fails to provide the required information with its proof of claim. See Bankruptcy Rule 3001(c)(2)(D)(i) and (ii).

proof of claim, filing of by debtor or trustee

If a creditor fails to timely file a proof of claim, the debtor or the trustee may file a proof of claim within 30 days after expiration of the time for filing claims. The clerk must forthwith give notice of the filing to the creditor, the debtor, and the trustee. See Bankruptcy Rule 3004 and 11 U.S.C. § 501(c). If there are assets in the estate, this can be a useful tactic for the debtor with respect to priority claims for nondischargeable debts, such as tax claims or divorce-related claims. If the creditor thereafter files a proof of claim, it supersedes the claim filed by the trustee or debtor on the creditor's behalf. See Bankruptcy Rule 3004.

proof of claim, filing of by codebtor or guarantor

If a creditor does not file a proof of claim, an entity who is or may be liable with the debtor to the creditor or who has secured the creditor may, within 30 days after the expiration of the time for filing claims, execute and file a proof of claim. However, no distribution may be made on the claim except on satisfactory proof that the original debt will be diminished by the amount distributed. See Bankruptcy Rule 3005(a) and 11 U.S.C. § 501(b).

subrogated claims, allowance of

An entity that is liable with the debtor on the claim of a creditor, or that has secured the claim of a creditor, and that pays such claim, is subrogated to the rights of the creditor to the extent of such payment. See 11 U.S.C. § 509(a). However, the entity is not subrogated to the rights of the creditor to the extent that (1) its claim for reimbursement is allowed as a separate claim, disallowed as a claim, or subordinated by agreement or otherwise, or (2) as between the debtor and the entity, the entity received consideration for the debt. See 11 U.S.C. § 509(b). Certain priority claims (i.e., unsecured claims for wages, salaries, commissions, contributions to employee benefit plans, the return of certain deposits, etc.) lose their priority if they are subrogated. See 11 U.S.C. § 507(d). It should be noted that subordination agreements are enforceable in chapter 7 cases to the same extent that they are enforceable under nonbankruptcy law. See 11 U.S.C. § 510(a).

transferred claims, proof of, filing requirements

If a claim has been transferred other than for purposes of security before proof of the claim is filed, the proof of claim may be filed only by the transferee or an indenture trustee. See Bankruptcy Rule 3001(e)(1). If a claim other than one based on a publicly traded note, bond or debenture, is transferred other than for purposes of security after the filing of a proof of claim, evidence of the transfer must be filed by the transferee and the clerk must notify the alleged transferor of the filing and of the time for filing objections. See Bankruptcy Rule 3001(e)(2).

claims transferred for security, filing requirements

If a claim, other than one based on a publicly traded note, bond or debenture, has been transferred for security before the filing of a proof of claim, either the transferor or the transferee, or both, may file a proof of claim in the full amount. See Bankruptcy Rule 3001(e)(3) for additional requirements. If a claim, other than one based on a publicly traded note, bond or debenture, is transferred for security after the filing of a proof of claim, evidence of the terms of the transfer must be filed by the transferee and the clerk must notify the alleged transferor of the filing and of the time for filing objections. See Bankruptcy Rule 3001(e)(4) for additional requirements. If an objection or motion is filed objecting to the transfer of a filed claim, a copy of the objection or motion, together with notice of the hearing, must be mailed or otherwise delivered to the transferor or transferee at least 30 days prior to the hearing. See Bankruptcy Rule 3001(e)(5).

objection to transfer of claim, procedure

A creditor may withdraw a claim as of right by filing a notice of withdrawal, except that if an objection to the claim or a complaint against the creditor in an adversary proceeding has been filed, the creditor may not withdraw the claim except on order of the court after a hearing on notice. See Bankruptcy Rule 3006.

withdrawal of claim, procedure

An objection to the allowance of a claim must be in writing and filed with the clerk of the bankruptcy court. A copy of the objection and a notice of the hearing thereon must be mailed or otherwise delivered to the claimant, the debtor, and the trustee at least 30 days prior to the hearing. If an objection is joined with a demand for relief of the kind specified in Bankruptcy Rule 7001 (i.e., to determine the validity or priority of a lien, etc.), it becomes an adversary proceeding. See Bankruptcy Rule 3007. The local rules may contain provisions dealing with objections to claims, and they should be checked in this regard.

objection to allowance of claim, procedure

A properly executed and filed proof of claim constitutes prima facie evidence of the validity and amount of the claim. See Bankruptcy Rule 3001(f). Unless a party in interest files an objection to a properly filed claim, it is deemed allowed. See 11 U.S.C. § 502(a). If an objection to a claim is properly made, the court, after a hearing on notice, must determine the amount of the claim as of the date of filing of the petition and allow the claim in that amount, unless the claim is of a type that is not allowable in a bankruptcy case. See 11 U.S.C. § 502(b).

proof of claim, effect of filing

In determining the allowability of claims, it should be noted that the Bankruptcy Code provides that the following types of claims are not allowable in bankruptcy cases.

claims not allowable in bankruptcy cases

(1) Claims that are unenforceable against the debtor or property of the debtor by reason of an agreement or applicable law for any reason other than because a claim is contingent or unliquidated, are not allowable. See 11 U.S.C. § 502(b)(1). This provision has the effect of giving the estate the benefit of any defenses to a claim that the debtor may possess. See 11 U.S.C. § 558.

(2) Claims for unmatured interest are not allowable. See 11 U.S.C. § 502(b)(2). This provision has the effect of denying unsecured creditors postpetition interest on their claims.

(3) Claims for taxes assessed against property of the estate are not allowable to the extent that the claim exceeds the value of the estate's interest in the property. See 11 U.S.C. § 502(b)(3).

(4) Claims of insiders or attorneys of the debtor are not allowable to the extent that the claim exceeds the reasonable value of such services. See 11 U.S.C. § 502(b)(4).

(5) Claims for unmatured domestic support obligations are not allowable to the extent that the claim is nondischargeable. See 11 U.S.C. § 502(b)(5).

(6) Claims of lessors for damages resulting from the termination of leases of real property are not allowable to the extent that the claim exceeds certain limits. See 11 U.S.C. § 502(b)(6) for the specific limits.

(7) Claims of employees for damages resulting from the termination of employment contracts are not allowable to the extent that the claim exceeds certain limits. See 11 U.S.C. § 502(b)(7) for the specific limits.

(8) Claims resulting from a reduction, due to late payment, in the amount of an otherwise applicable credit available to the debtor in connection with an employment tax on wages, salaries, or commissions earned from the debtor are not allowable. See 11 U.S.C. § 502(b)(8). This provision applies mainly to claims of governmental units for unemployment taxes.

(9) Claims for which a proof of claim was not timely filed, except to the extent that the tardy filing of the claim is permitted under 11 U.S.C. § 726(a)(1), (2), or (3) or by the Federal Rules of Bankruptcy Procedure. See 11 U.S.C. § 502(b)(9).

claims, when not allowable

contingent or unliquidated claims, allowance of

In addition, the claim of an entity from which property is recoverable by the trustee and the claim of an entity that is a transferee of a voidable transfer are not allowable, unless the entity has paid the amount or turned over the property for which it is liable. See 11 U.S.C. § 502(d). Certain claims for reimbursement or contribution are not allowable. See 11 U.S.C. § 502(e). Contingent or unliquidated claims, the liquidation of which would unduly delay the closing of the case, must be estimated by the court for purposes of allowance. See 11 U.S.C. § 502(c). It should be noted that proceedings to liquidate or estimate personal injury or wrongful death claims against the bankruptcy estate for purposes of distribution are not core proceedings. See 28 U.S.C. § 157(b)(2)(B). See 11 U.S.C. § 508 for the effect on a creditor's claim of payments or transfers received in another proceeding.

reconsideration of claims

A party in interest may move for the reconsideration of an order allowing or disallowing a claim, whereupon the court, after a hearing on notice, must enter an appropriate order. See Bankruptcy Rule 3008. See 11 U.S.C. § 502(j) for the effect of an order of reconsideration on the payment of claims.

setoff, definition, when exercisable

A creditor with a right of setoff is treated as a secured creditor to the extent of the amount of the setoff. See 11 U.S.C. § 506(a). A setoff is a right under nonbankruptcy law that exists between two parties to net (or setoff) their respective ascertainable debts that arose out of unrelated transactions. See In re Myers, 362 F.3d 667 (10th Cir. 2004). The general rule is that a creditor may offset a mutual debt owed by the creditor to the debtor that arose before the commencement of the case against a claim of the creditor against the debtor that arose before the commencement of the case, except to the extent that:

(1) the creditor's claim against the debtor is disallowed,

(2) the creditor's claim was transferred to the creditor by a person other than the debtor after the commencement of the case or within 90 days prior to the date of filing of the petition and while the debtor was insolvent, or

(3) the debt owed to the debtor by the creditor was incurred by the creditor within 90 days before the date of filing, while the debtor was insolvent, and for the purpose of obtaining a right of setoff against the debtor. See 11 U.S.C. § 553(a).

setoffs, general rules

In addition, the trustee is permitted to recover all or part of most setoffs that occur within 90 days prior to the filing of the petition. See 11 U.S.C. § 553(b). A debtor is presumed to have been insolvent during the 90 day-period preceding the filing of the petition. See 11 U.S.C. § 553(c). Creditors are precluded by the automatic stay from exercising a right of setoff after the commencement of the case. See 11 U.S.C. § 362(a)(7).

right of setoff, how to exercise

Subject to the provisions of 11 U.S.C. § 553 described above, a creditor may validly exercise a right of setoff prior to the commencement of the case, provided that the setoff is completed and that a verifiable record, such as a bookkeeping entry or letter, exists to indicate a completion of the setoff. See In re Tillery, 179 B.R. 576, 581 (Bankr. W. D. Ark. 1995). After the commencement of the case, a creditor with an unexercised right of setoff should file a proof of claim showing the setoff as its security and file a motion for relief from the automatic stay for the purpose of exercising its right of setoff. A creditor who does nothing to enforce or protect its unexercised right of setoff may lose the right of setoff and be required to pay over to the trustee the full amount of the debt that it owes to the debtor.

statute of limitations, effect of bankruptcy case on

It should be noted that if the debtor is denied a discharge, the statute of limitations will not have expired on claims against the debtor. 11 U.S.C. § 108(c) provides that if applicable law, an order entered in a proceeding, or an agreement fixes a period for commencing a civil action in a court other than a bankruptcy court on a claim against the debtor, and if such period has not expired before the filing of the petition, then such period shall not expire until the later of - (a) the end of such period, including any suspensions of such period occurring on or after the commencement of the case, or (b) 30 days after notice of the termination or expiration of the automatic stay with respect to such claim. Thus, the statute of limitations on claims against the debtor will expire either at the time it would have otherwise expired or 30 days after receipt of the order of discharge, the notice of no discharge, or the notice of dismissal of the case, whichever is later.

Priority expenses and claims must be paid before distributions to unsecured creditors can be made. See 11 U.S.C. § 726(a). Under 11 U.S.C. § 507(a), priority expenses and claims must be paid in the following order of priority:

priority claims and expenses, order of priority

(1) Allowed unsecured claims for domestic support obligations.

(2) Allowed administrative expenses (e.g., trustee's fees, etc.), and filing fees assessed against the bankruptcy estate.

(3) Certain unsecured claims arising before the appointment of a trustee in an involuntary case.

(4) Allowed unsecured claims for wages, salaries or commissions, including vacation, severance, and sick leave pay or sales commissions earned by independent contractors 75% or more of whose earnings were earned from the debtor, that were earned within 180 days before either the date of filing of the petition or the date of the cessation of the debtor's business, whichever occurred first, but only to the extent of $13,650 for each employee or independent contractor.

(5) Allowed unsecured claims for contributions to employee benefit plans up to a limit of $13,650 per employee.

(6) Certain allowed unsecured claims (up to a limit of $6,725 for each individual) of fishermen and persons engaged in the production or raising of grain.

(7) Allowed unsecured claims of individuals, to the extent of $3,025 each, arising from the deposit of money for the purchase, lease, or rental of property, or the purchase of services, for the personal, family, or household use of such individuals, that were not delivered or provided.

(8) Allowed unsecured claims of governmental units for certain taxes.

(9) Allowed unsecured claims based on a commitment by the debtor to a federal depository institution's regulatory agency to maintain the capital of an insured depository institution.

(10) Allowed claims for death or personal injury resulting from the operation of a motor vehicle or vessel if such operation was unlawful because the debtor was intoxicated from using alcohol, a drug, or another substance.

Distributions to unsecured creditors must be paid by the trustee in the form of dividends as promptly as practicable. Dividend checks must be made payable and mailed to each creditor whose claim has been allowed, unless a power of attorney authorizing another person to receive dividends has been executed and filed in accordance with Bankruptcy Rule 9010. In that event, dividend checks shall be made payable to the creditor and to the other person and shall be mailed to the other person. See Bankruptcy Rule 3009. However, no dividend in an amount of less than five dollars shall be distributed by the trustee to any creditor unless authorized by local rule or by order of the court. See Bankruptcy Rule 3010(a).

dividends to creditors, procedure

2.20 The Dismissal, Conversion, or Closing of a Chapter 7 Case

chapter 7 case, methods of termination

A chapter 7 case may end in any of the following scenarios: (1) by dismissal of the case under any of the Code sections listed below; (2) by conversion of the case to a case under another chapter of the Bankruptcy Code; (3) by the closing of the case after the granting of a discharge; or (4) by the closing of the case without the granting of a discharge.

dismissal of case, grounds for

A chapter 7 consumer case may be dismissed under any of the following Code sections: (1) under 11 U.S.C. § 109(g) for debtor ineligibility; (2) under 11 U.S.C. § 521(e)(2)(B) or (C) for failing to provide copies of the debtor's income tax returns to the trustee or to any requesting creditor; (3) under 11 U.S.C. § 521(j) for failing to file a tax return that becomes due after the commencement of the case; (4) under 11 U.S.C. § 707(a) for cause; (5) under 11 U.S.C. § 707(b)(1) for actual abuse of the chapter 7 provisions; (6) under 11 U.S.C. § 707(b)(2) for presumptive abuse of the chapter 7 provisions; and (7) under 11 U.S.C. § 707(c) for conviction of a crime of violence or a drug-trafficking crime. Each type of dismissal is discussed separately in paragraphs below.

dismissal of case under § 109(g), grounds for

11 U.S.C. § 109(g) provides that an individual is not eligible to be a debtor under any chapter of the Bankruptcy Code if he or she has been a debtor in a prior bankruptcy case at any time during the 180 day period immediately preceding the filing of the present case, if the prior case was either (1) dismissed by the court for willful failure of the debtor to abide by orders of the court or to appear before the court, or (2) voluntarily dismissed by the debtor after the filing of a request by a creditor for relief from the automatic stay. The chapter 7 case of a debtor who is ineligible under this Code provision is subject to dismissal. See In re Nix, 217 B.R. 237 (Bankr. W.D. Tenn. 1998). This Code provision is discussed briefly in section 2.04, supra. For further reading on this issue, see Williamson, The Bankruptcy Issues Handbook, supra, art. 1.01.

dismissal of case under § 521(e)(2), grounds for

11 U.S.C. § 521(e)(2)(B) provides that if the debtor fails to provide the trustee, not later than 7 days prior to the first date set for the first meeting of creditors, with a copy of the debtor's Federal income tax return for the most recent tax year for which a return was filed ending immediately before the commencement of the case (or with a transcript of such return), the court shall dismiss the case unless the debtor demonstrates that the failure to comply is due to circumstances beyond the control of the debtor. 11 U.S.C. § 521(e)(2)(C) provides a similar penalty of dismissal for debtors who fail to provide a copy of the tax return to any creditor who timely requests a copy thereof. See section 2.11, supra, for further reading on this matter. Presumably, most showings of the type enumerated in this paragraph will be the debtor's inability to obtain a copy of the applicable tax returns in time to meet the requirements.

dismissal of case under § 521(j), grounds for

11 U.S.C. § 521(j) provides that if the debtor fails to file a tax return that becomes due after the commencement of the case or obtain an extension of the due date for the filing thereof, the taxing authority may request the court to dismiss or convert the case and that if the debtor fails to file the return or obtain an extension within 90 days after the filing of the request to dismiss or convert by the taxing authority, the court shall dismiss or convert the case, whichever is in the best interests of creditors and the estate. However, this should not present a significant issue in chapter 7 cases because a discharge is usually granted within three or four months of filing.

dismissal for cause, requirements

voluntary dismissal, when permitted

The court may dismiss a chapter 7 case under 11 U.S.C. § 707(a) only after notice and a hearing, and only for cause, including nonpayment of the filing fee, unreasonable delay by the debtor that is prejudicial to creditors, and, on the motion of the United States trustee only, the failure of the debtor to timely file the required schedules and statements. It has been held that lack of good faith by the debtor in filing the case constitutes cause for dismissal under 11 U.S.C. § 707(a). See In Re Zick, 931 F.2d 1124 (6th Cir. 1990). The debtor may seek the voluntary dismissal of his or her chapter 7 case under this Code section upon a showing of good cause therefor. See In re Maixner, 288 B.R. 815 (BAP 8 2003). A proceeding to dismiss a chapter 7 case under 11 U.S.C. § 707(a), whether voluntary or involuntary, is governed by Bankruptcy Rule 9013. See Bankruptcy Rule 1017(f)(2). Proceedings to dismiss a case for nonpayment of the filing fee are governed by Bankruptcy Rule 1017(b), which provides that if any installment of the filing fee has not been paid, the court may, after a hearing on notice to the debtor and the trustee, dismiss the case. For further reading on the circumstances under which a chapter 7 case may be dismissed for cause, see Williamson, The Bankruptcy Issues Handbook, supra, Art. 2.01.

11 U.S.C. § 707(b)(1) provides that after notice and a hearing, the court, on its own motion or on a motion of the United States trustee or any party in interest, may dismiss the chapter 7 case of an individual debtor whose

debts are primarily consumer debts or, with the debtor's consent, convert the case to chapter 11 or 13, if it finds that the granting of relief under chapter 7 would be an abuse of the provisions of that chapter. This is the so-called "actual abuse" provision of section 707(b). In a proceeding on a motion to dismiss or convert under section 707(b)(1), the court must consider whether the case was filed in bad faith or whether under the totality of the debtor's financial circumstances abuse is demonstrated. See 11 U.S.C. § 707(b)(3). A party seeking dismissal or conversion for actual abuse under section 707(b)(1) must affirmatively establish one of these grounds.

dismissal for actual abuse, requirements

11 U.S.C. § 707(b)(2) is the so-called "means testing" and "presumptive abuse" provision of section 707(b). Under this provision a presumption of abuse arises if the debtor's current monthly disposable income multiplied by 60 is equal to or greater than the lesser of $13,650 or 25 percent of the debtor's nonpriority unsecured debts (or $8,125 if that figure is greater than the 25 percent figure). However, if the debtor's current monthly income multiplied by 12 is equal to or less than the median family income for the debtor's state and family size, as reported by U.S. Bureau of Census, then the debtor is not subject to means testing and a presumption of abuse cannot arise under section 707(b)(2). See 11 U.S.C. § 707(b)(6), (7)(A). Section 707(b) contains explicit rules for determining a debtor's current monthly income and disposable monthly income. A debtor who is a disabled veteran whose indebtedness occurred primarily while on active duty or while performing a homeland defense activity is also exempt from means testing under section 707(b)(2). See 11 U.S.C. § 707(b)(2)(D).

presumption of abuse, what constitutes

All chapter 7 debtors are now required to file with the petition a Statement of Current Monthly Income and Means Test Calculation on Official Form 122A-1. This document, when completed, contains the initial information needed for means testing. See section 2.07, supra, for further reading on the preparation and filing requirements of this document. If this document, when completed, indicates that a presumption of abuse has arisen in the case, the clerk is required to give written notice to all creditors within 10 days after the filing of the petition that a presumption of abuse has arisen in the case. See 11 U.S.C. § 342(d) and Bankruptcy Rule 5008. The United States trustee then has until 14 days after the date of the first meeting of creditors to file with the court a statement as to whether a presumption of abuse is deemed to have arisen in the case. Within 7 days after receiving the statement, the court must provide a copy thereof to all creditors. The United States trustee then has 30 days after the filing of the statement to file either a motion to dismiss or convert the case for presumptive abuse under 11 U.S.C. § 707(b)(2) or a statement setting forth the reasons why such a motion would not be appropriate. See 11 U.S.C. § 704(b)(1), (2).

presumption of abuse, procedure when arises

If, under means testing, the debtor's disposable monthly income is such that a presumption of abuse exists and a motion to dismiss or convert is filed, the presumption of abuse may be rebutted by the debtor only by showing that special circumstances exist, such as a serious medical condition or a call to active duty in the Armed Forces, and that the special circumstances justify additional expenses or adjustments of the debtor's current monthly income for which there is no reasonable alternative. In order to establish special circumstances, the debtor must itemize each additional expense or income adjustment and provide documentation and a detailed explanation thereof under oath. Even then, the presumption of abuse will be deemed rebutted only if the additional expenses or adjustments cause the debtor's current monthly income reduced by the allowed expenses listed above (i.e., the debtor's current disposable monthly income) multiplied by 60 to be less than the lesser of 25 percent of the debtor's nonpriority unsecured claims (or $8,125 if that figure is greater than the 25 percent figure), or $13,650. See 11 U.S.C. § 707(b)(2)(B).

presumption of abuse, rebutting of by debtor

Section 707(b) applies only to debtors whose debts are primarily consumer debts, which are debts incurred primarily for a personal, family, or household purpose. Business debts are not consumer debts, and Section 707(b) has been held not to apply to a debtor whose business debts constituted more than one-half of the total amount of debts, even though the number of consumer debts was substantially greater than the number of business debts. See In Re Kelly, 841 F. 2d 908 (9th Cir. 1988); In re Kempkers, 2012 WL 4953076 (Bankr. D. Idaho, Oct. 16 2012). For further reading on dismissals for abuse under Section 707(b), see Williamson, The Bankruptcy Issues Handbook, supra, Art. 2.02.

primarily consumer debts, what constitutes

A chapter 7 case may be dismissed for abuse under section 707(b) on the motion of the United States trustee or a party in interest, or on the court's own motion, after a hearing on notice to the debtor, the trustee, the United States trustee, and such other parties in interest as the court directs. The motion must be filed not later than 60 days

dismissal for abuse of chapter 7, procedure

after the first date set for the meeting of creditors, unless on a request filed before the time for filing has expired the court for cause extends the time for the filing of such motions. See Bankruptcy Rule 1017(e)(1). If the hearing is on the court's own motion, notice of the motion must be served on the debtor not later than 60 days after the first date set for the meeting of creditors. The motion or notice, as the case may be, must advise the debtor of all matters that will be submitted to or considered by the court at the hearing. See Bankruptcy Rule 1017(e)(2). Proceedings for dismissal under section 706(b) are contested matters governed by Bankruptcy Rule 9014. See Bankruptcy Rule 1017(f)(1). The requirements of Bankruptcy Rule 9014 are discussed below in this section.

dismissal of case, procedural requirements

dismissal of case by debtor, requirements

dismissal of case, notice requirements

Except for dismissals for abuse under 11 U.S.C. § 707(b), a chapter 7 case may not be dismissed, whether on the motion of the debtor, for want of prosecution, by the consent of the parties, or for any other cause, prior to a hearing on not less than 21 days notice by mail to the debtor, the trustee, and all creditors, a list of which, if not previously filed, must be provided by the debtor within the time fixed by the court. See Bankruptcy Rules 1017(a) and 2002(a). If dismissal is sought by the debtor, the debtor, too, must show cause, as a chapter 7 case may be dismissed only for cause and may not be dismissed solely because of a change of heart by the debtor or a desire to refile the case in order to include debts incurred after the filing of the present case. See In Re Sheets, 174 B.R. 254 (Bankr. N. D. Ohio 1994); In re Hopkins, 261 B.R. 822 (Bankr. E. D. Pa. 2001). Notice of the dismissal of a chapter 7 case must be mailed by the clerk to the debtor and all creditors. See Bankruptcy Rule 2002(f)(2).

conversion of case by debtor, procedure

conversion of case to chapter 11, filing fee

The debtor may, without cause, convert a chapter 7 case to a case under chapter 11, 12, or 13 at any time, provided that the case has not been previously converted to chapter 7 from chapter 11, 12 or 13, and provided that the debtor qualifies as a debtor under the chapter to which conversion is sought. See 11 U.S.C. § 706(a),(d). Any waiver of this right of conversion by the debtor is unenforceable. See 11 U.S.C. § 706(a). The voluntary conversion of a chapter 7 case under 11 U.S.C. § 706(a) is implemented by the filing and service of a motion under Bankruptcy Rule 9013. A hearing is not required on such a motion unless the court so directs. See Bankruptcy Rule 1017(f) and the Advisory Committee's Notes thereto. A debtor who converts a chapter 7 case to chapter 11 must pay an additional filing fee. See 28 U.S.C. § 1930(a).

involuntary conversion of case, general requirements

On the motion of a party in interest, and after notice and a hearing, the court may convert a chapter 7 case to a case under chapter 11 at any time. See 11 U.S.C. § 706(b). However, the court may not convert a chapter 7 case to a case under chapter 12 or chapter 13 unless the debtor requests such conversion. See 11 U.S.C. § 706(c). Thus, a chapter 7 case may be converted to chapter 11 over the objection of the debtor, but not to chapter 12 or 13. As noted above, a chapter 7 consumer case may also be converted, with the consent of the debtor, to a case under chapter 11 or 13 under the chapter 7 abuse provisions of 11 U.S.C. § 707(b).

proceedings to dismiss or convert case, procedure

Bankruptcy Rule 9014, requirements

dismissal for failure to file schedules

Voluntary conversions under 11 U.S.C. § 706(a), are governed by Bankruptcy Rule 9013. Involuntary conversion proceedings and proceedings to dismiss a chapter 7 case are governed by Bankruptcy Rule 9014. See Bankruptcy Rule 1017(f). Under Bankruptcy Rule 9014, the desired relief must be requested by motion and there must be reasonable notice and an opportunity for a hearing afforded the party against whom relief is sought. The motion must be in writing and must state with particularity the grounds therefor and set forth the relief or order sought. It must be served on the United States trustee, the trustee, and the persons specified in any applicable Bankruptcy Rule or by the court. See Bankruptcy Rules 9013 and 9034. In dismissal proceedings not less than 21 days notice by mail must be given to the debtor, the trustee, and all creditors, except that after 90 days following the first date set for the meeting of creditors, the court may direct that notices be mailed only to those creditors who have filed claims in the case or who may still legally do so. See Bankruptcy Rules 2002(a)(4), 2002(h). If dismissal is sought by the United States trustee for failure of the debtor to file the required schedules and statements, notice of the proceeding need only be given to the debtor, the trustee, and entities designated by the court. See Bankruptcy Rule 1017(c).

The conversion of a chapter 7 case to a case under another chapter constitutes an order for relief under the new chapter, but, with minor exceptions, does not change the date of the filing of the petition, the date of the commencement of the case, or the date of the order for relief. See 11 U.S.C. § 348(a). Notice of conversion of the case must be given by the clerk or such other person as the court may direct to the debtor, all creditors, and the United States trustee. See 11 U.S.C. § 348(c), Bankruptcy Rule 2002(f), and Bankruptcy Rule 2002(k). The conversion of a chapter 7 case to or a case under another chapter terminates the services of the trustee serving in the chapter 7 case.

conversion of case to another chapter, effect of

Unless the court, for cause, orders otherwise, the dismissal of a chapter 7 case - (1) reinstates any proceeding superseded by the case, reinstates certain transfers voided or preserved in the case, and reinstates certain liens voided in the case, (2) vacates certain orders, judgments, or transfers ordered in the case, and (3) revests the property of the bankruptcy estate in the entity in which such property was vested immediately before the commencement of the case. See 11 U.S.C. § 349(b). The dismissal of a case also causes the debtor to lose the postcase benefit of any exemptions claimed in the case, including the federal bankruptcy exemptions. See 11 U.S.C. § 522(c). Unless the court, for cause, orders otherwise, the dismissal of a chapter 7 case does not bar the discharge, in a later case under title 11, of debts that were dischargeable in the case dismissed. See 11 U.S.C. § 349(a). Finally, the dismissal of a case terminates the automatic stay. See 11 U.S.C. § 362(c)(2).

dismissal of case, effect of

Appeals from final orders, judgments, and decrees (and, with leave of the appellate court, of interlocutory orders and decrees) of bankruptcy judges must be taken to the United States district court in the district in which the bankruptcy court is located. See 28 U.S.C. § 158(a). However, if the circuit in which the district court sits has established a bankruptcy appellate panel, appeals from final orders, etc. of bankruptcy judges may, with the consent of all parties, be taken to the appellate panel, provided that the local district judges, by majority vote, have authorized the referral of such appeals to the appellate panel. See 28 U.S.C. § 158(b). The provisions of 28 U.S.C. § 158 are set forth in Appendix I, infra. Appellate procedures are contained in Part VIII of the Rules of Bankruptcy Procedure, which are set forth in Appendix II, infra.

appeals, procedures

The trustee must close the estate as expeditiously as is compatible with the best interests of the parties in interest. See 11 U.S.C. § 704(a)(1). The trustee must also make a final report and file a final account of the administration of the estate, if any, with the court. See 11 U.S.C. § 704(a)(9). If the net proceeds of the case exceed $1,500, the clerk, or such other person as the court may direct, must give the debtor and all creditors notice by mail of a summary of the trustee's final report and account. See Bankruptcy Rule 2002(f)(8). Otherwise, a chapter 7 case may be closed without notice to the debtor or the creditors, unless the local rules provide otherwise.

closing case, procedure

After the estate, if any, has been fully administered, the court must enter a final decree - (1) discharging the trustee, (2) making such provisions by way of injunction or otherwise as may be equitable, and (3) closing the case. See 11 U.S.C. § 350(a). If no objection is filed to the trustee's final report and account within 30 days after the filing thereof, it may be presumed that the estate has been fully administered. See Bankruptcy Rule 5009. The closing of a case terminates the automatic stay to the extent that it was not earlier terminated. See 11 U.S.C. § 362(c)(2).

final decree, contents

Upon the motion of the debtor or other party in interest, a chapter 7 case may be reopened in the court in which the case was closed to administer assets, to accord relief to the debtor, or for other cause. See 11 U.S.C. § 350(b). The reopening of a chapter 7 case lies in the discretion of the bankruptcy court. See In re Lopez, 283 B.R. 22 (BAP 9 2002). While the court will normally reopen a case if good cause is shown, if the debtor has been guilty of laches or if other equitable grounds exist for not reopening a case, the court may properly refuse to do so. See In re Tarkington, 301 B.R. 502 (E. D. Tenn. 2003). If a chapter 7 case is reopened, a trustee may not be appointed by the United States trustee unless the court determines that a trustee is necessary to protect the interests of creditors and the debtor or to insure the efficient administration of the case. See Bankruptcy Rule 5010.

reopening case, rules governing

Exhibit 2-A Disclosure of Compensation of Attorney for Debtor (Director's Form 2030)

B2030 (FORM 2030) (12/15)

UNITED STATES BANKRUPTCY COURT
Southern District of Ohio

In re: Sidney Samuel Smith and Sarah Arlene Smith,
Debtors

Case No. ____________________
Chapter 7

DISCLOSURE OF COMPENSATION OF ATTORNEY FOR DEBTOR(S)

1. Pursuant to 11 U .S.C. § 329(a) and Fed. Bankr. P. 2016(b), I certify that I am the attorney for the above named debtor(s) and that compensation paid to me within one year before the filing of the petition in bankruptcy, or agreed to be paid to me, for services rendered or to be rendered on behalf of the debtor(s) in contemplation of or in connection with the bankruptcy case is as follows:

For legal services, I have agreed to accept $950.00
Prior to the filing of this statement I have received.................................. $950.00
Balance Due $0.00

2. The source of the compensation paid to me was: the debtors.

3. The source of the compensation to be paid to me is: the debtors.

4. I have not agreed to share the above-disclosed compensation with any person unless they are members or associates of my law firm.

5. In return for the above-disclosed fee, I have agreed to render legal services for all aspects of the bankruptcy case, including:
   a. Analysis of the debtors' financial situation, and rendering advice to the debtors in determining whether to file a petition in bankruptcy;
   b. Preparation and filing of any petition, schedules, statement of affairs and plan which may be required;
   c. Representation of the debtors at the meeting of creditors and confirmation hearing, and any adjourned hearings thereof;
   d. Other provisions: N/A

6. By agreement with the debtors, the above-disclosed fee does not include the following services:

   representation of the debtors in any dischargeability actions; judicial lien avoidances; relief from automatic stay actions; any adversary proceedings.

CERTIFICATION

I certify that the foregoing is a complete statement of any agreement or arrangement for payment to me for representation of the debtors in this bankruptcy proceeding.

Dated: January 15, 2024

/s/ Alice B. Chase, Esq.
Alice B. Chase, #0009359
Chase & Chase, P.C.
2000 Market Street, Suite 1700
Columbus, OH 43222
614-333-3300
Alice@chase&chase.com

Exhibit 2-B Notices and Disclosures Under Section 527 (Director's Form 2010, Other Notices)

NOTICES AND DISCLOSURES TO ASSISTED PERSONS*

We are a debt relief agency and the notices and disclosures set forth in these documents are being provided to you pursuant to section 527 of the Bankruptcy Code. The purposes of these notices and disclosures are: (1) to make you aware of the various debt relief options that may be available to you; (2) to make you aware of the duties and obligations that are required of persons who file bankruptcy cases; (3) to make you aware of the various types of bankruptcy cases that may be available to you; and (4) to make you aware of the costs and fees (including attorneys' fees) that will be incurred should you decide to file a bankruptcy case.

Notice Required by 11 U.S.C. § 342(b) for Individuals Filing for Bankruptcy (Form 2010)

This notice is for you if:

You are an individual filing for bankruptcy, and

Your debts are primarily consumer debts. *Consumer debts* are defined in 11 U.S.C. § 101(8) as "incurred by an individual primarily for a personal, family, or household purpose."

The types of bankruptcy that are available to individuals

Individuals who meet the qualifications may file under one of four different chapters of the Bankruptcy Code:

- Chapter 7 — Liquidation
- Chapter 11— Reorganization
- Chapter 12— Voluntary repayment plan for family farmers or fishermen
- Chapter 13— Voluntary repayment plan for individuals with regular income

You should have an attorney review your decision to file for bankruptcy and the choice of chapter.

Chapter 7: Liquidation

	$245	filing fee
	$78	administrative fee
+	$15	trustee surcharge
	$338	total fee

Chapter 7 is for individuals who have financial difficulty preventing them from paying their debts and who are willing to allow their non-exempt property to be used to pay their creditors. The primary purpose of filing under chapter 7 is to have your debts discharged. The bankruptcy discharge relieves you after bankruptcy from having to pay many of your pre-bankruptcy debts. Exceptions exist for particular debts, and liens on property may still be enforced after discharge. For example, a creditor may have the right to foreclose a home mortgage or repossess an automobile.

However, if the court finds that you have committed certain kinds of improper conduct described in the Bankruptcy Code, the court may deny your discharge.

You should know that even if you file chapter 7 and you receive a discharge, some debts are not discharged under the law. Therefore, you may still be responsible to pay:

- most taxes;
- most student loans;
- domestic support and property settlement obligations;

- most fines, penalties, forfeitures, and criminal restitution obligations; and
- certain debts that are not listed in your bankruptcy papers.

You may also be required to pay debts arising from:

- fraud or theft;
- fraud or defalcation while acting in breach of fiduciary capacity;
- intentional injuries that you inflicted; and
- death or personal injury caused by operating a motor vehicle, vessel, or aircraft while intoxicated from alcohol or drugs.

If your debts are primarily consumer debts, the court can dismiss your chapter 7 case if it finds that you have enough income to repay creditors a certain amount. You must file *Chapter 7 Statement of Your Current Monthly Income* (Official Form 122A–1) if you are an individual filing for bankruptcy under chapter 7. This form will determine your current monthly income and compare whether your income is more than the median income that applies in your state.

If your income is not above the median for your state, you will not have to complete the other chapter 7 form, the *Chapter 7 Means Test Calculation* (Official Form 122A–2).

If your income is above the median for your state, you must file a second form —the *Chapter 7 Means Test Calculation* (Official Form 122A–2). The calculations on the form—sometimes called the *Means Test*—deduct from your income living expenses and payments on certain debts to determine any amount available to pay unsecured creditors. If your income is more than the median income for your state of residence and family size, depending on the results of the *Means Test*, the U.S. trustee, bankruptcy administrator, or creditors can file a motion to dismiss your case under § 707(b) of the Bankruptcy Code. If a motion is filed, the court will decide if your case should be dismissed. To avoid dismissal, you may choose to proceed under another chapter of the Bankruptcy Code.

If you are an individual filing for chapter 7 bankruptcy, the trustee may sell your property to pay your debts, subject to your right to exempt the property or a portion of the proceeds from the sale of the property. The property, and the proceeds from property that your bankruptcy trustee sells or liquidates that you are entitled to, is called *exempt property*. Exemptions may enable you to keep your home, a car, clothing, and household items or to receive some of the proceeds if the property is sold.

Exemptions are not automatic. To exempt property, you must list it on *Schedule C: The Property You Claim as Exempt* (Official Form 106C). If you do not list the property, the trustee may sell it and pay all of the proceeds to your creditors.

Chapter 11: Reorganization

	$1,167	filing fee
+	$571	administrative fee
	$1,738	total fee

Chapter 11 is often used for reorganizing a business, but is also available to individuals. The provisions of chapter 11 are too complicated to summarize briefly.

Read These Important Warnings

Because bankruptcy can have serious long-term financial and legal consequences, including loss of your property, you should hire an attorney and carefully consider all of your options before you file. Only an attorney can give you legal advice about what can happen as a result of filing for bankruptcy and what your options are. If you do file for bankruptcy, an attorney can help you fill out the forms properly and protect you, your family, your home, and your possessions.

Although the law allows you to represent yourself in bankruptcy court, you should understand that many people find it difficult to represent themselves successfully. The rules are technical, and a mistake or inaction may harm you. If you file without an attorney, you are still responsible for knowing and following all of the legal requirements.

You should not file for bankruptcy if you are not eligible to file or if you do not intend to file the necessary documents.

Bankruptcy fraud is a serious crime; you could be fined and imprisoned if you commit fraud in your bankruptcy case. Making a false statement, concealing property, or obtaining money or property by fraud in connection with a bankruptcy case can result in fines up to $250,000, or imprisonment for up to 20 years, or both. 18 U.S.C. §§ 152, 1341, 1519, and 3571.

Chapter 12: Repayment plan for family farmers or fishermen

	$200	filing fee
+	$78	administrative fee
	$278	total fee

Similar to chapter 13, chapter 12 permits family farmers and fishermen to repay their debts over a period of time using future earnings and to discharge some debts that are not paid.

Chapter 13: Repayment plan for individuals with regular income

	$235	filing fee
+	$78	administrative fee
	$313	total fee

Chapter 13 is for individuals who have regular income and would like to pay all or part of their debts in installments over a period of time and to discharge some debts that are not paid. You are eligible for chapter 13 only if your debts are not more than certain dollar amounts set forth in 11 U.S.C. § 109.

Under chapter 13, you must file with the court a plan to repay your creditors all or part of the money that you owe them, usually using your future earnings. If the court approves your plan, the court will allow you to repay your debts, as adjusted by the plan, within 3 years or 5 years, depending on your income and other factors.

After you make all the payments under your plan, many of your debts are discharged. The debts that are not discharged and that you may still be responsible to pay include:

- domestic support obligations,
- most student loans,
- certain taxes,
- debts for fraud or theft,
- debts for fraud or defalcation while acting in a fiduciary capacity,
- most criminal fines and restitution obligations,
- certain debts that are not listed in your bankruptcy papers,
- certain debts for acts that caused death or personal injury, and
- certain long-term secured debts.

Warning: File Your Forms on Time

Section 521(a)(1) of the Bankruptcy Code requires that you promptly file detailed information about your creditors, assets, liabilities, income, expenses and general financial condition. The court may dismiss your bankruptcy case if you do not file this information within the deadlines set by the Bankruptcy Code, the Bankruptcy Rules, and the local rules of the court.

For more information about the documents and their deadlines, go to: http://www.uscourts.gov/forms/bankruptcy-forms

Bankruptcy crimes have serious consequences

- If you knowingly and fraudulently conceal assets or make a false oath or statement under penalty of perjury—either orally or in writing—in connection with a bankruptcy case, you may be fined, imprisoned, or both.
- All information you supply in connection with a bankruptcy case is subject to examination by the Attorney General acting through the Office of the U.S. Trustee, the Office of the U.S. Attorney, and other offices and employees of the U.S. Department of Justice.

Make sure the court has your mailing address

The bankruptcy court sends notices to the mailing address you list on *Voluntary Petition for Individuals Filing for Bankruptcy* (Official Form 101). To ensure that you receive information about your case, Bankruptcy Rule 4002 requires that you notify the court of any changes in your address.

A married couple may file a bankruptcy case together—called a *joint case*. If you file a joint case and each spouse lists the same mailing address on the bankruptcy petition, the bankruptcy court generally will mail you and your spouse one copy of each notice, unless you file a statement with the court asking that each spouse receive separate copies.

Understand which services you could receive from credit counseling agencies

The law generally requires that you receive a credit counseling briefing from an approved credit counseling agency. 11 U.S.C. § 109(h). If you are filing a joint case, both spouses must receive the briefing. With limited exceptions, you must receive it within the 180 days ***before*** you file your bankruptcy petition. This briefing is usually conducted by telephone or on the Internet.

In addition, after filing a bankruptcy case, you generally must complete a financial management instructional course before you can receive a discharge. If you are filing a joint case, both spouses must complete the course.

You can obtain the list of agencies approved to provide both the briefing and the instructional course from: http://www.uscourts.gov/services-forms/bankruptcy/credit-counseling-and-debtor-education-courses.

In Alabama and North Carolina, go to: http://www.uscourts.gov/services-forms/bankruptcy/credit-counseling-and-debtor-education-courses.

If you do not have access to a computer, the clerk of the bankruptcy court may be able to help you obtain the list.

**IF WE PROVIDE BANKRUPTCY SERVICES FOR YOU,
YOU ARE HEREBY ADVISED AS FOLLOWS:**

1. All of the information that you provide for the purpose of preparing your bankruptcy petition and other documents must be complete, accurate and truthful.

2. All of the information that you may later provide after the filing of the bankruptcy case must also be complete, accurate and truthful.

3. All of your assets and all of your liabilities must be completely and accurately listed in the documents that are filed in your case. The replacement value of each asset must also be listed in the documents and you must make a reasonable effort and inquiry to establish the replacement value of each asset.

4. Your current monthly income and your allowed monthly expenses must be accurately stated in your bankruptcy documents and you must make a reasonable effort and inquiry to ascertain their correctness. In a chapter 13 case your disposable monthly income must also be accurately stated after reasonable inquiry.

5. Any information that you provide during the bankruptcy case may be audited and a failure to provide the required information may result in the dismissal of your bankruptcy case or other sanctions, including the filing of criminal charges against you.

IMPORTANT INFORMATION ABOUT BANKRUPTCY ASSISTANCE SERVICES FROM AN ATTORNEY OR BANKRUPTCY PETITION PREPARER.

If you decide to seek bankruptcy relief, you may represent yourself, you may hire an attorney to represent you, or you can get help in some localities from a bankruptcy petition preparer who is not an attorney. **THE LAW REQUIRES AN ATTORNEY OR BANKRUPTCY PETITION PREPARER TO GIVE YOU A WRITTEN CONTRACT SPECIFYING WHAT THE ATTORNEY OR BANKRUPTCY PREPARER WILL DO FOR YOU AND HOW MUCH IT WILL COST.** Ask to see the contract before you hire anyone.

The following information is intended to help you understand what must be done in a routine bankruptcy case and to help you evaluate how much legal service you need. Although a bankruptcy case can be complex and difficult to understand, many cases are routine and relatively simple.

Before filing a bankruptcy case, either you or your attorney should analyze your eligibility for the different forms of debt relief that are available under the Bankruptcy Code and which form of relief is likely to be most beneficial for you. Be sure you understand the type of relief that you can obtain and its limitations. To file a bankruptcy case, documents called a Petition, Schedules, a Statement of Financial Affairs, a Statement of Current Monthly Income, and in most chapter 7 cases a Statement of Intention must to be prepared correctly and filed with the bankruptcy court. Unless you qualify for a waiver of the filing fee, you will have to pay a filing fee to the bankruptcy court. Once your case starts, you will have to attend the required first meeting of creditors where you may be questioned by a court official called a "trustee" and by creditors.

If you choose to file a chapter 7 case, you may be asked by a creditor to reaffirm a debt. You may want help deciding whether to reaffirm a debt. A creditor is not permitted to coerce you into reaffirming a debt.

If you choose to file a chapter 13 case in which you repay your creditors what you can afford over a 3-to-5 year period, you may also want help with preparing your chapter 13 plan and with the confirmation hearing on your plan which will be held before a bankruptcy judge.

If you select a type of relief under the Bankruptcy Code other than chapter 7 or chapter 13, you will want to find out what should be done from someone familiar with that type of relief.

Your bankruptcy case may also involve litigation. You are generally permitted to represent yourself in litigation in bankruptcy court, but only attorneys, not bankruptcy petition preparers, can give you legal advice.

INSTRUCTIONS ON HOW TO OBTAIN THE INFORMATION NEEDED TO FULFILL YOUR DUTIES IN A BANKRUPTCY CASE

1. **INSTRUCTIONS ON HOW TO DETERMINE THE REPLACEMENT VALUE OF YOUR PERSONAL PROPERTY.** You will need to know the replacement value of any personal property that you own when your bankruptcy case is filed, even if the property is mortgaged, pledged, or otherwise subject to a lien. The replacement value of property that you acquired for a personal, family or household purpose is the price that a retail merchant would charge for property of that kind, considering the age and condition of the property at the time the bankruptcy case is filed. The value of personal property that is subject to a valid lien or mortgage is the replacement value of the property as of the date the bankruptcy case is filed without deducting anything for the cost of selling or marketing the property.

2. **INSTRUCTIONS ON HOW TO DETERMINE YOUR CURRENT MONTHLY INCOME.** Your current monthly income must be determined in order to file a bankruptcy case. In a chapter 7 case, your current monthly income is needed for means testing purposes; that is to determine your eligibility to proceed under chapter 7. In a chapter 13 case your current monthly income is needed to determine the monthly amount that you must pay to your creditors under a chapter 13 plan. Your current monthly income is the average monthly income from all sources for both you and your spouse (even if your spouse is not filing) for the six calendar months immediately preceding the filing of your bankruptcy case. If you are unmarried or if you and your spouse are legally separated or living in separate households, then only your income is counted. Income from all sources, regardless of whether the income is taxable, must be counted except that social security benefits and payments received as a victim of war crimes, crimes against humanity, or as a victim of international or domestic terrorism is not counted. Unemployment compensation is not counted to the extent that it is funded by the Federal Government under the Social Security Act. Income from the following sources must be counted:

   Gross income from wages, salary, tips, bonuses, overtime, and commissions.
   Net income from the operation of a business, profession or farm.
   Rent and other income from real property, less ordinary and necessary operating expenses.
   Interest, dividends and royalties.
   Pension and retirement income (other than Social Security income).
   Child or spousal support from a former spouse if received regularly.

3. **INSTRUCTIONS ON HOW TO DETERMINE YOUR ALLOWED MONTHLY EXPENSES AND YOUR MONTHLY DISPOSABLE INCOME.** If the amount of your current monthly income multiplied by 12 does not exceed the median annual family income for your state and household size, as determined by the U.S. Census Bureau, then you will not be subject to means testing and you will not be required to calculate your monthly disposable income, which means that you will not be required to determine the amounts of any deductions from your current monthly income. However, if the amount of your current monthly income multiplied by 12 exceeds the median annual family income for your state and household size, then the deductions from your current monthly income must be determined in order to calculate your disposable monthly income, which will be used to determine your eligibility to file a chapter 7 case or the amount of your monthly payment in a chapter 13 case. Many of these deductions are not the amounts that you actually spend each month, but the amounts calculated by the

Internal Revenue Service (the IRS) as being the standard allowable monthly living expenses for a household of your size and income level. These standard expenses include expenses for food, clothing, household supplies, personal care and similar expenses, housing and utility expenses, mortgage or rent expenses, transportation expenses, and other necessary expenses including taxes, payroll deductions, life insurance, child or spousal support payments, education, childcare, healthcare, and telecommunications. These standard expenses are listed on a Government website. Once we know your household size and the amount of your current monthly income, we will obtain this information for you.

In addition to the IRS standard expenses described in the paragraph above, you are allowed to deduct from your current monthly income, the average monthly amounts that you actually spend each month for (1) health insurance, disability insurance, and a health savings account, (2) the reasonable and necessary care and support of an elderly, chronically ill, or disabled member of your household or of your immediate family who is unable to pay for such services, (3) protection against family violence, and (4) for regular charitable contributions that your will continue to make after the bankruptcy case is filed.

In addition, if you can prove that your average monthly home energy costs exceed the amount specified in the IRS standards, then you may deduct the amount by which your monthly average exceeds the IRS standard. If you can prove that your average monthly expenses for food and clothing exceed the combined allowances for food and apparel set forth in the IRS standards, then you may deduct the amount by which your monthly expenses exceed the combined IRS standards for food and apparel, except that your deduction may not exceed 5% of the combined IRS standards. If you can prove that the expenses are reasonable and necessary and not already accounted for in the IRS standard expenses, you may deduct the average monthly amount, not to exceed $147.92 per child, that you spend for the educational expenses of your dependent children who are less than 18 years of age. In order to be able to deduct the actual expenses described in this paragraph you must provide the bankruptcy trustee with documents proving that you actually incur these expenses and spend these amounts. Statements, bills or receipts from utility companies, food and clothing providers, and educational providers should be obtained so that they can be given to the bankruptcy trustee. As indicated above, the total of all of your standard and permitted actual monthly expenses will be subtracted from your current monthly income to determine your monthly disposable income.

4. **INSTRUCTIONS ON HOW TO MAKE A LIST OF YOUR CREDITORS AND HOW TO DETERMINE THE AMOUNT THAT IS OWED TO EACH CREDITOR.** When a bankruptcy petition is filed, complete lists of the names and addresses of all of your secured creditors and unsecured creditors must also be filed. We will prepare and file those lists for you. However, to prepare the lists properly we will need to be provided with the name, address and account number (if one exists) of each of your secured and unsecured creditors. The names, addresses and account numbers of your commercial creditors may be obtained from the bills or statements that they send to you. Commercial creditors include banks, credit card companies, loan companies, stores, and other persons or companies that have extended commercial credit to you and have not been paid in full. The address that should be listed for each creditor is the address to which payments to the creditor are sent. If the account has been assigned to a collection agent, the name and address of the collection agent should also be listed. The names and addresses of any creditors who are not commercial creditors must also be provided to us.

Included here are creditors who are relatives or business associates, child or spousal support creditors, and persons who may have claims against you for any reason, including automobile accidents, contract or rent disputes, and business disputes. We must also be informed as to whether each debt is secured or unsecured. If a joint case is being filed we must be informed as to whether each debt was incurred by the husband, the wife, or jointly by both husband and wife. We must also be informed of the current amount owed to each creditor. For commercial creditors this amount can usually be obtained from the most recent bill or statement. If it is not clear how much is owed to a particular creditor, we will assist you in determining the amount that is owed.

5. **INSTRUCTIONS ON HOW TO DETERMINE WHAT PROPERTY IS EXEMPT AND HOW TO VALUE YOUR EXEMPT PROPERTY.** When a bankruptcy petition is filed, complete lists of your personal property and real property must be filed. A complete list of your exempt property must also be filed. We will prepare and file these lists for you. To do this we must be provided with a description of each item of personal and real property that you own and the value of each item of property. Once we are provided with this information, we will assist you in determining which of your property is exempt under applicable law. This will be accomplished by comparing your property with the property that is exempt under the State and Federal laws that are applicable to you. Your exempt personal property should be valued in the manner described in paragraph number 1 above in these instructions.

Exhibit 2-C Bankruptcy Worksheets

(These worksheets may be photocopied from this book or downloaded from our Bankruptcy Forms by an attorney for use in his or her practice.)

BANKRUPTCY WORKSHEETS

GENERAL INFORMATION: The questions in these work sheets should be answered by or on behalf of the debtor if a single case is to be filed or by or on behalf of both spouses if a joint case is to be filed. In these work sheets, a debtor is a person for whom a bankruptcy case is filed under chapter 7, chapter 12, or chapter 13 of the Bankruptcy Code. The DEBT FORM referred to below is located on the last page of these work sheets.

INSTRUCTIONS TO DEBTOR: Answer each question completely and truthfully. If more space is needed to completely answer a question, complete the answer on a separate sheet of paper or on the back of the work sheet. If you do not understand a question write "Don't Understand" after the question. Do not guess at the answer to any question. Except as otherwise directed below in these work sheets, the questions that are marked with an * should be answered only if a joint case is being filed, and the requested information related to your spouse in the other questions should be given only if a joint case is being filed. When indicating ownership of property or liability for a debt, use "H" for husband, "W" for wife, and "J" for joint ownership or liability by both husband and wife. The value listed for any item should be the estimated present market value of the item without regard to any lien, mortgage or exemption.

ADVISEMENT TO DEBTOR: Official Bankruptcy Forms will be completed using the information that you give in these work sheets and you will be required to sign a declaration stating under penalty of perjury that the information is true and correct. A failure to disclose assets in a bankruptcy case is a federal crime punishable by imprisonment for up to five years and by a fine of up to $500,000. In addition, a failure to provide complete and accurate information on your bankruptcy forms may result in the dismissal of your bankruptcy case or in a denial of your bankruptcy discharge, which means that your debts will not be discharged. It is also important to give the name and correct address for each of your creditors because a debt owed to a creditor who is not listed on your bankruptcy forms, or whose address on the forms is incorrect, might not be discharged, in which case you will remain liable to that creditor after the bankruptcy case.

Preliminary Information

1. List the name of the debtor, or the primary debtor if a joint case is to be filed. ______________________________
2. List the name of the spouse of the person listed above. ______________________________
3. List the date or dates upon which these work sheets were completed. ______________________________

Current Monthly Income and Means Testing Information

4. Are you a disabled veteran whose indebtedness occurred primarily during a period in which you were on active duty or while you were performing a homeland defense activity? __________ (If the answer is yes, do not complete items 5 through 13 below.)
5. Are you married? __________
6. If you are married, are you and your spouse living together? __________
7. If you and your spouse are not living together, are you and your spouse legally separated under state law or living in separate households? __________
8. If you are married, will you and your spouse be filing a joint bankruptcy petition? __________
9. List the amount of gross income from wages, salary, tips, bonuses, overtime and commissions that you and/or your spouse received during each of the last 6 calendar months.

Month	Yourself	Your Spouse
1.	$	$
2.	$	$
3.	$	$
4.	$	$
5.	$	$
6.	$	$

10. List the amount of gross receipts received and the amount of ordinary and necessary business expenses incurred by you and/or your spouse from the operation of a business, profession or farm during each of the last 6 calendar months.

	Gross Receipts		Business Expenses	
Month	Yourself	Your Spouse	Yourself	Your Spouse
1.	$	$	$	$
2.	$	$	$	$
3.	$	$	$	$
4.	$	$	$	$
5.	$	$	$	$
6.	$	$	$	$

11. List the amount of gross receipts received and the amount of ordinary and necessary operating expenses incurred by you and/or your spouse from rent and other real property income during each of the last 6 calendar months:

	Gross Receipts		Operating Expenses	
Month	Yourself	Your Spouse	Yourself	Your Spouse
1.	$	$	$	$
2.	$	$	$	$
3.	$	$	$	$
4.	$	$	$	$
5.	$	$	$	$
6.	$	$	$	$

12. List the amount of interest, dividends and royalties that you and/or your spouse received during each of the last 6 calendar months.

Month	Yourself	Your Spouse
1.	$	$
2.	$	$
3.	$	$
4.	$	$
5.	$	$
6.	$	$

13. List the amount of pension and retirement income, other than Social Security benefits, that you and/or your spouse received during each of the last 6 calendar months.

Month	Yourself	Your Spouse
1.	$	$
2.	$	$
3.	$	$
4.	$	$
5.	$	$
6.	$	$

14. List the amount of child or spousal support and other regular contributions to the household expenses of you and your dependents received by you and/or your spouse during each of the last 6 calendar months.

Month	Yourself	Your Spouse
1.	$	$
2.	$	$
3.	$	$
4.	$	$
5.	$	$
6.	$	$

15. List the amount of unemployment compensation received by you and/or your spouse during each of the last 6 calendar months and identify the source of the compensation.

Month	Yourself	Your Spouse
1.	$	$
2.	$	$
3.	$	$
4.	$	$
5.	$	$
6.	$	$

16. List the amount of income from any source not listed above received by you and /or your spouse during each of the last 6 calendar months and identify the source of any income listed. Do not list Social Security benefits or payments received as a war crime victim, as a victim of a crime against humanity, or as an international or domestic terrorism victim.

Month	Yourself	Your Spouse
1.	$	$
2.	$	$
3.	$	$
4.	$	$
5.	$	$
6.	$	$

17. In what state do you reside? ______________________

18. How many persons reside in your household? ____________

19. If you are married and not filing jointly with your spouse and if you and your spouse are not legally separated or living apart from one another, list the amount of your spouse's income during each of the last 6 calendar months that was contributed to your household expenses.

Month	Amount Not Contributed
1.	$
2.	$
3.	$
4.	$
5.	$
6.	$

20. List the amount of taxes, other than real estate taxes and sales taxes, that you paid or incurred during each of the last 6 calendar months. Include income taxes, self employment taxes, social security taxes, and Medicare taxes.

Month	Amount of Taxes Incurred
1.	$
2.	$
3.	$
4.	$
5.	$
6.	$

21. List the total amount of your mandatory payroll deductions during each of the last 6 calendar months. Include deductions for withholding taxes, union dues, uniform costs and mandatory retirement contributions. Do not include deductions for discretionary items such as non-mandatory 401(k) contributions.

Month	Amount Deducted
1.	$
2.	$
3.	$
4.	$
5.	$
6.	$

22. List the total amount of life insurance premiums that you paid or incurred during each of the last 6 calendar months for term life insurance for yourself. Do not include premiums for insurance on your dependents or premiums for whole life insurance or other forms of life insurance on yourself.

Month	Amount of Premiums
1.	$
2.	$
3.	$
4.	$
5.	$
6.	$

23. List the total monthly amount, if any, that you are required to pay pursuant to a court order, including spousal or child support payments. Do not include past due support obligations. $_______________.

24. List the total amount of expenses that you paid or incurred during each of the last 6 calendar months for education that was a condition of your employment and for education that is required for a physically or mentally challenged dependent child for whom no public education providing similar services is available.

Month	Amount of Expenses
1.	$
2.	$
3.	$
4.	$
5.	$
6.	$

25. List the total amount of expenses that you paid or incurred for child care during each of the last 6 calendar months. Do not include payments made for a child's education.

Month	Amount of Expenses
1.	$
2.	$
3.	$
4.	$
5.	$
6.	$

26. List the total amount that you paid or incurred during each of the last 6 calendar months for healthcare expenses that were not reimbursed by insurance or paid by a health savings account. Do not include health insurance premiums.

Month	Amount of Expenses
1.	$
2.	$
3.	$
4.	$
5.	$
6.	$

27. List the total amount of expenses that you paid or incurred during each of the last 6 calendar months for cell phones, pagers, call waiting, caller identification, special long distance or internet services that were necessary for the health and welfare of you and your dependents.

Month	Amount of Expenses
1.	$
2.	$
3.	$
4.	$
5.	$
6.	$

28. List the amount of expenses, if any, that you paid or incurred during each of the last 6 calendar months for health insurance, disability insurance, and health savings accounts.

Month	Health Insurance	Disability Insurance	Health Savings Accounts
1.	$	$	$
2.	$	$	$
3.	$	$	$
4.	$	$	$
5.	$	$	$
6.	$	$	$

29. List the amount of expenses, if any, that you paid or incurred during each of the last 6 calendar months for the reasonable and necessary care and support of an elderly, chronically ill, or disabled member of your household or your immediate family (including any of your parents, grandparents, siblings, children and grandchildren, any of your dependents, or your spouse if a joint case is being filed and he or she is not a dependent) who is unable to pay for these expenses.

Month	Amount of Expenses
1.	$
2.	$
3.	$
4.	$
5.	$
6.	$

Do you intend to continue paying these expenses after your bankruptcy case is filed? __________

30. List the total amount of expenses, if any, that you paid or incurred during each of the last 6 calendar months to maintain the safety of your family under the Family Violence Prevention and Services Act or other federal law.

Month	Amount of Expenses
1.	$
2.	$
3.	$
4.	$
5.	$
6.	$

31. List the total amount of expenses that you paid or incurred during each of the last 6 calendar months for your home energy costs.

Month	Home Energy Costs
1.	$
2.	$
3.	$
4.	$
5.	$
6.	$

If the average monthly amount exceeds $ ____________, which is the IRS Local Standard amount for your state and family size, attach statements, receipts and other documents verifying the amounts shown above.

32. List the total amount of expenses that you paid or incurred during each of the last 6 calendar months in providing elementary and secondary education for your dependent children who are less than 18 years of age.

Month	Amount of Expenses
1.	$
2.	$
3.	$
4.	$
5.	$
6.	$

Attach statements, receipts and other documents verifying the amounts shown above.

33. List the total amount of expenses that you paid or incurred during each of the last 6 calendar months for food and clothing.

Month	Amount of Expenses
1.	$
2.	$
3.	$
4.	$
5.	$
6.	$

If the average monthly amount exceeds $ ________ , which is the IRS National Standard amount for your family size and income level, attach statements, receipts and other documents verifying the amounts shown above.

34. List the total amount of charitable contributions that you paid during each of the last 6 calendar months.

Month	Amount of Contributions
1.	$
2.	$
3.	$
4.	$
5.	$
6.	$

Do you intend to continue making charitable contributions in these amounts after your bankruptcy case is filed?____

35. List the name of each of your creditors that is secured by a mortgage or lien on your property, identify the property securing the debt owed to each of these creditors, list the monthly amount that you are required to pay each creditor, and list the amount by which you are in default to each creditor.

Name of Creditor	Property Securing the Debt	Monthly Amount Due	Amount of Default
1.			
2.			
3.			
4.			
5.			
6.			

36. List the total amount that you owe on each of the following types of claims:

1. Past due and unpaid child support, alimony and other domestic support obligations. $ __________
2. Wages, salaries and commissions owed to employees. $ __________
3. Unpaid contributions owed to employee benefit plans. $ __________
4. Money owed to farmers or fisherman. $ __________
5. Money owed to individuals for deposits made for property or services that you failed to provide. $ __________
6. Amounts owed for federal, state or local taxes. $ __________

Petition Information

37. What is your full name? ____

*38. What is your spouse's full name? ____

39. What other names have you used in the last 6 years (include married or maiden names and names under which you have conducted business)? ____

____

*40. What other names has your spouse used in the last 6 years (include married or maiden names and names under which he or she has conducted business)? ____

____

41. What is your social security or tax identification number? ____________________________

* *Answer question only if a joint case is being filed.*

*42. What is your spouse's social security or tax identification number? ______________________

43. What is your street address? ______________________
no. & street city state zip code

44. In what county is your residence or principal place of business located? ______________________

*45. What is your spouse's street address? ______________________
no. & street city state zip code

*46. In what county is your spouse's residence or principal place of business located? ______________________

47. What is your mailing address? ______________________

*48. What is your spouse's mailing address? ______________________

49. Where are your principal business assets, if any, located? ______________________

50. Where have you resided for the last 180 days? ______________________

51. Are you engaged in a business other than as an employee? __________ If so, state the type or field of business that you are engaged in and briefly describe the nature of the business. ______________________

____

52. Has a bankruptcy case been filed by or against you within the last 8 years? __________ If so, when and where was the case filed, what was the case number, and what is the status of the case? ______________________

____

If the case was dismissed, give the date of and the grounds for the dismissal. ______________________

53. Is there a bankruptcy case now pending against your spouse or against a business partner or associate of yours? __________ If so, attach papers showing the particulars of the case.

54. Do you own or have possession of any property that poses or is alleged to pose a threat of imminent and identifiable harm to public health or safety? __________ If so, identify the property. ______________________

____

55. Do you live in rented property? __________ If so, have eviction proceedings been filed against you? __________

Schedule A/B Information - Your Real Estate

56. Do you or your spouse own or have an interest in any real estate? __________

57. If the answer to question 56 is yes, complete the following showing each parcel of real estate that you or your spouse own or have an interest in:

Address of the property	Legal description of the property	Nature of your interest in the property	Nature of your spouse's interest in the property	Date property acquired	Estimated current value of the property	Unpaid amount of each mortgage or lien against the property

Schedule A/B Information - Your Personal Property

58. How much cash do you now have? $__________

*59. How much cash does your spouse now have? $__________

* *Answer question only if a joint case is being filed.*

60. When do you next get paid? ____________________ How much do you expect to receive? $______________ To what date will you then be paid? ____________________

*61. When does your spouse next get paid? ____________________ How much will he or she receive? $______________ To what date will he or she then be paid ? ____________________

62. Are you owed any accrued and unpaid vacation, sick leave, or similar pay? ______________ If so, how much is owed and who owes it? $______________

*63. Is your spouse owed any accrued and unpaid vacation, sick leave, or similar pay? ______________ If so, how much is owed and who owes it? $______________ ____

64. Do you or your spouse have any checking, savings, or other accounts, certificates of deposit, or shares in any bank or financial institution? If so, complete the following for each account, deposit or share:

Name and address of financial institution	Name or names under which the account, deposit or shares are registered	Type of account, deposit, or shares	Amount of deposit or account, or value of shares

65. Do you or your spouse have any security deposits with a landlord, telephone company, utility company, or anyone else? ______________ If so, state who made each deposit and list the amount of each deposit and the name and address of the holder of each deposit. ____

____

____

66. Do you or your spouse own any household goods or furnishings, including audio, video, or computer equipment? ______________ If so, using a separate sheet of paper or the back of this sheet, list each item, or group of items and show the location and estimated replacement value of each without regard to any mortgage or lien, and state whether the items are owned by you, your spouse, or jointly. State the total replacement value of all of these items without regard to any mortgages or liens. $______________

67. Do you or your spouse own any books, pictures, art objects, antiques, stamp, coin, record, tape, compact disc, or other collections or collectibles? ______________ If so, describe them, list their location and estimated replacement value, and state whether they are owned by you, your spouse, or jointly. ____

____

68. What is the total replacement value of all of your wearing apparel? $______________ Using a separate sheet of paper or the back of this sheet, list each item of wearing apparel that has a replacement value of $20 or more. Include such items as watches and similar articles that are not made of gold or silver or set with gems.

*69. What is the total replacement value of all of your spouse's wearing apparel? $______________ Using a separate sheet of paper or the back of this sheet, list each item of wearing apparel that has a replacement value of $20 or more. Include such items as watches and similar articles that are not made of gold or silver or set with gems.

70. Do you or your spouse own any furs or jewelry? ______________ If so, identify each item, list its location and replacement value, and identify its owner. ____

____

71. Do you or your spouse own any firearms, sports equipment, photographic equipment, or other hobby equipment? ______________ If so, identify each item, list its location and estimated replacement value, and identify its owner.

____

72. Do you or your spouse own an interest in a life insurance policy? ______________ If so, identify each policy by policy number, owner, name of insurance company, amount of death benefit, and name of beneficiaries, and list the cash surrender or refund value of each policy. ____

____

** Answer question only if a joint case is being filed.*

73. Do you or your spouse own or have an interest in an annuity? ______________ If so, identify each annuity by number, owner, and issuer and list the value and terms of each annuity. ______________________________________

____

74. Do you or your spouse own an interest in an education IRA or under a state tuition plan? __________ If so, identify each IRA or plan and state the present value of your interest and when your interests were acquired. ______________

____

75. Do you or your spouse own an interest in an IRA, ERISA, Keogh, or other retirement, pension, or profit-sharing plan? ______________ If so, identify each plan and list the present value of the interest of you or your spouse in each plan.

____

76. Do you or your spouse own any stock in a corporation or an interest in any partnership, joint venture, or other business? ______________ If so, describe the stock or interest and list its owner and estimated value.

____

77. Do you or your spouse own any government or corporate bonds or similar instruments? ______________ If so, describe each instrument and list its owner, location, and value. ______________________________________

78. Do you or your spouse own any accounts receivable? ______________ If so, describe them and list their owner and estimated value. ____

79. Are you or your spouse owed any accrued and unpaid alimony, maintenance, support, or property settlement payments? ______________ If so, how much is owed, by and to whom is it owed, and what is the nature of the obligation? $______________ ____

80. Are you or your spouse entitled to any tax refunds or other money, the amount of which has been determined? ______________ If so, state the amount owed and identify the person to whom it is owed and the entity that owes it. $______________

81. Do you or your spouse own or have an equitable or future interest in any property? ______________ If so, describe each interest and list its owner and present value. ______________________________________

____

82. Do you or your spouse own or have an interest of any kind in the estate of a deceased person, in a death benefit plan, in the death benefits in a life insurance policy, or in a trust? ______________ If so, describe each interest and list its owner and present value. ____

____

83. Are you or your spouse entitled to any tax refunds or do you have any counterclaims or rights of setoff against other persons, the existence or amount of which is presently unclear or undetermined? ______________ If so, describe each one, identify its owners, and estimate its present value. ______________________________________

____

84. Do you or your spouse own or have an ownership interest in any patents, copyrights, or other intellectual property? ______________ If so, describe each interest, list its value, and identify the owners. ______________________

____

85. Do you or your spouse own or have an ownership interest in any license, franchise, or similar property? __________ If so, describe each interest and list its estimated value, and identify the owners. ______________________________

____

86. Do you or your spouse own or possess any customer lists or other compilations containing personally identifiable information that were obtained in connection with the sale of personal or household products or services? __________ If so, describe each list or compilation. ____

____

____

87. Do you or your spouse own or have an ownership interest in any automobiles, trucks, trailers, or other vehicles or accessories? ____________ If so, describe each vehicle or accessory, identify the owners, and list its location, vehicle identification number, if any, and estimated replacement value. ____________

____

____

88. Do you or your spouse own or have an ownership interest in any boats, motors, or accessories? ____________ If so, describe each item, list its location and replacement value, and identify the owners. ____________

____

89. Do you or your spouse own or have an ownership interest in any aircraft or accessories? ____________ If so, identify each item, list its location and replacement value, and identify the owners. ____________

____

90. Do you or your spouse own any office equipment, office furnishings, or office supplies? ____________ If so, using a separate sheet of paper or the back of this sheet, list each item or group of items, show the location and replacement value of each, and identify the owners.

91. Do you or your spouse own or have an ownership interest in any machinery, fixtures, equipment, or supplies used in business? ____________ If so, identify each item or group of items, list their location and replacement value, and identify the owners. ____________

____

92. Do you or your spouse own or have an ownership interest in any inventory? ____________ If so, describe the inventory, list its location and replacement value, and identify the owners. ____________

____

93. Do you or your spouse own or have an ownership interest in any animals? ____________ If so, describe each animal or group of animals, list their location and replacement value, and identify the owners. ____________

____

94. Do you or your spouse own or have an ownership interest in any growing or harvested crops? ____________ If so, describe the crops, list their value, and identify the owners. ____________

____

95. Do you or your spouse own or have an ownership interest in any farming equipment or implements? ____________ If so, using a separate sheet of paper or the back of this work sheet, describe each item, list its location and replacement value.

96. Do you or your spouse own any farm supplies, chemicals, or feed? ____________ If so, describe each item or group of items, list their replacement value and identify the owners. ____________

____

97. Do you or your spouse own or have an ownership interest in any other personal property of any kind that has not been listed above in these work sheets? ____________ If so, describe the property, list its location and replacement value, and identify the owners. ____________

____

Schedule C Information – Exempt Property

98. List the addresses of the places where you have resided during the last 730 days and dates during which you resided at each place. ____________

____

Schedule D Information - Your Secured Debts

99. Do any of your creditors have liens, mortgages, or other encumbrances against any of your property? ____________ If so, how many debts are owed to those creditors? __________. Fill out a DEBT FORM for each debt owed to those creditors and print the word "secured" at the top of each completed form.

*100. Do any of your spouse's creditors have liens, mortgages, or other encumbrances against any of his or her property other than those creditors for whom a form was filled out in response to question 98? ____________________________ If so, how may debts are owed to those creditors? __________ Fill out a DEBT FORM for each debt owed to those creditors and print the word "secured" at the top of each completed form.

Schedule E/F Information - Your Priority Unsecured Debts

101. Do you or your spouse owe any debts to a spouse, former spouse, son, daughter, or to the parent, legal guardian, or responsible relative of a son or daughter, or to a governmental agency, for child or spousal support or other domestic support obligation? __________ If so, fill out a DEBT FORM for each debt and print the word "priority" on the top of each completed form.

102. Do you or your spouse owe any debts to employees for wages, salaries, or commissions, including vacation, severance, or sick leave pay? ________ If so, fill out a DEBT FORM for each debt and print the word "priority" on the top of each completed form.

103. Do you or your spouse owe any debts for unpaid employer's contributions to employee benefit plans? _____________ If so, on the back of this sheet identify the employees, the plan, and the persons liable for each debt, and list the amount owed and the dates that the services were rendered that gave rise to the debt.

104. Do you or your spouse own or operate a grain storage facility or a fish produce storage or processing facility? _____ If so, on the back of this sheet describe each debt resulting from this operation and list the amount owed and the person liable for each debt.

105. Do you or your spouse owe any debts for the return of deposits made for the purchase, lease, or rental of property or services that were not provided? __________ If so, fill out a DEBT FORM for each debt and print the word "priority" on the top of each completed form.

106. Do you or your spouse owe any debts for local, state, or federal taxes, customs, duties, or penalties? _____________ If so, fill out a DEBT FORM for each of these debts and print the word "priority" on the top of each completed form.

107. Do you or your spouse have a commitment to the FDIC or another insuror to maintain the capital of a federally insured bank or savings and loan institution? _____________ If so, explain. ___________________________________

108. Do you or your spouse owe any debts for death or personal injury resulting from the operation of a motor vehicle or vessel while intoxicated? _________ If so, fill out a DEBT FORM for each debt and print the word "priority" on the top of each completed form.

Schedule E/F Information - Your Unsecured Nonpriority Debts

109. Fill out a DEBT FORM for each unsecured nonpriority debt that you owe (that is, for each debt that was not listed or described in response to questions 99-108). How many of these debts are there? ____________________________

*110. Fill out a DEBT FORM for each unsecured nonpriority debt that your spouse owes that has not been listed or described in response to questions 99-108. How many of these debts are there? ___________________________________

Schedule G Information - Your Existing Contracts and Leases

111. Are you or your spouse a party to any contracts or leases that are still in effect? _____________ If so, describe each contract or lease and list the name and address of all parties to each contract or lease. ______________________________

____

____

** Answer question only if a joint case is being filed.*

Schedule H Information - Codebtors

112. Is anyone beside yourself liable for any of your debts? ____________ If so, the name and address of each person that is liable with you for a particular debt should appear in items 4 and 5 of the DEBT FORM filled out for that debt. List the name and address of each of these persons. ____________

____

____

*113. Is anyone beside you and your spouse liable for any of your spouse's debts? ____________ If so, the name and address of each person that is liable with your spouse for a particular debt should appear in item 4 of the DEBT FORM filled out for that debt. List the name and address of each of these persons other than those listed in response to question 72.

____

Schedule I Information - Your Current Income

114. What is your marital status? ____________

115. List the name, age, and relationship to you of each of your dependents. ____________

____

____

116. What is your occupation? ____________

117. List the name and address of your employer. ____________

____

118. How long have you been employed by this employer? ____________

119. What is your spouse's occupation? ____________

120. List the name and address of your spouse's employer. ____________

____

121. How long has your spouse been employed by this employer? ____________

* *Answer question only if a joint case is being filed.*

122. Complete the following showing your current monthly income. If you are not paid on a monthly basis, either pro-rate your income to a monthly amount or enter the periodic amount and make an appropriate notation. The column labeled "Your Spouse's Income" must be completed if a joint case is being filed or if you are married and filing a single chapter 12 or 13 case, unless you and your spouse are separated.

	YOUR INCOME	YOUR SPOUSE'S INCOME
Current monthly gross wages, salary, and commissions	$ ________	$ ________
Estimated monthly overtime	$ ________	$ ________
SUBTOTAL	$ ________	$ ________
LESS PAYROLL DEDUCTIONS		
a. Payroll taxes and social security	$ ________	$ ________
b. Insurance	$ ________	$ ________
c. Union dues	$ ________	$ ________
d. Other (Specify:________________________)	$ ________	$ ________
SUBTOTAL OF PAYROLL DEDUCTIONS	$ ________	$ ________
TOTAL NET MONTHLY TAKE HOME PAY	$ ________	$ ________
Regular income from operation of business or profession or farm (attach detailed statement)	$ ________	$ ________
Income from real property	$ ________	$ ________
Interest and dividends	$ ________	$ ________
Alimony, maintenance or support payments payable to the debtor for the debtor's use or that of dependents listed above.	$ ________	$ ________
Social security or other government assistance (Specify) ________________________	$ ________	$ ________
Pension or retirement income	$ ________	$ ________
Other monthly income (Specify) ________________________	$ ________	$ ________
TOTAL MONTHLY INCOME	$ ________	$ ________

TOTAL COMBINED MONTHLY INCOME $________________

Describe any increase or decrease of more than 10% in any of the above categories anticipated to occur within the year following the filing of this document:

Schedule J Information - Your Current Expenditures

123. Complete the following by estimating the average monthly expenses of yourself and your family. Payments that are made other than monthly should be pro-rated to a monthly amount, if possible. Otherwise make an appropriate notation. If a joint petition is being filed and if your spouse maintains a separate household, make a separate list of expenditures for your spouse to the right of your list.

	YOUR EXPENDITURES
Rent or home mortgage payment (include lot rented for mobile home)	$________________
Are real estate taxes included? Yes _________ No ________	
Is property insurance included? Yes _________ No ________	
Utilities: Electricity and heating fuel	$________________
Water and sewer	$________________
Telephone	$________________
Other ______________________________	$________________
Home maintenance (repairs and upkeep)	$________________
Food	$________________
Clothing	$________________
Laundry and dry cleaning	$________________
Medical and dental expenses	$________________
Transportation (not including car payments)	$________________
Recreation, clubs and entertainment, newspapers, magazines, etc.	$________________
Charitable contributions	$________________
Insurance (not deducted from wages or included in home mortgage payments)	
Homeowner's or renter's	$________________
Life	$________________
Health	$________________
Auto	$________________
Other ______________________________	$________________
Taxes (not deducted from wages or included in home mortgage payments)	
(Specify) ______________________________	$________________
Installment payments: (In chapter 12 and 13 cases, do not list payments to be included in the plan)	
Auto	$________________
Other ______________________________	$________________
Other ______________________________	$________________
Other ______________________________	$________________
Alimony, maintenance, and support paid to others	$________________
Payments for support of additional dependents not living at your home	$________________
Regular expenses from operation of business, profession, or farm (attach detailed statement)	$________________
Other ______________________________	$________________
Other ______________________________	$________________
TOTAL MONTHLY EXPENSES	$________________

Statement of Financial Affairs Information

NOTE - If you are filing a chapter 12 or chapter 13 case and if you are married and living with your spouse, then the questions below pertaining to your spouse must be answered, and the requested information related to your spouse must be given, even if you are not filing a joint case.

124. How much gross income have you received from your employment or business in this calendar ** year? $______________

125. How much gross income have you received from your employment or business during each of the last two calendar ** years? Last year: $______________ Year before: $______________

*126. How much gross income has your spouse received from his or her employment or business in this calendar ** year? $______________

*127. How much gross income has your spouse received from his or her employment during each of the last two calendar ** years? Last year: $______________ Year before: $______________

128. How much income have you received other than from your employment or business during the last two years? $______________ What was the source of this income? ______________________________

*129. How much income has your spouse received other than from his or her employment or business during the last two years? $______________What was the source of this income? ______________________________

130. Complete the following showing each creditor to whom you or your spouse have paid more than $600 in the last 90 days.

Name and address of creditor	Date of payment	Maker of payment	Amount paid	Amount still owing

131. Complete the following showing each payment that you or your spouse have made within the last 365 days to (or for the benefit of) a relative or business associate of any kind.

Name and address of creditor	Relationship of creditor to you	Date of payment	Maker of payment	Amount paid	Amount still owing

132. Complete the following showing all lawsuits or other legal or administrative proceedings in which you or your spouse have been involved as a party during the last 365 days.

Name and number of case or proceeding	Nature of case or proceeding	Name of court or agency	Status or disposition of case or proceeding

* *Answer question only if a joint case is being filed, except as directed in the note at the top of this page.*

** *If you operate your business on a fiscal year other than the calendar year, substitute fiscal year for calendar year and identify your fiscal year.*

133. Complete the following showing all money or property of yourself or your spouse that has been attached, garnished or seized in a court proceeding within the last 365 days.

Name and address of creditor	Date of seizure	Owner of property seized	Description and value of property seized

134. Complete the following showing all property owned by yourself or your spouse that within the last 365 days has been repossessed by a creditor, foreclosed upon, or otherwise returned to the seller.

Name and address of creditor or seller	Date of repossession, foreclosure or return	Description and value of property	Owner of property

135. Have your or your spouse made an assignment for the benefit of creditors within the last 120 days? ______________ If so, attach copies of all papers relating to the assignment.

136. Has any of your property or your spouse's property been held by a custodian, receiver, or other court-appointed official during the last 365 days? ______________ If so, attach copies of all papers relating to the proceeding.

137. Complete the following showing all gifts or charitable contributions made by you or your spouse within the last 365 days, except ordinary gifts to family members totalling less than $200 per recipient and charitable contributions of less than $100 per recipient.

Name and address of recipient	Relationship of recipient to you	Date of gift	Description and value of gift	Person who made the gift

138. Complete the following showing any losses from fire, theft, or other casualty, or from gambling, that you or your spouse have incurred during the last 365 days.

Type of loss	Property lost	Date of loss	Amount of loss	Covered by insurance?	Person who incurred the loss

139. Complete the following showing all transfers of money or property within the last 365 days by or on behalf of you or your spouse to attorneys or other persons for consultation concerning debt consolidation or the filing of a bankruptcy case.

Name and address of person paid	Date of payment	Name of person who made payment	Amount paid or value and description of property transferred

140. Complete the following showing all transfers of money or property made by you or your spouse within the last 2 years that have not been listed above in these work sheets, other than transfers that were made in the ordinary course of your business or financial affairs.

Name and address of transferee	Relationship of transferee to you	Date of transfer	Description and value of property transferred	Owner of property transferred

141. Identify by trust name and by amount and date all property or money transferred by you or your spouse within the last 10 years to a trust created by you or your spouse of which you or your spouse is a beneficiary. ____________________

____

142. Complete the following showing all checking, savings, or other financial accounts, certificates of deposits, and shares in banks, credit unions or other financial institutions that you or your spouse have closed, transferred, or sold during the last 365 days.

Name and address of financial institution	Name of account, account number and type of account	Amount of final balance of account	Date of any sale and amount received

143. Complete the following showing all safe deposit boxes or other boxes or depositories in which you or your spouse have kept cash, securities, or other valuables within the last 365 days.

Name and address of bank or depository	Names and address of all persons with access to box or depository	Description of contents	Date of transfer or surrender, if any

144. Has any creditor, including a bank, made a setoff against a debt or deposit of you or your spouse within the last 90 days? ______________ If so, list the name and address of the creditor and the date and amount of the setoff.

____

145. Do you or your spouse hold or control any property owned by another person? ______________ If so, list the name and address of the owner, describe the property, and list its value and location. ____________________

____

____

146. Have you or your spouse moved during the last 24 months? ______________ If so, give the address of each place where either of you lived during that period, the name or names used at that address, and the dates of occupancy.

____

____

____

____

____

147. Have you or your spouse resided in a community property state within the past 6 years? ______ If so, list the name of the spouse or former spouse who resided with you or your spouse in that state. ______

148. Have you or your spouse ever been involved in Environmental Law litigation or received notice of an Environmental Law violation or provided notice to a government agency of a Hazardous Material release? ______ If so, list the particulars on the back of this sheet.

149. Have you or your spouse, within the last six years, been any of the following: (a) an officer, director, managing executive, or the owner of more than 5% of the voting stock of a corporation; (b) a general partner of a partnership; or (c) a sole proprietor or self-employed person? Yourself ______ Your spouse ______

If both answers are "no" or if your spouse is not filing and the answer for yourself is "no," then questions 150-155 need not be answered. Otherwise, each of the questions below must be answered.

150. Complete the following showing all business with which you or your spouse have been involved in the manner described in question 148 during the last two years.

Name and address of business	Nature of business	Dates of beginning and ending of business operation	Owner of business

Note: The following questions should be answered for any business listed in the answer to question 150.

151. List the names and addresses of, and the dates services were rendered by, any bookkeepers or accountants who kept or supervised the keeping of the books and records of your business within the last two years. ______

152. List the names and addresses of, and the dates services were rendered by, any firms or persons who, within the last two years, have audited the books and records of your business or prepared a financial statement for you or your business. ______

153. List the names and addresses of all firms or persons who now have possession of your business books and records, and if any of your business books and records are not available, explain why. ______

154. List the name and address of all banks, creditors, trade agencies, and other parties to whom you have issued a financial statement within the last two years and the date the statement was issued. ______

155. Complete the following showing the last two inventories taken of your business property.

Date of inventory	Inventory supervisor	Amount of inventory in dollars	Basis of inventory (cost, market value, etc.)	Name and address of person having custody of inventory records

DEBT FORM

Instructions to Debtor: Complete one of these forms for each debt of any kind. If possible, attach a copy of the creditor's most recent statement or bill to the completed form. Respond to every question on this form. Write "N/A" in the blank after each question that does not apply to a particular debt. If more space is needed to answer a question, use the back of the form.

1. List the complete name and address of the party to whom this debt is owed. ______________________
name
____
address city state zipcode
2. What is the creditor's account number for this debt? ______________
3. Is this debt covered or secured by a mortgage, lien, pledge, or other security interest on any property? ________
If so, is this property listed elsewhere in these Work Sheets? ________ In what question?__________
If it is not listed in these Work Sheets, describe the property and list its owner, value and location. __________
____
4. Which of the spouses is liable for this debt (check one)? Husband _______ Wife _______ Both _______
5. Is anyone beside you or your spouse liable for this debt? ________ If so, list the person's name and address.
____
6. Has this debt been turned over to another party for collection? _______ If so, to whom? ______________
name
____
address city state zipcode
7. When did you incur this debt? Month ___________ Year _______
8. What did you receive in consideration for this debt? ______________________
9. Does this creditor owe you a debt? _______ If so, can the creditor's debt be setoff against your debt? ________
10. Is this debt contingent upon anything? _______ If so, explain ______________________
11. Has the final amount of this debt been determined? _______
12. Do you admit that you are liable for the full amount of this debt? _______ If not, explain. ____________
____
13. Do you and the creditor agree on the amount of this debt? _______ If not, explain. ____________
____
14. What is the total amount of this debt? $____________
15. Have you given a written financial statement in connection with this debt? _______ If so, attach a copy of the statement to this form and state to whom and when the statement was given. ______________________
____
16. Do you wish to reaffirm (i.e., remain liable for after bankruptcy) all or any part of this debt? _______
17. If this debt is secured by any property, state your intention with regard to this debt (check one):
(a) I wish to turn the property over to the creditor. _______
(b) I wish to reaffirm this debt and retain the property. _______
(c) I wish to claim the property as exempt and redeem it from the creditor. _______
(d) I wish to claim the property as exempt and contest the lien against it. _______
18. Are the payments on this debt current or delinquent? _______ If delinquent, how many payments are you behind? _______ What is the total amount of the arrearage? $____________
19. Is this a debt of someone else that you have cosigned, guaranteed, secured, or otherwise became liable for? _______ If so, list the other person's name, address and relationship to you. ______________________
____

Exhibit 2-D Statement About Your Social Security Numbers (Official Form 121)

Fill in this information to identify your case:

United States Bankruptcy Court for the: Southern District of Ohio (State)

Case number *(If known)*: ____________

Official Form 121

Statement About Your Social Security Numbers

12/15

Use this form to tell the court about any Social Security or federal Individual Taxpayer Identification numbers you have used. Do not file this form as part of the public case file. This form must be submitted separately and must not be included in the court's public electronic records. Please consult local court procedures for submission requirements.

To protect your privacy, the court will not make this form available to the public. You should not include a full Social Security Number or Individual Taxpayer Number on any other document filed with the court. The court will make only the last four digits of your numbers known to the public. However, the full numbers will be available to your creditors, the U.S. Trustee or bankruptcy administrator, and the trustee assigned to your case.

Making a false statement, concealing property, or obtaining money or property by fraud in connection with a bankruptcy case can result in fines up to $250,000, or imprisonment for up to 20 years, or both. 18 U.S.C. §§ 152, 1341, 1519, and 3571.

Part 1: Tell the Court About Yourself and Your spouse if Your Spouse is Filing With You

	For Debtor 1:	For Debtor 2 (Only If Spouse Is Filing):
1. Your name	Sidney (First name)	Sarah (First name)
	Samuel (Middle name)	Arlene (Middle name)
	Smith (Last name)	Smith (Last name)

Part 2: Tell the Court About all of Your Social Security or Federal Individual Taxpayer Identification Numbers

	For Debtor 1:	For Debtor 2:
2. All Social Security Numbers you have used	544-44-4444	999-99-9999
	___-__-____	___-__-____
	☐ You do not have a Social Security number.	☐ You do not have a Social Security number.
3. All federal Individual Taxpayer Identification Numbers (ITIN) you have used	9__-__-____	9__-__-____
	9__-__-____	9__-__-____
	☒ You do not have an ITIN.	☒ You do not have an ITIN.

Part 3: Sign Below

Debtor 1	Debtor 2
Under penalty of perjury, I declare that the information I have provided in this form is true and correct.	Under penalty of perjury, I declare that the information I have provided in this form is true and correct.
✗ /s/ Sidney Samuel Smith Signature of Debtor 1	✗ /s/ Sarah Arlene Smith Signature of Debtor 2
Date 01/15/2024 MM / DD / YYYY	Date 01/15/2024 MM / DD / YYYY

Exhibit 2-E(1) Ch. 7 Statement of Your Current Monthly Income (Official Form 122A-1)

Fill in this information to identify your case:

Debtor 1 Smith, Sidney Samuel
First Name Middle Name Last Name

Debtor 2 (Spouse, if filing) Smight, Sarah Arlene
First Name Middle Name Last Name

United States Bankruptcy Court for the: Southern District of Ohio

Case number (If known) ____________________

Check one box only as directed in this form and in Form 122A-1Supp:

☒ 1. There is no presumption of abuse.

☐ 2. The calculation to determine if a presumption of abuse applies will be made under *Chapter 7 Means Test Calculation* (Official Form 122A–2).

☐ 3. The Means Test does not apply now because of qualified military service but it could apply later.

☐ Check if this is an amended filing

Official Form 122A–1

Chapter 7 Statement of Your Current Monthly Income

04/20

Be as complete and accurate as possible. If two married people are filing together, both are equally responsible for being accurate. If more space is needed, attach a separate sheet to this form. Include the line number to which the additional information applies. On the top of any additional pages, write your name and case number (if known). If you believe that you are exempted from a presumption of abuse because you do not have primarily consumer debts or because of qualifying military service, complete and file *Statement of Exemption from Presumption of Abuse Under § 707(b)(2)* (Official Form 122A-1Supp) with this form.

Part 1: Calculate Your Current Monthly Income

1. **What is your marital and filing status?** Check one only.
   - ☐ **Not married.** Fill out Column A, lines 2-11.
   - ☒ **Married and your spouse is filing with you.** Fill out both Columns A and B, lines 2-11.
   - ☐ **Married and your spouse is NOT filing with you. You and your spouse are:**
     - ☐ **Living in the same household and are not legally separated.** Fill out both Columns A and B, lines 2-11.
     - ☐ **Living separately or are legally separated.** Fill out Column A, lines 2-11; do not fill out Column B. By checking this box, you declare under penalty of perjury that you and your spouse are legally separated under nonbankruptcy law that applies or that you and your spouse are living apart for reasons that do not include evading the Means Test requirements. 11 U.S.C. § 707(b)(7)(B).

Fill in the average monthly income that you received from all sources, derived during the 6 full months before you file this bankruptcy case. 11 U.S.C. § 101(10A). For example, if you are filing on September 15, the 6-month period would be March 1 through August 31. If the amount of your monthly income varied during the 6 months, add the income for all 6 months and divide the total by 6. Fill in the result. Do not include any income amount more than once. For example, if both spouses own the same rental property, put the income from that property in one column only. If you have nothing to report for any line, write $0 in the space.

	Debtor 1	Debtor 2		*Column A* Debtor 1	*Column B* Debtor 2 or non-filing spouse
2. **Your gross wages, salary, tips, bonuses, overtime, and commissions** (before all payroll deductions).				$ 6,870.00	$ 1,730.00
3. **Alimony and maintenance payments.** Do not include payments from a spouse if Column B is filled in.				$_____	$_____
4. **All amounts from any source which are regularly paid for household expenses of you or your dependents, including child support.** Include regular contributions from an unmarried partner, members of your household, your dependents, parents, and roommates. Include regular contributions from a spouse only if Column B is not filled in. Do not include payments you listed on line 3.				$_____	$_____
5. **Net income from operating a business, profession, or farm**	Debtor 1	Debtor 2			
Gross receipts (before all deductions)	$_____	$_____			
Ordinary and necessary operating expenses	– $_____	– $_____			
Net monthly income from a business, profession, or farm	$_____	$_____	Copy here➔	$_____	$_____
6. **Net income from rental and other real property**	Debtor 1	Debtor 2			
Gross receipts (before all deductions)	$_____	$_____			
Ordinary and necessary operating expenses	– $_____	– $_____			
Net monthly income from rental or other real property	$_____	$_____	Copy here➔	$_____	$_____
7. **Interest, dividends, and royalties**				$_____	$_____

Debtor 1 Smith, Sidney Samuel
First Name Middle Name Last Name

Case number *(if known)*

	Column A **Debtor 1**	*Column B* **Debtor 2 or non-filing spouse**
8. **Unemployment compensation**	$	$
Do not enter the amount if you contend that the amount received was a benefit under the Social Security Act. Instead, list it here: ↓		
For you $		
For your spouse $		
9. **Pension or retirement income.** Do not include any amount received that was a benefit under the Social Security Act. Also, except as stated in the next sentence, do not include any compensation, pension, pay, annuity, or allowance paid by the United States Government in connection with a disability, combat-related injury or disability, or death of a member of the uniformed services. If you received any retired pay paid under chapter 61 of title 10, then include that pay only to the extent that it does not exceed the amount of retired pay to which you would otherwise be entitled if retired under any provision of title 10 other than chapter 61 of that title.	$	$
10. **Income from all other sources not listed above.** Specify the source and amount. Do not include any benefits received under the Social Security Act; payments made under the Federal law relating to the national emergency declared by the President under the National Emergencies Act (50 U.S.C. 1601 et seq.) with respect to the coronavirus disease 2019 (COVID-19); payments received as a victim of a war crime, a crime against humanity, or international or domestic terrorism; or compensation, pension, pay, annuity, or allowance paid by the United States Government in connection with a disability, combat-related injury or disability, or death of a member of the uniformed services. If necessary, list other sources on a separate page and put the total below.		
Bitcoin Mining	$ 100.00	$
	$	$
Total amounts from separate pages, if any.	+ $	+ $
11. **Calculate your total current monthly income.** Add lines 2 through 10 for each column. Then add the total for Column A to the total for Column B.	$ 6,970.00 +	$ 1,830.00 = $ 8,700.00 **Total current monthly income**

Part 2: Determine Whether the Means Test Applies to You

12. **Calculate your current monthly income for the year.** Follow these steps:

12a. Copy your total current monthly income from line 11. **Copy line 11 here➔** $ 8,700.00

Multiply by 12 (the number of months in a year). **x** 12

12b. The result is your annual income for this part of the form. 12b. $ 104,400.0(

13. **Calculate the median family income that applies to you.** Follow these steps:

Fill in the state in which you live. OH

Fill in the number of people in your household. 4

Fill in the median family income for your state and size of household. 13. $ 108,950.0(

To find a list of applicable median income amounts, go online using the link specified in the separate instructions for this form. This list may also be available at the bankruptcy clerk's office.

14. **How do the lines compare?**

14a. ☐ Line 12b is less than or equal to line 13. On the top of page 1, check box 1, *There is no presumption of abuse.* Go to Part 3. Do NOT fill out or file Official Form 122A-2

14b. ☐ Line 12b is more than line 13. On the top of page 1, check box 2, *The presumption of abuse is determined by Form 122A-2.* Go to Part 3 and fill out Form 122A–2.

Exhibit 2-E(2) Chapter 7 Means Test Calculation (Form 122A-2)

Fill in this information to identify your case:

Debtor 1 Samuel Sidney Smith
First Name Middle Name Last Name

Debtor 2 Sarah Arlene Smith
(Spouse, if filing) First Name Middle Name Last Name

United States Bankruptcy Court for the: __________ District of __________

Case number ______________________
(If known)

Check the appropriate box as directed in lines 40 or 42:

According to the calculations required by this Statement:

☒ 1. There is no presumption of abuse.

☐ 2. There is a presumption of abuse.

☐ Check if this is an amended filing

Official Form 122A–2

Chapter 7 Means Test Calculation

04/22

To fill out this form, you will need your completed copy of *Chapter 7 Statement of Your Current Monthly Income* (Official Form 122A-1).

Be as complete and accurate as possible. If two married people are filing together, both are equally responsible for being accurate. If more space is needed, attach a separate sheet to this form. Include the line number to which the additional information applies. On the top of any additional pages, write your name and case number (if known).

Part 1: Determine Your Adjusted Income

1. **Copy your total current monthly income.** .... **Copy line 11 from Official Form 122A-1 here→** .... $ 8,700.00

2. **Did you fill out Column B in Part 1 of Form 122A–1?**

   ☐ No. Fill in $0 for the total on line 3.

   ☒ Yes. Is your spouse filing with you?

   ☐ No. Go to line 3.

   ☒ Yes. Fill in $0 for the total on line 3.

3. **Adjust your current monthly income by subtracting any part of your spouse's income not used to pay for the household expenses of you or your dependents.** Follow these steps:

   On line 11, Column B of Form 122A–1, was any amount of the income you reported for your spouse NOT regularly used for the household expenses of you or your dependents?

   ☒ No. Fill in 0 for the total on line 3.

   ☐ Yes. Fill in the information below:

State each purpose for which the income was used For example, the income is used to pay your spouse's tax debt or to support people other than you or your dependents	**Fill in the amount you are subtracting from your spouse's income**
______________________	$______
______________________	$______
______________________	+ $______
Total.	$ 0.00

Copy total here .... → — $ 0.00

4. **Adjust your current monthly income.** Subtract the total on line 3 from line 1. $ 8,700.00

Debtor 1 Samuel Sidney Smith
First Name Middle Name Last Name

Case number *(if known)* ______

Part 2: Calculate Your Deductions from Your Income

The Internal Revenue Service (IRS) issues National and Local Standards for certain expense amounts. Use these amounts to answer the questions in lines 6-15. To find the IRS standards, go online using the link specified in the separate instructions for this form. This information may also be available at the bankruptcy clerk's office.

Deduct the expense amounts set out in lines 6-15 regardless of your actual expense. In later parts of the form, you will use some of your actual expenses if they are higher than the standards. Do not deduct any amounts that you subtracted from your spouse's income in line 3 and do not deduct any operating expenses that you subtracted from income in lines 5 and 6 of Form 122A–1.

If your expenses differ from month to month, enter the average expense.

Whenever this part of the form refers to *you*, it means both you and your spouse if Column B of Form 122A–1 is filled in.

5. **The number of people used in determining your deductions from income**

   Fill in the number of people who could be claimed as exemptions on your federal income tax return, plus the number of any additional dependents whom you support. This number may be different from the number of people in your household. **4**

National Standards You must use the IRS National Standards to answer the questions in lines 6-7.

6. **Food, clothing, and other items:** Using the number of people you entered in line 5 and the IRS National Standards, fill in the dollar amount for food, clothing, and other items. $ 1,993.00

7. **Out-of-pocket health care allowance:** Using the number of people you entered in line 5 and the IRS National Standards, fill in the dollar amount for out-of-pocket health care. The number of people is split into two categories—people who are under 65 and people who are 65 or older—because older people have a higher IRS allowance for health care costs. If your actual expenses are higher than this IRS amount, you may deduct the additional amount on line 22.

People who are under 65 years of age

7a. Out-of-pocket health care allowance per person $ 79.00

7b. Number of people who are under 65 X 4

7c. **Subtotal.** Multiply line 7a by line 7b. $ 316.00 **Copy here➔** $ 316.00

People who are 65 years of age or older

7d. Out-of-pocket health care allowance per person $ 0.00

7e. Number of people who are 65 or older X 0

7f. **Subtotal.** Multiply line 7d by line 7e. $ 0.00 **Copy here➔** + $ 0.00

7g. **Total.** Add lines 7c and 7f. .... $ 316.00 **Copy total here➔** $ 316.00

Debtor 1 Samuel Sidney Smith
First Name Middle Name Last Name

Case number *(if known)* ______

Local Standards You must use the IRS Local Standards to answer the questions in lines 8-15.

Based on information from the IRS, the U.S. Trustee Program has divided the IRS Local Standard for housing for bankruptcy purposes into two parts:

- **Housing and utilities – Insurance and operating expenses**
- **Housing and utilities – Mortgage or rent expenses**

To answer the questions in lines 8-9, use the U.S. Trustee Program chart.

To find the chart, go online using the link specified in the separate instructions for this form.
This chart may also be available at the bankruptcy clerk's office.

8. **Housing and utilities – Insurance and operating expenses:** Using the number of people you entered in line 5, fill in the dollar amount listed for your county for insurance and operating expenses. .... $ 0.00

9. **Housing and utilities – Mortgage or rent expenses:**

9a. Using the number of people you entered in line 5, fill in the dollar amount listed for your county for mortgage or rent expenses. .... $ 1,926.00

9b. Total average monthly payment for all mortgages and other debts secured by your home.

To calculate the total average monthly payment, add all amounts that are contractually due to each secured creditor in the 60 months after you file for bankruptcy. Then divide by 60.

Name of the creditor	Average monthly payment
X Y Bank	$ 3,350.00
	$
	+ $
Total average monthly payment	$ 3,350.00

Copy here➔ – $ 3,350.00 Repeat this amount on line 33a.

9c. Net mortgage or rent expense.
Subtract line 9b (*total average monthly payment*) from line 9a (*mortgage or rent expense*). If this amount is less than $0, enter $0. .... $ 0.00 Copy here➔ $ 0.00

10. **If you claim that the U.S. Trustee Program's division of the IRS Local Standard for housing is incorrect and affects the calculation of your monthly expenses, fill in any additional amount you claim.** $ ______

Explain why: ______

11. **Local transportation expenses:** Check the number of vehicles for which you claim an ownership or operating expense.

- ☐ 0. Go to line 14.
- ☐ 1. Go to line 12.
- ☒ 2 or more. Go to line 12.

12. **Vehicle operation expense:** Using the IRS Local Standards and the number of vehicles for which you claim the operating expenses, fill in the *Operating Costs* that apply for your Census region or metropolitan statistical area. $ 450.00

Debtor 1 Samuel Sidney Smith
First Name Middle Name Last Name

Case number *(if known)*

13. **Vehicle ownership or lease expense:** Using the IRS Local Standards, calculate the net ownership or lease expense for each vehicle below. You may not claim the expense if you do not make any loan or lease payments on the vehicle. In addition, you may not claim the expense for more than two vehicles.

Vehicle 1 **Describe Vehicle 1:** 2001 Chevrolet Impala

13a. Ownership or leasing costs using IRS Local Standard. .... $ 225.00

13b. Average monthly payment for all debts secured by Vehicle 1.
Do not include costs for leased vehicles.

To calculate the average monthly payment here and on line 13e, add all amounts that are contractually due to each secured creditor in the 60 months after you filed for bankruptcy. Then divide by 60.

Name of each creditor for Vehicle 1	Average monthly payment
B X Dealership	$ 229.00
	+ $
Total average monthly payment	$ 229.00

Copy here➔ – $ 229.00 Repeat this amount on line 33b.

13c. Net Vehicle 1 ownership or lease expense
Subtract line 13b from line 13a. If this amount is less than $0, enter $0. .... $ 0.00 **Copy net Vehicle 1 expense here..... ➔** $ 0.00

Vehicle 2 **Describe Vehicle 2:** 2009 Ford F-150

13d. Ownership or leasing costs using IRS Local Standard. .... $ 225.00

13e. Average monthly payment for all debts secured by Vehicle 2.
Do not include costs for leased vehicles.

Name of each creditor for Vehicle 2	Average monthly payment
M X Dealership	$ 112.00
	+ $
Total average monthly payment	$ 112.00

Copy here➔ – $ 112.00 Repeat this amount on line 33c.

13f. Net Vehicle 2 ownership or lease expense
Subtract line 13e from 13d. If this amount is less than $0, enter $0.................................... $ 113.00 **Copy net Vehicle 2 expense here ... ➔** $ 113.00

14. **Public transportation expense**: If you claimed 0 vehicles in line 11, using the IRS Local Standards, fill in the *Public Transportation* expense allowance regardless of whether you use public transportation. $________

15. **Additional public transportation expense:** If you claimed 1 or more vehicles in line 11 and if you claim that you may also deduct a public transportation expense, you may fill in what you believe is the appropriate expense, but you may not claim more than the IRS Local Standard for *Public Transportation.* $________

Debtor 1 Samuel Sidney Smith
First Name Middle Name Last Name

Case number *(if known)*

Other Necessary Expenses In addition to the expense deductions listed above, you are allowed your monthly expenses for the following IRS categories.

16. **Taxes:** The total monthly amount that you will actually owe for federal, state and local taxes, such as income taxes, self-employment taxes, Social Security taxes, and Medicare taxes. You may include the monthly amount withheld from your pay for these taxes. However, if you expect to receive a tax refund, you must divide the expected refund by 12 and subtract that number from the total monthly amount that is withheld to pay for taxes. $ 1,231.0(

    Do not include real estate, sales, or use taxes.

17. **Involuntary deductions:** The total monthly payroll deductions that your job requires, such as retirement contributions, union dues, and uniform costs.

    Do not include amounts that are not required by your job, such as voluntary 401(k) contributions or payroll savings. $________

18. **Life insurance:** The total monthly premiums that you pay for your own term life insurance. If two married people are filing together, include payments that you make for your spouse's term life insurance. Do not include premiums for life insurance on your dependents, for a non-filing spouse's life insurance, or for any form of life insurance other than term. $ 65.00

19. **Court-ordered payments:** The total monthly amount that you pay as required by the order of a court or administrative agency, such as spousal or child support payments.

    Do not include payments on past due obligations for spousal or child support. You will list these obligations in line 35. $________

20. **Education:** The total monthly amount that you pay for education that is either required:
    - as a condition for your job, or
    - for your physically or mentally challenged dependent child if no public education is available for similar services. $________

21. **Childcare:** The total monthly amount that you pay for childcare, such as babysitting, daycare, nursery, and preschool.

    Do not include payments for any elementary or secondary school education. $________

22. **Additional health care expenses, excluding insurance costs:** The monthly amount that you pay for health care that is required for the health and welfare of you or your dependents and that is not reimbursed by insurance or paid by a health savings account. Include only the amount that is more than the total entered in line 7.
    Payments for health insurance or health savings accounts should be listed only in line 25. $________

23. **Optional telephones and telephone services:** The total monthly amount that you pay for telecommunication services for you and your dependents, such as pagers, call waiting, caller identification, special long distance, or business cell phone service, to the extent necessary for your health and welfare or that of your dependents or for the production of income, if it is not reimbursed by your employer. + $________

    Do not include payments for basic home telephone, internet and cell phone service. Do not include self-employment expenses, such as those reported on line 5 of Official Form 122A-1, or any amount you previously deducted.

24. **Add all of the expenses allowed under the IRS expense allowances.**
    Add lines 6 through 23. $ 4,168.0(

Debtor 1 Samuel Sidney Smith
First Name Middle Name Last Name
Case number *(if known)*

Additional Expense Deductions These are additional deductions allowed by the Means Test.
Note: Do not include any expense allowances listed in lines 6-24.

25. **Health insurance, disability insurance, and health savings account expenses.** The monthly expenses for health insurance, disability insurance, and health savings accounts that are reasonably necessary for yourself, your spouse, or your dependents.

Health insurance	$ 498.00	
Disability insurance	$ 45.00	
Health savings account	+ $ 50.00	
Total	$ 593.00	**Copy total here➔** .... $ 593.00

Do you actually spend this total amount?

- ☐ No. How much do you actually spend? $________
- ☒ Yes

26. **Continuing contributions to the care of household or family members.** The actual monthly expenses that you will continue to pay for the reasonable and necessary care and support of an elderly, chronically ill, or disabled member of your household or member of your immediate family who is unable to pay for such expenses. These expenses may include contributions to an account of a qualified ABLE program. 26 U.S.C. § 529A(b). $________

27. **Protection against family violence.** The reasonably necessary monthly expenses that you incur to maintain the safety of you and your family under the Family Violence Prevention and Services Act or other federal laws that apply. $________
By law, the court must keep the nature of these expenses confidential.

28. **Additional home energy costs.** Your home energy costs are included in your insurance and operating expenses on line 8.
If you believe that you have home energy costs that are more than the home energy costs included in expenses on line 8, then fill in the excess amount of home energy costs.
You must give your case trustee documentation of your actual expenses, and you must show that the additional amount claimed is reasonable and necessary. $________

29. **Education expenses for dependent children who are younger than 18.** The monthly expenses (not more than $189.58* per child) that you pay for your dependent children who are younger than 18 years old to attend a private or public elementary or secondary school. $________
You must give your case trustee documentation of your actual expenses, and you must explain why the amount claimed is reasonable and necessary and not already accounted for in lines 6-23.
* Subject to adjustment on 4/01/25, and every 3 years after that for cases begun on or after the date of adjustment.

30. **Additional food and clothing expense.** The monthly amount by which your actual food and clothing expenses are higher than the combined food and clothing allowances in the IRS National Standards. That amount cannot be more than 5% of the food and clothing allowances in the IRS National Standards. $________
To find a chart showing the maximum additional allowance, go online using the link specified in the separate instructions for this form. This chart may also be available at the bankruptcy clerk's office.
You must show that the additional amount claimed is reasonable and necessary.

31. **Continuing charitable contributions.** The amount that you will continue to contribute in the form of cash or financial instruments to a religious or charitable organization. 26 U.S.C. § 170(c)(1)-(2). + $ 20.00

32. **Add all of the additional expense deductions.** $ 613.00
Add lines 25 through 31.

Debtor 1 Samuel Sidney Smith — First Name Middle Name Last Name — Case number *(if known)* ____

Deductions for Debt Payment

33. **For debts that are secured by an interest in property that you own, including home mortgages, vehicle loans, and other secured debt, fill in lines 33a through 33e.**

To calculate the total average monthly payment, add all amounts that are contractually due to each secured creditor in the 60 months after you file for bankruptcy. Then divide by 60.

Mortgages on your home: — **Average monthly payment**

33a. Copy line 9b here → $ 3,350.00

Loans on your first two vehicles:

33b. Copy line 13b here. → $ 229.00

33c. Copy line 13e here. → $ 112.00

33d. List other secured debts:

Name of each creditor for other secured debt	Identify property that secures the debt	Does payment include taxes or insurance?	
____	____	❑ No ❑ Yes	$ ____
____	____	❑ No ❑ Yes	$ ____
____	____	❑ No ❑ Yes	+ $ ____

33e. Total average monthly payment. Add lines 33a through 33d. $ 3,691.00 **Copy total here→** $ 3,691.00

34. **Are any debts that you listed in line 33 secured by your primary residence, a vehicle, or other property necessary for your support or the support of your dependents?**

❑ No. Go to line 35.

☒ Yes. State any amount that you must pay to a creditor, in addition to the payments listed in line 33, to keep possession of your property (called the *cure amount*). Next, divide by 60 and fill in the information below.

Name of the creditor	Identify property that secures the debt	Total cure amount		Monthly cure amount
XY Bank	House	$ 8,000.00	÷ 60 =	$ 133.33
BX Dealership`	Car	$ 0.00	÷ 60 =	$ 0.00
MZ Dealership	Truck	$ 1,230.00	÷ 60 =	+ $ 20.50
			Total	$ 153.83

Copy total here→ $ 153.83

35. **Do you owe any priority claims such as a priority tax, child support, or alimony — that are past due as of the filing date of your bankruptcy case?** 11 U.S.C. § 507.

☒ No. Go to line 36.

❑ Yes. Fill in the total amount of all of these priority claims. Do not include current or ongoing priority claims, such as those you listed in line 19.

Total amount of all past-due priority claims $ ____ ÷ 60 = $ ____

Debtor 1 Samuel Sidney Smith
First Name Middle Name Last Name

Case number *(if known)* ______

36. **Are you eligible to file a case under Chapter 13?** 11 U.S.C. § 109(e).
For more information, go online using the link for *Bankruptcy Basics* specified in the separate instructions for this form. *Bankruptcy Basics* may also be available at the bankruptcy clerk's office.

- ☒ No. Go to line 37.
- ☐ Yes. Fill in the following information.

Projected monthly plan payment if you were filing under Chapter 13 $______

Current multiplier for your district as stated on the list issued by the Administrative Office of the United States Courts (for districts in Alabama and North Carolina) or by the Executive Office for United States Trustees (for all other districts). x ______

To find a list of district multipliers that includes your district, go online using the link specified in the separate instructions for this form. This list may also be available at the bankruptcy clerk's office.

Average monthly administrative expense if you were filing under Chapter 13 $______ **Copy total here➔** $______

37. **Add all of the deductions for debt payment.**
Add lines 33e through 36. .... $3,844.80

Total Deductions from Income

38. **Add all of the allowed deductions.**

Copy line 24, *All of the expenses allowed under IRS expense allowances*	$ 4,168.00
Copy line 32, *All of the additional expense deductions*	$ 613.00
Copy line 37, *All of the deductions for debt payment*	+ $ 3,844.80
Total deductions	$ 8,625.80

Copy total here .... ➔ $ 8,625.80

Part 3: Determine Whether There Is a Presumption of Abuse

39. **Calculate monthly disposable income for 60 months**

39a. Copy line 4, *adjusted current monthly income* ..... $ 8,700.00

39b. Copy line 38, *Total deductions*.......... − $ 8,625.80

39c. Monthly disposable income. 11 U.S.C. § 707(b)(2). Subtract line 39b from line 39a. $ 74.20 **Copy here➔** $ 74.20

For the next 60 months (5 years).......... x 60

39d. **Total**. Multiply line 39c by 60.......... $ 4,452.00 **Copy here➔** $ 4,452.00

40. **Find out whether there is a presumption of abuse.** Check the box that applies:

- ☒ **The line 39d is less than $9,075*.** On the top of page 1 of this form, check box 1, *There is no presumption of abuse.* Go to Part 5.
- ☐ **The line 39d is more than $15,150*.** On the top of page 1 of this form, check box 2, *There is a presumption of abuse.* You may fill out Part 4 if you claim special circumstances. Then go to Part 5.
- ☐ **The line 39d is at least $9,075*, but not more than $15,150*.** Go to line 41.

* Subject to adjustment on 4/01/25, and every 3 years after that for cases filed on or after the date of adjustment.

Debtor 1 Samuel Sidney Smith
First Name Middle Name Last Name
Case number *(if known)* ____________

41. 41a. **Fill in the amount of your total nonpriority unsecured debt.** If you filled out *A Summary of Your Assets and Liabilities and Certain Statistical Information Schedules* (Official Form 106Sum), you may refer to line 3b on that form. .... $________

x .25

41b. **25% of your total nonpriority unsecured debt.** 11 U.S.C. § 707(b)(2)(A)(i)(I).
Multiply line 41a by 0.25. .... $________ **Copy here➔** $________

42. **Determine whether the income you have left over after subtracting all allowed deductions is enough to pay 25% of your unsecured, nonpriority debt.**
Check the box that applies:

☒ **Line 39d is less than line 41b.** On the top of page 1 of this form, check box 1, *There is no presumption of abuse.* Go to Part 5.

☐ **Line 39d is equal to or more than line 41b.** On the top of page 1 of this form, check box 2, *There is a presumption of abuse.* You may fill out Part 4 if you claim special circumstances. Then go to Part 5.

Part 4: Give Details About Special Circumstances

43. **Do you have any special circumstances that justify additional expenses or adjustments of current monthly income for which there is no reasonable alternative?** 11 U.S.C. § 707(b)(2)(B).

☒ No. Go to Part 5.

☐ Yes. Fill in the following information. All figures should reflect your average monthly expense or income adjustment for each item. You may include expenses you listed in line 25.

You must give a detailed explanation of the special circumstances that make the expenses or income adjustments necessary and reasonable. You must also give your case trustee documentation of your actual expenses or income adjustments.

Give a detailed explanation of the special circumstances	Average monthly expense or income adjustment
	$
	$
	$
	$

Part 5: Sign Below

By signing here, I declare under penalty of perjury that the information on this statement and in any attachments is true and correct.

✗ /s/ Sidney Samuel Smith
Signature of Debtor 1

Date 01/15/2024
MM / DD / YYYY

✗ /s/ Sarah Arlene Smith
Signature of Debtor 2

Date 01/15/2024
MM / DD / YYYY

EXHIBIT 2-F VOLUNTARY PETITION (OFFICIAL FORM 101)

Fill in this information to identify your case:

United States Bankruptcy Court for the:

__________ District of __________

Case number *(If known)*: ______________________

Chapter you are filing under:
- ☐ Chapter 7
- ☐ Chapter 11
- ☐ Chapter 12
- ☐ Chapter 13

☐ Check if this is an amended filing

Official Form 101

Voluntary Petition for Individuals Filing for Bankruptcy

12/22

The bankruptcy forms use *you* and *Debtor 1* to refer to a debtor filing alone. A married couple may file a bankruptcy case together—called a *joint case*—and in joint cases, these forms use *you* to ask for information from both debtors. For example, if a form asks, "Do you own a car," the answer would be *yes* if either debtor owns a car. When information is needed about the spouses separately, the form uses *Debtor 1* and *Debtor 2* to distinguish between them. In joint cases, one of the spouses must report information as *Debtor 1* and the other as *Debtor 2*. The same person must be *Debtor 1* in all of the forms.

Be as complete and accurate as possible. If two married people are filing together, both are equally responsible for supplying correct information. If more space is needed, attach a separate sheet to this form. On the top of any additional pages, write your name and case number (if known). Answer every question.

Part 1: Identify Yourself

	About Debtor 1:	About Debtor 2 (Spouse Only in a Joint Case):
1. **Your full name** Write the name that is on your government-issued picture identification (for example, your driver's license or passport). Bring your picture identification to your meeting with the trustee.	Sidney First name Samuel Middle name Smith Last name ______ Suffix (Sr., Jr., II, III)	Sarah First name Arlene Middle name Smith Last name ______ Suffix (Sr., Jr., II, III)
2. **All other names you have used in the last 8 years** Include your married or maiden names and any assumed, trade names and *doing business as* names. Do NOT list the name of any separate legal entity such as a corporation, partnership, or LLC that is not filing this petition.	______ First name ______ Middle name ______ Last name ______ First name ______ Middle name ______ Last name ______ Business name (if applicable) ______ Business name (if applicable)	Sarah First name Arlene Middle name Brooks Last name ______ First name ______ Middle name ______ Last name ______ Business name (if applicable) ______ Business name (if applicable)
3. **Only the last 4 digits of your Social Security number or federal Individual Taxpayer Identification number** (ITIN)	xxx – xx – 4 4 4 4 OR 9 xx – xx – ___ ___ ___ ___	xxx – xx – 9 9 9 9 OR 9 xx – xx – ___ ___ ___ ___

Debtor 1 Sidney Samuel Smith
First Name Middle Name Last Name

Case number (if known)________________

	About Debtor 1:	About Debtor 2 (Spouse Only in a Joint Case):
4. **Your Employer Identification Number (EIN), if any.**	__ __ – __ __ __ __ __ __ __ EIN __ __ – __ __ __ __ __ __ __ EIN	__ __ – __ __ __ __ __ __ __ EIN __ __ – __ __ __ __ __ __ __ EIN
5. **Where you live**	1234 Elm St. Number Street Columbus OH 43211 City State ZIP Code Franklin County **If your mailing address is different from the one above, fill it in here.** Note that the court will send any notices to you at this mailing address. Number Street P.O. Box City State ZIP Code	**If Debtor 2 lives at a different address:** Number Street City State ZIP Code County **If Debtor 2's mailing address is different from yours, fill it in here.** Note that the court will send any notices to this mailing address. Number Street P.O. Box City State ZIP Code
6. **Why you are choosing *this district* to file for bankruptcy**	*Check one:* ☐ Over the last 180 days before filing this petition, I have lived in this district longer than in any other district. ☐ I have another reason. Explain. (See 28 U.S.C. § 1408.) ________________ ________________ ________________ ________________	*Check one:* ☐ Over the last 180 days before filing this petition, I have lived in this district longer than in any other district. ☐ I have another reason. Explain. (See 28 U.S.C. § 1408.) ________________ ________________ ________________ ________________

Debtor 1 Sidney Samuel Smith
First Name Middle Name Last Name

Case number *(if known)*

Part 2: Tell the Court About Your Bankruptcy Case

7. The chapter of the Bankruptcy Code you are choosing to file under

Check one. (For a brief description of each, see *Notice Required by 11 U.S.C. § 342(b) for Individuals Filing for Bankruptcy* (Form 2010)). Also, go to the top of page 1 and check the appropriate box.

- ☒ Chapter 7
- ☐ Chapter 11
- ☐ Chapter 12
- ☐ Chapter 13

8. How you will pay the fee

- ☐ **I will pay the entire fee when I file my petition**. Please check with the clerk's office in your local court for more details about how you may pay. Typically, if you are paying the fee yourself, you may pay with cash, cashier's check, or money order. If your attorney is submitting your payment on your behalf, your attorney may pay with a credit card or check with a pre-printed address.
- ☒ **I need to pay the fee in installments**. If you choose this option, sign and attach the *Application for Individuals to Pay The Filing Fee in Installments* (Official Form 103A).
- ☐ **I request that my fee be waived** (You may request this option only if you are filing for Chapter 7. By law, a judge may, but is not required to, waive your fee, and may do so only if your income is less than 150% of the official poverty line that applies to your family size and you are unable to pay the fee in installments). If you choose this option, you must fill out the *Application to Have the Chapter 7 Filing Fee Waived* (Official Form 103B) and file it with your petition.

9. Have you filed for bankruptcy within the last 8 years?

- ☒ No
- ☐ Yes. District ______ When ______ MM / DD / YYYY Case number ______

  District ______ When ______ MM / DD / YYYY Case number ______

  District ______ When ______ MM / DD / YYYY Case number ______

10. Are any bankruptcy cases pending or being filed by a spouse who is not filing this case with you, or by a business partner, or by an affiliate?

- ☒ No
- ☐ Yes. Debtor ______ Relationship to you ______

  District ______ When ______ MM / DD / YYYY Case number, if known ______

  Debtor ______ Relationship to you ______

  District ______ When ______ MM / DD / YYYY Case number, if known ______

11. Do you rent your residence?

- ☒ No. Go to line 12.
- ☐ Yes. Has your landlord obtained an eviction judgment against you?
  - ☐ No. Go to line 12.
  - ☐ Yes. Fill out *Initial Statement About an Eviction Judgment Against You* (Form 101A) and file it as part of this bankruptcy petition.

Debtor 1 Sidney Samuel Smith
First Name Middle Name Last Name

Case number (*if known*) ____________

Part 3: Report About Any Businesses You Own as a Sole Proprietor

12. **Are you a sole proprietor of any full- or part-time business?**

A sole proprietorship is a business you operate as an individual, and is not a separate legal entity such as a corporation, partnership, or LLC.

If you have more than one sole proprietorship, use a separate sheet and attach it to this petition.

☒ No. Go to Part 4.

☐ Yes. Name and location of business

____
Name of business, if any

____
Number Street

____

____________ ____ ____________
City State ZIP Code

Check the appropriate box to describe your business:

☐ Health Care Business (as defined in 11 U.S.C. § 101(27A))

☐ Single Asset Real Estate (as defined in 11 U.S.C. § 101(51B))

☐ Stockbroker (as defined in 11 U.S.C. § 101(53A))

☐ Commodity Broker (as defined in 11 U.S.C. § 101(6))

☐ None of the above

13. **Are you filing under Chapter 11 of the Bankruptcy Code, and are you a *small business debtor* or a debtor as defined by 11 U.S. C. § 1182(1)?**

For a definition of *small business debtor*, see 11 U.S.C. § 101(51D).

If you are filing under Chapter 11, the court must know whether you are a small business debtor or a debtor choosing to proceed under Subchapter V so that it can set appropriate deadlines. If you indicate that you are a small business debtor or you are choosing to proceed under Subchapter V, you must attach your most recent balance sheet, statement of operations, cash-flow statement, and federal income tax return or if any of these documents do not exist, follow the procedure in 11 U.S.C. § 1116(1)(B).

☒ No. I am not filing under Chapter 11.

☐ No. I am filing under Chapter 11, but I am NOT a small business debtor according to the definition in the Bankruptcy Code.

☐ Yes. I am filing under Chapter 11, I am a small business debtor according to the definition in the Bankruptcy Code, and I do not choose to proceed under Subchapter V of Chapter 11.

☐ Yes. I am filing under Chapter 11, I am a debtor according to the definition in § 1182(1) of the Bankruptcy Code, and I choose to proceed under Subchapter V of Chapter 11.

Debtor 1 Sidney Samuel Smith
First Name Middle Name Last Name

Case number *(if known)* ______

Part 4: Report if You Own or Have Any Hazardous Property or Any Property That Needs Immediate Attention

14. **Do you own or have any property that poses or is alleged to pose a threat of imminent and identifiable hazard to public health or safety? Or do you own any property that needs immediate attention?**

For example, do you own perishable goods, or livestock that must be fed, or a building that needs urgent repairs?

☐ No

☐ Yes. What is the hazard? ______

If immediate attention is needed, why is it needed? ______

Where is the property? ______
Number Street

______
City State ZIP Code

Debtor 1 Sidney Samuel Smith
First Name Middle Name Last Name

Case number (if known)

Part 5: Explain Your Efforts to Receive a Briefing About Credit Counseling

15. Tell the court whether you have received a briefing about credit counseling.

The law requires that you receive a briefing about credit counseling before you file for bankruptcy. You must truthfully check one of the following choices. If you cannot do so, you are not eligible to file.

If you file anyway, the court can dismiss your case, you will lose whatever filing fee you paid, and your creditors can begin collection activities again.

About Debtor 1:

You must check one:

- ☒ **I received a briefing from an approved credit counseling agency within the 180 days before I filed this bankruptcy petition, and I received a certificate of completion.**

  Attach a copy of the certificate and the payment plan, if any, that you developed with the agency.

- ☐ **I received a briefing from an approved credit counseling agency within the 180 days before I filed this bankruptcy petition, but I do not have a certificate of completion.**

  Within 14 days after you file this bankruptcy petition, you MUST file a copy of the certificate and payment plan, if any.

- ☐ **I certify that I asked for credit counseling services from an approved agency, but was unable to obtain those services during the 7 days after I made my request, and exigent circumstances merit a 30-day temporary waiver of the requirement.**

  To ask for a 30-day temporary waiver of the requirement, attach a separate sheet explaining what efforts you made to obtain the briefing, why you were unable to obtain it before you filed for bankruptcy, and what exigent circumstances required you to file this case.

  Your case may be dismissed if the court is dissatisfied with your reasons for not receiving a briefing before you filed for bankruptcy.

  If the court is satisfied with your reasons, you must still receive a briefing within 30 days after you file. You must file a certificate from the approved agency, along with a copy of the payment plan you developed, if any. If you do not do so, your case may be dismissed.

  Any extension of the 30-day deadline is granted only for cause and is limited to a maximum of 15 days.

- ☐ **I am not required to receive a briefing about credit counseling because of:**

  - ☐ **Incapacity.** I have a mental illness or a mental deficiency that makes me incapable of realizing or making rational decisions about finances.
  - ☐ **Disability.** My physical disability causes me to be unable to participate in a briefing in person, by phone, or through the internet, even after I reasonably tried to do so.
  - ☐ **Active duty.** I am currently on active military duty in a military combat zone.

  If you believe you are not required to receive a briefing about credit counseling, you must file a motion for waiver of credit counseling with the court.

About Debtor 2 (Spouse Only in a Joint Case):

You must check one:

- ☒ **I received a briefing from an approved credit counseling agency within the 180 days before I filed this bankruptcy petition, and I received a certificate of completion.**

  Attach a copy of the certificate and the payment plan, if any, that you developed with the agency.

- ☐ **I received a briefing from an approved credit counseling agency within the 180 days before I filed this bankruptcy petition, but I do not have a certificate of completion.**

  Within 14 days after you file this bankruptcy petition, you MUST file a copy of the certificate and payment plan, if any.

- ☐ **I certify that I asked for credit counseling services from an approved agency, but was unable to obtain those services during the 7 days after I made my request, and exigent circumstances merit a 30-day temporary waiver of the requirement.**

  To ask for a 30-day temporary waiver of the requirement, attach a separate sheet explaining what efforts you made to obtain the briefing, why you were unable to obtain it before you filed for bankruptcy, and what exigent circumstances required you to file this case.

  Your case may be dismissed if the court is dissatisfied with your reasons for not receiving a briefing before you filed for bankruptcy.

  If the court is satisfied with your reasons, you must still receive a briefing within 30 days after you file. You must file a certificate from the approved agency, along with a copy of the payment plan you developed, if any. If you do not do so, your case may be dismissed.

  Any extension of the 30-day deadline is granted only for cause and is limited to a maximum of 15 days.

- ☐ **I am not required to receive a briefing about credit counseling because of:**

  - ☐ **Incapacity.** I have a mental illness or a mental deficiency that makes me incapable of realizing or making rational decisions about finances.
  - ☐ **Disability.** My physical disability causes me to be unable to participate in a briefing in person, by phone, or through the internet, even after I reasonably tried to do so.
  - ☐ **Active duty.** I am currently on active military duty in a military combat zone.

  If you believe you are not required to receive a briefing about credit counseling, you must file a motion for waiver of credit counseling with the court.

Debtor 1 Sidney Samuel Smith
First Name Middle Name Last Name

Case number *(if known)* ______

Part 6: Answer These Questions for Reporting Purposes

16. What kind of debts do you have?

16a. **Are your debts primarily consumer debts?** *Consumer debts* are defined in 11 U.S.C. § 101(8) as "incurred by an individual primarily for a personal, family, or household purpose."

- ☐ No. Go to line 16b.
- ☒ Yes. Go to line 17.

16b. **Are your debts primarily business debts?** *Business debts* are debts that you incurred to obtain money for a business or investment or through the operation of the business or investment.

- ☐ No. Go to line 16c.
- ☐ Yes. Go to line 17.

16c. State the type of debts you owe that are not consumer debts or business debts.

______

17. Are you filing under Chapter 7?

Do you estimate that after any exempt property is excluded and administrative expenses are paid that funds will be available for distribution to unsecured creditors?

- ☐ No. I am not filing under Chapter 7. Go to line 18.
- ☒ Yes. I am filing under Chapter 7. Do you estimate that after any exempt property is excluded and administrative expenses are paid that funds will be available to distribute to unsecured creditors?
  - ☒ No
  - ☐ Yes

18. How many creditors do you estimate that you owe?

☒ 1-49	☐ 1,000-5,000	☐ 25,001-50,000
☐ 50-99	☐ 5,001-10,000	☐ 50,001-100,000
☐ 100-199	☐ 10,001-25,000	☐ More than 100,000
☐ 200-999		

19. How much do you estimate your assets to be worth?

☐ $0-$50,000	☐ $1,000,001-$10 million	☐ $500,000,001-$1 billion
☐ $50,001-$100,000	☐ $10,000,001-$50 million	☐ $1,000,000,001-$10 billion
☒ $100,001-$500,000	☐ $50,000,001-$100 million	☐ $10,000,000,001-$50 billion
☐ $500,001-$1 million	☐ $100,000,001-$500 million	☐ More than $50 billion

20. How much do you estimate your liabilities to be?

☐ $0-$50,000	☐ $1,000,001-$10 million	☐ $500,000,001-$1 billion
☐ $50,001-$100,000	☐ $10,000,001-$50 million	☐ $1,000,000,001-$10 billion
☒ $100,001-$500,000	☐ $50,000,001-$100 million	☐ $10,000,000,001-$50 billion
☐ $500,001-$1 million	☐ $100,000,001-$500 million	☐ More than $50 billion

Part 7: Sign Below

For you

I have examined this petition, and I declare under penalty of perjury that the information provided is true and correct.

If I have chosen to file under Chapter 7, I am aware that I may proceed, if eligible, under Chapter 7, 11,12, or 13 of title 11, United States Code. I understand the relief available under each chapter, and I choose to proceed under Chapter 7.

If no attorney represents me and I did not pay or agree to pay someone who is not an attorney to help me fill out this document, I have obtained and read the notice required by 11 U.S.C. § 342(b).

I request relief in accordance with the chapter of title 11, United States Code, specified in this petition.

I understand making a false statement, concealing property, or obtaining money or property by fraud in connection with a bankruptcy case can result in fines up to $250,000, or imprisonment for up to 20 years, or both.
18 U.S.C. §§ 152, 1341, 1519, and 3571.

✘ /s/ Sidney Samuel Smith
Signature of Debtor 1

Executed on 01/15/2024
MM / DD / YYYY

✘ Sarah Arlene Smith
Signature of Debtor 2

Executed on 01/15/2024
MM / DD / YYYY

Debtor 1 Sidney Samuel Smith
First Name Middle Name Last Name

Case number *(if known)*

For your attorney, if you are represented by one

If you are not represented by an attorney, you do not need to file this page.

I, the attorney for the debtor(s) named in this petition, declare that I have informed the debtor(s) about eligibility to proceed under Chapter 7, 11, 12, or 13 of title 11, United States Code, and have explained the relief available under each chapter for which the person is eligible. I also certify that I have delivered to the debtor(s) the notice required by 11 U.S.C. § 342(b) and, in a case in which § 707(b)(4)(D) applies, certify that I have no knowledge after an inquiry that the information in the schedules filed with the petition is incorrect.

✘ /s/ Alice B. Chase
Signature of Attorney for Debtor

Date 01/15/2024
MM / DD / YYYY

Alice B Chase, Esq.
Printed name

Chase and Chase, P.C.
Firm name

200 Market St.
Number Street

Columbus
City

OH
State

43210
ZIP Code

Contact phone (624) 999-9999

Email address

123456
Bar number

OH
State

Exhibit 2-G Schedule A/B - Property (Official Form 106A/B)

Fill in this information to identify your case and this filing:

Debtor 1 Sidney Samuel Smith
First Name Middle Name Last Name

Debtor 2 (Spouse, if filing) Sarah Arlene Smith
First Name Middle Name Last Name

United States Bankruptcy Court for the: Southern District of Ohio

Case number ______________________

☐ Check if this is an amended filing

Official Form 106A/B

Schedule A/B: Property

12/15

In each category, separately list and describe items. List an asset only once. If an asset fits in more than one category, list the asset in the category where you think it fits best. Be as complete and accurate as possible. If two married people are filing together, both are equally responsible for supplying correct information. If more space is needed, attach a separate sheet to this form. On the top of any additional pages, write your name and case number (if known). Answer every question.

Part 1: Describe Each Residence, Building, Land, or Other Real Estate You Own or Have an Interest In

1. **Do you own or have any legal or equitable interest in any residence, building, land, or similar property?**

☐ No. Go to Part 2.
☒ Yes. Where is the property?

1.1. 1234 Elm Street
Street address, if available, or other description

Columbus OH 43211
City State ZIP Code

Franklin
County

What is the property? Check all that apply.
☒ Single-family home
☐ Duplex or multi-unit building
☐ Condominium or cooperative
☐ Manufactured or mobile home
☐ Land
☐ Investment property
☐ Timeshare
☐ Other ______________

Who has an interest in the property? Check one.
☐ Debtor 1 only
☐ Debtor 2 only
☒ Debtor 1 and Debtor 2 only
☐ At least one of the debtors and another

Other information you wish to add about this item, such as local property identification number: ______________

Do not deduct secured claims or exemptions. Put the amount of any secured claims on *Schedule D: Creditors Who Have Claims Secured by Property.*

Current value of the entire property? $ 120,000.00
Current value of the portion you own? $ 120,000.00

Describe the nature of your ownership interest (such as fee simple, tenancy by the entireties, or a life estate), if known.
fee simple

☐ **Check if this is community property** (see instructions)

If you own or have more than one, list here:

1.2. 700 Fox Street
Street address, if available, or other description

Elyria OH 43222
City State ZIP Code

Lorain
County

What is the property? Check all that apply.
☐ Single-family home
☐ Duplex or multi-unit building
☐ Condominium or cooperative
☐ Manufactured or mobile home
☒ Land
☐ Investment property
☐ Timeshare
☐ Other ______________

Who has an interest in the property? Check one.
☐ Debtor 1 only
☐ Debtor 2 only
☐ Debtor 1 and Debtor 2 only
☒ At least one of the debtors and another

Other information you wish to add about this item, such as local property identification number: ______________

Do not deduct secured claims or exemptions. Put the amount of any secured claims on *Schedule D: Creditors Who Have Claims Secured by Property.*

Current value of the entire property? $ 12,000.00
Current value of the portion you own? $ 6,000.00

Describe the nature of your ownership interest (such as fee simple, tenancy by the entireties, or a life estate), if known.
tenants in common

☐ **Check if this is community property** (see instructions)

Debtor 1 Sidney Samuel Smith
First Name Middle Name Last Name

Case number (if known)__________

1.3. __________
Street address, if available, or other description

____

City State ZIP Code

____
County

What is the property? Check all that apply.
- ❑ Single-family home
- ❑ Duplex or multi-unit building
- ❑ Condominium or cooperative
- ❑ Manufactured or mobile home
- ❑ Land
- ❑ Investment property
- ❑ Timeshare
- ❑ Other __________

Who has an interest in the property? Check one.
- ❑ Debtor 1 only
- ❑ Debtor 2 only
- ❑ Debtor 1 and Debtor 2 only
- ❑ At least one of the debtors and another

Other information you wish to add about this item, such as local property identification number: __________

Do not deduct secured claims or exemptions. Put the amount of any secured claims on *Schedule D: Creditors Who Have Claims Secured by Property.*

Current value of the entire property?	**Current value of the portion you own?**
$__________	$__________

Describe the nature of your ownership interest (such as fee simple, tenancy by the entireties, or a life estate), if known.
____

❑ **Check if this is community property** (see instructions)

2. **Add the dollar value of the portion you own for all of your entries from Part 1, including any entries for pages you have attached for Part 1. Write that number here.** .... → $ 126,000.00

Part 2: Describe Your Vehicles

Do you own, lease, or have legal or equitable interest in any vehicles, whether they are registered or not? Include any vehicles you own that someone else drives. If you lease a vehicle, also report it on *Schedule G: Executory Contracts and Unexpired Leases.*

3. **Cars, vans, trucks, tractors, sport utility vehicles, motorcycles**
- ❑ No
- ☒ Yes

3.1. Make: Chevrolet
Model: Impala
Year: 2001
Approximate mileage: 83000
Other information:

Who has an interest in the property? Check one.
- ❑ Debtor 1 only
- ❑ Debtor 2 only
- ☒ Debtor 1 and Debtor 2 only
- ❑ At least one of the debtors and another

❑ **Check if this is community property** (see instructions)

Do not deduct secured claims or exemptions. Put the amount of any secured claims on *Schedule D: Creditors Who Have Claims Secured by Property.*

Current value of the entire property?	**Current value of the portion you own?**
$ 2,100.00	$ 2,100.00

If you own or have more than one, describe here:

3.2. Make: Ford
Model: F-150
Year: 2009
Approximate mileage: 55000
Other information:

Who has an interest in the property? Check one.
- ❑ Debtor 1 only
- ❑ Debtor 2 only
- ☒ Debtor 1 and Debtor 2 only
- ❑ At least one of the debtors and another

❑ **Check if this is community property** (see instructions)

Do not deduct secured claims or exemptions. Put the amount of any secured claims on *Schedule D: Creditors Who Have Claims Secured by Property.*

Current value of the entire property?	**Current value of the portion you own?**
$ 14,000.00	$ 14,000.00

Debtor 1 Sidney Samuel Smith
First Name Middle Name Last Name

Case number *(if known)*____________________

3.3. Make: __________
Model: __________
Year: __________
Approximate mileage: __________
Other information:

Who has an interest in the property? Check one.
- ❑ Debtor 1 only
- ❑ Debtor 2 only
- ❑ Debtor 1 and Debtor 2 only
- ❑ At least one of the debtors and another

❑ **Check if this is community property** (see instructions)

Do not deduct secured claims or exemptions. Put the amount of any secured claims on *Schedule D: Creditors Who Have Claims Secured by Property.*

Current value of the entire property?	**Current value of the portion you own?**
$__________	$__________

3.4. Make: __________
Model: __________
Year: __________
Approximate mileage: __________
Other information:

Who has an interest in the property? Check one.
- ❑ Debtor 1 only
- ❑ Debtor 2 only
- ❑ Debtor 1 and Debtor 2 only
- ❑ At least one of the debtors and another

❑ **Check if this is community property** (see instructions)

Do not deduct secured claims or exemptions. Put the amount of any secured claims on *Schedule D: Creditors Who Have Claims Secured by Property.*

Current value of the entire property?	**Current value of the portion you own?**
$__________	$__________

4. **Watercraft, aircraft, motor homes, ATVs and other recreational vehicles, other vehicles, and accessories**
Examples: Boats, trailers, motors, personal watercraft, fishing vessels, snowmobiles, motorcycle accessories
- ☒ No
- ❑ Yes

4.1. Make: __________
Model: __________
Year: __________
Other information:

Who has an interest in the property? Check one.
- ❑ Debtor 1 only
- ❑ Debtor 2 only
- ❑ Debtor 1 and Debtor 2 only
- ❑ At least one of the debtors and another

❑ **Check if this is community property** (see instructions)

Do not deduct secured claims or exemptions. Put the amount of any secured claims on *Schedule D: Creditors Who Have Claims Secured by Property.*

Current value of the entire property?	**Current value of the portion you own?**
$__________	$__________

If you own or have more than one, list here:

4.2. Make: __________
Model: __________
Year: __________
Other information:

Who has an interest in the property? Check one.
- ❑ Debtor 1 only
- ❑ Debtor 2 only
- ❑ Debtor 1 and Debtor 2 only
- ❑ At least one of the debtors and another

❑ **Check if this is community property** (see instructions)

Do not deduct secured claims or exemptions. Put the amount of any secured claims on *Schedule D: Creditors Who Have Claims Secured by Property.*

Current value of the entire property?	**Current value of the portion you own?**
$__________	$__________

5. **Add the dollar value of the portion you own for all of your entries from Part 2, including any entries for pages you have attached for Part 2. Write that number here** .... ➔ $ 16,100.00

Debtor 1 Sidney Samuel Smith
First Name Middle Name Last Name

Case number *(if known)*____________________

Part 3: Describe Your Personal and Household Items

Do you own or have any legal or equitable interest in any of the following items?

Current value of the portion you own?
Do not deduct secured claims or exemptions.

6. **Household goods and furnishings**
Examples: Major appliances, furniture, linens, china, kitchenware
☐ No
☒ Yes. Describe......... 1 Kenmore Washing Machine, 1 Kenmore Dryer, 1 GE Range — $ 700.00

7. **Electronics**
Examples: Televisions and radios; audio, video, stereo, and digital equipment; computers, printers, scanners; music collections; electronic devices including cell phones, cameras, media players, games
☐ No
☒ Yes. Describe.......... 1 Sony TV — $ 200.00

8. **Collectibles of value**
Examples: Antiques and figurines; paintings, prints, or other artwork; books, pictures, or other art objects; stamp, coin, or baseball card collections; other collections, memorabilia, collectibles
☒ No
☐ Yes. Describe.......... — $________

9. **Equipment for sports and hobbies**
Examples: Sports, photographic, exercise, and other hobby equipment; bicycles, pool tables, golf clubs, skis; canoes and kayaks; carpentry tools; musical instruments
☐ No
☒ Yes. Describe.......... Nikon camera and fishing equipment — $ 100.00

10. **Firearms**
Examples: Pistols, rifles, shotguns, ammunition, and related equipment
☒ No
☐ Yes. Describe.......... — $________

11. **Clothes**
Examples: Everyday clothes, furs, leather coats, designer wear, shoes, accessories
☐ No
☒ Yes. Describe.......... Personal clothing — $ 100.00

12. **Jewelry**
Examples: Everyday jewelry, costume jewelry, engagement rings, wedding rings, heirloom jewelry, watches, gems, gold, silver
☐ No
☒ Yes. Describe.......... wedding bands — $ 900.00

13. **Non-farm animals**
Examples: Dogs, cats, birds, horses
☒ No
☐ Yes. Describe.......... — $________

14. **Any other personal and household items you did not already list, including any health aids you did not list**
☒ No
☐ Yes. Give specific information. .... — $________

15. **Add the dollar value of all of your entries from Part 3, including any entries for pages you have attached for Part 3. Write that number here** .... ➔ $ 2,000.00

Debtor 1 Sidney Samuel Smith
First Name Middle Name Last Name

Case number *(if known)*

Part 4: Describe Your Financial Assets

Do you own or have any legal or equitable interest in any of the following?

Current value of the portion you own?
Do not deduct secured claims or exemptions.

16. **Cash**
Examples: Money you have in your wallet, in your home, in a safe deposit box, and on hand when you file your petition

☐ No
☒ Yes .... Cash: .... $ 5.00

17. **Deposits of money**
Examples: Checking, savings, or other financial accounts; certificates of deposit; shares in credit unions, brokerage houses, and other similar institutions. If you have multiple accounts with the same institution, list each.

☐ No
☒ Yes .... Institution name:

	Institution name	
17.1. Checking account:	XY Bank	$ 1,200.00
17.2. Checking account:		$
17.3. Savings account:		$
17.4. Savings account:		$
17.5. Certificates of deposit:		$
17.6. Other financial account:		$
17.7. Other financial account:		$
17.8. Other financial account:		$
17.9. Other financial account:		$

18. **Bonds, mutual funds, or publicly traded stocks**
Examples: Bond funds, investment accounts with brokerage firms, money market accounts

☒ No
☐ Yes .... Institution or issuer name:

$
$
$

19. **Non-publicly traded stock and interests in incorporated and unincorporated businesses, including an interest in an LLC, partnership, and joint venture**

☒ No
☐ Yes. Give specific information about them..........

Name of entity:	% of ownership:	
	0% %	$
	0% %	$
	0% %	$

Debtor 1 Sidney Samuel Smith
First Name Middle Name Last Name

Case number *(if known)* ______

20. **Government and corporate bonds and other negotiable and non-negotiable instruments**

Negotiable instruments include personal checks, cashiers' checks, promissory notes, and money orders.
Non-negotiable instruments are those you cannot transfer to someone by signing or delivering them.

- ☒ No
- ☐ Yes. Give specific information about them.......................

Issuer name:

______	$______
______	$______
______	$______

21. **Retirement or pension accounts**

Examples: Interests in IRA, ERISA, Keogh, 401(k), 403(b), thrift savings accounts, or other pension or profit-sharing plans

- ☐ No
- ☒ Yes. List each account separately.

Type of account:	Institution name:	
401(k) or similar plan:	YZ Bank	$ 5,540.00
Pension plan:		$
IRA:	Ohio Bank	$ 4,720.00
Retirement account:		$
Keogh:		$
Additional account:		$
Additional account:		$

22. **Security deposits and prepayments**

Your share of all unused deposits you have made so that you may continue service or use from a company
Examples: Agreements with landlords, prepaid rent, public utilities (electric, gas, water), telecommunications companies, or others

- ☐ No
- ☒ Yes.........................

	Institution name or individual:	
Electric:	Ohio Utilities	$ 20.00
Gas:		$
Heating oil:		$
Security deposit on rental unit:		$
Prepaid rent:		$
Telephone:		$
Water:		$
Rented furniture:		$
Other:		$

23. **Annuities** (A contract for a periodic payment of money to you, either for life or for a number of years)

- ☒ No
- ☐ Yes.........................

Issuer name and description:

______	$______
______	$______
______	$______

Debtor 1 Sidney Samuel Smith
First Name Middle Name Last Name

Case number *(if known)*

24. **Interests in an education IRA, in an account in a qualified ABLE program, or under a qualified state tuition program.**
26 U.S.C. §§ 530(b)(1), 529A(b), and 529(b)(1).

☒ No
☐ Yes .... Institution name and description. Separately file the records of any interests.11 U.S.C. § 521(c):

$
$
$

25. **Trusts, equitable or future interests in property (other than anything listed in line 1), and rights or powers exercisable for your benefit**

☒ No
☐ Yes. Give specific information about them.... $

26. **Patents, copyrights, trademarks, trade secrets, and other intellectual property**
Examples: Internet domain names, websites, proceeds from royalties and licensing agreements

☒ No
☐ Yes. Give specific information about them.... $

27. **Licenses, franchises, and other general intangibles**
Examples: Building permits, exclusive licenses, cooperative association holdings, liquor licenses, professional licenses

☒ No
☐ Yes. Give specific information about them.... $

Money or property owed to you?

Current value of the portion you own?
Do not deduct secured claims or exemptions.

28. **Tax refunds owed to you**

☐ No
☒ Yes. Give specific information about them, including whether you already filed the returns and the tax years. ....

2016 federal income tax refund

Federal:	$ 410.00
State:	$ 20.00
Local:	$ 0.00

29. **Family support**
Examples: Past due or lump sum alimony, spousal support, child support, maintenance, divorce settlement, property settlement

☒ No
☐ Yes. Give specific information.............

Alimony:	$
Maintenance:	$
Support:	$
Divorce settlement:	$
Property settlement:	$

30. **Other amounts someone owes you**
Examples: Unpaid wages, disability insurance payments, disability benefits, sick pay, vacation pay, workers' compensation, Social Security benefits; unpaid loans you made to someone else

☒ No
☐ Yes. Give specific information.............. $

Debtor 1 Sidney Samuel Smith
First Name Middle Name Last Name

Case number *(if known)*

31. **Interests in insurance policies**
Examples: Health, disability, or life insurance; health savings account (HSA); credit, homeowner's, or renter's insurance

❑ No
❑ Yes. Name the insurance company of each policy and list its value. ...

Company name:	Beneficiary:	Surrender or refund value:
HS Bank HSA	Sarah Smith	$ 200.00
		$
		$

32. **Any interest in property that is due you from someone who has died**
If you are the beneficiary of a living trust, expect proceeds from a life insurance policy, or are currently entitled to receive property because someone has died.

❑ No
❑ Yes. Give specific information............. $

33. **Claims against third parties, whether or not you have filed a lawsuit or made a demand for payment**
Examples: Accidents, employment disputes, insurance claims, or rights to sue

❑ No
❑ Yes. Describe each claim. .... $

34. **Other contingent and unliquidated claims of every nature, including counterclaims of the debtor and rights to set off claims**

❑ No
❑ Yes. Describe each claim. .... $

35. **Any financial assets you did not already list**

❑ No
❑ Yes. Give specific information........... $

36. **Add the dollar value of all of your entries from Part 4, including any entries for pages you have attached for Part 4. Write that number here** .... ➔ $ 12,115.00

Part 5: Describe Any Business-Related Property You Own or Have an Interest In. List any real estate in Part 1.

37. **Do you own or have any legal or equitable interest in any business-related property?**

❑ No. Go to Part 6.
❑ Yes. Go to line 38.

Current value of the portion you own?
Do not deduct secured claims or exemptions.

38. **Accounts receivable or commissions you already earned**

❑ No
❑ Yes. Describe....... $

39. **Office equipment, furnishings, and supplies**
Examples: Business-related computers, software, modems, printers, copiers, fax machines, rugs, telephones, desks, chairs, electronic devices

❑ No
❑ Yes. Describe....... $

Debtor 1 Sidney Samuel Smith
First Name Middle Name Last Name

Case number *(if known)*____________________

40. **Machinery, fixtures, equipment, supplies you use in business, and tools of your trade**

- ☐ No
- ☐ Yes. Describe....... $__________

41. **Inventory**

- ☐ No
- ☐ Yes. Describe....... $__________

42. **Interests in partnerships or joint ventures**

- ☐ No
- ☐ Yes. Describe.......

Name of entity:	% of ownership:	
__________	____%	$__________
__________	____%	$__________
__________	____%	$__________

43. **Customer lists, mailing lists, or other compilations**

- ☐ No
- ☐ Yes. **Do your lists include personally identifiable information** (as defined in 11 U.S.C. § 101(41A))?
  - ☐ No
  - ☐ Yes. Describe....... $__________

44. **Any business-related property you did not already list**

- ☐ No
- ☐ Yes. Give specific information ....

$__________
$__________
$__________
$__________
$__________
$__________

45. **Add the dollar value of all of your entries from Part 5, including any entries for pages you have attached for Part 5. Write that number here** .... ➔ $__________

Part 6: Describe Any Farm- and Commercial Fishing-Related Property You Own or Have an Interest In.
If you own or have an interest in farmland, list it in Part 1.

46. **Do you own or have any legal or equitable interest in any farm- or commercial fishing-related property?**

- ☒ No. Go to Part 7.
- ☐ Yes. Go to line 47.

Current value of the portion you own?
Do not deduct secured claims or exemptions.

47. **Farm animals**
Examples: Livestock, poultry, farm-raised fish

- ☐ No
- ☐ Yes......................... $__________

Debtor 1 Sidney Samuel Smith
First Name Middle Name Last Name

Case number (if known) ____________

48. **Crops—either growing or harvested**

❑ No
❑ Yes. Give specific information. .... $________

49. **Farm and fishing equipment, implements, machinery, fixtures, and tools of trade**

❑ No
❑ Yes .... $________

50. **Farm and fishing supplies, chemicals, and feed**

❑ No
❑ Yes .... $________

51. **Any farm- and commercial fishing-related property you did not already list**

❑ No
❑ Yes. Give specific information. .... $________

52. **Add the dollar value of all of your entries from Part 6, including any entries for pages you have attached for Part 6. Write that number here** .... ➔ $________

Part 7: Describe All Property You Own or Have an Interest in That You Did Not List Above

53. **Do you have other property of any kind you did not already list?**
Examples: Season tickets, country club membership

☒ No
❑ Yes. Give specific information. .... $________ $________ $________

54. **Add the dollar value of all of your entries from Part 7. Write that number here** .... ➔ $________

Part 8: List the Totals of Each Part of this Form

55. **Part 1: Total real estate, line 2** .... ➔		$ 126,000.00
56. **Part 2: Total vehicles, line 5**	$ 16,100.00	
57. **Part 3: Total personal and household items, line 15**	$ 2,000.00	
58. **Part 4: Total financial assets, line 36**	$ 12,115.00	
59. **Part 5: Total business-related property, line 45**	$ 0.00	
60. **Part 6: Total farm- and fishing-related property, line 52**	$ 0.00	
61. **Part 7: Total other property not listed, line 54**	+ $ 0.00	
62. **Total personal property.** Add lines 56 through 61.	$ 30,215.00 Copy personal property total ➔	+ $ 30,215.00
63. **Total of all property on Schedule A/B.** Add line 55 + line 62........		$ 156,215.00

Exhibit 2-H Schedule C - The Property You Claim as Exempt (Official Form 106C)

Fill in this information to identify your case:

Debtor 1 Sidney Samuel Smith
First Name Middle Name Last Name

Debtor 2 Sarah Arlene Smith
(Spouse, if filing) First Name Middle Name Last Name

United States Bankruptcy Court for the: __________ District of __________

Case number (If known) ______________________

☐ Check if this is an amended filing

Official Form 106C

Schedule C: The Property You Claim as Exempt

04/22

Be as complete and accurate as possible. If two married people are filing together, both are equally responsible for supplying correct information. Using the property you listed on *Schedule A/B: Property* (Official Form 106A/B) as your source, list the property that you claim as exempt. If more space is needed, fill out and attach to this page as many copies of *Part 2: Additional Page* as necessary. On the top of any additional pages, write your name and case number (if known).

For each item of property you claim as exempt, you must specify the amount of the exemption you claim. One way of doing so is to state a specific dollar amount as exempt. Alternatively, you may claim the full fair market value of the property being exempted up to the amount of any applicable statutory limit. Some exemptions—such as those for health aids, rights to receive certain benefits, and tax-exempt retirement funds—may be unlimited in dollar amount. However, if you claim an exemption of 100% of fair market value under a law that limits the exemption to a particular dollar amount and the value of the property is determined to exceed that amount, your exemption would be limited to the applicable statutory amount.

Part 1: Identify the Property You Claim as Exempt

1. **Which set of exemptions are you claiming?** *Check one only, even if your spouse is filing with you.*
   - ☒ You are claiming state and federal nonbankruptcy exemptions. 11 U.S.C. § 522(b)(3)
   - ☐ You are claiming federal exemptions. 11 U.S.C. § 522(b)(2)

2. **For any property you list on *Schedule A/B* that you claim as exempt, fill in the information below.**

Brief description of the property and line on *Schedule A/B* that lists this property	Current value of the portion you own Copy the value from *Schedule A/B*	Amount of the exemption you claim *Check only one box for each exemption.*	Specific laws that allow exemption
Brief description: Family Home Line from *Schedule A/B*: 1.1	$120,000.00	☐ $ ______ ☒ 100% of fair market value, up to any applicable statutory limit	O.R.C. 2329.66(A)(1)
Brief description: Ford Truck Line from *Schedule A/B*: 3.2	$14,000.00	☐ $ ______ ☒ 100% of fair market value, up to any applicable statutory limit	O.R.C. 2329.66(A)(2)
Brief description: ______ Line from *Schedule A/B*: ______	$ ______	☐ $ ______ ☐ 100% of fair market value, up to any applicable statutory limit	

3. **Are you claiming a homestead exemption of more than $189,050?**
   (Subject to adjustment on 4/01/25 and every 3 years after that for cases filed on or after the date of adjustment.)
   - ☐ No
   - ☐ Yes. Did you acquire the property covered by the exemption within 1,215 days before you filed this case?
     - ☐ No
     - ☐ Yes

Debtor 1 Sidney Samuel Smith
First Name Middle Name Last Name

Case number (if known) ____________

Part 2: Additional Page

Brief description of the property and line on *Schedule A/B* that lists this property	**Current value of the portion you own** Copy the value from *Schedule A/B*	**Amount of the exemption you claim** *Check only one box for each exemption*	**Specific laws that allow exemption**
Brief description: Household Goods Line from *Schedule A/B:* ____	$ 700.00	☐ $ ____ ☒ 100% of fair market value, up to any applicable statutory limit	O.R.C. 2329.66(A)(4)
Brief description: Sports and Hobbies Line from *Schedule A/B:* 9	$ 100.00	☐ $ ____ ☒ 100% of fair market value, up to any applicable statutory limit	O.R.C. 2329.66(A)(4)
Brief description: Clothing Line from *Schedule A/B:* 11	$ 100.00	☐ $ ____ ☒ 100% of fair market value, up to any applicable statutory limit	O.R.C. 2329.66(A)(3)
Brief description: Jewelry Line from *Schedule A/B:* 12	$ 900.00	☐ $ ____ ☒ 100% of fair market value, up to any applicable statutory limit	O.R.C. 2329.66(A)(4)
Brief description: Cash Line from *Schedule A/B:* 16	$ 5.00	☐ $ ____ ☒ 100% of fair market value, up to any applicable statutory limit	O.R.C. 2329.66(A)(4)
Brief description: Checking Account Line from *Schedule A/B:* 17	$ 1,200.00	☐ $ ____ ☒ 100% of fair market value, up to any applicable statutory limit	O.R.C. 2329.66(A)(3), (18)
Brief description: 401k Line from *Schedule A/B:* ____	$ 5,540.00	☐ $ ____ ☒ 100% of fair market value, up to any applicable statutory limit	O.R.C. 2329.66(A)(10)
Brief description: IRA Line from *Schedule A/B:* 21	$ 4,720.00	☐ $ ____ ☒ 100% of fair market value, up to any applicable statutory limit	O.R.C. 2329.66(A)(10)
Brief description: Utilities Deposit Line from *Schedule A/B:* ____	$ 20.00	☐ $ 20.00 ☒ 100% of fair market value, up to any applicable statutory limit	O.R.C. 2329.66(A)(17)
Brief description: ____ Line from *Schedule A/B:* ____	$ ____	☐ $ ____ ☐ 100% of fair market value, up to any applicable statutory limit	____
Brief description: ____ Line from *Schedule A/B:* ____	$ ____	☐ $ ____ ☐ 100% of fair market value, up to any applicable statutory limit	____
Brief description: ____ Line from *Schedule A/B:* ____	$ ____	☐ $ ____ ☐ 100% of fair market value, up to any applicable statutory limit	____

Exhibit 2-I Creditors Who Have Claims Secured by Property (Official Form 106D)

Fill in this information to identify your case:

Debtor 1: Sidney Samuel Smith
First Name / Middle Name / Last Name

Debtor 2 (Spouse, if filing): Sarah Arlene Smith
First Name / Middle Name / Last Name

United States Bankruptcy Court for the: Southern District of Ohio

Case number (If known) ______________________

☐ Check if this is an amended filing

Official Form 106D

Schedule D: Creditors Who Have Claims Secured by Property

12/15

Be as complete and accurate as possible. If two married people are filing together, both are equally responsible for supplying correct information. If more space is needed, copy the Additional Page, fill it out, number the entries, and attach it to this form. On the top of any additional pages, write your name and case number (if known).

1. **Do any creditors have claims secured by your property?**
   - ☐ No. Check this box and submit this form to the court with your other schedules. You have nothing else to report on this form.
   - ☑ Yes. Fill in all of the information below.

Part 1: List All Secured Claims

2. **List all secured claims.** If a creditor has more than one secured claim, list the creditor separately for each claim. If more than one creditor has a particular claim, list the other creditors in Part 2. As much as possible, list the claims in alphabetical order according to the creditor's name.

	Column A **Amount of claim** Do not deduct the value of collateral.	Column B **Value of collateral that supports this claim**	Column C **Unsecured portion** If any
2.1 XY Bank	$ 98,000.00	$ 120,000.00	$
2.2 BX Dealership	$ 1,298.00	$ 2,100.00	$

2.1 XY Bank
Creditor's Name
1234 Main Street
Number Street

Columbus OH 43222
City State ZIP Code

Describe the property that secures the claim: Residence

As of the date you file, the claim is: Check all that apply.
- ☐ Contingent
- ☐ Unliquidated
- ☐ Disputed

Who owes the debt? Check one.
- ☐ Debtor 1 only
- ☐ Debtor 2 only
- ☑ Debtor 1 and Debtor 2 only
- ☐ At least one of the debtors and another

☐ **Check if this claim relates to a community debt**

Nature of lien. Check all that apply.
- ☑ An agreement you made (such as mortgage or secured car loan)
- ☐ Statutory lien (such as tax lien, mechanic's lien)
- ☐ Judgment lien from a lawsuit
- ☐ Other (including a right to offset) ______________

Date debt was incurred 09/20/2011

Last 4 digits of account number 2 2 9 8

2.2 BX Dealership
Creditor's Name
4567 West Road
Number Street

Columbus OH 43221
City State ZIP Code

Describe the property that secures the claim: Chevrolet Impala

As of the date you file, the claim is: Check all that apply.
- ☐ Contingent
- ☐ Unliquidated
- ☐ Disputed

Who owes the debt? Check one.
- ☐ Debtor 1 only
- ☐ Debtor 2 only
- ☑ Debtor 1 and Debtor 2 only
- ☐ At least one of the debtors and another

☐ **Check if this claim relates to a community debt**

Nature of lien. Check all that apply.
- ☑ An agreement you made (such as mortgage or secured car loan)
- ☐ Statutory lien (such as tax lien, mechanic's lien)
- ☐ Judgment lien from a lawsuit
- ☐ Other (including a right to offset) ______________

Date debt was incurred 05/01/2014

Last 4 digits of account number 2 2 1 6

Add the dollar value of your entries in Column A on this page. Write that number here: $ 99,298.00

Debtor 1 Sidney Samuel Smith
First Name Middle Name Last Name

Case number (if known) ______

Part 1: Additional Page

After listing any entries on this page, number them beginning with 2.3, followed by 2.4, and so forth.

	Column A **Amount of claim** Do not deduct the value of collateral.	Column B **Value of collateral that supports this claim**	Column C **Unsecured portion** If any
2.3 MZ Dealership	$ 13,290.00	$ 14,000.00	$

2.3 MZ Dealership
Creditor's Name
4456 Main Street
Number Street

Columbus OH 43221
City State ZIP Code

Describe the property that secures the claim: Ford F-150

As of the date you file, the claim is: Check all that apply.
- ☐ Contingent
- ☐ Unliquidated
- ☐ Disputed

Who owes the debt? Check one.
- ☐ Debtor 1 only
- ☐ Debtor 2 only
- ☒ Debtor 1 and Debtor 2 only
- ☐ At least one of the debtors and another

☐ **Check if this claim relates to a community debt**

Nature of lien. Check all that apply.
- ☒ An agreement you made (such as mortgage or secured car loan)
- ☐ Statutory lien (such as tax lien, mechanic's lien)
- ☐ Judgment lien from a lawsuit
- ☐ Other (including a right to offset) ______

Date debt was incurred 02/01/2014

Last 4 digits of account number 3 8 7 9

☐ ______
Creditor's Name
______
Number Street
______
______
City State ZIP Code

Describe the property that secures the claim: ______ $______ $______ $______

As of the date you file, the claim is: Check all that apply.
- ☐ Contingent
- ☐ Unliquidated
- ☐ Disputed

Who owes the debt? Check one.
- ☐ Debtor 1 only
- ☐ Debtor 2 only
- ☐ Debtor 1 and Debtor 2 only
- ☐ At least one of the debtors and another

☐ **Check if this claim relates to a community debt**

Nature of lien. Check all that apply.
- ☐ An agreement you made (such as mortgage or secured car loan)
- ☐ Statutory lien (such as tax lien, mechanic's lien)
- ☐ Judgment lien from a lawsuit
- ☐ Other (including a right to offset) ______

Date debt was incurred ______

Last 4 digits of account number ___ ___ ___ ___

☐ ______
Creditor's Name
______
Number Street
______
______
City State ZIP Code

Describe the property that secures the claim: ______ $______ $______ $______

As of the date you file, the claim is: Check all that apply.
- ☐ Contingent
- ☐ Unliquidated
- ☐ Disputed

Who owes the debt? Check one.
- ☐ Debtor 1 only
- ☐ Debtor 2 only
- ☐ Debtor 1 and Debtor 2 only
- ☐ At least one of the debtors and another

☐ **Check if this claim relates to a community debt**

Nature of lien. Check all that apply.
- ☐ An agreement you made (such as mortgage or secured car loan)
- ☐ Statutory lien (such as tax lien, mechanic's lien)
- ☐ Judgment lien from a lawsuit
- ☐ Other (including a right to offset) ______

Date debt was incurred ______

Last 4 digits of account number ___ ___ ___ ___

Add the dollar value of your entries in Column A on this page. Write that number here: $ 13,290.00

If this is the last page of your form, add the dollar value totals from all pages. Write that number here: $ 112,588.00

Debtor 1 Sidney Samuel Smith
First Name Middle Name Last Name

Case number *(if known)* ____________

Part 2: **List Others to Be Notified for a Debt That You Already Listed**

Use this page only if you have others to be notified about your bankruptcy for a debt that you already listed in Part 1. For example, if a collection agency is trying to collect from you for a debt you owe to someone else, list the creditor in Part 1, and then list the collection agency here. Similarly, if you have more than one creditor for any of the debts that you listed in Part 1, list the additional creditors here. If you do not have additional persons to be notified for any debts in Part 1, do not fill out or submit this page.

☐ ____________
Name
____
Number Street
____
____
City State ZIP Code

On which line in Part 1 did you enter the creditor? ____
Last 4 digits of account number ___ ___ ___ ___

☐ ____________
Name
____
Number Street
____
____
City State ZIP Code

On which line in Part 1 did you enter the creditor? ____
Last 4 digits of account number ___ ___ ___ ___

☐ ____________
Name
____
Number Street
____
____
City State ZIP Code

On which line in Part 1 did you enter the creditor? ____
Last 4 digits of account number ___ ___ ___ ___

☐ ____________
Name
____
Number Street
____
____
City State ZIP Code

On which line in Part 1 did you enter the creditor? ____
Last 4 digits of account number ___ ___ ___ ___

☐ ____________
Name
____
Number Street
____
____
City State ZIP Code

On which line in Part 1 did you enter the creditor? ____
Last 4 digits of account number ___ ___ ___ ___

☐ ____________
Name
____
Number Street
____
____
City State ZIP Code

On which line in Part 1 did you enter the creditor? ____
Last 4 digits of account number ___ ___ ___ ___

Print | Save As... | Add Attachment | Reset

EXHIBIT 2-J SCHEDULE E/F - CREDITORS WHO HAVE UNSECURED CLAIMS (OFFICIAL FORM 106E/F)

Fill in this information to identify your case:

Debtor 1 Sidney Samuel Smith
First Name Middle Name Last Name

Debtor 2 Sarah Arlene Smith
(Spouse, if filing) First Name Middle Name Last Name

United States Bankruptcy Court for the: Southern District of Ohio

Case number ____________
(If known)

❑ Check if this is an amended filing

Official Form 106E/F

Schedule E/F: Creditors Who Have Unsecured Claims

12/15

Be as complete and accurate as possible. Use Part 1 for creditors with PRIORITY claims and Part 2 for creditors with NONPRIORITY claims. List the other party to any executory contracts or unexpired leases that could result in a claim. Also list executory contracts on *Schedule A/B: Property* (Official Form 106A/B) and on *Schedule G: Executory Contracts and Unexpired Leases* (Official Form 106G). Do not include any creditors with partially secured claims that are listed in *Schedule D: Creditors Who Have Claims Secured by Property*. If more space is needed, copy the Part you need, fill it out, number the entries in the boxes on the left. Attach the Continuation Page to this page. On the top of any additional pages, write your name and case number (if known).

Part 1: List All of Your PRIORITY Unsecured Claims

1. **Do any creditors have priority unsecured claims against you?**
   - ☒ No. Go to Part 2.
   - ❑ Yes.

2. **List all of your priority unsecured claims.** If a creditor has more than one priority unsecured claim, list the creditor separately for each claim. For each claim listed, identify what type of claim it is. If a claim has both priority and nonpriority amounts, list that claim here and show both priority and nonpriority amounts. As much as possible, list the claims in alphabetical order according to the creditor's name. If you have more than two priority unsecured claims, fill out the Continuation Page of Part 1. If more than one creditor holds a particular claim, list the other creditors in Part 3.
   (For an explanation of each type of claim, see the instructions for this form in the instruction booklet.)

Total claim | **Priority amount** | **Nonpriority amount**

2.1

____________ Priority Creditor's Name

____________ Number Street

____

____________ City State ZIP Code

Who incurred the debt? Check one.
- ❑ Debtor 1 only
- ❑ Debtor 2 only
- ❑ Debtor 1 and Debtor 2 only
- ❑ At least one of the debtors and another
- ❑ **Check if this claim is for a community debt**

Is the claim subject to offset?
- ❑ No
- ❑ Yes

Last 4 digits of account number __ __ __ __ $________ $________ $________

When was the debt incurred? ________

As of the date you file, the claim is: Check all that apply
- ❑ Contingent
- ❑ Unliquidated
- ❑ Disputed

Type of PRIORITY unsecured claim:
- ❑ Domestic support obligations
- ❑ Taxes and certain other debts you owe the government
- ❑ Claims for death or personal injury while you were intoxicated
- ❑ Other. Specify ____________

2.2

____________ Priority Creditor's Name

____________ Number Street

____

____________ City State ZIP Code

Who incurred the debt? Check one.
- ❑ Debtor 1 only
- ❑ Debtor 2 only
- ❑ Debtor 1 and Debtor 2 only
- ❑ At least one of the debtors and another
- ❑ **Check if this claim is for a community debt**

Is the claim subject to offset?
- ❑ No
- ❑ Yes

Last 4 digits of account number __ __ __ __ $________ $________ $________

When was the debt incurred? ________

As of the date you file, the claim is: Check all that apply
- ❑ Contingent
- ❑ Unliquidated
- ❑ Disputed

Type of PRIORITY unsecured claim:
- ❑ Domestic support obligations
- ❑ Taxes and certain other debts you owe the government
- ❑ Claims for death or personal injury while you were intoxicated
- ❑ Other. Specify ____________

Debtor 1 Sidney Samuel Smith
First Name Middle Name Last Name

Case number *(if known)*__________

Part 1: Your PRIORITY Unsecured Claims – Continuation Page

After listing any entries on this page, number them beginning with 2.3, followed by 2.4, and so forth. | **Total claim** | **Priority amount** | **Nonpriority amount**

☐

____
Priority Creditor's Name

____
Number Street

____

____
City State ZIP Code

Who incurred the debt? Check one.

- ❑ Debtor 1 only
- ❑ Debtor 2 only
- ❑ Debtor 1 and Debtor 2 only
- ❑ At least one of the debtors and another

❑ **Check if this claim is for a community debt**

Is the claim subject to offset?

- ❑ No
- ❑ Yes

Last 4 digits of account number __ __ __ __ $______ $______ $______

When was the debt incurred? ________

As of the date you file, the claim is: Check all that apply.

- ❑ Contingent
- ❑ Unliquidated
- ❑ Disputed

Type of PRIORITY unsecured claim:

- ❑ Domestic support obligations
- ❑ Taxes and certain other debts you owe the government
- ❑ Claims for death or personal injury while you were intoxicated
- ❑ Other. Specify __________

☐

____
Priority Creditor's Name

____
Number Street

____

____
City State ZIP Code

Who incurred the debt? Check one.

- ❑ Debtor 1 only
- ❑ Debtor 2 only
- ❑ Debtor 1 and Debtor 2 only
- ❑ At least one of the debtors and another

❑ **Check if this claim is for a community debt**

Is the claim subject to offset?

- ❑ No
- ❑ Yes

Last 4 digits of account number __ __ __ __ $______ $______ $______

When was the debt incurred? ________

As of the date you file, the claim is: Check all that apply.

- ❑ Contingent
- ❑ Unliquidated
- ❑ Disputed

Type of PRIORITY unsecured claim:

- ❑ Domestic support obligations
- ❑ Taxes and certain other debts you owe the government
- ❑ Claims for death or personal injury while you were intoxicated
- ❑ Other. Specify __________

☐

____
Priority Creditor's Name

____
Number Street

____

____
City State ZIP Code

Who incurred the debt? Check one.

- ❑ Debtor 1 only
- ❑ Debtor 2 only
- ❑ Debtor 1 and Debtor 2 only
- ❑ At least one of the debtors and another

❑ **Check if this claim is for a community debt**

Is the claim subject to offset?

- ❑ No
- ❑ Yes

Last 4 digits of account number __ __ __ __ $______ $______ $______

When was the debt incurred? ________

As of the date you file, the claim is: Check all that apply.

- ❑ Contingent
- ❑ Unliquidated
- ❑ Disputed

Type of PRIORITY unsecured claim:

- ❑ Domestic support obligations
- ❑ Taxes and certain other debts you owe the government
- ❑ Claims for death or personal injury while you were intoxicated
- ❑ Other. Specify __________

Debtor 1 Sidney Samuel Smith
First Name Middle Name Last Name

Case number (if known)

Part 2: List All of Your NONPRIORITY Unsecured Claims

3. **Do any creditors have nonpriority unsecured claims against you?**
☐ No. You have nothing to report in this part. Submit this form to the court with your other schedules.
☒ Yes

4. **List all of your nonpriority unsecured claims in the alphabetical order of the creditor who holds each claim.** If a creditor has more than one nonpriority unsecured claim, list the creditor separately for each claim. For each claim listed, identify what type of claim it is. Do not list claims already included in Part 1. If more than one creditor holds a particular claim, list the other creditors in Part 3.If you have more than three nonpriority unsecured claims fill out the Continuation Page of Part 2.

Total claim

4.1 A-1 Bank
Nonpriority Creditor's Name
1145 West Smith Road
Number Street
Columbus OH 43215
City State ZIP Code

Last 4 digits of account number 6 6 3 9 — $ 10,556.00
When was the debt incurred? 12/11/2013

As of the date you file, the claim is: Check all that apply.
☐ Contingent
☐ Unliquidated
☐ Disputed

Who incurred the debt? Check one.
☒ Debtor 1 only
☐ Debtor 2 only
☐ Debtor 1 and Debtor 2 only
☐ At least one of the debtors and another

☐ **Check if this claim is for a community debt**

Is the claim subject to offset?
☒ No
☐ Yes

Type of NONPRIORITY unsecured claim:
☐ Student loans
☐ Obligations arising out of a separation agreement or divorce that you did not report as priority claims
☐ Debts to pension or profit-sharing plans, and other similar debts
☒ Other. Specify credit card

4.2 Charles Chase
Nonpriority Creditor's Name
11255 Westfield Road
Number Street
Columbus OH 43219
City State ZIP Code

Last 4 digits of account number n o n e — $ 5,689.00
When was the debt incurred? 05/11/2014

As of the date you file, the claim is: Check all that apply.
☐ Contingent
☐ Unliquidated
☐ Disputed

Who incurred the debt? Check one.
☒ Debtor 1 only
☐ Debtor 2 only
☐ Debtor 1 and Debtor 2 only
☐ At least one of the debtors and another

☐ **Check if this claim is for a community debt**

Is the claim subject to offset?
☒ No
☐ Yes

Type of NONPRIORITY unsecured claim:
☐ Student loans
☐ Obligations arising out of a separation agreement or divorce that you did not report as priority claims
☐ Debts to pension or profit-sharing plans, and other similar debts
☒ Other. Specify Personal loan

4.3 Home Goods Store
Nonpriority Creditor's Name
1249 Main Street
Number Street
Columbus OH 43211
City State ZIP Code

Last 4 digits of account number 4 5 6 7 — $ 1,289.00
When was the debt incurred? 05/05/2011

As of the date you file, the claim is: Check all that apply.
☐ Contingent
☐ Unliquidated
☐ Disputed

Who incurred the debt? Check one.
☐ Debtor 1 only
☐ Debtor 2 only
☒ Debtor 1 and Debtor 2 only
☐ At least one of the debtors and another

☐ **Check if this claim is for a community debt**

Is the claim subject to offset?
☒ No
☐ Yes

Type of NONPRIORITY unsecured claim:
☐ Student loans
☐ Obligations arising out of a separation agreement or divorce that you did not report as priority claims
☐ Debts to pension or profit-sharing plans, and other similar debts
☒ Other. Specify furniture purchased

Debtor 1 Sidney Samuel Smith
First Name Middle Name Last Name

Case number (if known) ______________________

Part 2: **Your NONPRIORITY Unsecured Claims – Continuation Page**

After listing any entries on this page, number them beginning with 4.4, followed by 4.5, and so forth. **Total claim**

4.4

Ohio Bank and Trust
Nonpriority Creditor's Name
235 East 2nd Avenue
Number Street
Columbus OH 43218
City State ZIP Code

Who incurred the debt? Check one.

- ☐ Debtor 1 only
- ☐ Debtor 2 only
- ☒ Debtor 1 and Debtor 2 only
- ☐ At least one of the debtors and another

☐ **Check if this claim is for a community debt**

Is the claim subject to offset?

- ☒ No
- ☐ Yes

Last 4 digits of account number 5 6 9 0

When was the debt incurred? 04/03/2011

As of the date you file, the claim is: Check all that apply.

- ☐ Contingent
- ☐ Unliquidated
- ☐ Disputed

Type of **NONPRIORITY** unsecured claim:

- ☐ Student loans
- ☐ Obligations arising out of a separation agreement or divorce that you did not report as priority claims
- ☐ Debts to pension or profit-sharing plans, and other similar debts
- ☒ Other. Specify Credit Card

$ 5,890.00

4.5

Student Loan Company
Nonpriority Creditor's Name
1389 Lincoln Avenue
Number Street
Washington DC 00123
City State ZIP Code

Who incurred the debt? Check one.

- ☒ Debtor 1 only
- ☐ Debtor 2 only
- ☐ Debtor 1 and Debtor 2 only
- ☐ At least one of the debtors and another

☐ **Check if this claim is for a community debt**

Is the claim subject to offset?

- ☒ No
- ☐ Yes

Last 4 digits of account number 3 4 8 0

When was the debt incurred? 03/20/2001

As of the date you file, the claim is: Check all that apply.

- ☐ Contingent
- ☐ Unliquidated
- ☐ Disputed

Type of **NONPRIORITY** unsecured claim:

- ☒ Student loans
- ☐ Obligations arising out of a separation agreement or divorce that you did not report as priority claims
- ☐ Debts to pension or profit-sharing plans, and other similar debts
- ☐ Other. Specify ______________

$ 12,890.00

☐

____
Nonpriority Creditor's Name
____
Number Street
____
City State ZIP Code

Who incurred the debt? Check one.

- ☐ Debtor 1 only
- ☐ Debtor 2 only
- ☐ Debtor 1 and Debtor 2 only
- ☐ At least one of the debtors and another

☐ **Check if this claim is for a community debt**

Is the claim subject to offset?

- ☐ No
- ☐ Yes

Last 4 digits of account number ___ ___ ___ ___

When was the debt incurred? ________

As of the date you file, the claim is: Check all that apply.

- ☐ Contingent
- ☐ Unliquidated
- ☐ Disputed

Type of **NONPRIORITY** unsecured claim:

- ☐ Student loans
- ☐ Obligations arising out of a separation agreement or divorce that you did not report as priority claims
- ☐ Debts to pension or profit-sharing plans, and other similar debts
- ☐ Other. Specify ______________

$ ________

Debtor 1 Sidney Samuel Smith
First Name Middle Name Last Name

Case number (if known)________________

Part 3: List Others to Be Notified About a Debt That You Already Listed

5. **Use this page only if you have others to be notified about your bankruptcy, for a debt that you already listed in Parts 1 or 2. For example, if a collection agency is trying to collect from you for a debt you owe to someone else, list the original creditor in Parts 1 or 2, then list the collection agency here. Similarly, if you have more than one creditor for any of the debts that you listed in Parts 1 or 2, list the additional creditors here. If you do not have additional persons to be notified for any debts in Parts 1 or 2, do not fill out or submit this page.**

Name
Number Street
City State ZIP Code

On which entry in Part 1 or Part 2 did you list the original creditor?

Line _____ of (*Check one*): ❑ Part 1: Creditors with Priority Unsecured Claims
❑ Part 2: Creditors with Nonpriority Unsecured Claims

Last 4 digits of account number __ __ __ __

Name
Number Street
City State ZIP Code

On which entry in Part 1 or Part 2 did you list the original creditor?

Line _____ of (*Check one*): ❑ Part 1: Creditors with Priority Unsecured Claims
❑ Part 2: Creditors with Nonpriority Unsecured Claims

Last 4 digits of account number __ __ __ __

Name
Number Street
City State ZIP Code

On which entry in Part 1 or Part 2 did you list the original creditor?

Line _____ of (*Check one*): ❑ Part 1: Creditors with Priority Unsecured Claims
❑ Part 2: Creditors with Nonpriority Unsecured Claims

Last 4 digits of account number __ __ __ __

Name
Number Street
City State ZIP Code

On which entry in Part 1 or Part 2 did you list the original creditor?

Line _____ of (*Check one*): ❑ Part 1: Creditors with Priority Unsecured Claims
❑ Part 2: Creditors with Nonpriority Unsecured Claims

Last 4 digits of account number __ __ __ __

Name
Number Street
City State ZIP Code

On which entry in Part 1 or Part 2 did you list the original creditor?

Line _____ of (*Check one*): ❑ Part 1: Creditors with Priority Unsecured Claims
❑ Part 2: Creditors with Nonpriority Unsecured Claims

Last 4 digits of account number __ __ __ __

Name
Number Street
City State ZIP Code

On which entry in Part 1 or Part 2 did you list the original creditor?

Line _____ of (*Check one*): ❑ Part 1: Creditors with Priority Unsecured Claims
❑ Part 2: Creditors with Nonpriority Unsecured Claims

Last 4 digits of account number __ __ __ __

Name
Number Street
City State ZIP Code

On which entry in Part 1 or Part 2 did you list the original creditor?

Line _____ of (*Check one*): ❑ Part 1: Creditors with Priority Unsecured Claims
❑ Part 2: Creditors with Nonpriority Unsecured Claims

Last 4 digits of account number __ __ __ __

Debtor 1 Sidney Samuel Smith
First Name Middle Name Last Name

Case number *(if known)*__________

Part 4: Add the Amounts for Each Type of Unsecured Claim

6. **Total the amounts of certain types of unsecured claims. This information is for statistical reporting purposes only. 28 U.S.C. § 159. Add the amounts for each type of unsecured claim.**

			Total claim
Total claims from Part 1	6a. **Domestic support obligations**	6a.	$ 0.00
	6b. **Taxes and certain other debts you owe the government**	6b.	$ 0.00
	6c. **Claims for death or personal injury while you were intoxicated**	6c.	$ 0.00
	6d. **Other.** Add all other priority unsecured claims. Write that amount here.	6d.	+ $ 0.00
	6e. **Total.** Add lines 6a through 6d.	6e.	$ 0.00

			Total claim
Total claims from Part 2	6f. **Student loans**	6f.	$ 12,890.00
	6g. **Obligations arising out of a separation agreement or divorce that you did not report as priority claims**	6g.	$ 0.00
	6h. **Debts to pension or profit-sharing plans, and other similar debts**	6h.	$ 0.00
	6i. **Other.** Add all other nonpriority unsecured claims. Write that amount here.	6i.	+ $ 23,424.00
	6j. **Total.** Add lines 6f through 6i.	6j.	$ 36,314.00

Print | Save As... | Add Attachment | Reset

Exhibit 2-K Schedule G - Executory Contracts and Unexpired Leases (Official Form 106G)

Fill in this information to identify your case:

Debtor: Sidney Samuel Smith
First Name / Middle Name / Last Name

Debtor 2 (Spouse If filing): Sarah Arlene Smith
First Name / Middle Name / Last Name

United States Bankruptcy Court for the: Southern District of Ohio

Case number (If known): ____________________

☐ Check if this is an amended filing

Official Form 106G

Schedule G: Executory Contracts and Unexpired Leases

12/15

Be as complete and accurate as possible. If two married people are filing together, both are equally responsible for supplying correct information. If more space is needed, copy the additional page, fill it out, number the entries, and attach it to this page. On the top of any additional pages, write your name and case number (if known).

1. **Do you have any executory contracts or unexpired leases?**
   - ☐ No. Check this box and file this form with the court with your other schedules. You have nothing else to report on this form.
   - ☒ Yes. Fill in all of the information below even if the contracts or leases are listed on *Schedule A/B: Property* (Official Form 106A/B).

2. **List separately each person or company with whom you have the contract or lease. Then state what each contract or lease is for (for example, rent, vehicle lease, cell phone).** See the instructions for this form in the instruction booklet for more examples of executory contracts and unexpired leases.

	Person or company with whom you have the contract or lease	State what the contract or lease is for
2.1	Morton Leasing Co. (Name) 2000 East Pine Avenue (Number Street) Columbus OH 43206 (City State ZIP Code)	Lease for copy machine dated 8/22/2014..
2.2	Lawn Care Specialists (Name) 14450 West 33rd Avenue (Number Street) Columbus OH 43227 (City State ZIP Code)	Lawn services contract for three years dated 4/6/2015.
2.3	Name Number Street City State ZIP Code	
2.4	Name Number Street City State ZIP Code	
2.5	Name Number Street City State ZIP Code	

Exhibit 2-L Schedule H - Your Codebtors (Official Form 106H)

Fill in this information to identify your case:

Debtor 1 Sidney Samuel Smith
First Name Middle Name Last Name

Debtor 2 (Spouse, if filing) Sarah Arlene Smith
First Name Middle Name Last Name

United States Bankruptcy Court for the: Southern District of Ohio

Case number ______________ (If known)

☐ Check if this is an amended filing

Official Form 106H

Schedule H: Your Codebtors

12/15

Codebtors are people or entities who are also liable for any debts you may have. Be as complete and accurate as possible. If two married people are filing together, both are equally responsible for supplying correct information. If more space is needed, copy the Additional Page, fill it out, and number the entries in the boxes on the left. Attach the Additional Page to this page. On the top of any Additional Pages, write your name and case number (if known). Answer every question.

1. **Do you have any codebtors?** (If you are filing a joint case, do not list either spouse as a codebtor.)
   - ☐ No
   - ☑ Yes

2. **Within the last 8 years, have you lived in a community property state or territory?** (*Community property states and territories* include Arizona, California, Idaho, Louisiana, Nevada, New Mexico, Puerto Rico, Texas, Washington, and Wisconsin.)
   - ☑ No. Go to line 3.
   - ☐ Yes. Did your spouse, former spouse, or legal equivalent live with you at the time?
     - ☐ No
     - ☐ Yes. In which community state or territory did you live? ______________. Fill in the name and current address of that person.

   Name of your spouse, former spouse, or legal equivalent

   Number Street

   City State ZIP Code

3. **In Column 1, list all of your codebtors. Do not include your spouse as a codebtor if your spouse is filing with you. List the person shown in line 2 again as a codebtor only if that person is a guarantor or cosigner. Make sure you have listed the creditor on *Schedule D* (Official Form 106D), *Schedule E/F* (Official Form 106E/F), or *Schedule G* (Official Form 106G). Use *Schedule D, Schedule E/F, or Schedule G* to fill out Column 2.**

	Column 1: **Your codebtor**	*Column 2:* **The creditor to whom you owe the debt** Check all schedules that apply:
3.1	Paul R. Smith (Name) 2240 Garrison Street (Number Street) Toledo (City) OH (State) 43614 (ZIP Code)	☐ Schedule D, line ______ ☐ Schedule E/F, line ______ ☑ Schedule G, line 2.1
3.2	Name Number Street City State ZIP Code	☐ Schedule D, line ______ ☐ Schedule E/F, line ______ ☐ Schedule G, line ______
3.3	Name Number Street City State ZIP Code	☐ Schedule D, line ______ ☐ Schedule E/F, line ______ ☐ Schedule G, line ______

Exhibit 2-M Schedule I - Your Income (Official Form 106I)

Fill in this information to identify your case:

Debtor 1 Sidney Samuel Smith
First Name Middle Name Last Name

Debtor 2 (Spouse, if filing) Sarah Arlene Smith
First Name Middle Name Last Name

United States Bankruptcy Court for the: Southern District of Ohio

Case number (If known) ____________

Check if this is:
- ❑ An amended filing
- ❑ A supplement showing postpetition chapter 13 income as of the following date:

____
MM / DD / YYYY

Official Form 106I

Schedule I: Your Income

12/15

Be as complete and accurate as possible. If two married people are filing together (Debtor 1 and Debtor 2), both are equally responsible for supplying correct information. If you are married and not filing jointly, and your spouse is living with you, include information about your spouse. If you are separated and your spouse is not filing with you, do not include information about your spouse. If more space is needed, attach a separate sheet to this form. On the top of any additional pages, write your name and case number (if known). Answer every question.

Part 1: Describe Employment

1. **Fill in your employment information.**

If you have more than one job, attach a separate page with information about additional employers.

Include part-time, seasonal, or self-employed work.

Occupation may include student or homemaker, if it applies.

	Debtor 1	Debtor 2 or non-filing spouse
Employment status	☑ Employed ❑ Not employed	☑ Employed ❑ Not employed
Occupation	Salesman	Receptionist
Employer's name	Jackson Sales, Inc.	Wilson Land Co.
Employer's address	4770 Federal Blvd. (Number Street) Columbus OH 43211 (City State ZIP Code)	2177 North Elm Street (Number Street) Columbus OH 43216 (City State ZIP Code)
How long employed there?	6 years	6 years

Part 2: Give Details About Monthly Income

Estimate monthly income as of the date you file this form. If you have nothing to report for any line, write $0 in the space. Include your non-filing spouse unless you are separated.

If you or your non-filing spouse have more than one employer, combine the information for all employers for that person on the lines below. If you need more space, attach a separate sheet to this form.

		For Debtor 1	For Debtor 2 or non-filing spouse
2. **List monthly gross wages, salary, and commissions** (before all payroll deductions). If not paid monthly, calculate what the monthly wage would be.	2.	$ 3,850.00	$ 1,830.00
3. **Estimate and list monthly overtime pay.**	3.	+ $ 0.00	+ $ 0.00
4. **Calculate gross income.** Add line 2 + line 3.	4.	$ 3,850.00	$ 1,830.00

Debtor 1 Sidney Samuel Smith
First Name Middle Name Last Name

Case number *(if known)*

		For Debtor 1	For Debtor 2 or non-filing spouse
Copy line 4 here →	4.	$ 3,850.00	$ 1,830.00
5. **List all payroll deductions:**			
5a. **Tax, Medicare, and Social Security deductions**	5a.	$ 770.00	$ 275.00
5b. **Mandatory contributions for retirement plans**	5b.	$ 0.00	$ 0.00
5c. **Voluntary contributions for retirement plans**	5c.	$ 0.00	$ 0.00
5d. **Required repayments of retirement fund loans**	5d.	$ 0.00	$ 0.00
5e. **Insurance**	5e.	$ 498.00	$ 0.00
5f. **Domestic support obligations**	5f.	$ 0.00	$ 0.00
5g. **Union dues**	5g.	$ 0.00	$ 0.00
5h. **Other deductions.** Specify: 0	5h.	+ $ 0.00	+ $ 0.00
6. **Add the payroll deductions.** Add lines 5a + 5b + 5c + 5d + 5e +5f + 5g + 5h.	6.	$ 1,268.00	$ 275.00
7. **Calculate total monthly take-home pay.** Subtract line 6 from line 4.	7.	$ 2,582.00	$ 1,555.00
8. **List all other income regularly received:**			
8a. **Net income from rental property and from operating a business, profession, or farm** Attach a statement for each property and business showing gross receipts, ordinary and necessary business expenses, and the total monthly net income.	8a.	$ 0.00	$ 0.00
8b. **Interest and dividends**	8b.	$ 0.00	$ 100.00
8c. **Family support payments that you, a non-filing spouse, or a dependent regularly receive** Include alimony, spousal support, child support, maintenance, divorce settlement, and property settlement.	8c.	$ 0.00	$ 0.00
8d. **Unemployment compensation**	8d.	$ 0.00	$ 0.00
8e. **Social Security**	8e.	$ 0.00	$ 0.00
8f. **Other government assistance that you regularly receive** Include cash assistance and the value (if known) of any non-cash assistance that you receive, such as food stamps (benefits under the Supplemental Nutrition Assistance Program) or housing subsidies. Specify:	8f.	$ 0.00	$ 0.00
8g. **Pension or retirement income**	8g.	$ 0.00	$ 0.00
8h. **Other monthly income.** Specify: Paper route	8h.	+ $ 140.00	+ $
9. **Add all other income.** Add lines 8a + 8b + 8c + 8d + 8e + 8f +8g + 8h.	9.	$ 140.00	$ 100.00
10. **Calculate monthly income.** Add line 7 + line 9. Add the entries in line 10 for Debtor 1 and Debtor 2 or non-filing spouse.	10.	$ 2,722.00 +	$ 1,655.00 = $ 4,377.00

11. **State all other regular contributions to the expenses that you list in *Schedule J*.**
Include contributions from an unmarried partner, members of your household, your dependents, your roommates, and other friends or relatives.
Do not include any amounts already included in lines 2-10 or amounts that are not available to pay expenses listed in *Schedule J*.
Specify: ______ 11. + $ 0.00

12. **Add the amount in the last column of line 10 to the amount in line 11.** The result is the combined monthly income. Write that amount on the *Summary of Your Assets and Liabilities and Certain Statistical Information,* if it applies 12. $ 4,377.00
Combined monthly income

13. **Do you expect an increase or decrease within the year after you file this form?**
☐ No.
☐ Yes. Explain:

Print Save As... Add Attachment Reset

Exhibit 2-N Schedule J - Your Expenses (Official Form 106J)

Fill in this information to identify your case:

Debtor 1 Sidney Samuel Smith
First Name Middle Name Last Name

Debtor 2 Sarah Arlene Smith
(Spouse, if filing) First Name Middle Name Last Name

United States Bankruptcy Court for the: Southern District of Ohio

Case number ______________________
(If known)

Check if this is:

☐ An amended filing

☐ A supplement showing postpetition chapter 13 expenses as of the following date:

____
MM / DD / YYYY

Official Form 106J

Schedule J: Your Expenses

12/15

Be as complete and accurate as possible. If two married people are filing together, both are equally responsible for supplying correct information. If more space is needed, attach another sheet to this form. On the top of any additional pages, write your name and case number (if known). Answer every question.

Part 1: Describe Your Household

1. **Is this a joint case?**

☐ No. Go to line 2.

☒ Yes. **Does Debtor 2 live in a separate household?**

☒ No

☐ Yes. Debtor 2 must file Official Form 106J-2, *Expenses for Separate Household of Debtor 2.*

2. **Do you have dependents?**

Do not list Debtor 1 and Debtor 2.

Do not state the dependents' names.

☐ No

☒ Yes. Fill out this information for each dependent..........................

Dependent's relationship to Debtor 1 or Debtor 2	Dependent's age	Does dependent live with you?
Son	9	☐ No ☒ Yes
Daughter	7	☐ No ☒ Yes
		☐ No ☐ Yes
		☐ No ☐ Yes
		☐ No ☐ Yes

3. **Do your expenses include expenses of people other than yourself and your dependents?**

☒ No

☐ Yes

Part 2: Estimate Your Ongoing Monthly Expenses

Estimate your expenses as of your bankruptcy filing date unless you are using this form as a supplement in a Chapter 13 case to report expenses as of a date after the bankruptcy is filed. If this is a supplemental *Schedule J*, check the box at the top of the form and fill in the applicable date.

Include expenses paid for with non-cash government assistance if you know the value of such assistance and have included it on *Schedule I: Your Income* (Official Form 106I.)

		Your expenses
4. **The rental or home ownership expenses for your residence.** Include first mortgage payments and any rent for the ground or lot.	4.	$ 1,329.00
If not included in line 4:		
4a. Real estate taxes	4a.	$ 120.00
4b. Property, homeowner's, or renter's insurance	4b.	$ 90.00
4c. Home maintenance, repair, and upkeep expenses	4c.	$ 85.00
4d. Homeowner's association or condominium dues	4d.	$ 70.00

Debtor 1 Sidney Samuel Smith
First Name Middle Name Last Name

Case number *(if known)*

		Your expenses
5. **Additional mortgage payments for your residence**, such as home equity loans	5.	$ 0.00
6. **Utilities:**		
6a. Electricity, heat, natural gas	6a.	$ 190.00
6b. Water, sewer, garbage collection	6b.	$ 60.00
6c. Telephone, cell phone, Internet, satellite, and cable services	6c.	$ 130.00
6d. Other. Specify:	6d.	$
7. **Food and housekeeping supplies**	7.	$ 700.00
8. **Childcare and children's education costs**	8.	$ 200.00
9. **Clothing, laundry, and dry cleaning**	9.	$ 150.00
10. **Personal care products and services**	10.	$ 50.00
11. **Medical and dental expenses**	11.	$ 50.00
12. **Transportation.** Include gas, maintenance, bus or train fare. Do not include car payments.	12.	$ 100.00
13. **Entertainment, clubs, recreation, newspapers, magazines, and books**	13.	$ 40.00
14. **Charitable contributions and religious donations**	14.	$ 20.00
15. **Insurance.** Do not include insurance deducted from your pay or included in lines 4 or 20.		
15a. Life insurance	15a.	$ 65.00
15b. Health insurance	15b.	$ 0.00
15c. Vehicle insurance	15c.	$ 90.00
15d. Other insurance. Specify: Disability	15d.	$ 45.00
16. **Taxes.** Do not include taxes deducted from your pay or included in lines 4 or 20. Specify:	16.	$ 0.00
17. **Installment or lease payments:**		
17a. Car payments for Vehicle 1	17a.	$ 329.00
17b. Car payments for Vehicle 2	17b.	$ 112.00
17c. Other. Specify: Copier Rental	17c.	$ 30.00
17d. Other. Specify: Lawn care	17d.	$ 20.00
18. **Your payments of alimony, maintenance, and support that you did not report as deducted from your pay on line 5, *Schedule I, Your Income* (Official Form 106I).**	18.	$ 0.00
19. **Other payments you make to support others who do not live with you.** Specify:	19.	$ 0.00
20. **Other real property expenses not included in lines 4 or 5 of this form or on *Schedule I: Your Income.***		
20a. Mortgages on other property	20a.	$
20b. Real estate taxes	20b.	$
20c. Property, homeowner's, or renter's insurance	20c.	$
20d. Maintenance, repair, and upkeep expenses	20d.	$
20e. Homeowner's association or condominium dues	20e.	$

Debtor 1 Sidney Samuel Smith
First Name Middle Name Last Name

Case number *(if known)*

21. **Other**. Specify: ______ 21. +$______

22. **Calculate your monthly expenses.**

22a. Add lines 4 through 21.	22a.	$ 4,075.00
22b. Copy line 22 (monthly expenses for Debtor 2), if any, from Official Form 106J-2	22b.	$ 0.00
22c. Add line 22a and 22b. The result is your monthly expenses.	22c.	$ 4,075.00

23. **Calculate your monthly net income.**

23a. Copy line 12 (*your combined monthly income*) from *Schedule I.*	23a.	$ 4,388.00
23b. Copy your monthly expenses from line 22c above.	23b.	– $ 4,075.00
23c. Subtract your monthly expenses from your monthly income. The result is your *monthly net income.*	23c.	$ 313.00

24. **Do you expect an increase or decrease in your expenses within the year after you file this form?**

For example, do you expect to finish paying for your car loan within the year or do you expect your mortgage payment to increase or decrease because of a modification to the terms of your mortgage?

☐ No.
☐ Yes. Explain here:

Exhibit 2-O Declaration About an Individual Debtor's Schedules (Official Form 106Dec)

Fill in this information to identify your case:

Debtor 1 Sidney Samuel Smith
First Name Middle Name Last Name

Debtor 2 Sarah Arlene Smith
(Spouse, if filing) First Name Middle Name Last Name

United States Bankruptcy Court for the: Southern District of Ohio

Case number ____________________
(If known)

☐ Check if this is an amended filing

Official Form 106Dec

Declaration About an Individual Debtor's Schedules

12/15

If two married people are filing together, both are equally responsible for supplying correct information.

You must file this form whenever you file bankruptcy schedules or amended schedules. Making a false statement, concealing property, or obtaining money or property by fraud in connection with a bankruptcy case can result in fines up to $250,000, or imprisonment for up to 20 years, or both. 18 U.S.C. §§ 152, 1341, 1519, and 3571.

Sign Below

Did you pay or agree to pay someone who is NOT an attorney to help you fill out bankruptcy forms?

☒ No

☐ Yes. Name of person____________________. Attach *Bankruptcy Petition Preparer's Notice, Declaration, and Signature* (Official Form 119).

Under penalty of perjury, I declare that I have read the summary and schedules filed with this declaration and that they are true and correct.

✘ /s/ Sidney Samuel Smith
Signature of Debtor 1

Date 01/15/2024
MM / DD / YYYY

✘ /s/ Sarah Arlene Smith
Signature of Debtor 2

Date 01/15/2024
MM / DD / YYYY

Exhibit 2-P Summ. of Your Assets and Liab. and Certain Statistical Info. (Off. Form 106Sum)

Fill in this information to identify your case:

Debtor 1 Sidney Samuel Smith
First Name Middle Name Last Name

Debtor 2 Sarah Arlene Smith
(Spouse, if filing) First Name Middle Name Last Name

United States Bankruptcy Court for the: Southern District of Ohio

Case number ____________
(If known)

☐ Check if this is an amended filing

Official Form 106Sum

Summary of Your Assets and Liabilities and Certain Statistical Information 12/15

Be as complete and accurate as possible. If two married people are filing together, both are equally responsible for supplying correct information. Fill out all of your schedules first; then complete the information on this form. If you are filing amended schedules after you file your original forms, you must fill out a new *Summary* and check the box at the top of this page.

Part 1: Summarize Your Assets

	Your assets Value of what you own
1. *Schedule A/B: Property* (Official Form 106A/B)	
1a. Copy line 55, Total real estate, from *Schedule A/B*	$ 126,000.00
1b. Copy line 62, Total personal property, from *Schedule A/B*	$ 30,215.00
1c. Copy line 63, Total of all property on *Schedule A/B*	$ 156,215.00

Part 2: Summarize Your Liabilities

	Your liabilities Amount you owe
2. *Schedule D: Creditors Who Have Claims Secured by Property* (Official Form 106D)	
2a. Copy the total you listed in Column A, *Amount of claim,* at the bottom of the last page of Part 1 of *Schedule D*	$ 112,588.00
3. *Schedule E/F: Creditors Who Have Unsecured Claims* (Official Form 106E/F)	
3a. Copy the total claims from Part 1 (priority unsecured claims) from line 6e of *Schedule E/F*	$ 0.00
3b. Copy the total claims from Part 2 (nonpriority unsecured claims) from line 6j of *Schedule E/F*	+ $ 36,314.00
Your total liabilities	$ 148,902.00

Part 3: Summarize Your Income and Expenses

4. *Schedule I: Your Income* (Official Form 106I) Copy your combined monthly income from line 12 of *Schedule I*	$ 4,377.00
5. *Schedule J: Your Expenses* (Official Form 106J) Copy your monthly expenses from line 22c of *Schedule J*	$ 4,075.00

Debtor 1 Sidney Samuel Smith — Case number (if known) ____

First Name / Middle Name / Last Name

Part 4: Answer These Questions for Administrative and Statistical Records

6. **Are you filing for bankruptcy under Chapters 7, 11, or 13?**

   ☐ No. You have nothing to report on this part of the form. Check this box and submit this form to the court with your other schedules.

   ☒ Yes

7. **What kind of debt do you have?**

   ☒ **Your debts are primarily consumer debts.** *Consumer debts* are those "incurred by an individual primarily for a personal, family, or household purpose." 11 U.S.C. § 101(8). Fill out lines 8-9g for statistical purposes. 28 U.S.C. § 159.

   ☐ **Your debts are not primarily consumer debts**. You have nothing to report on this part of the form. Check this box and submit this form to the court with your other schedules.

8. **From the *Statement of Your Current Monthly Income***: Copy your total current monthly income from Official Form 122A-1 Line 11; **OR**, Form 122B Line 11; **OR**, Form 122C-1 Line 14. — $ 5,820.00

9. **Copy the following special categories of claims from Part 4, line 6 of *Schedule E/F***:

From Part 4 on *Schedule E/F*, copy the following:	**Total claim**
9a. Domestic support obligations (Copy line 6a.)	$ 0.00
9b. Taxes and certain other debts you owe the government. (Copy line 6b.)	$ 0.00
9c. Claims for death or personal injury while you were intoxicated. (Copy line 6c.)	$ 0.00
9d. Student loans. (Copy line 6f.)	$ 12,890.00
9e. Obligations arising out of a separation agreement or divorce that you did not report as priority claims. (Copy line 6g.)	$ 0.00
9f. Debts to pension or profit-sharing plans, and other similar debts. (Copy line 6h.)	+ $ 0.00
9g. **Total.** Add lines 9a through 9f.	$ 12,890.00

Print | Save As... | Add Attachment | Reset

Exhibit 2-Q Stmt. of Financial Affairs for Individuals Filing for Bankruptcy (Off. Form 107)

Fill in this information to identify your case:

Debtor 1 Sidney Samuel Smith
First Name Middle Name Last Name

Debtor 2 Sarah Arlene Smith
(Spouse, if filing) First Name Middle Name Last Name

United States Bankruptcy Court for the: __________ District of __________

Case number ______________________
(If known)

❑ Check if this is an amended filing

Official Form 107

Statement of Financial Affairs for Individuals Filing for Bankruptcy

04/22

Be as complete and accurate as possible. If two married people are filing together, both are equally responsible for supplying correct information. If more space is needed, attach a separate sheet to this form. On the top of any additional pages, write your name and case number (if known). Answer every question.

Part 1: Give Details About Your Marital Status and Where You Lived Before

1. **What is your current marital status?**

☑ Married
❑ Not married

2. **During the last 3 years, have you lived anywhere other than where you live now?**

☑ No
❑ Yes. List all of the places you lived in the last 3 years. Do not include where you live now.

Debtor 1:	Dates Debtor 1 lived there	Debtor 2:	Dates Debtor 2 lived there
		❑ Same as Debtor 1	❑ Same as Debtor 1
Number Street City State ZIP Code	From ______ To ______	Number Street City State ZIP Code	From ______ To ______
		❑ Same as Debtor 1	❑ Same as Debtor 1
Number Street City State ZIP Code	From ______ To ______	Number Street City State ZIP Code	From ______ To ______

3. **Within the last 8 years, did you ever live with a spouse or legal equivalent in a community property state or territory?** (*Community property states and territories* include Arizona, California, Idaho, Louisiana, Nevada, New Mexico, Puerto Rico, Texas, Washington, and Wisconsin.)

❑ No
☑ Yes. Make sure you fill out *Schedule H: Your Codebtors* (Official Form 106H).

Part 2: Explain the Sources of Your Income

Debtor 1 Sidney Samuel Smith
First Name Middle Name Last Name

Case number *(if known)* ______

4. **Did you have any income from employment or from operating a business during this year or the two previous calendar years?**
Fill in the total amount of income you received from all jobs and all businesses, including part-time activities.
If you are filing a joint case and you have income that you receive together, list it only once under Debtor 1.

☐ No
☐ Yes. Fill in the details.

	Debtor 1		**Debtor 2**	
	Sources of income Check all that apply.	**Gross income** (before deductions and exclusions)	**Sources of income** Check all that apply.	**Gross income** (before deductions and exclusions)
From January 1 of current year until the date you filed for bankruptcy:	☑ Wages, commissions, bonuses, tips ☐ Operating a business	$ 1,995.00	☑ Wages, commissions, bonuses, tips ☐ Operating a business	$ 915.00
For last calendar year: (January 1 to December 31, 2023) YYYY	☑ Wages, commissions, bonuses, tips ☐ Operating a business	$ 47,880.00	☑ Wages, commissions, bonuses, tips ☐ Operating a business	$ 21,960.00
For the calendar year before that: (January 1 to December 31, 2023) YYYY	☑ Wages, commissions, bonuses, tips ☐ Operating a business	$ 47,280.00	☑ Wages, commissions, bonuses, tips ☐ Operating a business	$ 21,360.00

5. **Did you receive any other income during this year or the two previous calendar years?**
Include income regardless of whether that income is taxable. Examples of *other income* are alimony; child support; Social Security, unemployment, and other public benefit payments; pensions; rental income; interest; dividends; money collected from lawsuits; royalties; and gambling and lottery winnings. If you are filing a joint case and you have income that you received together, list it only once under Debtor 1.

List each source and the gross income from each source separately. Do not include income that you listed in line 4.

☐ No
☑ Yes. Fill in the details.

	Debtor 1		**Debtor 2**	
	Sources of income Describe below.	**Gross income from each source** (before deductions and exclusions)	**Sources of income** Describe below.	**Gross income from each source** (before deductions and exclusions)
From January 1 of current year until the date you filed for bankruptcy:		$	Stock Dividends	$ 50.00
		$		$
		$		$
For last calendar year: (January 1 to December 31, 2023) YYYY		$	Stock Dividends	$ 1,200.00
		$		$
		$		$
For the calendar year before that: (January 1 to December 31, 2023) YYYY		$	Stock Dividends	$ 1,200.00
		$		$
		$		$

Debtor 1 Sidney Samuel Smith
First Name Middle Name Last Name

Case number *(if known)*__________

Part 3: List Certain Payments You Made Before You Filed for Bankruptcy

6. Are either Debtor 1's or Debtor 2's debts primarily consumer debts?

☐ No. **Neither Debtor 1 nor Debtor 2 has primarily consumer debts.** *Consumer debts* are defined in 11 U.S.C. § 101(8) as "incurred by an individual primarily for a personal, family, or household purpose."

During the 90 days before you filed for bankruptcy, did you pay any creditor a total of $7,575* or more?

☐ No. Go to line 7.

☐ Yes. List below each creditor to whom you paid a total of $7,575* or more in one or more payments and the total amount you paid that creditor. Do not include payments for domestic support obligations, such as child support and alimony. Also, do not include payments to an attorney for this bankruptcy case.

* Subject to adjustment on 4/01/25 and every 3 years after that for cases filed on or after the date of adjustment.

☒ Yes. **Debtor 1 or Debtor 2 or both have primarily consumer debts.**

During the 90 days before you filed for bankruptcy, did you pay any creditor a total of $600 or more?

☐ No. Go to line 7.

☐ Yes. List below each creditor to whom you paid a total of $600 or more and the total amount you paid that creditor. Do not include payments for domestic support obligations, such as child support and alimony. Also, do not include payments to an attorney for this bankruptcy case.

	Dates of payment	Total amount paid	Amount you still owe	Was this payment for...
XY Bank Creditor's Name Number Street City State ZIP Code	01/01/2024 12/01/2023 11/01/2023	$ 3,987.00	$ 98,000.00	☒ Mortgage ☐ Car ☐ Credit card ☐ Loan repayment ☐ Suppliers or vendors ☐ Other ______
MZ Dealership Creditor's Name Number Street City State ZIP Code	01/01/2024 12/01/2023 11/01/2023	$ 687.00	$ 135,290.00	☐ Mortgage ☐ Car ☐ Credit card ☐ Loan repayment ☐ Suppliers or vendors ☐ Other ______
Creditor's Name Number Street City State ZIP Code		$	$	☐ Mortgage ☐ Car ☐ Credit card ☐ Loan repayment ☐ Suppliers or vendors ☐ Other ______

Debtor 1 Sidney Samuel Smith
First Name Middle Name Last Name

Case number *(if known)* ______

7. **Within 1 year before you filed for bankruptcy, did you make a payment on a debt you owed anyone who was an insider?**
Insiders include your relatives; any general partners; relatives of any general partners; partnerships of which you are a general partner; corporations of which you are an officer, director, person in control, or owner of 20% or more of their voting securities; and any managing agent, including one for a business you operate as a sole proprietor. 11 U.S.C. § 101. Include payments for domestic support obligations, such as child support and alimony.

☒ No
☐ Yes. List all payments to an insider.

	Dates of payment	Total amount paid	Amount you still owe	Reason for this payment
Insider's Name Number Street City State ZIP Code		$	$	
Insider's Name Number Street City State ZIP Code		$	$	

8. **Within 1 year before you filed for bankruptcy, did you make any payments or transfer any property on account of a debt that benefited an insider?**
Include payments on debts guaranteed or cosigned by an insider.

☒ No
☐ Yes. List all payments that benefited an insider.

	Dates of payment	Total amount paid	Amount you still owe	Reason for this payment Include creditor's name
Insider's Name Number Street City State ZIP Code		$	$	
Insider's Name Number Street City State ZIP Code		$	$	

Debtor 1 Sidney Samuel Smith
First Name Middle Name Last Name

Case number (if known)

Part 4: Identify Legal Actions, Repossessions, and Foreclosures

9. **Within 1 year before you filed for bankruptcy, were you a party in any lawsuit, court action, or administrative proceeding?**
List all such matters, including personal injury cases, small claims actions, divorces, collection suits, paternity actions, support or custody modifications, and contract disputes.

☐ No
☒ Yes. Fill in the details.

	Nature of the case	Court or agency	Status of the case
Case title Bill Collections, Inc. v Sarah Smith Case number	Collection Action	Franklin County District Court Court Name Number Street City State ZIP Code	☐ Pending ☐ On appeal ☒ Concluded
Case title Case number		Court Name Number Street City State ZIP Code	☐ Pending ☐ On appeal ☐ Concluded

10. **Within 1 year before you filed for bankruptcy, was any of your property repossessed, foreclosed, garnished, attached, seized, or levied?**
Check all that apply and fill in the details below.

☐ No. Go to line 11.
☒ Yes. Fill in the information below.

	Describe the property	Date	Value of the property
Home Goods Store Creditor's Name Number Street City State ZIP Code	Couch, Entertainment Center **Explain what happened** ☒ Property was repossessed. ☐ Property was foreclosed. ☐ Property was garnished. ☐ Property was attached, seized, or levied.	10/31/2022	$ 875.00
Creditor's Name Number Street City State ZIP Code	**Explain what happened** ☐ Property was repossessed. ☐ Property was foreclosed. ☐ Property was garnished. ☐ Property was attached, seized, or levied.		$

Debtor 1 Sidney Samuel Smith
First Name Middle Name Last Name

Case number *(if known)*______________________

11. Within 90 days before you filed for bankruptcy, did any creditor, including a bank or financial institution, set off any amounts from your accounts or refuse to make a payment because you owed a debt?

☒ No
☐ Yes. Fill in the details.

	Describe the action the creditor took	Date action was taken	Amount
______________________ Creditor's Name ______________________ Number Street ______________________ ______________________ City State ZIP Code		________	$________
	Last 4 digits of account number: XXXX–___ ___ ___ ___		

12. Within 1 year before you filed for bankruptcy, was any of your property in the possession of an assignee for the benefit of creditors, a court-appointed receiver, a custodian, or another official?

☒ No
☐ Yes

Part 5: List Certain Gifts and Contributions

13. Within 2 years before you filed for bankruptcy, did you give any gifts with a total value of more than $600 per person?

☒ No
☐ Yes. Fill in the details for each gift.

Gifts with a total value of more than $600 per person	Describe the gifts	Dates you gave the gifts	Value
______________________ Person to Whom You Gave the Gift ______________________ ______________________ Number Street ______________________ City State ZIP Code Person's relationship to you ________		________ ________	$________ $________

Gifts with a total value of more than $600 per person	Describe the gifts	Dates you gave the gifts	Value
______________________ Person to Whom You Gave the Gift ______________________ ______________________ Number Street ______________________ City State ZIP Code Person's relationship to you ________		________ ________	$________ $________

Debtor 1 Sidney Samuel Smith
First Name Middle Name Last Name

Case number *(if known)*

14. Within 2 years before you filed for bankruptcy, did you give any gifts or contributions with a total value of more than $600 to any charity?

❑ No
☑ Yes. Fill in the details for each gift or contribution.

Gifts or contributions to charities that total more than $600	Describe what you contributed	Date you contributed	Value
Ohio State University Charity's Name Number Street City State ZIP Code	Contribution to Scholarship Fund	09/15/2023	$ 1,000.00
			$

Part 6: List Certain Losses

15. Within 1 year before you filed for bankruptcy or since you filed for bankruptcy, did you lose anything because of theft, fire, other disaster, or gambling?

❑ No
☑ Yes. Fill in the details.

Describe the property you lost and how the loss occurred	Describe any insurance coverage for the loss Include the amount that insurance has paid. List pending insurance claims on line 33 of *Schedule A/B: Property.*	Date of your loss	Value of property lost
Car Stereo Theft	Insurance Paid $2,000	10/31/2022	$ 2,000.00

Part 7: List Certain Payments or Transfers

16. Within 1 year before you filed for bankruptcy, did you or anyone else acting on your behalf pay or transfer any property to anyone you consulted about seeking bankruptcy or preparing a bankruptcy petition?
Include any attorneys, bankruptcy petition preparers, or credit counseling agencies for services required in your bankruptcy.

❑ No
☑ Yes. Fill in the details.

	Description and value of any property transferred	Date payment or transfer was made	Amount of payment
Debt Counseling, Inc. Person Who Was Paid Number Street City State ZIP Code Email or website address Person Who Made the Payment, if Not You	Cash	10/15/2022	$ 500.00
			$

Debtor 1 Sidney Samuel Smith
First Name Middle Name Last Name

Case number *(if known)*__________

	Description and value of any property transferred	Date payment or transfer was made	Amount of payment
Person Who Was Paid Number Street City State ZIP Code Email or website address Person Who Made the Payment, if Not You		______ ______	$______ $______

17. **Within 1 year before you filed for bankruptcy, did you or anyone else acting on your behalf pay or transfer any property to anyone who promised to help you deal with your creditors or to make payments to your creditors?**
Do not include any payment or transfer that you listed on line 16.

☒ No
☐ Yes. Fill in the details.

	Description and value of any property transferred	Date payment or transfer was made	Amount of payment
Person Who Was Paid Number Street City State ZIP Code		______ ______	$______ $______

18. **Within 2 years before you filed for bankruptcy, did you sell, trade, or otherwise transfer any property to anyone, other than property transferred in the ordinary course of your business or financial affairs?**
Include both outright transfers and transfers made as security (such as the granting of a security interest or mortgage on your property).
Do not include gifts and transfers that you have already listed on this statement.

☒ No
☐ Yes. Fill in the details.

	Description and value of property transferred	Describe any property or payments received or debts paid in exchange	Date transfer was made
Person Who Received Transfer Number Street City State ZIP Code Person's relationship to you ______			______
Person Who Received Transfer Number Street City State ZIP Code Person's relationship to you ______			______

Debtor 1 Sidney Samuel Smith
First Name Middle Name Last Name

Case number *(if known)*

19. **Within 10 years before you filed for bankruptcy, did you transfer any property to a self-settled trust or similar device of which you are a beneficiary?** (These are often called *asset-protection devices.*)

☑ No
☐ Yes. Fill in the details.

	Description and value of the property transferred	Date transfer was made
Name of trust ______		______

Part 8: List Certain Financial Accounts, Instruments, Safe Deposit Boxes, and Storage Units

20. **Within 1 year before you filed for bankruptcy, were any financial accounts or instruments held in your name, or for your benefit, closed, sold, moved, or transferred?**
Include checking, savings, money market, or other financial accounts; certificates of deposit; shares in banks, credit unions, brokerage houses, pension funds, cooperatives, associations, and other financial institutions.

☑ **No**
☐ **Yes. Fill in the details.**

	Last 4 digits of account number	Type of account or instrument	Date account was closed, sold, moved, or transferred	Last balance before closing or transfer
Name of Financial Institution Number Street City State ZIP Code	XXXX–__ __ __ __	☐ Checking ☐ Savings ☐ Money market ☐ Brokerage ☐ Other______	______	$______
Name of Financial Institution Number Street City State ZIP Code	XXXX–__ __ __ __	☐ Checking ☐ Savings ☐ Money market ☐ Brokerage ☐ Other______	______	$______

21. **Do you now have, or did you have within 1 year before you filed for bankruptcy, any safe deposit box or other depository for securities, cash, or other valuables?**

☑ **No**
☐ **Yes. Fill in the details.**

	Who else had access to it?	Describe the contents	Do you still have it?
Name of Financial Institution Number Street City State ZIP Code	Name Number Street City State ZIP Code		☐ No ☐ Yes

Debtor 1 Sidney Samuel Smith
First Name Middle Name Last Name

Case number *(if known)*

22. Have you stored property in a storage unit or place other than your home within 1 year before you filed for bankruptcy?

☑ No

☐ Yes. Fill in the details.

	Who else has or had access to it?	Describe the contents	Do you still have it?
Name of Storage Facility Number Street City State ZIP Code	Name Number Street City State ZIP Code		☐ No ☐ Yes

Part 9: Identify Property You Hold or Control for Someone Else

23. Do you hold or control any property that someone else owns? Include any property you borrowed from, are storing for, or hold in trust for someone.

☑ No

☐ Yes. Fill in the details.

	Where is the property?	Describe the property	Value
Owner's Name Number Street City State ZIP Code	Number Street City State ZIP Code		$

Part 10: Give Details About Environmental Information

For the purpose of Part 10, the following definitions apply:

- *Environmental law* means any federal, state, or local statute or regulation concerning pollution, contamination, releases of hazardous or toxic substances, wastes, or material into the air, land, soil, surface water, groundwater, or other medium, including statutes or regulations controlling the cleanup of these substances, wastes, or material.
- *Site* means any location, facility, or property as defined under any environmental law, whether you now own, operate, or utilize it or used to own, operate, or utilize it, including disposal sites.
- *Hazardous material* means anything an environmental law defines as a hazardous waste, hazardous substance, toxic substance, hazardous material, pollutant, contaminant, or similar term.

Report all notices, releases, and proceedings that you know about, regardless of when they occurred.

24. Has any governmental unit notified you that you may be liable or potentially liable under or in violation of an environmental law?

☑ No

☐ Yes. Fill in the details.

	Governmental unit	Environmental law, if you know it	Date of notice
Name of site Number Street City State ZIP Code	Governmental unit Number Street City State ZIP Code		

Debtor 1 Sidney Samuel Smith
First Name Middle Name Last Name

Case number *(if known)*__________

25. Have you notified any governmental unit of any release of hazardous material?

☒ No
☐ Yes. Fill in the details.

	Governmental unit	Environmental law, if you know it	Date of notice
Name of site	Governmental unit		______
Number Street	Number Street		
	City State ZIP Code		
City State ZIP Code			

26. Have you been a party in any judicial or administrative proceeding under any environmental law? Include settlements and orders.

☒ No
☐ Yes. Fill in the details.

	Court or agency	Nature of the case	Status of the case
Case title__________	Court Name		☐ Pending ☐ On appeal ☐ Concluded
	Number Street		
Case number	City State ZIP Code		

Part 11: Give Details About Your Business or Connections to Any Business

27. Within 4 years before you filed for bankruptcy, did you own a business or have any of the following connections to any business?

- ☐ A sole proprietor or self-employed in a trade, profession, or other activity, either full-time or part-time
- ☐ A member of a limited liability company (LLC) or limited liability partnership (LLP)
- ☐ A partner in a partnership
- ☐ An officer, director, or managing executive of a corporation
- ☐ An owner of at least 5% of the voting or equity securities of a corporation

☒ No. None of the above applies. Go to Part 12.
☐ Yes. Check all that apply above and fill in the details below for each business.

	Describe the nature of the business	Employer Identification number Do not include Social Security number or ITIN.
Business Name		
Number Street		EIN: __ __ – __ __ __ __ __ __ __
	Name of accountant or bookkeeper	Dates business existed
City State ZIP Code		From ______ To ______

	Describe the nature of the business	Employer Identification number Do not include Social Security number or ITIN.
Business Name		
Number Street		EIN: __ __ – __ __ __ __ __ __ __
	Name of accountant or bookkeeper	Dates business existed
City State ZIP Code		From ______ To ______

Debtor 1 Sidney Samuel Smith
First Name Middle Name Last Name

Case number *(if known)* ____________

	Describe the nature of the business	Employer Identification number Do not include Social Security number or ITIN.
____________ Business Name ____________ Number Street ____________ ____________ City State ZIP Code		EIN: __ __ - __ __ __ __ __ __ __
	Name of accountant or bookkeeper	Dates business existed
		From ______ To ______

28. Within 2 years before you filed for bankruptcy, did you give a financial statement to anyone about your business? Include all financial institutions, creditors, or other parties.

- ☐ No
- ☐ Yes. Fill in the details below.

	Date issued
____________ Name ____________ Number Street ____________ ____________ City State ZIP Code	______ MM / DD / YYYY

Part 12: Sign Below

I have read the answers on this *Statement of Financial Affairs* and any attachments, and I declare under penalty of perjury that the answers are true and correct. I understand that making a false statement, concealing property, or obtaining money or property by fraud in connection with a bankruptcy case can result in fines up to $250,000, or imprisonment for up to 20 years, or both.
18 U.S.C. §§ 152, 1341, 1519, and 3571.

✘ /s/ Sidney Samuel Smith
Signature of Debtor 1

Date ____________

✘ Sara Arlene Smith
Signature of Debtor 2

Date ____________

Did you attach additional pages to *Your Statement of Financial Affairs for Individuals Filing for Bankruptcy* (Official Form 107)?

- ☐ No
- ☐ Yes

Did you pay or agree to pay someone who is not an attorney to help you fill out bankruptcy forms?

- ☐ No
- ☐ Yes. Name of person ____________________. Attach the *Bankruptcy Petition Preparer's Notice, Declaration, and Signature* (Official Form 119).

Exhibit 2-R Application for Individuals to Pay the Filing Fee in Installments (Off. Form 103A)

Fill in this information to identify your case:

Debtor 1: Sidney Samuel Smith
First Name / Middle Name / Last Name

Debtor 2 (Spouse, if filing): Sarah Arlene Smith
First Name / Middle Name / Last Name

United States Bankruptcy Court for the: Southern District of Ohio

Case number (If known): ______________________

☐ Check if this is an amended filing

Official Form 103A

Application for Individuals to Pay the Filing Fee in Installments

12/15

Be as complete and accurate as possible. If two married people are filing together, both are equally responsible for supplying correct information.

Part 1: Specify Your Proposed Payment Timetable

1. **Which chapter of the Bankruptcy Code are you choosing to file under?**

☒ Chapter 7
☐ Chapter 11
☐ Chapter 12
☐ Chapter 13

2. **You may apply to pay the filing fee in up to four installments. Fill in the amounts you propose to pay and the dates you plan to pay them. Be sure all dates are business days. Then add the payments you propose to pay.**

You must propose to pay the entire fee no later than 120 days after you file this bankruptcy case. If the court approves your application, the court will set your final payment timetable.

You propose to pay...		Date (MM / DD / YYYY)
$ 100.00	☒ With the filing of the petition ☐ On or before this date........	01/20/2024
$ 50.00	On or before this date...........	02/15/2024
$ 50.00	On or before this date...........	03/15/2024
+ $ 135.00	On or before this date...........	04/15/2024
Total $ 335.00	◀ Your total must equal the entire fee for the chapter you checked in line 1.	

Part 2: Sign Below

By signing here, you state that you are unable to pay the full filing fee at once, that you want to pay the fee in installments, and that you understand that:

- You must pay your entire filing fee before you make any more payments or transfer any more property to an attorney, bankruptcy petition preparer, or anyone else for services in connection with your bankruptcy case.
- You must pay the entire fee no later than 120 days after you first file for bankruptcy, unless the court later extends your deadline. Your debts will not be discharged until your entire fee is paid.
- If you do not make any payment when it is due, your bankruptcy case may be dismissed, and your rights in other bankruptcy proceedings may be affected.

✗ /s/ Sidney Samuel Smith	✗ /s/ Sarah Arlene Smith	✗ /s/ Alice B. Chase, Esq.
Signature of Debtor 1	Signature of Debtor 2	Your attorney's name and signature, if you used one
Date 01/15/2024 (MM / DD / YYYY)	Date 01/15/2024 (MM / DD / YYYY)	Date 01/15/2024 (MM / DD / YYYY)

Fill in this information to identify the case:

Debtor 1 Sidney Samuel Smith
First Name Middle Name Last Name

Debtor 2 Sarah Arlene Smith
(Spouse, if filing) First Name Middle Name Last Name

United States Bankruptcy Court for the: Southern District of Ohio

Case number ______________________
(If known)

Chapter filing under:

- ☐ Chapter 7
- ☐ Chapter 11
- ☐ Chapter 12
- ☐ Chapter 13

Order Approving Payment of Filing Fee in Installments

After considering the *Application for Individuals to Pay the Filing Fee in Installments* (Official Form 103A), the court orders that:

[ ] The debtor(s) may pay the filing fee in installments on the terms proposed in the application.

[ ] The debtor(s) must pay the filing fee according to the following terms:

	You must pay...	On or before this date...
	$__________	__________ Month / day / year
	$__________	__________ Month / day / year
	$__________	__________ Month / day / year
	+ $__________	__________ Month / day / year
Total	$__________	

Until the filing fee is paid in full, the debtor(s) must not make any additional payment or transfer any additional property to an attorney or to anyone else for services in connection with this case.

__________ Month / day / year

By the court: ______________________________
United States Bankruptcy Judge

Exhibit 2-S Application to Have the Chapter 7 Filing Fee Waived (Official Form 103B)

Fill in this information to identify your case:

Debtor 1 Sidney Samuel Smith
First Name Middle Name Last Name

Debtor 2 Sarah Arlene Smith
(Spouse, if filing) First Name Middle Name Last Name

United States Bankruptcy Court for the: Southern District of Ohio

Case number ______________________
(If known)

☐ Check if this is an amended filing

Official Form 103B

Application to Have the Chapter 7 Filing Fee Waived

12/15

Be as complete and accurate as possible. If two married people are filing together, both are equally responsible for supplying correct information. If more space is needed, attach a separate sheet to this form. On the top of any additional pages, write your name and case number (if known).

Part 1: Tell the Court About Your Family and Your Family's Income

1. **What is the size of your family?**
   Your family includes you, your spouse, and any dependents listed on *Schedule J: Your Expenses* (Official Form 106J).

   Check all that apply:
   - ☐ You
   - ☐ Your spouse
   - ☐ Your dependents 2 (How many dependents?) 4 (Total number of people)

2. **Fill in your family's average monthly income.**
   Include your spouse's income if your spouse is living with you, even if your spouse is not filing.
   Do not include your spouse's income if you are separated and your spouse is not filing with you.

   Add your income and your spouse's income. Include the value (if known) of any non-cash governmental assistance that you receive, such as food stamps (benefits under the Supplemental Nutrition Assistance Program) or housing subsidies.
   If you have already filled out *Schedule I: Your Income,* see line 10 of that schedule.

		That person's average monthly net income (take-home pay)
You		$ 2,722.00
Your spouse	+	$ 1,655.00
Subtotal		$ 4,377.00
Subtract any non-cash governmental assistance that you included above.	−	$ 0.00
Your family's average monthly net income Total		$ 4,377.00

3. **Do you receive non-cash governmental assistance?**
   - ☐ No
   - ☐ Yes. Describe.......... **Type of assistance** ______

4. **Do you expect your family's average monthly net income to increase or decrease by more than 10% during the next 6 months?**
   - ☐ No
   - ☐ Yes. Explain. .... ______

5. **Tell the court why you are unable to pay the filing fee in installments within 120 days.** If you have some additional circumstances that cause you to not be able to pay your filing fee in installments, explain them.

   Not enough disposable income to cover the cost.

Debtor 1 Sidney Samuel Smith
First Name Middle Name Last Name

Case number *(if known)* ______

Part 2: Tell the Court About Your Monthly Expenses

6. Estimate your average monthly expenses.
Include amounts paid by any government assistance that you reported on line 2. $ 4,075.00

If you have already filled out *Schedule J, Your Expenses,* copy line 22 from that form.

7. Do these expenses cover anyone who is not included in your family as reported in line 1?
☐ No
☐ Yes. Identify who........

8. Does anyone other than you regularly pay any of these expenses?
If you have already filled out *Schedule I: Your Income*, copy the total from line 11.
☐ No
☐ Yes. How much do you regularly receive as contributions? $________ monthly

9. Do you expect your average monthly expenses to increase or decrease by more than 10% during the next 6 months?
☐ No
☐ Yes. Explain ....

Part 3: Tell the Court About Your Property

If you have already filled out *Schedule A/B: Property (Official Form 106A/B)* attach copies to this application and go to Part 4.

10. How much cash do you have?
Examples: Money you have in your wallet, in your home, and on hand when you file this application

Cash: $______

11. Bank accounts and other deposits of money?
Examples: Checking, savings, money market, or other financial accounts; certificates of deposit; shares in banks, credit unions, brokerage houses, and other similar institutions. If you have more than one account with the same institution, list each. Do not include 401(k) and IRA accounts.

	Institution name:	Amount:
Checking account:	______	$______
Savings account:	______	$______
Other financial accounts:	______	$______
Other financial accounts:	______	$______

12. Your home? (if you own it outright or are purchasing it)
Examples: House, condominium, manufactured home, or mobile home

Number Street
City State ZIP Code

Current value: $______
Amount you owe on mortgage and liens: $______

13. Other real estate?

Number Street
City State ZIP Code

Current value: $______
Amount you owe on mortgage and liens: $______

14. The vehicles you own?
Examples: Cars, vans, trucks, sports utility vehicles, motorcycles, tractors, boats

Make: ______
Model: ______
Year: ______
Mileage ______

Current value: $______
Amount you owe on liens: $______

Make: ______
Model: ______
Year: ______
Mileage ______

Current value: $______
Amount you owe on liens: $______

Debtor 1 Sidney Samuel Smith
First Name Middle Name Last Name

Case number (*if known*) ______

15. Other assets?

Do not include household items and clothing.

Describe the other assets:

Current value: $______

Amount you owe on liens: $______

16. Money or property due you?

Examples: Tax refunds, past due or lump sum alimony, spousal support, child support, maintenance, divorce or property settlements, Social Security benefits, workers' compensation, personal injury recovery

Who owes you the money or property? ______

How much is owed? $______ $______

Do you believe you will likely receive payment in the next 180 days?

☐ No

☐ Yes. Explain:

Part 4: Answer These Additional Questions

17. Have you paid anyone for services for this case, including filling out this application, the bankruptcy filing package, or the schedules?

☐ No

☒ Yes. **Whom did you pay?** *Check all that apply:*

☒ An attorney

☐ A bankruptcy petition preparer, paralegal, or typing service

☐ Someone else ______

How much did you pay? $ 500.00

18. Have you promised to pay or do you expect to pay someone for services for your bankruptcy case?

☐ No

☒ Yes. **Whom do you expect to pay?** *Check all that apply:*

☒ An attorney

☐ A bankruptcy petition preparer, paralegal, or typing service

☐ Someone else ______

How much do you expect to pay? $ 500.00

19. Has anyone paid someone on your behalf for services for this case?

☒ No

☐ Yes. **Who was paid on your behalf?** *Check all that apply:*

☐ An attorney

☐ A bankruptcy petition preparer, paralegal, or typing service

☐ Someone else ______

Who paid? *Check all that apply:*

☐ Parent

☐ Brother or sister

☐ Friend

☐ Pastor or clergy

☐ Someone else ______

How much did someone else pay? $______

20. Have you filed for bankruptcy within the last 8 years?

☒ No

☐ Yes. District ______ When ______ (MM/ DD/ YYYY) Case number ______

District ______ When ______ (MM/ DD/ YYYY) Case number ______

District ______ When ______ (MM/ DD/ YYYY) Case number ______

Part 5: Sign Below

By signing here under penalty of perjury, I declare that I cannot afford to pay the filing fee either in full or in installments. I also declare that the information I provided in this application is true and correct.

✗ /s/ Sidney Samuel Smith
Signature of Debtor 1

Date 01/15/2024
MM / DD / YYYY

✗ /s/ Sarah Arlene Smith
Signature of Debtor 2

Date 01/15/2024
MM / DD / YYYY

Fill in this information to identify the case:

Debtor 1 Sidney Samuel Smith
First Name Middle Name Last Name

Debtor 2 Sarah Arlene Smith
(Spouse, if filing) First Name Middle Name Last Name

United States Bankruptcy Court for the: Southern District of Ohio

Case number ______________________
(If known)

Order on the Application to Have the Chapter 7 Filing Fee Waived

After considering the debtor's *Application to Have the Chapter 7 Filing Fee Waived* (Official Form 103B), the court orders that the application is:

[ ] **Granted.** However, the court may order the debtor to pay the fee in the future if developments in administering the bankruptcy case show that the waiver was unwarranted.

[ ] **Denied.** The debtor must pay the filing fee according to the following terms:

	You must pay...	On or before this date...
	$__________	__________ Month / day / year
	$__________	__________ Month / day / year
	$__________	__________ Month / day / year
	+ $__________	__________ Month / day / year
Total		

If the debtor would like to propose a different payment timetable, the debtor must file a motion promptly with a payment proposal. The debtor may use *Application for Individuals to Pay the Filing Fee in Installments* (Official Form 103A) for this purpose. The court will consider it.

The debtor must pay the entire filing fee before making any more payments or transferring any more property to an attorney, bankruptcy petition preparer, or anyone else in connection with the bankruptcy case. The debtor must also pay the entire filing fee to receive a discharge. If the debtor does not make any payment when it is due, the bankruptcy case may be dismissed and the debtor's rights in future bankruptcy cases may be affected.

[ ] **Scheduled for hearing.**

A hearing to consider the debtor's application will be held

on __________ at __________ AM / PM at ______________________________.
Month / day / year Address of courthouse

If the debtor does not appear at this hearing, the court may deny the application.

__________ **By the court:** ______________________________
Month / day / year United States Bankruptcy Judge

Exhibit 2-T Statement of Intention for Individuals Filing Under Ch. 7 (Off. Form 108)

Fill in this information to identify your case:

Debtor 1 Sidney Samuel Smith
First Name Middle Name Last Name

Debtor 2 Sarah Arlene Smith
(Spouse, if filing) First Name Middle Name Last Name

United States Bankruptcy Court for the: Southern District of Ohio

Case number ____________________
(If known)

☐ Check if this is an amended filing

Official Form 108

Statement of Intention for Individuals Filing Under Chapter 7

12/15

If you are an individual filing under chapter 7, you must fill out this form if:

- **creditors have claims secured by your property, or**
- **you have leased personal property and the lease has not expired.**

You must file this form with the court within 30 days after you file your bankruptcy petition or by the date set for the meeting of creditors, whichever is earlier, unless the court extends the time for cause. You must also send copies to the creditors and lessors you list on the form.

If two married people are filing together in a joint case, both are equally responsible for supplying correct information. Both debtors must sign and date the form.

Be as complete and accurate as possible. If more space is needed, attach a separate sheet to this form. On the top of any additional pages, write your name and case number (if known).

Part 1: List Your Creditors Who Have Secured Claims

1. **For any creditors that you listed in Part 1 of *Schedule D: Creditors Who Have Claims Secured by Property* (Official Form 106D), fill in the information below.**

Identify the creditor and the property that is collateral	What do you intend to do with the property that secures a debt?	Did you claim the property as exempt on Schedule C?
Creditor's name: XY Bank Description of property securing debt: Residence	☐ Surrender the property. ☐ Retain the property and redeem it. ☑ Retain the property and enter into a *Reaffirmation Agreement.* ☐ Retain the property and [explain]: __________	☐ No ☑ Yes
Creditor's name: BX Dealership Description of property securing debt: Chevrolet Impala	☐ Surrender the property. ☐ Retain the property and redeem it. ☑ Retain the property and enter into a *Reaffirmation Agreement.* ☐ Retain the property and [explain]: __________	☐ No ☑ Yes
Creditor's name: MZ Dealership Description of property securing debt: Ford F-150	☐ Surrender the property. ☐ Retain the property and redeem it. ☑ Retain the property and enter into a *Reaffirmation Agreement.* ☐ Retain the property and [explain]: __________	☐ No ☑ Yes
Creditor's name: Description of property securing debt:	☐ Surrender the property. ☐ Retain the property and redeem it. ☐ Retain the property and enter into a *Reaffirmation Agreement.* ☐ Retain the property and [explain]: __________	☐ No ☐ Yes

Debtor 1 Sidney Samuel Smith
First Name Middle Name Last Name

Case number (*If known*)

Part 2: List Your Unexpired Personal Property Leases

For any unexpired personal property lease that you listed in *Schedule G: Executory Contracts and Unexpired Leases* (Official Form 106G), fill in the information below. Do not list real estate leases. *Unexpired leases* are leases that are still in effect; the lease period has not yet ended. You may assume an unexpired personal property lease if the trustee does not assume it. 11 U.S.C. § 365(p)(2).

Describe your unexpired personal property leases	Will the lease be assumed?
Lessor's name: Morton Leasing Co. Description of leased property: copy machine	☐ No ☒ Yes
Lessor's name: Description of leased property:	☐ No ☐ Yes
Lessor's name: Description of leased property:	☐ No ☐ Yes
Lessor's name: Description of leased property:	☐ No ☐ Yes
Lessor's name: Description of leased property:	☐ No ☐ Yes
Lessor's name: Description of leased property:	☐ No ☐ Yes
Lessor's name: Description of leased property:	☐ No ☐ Yes

Part 3: Sign Below

Under penalty of perjury, I declare that I have indicated my intention about any property of my estate that secures a debt and any personal property that is subject to an unexpired lease.

✘ /s/ Sidney Samuel Smith
Signature of Debtor 1

Date 01/15/2024
MM / DD / YYYY

✘ /s/ Sarah Arlene Smith
Signature of Debtor 2

Date 01/15/2024
MM / DD / YYYY

Exhibit 2-U Notice Required for Individuals Filing for Bankruptcy (Director's Form 2010)

Notice Required by 11 U.S.C. § 342(b) for Individuals Filing for Bankruptcy (Form 2010)

This notice is for you if:

You are an individual filing for bankruptcy, and

Your debts are primarily consumer debts. *Consumer debts* are defined in 11 U.S.C. § 101(8) as "incurred by an individual primarily for a personal, family, or household purpose."

The types of bankruptcy that are available to individuals

Individuals who meet the qualifications may file under one of four different chapters of the Bankruptcy Code:

- Chapter 7 — Liquidation
- Chapter 11— Reorganization
- Chapter 12— Voluntary repayment plan for family farmers or fishermen
- Chapter 13— Voluntary repayment plan for individuals with regular income

You should have an attorney review your decision to file for bankruptcy and the choice of chapter.

Chapter 7: Liquidation

	$245	filing fee
	$78	administrative fee
+	$15	trustee surcharge
	$338	total fee

Chapter 7 is for individuals who have financial difficulty preventing them from paying their debts and who are willing to allow their non-exempt property to be used to pay their creditors. The primary purpose of filing under chapter 7 is to have your debts discharged. The bankruptcy discharge relieves you after bankruptcy from having to pay many of your pre-bankruptcy debts. Exceptions exist for particular debts, and liens on property may still be enforced after discharge. For example, a creditor may have the right to foreclose a home mortgage or repossess an automobile.

However, if the court finds that you have committed certain kinds of improper conduct described in the Bankruptcy Code, the court may deny your discharge.

You should know that even if you file chapter 7 and you receive a discharge, some debts are not discharged under the law. Therefore, you may still be responsible to pay:

- most taxes;
- most student loans;
- domestic support and property settlement obligations;

- most fines, penalties, forfeitures, and criminal restitution obligations; and
- certain debts that are not listed in your bankruptcy papers.

You may also be required to pay debts arising from:

- fraud or theft;
- fraud or defalcation while acting in breach of fiduciary capacity;
- intentional injuries that you inflicted; and
- death or personal injury caused by operating a motor vehicle, vessel, or aircraft while intoxicated from alcohol or drugs.

If your debts are primarily consumer debts, the court can dismiss your chapter 7 case if it finds that you have enough income to repay creditors a certain amount. You must file *Chapter 7 Statement of Your Current Monthly Income* (Official Form 122A–1) if you are an individual filing for bankruptcy under chapter 7. This form will determine your current monthly income and compare whether your income is more than the median income that applies in your state.

If your income is not above the median for your state, you will not have to complete the other chapter 7 form, the *Chapter 7 Means Test Calculation* (Official Form 122A–2).

If your income is above the median for your state, you must file a second form —the *Chapter 7 Means Test Calculation* (Official Form 122A–2). The calculations on the form—sometimes called the *Means Test*—deduct from your income living expenses and payments on certain debts to determine any amount available to pay unsecured creditors. If your income is more than the median income for your state of residence and family size, depending on the results of the *Means Test*, the U.S. trustee, bankruptcy administrator, or creditors can file a motion to dismiss your case under § 707(b) of the Bankruptcy Code. If a motion is filed, the court will decide if your case should be dismissed. To avoid dismissal, you may choose to proceed under another chapter of the Bankruptcy Code.

If you are an individual filing for chapter 7 bankruptcy, the trustee may sell your property to pay your debts, subject to your right to exempt the property or a portion of the proceeds from the sale of the property. The property, and the proceeds from property that your bankruptcy trustee sells or liquidates that you are entitled to, is called *exempt property*. Exemptions may enable you to keep your home, a car, clothing, and household items or to receive some of the proceeds if the property is sold.

Exemptions are not automatic. To exempt property, you must list it on *Schedule C: The Property You Claim as Exempt* (Official Form 106C). If you do not list the property, the trustee may sell it and pay all of the proceeds to your creditors.

Chapter 11: Reorganization

	$1,167	filing fee
+	$571	administrative fee
	$1,738	total fee

Chapter 11 is often used for reorganizing a business, but is also available to individuals. The provisions of chapter 11 are too complicated to summarize briefly.

Read These Important Warnings

Because bankruptcy can have serious long-term financial and legal consequences, including loss of your property, you should hire an attorney and carefully consider all of your options before you file. Only an attorney can give you legal advice about what can happen as a result of filing for bankruptcy and what your options are. If you do file for bankruptcy, an attorney can help you fill out the forms properly and protect you, your family, your home, and your possessions.

Although the law allows you to represent yourself in bankruptcy court, you should understand that many people find it difficult to represent themselves successfully. The rules are technical, and a mistake or inaction may harm you. If you file without an attorney, you are still responsible for knowing and following all of the legal requirements.

You should not file for bankruptcy if you are not eligible to file or if you do not intend to file the necessary documents.

Bankruptcy fraud is a serious crime; you could be fined and imprisoned if you commit fraud in your bankruptcy case. Making a false statement, concealing property, or obtaining money or property by fraud in connection with a bankruptcy case can result in fines up to $250,000, or imprisonment for up to 20 years, or both. 18 U.S.C. §§ 152, 1341, 1519, and 3571.

Chapter 12: Repayment plan for family farmers or fishermen

	$200	filing fee
+	$78	administrative fee
	$278	total fee

Similar to chapter 13, chapter 12 permits family farmers and fishermen to repay their debts over a period of time using future earnings and to discharge some debts that are not paid.

Chapter 13: Repayment plan for individuals with regular income

	$235	filing fee
+	$78	administrative fee
	$313	total fee

Chapter 13 is for individuals who have regular income and would like to pay all or part of their debts in installments over a period of time and to discharge some debts that are not paid. You are eligible for chapter 13 only if your debts are not more than certain dollar amounts set forth in 11 U.S.C. § 109.

Under chapter 13, you must file with the court a plan to repay your creditors all or part of the money that you owe them, usually using your future earnings. If the court approves your plan, the court will allow you to repay your debts, as adjusted by the plan, within 3 years or 5 years, depending on your income and other factors.

After you make all the payments under your plan, many of your debts are discharged. The debts that are not discharged and that you may still be responsible to pay include:

- domestic support obligations,
- most student loans,
- certain taxes,
- debts for fraud or theft,
- debts for fraud or defalcation while acting in a fiduciary capacity,
- most criminal fines and restitution obligations,
- certain debts that are not listed in your bankruptcy papers,
- certain debts for acts that caused death or personal injury, and
- certain long-term secured debts.

Warning: File Your Forms on Time

Section 521(a)(1) of the Bankruptcy Code requires that you promptly file detailed information about your creditors, assets, liabilities, income, expenses and general financial condition. The court may dismiss your bankruptcy case if you do not file this information within the deadlines set by the Bankruptcy Code, the Bankruptcy Rules, and the local rules of the court.

For more information about the documents and their deadlines, go to: http://www.uscourts.gov/forms/bankruptcy-forms

Bankruptcy crimes have serious consequences

- If you knowingly and fraudulently conceal assets or make a false oath or statement under penalty of perjury—either orally or in writing—in connection with a bankruptcy case, you may be fined, imprisoned, or both.
- All information you supply in connection with a bankruptcy case is subject to examination by the Attorney General acting through the Office of the U.S. Trustee, the Office of the U.S. Attorney, and other offices and employees of the U.S. Department of Justice.

Make sure the court has your mailing address

The bankruptcy court sends notices to the mailing address you list on *Voluntary Petition for Individuals Filing for Bankruptcy* (Official Form 101). To ensure that you receive information about your case, Bankruptcy Rule 4002 requires that you notify the court of any changes in your address.

A married couple may file a bankruptcy case together—called a *joint case*. If you file a joint case and each spouse lists the same mailing address on the bankruptcy petition, the bankruptcy court generally will mail you and your spouse one copy of each notice, unless you file a statement with the court asking that each spouse receive separate copies.

Understand which services you could receive from credit counseling agencies

The law generally requires that you receive a credit counseling briefing from an approved credit counseling agency. 11 U.S.C. § 109(h). If you are filing a joint case, both spouses must receive the briefing. With limited exceptions, you must receive it within the 180 days ***before*** you file your bankruptcy petition. This briefing is usually conducted by telephone or on the Internet.

In addition, after filing a bankruptcy case, you generally must complete a financial management instructional course before you can receive a discharge. If you are filing a joint case, both spouses must complete the course.

You can obtain the list of agencies approved to provide both the briefing and the instructional course from: http://www.uscourts.gov/services-forms/bankruptcy/credit-counseling-and-debtor-education-courses.

In Alabama and North Carolina, go to: http://www.uscourts.gov/services-forms/bankruptcy/credit-counseling-and-debtor-education-courses.

If you do not have access to a computer, the clerk of the bankruptcy court may be able to help you obtain the list.

Exhibit 2-V Declaration Regarding Electronic Filing

UNITED STATES BANKRUPTCY COURT
SOUTHERN DISTRICT OF OHIO

In re:	)	**Case No.** ____________
Sidney Samuel Smith and	)	
Sarah Arlene Smith	)	**Chapter** 7
	)	
Debtor(s)	)	**Judge** Tallman
	)	
	)	**DECLARATION RE: ELECTRONIC FILING OF DOCUMENTS AND STATEMENT OF SOCIAL SECURITY NUMBER**

Part I - Declaration of Petitioner

I [We] Sidney Samuel Smith and Sarah Arlene Smith, the undersigned debtor(s), ***hereby declare under penalty of perjury*** that the information I have given my attorney and the information provided in the electronically filed petition, statements, and schedules, as well as in any other documents that must contain original signatures, is true, correct, and complete. I consent to my attorney sending my petition, this declaration, statements, and schedules, and any other documents that must contain original signatures, to the United States Bankruptcy Court. I understand that this DECLARATION RE: ELECTRONIC FILING is to be filed with the Clerk once all schedules have been filed electronically but, in no event, no later than 7 days following the date the petition or other document that must contain original signatures was electronically filed.

I am aware that I may proceed under Chapter 7, 11, 12 or 13 of Title 11 of the United States Code, understand the relief available under each chapter, and choose to proceed under the chapter specified in the petition.

I [We] ***further declare under penalty of perjury*** that [*check appropriate box(es)*]:

- [x] The Social Security Number that I, the Debtor, have given to my attorney, which will be submitted to the Court as part of the electronic case opening process, is true, correct, and complete.
- [ ] I, the Debtor, do not have a Social Security Number.
- [x] The Social Security Number that I, the Joint Debtor, have given to my attorney, which will be submitted to the Court as part of the electronic case opening process, is true, correct, and complete.
- [ ] I, the Joint Debtor, do not have a Social Security Number.
- [ ] [Check box if petitioner is a corporation or partnership] I declare under penalty of perjury that the information provided in the petition is true, correct, and complete, and that I have been authorized to file the petition on behalf of the debtor. The debtor requests relief in accordance with the chapter specified in the petition.

Dated: 01/15/2023 Signed: ____________________ (Debtor) ____________________ (Co-Debtor)

Part II - Declaration of Attorney

I ***declare under penalty of perjury*** that I have reviewed the above debtor's petition and that the information is complete and correct to the best of my knowledge. The debtor(s) will have signed this form before I submit the petition, schedules, and statements, or any other documents that must contain original signatures. I will give the debtor(s) a copy of all forms and information to be filed with the United States Bankruptcy Court, and have followed all other requirements in the most recent exhibit to General Order No. 02-2. I further declare that I have examined the above debtor's petition, schedules, and statements, and any other documents that must contain original signatures, and to the best of my knowledge and belief, they are true, correct, and complete. If an individual, I further declare that I have informed the petitioner that [he or she] may proceed under chapter 7, 11, 12, or 13 of Title 11, United States Code and have explained the relief available under such chapter. This declaration is based on all information of which I have knowledge. I understand that failure to file the signed original of this DECLARATION will cause this case to be dismissed.

Dated: 01/15/2023 /s/ Alice B. Chase
Attorney for Debtor(s)

Exhibit 2-W Motion to Redeem Personal Property Under Section 722

UNITED STATES BANKRUPTCY COURT
FOR THE SOUTHERN DISTRICT OF OHIO

IN RE Sidney Samuel Smith and	)	
Sarah Arlene Smith	)	Case No. 23BR10986-SBB
	)	
Debtors	)	Chapter 7

MOTION TO REDEEM PERSONAL PROPERTY UNDER 11 U.S.C. § 722

The debtors, by their attorney, state and represent as follows:

1. That the property described in paragraph 4 below is tangible personal property intended primarily for personal, family or household use and such property is exempt to the debtors under the laws of the state of Ohio, to wit: Ohio Revised Code section 2329(A)(3), (4)(b).

2. That the lien of the creditor, Easy Loans, Inc., on such property secures a dischargeable debt that was incurred by the debtors primarily for a personal, family or household purpose, to wit: the purchase of food, supplies, and clothing used by the debtors and the debtors' family.

3. That pursuant to 11 U.S.C. 722, the debtors desire to redeem such property from the lien of the creditor by paying to the creditor the amount of the creditor's allowed secured claim secured by the lien on such property.

4. That the property to be redeemed by the debtors and the alleged value of such property is as follows:

Sharp Television Set #B444564	$	100.00
General Electric Refrigerator #F3452	$	50.00
Westinghouse Electric Range #R-44589	$	40.00
Beds, tables, and chairs described in item 4 of the debtors' Schedule B	$	500.00

5. That the amount of the secured claim of the creditor, Easy Loans, Inc., secured by its lien on such property is $690.00, which amount the debtors propose to pay to the creditor in redemption of such property.

WHEREFORE, the debtors move this honorable court to schedule a hearing on notice as provided in Fed.R.Bank.P. 6008 and thereafter enter an order fixing the amount of the allowed secured claim of the creditor, Easy Loans, Inc., secured by its lien on the property described in paragraph 4 above as $690.00, and permit the debtors to redeem the above-described property by paying to the said creditor the sum of $690.00 within a reasonable period.

Dated: January 30, 2024

____
Alice B. Chase
Attorney for Debtor
2000 Market Street, Columbus, OH 43222

Telephone: 614-333-3300

EXHIBIT 2-X Motion to Avoid Security Interest in Exempt Property Under Section 522(f)

UNITED STATES BANKRUPTCY COURT
FOR THE SOUTHERN DISTRICT OF OHIO

IN RE Sidney Samuel Smith and	)	
Sarah Arlene Smith	)	Case No. 23BR10986-SBB
	)	
Debtors	)	Chapter 7

<u>MOTION TO AVOID SECURITY INTEREST IN EXEMPT PROPERTY UNDER 11 U.S.C §522(f)</u>

The debtors, by their attorney, state and represent as follows:

1. That the creditor, Fast Finance Company, has a nonpossessory, nonpurchase-money security interest in the following described property of the debtors, which property is held primarily for the personal, family, and household use of the debtors and their dependents:

1 diamond wedding ring
1 gold wedding ring
1 Rolex wrist watch
1994 Ford Escort automobile (VIN # 7698764458R1927J742)

2. That the security interest of the creditor, Fast Finance Company, impairs an exemption to which the debtors would have been entitled under the laws of the State of Ohio, which exemptions have been claimed by the debtors in this case and have been allowed.

3. That the debtors are entitled to avoid the security interest of the creditor, Fast Finance Company, in the above-described property under the provisions of 11 U.S.C. §522(f).

WHEREFORE, the debtors move this honorable court to schedule a hearing on notice as provided in Fed.R.Bank.P. 4003(d) and 9014 and to thereafter enter an order avoiding the lien of the creditor, Fast Finance Company, in the property described in paragraph 1 above.

Dated: January 30, 2024

____
Alice B. Chase
Attorney for Debtor
2000 Market Street
Columbus, OH 43222
Telephone: 614-333-3300

EXHIBIT 2-Y Amended Schedule E/F (Official Form 106E/F, Amended)

Fill in this information to identify your case:

Debtor 1 Sidney Samuel Smith
First Name Middle Name Last Name

Debtor 2 (Spouse, if filing) Sarah Arlene Smith
First Name Middle Name Last Name

United States Bankruptcy Court for the: Southern District of Ohio

Case number (If known) 23BR10986-SBB

☒ Check if this is an amended filing

Official Form 106E/F

Schedule E/F: Creditors Who Have Unsecured Claims

12/15

Be as complete and accurate as possible. Use Part 1 for creditors with PRIORITY claims and Part 2 for creditors with NONPRIORITY claims. List the other party to any executory contracts or unexpired leases that could result in a claim. Also list executory contracts on *Schedule A/B: Property* (Official Form 106A/B) and on *Schedule G: Executory Contracts and Unexpired Leases* (Official Form 106G). Do not include any creditors with partially secured claims that are listed in *Schedule D: Creditors Who Have Claims Secured by Property*. If more space is needed, copy the Part you need, fill it out, number the entries in the boxes on the left. Attach the Continuation Page to this page. On the top of any additional pages, write your name and case number (if known).

Part 1: List All of Your PRIORITY Unsecured Claims

1. **Do any creditors have priority unsecured claims against you?**
   - ☒ No. Go to Part 2.
   - ☐ Yes.

2. **List all of your priority unsecured claims.** If a creditor has more than one priority unsecured claim, list the creditor separately for each claim. For each claim listed, identify what type of claim it is. If a claim has both priority and nonpriority amounts, list that claim here and show both priority and nonpriority amounts. As much as possible, list the claims in alphabetical order according to the creditor's name. If you have more than two priority unsecured claims, fill out the Continuation Page of Part 1. If more than one creditor holds a particular claim, list the other creditors in Part 3.
   (For an explanation of each type of claim, see the instructions for this form in the instruction booklet.)

		Total claim	Priority amount	Nonpriority amount
2.1	Last 4 digits of account number ___ ___ ___ ___	$________	$________	$________

2.1 ______ Priority Creditor's Name
______ Number Street
______
______ City State ZIP Code

Who incurred the debt? Check one.
- ☐ Debtor 1 only
- ☐ Debtor 2 only
- ☐ Debtor 1 and Debtor 2 only
- ☐ At least one of the debtors and another
- ☐ **Check if this claim is for a community debt**

Is the claim subject to offset?
- ☐ No
- ☐ Yes

Last 4 digits of account number ___ ___ ___ ___ $______ $______ $______

When was the debt incurred? ______

As of the date you file, the claim is: Check all that apply.
- ☐ Contingent
- ☐ Unliquidated
- ☐ Disputed

Type of PRIORITY unsecured claim:
- ☐ Domestic support obligations
- ☐ Taxes and certain other debts you owe the government
- ☐ Claims for death or personal injury while you were intoxicated
- ☐ Other. Specify ______

2.2 ______ Priority Creditor's Name
______ Number Street
______
______ City State ZIP Code

Who incurred the debt? Check one.
- ☐ Debtor 1 only
- ☐ Debtor 2 only
- ☐ Debtor 1 and Debtor 2 only
- ☐ At least one of the debtors and another
- ☐ **Check if this claim is for a community debt**

Is the claim subject to offset?
- ☐ No
- ☐ Yes

Last 4 digits of account number ___ ___ ___ ___ $______ $______ $______

When was the debt incurred? ______

As of the date you file, the claim is: Check all that apply.
- ☐ Contingent
- ☐ Unliquidated
- ☐ Disputed

Type of PRIORITY unsecured claim:
- ☐ Domestic support obligations
- ☐ Taxes and certain other debts you owe the government
- ☐ Claims for death or personal injury while you were intoxicated
- ☐ Other. Specify ______

NOTE TO READER:
Declaration sheet will be required for all amended schedules.

Debtor 1 Sidney Samuel Smith
First Name Middle Name Last Name

Case number (if known) 23BR10986-SBB

Part 2: Your NONPRIORITY Unsecured Claims — Continuation Page

After listing any entries on this page, number them beginning with 4.4, followed by 4.5, and so forth. **Total claim**

4.6

Glen's Garage
Nonpriority Creditor's Name
201 Side Street
Number Street
Columbus OH 43209
City State ZIP Code

Who incurred the debt? Check one.

- ☑ Debtor 1 only
- ☐ Debtor 2 only
- ☐ Debtor 1 and Debtor 2 only
- ☐ At least one of the debtors and another

☐ **Check if this claim is for a community debt**

Is the claim subject to offset?

- ☐ No
- ☐ Yes

Last 4 digits of account number n o n e

$ 697.00

When was the debt incurred? 02/13/2018

As of the date you file, the claim is: Check all that apply.

- ☐ Contingent
- ☐ Unliquidated
- ☐ Disputed

Type of **NONPRIORITY** unsecured claim:

- ☐ Student loans
- ☐ Obligations arising out of a separation agreement or divorce that you did not report as priority claims
- ☐ Debts to pension or profit-sharing plans, and other similar debts
- ☑ Other. Specify auto repair debt

4.7

XYZ Medical Supply
Nonpriority Creditor's Name
9777 Rolling Hills Drive
Number Street
Columbus OH 43229
City State ZIP Code

Who incurred the debt? Check one.

- ☐ Debtor 1 only
- ☑ Debtor 2 only
- ☐ Debtor 1 and Debtor 2 only
- ☐ At least one of the debtors and another

☐ **Check if this claim is for a community debt**

Is the claim subject to offset?

- ☐ No
- ☐ Yes

Last 4 digits of account number 2 4 5 1

$ 2,798.00

When was the debt incurred? 02/28/2018

As of the date you file, the claim is: Check all that apply.

- ☐ Contingent
- ☐ Unliquidated
- ☐ Disputed

Type of **NONPRIORITY** unsecured claim:

- ☐ Student loans
- ☐ Obligations arising out of a separation agreement or divorce that you did not report as priority claims
- ☐ Debts to pension or profit-sharing plans, and other similar debts
- ☑ Other. Specify medical services provided

☐

Nonpriority Creditor's Name
Number Street
City State ZIP Code

Who incurred the debt? Check one.

- ☐ Debtor 1 only
- ☐ Debtor 2 only
- ☐ Debtor 1 and Debtor 2 only
- ☐ At least one of the debtors and another

☐ **Check if this claim is for a community debt**

Is the claim subject to offset?

- ☐ No
- ☐ Yes

Last 4 digits of account number __ __ __ __

$________

When was the debt incurred? ________

As of the date you file, the claim is: Check all that apply.

- ☐ Contingent
- ☐ Unliquidated
- ☐ Disputed

Type of **NONPRIORITY** unsecured claim:

- ☐ Student loans
- ☐ Obligations arising out of a separation agreement or divorce that you did not report as priority claims
- ☐ Debts to pension or profit-sharing plans, and other similar debts
- ☐ Other. Specify________

Debtor 1 Sidney Samuel Smith
First Name Middle Name Last Name

Case number *(if known)* 23BR10986-SBB

Part 4: Add the Amounts for Each Type of Unsecured Claim

6. Total the amounts of certain types of unsecured claims. This information is for statistical reporting purposes only. 28 U.S.C. § 159. Add the amounts for each type of unsecured claim.

			Total claim
Total claims from Part 1	6a. **Domestic support obligations**	6a.	$ 0.00
	6b. **Taxes and certain other debts you owe the government**	6b.	$ 0.00
	6c. **Claims for death or personal injury while you were intoxicated**	6c.	$ 0.00
	6d. **Other.** Add all other priority unsecured claims. Write that amount here.	6d.	+ $ 0.00
	6e. **Total.** Add lines 6a through 6d.	6e.	$ 0.00

			Total claim
Total claims from Part 2	6f. **Student loans**	6f.	$ 12,890.00
	6g. **Obligations arising out of a separation agreement or divorce that you did not report as priority claims**	6g.	$ 0.00
	6h. **Debts to pension or profit-sharing plans, and other similar debts**	6h.	$ 0.00
	6i. **Other.** Add all other nonpriority unsecured claims. Write that amount here.	6i.	+ $ 26,919.00
	6j. **Total.** Add lines 6f through 6i.	6j.	$ 39,809.00

Print | Save As... | Add Attachment | Reset

Exhibit 2-Z(1) Reaffirmation Documents (Official Forms 427 and 2400A)

Fill in this information to identify your case:

Debtor 1 Sidney Samuel Smith
First Name Middle Name Last Name

Debtor 2 (Spouse, if filing) Sarah Arlene Smith
First Name Middle Name Last Name

United States Bankruptcy Court for the: Southern District of Ohio

Case number (If known) 23BR10986-SBB

Official Form 427

Cover Sheet for Reaffirmation Agreement

12/15

Anyone who is a party to a reaffirmation agreement may fill out and file this form. Fill it out completely, attach it to the reaffirmation agreement, and file the documents within the time set under Bankruptcy Rule 4008.

Part 1: Explain the Repayment Terms of the Reaffirmation Agreement

1. **Who is the creditor?**
MZ Dealership
Name of the creditor

2. **How much is the debt?**
On the date that the bankruptcy case is filed $ 13,290.00
To be paid under the reaffirmation agreement $ 13,290.00
$ 238.80 per month for 60 months (if fixed interest rate)

3. **What is the Annual Percentage Rate (APR) of interest? (See Bankruptcy Code § 524(k)(3)(E).)**
Before the bankruptcy case was filed 5.40 %
Under the reaffirmation agreement 3.00 % ☒ Fixed rate ☐ Adjustable rate

4. **Does collateral secure the debt?**
☐ No
☒ Yes. Describe the collateral. Ford F-150
Current market value $ 14,000.00

5. **Does the creditor assert that the debt is nondischargeable?**
☒ No
☐ Yes. Attach an explanation of the nature of the debt and the basis for contending that the debt is nondischargeable.

6. **Using information from *Schedule I: Your Income* (Official Form 106I) and *Schedule J: Your Expenses* (Official Form 106J), fill in the amounts.**

Income and expenses reported on Schedules I and J		Income and expenses stated on the reaffirmation agreement	
6a. Combined monthly income from line 12 of Schedule I	$ 4,377.00	6e. Monthly income from all sources after payroll deductions	$ 4,377.00
6b. Monthly expenses from line 22c of Schedule J	– $ 4,075.00	6f. Monthly expenses	– $ 3,575.00
6c. Monthly payments on all reaffirmed debts not listed on Schedule J	– $ 0.00	6g. Monthly payments on all reaffirmed debts not included in monthly expenses	– $ 0.00
6d. **Scheduled net monthly income** Subtract lines 6b and 6c from 6a. If the total is less than 0, put the number in brackets.	$ 302.00	6h. **Present net monthly income** Subtract lines 6f and 6g from 6e. If the total is less than 0, put the number in brackets.	$ 802.00

Debtor 1 Sidney Samuel Smith
First Name Middle Name Last Name

Case number (*if known*) 23BR10986-SBB

7. **Are the income amounts on lines 6a and 6e different?**	☑ No ☐ Yes.	Explain why they are different and complete line 10.
8. **Are the expense amounts on lines 6b and 6f different?**	☐ No ☑ Yes.	Explain why they are different and complete line 10. Debtors relinquished their cell phones and certain rented household furniture since filing of petition.
9. **Is the net monthly income in line 6h less than 0?**	☑ No ☐ Yes.	A presumption of hardship arises (unless the creditor is a credit union). Explain how the debtor will make monthly payments on the reaffirmed debt and pay other living expenses. Complete line 10.
10. **Debtor's certification about lines 7-9** If any answer on lines 7-9 is *Yes*, the debtor must sign here. If all the answers on lines 7-9 are *No*, go to line 11.		I certify that each explanation on lines 7-9 is true and correct. ✗ /s/ Sidney Samuel Smith Signature of Debtor 1 ✗ /s/ Sarah Arlene Smith Signature of Debtor 2 (Spouse Only in a Joint Case)
11. **Did an attorney represent the debtor in negotiating the reaffirmation agreement?**	☐ No ☑ Yes.	Has the attorney executed a declaration or an affidavit to support the reaffirmation agreement? ☐ No ☑ Yes

Part 2: Sign Here

Whoever fills out this form must sign here.

I certify that the attached agreement is a true and correct copy of the reaffirmation agreement between the parties identified on this *Cover Sheet for Reaffirmation Agreement.*

✗ /s/ Alice B. Chase
Signature

Date 02/01/2023
MM / DD / YYYY

Alice B. Chase
Printed Name

Check one:

☑ Debtor or Debtor's Attorney

☐ Creditor or Creditor's Attorney

Check one.
☐ **Presumption of Undue Hardship**
☒ **No Presumption of Undue Hardship**
See Debtor's Statement in Support of Reaffirmation, Part II below, to determine which box to check.

UNITED STATES BANKRUPTCY COURT

Southern District of Ohio

In re Sidney Samuel Smith,
Debtor

Case No. 24BR10986-SBB

Chapter 7

REAFFIRMATION DOCUMENTS

Name of Creditor: MZ Dealership

☐ Check this box if Creditor is a Credit Union

PART I. REAFFIRMATION AGREEMENT

Reaffirming a debt is a serious financial decision. Before entering into this Reaffirmation Agreement, you must review the important disclosures, instructions, and definitions found in Part V of this form.

A. Brief description of the original agreement being reaffirmed: auto loan
For example, auto loan

B. ***AMOUNT REAFFIRMED***: $ 13,290.00

The Amount Reaffirmed is the entire amount that you are agreeing to pay. This may include unpaid principal, interest, and fees and costs (if any) arising on or before 02/01/2024, which is the date of the Disclosure Statement portion of this form (Part V).

See the definition of "Amount Reaffirmed" in Part V, Section C below.

C. The ***ANNUAL PERCENTAGE RATE*** applicable to the Amount Reaffirmed is 3.0000 %.

See definition of "Annual Percentage Rate" in Part V, Section C below.

This is a *(check one)* ☒ Fixed rate ☐ Variable rate

If the loan has a variable rate, the future interest rate may increase or decrease from the Annual Percentage Rate disclosed here.

Form 2400A, Reaffirmation Documents Page 2

D. Reaffirmation Agreement Repayment Terms *(check and complete one)*:

☐ $ 238.80 per month for 60 months starting on 03/01/2023.

☐ Describe repayment terms, including whether future payment amount(s) may be different from the initial payment amount.

E. Describe the collateral, if any, securing the debt:

Description: Ford F-150
Current Market Value $ 14,000.00

F. Did the debt that is being reaffirmed arise from the purchase of the collateral described above?

☐ Yes. What was the purchase price for the collateral? $ 16,590.00

☐ No. What was the amount of the original loan? $______

G. Specify the changes made by this Reaffirmation Agreement to the most recent credit terms on the reaffirmed debt and any related agreement:

	Terms as of the Date of Bankruptcy	Terms After Reaffirmation
Balance due *(including fees and costs)*	$ 13,290.00	$ 13,290.00
Annual Percentage Rate	5.4000 %	3.0000 %
Monthly Payment	$ 329.00	$ 238.80

H.☐ Check this box if the creditor is agreeing to provide you with additional future credit in connection with this Reaffirmation Agreement. Describe the credit limit, the Annual Percentage Rate that applies to future credit and any other terms on future purchases and advances using such credit:

PART II. DEBTOR'S STATEMENT IN SUPPORT OF REAFFIRMATION AGREEMENT

A. Were you represented by an attorney during the course of negotiating this agreement?

Check one. ☐ Yes ☐ No

B. Is the creditor a credit union?

Check one. ☐ Yes ☐ No

C. If your answer to EITHER question A. or B. above is "No," complete 1. and 2. below.

1. Your present monthly income and expenses are:

a. Monthly income from all sources after payroll deductions (take-home pay plus any other income) $ 4,377.00

b. Monthly expenses (including all reaffirmed debts except this one) $ 3,575.00

c. Amount available to pay this reaffirmed debt (subtract b. from a.) $ 802.00

d. Amount of monthly payment required for this reaffirmed debt $ 238.80

If the monthly payment on this reaffirmed debt (line d.) ***is greater than*** *the amount you have available to pay this reaffirmed debt (line c.), you must check the box at the top of page one that says "Presumption of Undue Hardship." Otherwise, you must check the box at the top of page one that says "No Presumption of Undue Hardship."*

2. You believe that this reaffirmation agreement will not impose an undue hardship on you or your dependents because:

Check one of the two statements below, if applicable:

☐ You can afford to make the payments on the reaffirmed debt because your monthly income is greater than your monthly expenses even after you include in your expenses the monthly payments on all debts you are reaffirming, including this one.

☐ You can afford to make the payments on the reaffirmed debt even though your monthly income is less than your monthly expenses after you include in your expenses the monthly payments on all debts you are reaffirming, including this one, because:

Use an additional page if needed for a full explanation.

D. If your answers to BOTH questions A. and B. above were "Yes," check the following statement, if applicable:

☐ You believe this Reaffirmation Agreement is in your financial interest and you can afford to make the payments on the reaffirmed debt.

Also, check the box at the top of page one that says "No Presumption of Undue Hardship."

PART III. CERTIFICATION BY DEBTOR(S) AND SIGNATURES OF PARTIES

I hereby certify that:

(1) I agree to reaffirm the debt described above.

(2) Before signing this Reaffirmation Agreement, I read the terms disclosed in this Reaffirmation Agreement (Part I) and the Disclosure Statement, Instructions and Definitions included in Part V below;

(3) The Debtor's Statement in Support of Reaffirmation Agreement (Part II above) is true and complete;

(4) I am entering into this agreement voluntarily and am fully informed of my rights and responsibilities; and

(5) I have received a copy of this completed and signed Reaffirmation Documents form.

SIGNATURE(S) (If this is a joint Reaffirmation Agreement, both debtors must sign.):

Date 02/01/2024 Signature /s/ Sidney Samuel Smith
Debtor

Date 02/01/2024 Signature /s/ Sarah Arlene Smith
Joint Debtor, if any

Reaffirmation Agreement Terms Accepted by Creditor:

Creditor MZ Dealership — 4456 Main Street, Columbus, OH 43221
Print Name — *Address*

John R. Redstone — /s/ John R. Redstone — 02/01/2024
Print Name of Representative — *Signature* — *Date*

PART IV. CERTIFICATION BY DEBTOR'S ATTORNEY (IF ANY)

To be filed only if the attorney represented the debtor during the course of negotiating this agreement.

I hereby certify that: (1) this agreement represents a fully informed and voluntary agreement by the debtor; (2) this agreement does not impose an undue hardship on the debtor or any dependent of the debtor; and (3) I have fully advised the debtor of the legal effect and consequences of this agreement and any default under this agreement.

☐ A presumption of undue hardship has been established with respect to this agreement. In my opinion, however, the debtor is able to make the required payment.

Check box, if the presumption of undue hardship box is checked on page 1 and the creditor is not a Credit Union.

Date 02/01/2024 Signature of Debtor's Attorney /s/ Alice B. Chase

Print Name of Debtor's Attorney Alice B. Chase

PART V. DISCLOSURE STATEMENT AND INSTRUCTIONS TO DEBTOR(S)

Before agreeing to reaffirm a debt, review the terms disclosed in the Reaffirmation Agreement (Part I above) and these additional important disclosures and instructions.

Reaffirming a debt is a serious financial decision. The law requires you to take certain steps to make sure the decision is in your best interest. If these steps, which are detailed in the Instructions provided in Part V, Section B below, are not completed, the Reaffirmation Agreement is not effective, even though you have signed it.

A. DISCLOSURE STATEMENT

1. **What are your obligations if you reaffirm a debt?** A reaffirmed debt remains your personal legal obligation to pay. Your reaffirmed debt is not discharged in your bankruptcy case. That means that if you default on your reaffirmed debt after your bankruptcy case is over, your creditor may be able to take your property or your wages. Your obligations will be determined by the Reaffirmation Agreement, which may have changed the terms of the original agreement. If you are reaffirming an open end credit agreement, that agreement or applicable law may permit the creditor to change the terms of that agreement in the future under certain conditions.

2. **Are you required to enter into a reaffirmation agreement by any law?** No, you are not required to reaffirm a debt by any law. Only agree to reaffirm a debt if it is in your best interest. Be sure you can afford the payments that you agree to make.

3. **What if your creditor has a security interest or lien?** Your bankruptcy discharge does not eliminate any lien on your property. A ''lien'' is often referred to as a security interest, deed of trust, mortgage, or security deed. The property subject to a lien is often referred to as collateral. Even if you do not reaffirm and your personal liability on the debt is discharged, your creditor may still have a right under the lien to take the collateral if you do not pay or default on the debt. If the collateral is personal property that is exempt or that the trustee has abandoned, you may be able to redeem the item rather than reaffirm the debt. To redeem, you make a single payment to the creditor equal to the current value of the collateral, as the parties agree or the court determines.

4. **How soon do you need to enter into and file a reaffirmation agreement?** If you decide to enter into a reaffirmation agreement, you must do so before you receive your discharge. After you have entered into a reaffirmation agreement and all parts of this form that require a signature have been signed, either you or the creditor should file it as soon as possible. The signed agreement must be filed with the court no later than 60 days after the first date set for the meeting of creditors, so that the court will have time to schedule a hearing to approve the agreement if approval is required. However, the court may extend the time for filing, even after the 60-day period has ended.

5. **Can you cancel the agreement?** You may rescind (cancel) your Reaffirmation Agreement at any time before the bankruptcy court enters your discharge, or during the 60-day period that begins on the date your Reaffirmation Agreement is filed with the court, whichever occurs later. To rescind (cancel) your Reaffirmation Agreement, you must notify the creditor that your Reaffirmation Agreement is rescinded (or canceled). Remember that you can rescind the agreement, even if the court approves it, as long as you rescind within the time allowed.

6. **When will this Reaffirmation Agreement be effective?**

a. **If you *were* represented by an attorney during the negotiation of your Reaffirmation Agreement and**

i. **if the creditor is not a Credit Union**, your Reaffirmation Agreement becomes effective when it is filed with the court unless the reaffirmation is presumed to be an undue hardship. If the Reaffirmation Agreement is presumed to be an undue hardship, the court must review it and may set a hearing to determine whether you have rebutted the presumption of undue hardship.

ii. **if the creditor is a Credit Union**, your Reaffirmation Agreement becomes effective when it is filed with the court.

b. **If you *were not* represented by an attorney during the negotiation of your Reaffirmation Agreement**, the Reaffirmation Agreement will not be effective unless the court approves it. To have the court approve your agreement, you must file a motion. See Instruction 5, below. The court will notify you and the creditor of the hearing on your Reaffirmation Agreement. You must attend this hearing, at which time the judge will review your Reaffirmation Agreement. If the judge decides that the Reaffirmation Agreement is in your best interest, the agreement will be approved and will become effective. However, if your Reaffirmation Agreement is for a consumer debt secured by a mortgage, deed of trust, security deed, or other lien on your real property, like your home, you do not need to file a motion or get court approval of your Reaffirmation Agreement.

7. **What if you have questions about what a creditor can do?** If you have questions about reaffirming a debt or what the law requires, consult with the attorney who helped you negotiate this agreement. If you do not have an attorney helping you, you may ask the judge to explain the effect of this agreement to you at the hearing to approve the Reaffirmation Agreement. When this disclosure refers to what a creditor "may" do, it is not giving any creditor permission to do anything. The word "may" is used to tell you what might occur if the law permits the creditor to take the action.

B. INSTRUCTIONS

1. Review these Disclosures and carefully consider your decision to reaffirm. If you want to reaffirm, review and complete the information contained in the Reaffirmation Agreement (Part I above). If your case is a joint case, both spouses must sign the agreement if both are reaffirming the debt.

2. Complete the Debtor's Statement in Support of Reaffirmation Agreement (Part II above). Be sure that you can afford to make the payments that you are agreeing to make and that you have received a copy of the Disclosure Statement and a completed and signed Reaffirmation Agreement.

3. If you were represented by an attorney during the negotiation of your Reaffirmation Agreement, your attorney must sign and date the Certification By Debtor's Attorney (Part IV above).

4. You or your creditor must file with the court the original of this Reaffirmation Documents packet and a completed Reaffirmation Agreement Cover Sheet (Official Bankruptcy Form 427).

5. *If you are not represented by an attorney, you must also complete and file with the court a separate document entitled "Motion for Court Approval of Reaffirmation Agreement" unless your Reaffirmation Agreement is for a consumer debt secured by a lien on your real property, such as your home.* You can use Form 2400B to do this.

C. DEFINITIONS

1. **"Amount Reaffirmed"** means the total amount of debt that you are agreeing to pay (reaffirm) by entering into this agreement. The total amount of debt includes any unpaid fees and costs that you are agreeing to pay that arose on or before the date of disclosure, which is the date specified in the Reaffirmation Agreement (Part I, Section B above). Your credit agreement may obligate you to pay additional amounts that arise after the date of this disclosure. You should consult your credit agreement to determine whether you are obligated to pay additional amounts that may arise after the date of this disclosure.

2. **"Annual Percentage Rate"** means the interest rate on a loan expressed under the rules required by federal law. The annual percentage rate (as opposed to the "stated interest rate") tells you the full cost of your credit including many of the creditor's fees and charges. You will find the annual percentage rate for your original agreement on the disclosure statement that was given to you when the loan papers were signed or on the monthly statements sent to you for an open end credit account such as a credit card.

3. **"Credit Union"** means a financial institution as defined in 12 U.S.C. § 461(b)(1)(A)(iv). It is owned and controlled by and provides financial services to its members and typically uses words like "Credit Union" or initials like "C.U." or "F.C.U." in its name.

Exhibit 2-Z(2) Certification About Financial Management Course (Official Form 423)

Fill in this information to identify the case:	
Debtor 1	Sidney Samuel Smith (First Name / Middle Name / Last Name)
Debtor 2 (Spouse, if filing)	Sarah Arlene Smith (First Name / Middle Name / Last Name)
United States Bankruptcy Court for the:	Southern District of Ohio
Case number (If known)	23BR10986-SBB

* Note that one form is required per debtor.

Official Form 423

Certification About a Financial Management Course

12/15

If you are an individual, you must take an approved course about personal financial management if:

- **you filed for bankruptcy under chapter 7 or 13, or**
- **you filed for bankruptcy under chapter 11 and § 1141 (d)(3) does not apply.**

In a joint case, each debtor must take the course. 11 U.S.C. §§ 727(a)(11) and 1328(g).

After you finish the course, the provider will give you a certificate. The provider may notify the court that you have completed the course. If the provider does notify the court, you need not file this form. If the provider does not notify the court, then Debtor 1 and Debtor 2 must each file this form with the certificate number before your debts will be discharged.

- If you filed under chapter 7 and you need to file this form, file it within 60 days after the first date set for the meeting of creditors under § 341 of the Bankruptcy Code.
- If you filed under chapter 11 or 13 and you need to file this form, file it before you make the last payment that your plan requires or before you file a motion for a discharge under § 1141(d)(5)(B) or § 1328(b) of the Bankruptcy Code. Fed. R. Bankr. P. 1007(c).

In some cases, the court can waive the requirement to take the financial management course. To have the requirement waived, you must file a motion with the court and obtain a court order.

Part 1: Tell the Court About the Required Course

You must check one:

☐ **I completed an approved course in personal financial management:**

Date I took the course: 12/15/2023 (MM / DD / YYYY)

Name of approved provider: Ace Financial Managers

Certificate number: A45328

☐ **I am not required to complete a course in personal financial management because the court has granted my motion for a waiver of the requirement based on** *(check one)*:

- ☐ **Incapacity.** I have a mental illness or a mental deficiency that makes me incapable of realizing or making rational decisions about finances.
- ☐ **Disability.** My physical disability causes me to be unable to complete a course in personal financial management in person, by phone, or through the internet, even after I reasonably tried to do so.
- ☐ **Active duty.** I am currently on active military duty in a military combat zone.
- ☐ **Residence.** I live in a district in which the United States trustee (or bankruptcy administrator) has determined that the approved instructional courses cannot adequately meet my needs.

Part 2: Sign Here

I certify that the information I have provided is true and correct.

/s/ Sidney Samuel Smith	Sidney Samuel Smith	Date 01/15/2024
Signature of debtor named on certificate	Printed name of debtor	MM / DD / YYYY

EXHIBIT 2-Z(3) STATEMENT OF MILITARY SERVICE (DIRECTOR'S FORM 2020)

B2020 (Form 2020) (12/15)

United States Bankruptcy Court
____________________ District of ____________________

In re ________________________

Case Number ______________________
Chapter ______________________

STATEMENT OF MILITARY SERVICE

The Servicemembers' Civil Relief Act of 2003, Pub. L. No. 108-189, provides for the temporary suspension of certain judicial proceedings or transactions that may adversely affect military servicemembers, their dependents, and others. Each party to a bankruptcy case who might be eligible for relief under the act should complete this form and file it with the Bankruptcy Court.

IDENTIFICATION OF SERVICEMEMBER

❑ Self (Debtor, Codebtor, Creditor, Other)
❑ Non-Filing Spouse of Debtor (name)________________________
❑ Other (Name of servicemember)________________________
(Relationship of filer to servicemember)____________________
(Type of liability) ________________________

TYPE OF MILITARY SERVICE

U.S. Armed Forces (Army, Navy, Air Force, Marine Corps, or Coast Guard) or commissioned officer of the Public Health Service or the National Oceanic and Atmospheric Administration (specify type of service) ________________________

❑ Active Service since ____________________(date)
❑ Inductee - ordered to report on ____________________(date)
❑ Retired / Discharged ____________________(date)

U.S. Military Reserves and National Guard

❑ Active Service since ____________________(date)
❑ Impending Active Service -orders postmarked ____________________(date)
Ordered to report on ____________________(date)
❑ Retired /Discharged ____________________(date)

U.S. Citizen Serving with U.S. ally in war or military action (specify ally and war or action)

____

❑ Active Service since ____________________(date)
❑ Retired/Discharged ____________________(date)

DEPLOYMENT

❑ Servicemember deployed overseas on ____________________(date)
Anticipated completion of overseas tour-of-duty ____________________(date)

SIGNATURE

________________________ ____________________
Date

____
(print name)

This statement is for information use only. Filing this statement with the Bankruptcy Court does not constitute an application for or invoke the benefits and relief available under the Servicemembers' Civil Relief Act of 2003.

CHAPTER THREE
Adjustment of Debts Under Chapter 13

PART A - QUESTIONS AND ANSWERS ABOUT CHAPTER 13 CASES

1. What is a chapter 13 bankruptcy case and how does it work?

A chapter 13 bankruptcy case is a proceeding under federal law in which the debtor seeks relief under chapter 13 of the Bankruptcy Code. Chapter 13 is the chapter of the Bankruptcy Code which allows a person to repay all or a portion of his or her debts under the supervision and protection of the bankruptcy court. The Bankruptcy Code is the federal law that deals with bankruptcy. A person who files a chapter 13 case is called a debtor. In a chapter 13 case, the debtor must submit to the court a plan for the repayment of all or a portion of his or her debts. The plan must be approved by the court to become effective. If the court approves the debtor's plan, most creditors will be prohibited from collecting their claims from the debtor. The debtor must make regular payments to a person called the chapter 13 trustee, who collects the money paid by the debtor and disburses it to creditors in the manner called for in the plan. Upon completion of the payments called for in the plan, the debtor is released from liability for the remainder of his or her dischargeable debts.

2. How does a chapter 13 case differ from a chapter 7 case?

The basic difference between a chapter 7 case and a chapter 13 case is that in a chapter 7 case the debtor's nonexempt property (if any exists) is liquidated to pay as much as possible of the debtor's debts, while in chapter 13 cases a portion of the debtor's future income is used to pay as much of the debtor's debts as is feasible under the debtor's circumstances. As a practical matter, in a chapter 7 case the debtor loses all or most of his or her nonexempt property and receives a chapter 7 discharge, which releases the debtor from liability for most debts. In a chapter 13 case, the debtor usually retains his or her nonexempt property, but must pay off as much of his or her debts as the court deems feasible and receives a chapter 13 discharge, which is slightly broader than a chapter 7 discharge and releases the debtor from liability for a few types of debts that are not dischargeable under chapter 7. However, a chapter 13 case normally lasts much longer than a chapter 7 case and is usually more expensive for the debtor.

3. When is a chapter 13 case preferable to a chapter 7 case?

Chapter 13 is usually preferable for a person who - (1) wishes to repay all or most of his or her unsecured debts and has the income with which to do so within a reasonable time, (2) has valuable nonexempt property or has valuable exempt property securing debts, either of which would be lost in a chapter 7 case, (3) is not eligible under means testing to maintain a chapter 7 case, (4) is not eligible for a chapter 7 discharge, (5) has one or more substantial debts that are dischargeable under chapter 13 but not under chapter 7, or (6) has sufficient assets with which to repay most of his or her debts, but needs temporary relief from creditors in order to do so.

4. How does a chapter 13 case differ from a private debt consolidation service?

In a chapter 13 case, the bankruptcy court can provide relief to the debtor that a private debt consolidation service cannot provide. For example, the court has the authority to prohibit creditors from attaching or foreclosing on the debtor's property, to force unsecured creditors to accept a chapter 13 plan that pays only a portion of their claims, and to discharge a debtor from unpaid portions of debts. Private debt consolidation services have none of these powers.

5. What is a chapter 13 discharge?

It is a court order releasing a debtor from all of his or her dischargeable debts and ordering creditors not to collect them from the debtor. A debt that is discharged is one that the debtor is released from and does not have to pay. There are two types of chapter 13 discharges: (1) a full or successful plan discharge, which is granted to a debtor who completes all payments called for in the plan, and (2) a partial or unsuccessful plan discharge, which is granted to a debtor who is unable to complete the payments called for in the plan due to circumstances for which the debtor should not be held accountable. A full chapter 13 discharge discharges a few more debts than a chapter 7 discharge, while a partial chapter 13 discharge is similar to a chapter 7 discharge.

6. What types of debts are not dischargeable in chapter 13 cases?

A full chapter 13 discharge granted upon the completion of all payments required in the plan discharges a debtor from all debts except:

(1) debts that were paid outside of the plan and not covered in the plan,

(2) debts for domestic support obligations, which includes debts for child support and alimony,

(3) debts for death or personal injury caused by the debtor's operation of a motor vehicle, vessel or aircraft while intoxicated,

(4) most tax debts,

(5) debts for restitution or criminal fines included in a sentence imposed on the debtor for conviction of a crime,

(6) debts for fraud, embezzlement or larceny,

(7) debts for student loans or educational obligations unless a court rules that not discharging the debt would impose an undue hardship on the debtor and his or her dependents,

(8) debts for damages caused by willful or malicious conduct by the debtor,

(9) installment debts whose last payment is due after the completion of the plan,

(10) debts incurred while the plan was in effect that were not paid under the plan,

(11) debts owed to creditors who did not receive notice of the chapter 13 case, and

(12) long-term debts upon which payments were made under the plan.

A partial chapter 13 discharge, which is granted when a debtor is unable to complete the payments under a plan due to circumstances for which he or she should not be held accountable, discharges the debtor from all debts except:

(1) secured debts (i.e., debts secured by mortgages or liens),

(2) debts that were paid outside of the plan and not covered in the plan,

(3) installment debts whose last payment is due after the completion of the plan,

(4) debts incurred while the plan was in effect that were not paid under the plan,

(5) debts owed to creditors who did not receive notice of the chapter 13 case,

(6) debts that are not dischargeable in a chapter 7 case, and

(7) long-term debts upon which payments were made under the plan.

7. What is a chapter 13 plan?

It is a written plan presented to the bankruptcy court by a debtor that states how much money or property the debtor will pay to the chapter 13 trustee, how long the debtor's payments to the chapter 13 trustee will continue, how much will be paid to each of the debtor's creditors, and certain other matters.

8. What is a chapter 13 trustee?

A chapter 13 trustee is a person appointed by the United States trustee to collect payments from the debtor, make payments to creditors in the manner set forth in the debtor's plan, and administer the debtor's chapter 13 case until it is closed. In some cases the chapter 13 trustee is required to perform certain other duties. The debtor is required to cooperate with the chapter 13 trustee.

9. What debts may be paid under a chapter 13 plan?

Any debts whatsoever, whether they are secured or unsecured. Even debts that are nondischargeable, such as debts for student loans or child support, may be paid under a chapter 13 plan.

10. Must all debts be paid in full under a chapter 13 plan?

No. While priority debts, such as debts for domestic support obligations and taxes, and fully secured debts must be paid in full under a chapter 13 plan, only an amount that the debtor can reasonably afford must be paid on most debts. The unpaid balances of most debts that are not paid in full under a chapter 13 plan are discharged upon the completion or termination of the plan.

11. Must all unsecured debts be treated alike under a chapter 13 plan?

No. If there is a reasonable basis for doing so, unsecured debts (or claims) may be divided into separate classes and treated differently. It may be possible, therefore, to pay certain unsecured debts in full, while paying significantly less on others.

12. Is there a difference between a debt and a claim?

No, not in a practical sense. They are different terms for an obligation owed by the debtor to a creditor. A claim is the right of a creditor to the payment of an obligation by the debtor. A debt is a liability of a debtor on an obligation to a creditor. For example, if the debtor owes $1,000 to the bank, the $1,000 obligation is viewed as a debt by the debtor and as a claim by the bank.

13. How much of a debtor's income must be paid to the chapter 13 trustee under a chapter 13 plan?

Usually all of the disposable income of the debtor and the debtor's spouse for a 3 or 5 year period must be paid to the chapter 13 trustee. Disposable income is income received by the debtor and his or her spouse that is not deemed to be necessary for the support of the debtor and his or her dependents.

14. When must the debtor begin making payments to the chapter 13 trustee and how are the payments made?

The debtor must begin making payments to the chapter 13 trustee within 30 days after the chapter 13 case is filed with the court. The payments must be made regularly, usually on a weekly, bi-weekly, or monthly basis. If the debtor is employed, some courts require that the payments to be made directly to the chapter 13 trustee by the debtor's employer.

15. How long does a chapter 13 plan last?

The required length of a chapter 13 plan depends on the debtor's income. If the debtor's annual income is less than the median family income for the debtor's state and family size, the length of the plan must be 3 years, unless the debtor can justify a longer period, which may not exceed 5 years. If the debtor's annual income exceeds the median family income, the length of the plan must be 5 years unless all unsecured claims can be paid off in a shorter period. The debtor's annual income is his or her current monthly income multiplied by 12.

16. Is it necessary for all creditors to approve a chapter 13 plan?

No. To become effective, a chapter 13 plan must be approved by the court, not by the creditors. The court, however, cannot approve a plan unless each secured creditor is dealt with in the manner described in the answer to Question 18 below. Also, unsecured creditors are permitted to file objections to the debtor's plan, and these objections must be ruled on by the court before it can approve the debtor's chapter 13 plan.

17. What is the difference between a secured creditor and an unsecured creditor?

A secured creditor is a creditor whose claim against the debtor is secured by a valid mortgage, lien, or other security interest against property that is owned by the debtor. An unsecured creditor is a creditor whose claim against the debtor is not secured by a valid mortgage, lien or security interest against the debtor's property. In other words, a secured creditor has collateral for its claim and an unsecured creditor does not. The basic difference is that a secured creditor may collect all or a portion of its claim from its collateral, while an unsecured creditor may not. It is common for the amount of a secured creditor's claim to exceed the value of its collateral. This type of creditor is called a partially-secured (or undersecured) creditor. In chapter 13 cases the claims of most partially-secured creditors are divided into secured and unsecured portions. For example, a partially-secured creditor with a $2,000 claim against the debtor that is secured by collateral that is worth $1,500 has a $1,500 secured claim and a $500 unsecured claim. The only types of partially-secured creditors whose claim may not be treated in this manner are creditors secured by a mortgage on the debtor's home and certain creditors who advanced funds for the purchase of automobile or other personal property of the debtor. It is important to differentiate between secured and unsecured claims because they are treated quite differently in chapter 13 cases. Secured claims must be paid in full with interest, while only amounts that the debtor can reasonably afford need be paid to the holders of unsecured claims (except priority claims – see Question 36, infra).

18. How are the claims of secured creditors dealt with in chapter 13 cases?

There are four methods of dealing with secured claims in chapter 13 cases: (1) the creditor may accept the debtor's plan, (2) the creditor may retain its lien and be paid the full amount of its secured claim in equal monthly payments under the plan, (3) the debtor may surrender the collateral to the creditor, or (4) the creditor may be paid or dealt with outside the plan. It is important to understand that most partially-secured creditors have a secured claim only to the extent of the value of their collateral. If the debtor is in default to a secured creditor, the default must be cured (made current) within a reasonable time.

19. How are cosigned or guaranteed debts handled in chapter 13 cases?

A cosigned or guaranteed debt is a debt of the debtor that has been cosigned or guaranteed by another person. If a cosigned or guaranteed consumer debt is being paid in full under a chapter 13 plan, the creditor may not collect the debt from the cosigner or guarantor. However, if a consumer debt is not being paid in full under the plan, the creditor may collect the unpaid portion of the debt from the cosigner or guarantor. A consumer debt is a nonbusiness debt. Creditors may collect business debts from cosigners or guarantors even if the debts are to be paid in full under the debtor's plan.

20. Who is eligible to file a chapter 13 case?

Any individual (i.e., natural person) is eligible to file a chapter 13 case if he or she - (1) resides in, does business in, or owns property in the United States, (2) has regular income, (3) has unsecured debts of less than $419,275*, (4) has secured debts of less than $1,257,850*, (5) is not a stockbroker or a commodity broker, (6) has not intentionally dismissed another bankruptcy case within the last 180 days, and (7) has received a briefing from an approved credit counseling agency within the last 180 days (unless this requirement is not in effect in the local bankruptcy court). Corporations, partnerships, limited liability companies, and other business entities are not eligible to file a chapter 13 case.

* Subject to adjustment on April 1, 2022.

21. May a husband and wife file a joint chapter 13 case?

A husband and wife may file a joint chapter 13 case if each of them meets the requirements listed in the answer to Question 20 above, except that only one of them need have regular income and their combined debts must meet the debt limitations described in the answer to Question 20 above.

22. When should a husband and wife file a joint chapter 13 case?

If both spouses are liable for any significant debts, they should file a joint chapter 13 case, even if only one of them has income. Also, if both of them have regular income, they should file a joint case.

23. May a self-employed person file a chapter 13 case?

Yes. A self-employed person meeting the eligibility requirements listed in the answer to Question 20 above may file a chapter 13 case. A debtor engaged in business may continue to operate the business during his or her chapter 13 case.

24. May a chapter 7 case be converted to a chapter 13 case?

Yes. An existing chapter 7 case may be converted to a chapter 13 case at any time at the request of the debtor if the case has not previously been converted from chapter 13 to chapter 7.

25. Where is a chapter 13 case filed?

A chapter 13 case is filed in the office of the clerk of the bankruptcy court in the district where the debtor has lived or maintained a principal place of business for the greatest portion of the last 180 days. The bankruptcy court is a federal court and is a unit of the United States district court.

26. What fees are charged in a chapter 13 case?

There is a $318 fee charged when the case is filed, which may be paid in installments if necessary. In addition, the chapter 13 trustee assesses a fee of up to 10 percent on all payments made by the debtor under the plan (up to a certain cap based on a variety of factors). Thus, if a debtor pays a total of $5,000 under a chapter 13 plan, the total amount of fees charged in the case will be up to $810 (up to a $500 trustee's fee, plus the $318 filing fee). These fees are in addition to the fee charged by the debtor's attorney.

27. Will a person lose any property if he or she files a chapter 13 case?

Usually not. In a chapter 13 case, creditors are usually paid out of the debtor's income and not from the debtor's property. However, if a debtor has valuable nonexempt property and has insufficient income to pay enough to creditors to satisfy the court, some of the debtor's property may have to be used to pay creditors.

28. How does the filing of a chapter 13 case affect collection proceedings and foreclosures that are filed against the debtor?

The filing of a chapter 13 case automatically stays (stops) all lawsuits, attachments, garnishments, foreclosures, and other actions by creditors against the debtor or the debtor's property. This stay is called the automatic stay. A few days after the case is filed, the court will mail a notice to all creditors advising them of the automatic stay. Certain creditors may be notified sooner, if necessary. Most creditors are prohibited from proceeding against the debtor during the entire course of the chapter 13 case. If the debtor is later granted a chapter 13 discharge, the creditors will then be prohibited from collecting the discharged debts from the debtor after the case is closed. If the debtor has had a prior bankruptcy case dismissed within the past year, he or she may be denied the protection of the automatic stay.

29. May a person whose debts are being administered by a financial counselor file a chapter 13 case?

Yes. A financial counselor has no legal authority to prevent a person from filing any type of bankruptcy case, including a chapter 13 case.

30. How does filing a chapter 13 case affect a person's credit rating?

It may worsen it, at least temporarily. However, if most of a person's debts are ultimately paid off under a chapter 13 plan, that fact may be taken into account by credit reporting agencies. If very little is paid on most debts, the effect of a chapter 13 case on a person's credit rating may be similar to that of a chapter 7 case.

31. Are the names of persons who file chapter 13 cases published?

When a chapter 13 case is filed, it becomes a public record and the name of the debtor may be published by some credit reporting agencies. However, newspapers do not usually publish the names of persons who file chapter 13 cases.

32. Is a person's employer notified when he or she files a chapter 13 cas

In most cases, yes. Many courts require a debtor's employer to make payments to the chapter 13 trustee on the debtor's behalf. Also, the chapter 13 trustee may contact an employer to verify the debtor's income. However, if there are compelling reasons for not informing an employer in a particular case, it may be possible to make other arrangements for the required information and payments.

33. Does a person lose any legal rights by filing a chapter 13 case?

No. A chapter 13 case is a civil proceeding and not a criminal proceeding. Therefore, a person does not lose any legal or constitutional rights by filing a chapter 13 case.

34. May employers or government agencies discriminate against persons who file chapter 13 cases?

No. It is illegal for either private or governmental employers to discriminate against a person as to employment because that person has filed a chapter 13 case. It is also illegal for local, state, or federal governmental agencies to discriminate against a person as to the granting of licenses, permits, student loans, and similar grants because that person has filed a chapter 13 case.

35. What is required for court approval of a chapter 13 plan?

The court will approve and confirm a chapter 13 plan if it finds that: (1) all required fees, charges and deposits have been paid, (2) all priority claims will be paid in full under the plan, (3) if the plan creates different classes of claims, it provides the same treatment for each claim within a particular class, (4) the plan was proposed in good faith, (5) each unsecured creditor will receive under the plan at least as much as it would have received had the debtor filed a chapter 7 case, (6) the debtor will be able to make the required payments and comply with the plan, and (7) each secured creditor is dealt with in one of the four methods described in the answer to Question 18 above.

36. What is a priority claim?

A priority claim is an unsecured claim that is given priority of payment under the Bankruptcy Code. It is a claim that must be paid before other unsecured claims are paid. Examples of priority claims are tax claims, wage claims, and claims for alimony, maintenance or support. Claims for administrative fees, such as the chapter 13 trustee's fee, the filing fee, and the fee of the debtor's attorney, are also priority claims in chapter 13 cases.

37. When does the debtor have to appear in court in a chapter 13 case?

Most debtors have to appear in court at least twice: once for a hearing called the meeting of creditors, and once for a hearing on the confirmation of the debtor's chapter 13 plan. The meeting of creditors is usually held about a month after the case is filed. The confirmation hearing may be held on the same day as the meeting of creditors or at a later date, depending on the scheduling practices in the local court. If difficulties or unusual circumstances arise during the course of a case, additional court appearances may be necessary.

38. What if the court does not approve a debtor's chapter 13 plan?

If the court will not approve the plan initially proposed by a debtor, the debtor may modify the plan and seek court approval of the modified plan. If the court does not approve a plan, it will usually give its reasons for refusing to do so, and the plan may then be appropriately modified so as become acceptable to the court. A debtor who does not wish to modify a proposed plan may either convert the case to a chapter 7 case or dismiss the case.

39. How are the claims of unsecured creditors handled in chapter 13 cases?

Unsecured creditors, including those with priority claims, must file their claims with the bankruptcy court within 70 days after the first date set for the meeting of creditors in order for their claims to be allowed. Unsecured creditors who fail to file claims within that period are barred from doing so, and upon completion of the plan their claims will be discharged. The debtor may file a claim on behalf of a creditor, if desired. After the claims have been filed, the debtor may file objections to any claims that he or she disputes. When the claims have been approved by the court, the chapter 13 trustee begins paying unsecured creditors in the manner and in the amounts provided for in the debtor's chapter 13 plan. Payments to secured creditors, priority creditors, and special classes of unsecured creditors may begin earlier, if desired.

40. What if the debtor is temporarily unable to make the chapter 13 payments?

If the debtor is temporarily out of work, injured, or otherwise unable to make the payments required under a chapter 13 plan, the plan can usually be modified so as to enable the debtor to resume the payments when he or she is able to do so. If it appears that the debtor's inability to make the required payments will continue indefinitely or for an extended period, the case may be dismissed or converted to a chapter 7 case.

41. What if the debtor incurs new debts or needs credit during a chapter 13 case?

Only two types of credit obligations or debts incurred after the filing of the case may be included in a chapter 13 plan. These are: (1) debts for taxes that become payable while the case is pending, and (2) consumer debts arising after the filing of the case that are for property or services necessary for the debtor's performance under the plan and that are approved in advance by the chapter 13 trustee. All other debts or credit obligations incurred after the case is filed must be paid by the debtor outside the plan. Some courts issue an order prohibiting the debtor from incurring new debts during the case unless they are approved in advance by the chapter 13 trustee. Therefore, the approval of the chapter 13 trustee should be obtained before incurring credit or new debts after the case has been filed. The incurrence of regular debts, such as debts for telephone service or utilities, do not require the trustee's approval.

42. What should the debtor do if he or she moves while the case is pending?

The debtor should immediately notify the bankruptcy court and the chapter 13 trustee in writing of the new address. Most communications in a chapter 13 case are by mail, and if the debtor fails to receive an order of the court or a notice from the chapter 13 trustee because of an incorrect address, the case may be dismissed. Many courts have change-of-address forms that may be used if the debtor moves.

43. What if the debtor later decides to discontinue the chapter 13 case?

The debtor has the right to either dismiss a chapter 13 case or convert it to a chapter 7 case at any time for any reason. However, if the debtor simply stops making the required chapter 13 payments, the court may compel the debtor or the debtor's employer to make the payments and to comply with the orders of the court. Therefore, a debtor who wishes to discontinue a chapter 13 case should do so through his or her attorney.

44. What happens if a debtor is unable to complete the chapter 13 payments?

A debtor who is unable to complete the chapter 13 payments has three options: (1) dismiss the chapter 13 case, (2) convert the chapter 13 case to a chapter 7 case, or (3) if the debtor is unable to complete the payments due to circumstances for which he or she should not be held accountable, close the case and obtain a partial chapter 13 discharge as described in the answer to Question 6 above.

45. What is the role of the debtor's attorney in a chapter 13 case?

The debtor's attorney performs the following functions in a typical chapter 13 case:

(1) Examining the debtor's financial situation and determining whether a chapter 13 case is a feasible alternative for the debtor, and if so, whether a single or a joint case should be filed.

(2) Assist the debtor in obtaining the required prebankruptcy briefing on budget and credit counseling.

(3) Assisting the debtor in the preparation of a budget.

(4) Examining the liens or security interests of secured creditors to ascertain their validity or avoidability, and taking the legal steps necessary to protect the debtor's interest in such matters.

(5) Devising and implementing methods of dealing with secured creditors.

(6) Assisting the debtor in devising a chapter 13 plan that meets the needs of the debtor and is acceptable to the court.

(7) Preparing the necessary pleadings and chapter 13 forms.

(8) Filing the chapter 13 forms and pleadings with the court.

(9) Attending the meeting of creditors, the confirmation hearing, and any other court hearings required in the case.

(10) Assisting the debtor in obtaining court approval of a chapter 13 plan.

(11) Checking the claims filed in the case, filing objections to improper claims, and attending court hearings thereon.

(12) Assisting the debtor in overcoming any legal obstacles that may arise during the course of the case.

(13) Assisting the debtor in attending and completing the required instructional course on personal financial management.

(14) Assisting the debtor in obtaining a discharge upon the completion or termination of the plan.

The fee charged by an attorney for representing a debtor in a chapter 13 case must be reviewed and approved by the bankruptcy court. This rule is followed whether the fee is paid to the attorney prior to or after the filing of the case, and whether it is paid to the attorney directly by the debtor or by the chapter 13 trustee. The court will not approve a fee unless it finds the fee to be reasonable.

CHAPTER THREE

Part B - Preparing a Chapter 13 Case

3.01 Chapter 13 - A General Description

A chapter 13 case is initiated by the filing of a petition seeking relief under chapter 13 of the Bankruptcy Code with the clerk of the bankruptcy court in the proper district. The debtor must also file schedules and statements that contain the names and addresses of all creditors, a list of the debtor's assets and liabilities, and other financial information about the debtor. Unless the requirement is not in effect in the local district, the debtor must also file with the petition a certificate from an approved credit counseling agency stating, among other things, that the debtor has received credit counseling within the last 180 days. If a debt repayment plan was created for the debtor, a copy of the plan must also be filed with the petition. In addition, the debtor must file copies of records showing all payments received from his or her employer during the 60 day period prior to the filing of the bankruptcy case, records showing any interest that the debtor has in educational IRAs or qualified state tuition programs, a statement of current monthly income and disposable income calculation, and copies of the debtor's most recent federal income tax returns. In addition, a debtor must, within 14 days after the petition is filed, file a plan for the adjustment or repayment of his or her debts over a three-to-five year period. The debtor must usually apply all of his or her disposable income for the period of the plan toward the making of payments under the plan and must start making payments within 30 days after the case is filed in the amount called for in the plan. During the pendency of the case, most creditor actions against the debtor and the debtor's property are stayed.

chapter 13 case, general aspects

Unsecured creditors may file objections to the debtor's plan, but they must accept the plan if it is approved by the court. A secured creditor, however, cannot be forced to accept a chapter 13 plan unless its secured claim is to be paid in full under the plan or its collateral is surrendered. A secured creditor may be paid outside the plan if desired. Unsecured creditors may be paid all or a portion of their claims under the plan, but each unsecured creditor must receive at least as much as it would have received had the debtor filed a chapter 7 case. All creditors are notified of the filing of the case, and unsecured creditors must file their claims within 70 days after the first date set for the meeting of creditors or their claims will be barred.

creditors in chapter 13 cases, general aspects

If the court finds that a debtor's proposed plan satisfies the legal requirements as to the payment of both secured and unsecured creditors, that the plan has been proposed in good faith, that the debtor will be able to comply with the plan, and that all required fees and charges have been paid or provided for, it may confirm the plan, at which time the plan becomes effective. The debtor, must appear in court for the meeting of creditors and the confirmation hearing. The debtor must also complete an instructional course on personal financial management. The chapter 13 trustee collects the debtor's payments and pays the allowed fees and the creditors as provided in the plan.

chapter 13 plan, general aspects

Upon the successful completion of a chapter 13 plan, the debtor is granted a full chapter 13 discharge, which is slightly broader than a chapter 7 discharge. A debtor who is unable to complete the payments called for in the plan due to circumstances for which the debtor should not justly be held accountable, may be granted a partial chapter 13 discharge, which is similar to a chapter 7 discharge. Otherwise, an unsuccessful chapter 13 case may be either dismissed or converted to chapter 7.

chapter 13 discharge, general aspects

It should be noted that a bankruptcy court is a unit of the federal district court, and that limitations are imposed on the type and nature of proceedings and cases that a bankruptcy judge may hear. See section 2.01, supra, for a discussion of core vs. non-core proceedings. Generally, however, all proceedings arising in a chapter 13 case are core proceedings and may be heard and ruled upon by the bankruptcy judge.

bankruptcy court, general aspects

3.02 The Local Bankruptcy Rules and Forms

local rules, requirements and functions of

Bankruptcy Rule 9029(a) permits a local district to adopt rules governing the practice and procedure in bankruptcy cases, provided that such rules are consistent with the Bankruptcy Code and the Rules of Bankruptcy Procedure and do not prohibit or limit the use of the Official Forms. The Rules of Bankruptcy Procedure leave many administrative and procedural aspects of chapter 13 cases to the discretion of the local districts, and most districts have adopted local rules governing certain aspects of bankruptcy practice and procedure. Some districts have only limited local rules, and few, if any, local forms. Other districts have adopted extensive local rules and forms dealing with many aspects of chapter 13 cases, including the initial filing requirements. Many bankruptcy courts have adopted local rules or general orders dealing with electronic case management and the electronic filing of cases and documents. It is important to obtain a copy of the local rules prior to the commencement of a chapter 13 case. The clerk's office will usually provide copies of the local rules and forms upon request or they may be available on line from the local bankruptcy court's website.

procedure when there is no controlling law or rule

It should be noted here that if a particular matter is not governed by the Bankruptcy Code, the Rules of Bankruptcy Procedure, or the local rules of the district, a bankruptcy judge may regulate the matter in any manner consistent with federal law, the Rules of Bankruptcy Procedure, the Official Forms and the local rules of the district. However, no sanction or other disadvantage may be imposed for noncompliance with any such judge-imposed requirement unless the alleged violator has been furnished in the particular case with actual notice of the requirement. See Bankruptcy Rule 9029(b).

3.03 The Duties and Liabilities of the Debtor's Attorney

debt relief agency, debtor's attorney as

The Bankruptcy Reform Act of 2005 created an entity known as a "debt relief agency," which is defined as any person who provides bankruptcy assistance to an assisted person in return for the payment of money or other valuable consideration. See 11 U.S.C. § § 101(12A). An "assisted person" is defined as any person whose debts consist primarily of consumer debts and whose nonexempt property is valued at less than $226,850*. See 11 U.S.C. § 101(3). An attorney who represents a consumer debtor in a chapter 13 case qualifies as a debt relief agency. Therefore the debtor's attorney will have to comply with the restrictions, disclosures and requirements imposed on debt relief agencies by the Bankruptcy Code. See 11 U.S.C. § 526, 527, 528. These restrictions, requirements and disclosures are discussed in section 2.03, supra.

* Subject to adjustment on April 1, 2025

attorney's fee, allowance of by court

11 U.S.C. § 330(a)(4)(B) provides that in a chapter 13 case the court may allow reasonable compensation to the debtor's attorney for representing the interests of the debtor in connection with the bankruptcy case based on a consideration of the benefit and necessity of such services to the debtor and the other factors set forth in 11 U.S.C. § 330. These other factors include the amount of time spent by the attorney on the case, the rates charged by the attorney for his or her services, whether the compensation is reasonable based on customary compensation charged by comparably skilled practitioners in nonbankruptcy cases and whether the attorney is board certified or otherwise has demonstrated skill and experience in the bankruptcy field.

attorney's fee, review of by court

The fees charged by the debtor's attorney in a chapter 13 case, whether paid or agreed to be paid before or after the filing of the case, are subject to the review and approval of the bankruptcy court. See 11 U.S.C. § 329 and Bankruptcy Rule 2017. On the motion of a party in interest or on the court's own initiative, the court, after notice and a hearing, may determine whether any direct or indirect payment of money or transfer of property by the debtor to an attorney for services rendered or to be rendered in contemplation of the filing of a chapter 13 case by the debtor is excessive. See Bankruptcy Rule 2017(a).

On the motion of the debtor or the United States trustee, or on the court's own initiative, the court may, after notice and a hearing, determine whether any direct or indirect payment of money or transfer of property, or any agreement therefor, by the debtor to an attorney after the order for relief is excessive, if the payment or transfer, or agreement therefor, is for services in any way related to the case. See Bankruptcy Rule 2017(b). If the attorney's compensation exceeds the reasonable value of any such services, the court may cancel the fee agreement, or order that any payments received by the attorney, to the extent excessive, be returned to the entity that made the payments, or, if the payments were made under the chapter 13 plan or if the funds or property would otherwise have been property of the debtor's estate, order them turned over to the chapter 13 trustee. See 11 U.S.C. § 329(b).

attorney's fee, excessive amount, disposition of

Within 14 days after the date of the order for relief, or as otherwise directed by the court, the debtor's attorney must file with the court and transmit to the United States trustee a statement disclosing the compensation paid or to be paid to the attorney in the case. See Bankruptcy Rule 2016(b) and 11 U.S.C. § 329(a). Unless the local rules provide otherwise, Director's Form 2030, entitled Disclosure of Compensation of Attorney for Debtor, should be used for this statement. A sample of this statement may be found in Exhibit 2-A at the end of chapter 2, supra.

attorney's disclosure statement

In the disclosure statement, the attorney must disclose the entire compensation arrangement with the debtor, indicating the amount paid, the amount to be paid, and the source of the funds. The particulars of any agreement to share fees with other persons or attorneys, except members or regular associates of the attorney's law firm, must also be disclosed. See Bankruptcy Rule 2016(b). It should be remembered that an attorney's compensation may include not only the direct payment of money, but any direct or indirect payment of money or transfer of property, or agreement therefor, as long as the payment, transfer, or agreement is for services in any way related to the case. See Bankruptcy Rule 2017(b).

attorney's compensation, what constitutes

This does not mean that a reasonable fee cannot be charged and collected by an attorney representing a debtor in a chapter 13 case. To the contrary, unless the debtor makes no payments under the plan, the attorney is virtually assured of collecting a reasonable fee in the case because the fee is considered an administrative expense of the case and is treated as a priority claim, entitled to payment before the payment of other claims in the case. See 11 U.S.C. § 1326(a). All or a portion of the attorney's compensation may be paid in advance of filing, if the debtor is financially able to do so. However, the main portion of the attorney's fee is customarily paid by the chapter 13 trustee out of the first moneys paid by the debtor under the plan. If the debtor is unable to pay the filing fee when the case is filed and files an application to pay the filing fee in installments, no further payments may be made to the debtor's attorney by either the debtor or the chapter 13 trustee until the entire filing fee has been paid. See Bankruptcy Rule 1006(b)(3). It should be noted that the court has no authority to waive the filing fee in a chapter 13 case. See 28 U.S.C. § 1930(f)(1).

attorney's fee, when collected

While the amount of compensation approved for attorneys representing debtors in chapter 13 cases varies from district to district and from case to case, the amount generally runs about $3,000 in nonbusiness cases, depending on the district and the complexity of the case. Higher fees are generally allowed for attorneys representing debtors who are engaged in an active business.

attorney's fee, amount allowed

In some districts it may be necessary for the debtor's attorney to prepare, file, and transmit to the United States trustee an Application For Allowance of Compensation, a sample of which is set forth in Exhibit 3-A at the end of this chapter. A local form may be provided for this application in some districts. The local rules should be checked for the requirement of filing this application and for the time within which the application should be filed.

application for allowance of attorney's fee

The functions performed by the debtor's attorney in a typical chapter 13 case are set forth in the answer to Question 45 in Part A of this chapter, supra. In some districts the local rules specify the functions to be performed by the debtor's attorney in order to obtain court approval of his or her compensation. It should be noted that Director's Form 2030 (Exhibit 2-A, supra) also specifies certain functions to be performed by the debtor's attorney.

functions of attorney in chapter 13 case

3.04 The Chapter 13 Eligibility Requirements

To be eligible to file a chapter 13 case, a debtor must:

chapter 13 eligibility requirements

(1) be an individual (i.e., a natural person and not a corporation, partnership or limited liability company) or an individual and his or her spouse;

(2) have regular income;

(3) combined total secured and unsecured debts are less than $2,750,000 ;

(4) not be a stockbroker or a commodity broker;

(5) reside in the United States, or have a domicile, place of business or property in the United States; and

(6) not have been a debtor in a prior bankruptcy case that was dismissed by or on account of the debtor within the preceding 180 days. See, respectively, 11 U.S.C. § 109(e), (a), (g).

(7) have received an individual or group briefing from an approved nonprofit budget and credit counseling agency within 180 days prior to the filing of the case, unless this requirement is not applicable in the local district. See, respectively, 11 U.S.C. § 109(e), (a), (g), (h).

individual with regular income, definition

joint petition, eligibility requirements

An individual with regular income is defined as an individual whose income is sufficiently stable and regular to enable the individual to make payments under a chapter 13 plan. See 11 U.S.C. § 101(30). There is no requirement of regular employment, which means that self-employed persons, pensioners, farmers, and other persons with regular income are eligible to file under chapter 13. Any individual meeting the above requirements, and his or her spouse (if the spouse meets the requirements of (5), (6), (7) and (8) above), may file under chapter 13. Thus, a husband and wife may file a joint petition under chapter 13 even if only one of them has regular income, provided that their combined debts meet the requirements listed in (3) and (4) above. Stockbrokers and commodity brokers may not file under chapter 13. See 11 U.S.C. § 109(e).

contingent debt, what constitutes

In determining whether a debt is contingent or noncontingent for purposes of chapter 13 eligibility, it should be noted that a contingent debt is one which the debtor will be called upon to pay only upon the occurrence or happening of an extrinsic event which will trigger liability. A debt is not contingent merely because the debtor disputes his or her liability for the claim and an extrinsic event does not include a judicial determination of liability for the debt. The contingency must originate from outside of the claim itself. See In re Mazzeo, 131 F. 3d 295 (2nd Cir., 1997).

previous bankruptcy case, eligibility of debtor

An individual may not be a debtor under any chapter of the Bankruptcy Code, including chapter 13, if he or she has been a debtor in another bankruptcy case pending at any time during the preceding 180 days, if the prior case was - (1) dismissed by the court on account of the willful failure of the debtor to abide by orders of the court or to appear in court in the proper prosecution of the case, or (2) dismissed by the court at the request of the debtor following the filing of a request for relief from the automatic stay. See 11 U.S.C. § 109(g). The purpose of this requirement is to prevent serial bankruptcy filings by persons whose objective is to frustrate creditors by repeatedly taking advantage of the automatic stay and then causing the case to be dismissed. As indicated above, an individual must meet this title 11 eligibility requirement, as well as the chapter 13 eligibility requirements, in order to be eligible to file a chapter 13 case. For further reading on this requirement see Williamson, The Bankruptcy Issues Handbook, 7th Ed., 2015 (Argyle Pub. Co.) Art. 1.01.

credit counseling, requirement of for filing case

11 U.S.C. § 109(h)(1) provides that an individual may not be a debtor under any chapter of the Bankruptcy Code unless he or she has, during the 180 day period preceding the filing of the case, received from an approved nonprofit budget and credit counseling agency an individual or group briefing that outlined the opportunities for available credit counseling and assisted the debtor in performing a related budget analysis. However, this requirement is not in effect in districts where the United States trustee has determined that the approved agencies are unable to provide this service, and some persons are exempt from this requirement. See 11 U.S.C. § 109(h)(2), (4). See section 2.05, supra, for further reading on this requirement.

It should be noted that an individual is not eligible for a chapter 13 discharge if he or she has received a discharge in a chapter 7, 11 or 12 case filed within 4 years prior to the filing of the present case or if he or she has received a chapter 13 discharge in a case filed within 2 years prior to the filing of the present case. See 11 U.S.C.

§ 1328(f). However, debts dealt with in a prior bankruptcy case may be dealt with in a chapter 13 case, and, unless the court in the prior proceeding ordered otherwise, may be discharged. See 11 U.S.C. § 349(a). See section 3.18, infra, for further reading on chapter 13 discharges.

chapter 13 discharge, eligibility for

3.05 Interviewing the Debtor - Matters to Cover

It is important that the information collected from the debtor be both accurate and complete. Otherwise, the chapter 13 forms cannot be properly completed and the interests of the debtor will not be adequately served and the debtor's attorney could later be found to be in violation of 11 U.S.C. § 526 and Bankruptcy Rule 9011. (See section 2.03, supra.) To this end, it is usually better to interview both the debtor and the debtor's spouse, if one exists, even if a joint filing is not initially contemplated. In most cases, one of the matters to be resolved during the interview is whether the spouses should file jointly under chapter 13, and both spouses should have a voice in the resolution of this issue. Even if a joint filing is not warranted, the nonfiling spouse may be more familiar with the family financial situation than the filing spouse. Also, even in a single filing some of the information required in the chapter 13 forms involves the debtor's spouse. In any event, the debtor should be advised in advance of the nature of the information needed and of the documents and papers to bring to the interview.

chapter 13 case, who to interview

In order to properly prepare the chapter 13 forms and devise a chapter 13 plan, the information collected from the debtor must be both accurate and complete. The only proven method of gathering all of the needed information without repeated interviews and telephone calls is to use some form of work sheets that call for all of the required information and leave nothing to memory or chance. Some attorneys use an extra copy of the chapter 13 forms for this purpose; others have devised work sheets of their own.

accurate data, how to obtain

An attorney without work sheets will find the Bankruptcy Worksheets appearing in Exhibit 2-C at the end of chapter 2, supra, useful. Simply photocopy the work sheets and follow the instructions contained therein, and all of the required information will be assembled in the order appearing in the chapter 13 schedules and statements, except the Statement of Current Monthly Income and Disposable Income Calculation. However, much of the information required to complete this statement will appear in schedules I and J. It may be helpful to give a copy of the work sheets to the debtor prior to the interview. Once assembled, the information can easily be transferred from the work sheets to the appropriate schedules and statements, using the completed forms appearing in the exhibits at the end of chapter 2, supra, as guides.

bankruptcy work sheets, use of in chapter 13 case

To enable an attorney to properly plan and prepare a chapter 13 case, certain other important matters should be covered during the interview with the debtor. In addition to the gathering of data, the following matters should be covered when interviewing the debtor:

(1) The eligibility of the debtor for relief under chapter 13. It should be ascertained whether the debtor is eligible to file under chapter 13, and whether the debtor's debts are dischargeable under chapter 13. See section 3.04, supra, for a discussion of the chapter 13 eligibility requirements, and see section 3.18, infra, for a list of the debts that are not dischargeable in a chapter 13 case. It should be remembered, however, that even if a debt is nondischargeable under chapter 13, it may still be dealt with in a chapter 13 plan. This aspect of chapter 13 can be helpful to debtors with nondischargeable debts who are threatened with wage garnishments, property seizures, or contempt of court citations. The debtor's eligibility for a chapter 13 discharge should also be determined. See section 3.04, supra, and section 3.18, infra, for these requirements.

debtor's eligibility under chapter 13

(2) Whether a joint or single petition should be filed. The general rule is that if both spouses are liable for significant unsecured or partially-secured debts, a joint petition should be filed. Also, a joint petition should be filed if both spouses have significant regular income, unless there is a strong reason for not filing jointly.

Finally, if both spouses are liable on a secured debt that is significantly in default, a joint petition should be filed. When it is not clear whether both spouses are liable on an unsecured debt, the safest practice is to file jointly. The local rules may set forth instances when a joint filing is required, and they should be checked in this regard. Filing a joint petition normally entails no more legal or clerical work than a single filing, and the filing fee is the same. In practice, most chapter 13 cases of consumer debtors are joint filings. However, if the spouses are separated or involved in divorce proceedings, or if one spouse is engaged in business without the involvement of the other, a joint filing may not be advisable.

joint vs. single petition

(3) The debtor's primary reason for filing under chapter 13. Chapter 13 debtors can be divided into three general categories: (1) those who file under chapter 13 primarily to repay unsecured debts, (2) those who file primarily for the chapter 13 discharge, and (3) those who file under chapter 13 primarily for temporary injunctive relief, usually from secured creditors. The three classes of debtors have substantially different attitudes toward chapter 13. Debtors in the first category usually want to repay as much of their unsecured debts as possible, while debtors in the second category invariably want to repay as little of their unsecured debts as possible. Debtors in the third category are usually seeking temporary relief from aggressive creditors until their financial prospects improve or until they become eligible for a chapter 7 discharge.

categories of chapter 13 debtors

Debtors in the first category often want to adopt a plan that is too ambitious; that is, they want to pay more into the plan than they can reasonably afford. Such debtors often want to repay every dollar to every creditor, and if this appears impossible they tend to become discouraged and begin to think in terms of chapter 7. In such cases every attempt should be made to accommodate the repayment wishes of the debtor, but if it is obvious that a feasible plan calling for the repayment of all debts is impossible, they should be so advised. It will serve no purpose for such debtors to sink several thousand dollars into a plan, and then wind up converting to chapter 7. Such debtors should be advised that it is better to pay their creditors a portion of what is owed to them rather than to pay them nothing in a chapter 7 case.

advising category 1 debtors

Debtors in the second category usually file under chapter 13 because they are ineligible under means testing for a chapter 7 case, because they are ineligible for a chapter 7 discharge, or because they have debts that are dischargeable under chapter 13 but not under chapter 7. Occasionally debtors in this category file under chapter 13 because they have valuable nonexempt property that would be lost if they filed under chapter 7, but which they hope to retain in a chapter 13 case. Debtors in this category should be advised that enough of their income must be paid into the plan, and sufficient payments made to unsecured creditors, to satisfy the court that the plan is being proposed in good faith. Also, debtors in this category should be advised that all of their projected disposable income for a 3 or 5 year period must be applied to the plan. For an in-depth discussion on the issue of what constitutes "good faith" in the proposal of a chapter 13 plan, see Williamson, The Bankruptcy Issues Handbook, supra, Art. 3.03.

advising debtors who are ineligible for chapter 7 discharge

chapter 13 plan, good faith requirement

Debtors in the third category are often business debtors seeking temporary relief from a few creditors until funds can be obtained to repay their debts. Such debtors should be advised of the good faith requirements of filing under chapter 13, and of the necessity of filing a plan within 14 days after the petition is filed. Included in this category are debtors who are seeking a year or two of chapter 13 relief until they are again eligible for a chapter 7 discharge. These debtors should be advised of the provisions of 11 U.S.C. § 109(g), which is discussed in section 3.04, supra. Debtors with a heavy debt load who are ineligible for a chapter 7 discharge should be advised that they will be closely scrutinized by the court on the issue of good faith. Debtors seeking injunctive relief from nondischargeable debts for accumulated alimony or child support obligations are also included in this category. Such debtors should be advised that while debts of this nature can be repaid in an equitable manner under chapter 13, the bankruptcy court has no authority to change the amount of alimony or support that must ultimately be paid by the debtor, and that debts of this nature are not dischargeable.

advising debtors seeking temporary relief

(4) The necessity of avoiding liens and security interests. Under 11 U.S.C. § 522(f), the debtor may avoid (i.e., set aside) judicial liens against exempt property and nonpurchase-money, nonpossessory security interests in certain exempt personal property. See section 2.12, supra, for further reading on lien avoidance under Section 522(f) and for a full description of the type of property covered. If the debtor has property that is subject to a lien or security interest that may be avoidable under Section 522(f), the avoidability of such a lien or security interest could turn a secured creditor into an unsecured creditor and substantially affect the type of plan adopted by the debtor. It may be necessary, therefore, to determine the avoidability of such liens and security interests prior to the adoption of a plan. The procedure for avoiding such liens in chapter 13 cases is the same as in chapter 7 cases, and the reader is referred to section 2.12, supra, for further reading. The local rules may require motions to avoid liens under Section 522(f) to be filed with the petition or shortly thereafter. It should also be noted that if a lien or security interest of a creditor is avoidable by the trustee as a preferential or fraudulent transfer, it may be avoided in a chapter 13 case as well as in a chapter 7 case. See 11 U.S.C. § 103(a), 547-549. See sections 2.16, supra, and 3.08, infra, for further reading on the avoidance of such liens. See section 2.08, supra, for a discussion of the debtor's right to avoid involuntary transfers of exempt property under Section 522(h).

liens and security interests, necessity of avoiding

(5) Explaining the chapter 13 process to the debtor. A chapter 13 case will proceed more smoothly if the debtor understands the concepts and procedures involved. It is suggested that the debtor's attorney reproduce the questions and answers set forth in Part A of this chapter, supra, and give a copy of them to the debtor at the outset of the case. These questions and answers will answer most questions raised by typical chapter 13 debtors.

chapter 13 process, explaining to debtor

(6) Advising the debtor of his or her rights and duties in a chapter 13 case. The principal right of a debtor under chapter 13 is the right to propose a plan for the repayment or adjustment of his or her debts under the supervision and protection of the court. Upon the successful completion of a confirmed chapter 13 plan, a debtor has the right to a full chapter 13 discharge under 11 U.S.C. § 1328(a) (see section 3.18, infra). A chapter 13 debtor has many of the rights, powers, and duties of a trustee in regards to the possession of property and the running of a business during the case. See 11 U.S.C. § 1303. With only limited exceptions, the debtor has the right to dismiss a chapter 13 case or convert it to chapter 7 at any time (see section 3.17, infra). A debtor has the right to modify a chapter 13 plan at any time prior to confirmation and under certain conditions after confirmation (see sections 3.13 and 3.15, infra). See section 2.12, supra, for a list of the rights of debtors in bankruptcy cases.

rights of debtor under chapter 13

The primary duties of a debtor in a chapter 13 case are to file the appropriate schedules and statements, file and obtain confirmation of a chapter 13 plan, and make the payments and perform the acts required under the confirmed plan. The debtor must also comply with the prefiling credit counseling requirement, cooperate with the chapter 13 trustee, comply with the orders and rules of the bankruptcy court, and complete an instructional course on personal financial management. The debtor should be advised of his or her duty to file with the taxing authorities all tax returns that became due during the last 4 years. See 11 U.S.C. § 1308. See section 3.12, infra, for further reading on this duty. See section 2.11, supra, for a list of the duties of debtors in bankruptcy cases.

duties of debtor under chapter 13

(7) Drafting a budget and devising a chapter 13 plan. These matters are dealt with at length in sections 3.07 and 3.08, infra. While it is usually impossible to devise a final chapter 13 plan at the time of the interview, a preliminary plan should be devised so that the debtor will know what to expect in the case. If the debtor's income and expenses are known, it should be possible to draft a preliminary budget during the interview.

preliminary plan, use of

(8) Making arrangements for the payment of the filing fee, the attorney's fee, and any required deposit. The debtor should be advised that the filing fee must be paid, either when the case is filed or within the required period (see section 3.10, infra), or the case will be dismissed and a discharge will not be granted. For the protection of both the attorney and the debtor, there should be no misunderstanding as to either the amount or the terms of the fee to be charged by the attorney for handling the case, even if the fee is to be disbursed later by the chapter 13 trustee. The fee agreement must be in writing and signed by all parties. See sections 2.03 and 3.03, supra, for a discussion of the duties and requirements of the debtor's attorney with respect to attorney's fees.

payment of costs and fees, arrangements for

commencement of payments under plan, arrangements for

(9) Making arrangements for the commencement of payments under the plan. Unless the court orders otherwise, a debtor must begin making the payments proposed in the plan within 30 days after the chapter 13 case is filed. See 11 U.S.C. § 1326(a)(1)(A). In most cases payments to the chapter 13 trustee must begin before the plan is confirmed by the court. Should the debtor fail to commence making timely payments under a proposed plan, the case may be dismissed by the court. See 11 U.S.C. § 1307(c)(4). It is important, then, that arrangements be made for the commencement of payments within the required time. By whom the debtor's chapter 13 payments shall be made should also be discussed during the interview. Some courts have a rule or policy that if a debtor is employed, the chapter 13 payments must be forwarded by the debtor's employer directly to the chapter 13 trustee, a procedure enforceable by the court after confirmation under 11 U.S.C. § 1325(c). However, until a plan has been confirmed by the court and the final amount of the periodic payment determined, it is usually preferable for the debtor, rather than the employer, to make the payments.

3.06 Debtors Engaged in Business

engaged in business, what constitutes

operation of business during case

cash collateral, what constitutes

A debtor engaged in business may file a chapter 13 case if he or she is otherwise eligible (see section 3.04, supra). A self-employed debtor who incurs trade credit in the production of income from such employment is deemed to be engaged in business. See 11 U.S.C. § 1304(a). Unless the court orders otherwise, a debtor engaged in business may continue to operate the business during the case, and has many of the rights and powers of a trustee in so doing, subject to the limitations applicable to trustees generally and to any special limitations or conditions imposed by the court in a particular case. See 11 U.S.C. § 1304(b). However, the debtor may not, without court approval, use, sell, or lease cash collateral or obtain credit, other than unsecured credit in the ordinary course of business. See 11 U.S.C. § 1303, 364(a), (b). This means that the debtor must segregate and account for any cash collateral that may be in the debtor's possession or control at any time during the case. Cash collateral is cash, bank deposits, negotiable instruments, and other cash equivalents owned by the debtor that are subject to the lien or security interest of a creditor. See 11 U.S.C. § 363(a).

business debtor, required reports

A debtor engaged in business must file with the court, with the United States trustee, and with any governmental unit responsible for the collection or determination of any tax arising out of the operation of the debtor's business, periodic reports and summaries of the operation of the business, including a statement of receipts and disbursements, and such other information as the United States trustee or the court may require. See 11 U.S.C. § 1304(c). If the reports reflect payments to employees, the amount and location of any funds deducted or withheld for taxes must also be reported. See Bankruptcy Rule 2015(a)(3),(c)(1).

business debtor, duties of during case

A chapter 13 debtor engaged in business is also required to file a complete inventory of the debtor's property within 30 days after the case is filed (unless an inventory was previously filed or contained in the debtor's bankruptcy schedules), keep a record of the receipt and disposition of any money or property received during the case, and give notice of the case to every entity known to be holding money or property subject to the withdrawal or order of the debtor, including banks, insurance companies, and holders of deposits previously made by the debtor. See Bankruptcy Rule 2015(c)(1). Unless the court orders otherwise, the chapter 13 trustee is required to investigate and file a report on the acts, conduct, assets, liabilities, and financial condition of a debtor engaged in business, on the operation of the debtor's business, and on the desirability of continuing the business. See 11 U.S.C. § 1302(c). Many courts and United States trustees have local rules and forms pertaining to chapter 13 debtors that are engaged in business.

The preparation of a budget and a feasible chapter 13 plan is usually more complicated for a debtor engaged in business than for a consumer debtor. For example, a debtor engaged in business has to justify the expenditures necessary for the continuation, preservation, and operation of the business, which expenditures often include the debtor's personal compensation, which, in turn, may have to be separately justified. The same general rules apply, however, and the principles and procedures set forth in sections 3.07 and 3.08, infra, should be followed.

business debtor, budget and plan

The official schedules and statements, and any applicable local forms, should be appropriately modified and supplemented, if necessary, so as to give an accurate financial account of both the debtor and the debtor's business. A debtor engaged in business is required to attach detailed statements to Schedules I and J showing the debtor's income and expenses from the business.

business debtor, modification of forms

On the request of a party in interest or the United States trustee, the court, after notice and a hearing, may convert the chapter 13 case of a debtor engaged in business to chapter 11 or chapter 12 at any time before confirmation of the plan, except that the chapter 13 case of a farmer may not be so converted without the consent of the debtor. See 11 U.S.C. § 1307(d),(f).

business debtor, conversion to chapter 11

3.07 Determining and Providing for the Debtor's Disposable Income

A debtor's disposable income is defined as the debtor's current monthly income less the amounts reasonably necessary to be expended by the debtor for (1) the maintenance or support of the debtor and his or her dependents and for a domestic support obligation that first becomes payable after the chapter 13 case is filed, (2) contributions to qualified charities of up to 15 percent of the debtor's gross income, (3) if the debtor is engaged in business, the payment of expenditures necessary for the continuation, preservation and operation of the business. See 11 U.S.C. § 1325(b)(2). Also excluded from a debtor's disposable income are amounts withheld by the debtor's employer for contributions to tax-qualified employee benefit plans, deferred compensation plans and tax-deferred annuities and amounts required to repay loans from tax-qualified employee retirement plans. See 11 U.S.C. § 541(b)(7), 1322(f).

disposable income, definition of

A debtor's current monthly income is the average monthly income from all sources that the debtor (or both debtors in a joint case) receives, without regard as to whether the income is taxable, during the 6 month period ending on the last day of the calendar month immediately preceding the filing of the case. See 11 U.S.C. § 101(10A). However, for chapter 13 purposes, current monthly income does not include child support payments, foster care payments, and child disability payments. See 11 U.S.C. § 1325(b)(2).

current monthly income, what constitutes

Chapter 13 has its own version of means testing whereunder the type of expenses that may be used by the debtor to calculate his or her disposable income is determined by whether the debtor's annual income is above or below the median family income for the debtor's state and family size as determined by the U.S. Census Bureau. If the debtor's annualized current monthly income (i.e., current monthly income multiplied by 12) is equal to or less than the median family income for the debtor's state and family size, the debtor may use his or her actual expenses in calculating his or her disposable income for chapter 13 purposes and the debtor's disposable income must be calculated from the figures appearing in schedules I and J. If the debtor's annualized current monthly income exceeds the median family income for the debtor's state and family size, the debtor's expenses must be determined in accordance with the provisions of 11 U.S.C. § 707(b)(2)(A) and (B). See 11 U.S.C. § 1325(b)(2). These Code provisions require the debtor to use, in lieu of his or her actual expenses, expenses in the amounts specified in the National Standards and Local Standards established by the Internal Revenue Service (the IRS). See section 2.07, supra, for further reading on the IRS standards.

disposable income, expenses used

disposable income, use of IRS standard expenses

This means that if a debtor's annualized current monthly income exceeds the applicable median family income, the debtor's disposable income for chapter 13 purposes must be calculated using as his or her expenses the amounts specified in the IRS standards. These expenses may or may not be in accordance with the debtor's actual expenses. Most likely the IRS standard expenses will be less than the debtor's actual expenses, which means that the debtor's disposable income will be greater than it would be if his or her actual expenses were used. In many cases it may be necessary for the debtor to change his or her lifestyle in order to be able to pay into the plan the amount of disposable income that is calculated using the IRS standards. The debtor should understand that all of his or her disposable income, however calculated, must be paid into the plan for the entire period of the plan. See 11 U.S.C. § 1325(b)(1)(B).

disposable income, type of expenses used, how to determine

It is important to determine at the outset whether the debtor will be able to use his or her actual expenses or the IRS standards in calculating his or her disposable income. Therefore, one of the attorney's first functions should be to determine the amount of the debtor's current monthly income for means testing purpose. To do this, Official Forms 122C–1 and 122C–2 should be used. When these forms are completed the type of expenses the debtor must use will be indicated. Instructions on the completion of this form may be found in section 3.09, infra. If the debtor's annualized current monthly income is equal to or less than the applicable median family income, the debtor's disposable income can be calculated from the figures appearing in schedules I and J. If the debtor's annualized current monthly income is shown on Official Form 122C–1 to exceed the applicable median family income, the debtor's disposable income must be calculated under Official Form 122C–2.

debtor's budget, importance of

Regardless of the amount of the debtor's current monthly income and regardless of the type of expenses that the debtor must use in calculating disposable income, it is important to assist the debtor in devising a realistic and workable budget that will enable the debtor to make the required payments under the plan for the entire period of the plan. This function will usually be more difficult if the debtor is required to use the IRS standard expenses.

debtor's budget, requirements of

A workable budget must meet two requirements: it must be realistic for the debtor, and it must be justifiable to the court. If a budget is not realistic and workable for the debtor for the entire period of the plan, the plan is probably doomed to failure because sooner or later the debtor will be unable to make the payments required under the plan. If the budget, as it appears in the Schedules of Current Income and Current Expenditures, is not justifiable to the court because it is too restrictive on the debtor, the court will probably refuse to confirm the debtor's plan.

debtor's budget, data needed

To devise a realistic budget for a debtor, accurate information as to exactly how much money the debtor is taking in and spending each month must be obtained. It should be remembered that in devising a budget income such as child support payments may be used even though they are excluded in calculating disposable income. The expenses employed in the budget should always be the debtor's actual expenses, even if the debtor is required to use the IRS standards in calculating disposable income. The data gathered in completing the bankruptcy schedules and statements will supply most of the needed information. However, the surest method of ascertaining exactly what a debtor spends each month is to examine the entries in his or her checkbook, or other record of expenditures, for the previous several months. An effort should be made to look for quarterly, semiannual, or annual expenses for such items as insurance premiums and taxes. The expenses currently being deducted from the debtor's wages or salary should also be accounted for.

budget, method of preparation

The information appearing in the Statement of Current Income and Disposable Income Calculation and in the Schedules of Current Income and Current Expenditures (schedules I and J) may be used in preparing the debtor's budget. However, because each debtor's situation is unique and because it is important that the debtor understand the budget, labels and terms familiar to the debtor should be used, and the terms appearing on the schedules should be appropriately modified. The budget should show average figures for expenses that vary from month to month, such as water, telephone, or utility bills and credit card payments. If the debtor's income varies seasonally, a realistic average should be used if feasible, or separate budgets should be prepared for each season. As indicated above, income from all sources should be included in the budget, including alimony or child support payments, if received regularly. For budget-making purposes it does not matter whether the income is included in the debtor's current monthly income for means testing purposes. The impact of inflation on the items appearing in the budget over the period of the plan should also be considered, if appropriate.

It is important to include as expenses in the budget payments to creditors that the debtor intends to pay outside of the chapter 13 plan. It is usually preferable to pay fully secured claims upon which the debtor is not in default outside the plan, because by so doing the debtor will avoid the chapter 13 trustee's ten-percent fee that is assessed on payments made under the plan. Even if the debtor is in default on a fully secured claim (such as a home mortgage), it may be possible for the debtor to make the regular payments on the claim outside the plan and make only the payments necessary to cure the default under the plan. See section 3.08, infra, for further reading. Unless the debtor is in default on such a claim, it is also preferable for the debtor to pay nondischargeable claims outside the plan. See section 3.18, infra, for a list of debts (or claims) that are nondischargeable in a chapter 13 case. Payments on executory contracts or unexpired leases that are to be assumed by the debtor and that are not in default should also be paid outside the plan.

secured or nondischargeable claims, payment outside of plan

3.08 Devising a Confirmable Chapter 13 Plan

The statutory authority for the required and permissible provisions of chapter 13 plans is 11 U.S.C. § 1322. The confirmation requirements, which must also be complied with in the preparation of a plan, are found in 11 U.S.C. § 1325. Together, Sections 1322(a) and 1325 impose the following mandatory requirements for a chapter 13 plan:

chapter 13 plan, mandatory requirements

(1) The plan must provide for the submission of all or such portion of the future earnings or income of the debtor to the supervision and control of the chapter 13 trustee as is necessary for the execution of the plan.

(2) The plan must provide for the full payment, in deferred cash, of all priority claims, unless the holder of such a claim agrees otherwise, except that a plan may provide for less than full payment to claims for domestic support obligations that are owed to governmental units if the plan provides that all of the debtor's projected disposable income for a 5 year period will be applied to make payments under the plan.

(3) If the plan classifies claims, it must provide the same treatment for each claim within a particular class.

(4) The plan must provide for the payment of any fee, charge, or other amount required by law or by the plan to be paid prior to confirmation.

(5) The plan must be proposed in good faith and not by any means forbidden by law.

(6) The value, as of the effective date of the plan, of property to be distributed under the plan on the account of each allowed unsecured nonpriority claim must be not less than the amount that would be paid on such claim if the estate of the debtor was liquidated under chapter 7 on the same date.

(7) With respect to each allowed secured claim dealt with under the plan, the plan must provide for one of the following - (a) the holder of the claim has accepted the plan, (b) the creditor may retain the lien securing its claim until the claim is paid in full or a chapter 13 discharge is granted, whichever is earlier, and money or property will be distributed to the creditor in an amount that is at least equal to the allowed amount of the claim in equal monthly payments in amounts that will provide the claimholder with adequate protection during the period of the plan, or (c) the debtor surrenders the property securing the claim to the holder of the claim.

(8) It must appear to the court that the debtor will be able to make all payments called for under the plan and otherwise comply with the plan and that the petition was filed by the debtor in good faith.

(9) It must be shown that the debtor has paid all required amounts owed by the debtor under any domestic support obligation that first became payable after the chapter 13 case was filed.

(10) It must be shown that the debtor has filed with the taxing authorities all tax returns that were required to be filed for the 4 year period prior to the filing of the case.

priority claims, types of

divorce related claims, priority of

Priority claims are defined in 11 U.S.C. § 507(a) and a list of them is set forth in section 2.19, supra. The unpaid balance of the filing fee and the compensation allowed to the debtor's attorney are the most common priority claims in chapter 13 cases. Other common priority claims include claims for unpaid wages, salaries, commissions and employee benefits, claims for domestic support obligations, and tax claims. It should be noted that while domestic support obligations are priority claims, divorce related property settlement claims are not priority claims. See 11 U.S.C. § 101(14A) for the definition of a domestic support obligation. As indicated above, except for domestic support obligations owed to governmental units, priority claims must be paid in full under the plan unless a particular creditor agrees otherwise. See 11 U.S.C. § 1322(a)(2).

11 U.S.C. § 1322(b) provides that a chapter 13 plan may include provisions dealing with the following matters:

chapter 13 plan, permitted provisions

(1) The plan may designate one or more classes of unsecured claims, provided that if more than one class is designated, all claims within a particular class must be substantially similar and no class of claims may be unfairly discriminated against, except that a plan may treat claims for a consumer debt of the debtor for which another individual is also liable differently than other unsecured claims.

(2) The plan may modify the rights of holders of unsecured and secured claims, other than a claim secured only by a security interest in real property that is the debtor's principal residence.

(3) The plan may provide for the curing or waiving of any default.

(4) The plan may provide for the concurrent payment of secured and unsecured claims.

(5) The plan may provide for the curing of any default within a reasonable time and the maintenance of payments while the case is pending on any claim on which the last payment is due after the proposed date of the final payment under the plan.

(6) The plan may provide for the payment of postpetition claims.

(7) The plan may provide for the assumption or rejection of executory contracts or unexpired leases not previously rejected in the case.

(8) The plan may provide for the payment of claims from property of the debtor or the debtor's estate.

(9) The plan may provide for the vesting of property of the estate, on or after confirmation of the plan, in the debtor or in another entity.

(10) The plan may provide for the payment of postpetition interest on nondischargeable unsecured claims if all other allowed claims are paid in full under the plan

(11) The plan may include any other appropriate provision that is not inconsistent with the Bankruptcy Code.

11 U.S.C. § 1322(d)(2) specifies that if the debtor's annualized current monthly income (i.e., current monthly income multiplied by 12) is less than the median family income for the debtor's state and family size, the debtor's chapter 13 plan may not provide for payments over a period that is longer than three years, unless the court, for cause, approves a longer period, which may not exceed five years. If the debtor's annualized current monthly income is equal to or greater than the median family income for the debtor's state and family size, the applicable commitment period for the debtor's plan must be at least 3 years and may not provide for payments over a period that is longer than 5 years. See 11 U.S.C. § 1322(d)(1), 1325(b)(4). The applicable commitment period of a plan may be less than 3 years only if the plan provides for payment in full of all allowed unsecured claims over a shorter period. See 11 U.S.C. § 1325(b)(4)(B). It should be noted that if a plan is later modified so as to extend the period for making payments, the period may not be extended to a date more than five years after the date when the first payment under the original plan was due. See 11 U.S.C. § 1329(c).

chapter 13 plan, length of

In devising a chapter 13 plan, the following matters should be determined: (1) the debtor's primary reason for filing under chapter 13, (2) the length of the plan, (3) the total amount that can be paid on all claims under the plan, (4) the total amount, if any, that must be paid to the holders of priority claims under the plan, (5) the total amount, including interest, that must be paid to the holders of secured claims under the plan, (6) the total amount to be paid to the holders of special classes of unsecured claims under the plan, and (7) the total amount that can be paid to the holders of all other unsecured claims under the plan. While some of the items may be interdependent, each item should be determined separately. Each item is discussed separately below.

devising plan, factors to consider

It is important to determine the debtor's primary reason for filing under chapter 13 when preparing a plan because it is likely to affect the debtor's attitude toward the payment of his or her creditors. For example, a debtor whose primary reason for filing under chapter 13 is because he or she is not eligible for a chapter 7 discharge or who has converted to chapter 13 from chapter 7 because of means testing, will normally want to pay as little to creditors as possible for the shortest allowable period, while a debtor who is filing under chapter 13 primarily to repay debts will usually want to pay as much to creditors as possible for the longest allowable period. A debtor whose primary purpose in filing is to pay off a nondischargeable or priority debt will usually want to pay as much as possible on the nondischargeable or priority debt and as little as possible to other creditors. All of these factors will be considered by the court in determining whether the plan is being proposed in good faith by the debtor. See section 3.05, supra, for a discussion of the various categories of chapter 13 debtors. For further reading on the issue of what constitutes "good faith" in the proposal of a chapter 13 plan, see Williamson, The Bankruptcy Issues Handbook, supra, Art. 3.03.

reason for filing, importance of in plan

good faith, requirement of

For debtors whose annualized current monthly income is less than the applicable median family income, the rule is that the applicable commitment period of the plan must be 3 years unless the debtor can justify a longer period or can pay all unsecured claims in full over a shorter period. For debtors whose annualized current monthly income exceeds the applicable median family income, the applicable commitment period of the plan must be 5 years unless the debtor can justify a shorter period, which may not be less than 3 years unless all unsecured claims can be paid in a shorter period.

period of plan, types of debtors

Once the length of the plan has been determined, the total amount to be paid on all claims under the plan can usually be calculated by simply multiplying the number of periodic payments to be made by the debtor under the plan by the amount of the periodic payment, and subtracting the projected expenses of administration. The calculation may be more difficult if the plan does not call for the debtor to make uniform payments. The amount of the debtor's periodic payment to the chapter 13 trustee will normally be 100 percent of the debtor's disposable income, less the amounts of any payments made by the debtor to creditors outside the plan. See section 3.07, supra, for further reading on disposable income. The projected expenses of administration are usually the chapter 13 trustee's fee, which is ten percent of all payments made by the debtor under the plan, and any unpaid portions of the filing fee and the fee allowed to the debtor's attorney. The total amount to be paid on all claims under the plan must be calculated in order to determine the feasibility of the plan, both to the court and to the debtor.

determining total amount to be paid on all claims

contributing assets to plan

If, after calculating the total amount to be paid on all claims under the plan from the debtor's periodic payments, it appears that the amount will be insufficient to either obtain confirmation of the plan or satisfy the debtor's primary purpose in proposing the plan, it may be necessary for the debtor to contribute assets (or the proceeds therefrom) to the plan. This practice is permitted under 11 U.S.C. § 1322(b)(9). If the debtor wishes to proceed in this manner, the estimated amount to be realized from the contributed assets should be included in the total amount to be paid on all claims under the plan.

priority claims, determining amount to be paid on

If the debtor has tax, domestic support obligations, or other debts, the claims for which are priority claims, the plan must provide for the full payment of these claims (except domestic support obligations owed to governmental units), unless a particular creditor agrees otherwise (which is unlikely). Therefore, the total amount that must be paid on these claims is normally the total amount of the claims as of the date the case is filed. Postfiling interest does not normally have to be paid on priority claims. See In re Burnett, 646 F.3d 575 (8th Cir. 2011); In re Moore, 307 B.R. 394 (Bankr. S. D. N. Y. 2004).

paying secured claims outside of plan

Before the amount that must be paid to the holders of secured claims under the plan can be calculated, it must be determined which of the secured claims are to be paid or dealt with under the plan and the manner in which such claims are to be paid or dealt with under the plan must be resolved. It is generally preferable to pay fully secured claims upon which the debtor is not in default outside the plan, because by so doing the debtor will avoid paying the trustee's fee on the claim. If the debtor is in the early stages of default on a fully secured claim, it may still be possible to pay the claim outside the plan and make only the payments necessary to cure the default under the plan. Partially secured creditors must usually be paid under the plan, unless there is no dispute as to the amount of the secured portion of a particular creditor's claim. Fully secured creditors whose claims have accelerated or who have commenced foreclosure or repossession proceedings must be paid and dealt with under the plan in most instances.

secured claims, plan requirements

Once the secured claims that are to be paid or dealt with under the plan have been ascertained, the difficult task of deciding how to deal with the holders of such claims must be undertaken. Secured creditors have considerable leverage under chapter 13, at least to the extent of their secured interest. To permit confirmation of a chapter 13 plan, the holder of each secured claim dealt with in the plan must either - (1) accept the plan, (2) retain its lien and be paid the full amount of its allowed secured claim in equal monthly payments, or (3) be given the property securing its claim. See 11 U.S.C. § 1325(a)(5). Thus, while a chapter 13 plan may modify the rights of secured creditors (except home mortgage holders), such creditors cannot be forced to accept the plan and, unless the proposed plan satisfies one of the three alternatives described above, can either prevent confirmation of the plan or force the debtor to pay the claim outside the plan.

secured claims, interest requirements

In addition, interest must be paid on all secured claims, either at the rate called for in the agreement giving rise to the claim or, if no rate is specified, at a rate justifiable under the circumstances. Some courts have established interest rates or capitalization tables that must be used in cases where an interest rate is not otherwise specified or agreed upon, and the local rules should be checked in this regard. If the plan proposes to cure a default, the amount necessary to cure the default must be determined in accordance with the underlying agreement and applicable state law. See 11 U.S.C. § 1322(e).

secured claims, matters to check

The two principal functions that should be performed by the debtor's attorney in connection with secured claims are - (1) ascertaining the validity and extent of a creditor's lien or security interest, and (2) providing for the curing of any defaults. In ascertaining the validity and extent of a creditor's lien or security interest, the following aspects of the lien or security should be checked:

secured claim, validity of lien

(1) The validity of the lien or security interest under state law. It should be ascertained whether the recording and other acts required under state law to perfect the lien or security interest have been performed. While this can sometimes be accomplished by examining the proof of claim filed by the secured creditor (Bankruptcy Rule 3001(d) requires a proof of claim claiming a security interest in property of the debtor to be accompanied by evidence that the security interest has been perfected), the best practice is to check directly with the local recording office or official.

(2) The avoidability of the lien or security interest under Section 522(f). Under 11 U.S.C. § 522(f), a debtor may set aside judicial liens on exempt property and nonpurchase-money security interests in certain exempt personal property that is not in the possession of the creditor. Section 522(f) lien avoidance powers apply to chapter 13 debtors. See, e.g., In Re Hall, 752 F. 2d 582 (11th Cir. 1986). The procedure for avoiding such liens is the same under chapter 13 as under chapter 7, and the reader is referred to section 2.12, supra, for further reading. If a lien or security interest is avoidable under Section 522(f), the local rules should be checked for special provisions applicable to motions to avoid such liens in chapter 13 cases.

secured claim, avoidability of lien under Section 522(f)

(3) The avoidability of the lien or security interest by the trustee. Even if a lien or security interest is valid under local law and is not avoidable by the debtor under Section 522(f), it may be avoidable by the trustee as a preference under 11 U.S.C. § 547(b), or as a fraudulent transfer under 11 U.S.C. § 548(a). It may be possible to set aside recently created liens and recent repossessions of property by a secured creditor in this manner. See section 2.16, supra, for further reading. The chapter 13 trustee has lien avoidance powers and if the trustee refuses to act the debtor may act to avoid a preferential or fraudulent lien or other transfer. See generally In re Cerrato, 504 B.R. 23 (Bankr. E.D.N.Y. 2014). For further reading on the avoidability of prefiling transfers, see Williamson, The Bankruptcy Issues Handbook, supra, Art 1.14.

secured claim, avoidability of lien by trustee

(4) The extent to which the claim is secured. Determining the extent to which a claim is secured is usually necessary in dealing with partially-secured creditors. Under 11 U.S.C. § 506(a), an allowed claim secured by a lien on property of the debtor's estate is a secured claim only to the extent of the value of the creditor's interest in such property, and is an unsecured claim to the extent of the excess of the amount of the allowed claim over the value of the creditor's interest in the property. Of course, the value of a creditor's interest in property cannot exceed the value of the property. The valuation of the secured property is usually the main issue in such disputes because the secured portion of the creditor's claim is usually not equal to the value of the property. Not surprisingly, the creditor will often assign a higher value to the secured property than the debtor. If a partially secured creditor files a proof of claim claiming a security interest in property of the debtor that exceeds the debtor's estimate of the value of the secured property, an objection to the allowance of the claim should be filed in order to preserve the debtor's right to contest the amount of the secured claim. It should be noted that for confirmation purposes 11 U.S.C. § 506(a) does not apply to purchase-money security interests in automobiles acquired by the debtor for his or her personal use within 910 days of bankruptcy or to purchase-money security interests in other property if the debt was incurred within one year of bankruptcy. See 11 U.S.C. § 1325(a). This means that claims of this type are deemed to be fully secured regardless of the value of the secured property. The local rules and forms often contain provisions dealing with the valuation of secured or partially-secured claims and the bifurcation of partially-secured claims under 11 U.S.C. § 506(a), and they should be checked in this regard. See section 3.13, infra, for further reading on the handling of secured and partially-secured claims.

secured claim, determining extent of

claims secured by purchase-money security interest, extent secured

The curing of defaults can be a troublesome aspect of dealing with fully secured creditors in chapter 13 cases. If the debtor is in default on a secured claim dealt with under the plan, it will be necessary to provide a method in the plan for curing the default within a reasonable time in order to obtain confirmation of the plan. If the plan proposes to cure a default, the amount necessary to cure the default must be determined in accordance with the underlying agreement and applicable nonbankruptcy law. See 11 U.S.C. § 1322(e). If the underlying agreement requires periodic payments, it may be necessary to make double payments to the creditor (one on the underlying obligation and one curing the default) until the default is cured. Interest may also have to be paid on the arrearage if required by the underlying agreement or by state law.

curing defaults, importance of

The handling of defaulted home mortgages under a chapter 13 plan can be difficult because of the provision in 11 U.S.C. § 1322(b)(2) prohibiting a plan from modifying the rights of creditors secured only by a security interest in real property that is the debtor's principal residence. It should be noted initially that this prohibition is not applicable if the last payment on the mortgage is due prior to the end of the plan. See 11 U.S.C. § 1322(c)(2). The prohibition is also not applicable if the creditor's claim is also secured by a lien on other collateral, such as fixtures, household goods, a farm, or a life insurance policy. See In re Ferandos, 402 F.3d 147 (3rd Cir. 2005). In cases where the prohibition is applicable, it is clear that a defaulted home mortgage may be cured under a chapter 13 plan. See 11 U.S.C. § 1322(b)(5). A default on a home mortgage may be cured until the residence is sold at a foreclosure sale that is conducted in accordance with state law. See 11 U.S.C. § 1322(c)(1). If state law gives the debtor a period of redemption or other cure rights, the debtor may be permitted to cure the default until the expiration of the redemption or other cure period. See Annotation, 67 A.L.R. Fed. 217; the Congressional statement regarding section 301 of the Bankruptcy Reform Act of 1994.

curing defaults on home mortgages

under-secured home mortgage, bifurcation of claim, preclusion of

The practice of bifurcating the claim of the holder of an undersecured home mortgage has been effectively banned by the Supreme Court. In Nobleman v. American Savings Bank, 508 U.S. 324, 113 S.Ct. 2106 (1993), the Supreme Court held that the provisions of 11 U.S.C. § 1322(b)(2) preclude the debtor from bifurcating the claim of an undersecured home mortgagee into a secured claim and an unsecured claim and treating the claims differently. In essence the court held that a chapter 13 plan may not modify the secured or unsecured rights of a creditor who is secured only by a mortgage on the debtor's principal residence. This case should be noted when devising a chapter 13 plan for a debtor with a home mortgage holder that is undersecured.

second mortgage lien stripping

The prohibition against modification of a secured creditor's rights provided for in 11 U.S.C. § §1322(b)(2) does not protect a junior lien holder whose claim is wholly unsecured by virtue of the first mortgage balance equalling or exceeding the value of the residence. The practice of removing second mortgages from a debtor's principal residence and treating such claims as unsecured is commonly referred to as "lien stripping". Lien stripping renders second mortgages as totally unsecured claims when there is no equity to attach to them under 11 U.S.C. §506(a). The procedure is usually commenced by filing a motion to determine secured status and valuate real property under Fed.R.Bank.P. 3012 and 9014. If the court determines that the value of the first mortgage is equal to or greater than the value of the residence, all junior liens will be deemed to be unsecured and may be treated as an general unsecured nonpriority claims in the debtor's Chapter 13 plan. See Exhibit 3-M for an example of such a motion. Lien stripping is not available if there exists any security, however small, in the second mortgage.

acceleration clauses, validity of in chapter 13 case

Most home mortgages contain acceleration clauses permitting the lender to demand immediate payment of the entire unpaid balance of the obligation upon a default by the borrower. It often happens that the lender has exercised the acceleration option in the debtor's home mortgage prior to the filing of the chapter 13 case. It is clear, however, that under 11 U.S.C. § 1322(b)(5) an accelerated home mortgage obligation can be deaccelerated and cured under a chapter 13 plan despite the provision in 11 U.S.C. § 1322(b)(2) prohibiting the modification of home mortgages until a foreclosure sale is held. See In re Bailey, 468 B.R. 464 (Bankr. D. Mass. 2012); Grubbs v. Houston First Am. Savings Assoc., 730 F.2d 236 (5th Cir. 1984). For further reading on the extent to which defaults on secured obligations may be cured and dealt with in a chapter 13 plan, see Williamson, The Bankruptcy Issues Handbook, supra, Art. 3.01.

secured claims, total amount of

Once it is determined how each secured claim dealt with under the plan is to be paid, it should be possible to calculate the total amount, including interest, that must be paid to the holders of secured claims under the plan. If this amount plus the amount that must be paid to the holders of priority claims exceeds the total amount that can be paid on all claims under the plan, the plan will not be feasible and must be changed.

unsecured claims, special classes of

The next matter to determine is the total amount to be paid to the holders of special classes of unsecured claims under the plan. Whether special classes of unsecured claims are to be created under a plan is likely to depend on the debtor's reason for filing under chapter 13. If the debtor's reason for filing is to deal with a specific unsecured nonpriority debt, such as a student loan or other nondischargeable debt, it may be necessary to create a special class for the claim in order to carry out the debtor's purpose. Even debtors whose reason for filing under chapter 13 is to repay as many of their debts as possible often have valid reasons for paying more to certain creditors than others. In many cases, then, it will be necessary to establish special classes of unsecured claims in order to comply with the wishes of the debtor.

classes of unsecured claims, legal requirements

Under 11 U.S.C. § 1322(b)(1), a chapter 13 plan may designate one or more classes of unsecured claims, but may not discriminate unfairly against any class of claims. A plan may place a claim in a particular class only if the claim is substantially similar to the other claims in the class. See 11 U.S.C. § 1322(b)(1), 1122(a). Further, if the plan classifies such claims, the same treatment must be provided for each claim within a particular class. See 11 U.S.C. § 1322(a)(3). In construing these statutes, most courts invoke a basic fairness test wherein all similarly-situated claims must be given equal treatment unless there is a reasonable and good-faith basis for a proposed discrimination. See In re Leser, 939 F.2d 669 (8th Cir. 1991).

There must be a justifiable, if not always substantial, difference in the type or nature of a claim to warrant the creation of a separate class for the claim. Unsecured claims for consumer debts of the debtor for which another individual is also liable may, by statute, be treated differently than other unsecured claims, and may therefore constitute a separate class of claims. See 11 U.S.C. § 1322(b)(1). However, the unfair discrimination requirements of Section 1322(b)(1) are applicable to claims of this type, which means that the treatment given codebtor claims under a plan may not unfairly discriminate against other classes of unsecured claims. See In re Renteria, 470 B.R. 838 (BAP 9 2012). Claims for services or supplies needed by the debtor to remain in business may justify the creation of a separate class, as may claims for the services of a physician or hospital whose future services are needed by the debtor. See In Re Terry, 78 B.R. 171 (Bankr. E. D. Tenn. 1987). Unsecured priority claims, such as most domestic support obligations and most tax claims, are required by statute to be paid in full under the plan, so it is not necessary to create a special class for these claims. See 11 U.S.C. § 1322(a)(2).

permitted classes of unsecured claims

Generally, nondischargeable student loans may be put into a separate class, provided that the classification does not result in unfair discrimination. See In re Boscaccy, 442 B.R. 501 (Bankr. N. D. Miss. 2010). However, nondischargeability alone does not constitute a sufficient basis for according discriminatorily favorable treatment to a student loan debt. See In re Groves, 39 F. 3d 212 (8th Cir. 1994). Therefore, if student loan claims are classified separately in a chapter 13 plan, there must be a reason for doing so other than the fact that the debts are nondischargeable. See also In re Orawsky, 387 B.R. 128 (Bankr. E. D. Pa. 2008).

classification of student loan debts

A separate class may not be established for the claims of friends, relatives, or other favorites of the debtor. See In re Tennis, 232 B.R. 403 (Bankr. W. D. Mo. 1999). Further, the payment of an unsecured claim outside the plan constitutes the creation of a separate class of claims, and payments to such a creditor in excess of payments to other unsecured creditors are prohibited. See In re Green, 70 B.R. 164 (Bankr. W. D. Ark. 1986). For further reading on the extent to which unsecured claims may be treated unequally in a chapter 13 plan, see Williamson, The Bankruptcy Issues Handbook, supra, Art. 3.02.

unsecured claims, prohibited classes of

When the special classes of unsecured claims have been determined, the amount to be paid to the holders of such claims must be determined. The amount to be paid on such claims is usually determined by the type of claim and by the availability of funds under the plan. Certain claims, such as important business claims, claims which have been guaranteed by a special person, and nondischargeable claims, must usually be paid in full in order to accomplish the purpose of the plan. Other claims need not be paid in full in order to accomplish the purpose of the plan. Much depends on the type of claim, the purpose of the plan, and the availability of funds. Regardless of the purpose of the plan, if insufficient funds are available, after the payment of secured and priority claims, with which to pay a special class of claims in full, then the claims obviously cannot be paid in full. If the debtor has accrued and unpaid debts for domestic support obligations or for unpaid taxes, it is important to remember that these debts are usually priority claims that must be paid in full under the plan with interest, unless a particular creditor agrees otherwise. Further, in the absence of a justifiable reason for doing so, most courts will not permit significant payments to be made to special classes of unsecured creditors if little or nothing is paid to general unsecured creditors.

special classes of unsecured claims, determining amount to pay to

When the special classes of unsecured claims and the amount to be paid to the holders of such claims have been determined, the total amount to be paid to the holders of special classes of unsecured claims can be calculated. If this amount exceeds the amount remaining after the payment of secured and priority claims, the plan will not be feasible and must be changed.

special classes of unsecured claims, total amount paid to

The amount remaining after the payment of secured claims, priority claims and special classes of unsecured claims is the total amount that can be paid to the holders of all other (i.e., general) unsecured claims under the plan. It is necessary to ascertain the total amount to be paid to the holders of general unsecured claims for two reasons: (1) to determine whether each unsecured creditor will receive not less than what the creditor would have received had the debtor filed under chapter 7, and (2) to determine the acceptability of the plan to the court.

general unsecured claims, amount paid to

determining total amount of general unsecured claims

To determine the dividend payable to the holders of general unsecured claims under the plan, the total dollar amount of all such claims must be determined. For purposes of preparing the plan, the total dollar amount of such claims must usually be estimated, because the exact amount of each such claim is not usually known until later in the case. In making such an estimate, the unsecured portions of partially secured claims (other than claims secured solely by a mortgage on the debtor's home and claims secured by purchase-money security interests covered by 11 U.S.C. § 1325(a)) should be counted as unsecured claims.

executory contracts, damage claims from

Executory contracts and unexpired leases rejected in the debtor's plan under 11 U.S.C. § 1322(b)(7) are possible sources of unsecured claims. If such a contract or lease is rejected by the debtor, the contracting party becomes either a secured or an unsecured creditor, depending on the terms of the contract or lease, to the extent of any damages incurred as a result of the rejection, and such a claim is determined and allowed or disallowed as though the claim had arisen prior to the date of filing. See 11 U.S.C. § 502(g)(1). Unless the amount of the contracting party's damages can be agreed to, the extent and allowability of such damages must be determined by the court, and the total amount of unsecured claims to be dealt with under the plan will not be known until after the court rules on the matter.

general unsecured claims, categories of plans

In their treatment of general unsecured claims, chapter 13 plans may be categorized as follows: (1) 100 percent plans, where all general unsecured claims are paid in full; (2) 70 percent plans, where the debtor pays general unsecured claims enough (70 percent) to preserve the debtor's right to a chapter 7 discharge (see 11 U.S.C. § 727(a)(9) and section 2.17, supra); and (3) minimum payment plans, where the debtor pays as little as the court will allow to the holders of general unsecured claims. In practice, most plans are minimum payment plans.

treatment of unsecured claims, good faith requirements

While the courts vary in their approval of minimum payment plans, most courts will confirm such a plan if it is shown that the debtor is acting in good faith and that the plan constitutes the debtor's best effort. See, e.g., In re Warren, 89 B.R. 87 (BAP 9 1988); In re Nelson, 343 B.R. 671 (BAP 9 2006). It should be noted, however, that many courts have held that "good faith" is established when it is shown that the debtor has committed all of his or her disposable income to the plan for "an applicable commitment period" regardless of the amount paid to unsecured creditors under the plan. See 11 U.S.C. § 1325(b)(1); In re Henderson, 455 B.R. 203 (Bankr. D. Idaho 2011). For an in-depth discussion on what constitutes "good faith" in the proposal of a chapter 13 plan, see Williamson, The Bankruptcy Issues Handbook, supra, Art. 3.03.

unsecured claims, confirmation requirements

For a plan to be confirmed, the holder of each unsecured claim in every class must receive not less than what the holder would have received had the debtor been liquidated under chapter 7 on the same date. See 11 U.S.C. § 1325(a)(4). Therefore, if a debtor has significant nonexempt assets that would be used to pay dividends to creditors in a chapter 7 case, substantial payments to all unsecured creditors may be required under the plan.

general unsecured claims, payment of

If it appears under the above-described criteria that the amounts payable to the holders of general unsecured claims will be sufficient to satisfy the court, the plan should be prepared and submitted. Otherwise, the plan must be revised so as to provide more funds for general unsecured creditors. In many cases the best and simplest practice is for the debtor to propose to pay either a specified amount or the balance remaining after the payment of priority claims, secured claims, and special classes of unsecured claims ratably to the holders of general unsecured claims. See Exhibit 3-C, at the end of this chapter for an example of this type of provision.

3.09 Preparing the Chapter 13 Forms

Bankruptcy Rule 1001 provides that the Bankruptcy Rules and Official Forms shall govern the procedure in bankruptcy cases. Bankruptcy Rule 9009 provides that the Official Forms may be used with such alterations as may be appropriate and that the Official Forms may be combined and their contents rearranged to permit economies in their use. Bankruptcy Rule 9029 provides that the local bankruptcy rules may not prohibit or limit the use of the Official Forms. official bankruptcy forms, use of

11 U.S.C. § 521(a)(1) requires a chapter 13 debtor to file a list of creditors, and, unless the court orders otherwise, a schedule of assets and liabilities, a schedule of current income and current expenditures, a statement of the debtor's financial affairs, a certificate by the debtor's attorney that he has delivered to the debtor the notice required by 11 U.S.C. § 342(b), copies of all pay advices or other evidences of payment received by the debtor from any employer within 60 days prior to the date of filing, a statement of the amount of monthly net income, itemized to show how it was calculated, and a statement disclosing any reasonably anticipated increase in income or expenditures during the next 12 months. A list of creditors is contained in the debtor's schedules of liabilities and need not be filed separately unless the schedules of liabilities are not filed with the petition. statutory chapter 13 filing requirements

Bankruptcy Rule 1007(b)(1) requires a chapter 13 debtor to file schedules of assets and liabilities, a schedule of current income and expenditures, a schedule of executory contracts and unexpired leases, a statement of financial affairs, copies of all payment advices or other evidence of payment, if any, (with all but the last four digits of the debtor's social security number edited out), received by the debtor from an employer within 60 days prior to filing, a record of any interest that the debtor has in an education IRA or qualified state tuition program, each prepared as prescribed by the appropriate Official Form if one exists. In addition, unless the United States trustee has determined that the credit counseling requirement does not apply in the district, the debtor must file a certificate of credit counseling and any debt repayment plan prepared by the agency for the debtor, together with a statement of current monthly income prepared on an appropriate official form and, if the debtor has current monthly income greater than the applicable median family income for the applicable state and household size, the calculation of disposable income required by 11 U.S.C. § 1325(b)(3), prepared on the appropriate official form. See Bankruptcy Rule 1007(b)(3), (6). required schedules and statements

The following forms may be needed at the time of filing in a typical chapter 13 case: forms needed, typical chapter 13 case

Voluntary Petition for Individuals Filing for Bankruptcy (Official Form 101)

Chapter 13 Statement of Your Current Monthly Income and Calculation of Your Disposable Income (Official Forms 122C-1 and 122C-2)

Statement of Anticipated Increase in Income or Expenses (a local form, if needed)

Your Statement About Your Social Security Numbers (Official Form 121)

Certificate as to Credit Counseling

Debt Repayment Plan from credit counseling agency, if one exists

Schedules A/B, C, D, E/F, G, H, I, and J (Official Forms 106A/B, 106C, 106D, 106E/F, 106G, 106H, 106I, 106J, and 106J-2)

Your Statement of Financial Affairs for Individuals Filing for Bankruptcy (Official Form 107)

Application for Individuals to Pay the Filing Fee in Installments (Official Form 103A, if needed)

Disclosure of Compensation of Attorney for Debtor (Director's Form 2030 or a local form)

Notice to Individual Consumer Debtor (Director's Form 2010)

Copies of pay advices for last 60 days

Statement of Interest in Education IRA or Qualified State Tuition Program (a local form, if needed)

List of Names and Addresses of Persons to Receive Bankruptcy Notices

Declaration Regarding Electronic Filing (a local form that is needed for electronically filed cases)

chapter 13 forms, where to find

Some districts may require additional local forms to be completed and filed in chapter 13 cases, and the local rules should be checked for such requirements. The required local forms are usually supplied by the clerk of the bankruptcy court or may be downloaded from the local bankruptcy court's website. The local rules often contain copies of these forms. The official forms can be downloaded from the Argyle Publishing Company Bankruptcy Forms.

electronic filing, necessity of forms

If the case is being filed electronically, paper bankruptcy forms may not be needed because the required information can be transmitted via the internet directly from the debtor's attorney's computer to the electronic files in the clerk's office. If the case is not being filed electronically, care should be taken to ensure that the filed forms can be electronically scanned. This means that the forms should not be stapled together or contain notes or unwieldy attachments. In most districts the scanning is done by personnel in the clerk's office, but in some districts the filer must do the scanning. In many districts electronic filing is now required.

preparation of forms, use of work sheets

When the proper forms have been obtained and the necessary information assembled, the next task is that of preparing the chapter 13 forms for filing. The forms will be similar to those appearing in the exhibits at the end of chapter 2, and it is suggested that the exhibits be used as guides in preparing the forms for filing. If the Bankruptcy Worksheets appearing in Exhibit 2-C at the end of chapter 2 were used to assemble the information, the assembled data will be in the order required by with Schedules A/B through J and the Statement of Financial Affairs. Information for the Chapter 13 Statement of Your Current Monthly Income and Calculation of Your Disposable Income (Official Forms 122C-1 and 122C-2) is not contained in the work sheets, but much of the information needed for the statement will be contained in Schedules I and J.

verification of forms, when required

It is important that the chapter 13 bankruptcy forms be properly and completely prepared, both substantively and technically. If the forms are technically incomplete or incorrect, the clerk is likely to refuse to process them and return them to the debtor's attorney for corrections. It should be noted here that Bankruptcy Rule 1008 requires that all petitions, lists, schedules, statements, and amendments thereto be verified or contain an unsworn declaration as provided in 28 U.S.C. § 1746. This rule applies only to the original copy of each document. Other documents need not contain an unsworn declaration or be verified unless specifically required by a particular Bankruptcy Rule. See Bankruptcy Rule 9011(e), (f).

signature of attorney, effect of

filing of document by attorney, effect of, sanctions for violations

If the debtor is represented by an attorney, every petition, pleading, motion, and other paper filed in the case, other than a list, schedule, statement, or amendments thereto, must be signed by at least one attorney of record in the attorney's individual name, with the attorney's office address and telephone number stated. See Bankruptcy Rule 9011(a). An unrepresented debtor must personally sign each paper that requires a signature. An unsigned document will be stricken unless it is promptly signed. See Bankruptcy Rule 9011(a). Bankruptcy Rule 9011(b) and 11 U.S.C. § 707(b)(4) impose certification requirements on attorneys who sign bankruptcy petitions and document and liabilities for faulty certifications. For example, 11 U.S.C. § 707(b)(4)(D) provides that the signature of an attorney on the petition constitutes a certification that the attorney has no knowledge after an inquiry that the information in the schedules filed with the petition is incorrect. See section 2.03, supra, for further reading on the duties and liabilities of debtors' attorneys in bankruptcy cases.

signature requirements electronically filed documents

In most districts there are local rules or general orders that deal with the signature requirements of electronically-filed documents. Generally, documents, such as bankruptcy petitions, which must contain original signatures or which require verification under Bankruptcy Rule 1008 or an unsworn declaration under 28 U.S.C. § 1746, may be filed electronically using a facsimile imaged or electronic signature (e.g., "/s/John Doe"). The original signed document must be retained by the attorney of record or the party originating the document for the locally-required retention period. Upon request, the original document must be provided to other parties or to the court for review. In most districts the local rules or general orders provide that the use of an attorney's password to file a document electronically constitutes the signature of that attorney for purposes of Bankruptcy Rule 9011. The local rules and general orders should be checked in this regard. They are usually available on the website of the local bankruptcy court.

The preparation of each document normally required in a chapter 13 case is discussed separately below.

Statement of Your Current Monthly Income and Calculation of Your Disposable Income

Official Form 122C-1, is used for chapter 13 means testing and to calculate a qualifying debtor's monthly disposable income for chapter 13 purposes. This form must be completed and filed by every chapter 13 debtor, except that only a single form need be filed for both debtors in a joint case. A completed copy of this form appears in Exhibit 3-B(1) at the end of this chapter. This exhibit may be used as a guide in completing the form. statement of current monthly income, versions of

Except for the portion dealing with the debtor's marital status (which is simple in a chapter 13 case), Part 1 of Official Form 122C-1 is identical to Part 1 of the Chapter 7 Statement of Your Current Monthly Income (Official Form 122A-1) which is used in chapter 7 cases, the completion of which is covered in section 2.07. The reader is referred to section 2.07 for instructions on the completion of Part 1 of Official Form 122C-1. In completing Part 1 of Official Form 122C-1, figures should be entered in column B if the debtor is married, even if the case is not a joint case. statement of current monthly income, Part 1, preparation of

Official Form 122C-1 is where the debtor's applicable chapter 13 commitment period is calculated. 11 U.S.C. § 1325(b)(4) provides that the debtor's commitment period (i.e., the length of his or her chapter 13 plan) must be 3 years unless the combined current monthly income of the debtor and his or her spouse multiplied by 12 exceeds the highest median family income for debtor's state and family size, in which case the commitment period must be not less than 5 years, unless all unsecured claims can be paid off in a shorter period. If the debtor is married, if a joint case is not being filed, and if all of the spouse's income is not regularly contributed to the debtor's household expenses, the amount not contributed should be entered in line 13 of the form. If the required calculation (which is self explanatory on the form) shows that the debtor's commitment period is 3 years, Official 122C-2 is not necessary. applicable commitment period, calculation of

In completing line 16 of Form 122C-1 the median family income that is applicable to the debtor may be found at: https://www.justice.gov/ust/means-testing. It should be entered on line 16c. The appropriate marital adjustment, if any, should be entered in line 13. The debtor's annualized current monthly income should be entered on line 15. The appropriate box on line 17 should be checked. See sections 2.07 and 3.07, supra, for an explanation and discussion of median family income. statement of current monthly income, Part 2, preparation of

If the debtor's annualized current monthly income exceeds the applicable median family income and he or she is required to determine his or her disposable income using the IRS Standard expenses as provided in 11 U.S.C. § 1325(b)(3), Official Form 122C-2 must be completed. Part 1 of Official Form 122C-2 is identical to Part 2 of Official Form 122A-2, and the reader is referred to section 2.07, supra, for instructions on the completion of this part of the form. median family income, where to find

Official Form 122C-2 is where the type of monthly expenses to be used by the debtor in calculating his or her disposable income is determined. If the debtor's annualized current monthly income (i.e., current monthly income multiplied by 12) exceeds the median family income for the debtor's state and family size, the debtor is required by 11 U.S.C. § 1325(b)(3) to use the National and Local Standards prepared by the Internal Revenue Service (IRS) in determining his or her expenses for purposes of calculating disposable income. If the debtor's annualized current monthly income is less than the applicable median family income, the debtor may use his or her actual expenses in calculating disposable income and his or her disposable income will not appear in this form and must be calculated separately. See section 3.07, supra, for an explanation of actual versus IRS Standard expenses. IRS Standards, use of to calculate disposable income

calculation of disposable income

Official Form 122C-2 is where the debtor's monthly disposable income is calculated and is largely self explanatory and easy to complete. Again, it should be completed only if the debtor's annualized current monthly income exceeds the applicable median family income. The child support and retirement plan contribution figures entered in this part of the form are by statute not includable in disposable income and must be deducted from current monthly income (see section 3.07, supra). The figure appearing on line 45 is the debtor's monthly disposable income and is the amount that the debtor will most likely be required to pay under the plan to the chapter 13 trustee. See section 2.07, supra, for further reading on the completion of this part of the form, which is identical to Part 2 of Official Form 122A-2.

Voluntary Petition for Individuals Filing for Bankruptcy (Official Form 101)

voluntary petition, preparation of

Use Exhibit 2-F at the end of chapter two, supra, as a guide in preparing this document. The Voluntary Petition, as set forth in Official Form 101, is self-explanatory and relatively simple to complete. The instructions for completing a chapter 7 petition set forth in section 2.07, supra, should be followed in the preparation of a chapter 13 petition.

Your Statement About Your Social Security Numbers (Official Form 121)

statement of social security number, requirements and preparation of

Official Form 121 must be used for this statement. A completed sample of this form is set forth in Exhibit 2-D at the end of chapter two, supra. The form is self explanatory and simple to complete. The instructions for completing this form are set forth in section 2.07, supra, and should be followed.

Schedules A/B through J.

Schedules A/B through J, preparation requirements

Use Exhibits 2-G through 2-P at the end of chapter two, supra, as a guide in preparing these schedules (Official Forms 106A/B, 106C, 106D, 106E/F, 106G, 106H, 106I, 106J, and 106J-2). These schedules are prepared in substantially the same manner in a chapter 13 case as in a chapter 7 case and the instructions on their preparation set forth in section 2.07, supra, are equally applicable to chapter 13 cases and should be reviewed if necessary. When completing Schedule I (Your Income), the requested information pertaining to the debtor's spouse should be completed even if a joint petition is not being filed, unless the spouses are separated and maintain separate households. If the debtor is engaged in business, a detailed statement of the debtor's income and expenses from the business should be attached to Schedules I and J, respectively. The debtor's total projected monthly income and expenses and the total amount of the debtor's periodic payment under the plan should be calculated and inserted in the appropriate blanks at the bottom of Schedule J. These figures should be consistent with the figures appearing in the Statement of Your Current Monthly Income and Calculation of Your Disposable Income. The Declaration About an Individual Debtor's Schedules and the Summary of Your Assets and Liabilities and Certain Statistical Information (individuals) should be completed in the manner described in section 2.07, supra.

exempt property, how to list,

It is important to list the debtor's exemptions correctly on Schedule C because to confirm a chapter 13 plan the court must find that each unsecured creditor will receive under the plan not less than what it would have received had the debtor filed under chapter 7, and such a finding requires the court to consider the exemptions claimed by the debtor. Also, if the case is later converted to chapter 7, the exemptions may become important to the debtor. Complete lists of exempt property (both state and federal) may be found in Appendix III, infra. See section 2.08, supra, for further reading on the claiming of exemptions.

Your Statement of Financial Affairs for Individuals Filing for Bankruptcy

statement of financial affairs, preparation requirements

Use Exhibit 2-Q at the end of chapter two, supra, as a guide in preparing this statement. Official Form 107 must be used for the debtor's statement of financial affairs. The questions appearing in the statement of financial affairs are generally self-explanatory and a response should be made to each question. The instructions for completing the statement of financial affairs set forth in section 2.07, supra, are equally applicable to chapter 13 cases and should be reviewed if necessary.

Chapter 13 Plan and Related Documents.

chapter 13 plan, preparation of, when to file

As of December 1, 2017, Official Form 113 is now the official form for a chapter 13 plan. See Bankruptcy Rule 3015(c); Exhibit 3-C. This form must be used unless a local form has been adopted in compliance with Bankruptcy Rule 3015.1. Except as permitted by Rule 9009, alterations to the Official Form are prohibited. Additionally, per Rule 3015, nonstandard provisions are only effective if included in the designated section of the form. For assistance in filling out the official form, see the Committee Notes for Official Form 113, which are contained in the Argyle Official Bankruptcy Forms folder.

The Rules allow a local district to adopt its own form, so long as the form retains much of the key information in the official form. You should check the local rules prior to filing. The local rules often contain extensive requirements related to the preparation of chapter 13 plans and documents. A summary of the plan, a statement by the debtor, an analysis of the plan, and similar documents are often required. See section 3.08, supra, for further reading on the preparation of a chapter 13 plan. The plan must be filed either with the petition or within 14 days thereafter. See Bankruptcy Rule 3015(b). An advantage of filing the plan with the petition is that in most districts the confirmation hearing will be scheduled in conjunction with the meeting of creditors if this is done. If the plan is not filed with the petition, the confirmation hearing is likely to be scheduled for a different time and date, thus necessitating an additional court appearance by the debtor and his or her attorney.

Disclosure of Compensation of Attorney for Debtor (Director's Form 2030)

attorney's compensation documents, preparation of

Use Exhibit 2-A at the end of chapter 2, supra, as a guide in preparing this document. See section 3.03, supra, for the preparation requirements of this document. This document must be filed within 14 days after the order for relief.

Application For Allowance of Compensation.

Most districts require a local form for requesting compensation. If, however, no local form is required or available, use Exhibit 3-A at the end of this chapter as a guide in preparing this document. See section 3.03, supra, for a discussion of the necessity for and the preparation of this document.

other chapter 13 documents, preparation of

See section 2.07, supra, for instructions on the preparation of the Application for Individuals to Pay the Filing Fee in Installments (Official Form 103A), the Notice Required by 11 U.S.C. § 342(b) for Individuals Filing for Bankruptcy (Director's Form 2010), the List of Names and Addresses of Persons to Receive Notices, the Certificate as to Credit Counseling, and Declaration Regarding Electronic Filing. The local rules should be checked for additional documents or pleadings required to be filed with a chapter 13 petition. Motions to avoid liens under 11 U.S.C. § 522(f) and notices disputing the value of secured claims are often required to be filed with the petition or shortly thereafter. See sections 2.16, 3.05 and 3.08, supra, for further reading on the filing of motions to avoid liens.

CHAPTER THREE

Part C - Filing and Handling a Chapter 13 Case

3.10 Filing a Chapter 13 Case – Electronic Filing

venue requirements, chapter 13 case

A chapter 13 case should be filed in a district in which the domicile, residence, principal place of business, or principal assets of the debtor have been located for 180 days immediately preceding the commencement of the case, or for a longer portion of such 180 day period than the domicile, residence, principal place of business, or principal assets were located in any other district. See 28 U.S.C. § 1408. Thus, a debtor who has resided in two districts during the previous 180 days must reside (or maintain a principal place of business, etc.) in a particular district for a minimum of 91 days in order to satisfy the venue requirements for filing in that district. The change of venue requirements in chapter 13 cases are the same as those in chapter 7 cases, and the reader is referred to section 2.09, supra, for further reading.

chapter 13 forms, number of copies to file

Unless otherwise provided in the local rules, only one copy of any petition, schedule, statement, list or other document that is either filed electronically or converted to an electronic format upon filing (i.e., scanned) need be filed. The local rules should be checked in this regard. If the local court has adopted the electronic case file and management system, only one copy of each bankruptcy form need be filed, even if the case is not filed electronically.

chapter 13 plan, number of copies to file

Bankruptcy Rule 3015(d) requires the clerk to send a copy or summary of the chapter 13 plan with each notice of the confirmation hearing. The rule further states that if required by the court, the debtor shall furnish a sufficient number of copies of the plan to enable the clerk to include a copy with each such notice. Accordingly, many districts require the filing of a sufficient number of copies of the plan (or summaries of the plan in some districts) to permit the clerk to comply with Bankruptcy Rule 3015(d). The local rules should be checked for the specific filing requirements of not only the chapter 13 plan, but any related documents, such as summaries of the plan, statements of the debtor, or similar documents. If the local rules are silent on the subject, the safest practice is to contact the clerk's office in this regard.

filing fee, amount, necessity of payment

The total filing fee is $310 for either a single or a joint chapter 13 case. The $318 total filing fee consists of a $235 statutory filing fee plus a $78 administrative fee. See 28 U.S.C. § 1930(a)(1)(B). If an Application to Pay Filing Fee in Installments is filed, the filing fee may be paid in up to four installments, with the final installment payable not later than 120 days after the date of filing. For cause, however, the court may extend the time for any installment, provided that the last installment must be paid within 180 days of the date of filing. See Bankruptcy Rule 1006(b)(2). In chapter 13 cases the filing fee may not be waived and must normally be paid prior to confirmation of the plan. Any unpaid portion of the filing fee is usually paid out of the first payments made under the plan by the debtor. Plan payments must begin within 30 days after the plan is filed, unless the court orders otherwise. See 11 U.S.C. § 1326(a)(1).

chapter 13 forms, where to file

A chapter 13 case is commenced by filing a voluntary petition seeking relief under chapter 13 of the Bankruptcy Code with the clerk of the bankruptcy court in the proper district and division. If a bankruptcy clerk has not been appointed in the district, the petition (and all other documents in the case) should be filed with the clerk of the district court. If the case is not being filed on an emergency basis, the schedules, statements, plan, and other documents described in section 3.09, supra, should be filed with the petition.

If the debtor has an immediate need for the relief provided by the automatic stay and the case must be filed before the schedules, statements and other documents can be prepared, the case may be commenced by filing the petition accompanied by a list containing the names and addresses of all of the debtor's creditors and a certification under 11 U.S.C. § 109(h)(3) for a temporary exemption from the prefiling credit counseling requirement. See Bankruptcy Rule 1007(a)(1) and Bankruptcy Rule 1007(b)(3). If the filing fee is not paid in full when the petition is filed, an Application for Individuals to Pay the Filing Fee in Installments (Official Form 103A) must also be prepared and filed with the petition. The Notice Required by 11 U.S.C. § 342(b) for Individuals Filing for Bankruptcy (Director's Form 2010) should also be filed with the petition.

emergency filing procedure

If not filed with the petition, the schedules and statements must be filed within 14 days after the petition is filed. Any extension of the time for the filing of such statements and schedules may be granted by the court only on motion for cause shown and on notice to the United States trustee, the trustee or other party as the court may direct. See Bankruptcy Rule 1007(c). If not filed with the petition, the chapter 13 plan must also be filed within 14 days thereafter, and the time for filing may not be further extended except for cause and on such notice as the court may direct. See Bankruptcy Rule 3015(b).

chapter 13 forms, when to file

If it is important to deliver notice of the commencement of the case and of the automatic stay to certain creditors or other parties in advance of the mailing of the notice of commencement of case by the clerk, either a certified copy of the filed petition or a certificate of commencement of case signed by clerk (if available locally) may be used for this purpose and served upon the appropriate parties. A letter or other written notice from the debtor's attorney containing the bankruptcy case number and the date and time of filing will also suffice in most instances.

notice of commencement of case

Electronic Case Filing. The Administrative Office of the United States Courts has established a case management and electronic case file system for the U.S. Bankruptcy Courts whereby case files are maintained in an electronic format, rather than in a paper format as in the past. Under this system virtually all court documents must either be filed electronically or converted to an electronic format immediately upon filing by the electronic scanning of filed paper documents. In most districts a chapter 13 case may be filed either electronically or by the filing of paper documents as in the past. In the near future, however, it is expected that electronic filing will become mandatory in most districts. See section 2.09, supra, for further reading on the electronic case file system in the bankruptcy courts and on the electronic filing of bankruptcy cases.

Electronic case file

3.11 The Automatic Stay

automatic stay, effect of

The filing of a petition under chapter 13 operates as an automatic stay of acts, claims, and proceedings against the debtor and the debtor's property to the same extent as the filing of a petition under chapter 7. See 11 U.S.C. § 362(a),(b). Except as provided in the next paragraph, the statutory provisions dealing with relief from the automatic stay are the same under chapter 13 as under chapter 7. See 11 U.S.C. § 362(d). See section 2.10, supra, for a list of the acts stayed and not stayed by the automatic stay and for further reading on the automatic stay and the obtaining of relief therefrom.

section 1301 stay of actions against codebtor

Chapter 13 contains a special provision dealing with stays of actions against codebtors. See 11 U.S.C. § 1301. After an order for relief under chapter 13, which occurs with the filing of a chapter 13 petition, a creditor may not act or commence or continue a civil action to collect all or any part of a consumer debt of the debtor from any individual that is liable on the debt with the debtor, or that has secured the debt, unless the codebtor became liable on or secured the debt in the ordinary course of the codebtor's business, or unless the chapter 13 case is dismissed or converted to another chapter. See 11 U.S.C. § 1301(a). However, a creditor may present or give notice of dishonor of a negotiable instrument. See 11 U.S.C. § 1301(b). This stay is often referred to as the Section 1301 codebtor stay. See In re Lemma, 393 B.R. 299 (Bankr. E. D. N.Y. 2008).

section 1301 stay, relief from, grounds for

section 1301 stay, applicability to repossessions against codebtor

The court, after notice and hearing, may grant relief from the Section 1301 stay to a creditor to the extent that: (1) as between the debtor and the codebtor, the codebtor received the consideration for the creditor's claim, (2) the plan filed by the debtor proposes not to pay the claim, or (3) the creditor's interest would be irreparably harmed by the stay. See 11 U.S.C. § 1301(c). Twenty days after the filing of a request for relief from the stay on the grounds that the debtor's plan proposes not to pay the creditor's claim, the stay is terminated with respect to the requesting party unless the debtor or an individual liable on the debt with the debtor files and serves upon the requesting party a written objection to the proposed relief. See 11 U.S.C. § 1301(d). It should be noted that the Section 1301 stay applies to repossessions of property owned by a codebtor that is security for a debt owed by the debtor and is not limited to "in personam" collection actions against the codebtor. See In re King, 32 B.R. 226 (Bankr. D. Md. 2008).

secured creditors, obtaining relief from stay

stay of order granting relief

A secured creditor whose claim is not dealt with in the plan must obtain relief from the automatic stay in order to reclaim or foreclose on its security. See sections 2.10 and 2.19, supra, for further reading on this subject. Motions by such creditors for relief from the stay are normally granted if the debtor is in default on the creditor's claim. The court has discretion in the granting of such relief, however, and a debtor who disputes the alleged default or who can show extenuating circumstances should contest a motion for relief from stay. It should be noted that under Bankruptcy Rule 4001(a)(1), an order granting relief from the automatic stay (other than an order granting ex parte relief) is stayed until the expiration of 14 days after the entry of the order, unless the court orders otherwise.

prior bankruptcy case, effect of on stay

domestic support obligations, affect of stay on

Debtors who have filed or maintained a prior bankruptcy case within the past year may be denied all or part of the protection of the automatic stay. See 11 U.S.C. § 362(c)(3), (4). See section 2.10, supra, for further reading on this issue. It should be noted that the automatic stay does not stay actions or proceedings to collect domestic support obligations from property that is not property of the estate or from postpetition earnings of the debtor. See 11 U.S.C. § 362(b)(2)(B), (C).

defaulting debtor, creditors' remedies

Of concern to secured creditors in chapter 13 cases is the problem posed by the debtor who files under chapter 13, obtains the benefit of the automatic stay, and then abandons the plan after making few, if any, payments thereunder. In such instances the creditor may either seek relief from the automatic stay under 11 U.S.C. § 362(d) (see section 2.10, supra), or file a motion to dismiss the case under 11 U.S.C. § 1307(c) and Bankruptcy Rule 9014 (see section 3.17, infra). The dismissal of the case terminates the automatic stay and permits the creditor to proceed against its security. See 11 U.S.C. § 362(c)(1).

3.12 The Meeting of Creditors

The United States trustee must call a meeting of creditors to be held not less than 21 nor more than 50 days after the filing of a chapter 13 case. The meeting may be held at a regular place for holding court or at any other convenient place within the district designated by the United States trustee. If the place designated for the meeting is not regularly staffed by the United States trustee, the meeting may be held not more than 60 days after the filing of the case. See Bankruptcy Rule 2003.

meeting of creditors, when held, notice of

A central Bankruptcy Noticing Center (BNC) has been established in Reston, Virginia by the Administrative Office of the United States Courts. This center now sends most routine notices in bankruptcy cases, including the notice of commencement of case. The BNC processes about 300,000 bankruptcy notices per day. The BNC also provides a free Electronic Bankruptcy Noticing service (EBN) to attorneys who elect to participate in the service. In lieu of paper notices, an electing attorney may choose to receive bankruptcy notices:

Bankruptcy Noticing Center, functions of

(1) By E-mail.
(2) By EDI. This is for high volume recipients.

For more information on EBN and how to sign up for it, see the EBN website at ebn.uscourts.gov or call the EBN toll free help line at 877-837-3424. Those who do not elect to sign up for EBN will continue to receive notices by mail from the BNC.

The clerk, or such other person as the court may direct, must give the debtor, the trustee, and all creditors not less than 21 days notice of the meeting of creditors. See Bankruptcy Rule 2002(a). If the debtor's debts are primarily consumer debts, notice of the order for relief must be given to the trustee and all creditors within 21 days after the date of the order for relief. See Bankruptcy Rule 2002(o). The clerk, or such other person as the court may direct, must give the debtor, the trustee, and all creditors at least 28 days notice of the confirmation hearing and of the time fixed for filing objections to confirmation of the plan, and the notice must be accompanied by a copy or summary of the debtor's chapter 13 plan. See Bankruptcy Rules 2002(b) and 3015(d), and section 3.13, infra. Any notice given to creditors must contain the debtor's name, address and the last four digits of his or her taxpayer identification or social security number. See 11 U.S.C. § 342(c). In practice, a few days after the commencement of a chapter 13 case, a document entitled "Notice of Chapter 13 Bankruptcy Case, Meeting of Creditors, & Deadlines" is sent by the BNC to the debtor and all creditors and other parties in interest.

meeting of creditors, confirmation hearing, notice requirements

Not later than the day before the date on which the meeting of the creditors is first scheduled to be held, if the debtor was required to file a tax return under applicable nonbankruptcy law, the debtor must file with the appropriate tax authorities all tax returns for all taxable periods ending during the 4-year period preceding the filing of the case. If the required tax returns have not been filed by that date, the trustee may hold open the meeting of creditors for a reasonable period to allow the debtor additional time to file any unfiled returns. See 11 U.S.C. § 1308 for the particulars.

filing of prepetition tax returns by debtor, requirements

The United States trustee or a designee thereof must preside at the meeting of creditors. See Bankruptcy Rule 2003(b)(1). In most chapter 13 cases the United States trustee designates the standing chapter 13 trustee to preside over the meeting of creditors. The court may neither preside at nor attend the meeting of creditors. See 11 U.S.C. § 341(c). The meeting of creditors is often referred to as the Section 341(a) meeting. It should be noted that the hearing on confirmation of the debtor's plan is often held immediately after the meeting of creditors. This hearing, however, is presided over by a bankruptcy judge and not the chapter 13 trustee. See section 3.13, infra, for further reading on the confirmation hearing.

meeting of creditors, presiding officer

confirmation hearing, when held

meeting of creditors, order of business

The debtor may be examined under oath at the meeting of creditors. See Bankruptcy Rule 2003(b)(1). Especially if the confirmation hearing is scheduled for the same date and approximate time as the meeting of creditors, unsecured creditors who have filed objections to the debtor's plan are likely to attend the meeting, as are secured creditors who have not accepted the plan. Any creditor, as well as the trustee, may examine the debtor under oath if they so desire. See 11 U.S.C. § 343. In this regard it should be noted that a creditor holding a consumer debt or any representative of the creditor (which may include an entity or an employee of an entity and may be a representative for more than 1 creditor) is permitted to appear at and participate in the meeting of creditors, either alone or in conjunction with an attorney for the creditor. A creditor is not required to be represented by an attorney at the meeting of creditors. See 11 U.S.C. § 341(c). However, the examination of the debtor may relate only to the acts, conduct, property, liabilities or financial condition of the debtor, any matter that may affect the administration of the debtor's estate or the debtor's right to a discharge, or to the operation of the debtor's business and the desirability of its continuance, the source of any money or property acquired or to be acquired by the debtor for the purpose of consummating a plan and the consideration given or offered therefor, and any other matter relevant to the case or to the formulation of a plan. See Bankruptcy Rule 2004(b).

meeting of creditors, creditor representative

meeting of creditors, recording requirements, adjournment

Any examination under oath at the meeting of creditors must be recorded verbatim by the United States trustee using electronic sound recording equipment or other means of recording. Such record must be preserved by the United States trustee and made available for public access for two years thereafter. Upon request, the United States trustee must provide a certified copy or transcript of the recording at the expense of the person making the request. See Bankruptcy Rule 2003(c). The meeting may be adjourned from time to time by announcement at the meeting of the adjourned date and time, without further written notice. See Bankruptcy Rule 2003(e). It should be remembered that the debtor is required to provide the trustee and any requesting creditor with copies or transcripts of the debtor's most recent income tax returns at least 7 days prior to the meeting of creditors or the case is subject to dismissal under 11 U.S.C. § 521(e)(2)(B).

tax returns, providing of to trustee

The debtor is required under Bankruptcy Rule 4002(b) to bring the following items and documents to the meeting of creditors and make them available to the trustee or provide a written statement that the document or item either does not exist or is not in the debtor's possession:

meeting of creditors, items to bring to

(1) a picture identification issued by a governmental unit, or other personal identifying information that establishes the debtor's identity;

(2) evidence of the debtor's social security number;

(3) evidence of the debtor's income at the present time, such as the debtor's most recent pay stub;

(4) unless the trustee or the United States trustee instructs otherwise, statements for each of the debtor's depository and investment accounts (including checking accounts, savings accounts, money market accounts, mutual fund accounts and brokerage accounts) for the time period that includes the date of filing of the bankruptcy case; and

(5) if required under 11 U.S.C. § 707(b)(2)(A) or (B), documentation of the monthly expenses claimed by the debtor on the Statement of Current Monthly Income and Disposable Income Calculation filed by the debtor in the case.

meeting of creditors, required documents

In some districts written instructions are sent to the debtor, and often to the debtor's attorney, usually with the notice of commencement of case. These instructions may require the debtor to bring certain documents to the meeting. The debtor should, of course, bring the required documents to the meeting; otherwise the meeting may be postponed to a later date, necessitating another court appearance. The attorney's application for approval of compensation, if not combined with the attorney's disclosure statement, must be filed at or before this meeting in some districts.

meeting of creditors, procedure

In most districts the standing chapter 13 trustee presides at meetings of creditors in chapter 13 cases. Generally, meetings of creditors are informal and not lengthy, although the actual amount of time spent at a hearing may depend on when a particular case is called, as several cases are often scheduled for the same time period. If the confirmation hearing is held on the same date as the meeting of creditors, the amount of time spent at the hearings will depend on the dockets of both the chapter 13 trustee and the court. Disputes arising at the creditors' meeting may have to be taken before the court for resolution, either in conjunction with the confirmation hearing or separately.

If the addresses listed in the schedules for any of the creditors were incorrect, the notices mailed to those creditors will have been returned to the clerk's office by the Postal Service by the time of the meeting of creditors. If the matter is not brought to the attorney's attention by the hearing officer, the attorney should inquire or check the case file to insure that none have been returned. If one or more notices have been returned, it is important that a correct address be obtained for each creditor because the debt owed to a creditor who does not receive notice of the case will not be discharged. See 11 U.S.C. § 523(a)(3), and section 3.18, infra. Unless the court directs otherwise, an amended schedule should be filed listing the correct address for any such creditor. Notice of the case should be immediately mailed to any such creditors by the debtor's attorney.

incorrectly listed creditor, procedure

If an amended schedule is filed, only the corrected information need be shown, unless the local rules provide otherwise. It should be noted that a voluntary petition, list, schedule or statement may be amended by the debtor as a matter of course at any time before the case is closed. See Bankruptcy Rule 1009(a). If a creditor cannot be located, notice of the case may be served by publication under Bankruptcy Rule 2002(l). A fee is charged for amending a schedule of liabilities or a list of creditors. However, the court may waive the charge if the debtor's income is less than 150% of the poverty line. See 11 U.S.C. § 1930(f).

filing amended statement, procedure, fee

3.13 Obtaining Confirmation of a Chapter 13 Plan

The clerk of the bankruptcy court, or such other person as the court may direct, must give the debtor, the chapter 13 trustee, and all creditors not less than 28 days notice by mail of the time and place of the hearing on the confirmation of the debtor's plan and of the time fixed by the court for the filing of objections to confirmation of the plan. See Bankruptcy Rule 2002(b). A copy of the debtor's plan, or a summary thereof, must be included with this notice. See Bankruptcy Rule 3015(d).

confirmation hearing, notice requirements

Objections to confirmation of the debtor's plan must be filed in writing with the court within the time fixed by the court, and served on the debtor, the chapter 13 trustee, and the United States trustee within the time so fixed. Objections to confirmation are contested matters governed by Bankruptcy Rule 9014, which requires a hearing on reasonable notice and does not require the debtor to file a written response to the objection unless the court so orders. See Bankruptcy Rule 3015(f) and 11 U.S.C. § 1324(a).

objections to confirmation, filing requirements

If the debtor filed a chapter 13 plan with the petition, notice of date, time and place of the confirmation hearing and of the time fixed for the filing of objections to confirmation may be contained in the notice of commencement of case. Otherwise, a separate notice must be sent, often by the debtor under a local rule. This notice is especially important to unsecured creditors because the filing of objections to confirmation is their only method of opposing the debtor's plan. The local rules often contain extensive provisions dealing with the confirmation of chapter 13 plans. They may require the filing of a motion for confirmation and related documents using specified forms, as well as the mailing of notices to creditors by the debtor.

confirmation hearing, local rules

The court must hold a hearing on confirmation of a chapter 13 plan, after the giving of appropriate notice, not earlier than 20 days and not later than 45 days after the date of the meeting of creditors, unless the court determines that it would be in the best interests of the creditors and the estate to hold the hearing at an earlier date and there is no objection to the earlier date. See 11 U.S.C. § 1324(b). At the hearing the court will consider the plan proposed by the debtor, together with any accompanying documents and any proposed modifications, as well as any timely-filed objections to confirmation. Matters that must be resolved in order to finalize the plan, such as motions to avoid liens and the valuation of contested security interests, if not previously ruled on by the court, may also be ruled on at the confirmation hearing. Objections or disputes relating to the classification of claims in the plan may also be ruled on by the court at the confirmation hearing, although a separate hearing may be held under Bankruptcy Rule 3013, if desired.

confirmation hearing, when held, order of business

modifying plan prior to confirmation, procedure

The debtor may modify a chapter 13 plan at any time prior to confirmation as long as the plan, as modified, continues to meet the requirements of 11 U.S.C. § 1322, which are listed in section 3.08, supra. See 11 U.S.C. § 1323(a). If the debtor files a modified plan, the plan as modified becomes the chapter 13 plan. See 11 U.S.C. § 1323(b). However, every modification of a plan must be separately dated. See Bankruptcy Rule 3015(c). If a secured creditor has previously accepted or rejected the plan, the creditor will be deemed to have accepted or rejected the modified plan unless the modification changes the creditor's rights under the plan and the creditor changes its previous acceptance or rejection. See 11 U.S.C. § 1323(c). The court may find that a proposed modification does not change the treatment of a creditor's claim. The local rules should be checked for notice and other requirements relating to the modification of chapter 13 plans prior to confirmation.

valuation of security interest, procedure

An important aspect of many chapter 13 cases is the valuation of contested security interests. Such a valuation is often necessary in order to determine the amount of the allowed secured claim of a partially-secured creditor. In many districts the local rules govern the procedural aspects of valuation proceedings. Under such rules, the debtor may be required to list a value for the security interest of each secured claim (an amount that should appear on the debtor's Schedule D), with the creditor then required to file an objection to the value listed by the debtor within a specified period. If the local rules contain no such provisions, it may be necessary for the debtor to either file an objection to an excessive secured claim filed or asserted by a partially-secured creditor or file a motion under Bankruptcy Rule 3012 to determine the secured portion of a partially secured claim.

valuation of security interest, hearing

The value of a security interest must be determined in light of the purpose of the valuation and of any proposed use or disposition of the property. See 11 U.S.C. § 506(a)(1). However, the value of personal property securing an allowed claim must be determined based on the replacement value of the property as of the date of the filing of the petition without deduction for costs of sales or marketing. With respect to property acquired for personal, family, or household purposes, replacement value means the price a retail merchant would charge for property of that kind considering the age and condition of the property at the time value is determined. See 11 U.S.C. § 506(a)(2). It is usually in the debtor's interest to value secured property as low as possible because this will make the creditor's secured claim as small as possible. At the valuation hearing, whether held in conjunction with the confirmation hearing, under Bankruptcy Rule 3012, or otherwise, the debtor should be prepared to present evidence as to the replacement value of the property in question. Usually the debtor is competent to testify as to the value of his or her property. See Federal Rule of Evidence No. 701 and the cases cited thereunder. Therefore, with respect to personal property the debtor should be prepared to testify as to the price of comparable replacement property and the age and present condition of the debtor's property. It may be advisable to employ an appraiser or other expert, especially if the property is valuable and the discrepancy in asserted values is great. Recent photographs of the property may also be helpful.

personal property, valuation of

partially-secured creditor, cram-down

By seeking a judicial determination of the value of the security interest of a partially-secured creditor, the debtor can often prevent the creditor from blocking confirmation of the plan. This may be accomplished by proposing in the plan that the creditor retain its lien and be paid the secured portion of its claim, with interest, in an equitable manner under the plan. If the court accepts the debtor's proposal and confirms the plan, the creditor will be forced to accept the plan under 11 U.S.C. § 1325(a)(5)(B), and the unsecured balance of its claim will be treated under the plan as an unsecured claim. This is the so-called "cramdown" feature of chapter 13. It can be a useful tool for the debtor in dealing with partially secured creditors. It should be noted, however, that a "cramdown" may not be imposed on creditors holding certain purchase-money security interests (see next paragraph) or on a partially-secured creditor secured only by a mortgage on the debtor's residence. See Nobleman v. American Savings Bank, 508 U.S. 324, 113 S. CT. 2106 (1993), which is discussed in section 3.08, supra.

claims secured by purchase-money security interests, confirmation requirements

It should be noted that 11 U.S.C. § 506 does not apply to the partially-secured claim of (1) a creditor who has a purchase-money security interest in a motor vehicle that was acquired for the personal use of the debtor via a debt that was in incurred within 910 days prior to bankruptcy, or (2) a creditor who has a purchase-money security interest in any other property of value if the debt was incurred within 1 year prior to bankruptcy. See the clause at the end of 11 U.S.C. § 1325(a). What this means is that the partially-secured claim of such a creditor may not be bifurcated into secured and unsecured portions under Code section 506 and must therefore be treated under the plan as a fully secured claim regardless of the value of secured property. As indicated above, a cramdown under 11 U.S.C. § 1325(a)(5)(B) may not be imposed on such a creditor.

To confirm a chapter 13 plan, the court must find that the plan meets the requirements of 11 U.S.C. § 1322 and 1325(a), which are described in section 3.08, supra. However, in the absence of a timely filed objection to confirmation, the court may find, without receiving evidence, that the plan has been proposed in good faith and not by any means forbidden by law. See Bankruptcy Rule 3015(f). On most other matters, however, the burden of establishing the right to confirmation rests with the debtor, who should be prepared to show that the requirements of 11 U.S.C. § 1322 and 1325(a) have been met or complied with in the case. See In re Potgieter, 436 B.R. 739 (Bankr. M. D. Fla. 2010). Much of the required information will be contained in the court records and in the schedules, statements and other documents filed by the debtor. However, the court may require additional documentation or testimony from the debtor, especially if the plan appears to be difficult for the debtor to comply with or pays little or nothing to unsecured creditors or if there is a question as to whether the debtor's annualized current monthly income is below the applicable median family income.

confirmation hearing, procedure

The debtor should be prepared to justify the income and expense figures appearing in the schedules of current income and current expenditures or in the Statement of Current Monthly Income and Disposable Income Calculation. The debtor should also be prepared to show that all of his or her projected disposable income for the period of the plan will be applied to the plan. If the plan establishes special classes of unsecured claims, the debtor should be prepared to justify the classification and treatment of such claims. If assets are to be contributed to the plan by the debtor, the manner in which the assets are to be contributed and the amount to be realized from such assets should be established.

confirmation hearing, debtor's responsibilities

The order of confirmation must be entered by the court, and notice of the entry of the order will presumably be mailed or transmitted by the clerk to the debtor, the creditors, the trustee, the United States trustee, and other parties in interest, although the Bankruptcy Rules contain no such requirement. After entry of the order of confirmation, the court may enter any order necessary to administer the case and may compel any entity from whom the debtor receives income to pay all or any part of such income to the chapter 13 trustee. See 11 U.S.C. § 1325(c). A sample Order Confirming Chapter 13 Plan is set forth in Exhibit 3-D at the end of this chapter.

order of confirmation, form, notice

The provisions of a confirmed plan bind the debtor and each creditor, whether or not the claim of the creditor is dealt with under the plan and whether or not the creditor has objected to, accepted, or rejected the plan. See 11 U.S.C. § 1327(a). Except as otherwise provided in the plan or in the order confirming the plan, the confirmation of a plan vests the property of the estate in the debtor. See 11 U.S.C. § 1327(b). And, except as otherwise provided in the plan or in the order confirming the plan, the property vested in the debtor is free and clear of any claim or interest of any creditor dealt with under the plan. See 11 U.S.C. § 1327(c).

confirmed chapter 13 plan, effect of

Upon a complaint filed by a party in interest within 180 days after the order of confirmation, and after notice and a hearing, the court may revoke an order of confirmation if the order was procured by fraud. See 11 U.S.C. § 1330(a). A proceeding to revoke an order of confirmation is an adversary proceeding governed by Part VII of the Rules of Bankruptcy Procedure. See Bankruptcy Rule 7001. If an order of confirmation is revoked, the court may dismiss the case or convert it to chapter 7, unless the debtor modifies the plan and the modified plan is confirmed by the court. See 11 U.S.C. § 1330(b).

revocation of confirmation, grounds, procedure

3.14 The Chapter 13 Trustee

standing trustee, when appointed

If a sufficient number of chapter 13 cases are filed in a district, a standing trustee may be appointed to serve in chapter 13 cases filed in the district. See 28 U.S.C. § 586(b). If the standing trustee qualifies under 11 U.S.C. § 322, he or she will normally be appointed to serve as trustee in a chapter 13 case. Otherwise, a disinterested person must be appointed to serve as the trustee in the case. See 11 U.S.C. § 1302(a). The chapter 13 trustee is appointed by the United States trustee. See section 2.16, supra, for further reading on the powers and duties of the United States trustee.

chapter 13 trustee, duties, fee

The principal function of the chapter 13 trustee is to collect the payments made by the debtor and disburse the funds as provided in the plan, in the order confirming the plan, and by applicable law. The chapter 13 trustee must retain the payments made by the debtor until the ruling on confirmation of the plan. If the plan is confirmed, the trustee must begin making payments under the plan as soon as practicable. See 11 U.S.C. § 1326(a)(2). If the plan is not confirmed, the trustee must return any retained funds to the debtor after deducting administrative expenses therefrom. See 11 U.S.C. § 1326(a)(3). Before making payments under the plan, however, the trustee must pay any unpaid administrative expenses and fees assessed against the debtor's estate. Such fees and expenses normally include the unpaid portions of the filing fee and the fee allowed the debtor's attorney, the chapter 13 trustee's fee, which is usually ten percent of the amount received by the trustee under the plan, and, if a chapter 7 trustee has been allowed compensation due to the conversion or dismissal of the debtor's prior chapter 7 case for abuse under 11 U.S.C. § 707(b), the unpaid portion of that compensation, which must be prorated over the period of the plan in specified amounts. See 11 U.S.C. § 1326(b). Except as otherwise provided in the plan or in the order confirming the plan, the trustee must make all payments to creditors under the plan. See 11 U.S.C. § 1326(c).

The duties of the chapter 13 trustee are set forth in 11 U.S.C. § 1302 and Bankruptcy Rule 2015(c). In nonbusiness chapter 13 cases, the duties of the chapter 13 trustee include the following:

duties of trustee, nonbusiness case

(1) Ensure that the debtor commences making timely payments under the plan or proposed plan.

(2) Be accountable for all money and other property received.

(3) Keep a record of receipts and the disposition of money and property received.

(4) Investigate the financial affairs of the debtor.

(5) Examine proofs of claims and object to the allowance of any improper claim, if a purpose would be served.

(6) Oppose the discharge of the debtor, if advisable.

(7) Furnish such information concerning the estate and its administration as may be requested by a party in interest, unless the court orders otherwise.

(8) Appear and be heard at any hearing concerning the value of property subject to a lien, the confirmation of a plan, or the modification of a plan after confirmation.

(9) Advise (except on legal matters) and assist the debtor in his or her performance under the plan.

(10) Approve or disapprove postpetition claims for necessary consumer debts to be incurred by the debtor, if so requested under section 1305(c) of the Bankruptcy Code.

(11) If there is a claim for a domestic support obligation against the debtor, provide the written notice specified in 11 U.S.C. § 1302(d) to the holder of the claim and to the state child support enforcement agency.

(12) Make a final report and file a final account of the administration of the estate with the court and the United States trustee.

If the debtor is engaged in business, the duties of the chapter 13 trustee, in addition to the duties listed above, include the following:

duties of trustee, business case

(1) Unless ordered otherwise by the court, investigate the acts, conduct, assets, liabilities, and financial condition of the debtor, the operation of the debtor's business and desirability of its continuance, and any other matter relevant to the case or to the formulation of a plan.

(2) As soon as practical, file a statement of such investigation, including any finding of fraud, dishonesty, incompetence, misconduct, mismanagement, or irregularity in the management of the debtor's affairs, or the discovery of any cause of action available to the estate. See 11 U.S.C. § 1302(c).

powers of chapter 13 trustee

A chapter 13 trustee has the avoidance and other powers of a trustee under any other chapter of the Bankruptcy Code. See 11 U.S.C. § 103(a). See section 2.16, supra, for a discussion of these powers. While a chapter 13 trustee seldom takes possession of the debtor's estate (see 11 U.S.C. § 1306(b)), the trustee is charged with the duty of preserving the estate for the benefit of creditors should the chapter 13 plan fail. See In re Cohen, 305 B.R. 886 (BAP 9 2004). Under chapter 13, the debtor's estate includes, in addition to the estate that would have existed under chapter 7 (which is described in section 2.15, supra), property of the kind included under chapter 7 that is acquired by the debtor during the pendency of the chapter 13 case, and earnings from services performed by the debtor during the pendency of the chapter 13 case. See 11 U.S.C. § 1306(a). Except as provided in the plan or in the order confirming the plan, the debtor retains possession of all property of the estate. See 11 U.S.C. § 1306(b).

debtor's estate, what constitutes

payments made directly to creditor by debtor, when required

While the chapter 13 trustee normally pays all claims allowed under the plan, certain creditors must, by statute, be paid directly by the debtor. Postpetition lease payments on leases of personal property (e.g., automobile leases) and adequate protection payments to creditors holding a purchase-money security interest in personal property of the debtor must be paid by the debtor directly to the lessor or creditor. See 11 U.S.C. § 1326(a)(1)(B), (C). The amount of any such payment may be deducted by the debtor from the amount paid to the chapter 13 trustee and the debtor must provide the trustee with evidence of payment, including the amount and date of payment. Within 60 days after the case is filed the debtor must provide the lessor or creditor with evidence that any required insurance coverage on the property is being maintained. See 11 U.S.C. § 1326(a)(4).

evidence of insurance, when required

contacts with bankruptcy judge

All parties in interest, including the chapter 13 trustee and the United States trustee, and any attorney, accountant, or employee of a party in interest, must refrain from ex parte contacts, meetings, or communications with the bankruptcy judge concerning matters affecting a particular case or proceeding. See Bankruptcy Rule 9003.

3.15 Modifying a Chapter 13 Plan After Confirmation - Postpetition Debts

modification of plan, after confirmation, typical reasons

It often happens that at some point during the course of a chapter 13 case the debtor becomes unable to make the payments required under the plan. Unemployment, illness, injury, a divorce, a business setback, and the failure of the debtor to control his or her spending are the most common causes of a debtor's inability to comply with the plan. Other reasons for modifying a confirmed plan include the making of an outside payment on a claim dealt with under the plan, the incurrence by the debtor of an allowable postpetition debt, and a significant change in the debtor's income or expenses. For a variety of reasons, then, it often becomes necessary for a debtor to modify his or her plan after confirmation. Usually the alternative is dismissal or conversion to chapter 7.

modification of plan, grounds for

Modification of a chapter 13 plan after confirmation is governed by Bankruptcy Rule 3015(g) and by 11 U.S.C. § 1329(a), which provides that at any time after confirmation of a plan, but before the completion of payments under the plan, the plan may be modified, upon the request of the debtor, the trustee, or the holder of an allowed unsecured claim, so as to:

(1) increase or reduce the amount of payments on claims of a particular class provided under the plan,

(2) extend or reduce the time for such payments,

(3) alter the amount of the distribution to a creditor whose claim is provided for by the plan, to the extent necessary to take account of any payment of such claim other than under the plan, or

modification of plan to provide health insurance for debtor

(4) reduce amounts to be paid under the plan by the actual amount expended by the debtor to purchase health insurance for the debtor (and for any dependent of the debtor if he or she does not have health insurance) if the debtor documents the cost of the insurance and demonstrates (a) that the expenses are reasonable and necessary, (b) if the debtor had health insurance, that the amount is not materially larger than the cost the debtor previously paid or the cost necessary to maintain the lapsed policy, or if the debtor did not have health insurance that the amount is not materially larger than the reasonable cost that would be incurred by a debtor who purchases health insurance, who has similar income, expenses, age, and health status, and who lives in the same geographical location with the same number of dependents who do not otherwise have health insurance coverage, and (c) that the amount is not otherwise allowed for purposes of determining disposable income under section 11 U.S.C. § 1325(b). Upon the request of a party in interest, the debtor must file proof that a health insurance policy was purchased.

same, good cause, what constitutes

same, amending order of confirmation

A showing of good cause is required of any party seeking modification of a chapter 13 plan after confirmation. For the debtor to modify a confirmed plan under 11 U.S.C. § 1329(a), a substantial unanticipated change in the debtor's circumstances must be shown. See In re Mattson, 456 B.R. 75 (Bankr. W. D. Wash. 2011); but see In re Arnold, 869 F.2d 240 (4th Cir. 1989). Many courts, it should be noted, are reluctant to permit the debtor to modify a confirmed plan so as to include one or more additional unsecured creditors if the modification will prejudice the rights of existing creditors under the plan. See In re Plummer, 378 B.R. 569 (Bankr. C. D. Ill. 2007). Because of the limited instances under which a confirmed chapter 13 plan may be modified, it may be more practicable to amend the order of confirmation than to modify the plan, if the proposed change is not substantial.

same, at request of trustee or creditor

It should be understood that if the debtor's circumstances change so as to increase the amount of the debtor's disposable income, the chapter 13 trustee or an unsecured creditor may request modification of a confirmed plan under 11 U.S.C. § 1329(a). See In re Wetzel, 381 B.R. 247 (Bankr. E. D. Wis. 2008). Minor changes in the debtor's income or expenses, however, do not warrant modification of a confirmed plan.

same, plan requirements

The plan contents requirements described above for confirmation apply to the modification of a plan after confirmation. See 11 U.S.C. § 1329(b)(1), and section 3.08, supra. The confirmation requirements of 11 U.S.C. § 1325(a) also apply to the modification of a plan after confirmation. See 11 U.S.C. § 1329(b)(1). These requirements are also set forth in section 3.08, supra. The plan as modified becomes the debtor's chapter 13 plan unless, after notice and hearing, the proposed modification is disapproved by the court. See 11 U.S.C. § 1329(b)(2). Bankruptcy Rule 3015(c) requires any modification to be dated.

modified plan, maximum length

If a proposed modification seeks to extend the duration of a chapter 13 plan, it should be noted that a plan modified after confirmation may not provide for payments over a period that expires after the applicable commitment period beginning on the date that the first payment under the originally-confirmed plan was due, unless the court, for cause, approves a longer period, but the court may not approve a period that expires more than five years after such date. See 11 U.S.C. § 1329(c). Thus, a modified plan may not provide for payments by the debtor beyond five years after the date upon which the first payment was due under the originally-confirmed plan.

modified plan, rights of creditors

A secured creditor who has accepted or rejected the originally-confirmed plan will be deemed to have accepted or rejected the modified plan unless the modification changes the rights of the creditor under the plan and the creditor changes its previous acceptance or rejection. See 11 U.S.C. § 1323(c). If the rights of a secured creditor are found by the court to be changed by a proposed modification, the clerk or some other party as the court may direct must give the creditor at least 21 days notice of the time fixed by court for accepting or rejecting the proposed modification. See Bankruptcy Rule 2002(a)(6). If the rights of a class of unsecured creditors are found by the court to be changed by the proposed modification, the affected creditors must be given notice and an opportunity to file objections to the confirmation of the modified plan. See 11 U.S.C. § 1323(c) and Bankruptcy Rule 3015(g).

modifying plan, procedure

The procedure for modifying a plan after confirmation is a contested matter governed by Bankruptcy Rule 9014, which means that a proceeding to modify a confirmed plan is initiated by the filing of a motion, with reasonable notice and an opportunity for hearing afforded the parties against whom relief is sought. The local rules should be checked for notice and other requirements applicable to motions to modify a plan after confirmation. A sample Motion to Modify Chapter 13 Plan After Confirmation is set forth in Exhibit 3-E at the end of this chapter.

postpetition claims, allowance of

Chapter 13 debtors frequently encounter a need for credit during the course of a case. The need of money for medical, business, or other emergency purposes, and the need for a new or different automobile or household appliance are common causes of the need for such credit. Postpetition claims may be filed only for - (1) taxes that become payable to a governmental unit while the case is pending, and (2) consumer debts arising after the date of the order for relief under chapter 13 that are for property or services necessary for the debtor's performance under the plan. See 11 U.S.C. § 1305(a). However, claims for consumer debts are not allowable if the holder of the claim knew, or should have known, that the prior approval by the trustee of the incurrence of the obligation by the debtor was practicable and was not obtained. See 11 U.S.C. § 1305(c). A consumer debt is a debt incurred primarily for a personal, family, or household purpose. See 11 U.S.C. § 101(8). Qualifying postpetition claims are allowed or disallowed on the same basis as any other claims, but are determined as of the date the claim arose. See 11 U.S.C. § 1305(b).

postpetition claims, trustee's approval of

Even if a postpetition claim for a consumer debt is allowed by the court, the debt upon which the claim is based is not dischargeable in the case if the prior approval of the chapter 13 trustee was practicable and was not obtained. See 11 U.S.C. § 1328(d). It is important to the debtor, therefore, that the trustee's prior approval of such debts be obtained, and the burden of obtaining such approval usually rests with the debtor. A sample of a written request for the trustee's prior approval of a postpetition consumer debt may be found in Exhibit 3-F at the end of this chapter. In some districts the chapter 13 trustee may have forms for such requests.

3.16 Creditors - Claims and Payments

proofs of claims, filing and notice requirements

A creditor must file a proof of claim with the clerk of the bankruptcy court within 70 days after the first date set for the meeting of creditors for the claim to be allowed, unless the claim is filed on behalf of the creditor by the trustee, the debtor or a codebtor, or a guarantor. See Bankruptcy Rule 3002(a),(b),(c). There are four exceptions to the 70 day requirement for filing proofs of claims. These exceptions deal with claims by the governmental units, (who under 11 U.S.C. § 502(b)(9) have 180 days to file a claim), claims for infants or incompetents, claims that become allowable as a result of judgments, and claims arising from the rejection of executory contracts. See Bankruptcy Rule 3002(c). The clerk, or some other person as the court may direct, must give each creditor notice by mail of the time allowed for the filing of claims. See Bankruptcy Rule 2002(f)(3). This notice is normally contained in the notice of commencement of case.

proof of claim, by debtor or trustee

lien of creditor not dealt with in plan

If a creditor fails to file a claim on or before the first date set for the meeting of creditors, the debtor or the trustee may file a claim in the name of the creditor, a notice of which the clerk must forthwith mail to the creditor, the debtor, and the trustee. See Bankruptcy Rule 3004 and 11 U.S.C. § 501(c). This can be a useful provision for the debtor with respect to claims for nondischargeable debts and claims of partially-secured creditors which the debtor wishes to pay under the plan. If the creditor thereafter files a proof of claim, it supersedes the claim filed by the trustee or debtor on the creditor's behalf. See Bankruptcy Rule 3004. It should be noted that if no claim is filed on behalf of a secured creditor and if the creditor is not dealt with in the plan, the creditor's lien survives the chapter 13 case. See 11 U.S.C. § 506(d)(1).

proof of claim, by codebtor or guarantor

If a creditor fails to file a proof of claim, one who is liable with the debtor to the creditor, or one who has secured the creditor, may, within 30 days after the expiration of the 70 day period for filing claims, execute and file a proof of claim in the name of the creditor, if known, or if unknown, in the person's own name. However, no distribution can be made on the claim except on satisfactory proof that the original debt will be diminished by the amount distributed. The creditor may thereafter file a proof of claim, which shall supersede the proof of claim filed on its behalf. See Bankruptcy Rule 3005(a) and 11 U.S.C. § 501(b).

subrogated, transferred, offsetting, or improperly filed claims

See section 2.19, supra, for a discussion of subrogated claims, transferred claims, and offsetting claims. See section 3.15, supra, for a discussion of postpetition claims. See Bankruptcy Rule 5005(c) for the procedures when a claim is filed with the wrong official.

proof of claim, where filed, form and content

A proof of claim must be filed with the clerk of the bankruptcy court in the district where the case is pending. See Bankruptcy Rule 5005(a). The local rules often require a proof of claim to be filed in duplicate. A proof of claim is a written statement setting forth a creditor's claim. It must conform substantially to Official Form 410. See Bankruptcy Rule 3001(a). A proof of claim must be executed by the creditor or the creditor's authorized agent, unless it is filed on the creditor's behalf by the debtor, the trustee, a codebtor, or a guarantor. See Bankruptcy Rule 3001(b). If a claim, or an interest in property of the debtor securing a claim, is based on a writing, the original or a duplicate of the writing must be filed with the proof of claim, or its loss or destruction explained in a statement filed with the claim. See Bankruptcy Rule 3001(c). If a security interest in property of the debtor is claimed, the proof of claim must be accompanied by evidence that the security interest has been perfected. See Bankruptcy Rule 3001(d). A sample Proof of Claim is set forth in Exhibit 3-G at the end of this chapter.

withdrawal of claim

A creditor may withdraw a claim as of right by filing a notice of withdrawal, unless an objection to the claim or a complaint against the creditor in an adversary proceeding has been filed. Also, if a creditor has accepted the plan or otherwise participated significantly in the case, the creditor may not withdraw its claim except on order of the court after a hearing on notice. See Bankruptcy Rule 3006.

proof of claim, additional information required for individual consumer debtors

Bankruptcy Rule 3001(c)(2) requires additional information to be filed with the proof of claim in consumer debtor cases. This additional information includes: (1) an itemization of interest, fees, expenses, and other charges included in the claim which were incurred before the petition was filed; (2) a statement of the amount necessary to cure any prepetition default on a claim secured by a security interest in the debtor's property; and, (3) if a claim is secured by a security interest in the debtor's principal residence, an escrow account statement as of the petition date, if an escrow account has been established. Sanctions may be imposed on a creditor who fails to provide the required information with its proof of claim. See Bankruptcy Rule 3001(c)(2)(D)(i) and (ii).

An objection to the allowance of a claim must be in writing and filed with the clerk of the bankruptcy court. A copy of the objection and a notice of the hearing thereon must be mailed or otherwise delivered to the claimant, the debtor, and the trustee at least 30 days prior to the hearing. If an objection is joined with a demand for relief of the kind specified in Bankruptcy Rule 7001 (i.e., to determine the validity or priority of a lien, etc.), it becomes an adversary proceeding. See Bankruptcy Rule 3007. The local rules often contain provisions dealing with the filing of objections to claims in chapter 13 cases and they should be checked in this regard. objections to allowance of claims

A properly executed and filed proof of claim constitutes prima facie evidence of the validity and amount of the claim. See Bankruptcy Rule 3001(f). Unless a party in interest files an objection to a properly filed claim, it is deemed allowed. See 11 U.S.C. § 502(a). If an objection to a claim is timely filed, the court, after a hearing on notice, must determine the amount of the claim as of the date of filing of the petition, and must allow the claim in that amount, except to the extent that: proof of claim, effect of filing

(1) the claim is unenforceable against the debtor and the debtor's property under any agreement or applicable law for a reason other than because such claim is contingent or unmatured; claims, not allowable

(2) the claim is for unmatured interest;

(3) if the claim is for taxes assessed against property of the debtor's estate, the claim exceeds the reasonable value of the estate's interest in the property;

(4) if the claim is for services of an insider or attorney of the debtor, the claim exceeds the reasonable value of such services;

(5) the claim is for a debt for an unmatured and nondischargeable domestic support obligation;

(6) if the claim is for damages to a lessor for the termination of a lease of real property, the claim exceeds amounts specified in 11 U.S.C. § 502(b)(6);

(7) if the claim is for damages for the termination of an employment contract, the claim exceeds certain amounts specified in 11 U.S.C. § 502(b)(7);

(8) the claim results from a reduction, due to late payment, in the amount of an otherwise applicable credit available to the debtor in connection with an employment tax on wages, salaries or commissions earned from the debtor; or

(9) proof of the claim was not timely filed, unless a tardy filing of the claim is permitted by the Rules of Bankruptcy Procedure or is permitted under 11 U.S.C. § 502(b)(9). See 11 U.S.C. § 502(b).

In addition, the claim of an entity from which property is recoverable by the trustee or that is a transferee of a voidable transfer must be disallowed, unless the entity has paid the amount or turned over the property for which it is liable. See 11 U.S.C. § 502(d). Certain claims for reimbursement or contribution are also not allowable. See 11 U.S.C. § 502(e). Contingent or unliquidated claims, the liquidation of which would unduly delay the closing of the case, must be estimated by the court for purposes of allowance. See 11 U.S.C. § 502(c). It should be noted that a proceeding to liquidate or estimate personal injury or wrongful death claims against the estate for purposes of distribution is not a core proceeding and may not be heard by the bankruptcy judge unless the parties agree otherwise. See 28 U.S.C. § 152(b)(2)(B). Core proceedings are discussed in section 2.01, supra. claims, when disallowed contingent or unliquidated claims, allowance of

A party in interest may move for the reconsideration of an order allowing or disallowing a claim, whereupon the court, after a hearing on notice, must enter an appropriate order. See Bankruptcy Rule 3008. See 11 U.S.C. § 502(j) for the effect of an order of reconsideration on the payment of a claim. reconsideration of claim

A proof of claim filed by the holder of a claim that is secured by a security interest in the debtor's principal residence is timely filed if the proof of claim (Official Form 410) and the proof of claim attachment (Official Form 401A) and escrow analysis requires by Rule 3001(c)(2)(C) is filed no later than 70 days after the bankruptcy filing date; and any attachments required by Rule 3001(c)(1) and (d) are filed as a supplement to the holder's claim not later than 120 days after the bankruptcy filing date.

reduction of claim for refusing to negotiate

Creditors should be aware that the court, on the motion of the debtor and after a hearing, may reduce a claim based on an unsecured consumer debt by up to 20 percent of the claim, if (1) the claim was filed by a creditor who unreasonably refused to negotiate a reasonable alternative repayment schedule proposed on behalf of the debtor by an approved nonprofit budget and credit counseling agency, (2) the offer of the debtor was made at least 60 days before the date of the filing of the petition and provided for payment of at least 60 percent of the amount of the debt over a period not to exceed the repayment period of the loan, or a reasonable extension thereof, and (3) no part of the debt under the alternative repayment schedule is nondischargeable. See 11 U.S.C. § 502(k)(1). The debtor has the burden of proving, by clear and convincing evidence, that the creditor unreasonably refused to consider the debtor's proposal and that the proposed alternative repayment schedule was made prior to expiration of the 60 day period specified above.

claims, filing and allowance local rules

secured claim, allowance, valuation

The local rules in many districts contain special provisions dealing with the filing and allowance of both secured and unsecured claims in chapter 13 cases. In some districts a proof of claim form is printed on the reverse side of the notice of commencement of case. In some districts the claim form contains a ballot upon which a secured creditor can indicate its acceptance or rejection of the debtor's proposed plan. It should be noted that the valuation and allowance of secured claims is normally conducted prior to confirmation because of the confirmation requirements of 11 U.S.C. § 1325(a)(5). See section 3.13, supra, for further reading.

claims, examination of by debtor

The local rules may also contain provisions dealing with the debtor's rights and obligations with respect to claims and the filing of objections thereto. A procedure is often provided whereby either the clerk or the chapter 13 trustee sends the debtor a list of claims filed and the debtor is given a specific period within which to object to any disputed claims. It is important for the debtor's attorney to be aware of any such local rules.

secured claims, payment of

If a secured claim dealt with under a chapter 13 plan has been allowed, and if it so provided in the plan or in the order confirming the plan, payments on the claim may begin immediately upon confirmation, provided that the priority administrative expenses have been paid or the right to priority of payment waived. See 11 U.S.C. § 1326(b)(1). Priority administrative claims usually include the unpaid portions of the filing fee and the fee allowed to the debtor's attorney in the case. The chapter 13 trustee's fee is also collected prior to the payment of claims and any compensation awarded to a chapter 7 trustee in a prior case must be provided for. See 11 U.S.C. § 1326(b)(2), (3).

unsecured claims, payment of

While the trustee is required to begin making payments under the plan as soon as practicable after confirmation, payments to unsecured nonpriority creditors do not normally begin until after the period for filing claims has expired. This is because the debtor and the chapter 13 trustee must have an opportunity to examine the claims and file objections to any disputed claims and the court must enter an order allowing the approved claims. Many districts have local rules and procedures dealing with this aspect of chapter 13 cases. Payments to the holders of priority claims and special classes of unsecured nonpriority claims may begin earlier, however, if the plan so provides and if all claims in the class have been allowed. See Bankruptcy Rule 3021. Payments of $15 or less may not be distributed by the chapter 13 trustee unless authorized by local rule or an order of the court. See Bankruptcy Rule 3010(b).

required payments directly to creditor

required insurance on personal property

Postpetition lease payments by the debtor on a lease of personal property must be paid directly to the lessor. See 1326(a)(1)(B). Adequate protection payments must also be made directly to a creditor whose purchase-money claim is secured by personal property. See 11 U.S.C. § 1326(a)(1)(C). Further, within 60 days after the filing of the case, a debtor who retains leased personal property or personal property securing a purchase-money claim, must provide the lessor or secured creditor with evidence of the maintenance of any required insurance coverage on the property and must continue to do so as long as the debtor retains the property. See 11 U.S.C. § 1326(a)(4).

If a chapter 13 case is dismissed or if the debtor does not receive a discharge, the statute of limitations will not have expired on claims against the debtor or against codebtors protected under 11 U.S.C. § 1301. 11 U.S.C. § 108(c) provides that if applicable law, an order entered in a proceeding, or an agreement fixes a period for commencing a civil action in a court other than a bankruptcy court on a claim against the debtor, or against an individual with respect to which the individual is protected under 11 U.S.C 1301, and if such period has not expired before the filing of the petition, then such period does not expire until the later of - (1) the end of such period, including any suspensions of such period occurring on or after the commencement of the case, or (2) 30 days after notice of the termination or expiration of the automatic stay in the bankruptcy case with respect to such claim. Thus, the statute of limitations on claims against the debtor or a protected codebtor will expire either at the time it would have otherwise expired or 30 days after the order of discharge, the notice of no discharge, or the notice of dismissal of the case, whichever is last to occur.

Statute of limitations; effect of Chapter 13 case on

3.17 An Unsuccessful Chapter 13 Case - Dismissal or Conversion to Chapter 7

An unsuccessful chapter 13 case may either be dismissed or converted to a case under chapter 7, and such dismissal or conversion may be at the request of the debtor or upon the motion of a party in interest or the United States trustee. The debtor may, without cause, convert a chapter 13 case to a case under chapter 7 at any time, and any waiver of this right of conversion is unenforceable. See 11 U.S.C. § 1307(a). If the case has not been converted to chapter 13 from another chapter, the court is required to dismiss a chapter 13 case at any time upon the request of the debtor, and any waiver of this right of dismissal by the debtor is unenforceable. See 11 U.S.C. § 1307(b). If the case has been converted to chapter 13 from another chapter, it may be dismissed by the debtor only for cause. See In re Jacobsen, 609 F.3d 647 (5th Cir. 2010). The procedure for voluntary dismissals or conversions is discussed below in this section.

Voluntary dismissal or conversion of case

Upon the motion of a party in interest or the United States trustee, and upon notice and a hearing, the court may dismiss a chapter 13 case or convert it to a case under chapter 7, whichever is in the best interests of the creditors and the estate, for failure of the debtor to file a required tax return or for cause, except that the chapter 13 case of a farmer may not be converted to chapter 7 unless the debtor requests the conversion. See 11 U.S.C. § 1307(c), (e). Under 11 U.S.C. § 1307(c), cause for involuntary dismissal or conversion may include:

Involuntary dismissal or conversion of case, causes for

(1) unreasonable delay by the debtor that is prejudicial to the creditors;

(2) nonpayment of the filing fee;

(3) failure to timely file a plan;

(4) failure to commence making timely payments under the plan or proposed plan;

(5) denial of confirmation of a plan and denial of time for filing another plan or modifying the proposed plan;

(6) material default by the debtor with respect to a term of a confirmed plan;

(7) revocation of the order of confirmation and denial of confirmation of a modified plan;

(8) termination of a confirmed plan by reason of the occurrence of a condition specified in the plan, other than the completion of payments under the plan,

(9) only on the motion of the United States trustee, failure to timely file the schedules and other information required by 11 U.S.C. § 521; or

(10) failure of the debtor to pay a domestic support obligation that first became payable after the filing of the case.

death or incompetency of debtor, procedure

If the debtor dies or becomes incompetent during the pendency of a chapter 13 case, the case may be dismissed. However, if further administration is possible and in the best interest of the parties, the case may proceed in rem and be concluded in the same manner, so far as possible, as though the death or incompetency had not occurred. See Bankruptcy Rule 1016.

involuntary conversion of case to chapter 11 or 12

At any time before confirmation of a plan, on the motion of a party in interest or the United States trustee, and after notice and a hearing, the court may convert a chapter 13 case to a case under chapter 11 or chapter 12, if the debtor qualifies as a debtor under such chapter, except that the chapter 13 case of a farmer may be converted only on the request of the debtor. See 11 U.S.C. § 1307(d),(f), (g). A farmer is defined as a person who received more than 80 percent of his or her gross income during the tax year preceding the year in which the case was filed from a farming operation that was owned or operated by such person. See 11 U.S.C. § 101(20). Converting a chapter 13 case to a case under chapter 11 requires the payment of an additional filing fee. See 28 U.S.C. § 1930(a).

dismissal of case, notice and hearing requirements

Except for the above-described right of the debtor to dismiss a chapter 13 case without cause under 11 U.S.C. § 1307(b) and except for dismissals for nonpayment of the filing fee and for failure to file the required schedules and statements, a chapter 13 case may not be dismissed on the motion of the debtor, for want of prosecution, by consent of the parties, or for any other cause, prior to a hearing on notice to all creditors. For purposes of this notice, a list of creditors, if not previously filed, must be provided by the debtor (or by another entity if ordered by the court) within the time fixed by the court. See Bankruptcy Rule 1017(a).

dismissal for nonpayment of filing fee or failure to file schedules, procedure

After a hearing on notice to the debtor and the chapter 13 trustee, the court may dismiss a chapter 13 case for failure to pay any installment of the filing fee. See Bankruptcy Rule 1017(b)(1). After a hearing on notice served by the United States trustee on the debtor, the chapter 13 trustee, and any other entities designated by the court, the court may dismiss a chapter 13 case for failure to timely file a list of creditors and the required schedules and statements. See Bankruptcy Rule 1017(c).

involuntary dismissal, or conversion, procedure

notice of dismissal or conversion

The procedure for the involuntary dismissal or conversion of a chapter 13 case under 11 U.S.C. § 1307(c) is governed by Bankruptcy Rule 9014. See Bankruptcy Rule 1017(f). The party seeking dismissal or conversion must file a motion and give the debtor reasonable notice and an opportunity for a hearing. See Bankruptcy Rule 9014. The motion must set forth the relief or order sought and must state with particularity the grounds therefor. The motion should be served by the moving party on the chapter 13 trustee, the debtor, the United States trustee, and such other persons as the court may direct. See Bankruptcy Rules 9013, 9034, and 5005(b), which requires verification of transmittal to the United States trustee. A written response to the motion is not required unless ordered by the court. See Bankruptcy Rule 9014. The clerk or some other person as the court may direct must give the debtor and all creditors notice of the dismissal or conversion of a chapter 13 case. See Bankruptcy Rule 2002(f)(2).

voluntary conversion to chapter 7, procedure

The procedure for the voluntary conversion of a chapter 13 case to chapter 7 by the debtor under 11 U.S.C. § 1307(a) is governed by Bankruptcy Rule 1017(f)(3), which provides that a chapter 13 case shall be converted to chapter 7 without court order when the debtor files a notice of conversion under Section 1307(a). The filing date of the notice is the date of the conversion order for purposes of 11 U.S.C. § 348(c) and Bankruptcy Rule 1019. See Bankruptcy Rule 1017(f)(3). A sample Notice of Conversion of Chapter 13 Case to Chapter 7 Under Section 1307(a) is set forth in Exhibit 3-H at the end of this chapter.

voluntary dismissal, procedure

The voluntary dismissal of a chapter 13 case by the debtor under 11 U.S.C. § 1307(b) is effected by the filing and service of a motion under Bankruptcy Rule 9013. See Bankruptcy Rule 1017(f)(2). A copy of the motion must be served on the chapter 13 trustee, the United States trustee, and on such other entities as the court may direct. See Bankruptcy Rules 9013 and 9034. A hearing on the motion is not required unless the court so directs. See Advisory Committee's Notes to Bankruptcy Rule 1017(f). A sample Motion to Dismiss Case Under Section 1307(b) is set forth in Exhibit 3-I at the end of this chapter.

Unless the court, for cause, orders otherwise, the dismissal of a chapter 13 case does not bar the discharge in a later bankruptcy case of debts that were dischargeable in the case dismissed. See 11 U.S.C. § 349(a). Unless the court, for cause, orders otherwise, the dismissal of a chapter 13 case: (1) reinstates any proceeding superseded by the case, reinstates certain transfers avoided or preserved in the case, and reinstates certain liens avoided in the case, (2) vacates certain orders, judgments, or transfers ordered in the case, and (3) revests the property of the estate in the entity in which such property was vested immediately before the commencement of the case. See 11 U.S.C. § 349(b). The dismissal of the case also causes the debtor to lose the postcase benefit of any exemptions claimed in the case, including the federal bankruptcy exemptions. See 11 U.S.C. § 522(c). The dismissal of the case also terminates the automatic stay. See 11 U.S.C. § 362(c)(2), 1301(a)(2).

dismissal of case, effect of

The conversion of a chapter 13 case to chapter 7 is governed by 11 U.S.C. § 348 and Bankruptcy Rule 1019, together with any applicable local rules. The conversion of a chapter 13 case to a case under chapter 7 constitutes an order for relief under chapter 7, but, with only limited exceptions, does not change the dates of the filing of the petition, the commencement of the case, or the order for relief. See 11 U.S.C. § 348(a). As indicated above, the clerk or some other person as the court may direct must mail notice of the order converting a chapter 13 case to chapter 7 to the debtor and all creditors. See Bankruptcy Rule 2002(f)(2).

conversion to chapter 7, effect of, notice of

The property of the bankruptcy estate in the chapter 7 case is the property of the estate in the chapter 13 case as of the date the chapter 13 case was filed that remains in the possession or under the control of the debtor on the date of conversion. See 11 U.S.C. § 348(f)(1)(A). However, if the conversion to chapter 7 was made in bad faith the property of the estate in the chapter 7 case shall consist of the property of the estate in the chapter 13 case as of the date of conversion. See 11 U.S.C. § 348(f)(2). This means that unless the conversion to chapter 7 is found to be in bad faith, the debtor may retain any property acquired after the filing of the chapter 13 case and is not liable to the trustee for any increase in the value of any property of the estate. See In re Young, 66 F. 3d 376 (1st Cir. 1995).

property of estate in converted case, what constitutes

All lists, inventories, schedules, and statements of financial affairs filed in the chapter 13 case shall be deemed filed in the chapter 7 case, unless the court directs otherwise. If such documents have not been previously filed, they must be filed by the debtor within 14 days after entry of the order converting the case to chapter 7. See Bankruptcy Rule 1019(1)(A). A statement of intention, if required, must be filed within 30 days after the entry of the order for conversion or before the first date set for the meeting of creditors, whichever is earlier. See Bankruptcy Rule 1019(1)(B), which also provides that a motion for an extension of time to file a statement of intention must be made by written motion filed before the time expires or by oral request made at a hearing before the time expires.

conversion to chapter 7, procedure

Valuations of property and of allowed secured claims made in the chapter 13 case do not apply to the chapter 7 case. When a chapter 13 case is converted to a case under chapter 7, the claim of any creditor holding security as of the date the chapter 13 case was filed shall continue to be secured by that security unless the full amount of the claim, determined under applicable nonbankruptcy law, has been paid in full as of the date of conversion, notwithstanding any valuation or determination of the amount of an allowed secured claim made for purposes of the chapter 13 case. Further, unless a prebankruptcy default has been fully cured under the plan at the time of conversion, in the chapter 7 case the default shall have the effect given under applicable nonbankruptcy law. See 11 U.S.C. § 348(f)(1)(C). All claims filed in the chapter 13 case shall be deemed filed in the chapter 7 case. See Bankruptcy Rule 1019(3). New time periods are commenced for the filing of claims, complaints objecting to discharge, motions under 11 U.S.C. § 706(b) or (c), and complaints to determine the dischargeability of debts, except that if a chapter 7 case has been converted to chapter 13 and is thereafter reconverted to chapter 7, and if the time for filing claims or such complaints had expired in the original chapter 7 case, the time for filing is not revived or extended unless the court, for cause, had extended the time on a motion filed before the original time had expired. See Bankruptcy Rule 1019(2).

conversion to chapter 7, valuation and filing periods

conversion to chapter 7, duties of trustee

The conversion of a chapter 13 case to chapter 7 terminates the services of the chapter 13 trustee. See 11 U.S.C. § 348(e). After the qualification of, or the assumption of duties by, the trustee in the chapter 7 case, the chapter 13 trustee must forthwith turn over to the chapter 7 trustee all records and property of the estate in the possession and control of the chapter 13 trustee, unless the court orders otherwise. See Bankruptcy Rule 1019(4). Unless the court directs otherwise, the chapter 13 trustee must file with the clerk and transmit to the United States trustee a final report and account within 30 days after the entry of the order of conversion. Within 14 days after the order of conversion, the debtor must file a schedule of unpaid debts incurred after the commencement of the chapter 13 case. If the conversion to chapter 7 occurred after confirmation of the chapter 13 plan, the debtor must file with the court a schedule of property acquired after the filing of the original petition and before the order of conversion, a schedule of postpetition debts that were not included in the final report and account, and a schedule of executory contracts and unexpired leases entered into or assumed after the filing of the original petition and before the entry of the conversion order. See Bankruptcy Rule 1019(5).

conversion to chapter 7, postpetition claims

A claim against the debtor or the estate that arises after the order for relief in the chapter 13 case and prior to the conversion of the case, other than certain claims for administrative expenses, is treated as if the claim has arisen immediately before the filing of the petition. See 11 U.S.C. § 348(d). Upon the filing by the debtor of a schedule of unpaid debts incurred after commencement of the case and before conversion, the clerk or some other person as the court may direct, must give notice to those creditors of the time set by the court for filing claims for preconversion administrative expenses and, unless a notice of no dividend is mailed, of the time for filing claims for postpetition debts. See Bankruptcy Rule 1019(6). Postpetition claims arising from the rejection of executory contracts or unexpired leases may be filed within such time as the court may direct. See Bankruptcy Rule 3002(c)(4).

3.18 The Chapter 13 Discharges

Two types of discharges are available to chapter 13 debtors. One is a successful plan discharge that is granted to a debtor who has completed all payments under the plan. This discharge is provided for in 11 U.S.C 1328(a) and, not surprisingly, is referred to as a section 1328(a) discharge. The other type of chapter 13 discharge is a "best efforts" discharge that is granted to a debtor who was unable to complete the payments under the plan due to circumstances for which the debtor should not be held accountable. This discharge is provided for in 11 U.S.C. § 1328(b) and is referred to as a section 1328(b) discharge. However, the court may not grant a discharge under either section unless, after notice and a hearing held not more than 10 days before the date of the entry of the discharge order, the court finds that there is no reasonable cause to believe that the debtor has been convicted of a felony that rendered the filing of the case an abuse of the Bankruptcy Code or owes a debt that arose from a violation of the securities laws, or that there is pending a case under which the debtor could be found guilty of the crime or liable for the debt. See 11 U.S.C. § 1328(h). The debtor must also complete an instructional course in personal financial management and file the required certificate of completion before a discharge can be granted, unless this requirement is not applicable in the local district. See 11 U.S.C. § 1328(g). See Exhibit 2-Z(2) at the end of chapter 2, supra, for a sample of this certificate.

chapter 13 discharges, types of

instructional course on personal financial management, requirement of

As soon as practicable after the completion by the debtor of all payments under the plan, and, if the debtor is required to pay a domestic support obligation, the debtor certifies that all amounts payable under the obligation have been paid (see Director's Form 2830), and the requirements described in the paragraph above have been complied with, the court must grant the debtor a section 1328(a) discharge unless the court approves a written waiver of discharge executed by the debtor after the order for relief under chapter 13. See 11 U.S.C. § 1328(a). A section 1328(a) discharge is granted by the court as a matter of course without application upon the completion of all payments under the plan. A section 1328(a) discharge is slightly broader than either a chapter 7 discharge or a section 1328(b) discharge. A section 1328(a) discharge discharges a debtor from all debts except:

section 1328(a) discharge, when granted

(1) debts not provided for by the plan, including debts owed to unlisted or improperly listed creditors, but excluding debts for disallowed claims;

debts not discharged by section 1328(a) discharge

(2) debts whose last payment is due after the date of the final payment under the plan;

(3) most tax debts;

(4) debts obtained by fraud, false pretenses or false financial statements, if the court so rules under complaint to determine dischargeability;

(5) debts for embezzlement, larceny or fiduciary fraud;

(6) debts for domestic support obligations;

(7) debts for student loans or educational benefits, unless not discharging the debt would impose an undue hardship on the debtor or his or her dependents;

(8) debts for death or personal injury caused by the debtor's operation of a motor vehicle, vessel or aircraft while intoxicated;

(9) debts for restitution or a criminal fine included in a sentence on the debtor for conviction of a crime;

(10) debts for restitution or damages awarded in a civil action against the debtor as a result of willful or malicious injury by the debtor that caused personal injury or death to another; and

(11) postpetition debts not allowed under 11 U.S.C. § 1305, and allowed postpetition consumer debts, the prior approval of which by the trustee was practicable and was not obtained.

A section 1328(b) discharge is a narrower discharge that is granted to a debtor who is unable to complete the payments required under the plan. At any time after confirmation of the plan, and after notice and a hearing, the court may grant a discharge under section 1328(b) to a debtor who has not completed payments under the plan if - (1) the debtor's failure to complete such payments is due to circumstances for which the debtor should not justly be held accountable, (2) the value of the property actually distributed under the plan on the account of each allowed unsecured claim is not less than the amount that would have been paid on such claim had the debtor filed under chapter 7, and (3) modification of the plan is not practicable. See 11 U.S.C. § 1328(b).

section 1328(b) discharge, when granted, grounds for

unlisted debts, dischargeability of

A section 1328(b) discharge discharges a debtor from all debts except:

debts not discharged by section 1328(b) discharge

(1) secured debts;

(2) unsecured debts not provided for in the plan, including debts owed to unlisted or improperly listed unsecured creditors, but excluding debts for disallowed unsecured claims;

(3) unsecured debts whose last payment is due after the date of the final payment under the plan;

(4) postpetition debts not allowed under 11 U.S.C. § 1305, and allowed postpetition consumer debts, the prior approval of which by the trustee was practicable and was not obtained.

(5) debts specified in 11 U.S.C. § 523(a) (i.e., those not dischargeable in a chapter 7 case - see section 2.17, supra, for a list).

priority claims, dischargeability

student loans, dischargeability

It should be noted that while debts for priority claims are dischargeable under section 1328(a), the discharge of such debts is largely illusory because nearly all priority claims must be paid in full under a chapter 13 plan, unless the creditor agrees otherwise. See 11 U.S.C. § 1322(a)(2). Divorce-related debts that are not domestic support obligations (i.e., property settlement debts) are dischargeable under a section 1328(a) discharge but are not dischargeable under a section 1328(b) discharge. Debts for student loans and educational benefits are dischargeable under either a section 1328(a) discharge or a section 1328(b) discharge to the same extent that they are dischargeable in a chapter 7 case. See section 2.17, supra, for a discussion of the dischargeability of student loans in chapter 7 cases. Because their debts are not provided in the plan, debts owed to unlisted creditors are not discharged by either a section 1328(a) discharge or a section 1328(b) discharge. See In re Schuster, 428 B.R. 833 (Bankr. E. D. Wis. 2010); but see United Student Aid Funds, Inc. v. Espinosa, 130 S.Ct. 1367 (2010), (holding a student loan creditor who failed to object to a chapter 13 plan which proposed to discharge student loan interest after full payment of the underlying principal was barred from collecting the interest after completion of the plan payments despite no undue hardship hearing being held).

section 1328(b) discharge, procedure

To obtain a section 1328(b) discharge, the debtor must file a motion requesting that the discharge be granted. A sample of such a motion is set forth in Exhibit 3-J at the end of this chapter. Upon the filing of a motion by the debtor for a discharge under section 1328(b), the court must enter an order fixing a time for the filing of complaints to determine the dischargeability of debts under 11 U.S.C. § 523(c) and giving at least 30 days notice of the time so fixed to all creditors. The time for filing such complaints may be extended upon a motion filed before the time has expired. See Bankruptcy Rule 4007(d). Notice of the filing by the debtor of a motion for a section 1328(b) discharge must also be given. The local rules may also contain provisions dealing with the filing of such motions. If a complaint is filed either objecting to the discharge of the debtor or to determine the dischargeability of a debt, the proceeding thereunder is governed by Part VII of the Federal Rules of Bankruptcy Procedure. See Bankruptcy Rules 4004(d), 4007(e), and 7001. See section 2.17, supra, for further reading on dischargeability proceedings.

discharge and reaffirmation hearing

Regardless of whether a chapter 13 discharge is granted under section 1328(a) or section 1328(b), within 30 days following the grant or denial of a discharge and on not less than 14 days notice to the debtor and the trustee, the court may hold a discharge and reaffirmation hearing, which the debtor must attend if a discharge is denied or if a dischargeable debt is being reaffirmed under 11 U.S.C. § 524(c). See 11 U.S.C. § 524(d) and Bankruptcy Rule 4008. The local rules may also contain provisions dealing with discharge and reaffirmation hearings. Dischargeable debts may be reaffirmed in chapter 13 cases to the same extent as in chapter 7 cases unless payment of a reaffirmed debt is deemed to have created a forbidden class of claims. See section 3.08, supra, for further reading on the classification of claims. See section 2.18, supra, for further reading on the reaffirmation of dischargeable debts.

The order of discharge must conform to the appropriate Official Form. See Bankruptcy Rule 4004(e). The clerk must promptly mail a copy of the final order of discharge to all creditors, the United States trustee, and the trustee. See Bankruptcy Rule 4004(g). If so desired, a final order of discharge may be registered in another district by filing a certified copy of the order with the clerk of the bankruptcy court in the other district. When so registered, the order of discharge has the same effect as an order of the court in the district where it is registered. See Bankruptcy Rule 4004(f).

order of discharge, form, notice

On the request of a party in interest made within one year after a chapter 13 discharge is granted, and after notice and a hearing, the court may revoke a chapter 13 discharge if the discharge was obtained by the debtor through fraud and the requesting party did not know of the fraud until after the discharge was granted. See 11 U.S.C. § 1328(e). A proceeding to revoke a chapter 13 discharge must be initiated by the filing of a complaint and the proceedings thereunder are governed by Part VII of the Federal Rules of Bankruptcy Procedure. See Bankruptcy Rule 7001. If an order is entered denying or revoking a discharge, or if a waiver of discharge is filed and approved by the court, the clerk must promptly mail a notice of no discharge to all creditors. See Bankruptcy Rule 4006.

revocation of discharge, grounds, procedure

notice of denial or revocation of discharge

Regardless of whether a chapter 13 discharge is granted under Section 1328(a) or Section 1328(b), the debtor will not be eligible for a chapter 7 discharge for six years from the date of filing of the chapter 13 case unless the payments made under the plan totaled at least - (1) 100 percent of the allowed unsecured claims, or (2) 70 percent of such claims and the plan was proposed by the debtor in good faith and was the debtor's best effort. See 11 U.S.C. § 727(a)(9). See section 2.17, supra, for a discussion of the effect of a discharge on the debts and liabilities of the debtor and of the debtor's responsibilities should a creditor later attempt to collect a discharged debt. The effect of a discharge on community debts in community property states is also discussed in section 2.17, supra.

eligibility of debtor for chapter 7 discharge

effect of discharge

Appeals in chapter 13 cases, as in all title 11 cases, are governed by 28 U.S.C. § 158 and Part VIII of the Federal Rules of Bankruptcy Procedure. Final judgments, orders, and decrees of bankruptcy judges may be appealed as of right, while interlocutory orders may be appealed only with leave of the appellate court. Appeals from orders, judgments, and decrees of bankruptcy judges must be taken to the district court unless a bankruptcy appellate panel has been established in the local circuit and appeals thereto have been authorized in the local district. Even if appeals to the bankruptcy appellate panel have been authorized locally, an appeal to the panel may be taken only with the consent of all parties to the appeal. See 11 U.S.C. § 158.

appeals in chapter 13 cases

3.19 Closing a Chapter 13 Case

undistributed property, disposition of by trustee

Ninety days after the final distribution under a chapter 13 plan, the chapter 13 trustee must stop payment on any check remaining unpaid, and any remaining property of the estate must be paid into the court and disposed of under chapter 129 of title 28. See 11 U.S.C. § 347(a). The chapter 13 trustee must file with the clerk a list of the names and addresses of all known persons entitled to be paid under chapter 129 of title 28, together with the amounts that they are entitled to be paid from the remaining property of the estate that is paid into the court under 11 U.S.C. § 347(a). See Bankruptcy Rule 3011.

trustee's final report, notice requirements

When the administration of the estate has been completed, the chapter 13 trustee must make a final report and file a final account of the administration of the estate with the court. See 11 U.S.C. § 1302(b)(1), 704(a)(9). If with respect to the debtor there is a claim for a domestic support obligation, the trustee must provide the required notices to the claimholder and the state child support enforcement agency. See 11 U.S.C. § 1302(b)(1), 704(a)(10). If the trustee files a final report and final account and certifies that the estate has been fully administered, and if no objection thereto is filed within 30 days by the United States trustee or a party in interest, it is presumed that the estate has been fully administered. See Bankruptcy Rule 5009. The local rules often contain procedures governing the closing of chapter 13 cases. Normally, a chapter 13 case is closed as a matter of course without the assistance of the debtor or the debtor's attorney. A copy or summary of the trustee's final report or final accounting is customarily sent to the debtor and the debtor's attorney.

final decree, form and contents

After the estate has been fully administered, including the return or distribution of any deposit required by the plan, the court must enter a final decree discharging the chapter 13 trustee and closing the case. See 11 U.S.C. § 350(a). The closing of the case terminates the automatic stay to the extent that it was not earlier terminated. See 11 U.S.C. § 362(c)(2), 1301(a)(2).

reopening case, grounds for

Upon the motion of the debtor or other party in interest, a chapter 13 case may be reopened in the court in which the case was closed to administer assets, to accord relief to the debtor, or for other cause. See 11 U.S.C. § 350(b). If a chapter 13 case is reopened, a trustee shall not be appointed by the United States trustee unless the court determines that a trustee is necessary to protect the interests of creditors and the debtor or to insure an efficient administration of the case. See Bankruptcy Rule 5010.

Exhibit 3-A Application for Allowance of Compensation

UNITED STATES BANKRUPTCY COURT
CENTRAL DISTRICT OF CALIFORNIA

IN RE John Paul Jones and Shirley Ann Jones	)	
	)	Case No. 24B-00221-SRT
	)	
Debtors	)	Chapter 13

APPLICATION FOR ALLOWANCE OF COMPENSATION

The undersigned attorney for the debtors states and represents as follows:

1. The total fee to be charged by the attorney for legal services rendered or to be rendered for the debtors in this bankruptcy case, exclusive of costs, is $3,000.00, of which $2,000.00 has been paid, leaving a balance of $1,000.00.

2. The source of the compensation paid or to be paid is the debtors, which compensation shall, by agreement with the debtors, be paid by the Chapter 13 trustee as a priority administrative claim in the bankruptcy case, upon approval thereof by the court.

3. The attorney has filed a document entitled Disclosure of Compensation of Attorney for Debtor with the court, the provisions of which are incorporated by reference in this application.

4. The legal services rendered or to be rendered by the attorney in connection with this bankruptcy case include the following:

Assisting the debtor in attending the required briefing on budget and credit counseling.

Examining and analyzing the debtor's financial situation and advising the debtors thereon.

Preparing and filing the petition, schedules, statements, plan and other necessary documents and pleadings.

Representing the debtors at the meeting of creditors, the confirmation hearing, and all other court hearings.

Assisting the debtors in completing the instructional course on personal financial management.

Assisting the debtors in obtaining confirmation of the debtors' plan and in carrying out and consummating the plan.

5. The undersigned attorney is admitted to practice before this court and in the state of California, maintains a law practice at the address shown below on this application, is a disinterested person with respect to this bankruptcy case and does not hold or represent an interest adverse to the estate with respect to the matter for which the attorney has been employed, and is competent and experienced in the handling of Chapter 13 bankruptcy cases.

WHEREFORE, the undersigned attorney respectfully applies for allowance of the compensation described above in this application and requests that the unpaid balance of such compensation be approved by the court as a priority administrative claim in the case, to be paid by the Chapter 13 trustee out of the funds deposited with the trustee by the debtor.

Dated: February 10, 2024

____
John T. Smith
Attorney for Debtors
6200 Wilshire Blvd., Suite 3333
Los Angeles, CA 90012
John.smith@bklawyer.com
Telephone: 213-344-7666

Exhibit 3-B(1) Ch. 13 Stmt. of Your Current Monthly Income and Calc. of Commitment Period

(Official Form 122C-1)

Fill in this information to identify your case:

Debtor 1: John Paul Jones (First Name / Middle Name / Last Name)

Debtor 2 (Spouse, if filing): Shirley Ann Jones (First Name / Middle Name / Last Name)

United States Bankruptcy Court for the: Southern District of Ohio

Case number (If known) ______________

Check as directed in lines 17 and 21:

According to the calculations required by this Statement:

☐ 1. Disposable income is not determined under 11 U.S.C. § 1325(b)(3).

☐ 2. Disposable income is determined under 11 U.S.C. § 1325(b)(3).

☐ 3. The commitment period is 3 years.

☐ 4. The commitment period is 5 years.

☐ Check if this is an amended filing

Official Form 122C–1

Chapter 13 Statement of Your Current Monthly Income and Calculation of Commitment Period

04/20

Be as complete and accurate as possible. If two married people are filing together, both are equally responsible for being accurate. If more space is needed, attach a separate sheet to this form. Include the line number to which the additional information applies. On the top of any additional pages, write your name and case number (if known).

Part 1: Calculate Your Average Monthly Income

1. **What is your marital and filing status?** Check one only.

☐ **Not married.** Fill out Column A, lines 2-11.

☒ **Married.** Fill out both Columns A and B, lines 2-11.

Fill in the average monthly income that you received from all sources, derived during the 6 full months before you file this bankruptcy case. 11 U.S.C. § 101(10A). For example, if you are filing on September 15, the 6-month period would be March 1 through August 31. If the amount of your monthly income varied during the 6 months, add the income for all 6 months and divide the total by 6. Fill in the result. Do not include any income amount more than once. For example, if both spouses own the same rental property, put the income from that property in one column only. If you have nothing to report for any line, write $0 in the space.

	Debtor 1	Debtor 2		*Column A* Debtor 1	*Column B* Debtor 2 or non-filing spouse
2. **Your gross wages, salary, tips, bonuses, overtime, and commissions** (before all payroll deductions).				$ 3,350.00	$ 2,630.00
3. **Alimony and maintenance payments.** Do not include payments from a spouse.				$ 0.00	$ 0.00
4. **All amounts from any source which are regularly paid for household expenses of you or your dependents, including child support.** Include regular contributions from an unmarried partner, members of your household, your dependents, parents, and roommates. Do not include payments from a spouse. Do not include payments you listed on line 3.				$ 0.00	$ 0.00
5. **Net income from operating a business, profession, or farm**	Debtor 1	Debtor 2			
Gross receipts (before all deductions)	$ 0.00	$ 0.00			
Ordinary and necessary operating expenses	− $ 0.00	− $ 0.00			
Net monthly income from a business, profession, or farm	$ 0.00	$ 0.00	Copy here➔	$ 0.00	$ 0.00
6. **Net income from rental and other real property**	Debtor 1	Debtor 2			
Gross receipts (before all deductions)	$ 0.00	$ 0.00			
Ordinary and necessary operating expenses	− $ 0.00	− $ 0.00			
Net monthly income from rental or other real property	$ 0.00	$ 0.00	Copy here➔	$ 0.00	$ 0.00

Debtor 1 John Paul Jones
First Name Middle Name Last Name

Case number *(if known)*

	Column A **Debtor 1**	*Column B* **Debtor 2 or non-filing spouse**
7. **Interest, dividends, and royalties**	$ 0.00	$ 100.00
8. **Unemployment compensation**	$ 0.00	$ 0.00

Do not enter the amount if you contend that the amount received was a benefit under the Social Security Act. Instead, list it here: ↓

For you $ 0.00

For your spouse $ 0.00

	Column A	*Column B*
9. **Pension or retirement income.** Do not include any amount received that was a benefit under the Social Security Act. Also, except as stated in the next sentence, do not include any compensation, pension, pay, annuity, or allowance paid by the United States Government in connection with a disability, combat-related injury or disability, or death of a member of the uniformed services. If you received any retired pay paid under chapter 61 of title 10, then include that pay only to the extent that it does not exceed the amount of retired pay to which you would otherwise be entitled if retired under any provision of title 10 other than chapter 61 of that title.	$ 0.00	$ 0.00
10. **Income from all other sources not listed above.** Specify the source and amount. Do not include any benefits received under the Social Security Act; payments made under the Federal law relating to the national emergency declared by the President under the National Emergencies Act (50 U.S.C. 1601 et seq.) with respect to the coronavirus disease 2019 (COVID-19); payments received as a victim of a war crime, a crime against humanity, or international or domestic terrorism; or compensation, pension, pay, annuity, or allowance paid by the United States Government in connection with a disability, combat-related injury or disability, or death of a member of the uniformed services. If necessary, list other sources on a separate page and put the total below.		
Paper Route - Local Gazette	$ 140.00	$ 140.00
	$	$
Total amounts from separate pages, if any.	+ $ 0.00	+ $ 0.00
11. **Calculate your total average monthly income.** Add lines 2 through 10 for each column. Then add the total for Column A to the total for Column B.	$ 3,490.00	+ $ 2,730.00 = $ 6,220.00 (Total average monthly income)

Part 2: Determine How to Measure Your Deductions from Income

12. **Copy your total average monthly income from line 11.** $ 6,220.00

13. **Calculate the marital adjustment.** Check one:

☐ You are not married. Fill in 0 below.

☑ You are married and your spouse is filing with you. Fill in 0 below.

☐ You are married and your spouse is not filing with you.

Fill in the amount of the income listed in line 11, Column B, that was NOT regularly paid for the household expenses of you or your dependents, such as payment of the spouse's tax liability or the spouse's support of someone other than you or your dependents.

Below, specify the basis for excluding this income and the amount of income devoted to each purpose. If necessary, list additional adjustments on a separate page.

If this adjustment does not apply, enter 0 below.

$

$

+ $

Total $ 0.00 Copy here ➔ — 0.00

14. **Your current monthly income.** Subtract the total in line 13 from line 12. $ 6,220.00

Debtor 1 John Paul Jones
First Name Middle Name Last Name

Case number *(if known)*

15. **Calculate your current monthly income for the year.** Follow these steps:

15a. Copy line 14 here ➔ .... $ 6,220.00

Multiply line 15a by 12 (the number of months in a year). x 12

15b. The result is your current monthly income for the year for this part of the form. .... $ 74,640.00

16. **Calculate the median family income that applies to you.** Follow these steps:

16a. Fill in the state in which you live. CA

16b. Fill in the number of people in your household. 4

16c. Fill in the median family income for your state and size of household. .... $ 105,232.0(

To find a list of applicable median income amounts, go online using the link specified in the separate instructions for this form. This list may also be available at the bankruptcy clerk's office.

17. **How do the lines compare?**

17a. ☐ Line 15b is less than or equal to line 16c. On the top of page 1 of this form, check box 1, *Disposable income is not determined under 11 U.S.C. § 1325(b)(3).* **Go to Part 3.** Do NOT fill out *Calculation of Your Disposable Income* (Official Form 122C–2).

17b. ☐ Line 15b is more than line 16c. On the top of page 1 of this form, check box 2, *Disposable income is determined under 11 U.S.C. § 1325(b)(3).* **Go to Part 3 and fill out Calculation of Your Disposable Income (Official Form 122C–2).** On line 39 of that form, copy your current monthly income from line 14 above.

Part 3: Calculate Your Commitment Period Under 11 U.S.C. § 1325(b)(4)

18. **Copy your total average monthly income from line 11.** .... $ 6,220.00

19. **Deduct the marital adjustment if it applies.** If you are married, your spouse is not filing with you, and you contend that calculating the commitment period under 11 U.S.C. § 1325(b)(4) allows you to deduct part of your spouse's income, copy the amount from line 13.

19a. If the marital adjustment does not apply, fill in 0 on line 19a. .... – $ 0.00

19b. **Subtract line 19a from line 18.** $ 6,220.00

20. **Calculate your current monthly income for the year.** Follow these steps:

20a. Copy line 19b.. .... $ 6,220.00

Multiply by 12 (the number of months in a year). x 12

20b. The result is your current monthly income for the year for this part of the form. $ 74,640.00

20c. Copy the median family income for your state and size of household from line 16c. .... $ 105,232.0(

21. **How do the lines compare?**

☐ Line 20b is less than line 20c. Unless otherwise ordered by the court, on the top of page 1 of this form, check box 3, *The commitment period is 3 years.* Go to Part 4.

☐ Line 20b is more than or equal to line 20c. Unless otherwise ordered by the court, on the top of page 1 of this form, check box 4, *The commitment period is 5 years.* Go to Part 4.

Exhibit 3-B(2) Chapter 13 Calculation of Your Disposable Income (Official Form 122C-2)

Fill in this information to identify your case:

Debtor 1 John Paul Jones
First Name Middle Name Last Name

Debtor 2 (Spouse, if filing) Shirley Ann Jones
First Name Middle Name Last Name

United States Bankruptcy Court for the: __________ District of __________

Case number (if known) ______________________________

☐ Check if this is an amended filing

Official Form 122C-2

Chapter 13 Calculation of Your Disposable Income

04/22

To fill out this form, you will need your completed copy of *Chapter 13 Statement of Your Current Monthly Income and Calculation of Commitment Period* (Official Form 122C–1).

Be as complete and accurate as possible. If two married people are filing together, both are equally responsible for being accurate. If more space is needed, attach a separate sheet to this form. Include the line number to which the additional information applies. On the top of any additional pages, write your name and case number (if known).

Part 1: Calculate Your Deductions from Your Income

The Internal Revenue Service (IRS) issues National and Local Standards for certain expense amounts. Use these amounts to answer the questions in lines 6-15. To find the IRS standards, go online using the link specified in the separate instructions for this form. This information may also be available at the bankruptcy clerk's office.

Deduct the expense amounts set out in lines 6-15 regardless of your actual expense. In later parts of the form, you will use some of your actual expenses if they are higher than the standards. Do not include any operating expenses that you subtracted from income in lines 5 and 6 of Form 122C–1, and do not deduct any amounts that you subtracted from your spouse's income in line 13 of Form 122C–1.

If your expenses differ from month to month, enter the average expense.

Note: Line numbers 1-4 are not used in this form. These numbers apply to information required by a similar form used in chapter 7 cases.

5. **The number of people used in determining your deductions from income**
Fill in the number of people who could be claimed as exemptions on your federal income tax return, plus the number of any additional dependents whom you support. This number may be different from the number of people in your household. 4.00

National Standards You must use the IRS National Standards to answer the questions in lines 6-7.

6. **Food, clothing, and other items:** Using the number of people you entered in line 5 and the IRS National Standards, fill in the dollar amount for food, clothing, and other items. $ 1893

7. **Out-of-pocket health care allowance:** Using the number of people you entered in line 5 and the IRS National Standards, fill in the dollar amount for out-of-pocket health care. The number of people is split into two categories—people who are under 65 and people who are 65 or older—because older people have a higher IRS allowance for health care costs. If your actual expenses are higher than this IRS amount, you may deduct the additional amount on line 22.

Debtor 1 John Paul Jones
First Name Middle Name Last Name

Case number (if known) ____________________

People who are under 65 years of age

7a. Out-of-pocket health care allowance per person $ 79.00

7b. Number of people who are under 65 X 4

7c. Subtotal. Multiply line 7a by line 7b. $ 116.00 Copy here → $ 116.00

People who are 65 years of age or older

7d. Out-of-pocket health care allowance per person $ 0.00

7e. Number of people who are 65 or older X ____

7f. Subtotal. Multiply line 7d by line 7e. $ 0.00 Copy here → + $ 0.00

7g. **Total.** Add lines 7c and 7f. $ 116.00 Copy here → $ 116.00

Local Standards You must use the IRS Local Standards to answer the questions in lines 8-15.

Based on information from the IRS, the U.S. Trustee Program has divided the IRS Local Standard for housing for bankruptcy purposes into two parts:

- **Housing and utilities – Insurance and operating expenses**
- **Housing and utilities – Mortgage or rent expenses**

To answer the questions in lines 8-9, use the U.S. Trustee Program chart. To find the chart, go online using the link specified in the separate instructions for this form. This chart may also be available at the bankruptcy clerk's office.

8. **Housing and utilities – Insurance and operating expenses:** Using the number of people you entered in line 5, fill in the dollar amount listed for your county for insurance and operating expenses. $ 806.00

9. **Housing and utilities – Mortgage or rent expenses:**

9a. Using the number of people you entered in line 5, fill in the dollar amount listed for your county for mortgage or rent expenses. $ 2,638.00

9b. Total average monthly payment for all mortgages and other debts secured by your home.

To calculate the total average monthly payment, add all amounts that are contractually due to each secured creditor in the 60 months after you file for bankruptcy. Next divide by 60.

Name of the creditor	Average monthly payment
AB Bank	$ 3,000.00
	$
	+ $

9b. Total average monthly payment $ 3,000.00 Copy here → − $ 3,000.00 Repeat this amount on line 33a.

9c. Net mortgage or rent expense.

Subtract line 9b (*total average monthly payment*) from line 9a (*mortgage or rent expense*). If this number is less than $0, enter $0. $ 0.00 Copy here → $ 0.00

10. **If you claim that the U.S. Trustee Program's division of the IRS Local Standard for housing is incorrect and affects the calculation of your monthly expenses, fill in any additional amount you claim.** $ ____

Explain why: ____________________

Debtor 1 John Paul Jones Case number (if known)______
First Name Middle Name Last Name

11. **Local transportation expenses:** Check the number of vehicles for which you claim an ownership or operating expense.

- [ ] 0. Go to line 14.
- [x] 1. Go to line 12.
- [ ] 2 or more. Go to line 12.

12. **Vehicle operation expense:** Using the IRS Local Standards and the number of vehicles for which you claim the operating expenses, fill in the *Operating Costs* that apply for your Census region or metropolitan statistical area. $ 264.00

13. **Vehicle ownership or lease expense:** Using the IRS Local Standards, calculate the net ownership or lease expense for each vehicle below. You may not claim the expense if you do not make any loan or lease payments on the vehicle. In addition, you may not claim the expense for more than two vehicles.

Vehicle 1 Describe Vehicle 1: 2020 Impala

13a. Ownership or leasing costs using IRS Local Standard.................. $______

13b. Average monthly payment for all debts secured by Vehicle 1.
Do not include costs for leased vehicles.

To calculate the average monthly payment here and on line 13e, add all amounts that are contractually due to each secured creditor in the 60 months after you file for bankruptcy. Then divide by 60.

Name of each creditor for Vehicle 1	Average monthly payment
BC Bank	$ 800.00
	+ $
Total average monthly payment	$ 800.00

Copy here ➡ − $ 800.00 Repeat this amount on line 33b.

13c. Net Vehicle 1 ownership or lease expense
Subtract line 13b from line 13a. If this number is less than $0, enter $0. ...... $ 0.00 Copy net Vehicle 1 expense here ➡ $ 0.00

Vehicle 2 Describe Vehicle 2: ______

13d. Ownership or leasing costs using IRS Local Standard.................. $______

13e. Average monthly payment for all debts secured by Vehicle 2.
Do not include costs for leased vehicles.

Name of each creditor for Vehicle 2	Average monthly payment
	$
	+ $
Total average monthly payment	$

Copy here ➡ − $______ Repeat this amount on line 33c.

13f. Net Vehicle 2 ownership or lease expense
Subtract line 13e from 13d. If this number is less than $0, enter $0...... $______ Copy net Vehicle 2 expense here ➡ $______

14. **Public transportation expense:** If you claimed 0 vehicles in line 11, using the IRS Local Standards, fill in the *Public Transportation* expense allowance regardless of whether you use public transportation. $______

15. **Additional public transportation expense:** If you claimed 1 or more vehicles in line 11 and if you claim that you may also deduct a public transportation expense, you may fill in what you believe is the appropriate expense, but you may not claim more than the IRS Local Standard for *Public Transportation*. $______

Debtor 1 John Paul Jones
First Name Middle Name Last Name

Case number (if known) ____________________

Other Necessary Expenses In addition to the expense deductions listed above, you are allowed your monthly expenses for the following IRS categories.

16. **Taxes:** The total monthly amount that you actually pay for federal, state and local taxes, such as income taxes, self-employment taxes, social security taxes, and Medicare taxes. You may include the monthly amount withheld from your pay for these taxes. However, if you expect to receive a tax refund, you must divide the expected refund by 12 and subtract that number from the total monthly amount that is withheld to pay for taxes.
Do not include real estate, sales, or use taxes. $______

17. **Involuntary deductions:** The total monthly payroll deductions that your job requires, such as retirement contributions, union dues, and uniform costs.
Do not include amounts that are not required by your job, such as voluntary 401(k) contributions or payroll savings. $______

18. **Life insurance:** The total monthly premiums that you pay for your own term life insurance. If two married people are filing together, include payments that you make for your spouse's term life insurance.
Do not include premiums for life insurance on your dependents, for a non-filing spouse's life insurance, or for any form of life insurance other than term. $______

19. **Court-ordered payments:** The total monthly amount that you pay as required by the order of a court or administrative agency, such as spousal or child support payments.
Do not include payments on past due obligations for spousal or child support. You will list these obligations in line 35. $______

20. **Education:** The total monthly amount that you pay for education that is either required:
- as a condition for your job, or
- for your physically or mentally challenged dependent child if no public education is available for similar services. $______

21. **Childcare:** The total monthly amount that you pay for childcare, such as babysitting, daycare, nursery, and preschool.
Do not include payments for any elementary or secondary school education. $______

22. **Additional health care expenses, excluding insurance costs:** The monthly amount that you pay for health care that is required for the health and welfare of you or your dependents and that is not reimbursed by insurance or paid by a health savings account. Include only the amount that is more than the total entered in line 7.
Payments for health insurance or health savings accounts should be listed only in line 25. $______

23. **Optional telephones and telephone services:** The total monthly amount that you pay for telecommunication services for you and your dependents, such as pagers, call waiting, caller identification, special long distance, or business cell phone service, to the extent necessary for your health and welfare or that of your dependents or for the production of income, if it is not reimbursed by your employer.
Do not include payments for basic home telephone, internet or cell phone service. Do not include self-employment expenses, such as those reported on line 5 of Form 122C-1, or any amount you previously deducted. + $______

24. **Add all of the expenses allowed under the IRS expense allowances.**
Add lines 6 through 23. $______

Additional Expense Deductions These are additional deductions allowed by the Means Test.
Note: Do not include any expense allowances listed in lines 6-24.

25. **Health insurance, disability insurance, and health savings account expenses.** The monthly expenses for health insurance, disability insurance, and health savings accounts that are reasonably necessary for yourself, your spouse, or your dependents.

Health insurance $______

Disability insurance $______

Health savings account + $______

Total $______ Copy total here → $______

Do you actually spend this total amount?

☐ No. How much do you actually spend? $______

☐ Yes.

26. **Continuing contributions to the care of household or family members.** The actual monthly expenses that you will continue to pay for the reasonable and necessary care and support of an elderly, chronically ill, or disabled member of your household or member of your immediate family who is unable to pay for such expenses. These expenses may include contributions to an account of a qualified ABLE program. 26 U.S.C. § 529A(b). $______

27. **Protection against family violence.** The reasonably necessary monthly expenses that you incur to maintain the safety of you and your family under the Family Violence Prevention and Services Act or other federal laws that apply.
By law, the court must keep the nature of these expenses confidential. $______

Debtor 1 John Paul Jones
First Name Middle Name Last Name

Case number (if known) ____________________

28. **Additional home energy costs.** Your home energy costs are included in your insurance and operating expenses on line 8.
If you believe that you have home energy costs that are more than the home energy costs included in expenses on line 8, then fill in the excess amount of home energy costs. $______
You must give your case trustee documentation of your actual expenses, and you must show that the additional amount claimed is reasonable and necessary.

29. **Education expenses for dependent children who are younger than 18.** The monthly expenses (not more than $189.58* per child) that you pay for your dependent children who are younger than 18 years old to attend a private or public elementary or secondary school. $______
You must give your case trustee documentation of your actual expenses, and you must explain why the amount claimed is reasonable and necessary and not already accounted for in lines 6-23.

* Subject to adjustment on 4/01/25, and every 3 years after that for cases begun on or after the date of adjustment.

30. **Additional food and clothing expense.** The monthly amount by which your actual food and clothing expenses are higher than the combined food and clothing allowances in the IRS National Standards. That amount cannot be more than 5% of the food and clothing allowances in the IRS National Standards. $______
To find a chart showing the maximum additional allowance, go online using the link specified in the separate instructions for this form. This chart may also be available at the bankruptcy clerk's office.
You must show that the additional amount claimed is reasonable and necessary.

31. **Continuing charitable contributions.** The amount that you will continue to contribute in the form of cash or financial instruments to a religious or charitable organization. 11 U.S.C. § 548(d)(3) and (4). + $______
Do not include any amount more than 15% of your gross monthly income.

32. **Add all of the additional expense deductions.**
Add lines 25 through 31. $______

Deductions for Debt Payment

33. **For debts that are secured by an interest in property that you own, including home mortgages, vehicle loans, and other secured debt, fill in lines 33a through 33e.**
To calculate the total average monthly payment, add all amounts that are contractually due to each secured creditor in the 60 months after you file for bankruptcy. Then divide by 60.

	Average monthly payment
Mortgages on your home	
33a. Copy line 9b here	$ 3,000.00
Loans on your first two vehicles	
33b. Copy line 13b here.	$ 800.00
33c. Copy line 13e here.	$

33d. List other secured debts:

Name of each creditor for other secured debt	Identify property that secures the debt	Does payment include taxes or insurance?	
____________	____________	☐ No ☐ Yes	$______
____________	____________	☐ No ☐ Yes	$______
____________	____________	☐ No ☐ Yes	+ $______

33e. Total average monthly payment. Add lines 33a through 33d. ...... $______ Copy total here ➔ $______

Debtor 1 John Paul Jones
First Name Middle Name Last Name

Case number (if known) ______________

34. Are any debts that you listed in line 33 secured by your primary residence, a vehicle, or other property necessary for your support or the support of your dependents?

☒ **No.** Go to line 35.

☐ **Yes.** State any amount that you must pay to a creditor, in addition to the payments listed in line 33, to keep possession of your property (called the cure amount). Next, divide by 60 and fill in the information below.

Name of the creditor	Identify property that secures the debt	Total cure amount		Monthly cure amount
______	______	$______	÷ 60 =	$______
______	______	$______	÷ 60 =	$______
______	______	$______	÷ 60 =	+ $______

Total $______ Copy total here → $______

35. Do you owe any priority claims—such as a priority tax, child support, or alimony— that are past due as of the filing date of your bankruptcy case? 11 U.S.C. § 507.

☒ **No.** Go to line 36.

☐ **Yes.** Fill in the total amount of all of these priority claims. Do not include current or ongoing priority claims, such as those you listed in line 19.

Total amount of all past-due priority claims. ______ $______ ÷ 60 $______

36. Projected monthly Chapter 13 plan payment $______

Current multiplier for your district as stated on the list issued by the Administrative Office of the United States Courts (for districts in Alabama and North Carolina) or by the Executive Office for United States Trustees (for all other districts).

To find a list of district multipliers that includes your district, go online using the link specified in the separate instructions for this form. This list may also be available at the bankruptcy clerk's office. x ______

Average monthly administrative expense $______ Copy total here → $______

37. Add all of the deductions for debt payment. Add lines 33e through 36. $______

Total Deductions from Income

38. Add all of the allowed deductions.

Copy line 24, *All of the expenses allowed under IRS expense allowances* ______ $______

Copy line 32, *All of the additional expense deductions* ______ $______

Copy line 37, *All of the deductions for debt payment* ______ + $______

Total deductions ______ $______ Copy total here → $______

Debtor 1 John Paul Jones ______ Case number (if known) ______
First Name Middle Name Last Name

Part 2: Determine Your Disposable Income Under 11 U.S.C. § 1325(b)(2)

39. **Copy your total current monthly income from line 14 of Form 122C-1, *Chapter 13 Statement of Your Current Monthly Income and Calculation of Commitment Period.*** .... $______

40. **Fill in any reasonably necessary income you receive for support for dependent children.** The monthly average of any child support payments, foster care payments, or disability payments for a dependent child, reported in Part I of Form 122C-1, that you received in accordance with applicable nonbankruptcy law to the extent reasonably necessary to be expended for such child. $______

41. **Fill in all qualified retirement deductions.** The monthly total of all amounts that your employer withheld from wages as contributions for qualified retirement plans, as specified in 11 U.S.C. § 541(b)(7) plus all required repayments of loans from retirement plans, as specified in 11 U.S.C. § 362(b)(19). $______

42. **Total of all deductions allowed under 11 U.S.C. § 707(b)(2)(A).** Copy line 38 here ...... ➜ $______

43. **Deduction for special circumstances.** If special circumstances justify additional expenses and you have no reasonable alternative, describe the special circumstances and their expenses. You must give your case trustee a detailed explanation of the special circumstances and documentation for the expenses.

Describe the special circumstances	Amount of expense
______	$______
______	$______
______	+ $______
Total	$______

Copy here ➜ + $______

44. **Total adjustments.** Add lines 40 through 43. .... $______ Copy here ➜ − $______

45. **Calculate your monthly disposable income under § 1325(b)(2).** Subtract line 44 from line 39. $______

Part 3: Change in Income or Expenses

46. **Change in income or expenses.** If the income in Form 122C-1 or the expenses you reported in this form have changed or are virtually certain to change after the date you filed your bankruptcy petition and during the time your case will be open, fill in the information below. For example, if the wages reported increased after you filed your petition, check 122C-1 in the first column, enter line 2 in the second column, explain why the wages increased, fill in when the increase occurred, and fill in the amount of the increase.

Form	Line	Reason for change	Date of change	Increase or decrease?	Amount of change
☐ 122C-1 ☐ 122C-2	___	______	______	☐ Increase ☐ Decrease	$______
☐ 122C-1 ☐ 122C-2	___	______	______	☐ Increase ☐ Decrease	$______
☐ 122C-1 ☐ 122C-2	___	______	______	☐ Increase ☐ Decrease	$______
☐ 122C-1 ☐ 122C-2	___	______	______	☐ Increase ☐ Decrease	$______

Debtor 1 John Paul Jones
First Name Middle Name Last Name

Case number (if known) ____________________

Part 4: **Sign Below**

By signing here, under penalty of perjury you declare that the information on this statement and in any attachments is true and correct.

✗ ____________________ Signature of Debtor 1

✗ ____________________ Signature of Debtor 2

Date ____________ MM / DD / YYYY

Date ____________ MM / DD / YYYY

Print | Save As... | Add Attachment | Reset

EXHIBIT 3-C CHAPTER 13 PLAN

Fill in this information to identify your case:

Debtor 1 John Paul Jones
First Name Middle Name Last Name

Debtor 2 (Spouse, if filing) Shirley Ann Jones
First Name Middle Name Last Name

United States Bankruptcy Court for the: Central District of California (State)

Case number (If known) 21B-00221-SRT

☐ Check if this is an amended plan, and list below the sections of the plan that have been changed.

Official Form 113

Chapter 13 Plan

12/17

Part 1: Notices

To Debtors: **This form sets out options that may be appropriate in some cases, but the presence of an option on the form does not indicate that the option is appropriate in your circumstances or that it is permissible in your judicial district. Plans that do not comply with local rules and judicial rulings may not be confirmable.**

In the following notice to creditors, you must check each box that applies.

To Creditors: **Your rights may be affected by this plan. Your claim may be reduced, modified, or eliminated.**

You should read this plan carefully and discuss it with your attorney if you have one in this bankruptcy case. If you do not have an attorney, you may wish to consult one.

If you oppose the plan's treatment of your claim or any provision of this plan, you or your attorney must file an objection to confirmation at least 7 days before the date set for the hearing on confirmation, unless otherwise ordered by the Bankruptcy Court. The Bankruptcy Court may confirm this plan without further notice if no objection to confirmation is filed. See Bankruptcy Rule 3015. In addition, you may need to file a timely proof of claim in order to be paid under any plan.

The following matters may be of particular importance. ***Debtors must check one box on each line to state whether or not the plan includes each of the following items. If an item is checked as "Not Included" or if both boxes are checked, the provision will be ineffective if set out later in the plan.***

1.1	**A limit on the amount of a secured claim, set out in Section 3.2, which may result in a partial payment or no payment at all to the secured creditor**	☐ **Included**	■ **Not included**
1.2	**Avoidance of a judicial lien or nonpossessory, nonpurchase-money security interest, set out in Section 3.4**	☐ **Included**	■ **Not included**
1.3	**Nonstandard provisions, set out in Part 8**	☐ **Included**	■ **Not included**

Part 2: Plan Payments and Length of Plan

2.1 **Debtor(s) will make regular payments to the trustee as follows:**

$ 1,332.00 per month for 36 months

[and $ ________ per ______ for _____ months.] *Insert additional lines if needed.*

If fewer than 60 months of payments are specified, additional monthly payments will be made to the extent necessary to make the payments to creditors specified in this plan.

Debtor John Paul Jones Case number 21B-00221-SRT

2.2 Regular payments to the trustee will be made from future income in the following manner:

Check all that apply.

- ■ Debtor(s) will make payments pursuant to a payroll deduction order.
- ☐ Debtor(s) will make payments directly to the trustee.
- ☐ Other (specify method of payment):________________________.

2.3 Income tax refunds.

Check one.

- ☐ Debtor(s) will retain any income tax refunds received during the plan term.
- ■ Debtor(s) will supply the trustee with a copy of each income tax return filed during the plan term within 14 days of filing the return and will turn over to the trustee all income tax refunds received during the plan term.
- ☐ Debtor(s) will treat income tax refunds as follows:

____

____

2.4 Additional payments.

Check one.

- ■ **None.** *If "None" is checked, the rest of § 2.4 need not be completed or reproduced.*
- ☐ Debtor(s) will make additional payment(s) to the trustee from other sources, as specified below. Describe the source, estimated amount, and date of each anticipated payment.

____

____

2.5 The total amount of estimated payments to the trustee provided for in §§ 2.1 and 2.4 is $ 1,332.00/mo..

Part 3: Treatment of Secured Claims

3.1 Maintenance of payments and cure of default, if any.

Check one.

- ☐ **None.** *If "None" is checked, the rest of § 3.1 need not be completed or reproduced.*
- ■ The debtor(s) will maintain the current contractual installment payments on the secured claims listed below, with any changes required by the applicable contract and noticed in conformity with any applicable rules. These payments will be disbursed either by the trustee or directly by the debtor(s), as specified below. Any existing arrearage on a listed claim will be paid in full through disbursements by the trustee, with interest, if any, at the rate stated. Unless otherwise ordered by the court, the amounts listed on a proof of claim filed before the filing deadline under Bankruptcy Rule 3002(c) control over any contrary amounts listed below as to the current installment payment and arrearage. In the absence of a contrary timely filed proof of claim, the amounts stated below are controlling. If relief from the automatic stay is ordered as to any item of collateral listed in this paragraph, then, unless otherwise ordered by the court, all payments under this paragraph as to that collateral will cease, and all secured claims based on that collateral will no longer be treated by the plan. The final column includes only payments disbursed by the trustee rather than by the debtor(s).

Name of creditor	Collateral	Current installment payment (including escrow)	Amount of arrearage (if any)	Interest rate on arrearage (if applicable)	Monthly plan payment on arrearage	Estimated total payments by trustee
Bank of America	Home	$1,519.00 Disbursed by: ☐ Trustee ■ Debtor(s)	$6,983.07	18.00 %	$200.00	$1,719.00
______	______	$______ Disbursed by: ☐ Trustee ☐ Debtor(s)	$______	____%	$______	$______

Insert additional claims as needed.

Debtor John Paul Jones Case number 21B-00221-SRT

3.2 Request for valuation of security, payment of fully secured claims, and modification of undersecured claims. *Check one.*

■ **None.** *If "None" is checked, the rest of § 3.2 need not be completed or reproduced.*

The remainder of this paragraph will be effective only if the applicable box in Part 1 of this plan is checked.

☐ The debtor(s) request that the court determine the value of the secured claims listed below. For each non-governmental secured claim listed below, the debtor(s) state that the value of the secured claim should be as set out in the column headed *Amount of secured claim*. For secured claims of governmental units, unless otherwise ordered by the court, the value of a secured claim listed in a proof of claim filed in accordance with the Bankruptcy Rules controls over any contrary amount listed below. For each listed claim, the value of the secured claim will be paid in full with interest at the rate stated below.

The portion of any allowed claim that exceeds the amount of the secured claim will be treated as an unsecured claim under Part 5 of this plan. If the amount of a creditor's secured claim is listed below as having no value, the creditor's allowed claim will be treated in its entirety as an unsecured claim under Part 5 of this plan. Unless otherwise ordered by the court, the amount of the creditor's total claim listed on the proof of claim controls over any contrary amounts listed in this paragraph.

The holder of any claim listed below as having value in the column headed *Amount of secured claim* will retain the lien on the property interest of the debtor(s) or the estate(s) until the earlier of:

(a) payment of the underlying debt determined under nonbankruptcy law, or

(b) discharge of the underlying debt under 11 U.S.C. § 1328, at which time the lien will terminate and be released by the creditor.

Name of creditor	Estimated amount of creditor's total claim	Collateral	Value of collateral	Amount of claims senior to creditor's claim	Amount of secured claim	Interest rate	Monthly payment to creditor	Estimated total of monthly payments
______	$______	______	$______	$______	$______	___%	$______	$______
______	$______	______	$______	$______	$______	___%	$______	$______

Insert additional claims as needed.

3.3 Secured claims excluded from 11 U.S.C. § 506.

Check one.

☐ **None.** *If "None" is checked, the rest of § 3.3 need not be completed or reproduced.*

■ The claims listed below were either:

(1) incurred within 910 days before the petition date and secured by a purchase money security interest in a motor vehicle acquired for the personal use of the debtor(s), or

(2) incurred within 1 year of the petition date and secured by a purchase money security interest in any other thing of value.

These claims will be paid in full under the plan with interest at the rate stated below. These payments will be disbursed either by the trustee or directly by the debtor(s), as specified below. Unless otherwise ordered by the court, the claim amount stated on a proof of claim filed before the filing deadline under Bankruptcy Rule 3002(c) controls over any contrary amount listed below. In the absence of a contrary timely filed proof of claim, the amounts stated below are controlling. The final column includes only payments disbursed by the trustee rather than by the debtor(s).

Name of creditor	Collateral	Amount of claim	Interest rate	Monthly plan payment	Estimated total payments by trustee
XY Bank	2019 Toyota	$20,150	4.5%	$599.00 Disbursed by: ☐ Trustee ■ Debtor(s)	$21,564.00
______	______	$______	___%	$______ Disbursed by: ☐ Trustee ☐ Debtor(s)	$______

Insert additional claims as needed.

Debtor John Paul Jones Case number 19B-00221-SRT

3.4 Lien avoidance.

Check one.

■ **None.** *If "None" is checked, the rest of § 3.4 need not be completed or reproduced.*

The remainder of this paragraph will be effective only if the applicable box in Part 1 of this plan is checked.

☐ The judicial liens or nonpossessory, nonpurchase money security interests securing the claims listed below impair exemptions to which the debtor(s) would have been entitled under 11 U.S.C. § 522(b). Unless otherwise ordered by the court, a judicial lien or security interest securing a claim listed below will be avoided to the extent that it impairs such exemptions upon entry of the order confirming the plan. The amount of the judicial lien or security interest that is avoided will be treated as an unsecured claim in Part 5 to the extent allowed. The amount, if any, of the judicial lien or security interest that is not avoided will be paid in full as a secured claim under the plan. See 11 U.S.C. § 522(f) and Bankruptcy Rule 4003(d). *If more than one lien is to be avoided, provide the information separately for each lien.*

Information regarding judicial lien or security interest	Calculation of lien avoidance		Treatment of remaining secured claim
Name of creditor _______________	a. Amount of lien	$________	**Amount of secured claim after avoidance** (line a minus line f) $________
	b. Amount of all other liens	$________	
Collateral _______________	c. Value of claimed exemptions	+ $________	**Interest rate** (if applicable) _____ %
	d. Total of adding lines a, b, and c	$________	
Lien identification (such as judgment date, date of lien recording, book and page number) _______________ _______________	e. Value of debtor(s)' interest in property	− $________	**Monthly payment on secured claim** $________
	f. Subtract line e from line d.	$________	**Estimated total payments on secured claim** $________
	Extent of exemption impairment (*Check applicable box*): ☐ **Line f is equal to or greater than line a.** The entire lien is avoided. *(Do not complete the next column.)* ☐ **Line f is less than line a.** A portion of the lien is avoided. (*Complete the next column.)*		

Insert additional claims as needed.

3.5 Surrender of collateral.

Check one.

■ **None.** *If "None" is checked, the rest of § 3.5 need not be completed or reproduced.*

☐ The debtor(s) elect to surrender to each creditor listed below the collateral that secures the creditor's claim. The debtor(s) request that upon confirmation of this plan the stay under 11 U.S.C. § 362(a) be terminated as to the collateral only and that the stay under § 1301 be terminated in all respects. Any allowed unsecured claim resulting from the disposition of the collateral will be treated in Part 5 below.

Name of creditor	Collateral

Insert additional claims as needed.

Debtor John Paul Jones Case number 21B-00221-SRT

Part 4: Treatment of Fees and Priority Claims

4.1 General

Trustee's fees and all allowed priority claims, including domestic support obligations other than those treated in § 4.5, will be paid in full without postpetition interest.

4.2 Trustee's fees

Trustee's fees are governed by statute and may change during the course of the case but are estimated to be 11 % of plan payments; and during the plan term, they are estimated to total $4,752.00.

4.3 Attorney's fees

The balance of the fees owed to the attorney for the debtor(s) is estimated to be $1,000.

4.4 Priority claims other than attorney's fees and those treated in § 4.5.

Check one.

- ☐ **None.** *If "None" is checked, the rest of § 4.4 need not be completed or reproduced.*
- ■ The debtor(s) estimate the total amount of other priority claims to be $2,195.00.

4.5 Domestic support obligations assigned or owed to a governmental unit and paid less than full amount.

Check one.

- ■ **None.** *If "None" is checked, the rest of § 4.5 need not be completed or reproduced.*
- ☐ The allowed priority claims listed below are based on a domestic support obligation that has been assigned to or is owed to a governmental unit and will be paid less than the full amount of the claim under 11 U.S.C. § 1322(a)(4). *This plan provision requires that payments in § 2.1 be for a term of 60 months; see* 11 U.S.C. § 1322(a)(4).

Name of creditor	Amount of claim to be paid
	$
	$

Insert additional claims as needed.

Part 5: Treatment of Nonpriority Unsecured Claims

5.1 Nonpriority unsecured claims not separately classified.

Allowed nonpriority unsecured claims that are not separately classified will be paid, pro rata. If more than one option is checked, the option providing the largest payment will be effective. *Check all that apply.*

- ■ The sum of $169,605.00.
- ■ 11 % of the total amount of these claims, an estimated payment of $18,427.00.
- ■ The funds remaining after disbursements have been made to all other creditors provided for in this plan.

If the estate of the debtor(s) were liquidated under chapter 7, nonpriority unsecured claims would be paid approximately $0.00. Regardless of the options checked above, payments on allowed nonpriority unsecured claims will be made in at least this amount.

Debtor John Paul Jones Case number 21B-00221-SRT

5.2 **Maintenance of payments and cure of any default on nonpriority unsecured claims.** *Check one.*

■ **None.** *If "None" is checked, the rest of § 5.2 need not be completed or reproduced.*

❑ The debtor(s) will maintain the contractual installment payments and cure any default in payments on the unsecured claims listed below on which the last payment is due after the final plan payment. These payments will be disbursed either by the trustee or directly by the debtor(s), as specified below. The claim for the arrearage amount will be paid in full as specified below and disbursed by the trustee. The final column includes only payments disbursed by the trustee rather than by the debtor(s).

Name of creditor	Current installment payment	Amount of arrearage to be paid	Estimated total payments by trustee
____________	$______ Disbursed by: ❑ Trustee ❑ Debtor(s)	$______	$______
____________	$______ Disbursed by: ❑ Trustee ❑ Debtor(s)	$______	$______

Insert additional claims as needed.

5.3 **Other separately classified nonpriority unsecured claims.** *Check one.*

■ **None.** *If "None" is checked, the rest of § 5.3 need not be completed or reproduced.*

❑ The nonpriority unsecured allowed claims listed below are separately classified and will be treated as follows

Name of creditor	Basis for separate classification and treatment	Amount to be paid on the claim	Interest rate (if applicable)	Estimated total amount of payments
____________	____________	$______	____%	$______
____________	____________	$______	____%	$______

Insert additional claims as needed.

Part 6: Executory Contracts and Unexpired Leases

6.1 **The executory contracts and unexpired leases listed below are assumed and will be treated as specified. All other executory contracts and unexpired leases are rejected.** *Check one.*

■ **None.** *If "None" is checked, the rest of § 6.1 need not be completed or reproduced.*

❑ **Assumed items.** Current installment payments will be disbursed either by the trustee or directly by the debtor(s), as specified below, subject to any contrary court order or rule. Arrearage payments will be disbursed by the trustee. The final column includes only payments disbursed by the trustee rather than by the debtor(s).

Debtor John Paul Jones Case number 21B-00221-SRT

Name of creditor	Description of leased property or executory contract	Current installment payment	Amount of arrearage to be paid	Treatment of arrearage (Refer to other plan section if applicable)	Estimated total payments by trustee
________	________	$________ Disbursed by: ❑ Trustee ❑ Debtor(s)	$________	________ ________	$________
________	________	$________ Disbursed by: ❑ Trustee ❑ Debtor(s)	$________	________ ________	$________

Insert additional contracts or leases as needed.

Part 7: Vesting of Property of the Estate

7.1 Property of the estate will vest in the debtor(s) upon

Check the applicable box:

❑ plan confirmation.

■ entry of discharge.

❑ other: ________________________.

Part 8: Nonstandard Plan Provisions

8.1 Check "None" or List Nonstandard Plan Provisions

■ **None.** *If "None" is checked, the rest of Part 8 need not be completed or reproduced.*

Under Bankruptcy Rule 3015(c), nonstandard provisions must be set forth below. A nonstandard provision is a provision not otherwise included in the Official Form or deviating from it. Nonstandard provisions set out elsewhere in this plan are ineffective.

The following plan provisions will be effective only if there is a check in the box "Included" in § 1.3.

____

____

____

____

____

Debtor John Paul Jones Case number 21B-00221-SRT

Part 9: Signature(s):

9.1 Signatures of Debtor(s) and Debtor(s)' Attorney

If the Debtor(s) do not have an attorney, the Debtor(s) must sign below; otherwise the Debtor(s) signatures are optional. The attorney for the Debtor(s), if any, must sign below.

✘ /s/ John Paul Jones
Signature of Debtor 1
Executed on 02/15/2021
MM / DD / YYYY

✘ /s/ Shirley Ann Jones
Signature of Debtor 2
Executed on 02/15/2021
MM / DD / YYYY

✘ /s/ John T. Smith
Signature of Attorney for Debtor(s)

Date 02/15/2021
MM / DD / YYYY

By filing this document, the Debtor(s), if not represented by an attorney, or the Attorney for Debtor(s) also certify(ies) that the wording and order of the provisions in this Chapter 13 plan are identical to those contained in Official Form 113, other than any nonstandard provisions included in Part 8.

Exhibit: Total Amount of Estimated Trustee Payments

The following are the estimated payments that the plan requires the trustee to disburse. If there is any difference between the amounts set out below and the actual plan terms, the plan terms control.

a.	**Maintenance and cure payments on secured claims** (*Part 3, Section 3.1 total*)		$61,884.00
b.	**Modified secured claims** (*Part 3, Section 3.2 total*)		$0.00
c.	**Secured claims excluded from 11 U.S.C. § 506** (*Part 3, Section 3.3 total*)		$21,564.00
d.	**Judicial liens or security interests partially avoided** (*Part 3, Section 3.4 total*)		$0.00
e.	**Fees and priority claims** (*Part 4 total*)		$14,752
f.	**Nonpriority unsecured claims** (*Part 5, Section 5.1, highest stated amount*)		$18,427.00
g.	**Maintenance and cure payments on unsecured claims** (*Part 5, Section 5.2 total*)		$0.00
h.	**Separately classified unsecured claims** (*Part 5, Section 5.3 total*)		$0.00
i.	**Trustee payments on executory contracts and unexpired leases** (*Part 6, Section 6.1 total*)		$0.00
j.	**Nonstandard payments** (*Part 8, total*)	+	$0.00
	Total of lines a through j		$116,627.00

Exhibit 3-D Order Confirming Chapter 13 Plan

B2300B (Form 2300B) (12/15)

United States Bankruptcy Court

______________ District Of ______________

In re ____ Case No. _________

Debtor*

Address: _____________________________________ Chapter 13

Last four digits of Social-Security or Individual Taxpayer-
Identification (ITIN) No(s).,(if any):
Employer Tax-Identification (EIN) No(s).(if any):

ORDER CONFIRMING CHAPTER 13 PLAN

The debtor's plan was filed on ________________ (date), and was modified on _____________ (date). The plan or a summary of the plan was transmitted to creditors pursuant to Bankruptcy Rule 3015. The court finds that the plan meets the requirements of 11 U.S.C. § 1325.

IT IS ORDERED THAT:

The debtor's chapter 13 plan is confirmed, with the following provisions:

1. Payments:
Amount of each payment: $_________________

Due date of each payment: the ☐ ________day of each month, or
☐ _____________

Period of payments: ☐ _____________ months,
☐ until a _________% dividend is paid to creditors holding allowed unsecured claims, or
☐ ________________

Payable to:
____________________________________Standing Trustee
____
____

2. Attorney's Fees:
The debtor's attorney is awarded a fee in the amount of $_____________, of which $______________ is due and payable from the estate.

3. [Other provisions as needed] _____________________________

______________________________ ______________________________

Date *Bankruptcy Judge*

* *Set forth all names, including trade names, used by the debtor(s) within the last 8 years. For joint debtors, set forth the last four digits of both social-security numbers or individual taxpayer-identification numbers.*

Exhibit 3-E Motion to Modify Chapter 13 Plan After Confirmation

UNITED STATES BANKRUPTCY COURT
CENTRAL DISTRICT OF CALIFORNIA

IN RE John Paul Jones and	)	
Shirley Ann Jones	)	Case No. 21B-00221-SRT
	)	
Debtors	)	Chapter 13

MOTION TO MODIFY CHAPTER 13 PLAN AFTER CONFIRMATION

The debtors by their attorney, state and represent as follows:

1. That subsequent to the confirmation of their Chapter 13 plan on February 15, 2016, the debtor John Paul Jones has suffered a loss of income in the average monthly amount of $300.00 as a result of a decrease in sales by The Royal Sales Company, the company by whom the debtor is employed as a commission salesman.

2. That because of the reduction in the amount of income, the debtors are no longer able to pay the sum of $1,332.00 per month as required in the present Chapter 13 plan, but are able to pay the sum of $1,032.00 per month and propose, in the modified Chapter 13 plan, to extend the time for payments under the plan from 36 months to 47 months in order to compensate for the reduction in the amount of the monthly payment.

3. That the modification proposed by the debtor will not modify the rights of the holder of any secured claim being dealt with under the plan, and will modify the rights of only the holders of allowed Class B unsecured claims to the extent that the time of payment of their respective claims will be extended.

4. That a copy of the debtor's modified Chapter 13 plan dated April 10, 2018 is attached to this motion and that a copy of same, together with a copy of this motion, has been sent to the Chapter 13 trustee, the United States trustee and the holders of all allowed Class B unsecured claims.

WHEREFORE, the debtor moves this honorable court, to enter an order confirming the debtor's modified Chapter 13 plan dated April 10, 2018.

Date: April 10, 2021

John T. Smith
Attorney for Debtors
6200 Wilshire Blvd., Suite 3333
Los Angeles, CA 90012
John.smith@bklawyer.com
Telephone: 213-344-7666

Exhibit 3-F Request for Trustee's Prior Approval of Consumer Debt

UNITED STATES BANKRUPTCY COURT
CENTRAL DISTRICT OF CALIFORNIA

IN RE John Paul Jones and Shirley Ann Jones	)	
	)	Case No. 21B-00221-SRT
	)	
Debtors	)	Chapter 13

REQUEST FOR TRUSTEE'S PRIOR APPROVAL OF CONSUMER DEBT

The debtors, by their attorney, hereby request the Chapter 13 trustee's prior approval of the following consumer debt for the reasons set forth below:

1. The debt for which the Chapter 13 trustee's prior approval is sought is a proposed debt to the Friendly Finance Company for funds with which to purchase a used 2018 Buick Regal automobile.

2. The debtors' previous automobile was recently damaged in an accident and the cost of repairing the automobile would far exceed its value.

3. The debtors have made arrangements for the purchase of a 2001 Buick Regal automobile I.D. No. 333935JK33P884 from Better Buy Used Cars, 3333 Broadway, Englewood, California for the price of $8,700.00. $2,000.00 of the purchase price will be paid from the proceeds of the insurance on the debtor's previous automobile, and the debtors propose to borrow $6,700.00 from the Friendly Finance Company to pay the balance of the purchase price of the automobile.

4. The proposed loan from Friendly Finance Company will be payable at the rate of $100.00 per month for the duration of the plan and at the rate of $350.00 per month thereafter. The annual interest rate on the loan shall be 12 percent, and the debtors propose to pay the debt as a secured claim under the modified Chapter 13 plan and to reaffirm the unpaid balance of the claim upon completion of the plan.

5. The debtors need the automobile that is proposed to be purchased in order to maintain employment and continue performance under the Chapter 13 plan. The debtors will be able to maintain the Chapter 13 payments after the incurrence of the debt to Friendly Finance Company.

Dated: May 9, 2021

____
John Paul Jones, debtor

____
John T. Smith
Attorney for Debtors
6200 Wilshire Blvd. Suite 3333
Los Angeles, CA 90012
Telephone: 213-344-7666

____
Shirley Ann Jones, debtor

Debt approved: ______________________________
Chapter 13 Trustee Date

Debt disapproved: ______________________________
Chapter 13 Trustee Date

Exhibit 3-G Proof of Claim with Mortgage Attachment (Forms 410 & 410A)

Fill in this information to identify the case:

Debtor 1 John Paul Jones

Debtor 2 (Spouse, if filing) Shirley Ann Jones

United States Bankruptcy Court for the: __________ District of __________

Case number ____________________

Official Form 410

Proof of Claim

04/22

Read the instructions before filling out this form. This form is for making a claim for payment in a bankruptcy case. Do not use this form to make a request for payment of an administrative expense. Make such a request according to 11 U.S.C. § 503.

Filers must leave out or redact information that is entitled to privacy on this form or on any attached documents. Attach redacted copies of any documents that support the claim, such as promissory notes, purchase orders, invoices, itemized statements of running accounts, contracts, judgments, mortgages, and security agreements. **Do not send original documents;** they may be destroyed after scanning. If the documents are not available, explain in an attachment.

A person who files a fraudulent claim could be fined up to $500,000, imprisoned for up to 5 years, or both. 18 U.S.C. §§ 152, 157, and 3571.

Fill in all the information about the claim as of the date the case was filed. That date is on the notice of bankruptcy (Form 309) **that you received.**

Part 1: Identify the Claim

1. Who is the current creditor?

ABC Bank
Name of the current creditor (the person or entity to be paid for this claim)

Other names the creditor used with the debtor ____________________

2. Has this claim been acquired from someone else?

☑ No
☐ Yes. From whom? ____________________

3. Where should notices and payments to the creditor be sent?

Federal Rule of Bankruptcy Procedure (FRBP) 2002(g)

Where should notices to the creditor be sent?	Where should payments to the creditor be sent? (if different)
Steve James, Esq. (Name)	Name
12345 E 17th St, Suite 100A (Number Street)	Number Street
Los Angeles (City) CA (State) 90012 (ZIP Code)	City State ZIP Code
Contact phone __________	Contact phone __________
Contact email __________	Contact email __________

Uniform claim identifier for electronic payments in chapter 13 (if you use one):
123456898198

4. Does this claim amend one already filed?

☑ No
☐ Yes. Claim number on court claims registry (if known) ______ Filed on ________ MM / DD / YYYY

5. Do you know if anyone else has filed a proof of claim for this claim?

☑ No
☐ Yes. Who made the earlier filing? __________

Part 2: Give Information About the Claim as of the Date the Case Was Filed

6. Do you have any number you use to identify the debtor?

☒ No
☐ Yes. Last 4 digits of the debtor's account or any number you use to identify the debtor: ____ ____ ____ ____

7. How much is the claim?

$ 188,980.58. **Does this amount include interest or other charges?**

☐ No
☐ Yes. Attach statement itemizing interest, fees, expenses, or other charges required by Bankruptcy Rule 3001(c)(2)(A).

8. What is the basis of the claim?

Examples: Goods sold, money loaned, lease, services performed, personal injury or wrongful death, or credit card.

Attach redacted copies of any documents supporting the claim required by Bankruptcy Rule 3001(c).

Limit disclosing information that is entitled to privacy, such as health care information.

First mortgage on real property located at 34 1st Ave, Alameda, CA

9. Is all or part of the claim secured?

☐ No
☒ Yes. The claim is secured by a lien on property.

Nature of property:

☒ Real estate. If the claim is secured by the debtor's principal residence, file a *Mortgage Proof of Claim Attachment* (Official Form 410-A) with this *Proof of Claim.*
☐ Motor vehicle
☐ Other. Describe: ____________________

Basis for perfection: recorded first mortgage

Attach redacted copies of documents, if any, that show evidence of perfection of a security interest (for example, a mortgage, lien, certificate of title, financing statement, or other document that shows the lien has been filed or recorded.)

Value of property: $ 250,000.00

Amount of the claim that is secured: $ 188,980.58

Amount of the claim that is unsecured: $ 0.00 (The sum of the secured and unsecured amounts should match the amount in line 7.)

Amount necessary to cure any default as of the date of the petition: $ 10,499.67

Annual Interest Rate (when case was filed) 5.30 %

☒ Fixed
☐ Variable

10. Is this claim based on a lease?

☒ No
☐ Yes. **Amount necessary to cure any default as of the date of the petition.** $__________

11. Is this claim subject to a right of setoff?

☒ No
☐ Yes. Identify the property: ____________________

12. **Is all or part of the claim entitled to priority under 11 U.S.C. § 507(a)?** A claim may be partly priority and partly nonpriority. For example, in some categories, the law limits the amount entitled to priority.	☒ No ☐ Yes. *Check one:*	**Amount entitled to priority**
	☐ Domestic support obligations (including alimony and child support) under 11 U.S.C. § 507(a)(1)(A) or (a)(1)(B).	$__________
	☐ Up to $3,350* of deposits toward purchase, lease, or rental of property or services for personal, family, or household use. 11 U.S.C. § 507(a)(7).	$__________
	☐ Wages, salaries, or commissions (up to $15,150*) earned within 180 days before the bankruptcy petition is filed or the debtor's business ends, whichever is earlier. 11 U.S.C. § 507(a)(4).	$__________
	☐ Taxes or penalties owed to governmental units. 11 U.S.C. § 507(a)(8).	$__________
	☐ Contributions to an employee benefit plan. 11 U.S.C. § 507(a)(5).	$__________
	☐ Other. Specify subsection of 11 U.S.C. § 507(a)(__) that applies.	$__________
	* Amounts are subject to adjustment on 4/01/25 and every 3 years after that for cases begun on or after the date of adjustment.	

Part 3: Sign Below

The person completing this proof of claim must sign and date it. FRBP 9011(b).

If you file this claim electronically, FRBP 5005(a)(2) authorizes courts to establish local rules specifying what a signature is.

A person who files a fraudulent claim could be fined up to $500,000, imprisoned for up to 5 years, or both. 18 U.S.C. §§ 152, 157, and 3571.

Check the appropriate box:

☐ I am the creditor.
☒ I am the creditor's attorney or authorized agent.
☐ I am the trustee, or the debtor, or their authorized agent. Bankruptcy Rule 3004.
☐ I am a guarantor, surety, endorser, or other codebtor. Bankruptcy Rule 3005.

I understand that an authorized signature on this *Proof of Claim* serves as an acknowledgment that when calculating the amount of the claim, the creditor gave the debtor credit for any payments received toward the debt.

I have examined the information in this *Proof of Claim* and have a reasonable belief that the information is true and correct.

I declare under penalty of perjury that the foregoing is true and correct.

Executed on date 03/28/2024
MM / DD / YYYY

/s/ Steven James, Esq
Signature

Print the name of the person who is completing and signing this claim:

Name: Steven James, Esq.
First name Middle name Last name

Title: Attorney for Creditor

Company: James & James, P.C.
Identify the corporate servicer as the company if the authorized agent is a servicer.

Address: 12345 E. 17th St., Suite 100A
Number Street

Los Angeles CA 90012
City State ZIP Code

Contact phone 999*999*9999 Email

Print | Save As... | Add Attachment | Reset

Mortgage Proof of Claim Attachment

(12/15)

If you file a claim secured by a security interest in the debtor's principal residence, you must use this form as an attachment to your proof of claim. See separate instructions.

Part 1: Mortgage and Case Information

Case number:	17B-00221-SRT
Debtor 1:	John Paul Jones
Debtor 2:	Shirley Ann Jones
Last 4 digits to identify:	3 5 1 4
Creditor:	ABC Bank
Servicer:	Steve James Esq.
Fixed accrual/daily simple interest/other:	5.20%

Part 2: Total Debt Calculation

Principal balance:	$188,980.58
Interest due:	$6,520.89
Fees, costs due:	$3,196.50
Escrow deficiency for funds advanced:	
Less total funds on hand:	–
Total debt:	$198,697.97

Part 3: Arrearage as of Date of the Petition

Principal & interest due:	$6,983.07
Prepetition fees due:	$3,196.50
Escrow deficiency for funds advanced:	
Projected escrow shortage:	
Less funds on hand:	–
Total prepetition arrearage:	$10,179.57

Part 4: Monthly Mortgage Payment

Principal & interest:	$1,230.00
Monthly escrow:	$289.00
Private mortgage insurance:	0.00
Total monthly payment:	$1,519.00

Part 5 : Loan Payment History from First Date of Default

		Account Activity					How Funds Were Applied/Amount Incurred					Balance After Amount Received or Incurred				
A. Date	B. Contractual payment amount	C. Funds received	D. Amount incurred	E. Description	F. Contractual due date	G. Prin, int & esc past due balance	H. Amount to principal	I. Amount to interest	J. Amount to escrow	K. Amount to fees or charges	L. Unapplied funds	M. Principal balance	N. Accrued interest balance	O. Escrow balance	P. Fees / Charges balance	Q. Unapplied funds balance
12/2019	$1,519.00	0.00		12/1/2019		0				$300		$188,980.58				

Exhibit 3-H Notice of Conversion of Chapter 13 to Chapter 7 Under Section 1307(a)

UNITED STATES BANKRUPTCY COURT
CENTRAL DISTRICT OF CALIFORNIA

IN RE John Paul Jones and	)	
Shirley Ann Jones	)	Case No. 21B-00221-SRT
	)	
Debtors	)	Chapter 13

NOTICE OF CONVERSION OF CHAPTER 13 CASE TO CHAPTER 7 UNDER SECTION 1307(a)

The debtors, by their attorney, represent and state as follows:

1. The debtors are no longer able to comply with their Chapter 13 plan and do not desire to modify the plan.

2. The debtors qualify as debtors under Chapter 7 of the Bankruptcy Code.

3. Under section 1307(a) of the Bankruptcy Code, the debtors are entitled to convert their Chapter 13 case to a case under Chapter 7 at any time, and the debtors now wish to convert this Chapter 13 case to a case under Chapter 7.

4. The conversion to Chapter 7 is being made in good faith by the debtors.

WHEREFORE, the debtors, pursuant to Rule 1017(f)(3) of the Rules of Bankruptcy Procedure, hereby give notice of the conversion of this Chapter 13 case to a case under Chapter 7 of the Bankruptcy Code.

Dated: May 20, 2021

Approved:

____
John Paul Jones, debtor

____
Shirley Ann Jones, debtor

____
John T. Smith
Attorney for Debtors
6200 Wilshire Blvd. Suite 3333
Los Angeles, CA 90012
Telephone: 213-344-7666

Exhibit 3-I Motion to Dismiss Case Under Section 1307(b)

UNITED STATES BANKRUPTCY COURT
CENTRAL DISTRICT OF CALIFORNIA

IN RE John Paul Jones and	)	
Shirley Ann Jones	)	Case No. 21B-00221-SRT
	)	
Debtors	)	Chapter 13

<u>MOTION TO DISMISS CASE PURSUANT TO 11 U.S.C. SECTION 1307(b)</u>

The debtors, by their attorney, represent and state as follows:

1. The debtors are no longer able to comply with their Chapter 13 plan previously filed with this Court, and do not desire to modify the plan.

2. The above-captioned Chapter 13 case has not been converted to Chapter 13 from another chapter of the Bankruptcy Code.

3. Pursuant to 11 U.S.C. §1307(b), the debtors are entitled to have this Chapter 13 case dismissed at any time.

4. The debtors hereby respectfully request that the above-captioned case be dismissed and the estate closed as soon as practicable.

WHEREFORE, the debtors, pursuant to 11 U.S.C. §1307(b) of Fed.R.Bank.P. 1017(d), respectfully move this honorable Court to enter an order dismissing the above-captioned case and closing the estate as soon as practicable.

Dated: May 20, 2021

Approved:

____
John T. Smith
Attorney for Debtors
6200 Wilshire Blvd. Suite 3333
Los Angeles, CA 90012
Telephone: 213-344-7666

____
John Paul Jones, debtor

____
Shirley Ann Jones, debtor

Exhibit 3-J Motion for Discharge of Debtors Under Section 1328(a)

UNITED STATES BANKRUPTCY COURT
CENTRAL DISTRICT OF CALIFORNIA

IN RE John Paul Jones and	)	
Shirley Ann Jones	)	Case No. 21B-00221-SRT
	)	
Debtors	)	Chapter 13

MOTION FOR DISCHARGE OF DEBTORS UNDER SECTION 1328(b)

The debtors, by their attorney, represent and state as follows:

1. That the debtors will be unable to complete the payments required of them under the Chapter 13 plan due to circumstances for which they should not justly be held accountable; to wit: the debtor, John Paul Jones, has been discharged by his employer, The Royal Sales Company, and has been unable to find other employment despite diligent efforts on his part to do so, and the debtor, Shirley Ann Jones, is employed only part time, thus rendering the debtors unable to maintain the payments required of them under their Chapter 13 plan.

2. That because of the uncertainty as to when the debtor, John Paul Jones will find employment sufficient to permit the debtors to resume the Chapter 13 payments, a modification of the Chapter 13 plan is not practicable.

3. That the value of the property actually distributed under the debtors' Chapter 13 plan on the account of each allowed unsecured claim is greater than the amount that would have been distributed to the holders of such claims had the estates of the debtors been liquidated under Chapter 7 of the Bankruptcy Code.

WHEREFORE, the debtors move this honorable Court to enter an order granting the debtors a discharge under section 1328(b) of the Bankruptcy Code.

Dated: May 20, 2021

____
John T. Smith
Attorney for Debtors
6200 Wilshire Blvd. Suite 3333
Los Angeles, CA 90012
Telephone: 213-344-7666

Exhibit 3-K Order of Discharge After Completion of Ch. 13 Plan (Director's Form 3180W)

Information to identify the case:

Debtor 1 ______________________________ Last 4 digits of Social Security number or ITIN _ _ _ _
First Name Middle Name Last Name
EIN _ _ - _ _ _ _ _ _ _ _

Debtor 2 ______________________________ Last 4 digits of Social Security number or ITIN _ _ _ _
(Spouse, if filing) First Name Middle Name Last Name
EIN _ _ - _ _ _ _ _ _ _ _

United States Bankruptcy Court for the: ________ District of ____________
(State)

Case number: ______________________

Order of Discharge

IT IS ORDERED: A discharge under 11 U.S.C. § 1328(a) is granted to:

______________________ [______________________]

[include all names used by each debtor, including trade names, within the 8 years prior to the filing of the petition]

____
MM / DD / YYYY

By the court: ______________________
United States Bankruptcy Judge

Explanation of Bankruptcy Discharge in a Chapter 13 Case

This order does not close or dismiss the case.

Creditors cannot collect discharged debts

This order means that no one may make any attempt to collect a discharged debt from the debtors personally. For example, creditors cannot sue, garnish wages, assert a deficiency, or otherwise try to collect from the debtors personally on discharged debts. Creditors cannot contact the debtors by mail, phone, or otherwise in any attempt to collect the debt personally. Creditors who violate this order can be required to pay debtors damages and attorney's fees.

However, a creditor with a lien may enforce a claim against the debtors' property subject to that lien unless the lien was avoided or eliminated. For example, a creditor may have the right to foreclose a home mortgage or repossess an automobile.

This order does not prevent debtors from paying any debt voluntarily. 11 U.S.C. § 524(f).

Most debts are discharged

Most debts are covered by the discharge, but not all. Generally, a discharge removes the debtors' personal liability for debts provided for by the chapter 13 plan.

In a case involving community property: Special rules protect certain community property owned by the debtor's spouse, even if that spouse did not file a bankruptcy case.

Some debts are not discharged

Examples of debts that are not discharged are:

- debts that are domestic support obligations;
- debts for most student loans;
- debts for certain types of taxes specified in 11 U.S.C. §§ 507(a)(8)(C), 523(a)(1)(B), or 523(a)(1)(C) to the extent not paid in full under the plan;

For more information, see page 2 ▶

- debts that the bankruptcy court has decided or will decide are not discharged in this bankruptcy case;

- debts for most fines, penalties, forfeitures, or criminal restitution obligations;

- some debts which the debtors did not properly list;

- debts provided for under 11 U.S.C. § 1322(b)(5) and on which the last payment or other transfer is due after the date on which the final payment under the plan was due;

- debts for certain consumer purchases made after the bankruptcy case was filed if obtaining the trustee's prior approval of incurring the debt was practicable but was not obtained;

- debts for restitution, or damages, awarded in a civil action against the debtor as a result of malicious or willful injury by the debtor that caused personal injury to an individual or the death of an individual; and

- debts for death or personal injury caused by operating a vehicle while intoxicated.

In addition, this discharge does not stop creditors from collecting from anyone else who is also liable on the debt, such as an insurance company or a person who cosigned or guaranteed a loan.

This information is only a general summary of a chapter 13 discharge; some exceptions exist. Because the law is complicated, you should consult an attorney to determine the exact effect of the discharge in this case.

Exhibit 3-L Order of Discharge Before Completion of Ch. 13 Plan (Director's Form 3180WH)

Information to identify the case:

Debtor 1 ______________________________ Last 4 digits of Social Security number or ITIN _ _ _ _
First Name Middle Name Last Name
EIN __ - ________

Debtor 2 ______________________________ Last 4 digits of Social Security number or ITIN _ _ _ _
(Spouse, if filing) First Name Middle Name Last Name
EIN __ - ________

United States Bankruptcy Court for the: ________ District of ____________
(State)

Case number: ______________________

Order of Discharge

IT IS ORDERED: A discharge under 11 U.S.C. § 1328(b) is granted to:

______________________ [______________________]

[include all names used by each debtor, including trade names, within the 8 years prior to the filing of the petition]

____________ **By the court:** ______________________
MM / DD / YYYY United States Bankruptcy Judge

Explanation of Bankruptcy Discharge Before Completion of a Chapter 13 Plan

The court has determined that the debtors are entitled to a discharge pursuant to 11 U.S.C. § 1328(b) without completing all of the requirements under the chapter 13 plan. A discharge pursuant to § 1328(b) is referred to as a "hardship discharge."

This order does not close or dismiss the case.

Creditors cannot collect discharged debts

This order means that no one may make any attempt to collect a discharged debt from the debtors personally. For example, creditors cannot sue, garnish wages, assert a deficiency, or otherwise try to collect from the debtors personally on discharged debts. Creditors cannot contact the debtors by mail, phone, or otherwise in any attempt to collect the debt personally. Creditors who violate this order can be required to pay debtors damages and attorney's fees.

However, a creditor with a lien may enforce a claim against the debtors' property subject to that lien unless the lien was avoided or eliminated. For example, a creditor may have the right to foreclose a home mortgage or repossess an automobile.

This order does not prevent debtors from paying any debt voluntarily. 11 U.S.C. § 524(f).

Most debts are discharged

Most debts are covered by the discharge, but not all. Generally, a discharge removes the debtors' personal liability for debts provided for by the chapter 13 plan.

In a case involving community property: Special rules protect certain community property owned by the debtor's spouse, even if that spouse did not file a bankruptcy case.

Some debts are not discharged

Examples of debts that are not discharged are:

debts that are domestic support obligations;

debts for most student loans;

For more information, see page 2 ▶

debts for most taxes;

debts that the bankruptcy court has decided or will decide are not discharged in this bankruptcy case;

debts for most fines, penalties, forfeitures, or criminal restitution obligations;

some debts which the debtors did not properly list;

debts for certain types of loans owed to pension, profit sharing, stock bonus, or retirement plans;

debts provided for under 11 U.S.C. § 1322(b)(5) and on which the last payment or other transfer is due after the date on which the final payment under the plan was due;

debts for certain consumer purchases made after the bankruptcy case was filed if obtaining the trustee's prior approval of incurring the debt was practicable but was not obtained; and

debts for death or personal injury caused by operating a vehicle while intoxicated.

In addition, this discharge does not stop creditors from collecting from anyone else who is also liable on the debt, such as an insurance company or a person who cosigned or guaranteed a loan.

This information is only a general summary of a chapter 13 hardship discharge; some exceptions exist. Because the law is complicated, you should consult an attorney to determine the exact effect of the discharge in this case.

Exhibit 3-M Motion to Determine Secured Status Pursuant to 11 U.S.C. § 506(a)

UNITED STATES BANKRUPTCY COURT
CENTRAL DISTRICT OF CALIFORNIA

IN RE John Paul Jones and	)	
Shirley Ann Jones	)	Case No. 21B-00221-SRT
	)	
Debtors / Movants	)	Chapter 13
	)	
v.	)	
	)	
Second Place Bank, N.A.	)	
	)	
Creditor / Respondent	)	

MOTION TO DETERMINE SECURED STATUS PURSUANT TO 11 U.S.C. § 506

Comes now the Debtors/Movants, by and through their undersigned attorney, and submit this Motion to Determine Secured Status Pursuant to 11 U.S.C. §506 and Fed.R.Bank.P. 3012. As grounds for this motion, Debtors state the following:

1. The Court has jurisdiction over this case pursuant to 28 U.S.C. §1334(b). This is a core proceeding pursuant to 28 U.S.C. §157(a), §157(b)(1), (b)(2)(B) and (K) because this is an action to determine secured status of a lien secured by real property within the meaning of 11 U.S.C. §506, et. seq.

2. On January 15, 2021, Debtors filed for relief under Chapter 13 of the Bankruptcy Code in the United States Bankruptcy Court, Central District of California.

3. The principal asset of the Debtors' estate is real property located at 12345 West 3rd Ave., Santa Monica, CA 98876, Legal Description: Lot 2, Block 3 Perry's Addition Fling 4, County of Los Angeles, State of California (the "Debtors' Residence").

4. Respondent holds a second position deed of trust on Debtors' Residence as security for the payment of a loan, the alleged unpaid balance of which is $36,657.18. The Respondent's deed of trust was recorded on May 23, 2018 at reception number 2006125773410 with the Los Angeles County Clerk and Recorder.

5. Respondent's second position deed of trust is inferior to the deed of trust held by First Place Bank, which was recorded on May 23, 2018 at reception number 2018125773409 with Los Angeles County Clerk and Recorder. The First Place Bank Deed of Trust has priority over all other liens and encumbrances in a current amount of $343,750.00, except for unpaid real estate tax liens.

6. A current market analysis performed by The Real Estate Pros, LLC indicates that the current market value of the Debtors' Residence is $335,000.00. (*See Exhibit A.*). A second current market analysis performed by Daniel Helbig of Remax Alliance real estate brokerage indicates that a suggested current listing price for the Debtors' Residence would be $315,000.00. (*See Exhibit B.*) The 2019 Real Property Tax Assessment from the Los Angeles County Assessor places a value on the Debtors' Residence of $312,000. (*See Exhibit C..*)

7. The value of the Debtors' Residence is less than the lien secured by the first mortgage holder.

8. Pursuant to *In re Fisette*, 455 B.R. 177 (B.A.P. 8th Cir. 8011), the prohibition against the modification of a secured creditor's rights provided for in 11 U.S.C. 1322(b)(2) does not protect a junior lien holder whose claim is wholly unsecured by any equity in a debtor's primary residence.

9. Pursuant to 11 U.S.C. §506(a), Respondent has no allowable secured claim for the second mortgage loan on Debtors' Residence.

10. Any timely filed claim of the Respondent for the second mortgage loan is allowable only as an unsecured claim and to the extent that no such claim is filed, the Respondent has no claim against the Debtors' bankruptcy estate.

WHEREFORE, Debtors/Movants respectfully request:

A. That this Court determine the value of the Debtors' Residence to be less than $343,750.00.

B. That this Court determine that Respondent has no secured interest for the loan secured by the second deed of trust on Debtors' Residence;

C. That this Court order the Respondent to cancel and record a reconveyance of its second mortgage deed of trust against the Debtors' Residence pursuant to 11 U.S.C. §506(d) immediately upon the entry of a Discharge Order in this matter pursuant to 11 U.S.C. §1328, and deliver the same to counsel for the Debtors within 20 days from the date of the entry of the Discharge Order at no charge of fee for the aforesaid cancellation and delivery; and,

D. That this Court direct the Trustee serving in this matter that any timely filed proof of claim filed by Respondent for the second mortgage lien be treated as an unsecured nonpriority claim under the Debtors' Chapter 13 plan and any Court-approved modifications thereto.

Dated this 25th day of January, 2021

[/s/ John T. Smith]
John T. Smith
Attorney for Debtors
6200 Wilshire Blvd. Suite 3333
Los Angeles, CA 90012
Telephone: 213-344-7666

Exhibit 3-N Certification Regarding Domestic Support Obligations

B2830 (Form 2830) (12/15)

United States Bankruptcy Court

Central District Of California

In re John Paul Jones and Shirley Ann Jones
Debtor

Case No. 21B-00221-SRT

CHAPTER 13 DEBTOR'S CERTIFICATIONS REGARDING DOMESTIC SUPPORT OBLIGATIONS AND SECTION 522(q)

Part I. Certification Regarding Domestic Support Obligations (check no more than one)

Pursuant to 11 U.S.C. Section 1328(a), I certify that:

☒ I owed no domestic support obligation when I filed my bankruptcy petition, and I have not been required to pay any such obligation since then.

☐ I am or have been required to pay a domestic support obligation. I have paid all such amounts that my chapter 13 plan required me to pay. I have also paid all such amounts that became due between the filing of my bankruptcy petition and today.

Part II. If you checked the second box, you must provide the information below.

My current address: ______________________________

My current employer and my employer's address: ______________________________

____

Part III. Certification Regarding Section 522(q) (check no more than one)

Pursuant to 11 U.S.C. Section 1328(h), I certify that:

☒ I have not claimed an exemption pursuant to § 522(b)(3) and state or local law (1) in property that I or a dependent of mine uses as a residence, claims as a homestead, or acquired as a burial plot, as specified in § 522(p)(1), and (2) that exceeds $155,675* in value in the aggregate.

☐ I have claimed an exemption in property pursuant to § 522(b)(3) and state or local law (1) that I or a dependent of mine uses as a residence, claims as a homestead, or acquired as a burial plot, as specified in § 522(p)(1), and (2) that exceeds $155,675* in value in the aggregate.

* Amounts are subject to adjustment on 4/01/16, and every 3 years thereafter with respect to cases commenced on or after the date of adjustment.

B2830 (Form 2830) (page 2)

Part IV. Debtor's Signature

I certify under penalty of perjury that the information provided in these certifications is true and correct to the best of my knowledge and belief.

Executed on 03/18/2021
Date

/s/ John Paul Jones
Debtor

Appendix I

United States Bankruptcy Code (TITLE 11 UNITED STATES CODE)

(Current to January 1, 2024)

CONTENTS

Note: Chapters 9, 11, 12 and 15 have been omitted because they are inapplicable to cases under Chapters 7 and 13.

Chapter 1 - General Provisions

Sec.
101. Definitions
102. Rules of construction
103. Applicability of chapters
104. Adjustment of dollar amounts
105. Power of court
106. Waiver of sovereign immunity
107. Public access to papers
108. Extension of time
109. Who may be a debtor
110. Penalty for persons who negligently or fraudulently prepare bankruptcy petitions.
111. Nonprofit budget and credit counseling agencies; financial management instructional courses.
112. Prohibition on disclosure of name of minor children.

101. Definitions

In this title the following definitions shall apply:

(1) The term "accountant" means accountant authorized under applicable law to practice public accounting, and includes professional accounting association, corporation, or partnership, if so authorized.

(2) The term "affiliate" means -

(A) entity that directly or indirectly owns, controls, or holds with power to vote, 20 percent or more of the outstanding voting securities of the debtor, other than an entity that holds such securities -

(i) in a fiduciary or agency capacity without sole discretionary power to vote such securities; or

(ii) solely to secure a debt, if such entity has not in fact exercised such power to vote;

(B) corporation 20 percent or more of whose outstanding voting securities are directly or indirectly owned, controlled, or held with power to vote, by the debtor, or by an entity that directly or indirectly owns, controls, or holds with power to vote, 20 percent or more of the outstanding voting securities of the debtor, other than an entity that holds such securities -

(i) in a fiduciary or agency capacity without sole discretionary power to vote such securities; or

(ii) solely to secure a debt, if such entity has not in fact exercised such power to vote;

(C) person whose business is operated under a lease or operating agreement by a debtor, or person substantially all of whose property is operated under an operating agreement with the debtor; or

(D) entity that operates the business or substantially all of the property of the debtor under a lease or operating agreement.

(3) The term "assisted person" means any person whose debts consist primarily of consumer debts and the value of whose nonexempt property is less than $226,850.

(4) The term "attorney" means attorney, professional law association, corporation, or partnership, authorized under applicable law to practice law.

(4A) The term "bankruptcy assistance" means any goods or services sold or otherwise provided to an assisted person with the express or implied purpose of providing information, advice, counsel, document preparation, or filing, or attendance at a creditors' meeting or appearing in a case or proceeding on behalf of another or providing legal representation with respect to a case or proceeding under this title.

(5) The term "claim" means -

(A) right to payment, whether or not such right is reduced to judgment, liquidated, unliquidated, fixed, contingent, matured, unmatured, disputed, undisputed, legal, equitable, secured, or unsecured; or

(B) right to an equitable remedy for breach of performance if such breach gives rise to a right to payment, whether or not such right to an equitable remedy is reduced to judgment, fixed, contingent, matured, unmatured, disputed, undisputed, secured, or unsecured.

(6) The term "commodity broker" means futures commission merchant, foreign futures commission merchant, clearing organization, leverage transaction merchant, or commodity options dealer, as defined in section 761 of this title, with respect to which there is a customer, as defined in section 761 of this title.

(7) The term "community claim" means claim that arose before the commencement of the case concerning the debtor for which property of the kind specified in section 541(a)(2) of this title is liable, whether or not there is any such property at the time of the commencement of the case.

(7A) The term "commercial fishing operation" means -

(A) the catching or harvesting of fish, shrimp, lobsters, urchins, seaweed, shellfish, or other aquatic species or products of such species; or

(B) for purposes of section 109 and chapter 12, aquaculture activities consisting of raising for market any species or product described in subparagraph (A).

(7B) The term "commercial fishing vessel" means a vessel used by a family fisherman to carry out a commercial fishing operation.

(8) The term "consumer debt" means debt incurred by an individual primarily for a personal, family, or household purpose.

(9) The term "corporation" -

(A) includes -

(i) association having a power or privilege that a private corporation, but not an individual or a partnership, possesses;

(ii) partnership association organized under a law that makes only the capital subscribed responsible for the debts of such association;

(iii) joint-stock company;

(iv) unincorporated company or association; or

(v) business trust; but

(B) does not include limited partnership.

(10) The term "creditor" means -

(A) entity that has a claim against the debtor that arose at the time of or before the order for relief concerning the debtor;

(B) entity that has a claim against the estate of a kind specified in section 348(d), 502(f), 502(g), 502(h), or 502(i) of this title; or

(C) entity that has a community claim.

(10A) The term "current monthly income" -

(A) means the average monthly income from all sources that the debtor receives (or in a joint case the debtor and the debtor's spouse receive) without regard to whether such income is taxable income, derived during the 6-month period ending on –

(i) the last day of the calendar month immediately preceding the date of the commencement of the case if the debtor files the schedule of current income required by section 521(a)(1)(B)(ii); or

(ii) the date on which current income is determined by the court for purposes of this title if the debtor does not file the schedule of current income required by section 521(a)(1)(B)(ii); and

(B)(i) includes any amount paid by any entity other than the debtor (or in a joint case the debtor and the debtor's spouse), on a regular basis for the household expenses of the debtor or the debtor's dependents (and in a joint case the debtor's spouse if not otherwise a dependent); and

(ii) excludes--

(I) benefits received under the Social Security Act (42 U.S.C. 301 et seq.);

(II) payments to victims of war crimes or crimes against humanity on account of their status as victims of such crimes;

(III) payments to victims of international terrorism or domestic terrorism, as those terms are defined in section 2331 of title 18, on account of their status as victims of such terrorism; and

(IV) any monthly compensation, pension, pay, annuity, or allowance paid under title 10, 37, or 38 in connection with a disability, combat-related injury or disability, or death of a member of the uniformed services, except that any retired pay excluded under this subclause shall include retired pay paid under chapter 61 of title 10 only to the extent that such retired pay exceeds the amount of retired pay to which the debtor would otherwise be entitled if retired under any provision of title 10 other than chapter 61 of that title.

(V) [Repealed].

(11) The term "custodian" means -

(A) receiver or trustee of any of the property of the debtor, appointed in a case or proceeding not under this title;

(B) assignee under a general assignment for the benefit of the debtor's creditors; or

(C) trustee, receiver, or agent under applicable law, or under a contract, that is appointed or authorized to take charge of property of the debtor for the purpose of enforcing a lien against such property, or for the purpose of general administration of such property for the benefit of the debtor's creditors.

(12) The term "debt" means liability on a claim.

(12A) The term "debt relief agency" means any person who provides any bankruptcy assistance to an assisted person in return for the payment of money or other valuable consideration, or who is a bankruptcy petition preparer under section 110, but does not include –

(A) any person who is an officer, director, employee, or agent of a person who provides such assistance or of the bankruptcy petition preparer;

(B) a nonprofit organization that is exempt from taxation under section 501(c)(3) of the Internal Revenue Code of 1986;

(C) a creditor of such assisted person, to the extent that the creditor is assisting such assisted person to restructure any debt owed by such assisted person to the creditor;

(D) a depository institution (as defined in section 3 of the Federal Deposit Insurance Act) or any Federal credit union or State credit union (as those terms are defined in section 101 of the Federal Credit Union Act), or any affiliate or subsidiary of such depository institution or credit union; or

(E) an author, publisher, distributor, or seller of works subject to copyright protection under title 17, when acting in such capacity.

(13) The term "debtor" means person or municipality concerning which a case under this title has been commenced.

(13A) The term "debtor's principal residence" –

(A) means a residential structure if used as the principal residence by the debtor, including incidental property, without regard to whether that structure is attached to real property; and

(B) includes an individual condominium or cooperative unit, a mobile or manufactured home, or trailer if used as the principal residence by the debtor.

(14) The term "disinterested person" means a person that –

(A) is not a creditor, an equity security holder, or an insider;

(B) is not and was not, within 2 years before the date of the filing of the petition, a director, officer, or employee of the debtor; and

(C) does not have an interest materially adverse to the interest of the estate or of any class of creditors or equity security holders, by reason of any direct or indirect relationship to, connection with, or interest in, the debtor, or for any other reason.

(14A) The term "domestic support obligation" means a debt that accrues before, on, or after the date of the order for relief in a case under this title, including interest that accrues on that debt as provided under applicable nonbankruptcy law notwithstanding any other provision of this title, that is –

(A) owed to or recoverable by –

(i) a spouse, former spouse, or child of the debtor or such child's parent, legal guardian, or responsible relative; or

(ii) a governmental unit;

(B) in the nature of alimony, maintenance, or support (including assistance provided by a governmental unit) of such spouse, former spouse, or child of the debtor or such child's parent, without regard to whether such debt is expressly so designated;

(C) established or subject to establishment before, on, or after the date of the order for relief in a case under this title, by reason of applicable provisions of –

(i) a separation agreement, divorce decree, or property settlement agreement;

(ii) an order of a court of record; or

(iii) a determination made in accordance with applicable nonbankruptcy law by a governmental unit; and

(D) not assigned to a nongovernmental entity, unless that obligation is assigned voluntarily by the spouse, former spouse, child of the debtor, or such child's parent, legal guardian, or responsible relative for the purpose of collecting the debt.

(15) The term "entity" includes person, estate, trust, governmental unit, and United States trustee.

(16) The term "equity security" means -

(A) share in a corporation, whether or not transferable or denominated "stock", or similar security;

(B) interest of a limited partner in a limited partnership; or

(C) warrant or right, other than a right to convert, to purchase, sell, or subscribe to a share, security, or interest of a kind specified in subparagraph (A) or (B) of this paragraph.

(17) The term "equity security holder" means holder of an equity security of the debtor.

(18) The term "family farmer" means -

(A) individual or individual and spouse engaged in a farming operation whose aggregate debts do not exceed $11,097,350 and not less than 50 percent of whose aggregate noncontingent, liquidated debts (excluding a debt for the principal residence of such individual or such individual and spouse unless such debt arises out of a farming operation), on the date the case is filed, arise out of a farming operation owned or operated by such individual or such individual and spouse, and such individual or such individual and spouse receive from such farming operation more than 50 percent of such individual's or such individual and spouse's gross income for –

(i) the taxable year preceding; or

(ii) each of the 2d and 3d taxable years preceding;

the taxable year in which the case concerning such individual or such individual and spouse was filed; or

(B) corporation or partnership in which more than 50 percent of the outstanding stock or equity is held by one family, or by one family and the relatives of the members of such family, and such family or such relatives conduct the farming operation, and

(i) more than 80 percent of the value of its assets consists of assets related to the farming operation;

(ii) its aggregate debts do not exceed $11,097,350 and not less than 50 percent of its aggregate noncontingent, liquidated debts (excluding a debt for one dwelling which is owned by such corporation or partnership and which a shareholder or partner maintains as a principal residence, unless such debt arises out of a farming operation), on the date the case is filed, arise out of the farming operation owned or operated by such corporation or such partnership; and

(iii) if such corporation issues stock, such stock is not publicly traded.

(19) The term "family farmer with regular annual income" means family farmer whose annual income is sufficiently stable and regular to enable such family farmer to make payments under a plan under chapter 12 of this title.

(19A) The term "family fisherman" means –

(A) an individual or individual and spouse engaged in a commercial fishing operation –

(i) whose aggregate debts do not exceed $2,268,550 and not less than 80 percent of whose aggregate noncontingent, liquidated debts (excluding a debt for the principal residence of such individual or such individual and spouse, unless such debt arises out of a commercial fishing operation), on the date the case is filed, arise out of a commercial fishing operation owned or operated by such individual or such individual and spouse; and

(ii) who receive from such commercial fishing operation more than 50 percent of such individual's or such individual's and spouse's gross income for the taxable year preceding the taxable year in which the case concerning such individual or such individual and spouse was filed; or

(B) a corporation or partnership –

(i) in which more than 50 percent of the outstanding stock or equity is held by –

(I) 1 family that conducts the commercial fishing operation; or

(II) 1 family and the relatives of the members of such family, and such family or such relatives conduct the commercial fishing operation; and

(ii)(I) more than 80 percent of the value of its assets consists of assets related to the commercial fishing operation;

(II) its aggregate debts do not exceed $1,924,550 and not less than 80 percent of its aggregate noncontingent, liquidated debts (excluding a debt for 1 dwelling which is owned by such corporation or partnership and which a shareholder or partner maintains as a principal residence, unless such debt arises out of a commercial fishing operation), on the date the case is filed, arise out of a commercial fishing operation owned or operated by such corporation or such partnership; and

(III) if such corporation issues stock, such stock is not publicly traded.

(19B) The term "family fisherman with regular annual income" means a family fisherman whose annual income is sufficiently stable and regular to enable such family fisherman to make payments under a plan under chapter 12 of this title.

(20) The term "farmer" means (except when such term appears in the term "family farmer") person that received more than 80 percent of such person's gross income during the taxable year of such person immediately preceding the taxable year of such person during which the case under this title concerning such person was commenced from a farming operation owned or operated by such person.

(21) The term "farming operation" includes farming, tillage of the soil, dairy farming, ranching, production or raising of crops, poultry, or livestock, and production of poultry or livestock products in an unmanufactured state.

(21A) The term "farmout agreement" means a written agreement in which-

(A) the owner of a right to drill, produce, or operate liquid or gaseous hydrocarbons on property agrees or has agreed to transfer or assign all or a part of such right to another entity; and

(B) such other entity (either directly or through its agents or its assigns), as consideration, agrees to perform drilling, reworking, recompleting, testing, or similar or related operations, to develop or produce liquid or gaseous hydrocarbons on the property.

(21B) The term "Federal depository institutions regulatory agency" means-

(A) with respect to an insured depository institution (as defined in section 3(c)(2) of the Federal Deposit Insurance Act) for which no conservator or receiver has been appointed, the appropriate Federal banking agency (as defined in section 3(q) of such Act);

(B) with respect to an insured credit union (including an insured credit union for which the National Credit Union Administration has been appointed conservator or liquidating agent), the National Credit Union Administration;

(C) with respect to any insured depository institution for which the Resolution Trust Corporation has been appointed conservator or receiver, the Resolution Trust Corporation; and

(D) with respect to any insured depository institution for which the Federal Deposit Insurance Corporation has been appointed conservator or receiver, the Federal Deposit Insurance Corporation.

(22) The term "financial institution" means –

(A) a Federal reserve bank, or an entity that is a commercial or savings bank, industrial savings bank, savings and loan association, trust company, federally-insured credit union, or receiver, liquidating agent, or conservator for such entity and, when any such Federal reserve bank, receiver, liquidating agent, conservator or entity is acting as agent or custodian for a customer (whether or not a 'customer', as defined in section 741) in connection with a securities contract (as defined in section 741) such customer; or

(B) in connection with a securities contract (as defined in section 741) an investment company registered under the Investment Company Act of 1940.

(22A) The term "financial participant" means –

(A) an entity that, at the time it enters into a securities contract, commodity contract, swap agreement, repurchase agreement, or forward contract, or at the time of the date of the filing of the petition, has one or more agreements or transactions described in paragraph (1), (2), (3), (4), (5), or (6) of section 561(a) with the debtor or any other entity (other than an affiliate) of a total gross dollar value of not less than $1,100,000,000 in notional or actual principal amount outstanding (aggregated across counterparties) at such time or on any day during the 15-month period preceding the date of the filing of the petition, or has gross mark-to-market positions of not less than $100,000,000 (aggregated across counterparties) in one or more such agreements or transactions with the debtor or any other entity (other than an affiliate) at such time or on any day during the 15-month period preceding the date of the filing of the petition; or

(B) a clearing organization (as defined in section 402 of the Federal Deposit Insurance Corporation Improvement Act of 1991).

(23) The term "foreign proceeding" means a collective judicial or administrative proceeding in a foreign country, including an interim proceeding, under a law relating to insolvency or adjustment of debt in which proceeding the assets and affairs of the debtor are subject to control or supervision by a foreign court, for the purpose of reorganization or liquidation.

(24) The term "foreign representative" means a person or body, including a person or body appointed on an interim basis, authorized in a foreign proceeding to administer the reorganization or the liquidation of the debtor's assets or affairs or to act as a representative of such foreign proceeding.

(25) The term "forward contract" means –

(A) a contract (other than a commodity contract, as defined in section 761) for the purchase, sale, or transfer of a commodity, as defined in section 761(8) of this title, or any similar good, article, service, right, or interest which is presently or in the future becomes the subject of dealing in the forward contract trade, or product or byproduct thereof, with a maturity date more than two days after the date the contract is entered into, including, but not limited to, a repurchase or reverse repurchase transaction (whether or not such repurchase or reverse repurchase transaction is a 'repurchase agreement', as defined in this section), consignment, lease, swap, hedge transaction, deposit, loan, option, allocated transaction, unallocated transaction, or any other similar agreement;

(B) any combination of agreements or transactions referred to in subparagraphs (A) and (C);

(C) any option to enter into an agreement or transaction referred to in subparagraph (A) or (B);

(D) a master agreement that provides for an agreement or transaction referred to in subparagraph (A), (B), or (C), together with all supplements to any such master agreement, without regard to whether such master agreement provides for an agreement or transaction that is not a forward contract under this paragraph, except that such master agreement shall be considered to be a forward contract under this paragraph only with respect to each agreement or transaction under such master agreement that is referred to in subparagraph (A), (B), or (C); or

(E) any security agreement or arrangement, or other credit enhancement related to any agreement or transaction referred to in subparagraph (A), (B), (C), or (D), including any guarantee or reimbursement obligation by or to a forward contract merchant or financial participant in connection with any agreement or transaction referred to in any such subparagraph, but not to exceed the damages in connection with any such agreement or transaction, measured in accordance with section 562.

(26) The term "forward contract merchant" means a Federal reserve bank, or an entity the business of which consists in whole or in part of entering into forward contracts as or with merchants in a commodity (as defined in section 761) or any similar good, article, service, right, or interest which is presently or in the future becomes the subject of dealing in the forward contract trade.

(27) The term "governmental unit" means United States; State; Commonwealth; District; Territory; municipality; foreign state; department, agency, or instrumentality of the United States (but not a United States trustee while serving as a trustee in a case under this title), a State, a Commonwealth, a District, a Territory, a municipality, or a foreign state; or other foreign or domestic government.

(27A) The term "health care business" –

(A) means any public or private entity (without regard to whether that entity is organized for profit or not for profit) that is primarily engaged in

offering to the general public facilities and services for –
(i) the diagnosis or treatment of injury, deformity, or disease; and
(ii) surgical, drug treatment, psychiatric, or obstetric care; and
(B) includes –
(i) any –
(I) general or specialized hospital; (II) ancillary ambulatory, emergency, or surgical treatment facility;
(III) hospice;
(IV) home health agency; and
(V) other health care institution that is similar to an entity referred to in subclause (I), (II), (III), or (IV); and
(ii) any long-term care facility, including any –
(I) skilled nursing facility;
(II) intermediate care facility;
(III) assisted living facility;
(IV) home for the aged;
(V) domiciliary care facility; and
(VI) health care institution that is related to a facility referred to in subclause (I), (II), (III), (IV), or (V), if that institution is primarily engaged in offering room, board, laundry, or personal assistance with activities of daily living and incidentals to activities of daily living.

(27B) The term "incidental property" means, with respect to a debtor's principal residence –
(A) property commonly conveyed with a principal residence in the area where the real property is located;
(B) all easements, rights, appurtenances, fixtures, rents, royalties, mineral rights, oil or gas rights or profits, water rights, escrow funds, or insurance proceeds; and
(C) all replacements or additions.

(28) The term "indenture" means mortgage, deed of trust, or indenture, under which there is outstanding a security, other than a voting-trust certificate, constituting a claim against the debtor, a claim secured by a lien on any of the debtor's property, or an equity security of the debtor.

(29) The term "indenture trustee" means trustee under an indenture.

(30) The term "individual with regular income" means individual whose income is sufficiently stable and regular to enable such individual to make payments under a plan under chapter 13 of this title, other than a stockbroker or a commodity broker.

(31) The term "insider" includes -
(A) if the debtor is an individual -
(i) relative of the debtor or of a general partner of the debtor ;
(ii) partnership in which the debtor is a general partner;
(iii) general partner of the debtor; or
(iv) corporation of which the debtor is a director, officer, or person in control;
(B) if the debtor is a corporation -
(i) director of the debtor;
(ii) officer of the debtor;
(iii) person in control of the debtor;
(iv) partnership in which the debtor is a general partner;
(v) general partner of the debtor; or
(vi) relative of a general partner, director, officer, or person in control of the debtor;
(C) if the debtor is a partnership -
(i) general partner in the debtor;
(ii) relative of a general partner in, general partner of, or person in control of the debtor;
(iii) partnership in which the debtor is a general partner;
(iv) general partner of the debtor; or
(v) person in control of the debtor;
(D) if the debtor is a municipality, elected official of the debtor or relative of an elected official of the debtor;
(E) affiliate, or insider of an affiliate as if such affiliate were the debtor; and
(F) managing agent of the debtor.

(32) The term "insolvent" means -
(A) with reference to an entity other than a partnership and a municipality, financial condition such that the sum of such entity's debts is greater than all of such entity's property, at a fair valuation, exclusive of -
(i) property transferred, concealed, or removed with intent to hinder, delay, or defraud such entity's creditors; and
(ii) property that may be exempted from property of the estate under section 522 of this title;
(B) with reference to a partnership, financial condition such that the sum of such partnership's debts is greater than the aggregate of, at fair valuation -
(i) all of such partnership's property, exclusive of property of the kind specified in subparagraph (A)(i) of this paragraph; and
(ii) the sum of the excess of the value of each general partner's nonpartnership property, exclusive of property of the kind specified in subparagraph (A) of this paragraph, over such partner's nonpartnership debts; and
(C) with reference to a municipality, financial condition such that the municipality is -
(i) generally not paying its debts as they become due unless such debts are the subject of a bona fide dispute; or
(ii) unable to pay its debts as they become due.

(33) The term "institution-affiliated party"-
(A) with respect to an insured depository institution (as defined in section 3(c)(2) of the Federal Deposit Insurance Act), has the meaning given it in section 3(u) of the Federal Deposit Insurance Act; and
(B) with respect to an insured credit union, has the meaning given it in section 206(r) of the Federal Credit Union Act.

(34) The term "insured credit union" has the meaning given it in section 101(7) of the Federal Credit Union Act.

(35) The term "insured depository institution"-
(A) has the meaning given it in section 3(c)(2) of the Federal Deposit Insurance Act; and
(B) includes an insured credit union (except in the case of paragraphs (21B) and (33)(A) of this subsection).

(35A) The term "intellectual property" means -
(A) trade secret;
(B) invention, process, design, or plant protected under title 35;
(C) patent application;
(D) plant variety;
(E) work of authorship protected under title 17; or
(F) mask work protected under chapter 9 of title 17; to the extent protected by applicable nonbankruptcy law.

(36) The term "judicial lien" means lien obtained by judgment, levy, sequestration, or other legal or equitable process or proceeding.

(37) The term "lien" means charge against or interest in property to secure payment of a debt or performance of an obligation.

(38) The term "margin payment" means, for purposes of the forward contract provisions of this title, payment or deposit of cash, a security or other property, that is commonly known in the forward contract trade as original margin, initial margin, maintenance margin, or variation margin, including mark-to-market payments, or variation payments.

(38A) The term "master netting agreement" –
(A) means an agreement providing for the exercise of rights, including rights of netting, setoff, liquidation, termination, acceleration, or close out, under or in connection with one or more contracts that are described in any one or more of paragraphs (1) through (5) of section 561(a), or any security agreement or arrangement or other credit enhancement related to one or more of the foregoing, including any guarantee or reimbursement obligation related to 1 or more of the foregoing; and
(B) if the agreement contains provisions relating to agreements or transactions that are not contracts described in paragraphs (1) through (5) of section 561(a), shall be deemed to be a master netting agreement only with respect to those agreements or transactions that are described in any one or more of paragraphs (1) through (5) of section 561(a).

(38B) The term "master netting agreement participant" means an entity that, at any time before the date of the filing of the petition, is a party to an outstanding master netting agreement with the debtor.

(39) The term "mask work" has the meaning given it in section 901(a)(2) of title 17;

(39A) The term "median family income" means for any year –
(A) the median family income both calculated and reported by the Bureau of the Census in the then most recent year; and
(B) if not so calculated and reported in the then current year, adjusted annually after such most recent year until the next year in which median family income is both calculated and reported by the Bureau of the Census, to reflect the percentage change in the Consumer Price Index for All Urban Consumers during the period of years occurring after such most recent year and before such current year.

(40) The term "municipality" means political subdivision or public

agency or instrumentality of a State.

(40A) The term "patient" means any individual who obtains or receives services from a health care business.

(40B) The term "patient records" means any record relating to a patient, including a written document or a record recorded in a magnetic, optical, or other form of electronic medium.

(41) The term"person" includes individual, partnership, and corporation, but does not include governmental unit, except that a governmental unit that -

(A) acquires an asset from a person -

(i) as a result of the operation of a loan guarantee agreement; or

(ii) as receiver or liquidating agent of a person;

(B) is a guarantor of a pension benefit payable by or on behalf of the debtor or an affiliate of the debtor; or

(C) is the legal or beneficial owner of an asset of -

(i) an employee pension benefit plan that is a governmental plan, as defined in section 414(d) of the Internal Revenue Code of 1986; or

(ii) an eligible deferred compensation plan, as defined in section 457(b) of the Internal Revenue Code of 1986;

shall be considered, for purposes of section 1102 of this title, to be a person with respect to such asset or such benefit.

(41A) The term "personally identifiable information" means –

(A) if provided by an individual to the debtor in connection with obtaining a product or a service from the debtor primarily for personal, family, or household purposes –

(i) the first name (or initial) and last name of such individual, whether given at birth or time of adoption, or resulting from a lawful change of name;

(ii) the geographical address of a physical place of residence of such individual;

(iii) an electronic address (including an e-mail address) of such individual;

(iv) a telephone number dedicated to contacting such individual at such physical place of residence;

(v) a social security account number issued to such individual; or

(vi) the account number of a credit card issued to such individual; or

(B) if identified in connection with 1 or more of the items of information specified in subparagraph (A) –

(i) a birth date, the number of a certificate of birth or adoption, or a place of birth; or

(ii) any other information concerning an identified individual that, if disclosed, will result in contacting or identifying such individual physically or electronically.

(42) The term "petition" means petition filed under section 301, 302, 303 and 1504 of this title, as the case may be, commencing a case under this title.

(42A) The term "production payment" means a term overriding royalty satisfiable in cash or in kind -

(A) contingent on the production of a liquid or gaseous hydrocarbon from particular real property; and

(B) from a specified volume, or a specified value, from the liquid or gaseous hydrocarbon produced from such property, and determined without regard to production costs.

(43) The term "purchaser" means transferee of a voluntary transfer, and includes immediate or mediate transferee of such a transferee.

(44) The term "railroad" means common carrier by railroad engaged in the transportation of individuals or property or owner of trackage facilities leased by such a common carrier.

(45) The term "relative" means individual related by affinity or consanguinity within the third degree as determined by the common law, or individual in a step or adoptive relationship within such third degree.

(46) The term "repo participant" means an entity that, at any time before the filing of the petition, has an outstanding repurchase agreement with the debtor.

(47) The term "repurchase agreement" (which definition also applies to a reverse repurchase agreement) –

(A) means –

(i) an agreement, including related terms, which provides for the transfer of one or more certificates of deposit, mortgage related securities (as defined in section 3 of the Securities Exchange Act of 1934), mortgage loans, interests in mortgage related securities or mortgage loans, eligible bankers' acceptances, qualified foreign government securities (defined as a security that is a direct obligation of, or that is fully guaranteed by, the central government of a member of the Organization for Economic Cooperation and Development), or securities that are direct obligations of, or that are fully guaranteed by, the United States or any agency of the United States against the transfer of funds by the transferee of such certificates of deposit, eligible bankers' acceptances, securities, mortgage loans, or interests, with a simultaneous agreement by such transferee to transfer to the transferor thereof certificates of deposit, eligible bankers' acceptance, securities, mortgage loans, or interests of the kind described in this clause, at a date certain not later than 1 year after such transfer or on demand, against the transfer of funds;

(ii) any combination of agreements or transactions referred to in clauses (i) and (iii);

(iii) an option to enter into an agreement or transaction referred to in clause (i) or (ii);

(iv) a master agreement that provides for an agreement or transaction referred to in clause (i), (ii), or (iii), together with all supplements to any such master agreement, without regard to whether such master agreement provides for an agreement or transaction that is not a repurchase agreement under this paragraph, except that such master agreement shall be considered to be a repurchase agreement under this paragraph only with respect to each agreement or transaction under the master agreement that is referred to in clause (i), (ii), or (iii); or

(v) any security agreement or arrangement or other credit enhancement related to any agreement or transaction referred to in clause (i), (ii), (iii), or (iv), including any guarantee or reimbursement obligation by or to a repo participant or financial participant in connection with any agreement or transaction referred to in any such clause, but not to exceed the damages in connection with any such agreement or transaction, measured in accordance with section 562 of this title; and

(B) does not include a repurchase obligation under a participation in a commercial mortgage loan.

(48) The term "securities clearing agency" means person that is registered as a clearing agency under section 17A of the Securities Exchange Act of 1934, or exempt from such registration under such section pursuant to an order of the Securities and Exchange Commission, or whose business is confined to the performance of functions of a clearing agency with respect to exempted securities, as defined in section 3 (a)(12) of such Act for the purposes of such section 17A.

(48A) The term "securities self regulatory organization" means either a securities association registered with the Securities and Exchange Commission under section 15A of the Securities Exchange Act of 1934 or a national securities exchange registered with the Securities and Exchange Commission under section 6 of the Securities Exchange Act of 1934.

(49) The term "security" -

(A) includes -

(i) note;

(ii) stock;

(iii) treasury stock;

(iv) bond;

(v) debenture;

(vi) collateral trust certificate;

(vii) pre-organization certificate or subscription;

(viii) transferable share;

(ix) voting-trust certificate;

(x) certificate of deposit;

(xi) certificate of deposit for security;

(xii) investment contract or certificate of interest or participation in a profit-sharing agreement or in an oil, gas, or mineral royalty or lease, if such contract or interest is required to be the subject of a registration statement filed with the Securities and Exchange Commission under the provisions of the Securities Act of 1933, or is exempt under section 3(b) of such Act from the requirement to file such a statement;

(xiii) interest of a limited partner in a limited partnership;

(xiv) other claim or interest commonly known as "security"; and

(xv) certificate of interest or participation in, temporary or interim certificate for, receipt for, or warrant or right to subscribe to or purchase or sell, a security; but

(B) does not include -

(i) currency, check, draft, bill of exchange, or bank letter of credit;

(ii) leverage transaction, as defined in section 761 of this title;

(iii) commodity futures contract or forward contract;

(iv) option, warrant, or right to subscribe to or purchase or sell a commodity futures contract;

(v) option to purchase or sell a commodity;

(vi) contract or certificate of a kind specified in subparagraph (A)

(xii) of this paragraph that is not required to be the subject of a registration statement filed with the Securities and Exchange Commission and is not exempt under section 3(b) of the Securities Act of 1933 from the requirement to file such a statement; or

(vii) debt or evidence of indebtedness for goods sold and delivered or services rendered.

(50) The term "security agreement" means agreement that creates or provides for a security interest.

(51) The term "security interest" means lien created by an agreement.

(51A) The term "settlement payment" means, for purposes of the forward contract provisions of this title, a preliminary settlement payment, a partial settlement payment, an interim settlement payment, a settlement payment on account, a final settlement payment, a net settlement payment, or any other similar payment commonly used in the forward contract trade.

(51B) The term "single asset real estate" means real property constituting a single property or project, other than residential real property with fewer than 4 residential units, which generates substantially all of the gross income of a debtor who is not a family farmer and on which no substantial business is being conducted by a debtor other than the business of operating the real property and activities incidental thereto.

(51C) The term "small business case" means a case filed under chapter 11 of this title in which the debtor is a small business debtor and has not elected that subchpater V of chapter 11 of this title shall apply.

(51D) The term "small business debtor" –

(A) subject to subparagraph (B), means a person engaged in commercial or business activities (including any affiliate of such person that is also a debtor under this title and excluding a person whose primary activity is the business of owning single asset real estate) that has aggregate noncontingent liquidated secured and unsecured debts as of the date of the filing of the petition or the date of the order for relief in an amount not more than $3,024,800 (excluding debts owed to 1 or more affiliates or insiders) not less than 50 percent of which arose from the commercial or business activities of the debtor; and

(B) does not include---(i) any member of a group of affiliated debtors that has aggregate noncontingent liquidated secured and unsecured debts in an amount greater than $3,024,800 (excluding debt owed to 1 or more affiliates or insiders); (ii) any debtor that is a corporation subject to the reporting requirements under Section 13 or 15(d) of the Securities Exchange Act of 1934 (15 U.S.C. 78m, 78o(d)); or (iii) any debtor that is an affiliate of a corporation described in clause (ii).

(52) The term "State" includes the District of Columbia and Puerto Rico, except for the purpose of defining who may be a debtor under chapter 9 of this title.

(53) The term "statutory lien" means lien arising solely by force of a statute on specified circumstances or conditions, or lien of distress for rent, whether or not statutory, but does not include security interest or judicial lien, whether or not such interest or lien is provided by or is dependent on a statute and whether or not such interest or lien is made fully effective by statute.

(53A) The term "stockbroker" means person -

(A) with respect to which there is a customer, as defined in section 741 of this title; and

(B) that is engaged in the business of effecting transactions in securities-

(i) for the account of others; or

(ii) with members of the general public, from or for such person's own account.

(53B) The term "swap agreement" –

(A) means –

(i) any agreement, including the terms and conditions incorporated by reference in such agreement, which is –

(I) an interest rate swap, option, future, or forward agreement, including a rate floor, rate cap, rate collar, cross-currency rate swap, and basis swap;

(II) a spot, same day-tomorrow, tomorrow-next, forward, or other foreign exchange, precious metals, or other commodity agreement;

(III) a currency swap, option, future, or forward agreement;

(IV) an equity index or equity swap, option, future, or forward agreement;

(V) a debt index or debt swap, option, future, or forward agreement;

(VI) a total return, credit spread or credit swap, option, future, or forward agreement;

(VII) a commodity index or a commodity swap, option, future, or forward agreement;

(VIII) a weather swap, option, future, or forward agreement;

(IX) an emissions swap, option, future, or forward agreement; or

(X) an inflation swap, option, future, or forward agreement;

(ii) any agreement or transaction that is similar to any other agreement or transaction referred to in this paragraph and that –

(I) is of a type that has been, is presently, or in the future becomes, the subject of recurrent dealings in the swap or other derivatives markets (including terms and conditions incorporated by reference therein); and

(II) is a forward, swap, future, option, or spot transaction on one or more rates, currencies, commodities, equity securities, or other equity instruments, debt securities or other debt instruments, quantitative measures associated with an occurrence, extent of an occurrence, or contingency associated with a financial, commercial, or economic consequence, or economic or financial indices or measures of economic or financial risk or value;

(iii) any combination of agreements or transactions referred to in this subparagraph;

(iv) any option to enter into an agreement or transaction referred to in this subparagraph;

(v) a master agreement that provides for an agreement or transaction referred to in clause (i), (ii), (iii), or (iv), together with all supplements to any such master agreement, and without regard to whether the master agreement contains an agreement or transaction that is not a swap agreement under this paragraph, except that the master agreement shall be considered to be a swap agreement under this paragraph only with respect to each agreement or transaction under the master agreement that is referred to in clause (i), (ii), (iii), or (iv); or

(vi) any security agreement or arrangement or other credit enhancement related to any agreements or transactions referred to in clause (i) through (v), including any guarantee or reimbursement obligation by or to a swap participant or financial participant in connection with any agreement or transaction referred to in any such clause, but not to exceed the damages in connection with any such agreement or transaction, measured in accordance with section 562; and

(B) is applicable for purposes of this title only, and shall not be construed or applied so as to challenge or affect the characterization, definition, or treatment of any swap agreement under any other statute, regulation, or rule, including the Gramm-Leach-Bliley Act, the Legal Certainty for Bank Products Act of 2000, the securities laws (as such term is defined in section 3(a)(47) of the Securities Exchange Act of 1934) and the Commodity Exchange Act.

(53C) The term "swap participant" means an entity that, at any time before the filing of the petition, has an outstanding swap agreement with the debtor.

(53D) The term "timeshare plan" means and shall include that interest purchased in any arrangement, plan, scheme, or similar device, but not including exchange programs, whether by membership, agreement, tenancy in common, sale, lease, deed, rental agreement, license, right to use agreement, or by any other means, whereby a purchaser, in exchange for consideration, receives a right to use accommodations, facilities, or recreational sites, whether improved or unimproved, for a specific period of time less than a full year during any given year, but not necessarily for consecutive years, and which extends for a period of more than three years. A "timeshare interest" is that interest purchased in a timeshare plan which grants the purchaser the right to use and occupy accommodations, facilities, or recreational sites, whether improved or unimproved, pursuant to a timeshare plan.

(54) The term "transfer" means –

(A) the creation of a lien;

(B) the retention of title as a security interest;

(C) the foreclosure of a debtor's equity of redemption; or

(D) each mode, direct or indirect, absolute or conditional, voluntary or involuntary, of disposing of or parting with –

(i) property; or

(ii) an interest in property.

(54A) The term "uninsured State member bank" means a State member bank (as defined in section 3 of the Federal Deposit Insurance Act) the deposits of which are not insured by the Federal Deposit Insurance Corporation.

(55) The term "United States", when used in a geographical sense, includes all locations where the judicial jurisdiction of the United States extends, including territories and possessions of the United States.

(56A) The term "term overriding royalty" means an interest in liquid or gaseous hydrocarbons in place or to be produced from particular real property that entitles the owner thereof to a share of production, or the value thereof, for a term limited by time, quantity, or value realized.

102. Rules of construction

In this title -

(1) "after notice and a hearing", or a similar phrase -

(A) means after such notice as is appropriate in the particular circumstances, and such opportunity for a hearing as is appropriate in the particular circumstances; but

(B) authorizes an act without an actual hearing if such notice is given properly and if -

(i) such a hearing is not requested timely by a party in interest; or

(ii) there is insufficient time for a hearing to be commenced before such act must be done, and the court authorizes such act;

(2) "claim against the debtor" includes claim against property of the debtor;

(3) "includes" and "including" are not limiting;

(4) "may not" is prohibitive, and not permissive;

(5) "or" is not exclusive;

(6) "order for relief" means entry of an order for relief;

(7) the singular includes the plural;

(8) a definition, contained in a section of this title that refers to another section of this title, does not, for the purpose of such reference, affect the meaning of a term used in such other section; and

(9) "United States trustee" includes a designee of the United States trustee.

103. Applicability of chapters

(a) Except as provided in section 1161 of this title, chapters 1, 3, and 5 of this title apply in a case under chapter 7, 11, 12, or 13 of this title, and this chapter, sections 307, 362(o), 555 through 557, and 559 through 562 apply in a case under chapter 15.

(b) Subchapters I and II of chapter 7 of this title apply only in a case under such chapter.

(c) Subchapter III of chapter 7 of this title applies only in a case under such chapter concerning a stockbroker.

(d) Subchapter IV of chapter 7 of this title applies only in a case under such chapter concerning a commodity broker.

(e) SCOPE OF APPLICATION. – Subchapter V of chapter 7 of this title shall apply only in a case under such chapter concerning the liquidation of an uninsured State member bank, or a corporation organized under section 25A of the Federal Reserve Act, which operates, or operates as, a multilateral clearing organization pursuant to section 409 of the Federal Deposit Insurance Corporation Improvement Act of 1991.

(f) Except as provided in section 901 of this title, only chapters 1 and 9 of this title apply in a case under such chapter 9.

(g) Except as provided in section 901 of this title, subchapters I, II, and III of chapter 11 of this title apply only in a case under such chapter.

(h) Subchapter IV of chapter 11 of this title applies only in a case under such chapter concerning a railroad.

(i) Subchapter V of chapter 11 of this title applies only in a case under chapter 11 in which a debtor (as defined in section 1182) elects that subchapter V of chapter 11 shall apply.

(j) Chapter 13 of this title applies only in a case under such chapter.

(k) Chapter 12 of this title applies only in a case under such chapter.

(l) Chapter 15 applies only in a case under such chapter, except that –

(1) sections 1505, 1513, and 1514 apply in all cases under this title; and

(2) section 1509 applies whether or not a case under this title is pending.

104. Adjustment of dollar amounts

(a) On April 1, 1998, and at each 3-year interval ending on April 1 thereafter, each dollar amount in effect under sections 101(3), 101(18), 101(19A), 101(51D), 109(e), 303(b), 507(a), 522(d), 522(f)(3) and 522(f)(4), 522(n), 522(p), 522(q), 523(a)(2)(C), 541(b), 547(c)(9), 707(b), 1322(d), 1325(b), and 1326(b)(3) of this title and section 1409(b) of title 28 immediately before such April 1 shall be adjusted –

(1) to reflect the change in the Consumer Price Index for All Urban Consumers, published by the Department of Labor, for the most recent 3-year period ending immediately before January 1 preceding such April 1, and

(2) to round to the nearest $25 the dollar amount that represents such change.

(b) Not later than March 1, 1998, and at each 3-year interval ending on March 1 thereafter, the Judicial Conference of the United States shall publish in the Federal Register the dollar amounts that will become effective on such April 1 under sections 101(3), 101(18), 101(19A), 101(51D), 109(e), 303(b), 507(a), 522(d), 522(f)(3) and 522(f)(4), 522(n), 522(p), 522(q), 523(a)(2)(C), 541(b), 547(c)(9), 707(b), 1322(d), 1325(b), and 1326(b)(3) of this title and section 1409(b) of title 28.

(c) Adjustments made in accordance with subsection (a) shall not apply with respect to cases commenced before the date of such adjustments.

105. Power of court

(a) The court may issue any order, process, or judgment that is necessary or appropriate to carry out the provisions of this title. No provision of this title providing for the raising of an issue by a party in interest shall be construed to preclude the court from, sua sponte, taking any action or making any determination necessary or appropriate to enforce or implement court orders or rules, or to prevent an abuse of process.

(b) Notwithstanding subsection (a) of this section, a court may not appoint a receiver in a case under this title.

(c) The ability of any district judge or other officer or employee of a district court to exercise any of the authority or responsibilities conferred upon the court under this title shall be determined by reference to the provisions relating to such judge, officer, or employee set forth in title 28. This subsection shall not be interpreted to exclude bankruptcy judges and other officers or employees appointed pursuant to chapter 6 of title 28 from its operation.

(d) The court, on its own motion or on the request of a party in interest -

(1) shall hold such status conferences as are necessary to further the expeditious and economical resolution of the case; and

(2) unless inconsistent with another provision of this title or with applicable Federal Rules of Bankruptcy Procedure, may issue an order at any such conference prescribing such limitations and conditions as the court deems appropriate to ensure that the case is handled expeditiously and economically, including an order that -

(A) sets the date by which the trustee must assume or reject an executory contract or unexpired lease; or

(B) in a case under chapter 11 of this title -

(i) sets a date by which the debtor, or trustee if one has been appointed, shall file a disclosure statement and plan;

(ii) sets a date by which the debtor, or trustee if one has been appointed, shall solicit acceptances of a plan;

(iii) sets the date by which a party in interest other than a debtor may file a plan;

(iv) sets a date by which a proponent of a plan, other than the debtor, shall solicit acceptances of such plan;

(v) fixes the scope and format of the notice to be provided regarding the hearing on approval of the disclosure statement; or

(vi) provides that the hearing on approval of the disclosure statement may be combined with the hearing on confirmation of the plan.

106. Waiver of sovereign immunity

(a) Notwithstanding an assertion of sovereign immunity, sovereign immunity is abrogated as to a governmental unit to the extent set forth in this section with respect to the following:

(1) Sections 105, 106, 107, 108, 303, 346, 362, 363, 364, 365, 366, 502, 503, 505, 506, 510, 522, 523, 524, 525, 542, 543, 544, 545, 546, 547, 548, 549, 550, 551, 552, 553, 722, 724, 726, 744, 749, 764, 901, 922, 926, 928, 929, 944, 1107, 1141, 1142, 1143, 1146, 1201, 1203, 1205, 1206, 1227, 1231, 1301, 1303, 1305, and 1327 of this title.

(2) The court may hear and determine any issue arising with respect to the application of such sections to governmental units.

(3) The court may issue against a governmental unit an order, process, or judgment under such sections or the Federal Rules of Bankruptcy Procedure, including an order or judgment awarding a money recovery, but not including an award of punitive damages. Such order or judgment for costs or fees under this title or the Federal Rules of Bankruptcy Procedure

against any governmental unit shall be consistent with the provisions and limitations of section 2412(d)(2)(A) of title 28.

(4) The enforcement of any such order, process, or judgment against any governmental unit shall be consistent with appropriate nonbankruptcy law applicable to such governmental unit and, in the case of a money judgment against the United States, shall be paid as if it is a judgment rendered by a district court of the United States.

(5) Nothing in this section shall create any substantive claim for relief or cause of action not otherwise existing under this title, the Federal Rules of Bankruptcy Procedure, or nonbankruptcy law.

(b) A governmental unit that has filed a proof of claim in the case is deemed to have waived sovereign immunity with respect to a claim against such governmental unit that is property of the estate and that arose out of the same transaction or occurrence out of which the claim of such governmental unit arose.

(c) Notwithstanding any assertion of sovereign immunity by a governmental unit, there shall be offset against a claim or interest of a governmental unit any claim against such governmental unit that is property of the estate.

107. Public access to papers

(a) Except as provided in subsections (b) and (c) and subject to section 112, a paper filed in a case under this title and the dockets of a bankruptcy court are public records and open to examination by an entity at reasonable times without charge.

(b) On request of a party in interest, the bankruptcy court shall, and on the bankruptcy court's own motion, the bankruptcy court may -

(1) protect an entity with respect to a trade secret or confidential research, development, or commercial information; or

(2) protect a person with respect to scandalous or defamatory matter contained in a paper filed in a case under this title.

(c)(1) The bankruptcy court, for cause, may protect an individual, with respect to the following types of information to the extent the court finds that disclosure of such information would create undue risk of identity theft or other unlawful injury to the individual or the individual's property:

(A) Any means of identification (as defined in section 1028(d) of title 18) contained in a paper filed, or to be filed, in a case under this title.

(B) Other information contained in a paper described in subparagraph (A).

(2) Upon ex parte application demonstrating cause, the court shall provide access to information protected pursuant to paragraph (1) to an entity acting pursuant to the police or regulatory power of a domestic governmental unit.

(3) The United States trustee, bankruptcy administrator, trustee, and any auditor serving under section 586(f) of title 28 –

(A) shall have full access to all information contained in any paper filed or submitted in a case under this title; and

(B) shall not disclose information specifically protected by the court under this title.

108. Extension of time

(a) If applicable nonbankruptcy law, an order entered in a nonbankruptcy proceeding, or an agreement fixes a period within which the debtor may commence an action, and such period has not expired before the date of the filing of the petition, the trustee may commence such action only before the later of -

(1) the end of such period, including any suspension of such period occurring on or after the commencement of the case; or

(2) two years after the order for relief.

(b) Except as provided in subsection (a) of this section, if applicable nonbankruptcy law, an order entered in a nonbankruptcy proceeding, or an agreement fixes a period within which the debtor or an individual protected under section 1201 or 1301 of this title may file any pleading, demand, notice, or proof of claim or loss, cure a default, or perform any other similar act, and such period has not expired before the date of the filing of the petition, the trustee may only file, cure, or perform, as the case may be, before the later of

(1) the end of such period, including any suspension of such period occurring on or after the commencement of the case; or

(2) 60 days after the order for relief.

(c) Except as provided in section 524 of this title, if applicable nonbankruptcy law, an order entered in a nonbankruptcy proceeding, or an agreement fixes a period for commencing or continuing a civil action in a court other than a bankruptcy court on a claim against the debtor, or against an individual with respect to which such individual is protected under section 1201 or 1301 of this title, and such period has not expired before the date of the filing of the petition, then such period does not expire until the later of -

(1) the end of such period, including any suspension of such period occurring on or after the commencement of the case; or

(2) 30 days after notice of the termination or expiration of the stay under section 362, 922, 1201, or 1301 of this title, as the case may be, with respect to such claim.

109. Who may be a debtor

(a) Notwithstanding any other provision of this section, only a person that resides or has a domicile, a place of business, or property in the United States, or a municipality, may be a debtor under this title.

(b) A person may be a debtor under chapter 7 of this title only if such person is not -

(1) a railroad;

(2) a domestic insurance company, bank, savings bank, cooperative bank, savings and loan association, building and loan association, homestead association a New Markets Venture Capital company as defined in section 351 of the Small Business Investment Act of 1958, a small business investment company licensed by the Small Business Administration under section 301 of the Small Business Investment Act of 1958, credit union, or industrial bank or similar institution which is an insured bank as defined in section 3(h) of the Federal Deposit Insurance Act, except that an uninsured State member bank, or a corporation organized under section 25A of the Federal Reserve Act, which operates, or operates as, a multilateral clearing organization pursuant to section 409 of the Federal Deposit Insurance Corporation Improvement Act of 1991 may be a debtor if a petition is filed at the direction of the Board of Governors of the Federal Reserve System; or

(3)(A) a foreign insurance company, engaged in such business in the United States; or

(B) a foreign bank, savings bank, cooperative bank, savings and loan association, building and loan association, or credit union, that has a branch or agency (as defined in section 1(b) of the International Banking Act of 1978) in the United States.

(c) An entity may be a debtor under chapter 9 of this title if and only if such entity -

(1) is a municipality;

(2) is specifically authorized in its capacity as a municipality or by name, to be a debtor under such chapter by State law, or by a governmental officer or organization empowered by State law to authorize such entity to be a debtor under such chapter;

(3) is insolvent;

(4) desires to effect a plan to adjust such debts; and

(5)(A) has obtained the agreement of creditors holding at least a majority in amount of the claims of each class that such entity intends to impair under a plan in a case under such chapter;

(B) has negotiated in good faith with creditors and has failed to obtain the agreement of creditors holding at least a majority in amount of the claims of each class that such entity intends to impair under a plan in a case under such chapter;

(C) is unable to negotiate with creditors because such negotiation is impracticable; or

(D) reasonably believes that a creditor may attempt to obtain a transfer that is avoidable under section 547 of this title.

(d) Only a railroad, a person that may be a debtor under chapter 7 of this title (except a stockbroker or a commodity broker), and an uninsured State member bank, or a corporation organized under section 25A of the Federal Reserve Act, which operates, or operates as, a multilateral clearing organization pursuant to section 409 of the Federal Deposit Insurance Corporation Improvement Act of 1991 may be a debtor under chapter 11 of this title.

(e) Only an individual with regular income that owes, on the date of the filing of the petition, noncontingent, liquidated debts of less than $2,750,000 or an individual with regular income and such individual's spouse, except a stockbroker or a commodity broker, that owe, on the date of the filing of the petition, noncontingent, liquidated debts that aggregate less than $2,750,000 may be a debtor under chapter 13 of this title.

(f) Only a family farmer or family fisherman with regular annual income may be a debtor under chapter 12 of this title.

(g) Notwithstanding any other provision of this section, no individual or family farmer may be a debtor under this title who has been a debtor in a case pending under this title at any time in the preceding 180 days if -

(1) the case was dismissed by the court for willful failure of the debtor to abide by orders of the court, or to appear before the court in proper

prosecution of the case; or

(2) the debtor requested and obtained the voluntary dismissal of the case following the filing of a request for relief from the automatic stay provided by section 362 of this title.

(h)(1) Subject to paragraphs (2) and (3), and notwithstanding any other provision of this section other than paragraph (4) of this subsection, an individual may not be a debtor under this title unless such individual has, during the 180-day period ending on the date of filing of the petition by such individual, received from an approved nonprofit budget and credit counseling agency described in section 111(a) an individual or group briefing (including a briefing conducted by telephone or on the Internet) that outlined the opportunities for available credit counseling and assisted such individual in performing a related budget analysis.

(2)(A) Paragraph (1) shall not apply with respect to a debtor who resides in a district for which the United States trustee (or the bankruptcy administrator, if any) determines that the approved nonprofit budget and credit counseling agencies for such district are not reasonably able to provide adequate services to the additional individuals who would otherwise seek credit counseling from such agencies by reason of the requirements of paragraph (1).

(B) The United States trustee (or the bankruptcy administrator, if any) who makes a determination described in subparagraph (A) shall review such determination not later than 1 year after the date of such determination, and not less frequently than annually thereafter. Notwithstanding the preceding sentence, a nonprofit budget and credit counseling agency may be disapproved by the United States trustee (or the bankruptcy administrator, if any) at any time.

(3)(A) Subject to subparagraph (B), the requirements of paragraph (1) shall not apply with respect to a debtor who submits to the court a certification that –

(i) describes exigent circumstances that merit a waiver of the requirements of paragraph (1);

(ii) states that the debtor requested credit counseling services from an approved nonprofit budget and credit counseling agency, but was unable to obtain the services referred to in paragraph (1) during the 7-day period beginning on the date on which the debtor made that request; and

(iii) is satisfactory to the court.

(B) With respect to a debtor, an exemption under subparagraph (A) shall cease to apply to that debtor on the date on which the debtor meets the requirements of paragraph (1), but in no case may the exemption apply to that debtor after the date that is 30 days after the debtor files a petition, except that the court, for cause, may order an additional 15 days.

(4) The requirements of paragraph (1) shall not apply with respect to a debtor whom the court determines, after notice and hearing, is unable to complete those requirements because of incapacity, disability, or active military duty in a military combat zone. For the purposes of this paragraph, incapacity means that the debtor is impaired by reason of mental illness or mental deficiency so that he is incapable of realizing and making rational decisions with respect to his financial responsibilities; and "disability" means that the debtor is so physically impaired as to be unable, after reasonable effort, to participate in an in person, telephone, or Internet briefing required under paragraph (1).

110. Penalty for persons who negligently or fraudulently prepare bankruptcy petitions

(a) In this section -

(1) "bankruptcy petition preparer" means a person, other than an attorney for the debtor or an employee of such attorney under the direct supervision of such attorney, who prepares for compensation a document for filing; and

(2) "document for filing" means a petition or any other document prepared for filing by a debtor in a United States bankruptcy court or a United States district court in connection with a case under this title.

(b)(1) A bankruptcy petition preparer who prepares a document for filing shall sign the document and print on the document the preparer's name and address. If a bankruptcy petition preparer is not an individual, then an officer, principal, responsible person, or partner of the bankruptcy petition preparer shall be required to –

(A) sign the document for filing; and

(B) print on the document the name and address of that officer, principal, responsible person, or partner.

(2)(A) Before preparing any document for filing or accepting any fees from or on behalf of a debtor, the bankruptcy petition preparer shall provide to the debtor a written notice which shall be on an official form prescribed by the Judicial Conference of the United States in accordance with rule 9009 of the Federal Rules of Bankruptcy Procedure.

(B) The notice under the subparagraph (A) –

(i) shall inform the debtor in simple language that a bankruptcy petition preparer is not an attorney and may not practice law or give legal advice;

(ii) may contain a description of examples of legal advice that a bankruptcy petition preparer is not authorized to give, in addition to any advice that the preparer may not give by reason of subsection (e)(2); and

(iii) shall –

(I) be signed by the debtor and, under penalty of perjury, by the bankruptcy petition preparer; and

(II) be filed with any document for filing.

(c)(1) A bankruptcy petition preparer who prepares a document for filing shall place on the document, after the preparer's signature, an identifying number that identifies individuals who prepared the document.

(2)(A) Subject to subparagraph (B), for purposes of this section, the identifying number of a bankruptcy petition preparer shall be the Social Security account number of each individual who prepared the document or assisted in its preparation.

(B) If a bankruptcy petition preparer is not an individual, the identifying number of the bankruptcy petition preparer shall be the Social Security account number of the officer, principal, responsible person, or partner of the bankruptcy petition preparer.

(d) A bankruptcy petition preparer shall, not later than the time at which a document for filing is presented for the debtor's signature, furnish to the debtor a copy of the document.

(e)(1) A bankruptcy petition preparer shall not execute any document on behalf of a debtor.

(2)(A) A bankruptcy petition preparer may not offer a potential bankruptcy debtor any legal advice, including any legal advice described in subparagraph (B).

(B) The legal advice referred to in subparagraph (A) includes advising the debtor –

(i) whether –

(I) to file a petition under this title; or

(II) commencing a case under chapter 7, 11, 12, or 13 is appropriate;

(ii) whether the debtor's debts will be discharged in a case under this title;

(iii) whether the debtor will be able to retain the debtor's home, car, or other property after commencing a case under this title;

(iv) concerning –

(I) the tax consequences of a case brought under this title; or

(II) the dischargeability of tax claims;

(v) whether the debtor may or should promise to repay debts to a creditor or enter into a reaffirmation agreement with a creditor to reaffirm a debt;

(vi) concerning how to characterize the nature of the debtor's interests in property or the debtor's debts; or

(vii) concerning bankruptcy procedures and rights.

(f) A bankruptcy petition preparer shall not use the word "legal" or any similar term in any advertisements, or advertise under any category that includes the word "legal" or any similar term.

(g) A bankruptcy petition preparer shall not collect or receive any payment from the debtor or on behalf of the debtor for the court fees in connection with filing the petition.

(h)(1) The Supreme Court may promulgate rules under section 2075 of title 28, or the Judicial Conference of the United States may prescribe guidelines, for setting a maximum allowable fee chargeable by a bankruptcy petition preparer. A bankruptcy petition preparer shall notify the debtor of any such maximum amount before preparing any document for filing for the debtor or accepting any fee from or on behalf of the debtor.

(2) A declaration under penalty of perjury by the bankruptcy petition preparer shall be filed together with the petition, disclosing any fee received from or on behalf of the debtor within 12 months immediately prior to the filing of the case, and any unpaid fee charged to the debtor. If rules or guidelines setting a maximum fee for services have been promulgated or prescribed under paragraph (1), the declaration under this paragraph shall include a certification that the bankruptcy petition preparer complied with the notification requirement under paragraph (1).

(3)(A) The court shall disallow and order the immediate turnover to the bankruptcy trustee any fee referred to in paragraph (2) –

(i) found to be in excess of the value of any services rendered by the bankruptcy petition preparer during the 12-month period immediately preceding the date of the filing of the petition; or

(ii) found to be in violation of any rule or guideline promulgated or prescribed under paragraph (1).

(B) All fees charged by a bankruptcy petition preparer may be forfeited in any case in which the bankruptcy petition preparer fails to comply with this subsection or subsection (b), (c), (d), (e), (f), or (g).

(C) An individual may exempt any funds recovered under this paragraph under section 522(b).

(4) The debtor, the trustee, a creditor, the United States trustee (or the bankruptcy administrator, if any) or the court, on the initiative of the court, may file a motion for an order under paragraph (3).

(5) A bankruptcy petition preparer shall be fined not more than $500 for each failure to comply with a court order to turn over funds within 30 days of service of such order.

(i)(1) If a bankruptcy petition preparer violates this section or commits any act that the court finds to be fraudulent, unfair, or deceptive, on the motion of the debtor, trustee, United States trustee (or the bankruptcy administrator, if any), and after notice and a hearing, the court shall order the bankruptcy petition preparer to pay to the debtor –

(A) the debtor's actual damages;

(B) the greater of -

(i) $2,000; or

(ii) twice the amount paid by the debtor to the bankruptcy petition preparer for the preparer's services; and

(C) reasonable attorneys' fees and costs in moving for damages under this subsection.

(2) If the trustee or creditor moves for damages on behalf of the debtor under this subsection, the bankruptcy petition preparer shall be ordered to pay the movant the additional amount of $1,000 plus reasonable attorneys' fees and costs incurred.

(j)(1) A debtor for whom a bankruptcy petition preparer has prepared a document for filing, the trustee, a creditor, or the United States trustee in the district in which the bankruptcy petition preparer resides, has conducted business, or the United States trustee in any other district in which the debtor resides may bring a civil action to enjoin a bankruptcy petition preparer from engaging in any conduct in violation of this section or from further acting as a bankruptcy petition preparer.

(2)(A) In an action under paragraph (1), if the court finds that -

(i) a bankruptcy petition preparer has -

(I) engaged in conduct in violation of this section or of any provision of this title;

(II) misrepresented the preparer's experience or education as a bankruptcy petition preparer; or

(III) engaged in any other fraudulent, unfair, or deceptive conduct; and

(ii) injunctive relief is appropriate to prevent the recurrence of such conduct,

the court may enjoin the bankruptcy petition preparer from engaging in such conduct.

(B) If the court finds that a bankruptcy petition preparer has continually engaged in conduct described in subclause (I), (II), or (III) of clause (i) and that an injunction prohibiting such conduct would not be sufficient to prevent such person's interference with the proper administration of this title, has not paid a penalty imposed under this section, or failed to disgorge all fees ordered by the court, the court may enjoin the person from acting as a bankruptcy petition preparer.

(3) The court, as part of its contempt power, may enjoin a bankruptcy petition preparer that has failed to comply with a previous order issued under this section. The injunction under this paragraph may be issued on the motion of the court, the trustee, or the United States trustee (or the bankruptcy administrator, if any).

(4) The court shall award to a debtor, trustee, or creditor that brings a successful action under this subsection reasonable attorneys' fees and costs of the action, to be paid by the bankruptcy petition preparer.

(k) Nothing in this section shall be construed to permit activities that are otherwise prohibited by law, including rules and laws that prohibit the unauthorized practice of law.

(l)(1) A bankruptcy petition preparer who fails to comply with any provision of subsection (b), (c), (d), (e), (f), (g), or (h) may be fined not more than $500 for each such failure.

(2) The court shall triple the amount of a fine assessed under paragraph (1) in any case in which the court finds that a bankruptcy petition preparer –

(A) advised the debtor to exclude assets or income that should have been included on applicable schedules;

(B) advised the debtor to use a false Social Security account number;

(C) failed to inform the debtor that the debtor was filing for relief under this title; or

(D) prepared a document for filing in a manner that failed to disclose the identity of the bankruptcy petition preparer.

(3) A debtor, trustee, creditor, or United States trustee (or the bankruptcy administrator, if any) may file a motion for an order imposing a fine on the bankruptcy petition preparer for any violation of this section.

(4)(A) Fines imposed under this subsection in judicial districts served by United States trustees shall be paid to the United States trustees, who shall deposit an amount equal to such fines in the United States Trustee Fund.

(B) Fines imposed under this subsection in judicial districts served by bankruptcy administrators shall be deposited as offsetting receipts to the fund established under section 1931 of title 28, and shall remain available until expended to reimburse any appropriation for the amount paid out of such appropriation for expenses of the operation and maintenance of the courts of the United States.

111. Nonprofit budget and credit counseling agencies; financial management instructional courses

(a) The clerk shall maintain a publicly available list of –

(1) nonprofit budget and credit counseling agencies that provide 1 or more services described in section 109(h) currently approved by the United States trustee (or the bankruptcy administrator, if any); and

(2) instructional courses concerning personal financial management currently approved by the United States trustee (or the bankruptcy administrator, if any), as applicable.

(b) The United States trustee (or bankruptcy administrator, if any) shall only approve a nonprofit budget and credit counseling agency or an instructional course concerning personal financial management as follows:

(1) The United States trustee (or bankruptcy administrator, if any) shall have thoroughly reviewed the qualifications of the nonprofit budget and credit counseling agency or of the provider of the instructional course under the standards set forth in this section, and the services or instructional courses that will be offered by such agency or such provider, and may require such agency or such provider that has sought approval to provide information with respect to such review.

(2) The United States trustee (or bankruptcy administrator, if any) shall have determined that such agency or such instructional course fully satisfies the applicable standards set forth in this section.

(3) If a nonprofit budget and credit counseling agency or instructional course did not appear on the approved list for the district under subsection (a) immediately before approval under this section, approval under this subsection of such agency or such instructional course shall be for a probationary period not to exceed 6 months.

(4) At the conclusion of the applicable probationary period under paragraph (3), the United States trustee (or bankruptcy administrator, if any) may only approve for an additional 1-year period, and for successive 1-year periods thereafter, an agency or instructional course that has demonstrated during the probationary or applicable subsequent period of approval that such agency or instructional course –

(A) has met the standards set forth under this section during such period; and

(B) can satisfy such standards in the future.

(5) Not later than 30 days after any final decision under paragraph (4), an interested person may seek judicial review of such decision in the appropriate district court of the United States.

(c)(1) The United States trustee (or the bankruptcy administrator, if any) shall only approve a nonprofit budget and credit counseling agency that demonstrates that it will provide qualified counselors, maintain adequate provision for safekeeping and payment of client funds, provide adequate counseling with respect to client credit problems, and deal responsibly and effectively with other matters relating to the quality, effectiveness, and financial security of the services it provides.

(2) To be approved by the United States trustee (or the bankruptcy administrator, if any), a nonprofit budget and credit counseling agency shall, at a minimum –

(A) have a board of directors the majority of which –

(i) are not employed by such agency; and

(ii) will not directly or indirectly benefit financially from the outcome of the counseling services provided by such agency;

(B) if a fee is charged for counseling services, charge a reasonable fee, and provide services without regard to ability to pay the fee;

(C) provide for safekeeping and payment of client funds, including an annual audit of the trust accounts and appropriate employee bonding;

(D) provide full disclosures to a client, including funding sources, counselor qualifications, possible impact on credit reports, and any costs of such program that will be paid by such client and how such costs will be paid;

(E) provide adequate counseling with respect to a client's credit problems that includes an analysis of such client's current financial condition, factors that caused such financial condition, and how such client can develop a plan to respond to the problems without incurring negative amortization of debt;

(F) provide trained counselors who receive no commissions or bonuses based on the outcome of the counseling services provided by such agency, and who have adequate experience, and have been adequately trained to provide counseling services to individuals in financial difficulty, including the matters described in subparagraph (E);

(G) demonstrate adequate experience and background in providing credit counseling; and

(H) have adequate financial resources to provide continuing support services for budgeting plans over the life of any repayment plan.

(d) The United States trustee (or the bankruptcy administrator, if any) shall only approve an instructional course concerning personal financial management –

(1) for an initial probationary period under subsection (b)(3) if the course will provide at a minimum –

(A) trained personnel with adequate experience and training in providing effective instruction and services;

(B) learning materials and teaching methodologies designed to assist debtors in understanding personal financial management and that are consistent with stated objectives directly related to the goals of such instructional course;

(C) adequate facilities situated in reasonably convenient locations at which such instructional course is offered, except that such facilities may include the provision of such instructional course by telephone or through the Internet, if such instructional course is effective;

(D) the preparation and retention of reasonable records (which shall include the debtor's bankruptcy case number) to permit evaluation of the effectiveness of such instructional course, including any evaluation of satisfaction of instructional course requirements for each debtor attending such instructional course, which shall be available for inspection and evaluation by the Executive Office for United States Trustees, the United States trustee (or the bankruptcy administrator, if any), or the chief bankruptcy judge for the district in which such instructional course is offered; and

(E) if a fee is charged for the instructional course, charge a reasonable fee, and provide services without regard to ability to pay the fee; and

(2) for any 1-year period if the provider thereof has demonstrated that the course meets the standards of paragraph (1) and, in addition –

(A) has been effective in assisting a substantial number of debtors to understand personal financial management; and

(B) is otherwise likely to increase substantially the debtor's understanding of personal financial management.

(e) The district court may, at any time, investigate the qualifications of a nonprofit budget and credit counseling agency referred to in subsection (a), and request production of documents to ensure the integrity and effectiveness of such agency. The district court may, at any time, remove from the approved list under subsection (a) a nonprofit budget and credit counseling agency upon finding such agency does not meet the qualifications of subsection (b).

(f) The United States trustee (or the bankruptcy administrator, if any) shall notify the clerk that a nonprofit budget and credit counseling agency or an instructional course is no longer approved, in which case the clerk shall remove it from the list maintained under subsection (a).

(g)(1) No nonprofit budget and credit counseling agency may provide to a credit reporting agency information concerning whether a debtor has received or sought instruction concerning personal financial management from such agency.

(2) A nonprofit budget and credit counseling agency that willfully or negligently fails to comply with any requirement under this title with respect to a debtor shall be liable for damages in an amount equal to the sum of –

(A) any actual damages sustained by the debtor as a result of the violation; and

(B) any court costs or reasonable attorneys' fees (as determined by the court) incurred in an action to recover those damages.

112. Prohibition on disclosure of name of minor children

The debtor may be required to provide information regarding a minor child involved in matters under this title but may not be required to disclose in the public records in the case the name of such minor child. The debtor may be required to disclose the name of such minor child in a nonpublic record that is maintained by the court and made available by the court for examination by the United States trustee, the trustee, and the auditor (if any) serving under section 586(f) of title 28, in the case. The court, the United States trustee, the trustee, and such auditor shall not disclose the name of such minor child maintained in such nonpublic record.

Chapter 3 - Case Administration

Subchapter I - Commencement of a Case

Subchapter II - Officers

Subchapter III - Administration

Subchapter IV - Administrative Powers

SUBCHAPTER I - COMMENCEMENT OF A CASE

301. Voluntary cases

(a) A voluntary case under a chapter of this title is commenced by the filing with the bankruptcy court of a petition under such chapter by an entity that may be a debtor under such chapter.

(b) The commencement of a voluntary case under a chapter of this title constitutes an order for relief under such chapter.

302. Joint cases

(a) A joint case under a chapter of this title is commenced by the filing with the bankruptcy court of a single petition under such chapter by an individual that may be a debtor under such chapter and such individual's spouse. The commencement of a joint case under a chapter of this title constitutes an order for relief under such chapter.

(b) After the commencement of a joint case, the court shall determine the extent, if any, to which the debtors' estates shall be consolidated.

303. Involuntary cases

(a) An involuntary case may be commenced only under chapter 7 or 11 of this title, and only against a person, except a farmer, family farmer, or a corporation that is not a moneyed, business, or commercial corporation, that may be a debtor under the chapter under which such case is commenced.

(b) An involuntary case against a person is commenced by the filing with the bankruptcy court of a petition under chapter 7 or 11 of this title-

(1) by three or more entities, each of which is either a holder of a claim against such person that is not contingent as to liability or the subject of a bona fide dispute as to liability or amount, or an indenture trustee representing such a holder, if such noncontingent, undisputed claims aggregate at least $18,600 more than the value of any lien on property of the debtor securing such claims held by the holders of such claims;

(2) if there are fewer than 12 such holders, excluding any employee or insider of such person and any transferee of a transfer that is voidable under section 544, 545, 547, 548, 549, or 724(a) of this title, by one or more of such holders that hold in the aggregate at least $18,600 of such claims;

(3) if such person is a partnership-

(A) by fewer than all of the general partners in such partnership; or

(B) if relief has been ordered under this title with respect to all of the general partners in such partnership, by a general partner in such partnership, the trustee of such a general partner, or a holder of a claim against such partnership; or

(4) by a foreign representative of the estate in a foreign proceeding concerning such person.

(c) After the filing of a petition under this section but before the case is dismissed or relief is ordered, a creditor holding an unsecured claim that is not contingent, other than a creditor filing under subsection (b) of this section, may join in the petition with the same effect as if such joining creditor were a petitioning creditor under subsection (b) of this section.

(d) The debtor, or a general partner in a partnership debtor that did not join in the petition, may file an answer to a petition under this section.

(e) After notice and a hearing, and for cause, the court may require the petitioners under this section to file a bond to indemnify the debtor for such amounts as the court may later allow under subsection (i) of this section.

(f) Notwithstanding section 363 of this title, except to the extent that the court orders otherwise, and until an order for relief in the case, any business of the debtor may continue to operate, and the debtor may continue to use, acquire, or dispose of property as if an involuntary case concerning the debtor had not been commenced.

(g) At any time after the commencement of an involuntary case under chapter 7 of this title but before an order for relief in the case, the court, on request of a party in interest, after notice to the debtor and a hearing, and if necessary to preserve the property of the estate or to prevent loss to the estate, may order the United States trustee to appoint an interim trustee under section 701 of this title to take possession of the property of the estate and to operate any business of the debtor. Before an order for relief, the debtor may regain possession of property in the possession of a trustee ordered appointed under this subsection if the debtor files such bond as the court requires, conditioned on the debtor's accounting for and delivering to the trustee, if there is an order for relief in the case, such property, or the value, as of the date the debtor regains possession, of such property.

(h) If the petition is not timely controverted, the court shall order relief against the debtor in an involuntary case under the chapter under which the petition was filed. Otherwise, after trial, the court shall order relief against the debtor in an involuntary case under the chapter under which the petition was filed, only if-

(1) the debtor is generally not paying such debtor's debts as such debts become due unless such debts are the subject of a bona fide dispute as to liability or amount; or

(2) within 120 days before the date of the filing of the petition, a custodian, other than a trustee, receiver, or agent appointed or authorized to take charge of less than substantially all of the property of the debtor for the purpose of enforcing a lien against such property, was appointed or took possession.

(i) If the court dismisses a petition under this section other than on consent of all petitioners and the debtor, and if the debtor does not waive the right to judgment under this subsection, the court may grant judgment-

(1) against the petitioners and in favor of the debtor for-

(A) costs; or

(B) a reasonable attorney's fee; or

(2) against any petitioner that filed the petition in bad faith, for-

(A) any damages proximately caused by such filing; or

(B) punitive damages.

(j) Only after notice to all creditors and a hearing may the court dismiss a petition filed under this section-

(1) on the motion of a petitioner;

(2) on consent of all petitioners and the debtor; or

(3) for want of prosecution.

(k)(1) If –

(A) the petition under this section is false or contains any materially false, fictitious, or fraudulent statement;

(B) the debtor is an individual; and

(C) the court dismisses such petition,

the court, upon the motion of the debtor, shall seal all the records of the court relating to such petition, and all references to such petition.

(2) If the debtor is an individual and the court dismisses a petition under this section, the court may enter an order prohibiting all consumer reporting agencies (as defined in section 603(f) of the Fair Credit Reporting Act (15 U.S.C. 1681a(f))) from making any consumer report (as defined in section 603(d) of that Act) that contains any information relating to such petition or to the case commenced by the filing of such petition.

(3) Upon the expiration of the statute of limitations described in section 3282 of title 18, for a violation of section 152 or 157 of such title, the court, upon the motion of the debtor and for good cause, may expunge any records relating to a petition filed under this section.

305. Abstention

(a) The court, after notice and a hearing, may dismiss a case under this title, or may suspend all proceedings in a case under this title, at any time if -

(1) the interests of creditors and the debtor would be better served by such dismissal or suspension; or

(2)(A) a petition under section 1515 for recognition of a foreign proceeding has been granted; and

(B) the purposes of chapter 15 of this title would be best served by such dismissal or suspension.

(b) A foreign representative may seek dismissal or suspension under subsection(a)(2) of this section.

(c) An order under subsection (a) of this section dismissing a case or suspending all proceedings in a case, or a decision not so to dismiss or suspend, is not reviewable by appeal or otherwise by the court of appeals under section 158(d), 1291, or 1292 of title 28 or by the Supreme Court of the United States under section 1254 of title 28.

306. Limited appearance

An appearance in a bankruptcy court by a foreign representative in connection with a petition or request under section 303 or 305 of this title does not submit such foreign representative to the jurisdiction of any court in the United States for any other purpose, but the bankruptcy court may condition any order under section 303 or 305 of this title on compliance by such foreign representative with the orders of such bankruptcy court.

307. United States trustee

The United States trustee may raise and may appear and be heard on any issue in any case or proceeding under this title but may not file a plan pursuant to section 1121(c) of this title.

308. Debtor reporting requirements

(a) For purposes of this section, the term "profitability" means, with respect to a debtor, the amount of money that the debtor has earned or lost during current and recent fiscal periods.

(b) A debtor in a small business case shall file periodic financial and other reports containing information including –

(1) the debtor's profitability;

(2) reasonable approximations of the debtor's projected cash receipts and cash disbursements over a reasonable period;

(3) comparisons of actual cash receipts and disbursements with projections in prior reports;

(4) whether the debtor is –

(A) in compliance in all material respects with postpetition requirements imposed by this title and the Federal Rules of Bankruptcy Procedure; and

(B) timely filing tax returns and other required government filings and paying taxes and other administrative expenses when due;

(5) if the debtor is not in compliance with the requirements referred to in paragraph (4)(A) or filing tax returns and other required government filings and making the payments referred to in paragraph (4)(B), what the failures are and how, at what cost, and when the debtor intends to remedy such failures; and

(6) such other matters as are in the best interests of the debtor and creditors, and in the public interest in fair and efficient procedures under chapter 11 of this title.

SUBCHAPTER II - OFFICERS

321. Eligibility to serve as trustee

(a) A person may serve as trustee in a case under this title only if such person is-

(1) an individual that is competent to perform the duties of trustee and, in a case under chapter 7, 12, or 13 of this title, resides or has an office in the judicial district within which the case is pending, or in any judicial district adjacent to such district; or

(2) a corporation authorized by such corporation's charter or bylaws to act as trustee, and, in a case under chapter 7, 12, or 13 of this title, having an office in at least one of such districts.

(b) A person that has served as an examiner in the case may not serve as trustee in the case.

(c) The United States trustee for the judicial district in which the case is pending is eligible to serve as trustee in the case if necessary.

322. Qualification of trustee

(a) Except as provided in subsection (b)(1), a person selected under section 701, 702, 703, 1104, 1163, 1183, 1202, or 1302 of this title to serve as trustee in a case under this title qualifies if before seven days after such selection, and before beginning official duties, such person has filed with the court a bond in favor of the United States conditioned on the faithful performance of such official duties.

(b)(1) The United States trustee qualifies wherever such trustee serves as trustee in a case under this title.

(2) The United States trustee shall determine -

(A) the amount of a bond required to be filed under subsection (a) of this section; and

(B) the sufficiency of the surety on such bond.

(c) A trustee is not liable personally or on such trustee's bond in favor of the United States for any penalty or forfeiture incurred by the debtor.

(d) A proceeding on a trustee's bond may not be commenced after two years after the date on which such trustee was discharged.

323. Role and capacity of trustee

(a) The trustee in a case under this title is the representative of the estate.

(b) The trustee in a case under this title has capacity to sue and be sued.

324. Removal of trustee or examiner

(a) The court, after notice and a hearing, may remove a trustee, other than the United States trustee, or an examiner, for cause.

(b) Whenever the court removes a trustee or examiner under subsection (a) in a case under this title, such trustee or examiner shall thereby be removed in all other cases under this title in which such trustee or examiner is then serving unless the court orders otherwise.

325. Effect of vacancy

A vacancy in the office of trustee during a case does not abate any pending action or proceeding, and the successor trustee shall be substituted as a party in such action or proceeding.

326. Limitation on compensation of trustee

(a) In a case under chapter 7 or 11, other than a case under subchapter V of chapter 11, the court may allow reasonable compensation under section 330 of this title of the trustee for the trustee's services, payable after the trustee renders such services, not to exceed 25 percent on the first $5,000 or less, 10 percent on any amount in excess of $5,000 but not in excess of $50,000, 5 percent on any amount in excess of $50,000 but not in excess of $1,100,000, and reasonable compensation not to exceed 3 percent of such moneys in excess of $1,100,000, upon all moneys disbursed or turned over in the case by the trustee to parties in interest, excluding the debtor, but including holders of secured claims.

(b) In a case under subchapter V of chapter 11 or chapter 12 or 13 of this title, the court may not allow compensation for services or reimbursement of expenses of the United States trustee or of a standing trustee appointed under section 586(b) of title 28, but may allow reasonable compensation under section 330 of this title of a trustee appointed under section 1202(a) or 1302(a) of this title for the trustee's services, payable after the trustee renders such services, not to exceed five percent upon all payments under the plan.

(c) If more than one person serves as trustee in the case, the aggregate compensation of such persons for such service may not exceed the maximum compensation prescribed for a single trustee by subsection (a) or (b) of this section, as the case may be.

(d) The court may deny allowance of compensation for services or reimbursement of expenses of the trustee if the trustee failed to make diligent inquiry into facts that would permit denial of allowance under section 328(c) of this title or, with knowledge of such facts, employed a professional person under section 327 of this title.

327. Employment of professional persons

(a) Except as otherwise provided in this section, the trustee, with the court's approval, may employ one or more attorneys, accountants, appraisers, auctioneers, or other professional persons, that do not hold or represent an interest adverse to the estate, and that are disinterested persons, to represent or assist the trustee in carrying out the trustee's duties under this title.

(b) If the trustee is authorized to operate the business of the debtor under section 721, 1202, or 1108 of this title, and if the debtor has regularly employed attorneys, accountants, or other professional persons on salary, the trustee may retain or replace such professional persons if necessary in the operation of such business.

(c) In a case under chapter 7, 12, or 11 of this title, a person is not disqualified for employment under this section solely because of such person's employment by or representation of a creditor, unless there is objection by another creditor or the United States trustee, in which case the court shall disapprove such employment if there is an actual conflict of interest.

(d) The court may authorize the trustee to act as attorney or accountant for the estate if such authorization is in the best interest of the estate.

(e) The trustee, with the court's approval, may employ, for a specified special purpose, other than to represent the trustee in conducting the case, an attorney that has represented the debtor, if in the best interest of the estate, and if such attorney does not represent or hold any interest adverse to the debtor or to the estate with respect to the matter on which such attorney is to be employed.

(f) The trustee may not employ a person that has served as an examiner in the case.

328. Limitation on compensation of professional persons

(a) The trustee, or a committee appointed under section 1102 of this title, with the court's approval, may employ or authorize the employment of a professional person under section 327 or 1103 of this title, as the case may be, on any reasonable terms and conditions of employment, including on a retainer, on an hourly basis, on a fixed or percentage fee basis, or on a contingent fee basis. Notwithstanding such terms and conditions, the court may allow compensation different from the compensation provided under such terms and conditions after the conclusion of such employment, if such terms and conditions prove to have been improvident in light of developments not capable of being anticipated at the time of the fixing of such terms and conditions.

(b) If the court has authorized a trustee to serve as an attorney or accountant for the estate under section 327(d) of this title, the court may allow compensation for the trustee's services as such attorney or accountant only to the extent that the trustee performed services as attorney or accountant for the estate and not for performance of any of the trustee's duties that are generally performed by a trustee without the assistance of an attorney or accountant for the estate.

(c) Except as provided in section 327(c), 327(e), or 1107(b) of this title, the court may deny allowance of compensation for services and reimbursement of expenses of a professional person employed under section 327 or 1103 of this title if, at any time during such professional person's employment under section 327 or 1103 of this title, such professional person is not a disinterested person, or represents or holds an interest adverse to the interest of the estate with respect to the matter on which such professional person is employed.

329. Debtor's transactions with attorneys

(a) Any attorney representing a debtor in a case under this title, or in connection with such a case, whether or not such attorney applies for compensation under this title, shall file with the court a statement of the compensation paid or agreed to be paid, if such payment or agreement was made after one year before the date of the filing of the petition, for services rendered or to be rendered in contemplation of or in connection with the case by such attorney, and the source of such compensation.

(b) If such compensation exceeds the reasonable value of any such services, the court may cancel any such agreement, or order the return of any such payment, to the extent excessive, to -

(1) the estate, if the property transferred -

(A) would have been property of the estate; or

(B) was to be paid by or on behalf of the debtor under a plan under chapter 11, 12, or 13 of this title; or

(2) the entity that made such payment.

330. Compensation of officers

(a)(1) After notice to the parties in interest and the United States Trustee and a hearing, and subject to sections 326, 328, and 329, the court may award to a trustee, a consumer privacy ombudsman appointed under section 332, an examiner, an ombudsman appointed under section 333, or a professional person employed under section 327 or 1103 -

(A) reasonable compensation for actual, necessary services rendered by the trustee, examiner, ombudsman, professional person, or attorney and by any paraprofessional person employed by any such person; and

(B) reimbursement for actual, necessary expenses.

(2) The court may, on its own motion or on the motion of the United States Trustee, the United States Trustee for the District or Region, the trustee for the estate, or any other party in interest, award compensation that is less than the amount of compensation that is requested.

(3) In determining the amount of reasonable compensation to be awarded to an examiner, trustee under chapter 11, or professional person, the court shall consider the nature, the extent, and the value of such services, taking into account all relevant factors, including -

(A) the time spent on such services;

(B) the rates charged for such services;

(C) whether the services were necessary to the administration of, or beneficial at the time at which the service was rendered toward the completion of, a case under this title;

(D) whether the services were performed within a reasonable amount of time commensurate with the complexity, importance, and nature of the problem, issue, or task addressed;

(E) with respect to a professional person, whether the person is board certified or otherwise has demonstrated skill and experience in the bankruptcy field; and

(F) whether the compensation is reasonable based on the customary compensation charged by comparably skilled practitioners in cases other than cases under this title.

(4)(A) Except as provided in subparagraph (B), the court shall not allow compensation for -

(i) unnecessary duplication of services; or

(ii) services that were not -

(I) reasonably likely to benefit the debtor's estate; or

(II) necessary to the administration of the case.

(B) In a chapter 12 or chapter 13 case in which the debtor is an individual, the court may allow reasonable compensation to the debtor's attorney for representing the interests of the debtor in connection with the bankruptcy case based on a consideration of the benefit and necessity of such services to the debtor and the other factors set forth in this section.

(5) The court shall reduce the amount of compensation awarded under this section by the amount of any interim compensation awarded under section 331, and, if the amount of such interim compensation exceeds the amount of compensation awarded under this section, may order the return of the excess to the estate.

(6) Any compensation awarded for the preparation of a fee application shall be based on the level and skill reasonably required to prepare the application.

(7) In determining the amount of reasonable compensation to be awarded to a trustee, the court shall treat such compensation as a commission, based on section 326.

(b)(1) There shall be paid from the filing fee in a case under chapter 7 of this title $45 to the trustee serving in such case, after such trustee's services are rendered.

(2) The Judicial Conference of the United States -

(A) shall prescribe additional fees of the same kind as prescribed under section 1914(b) of title 28; and

(B) may prescribe notice of appearance fees and fees charged against distributions in cases under this title;

to pay $15 to trustees serving in cases after such trustees' services are rendered. Beginning 1 year after the date of the enactment of the Bankruptcy Reform Act of 1994, such $15 shall be paid in addition to the amount paid under paragraph (1).

(c) Unless the court orders otherwise, in a case under chapter 12 or 13 of this title the compensation paid to the trustee serving in the case shall not be less than $5 per month from any distribution under the plan during the administration of the plan.

(d) In a case in which the United States trustee serves as trustee, the compensation of the trustee under this section shall be paid to the clerk of the bankruptcy court and deposited by the clerk into the United States Trustee System Fund established by section 589a of title 28.

(e)(1) There is established a fund in the Treasury of the United States, to be known as the "Chapter 7 Trustee Fund", which shall be administered by the Director of the Administrative Office of the United States Courts.

(2) Deposits into the Chapter 7 Trustee Fund under section 589a(f)(1)(C) of title 28 shall be available until expended for the purposes described in paragraph (3).

(3) For fiscal years 2021 through 2026, the Chapter 7 Trustee Fund shall be available to pay the trustee serving in a case that is filed under chapter 7 or a case that is converted to a chapter 7 case in the most recent fiscal year (referred to in this subsection as a "chapter 7 case") the amount described in paragraph (4) for the chapter 7 case in which the trustee has rendered services.

(4) The amount described in this paragraph shall be the lesser of--

(A) $60; or

(B) a pro rata share, for each chapter 7 case, of the fees collected under section 1930(a)(6) of title 28 and deposited to the United States Trustee System Fund under section 589a(f)(1) of title 28, less the amounts specified in section 589a(f)(1)(A) and (B) of title 28.

(5) The payment received by a trustee under paragraph (3) shall be paid in addition to the amount paid under subsection (b).

(6) Not later than September 30, 2021, the Director of the Administrative Office of the United States Courts shall promulgate regulations for the administration of this subsection.

331. Interim compensation

A trustee, an examiner, a debtor's attorney, or any professional person employed under section 327 or 1103 of this title may apply to the court not more than once every 120 days after an order for relief in a case under this title, or more often if the court permits, for such compensation for services rendered before the date of such an application or reimbursement for expenses incurred before such date as is provided under section 330 of this title. After notice and a hearing, the court may allow and disburse to such applicant such compensation or reimbursement.

332. Consumer privacy ombudsman

(a) If a hearing is required under section 363(b)(1)(B), the court shall order the United States trustee to appoint, not later than 7 days before the commencement of the hearing, 1 disinterested person (other than the United States trustee) to serve as the consumer privacy ombudsman in the case and shall require that notice of such hearing be timely given to such ombudsman.

(b) The consumer privacy ombudsman may appear and be heard at such hearing and shall provide to the court information to assist the court in its consideration of the facts, circumstances, and conditions of the proposed sale or lease of personally identifiable information under section 363(b)(1)(B). Such information may include presentation of –

(1) the debtor's privacy policy;

(2) the potential losses or gains of privacy to consumers if such sale or such lease is approved by the court;

(3) the potential costs or benefits to consumers if such sale or such lease is approved by the court; and

(4) the potential alternatives that would mitigate potential privacy losses or potential costs to consumers.

(c) A consumer privacy ombudsman shall not disclose any personally identifiable information obtained by the ombudsman under this title.

333. Appointment of patient care ombudsman

(a)(1) If the debtor in a case under chapter 7, 9, or 11 is a health care business, the court shall order, not later than 30 days after the commencement of the case, the appointment of an ombudsman to monitor the quality of patient care and to represent the interests of the patients of the health care business unless the court finds that the appointment of such ombudsman is not necessary for the protection of patients under the specific facts of the case.

(2)(A) If the court orders the appointment of an ombudsman under paragraph(1), the United States trustee shall appoint 1 disinterested person (other than the United States trustee) to serve as such ombudsman.

(B) If the debtor is a health care business that provides long-term care, then the United States trustee may appoint the State Long-Term Care Ombudsman appointed under the Older Americans Act of 1965 for the State in which the case is pending to serve as the ombudsman required by paragraph (1).

(C) If the United States trustee does not appoint a State Long-Term Care Ombudsman under subparagraph (B), the court shall notify the State Long-Term Care Ombudsman appointed under the Older Americans Act of 1965 for the State in which the case is pending, of the name and address of the person who is appointed under subparagraph (A).

(b) An ombudsman appointed under subsection (a) shall –

(1) monitor the quality of patient care provided to patients of the debtor, to the extent necessary under the circumstances, including interviewing patients and physicians;

(2) not later than 60 days after the date of appointment, and not less frequently than at 60-day intervals thereafter, report to the court after notice to the parties in interest, at a hearing or in writing, regarding the quality of patient care provided to patients of the debtor; and

(3) if such ombudsman determines that the quality of patient care provided to patients of the debtor is declining significantly or is otherwise being materially compromised, file with the court a motion or a written report, with notice to the parties in interest immediately upon making such determination.

(c)(1) An ombudsman appointed under subsection (a) shall maintain any information obtained by such ombudsman under this section that relates to patients (including information relating to patient records) as confidential information. Such ombudsman may not review confidential patient records unless the court approves such review in advance and imposes restrictions on such ombudsman to protect the confidentiality of such records.

(2) An ombudsman appointed under subsection (a)(2)(B) shall have access to patient records consistent with authority of such ombudsman under the Older Americans Act of 1965 and under non-Federal laws governing the State Long-Term Care Ombudsman program.

SUBCHAPTER III - ADMINISTRATION

341. Meetings of creditors and equity security holders

(a) Within a reasonable time after the order for relief in a case under this title, the United States trustee shall convene and preside at a meeting of creditors.

(b) The United States trustee may convene a meeting of any equity security holders.

(c) The court may not preside at, and may not attend, any meeting under this section including any final meeting of creditors. Notwithstanding any local court rule, provision of a State constitution, any otherwise applicable nonbankruptcy law, or any other requirement that representation at the meeting of creditors under subsection (a) be by an attorney, a creditor holding a consumer debt or any representative of the creditor (which may include an entity or an employee of an entity and may be a representative for more than 1 creditor) shall be permitted to appear at and participate in the meeting of creditors in a case under chapter 7 or 13, either alone or in conjunction with an attorney for the creditor. Nothing in this subsection shall be construed to require any creditor to be represented by an attorney at any meeting of creditors.

(d) Prior to the conclusion of the meeting of creditors or equity security holders, the trustee shall orally examine the debtor to ensure that the debtor in a case under chapter 7 of this title is aware of –

(1) the potential consequences of seeking a discharge in bankruptcy, including the effects on credit history;

(2) the debtor's ability to file a petition under a different chapter of this title;

(3) the effect of receiving a discharge of debts under this title; and

(4) the effect of reaffirming a debt, including the debtor's knowledge of the provisions of section 524(d) of this title.

(e) Notwithstanding subsections (a) and (b), the court, on the request of a party in interest and after notice and a hearing, for cause may order that the United States trustee not convene a meeting of creditors or equity security holders if the debtor has filed a plan as to which the debtor solicited acceptances prior to the commencement of the case.

342. Notice

(a) There shall be given such notice as is appropriate, including notice to any holder of a community claim, of an order for relief in a case under this title.

(b) Before the commencement of a case under this title by an individual whose debts are primarily consumer debts, the clerk shall give to such individual written notice containing –

(1) a brief description of –

(A) chapters 7, 11, 12, and 13 and the general purpose, benefits, and costs of proceeding under each of those chapters; and

(B) the types of services available from credit counseling agencies; and

(2) statements specifying that –

(A) a person who knowingly and fraudulently conceals assets or makes a false oath or statement under penalty of perjury in connection with a case under this title shall be subject to fine, imprisonment, or both; and

(B) all information supplied by a debtor in connection with a case under this title is subject to examination by the Attorney General.

(c)(1) If notice is required to be given by the debtor to a creditor under this title, any rule, any applicable law, or any order of the court, such notice shall contain the name, address, and last 4 digits of the taxpayer identification number of the debtor. If the notice concerns an amendment that adds a creditor to the schedules of assets and liabilities, the debtor shall include the full taxpayer identification number in the notice sent to that creditor, but the debtor shall include only the last 4 digits of the taxpayer identification number in the copy of the notice filed with the court.

(2)(A) If, within the 90 days before the commencement of a voluntary case, a creditor supplies the debtor in at least 2 communications sent to the debtor with the current account number of the debtor and the address at which such creditor requests to receive correspondence, then any notice required by this title to be sent by the debtor to such creditor shall be sent to such address and shall include such account number.

(B) If a creditor would be in violation of applicable nonbankruptcy law by sending any such communication within such 90-day period and if such creditor supplies the debtor in the last 2 communications with the current account number of the debtor and the address at which such creditor requests to receive correspondence, then any notice required by this title to be sent by the debtor to such creditor shall be sent to such address and shall include such account number.

(d) In a case under chapter 7 of this title in which the debtor is an individual and in which the presumption of abuse arises under section 707(b), the clerk shall give written notice to all creditors not later than 10 days after the date of the filing of the petition that the presumption of abuse has arisen.

(e)(1) In a case under chapter 7 or 13 of this title of a debtor who is an individual, a creditor at any time may both file with the court and serve on the debtor a notice of address to be used to provide notice in such case to such creditor.

(2) Any notice in such case required to be provided to such creditor by the debtor or the court later than 7 days after the court and the debtor receive such creditor's notice of address, shall be provided to such address.

(f)(1) An entity may file with any bankruptcy court a notice of address to be used by all the bankruptcy courts or by particular bankruptcy courts, as so specified by such entity at the time such notice is filed, to provide notice to such entity in all cases under chapters 7 and 13 pending in the courts with respect to which such notice is filed, in which such entity is a creditor.

(2) In any case filed under chapter 7 or 13, any notice required to be provided by a court with respect to which a notice is filed under paragraph (1), to such entity later than 30 days after the filing of such notice under paragraph (1) shall be provided to such address unless with respect to a particular case a different address is specified in a notice filed and served in accordance with subsection (e).

(3) A notice filed under paragraph (1) may be withdrawn by such entity.

(g)(1) Notice provided to a creditor by the debtor or the court other than in accordance with this section (excluding this subsection) shall not be effective notice until such notice is brought to the attention of such creditor. If such creditor designates a person or an organizational subdivision of such creditor to be responsible for receiving notices under this title and establishes reasonable procedures so that such notices receivable by such creditor are to be delivered to such person or such subdivision, then a notice provided to such creditor other than in accordance with this section (excluding this subsection) shall not be considered to have been brought to the attention of such creditor until such notice is received by such person or such subdivision.

(2) A monetary penalty may not be imposed on a creditor for a violation of a stay in effect under section 362(a) (including a monetary penalty imposed under section 362(k)) or for failure to comply with section 542 or 543 unless the conduct that is the basis of such violation or of such failure occurs after such creditor receives notice effective under this section of the order for relief.

343. Examination of the debtor

The debtor shall appear and submit to examination under oath at the meeting of creditors under section 341(a) of this title. Creditors, any indenture trustee, any trustee or examiner in the case, or the United States trustee may examine the debtor. The United States trustee may administer the oath required under this section.

344. Self-incrimination; immunity

Immunity for persons required to submit to examination, to testify, or to provide information in a case under this title may be granted under part V of title 18.

345. Money of estates

(a) A trustee in a case under this title may make such deposit or investment of the money of the estate for which such trustee serves as will yield the maximum reasonable net return on such money, taking into account the safety of such deposit or investment.

(b) Except with respect to a deposit or investment that is insured or guaranteed by the United States or by a department, agency, or instrumentality of the United States or backed by the full faith and credit of the United States, the trustee shall require from an entity with which such money is deposited or invested -

(1) a bond-

(A) in favor of the United States;

(B) secured by the undertaking of a corporate surety approved by the United States trustee for the district in which the case is pending; and

(C) conditioned on -

(i) a proper accounting for all money so deposited or invested and for any return on such money;

(ii) prompt repayment of such money and return; and

(iii) faithful performance of duties as a depository; or

(2) the deposit of securities of the kind specified in section 9303 of title 31; unless the court for cause orders otherwise.

(c) An entity with which such moneys are deposited or invested is authorized to deposit or invest such moneys as may be required under this section.

346. Special provisions related to the treatment of State and local taxes

(a) Whenever the Internal Revenue Code of 1986 provides that a separate taxable estate or entity is created in a case concerning a debtor under this title, and the income, gain, loss, deductions, and credits of such estate shall be taxed to or claimed by the estate, a separate taxable estate is also created for purposes of any State and local law imposing a tax on or measured by income and such income, gain, loss, deductions, and credits shall be taxed to or claimed by the estate and may not be taxed to or claimed by the debtor. The preceding sentence shall not apply if the case is dismissed. The trustee shall make tax returns of income required under any such State or local law.

(b) Whenever the Internal Revenue Code of 1986 provides that no separate taxable estate shall be created in a case concerning a debtor under this title, and the income, gain, loss, deductions, and credits of an estate shall be taxed to or claimed by the debtor, such income, gain, loss, deductions, and credits shall be taxed to or claimed by the debtor under a State or local law imposing a tax on or measured by income and may not be taxed to or claimed by the estate. The trustee shall make such tax returns of income of corporations and of partnerships as are required under any State or local law, but with respect to partnerships, shall make such returns only to the extent such returns are also required to be made under such Code. The estate shall be liable for any tax imposed on such corporation or partnership, but not for any tax imposed on partners or members.(c) With respect to a partnership or any entity treated as a partnership under a State or local law imposing a tax on or measured by income that is a debtor in a case under this title, any gain or loss resulting from a distribution of property from such partnership, or any distributive share of any income, gain, loss, deduction, or credit of a partner or member that is distributed, or considered distributed, from such partnership, after the commencement of the case, is gain, loss, income, deduction, or credit, as the case may be, of the partner or member, and if such partner or member is a debtor in a case under this title, shall be subject to tax in accordance with subsection (a) or (b).

(d) For purposes of any State or local law imposing a tax on or measured by income, the taxable period of a debtor in a case under this title shall terminate only if and to the extent that the taxable period of such debtor terminates under the Internal Revenue Code of 1986.

(e) The estate in any case described in subsection (a) shall use the same accounting method as the debtor used immediately before the commencement of the case, if such method of accounting complies with applicable nonbankruptcy tax law.

(f) For purposes of any State or local law imposing a tax on or measured by income, a transfer of property from the debtor to the estate or from the estate to the debtor shall not be treated as a disposition for purposes of any provision assigning tax consequences to a disposition, except to the extent that such transfer is treated as a disposition under the Internal Revenue Code of 1986.

(g) Whenever a tax is imposed pursuant to a State or local law imposing a tax on or measured by income pursuant to subsection (a) or (b), such tax shall be imposed at rates generally applicable to the same types of entities under such State or local law.

(h) The trustee shall withhold from any payment of claims for wages, salaries, commissions, dividends, interest, or other payments, or collect, any amount required to be withheld or collected under applicable State or local tax law, and shall pay such withheld or collected amount to the appropriate governmental unit at the time and in the manner required by such tax law, and with the same priority as the claim from which such amount was withheld or collected was paid.

(i)(1) To the extent that any State or local law imposing a tax on or measured by income provides for the carryover of any tax attribute from one taxable period to a subsequent taxable period, the estate shall succeed to such tax attribute in any case in which such estate is subject to tax under subsection (a).

(2) After such a case is closed or dismissed, the debtor shall succeed to any tax attribute to which the estate succeeded under paragraph (1) to the extent consistent with the Internal Revenue Code of 1986.

(3) The estate may carry back any loss or tax attribute to a taxable period of the debtor that ended before the date of the order for relief under this title to the extent that –

(A) applicable State or local tax law provides for a carryback in the case of the debtor; and

(B) the same or a similar tax attribute may be carried back by the estate to such a taxable period of the debtor under the Internal Revenue Code of 1986.

(j)(1) For purposes of any State or local law imposing a tax on or measured by income, income is not realized by the estate, the debtor, or a successor to the debtor by reason of discharge of indebtedness in a case under this title, except to the extent, if any, that such income is subject to tax under the Internal Revenue Code of 1986.

(2) Whenever the Internal Revenue Code of 1986 provides that the amount excluded from gross income in respect of the discharge of indebtedness in a case under this title shall be applied to reduce the tax attributes of the debtor or the estate, a similar reduction shall be made under any State or local law imposing a tax on or measured by income to the extent such State or local law recognizes such attributes. Such State or local law may also provide for the reduction of other attributes to the extent that the full amount of income from the discharge of indebtedness has not been applied.

(k)(1) Except as provided in this section and section 505, the time and manner of filing tax returns and the items of income, gain, loss, deduction, and credit of any taxpayer shall be determined under applicable nonbankruptcy law.

(2) For Federal tax purposes, the provisions of this section are subject to the Internal Revenue Code of 1986 and other applicable Federal nonbankruptcy law.

347. Unclaimed property

(a) Ninety days after the final distribution under section 726, 1194, 1226, or 1326 of this title in a case under chapter 7, subchapter V of chapter 11, 12, or 13 of this title, as the case may be, the trustee shall stop payment on any check remaining unpaid, and any remaining property of the estate shall be paid into the court and disposed of under chapter 129 of title 28.

(b) Any security, money, or other property remaining unclaimed at the expiration of the time allowed in a case under chapter 9, 11, or 12 of this title for the presentation of a security or the performance of any other act as a condition to participation in the distribution under any plan confirmed under section 943(b), 1129, 1173, 1194, or 1225 of this title, as the case may be, becomes the property of the debtor or of the entity acquiring the assets of the debtor under the plan, as the case may be.

348. Effect of conversion

(a) Conversion of a case from a case under one chapter of this title to a case under another chapter of this title constitutes an order for relief under the chapter to which the case is converted, but, except as provided in subsections (b) and (c) of this section, does not effect a change in the date of the filing of the petition, the commencement of the case, or the order for relief.

(b) Unless the court for cause orders otherwise, in sections 701(a), 727(a)(10), 727(b), 1102(a), 1110(a)(1), 1121(b), 1121(c), 1141(d)(4), 1201(a), 1221, 1228(a), 1301(a), and 1305(a) of this title, "the order for relief under this chapter" in a chapter to which a case has been converted under section 706, 1112, 1208, or 1307 of this title means the conversion of such case to such chapter.

(c) Sections 342 and 365(d) of this title apply in a case that has been converted under section 706, 1112, 1208, or 1307 of this title, as if the conversion order were the order for relief.

(d) A claim against the estate or the debtor that arises after the order for relief but before conversion in a case that is converted under section 1112, 1208, or 1307 of this title, other than a claim specified in section 503(b) of this title, shall be treated for all purposes as if such claim had arisen immediately before the date of the filing of the petition.

(e) Conversion of a case under section 706, 1112, 1208, or 1307 of this title terminates the service of any trustee or examiner that is serving in the case before such conversion.

(f)(1) Except as provided in paragraph (2), when a case under chapter 13 of this title is converted to a case under another chapter under this title -

(A) property of the estate in the converted case shall consist of property of the estate, as of the date of filing of the petition, that remains in the possession of or is under the control of the debtor on the date of conversion;

(B) valuations of property and of allowed secured claims in the chapter 13 case shall apply only in a case converted to a case under chapter 11 or 12, but not in a case converted to a case under chapter 7, with allowed secured claims in cases under chapters 11 and 12 reduced to the extent that they have been paid in accordance with the chapter 13 plan; and

(C) with respect to cases converted from chapter 13 –

(i) the claim of any creditor holding security as of the date of the filing of the petition shall continue to be secured by that security unless the full amount of such claim determined under applicable nonbankruptcy law has been paid in full as of the date of conversion, notwithstanding any valuation or determination of the amount of an allowed secured claim made for the purposes of the case under chapter 13; and

(ii) unless a prebankruptcy default has been fully cured under the plan at the time of conversion, in any proceeding under this title or otherwise, the default shall have the effect given under applicable nonbankruptcy law.

(2) If the debtor converts a case under chapter 13 of this title to a case under another chapter under this title in bad faith, the property of the estate in the converted case shall consist of the property of the estate as of the date of conversion.

349. Effect of dismissal

(a) Unless the court, for cause, orders otherwise, the dismissal of a case under this title does not bar the discharge, in a later case under this title, of debts that were dischargeable in the case dismissed; nor does the dismissal of a case under this title prejudice the debtor with regard to the filing of a subsequent petition under this title, except as provided in section 109(g) of this title.

(b) Unless the court, for cause, orders otherwise, a dismissal of a case other than under section 742 of this title -

(1) reinstates -

(A) any proceeding or custodianship superseded under section 543 of this title;

(B) any transfer avoided under section 522, 544, 545, 547, 548, 549, or 724(a) of this title, or preserved under section 510(c)(2), 522(i)(2), or 551 of this title; and

(C) any lien voided under section 506(d) of this title;

(2) vacates any order, judgment, or transfer ordered, under section 522(i)(1), 542, 550, or 553 of this title; and

(3) revests the property of the estate in the entity in which such property was vested immediately before the commencement of the case under this title.

350. Closing and reopening cases

(a) After an estate is fully administered and the court has discharged the trustee, the court shall close the case.

(b) A case may be reopened in the court in which such case was closed to administer assets, to accord relief to the debtor, or for other cause.

351. Disposal of patient records

If a health care business commences a case under chapter 7, 9, or 11, and the trustee does not have a sufficient amount of funds to pay for the storage of patient records in the manner required under applicable Federal or State law, the following requirements shall apply:

(1) The trustee shall –

(A) promptly publish notice, in 1 or more appropriate newspapers, that if patient records are not claimed by the patient or an insurance provider (if applicable law permits the insurance provider to make that claim) by the date that is 365 days after the date of that notification, the trustee will destroy the patient records; and

(B) during the first 180 days of the 365-day period described in subparagraph (A), promptly attempt to notify directly each patient that is the subject of the patient records and appropriate insurance carrier concerning the patient records by mailing to the most recent known address of that patient, or a family member or contact person for that patient, and to the appropriate insurance carrier an appropriate notice regarding the claiming or disposing of patient records.

(2) If, after providing the notification under paragraph (1), patient records are not claimed during the 365-day period described under that paragraph, the trustee shall mail, by certified mail, at the end of such 365-day period a written request to each appropriate Federal agency to request permission from that agency to deposit the patient records with that agency,

except that no Federal agency is required to accept patient records under this paragraph.

(3) If, following the 365-day period described in paragraph (2) and after providing the notification under paragraph (1), patient records are not claimed by a patient or insurance provider, or request is not granted by a Federal agency to deposit such records with that agency, the trustee shall destroy those records by –

(A) if the records are written, shredding or burning the records; or

(B) if the records are magnetic, optical, or other electronic records, by otherwise destroying those records so that those records cannot be retrieved.

SUBCHAPTER IV - ADMINISTRATIVE POWERS

361. Adequate protection

When adequate protection is required under section 362, 363, or 364 of this title of an interest of an entity in property, such adequate protection may be provided by -

(1) requiring the trustee to make a cash payment or periodic cash payments to such entity, to the extent that the stay under section 362 of this title, use, sale, or lease under section 363 of this title, or any grant of a lien under section 364 of this title results in a decrease in the value of such entity's interest in such property;

(2) providing to such entity an additional or replacement lien to the extent that such stay, use, sale, lease, or grant results in a decrease in the value of such entity's interest in such property; or

(3) granting such other relief, other than entitling such entity to compensation allowable under section 503(b)(1) of this title as an administrative expense, as will result in the realization by such entity of the indubitable equivalent of such entity's interest in such property.

362. Automatic stay

(a) Except as provided in subsection (b) of this section, a petition filed under section 301, 302, or 303 of this title, or an application filed under section 5(a)(3) of the Securities Investor Protection Act of 1970, operates as a stay, applicable to all entities, of -

(1) the commencement or continuation, including the issuance or employment of process, of a judicial, administrative, or other action or proceeding against the debtor that was or could have been commenced before the commencement of the case under this title, or to recover a claim against the debtor that arose before the commencement of the case under this title;

(2) the enforcement, against the debtor or against property of the estate, of a judgment obtained before the commencement of the case under this title;

(3) any act to obtain possession of property of the estate or of property from the estate or to exercise control over property of the estate;

(4) any act to create, perfect, or enforce any lien against property of the estate;

(5) any act to create, perfect, or enforce against property of the debtor any lien to the extent that such lien secures a claim that arose before the commencement of the case under this title;

(6) any act to collect, assess, or recover a claim against the debtor that arose before the commencement of the case under this title;

(7) the setoff of any debt owing to the debtor that arose before the commencement of the case under this title against any claim against the debtor; and

(8) the commencement or continuation of a proceeding before the United States Tax Court concerning a tax liability of a debtor that is a corporation for a taxable period the bankruptcy court may determine or concerning the tax liability of a debtor who is an individual for a taxable period ending before the date of the order for relief under this title.

(b) The filing of a petition under section 301, 302, or 303 of this title, or of an application under section 5(a)(3) of the Securities Investor Protection Act of 1970, does not operate as a stay -

(1) under subsection (a) of this section, of the commencement or continuation of a criminal action or proceeding against the debtor;

(2) under subsection (a) –

(A) of the commencement or continuation of a civil action or proceeding –

(i) for the establishment of paternity;

(ii) for the establishment or modification of an order for domestic support obligations;

(iii) concerning child custody or visitation;

(iv) for the dissolution of a marriage, except to the extent that such proceeding seeks to determine the division of property that is property of the estate; or

(v) regarding domestic violence;

(B) of the collection of a domestic support obligation from property that is not property of the estate;

(C) with respect to the withholding of income that is property of the estate or property of the debtor for payment of a domestic support obligation under a judicial or administrative order or a statute;

(D) of the withholding, suspension, or restriction of a driver's license, a professional or occupational license, or a recreational license, under State law, as specified in section 466(a)(16) of the Social Security Act;

(E) of the reporting of overdue support owed by a parent to any consumer reporting agency as specified in section 466(a)(7) of the Social Security Act;

(F) of the interception of a tax refund, as specified in sections 464 and 466(a)(3) of the Social Security Act or under an analogous State law; or

(G) of the enforcement of a medical obligation, as specified under title IV of the Social Security Act;

(3) under subsection (a) of this section, of any act to perfect, or to maintain or continue the perfection of, an interest in property to the extent that the trustee's rights and powers are subject to such perfection under section 546(b) of this title or to the extent that such act is accomplished within the period provided under section 547(e)(2)(A) of this title;

(4) under paragraph (1), (2), (3), or (6) of subsection (a) of this section, of the commencement or continuation of an action or proceeding by a governmental unit or any organization exercising authority under the Convention on the Prohibition of the Development, Production, Stockpiling and Use of Chemical Weapons and on Their Destruction, opened for signature on January 13, 1993, to enforce such governmental unit's or organization's police and regulatory power, including the enforcement of a judgment other than a money judgment, obtained in an action or proceeding by the governmental unit to enforce such governmental unit's or organization's police or regulatory power;

(5) [Repealed Oct. 21, 1998; 112 Stat. 2681-886].

(6) under subsection (a) of this section, of the exercise by a commodity broker, forward contract merchant, stockbroker, financial institution, financial participant, or securities clearing agency of any contractual right (as defined in section 555 or 556) under any security agreement or arrangement or other credit enhancement forming a part of or related to any commodity contract, forward contract or securities contract, or of any contractual right (as defined in section 555 or 556) to offset or net out any termination value, payment amount, or other transfer obligation arising under or in connection with 1 or more such contracts, including any master agreement for such contracts;

(7) under subsection (a) of this section, of the exercise by a repo participant or financial participant of any contractual right (as defined in section 559) under any security agreement or arrangement or other credit enhancement forming a part of or related to any repurchase agreement, or of any contractual right (as defined in section 559) to offset or net out any termination value, payment amount, or other transfer obligation arising under or in connection with 1 or more such agreements, including any master agreement for such agreements;

(8) under subsection (a) of this section, of the commencement of any action by the Secretary of Housing and Urban Development to foreclose a mortgage or deed of trust in any case in which the mortgage or deed of trust held by the Secretary is insured or was formerly insured under the National Housing Act and covers property, or combinations of property, consisting of five or more living units;

(9) under subsection (a), of -

(A) an audit by a governmental unit to determine tax liability;

(B) the issuance to the debtor by a governmental unit of a notice of tax deficiency;

(C) a demand for tax returns; or

(D) the making of an assessment for any tax and issuance of a notice and demand for payment of such an assessment (but any tax lien that would otherwise attach to property of the estate by reason of such an assessment shall not take effect unless such tax is a debt of the debtor that will not be discharged in the case and such property or its proceeds are transferred out of the estate to, or otherwise revested in, the debtor).

(10) under subsection (a) of this section, of any act by a lessor to the debtor under a lease of nonresidential real property that has terminated by the expiration of the stated term of the lease before the commencement of or during a case under this title to obtain possession of such property;

(11) under subsection (a) of this section, of the presentment of a negotiable instrument and the giving of notice of and protesting dishonor of such an instrument;

(12) under subsection (a) of this section, after the date which is 90 days after the filing of such petition, of the commencement or continuation, and conclusion to the entry of final judgment, of an action which involves a debtor subject to reorganization pursuant to chapter 11 of this title and which was brought by the Secretary of Transportation under section 31325 of title 46 (including distribution of any proceeds of sale) to foreclose a preferred ship or fleet mortgage, or a security interest in or relating to a vessel or vessel under construction, held by the Secretary of Transportation under chapter 537 of title 46 or section 109(h) of title 49, or under applicable State law;

(13) under subsection (a) of this section, after the date which is 90 days after the filing of such petition, of the commencement or continuation, and conclusion to the entry of final judgment, of an action which involves a debtor subject to reorganization pursuant to chapter 11 of this title and which was brought by the Secretary of Commerce under section 31325 of title 46 (including distribution of any proceeds of sale) to foreclose a preferred ship or fleet mortgage in a vessel or a mortgage, deed of trust, or other security interest in a fishing facility held by the Secretary of Commerce under chapter 537 of title 46;

(14) under subsection (a) of this section, of any action by an accrediting agency regarding the accreditation status of the debtor as an educational institution;

(15) under subsection (a) of this section, of any action by a State licensing body regarding the licensure of the debtor as an educational institution;

(16) under subsection (a) of this section, of any action by a guaranty agency, as defined in section 435(j) of the Higher Education Act of 1965 or the Secretary of Education regarding the eligibility of the debtor to participate in programs authorized under such Act;

(17) under subsection (a) of this section, of the exercise by a swap participant or financial participant of any contractual right (as defined in section 560) under any security agreement or arrangement or other credit enhancement forming a part of or related to any swap agreement, or of any contractual right (as defined in section 560) to offset or net out any termination value, payment amount, or other transfer obligation arising under or in connection with 1 or more such agreements, including any master agreement for such agreements;

(18) under subsection (a) of the creation or perfection of a statutory lien for an ad valorem property tax, or a special tax or special assessment on real property whether or not ad valorem, imposed by a governmental unit, if such tax or assessment comes due after the date of the filing of the petition;

(19) under subsection (a), of withholding of income from a debtor's wages and collection of amounts withheld, under the debtor's agreement authorizing that withholding and collection for the benefit of a pension, profit-sharing, stock bonus, or other plan established under section 401, 403, 408, 408A, 414, 457, or 501(c) of the Internal Revenue Code of 1986, that is sponsored by the employer of the debtor, or an affiliate, successor, or predecessor of such employer –

(A) to the extent that the amounts withheld and collected are used solely for payments relating to a loan from a plan under section 408(b)(1) of the Employee Retirement Income Security Act of 1974 or is subject to section 72(p) of the Internal Revenue Code of 1986; or

(B) a loan from a thrift savings plan permitted under subchapter III of chapter 84 of title 5, that satisfies the requirements of section 8433(g) of such title;

but nothing in this paragraph may be construed to provide that any loan made under a governmental plan under section 414(d), or a contract or account under section 403(b), of the Internal Revenue Code of 1986 constitutes a claim or a debt under this title;

(20) under subsection (a), of any act to enforce any lien against or security interest in real property following entry of the order under subsection (d)(4) as to such real property in any prior case under this title, for a period of 2 years after the date of the entry of such an order, except that the debtor, in a subsequent case under this title, may move for relief from such order based upon changed circumstances or for other good cause shown, after notice and a hearing;

(21) under subsection (a), of any act to enforce any lien against or security interest in real property –

(A) if the debtor is ineligible under section 109(g) to be a debtor in a case under this title; or

(B) if the case under this title was filed in violation of a bankruptcy court order in a prior case under this title prohibiting the debtor from being a debtor in another case under this title;

(22) subject to subsection (l), under subsection (a)(3), of the continuation of any eviction, unlawful detainer action, or similar proceeding by a lessor against a debtor involving residential property in which the debtor resides as a tenant under a lease or rental agreement and with respect to which the lessor has obtained before the date of the filing of the bankruptcy petition, a judgment for possession of such property against the debtor;

(23) subject to subsection (m), under subsection (a)(3), of an eviction action that seeks possession of the residential property in which the debtor resides as a tenant under a lease or rental agreement based on endangerment of such property or the illegal use of controlled substances on such property, but only if the lessor files with the court, and serves upon the debtor, a certification under penalty of perjury that such an eviction action has been filed, or that the debtor, during the 30-day period preceding the date of the filing of the certification, has endangered property or illegally used or allowed to be used a controlled substance on the property;

(24) under subsection (a), of any transfer that is not avoidable under section 544 and that is not avoidable under section 549;

(25) under subsection (a), of –

(A) the commencement or continuation of an investigation or action by a securities self regulatory organization to enforce such organization's regulatory power;

(B) the enforcement of an order or decision, other than for monetary sanctions, obtained in an action by such securities self regulatory organization to enforce such organization's regulatory power; or

(C) any act taken by such securities self regulatory organization to delist, delete, or refuse to permit quotation of any stock that does not meet applicable regulatory requirements;

(26) under subsection (a), of the setoff under applicable nonbankruptcy law of an income tax refund, by a governmental unit, with respect to a taxable period that ended before the date of the order for relief against an income tax liability for a taxable period that also ended before the date of the order for relief, except that in any case in which the setoff of an income tax refund is not permitted under applicable nonbankruptcy law because of a pending action to determine the amount or legality of a tax liability, the governmental unit may hold the refund pending the resolution of the action, unless the court, on the motion of the trustee and after notice and a hearing, grants the taxing authority adequate protection (within the meaning of section 361) for the secured claim of such authority in the setoff under section 506(a);

(27) under subsection (a) of this section, of the exercise by a master netting agreement participant of any contractual right (as defined in section 555, 556, 559, or 560) under any security agreement or arrangement or other credit enhancement forming a part of or related to any master netting agreement, or of any contractual right (as defined in section 555, 556, 559, or 560) to offset or net out any termination value, payment amount, or other transfer obligation arising under or in connection with 1 or more such master netting agreements to the extent that such participant is eligible to exercise such rights under paragraph (6), (7), or (17) for each individual contract covered by the master netting agreement in issue; and

(28) under subsection (a), of the exclusion by the Secretary of Health and Human Services of the debtor from participation in the medicare program or any other Federal health care program (as defined in section 1128B(f) of the Social Security Act pursuant to title XI or XVIII of such Act); and

(29) under subsection (a)(1) of this section, of any action by--

(A) an amateur sports organization, as defined in section 220501(b) of title 36, to replace a national governing body, as defined in that section, under section 220528 of that title; or

(B) the corporation, as defined in section 220501(b) of title 36, to revoke the certification of a national governing body, as defined in that section, under section 220521 of that title.

The provisions of paragraphs (12) and (13) of this subsection shall apply with respect to any such petition filed on or before December 31, 1989.

(c) Except as provided in subsections (d), (e), (f), and (h) of this section -

(1) the stay of an act against property of the estate under subsection (a) of this section continues until such property is no longer property of the estate;

(2) the stay of any other act under subsection (a) of this section

continues until the earliest of -

(A) the time the case is closed;

(B) the time the case is dismissed; or

(C) if the case is a case under chapter 7 of this title concerning an individual or a case under chapter 9, 11, 12, or 13 of this title, the time a discharge is granted or denied;

(3) if a single or joint case is filed by or against a debtor who is an individual in a case under chapter 7, 11, or 13, and if a single or joint case of the debtor was pending within the preceding 1-year period but was dismissed, other than a case refiled under a chapter other than chapter 7 after dismissal under section 707(b) –

(A) the stay under subsection (a) with respect to any action taken with respect to a debt or property securing such debt or with respect to any lease shall terminate with respect to the debtor on the 30th day after the filing of the later case;

(B) on the motion of a party in interest for continuation of the automatic stay and upon notice and a hearing, the court may extend the stay in particular cases as to any or all creditors (subject to such conditions or limitations as the court may then impose) after notice and a hearing completed before the expiration of the 30-day period only if the party in interest demonstrates that the filing of the later case is in good faith as to the creditors to be stayed; and

(C) for purposes of subparagraph (B), a case is presumptively filed not in good faith (but such presumption may be rebutted by clear and convincing evidence to the contrary)-

(i) as to all creditors, if –

(I) more than 1 previous case under any of chapters 7, 11, and 13 in which the individual was a debtor was pending within the preceding 1-year period;

(II) a previous case under any of chapters 7, 11, and 13 in which the individual was a debtor was dismissed within such 1-year period, after the debtor failed to –

(aa) file or amend the petition or other documents as required by this title or the court without substantial excuse (but mere inadvertence or negligence shall not be a substantial excuse unless the dismissal was caused by the negligence of the debtor's attorney);

(bb) provide adequate protection as ordered by the court; or

(cc) perform the terms of a plan confirmed by the court, or

(III) there has not been a substantial change in the financial or personal affairs of the debtor since the dismissal of the next most previous case under chapter 7, 11, or 13 or any other reason to conclude that the later case will be concluded –

(aa) if a case under chapter 7, with a discharge; or

(bb) if a case under chapter 11 or 13, with a confirmed plan that will be fully performed; and

(ii) as to any creditor that commenced an action under subsection (d) in a previous case in which the individual was a debtor if, as of the date of dismissal of such case, that action was still pending or had been resolved by terminating, conditioning, or limiting the stay as to actions of such creditor; and

(4)(A)(i) if a single or joint case is filed by or against a debtor who is an individual under this title, and if 2 or more single or joint cases of the debtor were pending within the previous year but were dismissed, other than a case refiled under a chapter other than chapter 7 after dismissal under section 707(b), the stay under subsection (a) shall not go into effect upon the filing of the later case; and

(ii) on request of a party in interest, the court shall promptly enter an order confirming that no stay is in effect;

(B) if, within 30 days after the filing of the later case, a party in interest requests the court may order the stay to take effect in the case as to any or all creditors (subject to such conditions or limitations as the court may impose), after notice and a hearing, only if the party in interest demonstrates that the filing of the later case is in good faith as to the creditors to be stayed;

(C) a stay imposed under subparagraph (B) shall be effective on the date of the entry of the order allowing the stay to go into effect; and

(D) for purposes of subparagraph (B), a case is presumptively filed not in good faith (but such presumption may be rebutted by clear and convincing evidence to the contrary) –

(i) as to all creditors if –

(I) 2 or more previous cases under this title in which the individual was a debtor were pending within the 1-year period;

(II) a previous case under this title in which the individual was a debtor was dismissed within the time period stated in this paragraph after the debtor failed to file or amend the petition or other documents as required by this title or the court without substantial excuse (but mere inadvertence or negligence shall not be substantial excuse unless the dismissal was caused by the negligence of the debtor's attorney), failed to provide adequate protection as ordered by the court, or failed to perform the terms of a plan confirmed by the court; or

(III) there has not been a substantial change in the financial or personal affairs of the debtor since the dismissal of the next most previous case under this title, or any other reason to conclude that the later case will not be concluded, if a case under chapter 7, with a discharge, and if a case under chapter 11 or 13, with a confirmed plan that will be fully performed; or

(ii) as to any creditor that commenced an action under subsection (d) in a previous case in which the individual was a debtor if, as of the date of dismissal of such case, such action was still pending or had been resolved by terminating, conditioning, or limiting the stay as to such action of such creditor.

(d) On request of a party in interest and after notice and a hearing, the court shall grant relief from the stay provided under subsection (a) of this section, such as by terminating, annulling, modifying, or conditioning such stay-

(1) for cause, including the lack of adequate protection of an interest in property of such party in interest;

(2) with respect to a stay of an act against property under subsection (a) of this section, if -

(A) the debtor does not have an equity in such property; and

(B) such property is not necessary to an effective reorganization;

(3) with respect to a stay of an act against single asset real estate under subsection (a), by a creditor whose claim is secured by an interest in such real estate, unless, not later than the date that is 90 days after the entry of the order for relief (or such later date as the court may determine for cause by order entered within that 90-day period) or 30 days after the court determines that the debtor is subject to this paragraph, whichever is later –

(A) the debtor has filed a plan of reorganization that has a reasonable possibility of being confirmed within a reasonable time; or

(B) the debtor has commenced monthly payments that –

(i) may, in the debtor's sole discretion, notwithstanding section 363(c)(2), be made from rents or other income generated before, on, or after the date of the commencement of the case by or from the property to each creditor whose claim is secured by such real estate (other than a claim secured by a judgment lien or by an unmatured statutory lien); and

(ii) are in an amount equal to interest at the then applicable nondefault contract rate of interest on the value of the creditor's interest in the real estate; or

(4) with respect to a stay of an act against real property under subsection (a), by a creditor whose claim is secured by an interest in such real property, if the court finds that the filing of the petition was part of a scheme to delay, hinder, or defraud creditors that involved either –

(A) transfer of all or part ownership of, or other interest in, such real property without the consent of the secured creditor or court approval; or

(B) multiple bankruptcy filings affecting such real property.

If recorded in compliance with applicable State laws governing notices of interests or liens in real property, an order entered under paragraph (4) shall be binding in any other case under this title purporting to affect such real property filed not later than 2 years after the date of the entry of such order by the court, except that a debtor in a subsequent case under this title may move for relief from such order based upon changed circumstances or for good cause shown, after notice and a hearing. Any Federal, State, or local governmental unit that accepts notices of interests or liens in real property shall accept any certified copy of an order described in this subsection for indexing and recording.

(e)(1) Thirty days after a request under subsection (d) of this section for relief from the stay of any act against property of the estate under subsection (a) of this section, such stay is terminated with respect to the party in interest making such request, unless the court, after notice and a hearing, orders such stay continued in effect pending the conclusion of, or as a result of, a final hearing and determination under subsection (d) of this section. A hearing under this subsection may be a preliminary hearing, or may be consolidated with the final hearing under subsection (d) of this section. The court shall order such stay continued in effect pending the conclusion of the final hearing under subsection (d) of this section if there is a reasonable likelihood that the party opposing relief from such stay will prevail at the conclusion of such final hearing. If the hearing under this subsection is a preliminary hearing, then such final hearing shall be concluded not later than thirty days after the conclusion of such preliminary hearing, unless the 30-day period is extended with the consent of the parties in interest or for a specific time which the court finds is required by compelling circumstances.

(2) Notwithstanding paragraph (1), in a case under chapter 7, 11, or 13 in which the debtor is an individual, the stay under subsection (a) shall terminate on the date that is 60 days after a request is made by a party in interest under subsection (d), unless –

(A) a final decision is rendered by the court during the 60-day period beginning on the date of the request; or

(B) such 60-day period is extended –

(i) by agreement of all parties in interest; or

(ii) by the court for such specific period of time as the court finds is required for good cause, as described in findings made by the court.

(f) Upon request of a party in interest, the court, with or without a hearing, shall grant such relief from the stay provided under subsection (a) of this section as is necessary to prevent irreparable damage to the interest of an entity in property, if such interest will suffer such damage before there is an opportunity for notice and a hearing under subsection (d) or (e) of this section.

(g) In any hearing under subsection (d) or (e) of this section concerning relief from the stay of any act under subsection (a) of this section -

(1) the party requesting such relief has the burden of proof on the issue of the debtor's equity in property; and

(2) the party opposing such relief has the burden of proof on all other issues.

(h)(1) In a case in which the debtor is an individual, the stay provided by subsection (a) is terminated with respect to personal property of the estate or of the debtor securing in whole or in part a claim, or subject to an unexpired lease, and such personal property shall no longer be property of the estate if the debtor fails within the applicable time set by section 521(a)(2) –

(A) to file timely any statement of intention required under section 521(a)(2) with respect to such personal property or to indicate in such statement that the debtor will either surrender such personal property or retain it and, if retaining such personal property, either redeem such personal property pursuant to section 722, enter into an agreement of the kind specified in section 524(c) applicable to the debt secured by such personal property, or assume such unexpired lease pursuant to section 365(p) if the trustee does not do so, as applicable; and

(B) to take timely the action specified in such statement, as it may be amended before expiration of the period for taking action, unless such statement specifies the debtor's intention to reaffirm such debt on the original contract terms and the creditor refuses to agree to the reaffirmation on such terms.

(2) Paragraph (1) does not apply if the court determines, on the motion of the trustee filed before the expiration of the applicable time set by section 521(a)(2), after notice and a hearing, that such personal property is of consequential value or benefit to the estate, and orders appropriate adequate protection of the creditor's interest, and orders the debtor to deliver any collateral in the debtor's possession to the trustee. If the court does not so determine, the stay provided by subsection (a) shall terminate upon the conclusion of the hearing on the motion.

(i) If a case commenced under chapter 7, 11, or 13 is dismissed due to the creation of a debt repayment plan, for purposes of subsection (c)(3), any subsequent case commenced by the debtor under any such chapter shall not be presumed to be filed not in good faith.

(j) On request of a party in interest, the court shall issue an order under subsection (c) confirming that the automatic stay has been terminated.

(k)(1) Except as provided in paragraph (2), an individual injured by any willful violation of a stay provided by this section shall recover actual damages, including costs and attorneys' fees, and, in appropriate circumstances, may recover punitive damages.

(2) If such violation is based on an action taken by an entity in the good faith belief that subsection (h) applies to the debtor, the recovery under paragraph (1) of this subsection against such entity shall be limited to actual damages.

(l)(1) Except as otherwise provided in this subsection, subsection (b)(22) shall apply on the date that is 30 days after the date on which the bankruptcy petition is filed, if the debtor files with the petition and serves upon the lessor a certification under penalty of perjury that –

(A) under nonbankruptcy law applicable in the jurisdiction, there are circumstances under which the debtor would be permitted to cure the entire monetary default that gave rise to the judgment for possession, after that judgment for possession was entered; and

(B) the debtor (or an adult dependent of the debtor) has deposited with the clerk of the court, any rent that would become due during the 30-day period after the filing of the bankruptcy petition.

(2) If, within the 30-day period after the filing of the bankruptcy petition, the debtor (or an adult dependent of the debtor) complies with paragraph (1) and files with the court and serves upon the lessor a further certification under penalty of perjury that the debtor (or an adult dependent of the debtor) has cured, under nonbankruptcy law applicable in the jurisdiction, the entire monetary default that gave rise to the judgment under which possession is sought by the lessor, subsection (b)(22) shall not apply, unless ordered to apply by the court under paragraph (3).

(3)(A) If the lessor files an objection to any certification filed by the debtor under paragraph (1) or (2), and serves such objection upon the debtor, the court shall hold a hearing within 10 days after the filing and service of such objection to determine if the certification filed by the debtor under paragraph (1) or (2) is true.

(B) If the court upholds the objection of the lessor filed under subparagraph (A) –

(i) subsection (b)(22) shall apply immediately and relief from the stay provided under subsection (a)(3) shall not be required to enable the lessor to complete the process to recover full possession of the property; and

(ii) the clerk of the court shall immediately serve upon the lessor and the debtor a certified copy of the court's order upholding the lessor's objection.

(4) If a debtor, in accordance with paragraph (5), indicates on the petition that there was a judgment for possession of the residential rental property in which the debtor resides and does not file a certification under paragraph (1) or (2) –

(A) subsection (b)(22) shall apply immediately upon failure to file such certification, and relief from the stay provided under subsection (a)(3) shall not be required to enable the lessor to complete the process to recover full possession of the property; and

(B) the clerk of the court shall immediately serve upon the lessor and the debtor a certified copy of the docket indicating the absence of a filed certification and the applicability of the exception to the stay under subsection (b)(22).

(5)(A) Where a judgment for possession of residential property in which the debtor resides as a tenant under a lease or rental agreement has been obtained by the lessor, the debtor shall so indicate on the bankruptcy petition and shall provide the name and address of the lessor that obtained that pre-petition judgment on the petition and on any certification filed under this subsection.

(B) The form of certification filed with the petition, as specified in this subsection, shall provide for the debtor to certify, and the debtor shall certify –

(i) whether a judgment for possession of residential rental housing in which the debtor resides has been obtained against the debtor before the date of the filing of the petition; and

(ii) whether the debtor is claiming under paragraph (1) that under nonbankruptcy law applicable in the jurisdiction, there are circumstances under which the debtor would be permitted to cure the entire monetary default that gave rise to the judgment for possession, after that judgment of possession was entered, and has made the appropriate deposit with the court.

(C) The standard forms (electronic and otherwise) used in a bankruptcy proceeding shall be amended to reflect the requirements of this subsection.

(D) The clerk of the court shall arrange for the prompt transmittal of the rent deposited in accordance with paragraph (1)(B) to the lessor.

(m)(1) Except as otherwise provided in this subsection, subsection (b)(23) shall apply on the date that is 15 days after the date on which the lessor files and serves a certification described in subsection (b)(23).

(2)(A) If the debtor files with the court an objection to the truth or legal sufficiency of the certification described in subsection (b)(23) and serves such objection upon the lessor, subsection (b)(23) shall not apply, unless ordered to apply by the court under this subsection.

(B) If the debtor files and serves the objection under subparagraph (A), the court shall hold a hearing within 10 days after the filing and service of such objection to determine if the situation giving rise to the lessor's certification under paragraph (1) existed or has been remedied.

(C) If the debtor can demonstrate to the satisfaction of the court that the situation giving rise to the lessor's certification under paragraph (1) did not exist or has been remedied, the stay provided under subsection (a)(3) shall remain in effect until the termination of the stay under this section.

(D) If the debtor cannot demonstrate to the satisfaction of the court that the situation giving rise to the lessor's certification under paragraph (1) did not exist or has been remedied –

(i) relief from the stay provided under subsection (a)(3) shall not be required to enable the lessor to proceed with the eviction; and

(ii) the clerk of the court shall immediately serve upon the lessor and the debtor a certified copy of the court's order upholding the lessor's certification.

(3) If the debtor fails to file, within 15 days, an objection under paragraph (2)(A) –

(A) subsection (b)(23) shall apply immediately upon such failure and relief from the stay provided under subsection (a)(3) shall not be required to enable the lessor to complete the process to recover full possession of the property; and

(B) the clerk of the court shall immediately serve upon the lessor and the debtor a certified copy of the docket indicating such failure.

(n)(1) Except as provided in paragraph (2), subsection (a) does not apply in a case in which the debtor –

(A) is a debtor in a small business case pending at the time the petition is filed;

(B) was a debtor in a small business case that was dismissed for any reason by an order that became final in the 2-year period ending on the date of the order for relief entered with respect to the petition;

(C) was a debtor in a small business case in which a plan was confirmed in the 2-year period ending on the date of the order for relief entered with respect to the petition; or

(D) is an entity that has acquired substantially all of the assets or business of a small business debtor described in subparagraph (A), (B), or (C), unless such entity establishes by a preponderance of the evidence that such entity acquired substantially all of the assets or business of such small business debtor in good faith and not for the purpose of evading this paragraph.

(2) Paragraph (1) does not apply –

(A) to an involuntary case involving no collusion by the debtor with creditors; or

(B) to the filing of a petition if –

(i) the debtor proves by a preponderance of the evidence that the filing of the petition resulted from circumstances beyond the control of the debtor not foreseeable at the time the case then pending was filed; and

(ii) it is more likely than not that the court will confirm a feasible plan, but not a liquidating plan, within a reasonable period of time.

(o) The exercise of rights not subject to the stay arising under subsection (a) pursuant to paragraph (6), (7), (17), or (27) of subsection (b) shall not be stayed by any order of a court or administrative agency in any proceeding under this title.

363. Use, sale, or lease of property

(a) In this section, "cash collateral" means cash, negotiable instruments, documents of title, securities, deposit accounts, or other cash equivalents whenever acquired in which the estate and an entity other than the estate have an interest and includes the proceeds, products, offspring, rents, or profits of property and the fees, charges, accounts or other payments for the use or occupancy of rooms and other public facilities in hotels, motels, or other lodging properties subject to a security interest as provided in section 552(b) of this title, whether existing before or after the commencement of a case under this title.

(b)(1) The trustee, after notice and a hearing, may use, sell, or lease, other than in the ordinary course of business, property of the estate, except that if the debtor in connection with offering a product or a service discloses to an individual a policy prohibiting the transfer of personally identifiable information about individuals to persons that are not affiliated with the debtor and if such policy is in effect on the date of the commencement of the case, then the trustee may not sell or lease personally identifiable information to any person unless –

(A) such sale or such lease is consistent with such policy; or

(B) after appointment of a consumer privacy ombudsman in accordance with section 332, and after notice and a hearing, the court approves such sale or such lease –

(i) giving due consideration to the facts, circumstances, and conditions of such sale or such lease; and

(ii) finding that no showing was made that such sale or such lease would violate applicable nonbankruptcy law.

(2) If notification is required under subsection (a) of section 7A of the Clayton Act in the case of a transaction under this subsection, then -

(A) notwithstanding subsection (a) of such section, the notification required by such subsection to be given by the debtor shall be given by the trustee; and

(B) notwithstanding subsection (b) of such section, the required waiting period shall end on the 15th day after the date of the receipt, by the Federal Trade Commission and the Assistant Attorney General in charge of the Antitrust Division of the Department of Justice, of the notification required under such subsection (a), unless such waiting period is extended-

(i) pursuant to subsection (e)(2) of such section, in the same manner as such subsection (e)(2) applies to a cash tender offer;

(ii) pursuant to subsection (g)(2) of such section; or

(iii) by the court after notice and a hearing.

(c)(1) If the business of the debtor is authorized to be operated under section 721, 1108, 1183, 1184, 1203, 1204, or 1304 of this title and unless the court orders otherwise, the trustee may enter into transactions, including the sale or lease of property of the estate, in the ordinary course of business, without notice or a hearing, and may use property of the estate in the ordinary course of business without notice or a hearing.

(2) The trustee may not use, sell, or lease cash collateral under paragraph (1) of this subsection unless -

(A) each entity that has an interest in such cash collateral consents; or

(B) the court, after notice and a hearing, authorizes such use, sale, or lease in accordance with the provisions of this section.

(3) Any hearing under paragraph (2)(B) of this subsection may be a preliminary hearing or may be consolidated with a hearing under subsection (e) of this section, but shall be scheduled in accordance with the needs of the debtor. If the hearing under paragraph (2)(B) of this subsection is a preliminary hearing, the court may authorize such use, sale, or lease only if there is a reasonable likelihood that the trustee will prevail at the final hearing under subsection (e) of this section. The court shall act promptly on any request for authorization under paragraph (2)(B) of this subsection.

(4) Except as provided in paragraph (2) of this subsection, the trustee shall segregate and account for any cash collateral in the trustee's possession, custody, or control.

(d) The trustee may use, sell, or lease property under subsection (b) or (c) of this section –

(1) in the case of a debtor that is a corporation or trust that is not a moneyed business, commercial corporation, or trust, only in accordance with nonbankruptcy law applicable to the transfer of property by a debtor that is such a corporation or trust; and

(2) only to the extent not inconsistent with any relief granted under subsection (c), (d), (e), or (f) of section 362.

(e) Notwithstanding any other provision of this section, at any time, on request of an entity that has an interest in property used, sold, or leased, or proposed to be used, sold, or leased, by the trustee, the court, with or without a hearing, shall prohibit or condition such use, sale, or lease as is necessary to provide adequate protection of such interest. This subsection also applies to property that is subject to any unexpired lease of personal property (to the exclusion of such property being subject to an order to grant relief from the stay under section 362).

(f) The trustee may sell property under subsection (b) or (c) of this section free and clear of any interest in such property of an entity other than the estate, only if -

(1) applicable nonbankruptcy law permits sale of such property free and clear of such interest;

(2) such entity consents;

(3) such interest is a lien and the price at which such property is to be sold is greater than the aggregate value of all liens on such property;

(4) such interest is in bona fide dispute; or

(5) such entity could be compelled, in a legal or equitable proceeding, to accept a money satisfaction of such interest.

(g) Notwithstanding subsection (f) of this section, the trustee may sell property under subsection (b) or (c) of this section free and clear of any vested or contingent right in the nature of dower or curtesy.

(h) Notwithstanding subsection (f) of this section, the trustee may sell both the estate's interest, under subsection (b) or (c) of this section, and the interest of any co-owner in property in which the debtor had, at the time of the commencement of the case, an undivided interest as a tenant in common, joint tenant, or tenant by the entirety, only if -

(1) partition in kind of such property among the estate and such co-owners is impracticable;

(2) sale of the estate's undivided interest in such property would realize significantly less for the estate than sale of such property free of the interests of such co-owners;

(3) the benefit to the estate of a sale of such property free of the interests of co-owners outweighs the detriment, if any, to such co-owners; and

(4) such property is not used in the production, transmission, or distribution, for sale, of electric energy or of natural or synthetic gas for heat, light, or power.

(i) Before the consummation of a sale of property to which subsection (g) or (h) of this section applies, or of property of the estate that was community property of the debtor and the debtor's spouse immediately before the commencement of the case, the debtor's spouse, or a co-owner of such property, as the case may be, may purchase such property at the price at which such sale is to be consummated.

(j) After a sale of property to which subsection (g) or (h) of this section applies, the trustee shall distribute to the debtor's spouse or the co-owners of such property, as the case may be, and to the estate, the proceeds of such sale, less the costs and expenses, not including any compensation of the trustee, of such sale, according to the interests of such spouse or co-owners, and of the estate.

(k) At a sale under subsection (b) of this section of property that is subject to a lien that secures an allowed claim, unless the court for cause orders otherwise the holder of such claim may bid at such sale, and, if the holder of such claim purchases such property, such holder may offset such claim against the purchase price of such property.

(l) Subject to the provisions of section 365, the trustee may use, sell, or lease property under subsection (b) or (c) of this section, or a plan under chapter 11, 12, or 13 of this title may provide for the use, sale, or lease of property, notwithstanding any provision in a contract, a lease, or applicable law that is conditioned on the insolvency or financial condition of the debtor, on the commencement of a case under this title concerning the debtor, or on the appointment of or the taking possession by a trustee in a case under this title or a custodian, and that effects, or gives an option to effect, a forfeiture, modification, or termination of the debtor's interest in such property.

(m) The reversal or modification on appeal of an authorization under subsection (b) or (c) of this section of a sale or lease of property does not affect the validity of a sale or lease under such authorization to an entity that purchased or leased such property in good faith, whether or not such entity knew of the pendency of the appeal, unless such authorization and such sale or lease were stayed pending appeal.

(n) The trustee may avoid a sale under this section if the sale price was controlled by an agreement among potential bidders at such sale, or may recover from a party to such agreement any amount by which the value of the property sold exceeds the price at which such sale was consummated, and may recover any costs, attorneys' fees, or expenses incurred in avoiding such sale or recovering such amount. In addition to any recovery under the preceding sentence, the court may grant judgment for punitive damages in favor of the estate and against any such party that entered into such an agreement in willful disregard of this subsection.

(o) Notwithstanding subsection (f), if a person purchases any interest in a consumer credit transaction that is subject to the Truth in Lending Act or any interest in a consumer credit contract (as defined in section 433.1 of title 16 of the Code of Federal Regulations (January 1, 2004), as amended from time to time), and if such interest is purchased through a sale under this section, then such person shall remain subject to all claims and defenses that are related to such consumer credit transaction or such consumer credit contract, to the same extent as such person would be subject to such claims and defenses of the consumer had such interest been purchased at a sale not under this section.

(p) In any hearing under this section -

(1) the trustee has the burden of proof on the issue of adequate protection; and

(2) the entity asserting an interest in property has the burden of proof on the issue of the validity, priority, or extent of such interest.

364. Obtaining credit

(a) If the trustee is authorized to operate the business of the debtor under section 721, 1108, 1183, 1184, 1203, 1204, or 1304 of this title, unless the court orders otherwise, the trustee may obtain unsecured credit and incur unsecured debt in the ordinary course of business allowable under section 503(b)(1) of this title as an administrative expense.

(b) The court, after notice and a hearing, may authorize the trustee to obtain unsecured credit or to incur unsecured debt other than under subsection (a) of this section, allowable under section 503(b)(1) of this title as an administrative expense.

(c) If the trustee is unable to obtain unsecured credit allowable under section 503(b)(1) of this title as an administrative expense, the court, after notice and a hearing, may authorize the obtaining of credit or the incurring of debt -

(1) with priority over any or all administrative expenses of the kind specified in section 503(b) or 507(b) of this title;

(2) secured by a lien on property of the estate that is not otherwise subject to a lien; or

(3) secured by a junior lien on property of the estate that is subject to a lien.

(d)(1) The court, after notice and a hearing, may authorize the obtaining of credit or the incurring of debt secured by a senior or equal lien on property of the estate that is subject to a lien only if -

(A) the trustee is unable to obtain such credit otherwise; and(B) there is adequate protection of the interest of the holder of the lien on the property of the estate on which such senior or equal lien is proposed to be granted.

(2) In any hearing under this subsection, the trustee has the burden of proof on the issue of adequate protection.

(e) The reversal or modification on appeal of an authorization under this section to obtain credit or incur debt, or of a grant under this section of a priority or a lien, does not affect the validity of any debt so incurred, or any priority or lien so granted, to an entity that extended such credit in good faith, whether or not such entity knew of the pendency of the appeal, unless such authorization and the incurring of such debt, or the granting of such priority or lien, were stayed pending appeal.

(f) Except with respect to an entity that is an underwriter as defined in section 1145(b) of this title, section 5 of the Securities Act of 1933, the Trust Indenture Act of 1939, and any State or local law requiring registration for offer or sale of a security or registration or licensing of an issuer of, underwriter of, or broker or dealer in, a security does not apply to the offer or sale under this section of a security that is not an equity security.

365. Executory contracts and unexpired leases

(a) Except as provided in sections 765 and 766 of this title and in subsections (b), (c), and (d) of this section, the trustee, subject to the court's approval, may assume or reject any executory contract or unexpired lease of the debtor.

(b)(1) If there has been a default in an executory contract or unexpired lease of the debtor, the trustee may not assume such contract or lease unless, at the time of assumption of such contract or lease, the trustee -

(A) cures, or provides adequate assurance that the trustee will promptly cure, such default other than a default that is a breach of a provision relating to the satisfaction of any provision (other than a penalty rate or penalty provision) relating to a default arising from any failure to perform nonmonetary obligations under an unexpired lease of real property, if it is impossible for the trustee to cure such default by performing nonmonetary acts at and after the time of assumption, except that if such default arises from a failure to operate in accordance with a nonresidential real property lease, then such default shall be cured by performance at and after the time of assumption in accordance with such lease, and pecuniary losses resulting from such default shall be compensated in accordance with the provisions of this paragraph;

(B) compensates, or provides adequate assurance that the trustee will promptly compensate, a party other than the debtor to such contract or lease, for any actual pecuniary loss to such party resulting from such default; and

(C) provides adequate assurance of future performance under such contract or lease.

(2) Paragraph (1) of this subsection does not apply to a default that is a breach of a provision relating to -

(A) the insolvency or financial condition of the debtor at any time before the closing of the case;

(B) the commencement of a case under this title;

(C) the appointment of or taking possession by a trustee in a case under this title or a custodian before such commencement; or

(D) the satisfaction of any penalty rate or penalty provision relating to a default arising from any failure by the debtor to perform nonmonetary obligations under the executory contract or unexpired lease.

(3) For the purposes of paragraph (1) of this subsection and paragraph (2)(B) of subsection (f), adequate assurance of future performance of a lease of real property in a shopping center includes adequate assurance -

(A) of the source of rent and other consideration due under such lease, and in the case of an assignment, that the financial condition and operating performance of the proposed assignee and its guarantors, if any, shall be similar to the financial condition and operating performance of the debtor and its guarantors, if any, as of the time the debtor became the lessee under the lease;

(B) that any percentage rent due under such lease will not decline substantially;

(C) that assumption or assignment of such lease is subject to all the provisions thereof, including (but not limited to) provisions such as a radius, location, use, or exclusivity provision, and will not breach any such provision contained in any other lease, financing agreement, or master agreement relating to such shopping center; and

(D) that assumption or assignment of such lease will not disrupt any tenant mix or balance in such shopping center.

(4) Notwithstanding any other provision of this section, if there has been a default in an unexpired lease of the debtor, other than a default of a kind specified in paragraph (2) of this subsection, the trustee may not require a lessor to provide services or supplies incidental to such lease before assumption of such lease unless the lessor is compensated under the terms of such lease for any services and supplies provided under such lease before assumption of such lease.

(c) The trustee may not assume or assign any executory contract or unexpired lease of the debtor, whether or not such contract or lease prohibits or restricts assignment of rights or delegation of duties, if -

(1)(A) applicable law excuses a party, other than the debtor, to such contract or lease from accepting performance from or rendering performance to an entity other than the debtor or the debtor in possession whether or not such contract or lease prohibits or restricts assignment of rights or delegation of duties; and

(B) such party does not consent to such assumption or assignment; or

(2) such contract is a contract to make a loan, or extend other debt financing or financial accommodations, to or for the benefit of the debtor, or to issue a security of the debtor; or

(3) such lease is of nonresidential real property and has been terminated under applicable nonbankruptcy law prior to the order for relief.

(4) [Repealed April 20, 2005; 119 Stat. 100].

(d)(1) In a case under chapter 7 of this title, if the trustee does not assume or reject an executory contract or unexpired lease of residential real property or of personal property of the debtor within 60 days after the order for relief, or within such additional time as the court, for cause, within such 60-day period, fixes, then such contract or lease is deemed rejected.

(2) In a case under chapter 9, 11, 12, or 13 of this title, the trustee may assume or reject an executory contract or unexpired lease of residential real property or of personal property of the debtor at any time before the confirmation of a plan but the court, on the request of any party to such contract or lease, may order the trustee to determine within a specified period of time whether to assume or reject such contract or lease.

(3)(A) The trustee shall timely perform all the obligations of the debtor, except those specified in section 365(b)(2), arising from and after the order for relief under any unexpired lease of nonresidential real property, until such lease is assumed or rejected, notwithstanding section 503(b)(1) of this title. The court may extend, for cause, the time for performance of any such obligation that arises within 60 days after the date of the order for relief, but the time for performance shall not be extended beyond such 60-day period. This subsection shall not be deemed to affect the trustee's obligations under the provisions of subsection (b) or (f) of this section. Acceptance of any such performance does not constitute waiver or relinquishment of the lessor's rights under such lease or under this title.

(4)(A) Subject to subparagraph (B), an unexpired lease of nonresidential real property under which the debtor is the lessee shall be deemed rejected, and the trustee shall immediately surrender that nonresidential real property to the lessor, if the trustee does not assume or reject the unexpired lease by the earlier of –

(i) the date that is 120 days after the date of the order for relief; or

(ii) the date of the entry of an order confirming a plan.

(B)(i) The court may extend the period determined under subparagraph (A), prior to the expiration of the 120-day period, for 90 days on the motion of the trustee or lessor for cause.

(ii) If the court grants an extension under clause (i), the court may grant a subsequent extension only upon prior written consent of the lessor in each instance.

(5) The trustee shall timely perform all of the obligations of the debtor, except those specified in section 365(b)(2), first arising from or after 60 days after the order for relief in a case under chapter 11 of this title under an unexpired lease of personal property (other than personal property leased to an individual primarily for personal, family, or household purposes), until such lease is assumed or rejected notwithstanding section 503(b)(1) of this title, unless the court, after notice and a hearing and based on the equities of the case, orders otherwise with respect to the obligations or timely performance thereof. This subsection shall not be deemed to affect the trustee's obligations under the provisions of subsection (b) or (f). Acceptance of any such performance does not constitute waiver or relinquishment of the lessor's rights under such lease or under this title.

(6)-(9) [Repealed April 20, 2005; 119 Stat. 100. (10) redesignated to (5)].

(e)(1) Notwithstanding a provision in an executory contract or unexpired lease, or in applicable law, an executory contract or unexpired lease of the debtor may not be terminated or modified, and any right or obligation under such contract or lease may not be terminated or modified, at any time after the commencement of the case solely because of a provision in such contract or lease that is conditioned on -

(A) the insolvency or financial condition of the debtor at any time before the closing of the case;

(B) the commencement of a case under this title; or

(C) the appointment of or taking possession by a trustee in a case under this title or a custodian before such commencement.

(2) Paragraph (1) of this subsection does not apply to an executory contract or unexpired lease of the debtor, whether or not such contract or lease prohibits or restricts assignment of rights or delegation of duties, if -

(A)(i) applicable law excuses a party, other than the debtor, to such contract or lease from accepting performance from or rendering performance to the trustee or to an assignee of such contract or lease, whether or not such contract or lease prohibits or restricts assignment of rights or delegation of duties; and

(ii) such party does not consent to such assumption or assignment; or

(B) such contract is a contract to make a loan, or extend other debt financing or financial accommodations, to or for the benefit of the debtor, or to issue a security of the debtor.

(f)(1) Except as provided in subsections (b) and (c) of this section, notwithstanding a provision in an executory contract or unexpired lease of the debtor, or in applicable law, that prohibits, restricts, or conditions the assignment of such contract or lease, the trustee may assign such contract or lease under paragraph (2) of this subsection.

(2) The trustee may assign an executory contract or unexpired lease of the debtor only if -

(A) the trustee assumes such contract or lease in accordance with the provisions of this section; and

(B) adequate assurance of future performance by the assignee of such contract or lease is provided, whether or not there has been a default in such contract or lease.

(3) Notwithstanding a provision in an executory contract or unexpired lease of the debtor, or in applicable law that terminates or modifies, or permits a party other than the debtor to terminate or modify, such contract or lease or a right or obligation under such contract or lease on account of an assignment of such contract or lease, such contract, lease, right, or obligation may not be terminated or modified under such provision because of the assumption or assignment of such contract or lease by the trustee.

(g) Except as provided in subsections (h)(2) and (i)(2) of this section, the rejection of an executory contract or unexpired lease of the debtor constitutes a breach of such contract or lease -

(1) if such contract or lease has not been assumed under this section or under a plan confirmed under chapter 9, 11, 12, or 13 of this title, immediately before the date of the filing of the petition; or

(2) if such contract or lease has been assumed under this section or under a plan confirmed under chapter 9, 11, 12, or 13 of this title -

(A) if before such rejection the case has not been converted under section 1112, 1208, or 1307 of this title, at the time of such rejection; or

(B) if before such rejection the case has been converted under section 1112, 1208, or 1307 of this title -

(i) immediately before the date of such conversion, if such contract or lease was assumed before such conversion; or

(ii) at the time of such rejection, if such contract or lease was assumed after such conversion.

(h)(1)(A) If the trustee rejects an unexpired lease of real property under which the debtor is the lessor and -

(i) if the rejection by the trustee amounts to such a breach as would entitle the lessee to treat such lease as terminated by virtue of its terms, applicable nonbankruptcy law, or any agreement made by the lessee, then the lessee under such lease may treat such lease as terminated by the rejection; or

(ii) if the term of such lease has commenced, the lessee may retain its rights under such lease (including rights such as those relating to the amount and timing of payment of rent and other amounts payable by the lessee and any right of use, possession, quiet enjoyment, subletting, assignment, or hypothecation) that are in or appurtenant to the real property for the balance of the term of such lease and for any renewal or extension of such rights to the extent that such rights are enforceable under applicable nonbankruptcy law.

(B) If the lessee retains its rights under subparagraph (A)(ii), the lessee may offset against the rent reserved under such lease for the balance of the term after the date of the rejection of such lease and for the term of any renewal or extension of such lease, the value of any damage caused by the nonperformance after the date of such rejection, of any obligation of the debtor under such lease, but the lessee shall not have any other right against the estate or the debtor on account of any damage occurring after such date caused by such nonperformance.

(C) The rejection of a lease of real property in a shopping center with respect to which the lessee elects to retain its rights under subparagraph (A)(ii) does not affect the enforceability under applicable nonbankruptcy law of any provision in the lease pertaining to radius, location, use, exclusivity, or tenant mix or balance.

(D) In this paragraph, "lessee" includes any successor, assign, or mortgagee permitted under the terms of such lease.

(2)(A) If the trustee rejects a timeshare interest under a timeshare plan under which the debtor is the timeshare interest seller and -

(i) if the rejection amounts to such a breach as would entitle the timeshare interest purchaser to treat the timeshare plan as terminated under its terms, applicable nonbankruptcy law, or any agreement made by timeshare interest purchaser, the timeshare interest purchaser under the timeshare plan may treat the timeshare plan as terminated by such rejection; or

(ii) if the term of such timeshare interest has commenced, then the timeshare interest purchaser may retain its rights in such timeshare interest for the balance of such term and for any term of renewal or extension of such timeshare interest to the extent that such rights are enforceable under applicable nonbankruptcy law.

(B) If the timeshare interest purchaser retains its rights under subparagraph (A), such timeshare interest purchaser may offset against the moneys due for such timeshare interest for the balance of the term after the date of the rejection of such timeshare interest, and the term of any renewal or extension of such timeshare interest, the value of any damage caused by the nonperformance after the date of such rejection, of any obligation of the debtor under such timeshare plan, but the timeshare interest purchaser shall not have any right against the estate or the debtor on account of any damage occurring after such date caused by such nonperformance.

(i)(1) If the trustee rejects an executory contract of the debtor for the sale of real property or for the sale of a timeshare interest under a timeshare plan, under which the purchaser is in possession, such purchaser may treat such contract as terminated, or, in the alternative, may remain in possession of such real property or timeshare interest.

(2) If such purchaser remains in possession -

(A) such purchaser shall continue to make all payments due under such contract, but may, offset against such payments any damages occurring after the date of the rejection of such contract caused by the nonperformance of any obligation of the debtor after such date, but such purchaser does not have any rights against the estate on account of any damages arising after such date from such rejection, other than such offset; and

(B) the trustee shall deliver title to such purchaser in accordance with the provisions of such contract, but is relieved of all other obligations to perform under such contract.

(j) A purchaser that treats an executory contract as terminated under subsection (i) of this section, or a party whose executory contract to purchase real property from the debtor is rejected and under which such party is not in possession, has a lien on the interest of the debtor in such property for the recovery of any portion of the purchase price that such purchaser or party has paid.

(k) Assignment by the trustee to an entity of a contract or lease assumed under this section relieves the trustee and the estate from any liability for any breach of such contract or lease occurring after such assignment.

(l) If an unexpired lease under which the debtor is the lessee is assigned pursuant to this section, the lessor of the property may require a deposit or other security for the performance of the debtor's obligations under the lease substantially the same as would have been required by the landlord upon the initial leasing to a similar tenant.

(m) For purposes of this section 365 and sections 541(b)(2) and 362(b)(10), leases of real property shall include any rental agreement to use real property.

(n)(1) If the trustee rejects an executory contract under which the debtor is a licensor of a right to intellectual property, the licensee under such contract may elect -

(A) to treat such contract as terminated by such rejection if such rejection by the trustee amounts to such a breach as would entitle the licensee to treat such contract as terminated by virtue of its own terms, applicable nonbankruptcy law, or an agreement made by the licensee with another entity; or

(B) to retain its rights (including a right to enforce any exclusivity provision of such contract, but excluding any other right under applicable nonbankruptcy law to specific performance of such contract) under such contract and under any agreement supplementary to such contract, to such intellectual property (including any embodiment of such intellectual property to the extent protected by applicable nonbankruptcy law), as such rights existed immediately before the case commenced, for -

(i) the duration of such contract; and

(ii) any period for which such contract may be extended by the licensee as of right under applicable nonbankruptcy law.

(2) If the licensee elects to retain its rights, as described in paragraph (1)(B) of this subsection, under such contract -

(A) the trustee shall allow the licensee to exercise such rights;

(B) the licensee shall make all royalty payments due under such contract for the duration of such contract and for any period described in paragraph (1)(B) of this subsection for which the licensee extends such contract; and

(C) the licensee shall be deemed to waive -

(i) any right of setoff it may have with respect to such contract under this title or applicable nonbankruptcy law; and

(ii) any claim allowable under section 503(b) of this title arising from the performance of such contract.

(3) If the licensee elects to retain its rights, as described in paragraph (1)(B) of this subsection, then on the written request of the licensee the trustee shall -

(A) to the extent provided in such contract, or any agreement supplementary to such contract, provide to the licensee any intellectual property (including such embodiment) held by the trustee; and

(B) not interfere with the rights of the licensee as provided in such contract, or any agreement supplementary to such contract, to such intellectual property (including such embodiment) including any right to obtain such intellectual property (or such embodiment) from another entity.

(4) Unless and until the trustee rejects such contract, on the written request of the licensee the trustee shall -

(A) to the extent provided in such contract or any agreement supplementary to such contract -

(i) perform such contract; or

(ii) provide to the licensee such intellectual property (including any embodiment of such intellectual property to the extent protected by applicable nonbankruptcy law) held by the trustee; and

(B) not interfere with the rights of the licensee as provided in such contract, or any agreement supplementary to such contract, to such intellectual property (including such embodiment), including any right to obtain such intellectual property (or such embodiment) from another entity.

(o) In a case under chapter 11 of this title, the trustee shall be deemed to have assumed (consistent with the debtor's other obligations under section 507), and shall immediately cure any deficit under, any commitment by the debtor to a Federal depository institutions regulatory agency (or predecessor to such agency) to maintain the capital of an insured depository institution, and any claim for a subsequent breach of the obligations thereunder shall be entitled to priority under section 507. This subsection shall not extend any commitment that would otherwise be terminated by any act of such an agency.

(p)(1) If a lease of personal property is rejected or not timely assumed by the trustee under subsection (d), the leased property is no longer property of the estate and the stay under section 362(a) is automatically terminated.

(2)(A) If the debtor in a case under chapter 7 is an individual, the debtor may notify the creditor in writing that the debtor desires to assume the lease. Upon being so notified, the creditor may, at its option, notify the debtor that it is willing to have the lease assumed by the debtor and may condition such assumption on cure of any outstanding default on terms set by the contract.

(B) If, not later than 30 days after notice is provided under subparagraph (A), the debtor notifies the lessor in writing that the lease is assumed, the liability under the lease will be assumed by the debtor and not by the estate.

(C) The stay under section 362 and the injunction under section 524(a)(2) shall not be violated by notification of the debtor and negotiation of cure under this subsection.

(3) In a case under chapter 11 in which the debtor is an individual and in a case under chapter 13, if the debtor is the lessee with respect to personal property and the lease is not assumed in the plan confirmed by the court, the lease is deemed rejected as of the conclusion of the hearing on confirmation. If the lease is rejected, the stay under section 362 and any stay under section 1301 is automatically terminated with respect to the property subject to the lease.

366. Utility service

(a) Except as provided in subsections (b) and (c) of this section, a utility may not alter, refuse, or discontinue service to, or discriminate against, the trustee or the debtor solely on the basis of the commencement of a case under this title or that a debt owed by the debtor to such utility for service rendered before the order for relief was not paid when due.

(b) Such utility may alter, refuse, or discontinue service if neither the trustee nor the debtor, within 20 days after the date of the order for relief, furnishes adequate assurance of payment, in the form of a deposit or other security, for service after such date. On request of a party in interest and after notice and a hearing, the court may order reasonable modification of the amount of the deposit or other security necessary to provide adequate assurance of payment.

(c)(1)(A) For purposes of this subsection, the term "assurance of payment" means –

(i) a cash deposit;

(ii) a letter of credit;

(iii) a certificate of deposit;

(iv) a surety bond;

(v) a prepayment of utility consumption; or

(vi) another form of security that is mutually agreed on between the utility and the debtor or the trustee.

(B) For purposes of this subsection an administrative expense priority shall not constitute an assurance of payment.

(2) Subject to paragraphs (3) and (4), with respect to a case filed under chapter 11, a utility referred to in subsection (a) may alter, refuse, or discontinue utility service, if during the 30-day period beginning on the date of the filing of the petition, the utility does not receive from the debtor or the trustee adequate assurance of payment for utility service that is satisfactory to the utility.

(3)(A) On request of a party in interest and after notice and a hearing, the court may order modification of the amount of an assurance of payment under paragraph (2).

(B) In making a determination under this paragraph whether an assurance of payment is adequate, the court may not consider –

(i) the absence of security before the date of the filing of the petition;

(ii) the payment by the debtor of charges for utility service in a timely manner before the date of the filing of the petition; or

(iii) the availability of an administrative expense priority.

(4) Notwithstanding any other provision of law, with respect to a case subject to this subsection, a utility may recover or set off against a security deposit provided to the utility by the debtor before the date of the filing of the petition without notice or order of the court.

Chapter 5 - Creditors, the Debtor, and the Estate

Subchapter I - Creditors and Claims

Subchapter II - Debtor's Duties and Benefits

Subchapter III - The Estate

SUBCHAPTER I - CREDITORS AND CLAIMS

501. Filing of proofs of claims or interests

(a) A creditor or an indenture trustee may file a proof of claim. An equity security holder may file a proof of interest.

(b) If a creditor does not timely file a proof of such creditor's claim, an entity that is liable to such creditor with the debtor, or that has secured such creditor, may file a proof of such claim.

(c) If a creditor does not timely file a proof of such creditor's claim, the debtor or the trustee may file a proof of such claim.

(d) A claim of a kind specified in section 502(e)(2), 502(f), 502(g), 502(h) or 502(i) of this title may be filed under subsection (a), (b), or (c) of this section the same as if such claim were a claim against the debtor and had arisen before the date of the filing of the petition.

(e) A claim arising from the liability of a debtor for fuel use tax assessed consistent with the requirements of section 31705 of title 49 may be filed by the base jurisdiction designated pursuant to the International Fuel Tax Agreement (as defined in section 31701 of title 49) and, if so filed, shall be allowed as a single claim.

502. Allowance of claims or interests

(a) A claim or interest, proof of which is filed under section 501 of this title, is deemed allowed, unless a party in interest, including a creditor of a general partner in a partnership that is a debtor in a case under chapter 7 of this title, objects.

(b) Except as provided in subsections (e)(2), (f), (g), (h) and (i) of this section, if such objection to a claim is made, the court, after notice and a hearing, shall determine the amount of such claim in lawful currency of the United States as of the date of the filing of the petition, and shall allow such claim in such amount, except to the extent that -

(1) such claim is unenforceable against the debtor and property of the debtor, under any agreement or applicable law for a reason other than because such claim is contingent or unmatured;

(2) such claim is for unmatured interest;

(3) if such claim is for a tax assessed against property of the estate, such claim exceeds the value of the interest of the estate in such property;

(4) if such claim is for services of an insider or attorney of the debtor, such claim exceeds the reasonable value of such services;

(5) such claim is for a debt that is unmatured on the date of the filing of the petition and that is excepted from discharge under section 523(a)(5) of this title;

(6) if such claim is the claim of a lessor for damages resulting from the

termination of a lease of real property, such claim exceeds -

(A) the rent reserved by such lease, without acceleration, for the greater of one year, or 15 percent, not to exceed three years, of the remaining term of such lease, following the earlier of -

(i) the date of the filing of the petition; and

(ii) the date on which such lessor repossessed, or the lessee surrendered, the leased property; plus

(B) any unpaid rent due under such lease, without acceleration, on the earlier of such dates;

(7) if such claim is the claim of an employee for damages resulting from the termination of an employment contract, such claim exceeds -

(A) the compensation provided by such contract, without acceleration, for one year following the earlier of -

(i) the date of the filing of the petition; or

(ii) the date on which the employer directed the employee to terminate, or such employee terminated, performance under such contract; plus

(B) any unpaid compensation due under such contract, without acceleration, on the earlier of such dates;

(8) such claim results from a reduction, due to late payment, in the amount of an otherwise applicable credit available to the debtor in connection with an employment tax on wages, salaries, or commissions earned from the debtor; or

(9) proof of such claim is not timely filed, except to the extent tardily filed as permitted under paragraph (1), (2), or (3) of section 726(a) of this title or under the Federal Rules of Bankruptcy Procedure, except that a claim of a governmental unit shall be timely filed if it is filed before 180 days after the date of the order for relief or such later time as the Federal Rules of Bankruptcy Procedure may provide, and except that in a case under chapter 13, a claim of a governmental unit for a tax with respect to a return filed under section 1308 shall be timely if the claim is filed on or before the date that is 60 days after the date on which such return was filed as required.

(c) There shall be estimated for purpose of allowance under this section -

(1) any contingent or unliquidated claim, the fixing or liquidation of which, as the case may be, would unduly delay the administration of the case; or

(2) any right to payment arising from a right to an equitable remedy for breach of performance.

(d) Notwithstanding subsections (a) and (b) of this section, the court shall disallow any claim of any entity from which property is recoverable under section 542, 543, 550, or 553 of this title or that is a transferee of a transfer avoidable under section 522(f), 522(h), 544, 545, 547, 548, 549, or 724(a) of this title, unless such entity or transferee has paid the amount, or turned over any such property, for which such entity or transferee is liable under section 522(i), 542, 543, 550, or 553 of this title.

(e)(1) Notwithstanding subsections (a), (b), and (c) of this section and paragraph (2) of this subsection, the court shall disallow any claim for reimbursement or contribution of an entity that is liable with the debtor on or has secured the claim of a creditor, to the extent that -

(A) such creditor's claim against the estate is disallowed;

(B) such claim for reimbursement or contribution is contingent as of the time of allowance or disallowance of such claim for reimbursement or contribution; or

(C) such entity asserts a right of subrogation to the rights of such creditor under section 509 of this title.

(2) A claim for reimbursement or contribution of such an entity that becomes fixed after the commencement of the case shall be determined, and shall be allowed under subsection (a), (b), or (c) of this section, or disallowed under subsection (d) of this section, the same as if such claim had become fixed before the date of the filing of the petition.

(f) In an involuntary case, a claim arising in the ordinary course of the debtor's business or financial affairs after the commencement of the case but before the earlier of the appointment of a trustee and the order for relief shall be determined as of the date such claim arises, and shall be allowed under subsection (a), (b), or (c) of this section or disallowed under subsection (d) or (e) of this section, the same as if such claim had arisen before the date of the filing of the petition.

(g)(1) A claim arising from the rejection, under section 365 of this title or under a plan under chapter 9, 11, 12, or 13 of this title, of an executory contract or unexpired lease of the debtor that has not been assumed shall be determined, and shall be allowed under subsection (a), (b), or (c) of this section or disallowed under subsection (d) or (e) of this section, the same as if such claim had arisen before the date of the filing of the petition.

(2) A claim for damages calculated in accordance with section 562 shall be allowed under subsection (a), (b), or (c), or disallowed under subsection (d) or (e), as if such claim had arisen before the date of the filing of the petition.

(h) A claim arising from the recovery of property under section 522, 550, or 553 of this title shall be determined, and shall be allowed under subsection (a), (b), or (c) of this section, or disallowed under subsection (d) or (e) of this section, the same as if such claim had arisen before the date of the filing of the petition.

(i) A claim that does not arise until after the commencement of the case for a tax entitled to priority under section 507(a)(8) of this title shall be determined, and shall be allowed under subsection (a), (b), or (c) of this section, or disallowed under subsection (d) or (e) of this section, the same as if such claim had arisen before the date of the filing of the petition.

(j) A claim that has been allowed or disallowed may be reconsidered for cause. A reconsidered claim may be allowed or disallowed according to the equities of the case. Reconsideration of a claim under this subsection does not affect the validity of any payment or transfer from the estate made to a holder of an allowed claim on account of such allowed claim that is not reconsidered, but if a reconsidered claim is allowed and is of the same class as such holder's claim, such holder may not receive any additional payment or transfer from the estate on account of such holder's allowed claim until the holder of such reconsidered and allowed claim receives payment on account of such claim proportionate in value to that already received by such other holder. This subsection does not alter or modify the trustee's right to recover from a creditor any excess payment or transfer made to such creditor.

(k)(1) The court, on the motion of the debtor and after a hearing, may reduce a claim filed under this section based in whole on an unsecured consumer debt by not more than 20 percent of the claim, if –

(A) the claim was filed by a creditor who unreasonably refused to negotiate a reasonable alternative repayment schedule proposed on behalf of the debtor by an approved nonprofit budget and credit counseling agency described in section 111;

(B) the offer of the debtor under subparagraph (A) –

(i) was made at least 60 days before the date of the filing of the petition; and

(ii) provided for payment of at least 60 percent of the amount of the debt over a period not to exceed the repayment period of the loan, or a reasonable extension thereof; and

(C) no part of the debt under the alternative repayment schedule is nondischargeable.

(2) The debtor shall have the burden of proving, by clear and convincing evidence, that –

(A) the creditor unreasonably refused to consider the debtor's proposal; and

(B) the proposed alternative repayment schedule was made prior to expiration of the 60-day period specified in paragraph (1)(B)(i).

503. Allowance of administrative expenses

(a) An entity may timely file a request for payment of an administrative expense, or may tardily file such request if permitted by the court for cause.

(b) After notice and a hearing, there shall be allowed administrative expenses, other than claims allowed under section 502(f) of this title, including-

(1)(A) the actual, necessary costs and expenses of preserving the estate including –

(i) wages, salaries, and commissions for services rendered after the commencement of the case; and

(ii) wages and benefits awarded pursuant to a judicial proceeding or a proceeding of the National Labor Relations Board as back pay attributable to any period of time occurring after commencement of the case under this title, as a result of a violation of Federal or State law by the debtor, without regard to the time of the occurrence of unlawful conduct on which such award is based or to whether any services were rendered, if the court determines that payment of wages and benefits by reason of the operation of this clause will not substantially increase the probability of layoff or termination of current employees, or of nonpayment of domestic support obligations, during the case under this title;

(B) any tax -

(i) incurred by the estate, whether secured or unsecured, including property taxes for which liability is in rem, in personam, or both, except a tax of a kind specified in section 507(a)(8) of this title; or

(ii) attributable to an excessive allowance of a tentative carryback adjustment that the estate received, whether the taxable year to which such adjustment relates ended before or after the commencement of the case;

(C) any fine, penalty, or reduction in credit relating to a tax of a kind specified in subparagraph (B) of this paragraph; and

(D) notwithstanding the requirements of subsection (a), a governmental unit shall not be required to file a request for the payment of an expense described in subparagraph (B) or (C), as a condition of its being an allowed administrative expense;

(2) compensation and reimbursement awarded under section 330(a) of this title;

(3) the actual, necessary expenses, other than compensation and reimbursement specified in paragraph (4) of this subsection, incurred by -

(A) a creditor that files a petition under section 303 of this title;

(B) a creditor that recovers, after the court's approval, for the benefit of the estate any property transferred or concealed by the debtor;

(C) a creditor in connection with the prosecution of a criminal offense relating to the case or to the business or property of the debtor;

(D) a creditor, an indenture trustee, an equity security holder, or a committee representing creditors or equity security holders other than a committee appointed under section 1102 of this title, in making a substantial contribution in a case under chapter 9 or 11 of this title;

(E) a custodian superseded under section 543 of this title, and compensation for the services of such custodian; or

(F) a member of a committee appointed under section 1102 of this title, if such expenses are incurred in the performance of the duties of such committee;

(4) reasonable compensation for professional services rendered by an attorney or an accountant of an entity whose expense is allowable under subparagraph (A), (B), (C), (D), or (E) of paragraph (3) of this subsection, based on the time, the nature, the extent, and the value of such services, and the cost of comparable services other than in a case under this title, and reimbursement for actual, necessary expenses incurred by such attorney or accountant;

(5) reasonable compensation for services rendered by an indenture trustee in making a substantial contribution in a case under chapter 9 or 11 of this title, based on the time, the nature, the extent, and the value of such services, and the cost of comparable services other than in a case under this title;

(6) the fees and mileage payable under chapter 119 of title 28;

(7) with respect to a nonresidential real property lease previously assumed under section 365, and subsequently rejected, a sum equal to all monetary obligations due, excluding those arising from or relating to a failure to operate or a penalty provision, for the period of 2 years following the later of the rejection date or the date of actual turnover of the premises, without reduction or setoff for any reason whatsoever except for sums actually received or to be received from an entity other than the debtor, and the claim for remaining sums due for the balance of the term of the lease shall be a claim under section 502(b)(6);

(8) the actual, necessary costs and expenses of closing a health care business incurred by a trustee or by a Federal agency (as defined in section 551(1) of title 5) or a department or agency of a State or political subdivision thereof, including any cost or expense incurred –

(A) in disposing of patient records in accordance with section 351; or

(B) in connection with transferring patients from the health care business that is in the process of being closed to another health care business; and

(9) the value of any goods received by the debtor within 20 days before the date of commencement of a case under this title in which the goods have been sold to the debtor in the ordinary course of such debtor's business.

(c) Notwithstanding subsection (b), there shall neither be allowed, nor paid

(1) a transfer made to, or an obligation incurred for the benefit of, an insider of the debtor for the purpose of inducing such person to remain with the debtor's business, absent a finding by the court based on evidence in the record that –

(A) the transfer or obligation is essential to retention of the person because the individual has a bona fide job offer from another business at the same or greater rate of compensation;

(B) the services provided by the person are essential to the survival of the business; and

(C) either –

(i) the amount of the transfer made to, or obligation incurred for the benefit of, the person is not greater than an amount equal to 10 times the amount of the mean transfer or obligation of a similar kind given to nonmanagement employees for any purpose during the calendar year in which the transfer is made or the obligation is incurred; or

(ii) if no such similar transfers were made to, or obligations were incurred for the benefit of, such nonmanagement employees during such calendar year, the amount of the transfer or obligation is not greater than an amount equal to 25 percent of the amount of any similar transfer or obligation made to or incurred for the benefit of such insider for any purpose during the calendar year before the year in which such transfer is made or obligation is incurred;

(2) a severance payment to an insider of the debtor, unless –

(A) the payment is part of a program that is generally applicable to all full-time employees; and

(B) the amount of the payment is not greater than 10 times the amount of the mean severance pay given to nonmanagement employees during the calendar year in which the payment is made; or

(3) other transfers or obligations that are outside the ordinary course of business and not justified by the facts and circumstances of the case, including transfers made to, or obligations incurred for the benefit of, officers, managers, or consultants hired after the date of the filing of the petition.

504. Sharing of compensation

(a) Except as provided in subsection (b) of this section, a person receiving compensation or reimbursement under section 503(b)(2) or 503(b)(4) of this title may not share or agree to share -

(1) any such compensation or reimbursement with another person; or

(2) any compensation or reimbursement received by another person under such sections.

(b)(1) A member, partner, or regular associate in a professional association, corporation, or partnership may share compensation or reimbursement received under section 503(b)(2) or 503(b)(4) of this title with another member, partner, or regular associate in such association, corporation, or partnership, and may share in any compensation or reimbursement received under such sections by another member, partner, or regular associate in such association, corporation, or partnership.

(2) An attorney for a creditor that files a petition under section 303 of this title may share compensation and reimbursement received under section 503(b)(4) of this title with any other attorney contributing to the services rendered or expenses incurred by such creditor's attorney.

(c) This section shall not apply with respect to sharing, or agreeing to share, compensation with a bona fide public service attorney referral program that operates in accordance with non-Federal law regulating attorney referral services and with rules of professional responsibility applicable to attorney acceptance of referrals.

505. Determination of tax liability

(a)(1) Except as provided in paragraph (2) of this subsection, the court may determine the amount or legality of any tax, any fine or penalty relating to a tax, or any addition to tax, whether or not previously assessed, whether or not paid, and whether or not contested before and adjudicated by a judicial or administrative tribunal of competent jurisdiction.

(2) The court may not so determine-

(A) the amount or legality of a tax, fine, penalty, or addition to tax if such amount or legality was contested before and adjudicated by a judicial or administrative tribunal of competent jurisdiction before the commencement of the case under this title;

(B) any right of the estate to a tax refund, before the earlier of –

(i) 120 days after the trustee properly requests such refund from the governmental unit from which such refund is claimed; or

(ii) a determination by such governmental unit of such request; or

(C) the amount or legality of any amount arising in connection with an ad valorem tax on real or personal property of the estate, if the applicable period for contesting or redetermining that amount under applicable nonbankruptcy law has expired.

(b)(1)(A) The clerk shall maintain a list under which a Federal, State, or local governmental unit responsible for the collection of taxes within the district may –

(i) designate an address for service of requests under this subsection;

and

(ii) describe where further information concerning additional requirements for filing such requests may be found.

(B) If such governmental unit does not designate an address and provide such address to the clerk under subparagraph (A), any request made under this subsection may be served at the address for the filing of a tax return or protest with the appropriate taxing authority of such governmental unit.

(2) A trustee may request a determination of any unpaid liability of the estate for any tax incurred during the administration of the case by submitting a tax return for such tax and a request for such a determination to the governmental unit charged with responsibility for collection or determination of such tax at the address and in the manner designated in paragraph (1). Unless such return is fraudulent, or contains a material misrepresentation, the estate, the trustee, the debtor, and any successor to the debtor are discharged from any liability for such tax-

(A) upon payment of the tax shown on such return, if-

(i) such governmental unit does not notify the trustee, within 60 days after such request, that such return has been selected for examination; or

(ii) such governmental unit does not complete such an examination and notify the trustee of any tax due, within 180 days after such request or within such additional time as the court, for cause, permits;

(B) upon payment of the tax determined by the court, after notice and a hearing, after completion by such governmental unit of such examination; or

(C) upon payment of the tax determined by such governmental unit to be due.

(c) Notwithstanding section 362 of this title, after determination by the court of a tax under this section, the governmental unit charged with responsibility for collection of such tax may assess such tax against the estate, the debtor, or a successor to the debtor, as the case may be, subject to any otherwise applicable law.

506. Determination of secured status

(a)(1) An allowed claim of a creditor secured by a lien on property in which the estate has an interest, or that is subject to setoff under section 553 of this title, is a secured claim to the extent of the value of such creditor's interest in the estate's interest in such property, or to the extent of the amount subject to setoff, as the case may be, and is an unsecured claim to the extent that the value of such creditor's interest or the amount so subject to setoff is less than the amount of such allowed claim. Such value shall be determined in light of the purpose of the valuation and of the proposed disposition or use of such property, and in conjunction with any hearing on such disposition or use or on a plan affecting such creditor's interest.

(2) If the debtor is an individual in a case under chapter 7 or 13, such value with respect to personal property securing an allowed claim shall be determined based on the replacement value of such property as of the date of the filing of the petition without deduction for costs of sale or marketing. With respect to property acquired for personal, family, or household purposes, replacement value shall mean the price a retail merchant would charge for property of that kind considering the age and condition of the property at the time value is determined.

(b) To the extent that an allowed secured claim is secured by property the value of which, after any recovery under subsection (c) of this section, is greater than the amount of such claim, there shall be allowed to the holder of such claim, interest on such claim, and any reasonable fees, costs, or charges provided for under the agreement or State statute under which such claim arose.

(c) The trustee may recover from property securing an allowed secured claim the reasonable, necessary costs and expenses of preserving, or disposing of, such property to the extent of any benefit to the holder of such claim, including the payment of all ad valorem property taxes with respect to the property.

(d) To the extent that a lien secures a claim against the debtor that is not an allowed secured claim, such lien is void, unless -

(1) such claim was disallowed only under section 502(b)(5) or 502(e) of this title; or

(2) such claim is not an allowed secured claim due only to the failure of any entity to file a proof of such claim under section 501 of this title.

507. Priorities

(a) The following expenses and claims have priority in the following order:

(1) First:

(A) Allowed unsecured claims for domestic support obligations that, as of the date of the filing of the petition in a case under this title, are owed to or recoverable by a spouse, former spouse, or child of the debtor, or such child's parent, legal guardian, or responsible relative, without regard to whether the claim is filed by such person or is filed by a governmental unit on behalf of such person, on the condition that funds received under this paragraph by a governmental unit under this title after the date of the filing of the petition shall be applied and distributed in accordance with applicable nonbankruptcy law.

(B) Subject to claims under subparagraph (A), allowed unsecured claims for domestic support obligations that, as of the date of the filing of the petition, are assigned by a spouse, former spouse, child of the debtor, or such child's parent, legal guardian, or responsible relative to a governmental unit (unless such obligation is assigned voluntarily by the spouse, former spouse, child, parent, legal guardian, or responsible relative of the child for the purpose of collecting the debt) or are owed directly to or recoverable by a governmental unit under applicable nonbankruptcy law, on the condition that funds received under this paragraph by a governmental unit under this title after the date of the filing of the petition be applied and distributed in accordance with applicable nonbankruptcy law.

(C) If a trustee is appointed or elected under section 701, 702, 703, 1104, 1202, or 1302, the administrative expenses of the trustee allowed under paragraphs (1)(A), (2), and (6) of section 503(b) shall be paid before payment of claims under subparagraphs (A) and (B), to the extent that the trustee administers assets that are otherwise available for the payment of such claims.

(2) Second, administrative expenses allowed under section 503(b) of this title, unsecured claims of any federal reserve bank related to loans made through programs or facilities authorized under Section 13(3) of the Federal Reserve Act (12 U.S.C. 343), and any fees and charges assessed against the estate under chapter 123 of title 28.

(3) Third, unsecured claims allowed under section 502(f) of this title.

(4) Fourth, allowed unsecured claims, but only to the extent of $15,150 for each individual or corporation, as the case may be, earned within 180 days before the date of the filing of the petition or the date of the cessation of the debtor's business, whichever occurs first, for -

(A) wages, salaries, or commissions, including vacation, severance, and sick leave pay earned by an individual; or

(B) sales commissions earned by an individual or by a corporation with only 1 employee, acting as an independent contractor in the sale of goods or services for the debtor in the ordinary course of the debtor's business if, and only if, during the 12 months preceding that date, at least 75 percent of the amount that the individual or corporation earned by acting as an independent contractor in the sale of goods or services was earned from the debtor.

(5) Fifth, allowed unsecured claims for contributions to an employee benefit plan -

(A) arising from services rendered within 180 days before the date of the filing of the petition or the date of the cessation of the debtor's business, whichever occurs first; but only

(B) for each such plan, to the extent of -

(i) the number of employees covered by each such plan multiplied by $15,150; less

(ii) the aggregate amount paid to such employees under paragraph (4) of this subsection, plus the aggregate amount paid by the estate on behalf of such employees to any other employee benefit plan.

(6) Sixth, allowed unsecured claims of persons -

(A) engaged in the production or raising of grain, as defined in section 557(b) of this title, against a debtor who owns or operates a grain storage facility, as defined in section 557(b) of this title, for grain or the proceeds of grain, or

(B) engaged as a United States fisherman against a debtor who has acquired fish or fish produce from a fisherman through a sale or conversion, and who is engaged in operating a fish produce storage or processing facility -

but only to the extent of $7,475 for each such individual.

(7) Seventh, allowed unsecured claims of individuals, to the extent of $3,350 for each such individual, arising from the deposit, before the commencement of the case, of money in connection with the purchase, lease, or rental of property, or the purchase of services, for the personal, family, or household use of such individuals, that were not delivered or provided.

(8) Eighth, allowed unsecured claims of governmental units, only to

the extent that such claims are for -

(A) a tax on or measured by income or gross receipts for a taxable year ending on or before the date of the filing of the petition -

(i) for which a return, if required, is last due, including extensions, after three years before the date of the filing of the petition;

(ii) assessed within 240 days before the date of the filing of the petition, exclusive of –

(I) any time during which an offer in compromise with respect to that tax was pending or in effect during that 240-day period, plus 30 days; and

(II) any time during which a stay of proceedings against collections was in effect in a prior case under this title during that 240-day period, plus 90 days; or

(iii) other than a tax of a kind specified in section 523(a)(1)(B) or 523(a)(1)(C) of this title, not assessed before, but assessable, under applicable law or by agreement, after, the commencement of the case;

(B) a property tax incurred before the commencement of the case and last payable without penalty after one year before the date of the filing of the petition;

(C) a tax required to be collected or withheld and for which the debtor is liable in whatever capacity;

(D) an employment tax on a wage, salary, or commission of a kind specified in paragraph (4) of this subsection earned from the debtor before the date of the filing of the petition, whether or not actually paid before such date, for which a return is last due, under applicable law or under any extension, after three years before the date of the filing of the petition;

(E) an excise tax on -

(i) a transaction occurring before the date of the filing of the petition for which a return, if required, is last due, under applicable law or under any extension, after three years before the date of the filing of the petition; or

(ii) if a return is not required, a transaction occurring during the three years immediately preceding the date of the filing of the petition;

(F) a customs duty arising out of the importation of merchandise-

(i) entered for consumption within one year before the date of the filing of the petition;

(ii) covered by an entry liquidated or reliquidated within one year before the date of the filing of the petition; or

(iii) entered for consumption within four years before the date of the filing of the petition but unliquidated on such date, if the Secretary of the Treasury certifies that failure to liquidate such entry was due to an investigation pending on such date into assessment of antidumping or countervailing duties or fraud, or if information needed for the proper appraisement or classification of such merchandise was not available to the appropriate customs officer before such date;

or

(G) a penalty related to a claim of a kind specified in this paragraph and in compensation for actual pecuniary loss.

An otherwise applicable time period specified in this paragraph shall be suspended for any period during which a governmental unit is prohibited under applicable nonbankruptcy law from collecting a tax as a result of a request by the debtor for a hearing and an appeal of any collection action taken or proposed against the debtor, plus 90 days; plus any time during which the stay of proceedings was in effect in a prior case under this title or during which collection was precluded by the existence of 1 or more confirmed plans under this title, plus 90 days.

(9) Ninth, allowed unsecured claims based upon any commitment by the debtor to a Federal depository institutions regulatory agency (or predecessor to such agency) to maintain the capital of an insured depository institution.

(10) Tenth, allowed claims for death or personal injury resulting from the operation of a motor vehicle or vessel if such operation was unlawful because the debtor was intoxicated from using alcohol, a drug, or another substance.

(b) If the trustee, under section 362, 363, or 364 of this title, provides adequate protection of the interest of a holder of a claim secured by a lien on property of the debtor and if, notwithstanding such protection, such creditor has a claim allowable under subsection (a)(2) of this section arising from the stay of action against such property under section 362 of this title, from the use, sale, or lease of such property under section 363 of this title, or from the granting of a lien under section 364(d) of this title, then such creditor's claim under such subsection shall have priority over every other claim allowable under such subsection.

(c) For the purpose of subsection (a) of this section, a claim of a governmental unit arising from an erroneous refund or credit of a tax has the same priority as a claim for the tax to which such refund or credit relates.

(d) An entity that is subrogated to the rights of a holder of a claim of a kind specified in subsection (a)(1), (a)(4), (a)(5), (a)(6), (a)(7), (a)(8), or (a)(9) of this section is not subrogated to the right of the holder of such claim to priority under such subsection.

508. Effect of distribution other than under this title

If a creditor of a partnership debtor receives, from a general partner that is not a debtor in a case under chapter 7 of this title, payment of, or a transfer of property on account of, a claim that is allowed under this title and that is not secured by a lien on property of such partner, such creditor may not receive any payment under this title on account of such claim until each of the other holders of claims on account of which such holders are entitled to share equally with such creditor under this title has received payment under this title equal in value to the consideration received by such creditor from such general partner.

509. Claims of codebtors

(a) Except as provided in subsection (b) or (c) of this section, an entity that is liable with the debtor on, or that has secured, a claim of a creditor against the debtor, and that pays such claim, is subrogated to the rights of such creditor to the extent of such payment.

(b) Such entity is not subrogated to the rights of such creditor to the extent that -

(1) a claim of such entity for reimbursement or contribution on account of such payment of such creditor's claim is -

(A) allowed under section 502 of this title;

(B) disallowed other than under section 502(e) of this title; or

(C) subordinated under section 510 of this title; or

(2) as between the debtor and such entity, such entity received the consideration for the claim held by such creditor.

(c) The court shall subordinate to the claim of a creditor and for the benefit of such creditor an allowed claim, by way of subrogation under this section, or for reimbursement or contribution, of an entity that is liable with the debtor on, or that has secured, such creditor's claim, until such creditor's claim is paid in full, either through payments under this title or otherwise.

510. Subordination

(a) A subordination agreement is enforceable in a case under this title to the same extent that such agreement is enforceable under applicable nonbankruptcy law.

(b) For the purpose of distribution under this title, a claim arising from rescission of a purchase or sale of a security of the debtor or of an affiliate of the debtor, for damages arising from the purchase or sale of such a security, or for reimbursement or contribution allowed under section 502 on account of such a claim, shall be subordinated to all claims or interests that are senior to or equal the claim or interest represented by such security, except that if such security is common stock, such claim has the same priority as common stock.

(c) Notwithstanding subsections (a) and (b) of this section, after notice and a hearing, the court may -

(1) under principles of equitable subordination, subordinate for purposes of distribution all or part of an allowed claim to all or part of another allowed claim or all or part of an allowed interest to all or part of another allowed interest; or

(2) order that any lien securing such a subordinated claim be transferred to the estate.

511. Rate of interest on tax claims

(a) If any provision of this title requires the payment of interest on a tax claim or on an administrative expense tax, or the payment of interest to enable a creditor to receive the present value of the allowed amount of a tax claim, the rate of interest shall be the rate determined under applicable nonbankruptcy law.

(b) In the case of taxes paid under a confirmed plan under this title, the rate of interest shall be determined as of the calendar month in which the plan is confirmed.

SUBCHAPTER II - DEBTOR'S DUTIES AND BENEFITS

521. Debtor's duties

(a) The debtor shall -

(1) file –

(A) a list of creditors; and

(B) unless the court orders otherwise –

(i) a schedule of assets and liabilities;

(ii) a schedule of current income and current expenditures;

(iii) a statement of the debtor's financial affairs and, if section 342(b) applies, a certificate –

(I) of an attorney whose name is indicated on the petition as the attorney for the debtor, or a bankruptcy petition preparer signing the petition under section 110(b)(1), indicating that such attorney or the bankruptcy petition preparer delivered to the debtor the notice required by section 342(b); or

(II) if no attorney is so indicated, and no bankruptcy petition preparer signed the petition, of the debtor that such notice was received and read by the debtor;

(iv) copies of all payment advices or other evidence of payment received within 60 days before the date of the filing of the petition, by the debtor from any employer of the debtor;

(v) a statement of the amount of monthly net income, itemized to show how the amount is calculated; and

(vi) a statement disclosing any reasonably anticipated increase in income or expenditures over the 12-month period following the date of the filing of the petition;

(2) if an individual debtor's schedule of assets and liabilities includes debts which are secured by property of the estate -

(A) within thirty days after the date of the filing of a petition under chapter 7 of this title or on or before the date of the meeting of creditors, whichever is earlier, or within such additional time as the court, for cause, within such period fixes, file with the clerk a statement of his intention with respect to the retention or surrender of such property and, if applicable, specifying that such property is claimed as exempt, that the debtor intends to redeem such property, or that the debtor intends to reaffirm debts secured by such property; and

(B) within 30 days after the first date set for the meeting of creditors under section 341(a), or within such additional time as the court, for cause, within such 30-day period fixes, perform his intention with respect to such property, as specified by subparagraph (A) of this paragraph;except that nothing in subparagraphs (A) and (B) of this paragraph shall alter the debtor's or the trustee's rights with regard to such property under this title, except as provided in section 362(h);

(3) if a trustee is serving in the case or an auditor is serving under section 586(f) of title 28, cooperate with the trustee as necessary to enable the trustee to perform the trustee's duties under this title;

(4) if a trustee is serving in the case or an auditor is serving under section 586(f) of title 28, surrender to the trustee all property of the estate and any recorded information, including books, documents, records, and papers, relating to property of the estate, whether or not immunity is granted under section 344 of this title;

(5) appear at the hearing required under section 524(d) of this title;

(6) in a case under chapter 7 of this title in which the debtor is an individual, not retain possession of personal property as to which a creditor has an allowed claim for the purchase price secured in whole or in part by an interest in such personal property unless the debtor, not later than 45 days after the first meeting of creditors under section 341(a), either –

(A) enters into an agreement with the creditor pursuant to section 524(c) with respect to the claim secured by such property; or

(B) redeems such property from the security interest pursuant to section 722; and

(7) unless a trustee is serving in the case, continue to perform the obligations required of the administrator (as defined in section 3 of the Employee Retirement Income Security Act of 1974) of an employee benefit plan if at the time of the commencement of the case the debtor (or any entity designated by the debtor) served as such administrator.

If the debtor fails to so act within the 45-day period referred to in paragraph (6), the stay under section 362(a) is terminated with respect to the personal property of the estate or of the debtor which is affected, such property shall no longer be property of the estate, and the creditor may take whatever action as to such property as is permitted by applicable nonbankruptcy law, unless the court determines on the motion of the trustee filed before the expiration of such 45-day period, and after notice and a hearing, that such property is of consequential value or benefit to the estate, orders appropriate adequate protection of the creditor's interest, and orders the debtor to deliver any collateral in the debtor's possession to the trustee.

(b) In addition to the requirements under subsection (a), a debtor who is an individual shall file with the court –

(1) a certificate from the approved nonprofit budget and credit counseling agency that provided the debtor services under section 109(h) describing the services provided to the debtor; and

(2) a copy of the debt repayment plan, if any, developed under section 109(h) through the approved nonprofit budget and credit counseling agency referred to in paragraph (1).

(c) In addition to meeting the requirements under subsection (a), a debtor shall file with the court a record of any interest that a debtor has in an education individual retirement account (as defined in section 530(b)(1) of the Internal Revenue Code of 1986), an interest in an account in a qualified ABLE program (as defined in section 529A(b) of such Code,1 or under a qualified State tuition program (as defined in section 529(b)(1) of such Code).

(d) If the debtor fails timely to take the action specified in subsection (a)(6) of this section, or in paragraphs (1) and (2) of section 362(h), with respect to property which a lessor or bailor owns and has leased, rented, or bailed to the debtor or as to which a creditor holds a security interest not otherwise voidable under section 522(f), 544, 545, 547, 548, or 549, nothing in this title shall prevent or limit the operation of a provision in the underlying lease or agreement that has the effect of placing the debtor in default under such lease or agreement by reason of the occurrence, pendency, or existence of a proceeding under this title or the insolvency of the debtor. Nothing in this subsection shall be deemed to justify limiting such a provision in any other circumstance.

(e)(1) If the debtor in a case under chapter 7 or 13 is an individual and if a creditor files with the court at any time a request to receive a copy of the petition, schedules, and statement of financial affairs filed by the debtor, then the court shall make such petition, such schedules, and such statement available to such creditor.

(2)(A) The debtor shall provide –

(i) not later than 7 days before the date first set for the first meeting of creditors, to the trustee a copy of the Federal income tax return required under applicable law (or at the election of the debtor, a transcript of such return) for the most recent tax year ending immediately before the commencement of the case and for which a Federal income tax return was filed; and

(ii) at the same time the debtor complies with clause (i), a copy of such return (or if elected under clause (i), such transcript) to any creditor that timely requests such copy.

(B) If the debtor fails to comply with clause (i) or (ii) of subparagraph (A), the court shall dismiss the case unless the debtor demonstrates that the failure to so comply is due to circumstances beyond the control of the debtor.

(C) If a creditor requests a copy of such tax return or such transcript and if the debtor fails to provide a copy of such tax return or such transcript to such creditor at the time the debtor provides such tax return or such transcript to the trustee, then the court shall dismiss the case unless the debtor demonstrates that the failure to provide a copy of such tax return or such transcript is due to circumstances beyond the control of the debtor.

(3) If a creditor in a case under chapter 13 files with the court at any time a request to receive a copy of the plan filed by the debtor, then the court shall make available to such creditor a copy of the plan –

(A) at a reasonable cost; and

(B) not later than 7 days after such request is filed.

(f) At the request of the court, the United States trustee, or any party in interest in a case under chapter 7, 11, or 13, a debtor who is an individual shall file with the court –

(1) at the same time filed with the taxing authority, a copy of each Federal income tax return required under applicable law (or at the election of the debtor, a transcript of such tax return) with respect to each tax year of the debtor ending while the case is pending under such chapter;

(2) at the same time filed with the taxing authority, each Federal income tax return required under applicable law (or at the election of the debtor, a transcript of such tax return) that had not been filed with such authority as of the date of the commencement of the case and that was subsequently filed for

any tax year of the debtor ending in the 3-year period ending on the date of the commencement of the case;

(3) a copy of each amendment to any Federal income tax return or transcript filed with the court under paragraph (1) or (2); and

(4) in a case under chapter 13 –

(A) on the date that is either 90 days after the end of such tax year or 1 year after the date of the commencement of the case, whichever is later, if a plan is not confirmed before such later date; and

(B) annually after the plan is confirmed and until the case is closed, not later than the date that is 45 days before the anniversary of the confirmation of the plan;

a statement, under penalty of perjury, of the income and expenditures of the debtor during the tax year of the debtor most recently concluded before such statement is filed under this paragraph, and of the monthly income of the debtor, that shows how income, expenditures, and monthly income are calculated.

(g)(1) A statement referred to in subsection (f)(4) shall disclose –

(A) the amount and sources of the income of the debtor;

(B) the identity of any person responsible with the debtor for the support of any dependent of the debtor; and

(C) the identity of any person who contributed, and the amount contributed, to the household in which the debtor resides.

(2) The tax returns, amendments, and statement of income and expenditures described in subsections (e)(2)(A) and (f) shall be available to the United States trustee (or the bankruptcy administrator, if any), the trustee, and any party in interest for inspection and copying, subject to the requirements of section 315(c) of the Bankruptcy Abuse Prevention and Consumer Protection Act of 2005.

(h) If requested by the United States trustee or by the trustee, the debtor shall provide –

(1) a document that establishes the identity of the debtor, including a driver's license, passport, or other document that contains a photograph of the debtor; or

(2) such other personal identifying information relating to the debtor that establishes the identity of the debtor.

(i)(1) Subject to paragraphs (2) and (4) and notwithstanding section 707(a), if an individual debtor in a voluntary case under chapter 7 or 13 fails to file all of the information required under subsection (a)(1) within 45 days after the date of the filing of the petition, the case shall be automatically dismissed effective on the 46th day after the date of the filing of the petition.

(2) Subject to paragraph (4) and with respect to a case described in paragraph (1), any party in interest may request the court to enter an order dismissing the case. If requested, the court shall enter an order of dismissal not later than 7 days after such request.

(3) Subject to paragraph (4) and upon request of the debtor made within 45 days after the date of the filing of the petition described in paragraph (1), the court may allow the debtor an additional period of not to exceed 45 days to file the information required under subsection (a)(1) if the court finds justification for extending the period for the filing.

(4) Notwithstanding any other provision of this subsection, on the motion of the trustee filed before the expiration of the applicable period of time specified in paragraph (1), (2), or (3), and after notice and a hearing, the court may decline to dismiss the case if the court finds that the debtor attempted in good faith to file all the information required by subsection (a)(1)(B)(iv) and that the best interests of creditors would be served by administration of the case.

(j)(1) Notwithstanding any other provision of this title, if the debtor fails to file a tax return that becomes due after the commencement of the case or to properly obtain an extension of the due date for filing such return, the taxing authority may request that the court enter an order converting or dismissing the case.

(2) If the debtor does not file the required return or obtain the extension referred to in paragraph (1) within 90 days after a request is filed by the taxing authority under that paragraph, the court shall convert or dismiss the case, whichever is in the best interests of creditors and the estate.

522. Exemptions

(a) In this section -

(1) "dependent" includes spouse, whether or not actually dependent; and

(2) "value" means fair market value as of the date of the filing of the petition or, with respect to property that becomes property of the estate after such date, as of the date such property becomes property of the estate.

(b)(1) Notwithstanding section 541 of this title, an individual debtor may exempt from property of the estate the property listed in either paragraph (2) or, in the alternative, paragraph (3) of this subsection. In joint cases filed under section 302 of this title and individual cases filed under section 301 or 303 of this title by or against debtors who are husband and wife, and whose estates are ordered to be jointly administered under Rule 1015(b) of the Federal Rules of Bankruptcy Procedure, one debtor may not elect to exempt property listed in paragraph (2) and the other debtor elect to exempt property listed in paragraph (3) of this subsection. If the parties cannot agree on the alternative to be elected, they shall be deemed to elect paragraph (2), where such election is permitted under the law of the jurisdiction where the case is filed.

(2) Property listed in this paragraph is property that is specified under subsection (d), unless the State law that is applicable to the debtor under paragraph (3)(A) specifically does not so authorize.

(3) Property listed in this paragraph is –

(A) subject to subsections (o) and (p), any property that is exempt under Federal law, other than subsection (d) of this section, or State or local law that is applicable on the date of the filing of the petition to the place in which the debtor's domicile has been located for the 730 days immediately preceding the date of the filing of the petition or if the debtor's domicile has not been located in a single State for such 730-day period, the place in which the debtor's domicile was located for 180 days immediately preceding the 730-day period or for a longer portion of such 180-day period than in any other place;

(B) any interest in property in which the debtor had, immediately before the commencement of the case, an interest as a tenant by the entirety or joint tenant to the extent that such interest as a tenant by the entirety or joint tenant is exempt from process under applicable nonbankruptcy law; and

(C) retirement funds to the extent that those funds are in a fund or account that is exempt from taxation under section 401, 403, 408, 408A, 414, 457, or 501(a) of the Internal Revenue Code of 1986.

If the effect of the domiciliary requirement under subparagraph (A) is to render the debtor ineligible for any exemption, the debtor may elect to exempt property that is specified under subsection (d).

(4) For purposes of paragraph (3)(C) and subsection (d)(12), the following shall apply:

(A) If the retirement funds are in a retirement fund that has received a favorable determination under section 7805 of the Internal Revenue Code of 1986, and that determination is in effect as of the date of the filing of the petition in a case under this title, those funds shall be presumed to be exempt from the estate.

(B) If the retirement funds are in a retirement fund that has not received a favorable determination under such section 7805, those funds are exempt from the estate if the debtor demonstrates that –

(i) no prior determination to the contrary has been made by a court or the Internal Revenue Service; and

(ii)(I) the retirement fund is in substantial compliance with the applicable requirements of the Internal Revenue Code of 1986; or

(II) the retirement fund fails to be in substantial compliance with the applicable requirements of the Internal Revenue Code of 1986 and the debtor is not materially responsible for that failure.

(C) A direct transfer of retirement funds from 1 fund or account that is exempt from taxation under section 401, 403, 408, 408A, 414, 457, or 501(a) of the Internal Revenue Code of 1986, under section 401(a)(31) of the Internal Revenue Code of 1986, or otherwise, shall not cease to qualify for exemption under paragraph (3)(C) or subsection (d)(12) by reason of such direct transfer.

(D)(i) Any distribution that qualifies as an eligible rollover distribution within the meaning of section 402(c) of the Internal Revenue Code of 1986 or that is described in clause (ii) shall not cease to qualify for exemption under paragraph (3)(C) or subsection (d)(12) by reason of such distribution.

(ii) A distribution described in this clause is an amount that –

(I) has been distributed from a fund or account that is exempt from taxation under section 401, 403, 408, 408A, 414, 457, or 501(a) of the Internal Revenue Code of 1986; and

(II) to the extent allowed by law, is deposited in such a fund or account not later than 60 days after the distribution of such amount.

(c) Unless the case is dismissed, property exempted under this section is not liable during or after the case for any debt of the debtor that arose, or that is determined under section 502 of this title as if such debt had arisen, before the commencement of the case, except -

(1) a debt of a kind specified in paragraph (1) or (5) of section 523(a) (in which case, notwithstanding any provision of applicable nonbankruptcy law to the contrary, such property shall be liable for a debt of a kind specified

in such paragraph);

(2) a debt secured by a lien that is -

(A)(i) not avoided under subsection (f) or (g) of this section or under section 544, 545, 547, 548, 549, or 724(a) of this title; and

(ii) not void under section 506(d) of this title; or

(B) a tax lien, notice of which is properly filed;

(3) a debt of a kind specified in section 523(a)(4) or 523(a)(6) of this title owed by an institution-affiliated party of an insured depository institution to a Federal depository institutions regulatory agency acting in its capacity as conservator, receiver, or liquidating agent for such institution; or

(4) a debt in connection with fraud in the obtaining or providing of any scholarship, grant, loan, tuition, discount, award, or other financial assistance for purposes of financing an education at an institution of higher education (as that term is defined in section 101 of the Higher Education Act of 1965 (20 U.S.C. 1001)).

(d) The following property may be exempted under subsection (b)(2) of this section:

(1) The debtor's aggregate interest, not to exceed $27,900 in value, in real property or personal property that the debtor or a dependent of the debtor uses as a residence, in a cooperative that owns property that the debtor or a dependent of the debtor uses as a residence, or in a burial plot for the debtor or a dependent of the debtor.

(2) The debtor's interest, not to exceed $4,450 in value, in one motor vehicle.

(3) The debtor's interest, not to exceed $700 in value in any particular item or $14,875 in aggregate value, in household furnishings, household goods, wearing apparel, appliances, books, animals, crops, or musical instruments, that are held primarily for the personal, family, or household use of the debtor or a dependent of the debtor.

(4) The debtor's aggregate interest, not to exceed $1,825 in value, in jewelry held primarily for the personal, family, or household use of the debtor or a dependent of the debtor.

(5) The debtor's aggregate interest in any property, not to exceed in value $1,425 plus up to $13,950 of any unused amount of the exemption provided under paragraph (1) of this subsection.

(6) The debtor's aggregate interest, not to exceed $2,800 in value, in any implements, professional books, or tools, of the trade of the debtor or the trade of a dependent of the debtor.

(7) Any unmatured life insurance contract owned by the debtor, other than a credit life insurance contract.

(8) The debtor's aggregate interest, not to exceed in value $14,875 less any amount of property of the estate transferred in the manner specified in section 542(d) of this title, in any accrued dividend or interest under, or loan value of, any unmatured life insurance contract owned by the debtor under which the insured is the debtor or an individual of whom the debtor is a dependent.

(9) Professionally prescribed health aids for the debtor or a dependent of the debtor.

(10) The debtor's right to receive -

(A) a social security benefit, unemployment compensation, or a local public assistance benefit;

(B) a veterans' benefit;

(C) a disability, illness, or unemployment benefit;

(D) alimony, support, or separate maintenance, to the extent reasonably necessary for the support of the debtor and any dependent of the debtor;

(E) a payment under a stock bonus, pension, profitsharing, annuity, or similar plan or contract on account of illness, disability, death, age, or length of service, to the extent reasonably necessary for the support of the debtor and any dependent of the debtor, unless -

(i) such plan or contract was established by or under the auspices of an insider that employed the debtor at the time the debtor's rights under such plan or contract arose;

(ii) such payment is on account of age or length of service; and

(iii) such plan or contract does not qualify under section 401(a), 403(a), 403(b), or 408 of the Internal Revenue Code of 1986.

(11) The debtor's right to receive, or property that is traceable to -

(A) an award under a crime victim's reparation law;

(B) a payment on account of the wrongful death of an individual of whom the debtor was a dependent, to the extent reasonably necessary for the support of the debtor and any dependent of the debtor;

(C) a payment under a life insurance contract that insured the life of an individual of whom the debtor was a dependent on the date of such individual's death, to the extent reasonably necessary for the support of the debtor and any dependent of the debtor;

(D) a payment, not to exceed $27,900, on account of personal bodily injury, not including pain and suffering or compensation for actual pecuniary loss, of the debtor or an individual of whom the debtor is a dependent; or

(E) a payment in compensation of loss of future earnings of the debtor or an individual of whom the debtor is or was a dependent, to the extent reasonably necessary for the support of the debtor and any dependent of the debtor.

(12) Retirement funds to the extent that those funds are in a fund or account that is exempt from taxation under section 401, 403, 408, 408A, 414, 457, or 501(a) of the Internal Revenue Code of 1986.

(e) A waiver of an exemption executed in favor of a creditor that holds an unsecured claim against the debtor is unenforceable in a case under this title with respect to such claim against property that the debtor may exempt under subsection (b) of this section. A waiver by the debtor of a power under subsection (f) or (h) of this section to avoid a transfer, under subsection (g) or (i) of this section to exempt property, or under subsection (i) of this section to recover property or to preserve a transfer, is unenforceable in a case under this title

(f)(1) Notwithstanding any waiver of exemptions but subject to paragraph (3), the debtor may avoid the fixing of a lien on an interest of the debtor in property to the extent that such lien impairs an exemption to which the debtor would have been entitled under subsection (b) of this section, if such lien is -

(A) a judicial lien, other than a judicial lien that secures a debt of a kind that is specified in section 523(a)(5); or

(B) a nonpossessory, nonpurchase-money security interest in any -

(i) household furnishings, household goods, wearing apparel, appliances, books, animals, crops, musical instruments, or jewelry that are held primarily for the personal, family, or household use of the debtor or a dependent of the debtor;

(ii) implements, professional books, or tools, of the trade of the debtor or the trade of a dependent of the debtor; or

(iii) professionally prescribed health aids for the debtor or a dependent of the debtor.

(2)(A) For the purposes of this subsection, a lien shall be considered to impair an exemption to the extent that the sum of -

(i) the lien;

(ii) all other liens on the property; and

(iii) the amount of the exemption that the debtor could claim if there were no liens on the property;

exceeds the value that the debtor's interest in the property would have in the absence of any liens.

(B) In the case of a property subject to more than 1 lien, a lien that has been avoided shall not be considered in making the calculation under subparagraph (A) with respect to other liens.

(C) This paragraph shall not apply with respect to a judgment arising out of a mortgage foreclosure.

(3) In a case in which State law that is applicable to the debtor -

(A) permits a person to voluntarily waive a right to claim exemptions under subsection (d) or prohibits a debtor from claiming exemptions under subsection (d); and

(B) either permits the debtor to claim exemptions under State law without limitation in amount, except to the extent that the debtor has permitted the fixing of a consensual lien on any property or prohibits avoidance of a consensual lien on property otherwise eligible to be claimed as exempt property;

the debtor may not avoid the fixing of a lien on an interest of the debtor or a dependent of the debtor in property if the lien is a nonpossessory, nonpurchase-money security interest in implements, professional books, or tools of the trade of the debtor or a dependent of the debtor or farm animals or crops of the debtor or a dependent of the debtor to the extent the value of such implements, professional books, tools of the trade, animals, and crops exceeds $7,575.

(4)(A) Subject to subparagraph (B), for purposes of paragraph (1)(B), the term "household goods" means –

(i) clothing;

(ii) furniture;

(iii) appliances;

(iv) 1 radio;

(v) 1 television;

(vi) 1 VCR;

(vii) linens;

(viii) china;

(ix) crockery;

(x) kitchenware;

(xi) educational materials and educational equipment primarily for the use of minor dependent children of the debtor;

(xii) medical equipment and supplies;

(xiii) furniture exclusively for the use of minor children, or elderly or disabled dependents of the debtor;

(xiv) personal effects (including the toys and hobby equipment of minor dependent children and wedding rings) of the debtor and the dependents of the debtor; and

(xv) 1 personal computer and related equipment.

(B) The term "household goods" does not include –

(i) works of art (unless by or of the debtor, or any relative of the debtor);

(ii) electronic entertainment equipment with a fair market value of more than $800 in the aggregate (except 1 television, 1 radio, and 1 VCR);

(iii) items acquired as antiques with a fair market value of more than $800 in the aggregate;

(iv) jewelry with a fair market value of more than $800 in the aggregate (except wedding rings); and

(v) a computer (except as otherwise provided for in this section), motor vehicle (including a tractor or lawn tractor), boat, or a motorized recreational device, conveyance, vehicle, watercraft, or aircraft.

(g) Notwithstanding sections 550 and 551 of this title, the debtor may exempt under subsection (b) of this section property that the trustee recovers under section 510(c)(2), 542, 543, 550, 551, or 553 of this title, to the extent that the debtor could have exempted such property under subsection (b) of this section if such property had not been transferred, if -

(1)(A) such transfer was not a voluntary transfer of such property by the debtor; and

(B) the debtor did not conceal such property ; or

(2) the debtor could have avoided such transfer under subsection (f) (1)(B) of this section.

(h) The debtor may avoid a transfer of property of the debtor or recover a setoff to the extent that the debtor could have exempted such property under subsection (g)(1) of this section if the trustee had avoided such transfer, if -

(1) such transfer is avoidable by the trustee under section 544, 545, 547, 548, 549, or 724(a) of this title or recoverable by the trustee under section 553 of this title; and

(2) the trustee does not attempt to avoid such transfer.

(i)(1) If the debtor avoids a transfer or recovers a setoff under subsection (f) or (h) of this section, the debtor may recover in the manner prescribed by, and subject to the limitations of, section 550 of this title, the same as if the trustee had avoided such transfer, and may exempt any property so recovered under subsection (b) of this section.

(2) Notwithstanding section 551 of this title, a transfer avoided under section 544, 545, 547, 548, 549, or 724(a) of this title, under subsection (f) or (h) of this section, or property recovered under section 553 of this title, may be preserved for the benefit of the debtor to the extent that the debtor may exempt such property under subsection (g) of this section or paragraph (1) of this subsection.

(j) Notwithstanding subsections (g) and (i) of this section, the debtor may exempt a particular kind of property under subsections (g) and (i) of this section only to the extent that the debtor has exempted less property in value of such kind than that to which the debtor is entitled under subsection (b) of this section.

(k) Property that the debtor exempts under this section is not liable for payment of any administrative expense except -

(1) the aliquot share of the costs and expenses of avoiding a transfer of property that the debtor exempts under subsection (g) of this section, or of recovery of such property, that is attributable to the value of the portion of such property exempted in relation to the value of the property recovered; and

(2) any costs and expenses of avoiding a transfer under subsection (f) or (h) of this section, or of recovery of property under subsection (i)(1) of this section, that the debtor has not paid.

(l) The debtor shall file a list of property that the debtor claims as exempt under subsection (b) of this section. If the debtor does not file such a list, a dependent of the debtor may file such a list, or may claim property as exempt from property of the estate on behalf of the debtor. Unless a party in interest objects, the property claimed as exempt on such list is exempt.

(m) Subject to the limitation in subsection (b), this section shall apply separately with respect to each debtor in a joint case.

(n) For assets in individual retirement accounts described in section 408 or 408A of the Internal Revenue Code of 1986, other than a simplified employee pension under section 408(k) of such Code or a simple retirement account under section 408(p) of such Code, the aggregate value of such assets exempted under this section, without regard to amounts attributable to rollover contributions under section 402(c), 402(e)(6), 403(a)(4), 403(a)(5), and 403(b)(8) of the Internal Revenue Code of 1986, and earnings thereon, shall not exceed $1,512,350 in a case filed by a debtor who is an individual, except that such amount may be increased if the interests of justice so require.

(o) For purposes of subsection (b)(3)(A), and notwithstanding subsection (a), the value of an interest in –

(1) real or personal property that the debtor or a dependent of the debtor uses as a residence;

(2) a cooperative that owns property that the debtor or a dependent of the debtor uses as a residence;

(3) a burial plot for the debtor or a dependent of the debtor; or

(4) real or personal property that the debtor or a dependent of the debtor claims as a homestead;

shall be reduced to the extent that such value is attributable to any portion of any property that the debtor disposed of in the 10-year period ending on the date of the filing of the petition with the intent to hinder, delay, or defraud a creditor and that the debtor could not exempt, or that portion that the debtor could not exempt, under subsection (b), if on such date the debtor had held the property so disposed of.

(p)(1) Except as provided in paragraph (2) of this subsection and sections 544 and 548, as a result of electing under subsection (b)(3)(A) to exempt property under State or local law, a debtor may not exempt any amount of interest that was acquired by the debtor during the 1215-day period preceding the date of the filing of the petition that exceeds in the aggregate $189,050 in value in –

(A) real or personal property that the debtor or a dependent of the debtor uses as a residence;

(B) a cooperative that owns property that the debtor or a dependent of the debtor uses as a residence;

(C) a burial plot for the debtor or a dependent of the debtor; or

(D) real or personal property that the debtor or dependent of the debtor claims as a homestead.

(2)(A) The limitation under paragraph (1) shall not apply to an exemption claimed under subsection (b)(3)(A) by a family farmer for the principal residence of such farmer.

(B) For purposes of paragraph (1), any amount of such interest does not include any interest transferred from a debtor's previous principal residence (which was acquired prior to the beginning of such 1215-day period) into the debtor's current principal residence, if the debtor's previous and current residences are located in the same State.

(q)(1) As a result of electing under subsection (b)(3)(A) to exempt property under State or local law, a debtor may not exempt any amount of an interest in property described in subparagraphs (A), (B), (C), and (D) of subsection (p)(1) which exceeds in the aggregate $189,050 if –

(A) the court determines, after notice and a hearing, that the debtor has been convicted of a felony (as defined in section 3156 of title 18), which under the circumstances, demonstrates that the filing of the case was an abuse of the provisions of this title; or

(B) the debtor owes a debt arising from –

(i) any violation of the Federal securities laws (as defined in section 3(a)(47) of the Securities Exchange Act of 1934), any State securities laws, or any regulation or order issued under Federal securities laws or State securities laws;

(ii) fraud, deceit, or manipulation in a fiduciary capacity or in connection with the purchase or sale of any security registered under section 12 or 15(d) of the Securities Exchange Act of 1934 or under section 6 of the Securities Act of 1933;

(iii) any civil remedy under section 1964 of title 18; or

(iv) any criminal act, intentional tort, or willful or reckless misconduct that caused serious physical injury or death to another individual in the preceding 5 years.

(2) Paragraph (1) shall not apply to the extent the amount of an interest in property described in subparagraphs (A), (B), (C), and (D) of subsection (p) (1) is reasonably necessary for the support of the debtor and any dependent of the debtor.

523. Exceptions to discharge

(a) A discharge under section 727, 1141, 1192, 1228(a), 1228(b), or 1328(b) of this title does not discharge an individual debtor from any debt -

(1) for a tax or a customs duty -

(A) of the kind and for the periods specified in section 507(a)(3) or 507(a)(8) of this title, whether or not a claim for such tax was filed or allowed;

(B) with respect to which a return, or equivalent report or notice, if required -

(i) was not filed or given; or

(ii) was filed or given after the date on which such return, report, or notice was last due, under applicable law or under any extension, and after two years before the date of the filing of the petition; or

(C) with respect to which the debtor made a fraudulent return or willfully attempted in any manner to evade or defeat such tax;

(2) for money, property, services, or an extension, renewal, or refinancing of credit, to the extent obtained by -

(A) false pretenses, a false representation, or actual fraud, other than a statement respecting the debtor's or an insider's financial condition;

(B) use of a statement in writing -

(i) that is materially false;

(ii) respecting the debtor's or an insider's financial condition;

(iii) on which the creditor to whom the debtor is liable for such money, property, services, or credit reasonably relied; and

(iv) that the debtor caused to be made or published with intent to deceive; or

(C)(i) for purposes of subparagraph (A) –

(I) consumer debts owed to a single creditor and aggregating more than $800 for luxury goods or services incurred by an individual debtor on or within 90 days before the order for relief under this title are presumed to be nondischargeable; and

(II) cash advances aggregating more than $1,100 that are extensions of consumer credit under an open end credit plan obtained by an individual debtor on or within 70 days before the order for relief under this title, are presumed to be nondischargeable; and

(ii) for purposes of this subparagraph –

(I) the terms "consumer", "credit", and "open end credit plan" have the same meanings as in section 103 of the Truth in Lending Act; and

(II) the term "luxury goods or services" does not include goods or services reasonably necessary for the support or maintenance of the debtor or a dependent of the debtor;

(3) neither listed nor scheduled under section 521(a)(1) of this title, with the name, if known to the debtor, of the creditor to whom such debt is owed, in time to permit -

(A) if such debt is not of a kind specified in paragraph (2), (4), or (6) of this subsection, timely filing of a proof of claim, unless such creditor had notice or actual knowledge of the case in time for such timely filing; or

(B) if such debt is of a kind specified in paragraph (2), (4), or (6) of this subsection, timely filing of a proof of claim and timely request for a determination of dischargeability of such debt under one of such paragraphs, unless such creditor had notice or actual knowledge of the case in time for such timely filing and request;

(4) for fraud or defalcation while acting in a fiduciary capacity, embezzlement, or larceny;

(5) for a domestic support obligation;

(6) for willful and malicious injury by the debtor to another entity or to the property of another entity;

(7) to the extent such debt is for a fine, penalty, or forfeiture payable to and for the benefit of a governmental unit, and is not compensation for actual pecuniary loss, other than a tax penalty -

(A) relating to a tax of a kind not specified in paragraph (1) of this subsection; or

(B) imposed with respect to a transaction or event that occurred before three years before the date of the filing of the petition;

(8) unless excepting such debt from discharge under this paragraph would impose an undue hardship on the debtor and the debtor's dependents, for –

(A)(i) an educational benefit overpayment or loan made, insured, or guaranteed by a governmental unit, or made under any program funded in whole or in part by a governmental unit or nonprofit institution; or

(ii) an obligation to repay funds received as an educational benefit, scholarship, or stipend; or

(B) any other educational loan that is a qualified education loan, as defined in section 221(d)(1) of the Internal Revenue Code of 1986, incurred by a debtor who is an individual;

(9) for death or personal injury caused by the debtor's operation of a motor vehicle, vessel, or aircraft if such operation was unlawful because the debtor was intoxicated from using alcohol, a drug, or another substance;

(10) that was or could have been listed or scheduled by the debtor in a prior case concerning the debtor under this title or under the Bankruptcy Act in which the debtor waived discharge, or was denied a discharge under section 727(a)(2), (3), (4), (5), (6), or (7) of this title, or under section 14c(1), (2), (3), (4), (6), or (7) of such Act;

(11) provided in any final judgment, unreviewable order, or consent order or decree entered in any court of the United States or of any State, issued by a Federal depository institutions regulatory agency, or contained in any settlement agreement entered into by the debtor, arising from any act of fraud or defalcation while acting in a fiduciary capacity committed with respect to any depository institution or insured credit union;

(12) for malicious or reckless failure to fulfill any commitment by the debtor to a Federal depository institutions regulatory agency to maintain the capital of an insured depository institution, except that this paragraph shall not extend any such commitment which would otherwise be terminated due to any act of such agency;

(13) for any payment of an order of restitution issued under title 18, United States Code;

(14) incurred to pay a tax to the United States that would be nondischargeable pursuant to paragraph (1);

(14A) incurred to pay a tax to a governmental unit, other than the United States, that would be nondischargeable under paragraph (1);

(14B) incurred to pay fines or penalties imposed under Federal election law;

(15) to a spouse, former spouse, or child of the debtor and not of the kind described in paragraph (5) that is incurred by the debtor in the course of a divorce or separation or in connection with a separation agreement, divorce decree or other order of a court of record, or a determination made in accordance with State or territorial law by a governmental unit;

(16) for a fee or assessment that becomes due and payable after the order for relief to a membership association with respect to the debtor's interest in a unit that has condominium ownership, in a share of a cooperative corporation, or a lot in a homeowners association, for as long as the debtor or the trustee has a legal, equitable, or possessory ownership interest in such unit, such corporation, or such lot, but nothing in this paragraph shall except from discharge the debt of a debtor for a membership association fee or assessment for a period arising before entry of the order for relief in a pending or subsequent bankruptcy case;

(17) for a fee imposed on a prisoner by any court for the filing of a case, motion, complaint, or appeal, or for other costs and expenses assessed with respect to such filing, regardless of an assertion of poverty by the debtor under subsection (b) or (f)(2) of section 1915 of title 28 (or a similar non-Federal law), or the debtor's status as a prisoner, as defined in section 1915(h) of title 28 (or a similar non-Federal law);

(18) owed to a pension, profit-sharing, stock bonus, or other plan established under section 401, 403, 408, 408A, 414, 457, or 501(c) of the Internal Revenue Code of 1986, under –

(A) a loan permitted under section 408(b)(1) of the Employee Retirement Income Security Act of 1974, or subject to section 72(p) of the Internal Revenue Code of 1986; or

(B) a loan from a thrift savings plan permitted under subchapter III of chapter 84 of title 5, that satisfies the requirements of section 8433(g) of such title;

but nothing in this paragraph may be construed to provide that any loan made under a governmental plan under section 414(d), or a contract or account under section 403(b), of the Internal Revenue Code of 1986 constitutes a claim or a debt under this title; or

(19) that -

(A) is for –

(i) the violation of any of the Federal securities laws (as that term is defined in section 3(a)(47) of the Securities Exchange Act of 1934 [15 USC § 78c(a)(47)]), any of the State securities laws, or any regulation or order issued under such Federal or State securities laws; or

(ii) common law fraud, deceit, or manipulation in connection with the purchase or sale of any security; and

(B) results, before, on, or after the date on which the petition was filed, from -

(i) any judgment, order, consent order, or decree entered in any Federal or State judicial or administrative proceeding;

(ii) any settlement agreement entered into by the debtor; or

(iii) any court or administrative order for any damages, fine, penalty, citation, restitutionary payment, disgorgement payment, attorney fee, cost, or other payment owed by the debtor.

(20) for injury to an individual by the debtor relating to a violation of chapter 77 of title 18, including injury caused by an instance in which the debtor knowingly benefitted financially, or by receiving anything of value, from participation in a venture that the debtor knew or should have known engaged in an act in violation of chapter 77 of title 18.

For purposes of this subsection, the term "return" means a return that satisfies the requirements of applicable nonbankruptcy law (including applicable filing requirements). Such term includes a return prepared pursuant to section 6020(a) of the Internal Revenue Code of 1986, or similar State or local law, or a written stipulation to a judgment or a final order entered by a nonbankruptcy tribunal, but does not include a return made pursuant to section 6020(b) of the Internal Revenue Code of 1986, or a similar State or local law.

(b) Notwithstanding subsection (a) of this section, a debt that was excepted from discharge under subsection (a)(1), (a)(3), or (a)(8) of this section, under section 17a(1), 17a(3), or 17a(5) of the Bankruptcy Act, under section 439A of the Higher Education Act of 1965, or under section 733(g) of the Public Health Service Act in a prior case concerning the debtor under this title, or under the Bankruptcy Act, is dischargeable in a case under this title unless, by the terms of subsection (a) of this section, such debt is not dischargeable in the case under this title.

(c)(1) Except as provided in subsection (a)(3)(B) of this section, the debtor shall be discharged from a debt of a kind specified in paragraph (2), (4), or (6) of subsection (a) of this section, unless, on request of the creditor to whom such debt is owed, and after notice and a hearing, the court determines such debt to be excepted from discharge under paragraph (2), (4), or (6), as the case may be, of subsection (a) of this section.

(2) Paragraph (1) shall not apply in the case of a Federal depository institutions regulatory agency seeking, in its capacity as conservator, receiver, or liquidating agent for an insured depository institution, to recover a debt described in subsection (a)(2), (a)(4), (a)(6), or (a)(11) owed to such institution by an institution-affiliated party unless the receiver, conservator, or liquidating agent was appointed in time to reasonably comply, or for a Federal depository institutions regulatory agency acting in its corporate capacity as a successor to such receiver, conservator, or liquidating agent to reasonably comply, with subsection (a)(3)(B) as a creditor of such institution-affiliated party with respect to such debt.

(d) If a creditor requests a determination of dischargeability of a consumer debt under subsection (a)(2) of this section, and such debt is discharged, the court shall grant judgment in favor of the debtor for the costs of, and a reasonable attorney's fee for, the proceeding if the court finds that the position of the creditor was not substantially justified, except that the court shall not award such costs and fees if special circumstances would make the award unjust.

(e) Any institution-affiliated party of an insured depository institution shall be considered to be acting in a fiduciary capacity with respect to the purposes of subsection (a) (4) or (11).

524. Effect of discharge

(a) A discharge in a case under this title -

(1) voids any judgment at any time obtained, to the extent that such judgment is a determination of the personal liability of the debtor with respect to any debt discharged under section 727, 944, 1141, 1192, 1228 or 1328 of this title, whether or not discharge of such debt is waived;

(2) operates as an injunction against the commencement or continuation of an action, the employment of process, or an act, to collect, recover or offset any such debt as a personal liability of the debtor, whether or not discharge of such debt is waived; and

(3) operates as an injunction against the commencement or continuation of an action, the employment of process, or an act, to collect or recover from, or offset against, property of the debtor of the kind specified in section 541(a)(2) of this title that is acquired after the commencement of the case, on account of any allowable community claim, except a community claim that is excepted from discharge under section 523, 1192, 1228(a)(1), or 1328(a)(1), or that would be so excepted, determined in accordance with the provisions of sections 523(c) and 523(d) of this title, in a case concerning the debtor's spouse commenced on the date of the filing of the petition in the case concerning the debtor, whether or not discharge of the debt based on such community claim is waived.

(b) Subsection (a)(3) of this section does not apply if –

(1)(A) the debtor's spouse is a debtor in a case under this title, or a bankrupt or a debtor in a case under the Bankruptcy Act, commenced within six years of the date of the filing of the petition in the case concerning the debtor; and

(B) the court does not grant the debtor's spouse a discharge in such case concerning the debtor's spouse; or

(2)(A) the court would not grant the debtor's spouse a discharge in a case under chapter 7 of this title concerning such spouse commenced on the date of the filing of the petition in the case concerning the debtor; and

(B) a determination that the court would not so grant such discharge is made by the bankruptcy court within the time and in the manner provided for a determination under section 727 of this title of whether a debtor is granted a discharge.

(c) An agreement between a holder of a claim and the debtor, the consideration for which, in whole or in part, is based on a debt that is dischargeable in a case under this title is enforceable only to any extent enforceable under applicable nonbankruptcy law, whether or not discharge of such debt is waived, only if –

(1) such agreement was made before the granting of the discharge under section 727, 1141, 1192, 1228, or 1328 of this title;

(2) the debtor received the disclosures described in subsection (k) at or before the time at which the debtor signed the agreement;

(3) such agreement has been filed with the court and, if applicable, accompanied by a declaration or an affidavit of the attorney that represented the debtor during the course of negotiating an agreement under this subsection, which states that –

(A) such agreement represents a fully informed and voluntary agreement by the debtor;

(B) such agreement does not impose an undue hardship on the debtor or a dependent of the debtor; and

(C) the attorney fully advised the debtor of the legal effect and consequences of –

(i) an agreement of the kind specified in this subsection; and

(ii) any default under such an agreement;

(4) the debtor has not rescinded such agreement at any time prior to discharge or within sixty days after such agreement is filed with the court, whichever occurs later, by giving notice of rescission to the holder of such claim;

(5) the provisions of subsection (d) of this section have been complied with; and

(6)(A) in a case concerning an individual who was not represented by an attorney during the course of negotiating an agreement under this subsection, the court approves such agreement as –

(i) not imposing an undue hardship on the debtor or a dependent of the debtor; and

(ii) in the best interest of the debtor.

(B) Subparagraph (A) shall not apply to the extent that such debt is a consumer debt secured by real property.

(d) In a case concerning an individual, when the court has determined whether to grant or not to grant a discharge under section 727, 1141, 1192, 1228, or 1328 of this title, the court may hold a hearing at which the debtor shall appear in person. At any such hearing, the court shall inform the debtor that a discharge has been granted or the reason why a discharge has not been granted. If a discharge has been granted and if the debtor desires to make an agreement of the kind specified in subsection (c) of this section and was not represented by an attorney during the course of negotiating such agreement, then the court shall hold a hearing at which the debtor shall appear in person and at such hearing the court shall –

(1) inform the debtor –

(A) that such an agreement is not required under this title, under nonbankruptcy law, or under any agreement not made in accordance with the provisions of subsection (c) of this section; and

(B) of the legal effect and consequences of –

(i) an agreement of the kind specified in subsection (c) of this section; and

(ii) a default under such an agreement; and

(2) determine whether the agreement that the debtor desires to make complies with the requirements of subsection (c)(6) of this section, if the consideration for such agreement is based in whole or in part on a consumer debt that is not secured by real property of the debtor.

(e) Except as provided in subsection (a)(3) of this section, discharge of a debt of the debtor does not affect the liability of any other entity on, or the property of any other entity for, such debt.

(f) Nothing contained in subsection (c) or (d) of this section prevents a debtor from voluntarily repaying any debt.

(g)(1)(A) After notice and hearing, a court that enters an order confirming a plan of reorganization under chapter 11 may issue, in connection with such order, an injunction in accordance with this subsection to supplement the injunctive effect of a discharge under this section.

(B) An injunction may be issued under subparagraph (A) to enjoin entities from taking legal action for the purpose of directly or indirectly collecting, recovering, or receiving payment or recovery with respect to any claim or demand that, under a plan of reorganization, is to be paid in whole or in part by a trust described in paragraph (2)(B)(i), except such legal actions as are expressly allowed by the injunction, the confirmation order, or the plan of reorganization.

(2)(A) Subject to subsection (h), if the requirements of subparagraph (B) are met at the time an injunction described in paragraph (1) is entered, then after entry of such injunction, any proceeding that involves the validity, application, construction, or modification of such injunction, or of this subsection with respect to such injunction, may be commenced only in the district court in which such injunction was entered, and such court shall have exclusive jurisdiction over any such proceeding without regard to the amount in controversy.

(B) The requirements of this subparagraph are that –

(i) the injunction is to be implemented in connection with a trust that, pursuant to the plan of reorganization –

(I) is to assume the liabilities of a debtor which at the time of entry of the order for relief has been named as a defendant in personal injury, wrongful death, or property-damage actions seeking recovery for damages allegedly caused by the presence of, or exposure to, asbestos or asbestos-containing products;

(II) is to be funded in whole or in part by the securities of 1 or more debtors involved in such plan and by the obligation of such debtor or debtors to make future payments, including dividends;

(III) is to own, or by the exercise of rights granted under such plan would be entitled to own if specified contingencies occur, a majority of the voting shares of –

(aa) each such debtor;

(bb) the parent corporation of each such debtor; or

(cc) a subsidiary of each such debtor that is also a debtor; and

(IV) is to use its assets or income to pay claims and demands; and

(ii) subject to subsection (h), the court determines that –

(I) the debtor is likely to be subject to substantial future demands for payment arising out of the same or similar conduct or events that gave rise to the claims that are addressed by the injunction;

(II) the actual amounts, numbers, and timing of such future demands cannot be determined;

(III) pursuit of such demands outside the procedures prescribed by such plan is likely to threaten the plan's purpose to deal equitably with claims and future demands;

(IV) as part of the process of seeking confirmation of such plan-

(aa) the terms of the injunction proposed to be issued under paragraph (1)(A), including any provisions barring actions against third parties pursuant to paragraph (4)(A), are set out in such plan and in any disclosure statement supporting the plan; and

(bb) a separate class or classes of the claimants whose claims are to be addressed by a trust described in clause (i) is established and votes, by at least 75 percent of those voting, in favor of the plan; and

(V) subject to subsection (h), pursuant to court orders or otherwise, the trust will operate through mechanisms such as structured, periodic, or supplemental payments, pro rata distributions, matrices, or periodic review of estimates of the numbers and values of present claims and future demands, or other comparable mechanisms, that provide reasonable assurance that the trust will value, and be in a financial position to pay, present claims and future demands that involve similar claims in substantially the same manner.

(3)(A) If the requirements of paragraph (2)(B) are met and the order confirming the plan of reorganization was issued or affirmed by the district court that has jurisdiction over the reorganization case, then after the time for appeal of the order that issues or affirms the plan –

(i) the injunction shall be valid and enforceable and may not be revoked or modified by any court except through appeal in accordance with paragraph (6);

(ii) no entity that pursuant to such plan or thereafter becomes a direct or indirect transferee of, or successor to any assets of, a debtor or trust that is the subject of the injunction shall be liable with respect to any claim or demand made against such entity by reason of its becoming such a transferee or successor; and

(iii) no entity that pursuant to such plan or thereafter makes a loan to such a debtor or trust or to such a successor or transferee shall, by reason of making the loan, be liable with respect to any claim or demand made against such entity, nor shall any pledge of assets made in connection with such a loan be upset or impaired for that reason;

(B) Subparagraph (A) shall not be construed to –

(i) imply that an entity described in subparagraph (A)(ii) or (iii) would, if this paragraph were not applicable, necessarily be liable to any entity by reason of any of the acts described in subparagraph (A);

(ii) relieve any such entity of the duty to comply with, or of liability under, any Federal or State law regarding the making of a fraudulent conveyance in a transaction described in subparagraph (A)(ii) or (iii); or

(iii) relieve a debtor of the debtor's obligation to comply with the terms of the plan of reorganization, or affect the power of the court to exercise its authority under sections 1141 and 1142 to compel the debtor to do so.

(4)(A)(i) Subject to subparagraph (B), an injunction described in paragraph (1) shall be valid and enforceable against all entities that it addresses.

(ii) Notwithstanding the provisions of section 524(e), such an injunction may bar any action directed against a third party who is identifiable from the terms of such injunction (by name or as part of an identifiable group) and is alleged to be directly or indirectly liable for the conduct of, claims against, or demands on the debtor to the extent such alleged liability of such third party arises by reason of –

(I) the third party's ownership of a financial interest in the debtor, a past or present affiliate of the debtor, or a predecessor in interest of the debtor;

(II) the third party's involvement in the management of the debtor or a predecessor in interest of the debtor, or service as an officer, director or employee of the debtor or a related party;

(III) the third party's provision of insurance to the debtor or a related party; or

(IV) the third party's involvement in a transaction changing the corporate structure, or in a loan or other financial transaction affecting the financial condition, of the debtor or a related party, including but not limited to –

(aa) involvement in providing financing (debt or equity), or advice to an entity involved in such a transaction; or

(bb) acquiring or selling a financial interest in an entity as part of such a transaction.

(iii) As used in this subparagraph, the term "related party" means –

(I) a past or present affiliate of the debtor;

(II) a predecessor in interest of the debtor; or

(III) any entity that owned a financial interest in –

(aa) the debtor;

(bb) a past or present affiliate of the debtor, or

(cc) a predecessor in interest of the debtor.

(B) Subject to subsection (h), if, under a plan of reorganization, a kind of demand described in such plan is to be paid in whole or in part by a trust described in paragraph (2)(B)(i) in connection with which an injunction described in paragraph (1) is to be implemented, then such injunction shall be valid and enforceable with respect to a demand of such kind made, after such plan is confirmed against the debtor or debtors involved, or against a third party described in subparagraph (A)(ii), if –

(i) as part of the proceedings leading to issuance of such injunction, the court appoints a legal representative for the purpose of protecting the rights of persons that might subsequently assert demands of such kind, and

(ii) the court determines, before entering the order confirming such plan, that identifying such debtor or debtors, or such third party (by name or as part of an identifiable group), in such injunction with respect to such demands for purposes of this subparagraph is fair and equitable with respect to the persons that might subsequently assert such demands, in light of the benefits provided, or to be provided, to such trust on behalf of such debtor or debtors or such third party.

(5) In this subsection, the term "demand" means a demand for payment, present or future, that –

(A) was not a claim during the proceedings leading to the confirmation of a plan of reorganization;

(B) arises out of the same or similar conduct or events that gave rise to the claims addressed by the injunction issued under paragraph (1); and

(C) pursuant to the plan, is to be paid by a trust described in paragraph (2)(B)(i).

(6) Paragraph (3)(A)(i) does not bar an action taken by or at the direction of an appellate court on appeal of an injunction issued under paragraph (1) or of the order of confirmation that relates to the injunction.

(7) This subsection does not affect the operation of section 1144 or the power of the district court to refer a proceeding under section 157 of title 28 or any reference of a proceeding made prior to the date of the enactment of this subsection.

(h) Application to Existing Injunctions.- For purposes of subsection (g)-

(1) subject to paragraph (2), if an injunction of the kind described in subsection (g)(1)(B) was issued before the date of the enactment of this Act, as part of a plan of reorganization confirmed by an order entered before such date, then the injunction shall be considered to meet the requirements of subsection (g)(2)(B) for purposes of subsection (g)(2)(A), and to satisfy subsection (g)(4)(A)(ii), if –

(A) the court determined at the time the plan was confirmed that the plan was fair and equitable in accordance with the requirements of section 1129(b);

(B) as part of the proceedings leading to issuance of such injunction and confirmation of such plan, the court had appointed a legal representative for the purpose of protecting the rights of persons that might subsequently assert demands described in subsection (g)(4)(B) with respect to such plan; and

(C) such legal representative did not object to confirmation of such plan or issuance of such injunction; and

(2) for purposes of paragraph (1), if a trust described in subsection (g)(2)(B)(i) is subject to a court order on the date of the enactment of this Act staying such trust from settling or paying further claims –

(A) the requirements of subsection (g)(2)(B)(ii)(V) shall not apply with respect to such trust until such stay is lifted or dissolved; and

(B) if such trust meets such requirements on the date such stay is lifted or dissolved, such trust shall be considered to have met such requirements continuously from the date of the enactment of this Act.

(i) The willful failure of a creditor to credit payments received under a plan confirmed under this title, unless the order confirming the plan is revoked, the plan is in default, or the creditor has not received payments required to be made under the plan in the manner required by the plan (including crediting the amounts required under the plan), shall constitute a violation of an injunction under subsection (a)(2) if the act of the creditor to collect and failure to credit payments in the manner required by the plan caused material injury to the debtor.

(j) Subsection (a)(2) does not operate as an injunction against an act by a creditor that is the holder of a secured claim, if –

(1) such creditor retains a security interest in real property that is the principal residence of the debtor;

(2) such act is in the ordinary course of business between the creditor and the debtor; and

(3) such act is limited to seeking or obtaining periodic payments associated with a valid security interest in lieu of pursuit of in rem relief to enforce the lien.

(k)(1) The disclosures required under subsection (c)(2) shall consist of the disclosure statement described in paragraph (3), completed as required in that paragraph, together with the agreement specified in subsection (c), statement, declaration, motion and order described, respectively, in paragraphs (4) through (8), and shall be the only disclosures required in connection with entering into such agreement.

(2) Disclosures made under paragraph (1) shall be made clearly and conspicuously and in writing. The terms "Amount Reaffirmed" and "Annual Percentage Rate" shall be disclosed more conspicuously than other terms, data or information provided in connection with this disclosure, except that the phrases "Before agreeing to reaffirm a debt, review these important disclosures" and "Summary of Reaffirmation Agreement" may be equally conspicuous. Disclosures may be made in a different order and may use terminology different from that set forth in paragraphs (2) through (8), except that the terms "Amount Reaffirmed" and "Annual Percentage Rate" must be used where indicated.

(3) The disclosure statement required under this paragraph shall consist of the following:

(A) The statement: "Part A: Before agreeing to reaffirm a debt, review these important disclosures:";

(B) Under the heading "Summary of Reaffirmation Agreement", the statement: "This Summary is made pursuant to the requirements of the Bankruptcy Code";

(C) The "Amount Reaffirmed", using that term, which shall be –

(i) the total amount of debt that the debtor agrees to reaffirm by entering into an agreement of the kind specified in subsection (c), and

(ii) the total of any fees and costs accrued as of the date of the disclosure statement, related to such total amount.

(D) In conjunction with the disclosure of the "Amount Reaffirmed", the statements –

(i) "The amount of debt you have agreed to reaffirm"; and

(ii) "Your credit agreement may obligate you to pay additional amounts which may come due after the date of this disclosure. Consult your credit agreement.".

(E) The "Annual Percentage Rate", using that term, which shall be disclosed as –

(i) if, at the time the petition is filed, the debt is an extension of credit under an open end credit plan, as the terms "credit" and "open end credit plan" are defined in section 103 of the Truth in Lending Act, then –

(I) the annual percentage rate determined under paragraphs (5) and (6) of section 127(b) of the Truth in Lending Act, as applicable, as disclosed to the debtor in the most recent periodic statement prior to entering into an agreement of the kind specified in subsection (c) or, if no such periodic statement has been given to the debtor during the prior 6 months, the annual percentage rate as it would have been so disclosed at the time the disclosure statement is given to the debtor, or to the extent this annual percentage rate is not readily available or not applicable, then

(II) the simple interest rate applicable to the amount reaffirmed as of the date the disclosure statement is given to the debtor, or if different simple interest rates apply to different balances, the simple interest rate applicable to each such balance, identifying the amount of each such balance included in the amount reaffirmed, or

(III) if the entity making the disclosure elects, to disclose the annual percentage rate under subclause (I) and the simple interest rate under subclause (II); or

(ii) if, at the time the petition is filed, the debt is an extension of credit other than under an open end credit plan, as the terms "credit" and "open end credit plan" are defined in section 103 of the Truth in Lending Act, then –

(I) the annual percentage rate under section 128(a)(4) of the Truth in Lending Act, as disclosed to the debtor in the most recent disclosure statement given to the debtor prior to the entering into an agreement of the kind specified in subsection (c) with respect to the debt, or, if no such disclosure statement was given to the debtor, the annual percentage rate as it would have been so disclosed at the time the disclosure statement is given to the debtor, or to the extent this annual percentage rate is not readily available or not applicable, then

(II) the simple interest rate applicable to the amount reaffirmed as of the date the disclosure statement is given to the debtor, or if different simple interest rates apply to different balances, the simple interest rate applicable to each such balance, identifying the amount of such balance included in the amount reaffirmed, or

(III) if the entity making the disclosure elects, to disclose the annual percentage rate under (I) and the simple interest rate under (II).

(F) If the underlying debt transaction was disclosed as a variable rate transaction on the most recent disclosure given under the Truth in Lending Act, by stating "The interest rate on your loan may be a variable interest rate which changes from time to time, so that the annual percentage rate disclosed here may be higher or lower.".

(G) If the debt is secured by a security interest which has not been waived in whole or in part or determined to be void by a final order of the court at the time of the disclosure, by disclosing that a security interest or lien in goods or property is asserted over some or all of the debts the debtor is reaffirming and listing the items and their original purchase price that are subject to the asserted security interest, or if not a purchase-money security interest then listing by items or types and the original amount of the loan.

(H) At the election of the creditor, a statement of the repayment schedule using 1 or a combination of the following –

(i) by making the statement: "Your first payment in the amount of $XXX is due on XXX but the future payment amount may be different. Consult your reaffirmation agreement or credit agreement, as applicable.", and stating the amount of the first payment and the due date of that payment in the places provided;

(ii) by making the statement: "Your payment schedule will be:", and describing the repayment schedule with the number, amount, and due dates or period of payments scheduled to repay the debts reaffirmed to the extent then known by the disclosing party; or

(iii) by describing the debtor's repayment obligations with reasonable specificity to the extent then known by the disclosing party.

(I) The following statement: "Note: When this disclosure refers to what a creditor "may" do, it does not use the word "may" to give the creditor specific permission. The word "may" is used to tell you what might occur if the law permits the creditor to take the action. If you have questions about your reaffirming a debt or what the law requires, consult with the attorney who helped you negotiate this agreement reaffirming a debt. If you don't have an attorney helping you, the judge will explain the effect of your reaffirming a debt when the hearing on the reaffirmation agreement is held.".

(J)(i) The following additional statements:

"Reaffirming a debt is a serious financial decision. The law requires you to take certain steps to make sure the decision is in your best interest. If these steps are not completed, the reaffirmation agreement is not effective, even though you have signed it.

"1. Read the disclosures in this Part A carefully. Consider the decision to reaffirm carefully. Then, if you want to reaffirm, sign the reaffirmation agreement in Part B (or you may use a separate agreement you and your creditor agree on).

"2. Complete and sign Part D and be sure you can afford to make the payments you are agreeing to make and have received a copy of the disclosure statement and a completed and signed reaffirmation agreement.

"3. If you were represented by an attorney during the negotiation of your reaffirmation agreement, the attorney must have signed the certification in Part C.

"4. If you were not represented by an attorney during the negotiation of your reaffirmation agreement, you must have completed and signed Part E.

"5. The original of this disclosure must be filed with the court by you or your creditor. If a separate reaffirmation agreement (other than the one in Part B) has been signed, it must be attached.

"6. If you were represented by an attorney during the negotiation of your reaffirmation agreement, your reaffirmation agreement becomes effective upon filing with the court unless the reaffirmation is presumed to be an undue hardship as explained in Part D.

"7. If you were not represented by an attorney during the negotiation of your reaffirmation agreement, it will not be effective unless the court approves it. The court will notify you of the hearing on your reaffirmation agreement. You must attend this hearing in bankruptcy court where the judge will review your reaffirmation agreement. The bankruptcy court must approve your reaffirmation agreement as consistent with your best interests, except that no court approval is required if your reaffirmation agreement is for a consumer debt secured by a mortgage, deed of trust, security deed, or other lien on your real property, like your home.

"Your right to rescind (cancel) your reaffirmation agreement. You may rescind (cancel) your reaffirmation agreement at any time before the bankruptcy court enters a discharge order, or before the expiration of the 60-day period that begins on the date your reaffirmation agreement is filed with the court, whichever occurs later. To rescind (cancel) your reaffirmation agreement, you must notify the creditor that your reaffirmation agreement is rescinded (or canceled).

"What are your obligations if you reaffirm the debt? A reaffirmed debt remains your personal legal obligation. It is not discharged in your bankruptcy case. That means that if you default on your reaffirmed debt after your bankruptcy case is over, your creditor may be able to take your property or your wages. Otherwise, your obligations will be determined by the reaffirmation agreement which may have changed the terms of the original agreement. For example, if you are reaffirming an open end credit agreement, the creditor may be permitted by that agreement or applicable law to change the terms of that agreement in the future under certain conditions.

"Are you required to enter into a reaffirmation agreement by any law? No, you are not required to reaffirm a debt by any law. Only agree to reaffirm a debt if it is in your best interest. Be sure you can afford the payments you agree to make.

"What if your creditor has a security interest or lien? Your bankruptcy discharge does not eliminate any lien on your property. A "lien" is often referred to as a security interest, deed of trust, mortgage or security deed. Even if you do not reaffirm and your personal liability on the debt is discharged, because of the lien your creditor may still have the right to take the property securing the lien if you do not pay the debt or default on it. If the lien is on an item of personal property that is exempt under your State's law or that the trustee has abandoned, you may be able to redeem the item rather than reaffirm the debt. To redeem, you must make a single payment to the creditor equal to the amount of the allowed secured claim, as agreed by the parties or determined by the court.".

(ii) In the case of a reaffirmation under subsection (m)(2), numbered paragraph 6 in the disclosures required by clause (i) of this subparagraph shall read as follows:

"6. If you were represented by an attorney during the negotiation of your reaffirmation agreement, your reaffirmation agreement becomes effective upon filing with the court.".

(4) The form of such agreement required under this paragraph shall consist of the following:

"Part B: Reaffirmation Agreement. I (we) agree to reaffirm the debts arising under the credit agreement described below.

"Brief description of credit agreement:

"Description of any changes to the credit agreement made as part of this reaffirmation agreement:

"Signature: Date:

"Borrower:

"Co-borrower, if also reaffirming these debts:

"Accepted by creditor:

"Date of creditor acceptance:".

(5) The declaration shall consist of the following:

(A) The following certification:

"Part C: Certification by Debtor's Attorney (If Any).

"I hereby certify that (1) this agreement represents a fully informed and voluntary agreement by the debtor; (2) this agreement does not impose an undue hardship on the debtor or any dependent of the debtor; and (3) I have fully advised the debtor of the legal effect and consequences of this agreement and any default under this agreement.

"Signature of Debtor's Attorney: Date:".

(B) If a presumption of undue hardship has been established with respect to such agreement, such certification shall state that, in the opinion of the attorney, the debtor is able to make the payment.

(C) In the case of a reaffirmation agreement under subsection (m)(2), subparagraph (B) is not applicable.

(6)(A) The statement in support of such agreement, which the debtor shall sign and date prior to filing with the court, shall consist of the following:

"Part D: Debtor's Statement in Support of Reaffirmation Agreement.

"1. I believe this reaffirmation agreement will not impose an undue hardship on my dependents or me. I can afford to make the payments on the reaffirmed debt because my monthly income (take home pay plus any other income received) is $XXX, and my actual current monthly expenses including monthly payments on post-bankruptcy debt and other reaffirmation agreements total $XXX, leaving $XXX to make the required payments on this reaffirmed debt. I understand that if my income less my monthly expenses does not leave enough to make the payments, this reaffirmation agreement is presumed to be an undue hardship on me and must be reviewed by the court. However, this presumption may be overcome if I explain to the satisfaction of the court how I can afford to make the payments here: XXX.

"2. I received a copy of the Reaffirmation Disclosure Statement in Part A and a completed and signed reaffirmation agreement.".

(B) Where the debtor is represented by an attorney and is reaffirming a debt owed to a creditor defined in section 19(b)(1)(A)(iv) of the Federal Reserve Act, the statement of support of the reaffirmation agreement, which the debtor shall sign and date prior to filing with the court, shall consist of the following:

"I believe this reaffirmation agreement is in my financial interest. I can afford to make the payments on the reaffirmed debt. I received a copy of the Reaffirmation Disclosure Statement in Part A and a completed and signed reaffirmation agreement.".

(7) The motion that may be used if approval of such agreement by the court is required in order for it to be effective, shall be signed and dated by the movant and shall consist of the following:

"Part E: Motion for Court Approval (To be completed only if the debtor is not represented by an attorney.). I (we), the debtor(s), affirm the following to be true and correct:

"I am not represented by an attorney in connection with this reaffirmation agreement.

"I believe this reaffirmation agreement is in my best interest based on the income and expenses I have disclosed in my Statement in Support of this reaffirmation agreement, and because (provide any additional relevant reasons the court should consider):

"Therefore, I ask the court for an order approving this reaffirmation agreement.".

(8) The court order, which may be used to approve such agreement, shall

consist of the following:

"Court Order: The court grants the debtor's motion and approves the reaffirmation agreement described above.".

(l) Notwithstanding any other provision of this title the following shall apply:

(1) A creditor may accept payments from a debtor before and after the filing of an agreement of the kind specified in subsection (c) with the court.

(2) A creditor may accept payments from a debtor under such agreement that the creditor believes in good faith to be effective.

(3) The requirements of subsections (c)(2) and (k) shall be satisfied if disclosures required under those subsections are given in good faith.

(m)(1) Until 60 days after an agreement of the kind specified in subsection (c) is filed with the court (or such additional period as the court, after notice and a hearing and for cause, orders before the expiration of such period), it shall be presumed that such agreement is an undue hardship on the debtor if the debtor's monthly income less the debtor's monthly expenses as shown on the debtor's completed and signed statement in support of such agreement required under subsection (k)(6)(A) is less than the scheduled payments on the reaffirmed debt. This presumption shall be reviewed by the court. The presumption may be rebutted in writing by the debtor if the statement includes an explanation that identifies additional sources of funds to make the payments as agreed upon under the terms of such agreement. If the presumption is not rebutted to the satisfaction of the court, the court may disapprove such agreement. No agreement shall be disapproved without notice and a hearing to the debtor and creditor, and such hearing shall be concluded before the entry of the debtor's discharge.

(2) This subsection does not apply to reaffirmation agreements where the creditor is a credit union, as defined in section 19(b)(1)(A)(iv) of the Federal Reserve Act.

525. Protection against discriminatory treatment

(a) Except as provided in the Perishable Agricultural Commodities Act, 1930, the Packers and Stockyards Act, 1921, and section 1 of the Act entitled "An Act making appropriations for the Department of Agriculture for the fiscal year ending June 30, 1944, and for other purposes," approved July 12, 1943, a governmental unit may not deny, revoke, suspend, or refuse to renew a license, permit, charter, franchise, or other similar grant to, condition such a grant to, discriminate with respect to such a grant against, deny employment to, terminate the employment of, or discriminate with respect to employment against, a person that is or has been a debtor under this title or a bankrupt or a debtor under the Bankruptcy Act, or another person with whom such bankrupt or debtor has been associated, solely because such bankrupt or debtor is or has been a debtor under this title or a bankrupt or debtor under the Bankruptcy Act, has been insolvent before the commencement of the case under this title, or during the case but before the debtor is granted or denied a discharge, or has not paid a debt that is dischargeable in the case under this title or that was discharged under the Bankruptcy Act.

(b) No private employer may terminate the employment of, or discriminate with respect to employment against, an individual who is or has been a debtor under this title, a debtor or bankrupt under the Bankruptcy Act, or an individual associated with such debtor or bankrupt, solely because such debtor or bankrupt -

(1) is or has been a debtor under this title or a debtor or bankrupt under the Bankruptcy Act;

(2) has been insolvent before the commencement of a case under this title or during the case but before the grant or denial of a discharge; or

(3) has not paid a debt that is dischargeable in a case under this title or that was discharged under the Bankruptcy Act.

(c)(1) A governmental unit that operates a student grant or loan program and a person engaged in a business that includes the making of loans guaranteed or insured under a student loan program may not deny a student grant, loan, loan guarantee, or loan insurance to a person that is or has been a debtor under this title or a bankrupt or debtor under the Bankruptcy Act, or another person with whom the debtor or bankrupt has been associated, because the debtor or bankrupt is or has been a debtor under this title or a bankrupt or debtor under the Bankruptcy Act, has been insolvent before the commencement of a case under this title or during the pendency of the case but before the debtor is granted or denied a discharge, or has not paid a debt that is dischargeable in the case under this title or that was discharged under the Bankruptcy Act.

(2) In this section, "student loan program" means any program operated under title IV of the Higher Education Act of 1965 or a similar program operated under State or local law.

526. Restrictions on debt relief agencies

(a) A debt relief agency shall not –

(1) fail to perform any service that such agency informed an assisted person or prospective assisted person it would provide in connection with a case or proceeding under this title;

(2) make any statement, or counsel or advise any assisted person or prospective assisted person to make a statement in a document filed in a case or proceeding under this title, that is untrue or misleading, or that upon the exercise of reasonable care, should have been known by such agency to be untrue or misleading;

(3) misrepresent to any assisted person or prospective assisted person, directly or indirectly, affirmatively or by material omission, with respect to –

(A) the services that such agency will provide to such person; or

(B) the benefits and risks that may result if such person becomes a debtor in a case under this title; or

(4) advise an assisted person or prospective assisted person to incur more debt in contemplation of such person filing a case under this title or to pay an attorney or bankruptcy petition preparer a fee or charge for services performed as part of preparing for or representing a debtor in a case under this title.

(b) Any waiver by any assisted person of any protection or right provided under this section shall not be enforceable against the debtor by any Federal or State court or any other person, but may be enforced against a debt relief agency.

(c)(1) Any contract for bankruptcy assistance between a debt relief agency and an assisted person that does not comply with the material requirements of this section, section 527, or section 528 shall be void and may not be enforced by any Federal or State court or by any other person, other than such assisted person.

(2) Any debt relief agency shall be liable to an assisted person in the amount of any fees or charges in connection with providing bankruptcy assistance to such person that such debt relief agency has received, for actual damages, and for reasonable attorneys' fees and costs if such agency is found, after notice and a hearing, to have –

(A) intentionally or negligently failed to comply with any provision of this section, section 527, or section 528 with respect to a case or proceeding under this title for such assisted person;

(B) provided bankruptcy assistance to an assisted person in a case or proceeding under this title that is dismissed or converted to a case under another chapter of this title because of such agency's intentional or negligent failure to file any required document including those specified in section 521; or

(C) intentionally or negligently disregarded the material requirements of this title or the Federal Rules of Bankruptcy Procedure applicable to such agency.

(3) In addition to such other remedies as are provided under State law, whenever the chief law enforcement officer of a State, or an official or agency designated by a State, has reason to believe that any person has violated or is violating this section, the State –

(A) may bring an action to enjoin such violation;

(B) may bring an action on behalf of its residents to recover the actual damages of assisted persons arising from such violation, including any liability under paragraph (2); and

(C) in the case of any successful action under subparagraph (A) or (B), shall be awarded the costs of the action and reasonable attorneys' fees as determined by the court.

(4) The district courts of the United States for districts located in the State shall have concurrent jurisdiction of any action under subparagraph (A) or (B) of paragraph (3).

(5) Notwithstanding any other provision of Federal law and in addition to any other remedy provided under Federal or State law, if the court, on its own motion or on the motion of the United States trustee or the debtor, finds that a person intentionally violated this section, or engaged in a clear and consistent pattern or practice of violating this section, the court may –

(A) enjoin the violation of such section; or

(B) impose an appropriate civil penalty against such person.

(d) No provision of this section, section 527, or section 528 shall –

(1) annul, alter, affect, or exempt any person subject to such sections from complying with any law of any State except to the extent that such law is inconsistent with those sections, and then only to the extent of the inconsistency; or

(2) be deemed to limit or curtail the authority or ability –

(A) of a State or subdivision or instrumentality thereof, to determine and enforce qualifications for the practice of law under the laws of that State; or

(B) of a Federal court to determine and enforce the qualifications for the practice of law before that court.

527. Disclosures

(a) A debt relief agency providing bankruptcy assistance to an assisted person shall provide –

(1) the written notice required under section 342(b)(1); and

(2) to the extent not covered in the written notice described in paragraph (1), and not later than 3 business days after the first date on which a debt relief agency first offers to provide any bankruptcy assistance services to an assisted person, a clear and conspicuous written notice advising assisted persons that –

(A) all information that the assisted person is required to provide with a petition and thereafter during a case under this title is required to be complete, accurate, and truthful;

(B) all assets and all liabilities are required to be completely and accurately disclosed in the documents filed to commence the case, and the replacement value of each asset as defined in section 506 must be stated in those documents where requested after reasonable inquiry to establish such value;

(C) current monthly income, the amounts specified in section 707(b)(2), and, in a case under chapter 13 of this title, disposable income (determined in accordance with section 707(b)(2)), are required to be stated after reasonable inquiry; and

(D) information that an assisted person provides during their case may be audited pursuant to this title, and that failure to provide such information may result in dismissal of the case under this title or other sanction, including a criminal sanction.

(b) A debt relief agency providing bankruptcy assistance to an assisted person shall provide each assisted person at the same time as the notices required under subsection (a)(1) the following statement, to the extent applicable, or one substantially similar. The statement shall be clear and conspicuous and shall be in a single document separate from other documents or notices provided to the assisted person:

"IMPORTANT INFORMATION ABOUT BANKRUPTCY ASSISTANCE SERVICES FROM AN ATTORNEY OR BANKRUPTCY PETITION PREPARER.

"If you decide to seek bankruptcy relief, you can represent yourself, you can hire an attorney to represent you, or you can get help in some localities from a bankruptcy petition preparer who is not an attorney. THE LAW REQUIRES AN ATTORNEY OR BANKRUPTCY PETITION PREPARER TO GIVE YOU A WRITTEN CONTRACT SPECIFYING WHAT THE ATTORNEY OR BANKRUPTCY PETITION PREPARER WILL DO FOR YOU AND HOW MUCH IT WILL COST. Ask to see the contract before you hire anyone.

"The following information helps you understand what must be done in a routine bankruptcy case to help you evaluate how much service you need. Although bankruptcy can be complex, many cases are routine.

"Before filing a bankruptcy case, either you or your attorney should analyze your eligibility for different forms of debt relief available under the Bankruptcy Code and which form of relief is most likely to be beneficial for you. Be sure you understand the relief you can obtain and its limitations. To file a bankruptcy case, documents called a Petition, Schedules, and Statement of Financial Affairs, and in some cases a Statement of Intention, need to be prepared correctly and filed with the bankruptcy court. You will have to pay a filing fee to the bankruptcy court. Once your case starts, you will have to attend the required first meeting of creditors where you may be questioned by a court official called a "trustee" and by creditors.

"If you choose to file a chapter 7 case, you may be asked by a creditor to reaffirm a debt. You may want help deciding whether to do so. A creditor is not permitted to coerce you into reaffirming your debts.

"If you choose to file a chapter 13 case in which you repay your creditors what you can afford over 3 to 5 years, you may also want help with preparing your chapter 13 plan and with the confirmation hearing on your plan which will be before a bankruptcy judge.

"If you select another type of relief under the Bankruptcy Code other than chapter 7 or chapter 13, you will want to find out what should be done from someone familiar with that type of relief.

"Your bankruptcy case may also involve litigation. You are generally permitted to represent yourself in litigation in bankruptcy court, but only attorneys, not bankruptcy petition preparers, can give you legal advice.".

(c) Except to the extent the debt relief agency provides the required information itself after reasonably diligent inquiry of the assisted person or others so as to obtain such information reasonably accurately for inclusion on the petition, schedules or statement of financial affairs, a debt relief agency providing bankruptcy assistance to an assisted person, to the extent permitted by nonbankruptcy law, shall provide each assisted person at the time required for the notice required under subsection (a)(1) reasonably sufficient information (which shall be provided in a clear and conspicuous writing) to the assisted person on how to provide all the information the assisted person is required to provide under this title pursuant to section 521, including –

(1) how to value assets at replacement value, determine current monthly income, the amounts specified in section 707(b)(2) and, in a chapter 13 case, how to determine disposable income in accordance with section 707(b)(2) and related calculations;

(2) how to complete the list of creditors, including how to determine what amount is owed and what address for the creditor should be shown; and

(3) how to determine what property is exempt and how to value exempt property at replacement value as defined in section 506.

(d) A debt relief agency shall maintain a copy of the notices required under subsection (a) of this section for 2 years after the date on which the notice is given the assisted person.

528. Requirements for debt relief agencies

(a) A debt relief agency shall –

(1) not later than 5 business days after the first date on which such agency provides any bankruptcy assistance services to an assisted person, but prior to such assisted person's petition under this title being filed, execute a written contract with such assisted person that explains clearly and conspicuously –

(A) the services such agency will provide to such assisted person; and

(B) the fees or charges for such services, and the terms of payment;

(2) provide the assisted person with a copy of the fully executed and completed contract;

(3) clearly and conspicuously disclose in any advertisement of bankruptcy assistance services or of the benefits of bankruptcy directed to the general public (whether in general media, seminars or specific mailings, telephonic or electronic messages, or otherwise) that the services or benefits are with respect to bankruptcy relief under this title; and

(4) clearly and conspicuously use the following statement in such advertisement: "We are a debt relief agency. We help people file for bankruptcy relief under the Bankruptcy Code." or a substantially similar statement.

(b)(1) An advertisement of bankruptcy assistance services or of the benefits of bankruptcy directed to the general public includes –

(A) descriptions of bankruptcy assistance in connection with a chapter 13 plan whether or not chapter 13 is specifically mentioned in such advertisement; and

(B) statements such as "federally supervised repayment plan" or "Federal debt restructuring help" or other similar statements that could lead a reasonable consumer to believe that debt counseling was being offered when in fact the services were directed to providing bankruptcy assistance with a chapter 13 plan or other form of bankruptcy relief under this title.

(2) An advertisement, directed to the general public, indicating that the debt relief agency provides assistance with respect to credit defaults, mortgage foreclosures, eviction proceedings, excessive debt, debt collection pressure, or inability to pay any consumer debt shall –

(A) disclose clearly and conspicuously in such advertisement that the assistance may involve bankruptcy relief under this title; and

(B) include the following statement: "We are a debt relief agency. We help people file for bankruptcy relief under the Bankruptcy Code." or a substantially similar statement.

SUBCHAPTER III - THE ESTATE

541. Property of the estate

(a) The commencement of a case under section 301, 302, or 303 of this title creates an estate. Such estate is comprised of all the following property, wherever located and by whomever held:

(1) Except as provided in subsections (b) and (c)(2) of this section, all legal or equitable interests of the debtor in property as of the commencement of the case.

(2) All interests of the debtor and the debtor's spouse in community

property as of the commencement of the case that is -

(A) under the sole, equal, or joint management and control of the debtor; or

(B) liable for an allowable claim against the debtor, or for both an allowable claim against the debtor and an allowable claim against the debtor's spouse, to the extent that such interest is so liable.

(3) Any interest in property that the trustee recovers under section 329(b), 363(n), 543, 550, 553, or 723 of this title.

(4) Any interest in property preserved for the benefit of or ordered transferred to the estate under section 510(c) or 551 of this title.

(5) Any interest in property that would have been property of the estate if such interest had been an interest of the debtor on the date of the filing of the petition, and that the debtor acquires or becomes entitled to acquire within 180 days after such date -

(A) by bequest, devise, or inheritance;

(B) as a result of a property settlement agreement with the debtor's spouse, or of an interlocutory or final divorce decree; or

(C) as a beneficiary of a life insurance policy or of a death benefit plan.

(6) Proceeds, product, offspring, rents, or profits of or from property of the estate, except such as are earnings from services performed by an individual debtor after the commencement of the case.

(7) Any interest in property that the estate acquires after the commencement of the case.

(b) Property of the estate does not include -

(1) any power that the debtor may exercise solely for the benefit of an entity other than the debtor;

(2) any interest of the debtor as a lessee under a lease of nonresidential real property that has terminated at the expiration of the stated term of such lease before the commencement of the case under this title, and ceases to include any interest of the debtor as a lessee under a lease of nonresidential real property that has terminated at the expiration of the stated term of such lease during the case;

(3) any eligibility of the debtor to participate in programs authorized under the Higher Education Act of 1965 (20 U.S.C. 1001 et seq.; 42 U.S.C. 2751 et seq.), or any accreditation status or State licensure of the debtor as an educational institution;

(4) any interest of the debtor in liquid or gaseous hydrocarbons to the extent that -

(A)(i) the debtor has transferred or has agreed to transfer such interest pursuant to a farmout agreement or any written agreement directly related to a farmout agreement; and

(ii) but for the operation of this paragraph, the estate could include the interest referred to in clause (i) only by virtue of section 365 or 544(a)(3) of this title; or

(B)(i) the debtor has transferred such interest pursuant to a written conveyance of a production payment to an entity that does not participate in the operation of the property from which such production payment is transferred; and

(ii) but for the operation of this paragraph, the estate could include the interest referred to in clause (i) only by virtue of section 365 or 542 of this title;

(5) funds placed in an education individual retirement account (as defined in section 530(b)(1) of the Internal Revenue Code of 1986) not later than 365 days before the date of the filing of the petition in a case under this title, but –

(A) only if the designated beneficiary of such account was a child, stepchild, grandchild, or stepgrandchild of the debtor for the taxable year for which funds were placed in such account;

(B) only to the extent that such funds –

(i) are not pledged or promised to any entity in connection with any extension of credit; and

(ii) are not excess contributions (as described in section 4973(e) of the Internal Revenue Code of 1986); and

(C) in the case of funds placed in all such accounts having the same designated beneficiary not earlier than 720 days nor later than 365 days before such date, only so much of such funds as does not exceed $7,575;

(6) funds used to purchase a tuition credit or certificate or contributed to an account in accordance with section 529(b)(1)(A) of the Internal Revenue Code of 1986 under a qualified State tuition program (as defined in section 529(b)(1) of such Code) not later than 365 days before the date of the filing of the petition in a case under this title, but –

(A) only if the designated beneficiary of the amounts paid or contributed to such tuition program was a child, stepchild, grandchild, or stepgrandchild of the debtor for the taxable year for which funds were paid or contributed;

(B) with respect to the aggregate amount paid or contributed to such program having the same designated beneficiary, only so much of such amount as does not exceed the total contributions permitted under section 529(b)(6) of such Code with respect to such beneficiary, as adjusted beginning on the date of the filing of the petition in a case under this title by the annual increase or decrease (rounded to the nearest tenth of 1 percent) in the education expenditure category of the Consumer Price Index prepared by the Department of Labor; and

(C) in the case of funds paid or contributed to such program having the same designated beneficiary not earlier than 720 days nor later than 365 days before such date, only so much of such funds as does not exceed $7,575;

(7) any amount –

(A) withheld by an employer from the wages of employees for payment as contributions –

(i) to –

(I) an employee benefit plan that is subject to title I of the Employee Retirement Income Security Act of 1974 or under an employee benefit plan which is a governmental plan under section 414(d) of the Internal Revenue Code of 1986;

(II) a deferred compensation plan under section 457 of the Internal Revenue Code of 1986; or

(III) a tax-deferred annuity under section 403(b) of the Internal Revenue Code of 1986;

except that such amount under this subparagraph shall not constitute disposable income as defined in section 1325(b)(2); or

(ii) to a health insurance plan regulated by State law whether or not subject to such title; or

(B) received by an employer from employees for payment as contributions –

(i) to –

(I) an employee benefit plan that is subject to title I of the Employee Retirement Income Security Act of 1974 or under an employee benefit plan which is a governmental plan under section 414(d) of the Internal Revenue Code of 1986;

(II) a deferred compensation plan under section 457 of the Internal Revenue Code of 1986; or

(III) a tax-deferred annuity under section 403(b) of the Internal Revenue Code of 1986;

except that such amount under this subparagraph shall not constitute disposable income, as defined in section 1325(b)(2); or

(ii) to a health insurance plan regulated by State law whether or not subject to such title;

(8) subject to subchapter III of chapter 5, any interest of the debtor in property where the debtor pledged or sold tangible personal property (other than securities or written or printed evidences of indebtedness or title) as collateral for a loan or advance of money given by a person licensed under law to make such loans or advances, where –

(A) the tangible personal property is in the possession of the pledgee or transferee;

(B) the debtor has no obligation to repay the money, redeem the collateral, or buy back the property at a stipulated price; and

(C) neither the debtor nor the trustee have exercised any right to redeem provided under the contract or State law, in a timely manner as provided under State law and section 108(b); or

(9) any interest in cash or cash equivalents that constitute proceeds of a sale by the debtor of a money order that is made -

(A) on or after the date that is 14 days prior to the date on which the petition is filed; and

(B) under an agreement with a money order issuer that prohibits the commingling of such proceeds with property of the debtor (notwithstanding that, contrary to the agreement, the proceeds may have been commingled with property of the debtor),

unless the money order issuer had not taken action, prior to the filing of the petition, to require compliance with the prohibition.

(10) funds placed in an account of a qualified ABLE program (as defined in section 529A(b) of the Internal Revenue Code of 1986) not later than 365 days before the date of the filing of the petition in a case under this title, but--

(A) only if the designated beneficiary of such account was a child, stepchild, grandchild, or stepgrandchild of the debtor for the taxable year for which funds were placed in such account;

(B) only to the extent that such funds-- (i) are not pledged or promised to any entity in connection with any extension of credit; and (ii) are not excess contributions (as described in section 4973(h) of the Internal Revenue Code of 1986); and

(C) in the case of funds placed in all such accounts having the same designated beneficiary not earlier than 720 days nor later than 365 days before such date, only so much of such funds as does not exceed $7,575.

Paragraph (4) shall not be construed to exclude from the estate any consideration the debtor retains, receives, or is entitled to receive for transferring an interest in liquid or gaseous hydrocarbons pursuant to a farmout agreement.

(c)(1) Except as provided in paragraph (2) of this subsection, an interest of the debtor in property becomes property of the estate under subsection (a)(1), (a)(2), or (a)(5) of this section notwithstanding any provision in an agreement, transfer instrument, or applicable nonbankruptcy law -

(A) that restricts or conditions transfer of such interest by the debtor; or

(B) that is conditioned on the insolvency or financial condition of the debtor, on the commencement of a case under this title, or on the appointment of or taking possession by a trustee in a case under this title or a custodian before such commencement, and that effects or gives an option to effect a forfeiture, modification, or termination of the debtor's interest in property.

(2) A restriction on the transfer of a beneficial interest of the debtor in a trust that is enforceable under applicable nonbankruptcy law is enforceable in a case under this title.

(d) Property in which the debtor holds, as of the commencement of the case, only legal title and not an equitable interest, such as a mortgage secured by real property, or an interest in such a mortgage, sold by the debtor but as to which the debtor retains legal title to service or supervise the servicing of such mortgage or interest, becomes property of the estate under subsection (a)(1) or (2) of this section only to the extent of the debtor's legal title to such property, but not to the extent of any equitable interest in such property that the debtor does not hold.

(e) In determining whether any of the relationships specified in paragraph(5)(A) or (6)(A) of subsection (b) exists, a legally adopted child of an individual (and a child who is a member of an individual's household, if placed with such individual by an authorized placement agency for legal adoption by such individual), or a foster child of an individual (if such child has as the child's principal place of abode the home of the debtor and is a member of the debtor's household) shall be treated as a child of such individual by blood.

(f) Notwithstanding any other provision of this title, property that is held by a debtor that is a corporation described in section 501(c)(3) of the Internal Revenue Code of 1986 and exempt from tax under section 501(a) of such Code may be transferred to an entity that is not such a corporation, but only under the same conditions as would apply if the debtor had not filed a case under this title.

542. Turnover of property to the estate

(a) Except as provided in subsection (c) or (d) of this section, an entity, other than a custodian, in possession, custody, or control, during the case, of property that the trustee may use, sell, or lease under section 363 of this title, or that the debtor may exempt under section 522 of this title, shall deliver to the trustee, and account for, such property or the value of such property, unless such property is of inconsequential value or benefit to the estate.

(b) Except as provided in subsection (c) or (d) of this section, an entity that owes a debt that is property of the estate and that is matured, payable on demand, or payable on order, shall pay such debt to, or on the order of, the trustee, except to the extent that such debt may be offset under section 553 of this title against a claim against the debtor.

(c) Except as provided in section 362(a)(7) of this title, an entity that has neither actual notice nor actual knowledge of the commencement of the case concerning the debtor may transfer property of the estate, or pay a debt owing to the debtor, in good faith and other than in the manner specified in subsection

(d) of this section, to an entity other than the trustee, with the same effect as to the entity making such transfer or payment as if the case under this title concerning the debtor had not been commenced.

(d) A life insurance company may transfer property of the estate or property of the debtor to such company in good faith, with the same effect with respect to such company as if the case under this title concerning the debtor had not been commenced, if such transfer is to pay a premium or to carry out a nonforfeiture insurance option, and is required to be made automatically, under a life insurance contract with such company that was entered into before the date of the filing of the petition and that is property of the estate.

(e) Subject to any applicable privilege, after notice and a hearing, the court may order an attorney, accountant, or other person that holds recorded information, including books, documents, records, and papers, relating to the debtor's property or financial affairs, to turn over or disclose such recorded information to the trustee.

543. Turnover of property by a custodian

(a) A custodian with knowledge of the commencement of a case under this title concerning the debtor may not make any disbursement from, or take any action in the administration of, property of the debtor, proceeds, product, offspring, rents, or profits of such property, or property of the estate, in the possession, custody, or control of such custodian, except such action as is necessary to preserve such property.

(b) A custodian shall -

(1) deliver to the trustee any property of the debtor held by or transferred to such custodian, or proceeds, product, offspring, rents, or profits of such property, that is in such custodian's possession, custody, or control on the date that such custodian acquires knowledge of the commencement of the case; and

(2) file an accounting of any property of the debtor, or proceeds, product, offspring, rents, or profits of such property, that, at any time, came into the possession, custody, or control of such custodian.

(c) The court, after notice and a hearing, shall -

(1) protect all entities to which a custodian has become obligated with respect to such property or proceeds, product, offspring, rents, or profits of such property;

(2) provide for the payment of reasonable compensation for services rendered and costs and expenses incurred by such custodian; and

(3) surcharge such custodian, other than an assignee for the benefit of the debtor's creditors that was appointed or took possession more than 120 days before the date of the filing of the petition, for any improper or excessive disbursement, other than a disbursement that has been made in accordance with applicable law or that has been approved, after notice and a hearing, by a court of competent jurisdiction before the commencement of the case under this title.

(d) After notice and hearing, the bankruptcy court -

(1) may excuse compliance with subsection (a), (b), or (c) of this section if the interests of creditors and, if the debtor is not insolvent, of equity security holders would be better served by permitting a custodian to continue in possession, custody, or control of such property, and

(2) shall excuse compliance with subsections (a) and (b)(1) of this section if the custodian is an assignee for the benefit of the debtor's creditors that was appointed or took possession more than 120 days before the date of the filing of the petition, unless compliance with such subsections is necessary to prevent fraud or injustice.

544. Trustee as lien creditor and as successor to certain creditors and purchasers

(a) The trustee shall have, as of the commencement of the case, and without regard to any knowledge of the trustee or of any creditor, the rights and powers of, or may avoid any transfer of property of the debtor or any obligation incurred by the debtor that is voidable by -

(1) a creditor that extends credit to the debtor at the time of the commencement of the case, and that obtains, at such time and with respect to such credit, a judicial lien on all property on which a creditor on a simple contract could have obtained such a judicial lien, whether or not such a creditor exists;

(2) a creditor that extends credit to the debtor at the time of the commencement of the case, and obtains, at such time and with respect to such credit, an execution against the debtor that is returned unsatisfied at such time, whether or not such a creditor exists; or

(3) a bona fide purchaser of real property, other than fixtures, from the debtor, against whom applicable law permits such transfer to be perfected, that obtains the status of a bona fide purchaser and has perfected such transfer at the time of the commencement of the case, whether or not such a purchaser exists.

(b)(1) Except as provided in paragraph (2), the trustee may avoid any transfer of an interest of the debtor in property or any obligation incurred by the debtor that is voidable under applicable law by a creditor holding an unsecured claim that is allowable under section 502 of this title or that is not allowable only under section 502(e) of this title.

(2) Paragraph (1) shall not apply to a transfer of a charitable contribution (as that term is defined in section 548(d)(3)) that is not covered under section 548(a)(1)(B), by reason of section 548(a)(2). Any claim by any person to recover a transferred contribution described in the preceding sentence under Federal or State law in a Federal or State court shall be preempted by the commencement of the case.

545. Statutory liens

The trustee may avoid the fixing of a statutory lien on property of the debtor to the extent that such lien -

(1) first becomes effective against the debtor -

(A) when a case under this title concerning the debtor is commenced;

(B) when an insolvency proceeding other than under this title concerning the debtor is commenced;

(C) when a custodian is appointed or authorized to take or takes possession;

(D) when the debtor becomes insolvent;

(E) when the debtor's financial condition fails to meet a specified standard; or

(F) at the time of an execution against property of the debtor levied at the instance of an entity other than the holder of such statutory lien;

(2) is not perfected or enforceable at the time of the commencement of the case against a bona fide purchaser that purchases such property at the time of the commencement of the case, whether or not such a purchaser exists, except in any case in which a purchaser is a purchaser described in section 6323 of the Internal Revenue Code of 1986, or in any other similar provision of State or local law;

(3) is for rent; or

(4) is a lien of distress for rent.

546. Limitations on avoiding powers

(a) An action or proceeding under section 544, 545, 547, 548, or 553 of this title may not be commenced after the earlier of -

(1) the later of -

(A) 2 years after the entry of the order for relief; or

(B) 1 year after the appointment or election of the first trustee under section 702, 1104, 1163, 1202, or 1302 of this title if such appointment or such election occurs before the expiration of the period specified in subparagraph (A); or

(2) the time the case is closed or dismissed.

(b)(1) The rights and powers of a trustee under sections 544, 545, and 549 of this title are subject to any generally applicable law that -

(A) permits perfection of an interest in property to be effective against an entity that acquires rights in such property before the date of perfection; or

(B) provides for the maintenance or continuation of perfection of an interest in property to be effective against an entity that acquires rights in such property before the date on which action is taken to effect such maintenance or continuation.

(2) If -

(A) a law described in paragraph (1) requires seizure of such property or commencement of an action to accomplish such perfection, or maintenance or continuation of perfection of an interest in property; and

(B) such property has not been seized or such an action has not been commenced before the date of the filing of the petition;

such interest in such property shall be perfected, or perfection of such interest shall be maintained or continued, by giving notice within the time fixed by such law for such seizure or such commencement.

(c)(1) Except as provided in subsection (d) of this section and in section 507(c), and subject to the prior rights of a holder of a security interest in such goods or the proceeds thereof, the rights and powers of the trustee under sections 544(a), 545, 547, and 549 are subject to the right of a seller of goods that has sold goods to the debtor, in the ordinary course of such seller's business, to reclaim such goods if the debtor has received such goods while insolvent, within 45 days before the date of the commencement of a case under this title, but such seller may not reclaim such goods unless such seller demands in writing reclamation of such goods –

(A) not later than 45 days after the date of receipt of such goods by the debtor; or

(B) not later than 20 days after the date of commencement of the case, if the 45-day period expires after the commencement of the case.

(2) If a seller of goods fails to provide notice in the manner described in paragraph (1), the seller still may assert the rights contained in section 503(b)(9).

(d) In the case of a seller who is a producer of grain sold to a grain storage facility, owned or operated by the debtor, in the ordinary course of such seller's business (as such terms are defined in section 557 of this title) or in the case of a United States fisherman who has caught fish sold to a fish processing facility owned or operated by the debtor in the ordinary course of such fisherman's business, the rights and powers of the trustee under sections 544(a), 545, 547, and 549 of this title are subject to any statutory or common law right of such producer or fisherman to reclaim such grain or fish if the debtor has received such grain or fish while insolvent, but -

(1) such producer or fisherman may not reclaim any grain or fish unless such producer or fisherman demands, in writing, reclamation of such grain or fish before ten days after receipt thereof by the debtor; and

(2) the court may deny reclamation to such a producer or fisherman with a right of reclamation that has made such a demand only if the court secures such claim by a lien.

(e) Notwithstanding sections 544, 545, 547, 548(a)(1)(B), and 548(b) of this title, the trustee may not avoid a transfer that is a margin payment, as defined in section 101, 741 or 761 of this title, or settlement payment, as defined in section 101 or 741 of this title, made by or to (or for the benefit of) a commodity broker, forward contract merchant, stockbroker, financial institution, financial participant, or securities clearing agency, or that is a transfer made by or to (or for the benefit of) a commodity broker, forward contract merchant, stockbroker, financial institution, financial participant, or securities clearing agency, in connection with a securities contract, as defined in section 741(7), commodity contract, as defined in section 761(4), or forward contract, that is made before the commencement of the case, except under section 548(a)(1)(A) of this title.

(f) Notwithstanding sections 544, 545, 547, 548(a)(1)(B), and 548(b) of this title, the trustee may not avoid a transfer made by or to (or for the benefit of) a repo participant or financial participant, in connection with a repurchase agreement and that is made before the commencement of the case, except under section 548(a)(1)(A) of this title.

(g) Notwithstanding sections 544, 545, 547, 548(a)(1)(B) and 548(b) of this title, the trustee may not avoid a transfer, made by or to (or for the benefit of) a swap participant or financial participant, under or in connection with any swap agreement and that is made before the commencement of the case, except under section 548(a)(1)(A) of this title.

(h) Notwithstanding the rights and powers of a trustee under sections 544(a), 545, 547, 549, and 553, if the court determines on a motion by the trustee made not later than 120 days after the date of the order for relief in a case under chapter 11 of this title and after notice and a hearing, that a return is in the best interests of the estate, the debtor, with the consent of a creditor and subject to the prior rights of holders of security interests in such goods or the proceeds of such goods, may return goods shipped to the debtor by the creditor before the commencement of the case, and the creditor may offset the purchase price of such goods against any claim of the creditor against the debtor that arose before the commencement of the case.

(i)(1) Notwithstanding paragraphs (2) and (3) of section 545, the trustee may not avoid a warehouseman's lien for storage, transportation, or other costs incidental to the storage and handling of goods.

(2) The prohibition under paragraph (1) shall be applied in a manner consistent with any State statute applicable to such lien that is similar to section 7-209 of the Uniform Commercial Code, as in effect on the date of enactment of the Bankruptcy Abuse Prevention and Consumer Protection Act of 2005, or any successor to such section 7-209.

(j) Notwithstanding sections 544, 545, 547, 548(a)(1)(B), and 548(b) the trustee may not avoid a transfer made by or to (or for the benefit of) a master netting agreement participant under or in connection with any master netting agreement or any individual contract covered thereby that is made before the commencement of the case, except under section 548(a)(1)(A) and except to the extent that the trustee could otherwise avoid such a transfer made under an individual contract covered by such master netting agreement.

547. Preferences

(a) In this section -

(1) "inventory" means personal property leased or furnished, held for sale or lease, or to be furnished under a contract for service, raw materials,

work in process, or materials used or consumed in a business, including farm products such as crops or livestock, held for sale or lease;

(2) "new value" means money or money's worth in goods, services, or new credit, or release by a transferee of property previously transferred to such transferee in a transaction that is neither void nor voidable by the debtor or the trustee under any applicable law, including proceeds of such property, but does not include an obligation substituted for an existing obligation;

(3) "receivable" means right to payment, whether or not such right has been earned by performance; and

(4) a debt for a tax is incurred on the day when such tax is last payable without penalty, including any extension.

(b) Except as provided in subsections (c) and (i) of this section, the trustee may based on reasonable due diligence in the circumstances of the case and taking into account a party's known or reasonably knowable affirmative defenses under subsection (c) avoid any transfer of an interest of the debtor in property -

(1) to or for the benefit of a creditor;

(2) for or on account of an antecedent debt owed by the debtor before such transfer was made;

(3) made while the debtor was insolvent;

(4) made -

(A) on or within 90 days before the date of the filing of the petition; or

(B) between ninety days and one year before the date of the filing of the petition, if such creditor at the time of such transfer was an insider; and

(5) that enables such creditor to receive more than such creditor would receive if -

(A) the case were a case under chapter 7 of this title;

(B) the transfer had not been made; and

(C) such creditor received payment of such debt to the extent provided by the provisions of this title.

(c) The trustee may not avoid under this section a transfer -

(1) to the extent that such transfer was -

(A) intended by the debtor and the creditor to or for whose benefit such transfer was made to be a contemporaneous exchange for new value given to the debtor; and

(B) in fact a substantially contemporaneous exchange;

(2) to the extent that such transfer was in payment of a debt incurred by the debtor in the ordinary course of business or financial affairs of the debtor and the transferee, and such transfer was –

(A) made in the ordinary course of business or financial affairs of the debtor and the transferee; or

(B) made according to ordinary business terms;

(3) that creates a security interest in property acquired by the debtor-

(A) to the extent such security interest secures new value that was -

(i) given at or after the signing of a security agreement that contains a description of such property as collateral;

(ii) given by or on behalf of the secured party under such agreement;

(iii) given to enable the debtor to acquire such property; and

(iv) in fact used by the debtor to acquire such property; and

(B) that is perfected on or before 30 days after the debtor receives possession of such property;

(4) to or for the benefit of a creditor, to the extent that, after such transfer, such creditor gave new value to or for the benefit of the debtor -

(A) not secured by an otherwise unavoidable security interest; and

(B) on account of which new value the debtor did not make an otherwise unavoidable transfer to or for the benefit of such creditor;

(5) that creates a perfected security interest in inventory or a receivable or the proceeds of either, except to the extent that the aggregate of all such transfers to the transferee caused a reduction, as of the date of the filing of the petition and to the prejudice of other creditors holding unsecured claims, of any amount by which the debt secured by such security interest exceeded the value of all security interests for such debt on the later of -

(A)(i) with respect to a transfer to which subsection (b)(4)(A) of this section applies, 90 days before the date of the filing of the petition; or

(ii) with respect to a transfer to which subsection (b)(4)(B) of this section applies, one year before the date of the filing of the petition; or

(B) the date on which new value was first given under the security agreement creating such security interest;

(6) that is the fixing of a statutory lien that is not avoidable under section 545 of this title;

(7) to the extent such transfer was a bona fide payment of a debt for a domestic support obligation;

(8) if, in a case filed by an individual debtor whose debts are primarily consumer debts, the aggregate value of all property that constitutes or is affected by such transfer is less than $700; or

(9) if, in a case filed by a debtor whose debts are not primarily consumer debts, the aggregate value of all property that constitutes or is affected by such transfer is less than $7,575.

(d) The trustee may avoid a transfer of an interest in property of the debtor transferred to or for the benefit of a surety to secure reimbursement of such a surety that furnished a bond or other obligation to dissolve a judicial lien that would have been avoidable by the trustee under subsection (b) of this section. The liability of such surety under such bond or obligation shall be discharged to the extent of the value of such property recovered by the trustee or the amount paid to the trustee.

(e)(1) For the purposes of this section -

(A) a transfer of real property other than fixtures, but including the interest of a seller or purchaser under a contract for the sale of real property, is perfected when a bona fide purchaser of such property from the debtor against whom applicable law permits such transfer to be perfected cannot acquire an interest that is superior to the interest of the transferee; and

(B) a transfer of a fixture or property other than real property is perfected when a creditor on a simple contract cannot acquire a judicial lien that is superior to the interest of the transferee.

(2) For the purposes of this section, except as provided in paragraph (3) of this subsection, a transfer is made -

(A) at the time such transfer takes effect between the transferor and the transferee, if such transfer is perfected at, or within 30 days after, such time, except as provided in subsection (c)(3)(B);

(B) at the time such transfer is perfected, if such transfer is perfected after such 30 days; or

(C) immediately before the date of the filing of the petition, if such transfer is not perfected at the later of -

(i) the commencement of the case; or

(ii) 30 days after such transfer takes effect between the transferor and the transferee.

(3) For the purposes of this section, a transfer is not made until the debtor has acquired rights in the property transferred.

(f) For the purposes of this section, the debtor is presumed to have been insolvent on and during the 90 days immediately preceding the date of the filing of the petition.

(g) For the purposes of this section, the trustee has the burden of proving the avoidability of a transfer under subsection (b) of this section, and the creditor or party in interest against whom recovery or avoidance is sought has the burden of proving the nonavoidability of a transfer under subsection (c) of this section.

(h) The trustee may not avoid a transfer if such transfer was made as a part of an alternative repayment schedule between the debtor and any creditor of the debtor created by an approved nonprofit budget and credit counseling agency.

(i) If the trustee avoids under subsection (b) a transfer made between 90 days and 1 year before the date of the filing of the petition, by the debtor to an entity that is not an insider for the benefit of a creditor that is an insider, such transfer shall be considered to be avoided under this section only with respect to the creditor that is an insider.

(j) Repealed. Pub.L. 116-260, Div. FF, Title X, § 1001(g)(2)(A)(ii), Dec. 27, 2020, 134 Stat. 3220.

548. Fraudulent transfers and obligations

(a)(1) The trustee may avoid any transfer (including any transfer to or for the benefit of an insider under an employment contract) of an interest of the debtor in property, or any obligation (including any obligation to or for the benefit of an insider under an employment contract) incurred by the debtor, that was made or incurred on or within 2 years before the date of the filing of the petition, if the debtor voluntarily or involuntarily -

(A) made such transfer or incurred such obligation with actual intent to hinder, delay, or defraud any entity to which the debtor was or became, on or after the date that such transfer was made or such obligation was incurred, indebted; or

(B)(i) received less than a reasonably equivalent value in exchange for such transfer or obligation; and

(ii)(I) was insolvent on the date that such transfer was made or such obligation was incurred, or became insolvent as a result of such transfer or obligation;

(II) was engaged in business or a transaction, or was about to engage in business or a transaction, for which any property remaining with the debtor was an unreasonably small capital;

(III) intended to incur, or believed that the debtor would incur, debts that would be beyond the debtor's ability to pay as such debts matured; or

(IV) made such transfer to or for the benefit of an insider, or incurred such obligation to or for the benefit of an insider, under an employment contract and not in the ordinary course of business.

(2) A transfer of a charitable contribution to a qualified religious or charitable entity or organization shall not be considered to be a transfer covered under paragraph (1)(B) in any case in which -

(A) the amount of that contribution does not exceed 15 percent of the gross annual income of the debtor for the year in which the transfer of the contribution is made; or

(B) the contribution made by a debtor exceeded the percentage amount of gross annual income specified in subparagraph (A), if the transfer was consistent with the practices of the debtor in making charitable contributions.

(b) The trustee of a partnership debtor may avoid any transfer of an interest of the debtor in property, or any obligation incurred by the debtor, that was made or incurred on or within 2 years before the date of the filing of the petition, to a general partner in the debtor, if the debtor was insolvent on the date such transfer was made or such obligation was incurred, or became insolvent as a result of such transfer or obligation.

(c) Except to the extent that a transfer or obligation voidable under this section is voidable under section 544, 545, or 547 of this title, a transferee or obligee of such a transfer or obligation that takes for value and in good faith has a lien on or may retain any interest transferred or may enforce any obligation incurred, as the case may be, to the extent that such transferee or obligee gave value to the debtor in exchange for such transfer or obligation.

(d)(1) For the purposes of this section, a transfer is made when such transfer is so perfected that a bona fide purchaser from the debtor against whom applicable law permits such transfer to be perfected cannot acquire an interest in the property transferred that is superior to the interest in such property of the transferee, but if such transfer is not so perfected before the commencement of the case, such transfer is made immediately before the date of the filing of the petition.

(2) In this section -

(A) "value" means property, or satisfaction or securing of a present or antecedent debt of the debtor, but does not include an unperformed promise to furnish support to the debtor or to a relative of the debtor;

(B) a commodity broker, forward contract merchant, stockbroker, financial institution, financial participant, or securities clearing agency that receives a margin payment, as defined in section 101, 741 or 761 of this title, or settlement payment, as defined in section 101 or 741 of this title, takes for value to the extent of such payment;

(C) a repo participant or financial participant that receives a margin payment, as defined in section 741 or 761 of this title, or settlement payment, as defined in section 741 of this title, in connection with a repurchase agreement, takes for value to the extent of such payment;

(D) a swap participant or financial participant that receives a transfer in connection with a swap agreement takes for value to the extent of such transfer; and

(E) a master netting agreement participant that receives a transfer in connection with a master netting agreement or any individual contract covered thereby takes for value to the extent of such transfer, except that, with respect to a transfer under any individual contract covered thereby, to the extent that such master netting agreement participant otherwise did not take (or is otherwise not deemed to have taken) such transfer for value.

(3) In this section, the term "charitable contribution" means a charitable contribution, as that term is defined in section 170(c) of the Internal Revenue Code of 1986, if that contribution -

(A) is made by a natural person; and

(B) consists of -

(i) a financial instrument (as that term is defined in section 731(c)(2)(C) of the Internal Revenue Code of 1986); or

(ii) cash.

(4) In this section, the term "qualified religious or charitable entity or organization" means -

(A) an entity described in section 170(c)(1) of the Internal Revenue Code of 1986; or

(B) an entity or organization described in section 170(c)(2) of the Internal Revenue Code of 1986.

(e)(1) In addition to any transfer that the trustee may otherwise avoid, the trustee may avoid any transfer of an interest of the debtor in property that was made on or within 10 years before the date of the filing of the petition, if –

(A) such transfer was made to a self-settled trust or similar device;

(B) such transfer was by the debtor;

(C) the debtor is a beneficiary of such trust or similar device; and

(D) the debtor made such transfer with actual intent to hinder, delay, or defraud any entity to which the debtor was or became, on or after the date that such transfer was made, indebted.

(2) For the purposes of this subsection, a transfer includes a transfer made in anticipation of any money judgment, settlement, civil penalty, equitable order, or criminal fine incurred by, or which the debtor believed would be incurred by –

(A) any violation of the securities laws (as defined in section 3(a)(47) of the Securities Exchange Act of 1934 (15 U.S.C. 78c(a)(47))), any State securities laws, or any regulation or order issued under Federal securities laws or State securities laws; or

(B) fraud, deceit, or manipulation in a fiduciary capacity or in connection with the purchase or sale of any security registered under section 12 or 15(d) of the Securities Exchange Act of 1934 (15 U.S.C. 78l and 78o(d)) or under section 6 of the Securities Act of 1933 (15 U.S.C. 77f).

549. Postpetition transactions

(a) Except as provided in subsection (b) or (c) of this section, the trustee may avoid a transfer of property of the estate -

(1) that occurs after the commencement of the case; and

(2)(A) that is authorized only under section 303(f) or 542(c) of this title; or

(B) that is not authorized under this title or by the court.

(b) In an involuntary case, the trustee may not avoid under subsection (a) of this section a transfer made after the commencement of such case but before the order for relief to the extent any value, including services, but not including satisfaction or securing of a debt that arose before the commencement of the case, is given after the commencement of the case in exchange for such transfer, notwithstanding any notice or knowledge of the case that the transferee has.

(c) The trustee may not avoid under subsection (a) of this section a transfer of an interest in real property to a good faith purchaser without knowledge of the commencement of the case and for present fair equivalent value unless a copy or notice of the petition was filed, where a transfer of an interest in such real property may be recorded to perfect such transfer, before such transfer is so perfected that a bona fide purchaser of such real property, against whom applicable law permits such transfer to be perfected, could not acquire an interest that is superior to such interest of such good faith purchaser. A good faith purchaser without knowledge of the commencement of the case and for less than present fair equivalent value has a lien on the property transferred to the extent of any present value given, unless a copy or notice of the petition was so filed before such transfer was so perfected.

(d) An action or proceeding under this section may not be commenced after the earlier of -

(1) two years after the date of the transfer sought to be avoided; or

(2) the time the case is closed or dismissed.

550. Liability of transferee of avoided transfer

(a) Except as otherwise provided in this section, to the extent that a transfer is avoided under section 544, 545, 547, 548, 549, 553(b), or 724(a) of this title, the trustee may recover, for the benefit of the estate, the property transferred, or, if the court so orders, the value of such property, from -

(1) the initial transferee of such transfer or the entity for whose benefit such transfer was made; or

(2) any immediate or mediate transferee of such initial transferee.

(b) The trustee may not recover under section (a)(2) of this section from-

(1) a transferee that takes for value, including satisfaction or securing of a present or antecedent debt, in good faith, and without knowledge of the voidability of the transfer avoided; or

(2) any immediate or mediate good faith transferee of such transferee.

(c) If a transfer made between 90 days and one year before the filing of the petition -

(1) is avoided under section 547(b) of this title; and

(2) was made for the benefit of a creditor that at the time of such transfer was an insider; the trustee may not recover under subsection (a) from a transferee that is not an insider.

(d) The trustee is entitled to only a single satisfaction under subsection (a) of this section.

(e)(1) A good faith transferee from whom the trustee may recover under subsection (a) of this section has a lien on the property recovered to secure the lesser of -

(A) the cost, to such transferee, of any improvement made after the transfer, less the amount of any profit realized by or accruing to such transferee from such property; and

(B) any increase in the value of such property as a result of such improvement, of the property transferred.

(2) In this subsection, "improvement" includes -

(A) physical additions or changes to the property transferred;

(B) repairs to such property;

(C) payment of any tax on such property;

(D) payment of any debt secured by a lien on such property that is superior or equal to the rights of the trustee; and

(E) preservation of such property.

(f) An action or proceeding under this section may not be commenced after the earlier of -

(1) one year after the avoidance of the transfer on account of which recovery under this section is sought; or

(2) the time the case is closed or dismissed.

551. Automatic preservation of avoided transfer

Any transfer avoided under section 522, 544, 545, 547, 548, 549, or 724(a) of this title, or any lien void under section 506(d) of this title, is preserved for the benefit of the estate but only with respect to property of the estate.

552. Postpetition effect of security interest

(a) Except as provided in subsection (b) of this section, property acquired by the estate or by the debtor after the commencement of the case is not subject to any lien resulting from any security agreement entered into by the debtor before the commencement of the case.

(b)(1) Except as provided in sections 363, 506(c), 522, 544, 545, 547, and 548 of this title, if the debtor and an entity entered into a security agreement before the commencement of the case and if the security interest created by such security agreement extends to property of the debtor acquired before the commencement of the case and to proceeds, products, offspring, or profits of such property, then such security interest extends to such proceeds, products, offspring, or profits acquired by the estate after the commencement of the case to the extent provided by such security agreement and by applicable nonbankruptcy law, except to any extent that the court, after notice and a hearing and based on the equities of the case, orders otherwise.

(2) Except as provided in sections 363, 506(c), 522, 544, 545, 547, and 548 of this title, and notwithstanding section 546(b) of this title, if the debtor and an entity entered into a security agreement before the commencement of the case and if the security interest created by such security agreement extends to property of the debtor acquired before the commencement of the case and to amounts paid as rents of such property or the fees, charges, accounts, or other payments for the use or occupancy of rooms and other public facilities in hotels, motels, or other lodging properties, then such security interest extends to such rents and such fees, charges, accounts, or other payments acquired by the estate after the commencement of the case to the extent provided in such security agreement, except to any extent that the court, after notice and a hearing and based on the equities of the case, orders otherwise.

553. Setoff

(a) Except as otherwise provided in this section and in sections 362 and 363 of this title, this title does not affect any right of a creditor to offset a mutual debt owing by such creditor to the debtor that arose before the commencement of the case under this title against a claim of such creditor against the debtor that arose before the commencement of the case, except to the extent that -

(1) the claim of such creditor against the debtor is disallowed;

(2) such claim was transferred, by an entity other than the debtor, to such creditor -

(A) after the commencement of the case; or

(B)(i) after 90 days before the date of the filing of the petition; and

(ii) while the debtor was insolvent (except for a setoff of a kind described in section 362(b)(6), 362(b)(7), 362(b)(17), 362(b)(27), 555, 556, 559, 560, or 561); or

(3) the debt owed to the debtor by such creditor was incurred by such creditor -

(A) after 90 days before the date of the filing of the petition;

(B) while the debtor was insolvent; and

(C) for the purpose of obtaining a right of setoff against the debtor (except for a setoff of a kind described in section 362(b)(6), 362(b)(7), 362(b)(17), 362(b)(27), 555, 556, 559, 560, or 561).

(b)(1) Except with respect to a setoff of a kind described in section 362(b)(6), 362(b)(7), 362(b)(17), 362(b)(27), 555, 556, 559, 560, 561, 365(h), 546(h), or 365(i)(2) of this title, if a creditor offsets a mutual debt owing to the debtor against a claim against the debtor on or within 90 days before the date of the filing of the petition, then the trustee may recover from such creditor the amount so offset to the extent that any insufficiency on the date of such setoff is less than the insufficiency on the later of -

(A) 90 days before the date of the filing of the petition; and

(B) the first date during the 90 days immediately preceding the date of the filing of the petition on which there is an insufficiency.

(2) In this subsection, "insufficiency" means amount, if any, by which a claim against the debtor exceeds a mutual debt owing to the debtor by the holder of such claim.

(c) For the purposes of this section, the debtor is presumed to have been insolvent on and during the 90 days immediately preceding the date of the filing of the petition.

554. Abandonment of property of the estate

(a) After notice and a hearing, the trustee may abandon any property of the estate that is burdensome to the estate or that is of inconsequential value and benefit to the estate.

(b) On request of a party in interest and after notice and a hearing, the court may order the trustee to abandon any property of the estate that is burdensome to the estate or that is of inconsequential value and benefit to the estate.

(c) Unless the court orders otherwise, any property scheduled under section 521(a)(1) of this title not otherwise administered at the time of the closing of a case is abandoned to the debtor and administered for purposes of section 350 of this title.

(d) Unless the court orders otherwise, property of the estate that is not abandoned under this section and that is not administered in the case remains property of the estate.

555. Contractual right to liquidate, terminate, or accelerate a securities contract

The exercise of a contractual right of a stockbroker, financial institution, financial participant, or securities clearing agency to cause the liquidation, termination, or acceleration of a securities contract, as defined in section 741 of this title, because of a condition of the kind specified in section 365(e)(1) of this title shall not be stayed, avoided, or otherwise limited by operation of any provision of this title or by order of a court or administrative agency in any proceeding under this title unless such order is authorized under the provisions of the Securities Investor Protection Act of 1970 or any statute administered by the Securities and Exchange Commission. As used in this section, the term "contractual right" includes a right set forth in a rule or bylaw of a derivatives clearing organization (as defined in the Commodity Exchange Act), a multilateral clearing organization (as defined in the Federal Deposit Insurance Corporation Improvement Act of 1991), a national securities exchange, a national securities association, a securities clearing agency, a contract market designated under the Commodity Exchange Act, a derivatives transaction execution facility registered under the Commodity Exchange Act, or a board of trade (as defined in the Commodity Exchange Act), or in a resolution of the governing board thereof, and a right, whether or not in writing, arising under common law, under law merchant, or by reason of normal business practice.

556. Contractual right to liquidate, terminate, or accelerate a commodities contract or forward contract

The contractual right of a commodity broker, financial participant, or forward contract merchant to cause the liquidation, termination, or acceleration of a commodity contract, as defined in section 761 of this title, or forward contract because of a condition of the kind specified in section 365(e)(1) of this title, and the right to a variation or maintenance margin payment received from a trustee with respect to open commodity contracts or forward contracts, shall not be stayed, avoided, or otherwise limited by operation of any provision of this title or by the order of a court in any proceeding under this title. As used in this section, the term "contractual right" includes a right set forth in a rule or bylaw of a derivatives clearing organization (as defined in the Commodity Exchange Act), a multilateral clearing organization (as defined in the Federal Deposit Insurance Corporation Improvement Act of 1991), a national securities exchange, a national securities association, a securities clearing agency, a contract market designated under the Commodity Exchange Act, a derivatives transaction execution facility registered under the Commodity Exchange Act, or a board of trade (as defined in the Commodity Exchange Act) or in a resolution of the governing board thereof and a right, whether or not evidenced in writing, arising under common law, under law merchant or by reason of normal business practice.

557. Expedited determination of interests in, and abandonment or other disposition of grain assets

(a) This section applies only in a case concerning a debtor that owns or operates a grain storage facility and only with respect to grain and the proceeds of grain. This section does not affect the application of any other section of this title to property other than grain and proceeds of grain.

(b) In this section-

(1) "grain" means wheat, corn, flaxseed, grain sorghum, barley, oats, rye, soybeans, other dry edible beans, or rice;

(2) "grain storage facility" means a site or physical structure regularly used to store grain for producers, or to store grain acquired from producers for resale; and

(3) "producer" means an entity which engages in the growing of grain.

(c)(1) Notwithstanding sections 362, 363, 365, and 554 of this title, on the court's own motion the court may, and on the request of the trustee or an entity that claims an interest in grain or the proceeds of grain the court shall, expedite the procedures for the determination of interests in and the disposition of grain and the proceeds of grain, by shortening to the greatest extent feasible such time periods as are otherwise applicable for such procedures and by establishing, by order, a timetable having a duration of not to exceed 120 days for the completion of the applicable procedure specified in subsection (d) of this section. Such time periods and such timetable may be modified by the court, for cause, in accordance with subsection (f) of this section.

(2) The court shall determine the extent to which such time periods shall be shortened, based upon-

(A) any need of an entity claiming an interest in such grain or the proceeds of grain for a prompt determination of such interest;

(B) any need of such entity for a prompt disposition of such grain;

(C) the market for such grain;

(D) the conditions under which such grain is stored;

(E) the costs of continued storage or disposition of such grain;

(F) the orderly administration of the estate;

(G) the appropriate opportunity for an entity to assert an interest in such grain; and

(H) such other considerations as are relevant to the need to expedite such procedures in the case.

(d) The procedures that may be expedited under subsection (c) of this section include-

(1) the filing of and response to-

(A) a claim of ownership;

(B) a proof of claim;

(C) a request for abandonment;

(D) a request for relief from the stay of action against property under section 362(a) of this title;

(E) a request for determination of secured status;

(F) a request for determination of whether such grain or the proceeds of grain-

(i) is property of the estate;

(ii) must be turned over to the estate; or

(iii) may be used, sold, or leased; and

(G) any other request for determination of an interest in such grain or the proceeds of grain;

(2) the disposition of such grain or the proceeds of grain, before or after determination of interests in such grain or the proceeds of grain, by way of-

(A) sale of such grain;

(B) abandonment;

(C) distribution; or

(D) such other method as is equitable in the case;

(3) subject to sections 701, 702, 703, 1104, 1183, 1202, and 1302 of this title; the appointment of a trustee or examiner and the retention and compensation of any professional person required to assist with respect to matters relevant to the determination of interests in or disposition of such grain or the proceeds of grain; and

(4) the determination of any dispute concerning a matter specified in paragraph (1), (2), or (3) of this subsection.

(e)(1) Any governmental unit that has regulatory jurisdiction over the operation or liquidation of the debtor or the debtor's business shall be given notice of any request made or order entered under subsection (c) of this section.

(2) Any such governmental unit may raise, and may appear and be heard on, any issue relating to grain or the proceeds of grain in a case in which a request is made, or an order is entered, under subsection (c) of this section.

(3) The trustee shall consult with such governmental unit before taking any action relating to the disposition of grain in the possession, custody, or control of the debtor or the estate.

(f) The court may extend the period for final disposition of grain or the proceeds of grain under this section beyond 120 days if the court finds that-

(1) the interests of justice so require in light of the complexity of the case; and

(2) the interests of those claimants entitled to distribution of grain or the proceeds of grain will not be materially injured by such additional delay.

(g) Unless an order establishing an expedited procedure under subsection (c) of this section, or determining any interest in or approving any disposition of grain or the proceeds of grain, is stayed pending appeal-

(1) the reversal or modification of such order on appeal does not affect the validity of any procedure, determination, or disposition that occurs before such reversal or modification, whether or not any entity knew of the pendency of the appeal; and

(2) neither the court nor the trustee may delay, due to the appeal of such order, any proceeding in the case in which such order is issued.

(h)(1) The trustee may recover from grain and the proceeds of grain the reasonable and necessary costs and expenses allowable under section 503(b) of this title attributable to preserving or disposing of grain or the proceeds of grain, but may not recover from such grain or the proceeds of grain any other costs or expenses.

(2) Notwithstanding section 326(a) of this title, the dollar amounts of money specified in such section include the value, as of the date of disposition, of any grain that the trustee distributes in kind.

(i) In all cases where the quantity of a specific type of grain held by a debtor operating a grain storage facility exceeds ten thousand bushels, such grain shall be sold by the trustee and the assets thereof distributed in accordance with the provisions of this section.

558. Defenses of the estate

The estate shall have the benefit of any defense available to the debtor as against any entity other than the estate, including statutes of limitation, statutes of frauds, usury, and other personal defenses. A waiver of any such defense by the debtor after the commencement of the case does not bind the estate.

559. Contractual right to liquidate, terminate, or accelerate a repurchase agreement

The exercise of a contractual right of a repo participant or financial participant to cause the liquidation, termination, or acceleration of a repurchase agreement because of a condition of the kind specified in section 365(e)(1) of this title shall not be stayed, avoided, or otherwise limited by operation of any provision of this title or by order of a court or administrative agency in any proceeding under this title, unless, where the debtor is a stockbroker or securities clearing agency, such order is authorized under the provisions of the Securities Investor Protection Act of 1970 or any statute administered by the Securities and Exchange Commission. In the event that a repo participant or financial participant liquidates one or more repurchase agreements with a debtor and under the terms of one or more such agreements has agreed to deliver assets subject to repurchase agreements to the debtor, any excess of the market prices received on liquidation of such assets (or if any such assets are not disposed of on the date of liquidation of such repurchase agreements, at the prices available at the time of liquidation of such repurchase agreements from a generally recognized source or the most recent closing bid quotation from such a source) over the sum of the stated repurchase prices and all expenses in connection with the liquidation of such repurchase agreements shall be deemed property of the estate, subject to the available rights of setoff. As used in this section, the term "contractual right" includes a right set forth in a rule or bylaw, of a derivatives clearing organization (as defined in the Commodity Exchange Act), a multilateral clearing organization (as defined in the Federal Deposit Insurance Corporation Improvement Act of 1991), a national securities exchange, a national securities association, a securities clearing agency, a contract market designated under the Commodity Exchange Act, a derivatives transaction execution facility registered under the Commodity Exchange Act, or a board of trade (as defined in the Commodity Exchange Act) or in a resolution of the governing board thereof and a right, whether or not evidenced in writing, arising under common law, under law merchant or by reason of normal business practice.

560. Contractual right to liquidate, terminate, or accelerate a swap agreement

The exercise of any contractual right of any swap participant or financial participant to cause the liquidation, termination, or acceleration of one or more swap agreements because of a condition of the kind specified in section 365(e)(1) of this title or to offset or net out any termination values or payment amounts arising under or in connection with the termination, liquidation, or acceleration of one or more swap agreements shall not be stayed, avoided, or otherwise limited by operation of any provision of this title or by order of a court or administrative agency in any proceeding under this title. As used in this section, the term "contractual right" includes a right set forth in a rule or bylaw of a derivatives clearing organization (as defined in the Commodity Exchange Act), a multilateral clearing organization (as defined in the Federal Deposit Insurance Corporation Improvement Act of 1991), a national securities exchange, a national securities association, a securities clearing agency, a contract market designated under the Commodity Exchange Act, a derivatives transaction execution facility registered under the Commodity Exchange Act, or a board of trade (as defined in the Commodity Exchange Act) or in a resolution of the governing board thereof and a right, whether or not evidenced in writing, arising under common law, under law merchant, or by reason of normal business practice.

561. Contractual right to terminate, liquidate, accelerate, or offset under a master netting agreement and across contracts; proceedings under chapter 15

(a) Subject to subsection (b), the exercise of any contractual right, because of a condition of the kind specified in section 365(e)(1), to cause the termination, liquidation, or acceleration of or to offset or net termination values, payment amounts, or other transfer obligations arising under or in connection with one or more (or the termination, liquidation, or acceleration of one or more) –

(1) securities contracts, as defined in section 741(7);

(2) commodity contracts, as defined in section 761(4);

(3) forward contracts;

(4) repurchase agreements;

(5) swap agreements; or

(6) master netting agreements

shall not be stayed, avoided, or otherwise limited by operation of any provision of this title or by any order of a court or administrative agency in any proceeding under this title.

(b)(1) A party may exercise a contractual right described in subsection (a) to terminate, liquidate, or accelerate only to the extent that such party could exercise such a right under section 555, 556, 559, or 560 for each individual contract covered by the master netting agreement in issue.

(2) If a debtor is a commodity broker subject to subchapter IV of chapter 7 –

(A) a party may not net or offset an obligation to the debtor arising under, or in connection with, a commodity contract traded on or subject to the rules of a contract market designated under the Commodity Exchange Act or a derivatives transaction execution facility registered under the Commodity Exchange Act against any claim arising under, or in connection with, other instruments, contracts, or agreements listed in subsection (a) except to the extent that the party has positive net equity in the commodity accounts at the debtor, as calculated under such subchapter; and

(B) another commodity broker may not net or offset an obligation to the debtor arising under, or in connection with, a commodity contract entered into or held on behalf of a customer of the debtor and traded on or subject to the rules of a contract market designated under the Commodity Exchange Act or a derivatives transaction execution facility registered under the Commodity Exchange Act against any claim arising under, or in connection with, other instruments, contracts, or agreements listed in subsection (a).

(3) No provision of subparagraph (A) or (B) of paragraph (2) shall prohibit the offset of claims and obligations that arise under –

(A) a cross-margining agreement or similar arrangement that has been approved by the Commodity Futures Trading Commission or submitted to the Commodity Futures Trading Commission under paragraph (1) or (2) of section 5c(c) of the Commodity Exchange Act and has not been abrogated or rendered ineffective by the Commodity Futures Trading Commission; or

(B) any other netting agreement between a clearing organization (as defined in section 761) and another entity that has been approved by the Commodity Futures Trading Commission.

(c) As used in this section, the term "contractual right" includes a right set forth in a rule or bylaw of a derivatives clearing organization (as defined in the Commodity Exchange Act), a multilateral clearing organization (as defined in the Federal Deposit Insurance Corporation Improvement Act of 1991), a national securities exchange, a national securities association, a securities clearing agency, a contract market designated under the Commodity Exchange Act, a derivatives transaction execution facility registered under the Commodity Exchange Act, or a board of trade (as defined in the Commodity Exchange Act) or in a resolution of the governing board thereof, and a right, whether or not evidenced in writing, arising under common law, under law merchant, or by reason of normal business practice.

(d) Any provisions of this title relating to securities contracts, commodity contracts, forward contracts, repurchase agreements, swap agreements, or master netting agreements shall apply in a case under chapter 15, so that enforcement of contractual provisions of such contracts and agreements in accordance with their terms will not be stayed or otherwise limited by operation of any provision of this title or by order of a court in any case under this title, and to limit avoidance powers to the same extent as in a proceeding under chapter 7 or 11 of this title (such enforcement not to be limited based on the presence or absence of assets of the debtor in the United States).

562. Timing of damage measurement in connection with swap agreements, securities contracts, forward contracts, commodity contracts, repurchase agreements, and master netting agreements

(a) If the trustee rejects a swap agreement, securities contract (as defined in section 741), forward contract, commodity contract (as defined in section 761), repurchase agreement, or master netting agreement pursuant to section 365(a), or if a forward contract merchant, stockbroker, financial institution, securities clearing agency, repo participant, financial participant, master netting agreement participant, or swap participant liquidates, terminates, or accelerates such contract or agreement, damages shall be measured as of the earlier of –

(1) the date of such rejection; or

(2) the date or dates of such liquidation, termination, or acceleration.

(b) If there are not any commercially reasonable determinants of value as of any date referred to in paragraph (1) or (2) of subsection (a), damages shall be measured as of the earliest subsequent date or dates on which there are commercially reasonable determinants of value.

(c) For the purposes of subsection (b), if damages are not measured as of the date or dates of rejection, liquidation, termination, or acceleration, and the forward contract merchant, stockbroker, financial institution, securities clearing agency, repo participant, financial participant, master netting agreement participant, or swap participant or the trustee objects to the timing of the measurement of damages –

(1) the trustee, in the case of an objection by a forward contract merchant, stockbroker, financial institution, securities clearing agency, repo participant, financial participant, master netting agreement participant, or swap participant; or

(2) the forward contract merchant, stockbroker, financial institution, securities clearing agency, repo participant, financial participant, master netting agreement participant, or swap participant, in the case of an objection by the trustee,

has the burden of proving that there were no commercially reasonable determinants of value as of such date or dates.

Chapter 7 - Liquidation

Subchapter I - Officers and Administration

* Indicated subchapter does not pertain to chapter 7 consumer cases and is not included below.

SUBCHAPTER I - OFFICERS AND ADMINISTRATION

701. Interim trustee

(a)(1) Promptly after the order for relief under this chapter, the United States trustee shall appoint one disinterested person that is a member of the panel of private trustees established under section 586(a)(1) of title 28 or that is serving as trustee in the case immediately before the order for relief under this chapter to serve as interim trustee in the case.

(2) If none of the members of such panel is willing to serve as interim trustee in the case, then the United States trustee may serve as interim trustee in the case.

(b) The service of an interim trustee under this section terminates when a trustee elected or designated under section 702 of this title to serve as trustee in the case qualifies under section 322 of this title.

(c) An interim trustee serving under this section is a trustee in a case under this title.

702. Election of trustee

(a) A creditor may vote for a candidate for trustee only if such creditor -

(1) holds an allowable, undisputed, fixed, liquidated, unsecured claim of a kind entitled to distribution under section 726(a)(2), 726(a)(3),726(a)(4), 752(a), 766(h), or 766(i) of this title;

(2) does not have an interest materially adverse, other than an equity interest that is not substantial in relation to such creditor's interest as a creditor, to the interest of creditors entitled to such distribution; and

(3) is not an insider.

(b) At the meeting of creditors held under section 341 of this title, creditors may elect one person to serve as trustee in the case if election of a trustee is requested by creditors that may vote under subsection (a) of this section, and that hold at least 20 percent in amount of the claims specified in subsection (a)(1) of this section that are held by creditors that may vote under subsection (a) of this section.

(c) A candidate for trustee is elected trustee if -

(1) creditors holding at least 20 percent in amount of the claims of a kind specified in subsection (a)(1) of this section that are held by creditors that may vote under subsection (a) of this section vote; and

(2) such candidate receives the votes of creditors holding a majority in amount of claims specified in subsection (a)(1) of this section that are held by creditors that vote for a trustee.

(d) If a trustee is not elected under this section, then the interim trustee shall serve as trustee in the case.

703. Successor trustee

(a) If a trustee dies or resigns during a case, fails to qualify under section 322 of this title, or is removed under section 324 of this title, creditors may elect, in the manner specified in section 702 of this title, a person to fill the vacancy in the office of trustee.

(b) Pending election of a trustee under subsection (a) of this section, if necessary to preserve or prevent loss to the estate, the United States trustee may appoint an interim trustee in the manner specified in section 701(a).

(c) If creditors do not elect a successor trustee under subsection (a) of this section or if a trustee is needed in a case reopened under section 350 of this title, then the United States trustee -

(1) shall appoint one disinterested person that is a member of the panel of private trustees established under section 586(a)(1) of title 28 to serve as trustee in the case; or

(2) may, if none of the disinterested members of such panel is willing to serve as trustee, serve as trustee in the case.

704. Duties of trustee

(a) The trustee shall -

(1) collect and reduce to money the property of the estate for which such trustee serves, and close such estate as expeditiously as is compatible with the best interests of parties in interest;

(2) be accountable for all property received;

(3) ensure that the debtor shall perform his intention as specified in section 521(a)(2)(B) of this title;

(4) investigate the financial affairs of the debtor;

(5) if a purpose would be served, examine proofs of claims and object to the allowance of any claim that is improper;

(6) if advisable, oppose the discharge of the debtor;

(7) unless the court orders otherwise, furnish such information concerning the estate and the estate's administration as is requested by a party in interest;

(8) if the business of the debtor is authorized to be operated, file with the court, with the United States trustee, and with any governmental unit charged with responsibility for collection or determination of any tax arising out of such operation, periodic reports and summaries of the operation of such business, including a statement of receipts and disbursements, and such other information as the United States trustee or the court requires;

(9) make a final report and file a final account of the administration of the estate with the court and with the United States trustee;

(10) if with respect to the debtor there is a claim for a domestic support obligation, provide the applicable notice specified in subsection (c);

(11) if, at the time of the commencement of the case, the debtor (or any entity designated by the debtor) served as the administrator (as defined in section 3 of the Employee Retirement Income Security Act of 1974) of an employee benefit plan, continue to perform the obligations required of the administrator; and

(12) use all reasonable and best efforts to transfer patients from a health care business that is in the process of being closed to an appropriate health care business that –

(A) is in the vicinity of the health care business that is closing;

(B) provides the patient with services that are substantially similar to those provided by the health care business that is in the process of being closed; and

(C) maintains a reasonable quality of care.

(b)(1) With respect to a debtor who is an individual in a case under this chapter –

(A) the United States trustee (or the bankruptcy administrator, if any) shall review all materials filed by the debtor and, not later than 10 days after the date of the first meeting of creditors, file with the court a statement as to whether the debtor's case would be presumed to be an abuse under section 707(b); and

(B) not later than 7 days after receiving a statement under subparagraph (A), the court shall provide a copy of the statement to all creditors.

(2) The United States trustee (or bankruptcy administrator, if any) shall, not

later than 30 days after the date of filing a statement under paragraph (1), either file a motion to dismiss or convert under section 707(b) or file a statement setting forth the reasons the United States trustee (or the bankruptcy administrator, if any) does not consider such a motion to be appropriate, if the United States trustee (or the bankruptcy administrator, if any) determines that the debtor's case should be presumed to be an abuse under section 707(b) and the product of the debtor's current monthly income, multiplied by 12 is not less than –

(A) in the case of a debtor in a household of 1 person, the median family income of the applicable State for 1 earner; or

(B) in the case of a debtor in a household of 2 or more individuals, the highest median family income of the applicable State for a family of the same number or fewer individuals.

(c)(1) In a case described in subsection (a)(10) to which subsection (a)(10) applies, the trustee shall –

(A)(i) provide written notice to the holder of the claim described in subsection (a)(10) of such claim and of the right of such holder to use the services of the State child support enforcement agency established under sections 464 and 466 of the Social Security Act for the State in which such holder resides, for assistance in collecting child support during and after the case under this title;

(ii) include in the notice provided under clause (i) the address and telephone number of such State child support enforcement agency; and

(iii) include in the notice provided under clause (i) an explanation of the rights of such holder to payment of such claim under this chapter;

(B)(i) provide written notice to such State child support enforcement agency of such claim; and

(ii) include in the notice provided under clause (i) the name, address, and telephone number of such holder; and

(C) at such time as the debtor is granted a discharge under section 727, provide written notice to such holder and to such State child support enforcement agency of –

(i) the granting of the discharge;

(ii) the last recent known address of the debtor;

(iii) the last recent known name and address of the debtor's employer; and

(iv) the name of each creditor that holds a claim that –

(I) is not discharged under paragraph (2), (4), or (14A) of section 523(a); or

(II) was reaffirmed by the debtor under section 524(c).

(2)(A) The holder of a claim described in subsection (a)(10) or the State child support enforcement agency of the State in which such holder resides may request from a creditor described in paragraph (1)(C)(iv) the last known address of the debtor.

(B) Notwithstanding any other provision of law, a creditor that makes a disclosure of a last known address of a debtor in connection with a request made under subparagraph (A) shall not be liable by reason of making such disclosure.

705. Creditors' committee

(a) At the meeting under section 341(a) of this title, creditors that may vote for a trustee under section 702(a) of this title may elect a committee of not fewer than three, and not more than eleven, creditors, each of whom holds an allowable unsecured claim of a kind entitled to distribution under section 726(a)(2) of this title.

(b) A committee elected under subsection (a) of this section may consult with the trustee or the United States trustee in connection with the administration of the estate, make recommendations to the trustee or the United States trustee respecting the performance of the trustee's duties, and submit to the court or the United States trustee any question affecting the administration of the estate.

706. Conversion

(a) The debtor may convert a case under this chapter to a case under chapter 11, 12, or 13 of this title at any time, if the case has not been converted under section 1112, 1208, or 1307 of this title. Any waiver of the right to convert a case under this subsection is unenforceable.

(b) On request of a party in interest and after notice and a hearing, the court may convert a case under this chapter to a case under chapter 11 of this title at any time.

(c) The court may not convert a case under this chapter to a case under chapter 12 or 13 of this title unless the debtor requests or consents to such conversion.

(d) Notwithstanding any other provision of this section, a case may not be converted to a case under another chapter of this title unless the debtor may be a debtor under such chapter.

707. Dismissal of a case or conversion to a case under chapter 11 or 13

(a) The court may dismiss a case under this chapter only after notice and a hearing and only for cause, including -

(1) unreasonable delay by the debtor that is prejudicial to creditors;

(2) nonpayment of any fees or charges required under chapter 123 of title 28; and

(3) failure of the debtor in a voluntary case to file, within fifteen days or such additional time as the court may allow after the filing of the petition commencing such case, the information required by paragraph (1) of section 521(a), but only on a motion by the United States trustee.

(b)(1) After notice and a hearing, the court, on its own motion or on a motion by the United States trustee, trustee (or bankruptcy administrator, if any), or any party in interest, may dismiss a case filed by an individual debtor under this chapter whose debts are primarily consumer debts, or, with the debtor's consent, convert such a case to a case under chapter 11 or 13 of this title if it finds that the granting of relief would be an abuse of the provisions of this chapter. In making a determination whether to dismiss a case under this section, the court may not take into consideration whether a debtor has made, or continues to make, charitable contributions (that meet the definition of "charitable contribution" under section 548(d)(3)) to any qualified religious or charitable entity or organization (as that term is defined in section 548(d)(4)).

(2)(A)(i) In considering under paragraph (1) whether the granting of relief would be an abuse of the provisions of this chapter, the court shall presume abuse exists if the debtor's current monthly income reduced by the amounts determined under clauses (ii), (iii), and (iv), and multiplied by 60 is not less than the lesser of –

(I) 25 percent of the debtor's nonpriority unsecured claims in the case, or $9,075, whichever is greater; or

(II) $15,150.

(ii)(I) The debtor's monthly expenses shall be the debtor's applicable monthly expense amounts specified under the National Standards and Local Standards, and the debtor's actual monthly expenses for the categories specified as Other Necessary Expenses issued by the Internal Revenue Service for the area in which the debtor resides, as in effect on the date of the order for relief, for the debtor, the dependents of the debtor, and the spouse of the debtor in a joint case, if the spouse is not otherwise a dependent. Such expenses shall include reasonably necessary health insurance, disability insurance, and health savings account expenses for the debtor, the spouse of the debtor, or the dependents of the debtor. Notwithstanding any other provision of this clause, the monthly expenses of the debtor shall not include any payments for debts. In addition, the debtor's monthly expenses shall include the debtor's reasonably necessary expenses incurred to maintain the safety of the debtor and the family of the debtor from family violence as identified under section 302 of the Family Violence Prevention and Services Act, or other applicable Federal law. The expenses included in the debtor's monthly expenses described in the preceding sentence shall be kept confidential by the court. In addition, if it is demonstrated that it is reasonable and necessary, the debtor's monthly expenses may also include an additional allowance for food and clothing of up to 5 percent of the food and clothing categories as specified by the National Standards issued by the Internal Revenue Service.

(II) In addition, the debtor's monthly expenses may include, if applicable, the continuation of actual expenses paid by the debtor that are reasonable and necessary for care and support of an elderly, chronically ill, or disabled household member or member of the debtor's immediate family (including parents, grandparents, siblings, children, and grandchildren of the debtor, the dependents of the debtor, and the spouse of the debtor in a joint case who is not a dependent) and who is unable to pay for such reasonable and necessary expenses. Such monthly expenses may include, if applicable, contributions to an account of a qualified ABLE program to the extent such contributions are not excess contributions (as described in section 4973(h) of the Internal Revenue Code of 1986) and if the designated beneficiary of such account is a child, stepchild, grandchild, or stepgrandchild of the debtor.

(III) In addition, for a debtor eligible for chapter 13, the debtor's monthly expenses may include the actual administrative expenses of administering a chapter 13 plan for the district in which the debtor resides, up to an amount of 10 percent of the projected plan payments, as determined under schedules issued by the Executive Office for United States Trustees.

(IV) In addition, the debtor's monthly expenses may include the actual expenses for each dependent child less than 18 years of age, not to exceed $2,275 per year per child, to attend a private or public elementary or secondary school if the debtor provides documentation of such expenses and a detailed explanation of why such expenses are reasonable and necessary, and why such expenses are not already accounted for in the National Standards, Local Standards, or Other Necessary Expenses referred to in subclause (I).

(V) In addition, the debtor's monthly expenses may include an allowance for housing and utilities, in excess of the allowance specified by the Local Standards for housing and utilities issued by the Internal Revenue Service, based on the actual expenses for home energy costs if the debtor provides documentation of such actual expenses and demonstrates that such actual expenses are reasonable and necessary.

(iii) The debtor's average monthly payments on account of secured debts shall be calculated as the sum of –

(I) the total of all amounts scheduled as contractually due to secured creditors in each month of the 60 months following the date of the filing of the petition; and

(II) any additional payments to secured creditors necessary for the debtor, in filing a plan under chapter 13 of this title, to maintain possession of the debtor's primary residence, motor vehicle, or other property necessary for the support of the debtor and the debtor's dependents, that serves as collateral for secured debts;

divided by 60.

(iv) The debtor's expenses for payment of all priority claims (including priority child support and alimony claims) shall be calculated as the total amount of debts entitled to priority, divided by 60.

(B)(i) In any proceeding brought under this subsection, the presumption of abuse may only be rebutted by demonstrating special circumstances, such as a serious medical condition or a call or order to active duty in the Armed Forces, to the extent such special circumstances that justify additional expenses or adjustments of current monthly income for which there is no reasonable alternative.

(ii) In order to establish special circumstances, the debtor shall be required to itemize each additional expense or adjustment of income and to provide –

(I) documentation for such expense or adjustment to income; and

(II) a detailed explanation of the special circumstances that make such expenses or adjustment to income necessary and reasonable.

(iii) The debtor shall attest under oath to the accuracy of any information provided to demonstrate that additional expenses or adjustments to income are required.

(iv) The presumption of abuse may only be rebutted if the additional expenses or adjustments to income referred to in clause (i) cause the product of the debtor's current monthly income reduced by the amounts determined under clauses (ii), (iii), and (iv) of subparagraph (A) when multiplied by 60 to be less than the lesser of –

(I) 25 percent of the debtor's nonpriority unsecured claims, or $9,075, whichever is greater; or

(II) $15,150.

(C) As part of the schedule of current income and expenditures required under section 521, the debtor shall include a statement of the debtor's current monthly income, and the calculations that determine whether a presumption arises under subparagraph (A)(i), that show how each such amount is calculated.

(D) Subparagraphs (A) through (C) shall not apply, and the court may not dismiss or convert a case based on any form of means testing –

(i) if the debtor is a disabled veteran (as defined in section 3741(1) of title 38), and the indebtedness occurred primarily during a period during which he or she was -

(I) on active duty (as defined in section 101(d)(1) of title 10); or

(II) performing a homeland defense activity (as defined in section 901(1) of title 32); or

(ii) with respect to the debtor, while the debtor is –

(I) on, and during the 540-day period beginning immediately after the debtor is released from, a period of active duty (as defined in section 101(d)(1) of title 10) of not less than 90 days; or

(II) performing, and during the 540-day period beginning immediately after the debtor is no longer performing, a homeland defense activity (as defined in section 901(1) of title 32) performed for a period of not less than 90 days:

if after September 11, 2001, the debtor while a member of a reserve component of the Armed Forces or a member of the National Guard, was called to such active duty or performed such homeland defense activity.

(3) In considering under paragraph (1) whether the granting of relief would be an abuse of the provisions of this chapter in a case in which the presumption in paragraph (2)(A)(i) does not arise or is rebutted, the court shall consider –

(A) whether the debtor filed the petition in bad faith; or

(B) the totality of the circumstances (including whether the debtor seeks to reject a personal services contract and the financial need for such rejection as sought by the debtor) of the debtor's financial situation demonstrates abuse.

(4)(A) The court, on its own initiative or on the motion of a party in interest, in accordance with the procedures described in rule 9011 of the Federal Rules of Bankruptcy Procedure, may order the attorney for the debtor to reimburse the trustee for all reasonable costs in prosecuting a motion filed under section 707(b), including reasonable attorneys' fees, if –

(i) a trustee files a motion for dismissal or conversion under this subsection; and

(ii) the court –

(I) grants such motion; and

(II) finds that the action of the attorney for the debtor in filing a case under this chapter violated rule 9011 of the Federal Rules of Bankruptcy Procedure.

(B) If the court finds that the attorney for the debtor violated rule 9011 of the Federal Rules of Bankruptcy Procedure, the court, on its own initiative or on the motion of a party in interest, in accordance with such procedures, may order –

(i) the assessment of an appropriate civil penalty against the attorney for the debtor; and

(ii) the payment of such civil penalty to the trustee, the United States trustee (or the bankruptcy administrator, if any).

(C) The signature of an attorney on a petition, pleading, or written motion shall constitute a certification that the attorney has –

(i) performed a reasonable investigation into the circumstances that gave rise to the petition, pleading, or written motion; and

(ii) determined that the petition, pleading, or written motion –

(I) is well grounded in fact; and

(II) is warranted by existing law or a good faith argument for the extension, modification, or reversal of existing law and does not constitute an abuse under paragraph (1).

(D) The signature of an attorney on the petition shall constitute a certification that the attorney has no knowledge after an inquiry that the information in the schedules filed with such petition is incorrect.

(5)(A) Except as provided in subparagraph (B) and subject to paragraph (6), the court, on its own initiative or on the motion of a party in interest, in accordance with the procedures described in rule 9011 of the Federal Rules of Bankruptcy Procedure, may award a debtor all reasonable costs (including reasonable attorneys' fees) in contesting a motion filed by a party in interest (other than a trustee or United States trustee (or bankruptcy administrator, if any)) under this subsection if –

(i) the court does not grant the motion; and

(ii) the court finds that –

(I) the position of the party that filed the motion violated rule 9011 of the Federal Rules of Bankruptcy Procedure; or

(II) the attorney (if any) who filed the motion did not comply with the requirements of clauses (i) and (ii) of paragraph (4)(C), and the motion was made solely for the purpose of coercing a debtor into waiving a right guaranteed to the debtor under this title.

(B) A small business that has a claim of an aggregate amount less than $1,525 shall not be subject to subparagraph (A)(ii)(I).

(C) For purposes of this paragraph –

(i) the term "small business" means an unincorporated business, partnership, corporation, association, or organization that –

(I) has fewer than 25 full-time employees as determined on the date on which the motion is filed; and

(II) is engaged in commercial or business activity; and

(ii) the number of employees of a wholly owned subsidiary of a corporation includes the employees of –

(I) a parent corporation; and

(II) any other subsidiary corporation of the parent corporation.

(6) Only the judge or United States trustee (or bankruptcy administrator, if any) may file a motion under section 707(b), if the current monthly income of the debtor, or in a joint case, the debtor and the debtor's spouse, as of the date of the order for relief, when multiplied by 12, is equal to or less than –

(A) in the case of a debtor in a household of 1 person, the median family income of the applicable State for 1 earner;

(B) in the case of a debtor in a household of 2, 3, or 4 individuals, the highest median family income of the applicable State for a family of the same number or fewer individuals; or

(C) in the case of a debtor in a household exceeding 4 individuals, the highest median family income of the applicable State for a family of 4 or fewer individuals, plus $825 per month for each individual in excess of 4.

(7)(A) No judge, United States trustee (or bankruptcy administrator, if any), trustee, or other party in interest may file a motion under paragraph (2) if the current monthly income of the debtor, including a veteran (as that term is defined in section 101 of title 38), and the debtor's spouse combined, as of the date of the order for relief when multiplied by 12, is equal to or less than –

(i) in the case of a debtor in a household of 1 person, the median family income of the applicable State for 1 earner;

(ii) in the case of a debtor in a household of 2, 3, or 4 individuals, the highest median family income of the applicable State for a family of the same number or fewer individuals; or

(iii) in the case of a debtor in a household exceeding 4 individuals, the highest median family income of the applicable State for a family of 4 or fewer individuals, plus $825 per month for each individual in excess of 4.

(B) In a case that is not a joint case, current monthly income of the debtor's spouse shall not be considered for purposes of subparagraph (A) if –

(i)(I) the debtor and the debtor's spouse are separated under applicable nonbankruptcy law; or

(II) the debtor and the debtor's spouse are living separate and apart, other than for the purpose of evading subparagraph (A); and

(ii) the debtor files a statement under penalty of perjury –

(I) specifying that the debtor meets the requirement of subclause (I) or (II) of clause (i); and

(II) disclosing the aggregate, or best estimate of the aggregate, amount of any cash or money payments received from the debtor's spouse attributed to the debtor's current monthly income.

(c)(1) In this subsection –

(A) the term "crime of violence" has the meaning given such term in section 16 of title 18; and

(B) the term "drug trafficking crime" has the meaning given such term in section 924(c)(2) of title 18.

(2) Except as provided in paragraph (3), after notice and a hearing, the court, on a motion by the victim of a crime of violence or a drug trafficking crime, may when it is in the best interest of the victim dismiss a voluntary case filed under this chapter by a debtor who is an individual if such individual was convicted of such crime.

(3) The court may not dismiss a case under paragraph (2) if the debtor establishes by a preponderance of the evidence that the filing of a case under this chapter is necessary to satisfy a claim for a domestic support obligation.

SUBCHAPTER II - COLLECTION, LIQUIDATION, AND DISTRIBUTION OF THE ESTATE

721. Authorization to operate business

The court may authorize the trustee to operate the business of the debtor for a limited period, if such operation is in the best interest of the estate and consistent with the orderly liquidation of the estate.

722. Redemption

An individual debtor may, whether or not the debtor has waived the right to redeem under this section, redeem tangible personal property intended primarily for personal, family, or household use, from a lien securing a dischargeable consumer debt, if such property is exempted under section 522 of this title or has been abandoned under section 554 of this title, by paying the holder of such lien the amount of the allowed secured claim of such holder that is secured by such lien in full at the time of redemption.

723. Rights of partnership trustee against general partners

(a) If there is a deficiency of property of the estate to pay in full all claims which are allowed in a case under this chapter concerning a partnership and with respect to which a general partner of the partnership is personally liable, the trustee shall have a claim against such general partner to the extent that under applicable nonbankruptcy law such general partner is personally liable for such deficiency.

(b) To the extent practicable, the trustee shall first seek recovery of such deficiency from any general partner in such partnership that is not a debtor in a case under this title. Pending determination of such deficiency, the court may order any such partner to provide the estate with indemnity for, or assurance of payment of, any deficiency recoverable from such partner, or not to dispose of property.

(c) The trustee has a claim against the estate of each general partner in such partnership that is a debtor in a case under this title for the full amount of all claims of creditors allowed in the case concerning such partnership. Notwithstanding section 502 of this title, there shall not be allowed in such partner's case a claim against such partner on which both such partner and such partnership are liable, except to any extent that such claim is secured only by property of such partner and not by property of such partnership. The claim of the trustee under this subsection is entitled to distribution in such partner's case under section 726(a) of this title the same as any other claim of a kind specified in such section.

(d) If the aggregate that the trustee recovers from the estates of general partners under subsection (c) of this section is greater than any deficiency not recovered under subsection (b) of this section, the court, after notice and a hearing, shall determine an equitable distribution of the surplus so recovered, and the trustee shall distribute such surplus to the estates of the general partners in such partnership according to such determination.

724. Treatment of certain liens

(a) The trustee may avoid a lien that secures a claim of a kind specified in section 726(a)(4) of this title.

(b) Property in which the estate has an interest and that is subject to a lien that is not avoidable under this title (other than to the extent that there is a properly perfected unavoidable tax lien arising in connection with an ad valorem tax on real or personal property of the estate) and that secures an allowed claim for a tax, or proceeds of such property, shall be distributed -

(1) first, to any holder of an allowed claim secured by a lien on such property that is not avoidable under this title and that is senior to such tax lien;

(2) second, to any holder of a claim of a kind specified in section 507(a)(1)(C) or 507 (a)(2) (except that such expenses under each such section, other than claims for wages, salaries, or commissions that arise after the date of the filing of the petition, shall be limited to expenses incurred under this chapter and shall not include expenses incurred under chapter 11 of this title), 507(a)(1)(A), 507(a)(1)(B), 507(a)(3), 507(a)(4), 507(a)(5), 507(a)(6), or 507(a)(7) of this title, to the extent of the amount of such allowed tax claim that is secured by such tax lien;

(3) third, to the holder of such tax lien, to any extent that such holder's allowed tax claim that is secured by such tax lien exceeds any amount distributed under paragraph (2) of this subsection;

(4) fourth, to any holder of an allowed claim secured by a lien on such property that is not avoidable under this title and that is junior to such tax lien;

(5) fifth, to the holder of such tax lien, to the extent that such holder's allowed claim secured by such tax lien is not paid under paragraph (3) of this subsection; and

(6) sixth, to the estate.

(c) If more than one holder of a claim is entitled to distribution under a particular paragraph of subsection (b) of this section, distribution to such holders under such paragraph shall be in the same order as distribution to such holders would have been other than under this section.

(d) A statutory lien the priority of which is determined in the same manner as the priority of a tax lien under section 6323 of the Internal Revenue Code of 1986 shall be treated under subsection (b) of this section the same as if such lien were a tax lien.

(e) Before subordinating a tax lien on real or personal property of the estate, the trustee shall –

(1) exhaust the unencumbered assets of the estate; and

(2) in a manner consistent with section 506(c), recover from property securing an allowed secured claim the reasonable, necessary costs and expenses of preserving or disposing of such property.

(f) Notwithstanding the exclusion of ad valorem tax liens under this section and subject to the requirements of subsection (e), the following may be paid from property of the estate which secures a tax lien, or the proceeds of such property:

(1) Claims for wages, salaries, and commissions that are entitled to priority under section 507(a)(4).

(2) Claims for contributions to an employee benefit plan entitled to priority under section 507(a)(5).

800. Disposition of certain property

After the commencement of a case under this chapter, but before final distribution of property of the estate under section 726 of this title, the trustee, after notice and a hearing, shall dispose of any property in which an entity other than the estate has an interest, such as a lien, and that has not been disposed of under another section of this title.

726. Distribution of property of the estate

(a) Except as provided in section 510 of this title, property of the estate shall be distributed -

(1) first, in payment of claims of the kind specified in, and in the order specified in, section 507 of this title, proof of which is timely filed under section 501 of this title or tardily filed on or before the earlier of –

(A) the date that is 10 days after the mailing to creditors of the summary of the trustee's final report; or

(B) the date on which the trustee commences final distribution under this section;

(2) second, in payment of any allowed unsecured claim, other than a claim of a kind specified in paragraph (1), (3), or (4) of this subsection, proof of which is -

(A) timely filed under section 501(a) of this title;

(B) timely filed under section 501(b) or 501(c) of this title; or

(C) tardily filed under section 501(a) of this title, if -

(i) the creditor that holds such claim did not have notice or actual knowledge of the case in time for timely filing of a proof of such claim under section 501(a) of this title; and

(ii) proof of such claim is filed in time to permit payment of such claim;

(3) third, in payment of any allowed unsecured claim proof of which is tardily filed under section 501(a) of this title, other than a claim of the kind specified in paragraph (2)(C) of this subsection;

(4) fourth, in payment of any allowed claim, whether secured or unsecured, for any fine, penalty, or forfeiture, or for multiple, exemplary, or punitive damages, arising before the earlier of the order for relief or the appointment of a trustee, to the extent that such fine, penalty, forfeiture, or damages are not compensation for actual pecuniary loss suffered by the holder of such claim;

(5) fifth, in payment of interest at the legal rate from the date of the filing of the petition, on any claim paid under paragraph (1), (2), (3), or (4) of this subsection; and

(6) sixth, to the debtor.

(b) Payment on claims of a kind specified in paragraph (1), (2), (3), (4), (5), (6), (7), (8), (9), or (10) of section 507(a) of this title, or in paragraph (2), (3), (4), or (5) of subsection (a) of this section, shall be made pro rata among claims of the kind specified in each such particular paragraph, except that in a case that has been converted to this chapter under section 1112, 1208, or 1307 of this title, a claim allowed under section 503(b) of this title incurred under this chapter after such conversion has priority over a claim allowed under section 503(b) of this title incurred under any other chapter of this title or under this chapter before such conversion and over any expenses of a custodian superseded under section 543 of this title.

(c) Notwithstanding subsections (a) and (b) of this section, if there is property of the kind specified in section 541(a)(2) of this title, or proceeds of such property, in the estate, such property or proceeds shall be segregated from other property of the estate, and such property or proceeds and other property of the estate shall be distributed as follows:

(1) Claims allowed under section 503 of this title shall be paid either from property of the kind specified in section 541(a)(2) of this title, or from other property of the estate, as the interest of justice requires.

(2) Allowed claims, other than claims allowed under section 503 of this title, shall be paid in the order specified in subsection (a) of this section, and, with respect to claims of a kind specified in a particular paragraph of section 507 of this title or subsection (a) of this section, in the following order and manner:

(A) First, community claims against the debtor or the debtor's spouse shall be paid from property of the kind specified in section 541(a)(2) of this title, except to the extent that such property is solely liable for debts of the debtor.

(B) Second, to the extent that community claims against the debtor are not paid under subparagraph (A) of this paragraph, such community claims shall be paid from property of the kind specified in section 541(a)(2) of this title that is solely liable for debts of the debtor.

(C) Third, to the extent that all claims against the debtor including community claims against the debtor are not paid under subparagraph (A) or (B) of this paragraph such claims shall be paid from property of the estate other than property of the kind specified in section 541(a)(2) of this title.

(D) Fourth, to the extent that community claims against the debtor or the debtor's spouse are not paid under subparagraph (A), (B), or (C) of this paragraph, such claims shall be paid from all remaining property of the estate.

727. Discharge

(a) The court shall grant the debtor a discharge unless -

(1) the debtor is not an individual;

(2) the debtor, with intent to hinder, delay, or defraud a creditor or an officer of the estate charged with custody of property under this title, has transferred, removed, destroyed, mutilated, or concealed, or has permitted to be transferred, removed, destroyed, mutilated, or concealed -

(A) property of the debtor, within one year before the date of the filing of the petition; or

(B) property of the estate, after the date of the filing of the petition;

(3) the debtor has concealed, destroyed, mutilated, falsified, or failed to keep or preserve any recorded information, including books, documents, records, and papers, from which the debtor's financial condition or business transactions might be ascertained, unless such act or failure to act was justified under all of the circumstances of the case;

(4) the debtor knowingly and fraudulently, in or in connection with the case -

(A) made a false oath or account;

(B) presented or used a false claim;

(C) gave, offered, received, or attempted to obtain money, property, or advantage, or a promise of money, property, or advantage, for acting or forbearing to act; or

(D) withheld from an officer of the estate entitled to possession under this title, any recorded information, including books, documents, records, and papers, relating to the debtor's property or financial affairs;

(5) the debtor has failed to explain satisfactorily, before determination of denial of discharge under this paragraph, any loss of assets or deficiency of assets to meet the debtor's liabilities;

(6) the debtor has refused, in the case -

(A) to obey any lawful order of the court, other than an order to respond to a material question or to testify;

(B) on the ground of privilege against self-incrimination, to respond to a material question approved by the court or to testify, after the debtor has been granted immunity with respect to the matter concerning which such privilege was invoked; or

(C) on a ground other than the properly invoked privilege against self-incrimination, to respond to a material question approved by the court or to testify;

(7) the debtor has committed any act specified in paragraph (2), (3), (4), (5), or (6) of this subsection, on or within one year before the date of the filing of the petition, or during the case, in connection with another case, under this title or under the Bankruptcy Act, concerning an insider;

(8) the debtor has been granted a discharge under this section, under section 1141 of this title, or under section 14, 371, or 476 of the Bankruptcy Act, in a case commenced within 8 years before the date of the filing of the petition;

(9) the debtor has been granted a discharge under section 1228 or 1328 of this title, or under section 660 or 661 of the Bankruptcy Act, in a case commenced within six years before the date of the filing of the petition, unless payments under the plan in such case totaled at least -

(A) 100 percent of the allowed unsecured claims in such case; or

(B)(i) 70 percent of such claims; and

(ii) the plan was proposed by the debtor in good faith, and was the debtor's best effort;

(10) the court approves a written waiver of discharge executed by the debtor after the order for relief under this chapter;

(11) after filing the petition, the debtor failed to complete an instructional course concerning personal financial management described in section 111, except that this paragraph shall not apply with respect to a debtor who is a person described in section 109(h)(4) or who resides in a district for which the United States trustee (or the bankruptcy administrator, if any) determines that the approved instructional courses are not adequate to service the additional individuals who would otherwise be required to complete such instructional

courses under this section (The United States trustee (or the bankruptcy administrator, if any) who makes a determination described in this paragraph shall review such determination not later than 1 year after the date of such determination, and not less frequently than annually-- thereafter.); or

(12) the court after notice and a hearing held not more than 10 days before the date of the entry of the order granting the discharge finds that there is reasonable cause to believe that –

(A) section 522(q)(1) may be applicable to the debtor; and

(B) there is pending any proceeding in which the debtor may be found guilty of a felony of the kind described in section 522(q)(1)(A) or liable for a debt of the kind described in section 522(q)(1)(B).

(b) Except as provided in section 523 of this title, a discharge under subsection (a) of this section discharges the debtor from all debts that arose before the date of the order for relief under this chapter, and any liability on a claim that is determined under section 502 of this title as if such claim had arisen before the commencement of the case, whether or not a proof of claim based on any such debt or liability is filed under section 501 of this title, and whether or not a claim based on any such debt or liability is allowed under section 502 of this title.

(c)(1) The trustee, a creditor, or the United States trustee may object to the granting of a discharge under subsection (a) of this section.

(2) On request of a party in interest, the court may order the trustee to examine the acts and conduct of the debtor to determine whether a ground exists for denial of discharge.

(d) On request of the trustee, a creditor, or the United States trustee, and after notice and a hearing, the court shall revoke a discharge granted under subsection (a) of this section if -

(1) such discharge was obtained through the fraud of the debtor, and the requesting party did not know of such fraud until after the granting of such discharge;

(2) the debtor acquired property that is property of the estate, or became entitled to acquire property that would be property of the estate, and knowingly and fraudulently failed to report the acquisition of or entitlement to such property, or to deliver or surrender such property to the trustee;

(3) the debtor committed an act specified in subsection (a)(6) of this section; or

(4) the debtor has failed to explain satisfactorily –

(A) a material misstatement in an audit referred to in section 586(f) of title 28; or

(B) a failure to make available for inspection all necessary accounts, papers, documents, financial records, files, and all other papers, things, or property belonging to the debtor that are requested for an audit referred to in section 586(f) of title 28.

(e) The trustee, a creditor, or the United States trustee may request a revocation of a discharge -

(1) under subsection (d)(1) of this section within one year after such discharge is granted; or

(2) under subsection (d)(2) or (d)(3) of this section before the later of -

(A) one year after the granting of such discharge; and

(B) the date the case is closed.

Chapter 13 - Adjustment of Debts of an Individual with Regular Income

Subchapter I - Officers, Administration, and the Estate

Subchapter II - The Plan

SUBCHAPTER I - OFFICERS, ADMINISTRATION, AND THE ESTATE

1301. Stay of action against codebtor

(a) Except as provided in subsections (b) and (c) of this section, after the order for relief under this chapter, a creditor may not act, or commence or continue any civil action, to collect all or any part of a consumer debt of the debtor from any individual that is liable on such debt with the debtor, or that secured such debt, unless -

(1) such individual became liable on or secured such debt in the ordinary course of such individual's business; or

(2) the case is closed, dismissed, or converted to a case under chapter 7 or 11 of this title.

(b) A creditor may present a negotiable instrument, and may give notice of dishonor of such an instrument.

(c) On request of a party in interest and after notice and a hearing, the court shall grant relief from the stay provided by subsection (a) of this section with respect to a creditor, to the extent that -

(1) as between the debtor and the individual protected under subsection (a) of this section, such individual received the consideration for the claim held by such creditor;

(2) the plan filed by the debtor proposes not to pay such claim; or

(3) such creditor's interest would be irreparably harmed by continuation of such stay.

(d) Twenty days after the filing of a request under subsection (c)(2) of this section for relief from the stay provided by subsection (a) of this section, such stay is terminated with respect to the party in interest making such request, unless the debtor or any individual that is liable on such debt with the debtor files and serves upon such party in interest a written objection to the taking of the proposed action.

1302. Trustee

(a) If the United States trustee appoints an individual under section 586(b) of title 28 to serve as standing trustee in cases under this chapter and if such individual qualifies under section 322 of this title, then such individual shall serve as trustee in the case. Otherwise, the United States trustee shall appoint one disinterested person to serve as trustee in the case or the United States trustee may serve as a trustee in the case.

(b) The trustee shall -

(1) perform the duties specified in sections 704(a)(2), 704(a)(3), 704(a)(4), 704(a)(5), 704(a)(6), 704(a)(7), and 704(a)(9) of this title;

(2) appear and be heard at any hearing that concerns -

(A) the value of property subject to a lien;

(B) confirmation of a plan; or

(C) modification of the plan after confirmation;

(3) dispose of, under regulations issued by the Director of the Administrative Office of the United States Courts, moneys received or to be received in a case under chapter XIII of the Bankruptcy Act;

(4) advise, other than on legal matters, and assist the debtor in performance under the plan;

(5) ensure that the debtor commences making timely payments under section 1326 of this title; and

(6) if with respect to the debtor there is a claim for a domestic support obligation, provide the applicable notice specified in subsection (d).

(c) If the debtor is engaged in business, then in addition to the duties specified in subsection (b) of this section, the trustee shall perform the duties specified in sections 1106(a)(3) and 1106(a)(4) of this title.

(d)(1) In a case described in subsection (b)(6) to which subsection (b)(6) applies, the trustee shall –

(A)(i) provide written notice to the holder of the claim described in subsection (b)(6) of such claim and of the right of such holder to use the services of the State child support enforcement agency established under sections 464 and 466 of the Social Security Act for the State in which such holder resides, for assistance in collecting child support during and after the case under this title; and

(ii) include in the notice provided under clause (i) the address and telephone number of such State child support enforcement agency;

(B)(i) provide written notice to such State child support enforcement agency of such claim; and

(ii) include in the notice provided under clause (i) the name, address, and telephone number of such holder; and

(C) at such time as the debtor is granted a discharge under section 1328, provide written notice to such holder and to such State child support enforcement agency of –

(i) the granting of the discharge;

(ii) the last recent known address of the debtor;

(iii) the last recent known name and address of the debtor's employer; and

(iv) the name of each creditor that holds a claim that –

(I) is not discharged under paragraph (2) or (4) of section 523(a); or

(II) was reaffirmed by the debtor under section 524(c).

(2)(A) The holder of a claim described in subsection (b)(6) or the State child support enforcement agency of the State in which such holder resides may request from a creditor described in paragraph (1)(C)(iv) the last known address of the debtor.

(B) Notwithstanding any other provision of law, a creditor that makes a disclosure of a last known address of a debtor in connection with a request made under subparagraph (A) shall not be liable by reason of making that disclosure.

1303. Rights and powers of debtor

Subject to any limitations on a trustee under this chapter, the debtor shall have, exclusive of the trustee, the rights and powers of a trustee under sections 363(b), 363(d), 363(e), 363(f), and 363(l), of this title.

1304. Debtor engaged in business

(a) A debtor that is self-employed and incurs trade credit in the production of income from such employment is engaged in business.

(b) Unless the court orders otherwise, a debtor engaged in business may operate the business of the debtor and, subject to any limitations on a trustee under sections 363(c) and 364 of this title and to such limitations or conditions as the court prescribes, shall have, exclusive of the trustee, the rights and powers of the trustee under such sections.

(c) A debtor engaged in business shall perform the duties of the trustee specified in section 704(a)(8) of this title.

1305. Filing and allowance of postpetition claims

(a) A proof of claim may be filed by any entity that holds a claim against the debtor -

(1) for taxes that become payable to a governmental unit while the case is pending; or

(2) that is a consumer debt, that arises after the date of the order for

relief under this chapter, and that is for property or services necessary for the debtor's performance under the plan.

(b) Except as provided in subsection (c) of this section, a claim filed under subsection (a) of this section shall be allowed or disallowed under section 502 of this title, but shall be determined as of the date such claim arises, and shall be allowed under section 502(a), 502(b), or 502(c) of this title, or disallowed under section 502(d) or 502(e) of this title, the same as if such claim had arisen before the date of the filing of the petition.

(c) A claim filed under subsection (a)(2) of this section shall be disallowed if the holder of such claim knew or should have known that prior approval by the trustee of the debtor's incurring the obligation was practicable and was not obtained.

1306. Property of the estate

(a) Property of the estate includes, in addition to the property specified in section 541 of this title -

(1) all property of the kind specified in such section that the debtor acquires after the commencement of the case but before the case is closed, dismissed, or converted to a case under chapter 7, 11, or 12 of this title, whichever occurs first; and

(2) earnings from services performed by the debtor after the commencement of the case but before the case is closed, dismissed, or converted to a case under chapter 7, 11, or 12 of this title, whichever occurs first.

(b) Except as provided in a confirmed plan or order confirming a plan, the debtor shall remain in possession of all property of the estate.

1307. Conversion or dismissal

(a) The debtor may convert a case under this chapter to a case under chapter 7 of this title at any time. Any waiver of the right to convert under this subsection is unenforceable.

(b) On request of the debtor at any time, if the case has not been converted under section 706, 1112, or 1208 of this title, the court shall dismiss a case under this chapter. Any waiver of the right to dismiss under this subsection is unenforceable.

(c) Except as provided in subsection (f) of this section, on request of a party in interest or the United States trustee and after notice and a hearing, the court may convert a case under this chapter to a case under chapter 7 of this title, or may dismiss a case under this chapter, whichever is in the best interests of creditors and the estate, for cause, including -

(1) unreasonable delay by the debtor that is prejudicial to creditors;

(2) nonpayment of any fees and charges required under chapter 123 of title 28;

(3) failure to file a plan timely under section 1321 of this title;

(4) failure to commence making timely payments under section 1326 of this title;

(5) denial of confirmation of a plan under section 1325 of this title and denial of a request made for additional time for filing another plan or a modification of a plan;

(6) material default by the debtor with respect to a term of a confirmed plan;

(7) revocation of the order of confirmation under section 1330 of this title, and denial of confirmation of a modified plan under section 1329 of this title;

(8) termination of a confirmed plan by reason of the occurrence of a condition specified in the plan other than completion of payments under the plan;

(9) only on request of the United States trustee, failure of the debtor to file, within fifteen days, or such additional time as the court may allow, after the filing of the petition commencing such case, the information required by paragraph (1) of section 521(a);

(10) only on request of the United States trustee, failure to timely file the information required by paragraph (2) of section 521(a); or

(11) failure of the debtor to pay any domestic support obligation that first becomes payable after the date of the filing of the petition.

(d) Except as provided in subsection (f) of this section, at any time before the confirmation of a plan under section 1325 of this title, on request of a party in interest or the United States trustee and after notice and a hearing, the court may convert a case under this chapter to a case under chapter 11 or 12 of this title.

(e) Upon the failure of the debtor to file a tax return under section 1308, on request of a party in interest or the United States trustee and after notice and a hearing, the court shall dismiss a case or convert a case under this chapter to a case under chapter 7 of this title, whichever is in the best interest of the creditors and the estate.

(f) The court may not convert a case under this chapter to a case under chapter 7, 11, or 12 of this title if the debtor is a farmer, unless the debtor requests such conversion.

(g) Notwithstanding any other provision of this section, a case may not be converted to a case under another chapter of this title unless the debtor may be a debtor under such chapter.

1308. Filing of prepetition tax returns

(a) Not later than the day before the date on which the meeting of the creditors is first scheduled to be held under section 341(a), if the debtor was required to file a tax return under applicable nonbankruptcy law, the debtor shall file with appropriate tax authorities all tax returns for all taxable periods ending during the 4-year period ending on the date of the filing of the petition.

(b)(1) Subject to paragraph (2), if the tax returns required by subsection (a) have not been filed by the date on which the meeting of creditors is first scheduled to be held under section 341(a), the trustee may hold open that meeting for a reasonable period of time to allow the debtor an additional period of time to file any unfiled returns, but such additional period of time shall not extend beyond –

(A) for any return that is past due as of the date of the filing of the petition, the date that is 120 days after the date of that meeting; or

(B) for any return that is not past due as of the date of the filing of the petition, the later of –

(i) the date that is 120 days after the date of that meeting; or

(ii) the date on which the return is due under the last automatic extension of time for filing that return to which the debtor is entitled, and for which request is timely made, in accordance with applicable nonbankruptcy law.

(2) After notice and a hearing, and order entered before the tolling of any applicable filing period determined under paragraph (1), if the debtor demonstrates by a preponderance of the evidence that the failure to file a return as required under paragraph (1) is attributable to circumstances beyond the control of the debtor, the court may extend the filing period established by the trustee under paragraph (1) for –

(A) a period of not more than 30 days for returns described in paragraph (1)(A); and

(B) a period not to extend after the applicable extended due date for a return described in paragraph (1)(B).

(c) For purposes of this section, the term "return" includes a return prepared pursuant to subsection (a) or (b) of section 6020 of the Internal Revenue Code of 1986, or a similar State or local law, or a written stipulation to a judgment or a final order entered by a nonbankruptcy tribunal.

SUBCHAPTER II - THE PLAN

1321. Filing of plan

The debtor shall file a plan.

1322. Contents of plan

(a) The plan -

(1) shall provide for the submission of all or such portion of future earnings or other future income of the debtor to the supervision and control of the trustee as is necessary for the execution of the plan;

(2) shall provide for the full payment, in deferred cash payments, of all claims entitled to priority under section 507 of this title, unless the holder of a particular claim agrees to a different treatment of such claim;

(3) if the plan classifies claims, shall provide the same treatment for each claim within a particular class; and

(4) notwithstanding any other provision of this section, may provide for less than full payment of all amounts owed for a claim entitled to priority under section 507(a)(1)(B) only if the plan provides that all of the debtor's projected disposable income for a 5-year period beginning on the date that the first payment is due under the plan will be applied to make payments under the plan.

(b) Subject to subsections (a) and (c) of this section, the plan may -

(1) designate a class or classes of unsecured claims, as provided in section 1122 of this title, but may not discriminate unfairly against any class

so designated; however, such plan may treat claims for a consumer debt of the debtor if an individual is liable on such consumer debt with the debtor differently than other unsecured claims;

(2) modify the rights of holders of secured claims, other than a claim secured only by a security interest in real property that is the debtor's principal residence, or of holders of unsecured claims, or leave unaffected the rights of holders of any class of claims;

(3) provide for the curing or waiving of any default;

(4) provide for payments on any unsecured claim to be made concurrently with payments on any secured claim or any other unsecured claim;

(5) notwithstanding paragraph (2) of this subsection, provide for the curing of any default within a reasonable time and maintenance of payments while the case is pending on any unsecured claim or secured claim on which the last payment is due after the date on which the final payment under the plan is due;

(6) provide for the payment of all or any part of any claim allowed under section 1305 of this title;

(7) subject to section 365 of this title, provide for the assumption, rejection, or assignment of any executory contract or unexpired lease of the debtor not previously rejected under such section;

(8) provide for the payment of all or part of a claim against the debtor from property of the estate or property of the debtor;

(9) provide for the vesting of property of the estate, on confirmation of the plan or at a later time, in the debtor or in any other entity;

(10) provide for the payment of interest accruing after the date of the filing of the petition on unsecured claims that are nondischargeable under section 1328(a), except that such interest may be paid only to the extent that the debtor has disposable income available to pay such interest after making provision for full payment of all allowed claims; and

(11) include any other appropriate provision not inconsistent with this title.

(c) Notwithstanding subsection (b)(2) and applicable nonbankruptcy law-

(1) a default with respect to, or that gave rise to, a lien on the debtor's principal residence may be cured under paragraph (3) or (5) of subsection (b) until such residence is sold at a foreclosure sale that is conducted in accordance with applicable nonbankruptcy law; and

(2) in a case in which the last payment on the original payment schedule for a claim secured only by a security interest in real property that is the debtor's principal residence is due before the date on which the final payment under the plan is due, the plan may provide for the payment of the claim as modified pursuant to section 1325(a)(5) of this title.

(d)(1) If the current monthly income of the debtor and the debtor's spouse combined, when multiplied by 12, is not less than –

(A) in the case of a debtor in a household of 1 person, the median family income of the applicable State for 1 earner;

(B) in the case of a debtor in a household of 2, 3, or 4 individuals, the highest median family income of the applicable State for a family of the same number or fewer individuals; or

(C) in the case of a debtor in a household exceeding 4 individuals, the highest median family income of the applicable State for a family of 4 or fewer individuals, plus $825 per month for each individual in excess of 4,

the plan may not provide for payments over a period that is longer than 5 years.

(2) If the current monthly income of the debtor and the debtor's spouse combined, when multiplied by 12, is less than –

(A) in the case of a debtor in a household of 1 person, the median family income of the applicable State for 1 earner;

(B) in the case of a debtor in a household of 2, 3, or 4 individuals, the highest median family income of the applicable State for a family of the same number or fewer individuals; or

(C) in the case of a debtor in a household exceeding 4 individuals, the highest median family income of the applicable State for a family of 4 or fewer individuals, plus $825 per month for each individual in excess of 4,

the plan may not provide for payments over a period that is longer than 3 years, unless the court, for cause, approves a longer period, but the court may not approve a period that is longer than 5 years.

(e) Notwithstanding subsection (b)(2) of this section and sections 506(b) and 1325(a)(5) of this title, if it is proposed in a plan to cure a default, the amount necessary to cure the default, shall be determined in accordance with the underlying agreement and applicable nonbankruptcy law.

(f) A plan may not materially alter the terms of a loan described in section 362(b)(19) and any amounts required to repay such loan shall not constitute "disposable income" under section 1325.

1323. Modification of plan before confirmation

(a) The debtor may modify the plan at any time before confirmation, but may not modify the plan so that the plan as modified fails to meet the requirements of section 1322 of this title.

(b) After the debtor files a modification under this section, the plan as modified becomes the plan.

(c) Any holder of a secured claim that has accepted or rejected the plan is deemed to have accepted or rejected, as the case may be, the plan as modified, unless the modification provides for a change in the rights of such holder from what such rights were under the plan before modification, and such holder changes such holder's previous acceptance or rejection.

1324. Confirmation hearing

(a) Except as provided in subsection (b) and after notice, the court shall hold a hearing on confirmation of the plan. A party in interest may object to confirmation of the plan.

(b) The hearing on confirmation of the plan may be held not earlier than 20 days and not later than 45 days after the date of the meeting of creditors under section 341(a), unless the court determines that it would be in the best interests of the creditors and the estate to hold such hearing at an earlier date and there is no objection to such earlier date.

1325. Confirmation of plan

(a) Except as provided in subsection (b), the court shall confirm a plan if-

(1) the plan complies with the provisions of this chapter and with the other applicable provisions of this title;

(2) any fee, charge, or amount required under chapter 123 of title 28, or by the plan, to be paid before confirmation, has been paid;

(3) the plan has been proposed in good faith and not by any means forbidden by law;

(4) the value, as of the effective date of the plan, of property to be distributed under the plan on account of each allowed unsecured claim is not less than the amount that would be paid on such claim if the estate of the debtor were liquidated under chapter 7 of this title on such date;

(5) with respect to each allowed secured claim provided for by the plan-

(A) the holder of such claim has accepted the plan;

(B)(i) the plan provides that –

(I) the holder of such claim retain the lien securing such claim until the earlier of –

(aa) the payment of the underlying debt determined under nonbankruptcy law; or

(bb) discharge under section 1328; and

(II) if the case under this chapter is dismissed or converted without completion of the plan, such lien shall also be retained by such holder to the extent recognized by applicable nonbankruptcy law;

(ii) the value, as of the effective date of the plan, of property to be distributed under the plan on account of such claim is not less than the allowed amount of such claim; and

(iii) if –

(I) property to be distributed pursuant to this subsection is in the form of periodic payments, such payments shall be in equal monthly amounts; and

(II) the holder of the claim is secured by personal property, the amount of such payments shall not be less than an amount sufficient to provide to the holder of such claim adequate protection during the period of the plan; or

(C) the debtor surrenders the property securing such claim to such holder;

(6) the debtor will be able to make all payments under the plan and to comply with the plan;

(7) the action of the debtor in filing the petition was in good faith;

(8) the debtor has paid all amounts that are required to be paid under a domestic support obligation and that first become payable after the date of the filing of the petition if the debtor is required by a judicial or administrative order, or by statute, to pay such domestic support obligation; and

(9) the debtor has filed all applicable Federal, State, and local tax returns as required by section 1308.

For purposes of paragraph (5), section 506 shall not apply to a claim described in that paragraph if the creditor has a purchase money security interest securing the debt that is the subject of the claim, the debt was incurred within the 910-day period preceding the date of the filing of the petition, and the collateral for that debt consists of a motor vehicle (as defined in section 30102 of title 49) acquired for the personal use of the debtor, or if collateral for that debt consists of any other thing of value, if the debt was incurred during the 1-year period preceding that filing.

(b)(1) If the trustee or the holder of an allowed unsecured claim objects to the confirmation of the plan, then the court may not approve the plan unless, as of the effective date of the plan -

(A) the value of the property to be distributed under the plan on account of such claim is not less than the amount of such claim; or

(B) the plan provides that all of the debtor's projected disposable income to be received in the applicable commitment period beginning on the date that the first payment is due under the plan will be applied to make payments to unsecured creditors under the plan.

(2) For purposes of this subsection, the term "disposable income" means current monthly income received by the debtor (other than payments made under Federal law relating to the national emergency declared by the President under the National Emergencies Act (50 U.S.C. 1601 et seq.) with respect to the coronavirus disease 2019 (COVID-19), child support payments, foster care payments, or disability payments for a dependent child made in accordance with applicable nonbankruptcy law to the extent reasonably necessary to be expended for such child) less amounts reasonably necessary to be expended –

(A)(i) for the maintenance or support of the debtor or a dependent of the debtor, or for a domestic support obligation, that first becomes payable after the date the petition is filed; and

(ii) for charitable contributions (that meet the definition of "charitable contribution" under section 548(d)(3)) to a qualified religious or charitable entity or organization (as defined in section 548(d)(4)) in an amount not to exceed 15 percent of gross income of the debtor for the year in which the contributions are made; and

(B) if the debtor is engaged in business, for the payment of expenditures necessary for the continuation, preservation, and operation of such business.

(3) Amounts reasonably necessary to be expended under paragraph (2), other than subparagraph (A)(ii) of paragraph (2), shall be determined in accordance with subparagraphs (A) and (B) of section 707(b)(2), if the debtor has current monthly income, when multiplied by 12, greater than –

(A) in the case of a debtor in a household of 1 person, the median family income of the applicable State for 1 earner;

(B) in the case of a debtor in a household of 2, 3, or 4 individuals, the highest median family income of the applicable State for a family of the same number or fewer individuals; or

(C) in the case of a debtor in a household exceeding 4 individuals, the highest median family income of the applicable State for a family of 4 or fewer individuals, plus $825 per month for each individual in excess of 4.

(4) For purposes of this subsection, the "applicable commitment period"-

(A) subject to subparagraph (B), shall be –

(i) 3 years; or

(ii) not less than 5 years, if the current monthly income of the debtor and the debtor's spouse combined, when multiplied by 12, is not less than –

(I) in the case of a debtor in a household of 1 person, the median family income of the applicable State for 1 earner;

(II) in the case of a debtor in a household of 2, 3, or 4 individuals, the highest median family income of the applicable State for a family of the same number or fewer individuals; or

(III) in the case of a debtor in a household exceeding 4 individuals, the highest median family income of the applicable State for a family of 4 or fewer individuals, plus $825 per month for each individual in excess of 4; and

(B) may be less than 3 or 5 years, whichever is applicable under subparagraph (A), but only if the plan provides for payment in full of all allowed unsecured claims over a shorter period.

(c) After confirmation of a plan, the court may order any entity from whom the debtor receives income to pay all or any part of such income to the trustee.

1326. Payments

(a)(1) Unless the court orders otherwise, the debtor shall commence making payments not later than 30 days after the date of the filing of the plan or the order for relief, whichever is earlier, in the amount –

(A) proposed by the plan to the trustee;

(B) scheduled in a lease of personal property directly to the lessor for that portion of the obligation that becomes due after the order for relief, reducing the payments under subparagraph (A) by the amount so paid and providing the trustee with evidence of such payment, including the amount and date of payment; and

(C) that provides adequate protection directly to a creditor holding an allowed claim secured by personal property to the extent the claim is attributable to the purchase of such property by the debtor for that portion of the obligation that becomes due after the order for relief, reducing the payments under subparagraph (A) by the amount so paid and providing the trustee with evidence of such payment, including the amount and date of payment.

(2) A payment made under paragraph (1)(A) shall be retained by the trustee until confirmation or denial of confirmation. If a plan is confirmed, the trustee shall distribute any such payment in accordance with the plan as soon as is practicable. If a plan is not confirmed, the trustee shall return any such payments not previously paid and not yet due and owing to creditors pursuant to paragraph (3) to the debtor, after deducting any unpaid claim allowed under section 503(b).

(3) Subject to section 363, the court may, upon notice and a hearing, modify, increase, or reduce the payments required under this subsection pending confirmation of a plan.

(4) Not later than 60 days after the date of filing of a case under this chapter, a debtor retaining possession of personal property subject to a lease or securing a claim attributable in whole or in part to the purchase price of such property shall provide the lessor or secured creditor reasonable evidence of the maintenance of any required insurance coverage with respect to the use or ownership of such property and continue to do so for so long as the debtor retains possession of such property.

(b) Before or at the time of each payment to creditors under the plan, there shall be paid -

(1) any unpaid claim of the kind specified in section 507(a)(2) of this title;

(2) if a standing trustee appointed under section 586(b) of title 28 is serving in the case, the percentage fee fixed for such standing trustee under section 586(e)(1)(B) of title 28; and

(3) if a chapter 7 trustee has been allowed compensation due to the conversion or dismissal of the debtor's prior case pursuant to section 707(b), and some portion of that compensation remains unpaid in a case converted to this chapter or in the case dismissed under section 707(b) and refiled under this chapter, the amount of any such unpaid compensation, which shall be paid monthly –

(A) by prorating such amount over the remaining duration of the plan; and

(B) by monthly payments not to exceed the greater of –

(i) $25; or

(ii) the amount payable to unsecured nonpriority creditors, as provided by the plan, multiplied by 5 percent, and the result divided by the number of months in the plan.

(c) Except as otherwise provided in the plan or in the order confirming the plan, the trustee shall make payments to creditors under the plan.

(d) Notwithstanding any other provision of this title –

(1) compensation referred to in subsection (b)(3) is payable and may be collected by the trustee under that paragraph, even if such amount has been discharged in a prior case under this title; and

(2) such compensation is payable in a case under this chapter only to the extent permitted by subsection (b)(3).

1327. Effect of confirmation

(a) The provisions of a confirmed plan bind the debtor and each creditor, whether or not the claim of such creditor is provided for by the plan, and whether or not such creditor has objected to, has accepted, or has rejected the plan.

(b) Except as otherwise provided in the plan or the order confirming the plan, the confirmation of a plan vests all of the property of the estate in the debtor.

(c) Except as otherwise provided in the plan or in the order confirming the plan, the property vesting in the debtor under subsection (b) of this section is free and clear of any claim or interest of any creditor provided for by the plan.

1328. Discharge

(a) Subject to subsection (d), as soon as practicable after completion by the debtor of all payments under the plan, and in the case of a debtor who is required by a judicial or administrative order, or by statute, to pay a domestic support obligation, after such debtor certifies that all amounts payable under such order or such statute that are due on or before the date of the certification (including amounts due before the petition was filed, but only to the extent provided for by the plan) have been paid, unless the court approves a written waiver of discharge executed by the debtor after the order for relief under this chapter, the court shall grant the debtor a discharge of all debts provided for by the plan or disallowed under section 502 of this title, except any debt -

(1) provided for under section 1322(b)(5);

(2) of the kind specified in section 507(a)(8)(C) or in paragraph (1)(B), (1)(C), (2), (3), (4), (5), (8), or (9) of section 523(a);

(3) for restitution, or a criminal fine, included in a sentence on the debtor's conviction of a crime; or

(4) for restitution, or damages, awarded in a civil action against the debtor as a result of willful or malicious injury by the debtor that caused personal injury to an individual or the death of an individual.

(b) Subject to subsection (d), at any time after the confirmation of the plan and after notice and a hearing, the court may grant a discharge to a debtor that has not completed payments under the plan only if -

(1) the debtor's failure to complete such payments is due to circumstances for which the debtor should not justly be held accountable;

(2) the value, as of the effective date of the plan, of property actually distributed under the plan on account of each allowed unsecured claim is not less than the amount that would have been paid on such claim if the estate of the debtor had been liquidated under chapter 7 of this title on such date; and

(3) modification of the plan under section 1329 of this title is not practicable.

(c) A discharge granted under subsection (b) of this section discharges the debtor from all unsecured debts provided for by the plan or disallowed under section 502 of this title, except any debt -

(1) provided for under section 1322(b)(5) of this title; or

(2) of a kind specified in section 523(a) of this title.

(d) Notwithstanding any other provision of this section, a discharge granted under this section does not discharge the debtor from any debt based on an allowed claim filed under section 1305(a)(2) of this title if prior approval by the trustee of the debtor's incurring such debt was practicable and was not obtained.

(e) On request of a party in interest before one year after a discharge under this section is granted, and after notice and a hearing, the court may revoke such discharge only if -

(1) such discharge was obtained by the debtor through fraud; and

(2) the requesting party did not know of such fraud until after such discharge was granted.

(f) Notwithstanding subsections (a) and (b), the court shall not grant a discharge of all debts provided for in the plan or disallowed under section 502, if the debtor has received a discharge –

(1) in a case filed under chapter 7, 11, or 12 of this title during the 4-year period preceding the date of the order for relief under this chapter, or

(2) in a case filed under chapter 13 of this title during the 2-year period preceding the date of such order.

(g)(1) The court shall not grant a discharge under this section to a debtor unless after filing a petition the debtor has completed an instructional course concerning personal financial management described in section 111.

(2) Paragraph (1) shall not apply with respect to a debtor who is a person described in section 109(h)(4) or who resides in a district for which the United States trustee (or the bankruptcy administrator, if any) determines that the approved instructional courses are not adequate to service the additional individuals who would otherwise be required to complete such instructional course by reason of the requirements of paragraph (1).

(3) The United States trustee (or the bankruptcy administrator, if any) who makes a determination described in paragraph (2) shall review such determination not later than 1 year after the date of such determination, and not less frequently than annually thereafter.

(h) The court may not grant a discharge under this chapter unless the court after notice and a hearing held not more than 10 days before the date of the entry of the order granting the discharge finds that there is no reasonable cause to believe that –

(1) section 522(q)(1) may be applicable to the debtor; and

(2) there is pending any proceeding in which the debtor may be found guilty of a felony of the kind described in section 522(q)(1)(A) or liable for a debt of the kind described in section 522(q)(1)(B).

1329. Modification of plan after confirmation

(a) At any time after confirmation of the plan but before the completion of payments under such plan, the plan may be modified, upon request of the debtor, the trustee, or the holder of an allowed unsecured claim, to -

(1) increase or reduce the amount of payments on claims of a particular class provided for by the plan;

(2) extend or reduce the time for such payments;

(3) alter the amount of the distribution to a creditor whose claim is provided for by the plan to the extent necessary to take account of any payment of such claim other than under the plan; or

(4) reduce amounts to be paid under the plan by the actual amount expended by the debtor to purchase health insurance for the debtor (and for any dependent of the debtor if such dependent does not otherwise have health insurance coverage) if the debtor documents the cost of such insurance and demonstrates that –

(A) such expenses are reasonable and necessary;

(B)(i) if the debtor previously paid for health insurance, the amount is not materially larger than the cost the debtor previously paid or the cost necessary to maintain the lapsed policy; or

(ii) if the debtor did not have health insurance, the amount is not materially larger than the reasonable cost that would be incurred by a debtor who purchases health insurance, who has similar income, expenses, age, and health status, and who lives in the same geographical location with the same number of dependents who do not otherwise have health insurance coverage; and

(C) the amount is not otherwise allowed for purposes of determining disposable income under section 1325(b) of this title;

and upon request of any party in interest, files proof that a health insurance policy was purchased.

(b)(1) Sections 1322(a), 1322(b), and 1323(c) of this title and the requirements of section 1325(a) of this title apply to any modification under subsection (a) of this section.

(2) The plan as modified becomes the plan unless, after notice and a hearing, such modification is disapproved.

(c) A plan modified under this section may not provide for payments over a period that expires after the applicable commitment period under section 1325(b)(1)(B) after the time that the first payment under the original confirmed plan was due, unless the court, for cause, approves a longer period, but the court may not approve a period that expires after five years after such time.

1330. Revocation of an order of confirmation

(a) On request of a party in interest at any time within 180 days after the date of the entry of an order of confirmation under section 1325 of this title, and after notice and a hearing, the court may revoke such order if such order was procured by fraud.

(b) If the court revokes an order of confirmation under subsection (a) of this section, the court shall dispose of the case under section 1307 of this title, unless, within the time fixed by the court, the debtor proposes and the court confirms a modification of the plan under section 1329 of this title.

Miscellaneous Statutes

28 U.S.C. § 157. Procedures

(a) Each district court may provide that any or all cases under title 11 and any or all proceedings arising under title 11 or arising in or related to a case under title 11 shall be referred to the bankruptcy judges for the district.

(b)(1) Bankruptcy judges may hear and determine all cases under title 11 and all core proceedings arising under title 11, or arising in a case under title 11, referred under subsection (a) of this section, and may enter appropriate orders and judgments, subject to review under section 158 of this title.

(2) Core proceedings include, but are not limited to -

(A) matters concerning the administration of the estate;

(B) allowance or disallowance of claims against the estate or exemptions from property of the estate, and estimation of claims or interests for the purposes of confirming a plan under chapter 11, 12, or 13 of title 11 but not the liquidation or estimation of contingent or unliquidated personal injury tort or wrongful death claims against the estate for purposes of distribution in a case under title 11;

(C) counterclaims by the estate against persons filing claims against the estate;

(D) orders in respect to obtaining credit;

(E) orders to turn over property of the estate;

(F) proceedings to determine, avoid, or recover preferences;

(G) motions to terminate, annul, or modify the automatic stay;

(H) proceedings to determine, avoid, or recover fraudulent conveyances;

(I) determinations as to the dischargeability of particular debts;

(J) objections to discharges;

(K) determinations of the validity, extent, or priority of liens;

(L) confirmations of plans;

(M) orders approving the use or lease of property, including the use of cash collateral;

(N) orders approving the sale of property other than property resulting from claims brought by the estate against persons who have not filed claims against the estate;

(O) other proceedings affecting the liquidation of the assets of the estate or the adjustment of the debtor-creditor or the equity security holder relationship, except personal injury tort or wrongful death claims; and

(P) recognition of foreign proceedings and other matters under chapter 15 of title 11.

(3) The bankruptcy judge shall determine, on the judge's own motion or on timely motion of a party, whether a proceeding is a core proceeding under this subsection or is a proceeding that is otherwise related to a case under title 11. A determination that a proceeding is not a core proceeding shall not be made solely on the basis that its resolution may be affected by State law.

(4) Non-core proceedings under section 157(b)(2)(B) of title 28, United States Code, shall not be subject to the mandatory abstention provisions of section 1334(c)(2).

(5) The district court shall order that personal injury tort and wrongful death claims shall be tried in the district court in which the bankruptcy case is pending, or in the district court in the district in which the claim arose, as determined by the district court in which the bankruptcy case is pending.

(c)(1) A bankruptcy judge may hear a proceeding that is not a core proceeding but that is otherwise related to a case under title 11. In such proceeding, the bankruptcy judge shall submit proposed findings of fact and conclusions of law to the district court, and any final order or judgment shall be entered by the district judge after considering the bankruptcy judge's proposed findings and conclusions and after reviewing de novo those matters to which any party has timely and specifically objected.

(2) Notwithstanding the provisions of paragraph (1) of this subsection, the district court, with the consent of all the parties to the proceeding, may refer a proceeding related to a case under title 11 to a bankruptcy judge to hear and determine and to enter appropriate orders and judgments, subject to review under section 158 of this title.

(d) The district court may withdraw, in whole or in part, any case or proceeding referred under this section, on its own motion or on timely motion of any party, for cause shown. The district court shall, on timely motion of a party, so withdraw a proceeding if the court determines that resolution of the proceeding requires consideration of both title 11 and other laws of the United States regulating organizations or activities affecting interstate commerce.

(e) If the right to a jury trial applies in a proceeding that may be heard under this section by a bankruptcy judge, the bankruptcy judge may conduct the jury trial if specially designated to exercise such jurisdiction by the district court and with the express consent of all the parties.

28 U.S.C. § 158. Appeals

(a) The district courts of the United States shall have jurisdiction to hear appeals

(1) from final judgments, orders, and decrees;

(2) from interlocutory orders and decrees issued under section 1121(d) of title 11 increasing or reducing the time periods referred to in section 1121 of such title; and

(3) with leave of the court, from other interlocutory orders and decrees;

and, with leave of the court, from interlocutory orders and decrees, of bankruptcy judges entered in cases and proceedings referred to the bankruptcy judges under section 157 of this title. An appeal under this subsection shall be taken only to the district court for the judicial district in which the bankruptcy judge is serving.

(b)(1) The judicial council of a circuit shall establish a bankruptcy appellate panel service composed of bankruptcy judges of the districts in the circuit who are appointed by the judicial council in accordance with paragraph (3), to hear and determine, with the consent of all the parties, appeals under subsection (a) unless the judicial council finds that -

(A) there are insufficient judicial resources available in the circuit; or

(B) establishment of such service would result in undue delay or increased cost to parties in cases under title 11.

Not later than 90 days after making the finding, the judicial council shall submit to the Judicial Conference of the United States a report containing the factual basis of such finding.

(2)(A) A judicial council may reconsider, at any time, the finding described in paragraph (1).

(B) On the request of a majority of the district judges in a circuit for which a bankruptcy appellate panel service is established under paragraph (1), made after the expiration of the 1-year period beginning on the date such service is established, the judicial council of the circuit shall determine whether a circumstance specified in subparagraph (A) or (B) of such paragraph exists.

(C) On its own motion, after the expiration of the 3-year period beginning on the date a bankruptcy appellate panel service is established under paragraph (1), the judicial council of the circuit may determine whether a circumstance specified in subparagraph (A) or (B) of such paragraph exists.

(D) If the judicial council finds that either of such circumstances exists, the judicial council may provide for the completion of the appeals then pending before such service and the orderly termination of such service.

(3) Bankruptcy judges appointed under paragraph (1) shall be appointed and may be reappointed under such paragraph.

(4) If authorized by the Judicial Conference of the United States, the judicial councils of 2 or more circuits may establish a joint bankruptcy appellate panel comprised of bankruptcy judges from the districts within the circuits for which such panel is established, to hear and determine, upon the consent of all the parties, appeals under subsection (a) of this section.

(5) An appeal to be heard under this subsection shall be heard by a panel of 3 members of the bankruptcy appellate panel service, except that a member of such service may not hear an appeal originating in the district for which such member is appointed or designated under section 152 of this title.

(6) Appeals may not be heard under this subsection by a panel of the bankruptcy appellate panel service unless the district judges for the district in which the appeals occur, by majority vote, have authorized such service to hear and determine appeals originating in such district.

(c)(1) Subject to subsections (b), and (d)(2), each appeal under subsection (a) shall be heard by a 3-judge panel of the bankruptcy appellate panel service established under subsection (b)(1) unless -

(A) the appellant elects at the time of filing the appeal; or

(B) any other party elects, not later than 30 days after service of notice of the appeal;

to have such appeal heard by the district court.

(2) An appeal under subsections (a) and (b) of this section shall be taken in the same manner as appeals in civil proceedings generally are taken to the courts of appeals from the district courts and in the time provided by Rule 8002 of the Bankruptcy Rules.

(d)(1) The courts of appeals shall have jurisdiction of appeals from all final decisions, judgments, orders, and decrees entered under subsections (a) and (b) of this section.

(2)(A) The appropriate court of appeals shall have jurisdiction of appeals described in the first sentence of subsection (a) if the bankruptcy court, the district court, or the bankruptcy appellate panel involved, acting on its own motion or on the request of a party to the judgment, order, or decree described in such first sentence, or all the appellants and appellees (if any) acting jointly, certify that –

(i) the judgment, order, or decree involves a question of law as to which there is no controlling decision of the court of appeals for the circuit or of the Supreme Court of the United States, or involves a matter of public importance;

(ii) the judgment, order, or decree involves a question of law requiring resolution of conflicting decisions; or

(iii) an immediate appeal from the judgment, order, or decree may materially advance the progress of the case or proceeding in which the appeal is taken; and if the court of appeals authorizes the direct appeal of the judgment, order, or decree.

(B) If the bankruptcy court, the district court, or the bankruptcy appellate panel –

(i) on its own motion or on the request of a party, determines that a circumstance specified in clause (i), (ii), or (iii) of subparagraph (A) exists; or

(ii) receives a request made by a majority of the appellants and a majority of appellees (if any) to make the certification described in subparagraph (A); then the bankruptcy court, the district court, or the bankruptcy appellate panel shall make the certification described in subparagraph (A).

(C) The parties may supplement the certification with a short statement of the basis for the certification.

(D) An appeal under this paragraph does not stay any proceeding of the bankruptcy court, the district court, or the bankruptcy appellate panel from which the appeal is taken, unless the respective bankruptcy court, district court, or bankruptcy appellate panel, or the court of appeals in which the appeal is pending, issues a stay of such proceeding pending the appeal.

(E) Any request under subparagraph (B) for certification shall be made not later than 60 days after the entry of the judgment, order, or decree.

Appendix II - Federal Rules of Bankruptcy Procedure

(Current to January 1, 2024)

CONTENTS

RULES OF PRACTICE AND PROCEDURE IN BANKRUPTCY

Rule 1001. Scope of Rules and Forms; Short Title

The Bankruptcy Rules and Forms govern procedure in cases under title 11 of the United States Code. The rules shall be cited as the Federal Rules of Bankruptcy Procedure and the forms as the Official Bankruptcy Forms. These rules shall be construed, administered, and employed by the court and the parties to secure the just, speedy, and inexpensive determination of every case and proceeding.

PART I

COMMENCEMENT OF CASE; PROCEEDINGS RELATING TO PETITION AND ORDER FOR RELIEF

Rule 1002. Commencement of Case

(a) PETITION. A petition commencing a case under the Code shall be filed with the clerk.

(b) TRANSMISSION TO UNITED STATES TRUSTEE. The clerk shall forthwith transmit to the United States trustee a copy of the petition filed pursuant to subdivision (a) of this rule.

Rule 1003. Involuntary Petition

(a) TRANSFEROR OR TRANSFEREE OF CLAIM. A transferor or transferee of a claim shall annex to the original and each copy of the petition a copy of all documents evidencing the transfer, whether transferred unconditionally, for security, or otherwise, and a signed statement that the claim was not transferred for the purpose of commencing the case and setting forth the consideration for and terms of the transfer. An entity that has transferred or acquired a claim for the purpose of commencing a case for liquidation under chapter 7 or for reorganization under chapter 11 shall not be a qualified petitioner.

(b) JOINDER OF PETITIONERS AFTER FILING. If the answer to an involuntary petition filed by fewer than three creditors avers the existence of 12 or more creditors, the debtor shall file with the answer a list of all creditors with their addresses, a brief statement of the nature of their claims, and the amounts thereof. If it appears that there are 12 or more creditors as provided in Section 303(b) of the Code, the court shall afford a reasonable opportunity for other creditors to join in the petition before a hearing is held thereon.

Rule 1004. Involuntary Petition Against a Partnership

After filing of an involuntary petition under § 303(b)(3) of the Code, (1) the petitioning partners or other petitioners shall promptly send to or serve on each general partner who is not a petitioner a copy of the petition; and (2) the clerk shall promptly issue a summons for service on each general partner who is not a petitioner. Rule 1010 applies to the form and service of the summons.

Rule 1004.1. Petition for an Infant or Incompetent Person

If an infant or incompetent person has a representative, including a general guardian, committee, conservator, or similar fiduciary, the representative may file a voluntary petition on behalf of the infant or incompetent person. An infant or incompetent person who does not have a duly appointed representative may file a voluntary petition by next friend or guardian ad litem. The court shall appoint a guardian ad litem for an infant or incompetent person who is a debtor and is not otherwise represented or shall make any other order to protect the infant or incompetent debtor.

Rule 1004.2 Petition in Chapter 15 Cases

(a) DESIGNATING CENTER OF MAIN INTERESTS. A petition for recognition of a foreign proceeding under chapter 15 of the Code shall state the country where the debtor has its center of main interests. The petition shall also identify each country in which a foreign proceeding by, regarding, or against the debtor is pending.

(b) CHALLENGING DESIGNATION. The United States trustee or a party in interest may file a motion for a determination that the debtor's center of main interests is other than as stated in the petition for recognition commencing the chapter 15 case. Unless the court orders otherwise, the motion shall be filed no later than seven days before the date set for the hearing on the petition. The motion shall be transmitted to the United States trustee and served on the debtor, all persons or bodies authorized to administer foreign proceedings of the debtor, all entities against whom provisional relief is being sought under §1519 of the Code, all parties to litigation pending in the United States in which the debtor was a party as of the time the petition was filed, and such other entities as the court may direct.

Rule 1005. Caption of Petition

The caption of a petition commencing a case under the Code shall contain the name of the court, the title of the case, and the docket number. The title of the case shall include the following information about the debtor: name, employer identification number, last four digits of the social-security number or individual debtor's taxpayer-identification number, any other federal taxpayer-identification number, and all other names used within eight years before filing the petition. If the petition is not filed by the debtor, it shall include all names used by the debtor which are known to the petitioners.

Rule 1006. Filing Fee

(a) GENERAL REQUIREMENT. Every petition shall be accompanied by the filing fee except as provided in subdivisions (b) and (c) of this rule. For the purpose of this rule, "filing fee" means the filing fee prescribed by 28 U.S.C. § 1930(a)(1)-(a)(5) and any other fee prescribed by the Judicial Conference of the United States under 28 U.S.C. § 1930(b) that is payable to the clerk upon the commencement of a case under the Code.

(b) PAYMENT OF FILING FEE IN INSTALLMENTS.

(1) Application to Pay Filing Fee in Installments. A voluntary petition by an individual shall be accepted for filing, regardless of whether any portion of the filing fee is paid, if accompanied by the debtor's signed application, prepared as prescribed by the appropriate Official Form, stating that the debtor is unable to pay the filing fee except in installments.

(2) Action on Application. Prior to the meeting of creditors, the court may order the filing fee paid to the clerk or grant leave to pay in installments

and fix the number, amount and dates of payment. The number of installments shall not exceed four, and the final installment shall be payable not later than 120 days after filing the petition. For cause shown, the court may extend the time of any installment, provided the last installment is paid not later than 180 days after filing the petition.

(3) Postponement of Attorney's Fees. All installments of the filing fee must be paid in full before the debtor or chapter 13 trustee may make further payments to an attorney or any other person who renders services to the debtor in connection with the case.

(c) WAIVER OF FILING FEE. A voluntary chapter 7 petition filed by an individual shall be accepted for filing if accompanied by the debtor's application requesting a waiver under 28 U.S.C. § 1930(f), prepared as prescribed by the appropriate Official Form.

Rule 1007. Lists, Schedules, Statements, and Other Documents; Time Limits

(a) CORPORATE OWNERSHIP STATEMENT, LIST OF CREDITORS AND EQUITY SECURITY HOLDERS, AND OTHER LISTS.

(1) Voluntary Case. In a voluntary case, the debtor shall file with the petition a list containing the name and address of each entity included or to be included on Schedules D, E, F, G, and H as prescribed by the Official Forms. If the debtor is a corporation, other than a governmental unit, the debtor shall file with the petition a corporate ownership statement containing the information described in Rule 7007.1. The debtor shall file a supplemental statement promptly upon any change in circumstances that renders the corporate ownership statement inaccurate.

(2) Involuntary Case. In an involuntary case, the debtor shall file within seven days after entry of the order for relief, a list containing the name and address of each entity included or to be included on Schedules D, E, F, G, and H as prescribed by the Official Forms.

(3) Equity Security Holders. In a chapter 11 reorganization case, unless the court orders otherwise, the debtor shall file within 14 days after entry of the order for relief a list of the debtor's equity security holders of each class showing the number and kind of interests registered in the name of each holder, and the last known address or place of business of each holder.

(4) Chapter 15 Case. In addition to the documents required under § 1515 of the Code, a foreign representative filing a petition for recognition under chapter 15 shall file with the petition: (A) a corporate ownership statement containing the information described in Rule 7007.1; and (B) unless the court orders otherwise, a list containing the names and addresses of all persons or bodies authorized to administer foreign proceedings of the debtor, all parties to litigation pending in the United States in which the debtor is a party at the time of the filing of the petition, and all entities against whom provisional relief is being sought under § 1519 of the Code.

(5) Extension of Time. Any extension of time for the filing of the lists required by this subdivision may be granted only on motion for cause shown and on notice to the United States trustee and to any trustee, committee elected under § 705 or appointed under § 1102 of the Code, or other party as the court may direct.

(b) SCHEDULES, STATEMENTS, AND OTHER DOCUMENTS REQUIRED.

(1) Except in a chapter 9 municipality case, the debtor, unless the court orders otherwise, shall file the following schedules, statements, and other documents, prepared as prescribed by the appropriate Official Forms, if any:

(A) schedules of assets and liabilities;

(B) a schedule of current income and expenditures;

(C) a schedule of executory contracts and unexpired leases;

(D) a statement of financial affairs;

(E) copies of all payment advices or other evidence of payment, if any, received by the debtor from an employer within 60 days before the filing of the petition, with redaction of all but the last four digits of the debtor's social-security number or individual taxpayer-identification number; and

(F) a record of any interest that the debtor has in an account or program of the type specified in § 521(c) of the Code.

(2) An individual debtor in a chapter 7 case shall file a statement of intention as required by § 521(a) of the Code, prepared as prescribed by the appropriate Official Form. A copy of the statement of intention shall be served on the trustee and the creditors named in the statement on or before the filing of the statement.

(3) Unless the United States trustee has determined that the credit counseling requirement of § 109(h) does not apply in the district, an individual debtor must file a statement of compliance with the credit counseling requirement, prepared as prescribed by the appropriate Official Form which must include one of the following:

(A) an attached certificate and debt repayment plan, if any, required by § 521(b);

(B) a statement that the debtor has received the credit counseling briefing required by § 109(h)(1) but does not have the certificate required by § 521(b);

(C) a certification under § 109(h)(3); or

(D) a request for a determination by the court under § 109(h)(4).

(4) Unless § 707(b)(2)(D) applies, an individual debtor in a chapter 7 case shall file a statement of current monthly income prepared as prescribed by the appropriate Official Form, and, if the current monthly income exceeds the median family income for the applicable state and household size, the information, including calculations, required by § 707(b), prepared as prescribed by the appropriate Official Form.

(5) An individual debtor in a chapter 11 case shall file a statement of current monthly income, prepared as prescribed by the appropriate Official Form.

(6) A debtor in a chapter 13 case shall file a statement of current monthly income, prepared as prescribed by the appropriate Official Form, and, if the current monthly income exceeds the median family income for the applicable state and household size, a calculation of disposable income made in accordance with § 1325(b)(3), prepared as prescribed by the appropriate Official Form.

(7) Unless an approved provider of an instructional course concerning personal financial management has notified the court that a debtor has completed the course after filing the petition:

(A) An individual debtor in a chapter 7 or chapter 13 case shall file a statement of completion of the course, prepared as prescribed by the appropriate Official Form; and

(B) An individual debtor in a chapter 11 case shall file the statement if § 1141(d)(3) applies.

(8) If an individual debtor in a chapter 11, 12, or 13 case has claimed an exemption under § 522(b)(3)(A) in property of the kind described in § 522(p)(1) with a value in excess of the amount set out in § 522(q)(1), the debtor shall file a statement as to whether there is any proceeding pending in which the debtor may be found guilty of a felony of a kind described in § 522(q)(1)(A) or found liable for a debt of the kind described in § 522(q)(1)(B).

(c) TIME LIMITS. In a voluntary case, the schedules, statements, and other documents required by subdivision (b)(1), (4), (5), and (6) shall be filed with the petition or within 14 days thereafter, except as otherwise provided in subdivisions(d), (e), (f), and (h) of this rule. In an involuntary case, the schedules, statements, and other documents required by subdivision (b)(1) shall be filed by the debtor within 14 days after the entry of the order for relief. In a voluntary case, the documents required by paragraphs (A), (C), and (D) of subdivision (b)(3) shall be filed with the petition. Unless the court orders otherwise, a debtor who has filed a statement under subdivision (b)(3)(B), shall file the documents required by subdivision (b)(3)(A) within 14 days of the order for relief. In a chapter 7 case, the debtor shall file the statement required by subdivision (b)(7) within 60 days after the first date set for the meeting of creditors under § 341 of the Code, and in a chapter 11 or 13 case no later than the date when the last payment was made by the debtor as required by the plan or the filing of a motion for a discharge under § 1141(d)(5)(B) or § 1328(b) of the Code. The court may, at any time and in its discretion, enlarge the time to file the statement required by subdivision (b)(7). The debtor shall file the statement required by subdivision (b)(8) no earlier than the date of the last payment made under the plan or the date of the filing of a motion for a discharge under §§ 1141(d)(5)(B), 1228(b), or 1328(b) of the Code. Lists, schedules, statements, and other documents filed prior to the conversion of a case to another chapter shall be deemed filed in the converted case unless the court directs otherwise. Except as provided in § 1116(3), any extension of time to file schedules, statements, and other documents required under this rule may be granted only on motion for cause shown and on notice to the United States trustee, any committee elected under § 705 or appointed under § 1102 of the Code, trustee, examiner, or other party as the court may direct. Notice of an extension shall be given to the United States trustee and to any committee, trustee, or other party as the court may direct.

(d) LIST OF 20 LARGEST CREDITORS IN CHAPTER 9 MUNICIPALITY CASE OR CHAPTER 11 REORGANIZATION CASE. In addition to the list required by subdivision (a) of this rule, a debtor in a chapter 9 municipality case or a debtor in a voluntary chapter 11 reorganization case shall file with the petition a list containing the name, address and claim of the creditors that hold the

20 largest unsecured claims, excluding insiders, as prescribed by the appropriate Official Form. In an involuntary chapter 11 reorganization case, such list shall be filed by the debtor within 2 days after entry of the order for relief under Section 303(h) of the Code.

(e) LIST IN CHAPTER 9 MUNICIPALITY CASES. The list required by subdivision (a) of this rule shall be filed by the debtor in a chapter 9 municipality case within such time as the court shall fix. If a proposed plan requires a revision of assessments so that the proportion of special assessments or special taxes to be assessed against some real property will be different from the proportion in effect at the date the petition is filed, the debtor shall also file a list showing the name and address of each known holder of title, legal or equitable, to real property adversely affected. On motion for cause shown, the court may modify the requirements of this subdivision and subdivision (a) of this rule.

(f) STATEMENT OF SOCIAL SECURITY NUMBER. An individual debtor shall submit a verified statement that sets out the debtor's social security number, or states that the debtor does not have a social security number. In a voluntary case, the debtor shall submit the statement with the petition. In an involuntary case, the debtor shall submit the statement within 14 days after the entry of the order for relief.

(g) PARTNERSHIP AND PARTNERS. The general partners of a debtor partnership shall prepare and file the list required under subdivision (a), the schedules of the assets and liabilities, schedule of current income and expenditures, schedule of executory contracts and unexpired leases, and statement of financial affairs of the partnership. The court may order any general partner to file a statement of personal assets and liabilities within such time as the court may fix.

(h) INTERESTS ACQUIRED OR ARISING AFTER PETITION. If, as provided by Section 541(a)(5) of the Code, the debtor acquires or becomes entitled to acquire any interest in property, the debtor shall within 14 days after the information comes to the debtor's knowledge or within such further time the court may allow, file a supplemental schedule in the chapter 7 liquidation case, chapter 11 reorganization case, chapter 12 family farmer's debt adjustment case, or chapter 13 individual debt adjustment case. If any of the property required to be reported under this subdivision is claimed by the debtor as exempt, the debtor shall claim the exemptions in the supplemental schedule. The duty to file a supplemental schedule in accordance with this subdivision continues notwithstanding the closing of the case, except that the schedule need not be filed in a chapter 11, chapter 12, or chapter 13 case with respect to property acquired after entry of the order confirming a chapter 11 plan or discharging the debtor in a chapter 12 or chapter 13 case.

(i) DISCLOSURE OF LIST OF SECURITY HOLDERS. After notice and hearing and for cause shown, the court may direct an entity other than the debtor or trustee to disclose any list of security holders of the debtor in its possession or under its control, indicating the name, address and security held by any of them. The entity possessing this list may be required either to produce the list or a true copy thereof, or permit inspection or copying, or otherwise disclose the information contained on the list.

(j) IMPOUNDING OF LISTS. On motion of a party in interest and for cause shown the court may direct the impounding of the lists filed under this rule, and may refuse to permit inspection by any entity. The court may permit inspection or use of the lists, however, by any party in interest on terms prescribed by the court.

(k) PREPARATION OF LIST, SCHEDULES, OR STATEMENTS ON DEFAULT OF DEBTOR. If a list, schedule, or statement, other than a statement of intention, is not prepared and filed as required by this rule, the court may order the trustee, a petitioning creditor, committee, or other party to prepare and file any of these papers within a time fixed by the court. The court may approve reimbursement of the cost incurred in complying with such an order as an administrative expense.

(l) TRANSMISSION TO UNITED STATES TRUSTEE. The clerk shall forthwith transmit to the United States trustee a copy of every list, schedule, and statement filed pursuant to subdivision (a)(1), (a)(2), (b), (d), or (h) of this rule.

(m) INFANTS AND INCOMPETENT PERSONS. If the debtor knows that a person on the list of creditors or schedules is an infant or incompetent person, the debtor also shall include the name, address, and legal relationship of any person upon whom process would be served in an adversary proceeding against the infant or incompetent person in accordance with Rule 7004(b)(2).

Rule 1008. Verification of Petitions and Accompanying Papers

All petitions, lists, schedules, statements and amendments thereto shall be verified or contain an unsworn declaration as provided in 28 U.S.C. Section 1746.

Rule 1009. Amendments of Voluntary Petitions, Lists, Schedules and Statements

(a) GENERAL RIGHT TO AMEND. A voluntary petition, list, schedule, or statement may be amended by the debtor as a matter of course at any time before the case is closed. The debtor shall give notice of the amendment to the trustee and to any entity affected thereby. On motion of a party in interest, after notice and a hearing, the court may order any voluntary petition, list, schedule, or statement to be amended and the clerk shall give notice of the amendment to entities designated by the court.

(b) STATEMENT OF INTENTION. The statement of intention may be amended by the debtor at any time before the expiration of the period provided in § 521(a) of the Code. The debtor shall give notice of the amendment to the trustee and to any entity affected thereby.

(c) STATEMENT OF SOCIAL SECURITY NUMBER. If a debtor becomes aware that the statement of social security number submitted under Rule 1007(f) is incorrect, the debtor shall promptly submit an amended verified statement setting forth the correct social security number. The debtor shall give notice of the amendment to all of the entities required to be included on the list filed under Rule 1007(a)(1) or (a)(2).

(d) TRANSMISSION TO UNITED STATES TRUSTEE. The clerk shall promptly transmit to the United States trustee a copy of every amendment filed or submitted under subdivision (a), (b) or (c) of this rule.

Rule 1010. Service of Involuntary Petition and Summons; Petition For Recognition of a Foreign Nonmain Proceeding

(a) SERVICE OF INVOLUNTARY PETITION AND SUMMONS; SERVICE OF PETITION FOR RECOGNITION OF FOREIGN NONMAIN PROCEEDING. On the filing of an involuntary petition the clerk shall forthwith issue a summons for service. When an involuntary petition is filed, service shall be made on the debtor. The summons shall be served with a copy of the petition in the manner provided for service of a summons and complaint by Rule 7004(a) or (b). If service cannot be so made, the court may order that the summons and petition be served by mailing copies to the party's last known address, and by at least one publication in a manner and form directed by the court. The summons and petition may be served on the party anywhere. Rule 7004(e) and Rule 4(l) F.R.Civ.P. apply when service is made or attempted under this rule.

(b) CORPORATE OWNERSHIP STATEMENT. Each petitioner that is a corporation shall file with the involuntary petition a corporate ownership statement containing the information described in Rule 7007.1.

Rule 1011. Responsive Pleading or Motion in Involuntary and Cross-Border Cases

(a) WHO MAY CONTEST PETITION. The debtor named in an involuntary petition may contest the petition. In the case of a petition against a partnership under Rule 1004, a nonpetitioning general partner, or a person who is alleged to be a general partner but denies the allegation, may contest the petition.

(b) DEFENSES AND OBJECTIONS; WHEN PRESENTED. Defenses and objections to the petition shall be presented in the manner prescribed by Rule 12 F. R. Civ. P. and shall be filed and served within 21 days after service of the summons, except that if service is made by publication on a party or partner not residing or found within the state in which the court sits, the court shall prescribe the time for filing and serving the response.

(c) EFFECT OF MOTION. Service of a motion under Rule 12(b) F. R. Civ. P. shall extend the time for filing and serving a responsive pleading as permitted by Rule 12(a) F. R. Civ. P.

(d) CLAIMS AGAINST PETITIONERS. A claim against a petitioning creditor may not be asserted in the answer except for the purpose of defeating the petition.

(e) OTHER PLEADINGS. No other pleadings shall be permitted, except that the court may order a reply to an answer and prescribe the time for filing and service.

(f) CORPORATE OWNERSHIP STATEMENT. If the entity responding to the involuntary petition is a corporation, the entity shall file with its first appearance, pleading, motion, response, or other request addressed to the court a corporate ownership statement containing the information described in Rule 7007.1.

Rule 1012. [Abrogated]

Rule 1013. Hearing and Disposition of Petition in Involuntary Cases

(a) CONTESTED PETITION. The court shall determine the issues of a contested petition at the earliest practicable time and forthwith enter an order for relief, dismiss the petition, or enter any other appropriate order.

(b) DEFAULT. If no pleading or other defense to a petition is filed within the time provided by Rule 1011, the court, on the next day, or as soon thereafter as practicable, shall enter an order for the relief requested in the petition

Rule 1014. Dismissal and Change of Venue

(a) DISMISSAL AND TRANSFER OF CASES.

(1) Cases Filed in Proper District. If a petition is filed in the proper district, the court, on the timely motion of a party in interest or on its own motion, and after hearing on notice to the petitioners, the United States trustee, and other entities as directed by the court, may transfer the case to any other district if the court determines that the transfer is in the interest of justice or for the convenience of the parties.

(2) Cases Filed in Improper District. If a petition is filed in an improper district, the court, on the timely motion of a party in interest or on its own motion, and after hearing on notice to the petitioners, the United States trustee, and other entities as directed by the court, may dismiss the case or transfer it to any other district if the court determines that transfer is in the interest of justice or for the convenience of the parties.

(b) PROCEDURE WHEN PETITIONS INVOLVING THE SAME DEBTOR OR RELATED DEBTORS ARE FILED IN DIFFERENT COURTS. If petitions commencing cases under the Code or seeking recognition under chapter 15 are filed in different districts by, regarding, or against (1) the same debtor, (2) a partnership and one or more of its general partners, (3) two or more general partners, or (4) a debtor and an affiliate, the court in the district in which the first-filed petition is pending may determine, in the interest of justice or for the convenience of the parties, the district or districts in which any of the cases should proceed. The court may so determine on motion and after a hearing, with notice to the following entities in the affected cases: the United States trustee, entities entitled to notice under Rule 2002(a), and other entities as the court directs. The court may order the parties to the later-filed cases not to proceed further until it makes the determination.

Rule 1015. Consolidation or Joint Administration of Cases Pending in Same Court

(a) CASES INVOLVING SAME DEBTOR. If two or more petitions by, regarding, or against the same debtor are pending in the same court, the court may order consolidation of the cases.

(b) CASES INVOLVING TWO OR MORE RELATED DEBTORS. If a joint petition or two or more petitions are pending in the same court by or against (1) spouses, or (2) a partnership and one or more of its general partners, or (3) two or more general partners, or (4) a debtor and an affiliate, the court may order a joint administration of the estates. Prior to entering an order the court shall give consideration to protecting creditors of different estates against potential conflicts of interest. An order directing joint administration of individual cases of spouses shall, if one spouse has elected the exemptions under § 522(b)(2) of the Code and the other has elected the exemptions under § 522(b)(3), fix a reasonable time within which either may amend the election so that both shall have elected the same exemptions. The order shall notify the debtors that unless they elect the same exemptions within the time fixed by the court, they will be deemed to have elected the exemptions provided by § 522(b)(2).

(c) EXPEDITING AND PROTECTIVE ORDERS. When an order for consolidation or joint administration of a joint case or two or more cases is entered pursuant to this rule, while protecting the rights of the parties under the Code, the court may enter orders as may tend to avoid unnecessary costs and delay.

Rule 1016. Death or Incompetency of Debtor

Death or incompetency of the debtor shall not abate a liquidation case under chapter 7 of the Code. In such event the estate shall be administered and the case concluded in the same manner, so far as possible, as though the death or incompetency had not occurred. If a reorganization, family farmer's debt adjustment, or individual's debt adjustment case is pending under chapter 11, chapter 12, or chapter 13, the case may be dismissed; or if further administration is possible and in the best interest of the parties, the case may proceed and be concluded in the same manner, so far as possible, as though the death or incompetency had not occurred.

Rule 1017. Dismissal or Conversion of Case; Suspension

(a) VOLUNTARY DISMISSAL; DISMISSAL FOR WANT OF PROSECUTION OR OTHER CAUSE. Except as provided in §§707(a)(3), 707(b), 1208(b), and 1307(b) of the Code, and in Rule 1017(b), (c), and (e), a case shall not be dismissed on motion of the petitioner, for want of prosecution or other cause, or by consent of the parties, before a hearing on notice as provided in Rule 2002. For the purpose of the notice, the debtor shall file a list of creditors with their addresses within the time fixed by the court unless the list was previously filed. If the debtor fails to file the list, the court may order the debtor or another entity to prepare and file it.

(b) DISMISSAL FOR FAILURE TO PAY FILING FEE.

(1) If any installment of the filing fee has not been paid, the court may, after a hearing on notice to the debtor and the trustee, dismiss the case.

(2) If the case is dismissed or closed without full payment of the filing fee, the installments collected shall be distributed in the same manner and proportions as if the filing fee had been paid in full.

(c) DISMISSAL OF VOLUNTARY CHAPTER 7 OR CHAPTER 13 CASE FOR FAILURE TO TIMELY FILE LIST OF CREDITORS, SCHEDULES, AND STATEMENT OF FINANCIAL AFFAIRS. The court may dismiss a voluntary chapter 7 or chapter 13 case under §707(a)(3) or §1307(c)(9) after a hearing on notice served by the United States trustee on the debtor, the trustee, and any other entities as the court directs.

(d) SUSPENSION. The court shall not dismiss a case or suspend proceedings under §305 before a hearing on notice as provided in Rule 2002(a).

(e) DISMISSAL OF AN INDIVIDUAL DEBTOR'S CHAPTER 7 CASE, OR CONVERSION TO A CASE UNDER CHAPTER 11 OR 13, FOR ABUSE. The court may dismiss or, with the debtor's consent, convert an individual debtor's case for abuse under § 707(b) only on motion and after a hearing on notice to the debtor, the trustee, the United States trustee, and any other entity as the court directs.

(1) Except as otherwise provided in § 704(b)(2), a motion to dismiss a case for abuse under § 707(b) or (c) may be filed only within 60 days after the first date set for the meeting of creditors under § 341(a), unless, on request filed before the time has expired, the court for cause extends the time for filing the motion to dismiss. The party filing the motion shall set forth in the motion all matters to be considered at the hearing. In addition, a motion to dismiss under § 707(b)(1) and (3) shall state with particularity the circumstances alleged to constitute abuse.

(2) If the hearing is set on the court's own motion, notice of the hearing shall be served on the debtor no later than 60 days after the first date set for the meeting of creditors under §341(a). The notice shall set forth all matters to be considered by the court at the hearing.

(f) PROCEDURE FOR DISMISSAL, CONVERSION OR SUSPENSION.

(1) Rule 9014 governs a proceeding to dismiss or suspend a case, or to convert a case to another chapter, except under §§706(a), 1112(a), 1208(a) or (b), or 1307(a) or (b),

(2) Conversion or dismissal under §§706(a), 1112(a), 1208(b), or 1307(b) shall be on motion filed and served as required by Rule 9013.

(3) A chapter 12 or chapter 13 case shall be converted without court order when the debtor files a notice of conversion under §§1208(a) or 1307(a). The filing date of the notice becomes the date of the conversion order for the purposes of applying §348(c) and Rule 1019. The clerk shall promptly transmit a copy of the notice to the United States trustee.

Rule 1018. Contested Involuntary Petitions; Contested Petitions Commencing Chapter 15 Cases; Proceedings to Vacate Order for Relief; Applicability of Rules in Part VII Governing Adversary Proceedings

Unless the court otherwise directs and except as otherwise prescribed in Part I of these rules, the following rules in Part VII apply to all proceedings contesting an involuntary petition or a chapter 15 petition for recognition, and to all proceedings to vacate an order for relief: Rules 7005, 7008-7010, 7015, 7016, 7024-7026, 7028-7037, 7052, 7054, 7056, and 7062. The court may direct that other rules in Part VII shall also apply. For the purposes of this rule a reference in the Part VII rules to adversary proceedings shall be read as a reference to proceedings contesting an involuntary petition or a chapter 15 petition for recognition, or proceedings to vacate an order for relief. Reference in the Federal Rules of Civil Procedure to the complaint shall be read as a reference to the petition.

Rule 1019. Conversion of Chapter 11 Reorganization Case, Chapter 12 Family Farmer's Debt Adjustment Case, or Chapter 13 Individual's Debt Adjustment Case to Chapter 7 Liquidation Case

When a chapter 11, chapter 12, or chapter 13 case has been converted or reconverted to a chapter 7 case:

(1) Filing of Lists, Inventories, Schedules, Statements.

(A) Lists, inventories, schedules, and statements of financial affairs theretofore filed shall be deemed to be filed in the chapter 7 case, unless the court directs otherwise. If they have not been previously filed, the debtor shall comply with Rule 1007 as if an order for relief had been entered on an involuntary petition on the date of the entry of the order directing that the case continue under chapter 7.

(B) If a statement of intention is required, it shall be filed within 30 days after entry of the order of conversion or before the first date set for the meeting of creditors, whichever is earlier. The court may grant an extension of time for cause only on written motion filed, or oral request made during a hearing, before the time has expired. Notice of an extension shall be given to the United States trustee and to any committee, trustee, or other party as the court may direct.

(2) New Filing Periods.

(A) A new time period for filing a motion under § 707(b) or (c), a claim, a complaint objecting to discharge, or a complaint to obtain a determination of dischargeability of any debt shall commence under Rules 1017, 3002, 4004, or 4007, but a new time period shall not commence if a chapter 7 case had been converted to a chapter 11, 12, or 13 case and thereafter reconverted to a chapter 7 case and the time for filing a motion under § 707(b) or (c), a claim, a complaint objecting to discharge, or a complaint to obtain a determination of the dischargeability of any debt, or any extension thereof, expired in the original chapter 7 case.

(B) A new time period for filing an objection to a claim of exemptions shall commence under Rule 4003(b) after conversion of a case to chapter 7 unless:

(i) the case was converted to chapter 7 more than one year after the entry of the first order confirming a plan under chapter 11, 12, or 13; or

(ii) the case was previously pending in chapter 7 and the time to object to a claimed exemption had expired in the original chapter 7 case.

(3) Claims Filed Before Conversion. All claims actually filed by a creditor before conversion of the case are deemed filed in the chapter 7 case.

(4) Turnover of Records And Property. After qualification of, or assumption of duties by the chapter 7 trustee, any debtor in possession or trustee previously acting in the chapter 11, 12, or 13 case shall, forthwith, unless otherwise ordered, turn over to the chapter 7 trustee all records and property of the estate in the possession or control of the debtor in possession or trustee.

(5) Filing Final Report and Schedule of Postpetition Debts.

(A) Conversion of Chapter 11 or Chapter 12 Case. Unless the court directs otherwise, if a chapter 11 or chapter 12 case is converted to chapter 7, the debtor in possession or, if the debtor is not a debtor in possession, the trustee serving at the time of conversion, shall:

(i) not later than 14 days after conversion of the case, file a schedule of unpaid debts incurred after the filing of the petition and before conversion of the case, including the name and address of each holder of a claim; and

(ii) not later than 30 days after conversion of the case, file and transmit to the United States trustee a final report and account;

(B) Conversion of Chapter 13 Case. Unless the court directs otherwise, if a chapter 13 case is converted to chapter 7,

(i) the debtor, not later than 14 days after conversion of the case, shall file a schedule of unpaid debts incurred after the filing of the petition and before conversion of the case, including the name and address of each holder of a claim; and

(ii) the trustee, not later than 30 days after conversion of the case, shall file and transmit to the United States trustee a final report and account;

(C) Conversion After Confirmation of a Plan. Unless the court orders otherwise, if a chapter 11, chapter 12, or chapter 13 case is converted to chapter 7 after confirmation of a plan, the debtor shall file:

(i) a schedule of property not listed in the final report and account acquired after the filing of the petition but before conversion, except if the case is converted from chapter 13 to chapter 7 and §348(f)(2) does not apply;

(ii) a schedule of unpaid debts not listed in the final report and account incurred after confirmation but before the conversion; and

(iii) a schedule of executory contracts and unexpired leases entered into or assumed after the filing of the petition but before conversion.

(D) Transmission to United States Trustee. The clerk shall forthwith transmit to the United States trustee a copy of every schedule filed pursuant to Rule 1019(5).

(6) Postpetition claims; preconversion administrative expenses; notice. A request for payment of an administrative expense incurred before conversion of the case is timely filed under §503(a) of the Code if it is filed before conversion or a time fixed by the court. If the request is filed by a governmental unit, it is timely if it is filed before conversion or within the later of a time fixed by the court or 180 days after the date of the conversion. A claim of a kind specified in §348(d) may be filed in accordance with Rules 3001(a)-(d) and 3002. Upon the filing of the schedule of unpaid debts incurred after commencement of the case and before conversion, the clerk, or some other person as the court may direct, shall give notice to those entities listed on the schedule of the time for filing a request for payment of an administrative expense and, unless a notice of insufficient assets to pay a dividend is mailed in accordance with Rule 2002(e), the time for filing a claim of a kind specified in §348(d).

Rule 1020. Small Business Chapter 11 Reorganization Case

(a) Small business debtor designation

In a voluntary chapter 11 case, the debtor shall state in the petition whether the debtor is a small business debtor and, if so, whether the debtor elects to have subchapter V of chapter 11 apply. In an involuntary chapter 11 case, the debtor shall file within 14 days after entry of the order for relief a statement as to whether the debtor is a small business debtor and, if so, whether the debtor elects to have subchapter V of chapter 11 apply. The status of the case as a small business case or a case under subchapter V of chapter 11 shall be in accordance with the debtor's statement under this subdivision, unless and until the court enters an order finding that the debtor's statement is incorrect.

(b) Objecting to designation

The United States trustee or a party in interest may file an objection to the debtor's statement under subdivision (a) no later than 30 days after the conclusion of the meeting of creditors held under § 341(a) of the Code, or within 30 days after any amendment to the statement, whichever is later.

(c) Procedure for objection or determination

Any objection or request for a determination under this rule shall be governed by Rule 9014 and served on: the debtor; the debtor's attorney; the United States trustee; the trustee; the creditors included on the list filed under Rule 1007(d) or, if a committee has been appointed under § 1102(a)(3), the committee or its authorized agent; and any other entity as the court directs.

Rule 1021. Health Care Business Case

(a) HEALTH CARE BUSINESS DESIGNATION. Unless the court orders otherwise, if a petition in a case under chapter 7, chapter 9, or chapter 11 states that the debtor is a health care business, the case shall proceed as a case in which the debtor is a health care business.

(b) MOTION. The United States trustee or a party in interest may file a motion to determine whether the debtor is a health care business. The motion shall be transmitted to the United States trustee and served on: the debtor; the trustee; any committee elected under § 705 or appointed under § 1102 of the Code or its authorized agent, or, if the case is a chapter 9 municipality case or a chapter 11 reorganization case and no committee of unsecured creditors has been appointed under § 1102, the creditors included on the list filed under Rule 1007(d); and any other entity as the court directs. The motion shall be governed by Rule 9014.

PART II

OFFICERS AND ADMINISTRATION; NOTICES; MEETINGS; EXAMINATIONS; ELECTIONS; ATTORNEYS AND ACCOUNTANTS

Rule 2001. Appointment of Interim Trustee Before Order for Relief in a Chapter 7 Liquidation Case

(a) APPOINTMENT. At any time following the commencement of an involuntary liquidation case and before an order for relief, the court on written motion of a party in interest may order the appointment of an interim trustee under Section 303(g) of the Code. The motion shall set forth the necessity for the appointment and may be granted only after hearing on notice to the debtor, the petitioning creditors, the United States trustee, and other parties in interest as the court may designate.

(b) BOND OF MOVANT. An interim trustee may not be appointed under this rule unless the movant furnishes a bond in an amount approved by the court, conditioned to indemnify the debtor for costs, attorney's fee, expenses, and damages allowable under Section 303(i) of the Code.

(c) ORDER OF APPOINTMENT. The order directing the appointment of an interim trustee shall state the reason the appointment is necessary and shall specify the trustee's duties.

(d) TURNOVER AND REPORT. Following qualification of the trustee selected under Section 702 of the Code, the interim trustee, unless otherwise ordered, shall (1) forthwith deliver to the trustee all the records and property of the estate in possession or subject to control of the interim trustee and, (2) within 30 days thereafter file a final report and account.

Rule 2002. Notices to Creditors, Equity Security Holders, Administrators in Foreign Proceedings, Persons Against Whom Provisional Relief is Sought in Ancillary and Other Cross-Border Cases, United States, and United States Trustee

(a) TWENTY-ONE-DAY NOTICES TO PARTIES IN INTEREST. Except as provided in subdivisions (h), (i), (l), (p), and (q) of this rule, the clerk, or some other person as the court may direct, shall give the debtor, the trustee, all creditors and indenture trustees at least 21 days' notice by mail of:

(1) the meeting of creditors under §341 or §1104(b) of the Code; which notice, unless the court orders otherwise, shall include the debtor's employer identification number, social security number, and any other federal taxpayer identification number.

(2) a proposed use, sale, or lease of property of the estate other than in the ordinary course of business, unless the court for cause shown shortens the time or directs another method of giving notice;

(3) the hearing on approval of a compromise or settlement of a controversy other than approval of an agreement pursuant to Rule 4001(d), unless the court for cause shown directs that notice not be sent;

(4) in a chapter 7 liquidation, a chapter 11 reorganization case, or a chapter 12 family farmer debt adjustment case, the hearing on the dismissal of the case or the conversion of the case to another chapter, unless the hearing is under §707(a)(3) or §707(b) or is on dismissal of the case for failure to pay the filing fee;

(5) the time fixed to accept or reject a proposed modification of a plan;

(6) a hearing on any entity's request for compensation or reimbursement of expenses if the request exceeds $1,000;

(7) the time fixed for filing proofs of claims pursuant to Rule 3003(c);

(8) the time fixed for filing objections and the hearing to consider confirmation of a chapter 12 plan; and

(9) the time fixed for filing objections to confirmation of a chapter 13 plan.

(b) TWENTY-EIGHT-DAY NOTICES TO PARTIES IN INTEREST. Except as provided in subdivision (l) of this rule, the clerk, or some other person as the court may direct, shall give the debtor, the trustee, all creditors and indenture trustees not less than 28 days' notice by mail of the time fixed (1) for filing objections and the hearing to consider approval of a disclosure statement or, under § 1125(f), to make a final determination whether the plan provides adequate information so that a separate disclosure statement is not necessary; (2) for filing objections and the hearing to consider confirmation of a chapter 9 or chapter 11 plan; and (3) for the hearing to consider confirmation of a chapter 13 plan..

(c) CONTENT OF NOTICE.

(1) Proposed Use, Sale, or Lease of Property. Subject to Rule 6004, the notice of a proposed use, sale, or lease of property required by subdivision (a)(2) of this rule shall include the time and place of any public sale, the terms and conditions of any private sale and the time fixed for filing objections. The notice of a proposed use, sale, or lease of property, including real estate, is sufficient if it generally describes the property. The notice of a proposed sale or lease of personally identifiable information under § 363(b)(1) of the Code shall state whether the sale is consistent with any policy prohibiting the transfer of the information.

(2) Notice of Hearing on Compensation. The notice of a hearing on an application for compensation or reimbursement of expenses required by subdivision (a)(6) of this rule shall identify the applicant and the amounts requested.

(3) Notice of Hearing on Confirmation When Plan Provides for an Injunction. If a plan provides for an injunction against conduct not otherwise enjoined under the Code, the notice required under Rule 2002(b)(2) shall:

(A) include in conspicuous language (bold, italic, or underlined text) a statement that the plan proposes an injunction;

(B) describe briefly the nature of the injunction; and

(C) identify the entities that would be subject to the injunction.

(d) NOTICE TO EQUITY SECURITY HOLDERS. In a chapter 11 reorganization case, unless otherwise ordered by the court, the clerk, or some other person as the court may direct, shall in the manner and form directed by the court give notice to all equity security holders of (1) the order for relief; (2) any meeting of equity security holders held pursuant to Section 341 of the Code; (3) the hearing on the proposed sale of all or substantially all of the debtor's assets; (4) the hearing on the dismissal or conversion of a case to another chapter; (5) the time fixed for filing objections to and the hearing to consider approval of a disclosure statement; (6) the time fixed for filing objections to and the hearing to consider confirmation of a plan; and (7) the time fixed to accept or reject a proposed modification of a plan.

(e) NOTICE OF NO DIVIDEND. In a chapter 7 liquidation case, if it appears from the schedules that there are no assets from which a dividend can be paid, the notice of the meeting of creditors may include a statement to that effect; that it is unnecessary to file claims; and that if sufficient assets become available for the payment of a dividend, further notice will be given for the filing of claims.

(f) OTHER NOTICES. Except as provided in subdivision (l) of this rule, the clerk, or some other person as the court may direct, shall give the debtor, all creditors, and indenture trustees notice by mail of:

(1) the order for relief;

(2) the dismissal or the conversion of the case to another chapter, or the suspension of proceedings under § 305;

(3) the time allowed for filing claims pursuant to Rule 3002;

(4) the time fixed for filing a complaint objecting to the debtor's discharge pursuant to § 727 of the Code as provided in Rule 4004;

(5) the time fixed for filing a complaint to determine the dischargeability of a debt pursuant to § 523 of the Code as provided in Rule 4007;

(6) the waiver, denial, or revocation of a discharge as provided in Rule 4006;

(7) entry of an order confirming a chapter 9, 11, or 12 plan;

(8) a summary of the trustee's final report in a chapter 7 case if the net proceeds realized exceed $1,500;

(9) a notice under Rule 5008 regarding the presumption of abuse;

(10) a statement under § 704(b)(1) as to whether the debtor's case would be presumed to be an abuse under § 707(b); and

(11) the time to request a delay in the entry of the discharge under §§ 1141(d)(5)(C), 1228(f), and 1328(h). Notice of the time fixed for accepting or rejecting a plan pursuant to Rule 3017(c) shall be given in accordance with Rule 3017(d).

(g) ADDRESSING NOTICES.

(1) Notices required to be mailed under Rule 2002 to a creditor, indenture trustee, or equity security holder shall be addressed as such entity or an authorized agent has directed in its last request filed in the particular case. For the purposes of this subdivision –

(A) a proof of claim filed by a creditor or indenture trustee that designates a mailing address constitutes a filed request to mail notices to that address, unless a notice of no dividend has been given under Rule 2002(e) and a later notice of possible dividend under Rule 3002(c)(5) has not been given; and

(B) a proof of interest filed by an equity security holder that designates a mailing address constitutes a filed request to mail notices to that address.

(2) Except as provided in § 342(f) of the Code, if a creditor or indenture trustee has not filed a request designating a mailing address under Rule 2002(g)(1) or Rule 5003(e), the notices shall be mailed to the address shown on the list of creditors or schedule of liabilities, whichever is filed later. If an equity security holder has not filed a request designating a mailing address under Rule 2002(g)(1) or Rule 5003(e), the notices shall be mailed to the address shown on the list of equity security holders.

(3) If a list or schedule filed under Rule 1007 includes the name and address of a legal representative of an infant or incompetent person, and a person other than that representative files a request or proof of claim designating a name and mailing address that differs from the name and address of the representative included in the list or schedule, unless the court orders otherwise, notices under Rule 2002 shall be mailed to the representative included in the list or schedules and to the name and address

designated in the request or proof of claim.

(4) Notwithstanding Rule 2002(g)(1)-(3), an entity and a notice provider may agree that when the notice provider is directed by the court to give a notice, the notice provider shall give the notice to the entity in the manner agreed to and at the address or addresses the entity supplies to the notice provider. That address is conclusively presumed to be a proper address for the notice. The notice provider's failure to use the supplied address does not invalidate any notice that is otherwise effective under applicable law.

(5) A creditor may treat a notice as not having been brought to the creditor's attention under § 342(g)(1) only if, prior to issuance of the notice, the creditor has filed a statement that designates the name and address of the person or organizational subdivision of the creditor responsible for receiving notices under the Code, and that describes the procedures established by the creditor to cause such notices to be delivered to the designated person or subdivision.

(h) Notices to creditors whose claims are filed

(1) Voluntary case. In a voluntary chapter 7 case, chapter 12 case, or chapter 13 case, after 70 days following the order for relief under that chapter or the date of the order converting the case to chapter 12 or chapter 13, the court may direct that all notices required by subdivision (a) of this rule be mailed only to:

- the debtor;
- the trustee;
- all indenture trustees;
- creditors that hold claims for which proofs of claim have been filed; and
- creditors, if any, that are still permitted to file claims because an extension was granted under Rule 3002(c)(1) or (c)(2).

(2) Involuntary case. In an involuntary chapter 7 case, after 90 days following the order for relief under that chapter, the court may direct that all notices required by subdivision (a) of this rule be mailed only to:

- the debtor;
- the trustee;
- all indenture trustees;
- creditors that hold claims for which proofs of claim have been filed; and
- creditors, if any, that are still permitted to file claims because an extension was granted under Rule 3002(c)(1) or (c)(2).

(3) Insufficient assets. In a case where notice of insufficient assets to pay a dividend has been given to creditors under subdivision (e) of this rule, after 90 days following the mailing of a notice of the time for filing claims under Rule 3002(c)(5), the court may direct that notices be mailed only to the entities specified in the preceding sentence.

(i) NOTICES TO COMMITTEES. Copies of all notices required to be mailed pursuant to this rule shall be mailed to the committees elected under Section 705 or appointed under Section 1102 of the Code or to their authorized agents. Notwithstanding the foregoing subdivisions, the court may order that notices required by subdivision (a)(2), (3) and (6) of this rule be transmitted to the United States trustee and be mailed only to the committees elected under Section 705 or appointed under Section 1102 of the Code or to their authorized agents and to the creditors and equity security holders who serve on the trustee or debtor in possession and file a request that all notices be mailed to them. A committee appointed under Section 1114 shall receive copies of all notices required by subdivisions (a)(1), (a)(5), (b), (f)(2), and (f)(7), and such other notices as the court may direct.

(j) NOTICES TO THE UNITED STATES. Copies of notices required to be mailed to all creditors under this rule shall be mailed (1) in a chapter 11 reorganization case to the Securities and Exchange Commission at any place the Commission designates, if the Commission has filed either a notice of appearance in the case or a written request to receive notices; (2) in a commodity broker case, to the Commodity Futures Trading Commission at Washington, D.C.; (3) in a chapter 11 case to the Internal Revenue Service at its address set out in the register maintained under Rule 5003(e) for the district in which the case is pending; (4) if the papers in the case disclose a debt to the United States other than for taxes, to the United States attorney for the district in which the case is pending and to the department, agency, or instrumentality of the United States through which the debtor became indebted; or if the filed papers disclose a stock interest of the United States, to the Secretary of the Treasury at Washington, D.C.

(k) NOTICES TO UNITED STATES TRUSTEE. Unless the case is a chapter 9 municipality case or unless the United States trustee requests otherwise, the clerk, or some other person as the court may direct, shall transmit to the United States trustee notice of the matters described in subdivisions (a)(2), (a)(3), (a)(4), (a)(8), (b), (f)(1), (f)(2), (f)(4), (f)(6), (f)(7), (f)(8), and (q) of this rule and notice of hearings on all applications for compensation or reimbursement of expenses. Notices to the United States trustee shall be transmitted within the time prescribed in subdivision (a) or (b) of this rule. The United States trustee shall also receive notice of any other matter if such notice is requested by the United States trustee or ordered by the court. Nothing in these rules requires the clerk or any other person to transmit to the United States trustee any notice, schedule, report, application or other document in a case under the Securities Investor Protection Act, 15 U.S.C. § 78aaa et. seq.

(l) NOTICE BY PUBLICATION. The court may order notice by publication if it finds that notice by mail is impracticable or that it is desirable to supplement the notice.

(m) ORDERS DESIGNATING MATTER OF NOTICES. The court may from time to time enter orders designating the matters in respect to which, the entity to whom, and the form and manner in which notices shall be sent except as otherwise provided by these rules.

(n) CAPTION. The caption of every notice given under this rule shall comply with Rule 1005. The caption of every notice required to be given by the debtor to a creditor shall include the information required to be in the notice by §342(c) of the Code.

(o) NOTICE OF ORDER FOR RELIEF IN CONSUMER CASE. In a voluntary case commenced by an individual debtor whose debts are primarily consumer debts, the clerk or some other person as the court may direct shall give the trustee and all creditors notice by mail of the order for relief within 21 days from the date thereof.

(p) NOTICE TO A CREDITOR WITH A FOREIGN ADDRESS.

(1) If, at the request of the United States trustee or a party in interest, or on its own initiative, the court finds that a notice mailed within the time prescribed by these rules would not be sufficient to give a creditor with a foreign address to which notices under these rules are mailed reasonable notice under the circumstances, the court may order that the notice be supplemented with notice by other means or that the time prescribed for the notice by mail be enlarged.

(2) Unless the court for cause orders otherwise, a creditor with a foreign address to which notices under this rule are mailed shall be given at least 30 days' notice of the time fixed for filing a proof of claim under Rule 3002(c) or Rule 3003(c).

(3) Unless the court for cause orders otherwise, the mailing address of a creditor with a foreign address shall be determined under Rule 2002(g).

(q) NOTICE OF PETITION FOR RECOGNITION OF FOREIGN PROCEEDING AND OF COURT'S INTENTION TO COMMUNICATE WITH FOREIGN COURTS AND FOREIGN REPRESENTATIVES.

(1) Notice of Petition for Recognition. After the filing of a petition for recognition in a foreign proceeding, the court shall promptly schedule and hold a hearing on the petition. The clerk, or some other person as the court may direct, shall forthwith give the debtor, all persons or bodies authorized to administer foreign proceedings of the debtor, all entities against whom provisional relief is being sought under § 1519 of the Code, all parties to litigation pending in the United States in which the debtor is a party at the time of the filing of the petition, and such other entities as the court may direct, at least 21 days' notice by mail of the hearing on the petition for recognition of a foreign proceeding. The notice shall state whether the petition seeks recognition as a foreign main proceeding or foreign nonmain proceeding and shall include the petition and any other document the court may require. If the court consolidates the hearing on the petition with the hearing on a request for provisional relief, the court may set a shorter notice period, with notice to the entities listed in this subdivision.

(2) Notice of Court's Intention to Communicate with Foreign Courts and Foreign Representatives. The clerk, or some other person as the court may direct, shall give the debtor, all persons or bodies authorized to administer foreign proceedings of the debtor, all entities against whom provisional relief is being sought under § 1519 of the Code, all parties to litigation pending in the United States in which the debtor is a party at the time of the filing of the petition, and such other entities as the court may direct, notice by mail of the court's intention to communicate with a foreign court or foreign representative.

Rule 2003. Meeting of Creditors or Equity Security Holders

(a) DATE AND PLACE. Except as otherwise provided in § 341(e) of the Code, in a chapter 7 liquidation or a chapter 11 reorganization case, the United States trustee shall call a meeting of creditors to be held no fewer than 21 and no more than 40 days after the order for relief. In a chapter 12 family farmer debt adjustment case, the United States trustee shall call a meeting of creditors to be held no fewer than 21 and no more than 35 days after the order for relief. In a chapter 13 individual's debt adjustment case, the United States trustee shall call a meeting of creditors to be held no fewer than 21 and no more than 50 days after the order for relief. If there is an appeal from or a motion to vacate the order for relief, or if there is a motion to dismiss the case, the United States trustee may set a later date for the meeting. The meeting may be held at a regular place for holding court or at any other place designated by the United States trustee within the district convenient for the parties in interest. If the United States trustee designates a place for the meeting which is not regularly staffed by the United States trustee or an assistant who may preside at the meeting, the meeting may be held not more than 60 days after the order for relief.

(b) ORDER OF MEETING.

(1) Meeting of Creditors. The United States trustee shall preside at the meeting of creditors. The business of the meeting shall include the examination of the debtor under oath and, in a chapter 7 liquidation case, may include the election of a creditors' committee and, if the case is not under subchapter V of Chapter 7, the election of a trustee. The presiding officer shall have the authority to administer oaths.

(2) Meeting of Equity Security Holders. If the United States trustee convenes a meeting of equity security holders pursuant to Section 341(b) of the Code, the United States trustee shall fix a date for the meeting and shall preside.

(3) Right to Vote. In a chapter 7 liquidation case, a creditor is entitled to vote at a meeting if, at or before the meeting, the creditor has filed a proof of claim or a writing setting forth facts evidencing a right to vote pursuant to Section 702(a) of the Code unless objection is made to the claim or the proof of claim is insufficient on its face. A creditor of a partnership may file a proof of claim or writing evidencing a right to vote for the trustee for the estate of a general partner notwithstanding that a trustee for the estate of the partnership has previously qualified. In the event of an objection to the amount or allowability of a claim for the purpose of voting, unless the court orders otherwise, the United States trustee shall tabulate the votes for each alternative presented by the dispute and, if resolution of such dispute is necessary to determine the result of the election, the tabulations for each alternative shall be reported to the court.

(c) RECORD OF MEETING. Any examination under oath at the meeting of creditors held pursuant to Section 341(a) of the Code shall be recorded verbatim by the United States trustee using electronic sound recording equipment or other means of recording, and such record shall be preserved by the United States trustee and available for public access until two years after the conclusion of the meeting of creditors. Upon request of any entity, the United States trustee shall certify and provide a copy or transcript of such recording at the entity's expense.

(d) REPORT OF ELECTION AND RESOLUTION OF DISPUTES IN A CHAPTER 7 CASE.

(1) Report of undisputed election. In a chapter 7 case, if the election of a trustee or a member of a creditors' committee is not disputed, the United States trustee shall promptly file a report of the election, including the name and address of the person or entity elected and a statement that the election is undisputed.

(2) Disputed election. If the election is disputed, the United States trustee shall promptly file a report stating that the election is disputed, informing the court of the nature of the dispute, and listing the name and address of any candidate elected under any alternative presented by the dispute. No later than the date on which the report is filed, the United States trustee shall mail a copy of the report to any party in interest that has made a request to receive a copy of the report. Pending disposition by the court of a disputed election for trustee, the interim trustee shall continue in office. Unless a motion for the resolution of the dispute is filed no later than 14 days after the United States trustee files a report of disputed election for trustee, the interim trustee shall serve as trustee in the case.

(e) ADJOURNMENT. The meeting may be adjourned from time to time by announcement at the meeting of the adjourned date and time. The presiding official shall promptly file a statement specifying the date and time to which the meeting is adjourned.

(f) SPECIAL MEETINGS. The United States trustee may call a special meeting of creditors on request of a party in interest or on the United States trustee's own initiative.

(g) FINAL MEETING. If the United States trustee calls a final meeting of creditors in a case in which the net proceeds realized exceed $1,500, the clerk shall mail a summary of the trustee's final account to the creditors with a notice of the meeting, together with a statement of the amount of the claims allowed. The trustee shall attend the final meeting and shall, if requested, report on the administration of the estate.

Rule 2004. Examination

(a) EXAMINATION ON MOTION. On motion of any party in interest, the court may order the examination of any entity.

(b) SCOPE OF EXAMINATION. The examination of an entity under this rule or of the debtor under Section 343 of the Code may relate only to the acts, conduct, or property or to the liabilities and financial condition of the debtor, or to any matter which may affect the administration of the debtor's estate, or to the debtor's right to a discharge. In a family farmer's debt adjustment case under chapter 12, an individual's debt adjustment case under chapter 13, or a reorganization case under chapter 11 of the Code, other than for the reorganization of a railroad, the examination may also relate to the operation of any business and the desirability of its continuance, the source of any money or property acquired or to be acquired by the debtor for purposes of consummating a plan and the consideration given or offered therefor, and any other matter relevant to the case or to the formulation of a plan.

(c) COMPELLING ATTENDANCE AND PRODUCTION OF DOCUMENTS. The attendance of an entity for examination and for the production of documents, whether the examination is to be conducted within or without the district in which the case is pending, may be compelled as provided in Rule 9016 for the attendance of a witness at a hearing or trial. As an officer of the court, an attorney may issue and sign a subpoena on behalf of the court for the district in which the examination is to be held if the attorney is admitted to practice in that court or in the court in which the case is pending.

(d) TIME AND PLACE OF EXAMINATION OF DEBTOR. The court may for cause shown and on terms as it may impose order the debtor to be examined under this rule at any time or place it designates, whether within or without the district wherein the case is pending.

(e) MILEAGE. An entity other than a debtor shall not be required to attend as a witness unless lawful mileage and witness fee for one day's attendance shall be first tendered. If the debtor resides more than 100 miles from the place of examination when required to appear for an examination under this rule, the mileage allowed by law to a witness shall be tendered for any distance more than 100 miles from the debtor's residence at the date of the filing of the first petition commencing a case under the Code or the residence at the time the debtor is required to appear for the examination, whichever is the lesser.

Rule 2005. Apprehension and Removal of Debtor to Compel Attendance for Examination

(a) ORDER TO COMPEL ATTENDANCE FOR EXAMINATION. On motion of any party in interest supported by an affidavit alleging (1) that the examination of the debtor is necessary for the proper administration of the estate and that there is reasonable cause to believe that the debtor is about to leave or has left the debtor's residence or principal place of business to avoid examination, or (2) that the debtor has evaded service of a subpoena or of an order to attend for examination, or (3) that the debtor has willfully disobeyed a subpoena or order to attend for examination, duly served, the court may issue to the marshal, or some other officer authorized by law, an order directing the officer to bring the debtor before the court without unnecessary delay. If, after hearing, the court finds the allegations to be true, the court shall thereupon cause the debtor to be examined forthwith. If necessary, the court shall fix conditions for further examination and for the debtor's obedience to all orders made in reference thereto.

(b) REMOVAL. Whenever any order to bring the debtor before the court is issued under this rule and the debtor is found in a district other than that of the court issuing the order, the debtor may be taken into custody under the order and removed in accordance with the following rules:

(1) If the debtor is taken into custody under the order at a place less than 100 miles from the place of issue of the order, the debtor shall be brought forthwith before the court that issued the order.

(2) If the debtor is taken into custody under the order at a place 100 miles or more from the place of issue of the order, the debtor shall be brought without unnecessary delay before the nearest available United States magistrate judge, bankruptcy judge, or district judge. If, after hearing, the magistrate judge, bankruptcy judge, or district judge finds that an order has issued under this rule and that the person in custody is the debtor, or if the person in custody waives a hearing, the magistrate judge, bankruptcy judge, or district judge shall order removal, and the person in custody shall be released on conditions ensuring prompt appearance before the court that issued the order to compel the attendance.

(c) CONDITIONS OF RELEASE. In determining what conditions will reasonably assure attendance or obedience under subdivision (a) of this rule or appearance under subdivision (b) of this rule, the court shall be governed by the provisions and policies of title 18, U. S. C., Section 3146(a) and (b).

Rule 2006. Solicitation and Voting of Proxies in Chapter 7 Liquidation Cases

(a) APPLICABILITY. This rule applies only in a liquidation case pending under chapter 7 of the Code.

(b) DEFINITIONS.

(1) Proxy. A proxy is a written power of attorney authorizing any entity to vote the claim or otherwise act as the owner's attorney in fact in connection with the administration of the estate.

(2) Solicitation of Proxy. The solicitation of a proxy is any communication, other than one from an attorney to a regular client who owns a claim or from an attorney to the owner of a claim who has requested the attorney to represent the owner, by which a creditor is asked, directly or indirectly, to give a proxy after or in contemplation of the filing of a petition by or against the debtor.

(c) AUTHORIZED SOLICITATION.

(1) A proxy may be solicited only by (A) a creditor owning an allowable unsecured claim against the estate on the date of the filing of the petition; (B) a committee elected pursuant to Section 705 of the Code; (C) a committee of creditors selected by a majority in number and amount of claims of creditors (i) whose claims are not contingent or unliquidated, (ii) who are not disqualified from voting under Section 702(a) of the Code and (iii) who were present or represented at a meeting of which all creditors having claims of over $500 or the 100 creditors having the largest claims had at least seven days notice in writing and of which meeting written minutes were kept and are available reporting the names of the creditors present or represented and voting and the amounts of their claims; or (D) a bona fide trade or credit association, but such association may solicit only creditors who were its members or subscribers in good standing and had allowable unsecured claims on the date of the filing of the petition.

(2) A proxy may be solicited only in writing.

(d) SOLICITATION NOT AUTHORIZED. This rule does not permit solicitation (1) in any interest other than that of general creditors; (2) by or on behalf of any custodian; (3) by the interim trustee or by or on behalf of any entity not qualified to vote under Section 702(a) of the Code; (4) by or on behalf of an attorney at law; or (5) by or on behalf of a transferee of a claim for collection only.

(e) DATA REQUIRED FROM HOLDERS OF MULTIPLE PROXIES. At any time before the voting commences at any meeting of creditors pursuant to Section 341(a) of the Code, or at any other time as the court may direct, a holder of two or more proxies shall file and transmit to the United States trustee a verified list of the proxies to be voted and a verified statement of the pertinent facts and circumstances in connection with the execution and delivery of each proxy, including:

(1) a copy of the solicitation;

(2) identification of the solicitor, the forwarder, if the forwarder is neither the solicitor nor the owner of the claim, and the proxyholder, including their connections with the debtor and with each other. If the solicitor, forwarder, or proxyholder is an association, there shall also be included a statement that the creditors whose claims have been solicited and the creditors whose claims are to be voted were members or subscribers in good standing and had allowable unsecured claims on the date of the filing of the petition. If the solicitor, forwarder, or proxyholder is a committee of creditors, the statement shall also set forth the date and place the committee was organized, that the committee was organized in accordance with clause (B) or (C) of paragraph (c)(1) of this rule, the members of the committee, the amounts of their claims, when the claims were acquired, the amounts paid therefor, and the extent to which the claims of the committee members are secured or entitled to priority;

(3) a statement that no consideration has been paid or promised by the proxyholder for the proxy;

(4) a statement as to whether there is any agreement and, if so, the particulars thereof, between the proxyholder and any other entity for the payment of any consideration in connection with voting the proxy, or for the sharing of compensation with any entity, other than a member or regular associate of the proxyholder's law firm, which may be allowed the trustee or any entity for services rendered in the case, or for the employment of any person as attorney, accountant, appraiser, auctioneer, or other employee for the estate;

(5) if the proxy was solicited by an entity other than the proxyholder, or forwarded to the holder by an entity who is neither a solicitor of the proxy nor the owner of the claim, a statement signed and verified by the solicitor or forwarder that no consideration has been paid or promised for the proxy, and whether there is any agreement, and, if so, the particulars thereof, between the solicitor or forwarder and any other entity for the payment of any consideration in connection with voting the proxy, or for sharing compensation with any entity other than a member or regular associate of the solicitor's or forwarder's law firm which may be allowed the trustee or any entity for services rendered in the case, or for the employment of any person as attorney, accountant, appraiser, auctioneer, or other employee for the estate;

(6) if the solicitor, forwarder, or proxyholder is a committee, a statement signed and verified by each member as to the amount and source of any consideration paid or to be paid to such member in connection with the case other than by way of dividend on the member's claim.

(f) ENFORCEMENT OF RESTRICTIONS ON SOLICITATION. On motion of any party in interest or on its own initiative, the court may determine whether there has been a failure to comply with the provisions of this rule or any other impropriety in connection with the solicitation or voting of a proxy. After notice and a hearing the court may reject any proxy for cause, vacate any order entered in consequence of the voting of any proxy which should have been rejected, or take any other appropriate action.

Rule 2007. Review of Appointment of Creditors' Committee Organized Before Commencement of the Case

(a) MOTION TO REVIEW APPOINTMENT. If a committee appointed by the United States trustee pursuant to Section 1102(a) of the Code consists of the members of a committee organized by creditors before the commencement of a chapter 9 or chapter 11 case, on motion of a party in interest and after a hearing on notice to the United States trustee and other entities as the court may direct, the court may determine whether the appointment of the committee satisfies the requirements of Section 1102(b)(1) of the Code.

(b) SELECTION OF MEMBERS OF COMMITTEE. The court may find that a committee organized by unsecured creditors before the commencement of a chapter 9 or chapter 11 case was fairly chosen if:

(1) it was selected by a majority in number and amount of claims of unsecured creditors who may vote under Section 702(a) of the Code and were present in person or represented at a meeting of which all creditors having unsecured claims of over $1,000 or the 100 unsecured creditors having the largest claims had at least seven days' notice in writing, and of which meeting written minutes reporting the names of the creditors present or represented and voting and the amounts of their claims were kept and are available for inspection;

(2) all proxies voted at the meeting for the elected committee were solicited pursuant to Rule 2006 and the lists and statements required by subdivision (e) thereof have been transmitted to the United States trustee; and

(3) the organization of the committee was in all other respects fair and proper.

(c) FAILURE TO COMPLY WITH REQUIREMENTS FOR APPOINTMENT. After a hearing on notice pursuant to subdivision (a) of this rule, the court shall direct the United States trustee to vacate the appointment of the committee and may order other appropriate action if the court finds that such appointment failed to satisfy the requirements of Section 1102(b)(1) of the Code.

Rule 2007.1. Appointment of Trustee or Examiner in a Chapter 11 Reorganization Case

(a) ORDER TO APPOINT TRUSTEE OR EXAMINER. In a chapter 11 reorganization case, a motion for an order to appoint a trustee or an exam-iner under Section 1104(a) or Section 1104(c) of the Code shall be made in accordance with Rule 9014.

(b) ELECTION OF TRUSTEE.

(1) Request for an Election. A request to convene a meeting of creditors for the purpose of electing a trustee in a chapter 11 reorganization case shall be filed and transmitted to the United States trustee in accordance with Rule 5005 within the time prescribed by §1104(b) of the Code. Pending court approval of the person elected, any person appointed by the United States trustee under §1104(d) and approved in accordance with subdivision (c) of this rule shall serve as trustee.

(2) Manner of Election and Notice. An election of a trustee under §1104(b) of the Code shall be conducted in the manner provided in Rules 2003(b)(3) and 2006. Notice of the meeting of creditors convened under §1104(b) shall be given as provided in Rule 2002. The United States trustee shall preside at the meeting. A proxy for the purpose of voting in the election

may be solicited only by a committee of creditors appointed under § 1102 of the Code or by any other party entitled to solicit a proxy pursuant to Rule 2006.

(3) Report of Election and Resolution of Disputes.

(A) Report of Undisputed Election. If no dispute arises out of the election, the United States trustee shall promptly file a report certifying the election, including the name and address of the person elected and a statement that the election is undisputed. The report shall be accompanied by a verified statement of the person elected setting forth that person's connections with the debtor, creditors, any other party in interest, their respective attorneys and accountants, the United States trustee, or any person employed in the office of the United States trustee.

(B) Dispute Arising Out of an Election. If a dispute arises out of an election, the United States trustee shall promptly file a report stating that the election is disputed, informing the court of the nature of the dispute, and listing the name and address of any candidate elected under any alternative presented by the dispute. The report shall be accompanied by a verified statement by each candidate elected under each alternative presented by the dispute, setting forth the person's connections with the debtor, creditors, any other party in interest, their respective attorneys and accountants, the United States trustee, or any person employed in the office of the United States trustee. Not later than the date on which the report of the disputed election is filed, the United States trustee shall mail a copy of the report and each verified statement to any party in interest that has made a request to convene a meeting under § 1104(b) or to receive a copy of the report, and to any committee appointed under § 1102 of the Code.

(c) APPROVAL OF APPOINTMENT. An order approving the appointment of a trustee or an examiner under §1104(d) of the Code shall be made on application of the United States trustee. The application shall state the name of the person appointed and, to the best of the applicant's knowledge, all the person's connections with the debtor, creditors, any other parties in interest, their respective attorneys and accountants, the United States trustee, or persons employed in the office of the United States trustee. The application shall state the names of the parties in interest with whom the United States trustee consulted regarding the appointment. The application shall be accompanied by a verified statement of the person appointed setting forth the person's connections with the debtor, creditors, any other party in interest, their respective attorneys and accountants, the United States trustee, or any person employed in the office of the United States trustee.

Rule 2007.2. Appointment of Patient Care Ombudsman in a Health Care Business Case

(a) ORDER TO APPOINT PATIENT CARE OMBUDSMAN. In a chapter 7, chapter 9, or chapter 11 case in which the debtor is a health care business, the court shall order the appointment of a patient care ombudsman under § 333 of the Code, unless the court, on motion of the United States trustee or a party in interest filed no later than 21 days after the commencement of the case or within another time fixed by the court, finds that the appointment of a patient care ombudsman is not necessary under the specific circumstances of the case for the protection of patients.

(b) MOTION FOR ORDER TO APPOINT OMBUDSMAN. If the court has found that the appointment of an ombudsman is not necessary, or has terminated the appointment, the court, on motion of the United States trustee or a party in interest, may order the appointment at a later time if it finds that the appointment has become necessary to protect patients.

(c) NOTICE OF APPOINTMENT. If a patient care ombudsman is appointed under § 333, the United States trustee shall promptly file a notice of the appointment, including the name and address of the person appointed. Unless the person appointed is a State Long-Term Care Ombudsman, the notice shall be accompanied by a verified statement of the person appointed setting forth the person's connections with the debtor, creditors, patients, any other party in interest, their respective attorneys and accountants, the United States trustee, and any person employed in the office of the United States trustee.

(d) TERMINATION OF APPOINTMENT. On motion of the United States trustee or a party in interest, the court may terminate the appointment of a patient care ombudsman if the court finds that the appointment is not necessary to protect patients.

(e) MOTION. A motion under this rule shall be governed by Rule 9014. The motion shall be transmitted to the United States trustee and served on: the debtor; the trustee; any committee elected under § 705 or appointed under § 1102 of the Code or its authorized agent, or, if the case is a chapter 9 municipality case or a chapter 11 reorganization case and no committee of unsecured creditors has been appointed under § 1102, on the creditors included on the list filed under Rule 1007(d); and such other entities as the court may direct.

Rule 2008. Notice to Trustee of Selection

The United States trustee shall immediately notify the person selected as trustee how to qualify and, if applicable, the amount of the trustee's bond. A trustee that has filed a blanket bond pursuant to Rule 2010 and has been selected as trustee in a chapter 7, chapter 12, or chapter 13 case that does not notify the court and the United States trustee in writing of rejection of the office within seven days after receipt of notice of selection shall be deemed to have accepted the office. Any other person selected as trustee shall notify the court and the United States trustee in writing of acceptance of the office within seven days after receipt of notice of selection or shall be deemed to have rejected the office.

Rule 2009. Trustee for Estates When Joint Administration Ordered

(a) ELECTION OF SINGLE TRUSTEE FOR ESTATES BEING JOINTLY ADMINISTERED. If the court orders a joint administration of two or more estates under Rule 1015(b), creditors may elect a single trustee for the estates being jointly administered, unless the case is under subchapter V of chapter 7 of the Code.

(b) RIGHT OF CREDITORS TO ELECT SEPARATE TRUSTEE. Notwithstanding entry of an order for joint administration under Rule 1015(b), the creditors of any debtor may elect a separate trustee for the estate of the debtor as provided in Section 702 of the Code, unless the case is under subchapter V of chapter 7 of the Code.

(c) APPOINTMENT OF TRUSTEES FOR ESTATES BEING JOINTLY ADMINISTERED.

(1) Chapter 7 Liquidation Cases. Except in a case governed by subchapter V of chapter 7, the United States trustee may appoint one or more interim trustees for estates being jointly administered in chapter 7 cases.

(2) Chapter 11 Reorganization Cases. If the appointment of a trustee is ordered, the United States trustee may appoint one or more trustees for estates being jointly administered in chapter 11 cases.

(3) Chapter 12 Family Farmer's Debt Adjustment Cases. The United States trustee may appoint one or more trustees for estates being jointly administered in chapter 12 cases.

(4) Chapter 13 Individual's Debt Adjustment Cases. The United States trustee may appoint one or more trustees for estates being jointly administered in chapter 13 cases.

(d) POTENTIAL CONFLICTS OF INTEREST. On a showing that creditors or equity security holders of the different estates will be prejudiced by conflicts of interest of a common trustee who has been elected or appointed, the court shall order the selection of separate trustees for estates being jointly administered.

(e) SEPARATE ACCOUNTS. The trustee or trustees of estates being jointly administered shall keep separate accounts of the property and distribution of each estate.

Rule 2010. Qualification by Trustee; Proceeding on Bond

(a) BLANKET BOND. The United States trustee may authorize a blanket bond in favor of the United States conditioned on the faithful performance of official duties by the trustee or trustees to cover (1) a person who qualifies as trustee in a number of cases, and (2) a number of trustees each of whom qualifies in a different case.

(b) PROCEEDING ON BOND. A proceeding on the trustee's bond may be brought by any party in interest in the name of the United States for the use of the entity injured by the breach of the condition.

Rule 2011. Evidence of Debtor in Possession or Qualification of Trustee

(a) Whenever evidence is required that a debtor is a debtor in possession or that a trustee has qualified, the clerk may so certify and the certificate shall constitute conclusive evidence of that fact.

(b) If a person elected or appointed as trustee does not qualify within the time prescribed by Section 322(a) of the Code, the clerk shall so notify the court and the United States trustee.

Rule 2012. Substitution of Trustee or Successor Trustee; Accounting

(a) TRUSTEE. If a trustee is appointed in a chapter 11 case (other than under subchapter V), or the debtor is removed as debtor in possession in a chapter 12 case or in a case under subchapter V of chapter 11, the trustee is substituted automatically for the debtor in possession as a party in any pending action, proceeding, or matter.

(b) SUCCESSOR TRUSTEE. When a trustee dies, resigns, is removed, or otherwise ceases to hold office during the pendency of a case under the Code (1) the successor is automatically substituted as a party in any pending action, proceeding, or matter; and (2) the successor trustee shall prepare, file, and transmit to the United States trustee an accounting of the prior administration of the estate.

Rule 2013. Public Record of Compensation Awarded to Trustees, Examiners, and Professionals

(a) RECORD TO BE KEPT. The clerk shall maintain a public record listing fees awarded by the court (1) to trustees and attorneys, accountants, appraisers, auctioneers and other professionals employed by trustees, and (2) to examiners. The record shall include the name and docket number of the case, the name of the individual or firm receiving the fee and the amount of the fee awarded. The record shall be maintained chronologically and shall be kept current and open to examination by the public without charge. "Trustees," as used in this rule, does not include debtors in possession.

(b) SUMMARY OF RECORD. At the close of each annual period, the clerk shall prepare a summary of the public record by individual or firm name, to reflect total fees awarded during the preceding year. The summary shall be open to examination by the public without charge. The clerk shall transmit a copy of the summary to the United States trustee.

Rule 2014. Employment of Professional Persons

(a) APPLICATION FOR AN ORDER OF EMPLOYMENT. An order approving the employment of attorneys, accountants, appraisers, auctioneers, agents, or other professionals pursuant to Section 327, Section 1103, or Section 1114 of the Code shall be made only on application of the trustee or committee. The application shall be filed and, unless the case is a chapter 9 municipality case, a copy of the application shall be transmitted by the applicant to the United States trustee. The application shall state the specific facts showing the necessity for the employment, the name of the person to be employed, the reasons for the selection, the professional services to be rendered, any proposed arrangement for compensation, and, to the best of the applicant's knowledge, all of the person's connections with the debtor, creditors, any other party in interest, their respective attorneys and accountants, the United States trustee, or any person employed in the office of the United States trustee. The application shall be accompanied by a verified statement of the person to be employed setting forth the person's connections with the debtor, creditors, any other party in interest, their respective attorneys and accountants, the United States trustee, or any person employed in the office of the United States trustee.

(b) SERVICES RENDERED BY MEMBER OR ASSOCIATE OF FIRM OF ATTORNEYS OR ACCOUNTANTS. If, under the Code and this rule, a law partnership or corporation is employed as an attorney, or an accounting partnership or corporation is employed as an accountant, or if a named attorney or accountant is employed, any partner, member, or regular associate of the partnership, corporation or individual may act as attorney or accountant so employed, without further order of the court.

Rule 2015. Duty to Keep Records, Make Reports, and Give Notice of Case or Change of Status

(a) TRUSTEE OR DEBTOR IN POSSESSION. A trustee or debtor in possession shall:

(1) in a chapter 7 liquidation case and, if the court directs, in a chapter 11 reorganization case (other than under subchapter V), file and transmit to the United States trustee a complete inventory of the property of the debtor within 30 days after qualifying as a trustee or debtor in possession, unless such an inventory has already been filed;

(2) keep a record of receipts and the disposition of money and property received;

(3) file the reports and summaries required by § 704(a)(8) of the Code which shall include a statement, if payments are made to employees, of the amounts of deductions for all taxes required to be withheld or paid for and in behalf of employees and the place where these amounts are deposited;

(4) as soon as possible after the commencement of the case, give notice of the case to every entity known to be holding money or property subject to withdrawal or order of the debtor, including every bank, savings or building and loan association, public utility company, and landlord with whom the debtor has a deposit, and to every insurance company which has issued a policy having a cash surrender value payable to the debtor, except that notice need not be given to any entity who has knowledge or has previously been notified of the case;

(5) (5) in a chapter 11 reorganization case (other than under subchapter V), on or before the last day of the month after each calendar quarter during which there is a duty to pay fees under 28 U.S.C. § 1930(a)(6), file and transmit to the United States trustee a statement of any disbursements made during that quarter and of any fees payable under 28 U.S.C. § 1930(a)(6) for that quarter; and

(6) in a chapter 11 small business case, unless the court, for cause, sets another reporting interval, file and transmit to the United States trustee for each calendar month after the order for relief, on the appropriate Official Form, the report required by § 308. If the order for relief is within the first 15 days of a calendar month, a report shall be filed for the portion of the month that follows the order for relief. If the order for relief is after the 15th day of a calendar month, the period for the remainder of the month shall be included in the report for the next calendar month. Each report shall be filed no later than 21 days after the last day of the calendar month following the month covered by the report. The obligation to file reports under this subparagraph terminates on the effective date of the plan, or conversion or dismissal of the case.

(b) CHAPTER 12 TRUSTEE AND DEBTOR IN POSSESSION. In a chapter 12 family farmer's debt adjustment case, the debtor in possession shall perform the duties prescribed in clauses (2)-(4) of subdivision (a) of this rule and, if the court directs, shall file and transmit to the United States trustee a complete inventory of the property of the debtor within the time fixed by the court. If the debtor is removed as debtor in possession, the trustee shall perform the duties of the debtor in possession prescribed in this paragraph.

(c) CHAPTER 13 TRUSTEE AND DEBTOR.

(1) Business Cases. In a chapter 13 individual's debt adjustment case, when the debtor is engaged in business, the debtor shall perform the duties prescribed by clauses (2)-(4) of subdivision (a) of this rule and, if the court directs, shall file and transmit to the United States trustee a complete inventory of the property of the debtor within the time fixed by the court.

(2) Nonbusiness Cases. In a chapter 13 individual's debt adjustment case, when the debtor is not engaged in business, the trustee shall perform the duties prescribed by clause (2) of subdivision (a) of this rule.

(d) FOREIGN REPRESENTATIVE. In a case in which the court has granted recognition of a foreign proceeding under chapter 15, the foreign representative shall file any notice required under § 1518 of the Code within 14 days after the date when the representative becomes aware of the subsequent information.

(e) TRANSMISSION OF REPORTS. In a chapter 11 case the court may direct that copies or summaries of annual reports and copies or summaries of other reports shall be mailed to the creditors, equity security holders, and indenture trustees. The court may also direct the publication of summaries of any such reports. A copy of every report or summary mailed or published pursuant to this subdivision shall be transmitted to the United States trustee.

Rule 2015.1. Patient Care Ombudsman

(a) REPORTS. A patient care ombudsman, at least 14 days before making a report under § 333(b)(2) of the Code, shall give notice that the report will be made to the court, unless the court orders otherwise. The notice shall be transmitted to the United States trustee, posted conspicuously at the health care facility that is the subject of the report, and served on: the debtor; the trustee; all patients; and any committee elected under § 705 or appointed under § 1102 of the Code or its authorized agent, or, if the case is a chapter 9 municipality case or a chapter 11 reorganization case and no committee of unsecured creditors has been appointed under § 1102, on the creditors included on the list filed under Rule 1007(d); and such other entities as the court may direct. The notice shall state the date and time when the report will be made, the manner in which the report will be made, and, if the report is in writing, the name, address, telephone number, email address, and website, if any, of the person from whom a copy of the report may be obtained at the debtor's expense.

(b) AUTHORIZATION TO REVIEW CONFIDENTIAL PATIENT RECORDS. A motion by a patient care ombudsman under § 333(c) to review confidential patient records shall be governed by Rule 9014, served on the patient and any family member or other contact person whose name and address have been given to the trustee or the debtor for the purpose of providing information regarding the patient's health care, and transmitted to the United States trustee subject to applicable nonbankruptcy law relating to patient privacy. Unless the court orders otherwise, a hearing on the motion may not be commenced earlier than 14 days after service of the motion.

Rule 2015.2. Transfer of Patient in Health Care Business Case

Unless the court orders otherwise, if the debtor is a health care business, the trustee may not transfer a patient to another health care business under § 704(a)(12) of the Code unless the trustee gives at least 14 days' notice of the transfer to the patient care ombudsman, if any, the patient, and any family member or other contact person whose name and address has been given to the trustee or the debtor for the purpose of providing information regarding the patient's health care. The notice is subject to applicable nonbankruptcy law relating to patient privacy.

Rule 2015.3. Reports of Financial Information on Entities in Which a Chapter 11 Estate Holds a Controlling or Substantial Interest

(a) REPORTING REQUIREMENT. In a chapter 11 case, the trustee or debtor in possession shall file periodic financial reports of the value, operations, and profitability of each entity that is not a publicly traded corporation or a debtor in a case under title 11, and in which the estate holds a substantial or controlling interest. The reports shall be prepared as prescribed by the appropriate Official Form, and shall be based upon the most recent information reasonably available to the trustee or debtor in possession.

(b) TIME FOR FILING; SERVICE. The first report required by this rule shall be filed no later than seven days before the first date set for the meeting of creditors under § 341 of the Code. Subsequent reports shall be filed no less frequently than every six months thereafter, until the effective date of a plan or the case is dismissed or converted. Copies of the report shall be served on the United States trustee, any committee appointed under § 1102 of the Code, and any other party in interest that has filed a request therefor.

(c) PRESUMPTION OF SUBSTANTIAL OR CONTROLLING INTEREST; JUDICIAL DETERMINATION. For purposes of this rule, an entity of which the estate controls or owns at least a 20 percent interest, shall be presumed to be an entity in which the estate has a substantial or controlling interest. An entity in which the estate controls or owns less than a 20 percent interest shall be presumed not to be an entity in which the estate has a substantial or controlling interest. Upon motion, the entity, any holder of an interest therein, the United States trustee, or any other party in interest may seek to rebut either presumption, and the court shall, after notice and a hearing, determine whether the estate's interest in the entity is substantial or controlling.

(d) MODIFICATION OF REPORTING REQUIREMENT. The court may, after notice and a hearing, vary the reporting requirement established by subdivision (a) of this rule for cause, including that the trustee or debtor in possession is not able, after a good faith effort, to comply with those reporting requirements, or that the information required by subdivision (a) is publicly available.

(e) NOTICE AND PROTECTIVE ORDERS. No later than 14 days before filing the first report required by this rule, the trustee or debtor in possession shall send notice to the entity in which the estate has a substantial or controlling interest, and to all holders – known to the trustee or debtor in possession – of an interest in that entity, that the trustee or debtor in possession expects to file and serve financial information relating to the entity in accordance with this rule. The entity in which the estate has a substantial or controlling interest, or a person holding an interest in that entity, may request protection of the information under § 107 of the Code.

(f) EFFECT OF REQUEST. Unless the court orders otherwise, the pendency of a request under subdivisions (c), (d), or (e) of this rule shall not alter or stay the requirements of subdivision (a).

Rule 2016. Compensation for Services Rendered and Reimbursement of Expenses

(a) APPLICATION FOR COMPENSATION OR REIMBURSEMENT. An entity seeking interim or final compensation for services, or reimbursement of necessary expenses, from the estate shall file an application setting forth a detailed statement of (1) the services rendered, time expended and expenses incurred, and (2) the amounts requested. An application for compensation shall include a statement as to what payments have theretofore been made or promised to the applicant for services rendered or to be rendered in any capacity whatsoever in connection with the case, the source of the compensation so paid or promised, whether any compensation previously received has been shared and whether an agreement or understanding exists between the applicant and any other entity for the sharing of compensation received or to be received for services rendered in or in connection with the case, and the particulars of any sharing of compensation or agreement or understanding therefor, except that details of any agreement by the applicant for the sharing of compensation as a member or regular associate of a firm of lawyers or accountants shall not be required. The requirements of this subdivision shall apply to an application for compensation for services rendered by an attorney or accountant even though the application is filed by a creditor or other entity. Unless the case is a chapter 9 municipality case, the applicant shall transmit to the United States trustee a copy of the application.

(b) DISCLOSURE OF COMPENSATION PAID OR PROMISED TO ATTORNEY FOR DEBTOR. Every attorney for a debtor, whether or not the attorney applies for compensation, shall file and transmit to the United States trustee within 14 days after the order for relief, or at another time as the court may direct, the statement required by Section 329 of the Code including whether the attorney has shared or agreed to share the compensation with any other entity. The statement shall include the particulars of any such sharing or agreement to share by the attorney, but the details of any agreement for the sharing of the compensation with a member or regular associate of the attorney's law firm shall not be required. A supplemental statement shall be filed and transmitted to the United States trustee within 14 days after any payment or agreement not previously disclosed.

(c) DISCLOSURE OF COMPENSATION PAID OR PROMISED TO BANKRUPTCY PETITION PREPARER. Before a petition is filed, every bankruptcy petition preparer for a debtor shall deliver to the debtor, the declaration under penalty of perjury required by § 110(h)(2). The declaration shall disclose any fee, and the source of any fee, received from or on behalf of the debtor within 12 months of the filing of the case and all unpaid fees charged to the debtor. The declaration shall also describe the services performed and documents prepared or caused to be prepared by the bankruptcy petition preparer. The declaration shall be filed with the petition. The petition preparer shall file a supplemental statement within 14 days after any payment or agreement not previously disclosed.

Rule 2017. Examination of Debtor's Transactions with Debtor's Attorney

(a) PAYMENT OR TRANSFER TO ATTORNEY BEFORE ORDER FOR RELIEF. On motion by any party in interest or on the court's own initiative, the court after notice and a hearing may determine whether any payment of money or any transfer of property by the debtor, made directly or indirectly and in contemplation of the filing of a petition under the Code by or against the debtor or before entry of the order for relief in an involuntary case, to an attorney for services rendered or to be rendered is excessive.

(b) PAYMENT OR TRANSFER TO ATTORNEY AFTER ORDER FOR RELIEF. On motion by the debtor, the United States trustee, or on the court's own initiative, the court after notice and a hearing may determine whether any payment of money or any transfer of property, or any agreement therefor, by the debtor to an attorney after entry of an order for relief in a case under the Code is excessive, whether the payment or transfer is made or is to be made directly or indirectly, if the payment, transfer, or agreement therefor is for services in any way related to the case.

Rule 2018. Intervention; Right to be Heard

(a) PERMISSIVE INTERVENTION. In a case under the Code, after hearing on such notice as the court directs and for cause shown, the court may permit any interested entity to intervene generally or with respect to any specified matter.

(b) INTERVENTION BY ATTORNEY GENERAL OF A STATE. In a chapter 7, 11, 12, or 13 case, the Attorney General of a State may appear and be heard on behalf of consumer creditors if the court determines the appearance is in the public interest, but the Attorney General may not appeal from any judgment, order, or decree in the case.

(c) CHAPTER 9 MUNICIPALITY CASE. The Secretary of the Treasury of the United States may, or if requested by the court shall, intervene in a chapter 9 case. Representatives of the state in which the debtor is located may intervene in a chapter 9 case with respect to matters specified by the court.

(d) LABOR UNIONS. In a chapter 9, 11, or 12 case, a labor union or employees' association, representative of employees of the debtor, shall have the right to be heard on the economic soundness of a plan affecting the interests of the employees. A labor union or employees' association which exercises its right to be heard under this subdivision shall not be entitled to appeal any judgment, order, or decree relating to the plan, unless otherwise permitted by law.

(e) SERVICE ON ENTITIES COVERED BY THIS RULE. The court may enter orders governing the service of notice and papers on entities permitted to intervene or be heard pursuant to this rule

Rule 2019. Disclosure Regarding Creditors and Equity Security Holders in Chapter 9 and Chapter 11 Cases

(a) DEFINITIONS. In this rule the following terms have the meanings indicated:

(1) "Disclosable economic interest" means any claim, interest, pledge, lien, option, participation, derivative instrument, or any other right or derivative right granting the holder an economic interest that is affected by the value, acquisition, or disposition of a claim or interest.

(2)"Represent" or "represents" means to take a position before the court or to solicit votes regarding the confirmation of a plan on behalf of another.

(b) DISCLOSURE BY GROUPS, COMMITTEES, AND ENTITIES.

(1) In a chapter 9 or 11 case, a verified statement setting forth the information specified in subdivision (c) of this rule shall be filed by every group or committee that consists of or represents, and every entity that represents, multiple creditors or equity security holders that are (A) acting in concert to advance their common interests, and (B) not composed entirely of affiliates or insiders of one another.

(2) Unless the court orders otherwise, an entity is not required to file the verified statement described in paragraph (1) of this subdivision solely because of its status as:

(A) an indenture trustee;

(B) an agent for one or more other entities under an agreement for the extension of credit;

(C) a class action representative; or

(D) a governmental unit that is not a person.

(c) INFORMATION REQUIRED. The verified statement shall include:

(1) the pertinent facts and circumstances concerning:

(A) with respect to a group or committee, other than a committee appointed under § 1102 or § 1114 of the Code, the formation of the group or committee, including the name of each entity at whose instance the group or committee was formed or for whom the group or committee has agreed to act; or

(B) with respect to an entity, the employment of the entity, including the name of each creditor or equity security holder at whose instance the employment was arranged;

(2) if not disclosed under subdivision (c)(1), with respect to an entity, and with respect to each member of a group or committee;

(A) name and address

(B) the nature and amount of each disclosable economic interest held in relation to the debtor as of the date the entity was employed or the group or committee was formed; and

(C) with respect to each member of a group or committee that claims to represent any entity in addition to the members of the group or committee, other than a committee appointed under § 1102 or § 1114 of the Code, the date of acquisition by quarter and year of each disclosable economic interest, unless acquired more than one year before the petition was filed;

(3) if not disclosed under subdivision (c)(1) or (c)(2), with respect to each creditor or equity security holder represented by an entity, group, or committee, other than a committee appointed under § 1102 or § 1114 of the Code;

(A) name and address; and

(B) the nature and amount of each disclosable economic interest held in relation to the debtor as of the date of the statement; and

(4) a copy of the instrument, if any, authorizing the entity, group, or committee to act on behalf of creditors or equity security holders.

(d) SUPPLEMENTAL STATEMENTS. If any fact disclosed in its most recently filed statement has changed materially, an entity, group, or committee shall file a verified supplemental statement whenever it takes a position before the court or solicits votes on the confirmation of a plan. The supplemental statement shall set forth the material changes in the facts required by subdivision (c) to be disclosed.

(e) DETERMINATION OF FAILURE TO COMPLY; SANCTIONS.

(1) On motion of any party in interest , or on its own motion, the court may determine whether there has been a failure to comply with any provision of this rule.

(2) If the court finds such a failure to comply, it may:

(A) refuse to permit the entity, group, or committee to be heard or to intervene in the case;

(B) hold invalid any authority, acceptance, rejection, or objection given, procured, or received by the entity, group, or committee; or

(C) grant other appropriate relief.

Rule 2020. Review of Acts by United States Trustee

A proceeding to contest any act or failure to act by the United States trustee is governed by Rule 9014.

PART III

CLAIMS AND DISTRIBUTION TO CREDITORS AND EQUITY INTEREST HOLDERS; PLANS

Rule 3001. Proof of Claim.

(a) FORM AND CONTENT. A proof of claim is a written statement setting forth a creditor's claim. A proof of claim shall conform substantially to the appropriate Official Form.

(b) WHO MAY EXECUTE. A proof of claim shall be executed by the creditor or the creditor's authorized agent except as provided in Rules 3004 and 3005.

(c) SUPPORTING INFORMATION.

(1) Claim Based on a Writing. Except for a claim governed by paragraph (3) of this subdivision, when a claim, or an interest in property of the debtor securing the claim, is based on a writing, a copy of the writing shall be filed with the proof of claim. If the writing has been lost or destroyed, a statement of the circumstances of the loss or destruction shall be filed with the claim.

(2) Additional Requirements in an Individual Debtor Case; Sanctions for Failure to Comply. In a case in which the debtor is an individual:

(A) If, in addition to its principal amount, a claim includes interest, fees, expenses, or other charges incurred before the petition was filed, an itemized statement of the interest, fees, expenses, or charges shall be filed with the proof of claim.

(B) If a security interest is claimed in the debtor's property, a statement of the amount necessary to cure any default as of the date of the petition shall be filed with the proof of claim.

(C) If a security interest is claimed in property that is the debtor's principal residence, the attachment prescribed by the appropriate Official Form shall be filed with the proof of claim. If an escrow account has been established in connection with the claim, an escrow account statement prepared as of the date the petition was filed and in a form consistent with applicable nonbankruptcy law shall be filed with the attachment to the proof of claim.

(D) If the holder of a claim fails to provide any information required by this subdivision (c), the court may, after notice and hearing, take either or both of the following actions:

(i) preclude the holder from presenting the omitted information, in any form, as evidence in any contested matter or adversary proceeding in the case, unless the court determines that the failure was substantially justified or is harmless, or

(ii) award other appropriate relief, including reasonable expenses and attorney's fees caused by the failure.

(3) **Claim based on an open-end or revolving consumer credit agreement.**

(A) When a claim is based on an open-end or revolving consumer credit agreement--except one for which a security interest is claimed in the debtor's real property--a statement shall be filed with the proof of claim, including all of the following information that applies to the account:

(i) the name of the entity from whom the creditor purchased the account;

(ii) the name of the entity to whom the debt was owed at the time of an account holder's last transaction on the account;

(iii) the date of an account holder's last transaction;

(iv) the date of the last payment on the account; and

(v) the date on which the account was charged to profit and loss.

(B) On written request by a party in interest, the holder of a claim based on an open-end or revolving consumer credit agreement shall, within 30 days after the request is sent, provide the requesting party a copy of the writing specified in paragraph (1) of this subdivision.

(d) EVIDENCE OF PERFECTION OF SECURITY INTEREST. If a security interest in property of the debtor is claimed, the proof of claim shall be accompanied by evidence that the security interest has been perfected.

(e) TRANSFERRED CLAIM.

(1) Transfer of Claim Other Than for Security Before Proof Filed. If a claim has been transferred other than for security before proof of the claim has been filed, the proof of claim may be filed only by the transferee or an indenture trustee.

(2) Transfer of Claim Other Than for Security After Proof Filed. If a claim other than one based on a publicly traded note, bond, or debenture has been transferred other than for security after the proof of claim has been filed, evidence of the transfer shall be filed by the transferee. The clerk shall immediately notify the alleged transferor by mail of the filing of the evidence of transfer and that objection thereto, if any, must be filed within 21 days of the mailing of the notice or within any additional time allowed by the court. If the alleged transferor files a timely objection and the court finds, after notice and a hearing, that the claim has been transferred other than for security, it shall enter an order substituting the transferee for the transferor. If a timely objection is not filed by the alleged transferor, the transferee shall be substituted for the transferor.

(3) Transfer of Claim for Security Before Proof Filed. If a claim other than one based on a publicly traded note, bond, or debenture has been transferred for security before proof of the claim has been filed, the transferor or transferee or both may file a proof of claim for the full amount. The proof shall be supported by a statement setting forth the terms of the transfer. If either the transferor or the transferee files a proof of claim, the clerk shall immediately notify the other by mail of the right to join in the filed claim. If both transferor and transferee file proofs of the same claim, the proofs shall be consolidated. If the transferor or transferee does not file an agreement regarding its relative rights respecting voting of the claim, payment of dividends thereon, or participation in the administration of the estate, on motion by a party in interest and after notice and a hearing, the court shall enter such orders respecting these matters as may be appropriate.

(4) Transfer of Claim for Security After Proof Filed. If a claim other than one based on a publicly traded note, bond, or debenture has been transferred for security after the proof of claim has been filed, evidence of the terms of the transfer shall be filed by the transferee. The clerk shall immediately notify the alleged transferor by mail of the filing of the evidence of transfer and that objection thereto, if any, must be filed within 21 days of the mailing of the notice or within any additional time allowed by the court. If a timely objection is filed by the alleged transferor, the court, after notice and a hearing, shall determine whether the claim has been transferred for security. If the transferor or transferee does not file an agreement regarding its relative rights respecting voting of the claim, payment of dividends thereon, or participation in the administration of the estate, on motion by a party in interest and after notice and a hearing, the court shall enter such orders respecting these matters as may be appropriate.

(5) Service of Objection or Motion; Notice of Hearing. A copy of an objection filed pursuant to paragraph (2) or (4) or a motion filed pursuant to paragraph (3) or (4) of this subdivision together with a notice of a hearing shall be mailed or otherwise delivered to the transferor or transferee, whichever is appropriate, at least 30 days prior to the hearing.

(f) EVIDENTIARY EFFECT. A proof of claim executed and filed in accordance with these rules shall constitute prima facie evidence of the validity and amount of the claim.

(g) To the extent not inconsistent with the United States Warehouse Act or applicable State law, a warehouse receipt, scale ticket, or similar document of the type routinely issued as evidence of title by a grain storage facility, as defined in Section 557 of title 11, shall constitute prima facie evidence of the validity and amount of a claim of ownership of a quantity of grain.

Rule 3002. Filing Proof of Claim or Interest

(a) NECESSITY FOR FILING. A secured creditor, unsecured creditor, or equity security holder must file a proof of claim or interest for the claim or interest to be allowed, except as provided in Rules 1019(3), 3003, 3004, and 3005. A lien that secures a claim against the debtor is not void due only to the failure of any entity to file a proof of claim.

(b) PLACE OF FILING. A proof of claim or interest shall be filed in accordance with Rule 5005.

(c) TIME FOR FILING. In a voluntary chapter 7 case, chapter 12 case, or chapter 13 case, a proof of claim is timely filed if it is filed not later than 70 days after the order for relief under that chapter or the date of the order of conversion to a case under chapter 12 or chapter 13. In an involuntary chapter 7 case, a proof of claim is timely filed if it is filed not later than 90 days after the order for relief under that chapter is entered. But in all these cases, the following exceptions apply:

(1) A proof of claim filed by a governmental unit, other than for a claim resulting from a tax return filed under § 1308, is timely filed if it is filed not later than 180 days after the date of the order for relief. A proof of claim filed by a governmental unit for a claim resulting from a tax return filed under § 1308 is timely filed if it is filed no later than 180 days after the date of the order for relief or 60 days after the date of the filing of the tax return. The court may, for cause, enlarge the time for a governmental unit to file a proof of claim only upon motion of the governmental unit made before expiration of the period for filing a timely proof of claim.

(2) In the interest of justice and if it will not unduly delay the administration of the case, the court may extend the time for filing a proof of claim by an infant or incompetent person or the representative of either.

(3) An unsecured claim which arises in favor of an entity or becomes allowable as a result of a judgment may be filed within 30 days after the judgment becomes final if the judgment is for the recovery of money or property from that entity or denies or avoids the entity's interest in property. If the judgment imposes a liability which is not satisfied, or a duty which is not performed within such period or such further time as the court may permit, the claim shall not be allowed.

(4) A claim arising from the rejection of an executory contract or unexpired lease of the debtor may be filed within such time as the court may direct.

(5) If notice of insufficient assets to pay a dividend was given to creditors under Rule 2002(e), and subsequently the trustee notifies the court that payment of a dividend appears possible, the clerk shall give at least 90 days' notice by mail to creditors of that fact and of the date by which proofs of claim must be filed.

(6) On motion filed by a creditor before or after the expiration of the time to file a proof of claim, the court may extend the time by not more than 60 days from the date of the order granting the motion. The motion may be granted if the court finds that: (A) the notice was insufficient under the circumstances to give the creditor a reasonable time to file a proof of claim because the debtor failed to timely file the list of creditors' names and addresses required by Rule 1007(a); or (B) the notice was insufficient under the circumstances to give the creditor a reasonable time to file a proof of claim, and the notice was mailed to the creditor at a foreign address.

(7) A proof of claim filed by the holder of a claim that is secured by a security interest in the debtor's principal residence is timely filed if: (A) the proof of claim, together with the attachments required by Rule 3001(c)(2)(C), is filed not later than 70 days after the order for relief is entered; and (B) any attachments required by Rule 3001(c)(1) and (d) are filed as a supplement to the holder's claim not later than 120 days after the order for relief is entered.

Rule 3002.1 Notice Relating to Claims Secured by Security Interest in the Debtor's Principal Residence

(a) In general

This rule applies in a chapter 13 case to claims (1) that are secured by a security interest in the debtor's principal residence, and (2) for which the plan provides that either the trustee or the debtor will make contractual installment payments. Unless the court orders otherwise, the notice requirements of this rule cease to apply when an order terminating or annulling the automatic stay becomes effective with respect to the residence that secures the claim.

(b) Notice of payment changes; objection

(1) Notice

The holder of the claim shall file and serve on the debtor, debtor's counsel, and the trustee a notice of any change in the payment amount, including any change that results from an interest-rate or escrow-account adjustment, no later than 21 days before a payment in the new amount is due. If the claim arises from a home-equity line of credit, this requirement may be modified by court order.

(2) Objection

A party in interest who objects to the payment change may file a motion to determine whether the change is required to maintain payments in accordance with § 1322(b)(5) of the Code. If no motion is filed by the day before the new amount is due, the change goes into effect, unless the court orders otherwise.

(c) Notice of fees, expenses, and charges

The holder of the claim shall file and serve on the debtor, debtor's counsel, and the trustee a notice itemizing all fees, expenses, or charges (1) that were incurred in connection with the claim after the bankruptcy case was filed, and (2) that the holder asserts are recoverable against the debtor or against the debtor's principal residence. The notice shall be served within 180 days after the date on which the fees, expenses, or charges are incurred.

(d) Form and content

A notice filed and served under subdivision (b) or (c) of this rule shall be prepared as prescribed by the appropriate Official Form, and filed as a supplement to the holder's proof of claim. The notice is not subject to Rule 3001(f).

(e) Determination of fees, expenses, or charges

On motion of a party in interest filed within one year after service of a notice under subdivision (c) of this rule, the court shall, after notice and hearing, determine whether payment of any claimed fee, expense, or charge is required by the underlying agreement and applicable nonbankruptcy law to cure a default or maintain payments in accordance with § 1322(b)(5) of the Code.

(f) Notice of final cure payment

Within 30 days after the debtor completes all payments under the plan, the trustee shall file and serve on the holder of the claim, the debtor, and debtor's counsel a notice stating that the debtor has paid in full the amount required to cure any default on the claim. The notice shall also inform the holder of its obligation to file and serve a response under subdivision (g). If the debtor contends that final cure payment has been made and all plan payments have been completed, and the trustee does not timely file and serve the notice required by this subdivision, the debtor may file and serve the notice.

(g) Response to notice of final cure payment

Within 21 days after service of the notice under subdivision (f) of this rule, the holder shall file and serve on the debtor, debtor's counsel, and the trustee a statement indicating (1) whether it agrees that the debtor has paid in full the amount required to cure the default on the claim, and (2) whether the debtor is otherwise current on all payments consistent with § 1322(b)(5) of the Code. The statement shall itemize the required cure or postpetition amounts, if any, that the holder contends remain unpaid as of the date of the statement. The statement shall be filed as a supplement to the holder's proof of claim and is not subject to Rule 3001(f).

(h) Determination of final cure and payment

On motion of the debtor or trustee filed within 21 days after service of the statement under subdivision (g) of this rule, the court shall, after notice and hearing, determine whether the debtor has cured the default and paid all required postpetition amounts.

(i) Failure to notify

If the holder of a claim fails to provide any information as required by subdivision (b), (c), or (g) of this rule, the court may, after notice and hearing, take either or both of the following actions:

(1) preclude the holder from presenting the omitted information, in any form, as evidence in any contested matter or adversary proceeding in the case, unless the court determines that the failure was substantially justified or is harmless; or

(2) award other appropriate relief, including reasonable expenses and attorney's fees caused by the failure.

Rule 3003. Filing Proof of Claim or Equity Security Interest in Chapter 9 Municipality or Chapter 11 Reorganization Cases

(a) APPLICABILITY OF RULE. This rule applies in chapter 9 and 11 cases.

(b) SCHEDULE OF LIABILITIES AND LIST OF EQUITY SECURITY HOLDERS.

(1) Schedule of Liabilities. The schedule of liabilities filed pursuant to Section 521(1) of the Code shall constitute prima facie evidence of the validity and amount of the claims of creditors, unless they are scheduled as disputed, contingent, or unliquidated. It shall not be necessary for a creditor or equity security holder to file a proof of claim or interest except as provided in subdivision (c)(2) of this rule.

(2) List of Equity Security Holders. The list of equity security holders filed pursuant to Rule 1007(a)(3) shall constitute prima facie evidence of the validity and amount of the equity security interests and it shall not be necessary for the holders of such interests to file a proof of interest.

(c) FILING PROOF OF CLAIM.

(1) Who May File. Any creditor or indenture trustee may file a proof of claim within the time prescribed by subdivision (c)(3) of this rule.

(2) Who Must File. Any creditor or equity security holder whose claim or interest is not scheduled or scheduled as disputed, contingent, or unliquidated shall file a proof of claim or interest within the time prescribed by subdivision (c)(3) of this rule; any creditor who fails to do so shall not be treated as a creditor with respect to such claim for the purposes of voting and distribution.

(3) Time for Filing. The court shall fix and for cause shown may extend the time within which proofs of claim or interest may be filed. Notwithstanding the expiration of such time, a proof of claim may be filed to the extent and under the conditions stated in Rule 3002(c)(2), (c)(3), (c)(4), and (c)(6).

(4) Effect of Filing Claim or Interest. A proof of claim or interest executed and filed in accordance with this subdivision shall supersede any scheduling of that claim or interest pursuant to § 521(a)(1) of the Code.

(5) Filing by Indenture Trustee. An indenture trustee may file a claim on behalf of all known or unknown holders of securities issued pursuant to the trust instrument under which it is trustee.

(d) PROOF OF RIGHT TO RECORD STATUS. For the purposes of Rules 3017, 3018 and 3021 and for receiving notices, an entity who is not the record holder of a security may file a statement setting forth facts which entitle that entity to be treated as the record holder. An objection to the statement may be filed by any party in interest.

Rule 3004. Filing of Claims by Debtor or Trustee

If a creditor does not timely file a proof of claim under Rule 3002(c) or 3003(c), the debtor or trustee may file a proof of the claim within 30 days after the expiration of the time for filing claims prescribed by Rule 3002(c) or 3003(c), whichever is applicable. The clerk shall forthwith give notice of the filing to the creditor, the debtor and the trustee.

Rule 3005. Filing of Claim, Acceptance, or Rejection by Guarantor, Surety, Indorser, or Other Codebtor

(a) FILING OF CLAIM. If a creditor does not timely file a proof of claim under Rule 3002(c) or 3003(c), any entity that is or may be liable with the debtor to that creditor, or who has secured that creditor, may file a proof of the claim within 30 days after the expiration of the time for filing claims prescribed by Rule 3002(c) or Rule 3003(c) whichever is applicable. No distribution shall be made on the claim except on satisfactory proof that the original debt will be diminished by the amount of distribution.

(b) FILING OF ACCEPTANCE OR REJECTION; SUBSTITUTION OF CREDITOR. An entity which has filed a claim pursuant to the first sentence of subdivision (a) of this rule may file an acceptance or rejection of a plan in the name of the creditor, if known, or if unknown, in the entity's own name but if the creditor files a proof of claim within the time permitted by Rule 3003(c) or files a notice prior to confirmation of a plan of the creditor's intention to act in the creditor's own behalf, the creditor shall be substituted for the obligor with respect to that claim.

Rule 3006. Withdrawal of Claim; Effect on Acceptance or Rejection of Plan

A creditor may withdraw a claim as of right by filing a notice of withdrawal, except as provided in this rule. If after a creditor has filed a proof of claim an objection is filed thereto or a complaint is filed against that creditor in an adversary proceeding, or the creditor has accepted or rejected the plan or otherwise has participated significantly in the case, the creditor may not withdraw the claim except on order of the court after a hearing on notice to the trustee or debtor in possession, and any creditors' committee elected pursuant to Section 705(a) or appointed pursuant to Section 1102 of the Code. The order of the court shall contain such terms and conditions as the court deems proper. Unless the court orders otherwise, an authorized withdrawal of a claim shall constitute withdrawal of any related acceptance or rejection of a plan.

Rule 3007. Objections to Claims

(a) TIME AND MANNER OF SERVICE.

(1) Time of Service. An objection to the allowance of a claim and a notice of objection that substantially conforms to the appropriate Official Form shall be filed and served at least 30 days before any scheduled hearing on the objection or any deadline for the claimant to request a hearing.

(2) Manner of Service.

(A) The objection and notice shall be served on a claimant by first-class mail to the person most recently designated on the claimant's original or amended proof of claim as the person to receive notices, at the address so indicated; and

(i) if the objection is to a claim of the United States, or any of its officers or agencies, in the manner provided for service of a summons and complaint by Rule 7004(b)(4) or (5); or

(ii) if the objection is to a claim of an insured depository institution, in the manner provided by Rule 7004(h).

(B) Service of the objection and notice shall also be made by first-class mail or other permitted means on the debtor or debtor in possession, the trustee, and, if applicable, the entity filing the proof of claim under Rule 3005.

(b) DEMAND FOR RELIEF REQUIRING AN ADVERSARY PROCEEDING. A party in interest shall not include a demand for relief of a kind specified in Rule 7001 in an objection to the allowance of a claim, but may include the objection in an adversary proceeding.

(c) LIMITATION ON JOINDER OF CLAIMS OBJECTIONS. Unless otherwise ordered by the court, or permitted by subdivision (d), objections to more than one claim shall not be joined in a single objection.

(d) OMNIBUS OBJECTION. Subject to subdivision (e), objections to more than one claim may be joined in an omnibus objection if all the claims were filed by the same entity, or the objections are based solely on the grounds that the claims should be disallowed, in whole or in part, because:

(1) they duplicate other claims;

(2) they have been filed in the wrong case;

(3) they have been amended by subsequently filed proofs of claim;

(4) they were not timely filed;

(5) they have been satisfied or released during the case in accordance with the Code, applicable rules, or a court order;

(6) they were presented in a form that does not comply with applicable rules, and the objection states that the objector is unable to determine the validity of the claim because of the noncompliance;

(7) they are interests, rather than claims; or

(8) they assert priority in an amount that exceeds the maximum amount under § 507 of the Code.

(e) REQUIREMENTS FOR OMNIBUS OBJECTION. An omnibus objection shall:

(1) state in a conspicuous place that claimants receiving the objection should locate their names and claims in the objection;

(2) list claimants alphabetically, provide a cross-reference to claim numbers, and, if appropriate, list claimants by category of claims;

(3) state the grounds of the objection to each claim and provide a cross-reference to the pages in the omnibus objection pertinent to the stated grounds;

(4) state in the title the identity of the objector and the grounds for the objections;

(5) be numbered consecutively with other omnibus objections filed by the same objector; and

(6) contain objections to no more than 100 claims.

(f) FINALITY OF OBJECTION. The finality of any order regarding a claim objection included in an omnibus objection shall be determined as though the claim had been subject to an individual objection.

Rule 3008. Reconsideration of Claims

A party in interest may move for reconsideration of an order allowing or disallowing a claim against the estate. The court after a hearing on notice shall enter an appropriate order.

Rule 3009. Declaration and Payment of Dividends in a Chapter 7 Liquidation Case

In chapter 7 cases, dividends to creditors shall be paid as promptly as practicable. Dividend checks shall be made payable to and mailed to each creditor whose claim has been allowed, unless a power of attorney authorizing another entity to receive dividends has been executed and filed in accordance with Rule 9010. In that event, dividend checks shall be made payable to the creditor and to the other entity and shall be mailed to the other entity.

Rule 3010. Small Dividends and Payments in Chapter 7 Liquidation, Chapter 12 Family Farmer's Debt Adjustment, and Chapter 13 Individual's Debt Adjustment Cases

(a) Chapter 7 cases. In a chapter 7 case no dividend in an amount less than $5 shall be distributed by the trustee to any creditor unless authorized by local rule or order of the court. Any dividend not distributed to a creditor shall be treated in the same manner as unclaimed funds as provided in § 347 of the Code.

(b) Cases under subchapter V of chapter 11, chapter 12, and chapter 13

In a case under subchapter V of chapter 11, chapter 12, or chapter 13, no payment in an amount less than $15 shall be distributed by the trustee to any creditor unless authorized by local rule or order of the court. Funds not distributed because of this subdivision shall accumulate and shall be paid whenever the accumulation aggregates $15. Any funds remaining shall be distributed with the final payment.

Rule 3011. Unclaimed Funds in Chapter 7 Liquidation, Chapter 12 Family Farmer's Debt Adjustment, and Chapter 13 Individual's Debt Adjustment Cases

(a) The trustee shall file a list of all known names and addresses of the entities and the amounts which they are entitled to be paid from remaining property of the estate that is paid into court pursuant to Section 347(a) of the Code.

(b) On the court's website, the clerk must provide searchable access to information about funds deposited under § 347(a). The court may, for cause, limit access to information about funds in a specific case.

Rule 3012. Determining the Amount of Secured and Priority Claims

(a) DETERMINATION OF AMOUNT OF CLAIM. On request by a party in interest and after notice—to the holder of the claim and any other entity the court designates—and a hearing, the court may determine:

(1) the amount of a secured claim under § 506(a) of the Code; or

(2) the amount of a claim entitled to priority under § 507 of the Code.

(b) REQUEST FOR DETERMINATION; HOW MADE. Except as provided in subdivision (c), a request to determine the amount of a secured claim may be made by motion, in a claim objection, or in a plan filed in a chapter 12 or chapter 13 case. When the request is made in a chapter 12 or chapter 13 plan, the plan shall be served on the holder of the claim and any other entity the court designates in the manner provided for service of a summons and complaint by Rule 7004. A request to determine the amount of a claim entitled to priority may be made only by motion after a claim is filed or in a claim objection.

(c) CLAIMS OF GOVERNMENTAL UNITS. A request to determine the amount of a secured claim of a governmental unit may be made only by motion or in a claim objection after the governmental unit files a proof of claim or after the time for filing one under Rule 3002(c)(1) has expired.

Rule 3013. Classification of Claims and Interests

For the purposes of the plan and its acceptance, the court may, on motion after hearing on notice as the court may direct, determine classes of creditors and equity security holders pursuant to Sections 1122, 1222(b)(1), and 1322(b)(1) of the Code.

Rule 3014. Election Pursuant to Section 1111(b) by Secured Creditor in Chapter 9 Municipality and Chapter 11 Reorganization Case

An election of application of §1111(b)(2) of the Code by a class of secured creditors in a chapter 9 or 11 case may be made at any time prior to the conclusion of the hearing on the disclosure statement or within such later time as the court may fix. If the disclosure statement is conditionally approved pursuant to Rule 3017.1, and a final hearing on the disclosure statement is not held, the election of application of 1111(b)(2) may be made not later than the date fixed pursuant to Rule 3017.1(a)(2) or another date the court may fix. The election shall be in writing and signed unless made at the hearing on the disclosure statement. The election, if made by the majorities required by §1111(b)(1)(A)(i), shall be binding on all members of the class with respect to the plan.

Rule 3015. Filing, Objection to Confirmation, Effect of Confirmation, and Modification of a Plan in a Chapter 12 or a Chapter 13 Case

(a) FILING A CHAPTER 12 PLAN. The debtor may file a chapter 12 plan with the petition. If a plan is not filed with the petition, it shall be filed within the time prescribed by § 1221 of the Code.

(b) FILING A CHAPTER 13 PLAN. The debtor may file a chapter 13 plan with the petition. If a plan is not filed with the petition, it shall be filed within 14 days thereafter, and such time may not be further extended except for cause shown and on notice as the court may direct. If a case is converted to chapter 13, a plan shall be filed within 14 days thereafter, and such time may not be further extended except for cause shown and on notice as the court may direct.

(c) FORM OF CHAPTER 13 PLAN. If there is an Official Form for a plan filed in a chapter 13 case, that form must be used unless a Local Form has been adopted in compliance with Rule 3015.1. With either the Official Form or a Local Form, a nonstandard provision is effective only if it is included in a section of the form designated for nonstandard provisions and is also identified in accordance with any other requirements of the form. As used in this rule and the Official Form or a Local Form, "nonstandard provision" means a provision not otherwise included in the Official or Local Form or deviating from it.

(d) NOTICE. If the plan is not included with the notice of the hearing on confirmation mailed under Rule 2002, the debtor shall serve the plan on the trustee and all creditors when it is filed with the court.

(e) TRANSMISSION TO UNITED STATES TRUSTEE. The clerk shall forthwith transmit to the United States trustee a copy of the plan and any modification thereof filed under subdivision (a) or (b) of this rule.

(f) OBJECTION TO CONFIRMATION; DETERMINATION OF GOOD FAITH IN THE ABSENCE OF AN OBJECTION. An objection to confirmation of a plan shall be filed and served on the debtor, the trustee, and any other entity designated by the court, and shall be transmitted to the United States trustee, at least seven days before the date set for the hearing on confirmation, unless the court orders otherwise. An objection to confirmation is governed by Rule 9014. If no objection is timely filed, the court may determine that the plan has been proposed in good faith and not by any means forbidden by law without receiving evidence on such issues.

(g) EFFECT OF CONFIRMATION. Upon the confirmation of a chapter 12 or chapter 13 plan:

(1) any determination in the plan made under Rule 3012 about the amount of a secured claim is binding on the holder of the claim, even if the holder files a contrary proof of claim or the debtor schedules that claim, and regardless of whether an objection to the claim has been filed; and

(2) any request in the plan to terminate the stay imposed by § 362(a), § 1201(a), or § 1301(a) is granted.

(h) MODIFICATION OF PLAN AFTER CONFIRMATION. A request to modify a plan under § 1229 or § 1329 of the Code shall identify the proponent and shall be filed together with the proposed modification. The clerk, or some other person as the court may direct, shall give the debtor, the trustee, and all creditors not less than 21 days' notice by mail of the time fixed for filing objections and, if an objection is filed, the hearing to consider the proposed modification, unless the court orders otherwise with respect to creditors who are not affected by the proposed modification. A copy of the notice shall be transmitted to the United States trustee. A copy of the proposed modification, or a summary thereof, shall be included with the notice. Any objection to the proposed modification shall be filed and served on the debtor, the trustee, and any other entity designated by the court, and shall be transmitted to the United States trustee. An objection to a proposed modification is governed by Rule 9014.

Rule 3015.1. Requirements for a Local Form for Plans Filed in a Chapter 13 Case

Notwithstanding Rule 9029(a)(1), a district may require that a Local Form for a plan filed in a chapter 13 case be used instead of an Official Form adopted for that purpose if the following conditions are satisfied:

(a) a single Local Form is adopted for the district after public notice and an opportunity for public comment;

(b) each paragraph is numbered and labeled in boldface type with a heading stating the general subject matter of the paragraph;

(c) the Local Form includes an initial paragraph for the debtor to indicate that the plan does or does not:

(1) contain any nonstandard provision;

(2) limit the amount of a secured claim based on a valuation of the collateral for the claim; or

(3) avoid a security interest or lien;

(d) the Local Form contains separate paragraphs for:

(1) curing any default and maintaining payments on a claim secured by the debtor's principal residence;

(2) paying a domestic-support obligation;

(3) paying a claim described in the final paragraph of § 1325(a) of the Bankruptcy Code; and

(4) surrendering property that secures a claim with a request that the stay under §§ 362(a) and 1301(a) be terminated as to the surrendered collateral; and

(e) the Local Form contains a final paragraph for:

(1) the placement of nonstandard provisions, as defined in Rule 3015(c), along with a statement that any nonstandard provision placed elsewhere in the plan is void; and

(2) certification by the debtor's attorney or by an unrepresented debtor that the plan contains no nonstandard provision other than those set out in the final paragraph.

Rule 3016. Filing of Plan and Disclosure Statement in a Chapter 9 Municipality or Chapter 11 Reorganization Case

(a) IDENTIFICATION OF PLAN. Every proposed plan and any modification thereof shall be dated and, in a chapter 11 case, identified with the name of the entity or entities submitting or filing it.

(b) DISCLOSURE STATEMENT. In a chapter 9 or 11 case, a disclosure statement under § 1125 of the Code or evidence showing compliance with § 1126(b) shall be filed with the plan or within a time fixed by the court, unless the plan is intended to provide adequate information under § 1125(f)(1). If the plan is intended to provide adequate information under § 1125(f)(1), it shall be so designated and Rule 3017.1 shall apply as if the plan is a disclosure statement.

(c) INJUNCTION UNDER A PLAN. If a plan provides for an injunction against conduct not otherwise enjoined under the Code, the plan and disclosure statement shall describe in specific and conspicuous language (bold, italic, or underlined text) all acts to be enjoined and identify the entities that would be subject to the injunction.

(d) STANDARD FORM SMALL BUSINESS DISCLOSURE STATEMENT AND PLAN. In a small business case or a case under subchapter V of chapter 11, the court may approve a disclosure statement and may confirm a plan that conform substantially to the appropriate Official Forms or other standard forms approved by the court.

Rule 3017. Court Consideration of Disclosure Statement in a Chapter 9 Municipality or Chapter 11 Reorganization Case

(a) HEARING ON DISCLOSURE STATEMENT AND OBJECTIONS. Except as provided in Rule 3017.1, after a disclosure statement is filed in accordance with Rule 3016(b), the court shall hold a hearing on at least 28 days' notice to the debtor, creditors, equity security holders and other parties in interest as provided in Rule 2002 to consider the disclosure statement and any objections or modifications thereto. The plan and the disclosure statement shall be mailed with the notice of the hearing only to the debtor, any trustee or committee appointed under the Code, the Securities and Exchange Commission, and any party in interest who requests in writing a copy of the statement or plan. Objections to the disclosure statement shall be filed and served on the debtor, the trustee, any committee appointed under the Code, and any other entity designated by the court, at any time before the disclosure statement is approved or by an earlier date as the court may fix. In a chapter 11 reorganization case, every notice, plan, disclosure statement, and objection required to be served or mailed pursuant to this subdivision shall be transmitted to the United States trustee within the time provided in this subdivision.

(b) DETERMINATION ON DISCLOSURE STATEMENT. Following the hearing the court shall determine whether the disclosure statement should be approved.

(c) DATES FIXED FOR VOTING ON PLAN AND CONFIRMATION. On or before approval of the disclosure statement, the court shall fix a time within which the holders of claims and interests may accept or reject the plan and may fix a date for the hearing on confirmation.

(d) TRANSMISSION AND NOTICE TO UNITED STATES TRUSTEE, CREDITORS AND EQUITY SECURITY HOLDERS. Upon approval of a disclosure statement, - except to the extent that the court orders otherwise with respect to one or more unimpaired classes of creditors or equity security holders - the debtor in possession, trustee, proponent of the plan, or clerk as the court orders shall mail to all creditors and equity security holders, and in a chapter 11 reorganization case shall transmit to the United States trustee:

(1) the plan or a court-approved summary of the plan;

(2) the disclosure statement approved by the court;

(3) notice of the time within which acceptances and rejections of the plan may be filed; and

(4) any other information as the court may direct, including any court

opinion approving the disclosure statement or a court-approved summary of the opinion.

In addition, notice of the time fixed for filing objections and the hearing on confirmation shall be mailed to all creditors and equity security holders in accordance with Rule 2002(b), and a form of ballot conforming to the appropriate Official Form shall be mailed to creditors and equity security holders entitle to vote on the plan. If the court opinion is not transmitted or only a summary of the plan is transmitted, the court opinion or the plan shall be provided on request of a party in interest at the plan proponent's expense. If the court orders that the disclosure statement and the plan or a summary of the plan shall not be mailed to any unimpaired class, notice that the class is designated in the plan as unimpaired and notice of the name and address of the person from whom the plan or summary of the plan and disclosure statement may be obtained upon request and at the plan proponent's expense, shall be mailed to members of the unimpaired class together with the notice of the time fixed for filing objections to and the hearing on confirmation. For the purposes of this subdivision, creditors and equity security holders shall include holders of stock, bonds, debentures, notes, and other securities of record on the date the order approving the disclosure statement is entered or another date fixed by the court, for cause, after notice and a hearing.

(e) TRANSMISSION TO BENEFICIAL HOLDERS OF SECURITIES. At the hearing held pursuant to subdivision (a) of this rule, the court shall consider the procedures for transmitting the documents and information required by subdivision (d) of this rule to beneficial holders of stock, bonds, debentures, notes, and other securities, determine the adequacy of the procedures, and enter any orders the court deems appropriate.

(f) NOTICE AND TRANSMISSION OF DOCUMENTS TO ENTITIES SUBJECT TO AN INJUNCTION UNDER A PLAN. If a plan provides for an injunction against conduct not otherwise enjoined under the Code and an entity that would be subject to the injunction is not a creditor or equity security holder, at the hearing held under Rule 3017(a), the court shall consider procedures for providing the entity with:

(1) at least 28 days' notice of the time fixed for filing objections and the hearing on confirmation of the plan containing the information described in Rule 2002(c)(3); and

(2) to the extent feasible, a copy of the plan and disclosure statement.

Rule 3017.1. Court Consideration of Disclosure Statement in a Small Business Case

(a) CONDITIONAL APPROVAL OF DISCLOSURE STATEMENT. In a small business case or in a case under subchapter V of chapter 11 in which the court has ordered that § 1125 applies, the court may, on application of the plan proponent or on its own initiative, conditionally approve a disclosure statement filed in accordance with Rule 3016. On or before conditional approval of the disclosure statement, the court shall:

(1) fix a time within which the holders of claims and interests may accept or reject the plan;

(2) fix a time for filing objections to the disclosure statement;

(3) fix a date for the hearing on final approval of the disclosure statement to be held if a timely objection is filed; and

(4) fix a date for the hearing on confirmation.

(b) APPLICATION OF RULE 3017. Rule 3017(a), (b), (c), and (e) do not apply to a conditionally approved disclosure statement. Rule 3017(d) applies to a conditionally approved disclosure statement, except that conditional approval is considered approval of the disclosure statement for the purpose of applying Rule 3017(d).

(c) FINAL APPROVAL

(1) Notice. Notice of the time fixed for filing objections and the hearing to consider final approval of the disclosure statement shall be given in accordance with Rule 2002 and may be combined with notice of the hearing on confirmation of the plan.

(2) Objections. Objections to the disclosure statement shall be filed, transmitted to the United States trustee, and served on the debtor, the trustee, any committee appointed under the Code and any other entity designated by the court at any time before final approval of the disclosure statement or by an earlier date as the court may fix.

(3) Hearing. If a timely objection to the disclosure statement is filed, the court shall hold a hearing to consider final approval before or combined with the hearing on confirmation of the plan.

Rule 3017.2. Fixing of Dates by the Court in Subchapter V Cases in Which There Is No Disclosure Statement.

In a case under subchapter V of chapter 11 in which § 1125 does not apply, the court shall:

(a) fix a time within which the holders of claims and interests may accept or reject the plan;

(b) fix a date on which an equity security holder or creditor whose claim is based on a security must be the holder of record of the security in order to be eligible to accept or reject the plan;

(c) fix a date for the hearing on confirmation; and

(d) fix a date for transmitting the plan, notice of the time within which the holders of claims and interests may accept or reject it, and notice of the date for the hearing on confirmation.

Rule 3018. Acceptance or Rejection of Plan in a Chapter 9 Municipality or a Chapter 11 Reorganization Case

(a) ENTITIES ENTITLED TO ACCEPT OR REJECT PLAN; TIME FOR ACCEPTANCE OR REJECTION. A plan may be accepted or rejected in accordance with Section 1126 of the Code within the time fixed by the court pursuant to Rule 3017. Subject to subdivision (b) of this rule, an equity security holder or creditor whose claim is based on a security of record shall not be entitled to accept or reject a plan unless the equity security holder or creditor is the holder of record of the security on the date the order approving the disclosure statement is entered or on another date fixed by the court, for cause, after notice and a hearing. For cause shown, the court after notice and hearing may permit a creditor or equity security holder to change or withdraw an acceptance or rejection. Notwithstanding objection to a claim or interest, the court after notice and hearing may temporarily allow the claim or interest in an amount which the court deems proper for the purpose of accepting or rejecting a plan.

(b) ACCEPTANCES OR REJECTIONS OBTAINED BEFORE PETITION. An equity security holder or creditor whose claim is based on a security of record who accepted or rejected the plan before the commencement of the case shall not be deemed to have accepted or rejected the plan pursuant to Section 1126(b) of the Code unless the equity security holder or creditor was the holder of record of the security on the date specified in the solicitation of such acceptance or rejection for the purposes of such solicitation. A holder of a claim or interest who has accepted or rejected a plan before the commencement of the case under the Code shall not be deemed to have accepted or rejected the plan if the court finds after notice and hearing that the plan was not transmitted to substantially all creditors and equity security holders of the same class, that an unreasonably short time was prescribed for such creditors and equity security holders to accept or reject the plan, or that the solicitation was not in compliance with Section 1126(b) of the Code.

(c) FORM OF ACCEPTANCE OR REJECTION. An acceptance or rejection shall be in writing, identify the plan or plans accepted or rejected, be signed by the creditor or equity security holder or an authorized agent, and conform to the appropriate Official Form. If more than one plan is transmitted pursuant to Rule 3017, an acceptance or rejection may be filed by each creditor or equity security holder for any number of plans transmitted and if acceptances are filed for more than one plan, the creditor or equity security holder may indicate a preference or preferences among the plans so accepted.

(d) ACCEPTANCE OR REJECTION BY PARTIALLY SECURED CREDITOR. A creditor whose claim has been allowed in part as a secured claim and in part as an unsecured claim shall be entitled to accept or reject a plan in both capacities.

Rule 3019. Modification of Accepted Plan in a Chapter 9 Municipality or a Chapter 11 Reorganization Case

(a) MODIFICATION OF PLAN BEFORE CONFIRMATION. In a chapter 9 or chapter 11 case, after a plan has been accepted and before its confirmation, the proponent may file a modification of the plan. If the court finds after hearing on notice to the trustee, any committee appointed under the Code, and any other entity designated by the court that the proposed modification does not adversely change the treatment of the claim of any creditor or the interest of any equity security holder who has not accepted in writing the modification, it shall be deemed accepted by all creditors and equity security holders who have previously accepted the plan.

(b) MODIFICATION OF PLAN AFTER CONFIRMATION IN INDIVIDUAL DEBTOR CASE. If the debtor is an individual, a request to modify the plan under § 1127(e) of the Code is governed by Rule 9014. The request shall identify the proponent and shall be filed together with the proposed modification. The clerk, or some other person as the court may direct, shall give the debtor, the trustee, and all creditors not less than 21 days' notice by mail of the time fixed to file objections and, if an objection is filed, the hearing to consider the proposed modification, unless the court orders otherwise with respect to creditors who are not affected by the proposed modification. A copy of the notice shall be transmitted to the United States trustee, together with a copy of the proposed modification. Any objection to the proposed modification shall be filed and served on the debtor, the proponent of the modification, the trustee, and any other entity designated by the court, and shall be transmitted to the United States trustee.

Rule 3020. Deposit; Confirmation of Plan in a Chapter 9 Municipality or Chapter 11 Reorganization Case

(a) DEPOSIT. In a chapter 11 case, prior to entry of the order confirming the plan, the court may order the deposit with the trustee or debtor in possession of the consideration required by the plan to be distributed on confirmation. Any money deposited shall be kept in a special account established for the exclusive purpose of making the distribution.

(b) OBJECTIONS TO AND HEARING ON CONFIRMATION IN A CHAPTER 9 OR CHAPTER 11 CASE.

(1) Objection. An objection to confirmation of the plan shall be filed and served on the debtor, the trustee, the proponent of the plan, any committee appointed under the Code and on any other entity designated by the court, within a time fixed by the court. Unless the case is a chapter 9 municipality case, a copy of every objection to confirmation shall be transmitted by the objecting party to the United States trustee within the time fixed for the filing of objections. An objection to confirmation is governed by Rule 9014.

(2) Hearing. The court shall rule on confirmation of the plan after notice and hearing as provided in Rule 2002. If no objection is timely filed, the court may determine that the plan has been proposed in good faith and not by any means forbidden by law without receiving evidence on such issues.

(c) ORDER OF CONFIRMATION.

(1) The order of confirmation shall conform to the appropriate Official Form. If the plan provides for an injunction against conduct not otherwise enjoined under the Code, the order of confirmation shall (1) describe in reasonable detail all acts enjoined; (2) be specific in its terms regarding the injunction; and (3) identify the entities subject to the injunction.

(2)Notice of entry of the order of confirmation shall be mailed promptly to the debtor, the trustee, creditors, equity security holders, other parties in interest, and, if known, to any identified entity subject to an injunction provided for in the plan against conduct not otherwise enjoined under the Code.

(3) Except in a chapter 9 municipality case, notice of entry of the order of confirmation shall be transmitted to the United States trustee as provided in Rule 2002(k).

(d) RETAINED POWER. Notwithstanding the entry of the order of confirmation, the court may issue any other order necessary to administer the estate.

(e) STAY OF CONFIRMATION ORDER. An order confirming a plan is stayed until the expiration of 14 days after the entry of the order, unless the court orders otherwise.

Rule 3021. Distribution Under Plan

Except as provided in Rule 3020(e), after a plan is confirmed, distribution shall be made to creditors whose claims have been allowed, to interest holders whose interests have not been disallowed, and to indenture trustees who have filed claims under Rule 3003(c)(5) that have been allowed. For purposes of this rule, creditors include holders of bonds, debentures, notes, and other debt securities, and interest holders include the holders of stock and other equity securities, of record at the time of commencement of distribution, unless a different time is fixed by the plan or the order confirming the plan.

Rule 3022. Final Decree in Chapter 11 Reorganization Case

After an estate is fully administered in a chapter 11 reorganization case, the court, on its own motion or on motion of a party in interest, shall enter a final decree closing the case.

PART IV

THE DEBTOR: DUTIES AND BENEFITS

Rule 4001. Relief from Automatic Stay; Prohibiting or Conditioning the Use, Sale, or Lease of Property; Use of Cash Collateral; Obtaining Credit; Agreements

(a) RELIEF FROM STAY; PROHIBITING OR CONDITIONING THE USE, SALE, OR LEASE OF PROPERTY.

(1) Motion. A motion for relief from an automatic stay provided by the Code or a motion to prohibit or condition the use, sale, or lease of property pursuant to Section 363(e) shall be made in accordance with Rule 9014 and shall be served on any committee elected pursuant to Section 705 or appointed pursuant to Section 1102 of the Code or its authorized agent, or, if the case is a chapter 9 municipality case or a chapter 11 reorganization case and no committee of unsecured creditors has been appointed pursuant to Section 1102, on the creditors included on the list filed pursuant to Rule 1007(d), and on such other entities as the court may direct.

(2) Ex Parte Relief. Relief from a stay under Section 362(a) or a request to prohibit or condition the use, sale, or lease of property pursuant to Section 363(e) may be granted without prior notice only if (A) it clearly appears from specific facts shown by affidavit or by a verified motion that immediate and irreparable injury, loss, or damage will result to the movant before the adverse party or the attorney for the adverse party can be heard in opposition, and (B) the movant's attorney certifies to the court in writing the efforts, if any, which have been made to give notice and the reasons why notice should not be required. The party obtaining relief under this subdivision and Section 362(f) or Section 363(e) shall immediately give oral notice thereof to the trustee or debtor in possession and to the debtor and forthwith mail or otherwise transmit to such adverse party or parties a copy of the order granting relief. On two days notice to the party who obtained relief from the stay without notice or on shorter notice to that party as the court may prescribe, the adverse party may appear and move reinstatement of the stay or reconsideration of the order prohibiting or conditioning the use, sale, or lease of property. In that event, the court shall proceed expeditiously to hear and determine the motion.

(3) Stay of Order. An order granting a motion for relief from an automatic stay made in accordance with Rule 4001(a)(1) is stayed until the expiration of 14 days after the entry of the order, unless the court orders otherwise.

(b) USE OF CASH COLLATERAL.

(1) Motion; Service.

(A) Motion. A motion for authority to use cash collateral shall be made in accordance with Rule 9014 and shall be accompanied by a proposed form of order.

(B) Contents. The motion shall consist of or (if the motion is more than five pages in length) begin with a concise statement of the relief requested, not to exceed five pages, that lists or summarizes, and sets out the location within the relevant documents of, all material provisions, including:

(i) the name of each entity with an interest in the cash collateral;

(ii) the purposes for the use of the cash collateral;

(iii) the material terms, including duration, of the use of the cash collateral; and

(iv) any liens, cash payments, or other adequate protection that will be provided to each entity with an interest in the cash collateral or, if no additional adequate protection is proposed, an explanation of why each entity's interest is adequately protected.

(C) Service. The motion shall be served on: (1) any entity with an interest in the cash collateral; (2) any committee elected under § 705 or appointed under § 1102 of the Code, or its authorized agent, or, if the case is a chapter 9 municipality case or a chapter 11 reorganization case and no committee of unsecured creditors has been appointed under § 1102, the creditors included on the list filed under Rule 1007(d); and (3) any other entity that the court directs.

(2) Hearing. The court may commence a final hearing on a motion for authorization to use cash collateral no earlier than 14 days after service of the motion. If the motion so requests, the court may conduct a preliminary hearing before such 14 day period expires, but the court may authorize the use of only that amount of cash collateral as is necessary to avoid immediate and irreparable harm to the estate pending a final hearing.

(3) Notice. Notice of hearing pursuant to this subdivision shall be given to the parties on whom service of the motion is required by paragraph (1) of this subdivision and to such other entities as the court may direct.

(c) OBTAINING CREDIT.

(1) Motion; Service.

(A) Motion. A motion for authority to obtain credit shall be made in accordance with Rule 9014 and shall be accompanied by a copy of the credit agreement and a proposed form of order.

(B) Contents. The motion shall consist of or (if the motion is more than five pages in length) begin with a concise statement of the relief requested, not to exceed five pages, that lists or summarizes, and sets out the location within the relevant documents of, all material provisions of the proposed credit agreement and form of order, including interest rate, maturity, events of default, liens, borrowing limits, and borrowing conditions. If the proposed credit agreement or form of order includes any of the provisions listed below, the concise statement shall also: briefly list or summarize each one; identify its specific location in the proposed agreement and form of order; and identify any such provision that is proposed to remain in effect if interim approval is granted, but final relief is denied, as provided under Rule 4001(c)(2). In addition, the motion shall describe the nature and extent of each provision listed below:

(i) a grant of priority or a lien on property of the estate under § 364(c) or (d);

(ii) the providing of adequate protection or priority for a claim that arose before the commencement of the case, including the granting of a lien on property of the estate to secure the claim, or the use of property of the estate or credit obtained under § 364 to make cash payments on account of the claim;

(iii) a determination of the validity, enforceability, priority, or amount of a claim that arose before the commencement of the case, or of any lien securing the claim;

(iv) a waiver or modification of Code provisions or applicable rules relating to the automatic stay;

(v) a waiver or modification of any entity's authority or right to file a plan, seek an extension of time in which the debtor has the exclusive right to file a plan, request the use of cash collateral under § 363(c), or request authority to obtain credit under § 364;

(vi) the establishment of deadlines for filing a plan of reorganization, for approval of a disclosure statement, for a hearing on confirmation, or for entry of a confirmation order;

(vii) a waiver or modification of the applicability of nonbankruptcy law relating to the perfection of a lien on property of the estate, or on the foreclosure or other enforcement of the lien;

(viii) a release, waiver, or limitation on any claim or other cause of action belonging to the estate or the trustee, including any modification of the statute of limitations or other deadline to commence an action;

(ix) the indemnification of any entity;

(x) a release, waiver, or limitation of any right under § 506(c); or

(xi) the granting of a lien on any claim or cause of action arising under §§ 544, 545, 547, 548, 549, 553(b), 723(a), or 724(a).

(C) Service. The motion shall be served on: (1) any committee elected under § 705 or appointed under § 1102 of the Code, or its authorized agent, or, if the case is a chapter 9 municipality case or a chapter 11 reorganization case and no committee of unsecured creditors has been appointed under § 1102, on the creditors included on the list filed under Rule 1007(d); and (2) on any other entity that the court directs.

(2) Hearing. The court may commence a final hearing on a motion for authority to obtain credit no earlier than 14 days after service of the motion. If the motion so requests, the court may conduct a hearing before such 14 day period expires, but the court may authorize the obtaining of credit only to the extent necessary to avoid immediate and irreparable harm to the estate pending a final hearing.

(3) Notice. Notice of hearing pursuant to this subdivision shall be given to the parties on whom service of the motion is required by paragraph (1) of this subdivision and to such other entities as the court may direct.

(4) Inapplicability in a Chapter 13 Case. This subdivision (c) does not apply in a chapter 13 case.

(d) AGREEMENT RELATING TO RELIEF FROM THE AUTOMATIC STAY, PROHIBITING OR CONDITIONING THE USE, SALE, OR LEASE OF PROPERTY, PROVIDING ADEQUATE PROTECTION, USE OF CASH COLLATERAL, AND OBTAINING CREDIT.

(1) Motion; Service.

(A) Motion. A motion for approval of any of the following shall be accompanied by a copy of the agreement and a proposed form of order:

(i) an agreement to provide adequate protection;

(ii) an agreement to prohibit or condition the use, sale, or lease of property;

(iii) an agreement to modify or terminate the stay provided for in § 362;

(iv) an agreement to use cash collateral; or

(v) an agreement between the debtor and an entity that has a lien or interest in property of the estate pursuant to which the entity consents to the creation of a lien senior or equal to the entity's lien or interest in such property.

(B) Contents. The motion shall consist of or (if the motion is more than five pages in length) begin with a concise statement of the relief requested, not to exceed five pages, that lists or summarizes, and sets out the location within the relevant documents of, all material provisions of the agreement. In addition, the concise statement shall briefly list or summarize, and identify the specific location of, each provision in the proposed form of order, agreement, or other document of the type listed in subdivision (c)(1)(B). The motion shall also describe the nature and extent of each such provision.

(C) Service. The motion shall be served on: (1) any committee elected under § 705 or appointed under § 1102 of the Code, or its authorized agent, or, if the case is a chapter 9 municipality case or a chapter 11 reorganization case and no committee of unsecured creditors has been appointed under § 1102, on the creditors included on the list filed under Rule 1007(d); and (2) on any other entity the court directs.

(2) Objection. Notice of the motion and the time within which objections may be filed and served on the debtor in possession or trustee shall be mailed to the parties on whom service is required by paragraph (1) of this subdivision and to such other entities as the court may direct. Unless the court fixes a different time, objections may be filed within 14 days of the mailing of the notice.

(3) Disposition; Hearing. If no objection is filed, the court may enter an order approving or disapproving the agreement without conducting a hearing. If an objection is filed or if the court determines a hearing is appropriate, the court shall hold a hearing on no less than seven days' notice to the objector, the movant, the parties on whom service is required by paragraph (1) of this subdivision and such other entities as the court may direct.

(4) Agreement in Settlement of Motion. The court may direct that the procedures prescribed in paragraphs (1), (2), and (3) of this subdivision shall not apply and the agreement may be approved without further notice if the court determines that a motion made pursuant to subdivisions (a), (b), or (c) of this rule was sufficient to afford reasonable notice of the material provisions of the agreement and opportunity for a hearing.

Rule 4002. Duties of Debtor

(a) IN GENERAL. In addition to performing other duties prescribed by the Code and rules, the debtor shall:

(1) attend and submit to an examination at the times ordered by the court;

(2) attend the hearing on a complaint objecting to discharge and testify, if called as a witness;

(3) inform the trustee immediately in writing as to the location of real property in which the debtor has an interest and the name and address of every person holding money or property subject to the debtor's withdrawal or order if a schedule of property has not yet been filed pursuant to Rule 1007;

(4) cooperate with the trustee in the preparation of an inventory, the examination of proofs of claim, and the administration of the estate; and

(5) file a statement of any change of the debtor's address.

(b) INDIVIDUAL DEBTOR'S DUTY TO PROVIDE DOCUMENTATION.

(1) Personal Identification. Every individual debtor shall bring to the meeting of creditors under § 341:

(A) a picture identification issued by a governmental unit, or other personal identifying information that establishes the debtor's identity; and

(B) evidence of social-security number(s), or a written statement that such documentation does not exist.

(2) Financial Information. Every individual debtor shall bring to the meeting of creditors under § 341, and make available to the trustee, the following documents or copies of them, or provide a written statement that the documentation does not exist or is not in the debtor's possession:

(A) evidence of current income such as the most recent payment advice;

(B) unless the trustee or the United States trustee instructs otherwise, statements for each of the debtor's depository and investment accounts, including checking, savings, and money market accounts, mutual funds and brokerage accounts for the time period that includes the date of the filing of the petition; and

(C) documentation of monthly expenses claimed by the debtor if required by § 707(b)(2)(A) or (B).

(3) Tax Return. At least 7 days before the first date set for the meeting of creditors under § 341, the debtor shall provide to the trustee a copy of the debtor's federal income tax return for the most recent tax year ending immediately before the commencement of the case and for which a return was filed, including any attachments, or a transcript of the tax return, or provide a written statement that the documentation does not exist.

(4) Tax Returns Provided to Creditors. If a creditor, at least 14 days before the first date set for the meeting of creditors under § 341, requests a copy of the debtor's tax return that is to be provided to the trustee under subdivision (b)(3), the debtor, at least 7 days before the first date set for the meeting of creditors under § 341, shall provide to the requesting creditor a copy of the return, including any attachments, or a transcript of the tax return, or provide a written statement that the documentation does not exist.

(5) Confidentiality of Tax Information. The debtor's obligation to provide tax returns under Rule 4002(b)(3) and (b)(4) is subject to procedures for safeguarding the confidentiality of tax information established by the Director of the Administrative Office of the United States Courts.

Rule 4003. Exemptions

(a) CLAIM OF EXEMPTIONS. A debtor shall list the property claimed as exempt under Section 522 of the Code on the schedule of assets required to be filed by Rule 1007. If the debtor fails to claim exemptions or file the schedule within the time specified in Rule 1007, a dependent of the debtor may file the list within 30 days thereafter.

(b) OBJECTING TO A CLAIM OF EXEMPTIONS.

(1) Except as provided in paragraphs (2) and (3), a party in interest may file an objection to the list of property claimed as exempt within 30 days after the meeting of creditors held under § 341(a) is concluded or within 30 days after any amendment to the list or supplemental schedules is filed, whichever is later. The court may, for cause, extend the time for filing objections if, before the time to object expires, a party in interest files a request for an extension.

(2) The trustee may file an objection to a claim of exemption at any time prior to one year after the closing of the case if the debtor fraudulently asserted the claim of exemption. The trustee shall deliver or mail the objection to the debtor and the debtor's attorney, and to any person filing the list of exempt property and that person's attorney.

(3) An objection to a claim of exemption based on § 522(q) shall be filed before the closing of the case. If an exemption is first claimed after a case is reopened, an objection shall be filed before the reopened case is closed.

(4) A copy of any objection shall be delivered or mailed to the trustee, the debtor and the debtor's attorney, and the person filing the list and that person's attorney.

(c) BURDEN OF PROOF. In any hearing under this rule, the objecting party has the burden of proving that the exemptions are not properly claimed. After hearing on notice, the court shall determine the issues presented by the objections.

(d) AVOIDANCE BY DEBTOR OF TRANSFERS OF EXEMPT PROPERTY. A proceeding under § 522(f) to avoid a lien or other transfer of property exempt under the Code shall be commenced by motion in the manner provided by Rule 9014, or by serving a chapter 12 or chapter 13 plan on the affected creditors in the manner provided by Rule 7004 for service of a summons and complaint. Notwithstanding the provisions of subdivision (b), a creditor may object to a request under § 522(f) by challenging the validity of the exemption asserted to be impaired by the lien.

Rule 4004. Grant Or Denial of Discharge

(a) TIME FOR OBJECTING TO DISCHARGE; NOTICE OF TIME FIXED. In a chapter 7 case, a complaint, or a motion under § 727(a)(8) or (a)(9) of the Code, objecting to the debtor's discharge shall be filed no later than 60 days after the first date set for the meeting of creditors under Section 341(a). In a chapter 11 case, the complaint shall be filed no later than the first date set for the hearing on confirmation. In a Chapter 13 case, a motion objecting to the debtor's discharge under § 1328(f) shall be filed no later than 60 days after the first date set for the meeting of creditors under § 341(a). At least 28 days' notice of the time so fixed shall be given to the United States trustee and all creditors as provided in Rule 2002(f) and (k), and to the trustee and the trustee's attorney.

(b) EXTENSION OF TIME.

(1) On motion of any party in interest, after notice and hearing, the court may for cause extend the time to object to discharge. Except as provided in subdivision (b)(2), the motion shall be filed before the time has expired.

(2) A motion to extend the time to object to discharge may be filed after the time for objection has expired and before discharge is granted if (A) the objection is based on facts that, if learned after the discharge, would provide a basis for revocation under § 727 (d) of the Code, and (B) the movant did not have knowledge of those facts in time to permit an objection. The motion shall be filed promptly after the movant discovers the facts on which the objection is based.

(c) GRANT OF DISCHARGE.

(1) In a chapter 7 case, on expiration of the times fixed for objecting to discharge and for filing a motion to dismiss the case under Rule 1017(e), the court shall forthwith grant the discharge, except that the court shall not grant the discharge if:

(A) the debtor is not an individual;

(B) a complaint, or a motion under § 727(a)(8) or (a)(9), objecting to the discharge has been filed and not decided in the debtor's favor;

(C) the debtor has filed a waiver under § 727(a)(10);

(D) a motion to dismiss the case under § 707 is pending;

(E) a motion to extend the time for filing a complaint objecting to the discharge is pending;

(F) a motion to extend the time for filing a motion to dismiss the case under Rule 1017(e)(1) is pending;

(G) the debtor has not paid in full the filing fee prescribed by 28 U.S.C. § 1930(a) and any other fee prescribed by the Judicial Conference of the United States under 28 U.S.C. § 1930(b) that is payable to the clerk upon the commencement of a case under the Code, unless the court has waived the fees under 28 U.S.C. § 1930(f);

(H) the debtor has not filed with the court a statement of completion of a course concerning personal financial management if required by Rule 1007(b)(7);

(I) a motion to delay or postpone discharge under § 727(a)(12) is pending;

(J) a motion to enlarge the time to file a reaffirmation agreement under Rule 4008(a) is pending;

(K) a presumption is in effect under § 524(m) that a reaffirmation agreement is an undue hardship and the court has not concluded a hearing on the presumption; or

(L) a motion is pending to delay discharge because the debtor has not filed with the court all tax documents required to be filed under § 521(f).

(2) Notwithstanding Rule 4004(c)(1), on motion of the debtor, the court may defer the entry of an order granting a discharge for 30 days and, on motion within that period, the court may defer entry of the order to a date certain.

(3) If the debtor is required to file a statement under Rule 1007(b)(8), the court shall not grant a discharge earlier than 30 days after the statement is filed.

(4) In a chapter 11 case in which the debtor is an individual, or a chapter 13 case, the court shall not grant a discharge if the debtor has not filed any statement required by Rule 1007(b)(7).

(d) APPLICABILITY OF RULES IN PART VII AND RULE 9014. An objection to discharge is governed by Part VII of these rules, except that an objection to discharge under §§ 727(a)(8), (a)(9), or 1328(f) is commenced by motion and governed by Rule 9014.

(e) ORDER OF DISCHARGE. An order of discharge shall conform to the appropriate Official Form.

(f) REGISTRATION IN OTHER DISTRICTS. An order of discharge that has become final may be registered in any other district by filing a certified copy of the order in the office of the clerk of that district. When so registered the order of discharge shall have the same effect as an order of the court of the district where registered.

(g) NOTICE OF DISCHARGE. The clerk shall promptly mail a copy of the final order of discharge to those specified in subdivision (a) of this rule.

Rule 4005. Burden of Proof in Objecting to Discharge

At the trial on a complaint objecting to a discharge, the plaintiff has the burden of proving the objection.

Rule 4006. Notice of No Discharge

If an order is entered: denying a discharge; revoking a discharge; approving a waiver of discharge; or, in the case of an individual debtor, closing the case without the entry of a discharge, the clerk shall promptly notify all parties in interest in the manner provided by Rule 2002.

Rule 4007. Determination of Dischargeability of a Debt

(a) PERSONS ENTITLED TO FILE COMPLAINT. A debtor or any creditor may file a complaint to obtain a determination of the dischargeability of any debt.

(b) TIME FOR COMMENCING PROCEEDING OTHER THAN UNDER SECTION 523(c) OF THE CODE. A complaint other than under Section 523(c) may be filed at any time. A case may be reopened without payment of an additional filing fee for the purpose of filing a complaint to obtain a determination under this rule.

(c) TIME FOR FILING COMPLAINT UNDER § 523(c) IN A CHAPTER 7 LIQUIDATION, CHAPTER 11 REORGANIZATION, CHAPTER 12 FAMILY FARMER'S DEBT ADJUSTMENT CASE, OR CHAPTER 13 INDIVIDUAL'S DEBT ADJUSTMENT CASE; NOTICE OF TIME FIXED. Except as otherwise provided in subdivision (d), a complaint to determine the dischargeability of a debt under § 523(c) shall be filed no later than 60 days after the first date set for the meeting of creditors under § 341(a). The court shall give all creditors no less than 30 days' notice of the time so fixed in the manner provided in Rule 2002. On motion of a party in interest, after hearing on notice, the court may for cause extend the time fixed under this subdivision. The motion shall be filed before the time has expired.

(d) TIME FOR FILING COMPLAINT UNDER § 523(a)(6) IN A CHAPTER 13 INDIVIDUAL'S DEBT ADJUSTMENT CASE; NOTICE OF TIME FIXED. On motion by a debtor for a discharge under § 1328(b), the court shall enter an order fixing the time to file a complaint to determine the dischargeability of any debt under § 523(a)(6) and shall give no less than 30 days' notice of the time fixed to all creditors in the manner provided in Rule 2002. On motion of any party in interest, after hearing on notice, the court may for cause extend the time fixed under this subdivision. The motion shall be filed before the time has expired.

(e) APPLICABILITY OF RULES IN PART VII. A proceeding commenced by a complaint filed under this rule is governed by Part VII of these rules.

Rule 4008. Filing of Reaffirmation Agreement; Statement in Support of Reaffirmation Agreement

(a) FILING OF REAFFIRMATION AGREEMENT. A reaffirmation agreement shall be filed no later than 60 days after the first date set for the meeting of creditors under § 341(a) of the Code. The reaffirmation agreement shall be accompanied by a cover sheet, prepared as prescribed by the appropriate Official Form. The court may, at any time and in its discretion, enlarge the time to file a reaffirmation agreement.

(b) STATEMENT IN SUPPORT OF REAFFIRMATION AGREEMENT. The debtor's statement required under § 524(k)(6)(A) of the Code shall be accompanied by a statement of the total income and expenses stated on schedules I and J. If there is a difference between the total income and expenses stated on those schedules and the statement required under § 524(k)(6)(A), the statement required by this subdivision shall include an explanation of the difference.

PART V
COURTS AND CLERKS

Rule 5001. Courts and Clerks' Offices

(a) COURTS ALWAYS OPEN. The courts shall be deemed always open for the purpose of filing any pleading or other proper paper, issuing and returning process, and filing, making, or entering motions, orders and rules.

(b) TRIALS AND HEARINGS; ORDERS IN CHAMBERS. All trials and hearings shall be conducted in open court and so far as convenient in a regular court room. Except as otherwise provided in 28 U.S.C. § 152(c), all other acts or proceedings may be done or conducted by a judge in chambers and at any place either within or without the district; but no hearing, other than one ex parte, shall be conducted outside the district without the consent of all parties affected thereby.

(c) CLERK'S OFFICE. The clerk's office with the clerk or a deputy in attendance shall be open during business hours on all days except Saturdays, Sundays and the legal holidays listed in Rule 9006(a).

Rule 5002. Restrictions on Approval of Appointments

(a) APPROVAL OF APPOINTMENT OF RELATIVES PROHIBITED. The appointment of an individual as a trustee or examiner pursuant to Section 1104 of the Code shall not be approved by the court if the individual is a relative of the bankruptcy judge approving the appointment or the United States trustee in the region in which the case is pending. The employment of an individual as attorney, accountant, appraiser, auctioneer, or other professional person pursuant to Sections 327, 1103, or 1114 shall not be approved by the court if the individual is a relative of the bankruptcy judge approving the employment. The employment of an individual as attorney, accountant, appraiser, auctioneer, or other professional person pursuant to Sections 327, 1103, or 1114 may be approved by the court if the individual is a relative of the United States trustee in the region in which the case is pending, unless the court finds that the relationship with the United States trustee renders the employment improper under the circumstances of the case. Whenever under this subdivision an individual may not be approved for appointment or employment, the individual's firm, partnership, corporation, or any other form of business association or relationship, and all members, associates and professional employees thereof also may not be approved for appointment or employment.

(b) JUDICIAL DETERMINATION THAT APPROVAL OF APPOINTMENT OR EMPLOYMENT IS IMPROPER. A bankruptcy judge may not approve the appointment of a person as a trustee or examiner pursuant to Section 1104 of the Code or approve the employment of a person as an attorney, accountant, appraiser, auctioneer, or other professional person pursuant to Sections 327, 1103, or 1114 of the Code if that person is or has been so connected with such judge or the United States trustee as to render the appointment or employment improper.

Rule 5003. Records Kept By the Clerk

(a) BANKRUPTCY DOCKETS. The clerk shall keep a docket in each case under the Code and shall enter thereon each judgment, order, and activity in that case as prescribed by the Director of the Administrative Office of the United States Courts. The entry of a judgment or order in a docket shall show the date the entry is made.

(b) CLAIMS REGISTER. The clerk shall keep in a claims register a list of claims filed in a case when it appears that there will be a distribution to unsecured creditors.

(c) JUDGMENTS AND ORDERS. The clerk shall keep, in the form and manner as the Director of the Administrative Office of the United States Courts may prescribe, a correct copy of every final judgment or order affecting title to or lien on real property or for the recovery of money or property, and any other order which the court may direct to be kept. On request of the prevailing party, a correct copy of every judgment or order affecting title to or lien upon real or personal property or for the recovery of money or property shall be kept and indexed with the civil judgments of the district court.

(d) INDEX OF CASES; CERTIFICATE OF SEARCH. The clerk shall keep indices of all cases and adversary proceedings as prescribed by the Director of the Administrative Office of the United States Courts. On request, the clerk shall make a search of any index and papers in the clerk's custody and certify whether a case or proceeding has been filed in or transferred to the court or if a discharge has been entered in its records.

(e) REGISTER OF MAILING ADDRESSES OF FEDERAL AND STATE GOVERNMENTAL UNITS AND CERTAIN TAXING AUTHORITIES. The United States or the state or territory in which the court is located may file a statement designating its mailing address. The United States, state, territory, or local governmental unit responsible for collecting taxes within the district in which the case is pending may also file a statement designating an address for service of requests under § 505(b) of the Code, and the designation shall describe where further information concerning additional requirements for filing such requests may be found. The clerk shall keep, in the form and manner as the Director of the Administrative Office of the United States Courts may prescribe, a register that includes the mailing addresses designated under the first sentence of this subdivision, and a separate register of the addresses designated for the service of requests under § 505(b) of the Code. The clerk is not required to include in any single register more than one mailing address for each department, agency, or instrumentality of the United States or the state or territory. If more than one address for a department, agency, or instrumentality is included in the register, the clerk shall also include information that would enable a user of the register to determine the circumstances when each address is applicable, and mailing notice to only one applicable address is sufficient to provide effective notice. The clerk shall update the register annually, effective January 2 of each year. The mailing address in the register is conclusively presumed to be a proper address for the governmental unit, but the failure to use that mailing address does not invalidate any notice that is otherwise effective under applicable law.

(f) OTHER BOOKS AND RECORDS OF THE CLERK. The clerk shall keep any other books and records required by the Director of the Administrative Office of the United States Courts.

Rule 5004. Disqualification

(a) DISQUALIFICATION OF JUDGE. A bankruptcy judge shall be governed by 28 U. S. C. Section 455, and disqualified from presiding over the proceeding or contested matter in which the disqualifying circumstance arises or, if appropriate, shall be disqualified from presiding over the case.

(b) DISQUALIFICATION OF JUDGE FROM ALLOWING COMPENSATION. A bankruptcy judge shall be disqualified from allowing compensation to a person who is a relative of the bankruptcy judge or with whom the judge is so connected as to render it improper for the judge to authorize such compensation.

Rule 5005. Filing and Transmittal of Papers

(a) FILING.

(1) Place of Filing. The lists, schedules, statements, proofs of claim or interest, complaints, motions, applications, objections and other papers required to be filed by these rules, except as provided in 28 U.S.C. § 1409, shall be filed with the clerk in the district where the case under the Code is pending. The judge of that court may permit the papers to be filed with the judge, in which event the filing date shall be noted thereon, and they shall be forthwith transmitted to the clerk. The clerk shall not refuse to accept for filing any petition or other paper presented for the purpose of filing solely because it is not presented in proper form as required by these rules or any local rules or practices.

(2) Electronic filing and signing

(A) By a Represented Entity--Generally Required; Exceptions. An entity represented by an attorney shall file electronically, unless nonelectronic filing is allowed by the court for good cause or is allowed or required by local rule.

(B) By an Unrepresented Individual--When Allowed or Required. An individual not represented by an attorney:

(i) may file electronically only if allowed by court order or by local rule; and

(ii) may be required to file electronically only by court order, or by a local rule that includes reasonable exceptions.

(C) Signing. A filing made through a person's electronic-filing account and authorized by that person, together with that person's name on a signature block, constitutes the person's signature.

(D) Same as a Written Paper. A paper filed electronically is a written paper for purposes of these rules, the Federal Rules of Civil Procedure made applicable by these rules, and § 107 of the Code

(b) TRANSMITTAL TO THE UNITED STATES TRUSTEE.

(1) The complaints, notices, motions, applications, objections and other papers required to be transmitted to the United States trustee may be sent by filing with the court's electronic-filing system in accordance with Rule 9036, unless a court order or local rule provides otherwise.

(2) The entity, other than the clerk, transmitting a paper to the United States trustee other than through the court's electronic-filing system shall promptly file as proof of such transmittal a statement identifying the paper and stating the manner by which and the date on which it was transmitted to the United States trustee.

(3) Nothing in these rules shall require the clerk to transmit any paper to the United States trustee if the United States trustee requests in writing that the paper not be transmitted.

(c) ERROR IN FILING OR TRANSMITTAL. A paper intended to be filed with the clerk but erroneously delivered to the United States trustee, the trustee, the attorney for the trustee, a bankruptcy judge, a district judge, the clerk of the bankruptcy appellate panel, or the clerk of the district court shall, after the date of its receipt has been noted thereon, be transmitted forthwith to the clerk of the bankruptcy court. A paper intended to be transmitted to the United States trustee but erroneously delivered to the clerk, the trustee, the attorney for the trustee, a bankruptcy judge, a district judge, the clerk of the bankruptcy appellate panel, or the clerk of the district court shall, after the date of its receipt has been noted thereon, be transmitted forthwith to the United States trustee. In the interest of justice, the court may order that a paper erroneously delivered shall be deemed filed with the clerk or transmitted to the United States trustee as of the date of its original delivery.

Rule 5006. Certification of Copies of Papers

The clerk shall issue a certified copy of the record of any proceeding in a case under the Code or of any paper filed with the clerk on payment of any prescribed fee.

Rule 5007. Record of Proceedings and Transcripts

(a) FILING OF RECORD OR TRANSCRIPT. The reporter or operator of a recording device shall certify the original notes of testimony, tape recording, or other original record of the proceeding and promptly file them with the clerk. The person preparing any transcript shall promptly file a certified copy.

(b) TRANSCRIPT FEES. The fees for copies of transcripts shall be charged at rates prescribed by the Judicial Conference of the United States. No fee may be charged for the certified copy filed with the clerk.

(c) ADMISSIBILITY OF RECORD IN EVIDENCE. A certified sound recording or a transcript of a proceeding shall be admissible as prima facie evidence to establish the record.

Rule 5008. Notice Regarding Presumption of Abuse in Chapter 7 Cases of Individual Debtors

If a presumption of abuse has arisen under § 707(b) in a chapter 7 case of an individual with primarily consumer debts, the clerk shall within 10 days after the date of the filing of the petition notify creditors of the presumption of abuse in accordance with Rule 2002. If the debtor has not filed a statement indicating whether a presumption of abuse has arisen, the clerk shall within 10 days after the date of the filing of the petition notify creditors that the debtor has not filed the statement and that further notice will be given if a later filed statement indicates that a presumption of abuse has arisen. If a debtor later files a statement indicating that a presumption of abuse has arisen, the clerk shall notify creditors of the presumption of abuse as promptly as practicable.

Rule 5009. Closing Chapter 7, Chapter 12, Chapter 13, and Chapter 15 Cases; Order Declaring Lien Satisfied

(a) CLOSING OF CASES UNDER CHAPTERS 7, 12, AND 13. If in a chapter 7, chapter 12, or chapter 13 case the trustee has filed a final report and final account and has certified that the estate has been fully administered, and if within 30 days no objection has been filed by the United States trustee or a party in interest, there shall be a presumption that the estate has been fully administered.

(b) NOTICE OF FAILURE TO FILE RULE 1007(b)(7) STATEMENT. If an individual debtor in a chapter 7 or 13 case is required to file a statement under Rule 1007(b)(7) and fails to do so within 45 days after the first date set for the meeting of creditors under § 341(a) of the Code, the clerk shall promptly notify the debtor that the case will be closed without entry of a discharge unless the required statement is filed within the applicable time limit under Rule 1007(c).

(c) CASES UNDER CHAPTER 15. A foreign representative in a proceeding recognized under § 1517 of the Code shall file a final report when the purpose of the representative's appearance in the court is completed. The report shall describe the nature and results of the representative's activities in the court. The foreign representative shall transmit the report to the United States trustee, and give notice of its filing to the debtor, all persons or bodies authorized to administer foreign proceedings of the debtor, all parties to litigation pending in the United States in which the debtor was a party at the time of the filing of the petition, and such other entities as the court may direct. The foreign representative shall file a certificate with the court that notice has been given. If no objection has been filed by the United States trustee or a party in interest within 30 days after the certificate is filed, there shall be a presumption that the case has been fully administered.

(d) ORDER DECLARING LIEN SATISFIED. In a chapter 12 or chapter

13 case, if a claim that was secured by property of the estate is subject to a lien under applicable nonbankruptcy law, the debtor may request entry of an order declaring that the secured claim has been satisfied and the lien has been released under the terms of a confirmed plan. The request shall be made by motion and shall be served on the holder of the claim and any other entity the court designates in the manner provided by Rule 7004 for service of a summons and complaint.

Rule 5010. Reopening Cases

A case may be reopened on motion of the debtor or other party in interest pursuant to Section 350(b) of the Code. In a chapter 7, 12, or 13 case a trustee shall not be appointed by the United States trustee unless the court determines that a trustee is necessary to protect the interests of creditors and the debtor or to insure efficient administration of the case.

Rule 5011. Withdrawal and Abstention from Hearing a Proceeding

(a) WITHDRAWAL. A motion for withdrawal of a case or proceeding shall be heard by a district judge.

(b) ABSTENTION FROM HEARING A PROCEEDING. A motion for abstention pursuant to 28 U. S. C. Section 1334(c) shall be governed by Rule 9014 and shall be served on the parties to the proceeding.

(c) EFFECT OF FILING OF MOTION FOR WITHDRAWAL OR ABSTENTION. The filing of a motion for withdrawal of a case or proceeding or for abstention pursuant to 28 U. S. C. Section 1334(c) shall not stay the administration of the case or any proceeding therein before the bankruptcy judge except that the bankruptcy judge may stay, on such terms and conditions as are proper, proceedings pending disposition of the motion. A motion for a stay ordinarily shall be presented first to the bankruptcy judge. A motion for a stay or relief from a stay filed in the district court shall state why it has not been presented to or obtained from the bankruptcy judge. Relief granted by the district judge shall be on such terms and conditions as the judge deems proper.

Rule 5012. Agreements Concerning Coordination of Proceedings in Chapter 15 Cases

Approval of an agreement under § 1527(4) of the Code shall be sought by motion. The movant shall attach to the motion a copy of the proposed agreement or protocol and, unless the court directs otherwise, give at least 30 days' notice of any hearing on the motion by transmitting the motion to the United States trustee, and serving it on the debtor, all persons or bodies authorized to administer foreign proceedings of the debtor, all entities against whom provisional relief is being sought under § 1519, all parties to litigation pending in the United States in which the debtor was a party at the time of the filing of the petition, and such other entities as the court may direct.

PART VI

COLLECTION AND LIQUIDATION OF THE ESTATE

Rule 6001. Burden of Proof As to Validity of Postpetition Transfer

Any entity asserting the validity of a transfer under Section 549 of the Code shall have the burden of proof.

Rule 6002. Accounting by Prior Custodian of Property of the Estate

(a) ACCOUNTING REQUIRED. Any custodian required by the Code to deliver property in the custodian's possession or control to the trustee shall promptly file and transmit to the United States trustee a report and account with respect to the property of the estate and the administration thereof.

(b) EXAMINATION OF ADMINISTRATION. On the filing and transmittal of the report and account required by subdivision (a) of this rule and after an examination has been made into the superseded administration, after notice and a hearing, the court shall determine the propriety of the administration, including the reasonableness of all disbursements.

Rule 6003. Interim and Final Relief Immediately Following the Commencement of the Case – Applications for Employment; Motions for Use, Sale, or Lease of Property; and Motions for Assumption or Assignment of Executory Contracts

Except to the extent that relief is necessary to avoid immediate and irreparable harm, the court shall not, within 21 days after the filing of the petition, issue an order granting the following:

(a) an application under Rule 2014;

(b) a motion to use, sell, lease, or otherwise incur an obligation regarding property of the estate, including a motion to pay all or part of a claim that arose before the filing of the petition, but not a motion under Rule 4001; or

(c) a motion to assume or assign an executory contract or unexpired lease in accordance with § 365.

Rule 6004. Use, Sale, or Lease of Property

(a) NOTICE OF PROPOSED USE, SALE, OR LEASE OF PROPERTY. Notice of a proposed use, sale, or lease of property, other than cash collateral, not in the ordinary course of business shall be given pursuant to Rule 2002(a)(2), (c)(1), (i), and (k) and, if applicable, in accordance with Section 363(b)(2) of the Code.

(b) OBJECTION TO PROPOSAL. Except as provided in subdivisions (c) and (d) of this rule, an objection to a proposed use, sale, or lease of property shall be filed and served not less than seven days before the date set for the proposed action or within the time fixed by the court. An objection to the proposed use, sale, or lease of property is governed by Rule 9014.

(c) SALE FREE AND CLEAR OF LIENS AND OTHER INTERESTS. A motion for authority to sell property free and clear of liens or other interests shall be made in accordance with Rule 9014 and shall be served on the parties who have liens or other interests in the property to be sold. The notice required by subdivision (a) of this rule shall include the date of the hearing on the motion and the time within which objections may be filed and served on the debtor in possession or trustee.

(d) SALE OF PROPERTY UNDER $2,500. Notwithstanding subdivision (a) of this rule, when all of the nonexempt property of the estate has an aggregate gross value less than $2,500, it shall be sufficient to give a general notice of intent to sell such property other than in the ordinary course of business to all creditors, indenture trustees, committees appointed or elected pursuant to the Code, the United States trustee and other persons as the court may direct. An objection to any such sale may be filed and served by a party in interest within 14 days of the mailing of the notice, or within the time fixed by the court. An objection is governed by Rule 9014.

(e) HEARING. If a timely objection is made pursuant to subdivision (b) or (d) of this rule, the date of the hearing thereon may be set in the notice given pursuant to subdivision (a) of this rule.

(f) CONDUCT OF SALE NOT IN THE ORDINARY COURSE OF BUSINESS.

(1) Public or Private Sale. All sales not in the ordinary course of business may be by private sale or by public auction. Unless it is impracticable, an itemized statement of the property sold, the name of each purchaser, and the price received for each item or lot or for the property as a whole if sold in bulk shall be filed on completion of a sale. If the property is sold by an auctioneer, the auctioneer shall file the statement, transmit a copy thereof to the United States trustee, and furnish a copy to the trustee, debtor in possession, or chapter 13 debtor. If the property is not sold by an auctioneer, the trustee, debtor in possession, or chapter 13 debtor shall file the statement and transmit a copy thereof to the United States trustee.

(2) Execution of Instruments. After a sale in accordance with this rule the debtor, the trustee, or debtor in possession, as the case may be, shall execute any instrument necessary or ordered by the court to effectuate the transfer to the purchaser.

(g) SALE OF PERSONALLY IDENTIFIABLE INFORMATION.

(1) Motion. A motion for authority to sell or lease personally identifiable information under § 363(b)(1)(B) shall include a request for an order directing the United States trustee to appoint a consumer privacy ombudsman under § 332. Rule 9014 governs the motion which shall be served on: any committee elected under § 705 or appointed under § 1102 of the Code, or if the case is a chapter 11 reorganization case and no committee of unsecured creditors has been appointed under § 1102, on the creditors included on the list of creditors filed under Rule 1007(d); and on such other entities as the court may direct. The motion shall be transmitted to the United States trustee.

(2) Appointment. If a consumer privacy ombudsman is appointed under § 332, no later than seven days before the hearing on the motion under § 363(b)(1)(B), the United States trustee shall file a notice of the appointment, including the name and address of the person appointed. The United States trustee's notice shall be accompanied by a verified statement of the person

appointed setting forth the person's connections with the debtor, creditors, any other party in interest, their respective attorneys and accountants, the United States trustee, or any person employed in the office of the United States trustee.

(h) STAY OF ORDER AUTHORIZING USE, SALE, OR LEASE OF PROPERTY. An order authorizing the use, sale, or lease of property other than cash collateral is stayed until the expiration of 14 days after entry of the order, unless the court orders otherwise.

Rule 6005. Appraisers and Auctioneers

The order of the court approving the employment of an appraiser or auctioneer shall fix the amount or rate of compensation. No officer or employee of the Judicial Branch of the United States or the United States Department of Justice shall be eligible to act as appraiser or auctioneer. No residence or licensing requirement shall disqualify an appraiser or auctioneer from employment.

Rule 6006. Assumption, Rejection or Assignment of an Executory Contract or Unexpired Lease

(a) PROCEEDING TO ASSUME, REJECT OR ASSIGN. A proceeding to assume, reject, or assign an executory contract or unexpired lease, other than as part of a plan, is governed by Rule 9014.

(b) PROCEEDING TO REQUIRE TRUSTEE TO ACT. A proceeding by a party to an executory contract or unexpired lease in a chapter 9 municipality case, chapter 11 reorganization case, chapter 12 family farmer's debt adjustment case, or chapter 13 individual's debt adjustment case, to require the trustee, debtor in possession, or debtor to determine whether to assume or reject the contract or lease is governed by Rule 9014.

(c) NOTICE. Notice of a motion made pursuant to subdivision (a) or (b) of this rule shall be given to the other party to the contract or lease, to other parties in interest as the court may direct, and, except in a chapter 9 municipality case, to the United States trustee.

(d) STAY OF ORDER AUTHORIZING ASSIGNMENT. An order authorizing the trustee to assign an executory contract or unexpired lease under §365(f) is stayed until the expiration of 14 days after the entry of the order, unless the court orders otherwise.

(e) LIMITATIONS. The trustee shall not seek authority to assume or assign multiple executory contracts or unexpired leases in one motion unless: (1) all executory contracts or unexpired leases to be assumed or assigned are between the same parties or are to be assigned to the same assignee; (2) the trustee seeks to assume, but not assign to more than one assignee, unexpired leases of real property; or (3) the court otherwise authorizes the motion to be filed. Subject to subdivision (f), the trustee may join requests for authority to reject multiple executory contracts or unexpired leases in one motion.

(f) OMNIBUS MOTIONS. A motion to reject or, if permitted under subdivision (e), a motion to assume or assign multiple executory contracts or unexpired leases that are not between the same parties shall:

(1) state in a conspicuous place that parties receiving the omnibus motion should locate their names and their contracts or leases listed in the motion;

(2) list parties alphabetically and identify the corresponding contract or lease;

(3) specify the terms, including the curing of defaults, for each requested assumption or assignment;

(4) specify the terms, including the identity of each assignee and the adequate assurance of future performance by each assignee, for each requested assignment;

(5) be numbered consecutively with other omnibus motions to assume, assign, or reject executory contracts or unexpired leases; and

(6) be limited to no more than 100 executory contracts or unexpired leases.

(g) FINALITY OF DETERMINATION. The finality of any order respecting an executory contract or unexpired lease included in an omnibus motion shall be determined as though such contract or lease had been the subject of a separate motion.

Rule 6007. Abandonment or Disposition of Property

(a) NOTICE OF PROPOSED ABANDONMENT OR DISPOSITION; OBJECTIONS; HEARING. Unless otherwise directed by the court, the trustee or debtor in possession shall give notice of a proposed abandonment or disposition of property to the United States trustee, all creditors, indenture trustees, and committees elected pursuant to Section 705 or appointed pursuant to Section 1102 of the Code. A party in interest may file and serve an objection within 14 days of the mailing of the notice, or within the time fixed by the court. If a timely objection is made, the court shall set a hearing on notice to the United States trustee and to other entities as the court may direct.

(b) MOTION BY PARTY IN INTEREST. A party in interest may file and serve a motion requiring the trustee or debtor in possession to abandon property of the estate. Unless otherwise directed by the court, the party filing the motion shall serve the motion and any notice of the motion on the trustee or debtor in possession, the United States trustee, all creditors, indenture trustees, and committees elected pursuant to section 705 or appointed pursuant to section 1102 of this Code. A party in interest may file and serve an objection within 14 days of service, or within the time fixed by the court. If a timely objection is made, the court shall set a hearing on notice to the United States trustee and to other entities as the court may direct. If the court grants the motion, the order effects the trustee's or debtor in possession's abandonment without further notice, unless otherwise directed by the court.

Rule 6008. Redemption of Property from Lien or Sale

On motion by the debtor, trustee, or debtor in possession and after hearing on notice as the court may direct, the court may authorize the redemption of property from a lien or from a sale to enforce a lien in accordance with applicable law.

Rule 6009. Prosecution and Defense of Proceedings by Trustee or Debtor in Possession

With or without court approval, the trustee or debtor in possession may prosecute or may enter an appearance and defend any pending action or proceeding by or against the debtor, or commence and prosecute any action or proceeding in behalf of the estate before any tribunal.

Rule 6010. Proceeding to Avoid Indemnifying Lien or Transfer to Surety

If a lien voidable under Section 547 of the Code has been dissolved by the furnishing of a bond or other obligation and the surety thereon has been indemnified by the transfer of, or the creation of a lien upon, nonexempt property of the debtor, the surety shall be joined as a defendant in any proceeding to avoid the indemnifying transfer or lien. Such proceeding is governed by the rules in Part VII.

Rule 6011. Disposal of Patient Records in Health Care Business Case

(a) NOTICE BY PUBLICATION UNDER § 351(1)(A). A notice regarding the claiming or disposing of patient records under § 351(1)(A) shall not identify any patient by name or other identifying information, but shall:

(1) identify with particularity the health care facility whose patient records the trustee proposes to destroy;

(2) state the name, address, telephone number, email address, and website, if any, of a person from whom information about the patient records may be obtained;

(3) state how to claim the patient records; and

(4) state the date by which patient records must be claimed, and that if they are not so claimed the records will be destroyed.

(b) NOTICE BY MAIL UNDER § 351(1)(B). Subject to applicable nonbankruptcy law relating to patient privacy, a notice regarding the claiming or disposing of patient records under § 351(1)(B) shall, in addition to including the information in subdivision (a), direct that a patient's family member or other representative who receives the notice inform the patient of the notice. Any notice under this subdivision shall be mailed to the patient and any family member or other contact person whose name and address have been given to the trustee or the debtor for the purpose of providing information regarding the patient's health care, to the Attorney General of the State where the health care facility is located, and to any insurance company known to have provided health care insurance to the patient.

(c) PROOF OF COMPLIANCE WITH NOTICE REQUIREMENT. Unless the court orders the trustee to file proof of compliance with § 351(1)(B) under seal, the trustee shall not file, but shall maintain, the proof of compliance for a reasonable time.

(d) REPORT OF DESTRUCTION OF RECORDS. The trustee shall file, no later than 30 days after the destruction of patient records under § 351(3), a report certifying that the unclaimed records have been destroyed and explaining the method used to effect the destruction. The report shall not identify any patient by name or other identifying information.

PART VII
ADVERSARY PROCEEDINGS

Rule 7001. Scope of Rules of Part VII

An adversary proceeding is governed by the rules of this Part VII. The following are adversary proceedings:

(1) a proceeding to recover money or property, other than a proceeding to compel the debtor to deliver property to the trustee, or a proceeding under §554(b) or §725 of the Code, Rule 2017, or Rule 6002;

(2) a proceeding to determine the validity, priority, or extent of a lien or other interest in property, but not a proceeding under Rule 3012 or Rule 4003(d);

(3) a proceeding to obtain approval under §363(h) for the sale of both the interest of the estate and of a co-owner in property;

(4) a proceeding to object to or revoke a discharge, other than an objection to discharge under §§ 727(a)(8), (a)(9), or 1328(f);

(5) a proceeding to revoke an order of confirmation of a chapter 11, chapter 12, or chapter 13 plan;

(6) a proceeding to determine the dischargeability of a debt;

(7) a proceeding to obtain an injunction or other equitable relief, except when a chapter 9, chapter 11, chapter 12, or chapter 13 plan provides for the relief;

(8) a proceeding to subordinate any allowed claim or interest, except when a chapter 9, chapter 11, chapter 12, or chapter 13 plan provides for subordination;

(9) a proceeding to obtain a declaratory judgment relating to any of the foregoing; or

(10) a proceeding to determine a claim or cause of action removed under 28 U.S.C. §1452.

Rule 7002. References to Federal Rules of Civil Procedure

Whenever a Federal Rule of Civil Procedure applicable to adversary proceedings makes reference to another Federal Rule of Civil Procedure, the reference shall be read as a reference to the Federal Rule of Civil Procedure as modified in this Part VII.

Rule 7003. Commencement of Adversary Proceeding

Rule 3 F. R. Civ. P. applies in adversary proceedings.

Rule 7004. Process; Service of Summons, Complaint

(a) SUMMONS; SERVICE; PROOF OF SERVICE. (1) Except as provided in Rule 7004(a)(2), Rule 4(a), (b), (c)(1), (d)(5), (e)-(j), (l), and (m) F.R.Civ.P. applies in adversary proceedings. Personal service under Rule 4(e)-(j) F.R.Civ.P. may be made by any person at least 18 years of age who is not a party, and the summons may be delivered by the clerk to any such person.

(2) The clerk may sign, seal, and issue a summons electronically by putting an "s/" before the clerk's name and including the court's seal on the summons.

(b) Service by first class mail

Except as provided in subdivision (h), in addition to the methods of service authorized by Rule 4(e)-(j) F.R.Civ.P., service may be made within the United States by first class mail postage prepaid as follows:

(1) Upon an individual other than an infant or incompetent, by mailing a copy of the summons and complaint to the individual's dwelling house or usual place of abode or to the place where the individual regularly conducts a business or profession.

(2) Upon an infant or an incompetent person, by mailing a copy of the summons and complaint to the person upon whom process is prescribed to be served by the law of the state in which service is made when an action is brought against such a defendant in the courts of general jurisdiction of that state. The summons and complaint in that case shall be addressed to the person required to be served at that person's dwelling house or usual place of abode or at the place where the person regularly conducts a business or profession.

(3) Upon a domestic or foreign corporation or upon a partnership or other unincorporated association, by mailing a copy of the summons and complaint to the attention of an officer, a managing or general agent, or to any other agent authorized by appointment or by law to receive service of process and, if the agent is one authorized by statute to receive service and the statute so requires, by also mailing a copy to the defendant.

(4) Upon the United States, by mailing a copy of the summons and complaint addressed to the civil process clerk at the office of the United States attorney for the district in which the action is brought and by mailing a copy of the summons and complaint to the Attorney General of the United States at Washington, District of Columbia, and in any action attacking the validity of an order of an officer or an agency of the United States not made a party, by also mailing a copy of the summons and complaint to that officer or agency. The court shall allow a reasonable time for service pursuant to this subdivision for the purpose of curing the failure to mail a copy of the summons and complaint to multiple officers, agencies, or corporations of the United States if the plaintiff has mailed a copy of the summons and complaint either to the civil process clerk at the office of the United States attorney or to the Attorney General of the United States.

(5) Upon any officer or agency of the United States, by mailing a copy of the summons and complaint to the United States as prescribed in paragraph (4) of this subdivision and also to the officer or agency. If the agency is a corporation, the mailing shall be as prescribed in paragraph (3) of this subdivision of this rule. The court shall allow a reasonable time for service pursuant to this subdivision for the purpose of curing the failure to mail a copy of the summons and complaint to multiple officers, agencies, or corporations of the United States if the plaintiff has mailed a copy of the summons and complaint either to the civil process clerk at the office of the United States attorney or to the Attorney General of the United States. If the United States trustee is the trustee in the case and service is made upon the United States trustee solely as trustee, service may be made as prescribed in paragraph (10) of this subdivision of this rule.

(6) Upon a state or municipal corporation or other governmental organization thereof subject to suit, by mailing a copy of the summons and complaint to the person or office upon whom process is prescribed to be served by the law of the state in which service is made when an action is brought against such a defendant in the courts of general jurisdiction of that state, or in the absence of the designation of any such person or office by state law, then to the chief executive officer thereof.

(7) Upon a defendant of any class referred to in paragraph (1) or (3) of this subdivision of this rule, it is also sufficient if a copy of the summons and complaint is mailed to the entity upon whom service is prescribed to be served by any statute of the United States or by the law of the state in which service is made when an action is brought against such a defendant in the court of general jurisdiction of that state.

(8) Upon any defendant, it is also sufficient if a copy of the summons and complaint is mailed to an agent of such defendant authorized by appointment or by law to receive service of process, at the agent's dwelling house or usual place of abode or at the place where the agent regularly carries on a business or profession and, if the authorization so requires, by mailing also a copy of the summons and complaint to the defendant as provided in this subdivision.

(9) Upon the debtor, after a petition has been filed by or served upon the debtor and until the case is dismissed or closed, by mailing a copy of the summons and complaint to the debtor at the address shown in the petition or to such other address as the debtor may designate in a filed writing.

(10) Upon the United States trustee, when the United States trustee is the trustee in the case and service is made upon the United States trustee solely as trustee, by mailing a copy of the summons and complaint to an office of the United States trustee or another place designated by the United States trustee in the district where the case under the Code is pending.

(c) Service by publication

If a party to an adversary proceeding to determine or protect rights in property in the custody of the court cannot be served as provided in Rule 4(e)-(j) F.R.Civ.P. or subdivision (b) of this rule, the court may order the summons and complaint to be served by mailing copies thereof by first class mail, postage prepaid, to the party's last known address, and by at least one publication in such manner and form as the court may direct.

(d) Nationwide service of process

The summons and complaint and all other process except a subpoena may be served anywhere in the United States.

(e) Summons: time limit for service within the United States

Service made under Rule 4(e), (g), (h)(1), (i), or (j)(2) F.R.Civ.P. shall be by delivery of the summons and complaint within 7 days after the summons is issued. If service is by any authorized form of mail, the summons and complaint shall be deposited in the mail within 7 days after the summons is issued. If a summons is not timely delivered or mailed, another summons will be issued for service. This subdivision does not apply to service in a foreign country.

(f) Personal jurisdiction

If the exercise of jurisdiction is consistent with the Constitution and laws of the United States, serving a summons or filing a waiver of service in accordance with this rule or the subdivisions of Rule 4 F.R.Civ.P. made applicable by these rules is effective to establish personal jurisdiction over the person of any defendant with respect to a case under the Code or a civil proceeding arising under the Code, or arising in or related to a case under the Code.

(g) Service on debtor's attorney

If the debtor is represented by an attorney, whenever service is made upon the debtor under this Rule, service shall also be made upon the debtor's attorney by any means authorized under Rule 5(b) F.R.Civ.P.

(h) Service of process on an insured depository institution

Service on an insured depository institution (as defined in section 3 of the Federal Deposit Insurance Act) in a contested matter or adversary proceeding shall be made by certified mail addressed to an officer of the institution unless--

(1) the institution has appeared by its attorney, in which case the attorney shall be served by first class mail;

(2) the court orders otherwise after service upon the institution by certified mail of notice of an application to permit service on the institution by first class mail sent to an officer of the institution designated by the institution; or

(3) the institution has waived in writing its entitlement to service by certified mail by designating an officer to receive service.

(i) Service of process by title

This subdivision (i) applies to service on a domestic or foreign corporation or partnership or other unincorporated association under Rule 7004(b)(3) or on an officer of an insured depository institution under Rule 7004(h). The defendant's officer or agent need not be correctly named in the address--or even be named--if the envelope is addressed to the defendant's proper address and directed to the attention of the officer's or agent's position or title.

Rule 7005. Service and Filing of Pleadings and Other Papers

Rule 5 F. R. Civ. P. applies in adversary proceedings.

Rule 7007. Pleadings Allowed

Rule 7 F. R. Civ. P. applies in adversary proceedings.

Rule 7007.1. Corporate Ownership Statement

(a) REQUIRED DISCLOSURE. Any corporation that is a party to an adversary proceeding, other than the debtor or a governmental unit, shall file two copies of a statement that identifies any corporation, other than a governmental unit, that directly or indirectly owns 10% or more of any class of the corporation's equity interests, or states that there are no entities to report under this subdivision.

(b) TIME FOR FILING. A party shall file the statement required under Rule 7007.1(a) with its first appearance, pleading, motion, response, or other request addressed to the court. A party shall file a supplemental statement promptly upon any change in circumstances that this rule requires the party to identify or disclose.

Rule 7008. General Rules of Pleading

Rule 8 F.R.Civ.P. applies in adversary proceedings. The allegation of jurisdiction required by Rule 8(a) shall also contain a reference to the name, number, and chapter of the case under the Code to which the adversary proceeding relates and to the district and division where the case under the Code is pending. In an adversary proceeding before a bankruptcy court, the complaint, counterclaim, cross-claim, or third-party complaint shall contain a statement that the pleader does or does not consent to entry of final orders or judgment by the bankruptcy court.

Rule 7009. Pleading Special Matters

Rule 9 F. R. Civ. P. applies in adversary proceedings.

Rule 7010. Form of Pleadings

Rule 10 F. R. Civ. P. applies in adversary proceedings, except that the caption of each pleading in such a proceeding shall conform substantially to the appropriate Official Form.

Rule 7012. Defenses and Objections — When and How Presented — By Pleading or Motion — Motion for Judgment on the Pleadings

(a) WHEN PRESENTED. If a complaint is duly served, the defendant shall serve an answer within 30 days after the issuance of the summons, except when a different time is prescribed by the court. The court shall prescribe the time for service of the answer when service of a complaint is made by publication or upon a party in a foreign country. A party served with a pleading stating a cross-claim shall serve an answer thereto within 21 days after service. The plaintiff shall serve a reply to a counterclaim in the answer within 21 days after service of the answer or, if a reply is ordered by the court, within 21 days after service of the order, unless the order otherwise directs. The United States or an officer or agency thereof shall serve an answer to a complaint within 35 days after the issuance of the summons, and shall serve an answer to a cross-claim, or a reply to a counterclaim, within 35 days after service upon the United States attorney of the pleading in which the claim is asserted. The service of a motion permitted under this rule alters these periods of time as follows, unless a different time is fixed by order of the court: (1) if the court denies the motion or postpones its disposition until the trial on the merits, the responsive pleading shall be served within 14 days after notice of the court's action; (2) if the court grants a motion for a more definite statement, the responsive pleading shall be served within 14 days after the service of a more definite statement.

(b) APPLICABILITY OF RULE 12(b)-(i) F.R.CIV.P. Rule 12(b)-(i) F.R.Civ.P. applies in adversary proceedings. A responsive pleading shall include a statement that the party does or does not consent to entry of final orders or judgment by the bankruptcy court.

Rule 7013. Counterclaim and Cross-Claim

Rule 13 F. R. Civ. P. applies in adversary proceedings, except that a party sued by a trustee or debtor in possession need not state as a counterclaim any claim that the party has against the debtor, the debtor's property, or the estate, unless the claim arose after the entry of an order for relief. A trustee or debtor in possession who fails to plead a counterclaim through oversight, inadvertence, or excusable neglect, or when justice so requires, may by leave of court amend the pleading, or commence a new adversary proceeding or separate action.

Rule 7014. Third-Party Practice

Rule 14 F. R. Civ. P. applies in adversary proceedings.

Rule 7015. Amended and Supplemental Pleadings

Rule 15 F. R. Civ. P. applies in adversary proceedings.

Rule 7016. Pre-Trial Procedure; Formulating Issues

Rule 16 F. R. Civ. P. applies in adversary proceedings.

Rule 7017. Parties Plaintiff and Defendant; Capacity

Rule 17 F. R. Civ. P. applies in adversary proceedings, except as provided in Rule 2010(b).

Rule 7018. Joinder of Claims and Remedies

Rule 18 F. R. Civ. P. applies in adversary proceedings.

Rule 7019. Joinder of Persons Needed for Just Determination

Rule 19 F. R. Civ. P. applies in adversary proceedings, except that (1) if an entity joined as a party raises the defense that the court lacks jurisdiction over the subject matter and the defense is sustained, the court shall dismiss such entity from the adversary proceeding and (2) if an entity joined as a party properly and timely raises the defense of improper venue, the court shall determine, as provided in 28 U. S. C. Section 1412, whether that part of the proceeding involving the joined party shall be transferred to another district, or whether the entire adversary proceeding shall be transferred to another district.

Rule 7020. Permissive Joinder of Parties

Rule 20 F. R. Civ. P. applies in adversary proceedings.

Rule 7021. Misjoinder and Non-Joinder of Parties

Rule 21 F. R. Civ. P. applies in adversary proceedings.

Rule 7022. Interpleader

Rule 22(a) F.R.Civ.P. applies in adversary proceedings. This rule supplements – and does not limit – the joinder of parties allowed by Rule 7020.

Rule 7023. Class Proceedings

Rule 23 F. R. Civ. P. applies in adversary proceedings.

Rule 7023.1. Derivative Actions

Rule 23.1 F. R. Civ. P. applies in adversary proceedings.

Rule 7023.2. Adversary Proceedings Relating to Unincorporated Associations

Rule 23.2 F. R. Civ. P. applies in adversary proceedings.

Rule 7024. Intervention

Rule 24 F. R. Civ. P. applies in adversary proceedings.

Rule 7025. Substitution of Parties

Subject to the provisions of Rule 2012, Rule 25 F. R. Civ. P. applies in adversary proceedings.

Rule 7026. General Provisions Governing Discovery

Rule 26 F. R. Civ. P. applies in adversary proceedings.

Rule 7027. Depositions Before Adversary Proceedings or Pending Appeal

Rule 27 F. R. Civ. P. applies in adversary proceedings.

Rule 7028. Persons Before Whom Depositions May Be Taken

Rule 28 F. R. Civ. P. applies in adversary proceedings.

Rule 7029. Stipulations Regarding Discovery Procedure

Rule 29 F. R. Civ. P. applies in adversary proceedings.

Rule 7030. Depositions Upon Oral Examination

Rule 30 F. R. Civ. P. applies in adversary proceedings.

Rule 7031. Deposition Upon Written Questions

Rule 31 F. R. Civ. P. applies in adversary proceedings.

Rule 7032. Use of Depositions in Adversary Proceedings

Rule 32 F. R. Civ. P. applies in adversary proceedings.

Rule 7033. Interrogatories to Parties

Rule 33 F. R. Civ. P. applies in adversary proceedings.

Rule 7034. Production of Documents and Things and Entry Upon Land for Inspection and Other Purposes

Rule 34 F. R. Civ. P. applies in adversary proceedings.

Rule 7035. Physical and Mental Examination of Persons

Rule 35 F. R. Civ. P. applies in adversary proceedings.

Rule 7036. Requests for Admission

Rule 36 F. R. Civ. P. applies in adversary proceedings.

Rule 7037. Failure to Make Discovery: Sanctions

Rule 37 F. R. Civ. P. applies in adversary proceedings.

Rule 7040. Assignment of Cases for Trial

Rule 40 F. R. Civ. P. applies in adversary proceedings.

Rule 7041. Dismissal of Adversary Proceedings

Rule 41 F. R. Civ. P. applies in adversary proceedings, except that a complaint objecting to the debtor's discharge shall not be dismissed at the plaintiff's instance without notice to the trustee, the United States trustee, and such other persons as the court may direct, and only on order of the court containing terms and conditions which the court deems proper.

Rule 7042. Consolidation of Adversary Proceedings; Separate Trials

Rule 42 F. R. Civ. P. applies in adversary proceedings.

Rule 7052. Findings by the Court

Rule 52 F. R. Civ. P. applies in adversary proceedings, except that any motion under subdivision (b) of that rule for amended or additional findings shall be filed no later than 14 days after entry of judgment. In these proceedings, the reference in Rule 52 F.R. Civ. P. to the entry of judgment under Rule 58 F.R. Civ. P. shall be read as a reference to the entry of a judgment or order under Rule 5003(a).

Rule 7054. Judgments; Costs

(a) JUDGMENTS. Rule 54(a)-(c) F.R.Civ.P. applies in adversary proceedings.

(b) COSTS; ATTORNEY FEES.

(1) Costs Other Than Attorney's Fees. The court may allow costs to the prevailing party except when a statute of the United States or these rules otherwise provides. Costs against the United States, its officers and agencies shall be imposed only to the extent permitted by law. Costs may be taxed by the clerk on 14 days' notice; on motion served within seven days thereafter, the action of the clerk may be reviewed by the court.

(2) Attorney's Fees.

(A) Rule 54(d)(2)(A)-(C) and (E) F.R.Civ.P. applies in adversary proceedings except for the reference in Rule 54(d)(2)(C) to Rule 78.

(B) By local rule, the court may establish special procedures to resolve fee-related issues without extensive evidentiary hearings.

Rule 7055. Default

Rule 55 F. R. Civ. P. applies in adversary proceedings.

Rule 7056. Summary Judgment

Rule 56 F. R. Civ. P. applies in adversary proceedings.

Rule 7058. Entering Judgment in Adversary Proceeding

Rule 58 F.R. Civ. P. applies in adversary proceedings. In these proceedings, the reference in Rule 58 F.R. Civ. P. to the civil docket shall be read as a reference to the docket maintained by the clerk under Rule 5003(a).

Rule 7062. Stay of Proceedings to Enforce a Judgment

Rule 62 F. R. Civ. P. applies in adversary proceedings, except that proceedings to enforce a judgment are stayed for 14 days after its entry..

Rule 7064. Seizure of Person or Property

Rule 64 F. R. Civ. P. applies in adversary proceedings.

Rule 7065. Injunctions

Rule 65 F. R. Civ. P. applies in adversary proceedings, except that a temporary restraining order or preliminary injunction may be issued on application of a debtor, trustee, or debtor in possession without compliance with Rule 65(c).

Rule 7067. Deposit in Court

Rule 67 F. R. Civ. P. applies in adversary proceedings.

Rule 7068. Offer of Judgment

Rule 68 F. R. Civ. P. applies in adversary proceedings.

Rule 7069. Execution

Rule 69 F. R. Civ. P. applies in adversary proceedings.

Rule 7070. Judgment for Specific Acts; Vesting Title

Rule 70 F. R. Civ. P. applies in adversary proceedings and the court may enter a judgment divesting the title of any party and vesting title in others whenever the real or personal property involved is within the jurisdiction of the court.

Rule 7071. Process in Behalf of and Against Persons Not Parties

Rule 71 F. R. Civ. P. applies in adversary proceedings.

Rule 7087. Transfer of Adversary Proceeding

On motion and after a hearing, the court may transfer an adversary proceeding or any part thereof to another district pursuant to 28 U. S. C. Section 1412, except as provided in Rule 7019(2).

PART VIII

APPEALS TO DISTRICT COURT OR BANKRUPTCY APPELLATE PANEL

Rule 8001. Scope of Part VIII Rules; Definition of "BAP"; Method of Transmission

(a) GENERAL SCOPE. These Part VIII rules govern the procedure in a United States district court and a bankruptcy appellate panel on appeal from a judgment, order, or decree of a bankruptcy court. They also govern certain procedures on appeal to a United States court of appeals under 28 U.S.C. § 158(d).

(b) DEFINITION OF "BAP." "BAP" means a bankruptcy appellate panel established by a circuit's judicial council and authorized to hear appeals from a bankruptcy court under 28 U.S.C. § 158.

(c) METHOD OF TRANSMITTING DOCUMENTS. A document must be sent electronically under these Part VIII rules, unless it is being sent by or to an individual who is not represented by counsel or the court's governing rules permit or require mailing or other means of delivery.

Rule 8002. Time for Filing Notice of Appeal

(a) IN GENERAL.

(1) Fourteen-Day Period. Except as provided in subdivisions (b) and (c), a notice of appeal must be filed with the bankruptcy clerk within 14 days after entry of the judgment, order, or decree being appealed.

(2) Filing before the entry of judgment

A notice of appeal filed after the bankruptcy court announces a decision or order--but before entry of the judgment, order, or decree--is treated as filed on the date of and after the entry.

(3) Multiple appeals

If one party files a timely notice of appeal, any other party may file a notice of appeal within 14 days after the date when the first notice was filed, or within the time otherwise allowed by this rule, whichever period ends later.

(4) Mistaken filing in another court

If a notice of appeal is mistakenly filed in a district court, BAP, or court of appeals, the clerk of that court must state on the notice the date on which it was received and transmit it to the bankruptcy clerk. The notice of appeal is then considered filed in the bankruptcy court on the date so stated.

(5) Entry defined

(A) A judgment, order, or decree is entered for purposes of this Rule 8002(a):

(i) when it is entered in the docket under Rule 5003(a), or

(ii) if Rule 7058 applies and Rule 58(a) F.R.Civ.P. requires a separate document, when the judgment, order, or decree is entered in the docket under Rule 5003(a) and when the earlier of these events occurs:

• the judgment, order, or decree is set out in a separate document; or

• 150 days have run from entry of the judgment, order, or decree in the docket under Rule 5003(a).

(B) A failure to set out a judgment, order, or decree in a separate document when required by Rule 58(a) F.R.Civ.P. does not affect the validity of an appeal from that judgment, order, or decree.

(b) Effect of a motion on the time to appeal

(1) In general

If a party files in the bankruptcy court any of the following motions and does so within the time allowed by these rules, the time to file an appeal runs for all parties from the entry of the order disposing of the last such remaining motion:

(A) to amend or make additional findings under Rule 7052, whether or not granting the motion would alter the judgment;

(B) to alter or amend the judgment under Rule 9023;

(C) for a new trial under Rule 9023; or

(D) for relief under Rule 9024 if the motion is filed within 14 days after the judgment is entered.

(2) Filing an appeal before the motion is decided

If a party files a notice of appeal after the court announces or enters a judgment, order, or decree--but before it disposes of any motion listed in subdivision (b)(1)--the notice becomes effective when the order disposing of the last such remaining motion is entered.

(3) Appealing the ruling on the motion

If a party intends to challenge an order disposing of any motion listed in subdivision (b)(1)--or the alteration or amendment of a judgment, order, or decree upon the motion--the party must file a notice of appeal or an amended notice of appeal. The notice or amended notice must comply with Rule 8003 or 8004 and be filed within the time prescribed by this rule, measured from the entry of the order disposing of the last such remaining motion.

(4) No additional fee

No additional fee is required to file an amended notice of appeal.

(c) Appeal by an inmate confined in an institution

(1) In general

If an institution has a system designed for legal mail, an inmate confined there must use that system to receive the benefit of this Rule 8002(c)(1). If an inmate files a notice of appeal from a judgment, order, or decree of a bankruptcy court, the notice is timely if it is deposited in the institution's internal mail system on or before the last day for filing and:

(A) it is accompanied by:

(i) a declaration in compliance with 28 U.S.C. § 1746--or a notarized statement--setting out the date of deposit and stating that first-class postage is being prepaid; or

(ii) evidence (such as a postmark or date stamp) showing that the notice was so deposited and that postage was prepaid; or

(B) the appellate court exercises its discretion to permit the later filing of a declaration or notarized statement that satisfies Rule 8002(c)(1)(A)(i).

(2) Multiple appeals

If an inmate files under this subdivision the first notice of appeal, the 14-day period provided in subdivision (a)(3) for another party to file a notice of appeal runs from the date when the bankruptcy clerk dockets the first notice.

(d) Extending the time to appeal

(1) When the time may be extended

Except as provided in subdivision (d)(2), the bankruptcy court may extend the time to file a notice of appeal upon a party's motion that is filed:

(A) within the time prescribed by this rule; or

(B) within 21 days after that time, if the party shows excusable neglect.

(2) When the time may not be extended

The bankruptcy court may not extend the time to file a notice of appeal if the judgment, order, or decree appealed from:

(A) grants relief from an automatic stay under § 362, 922, 1201, or 1301 of the Code;

(B) authorizes the sale or lease of property or the use of cash collateral under § 363 of the Code;

(C) authorizes the obtaining of credit under § 364 of the Code;

(D) authorizes the assumption or assignment of an executory contract or unexpired lease under § 365 of the Code;

(E) approves a disclosure statement under § 1125 of the Code; or

(F) confirms a plan under § 943, 1129, 1225, or 1325 of the Code.

(3) Time limits on an extension

No extension of time may exceed 21 days after the time prescribed by this rule, or 14 days after the order granting the motion to extend time is entered, whichever is later.

Rule 8003. Appeal as of Right—How Taken; Docketing the Appeal

(a) FILING THE NOTICE OF APPEAL.

(1) In General. An appeal from a judgment, order, or decree of a bankruptcy court to a district court or BAP under 28 U.S.C. § 158(a)(1) or (a)(2) may be taken only by filing a notice of appeal with the bankruptcy clerk within the time allowed by Rule 8002.

(2) Effect of Not Taking Other Steps. An appellant's failure to take any step other than the timely filing of a notice of appeal does not affect the validity of the appeal, but is ground only for the district court or BAP to act as it considers appropriate, including dismissing the appeal.

(3) Contents. The notice of appeal must:

(A) conform substantially to the appropriate Official Form;

(B) be accompanied by the judgment, order, or decree, or the part of it, being appealed; and

(C) be accompanied by the prescribed fee.

(4) Merger. The notice of appeal encompasses all orders that, for purposes of appeal, merge into the identified judgment or appealable order or decree. It is not necessary to identify those orders in the notice of appeal.

(5) Final judgment. The notice of appeal encompasses the final judgment, whether or not that judgment is set out in a separate document under Rule 7058, if the notice identifies:

(A) an order that adjudicates all remaining claims and the rights and liabilities of all remaining parties; or

(B) an order described in Rule 8002(b)(1).

(6) Limited appeal

An appellant may identify only part of a judgment or appealable order or decree by expressly stating that the notice of appeal is so limited. Without such an express statement, specific identifications do not limit the scope of the notice of appeal.

(7) Impermissible ground for dismissal

An appeal must not be dismissed for failure to properly identify the judgment or appealable order or decree if the notice of appeal was filed after entry of the judgment or appealable order or decree and identifies an order that merged into that judgment or appealable order or decree.

(8) Additional copies

If requested to do so, the appellant must furnish the bankruptcy clerk with enough copies of the notice to enable the clerk to comply with subdivision (c).

(b) JOINT OR CONSOLIDATED APPEALS.

(1) Joint Notice of Appeal. When two or more parties are entitled to appeal from a judgment, order, or decree of a bankruptcy court and their interests make joinder practicable, they may file a joint notice of appeal. They may then proceed on appeal as a single appellant.

(2) Consolidating Appeals. When parties have separately filed timely notices of appeal, the district court or BAP may join or consolidate the appeals.

(c) SERVING THE NOTICE OF APPEAL.

(1) Serving Parties and Transmitting to the United States Trustee. The bankruptcy clerk must serve the notice of appeal on counsel of record for each party to the appeal, excluding the appellant, and transmit it to the United States trustee. If a party is proceeding pro se, the clerk must send the notice of appeal to the party's last known address. The clerk must note, on each copy, the date when the notice of appeal was filed.

(2) Effect of Failing to Serve or Transmit Notice. The bankruptcy clerk's failure to serve notice on a party or transmit notice to the United States trustee does not affect the validity of the appeal.

(3) Noting Service on the Docket. The clerk must note on the

docket the names of the parties served and the date and method of the service.

(d) TRANSMITTING THE NOTICE OF APPEAL TO THE DISTRICT COURT OR BAP; DOCKETING THE APPEAL.

(1) Transmitting the Notice. The bankruptcy clerk must promptly transmit the notice of appeal to the BAP clerk if a BAP has been established for appeals from that district and the appellant has not elected to have the district court hear the appeal. Otherwise, the bankruptcy clerk must promptly transmit the notice to the district clerk.

(2) Docketing in the District Court or BAP. Upon receiving the notice of appeal, the district or BAP clerk must docket the appeal under the title of the bankruptcy case and the title of any adversary proceeding, and must identify the appellant, adding the appellant's name if necessary.

Rule 8004. Appeal by Leave—How Taken; Docketing the Appeal

(a) NOTICE OF APPEAL AND MOTION FOR LEAVE TO APPEAL. To appeal from an interlocutory order or decree of a bankruptcy court under 28 U.S.C. § 158(a)(3), a party must file with the bankruptcy clerk a notice of appeal as prescribed by Rule 8003(a). The notice must:

(1) be filed within the time allowed by Rule 8002;

(2) be accompanied by a motion for leave to appeal prepared in accordance with subdivision (b); and

(3) unless served electronically using the court's transmission equipment, include proof of service in accordance with Rule 8011(d).

(b) CONTENTS OF THE MOTION; RESPONSE.

(1) Contents. A motion for leave to appeal under 28 U.S.C. § 158(a)(3) must include the following:

(A) the facts necessary to understand the question presented;

(B) the question itself;

(C) the relief sought;

(D) the reasons why leave to appeal should be granted; and

(E) a copy of the interlocutory order or decree and any related opinion or memorandum.

(2) Response. A party may file with the district or BAP clerk a response in opposition or a cross-motion within 14 days after the motion is served.

(c) TRANSMITTING THE NOTICE OF APPEAL AND THE MOTION; DOCKETING THE APPEAL; DETERMINING THE MOTION.

(1) Transmitting to the District Court or BAP. The bankruptcy clerk must promptly transmit the notice of appeal and the motion for leave to the BAP clerk if a BAP has been established for appeals from that district and the appellant has not elected to have the district court hear the appeal. Otherwise, the bankruptcy clerk must promptly transmit the notice and motion to the district clerk.

(2) Docketing in the District Court or BAP. Upon receiving the notice and motion, the district or BAP clerk must docket the appeal under the title of the bankruptcy case and the title of any adversary proceeding, and must identify the appellant, adding the appellant's name if necessary.

(3) Oral Argument Not Required. The motion and any response or cross-motion are submitted without oral argument unless the district court or BAP orders otherwise.

(d) FAILURE TO FILE A MOTION WITH A NOTICE OF APPEAL. If an appellant timely files a notice of appeal under this rule but does not include a motion for leave, the district court or BAP may order the appellant to file a motion for leave, or treat the notice of appeal as a motion for leave and either grant or deny it. If the court orders that a motion for leave be filed, the appellant must do so within 14 days after the order is entered, unless the order provides otherwise.

(e) DIRECT APPEAL TO A COURT OF APPEALS. If leave to appeal an interlocutory order or decree is required under 28 U.S.C. § 158(a)(3), an authorization of a direct appeal by the court of appeals under 28 U.S.C. § 158(d)(2) satisfies the requirement.

Rule 8005. Election to Have an Appeal Heard by the District Court Instead of the BAP

(a) FILING OF A STATEMENT OF ELECTION. To elect to have an appeal heard by the district court, a party must:

(1) file a statement of election that conforms substantially to the appropriate Official Form; and

(2) do so within the time prescribed by 28 U.S.C. § 158(c)(1).

(b) TRANSMITTING THE DOCUMENTS RELATED TO THE APPEAL. Upon receiving an appellant's timely statement of election, the bankruptcy clerk must transmit to the district clerk all documents related to the appeal. Upon receiving a timely statement of election by a party other than the appellant, the BAP clerk must transmit to the district clerk all documents related to the appeal and notify the bankruptcy clerk of the transmission.

(c) DETERMINING THE VALIDITY OF AN ELECTION. A party seeking a determination of the validity of an election must file a motion in the court where the appeal is then pending. The motion must be filed within 14 days after the statement of election is filed.

(d) MOTION FOR LEAVE WITHOUT A NOTICE OF APPEAL—EFFECT ON THE TIMING OF AN ELECTION. If an appellant moves for leave to appeal under Rule 8004 but fails to file a separate notice of appeal with the motion, the motion must be treated as a notice of appeal for purposes of determining the timeliness of a statement of election.

Rule 8006. Certifying a Direct Appeal to the Court of Appeals

(a) EFFECTIVE DATE OF A CERTIFICATION. A certification of a judgment, order, or decree of a bankruptcy court for direct review in a court of appeals under 28 U.S.C. § 158(d)(2) is effective when:

(1) the certification has been filed;

(2) a timely appeal has been taken under Rule 8003 or 8004; and

(3) the notice of appeal has become effective under Rule 8002.

(b) Filing the certification

The certification must be filed with the clerk of the court where the matter is pending. For purposes of this rule, a matter remains pending in the bankruptcy court for 30 days after the effective date under Rule 8002 of the first notice of appeal from the judgment, order, or decree for which direct review is sought. A matter is pending in the district court or BAP thereafter.

(c) Joint certification by all appellants and appellees

(1) How accomplished

A joint certification by all the appellants and appellees under 28 U.S.C. § 158(d)(2)(A) must be made by using the appropriate Official Form. The parties may supplement the certification with a short statement of the basis for the certification, which may include the information listed in subdivision (f)(2).

(2) Supplemental statement by the court

Within 14 days after the parties' certification, the bankruptcy court or the court in which the matter is then pending may file a short supplemental statement about the merits of the certification.

(d) The court that may make the certification

Only the court where the matter is pending, as provided in subdivision (b), may certify a direct review on request of parties or on its own motion.

(e) Certification on the court's own motion

(1) How accomplished

A certification on the court's own motion must be set forth in a separate document. The clerk of the certifying court must serve it on the parties to the appeal in the manner required for service of a notice of appeal under Rule 8003(c)(1). The certification must be accompanied by an opinion or memorandum that contains the information required by subdivision (f)(2)(A)-(D).

(2) Supplemental statement by a party

Within 14 days after the court's certification, a party may file with the clerk of the certifying court a short supplemental statement regarding the merits of certification.

(f) Certification by the court on request

(1) How requested

A request by a party for certification that a circumstance specified in 28 U.S.C. §158(d)(2)(A)(i)-(iii) applies--or a request by a majority of the appellants and a majority of the appellees--must be filed with the clerk of the court where the matter is pending within 60 days after the entry of the judgment, order, or decree.

(2) Service and contents

The request must be served on all parties to the appeal in the manner required for service of a notice of appeal under Rule 8003(c)(1), and it must include the following:

(A) the facts necessary to understand the question presented;

(B) the question itself;

(C) the relief sought;

(D) the reasons why the direct appeal should be allowed, including which circumstance specified in 28 U.S.C. § 158(d)(2)(A)(i)-(iii) applies; and

(E) a copy of the judgment, order, or decree and any related opinion or memorandum.

(3) Time to file a response or a cross-request
A party may file a response to the request within 14 days after the request is served, or such other time as the court where the matter is pending allows. A party may file a cross-request for certification within 14 days after the request is served, or within 60 days after the entry of the judgment, order, or decree, whichever occurs first.
(4) Oral argument not required
The request, cross-request, and any response are submitted without oral argument unless the court where the matter is pending orders otherwise.
(5) Form and service of the certification
If the court certifies a direct appeal in response to the request, it must do so in a separate document. The certification must be served on the parties to the appeal in the manner required for service of a notice of appeal under Rule 8003(c)(1).
(g) Proceeding in the court of appeals following a certification
Within 30 days after the date the certification becomes effective under subdivision (a), a request for permission to take a direct appeal to the court of appeals must be filed with the circuit clerk in accordance with F.R.App.P. 6(c).

Rule 8007. Stay Pending Appeal; Bonds; Suspension of Proceedings

(a) INITIAL MOTION IN THE BANKRUPTCY COURT.
(1) In general
Ordinarily, a party must move first in the bankruptcy court for the following relief:
(A) a stay of a judgment, order, or decree of the bankruptcy court pending appeal;
(B) the approval of a bond or other security provided to obtain a stay of judgment;
(C) an order suspending, modifying, restoring, or granting an injunction while an appeal is pending; or
(D) the suspension or continuation of proceedings in a case or other relief permitted by subdivision (e).
(2) Time to file
The motion may be made either before or after the notice of appeal is filed.
(b) Motion in the district court, the BAP, or the Court of Appeals on direct appeal
(1) Request for relief
A motion for the relief specified in subdivision (a)(1)--or to vacate or modify a bankruptcy court's order granting such relief--may be made in the court where the appeal is pending.
(2) Showing or statement required
The motion must:
(A) show that moving first in the bankruptcy court would be impracticable; or
(B) if a motion was made in the bankruptcy court, either state that the court has not yet ruled on the motion, or state that the court has ruled and set out any reasons given for the ruling.
(3) Additional content
The motion must also include:
(A) the reasons for granting the relief requested and the facts relied upon;
(B) affidavits or other sworn statements supporting facts subject to dispute; and
(C) relevant parts of the record.
(4) Serving notice
The movant must give reasonable notice of the motion to all parties.
(c) Filing a bond or other security
The district court, BAP, or court of appeals may condition relief on filing a bond or other security with the bankruptcy court.
(d) Bond or other security for a trustee or the United States
The court may require a trustee to file a bond or other security when the trustee appeals. A bond or other security is not required when an appeal is taken by the United States, its officer, or its agency or by direction of any department of the federal government.
(e) Continuation of proceedings in the bankruptcy court
Despite Rule 7062 and subject to the authority of the district court, BAP, or court of appeals, the bankruptcy court may:
(1) suspend or order the continuation of other proceedings in the case; or
(2) issue any other appropriate orders during the pendency of an appeal to protect the rights of all parties in interest.

Rule 8008. Indicative Rulings.

(a) Relief pending appeal
If a party files a timely motion in the bankruptcy court for relief that the court lacks authority to grant because of an appeal that has been docketed and is pending, the bankruptcy court may:
(1) defer considering the motion;
(2) deny the motion; or
(3) state that the court would grant the motion if the court where the appeal is pending remands for that purpose, or state that the motion raises a substantial issue.
(b) Notice to the court where the appeal is pending
The movant must promptly notify the clerk of the court where the appeal is pending if the bankruptcy court states that it would grant the motion or that the motion raises a substantial issue.
(c) Remand after an indicative ruling
If the bankruptcy court states that it would grant the motion or that the motion raises a substantial issue, the district court or BAP may remand for further proceedings, but it retains jurisdiction unless it expressly dismisses the appeal. If the district court or BAP remands but retains jurisdiction, the parties must promptly notify the clerk of that court when the bankruptcy court has decided the motion on remand.

Rule 8009. Record on Appeal; Sealed Documents

(a) DESIGNATING THE RECORD ON APPEAL; STATEMENT OF THE ISSUES.
(1) Appellant.
(A) The appellant must file with the bankruptcy clerk and serve on the appellee a designation of the items to be included in the record on appeal and a statement of the issues to be presented.
(B) The appellant must file and serve the designation and statement within 14 days after:
(i) the appellant's notice of appeal as of right becomes effective under Rule 8002; or
(ii) an order granting leave to appeal is entered.
A designation and statement served prematurely must be treated as served on the first day on which filing is timely.
(2) Appellee and Cross-Appellant. Within 14 days after being served, the appellee may file with the bankruptcy clerk and serve on the appellant a designation of additional items to be included in the record. An appellee who files a cross-appeal must file and serve a designation of additional items to be included in the record and a statement of the issues to be presented on the cross-appeal.
(3) Cross-Appellee. Within 14 days after service of the cross-appellant's designation and statement, a cross-appellee may file with the bankruptcy clerk and serve on the cross-appellant a designation of additional items to be included in the record.
(4) Record on Appeal. The record on appeal must include the following:

- docket entries kept by the bankruptcy clerk;
- items designated by the parties;
- the notice of appeal;
- the judgment, order, or decree being appealed;
- any order granting leave to appeal;
- any certification required for a direct appeal to the court of appeals;
- any opinion, findings of fact, and conclusions of law relating to the issues on appeal, including transcripts of all oral rulings;
- any transcript ordered under subdivision (b);
- any statement required by subdivision (c); and
- any additional items from the record that the court where the appeal is pending orders.

(5) Copies for the Bankruptcy Clerk. If paper copies are needed, a party filing a designation of items must provide a copy of any of those items that the bankruptcy clerk requests. If the party fails to do so, the bankruptcy clerk must prepare the copy at the party's expense.
(b) TRANSCRIPT OF PROCEEDINGS.
(1) Appellant's Duty to Order. Within the time period prescribed by subdivision (a)(1), the appellant must:
(A) order in writing from the reporter, as defined in Rule 8010(a)(1), a transcript of such parts of the proceedings not already on file as the appellant considers necessary for the appeal, and file a copy of the order with the bankruptcy clerk; or

(B) file with the bankruptcy clerk a certificate stating that the appellant is not ordering a transcript.

(2) Cross-Appellant's Duty to Order. Within 14 days after the appellant files a copy of the transcript order or a certificate of not ordering a transcript, the appellee as cross-appellant must:

(A) order in writing from the reporter, as defined in Rule 8010(a)(1), a transcript of such additional parts of the proceedings as the cross-appellant considers necessary for the appeal, and file a copy of the order with the bankruptcy clerk; or

(B) file with the bankruptcy clerk a certificate stating that the cross-appellant is not ordering a transcript.

(3) Appellee's or Cross-Appellee's Right to Order. Within 14 days after the appellant or cross-appellant files a copy of a transcript order or certificate of not ordering a transcript, the appellee or cross-appellee may order in writing from the reporter a transcript of such additional parts of the proceedings as the appellee or cross-appellee considers necessary for the appeal. A copy of the order must be filed with the bankruptcy clerk.

(4) Payment. At the time of ordering, a party must make satisfactory arrangements with the reporter for paying the cost of the transcript.

(5) Unsupported Finding or Conclusion. If the appellant intends to argue on appeal that a finding or conclusion is unsupported by the evidence or is contrary to the evidence, the appellant must include in the record a transcript of all relevant testimony and copies of all relevant exhibits.

(c) STATEMENT OF THE EVIDENCE WHEN A TRANSCRIPT IS UNAVAILABLE. If a transcript of a hearing or trial is unavailable, the appellant may prepare a statement of the evidence or proceedings from the best available means, including the appellant's recollection. The statement must be filed within the time prescribed by subdivision (a)(1) and served on the appellee, who may serve objections or proposed amendments within 14 days after being served. The statement and any objections or proposed amendments must then be submitted to the bankruptcy court for settlement and approval. As settled and approved, the statement must be included by the bankruptcy clerk in the record on appeal.

(d) AGREED STATEMENT AS THE RECORD ON APPEAL. Instead of the record on appeal as defined in subdivision (a), the parties may prepare, sign, and submit to the bankruptcy court a statement of the case showing how the issues presented by the appeal arose and were decided in the bankruptcy court. The statement must set forth only those facts alleged and proved or sought to be proved that are essential to the court's resolution of the issues. If the statement is accurate, it—together with any additions that the bankruptcy court may consider necessary to a full presentation of the issues on appeal—must be approved by the bankruptcy court and must then be certified to the court where the appeal is pending as the record on appeal. The bankruptcy clerk must then transmit it to the clerk of that court within the time provided by Rule 8010. A copy of the agreed statement may be filed in place of the appendix required by Rule 8018(b) or, in the case of a direct appeal to the court of appeals, by F.R.App.P. 30.

(e) CORRECTING OR MODIFYING THE RECORD.

(1) Submitting to the Bankruptcy Court. If any difference arises about whether the record accurately discloses what occurred in the bankruptcy court, the difference must be submitted to and settled by the bankruptcy court and the record conformed accordingly. If an item has been improperly designated as part of the record on appeal, a party may move to strike that item.

(2) Correcting in Other Ways. If anything material to either party is omitted from or misstated in the record by error or accident, the omission or misstatement may be corrected, and a supplemental record may be certified and transmitted:

(A) on stipulation of the parties;

(B) by the bankruptcy court before or after the record has been forwarded; or

(C) by the court where the appeal is pending.

(3) Remaining Questions. All other questions as to the form and content of the record must be presented to the court where the appeal is pending.

(f) SEALED DOCUMENTS. A document placed under seal by the bankruptcy court may be designated as part of the record on appeal. In doing so, a party must identify it without revealing confidential or secret information, but the bankruptcy clerk must not transmit it to the clerk of the court where the appeal is pending as part of the record. Instead, a party must file a motion with the court where the appeal is pending to accept the document under seal. If the motion is granted, the movant must notify the bankruptcy court of the ruling, and the bankruptcy clerk must promptly transmit the sealed document to the clerk of the court where the appeal is pending.

(g) OTHER NECESSARY ACTIONS. All parties to an appeal must take any other action necessary to enable the bankruptcy clerk to assemble and transmit the record.

Rule 8010. Completing and Transmitting the Record

(a) REPORTER'S DUTIES.

(1) Proceedings recorded without a reporter present

If proceedings were recorded without a reporter being present, the person or service selected under bankruptcy court procedures to transcribe the recording is the reporter for purposes of this rule.

(2) Preparing and filing the transcript

The reporter must prepare and file a transcript as follows:

(A) Upon receiving an order for a transcript in accordance with Rule 8009(b), the reporter must file in the bankruptcy court an acknowledgment of the request that shows when it was received, and when the reporter expects to have the transcript completed.

(B) After completing the transcript, the reporter must file it with the bankruptcy clerk, who will notify the district, BAP, or circuit clerk of its filing.

(C) If the transcript cannot be completed within 30 days after receiving the order, the reporter must request an extension of time from the bankruptcy clerk. The clerk must enter on the docket and notify the parties whether the extension is granted.

(D) If the reporter does not file the transcript on time, the bankruptcy clerk must notify the bankruptcy judge.

(b) Clerk's duties

(1) Transmitting the record--in general

Subject to Rule 8009(f) and subdivision (b)(5) of this rule, when the record is complete, the bankruptcy clerk must transmit to the clerk of the court where the appeal is pending either the record or a notice that the record is available electronically.

(2) Multiple appeals

If there are multiple appeals from a judgment, order, or decree, the bankruptcy clerk must transmit a single record.

(3) Receiving the record

Upon receiving the record or notice that it is available electronically, the district, BAP, or circuit clerk must enter that information on the docket and promptly notify all parties to the appeal.

(4) If paper copies are ordered

If the court where the appeal is pending directs that paper copies of the record be provided, the clerk of that court must so notify the appellant. If the appellant fails to provide them, the bankruptcy clerk must prepare them at the appellant's expense.

(5) When leave to appeal is requested

Subject to subdivision (c), if a motion for leave to appeal has been filed under Rule 8004, the bankruptcy clerk must prepare and transmit the record only after the district court, BAP, or court of appeals grants leave.

(c) Record for a preliminary motion in the district court, BAP, or court of appeals

This subdivision (c) applies if, before the record is transmitted, a party moves in the district court, BAP, or court of appeals for any of the following relief:

- leave to appeal;
- dismissal;
- a stay pending appeal;
- approval of a bond or other security provided to obtain a stay of judgment; or
- any other intermediate order.

The bankruptcy clerk must then transmit to the clerk of the court where the relief is sought any parts of the record designated by a party to the appeal or a notice that those parts are available electronically

Rule 8011. Filing and Service; Signature

(a) FILING.

(1) With the clerk

A document required or permitted to be filed in a district court or BAP must be filed with the clerk of that court.

(2) Method and timeliness

(A) Nonelectronic filing

(i) In general

For a document not filed electronically, filing may be accomplished by mail addressed to the clerk of the district court or BAP. Except as provided in subdivision (a)(2)(A)(ii) and (iii), filing is timely only if the clerk receives the

document within the time fixed for filing.
(ii) Brief or appendix
A brief or appendix not filed electronically is also timely filed if, on or before the last day for filing, it is:
• mailed to the clerk by first-class mail--or other class of mail that is at least as expeditious--postage prepaid; or
• dispatched to a third-party commercial carrier for delivery within 3 days to the clerk.
(iii) Inmate filing
If an institution has a system designed for legal mail, an inmate confined there must use that system to receive the benefit of this Rule 8011(a)(2)(A)(iii). A document not filed electronically by an inmate confined in an institution is timely if it is deposited in the institution's internal mailing system on or before the last day for filing and:
• it is accompanied by a declaration in compliance with 28 U.S.C. § 1746--or a notarized statement--setting out the date of deposit and stating that first-class postage is being prepaid; or evidence (such as a postmark or date stamp) showing that the notice was so deposited and that postage was prepaid; or
• the appellate court exercises its discretion to permit the later filing of a declaration or notarized statement that satisfies this Rule 8011(a)(2)(A)(iii).
(B) Electronic filing
(i) By a represented person--generally required; exceptions
An entity represented by an attorney must file electronically, unless nonelectronic filing is allowed by the court for good cause or is allowed or required by local rule.
(ii) By an unrepresented individual--when allowed or required
An individual not represented by an attorney:
• may file electronically only if allowed by court order or by local rule; and
• may be required to file electronically only by court order, or by a local rule that includes reasonable exceptions.
(iii) Same as a written paper
A document filed electronically is a written paper for purposes of these rules.
(C) Copies
If a document is filed electronically, no paper copy is required. If a document is filed by mail or delivery to the district court or BAP, no additional copies are required. But the district court or BAP may require by local rule or by order in a particular case the filing or furnishing of a specified number of paper copies.
(3) Clerk's refusal of documents
The court's clerk must not refuse to accept for filing any document transmitted for that purpose solely because it is not presented in proper form as required by these rules or by any local rule or practice.
(b) Service of all documents required
Unless a rule requires service by the clerk, a party must, at or before the time of the filing of a document, serve it on the other parties to the appeal. Service on a party represented by counsel must be made on the party's counsel.
(c) Manner of service
(1) Nonelectronic service
Nonelectronic service may be by any of the following:
(A) personal delivery;
(B) mail; or
(C) third-party commercial carrier for delivery within 3 days.
(2) Electronic service
Electronic service may be made by sending a document to a registered user by filing it with the court's electronic-filing system or by using other electronic means that the person served consented to in writing.
(3) When service is complete
Service by electronic means is complete on filing or sending, unless the person making service receives notice that the document was not received by the person served. Service by mail or by commercial carrier is complete on mailing or delivery to the carrier.
(d) Proof of service
(1) What is required
A document presented for filing must contain either of the following if it was served other than through the court's electronic-filing system:
(A) an acknowledgment of service by the person served; or
(B) proof of service consisting of a statement by the person who made service certifying:
(i) the date and manner of service;
(ii) the names of the persons served; and
(iii) the mail or electronic address, the fax number, or the address of the place of delivery, as appropriate for the manner of service, for each person served.
(2) Delayed proof
The district or BAP clerk may permit documents to be filed without acknowledgment or proof of service, but must require the acknowledgment or proof to be filed promptly thereafter.
(3) Brief or appendix
When a brief or appendix is filed, the proof of service must also state the date and manner by which it was filed.
(e) Signature
Every document filed electronically must include the electronic signature of the person filing it or, if the person is represented, the electronic signature of counsel. A filing made through a person's electronic-filing account and authorized by that person, together with that person's name on a signature block, constitutes the person's signature. Every document filed in paper form must be signed by the person filing the document or, if the person is represented, by counsel.

Rule 8012. Corporate Disclosure Statement

(a) Nongovernmental corporations. Any nongovernmental corporation that is a party to a proceeding in the district court or BAP must file a statement that identifies any parent corporation and any publicly held corporation that owns 10% or more of its stock or states that there is no such corporation. The same requirement applies to a nongovernmental corporation that seeks to intervene.
(b) Disclosure about the debtor. The debtor, the trustee, or, if neither is a party, the appellant must file a statement that:
(1) identifies each debtor not named in the caption; and
(2) for each debtor that is a corporation, discloses the information required by Rule 8012(a).
(c) Time to file; supplemental filing
A Rule 8012 statement must:
(1) be filed with the principal brief or upon filing a motion, response, petition, or answer in the district court or BAP, whichever occurs first, unless a local rule requires earlier filing;
(2) be included before the table of contents in the principal brief; and
(3) be supplemented whenever the information required by Rule 8012 changes.

Rule 8013. Motions; Intervention

(1) Request for relief
A request for an order or other relief is made by filing a motion with the district or BAP clerk, with proof of service on the other parties to the appeal.
(2) Contents of a motion
(A) Grounds and the relief sought
A motion must state with particularity the grounds for the motion, the relief sought, and the legal argument necessary to support it.
(B) Motion to expedite an appeal
A motion to expedite an appeal must explain what justifies considering the appeal ahead of other matters. If the district court or BAP grants the motion, it may accelerate the time to transmit the record, the deadline for filing briefs and other documents, oral argument, and the resolution of the appeal. A motion to expedite an appeal may be filed as an emergency motion under subdivision (d).
(C) Accompanying documents
(i) Any affidavit or other document necessary to support a motion must be served and filed with the motion.
(ii) An affidavit must contain only factual information, not legal argument.
(iii) A motion seeking substantive relief must include a copy of the bankruptcy court's judgment, order, or decree, and any accompanying opinion as a separate exhibit.
(D) Documents barred or not required
(i) A separate brief supporting or responding to a motion must not be filed.
(ii) Unless the court orders otherwise, a notice of motion or a proposed order is not required.
(3) Response and reply; time to file
Unless the district court or BAP orders otherwise,
(A) any party to the appeal may file a response to the motion within 7 days after service of the motion; and
(B) the movant may file a reply to a response within 7 days after service of the response, but may only address matters raised in the response.
(b) Disposition of a motion for a procedural order
The district court or BAP may rule on a motion for a procedural order--including a motion under Rule 9006(b) or (c)--at any time without awaiting a response. A party adversely affected by the ruling may move to reconsider, vacate, or modify it within 7 days after the procedural order is served.
(c) Oral argument

A motion will be decided without oral argument unless the district court or BAP orders otherwise.
(d) Emergency motion
(1) Noting the emergency
When a movant requests expedited action on a motion because irreparable harm would occur during the time needed to consider a response, the movant must insert the word "Emergency" before the title of the motion.
(2) Contents of the motion
The emergency motion must
(A) be accompanied by an affidavit setting out the nature of the emergency;
(B) state whether all grounds for it were submitted to the bankruptcy court and, if not, why the motion should not be remanded for the bankruptcy court to consider;
(C) include the e-mail addresses, office addresses, and telephone numbers of moving counsel and, when known, of opposing counsel and any unrepresented parties to the appeal; and
(D) be served as prescribed by Rule 8011.
(3) Notifying opposing parties
Before filing an emergency motion, the movant must make every practicable effort to notify opposing counsel and any unrepresented parties in time for them to respond. The affidavit accompanying the emergency motion must state when and how notice was given or state why giving it was impracticable.
(e) Power of a single BAP judge to entertain a motion
(1) Single judge's authority
A BAP judge may act alone on any motion, but may not dismiss or otherwise determine an appeal, deny a motion for leave to appeal, or deny a motion for a stay pending appeal if denial would make the appeal moot.
(2) Reviewing a single judge's action
The BAP may review a single judge's action, either on its own motion or on a party's motion.
(f) Form of documents; length limits; number of copies
(1) Format of a paper document
Rule 27(d)(1) F.R.App.P. applies in the district court or BAP to a paper version of a motion, response, or reply.
(2) Format of an electronically filed document
A motion, response, or reply filed electronically must comply with the requirements for a paper version regarding covers, line spacing, margins, typeface, and type style. It must also comply with the length limits under paragraph (3).
(3) Length limits
Except by the district court's or BAP's permission, and excluding the accompanying documents authorized by subdivision (a)(2)(C):
(A) a motion or a response to a motion produced using a computer must include a certificate under Rule 8015(h) and not exceed 5,200 words;
(B) a handwritten or typewritten motion or a response to a motion must not exceed 20 pages;
(C) a reply produced using a computer must include a certificate under Rule 8015(h) and not exceed 2,600 words; and
(D) a handwritten or typewritten reply must not exceed 10 pages.
(4) Paper copies
Paper copies must be provided only if required by local rule or by an order in a particular case.
(g) Intervening in an appeal
Unless a statute provides otherwise, an entity that seeks to intervene in an appeal pending in the district court or BAP must move for leave to intervene and serve a copy of the motion on the parties to the appeal. The motion or other notice of intervention authorized by statute must be filed within 30 days after the appeal is docketed. It must concisely state the movant's interest, the grounds for intervention, whether intervention was sought in the bankruptcy court, why intervention is being sought at this stage of the proceeding, and why participating as an amicus curiae would not be adequate.

Rule 8014. Briefs

(a) APPELLANT'S BRIEF. The appellant's brief must contain the following under appropriate headings and in the order indicated:

(1) a corporate disclosure statement, if required by Rule 8012;

(2) a table of contents, with page references;

(3) a table of authorities—cases (alphabetically arranged), statutes, and other authorities—with references to the pages of the brief where they are cited;

(4) a jurisdictional statement, including:

(A) the basis for the bankruptcy court's subject-matter jurisdiction, with citations to applicable statutory provisions and stating relevant facts establishing jurisdiction;

(B) the basis for the district court's or BAP's jurisdiction, with citations to applicable statutory provisions and stating relevant facts establishing jurisdiction;

(C) the filing dates establishing the timeliness of the appeal; and

(D) an assertion that the appeal is from a final judgment, order, or decree, or information establishing the district court's or BAP's jurisdiction on another basis;

(5) a statement of the issues presented and, for each one, a concise statement of the applicable standard of appellate review;

(6) a concise statement of the case setting out the facts relevant to the issues submitted for review, describing the relevant procedural history, and identifying the rulings presented for review, with appropriate references to the record;

(7) a summary of the argument, which must contain a succinct, clear, and accurate statement of the arguments made in the body of the brief, and which must not merely repeat the argument headings;

(8) the argument, which must contain the appellant's contentions and the reasons for them, with citations to the authorities and parts of the record on which the appellant relies;

(9) a short conclusion stating the precise relief sought; and

(10) the certificate of compliance, if required by Rule 8015(a)(7) or (b).

(b) APPELLEE'S BRIEF. The appellee's brief must conform to the requirements of subdivision (a)(1)-(8) and (10), except that none of the following need appear unless the appellee is dissatisfied with the appellant's statement:

(1) the jurisdictional statement;

(2) the statement of the issues and the applicable standard of appellate review; and

(3) the statement of the case.

(c) REPLY BRIEF. The appellant may file a brief in reply to the appellee's brief. A reply brief must comply with the requirements of subdivision (a)(2)-(3).

(d) STATUTES, RULES, REGULATIONS, OR SIMILAR AUTHORITY. If the court's determination of the issues presented requires the study of the Code or other statutes, rules, regulations, or similar authority, the relevant parts must be set out in the brief or in an addendum.

(e) BRIEFS IN A CASE INVOLVING MULTIPLE APPELLANTS OR APPELLEES. In a case involving more than one appellant or appellee, including consolidated cases, any number of appellants or appellees may join in a brief, and any party may adopt by reference a part of another's brief. Parties may also join in reply briefs.

(f) CITATION OF SUPPLEMENTAL AUTHORITIES. If pertinent and significant authorities come to a party's attention after the party's brief has been filed—or after oral argument but before a decision—a party may promptly advise the district or BAP clerk by a signed submission setting forth the citations. The submission, which must be served on the other parties to the appeal, must state the reasons for the supplemental citations, referring either to the pertinent page of a brief or to a point argued orally. The body of the submission must not exceed 350 words. Any response must be made within 7 days after the party is served, unless the court orders otherwise, and must be similarly limited.

Rule 8015. Form and Length of Briefs; Form of Appendices and Other Papers

(a) PAPER COPIES OF A BRIEF. If a paper copy of a brief may or must be filed, the following provisions apply:
(1) Reproduction
(A) A brief may be reproduced by any process that yields a clear black image on light paper. The paper must be opaque and unglazed. Only one side of the paper may be used.
(B) Text must be reproduced with a clarity that equals or exceeds the output of a laser printer.
(C) Photographs, illustrations, and tables may be reproduced by any method that results in a good copy of the original. A glossy finish is acceptable if the original is glossy.
(2) Cover
The front cover of a brief must contain:
(A) the number of the case centered at the top;

(B) the name of the court;
(C) the title of the case as prescribed by Rule 8003(d)(2) or 8004(c)(2);
(D) the nature of the proceeding and the name of the court below;
(E) the title of the brief, identifying the party or parties for whom the brief is filed; and
(F) the name, office address, telephone number, and e-mail address of counsel representing the party for whom the brief is filed.
(3) Binding
The brief must be bound in any manner that is secure, does not obscure the text, and permits the brief to lie reasonably flat when open.
(4) Paper size, line spacing, and margins
The brief must be on 8 1/2-by-11 inch paper. The text must be double-spaced, but quotations more than two lines long may be indented and single-spaced. Headings and footnotes may be single-spaced. Margins must be at least one inch on all four sides. Page numbers may be placed in the margins, but no text may appear there.
(5) Typeface
Either a proportionally spaced or monospaced face may be used.
(A) A proportionally spaced face must include serifs, but sans-serif type may be used in headings and captions. A proportionally spaced face must be 14-point or larger.
(B) A monospaced face may not contain more than 10 1/2 characters per inch.
(6) Type styles
A brief must be set in plain, roman style, although italics or boldface may be used for emphasis. Case names must be italicized or underlined.
(7) Length
(A) Page limitation
A principal brief must not exceed 30 pages, or a reply brief 15 pages, unless it complies with subparagraph (B).
(B) Type-volume limitation
(i) A principal brief is acceptable if it contains a certificate under Rule 8015(h) and:
• contains no more than 13,000 words; or
• uses a monospaced face and contains no more than 1,300 lines of text.
(ii) A reply brief is acceptable if it includes a certificate under Rule 8015(h) and contains no more than half of the type volume specified in item (i).
(b) Electronically filed briefs
A brief filed electronically must comply with subdivision (a), except for (a)(1), (a)(3), and the paper requirement of (a)(4).
(c) Paper copies of appendices
A paper copy of an appendix must comply with subdivision (a)(1), (2), (3), and (4), with the following exceptions:
(1) An appendix may include a legible photocopy of any document found in the record or of a printed decision.
(2) When necessary to facilitate inclusion of odd-sized documents such as technical drawings, an appendix may be a size other than 8 1/2-by-11 inches, and need not lie reasonably flat when opened.
(d) Electronically filed appendices
An appendix filed electronically must comply with subdivision (a)(2) and (4), except for the paper requirement of (a)(4).
(e) Other documents
(1) Motion
Rule 8013(f) governs the form of a motion, response, or reply.
(2) Paper copies of other documents
A paper copy of any other document, other than a submission under Rule 8014(f), must comply with subdivision (a), with the following exceptions:
(A) A cover is not necessary if the caption and signature page together contain the information required by subdivision (a)(2).
(B) Subdivision (a)(7) does not apply.
(3) Other documents filed electronically
Any other document filed electronically, other than a submission under Rule 8014(f), must comply with the appearance requirements of paragraph (2).
(f) Local variation
A district court or BAP must accept documents that comply with the form requirements of this rule and the length limits set by Part VIII of these rules. By local rule or order in a particular case, a district court or BAP may accept documents that do not meet all the form requirements of this rule or the length limits set by Part VIII of these rules.
(g) Items excluded from length
In computing any length limit, headings, footnotes, and quotations count toward the limit, but the following items do not:
• the cover page;
• a corporate disclosure statement;
• a table of contents;
• a table of citations;
• a statement regarding oral argument;
• an addendum containing statutes, rules, or regulations;
• certificates of counsel;
• the signature block;
• the proof of service; and
• any item specifically excluded by these rules or by local rule.
(h) Certificate of compliance
(1) Briefs and documents that require a certificate
A brief submitted under Rule 8015(a)(7)(B), 8016(d)(2), or 8017(b)(4)--and a document submitted under Rule 8013(f)(3)(A), 8013(f)(3)(C), or 8022(b)(1)--must include a certificate by the attorney, or an unrepresented party, that the document complies with the type-volume limitation. The individual preparing the certificate may rely on the word or line count of the word-processing system used to prepare the document. The certificate must state the number of words--or the number of lines of monospaced type--in the document.
(2) Acceptable form
The certificate requirement is satisfied by a certificate of compliance that conforms substantially to the appropriate Official Form.

Rule 8016. Cross-Appeals

(a) APPLICABILITY. This rule applies to a case in which a cross-appeal is filed. Rules 8014(a)-(c), 8015(a)(7)(A)-(B), and 8018(a)(1)-(3) do not apply to such a case, except as otherwise provided in this rule.
(b) Designation of appellant
The party who files a notice of appeal first is the appellant for purposes of this rule and Rule 8018(a)(4) and (b) and Rule 8019. If notices are filed on the same day, the plaintiff, petitioner, applicant, or movant in the proceeding below is the appellant. These designations may be modified by the parties' agreement or by court order.
(c) Briefs
In a case involving a cross-appeal:
(1) Appellant's principal brief
The appellant must file a principal brief in the appeal. That brief must comply with Rule 8014(a).
(2) Appellee's principal and response brief
The appellee must file a principal brief in the cross-appeal and must, in the same brief, respond to the principal brief in the appeal. That brief must comply with Rule 8014(a), except that the brief need not include a statement of the case unless the appellee is dissatisfied with the appellant's statement.
(3) Appellant's response and reply brief
The appellant must file a brief that responds to the principal brief in the cross-appeal and may, in the same brief, reply to the response in the appeal. That brief must comply with Rule 8014(a)(2)-(8) and (10), except that none of the following need appear unless the appellant is dissatisfied with the appellee's statement in the cross-appeal:
(A) the jurisdictional statement;
(B) the statement of the issues and the applicable standard of appellate review; and
(C) the statement of the case.
(4) Appellee's reply brief
The appellee may file a brief in reply to the response in the cross-appeal. That brief must comply with Rule 8014(a)(2)-(3) and (10) and must be limited to the issues presented by the cross-appeal.
(d) Length
(1) Page limitation
Unless it complies with paragraph (2), the appellant's principal brief must not exceed 30 pages; the appellee's principal and response brief, 35 pages; the appellant's response and reply brief, 30 pages; and the appellee's reply brief, 15 pages.
(2) Type-volume limitation
(A) The appellant's principal brief or the appellant's response and reply brief is acceptable if it includes a certificate under Rule 8015(h) and:
(i) contains no more than 13,000 words; or
(ii) uses a monospaced face and contains no more than 1,300 lines of text.
(B) The appellee's principal and response brief is acceptable if it includes a certificate under Rule 8015(h) and:
(i) contains no more than 15,300 words; or
(ii) uses a monospaced face and contains no more than 1,500 lines of text.
(C) The appellee's reply brief is acceptable if it includes a certificate under Rule 8015(h) and contains no more than half of the type volume specified in

subparagraph (A).
(e) Time to serve and file a brief
Briefs must be served and filed as follows, unless the district court or BAP by order in a particular case excuses the filing of briefs or specifies different time limits:
(1) the appellant's principal brief, within 30 days after the docketing of notice that the record has been transmitted or is available electronically;
(2) the appellee's principal and response brief, within 30 days after the appellant's principal brief is served;
(3) the appellant's response and reply brief, within 30 days after the appellee's principal and response brief is served; and
(4) the appellee's reply brief, within 14 days after the appellant's response and reply brief is served, but at least 7 days before scheduled argument unless the district court or BAP, for good cause, allows a later filing.

Rule 8017. Brief of an Amicus Curiae

(a) During initial consideration of a case on the merits. (1) Applicability
This Rule 8017(a) governs amicus filings during a court's initial consideration of a case on the merits.
(2) When permitted
The United States or its officer or agency or a state may file an amicus brief without the consent of the parties or leave of court. Any other amicus curiae may file a brief only by leave of court or if the brief states that all parties have consented to its filing, but a district court or BAP may prohibit the filing of or may strike an amicus brief that would result in a judge's disqualification. On its own motion, and with notice to all parties to an appeal, the district court or BAP may request a brief by an amicus curiae.
(3) Motion for leave to file
The motion must be accompanied by the proposed brief and state:
(A) the movant's interest; and
(B) the reason why an amicus brief is desirable and why the matters asserted are relevant to the disposition of the appeal.
(4) Contents and form
An amicus brief must comply with Rule 8015. In addition to the requirements of Rule 8015, the cover must identify the party or parties supported and indicate whether the brief supports affirmance or reversal. If an amicus curiae is a corporation, the brief must include a disclosure statement like that required of parties by Rule 8012. An amicus brief need not comply with Rule 8014, but must include the following:
(A) a table of contents, with page references;
(B) a table of authorities--cases (alphabetically arranged), statutes, and other authorities--with references to the pages of the brief where they are cited;
(C) a concise statement of the identity of the amicus curiae, its interest in the case, and the source of its authority to file;
(D) unless the amicus curiae is one listed in the first sentence of subdivision (a)(2), a statement that indicates whether:
(i) a party's counsel authored the brief in whole or in part;
(ii) a party or a party's counsel contributed money that was intended to fund preparing or submitting the brief; and
(iii) a person--other than the amicus curiae, its members, or its counsel--contributed money that was intended to fund preparing or submitting the brief and, if so, identifies each such person;
(E) an argument, which may be preceded by a summary and need not include a statement of the applicable standard of review; and
(F) a certificate of compliance, if required by Rule 8015(h).
(5) Length
Except by the district court's or BAP's permission, an amicus brief must be no more than one-half the maximum length authorized by these rules for a party's principal brief. If the court grants a party permission to file a longer brief, that extension does not affect the length of an amicus brief.
(6) Time for filing
An amicus curiae must file its brief, accompanied by a motion for filing when necessary, no later than 7 days after the principal brief of the party being supported is filed. An amicus curiae that does not support either party must file its brief no later than 7 days after the appellant's principal brief is filed. The district court or BAP may grant leave for later filing, specifying the time within which an opposing party may answer.
(7) Reply brief
Except by the district court's or BAP's permission, an amicus curiae may not file a reply brief.
(8) Oral argument
An amicus curiae may participate in oral argument only with the district court's or BAP's permission.
(b) During consideration of whether to grant rehearing
(1) Applicability
This Rule 8017(b) governs amicus filings during a district court's or BAP's consideration of whether to grant rehearing, unless a local rule or order in a case provides otherwise.
(2) When permitted
The United States or its officer or agency or a state may file an amicus brief without the consent of the parties or leave of court. Any other amicus curiae may file a brief only by leave of court.
(3) Motion for leave to file
Rule 8017(a)(3) applies to a motion for leave.
(4) Contents, form, and length
Rule 8017(a)(4) applies to the amicus brief. The brief must include a certificate under Rule 8015(h) and not exceed 2,600 words.
(5) Time for filing
An amicus curiae supporting the motion for rehearing or supporting neither party must file its brief, accompanied by a motion for filing when necessary, no later than 7 days after the motion is filed. An amicus curiae opposing the motion for rehearing must file its brief, accompanied by a motion for filing when necessary, no later than the date set by the court for the response..

Rule 8018. Serving and Filing Briefs; Appendices

(a) TIME TO SERVE AND FILE A BRIEF. The following rules apply unless the district court or BAP by order in a particular case excuses the filing of briefs or specifies different time limits:

(1) The appellant must serve and file a brief within 30 days after the docketing of notice that the record has been transmitted or is available electronically.

(2) The appellee must serve and file a brief within 30 days after service of the appellant's brief.

(3) The appellant may serve and file a reply brief within 14 days after service of the appellee's brief, but a reply brief must be filed at least 7 days before scheduled argument unless the district court or BAP, for good cause, allows a later filing.

(4) If an appellant fails to file a brief on time or within an extended time authorized by the district court or BAP, an appellee may move to dismiss the appeal—or the district court or BAP, after notice, may dismiss the appeal on its own motion. An appellee who fails to file a brief will not be heard at oral argument unless the district court or BAP grants permission.

(b) DUTY TO SERVE AND FILE AN APPENDIX TO THE BRIEF.

(1) Appellant. Subject to subdivision (e) and Rule 8009(d), the appellant must serve and file with its principal brief excerpts of the record as an appendix. It must contain the following:

(A) the relevant entries in the bankruptcy docket;
(B) the complaint and answer, or other equivalent filings;
(C) the judgment, order, or decree from which the appeal is taken;
(D) any other orders, pleadings, jury instructions, findings, conclusions, or opinions relevant to the appeal;
(E) the notice of appeal; and
(F) any relevant transcript or portion of it.

(2) Appellee. The appellee may also serve and file with its brief an appendix that contains material required to be included by the appellant or relevant to the appeal or cross-appeal, but omitted by the appellant.

(3) Cross-Appellee. The appellant as cross-appellee may also serve and file with its response an appendix that contains material relevant to matters raised initially by the principal brief in the cross-appeal, but omitted by the cross-appellant.

(c) FORMAT OF THE APPENDIX. The appendix must begin with a table of contents identifying the page at which each part begins. The relevant docket entries must follow the table of contents. Other parts of the record must follow chronologically. When pages from the transcript of proceedings are placed in the appendix, the transcript page numbers must be shown in brackets immediately before the included pages. Omissions in the text of documents or of the transcript must be indicated by asterisks. Immaterial formal matters (captions, subscriptions, acknowledgments, and the like) should be omitted.

(d) EXHIBITS. Exhibits designated for inclusion in the appendix may be reproduced in a separate volume or volumes, suitably indexed.

(e) APPEAL ON THE ORIGINAL RECORD WITHOUT AN

APPENDIX. The district court or BAP may, either by rule for all cases or classes of cases or by order in a particular case, dispense with the appendix and permit an appeal to proceed on the original record, with the submission of any relevant parts of the record that the district court or BAP orders the parties to file.

Rule 8018.1. District-Court Review of a Judgment that the Bankruptcy Court Lacked the Constitutional Authority to Enter

If, on appeal, a district court determines that the bankruptcy court did not have the power under Article III of the Constitution to enter the judgment, order, or decree appealed from, the district court may treat it as proposed findings of fact and conclusions of law.

Rule 8019. Oral Argument

(a) PARTY'S STATEMENT. Any party may file, or a district court or BAP may require, a statement explaining why oral argument should, or need not, be permitted.

(b) PRESUMPTION OF ORAL ARGUMENT AND EXCEPTIONS. Oral argument must be allowed in every case unless the district judge—or all the BAP judges assigned to hear the appeal—examine the briefs and record and determine that oral argument is unnecessary because

(1) the appeal is frivolous;

(2) the dispositive issue or issues have been authoritatively decided; or

(3) the facts and legal arguments are adequately presented in the briefs and record, and the decisional process would not be significantly aided by oral argument.

(c) NOTICE OF ARGUMENT; POSTPONEMENT. The district court or BAP must advise all parties of the date, time, and place for oral argument, and the time allowed for each side. A motion to postpone the argument or to allow longer argument must be filed reasonably in advance of the hearing date.

(d) ORDER AND CONTENTS OF ARGUMENT. The appellant opens and concludes the argument. Counsel must not read at length from briefs, the record, or authorities.

(e) CROSS-APPEALS AND SEPARATE APPEALS. If there is a cross-appeal, Rule 8016(b) determines which party is the appellant and which is the appellee for the purposes of oral argument. Unless the district court or BAP directs otherwise, a cross-appeal or separate appeal must be argued when the initial appeal is argued. Separate parties should avoid duplicative argument.

(f) NONAPPEARANCE OF A PARTY. If the appellee fails to appear for argument, the district court or BAP may hear the appellant's argument. If the appellant fails to appear for argument, the district court or BAP may hear the appellee's argument. If neither party appears, the case will be decided on the briefs unless the district court or BAP orders otherwise.

(g) SUBMISSION ON BRIEFS. The parties may agree to submit a case for decision on the briefs, but the district court or BAP may direct that the case be argued.

(h) USE OF PHYSICAL EXHIBITS AT ARGUMENT; REMOVAL. Counsel intending to use physical exhibits other than documents at the argument must arrange to place them in the courtroom on the day of the argument before the court convenes. After the argument, counsel must remove the exhibits from the courtroom unless the district court or BAP directs otherwise. The clerk may destroy or dispose of the exhibits if counsel does not reclaim them within a reasonable time after the clerk gives notice to remove them.

Rule 8020. Frivolous Appeal and Other Misconduct

(a) FRIVOLOUS APPEAL—DAMAGES AND COSTS. If the district court or BAP determines that an appeal is frivolous, it may, after a separately filed motion or notice from the court and reasonable opportunity to respond, award just damages and single or double costs to the appellee.

(b) OTHER MISCONDUCT. The district court or BAP may discipline or sanction an attorney or party appearing before it for other misconduct, including failure to comply with any court order. First, however, the court must afford the attorney or party reasonable notice, an opportunity to show cause to the contrary, and, if requested, a hearing.

Rule 8021. Costs

(a) Against whom assessed

The following rules apply unless the law provides or the district court or BAP orders otherwise:

(1) if an appeal is dismissed, costs are taxed against the appellant, unless the parties agree otherwise;

(2) if a judgment, order, or decree is affirmed, costs are taxed against the appellant;

(3) if a judgment, order, or decree is reversed, costs are taxed against the appellee;

(4) if a judgment, order, or decree is affirmed or reversed in part, modified, or vacated, costs are taxed only as the district court or BAP orders.

(b) Costs for and against the United States

Costs for or against the United States, its agency, or its officer may be assessed under subdivision (a) only if authorized by law.

(c) Costs on appeal taxable in the bankruptcy court

The following costs on appeal are taxable in the bankruptcy court for the benefit of the party entitled to costs under this rule:

(1) the production of any required copies of a brief, appendix, exhibit, or the record;

(2) the preparation and transmission of the record;

(3) the reporter's transcript, if needed to determine the appeal;

(4) premiums paid for a bond or other security to preserve rights pending appeal; and

(5) the fee for filing the notice of appeal.

(d) Bill of costs; objections

A party who wants costs taxed must, within 14 days after entry of judgment on appeal, file with the bankruptcy clerk, with proof of service, an itemized and verified bill of costs. Objections must be filed within 14 days after service of the bill of costs, unless the bankruptcy court extends the time.

Rule 8022. Motion for Rehearing

(a) Time to file; contents; response; action by the district court or BAP if granted

(1) Time

Unless the time is shortened or extended by order or local rule, any motion for rehearing by the district court or BAP must be filed within 14 days after entry of judgment on appeal.

(2) Contents

The motion must state with particularity each point of law or fact that the movant believes the district court or BAP has overlooked or misapprehended and must argue in support of the motion. Oral argument is not permitted.

(3) Response

Unless the district court or BAP requests, no response to a motion for rehearing is permitted. But ordinarily, rehearing will not be granted in the absence of such a request.

(4) Action by the district court or BAP

If a motion for rehearing is granted, the district court or BAP may do any of the following:

(A) make a final disposition of the appeal without reargument;

(B) restore the case to the calendar for reargument or resubmission; or

(C) issue any other appropriate order.

(b) Form of the motion; length

The motion must comply in form with Rule 8013(f)(1) and (2). Copies must be served and filed as provided by Rule 8011. Except by the district court's or BAP's permission:

(1) a motion for rehearing produced using a computer must include a certificate under Rule 8015(h) and not exceed 3,900 words; and

(2) a handwritten or typewritten motion must not exceed 15 pages.

Rule 8023. Voluntary Dismissal

(a) Stipulated dismissal. The clerk of the district court or BAP must dismiss an appeal if the parties file a signed dismissal agreement specifying how costs are to be paid and pay any court fees that are due.

(b) Appellant's motion to dismiss. An appeal may be dismissed on the appellant's motion on terms agreed to by the parties or fixed by the district court or BAP.

(c) Other relief. A court order is required for any relief under Rule 8023(a) or (b) beyond the dismissal of an appeal--including approving a settlement, vacating an action of the bankruptcy court, or remanding the case to it.

(d) Court approval. This rule does not alter the legal requirements governing court approval of a settlement, payment, or other consideration.

Rule 8024. Clerk's Duties on Disposition of the Appeal

(a) JUDGMENT ON APPEAL. The district or BAP clerk must prepare, sign, and enter the judgment after receiving the court's opinion or, if there is no opinion, as the court instructs. Noting the judgment on the docket constitutes entry of judgment.
(b) NOTICE OF A JUDGMENT. Immediately upon the entry of a judgment, the district or BAP clerk must:
(1) transmit a notice of the entry to each party to the appeal, to the United States trustee, and to the bankruptcy clerk, together with a copy of any opinion; and
(2) note the date of the transmission on the docket.
(c) RETURNING PHYSICAL ITEMS. If any physical items were transmitted as the record on appeal, they must be returned to the bankruptcy clerk on disposition of the appeal.

Rule 8025. Stay of a District Court or BAP Judgment

(a) AUTOMATIC STAY OF JUDGMENT ON APPEAL. Unless the district court or BAP orders otherwise, its judgment is stayed for 14 days after entry.
(b) STAY PENDING APPEAL TO THE COURT OF APPEALS.
(1) In General. On a party's motion and notice to all other parties to the appeal, the district court or BAP may stay its judgment pending an appeal to the court of appeals.
(2) Time Limit. The stay must not exceed 30 days after the judgment is entered, except for cause shown.
(3) Stay Continued. If, before a stay expires, the party who obtained the stay appeals to the court of appeals, the stay continues until final disposition by the court of appeals.
(4) Bond or Other Security. A bond or other security may be required as a condition for granting or continuing a stay of the judgment. A bond or other security may be required if a trustee obtains a stay, but not if a stay is obtained by the United States or its officer or agency or at the direction of any department of the United States government.
(c) AUTOMATIC STAY OF AN ORDER, JUDGMENT, OR DECREE OF A BANKRUPTCY COURT. If the district court or BAP enters a judgment affirming an order, judgment, or decree of the bankruptcy court, a stay of the district court's or BAP's judgment automatically stays the bankruptcy court's order, judgment, or decree for the duration of the appellate stay.
(d) POWER OF A COURT OF APPEALS NOT LIMITED. This rule does not limit the power of a court of appeals or any of its judges to do the following:
(1) stay a judgment pending appeal;
(2) stay proceedings while an appeal is pending;
(3) suspend, modify, restore, vacate, or grant a stay or an injunction while an appeal is pending; or
(4) issue any order appropriate to preserve the status quo or the effectiveness of any judgment to be entered.

Rule 8026. Rules by Circuit Councils and District Courts; Procedure When There is No Controlling Law

(a) LOCAL RULES BY CIRCUIT COUNCILS AND DISTRICT COURTS.
(1) Adopting Local Rules. A circuit council that has authorized a BAP under 28 U.S.C. § 158(b) may make and amend rules governing the practice and procedure on appeal from a judgment, order, or decree of a bankruptcy court to the BAP. A district court may make and amend rules governing the practice and procedure on appeal from a judgment, order, or decree of a bankruptcy court to the district court. Local rules must be consistent with, but not duplicative of, Acts of Congress and these Part VIII rules. Rule 83 F.R.Civ.P. governs the procedure for making and amending rules to govern appeals.
(2) Numbering. Local rules must conform to any uniform numbering system prescribed by the Judicial Conference of the United States.
(3) Limitation on Imposing Requirements of Form. A local rule imposing a requirement of form must not be enforced in a way that causes a party to lose any right because of a nonwillful failure to comply.
(b) PROCEDURE WHEN THERE IS NO CONTROLLING LAW.
(1) In General. A district court or BAP may regulate practice in any manner consistent with federal law, applicable federal rules, the Official Forms, and local rules.
(2) Limitation on Sanctions. No sanction or other disadvantage may be imposed for noncompliance with any requirement not in federal law, applicable federal rules, the Official Forms, or local rules unless the alleged violator has been furnished in the particular case with actual notice of the requirement.

Rule 8027. Notice of a Mediation Procedure
If the district court or BAP has a mediation procedure applicable to bankruptcy appeals, the clerk must notify the parties promptly after docketing the appeal of:
(a) the requirements of the mediation procedure; and
(b) any effect the mediation procedure has on the time to file briefs.

Rule 8028. Suspension of Rules in Part VIII
In the interest of expediting decision or for other cause in a particular case, the district court or BAP, or where appropriate the court of appeals, may suspend the requirements or provisions of the rules in Part VIII, except Rules 8001, 8002, 8003, 8004, 8005, 8006, 8007, 8012, 8020, 8024, 8025, 8026, and 8028.

PART IX
GENERAL PROVISIONS

Rule 9001. General Definitions
The definitions of words and phrases in §§ 101, 902, 1101, and 1502 of the Code, and the rules of construction in § 102 govern their use in these rules. In addition, the following words and phrases used in these rules have the meanings indicated:
(1) "Bankruptcy clerk" means a clerk appointed pursuant to 28 U. S. C. Section 156(b).
(2) "Bankruptcy Code" or "Code" means title 11 of the United States Code.
(3) "Clerk" means bankruptcy clerk, if one has been appointed, otherwise clerk of the district court.
(4) "Court" or "judge" means the judicial officer before whom a case or proceeding is pending.
(5) "Debtor." When any act is required by these rules to be performed by a debtor or when it is necessary to compel attendance of a debtor for examination and the debtor is not a natural person: (A) if the debtor is a corporation, "debtor" includes, if designated by the court, any or all of its officers, members of its board of directors or trustees or of a similar controlling body, a controlling stockholder or member, or any other person in control; (B) if the debtor is a partnership, "debtor" includes any or all of its general partners or, if designated by the court, any other person in control.
(6) "Firm" includes a partnership or professional corporation of attorneys or accountants.
(7) "Judgment" means any appealable order.
(8) "Mail" means first class, postage prepaid.
(9) "Notice provider" means any entity approved by the Administrative Office of the United States Courts to give notice to creditors under Rule 2002(g)(4).
(10) "Regular associate" means any attorney regularly employed by, associated with, or counsel to an individual or firm.
(11) "Trustee" includes a debtor in possession in a chapter 11 case.
(12) "United States trustee" includes an assistant United States trustee and any designee of the United States trustee.

Rule 9002. Meanings of Words in the Federal Rules of Civil Procedure When Applicable to Cases Under The Code

The following words and phrases used in the Federal Rules of Civil Procedure made applicable to cases under the Code by these rules have the meanings indicated unless they are inconsistent with the context:
(1) "Action" or "civil action" means an adversary proceeding or, when appropriate, a contested petition, or proceedings to vacate an order for relief or to determine any other contested matter.
(2) "Appeal" means an appeal as provided by 28 U. S. C. Section 158.
(3) "Clerk" or "clerk of the district court" means the court officer

responsible for the bankruptcy records in the district.

(4) "District court," "trial court," "court," "district judge," or "judge" means bankruptcy judge if the case or proceeding is pending before a bankruptcy judge.

(5) "Judgment" includes any order appealable to an appellate court.

Rule 9003. Prohibition of Ex Parte Contacts

(a) GENERAL PROHIBITION. Except as otherwise permitted by applicable law, any examiner, any party in interest, and any attorney, accountant, or employee of a party in interest shall refrain from ex parte meetings and communications with the court concerning matters affecting a particular case or proceeding.

(b) UNITED STATES TRUSTEE. Except as otherwise permitted by applicable law, the United States trustee and assistants to and employees or agents of the United States trustee shall refrain from ex parte meetings and communications with the court concerning matters affecting a particular case or proceeding. This rule does not preclude communications with the court to discuss general problems of administration and improvement of bankruptcy administration, including the operation of the United States trustee system.

Rule 9004. General Requirements of Form

(a) LEGIBILITY; ABBREVIATIONS. All petitions, pleadings, schedules and other papers shall be clearly legible. Abbreviations in common use in the English language may be used.

(b) CAPTION. Each paper filed shall contain a caption setting forth the name of the court, the title of the case, the bankruptcy docket number, and a brief designation of the character of the paper.

Rule 9005. Harmless Error

Rule 61 F. R. Civ. P. applies in cases under the Code. When appropriate, the court may order the correction of any error or defect or the cure of any omission which does not affect substantial rights.

Rule 9005.1. Constitutional Challenge to a Statute – Notice, Certification, and Intervention

Rule 5.1 F.R.Civ.P. applies in cases under the Code.

Rule 9006. Computing and Extending Time

(a) COMPUTING TIME. The following rules apply in computing any time period specified in these rules, in the Federal Rules of Civil Procedure, in any local rule or court order, or in any statute that does not specify a method of computing time.

(1) Period Stated in Days or a Longer Unit. When the period is stated in days or a longer unit of time:

(A) exclude the day of the event that triggers the period;

(B) count every day, including intermediate Saturdays, Sundays, and legal holidays; and

(C) include the last day of the period, but if the last day is a Saturday, Sunday, or legal holiday, the period continues to run until the end of the next day that is not a Saturday, Sunday, or legal holiday.

(2) Period Stated in Hours. When the period is stated in hours:

(A) begin counting immediately on the occurrence of the event that triggers the period;

(B) count every hour, including hours during intermediate Saturdays, Sundays, and legal holidays; and

(C) if the period would end on a Saturday, Sunday, or legal holiday, then continue the period until the same time on the next day that is not a Saturday, Sunday, or legal holiday.

(3) Inaccessibility of Clerk's Office. Unless the court orders otherwise, if the clerk's office is inaccessible:

(A) on the last day for filing under Rule 9006(a)(1), then the time for filing is extended to the first accessible day that is not a Saturday, Sunday, or legal holiday; or

(B) during the last hour for filing under Rule 9006(a)(2), then the time for filing is extended to the same time on the first accessible day that is not a Saturday, Sunday, or legal holiday.

(4) "Last Day" Defined. Unless a different time is set by a statute, local rule, or order in the case, the last day ends:

(A) for electronic filing, at midnight in the court's time zone; and

(B) for filing by other means, when the clerk's office is scheduled to close.

(5) "Next Day" Defined. The "next day" is determined by continuing to count forward when the period is measured after an event and backward when measured before an event.

(6) "Legal Holiday" Defined. "Legal holiday" means:

(A) the day set aside by statute for observing New Year's Day, Martin Luther King Jr.'s Birthday, Washington's Birthday, Memorial Day, Independence Day, Labor Day, Columbus Day, Veterans' Day, Thanksgiving Day, or Christmas Day;

(B) any day declared a holiday by the President or Congress; and

(C) for periods that are measured after an event, any other day declared a holiday by the state where the district court is located. (In this rule, "state" includes the District of Columbia and any United States commonwealth or territory.)

(b) ENLARGEMENT.

(1) In General. Except as provided in paragraphs (2) and (3) of this subdivision, when an act is required or allowed to be done at or within a specified period by these rules or by a notice given thereunder or by order of court, the court for cause shown may at any time in its discretion (1) with or without motion or notice order the period enlarged if the request therefor is made before the expiration of the period originally prescribed or as extended by a previous order or (2) on motion made after the expiration of the specified period permit the act to be done where the failure to act was the result of excusable neglect.

(2) Enlargement Not Permitted. The court may not enlarge the time for taking action under Rules 1007(d), 2003(a) and (d), 7052, 9023, and 9024.

(3) Enlargement Governed By Other Rules. The court may enlarge the time for taking action under Rules 1006(b)(2), 1017(e), 3002(c), 4003(b), 4004(a), 4007(c), 4008(a), 8002, and 9033, only to the extent and under the conditions stated in those rules. In addition, the court may enlarge the time to file the statement required under Rule 1007(b)(7), and to file schedules and statements in a small business case under § 1116(3) of the Code, only to the extent and under the conditions stated in Rule 1007(c).

(c) REDUCTION.

(1) In General. Except as provided in paragraph (2) of this subdivision, when an act is required or allowed to be done at or within a specified time by these rules or by a notice given thereunder or by order of court, the court for cause shown may in its discretion with or without motion or notice order the period reduced.

(2) Reduction Not Permitted. The court may not reduce the time for taking action under Rules 2002(a)(7), 2003(a), 3002(c), 3014, 3015, 4001(b)(2), (c)(2), 4003(a), 4004(a), 4007(c), 4008(a), 8002, and 9033(b). In addition, the court may not reduce the time under Rule 1007(c) to file the statement required by Rule 1007(b)(7).

(d) MOTION PAPERS. A written motion, other than one which may be heard ex parte, and notice of any hearing shall be served not later than seven days before the time specified for such hearing, unless a different period is fixed by these rules or by order of the court. Such an order may for cause shown be made on ex parte application. When a motion is supported by affidavit, the affidavit shall be served with the motion. Except as otherwise provided in Rule 9023, any written response shall be served not later than one day before the hearing, unless the court permits otherwise.

(e) TIME OF SERVICE. Service of process and service of any paper other than process or of notice by mail is complete on mailing.

(f) ADDITIONAL TIME AFTER SERVICE BY MAIL OR UNDER RULE 5(b)(2)(D), (E), or (F) F.R.Civ.P. When there is a right or requirement to act or undertake some proceedings within a prescribed period after being served and that service is by mail or under Rule 5(b)(2)(D) (leaving with the clerk) or (F) (other means consented to) F.R.Civ.P., three days are added after the prescribed period would otherwise expire under Rule 9006(a).

(g) GRAIN STORAGE FACILITY CASES. This rule shall not limit the court's authority under Section 557 of the Code to enter orders governing procedures in cases in which the debtor is an owner or operator of a grain storage facility.

Rule 9007. General Authority to Regulate Notices

When notice is to be given under these rules, the court shall designate, if not otherwise specified herein, the time within which, the entities to whom, and the form and manner in which the notice shall be given. When feasible, the court may order any notices under these rules to be combined.

Rule 9008. Service or Notice by Publication

Whenever these rules require or authorize service or notice by publication, the court shall, to the extent not otherwise specified in these rules, determine the form and manner thereof, including the newspaper or other medium to be used and the number of publications.

Rule 9009. Forms

(a) OFFICIAL FORMS. The Official Forms prescribed by the Judicial Conference of the United States shall be used without alteration, except as otherwise provided in these rules, in a particular Official Form, or in the national instructions for a particular Official Form. Official Forms may be modified to permit minor changes not affecting wording or the order of presenting information, including changes that:

(1) expand the prescribed areas for responses in order to permit complete responses;

(2) delete space not needed for responses; or

(3) delete items requiring detail in a question or category if the filer indicates—either by checking "no" or "none" or by stating in words—that there is nothing to report on that question or category.

(b) DIRECTOR'S FORMS. The Director of the Administrative Office of the United States Courts may issue additional forms for use under the Code.

(c) CONSTRUCTION. The forms shall be construed to be consistent with these rules and the Code.

Rule 9010. Representation and Appearances; Powers of Attorney

(a) AUTHORITY TO ACT PERSONALLY OR BY ATTORNEY. A debtor, creditor, equity security holder, indenture trustee, committee or other party may (1) appear in a case under the Code and act either in the entity's own behalf or by an attorney authorized to practice in the court, and (2) perform any act not constituting the practice of law, by an authorized agent, attorney in fact, or proxy.

(b) NOTICE OF APPEARANCE. An attorney appearing for a party in a case under the Code shall file a notice of appearance with the attorney's name, office address and telephone number, unless the attorney's appearance is otherwise noted in the record.

(c) POWER OF ATTORNEY. The authority of any agent, attorney in fact, or proxy to represent a creditor for any purpose other than the execution and filing of a proof of claim or the acceptance or rejection of a plan shall be evidenced by a power of attorney conforming substantially to the appropriate Official Form. The execution of any such power of attorney shall be acknowledged before one of the officers enumerated in 28 U. S. C. Section 459, Section 953, Rule 9012, or a person authorized to administer oaths under the laws of the state where the oath is administered.

Rule 9011. Signing of Papers; Representations to the Court; Sanctions; Verification and Copies of Papers

(a) SIGNING OF PAPERS. Every petition, pleading, written motion, and other paper, except a list, schedule, or statement, or amendments thereto, shall be signed by at least one attorney of record in the attorney's individual name. A party who is not represented by an attorney shall sign all papers. Each paper shall state the signer's address and telephone number, if any. An unsigned paper shall be stricken unless omission of the signature is corrected promptly after being called to the attention of the attorney or party.

(b) REPRESENTATIONS TO THE COURT. By presenting to the court (whether by signing, filing, submitting, or later advocating) a petition, pleading, written motion, or other paper, an attorney or unrepresented party is certifying that to the best of the person's knowledge, information, and belief, formed after an inquiry reasonable under the circumstances,-

(1) it is not being presented for any improper purpose, such as to harass or to cause unnecessary delay or needless increase in the cost of litigation;

(2) the claims, defenses, and other legal contentions therein are warranted by existing law or by a nonfrivolous argument for the extension, modification, or reversal of existing law or the establishment of new law;

(3) the allegations and other factual contentions have evidentiary support or, if specifically so identified, are likely to have evidentiary support after a reasonable opportunity for further investigation or discovery; and

(4) the denials of factual contentions are warranted on the evidence or, if specifically so identified, are reasonably based on a lack of information or belief.

(c) SANCTIONS. If, after notice and a reasonable opportunity to respond, the court determines that subdivision (b) has been violated, the court may, subject to the conditions stated below, impose an appropriate sanction upon the attorneys, law firms, or parties that have violated subdivision (b) or are responsible for the violation.

(1) How Initiated.

(A) By Motion. A motion for sanctions under this rule shall be made separately from other motions or requests and shall describe the specific conduct alleged to violate subdivision (b). It shall be served as provided in Rule 7004. The motion for sanctions may not be filed with or presented to the court unless, within 21 days after service of the motion (or such other period as the court may prescribe), the challenged paper, claim, defense, contention, allegation, or denial is not withdrawn or appropriately corrected, except that this limitation shall not apply if the conduct alleged is the filing of a petition in violation of subdivision (b). If warranted, the court may award to the party prevailing on the motion the reasonable expenses and attorney's fees incurred in presenting or opposing the motion. Absent exceptional circumstances, a law firm shall be held jointly responsible for violations committed by its partners, associates, and employees.

(B) On Court's Initiative. On its own initiative, the court may enter an order describing the specific conduct that appears to violate subdivision (b) and directing an attorney, law firm, or party to show cause why it has not violated subdivision (b) with respect thereto.

(2) Nature of Sanction; Limitations. A sanction imposed for violation of this rule shall be limited to what is sufficient to deter repetition of such conduct or comparable conduct by others similarly situated. Subject to the limitations in subparagraphs (A) and (B), the sanction may consist of, or include, directives of a nonmonetary nature, an order to pay a penalty into court, or, if imposed on motion and warranted for effective deterrence, an order directing payment to the movant of some or all of the reasonable attorneys' fees and other expenses incurred as a direct result of the violation.

(A) Monetary sanctions may not be awarded against a represented party for a violation of subdivision (b)(2).

(B) Monetary sanctions may not be awarded on the court's initiative unless the court issues its order to show cause before a voluntary dismissal or settlement of the claims made by or against the party which is, or whose attorneys are, to be sanctioned.

(3) Order. When imposing sanctions, the court shall describe the conduct determined to constitute a violation of this rule and explain the basis for the sanction imposed.

(d) INAPPLICABILITY TO DISCOVERY. Subdivisions (a) through (c) of this rule do not apply to disclosures and discovery requests, responses, objections, and motions that are subject to the provisions of Rules 7026 through 7037.

(e) VERIFICATION. Except as otherwise specifically provided by these rules, papers filed in a case under the Code need not be verified. Whenever verification is required by these rules, an unsworn declaration as provided in 28 U. S. C. Section 1746 satisfies the requirement of verification.

(f) COPIES OF SIGNED OR VERIFIED PAPERS. When these rules require copies of a signed or verified paper, it shall suffice if the original is signed or verified and the copies are conformed to the original.

Rule 9012. Oaths and Affirmations

(a) PERSONS AUTHORIZED TO ADMINISTER OATHS. The following persons may administer oaths and affirmations and take acknowledgements: a bankruptcy judge, clerk, deputy clerk, United States trustee, officer authorized to administer oaths in proceedings before the courts of the United States or under the laws of the state where the oath is to be taken, or a diplomatic or consular officer of the United States in any foreign country.

(b) AFFIRMATION IN LIEU OF OATH. When in a case under the Code an oath is required to be taken, a solemn affirmation may be accepted in lieu thereof.

Rule 9013. Motions: Form and Service

A request for an order, except when an application is authorized by the rules, shall be by written motion, unless made during a hearing. The motion shall state with particularity the grounds therefor, and shall set forth the relief or order sought. Every written motion, other than one which may be considered ex parte, shall be served by the moving party within the time determined under Rule 9006(d). The moving party shall serve the motion on:

(a) the trustee or debtor in possession and on those entities specified by these rules; or

(b) the entities the court directs if these rules do not require service or specify the entities to be served.

Rule 9014. Contested Matters

(a) MOTION. In a contested matter not otherwise governed by these rules, relief shall be requested by motion, and reasonable notice and opportunity for hearing shall be afforded the party against whom relief is sought. No response is required under this rule unless the court directs otherwise.

(b) SERVICE. The motion shall be served in the manner provided for service of a summons and complaint by Rule 7004 and within the time determined under Rule 9006(d). Any written response to the motion shall be served within the time determined under Rule 9006(d). Any paper served after the motion shall be served in the manner provided by Rule 5(b) F.R. Civ. P.

(c) APPLICATION OF PART VII RULES. Except as otherwise provided in this rule, and unless the court directs otherwise, the following rules shall apply: 7009, 7017, 7021, 7025, 7026, 7028-7037, 7041, 7042, 7052, 7054-7056, 7064, 7069, anD 7071. The following subdivisions of Fed. R. Civ. P. 26, as incorporated by Rule 7026, shall not apply in a contested matter unless the court directs otherwise: 26(a)(1) (mandatory disclosure), 26(a)(2) (disclosures regarding expert testimony) and 26(a)(3) (additional pre-trial disclosure), and 26(f) (mandatory meeting before scheduling conference/discovery plan). An entity that desires to perpetuate testimony may proceed in the same manner as provided in Rule 7027 for the taking of a deposition before an adversary proceeding. The court may at any stage in a particular matter direct that one or more of the other rules in Part VII shall apply. The court shall give the parties notice of any order issued under this paragraph to afford them a reasonable opportunity to comply with the procedures prescribed by the order.

(d) TESTIMONY OF WITNESSES. Testimony of witnesses with respect to disputed material factual issues shall be taken in the same manner as testimony in an adversary proceeding.

(e) ATTENDANCE OF WITNESSES. The court shall provide procedures that enable parties to ascertain at a reasonable time before any scheduled hearing whether the hearing will be an evidentiary hearing at which witnesses may testify.

Rule 9015. Jury Trials.

(a) APPLICABILITY OF CERTAIN FEDERAL RULES OF CIVIL PROCEDURE. Rules 38, 39, 47, 49, and 51, F.R.Civ.P., and Rule 81(c) F.R.Civ.P. insofar as it applies to jury trials, apply in cases and proceedings, except that a demand made under Rule 38(b) F.R.Civ.P. shall be filed in accordance with Rule 5005.

(b) CONSENT TO HAVE TRIAL CONDUCTED BY BANKRUPTCY JUDGE. If the right to a jury trial applies, a timely demand has been filed pursuant to Rule 38(b) F.R.Civ.P., and the bankruptcy judge has been specially designated to conduct the jury trial, the parties may consent to have a jury trial conducted by a bankruptcy judge under 28 U.S.C. §157(e) by jointly or separately filing a statement of consent within any applicable time limits specified by local rule.

(c) APPLICABILITY OF RULE 50 F.R. CIV. P. Rule 50 F.R. Civ. P. applies in cases and proceedings, except that any renewed motion for judgment or request for a new trial shall be filed no later than 14 days after the entry of judgment.

Rule 9016. Subpoena

Rule 45 F. R. Civ. P. applies in cases under the Code.

Rule 9017. Evidence

The Federal Rules of Evidence and Rules 43, 44, and 44.1 F. R. Civ. P. apply in cases under the Code.

Rule 9018. Secret, Confidential, Scandalous, or Defamatory Matter

On motion or on its own initiative, with or without notice, the court may make any order which justice requires (1) to protect the estate or any entity in respect of a trade secret or other confidential research, development, or commercial information, (2) to protect any entity against scandalous or defamatory matter contained in any paper filed in a case under the Code, or (3)to protect governmental matters that are made confidential by statute or regulation. If an order is entered under this rule without notice, any entity affected thereby may move to vacate or modify the order, and after a hearing on notice the court shall determine the motion.

Rule 9019. Compromise and Arbitration

(a) COMPROMISE. On motion by the trustee and after notice and a hearing, the court may approve a compromise or settlement. Notice shall be given to creditors, the United States trustee, the debtor, and indenture trustees as provided in Rule 2002 and to any other entity as the court may direct.

(b) AUTHORITY TO COMPROMISE OR SETTLE CONTROVERSIES WITHIN CLASSES. After a hearing on such notice as the court may direct, the court may fix a class or classes of controversies and authorize the trustee to compromise or settle controversies within such class or classes without further hearing or notice.

(c) ARBITRATION. On stipulation of the parties to any controversy affecting the estate the court may authorize the matter to be submitted to final and binding arbitration.

Rule 9020. Contempt Proceedings

Rule 9014 governs a motion for an order of contempt made by the United States trustee or a party in interest.

Rule 9021. Entry of Judgment

A judgment or order is effective when entered under Rule 5003.

Rule 9022. Notice of Judgment or Order

(a) JUDGMENT OR ORDER OF BANKRUPTCY JUDGE. Immediately on the entry of a judgment or order the clerk shall serve a notice of entry in the manner provided in Rule 5(b) F.R.Civ.P. on the contesting parties and on other entities as the court directs. Unless the case is a chapter 9 municipality case, the clerk shall forthwith transmit to the United States trustee a copy of the judgment or order. Service of the notice shall be noted in the docket. Lack of notice of the entry does not affect the time to appeal or relieve or authorize the court to relieve a party for failure to appeal within the time allowed, except as permitted in Rule 8002.

(b) JUDGMENT OR ORDER OF DISTRICT JUDGE. Notice of a judgment or order entered by a district judge is governed by Rule 77(d) F. R. Civ. P. Unless the case is a chapter 9 municipality case, the clerk shall forthwith transmit to the United States trustee a copy of a judgment or order entered by a district judge.

Rule 9023. New Trials; Amendment Of Judgments

Except as provided in this rule and Rule 3008, Rule 59 F.R.Civ.P. applies in cases under the Code. A motion for a new trial or to alter or amend a judgment shall be filed, and a court may on its own order a new trial, no later than 14 days after entry of judgment. In some circumstances, Rule 8008 governs post-judgment motion practice after an appeal has been docketed and is pending.

Rule 9024. Relief from Judgment or Order

Rule 60 F.R.Civ.P. applies in cases under the Code except that (1) a motion to reopen a case under the Code or for the reconsideration of an order allowing or disallowing a claim against the estate entered without a contest is not subject to the one year limitation prescribed in Rule 60(c), (2) a complaint to revoke a discharge in a chapter 7 liquidation case may be filed only within the time allowed by § 727(e) of the Code, and (3) a complaint to revoke an order confirming a plan may be filed only within the time allowed by § 1144, § 1230, or § 1330. In some circumstances, Rule 8008 governs post-judgment motion practice after an appeal has been docketed and is pending.

Rule 9025. Security: Proceedings Against Sureties

Whenever the Code or these rules require or permit a party to give security, and security is given with one or more security providers, each provider submits to the jurisdiction of the court, and liability may be determined in an adversary proceeding governed by the rules in Part VII.

Rule 9026. Exceptions Unnecessary

Rule 46 F. R. Civ. P. applies in cases under the Code.

Rule 9027. Removal

(a) NOTICE OF REMOVAL.

(1) WHERE FILED; FORM AND CONTENT. A notice of removal shall be filed with the clerk for the district and division within which is located the state or federal court where the civil action is pending. The notice shall be signed pursuant to Rule 9011 and contain a short and plain statement of the facts which entitle the party filing the notice to remove, contain a statement that upon removal of the claim or cause of action the proceeding is

core or non-core and, if non-core, that the party filing the notice does or does not consent to entry of final orders or judgment by the bankruptcy judge, and be accompanied by a copy of all process and pleadings.

(2) TIME FOR FILING; CIVIL ACTION INITIATED BEFORE COMMENCEMENT OF THE CASE UNDER THE CODE. If the claim or cause of action in a civil action is pending when a case under the Code is commenced, a notice of removal may be filed only within the longest of (A) 90 days after the order for relief in the case under the Code, (B) 30 days after entry of an order terminating a stay, if the claim or cause of action in a civil action has been stayed under Section 362 of the Code, or (C) 30 days after a trustee qualifies in a chapter 11 reorganization case but not later than 180 days after the order for relief.

(3) TIME FOR FILING; CIVIL ACTION INITIATED AFTER COMMENCEMENT OF THE CASE UNDER THE CODE. If a claim or cause of action is asserted in another court after the commencement of a case under the Code, a notice of removal may be filed with the clerk only within the shorter of (A) 30 days after receipt, through service or otherwise, of a copy of the initial pleading setting forth the claim or cause of action sought to be removed or (B) 30 days after receipt of the summons if the initial pleading has been filed with the court but not served with the summons.

(b) NOTICE. Promptly after filing the notice of removal, the party filing the notice shall serve a copy of it on all parties to the removed claim or cause of action.

(c) FILING IN NON-BANKRUPTCY COURT. Promptly after filing the notice of removal, the party filing the notice shall file a copy of it with the clerk of the court from which the claim or cause of action is removed. Removal of the claim or cause of action is effected on such filing of a copy of the notice of removal. The parties shall proceed no further in that court unless and until the claim or cause of action is remanded.

(d) REMAND. A motion for remand of the removed claim or cause of action shall be governed by Rule 9014 and served on the parties to the removed claim or cause of action.

(e) PROCEDURE AFTER REMOVAL.

(1) After removal of a claim or cause of action to a district court the district court or, if the case under the Code has been referred to a bankruptcy judge of the district, the bankruptcy judge, may issue all necessary orders and process to bring before it all proper parties whether served by process issued by the court from which the claim or cause of action was removed or otherwise.

(2) The district court or, if the case under the Code has been referred to a bankruptcy judge of the district, the bankruptcy judge, may require the party filing the notice of removal to file with the clerk copies of all records and proceedings relating to the claim or cause of action in the court from which the claim or cause of action was removed.

(3) Any party who has filed a pleading in connection with the removed claim or cause of action, other than the party filing the notice of removal, shall file a statement that the party does or does not consent to entry of final orders or judgment by the bankruptcy judge. A statement required by this paragraph shall be signed pursuant to Rule 9011 and shall be filed not later than 14 days after the filing of the notice of removal. Any party who files a statement pursuant to this paragraph shall mail a copy to every other party to the removed claim or cause of action.

(f) PROCESS AFTER REMOVAL. If one or more of the defendants has not been served with process, the service has not been perfected prior to removal, or the process served proves to be defective, such process or service may be completed or new process issued pursuant to Part VII of these rules. This subdivision shall not deprive any defendant on whom process is served after removal of the defendant's right to move to remand the case.

(g) APPLICABILITY OF PART VII. The rules of Part VII apply to a claim or cause of action removed to a district court from a federal or state court and govern procedure after removal. Repleading is not necessary unless the court so orders. In a removed action in which the defendant has not answered, the defendant shall answer or present the other defenses or objections available under the rules of Part VII within 21 days following the receipt through service or otherwise of a copy of the initial pleading setting forth the claim for relief on which the action or proceeding is based, or within 21 days following the service of summons on such initial pleading, or within seven days following the filing of the notice of removal, whichever period is longest.

(h) RECORD SUPPLIED. When a party is entitled to copies of the records and proceedings in any civil action or proceeding in a federal or state court, to be used in the removed civil action or proceeding, and the clerk of the federal or state court, on demand accompanied by payment or tender of the lawful fees, fails to deliver certified copies, the court may, on affidavit reciting the facts, direct such record to be supplied by affidavit or otherwise. Thereupon the proceedings, trial and judgment may be had in the court, and all process awarded, as if certified copies had been filed.

(i) ATTACHMENT OR SEQUESTRATION; SECURITIES. When a claim or cause of action is removed to a district court, any attachment or sequestration of property in the court from which the claim or cause of action was removed shall hold the property to answer the final judgment or decree in the same manner as the property would have been held to answer final judgment or decree had it been rendered by the court from which the claim or cause of action was removed. All bonds, undertakings, or security given by either party to the claim or cause of action prior to its removal shall remain valid and effectual notwithstanding such removal. All injunctions issued, orders entered and other proceedings had prior to removal shall remain in full force and effect until dissolved or modified by the court.

Rule 9028. Disability of a Judge

Rule 63 F.R. Civ. P. applies in cases under the Code.

Rule 9029. Local Bankruptcy Rules; Procedure When There is No Controlling Law

(a) LOCAL BANKRUPTCY RULES.

(1) Each district court acting by a majority of its district judges may make and amend rules governing practice and procedure in all cases and proceedings within the district court's bankruptcy jurisdiction which are consistent with - but not duplicative of - Acts of Congress and these rules and which do not prohibit or limit the use of the Official Forms. Rule 83 F.R.Civ.P. governs the procedure for making local rules. A district court may authorize the bankruptcy judges of the district, subject to any limitation or condition it may prescribe and the requirements of 83 F.R.Civ.P., to make and amend rules of practice and procedure which are consistent with - but not duplicative of - Acts of Congress and these rules and which do not prohibit or limit the use of the Official Forms. Local rules shall conform to any uniform numbering system prescribed by the Judicial Conference of the United States.

(2) A local rule imposing a requirement of form shall not be enforced in a manner that causes a party to lose rights because of a nonwillful failure to comply with the requirement.

(b) PROCEDURE WHEN THERE IS NO CONTROLLING LAW. A judge may regulate practice in any manner consistent with federal law, these rules, Official Forms, and local rules of the district. No sanction or other disadvantage may be imposed for noncompliance with any requirement not in federal law, federal rules, Official Forms, or the local rules of the district unless the alleged violator has been furnished in the particular case with actual notice of the requirement.

Rule 9030. Jurisdiction and Venue Unaffected

These rules shall not be construed to extend or limit the jurisdiction of the courts or the venue of any matters therein.

Rule 9031. Masters Not Authorized

Rule 53 F. R. Civ. P. does not apply in cases under the Code.

Rule 9032. Effect of Amendment of Federal Rules of Civil Procedure

The Federal Rules of Civil Procedure which are incorporated by reference and made applicable by these rules shall be the Federal Rules of Civil Procedure in effect on the effective date of these rules and as thereafter amended, unless otherwise provided by such amendment or by these rules.

Rule 9033. Review of Proposed Findings of Fact and Conclusions of Law in Non-Core Proceedings

(a) SERVICE. In a proceeding in which the bankruptcy court has issued proposed findings of fact and conclusions of law, the clerk shall serve forthwith copies on all parties by mail and note the date of mailing on the docket.

(b) OBJECTIONS: TIME FOR FILING. Within 14 days after being served with a copy of the proposed findings of fact and conclusions of law a party may serve and file with the clerk written objections which identify the specific proposed findings or conclusions objected to and state the grounds for such objection. A party may respond to another party's objections within 14 days after being served with a copy thereof. A party objecting to the bankruptcy judge's proposed findings or conclusions shall arrange promptly for the transcription of the record, or such portions of it as all parties may agree upon or the bankruptcy judge deems sufficient, unless the district judge otherwise directs.

(c) EXTENSION OF TIME. The bankruptcy judge may for cause extend the time for filing objections by any party for a period not to exceed 21 days from the expiration of the time otherwise prescribed by this rule. A request to extend the time for filing objections must be made before the time for filing objections has expired, except that a request made no more than 21 days after the expiration of the time for filing objections may be granted upon a showing of excusable neglect.

(d) STANDARD OF REVIEW. The district judge shall make a de novo review upon the record or, after additional evidence, of any portion of the bankruptcy judge's findings of fact or conclusions of law to which specific written objection has been made in accordance with this rule. The district judge may accept, reject, or modify the proposed findings of fact or conclusions of law, receive further evidence, or recommit the matter to the bankruptcy judge with instructions.

Rule 9034. Transmittal of Pleadings, Motion Papers, Objections, and Other Papers to the United States Trustee

Unless the United States trustee requests otherwise or the case is a chapter 9 municipality case, any entity that files a pleading, motion, objection, or similar paper relating to any of the following matters shall transmit a copy thereof to the United States trustee within the time required by these rules for service of the paper:

(a) a proposed use, sale, or lease of property of the estate other than in the ordinary course of business;

(b) the approval of a compromise or settlement of a controversy;

(c) the dismissal or conversion of a case to another chapter;

(d) the employment of professional persons;

(e) an application for compensation or reimbursement of expenses;

(f) a motion for, or approval of an agreement relating to, the use of cash collateral or authority to obtain credit;

(g) the appointment of a trustee or examiner in a chapter 11 reorganization case;

(h) the approval of a disclosure statement;

(i) the confirmation of a plan;

(j) an objection to, or waiver or revocation of, the debtor's discharge;

(k) any other matter in which the United States trustee requests copies of filed papers or the court orders copies transmitted to the United States trustee.

Rule 9035. Applicability of Rules in Judicial Districts in Alabama and NC

In any case under the Code that is filed in or transferred to a district in the State of Alabama or the State of North Carolina and in which a United States trustee is not authorized to act, these rules apply to the extent that they are not inconsistent with any federal statute effective in the case.

Rule 9036. Notice by Electronic Transmission

(a) In general. This rule applies whenever these rules require or permit sending a notice or serving a paper by mail or other means.

(b) Notices from and service by the court

(1) Registered users

The clerk may send notice to or serve a registered user by filing the notice or paper with the court's electronic-filing system.

(2) All recipients

For any recipient, the clerk may send notice or serve a paper by electronic means that the recipient consented to in writing, including by designating an electronic address for receipt of notices. But these exceptions apply:

(A) if the recipient has registered an electronic address with the Administrative Office of the United States Courts' bankruptcy-noticing program, the clerk shall send the notice to or serve the paper at that address; and

(B) if an entity has been designated by the Director of the Administrative Office of the United States Courts as a high-volume paper-notice recipient, the clerk may send the notice to or serve the paper electronically at an address designated by the Director, unless the entity has designated an address under § 342(e) or (f) of the Code.

(c) Notices from and service by an entity

An entity may send notice or serve a paper in the same manner that the clerk does under (b), excluding (b)(2)(A) and (B).

(d) Completing notice or service

Electronic notice or service is complete upon filing or sending but is not effective if the filer or sender receives notice that it did not reach the person to be served. It is the recipient's responsibility to keep its electronic address current with the clerk.

(e) Inapplicability

This rule does not apply to any paper required to be served in accordance with Rule 7004.

Rule 9037. Privacy Protection For Filings Made with the Court

(a) REDACTED FILINGS. Unless the court orders otherwise, in an electronic or paper filing made with the court that contains an individual's social-security number, taxpayer-identification number, or birth date, the name of an individual, other than the debtor, known to be and identified as a minor, or a financial-account number, a party or nonparty making the filing may include only:

(1) the last four digits of the social-security number and taxpayer-identification number;

(2) the year of the individual's birth;

(3) the minor's initials; and

(4) the last four digits of the financial-account number.

(b) EXEMPTIONS FROM THE REDACTION REQUIREMENT. The redaction requirement does not apply to the following:

(1) a financial-account number that identifies the property allegedly subject to forfeiture in a forfeiture proceeding;

(2) the record of an administrative or agency proceeding unless filed with a proof of claim;

(3) the official record of a state-court proceeding;

(4) the record of a court or tribunal, if that record was not subject to the redaction requirement when originally filed;

(5) a filing covered by subdivision (c) of this rule; and

(6) a filing that is subject to § 110 of the Code.

(c) FILINGS MADE UNDER SEAL. The court may order that a filing be made under seal without redaction. The court may later unseal the filing or order the entity that made the filing to file a redacted version for the public record.

(d) PROTECTIVE ORDERS. For cause, the court may by order in a case under the Code:

(1) require redaction of additional information; or

(2) limit or prohibit a nonparty's remote electronic access to a document filed with the court.

(e) OPTION FOR ADDITIONAL UNREDACTED FILING UNDER SEAL. An entity making a redacted filing may also file an unredacted copy under seal. The court must retain the unredacted copy as part of the record.

(f) OPTION FOR FILING A REFERENCE LIST. A filing that contains redacted information may be filed together with a reference list that identifies each item of redacted information and specifies an appropriate identifier that uniquely corresponds to each item listed. The list must be filed under seal and may be amended as of right. Any reference in the case to a listed identifier will be construed to refer to the corresponding item of information.

(g) WAIVER OF PROTECTION OF IDENTIFIERS. An entity waives the protection of subdivision (a) as to the entity's own information by filing it without redaction and not under seal

(h) Motion to redact a previously filed document

(1) Content of the motion; service

Unless the court orders otherwise, if an entity seeks to redact from a previously filed document information that is protected under subdivision (a), the entity must:

(A) file a motion to redact identifying the proposed redactions;

(B) attach to the motion the proposed redacted document;

(C) include in the motion the docket or proof-of-claim number of the previously filed document; and

(D) serve the motion and attachment on the debtor, debtor's attorney, trustee (if any), United States trustee, filer of the unredacted document, and any individual whose personal identifying information is to be redacted.

(2) Restricting public access to the unredacted document; docketing the redacted document

The court must promptly restrict public access to the motion and the unredacted document pending its ruling on the motion. If the court grants it, the court must docket the redacted document. The restrictions on public access to the motion and unredacted document remain in effect until a further court order. If the court denies it, the restrictions must be lifted, unless the court orders otherwise.

PART X [Abrogated]

APPENDIX III - EXEMPT PROPERTY: FEDERAL AND ALL 50 STATES

Contents

FEDERAL BANKRUPTCY EXEMPTIONS

Type of Property	Amount of Exemption	Statute Creating Exemption
Debtor's aggregate interest in real or personal property that the debtor or a dependent of the debtor uses as a residence; or in a cooperative that owns property that the debtor or a dependent of the debtor uses as a residence; or in a burial lot for the debtor or a dependent of the debtor	$27,900	11 USC § 522(d)(1)
1 motor vehicle	$4,450	11 USC § 522(d)(2)
household furnishings, household goods, wearing apparel, appliances, books, animals, crops, or musical instruments held primarily for the personal, family, or household use of the debtor or a dependent of the debtor.	$124,875 aggregate value limitations with $700 limitation on value of each item.	11 USC § 522(d)(3)
Jewelry held primarily for personal, family, or household use of debtor or a dependent of the debtor	$1,875	11 USC § 522(d)(4)
Any property selected by debtor	$1,475 plus up to $14,875 of unused portion of § 522(d)(1) exemption	11 USC § 522(d)(5)
Implements, professional books, or tools, of the trade of debtor or a dependent of the debtor	$2,800	11 USC § 522(d)(6)
Unmatured life insurance contracts owned by debtor, except credit life insurance contracts	100%	11 USC § 522(d)(7)
Accrued dividends or interest under, or loan value of, any unmatured life insurance contract owned by debtor in which the insured is the debtor or a person of whom the debtor is a dependent	$14,8775 less any amounts transferred by insurer from cash reserve for payment of premiums	11 USC § 522(d)(8)
Professionally prescribed health aids of debtor and dependents	100%	11 USC § 522 (d)(9)
Social security, unemployment compensation, or public assistance benefits	100%	11 USC § 522(d)(10)(A)
Veterans' benefits	100%	11 USC § 522(d)(10)(B)
Disability, illness, or unemployment benefits	100%	11 USC § 522(d)(10)(C)
Alimony, support, or separate maintenance	100% of amount reasonably necessary for support of debtor and dependents	11 USC § 522(d)(10)(D)
Payments under stock bonus, pension, profit sharing, annuity, or similar plan or contract on account of illness, disability, death, age, or length of service	100% of amount reasonably necessary for support of debtor and dependents	11 USC § 522(d)(10)(E)
	NOTE - Exemption does not apply if: plan or contract was established under auspices of insider that employed debtor at time plan or contract arose; such payment is on account of age or length of service; and such plan or contract does not qualify under Internal Revenue Code.	
Crime victim's reparation law benefits or awards	100%	11 USC § 522(d)(11)(A)
Payments on account of the wrongful death of individual of whom debtor was a dependent	100% of amount reasonably necessary for support of debtor and independents	11 USC § 522(d)(11)(B)
Payments under life insurance contract insuring life of an individual of whom debtor was a dependent	100% of amount reasonably necessary for support of debtor and dependent	11 USC § 522(d)(11)(C)
Payments on account of personal bodily injury of debtor or person of whom debtor is a dependent (does not include compensation for pain and suffering or actual pecuniary loss)	$27,900	11 USC § 522(d)(11)(D)
Payments in compensation for loss of future earnings of debtor or person of whom debtor is a dependent	100% of amount reasonably necessary for support of debtor and dependents	11 USC § 522(d)(11)(E)
Retirement funds and IRAs that are tax-qualified under the I.R.C.	100%	11 USC § 522(d)(12)

FEDERAL - NONBANKRUPTCY

Type of Property	Amount of Exemption	Statute Creating Exemption
Retirement funds and IRAs that are tax-qualified under the I.R.C	100%	11 USC 522(b)(3)(C)
Disposable earnings (earnings after deductions required by law)	75% OR 30 times the federal minimum hourly wage per week.* WHICHEVER IS GREATER	15 USC § 1673
Wages due masters, seamen and apprentices	100% (does not apply to claims for maintenance and support of spouse and dependent children)	46 USC § 11109(a)
Veterans Administration benefits (includes pensions, life insurance and disability benefits)	100%	38 USC § 5301
Social Security benefits (includes retirement, death and disability benefits)	100%	42 USC § 407
Longshoremen and harbor workers' medical, disability and death benefits	100%	33 USC § 916
Railroad employees retirement and disability annuities	100%	45 USC § 231
Federal civil service disability and death benefits	100%	5 USC § 8130
Federal civil service retirement benefits	100%	5 USC § 8346(a)
Military Survivor Benefit Plan annuities	100%	10 USC § 1450(i)
Annuities paid to widows and dependent children of Federal Justices and Judges	100%	28 USC § 376(n)
Servicemen's group life insurance benefits	100%	38 USC § 1970(g)
Veteran's group life insurance benefits	100%	38 USC § 1970(g)
Deposits made in U.S. servicemen's savings institutions by servicemen while on permanent duty assignment outside U.S. and its possessions	no limit	10 USC § 1035(d)
Debtor's interest in ERISA-qualified retirement and other employee benefit plans and IRAs**	$1,512,350	11 USC § 522(n)
Compensation paid for injury or death resulting from war risk hazard	100%	42 USC § 1717
Railroad unemployment benefits	100%	45 USC § 352(e)
U.S. Servicemember annuities	100%	10 USC § 1440
Certain benefits protected from collections by the US under the Debt Collection Improvement Act of 1996	$9000	31 USC § 3716(c)(3)(A)
Exemptions provided for in suits by the US against individual defendants under the Federal Debt Collections Procedure Act	See statue for details	28 USC § 3001(a)
Benefits, annuities or payments to survivors of foreign service employees	100%	22 USC § 4060(c)
Any monies accruing from any lease or sale of lands held in trust by the US for any Indian	100%	25 USC § 410
Pensions paid to Medal of Honor recipients	100%	38 USC §1562(c)
Protections from entry of judgment, attachment or garnishment under Servicemembers Civil Rights Act	See statute for details	50 USC § 501
Federal employees' limitation on garnishment for debts owed to the US	85% of disposable income	5 USC § 5514
Exemptions from levy by the IRS	See statute for details	26 USC § 6334(a)

* This exemption does not apply to state and federal tax claims and smaller amounts are exempt against support claims. The federal minimum hourly wage is $7.25 per hour. See 29 USC § 206(a)(1). NOTE: This exemption may not apply in certain states.

** For an in-depth discussion on the extent to which a debtor's retirement funds and IRAs are protectable in bankruptcy, see *Williamson, The Bankruptcy Issues Handbook*, 7th Ed., 2016 (Argyle Pub.), Art. 1.13 .

*** Amounts set forth above relating to 11 USC 522(d) and (n) are subject to change as of April 1, 2022 to reflect changes in CPI. (See 11 USC §104(a)).

ALABAMA

Federal bankruptcy exemptions not permitted. See ALA. CODE § 6-10-11.

Type of Property	Amount of Exemption	Statute Creating Exemption
Homestead of resident (includes mobile home)	$16,450 per individual (cannot exceed 160 acres)	ALA. CODE § 6-10-2
NOTE - Homestead and other personal exemptions must be filed with Probate Court to be effective (ALA. CODE §§6-10-20 & 21)		
Burial lots and seat or pew in place of public worship	100%	ALA. CODE § 6-10-5
Personal property of resident, except wages, salaries and compensation	$7,500	ALA. CODE § 6-10-6**
Necessary wearing apparel of resident debtor and family	100%	ALA. CODE § 6-10-6
Family portraits or pictures and all books used by family	100%	ALA. CODE § 6-10-6
Wages, salaries and compensation for personal services	75%	ALA. CODE § 6-10-7
Proceeds and avails of life insurance policies payable to person other than the insured (includes cash surrender value, loan value and dividends)	100%	ALA. CODE §§ 6-10-8, 27-14-29
Disposable earnings (earnings less deductions required by law and deductions as periodic payments to pension, retirement or disability programs)	75% or 30 times the federal minimum hourly wage per week, whichever is greater	ALA. CODE § 5-19-15
Growing or ungathered crops	100%	ALA. CODE § 6-9-41
Public assistance payments	100%	ALA. CODE § 38-4-8, 38-5-5
Workmen's compensation benefits	100%	ALA. CODE § 25-5-86
Unemployment compensation benefits	100%	ALA. CODE § 25-4-140
Proceeds and avails of disability insurance contracts & annuity contracts	$250 per month	ALA. CODE § 27-14-31 & 32
Fraternal Benefit Society benefits	100%	ALA. CODE § 27-34-27
Teachers' retirement system benefits	100%	ALA. CODE § 16-25-23
State employees retirement system benefits	100%	ALA. CODE § 36-27-28
Peace officers retirement and disability benefits	100%	ALA. CODE § 36-21-77
Partner's interest in specific partnership property	100%	ALA. CODE § 6-10-9,10A-8-2.03
Household goods and furnishings: Cooking utensils, stove, tablewear, table, chairs, bed, bedding in use by family	100%	ALA. CODE § 6-10-126
Vehicle essential to debtor's business	100%	ALA. CODE § 6-10-126
Tools essential to debtor's business	100%	ALA. CODE § 6-10-126
Retirement and disability benefits-judges	100%	ALA. CODE § 12-18-10
Crime Victims' Compensation	100% (support claims excepted)	ALA. CODE § 15-23-15(e)
"Qualified trusts" under Internal Revenue Code (spendthrift trust)	100%	ALA. CODE § 19-3B-508
Insurance: Interest of resident members and policyholders of mutual aid associations	100%	ALA. CODE § 27-30-25
Military: personally owned uniformed, arms, equipment, etc. retirement plans	100%	ALA. CODE § 31-2-78
Southeast Asian War prisoners: security for loan or bonuses	$500	ALA. CODE §§ 31-7-1, 31-7-2

*Ala. Code stands for Code of Alabama

** Adjusted every 3 years beginning July 1, 2017 per CPI (ALA. CODE § 6-10-12)

ALASKA

Use of federal bankruptcy exemption **not permitted in this state.** ALASKA STAT. § 9.38.055

Type of Property	Amount of Exemption	Statute Creating Exemption
Property used as principal residence of debtor or dependents	$72,900 (exemption may be claimed pro rata by joint or multiple owners)	ALASKA STAT. § 9.38.010
Burial plots, health aids, medical benefits, crime victim's reparation awards, longevity bonuses, benefits exempt under federal law, liquor licenses, tuition credits or savings account authorized under ALASKA STAT. § 14.40.809(a), permanent fund dividends allowed under ALASKA STAT. § 43.23.065, and senior care benefits payable under ALASKA STAT. § 47.45.301–309.	100%	ALASKA STAT. § 9.38.015(a)
State disability, unemployment or illness benefits; teachers'; judges'; and public employees' retirement benefits; elected public officials retirement benefits; and state child support collections	100%	ALASKA STAT. § 9.38.015(b) ALASKA STAT. § 14.25.200 ALASKA STAT. § 23.20.405 ALASKA STAT. § 22.25.100
Assets and benefits of retirement plans that are qualified under I.R.C., except contributions made within 120 days of bankruptcy.	100%	ALASKA STAT. § 9.38.017(a)
Household goods, wearing apparel, personal books and musical instruments, and family portraits and heirlooms	$4,050 aggregate value	ALASKA STAT. § 9.38.020(a)
Personal jewelry of debtor and dependents	$1,350	ALASKA STAT. § 9.38.020(b)
Implements, professional books and tools of trade	$3,780	ALASKA STAT. § 9.38.020(c)
Pets	$1,350	ALASKA STAT. § 9.38.020(d)
One motor vehicle not exceeding $27,000 in value	$4,050	ALASKA STAT. § 9.38.020(e)
Unmatured life insurance and annuity contracts, including accrued dividends and loan value	$500,500	ALASKA STAT. § 9.38.025(a)
Periodic earnings or benefits of debtor	$473 per week or equivalent ($743 if debtor is sole support of household)	ALASKA STAT. § 9.38.030(a), (e) & §9.38.050(b)
Cash and liquid assets of debtor without periodic earnings	$1,890 per month ($2,970 if debtor is sole support of household) (does not include permanent fund dividends)	ALASKA STAT. § 9.38.030 (b) ALASKA STAT. §9.38.050 (b)
Partner's interest in specific partnership property	100%	ALASKA STAT. § 9.38.100(b)
Aid to dependent children and public assistance payments	As provided in § 9.38 above	ALASKA STAT. § 47.25.210 ALASKA STAT. § 47.25.550
Workmen's compensation benefits	As provided in § 9.38 above	ALASKA STAT. § 23.30.160(b)
Child support installments paid directly by debtor's employer	100%	ALASKA STAT. § 9.55.210 (2)
Fraternal Benefit Society benefits	100%	ALASKA STAT. § 21.84.240
Materials furnished by mechanics for construction of buildings	100%	ALASKA STAT. § 34.35.105
Tenancies by the entireties	100%	ALASKA STAT. § 34.15.140& 11 USC § 522(b)(3)(B)
Benefits paid by reason of disability, illness, or unemployment	100%	ALASKA STAT. § 09.38.030(e)(1)
Alimony	100%	ALASKA STAT. § 9.38.030(e)(2)
Personal injury/wrongful death recoveries	100%	ALASKA STAT. § 9.38.030(e)(3)
Life insurance proceeds payable to spouse or dependent	100%	ALASKA STAT. § 9.38.030(e)(4)
Payments being received from other pensions	100%	ALASKA STAT. § 9.38.030(e)(5)
Increased exemption amounts where individual's earnings alone support the household	$743/week if claiming liquid asset under ALASKA STAT. §9.38.030(b) (continues on next page)	ALASKA STAT. §9.38.050(b); 8AAC 95.030(e)(1); 8AAC 95.030(e)(2)

(continued from previous page)

Type of Property	Amount of Exemption	Statute Creating Exemption
Household goods, clothes, books, musical instruments, family heirlooms	$3000 (as against awards against crime victim)	ALASKA STAT. § 09.38.065(a)(3)(A)
Professional books, implements, tools of trade	$2800 (as against awards against crime victim)	ALASKA STAT. § 09.38.065(a)(3)(B)
80 acres of land owned by a cemetery association	100%	ALASKA STAT. § 10.30.060,09.38.015(d)
Lots sold by cemetery associations for interment	100%	ALASKA STAT. § 10.30.120
Relief assistance granted under ALASKA STAT. § 47.25.120-47.25.300	100%	ALASKA STAT. § 47.25.210
Benefits from Alaska Longevity Bonus	100%	ALASKA STAT. § 47.45.120
Commercial fishing privileges	100%	ALASKA STAT. § 16.43.945
Increased exemption amounts for personal injury or disability payments	available at the court's discretion	ALASKA STAT. § 9.38.050 (a)
Proceeds from lost, damaged, destroyed exempt property for 12 months or 6 months if homestead	100%	ALASKA STAT. § 9.38.060

NOTES: ALASKA STAT. § 9.38.055 provides that only the exemptions in ALASKA STAT. §§ 9.38.010, 9.38.015(a), 9.38.017, 9.38.020, 9.38.025 and 9.38.030 apply in bankruptcy proceedings. ALASKA STAT. § 9.38.115 provides that the dollar amounts in ALASKA STAT. § 9.38 are to be adjusted on October 1 in the even numbered years to reflect cost of living changes. These changes are published at 8 AAC § 95.030.

ARIZONA

Use of federal bankruptcy **not** permitted in AZ. See ARIZ. REV. STAT. § 33-1133(B)

Type of Property	Amount of Exemption	Statute Creating Exemption
Homestead, consisting of debtor's interest in real property used as residence, in a condominium or cooperative, or in a mobile home and land upon which it is located	$150,000 NOTE - The total exemption claimed by both spouses may not exceed $150,000. The exemption applies to identifiable cash proceeds of a homestead sale for 18 months after the sale	ARIZ. REV. STAT. § 33-1101(A)
1 kitchen table, 1 dining room table, 4 chairs for each table (plus 1 chair per table for each dependent residing in household exceeding 4) 1 living, room couch, 1 living room chair plus 1 per dependent residing in household, 3 living room coffee or end tables, 3 living room lamps, 1 living room carpet or rug, 2 beds plus 1 per dependent residing in household, 1 bed table, dresser and lamp per each allowed bed, bedding for each allowed bed, pictures, oil paintings and drawings made by debtor, family portraits and frames, 1 television set, 1 radio, 1 stove, 1 refrigerator, 1 washing machine, 1 clothes dryer, 1 vacuum cleaner.	$6,000 aggregate value	ARIZ. REV. STAT. § 33-1123
Food, fuel and provisions for 6 months	100%	ARIZ. REV. STAT. § 33-1124
Wearing apparel	$500	ARIZ. REV. STAT. § 33-1125(1)
Musical instruments of debtor & family	$400	ARIZ. REV. STAT. § 33-1125(2)
Pets, horses, milk cows, and poultry	$1,000	ARIZ. REV. STAT. § 33-1125(3)
Engagement and wedding rings	$2,000	ARIZ. REV. STAT. § 33-1125(4)
Library	$250	ARIZ. REV. STAT. § 33-1125(5)
1 typewriter, 1 bicycle, 1 sewing machine, a family bible, a lot in burying ground, 1 rifle, shotgun, or pistol	$2,000 aggregate value	ARIZ. REV. STAT. § 33-1125(7)
1 watch	$250	ARIZ. REV. STAT. § 33-1125(6)
1 motor vehicle used primarily for personal, family or household purpose. (In case of married persons, each spouse may claim exemption, which may be combined with other spouses' exemption in same property.)	$6,000 ($12,000 if debtor physically disabled)	ARIZ. REV. STAT. § 33-1125(8)
Professionally prescribed prostheses, including a wheelchair	100%	ARIZ. REV. STAT. § 33-1125(9)
Interest of debtor as participant or alternate payee in retirement or deferred compensation plan qualified under Internal Revenue Code	100% (contributions by participant made within 120 days of filing of petition are not exempt)	ARIZ. REV. STAT. § 33-1126B.
Prepaid rent and security deposits for debtor's residence	Lesser of $2,000 or 1 1/2 months rent (except child support obligation) (cannot be claimed if homestead exemption is claimed	ARIZ. REV. STAT. § 33-1126C.
Life insurance proceeds paid or payable to surviving spouse or child	$20,000 (except child support obligations) (excludes cash value increases caused by excessive payments in previous 2 years)	ARIZ. REV. STAT. § 33-1126A(1)
Earnings of minor child	100% (except child support obligations)	ARIZ. REV. STAT. § 33-1126A(2)
Funds received by or payable to debtor as child support or spousal maintenance under court order	100% (except child support obligations)	ARIZ. REV. STAT. § 33-1126A(3)
Health, accident or disability insurance benefits	100% (except child support obligations) (certain debts excepted)	ARIZ. REV. STAT. § 33-1126A(4)
Insurance proceeds for damage or destruction of exempt property	100% of exemption given for damaged or destroyed property	ARIZ. REV. STAT. § 33-1126A(5)
Cash surrender value of debtor's life insurance policies payable to debtor's spouse, child, parent, siblings or dependent	100% (except child support obligations) (debtor must own policies for at least 2 years)	ARIZ. REV. STAT. § 33-1126A(6) ARIZ. REV. STAT. § 20-1131(D)
Proceeds from annuity contract owned by debtor for 2 years or more	100% (except child support obligations)	ARIZ. REV. STAT. § 33-1126A(7)
Damages for wrongful levy or execution	100% (except child support obligations)	ARIZ. REV. STAT. § 33-1126A(8)
One single bank account	$300 (except child support obligations)	ARIZ. REV. STAT. § 33-1126A(9)
Necessary tools, equipment, instruments and books used in business or profession by debtor or spouse	$5,000 (does not include personal motor vehicle)	ARIZ. REV. STAT. § 33-1130(1)
Machinery, utensils, feed, grain, seed and animals of farmer	$ 2,500	ARIZ. REV. STAT. § 33-1130(2)
Arms, uniforms and accoutrements required by law to be kept by debtor	100%	ARIZ. REV. STAT. § 33-1130(3)
Disposable earnings (earnings less deduction required by law) - includes pension, retirement and deferred compensation payments * Does not apply to Chapter 13 proceedings.	75% or 30 times the federal minimum hourly wage per week, whichever is greater.	ARIZ. REV. STAT. § 33-1131(B)
Fraternal Benefit Society benefits	100%	ARIZ. REV. STAT. § 20-877

(continued on next page)

ARIZONA

Type of Property	Amount of exemption	Statute Creating Exemption
All property of judgment debtor	100% exempt from execution in favor of another state for failure to pay that state's income tax on pension or retirement benefits received while the debtor was an AZ resident	Ariz. Rev. Stat. § 33-1151
Firemen's relief and pension benefits	100%	Ariz. Rev. Stat. § 9-968
Police pension benefits	100%	Ariz. Rev. Stat. § 9-931
Teachers' retirement benefits	100%	Ariz. Rev. Stat. § 38-792
State employees' retirement benefits	100%	Ariz. Rev. Stat. § 38-792
Specific partnership property	100% of partner's interest	Ariz. Rev. Stat. § 29-1041
Wrongful death benefits	100%*	Ariz. Rev. Stat. § 12-592
Group life insurance policy or proceeds	100%	Ariz. Rev. Stat. § 20-1132
Wages	$50/week +$15/wk. for each dependent	Ariz. Rev. Stat. § 23-755(D)
Retirement benefits-Elected officials	100%	Ariz. Rev. Stat. § 38-809(B)
Retirement benefits--Public safety personnel	100%	Ariz. Rev. Stat. § 38-850(C)
Retirement benefits--Corrections officers'	100%	Ariz. Rev. Stat. § 38-897(B)
Retirement benefits-Rangers	100%	Ariz. Rev. Stat. § 41-955
Taxing district employee retirement benefits	100%	Ariz. Rev. Stat. § 48-227
Public officers long term disability benefits	100%	Ariz. Rev. Stat. § 38-797.11
School equipment, books, and teaching aids	100%	Ariz. Rev. Stat. § 33-1127
Prearranged funeral benefits	$5,000	Ariz. Rev. Stat. § 32-1391.05(C)(4)
Workmen's compensation benefits	100%	Ariz. Rev. Stat. § 23-1068(B)
Unemployment compensation benefits	100% (except child support obligations)	Ariz. Rev. Stat. § 23-783(A)
Welfare assistance	100%	Ariz. Rev. Stat. § 46-208
Domestic Pets	100%	Ariz. Rev. Stat. § 33-1125(11)
Firearms	$2,000	Ariz. Rev. Stat. § 33-1125(10)

* But See Smith v. Myers, 181 Ariz. 11 (Ariz. 1994).

ARKANSAS

Use of federal bankruptcy exemptions permitted. ARK. CODE. ANN. § 16-66-217

Type of Property	Amount of Exemption	Statute Creating Exemption
Wearing apparel of debtor and family	100%	ARK. CONST. ART. 9, §§ 1 & 2
Personal property of unmarried resident debtor who is not head of family	$200	ARK. CONST. ART. 9, § 1 ACA § 16-66-218(b)(1)
Personal property of resident debtor who is married or head of family	$500	ARK. CONST. ART. 9, § 2
Homestead of resident who is married or head of family (Homestead must be owned and occupied as residence by debtor; except purchase money liens)	$2,500 or entire value of 80 to 160 acres of rural land or ¼ to 1 acre of urban land	ARK. CONST. ART. 9, §§ 3, 4, 5 ACA § 16-66-210
Homestead of deceased homesteader leaving widow or minor children	100% of value of homestead plus rents and profits there from for life of widow or children during minority.	ARK. CONST. ART. 9, § 6
Earned but unpaid earnings for 60 days	$25 per week (may include excess earnings in personal property exemption)	ARK. CODE. ANN. § 16-66-208(b)(1)
Family burial grounds	100% (5 acre limit)	ARK. CODE. ANN. § 16-66-207
Proceeds of life, accident, or disability insurance policies & cash surrender up to $200 (single) and $500 (married)	100% (to the extent permitted by the Arkansas constitution)	ARK. CODE. ANN. § 16-66-209
Contributions to Individual Retirement Account made more than one year prior to filing of bankruptcy case	$20,000 (limit applies to individual debtor and to husband and wife combined)	ARK. CODE. ANN. § 16-66-218(b)(16)
Wedding rings	100%	ARK. CODE. ANN. § 16-66-219
Assets held in and payments receivable from IRC-qualified pension, profit-sharing, or similar retirement plans or contracts including self-employed retirement plans, regular and Roth IRAs	100% of IRC qualified contributions + 100% of amounts in Roth IRAs	ARK. CODE. ANN. § 16-66-220
Proceeds of annuity contracts	100%	ARK. CODE. ANN. § 23-79-134
Unemployment compensation benefits	100% (support claims excepted)	ARK. CODE. ANN. § 11-10-109
Worker's compensation benefits	100%	ARK. CODE. ANN. § 11-9-110
Disability insurance benefits	100%	ARK. CODE. ANN. § 23-79-133
Stipulated premium insurance benefits	100%	ARK. CODE. ANN. § 23-71-112
Mutual assessment life insurance benefits	$1,000	ARK. CODE. ANN. § 23-72-114
Group life insurance proceeds	100%	ARK. CODE. ANN. § 23-79-132
Teachers' retirement benefits	100%	ARK. CODE. ANN. § 24-7-715
State police retirement benefits	100%	ARK. CODE. ANN. § 24-6-223
Firemen's relief & pension benefits	100%	ARK. CODE. ANN. § 24-11-814
Policemen's pension & relief benefits	100%	ARK. CODE. ANN. § 24-11-417
Local police & fire retirement benefits	100%	ARK. CODE. ANN. § 24-10-616
Specific partnership property	100%	ARK. CODE. ANN. § 4-46-307(d)

NOTE: The following exemptions apply only to bankruptcy proceedings and are in addition to any other applicable state exemptions.

The debtor's aggregate interest in real or personal property used by the debtor or a dependent of the debtor as a residence or as a burial plot	$800 for unmarried debtor $1,250 for married debtor	ARK. CODE. ANN. § 16-66-218(a)(1)
One motor vehicle	$1,200 (See Ark. Const.)	[ARK. CODE. ANN. § 16-66-218(a)(2)]*
Wedding bands, including diamonds of 1/2 carat or less	100%	ARK. CODE. ANN. § 16-66-218(a)(3)
Implements, professional books, or tools of trade of debtor or a dependent of the debtor	$750	ARK. CODE. ANN. § 16-66-218(a)(4)*

* See In re Kelley, 455 B.R. 710 (Bank. E. D. Ark. 2011) (holding Section 16-66-218(2) & (4) unconstitutional to the extent they exceed Arkansas's constitutional exemptions); see also *Re:Holt,* 894 F2d 1005 (8th Cir., 1990) and *In re Giller*, 127 BR 215 (Bankr. W.D. Ark. 1990) (questioning statutory exemptions).

Use of federal bankruptcy exemptions **not permitted.** See CAL. CIV. PROC. CODE § 703.130

CALIFORNIA

Type of Property	Amount of Exemption	Statute Creating Exemption
Earnings of debtor	Amount necessary for support of debtor or debtor's family	CAL. CIV. PROC. CODE § 706.051
Homestead exemption. Includes house and outbuildings, land, or mobile home, or boat; and includes proceeds from sale, damage or taking thereof	$100,000 for family unit member living with 1 or more non-owner family unit members. $175,000 for person who is 65 or older, disabled, or over 55 with annual gross income of $25,000 or less if single or $35,000 or less if married. $75,000 for any other person	* CAL. CIV. PROC. CODE § 704.730 *NOTE- Debtor or spouse must reside in homestead and the exemption must be apportioned between the spouses if both are entitled to the exemption.
Necessary personal household furnishings, provisions, appliances, wearing apparel and personal effects of debtor and family	100%	CAL. CIV. PROC. CODE § 704.020
Equity in motor vehicles, including insurance or execution sale proceeds for 90 days under § 704.010	$3,325	CAL. CIV. PROC. CODE § 704.010
Tools, implements, materials, books and equipment used in trade or business (can include motor vehicle if not claimed under C.C.P. § 704.010)	$17,450 combined for debtor & spouse if each is engaged in trade or business (motor vehicle limit is $9,700); if only one is engaged in trade or business, limits are $8,725 and $4,850	CAL. CIV. PROC. CODE § 704.060
Prosthetic and orthopedic appliances and health aids	100%	CAL. CIV. PROC. CODE § 704.050
Jewelry, heirlooms and works of art	$8,725	CAL. CIV. PROC. CODE § 704.040
Residential building materials	$3,500	CAL. CIV. PROC. CODE § 704.030
Prisoners' funds in inmates' trust accounts	$1,750	CAL. CIV. PROC. CODE § 704.090
Bank accounts used for direct deposit of Social Security or public benefit funds	$1,750 for one public benefit depositor $3,500 for one social security depositor $2,600 for 2 or more public benefit depositors $5,250 for 2 or more social security depositors	CAL. CIV. PROC. CODE § 704.080 (all traceable social security and benefit funds in account are exempt)
Earnings in deposit accounts or in cash or its equivalent	75%, except that all earnings subject support orders or assignments are exempt	CAL. CIV. PROC. CODE § 704.070
Unmatured life insurance policies	100%	CAL. CIV. PROC. CODE § 704.100(a)
Aggregate loan values of unmatured life insurance policies	$13,975 each for debtor and spouse	CAL. CIV. PROC. CODE § 704.100(b)
Proceeds of matured life insurance policies	Amount reasonably necessary to support debtor and dependents	CAL. CIV. PROC. CODE § 704.100(c)
Retirement funds and benefits held or payable by a public entity	100% (support claims excepted)	CAL. CIV. PROC. CODE § 704.110(b) CAL. GOV'T. CODE § 21201
Public retirement benefits received	100%	CAL. CIV. PROC. CODE § 704.110(d)
State and public employees' vacation credits	100% (lump sum payments subject to federal earnings exemptions)	CAL. CIV. PROC. CODE § 704.113
Funds and benefits of private retirement plans, except self-employed retirement plans	100% (support claims excepted)	CAL. CIV. PROC. CODE §704.115(b)
Funds and benefits of self employed retirement plans, including IRAs and Roth IRAs	Funds - Amounts necessary to support debtor and dependents upon retirement Periodic benefits - Amount necessary for support of debtor or debtor's family	CAL. CIV. PROC. CODE § 704.115(e)(f) §704.115(a)(3),(b),(e),(f)
Health and disability insurance benefits	100% - health care and support claims excepted	CAL. CIV. PROC. CODE § 704.130
Personal injury and wrongful death claims	100%	CAL. CIV. PROC. CODE §§ 704.140(a), 704.150(a)
Proceeds of personal injury and wrongful death claims	Amount necessary to support debtor and dependents (periodic payments subject only to federal earnings exemption)	CAL. CIV. PROC. CODE §§ 704.140(d), 704.150(c)

(continued on next page)

(Continued from previous page)

Type of Property	Amount of Exemption	Statute Creating Exemption
Workmen's compensation benefits	100% (support claims excepted)	CAL. CIV. PROC. CODE § 704.160
Unemployment insurance contributions and benefits	100% (support claims excepted)	CAL. CIV. PROC. CODE § 704.120
Relocation payments	100%	CAL. CIV. PROC. CODE § 704.180
Welfare and Fraternal Benefit Society benefits	100%	CAL. CIV. PROC. CODE § 704.170
Students' financial aid from institution of higher learnings	100%	CAL. CIV. PROC. CODE § 704.190
Burial plots of debtor and spouse	100%	CAL. CIV. PROC. CODE § 704.200
Specific partnership property	100% of partner's interest	CAL. CORP. CODE § 16501
Business or professional license	100%	CAL. CIV. PROC. CODE § 695.060
Cash employment bonds (all)	100%	CAL. LAB. CODE § 404
Public aid	100%	CAL. WELF. & INST. § 11002
Property not subject to enforcement of a money judgment	100%	CAL. CIV. PROC. CODE § 704.210

NOTE: The exemptions listed below apply only to bankruptcy cases and may only be used in lieu of the exemptions listed above. The exemptions listed below may be used as follows: (1) if a husband and wife file a joint petition, they must both use either the exemptions listed above or the exemptions listed below, but not both; (2) if a married person files a single petition, the exemptions listed above must be used unless both spouses sign a written waiver waiving the above exemptions for the period in which the case is pending; (3) a single person may use either the exemptions listed above or the exemptions listed below, but not both. See CAL. CIV. PROC. CODE § 703.140(a). The exemptions listed above and below apply jointly to both debtors in a joint case and may not be claimed separately by each debtor in a joint case. See CAL. CIV. PROC. CODE § 703.110 and In Re Talmadge, 832 F. 2d 1120.

Type of Property	Amount of Exemption*	Statute Creating Exemption
Debtor's aggregate interest in real or personal property that the debtor or a dependent of the debtor uses as a residence; or in a cooperative that owns property that the debtor or a dependent of the debtor uses as a residence; or in a burial lot for the debtor or a dependent of the debtor	$29,725	CAL. CIV. PROC. CODE § 703.140(b)(1)
1 motor vehicle	$5,850	CAL. CIV. PROC. CODE § 703.140(b)(2)
Household furnishings, household goods, wearing apparel, appliances, books, animals, crops, or musical instruments held primarily for the personal, family, or household use of the debtor or a dependent of the debtor	$725 per item (no aggregate limit)	CAL. CIV. PROC. CODE § 703.140(b)(3)
Jewelry held primarily for personal, family, or household use of debtor or a dependent of the debtor	$1,750	CAL. CIV. PROC. CODE. § 703.140(b)(4)
Any property selected by debtor	$1,550 plus unused portion of § 703.140(b)(1) exemption ($26,800 if not a homeowner)	CAL. CIV. PROC. CODE § 703.140(b)(5)
Implements, professional books, or tools, of the trade of debtor or a dependent of the debtor	$8,000	CAL. CIV. PROC. CODE § 703.140(b)(6)
Unmatured life insurance contracts owned by debtor, except credit life insurance contracts	100%	CAL. CIV. PROC. CODE § 703.140(b)(7)
Accrued dividends or interest under, or loan value of, any unmatured life insurance contract owned by debtor in which the insured is the debtor or a person of whom the debtor is a dependent	$15,560	CAL. CIV. PROC. CODE § 703.140(b)(8)
Professionally prescribed health aids of debtor and dependents	100%	CAL. CIV. PROC. CODE § 703.140(b)(9)
Social security, unemployment compensation, or public assistance benefits	100%	CAL. CIV. PROC. CODE § 703.140(b)(10)(A)

(Continued on next page)

* Amounts Readjust April 1, 2022

(Continued from previous page)

CALIFORNIA

Type of Property	Amount of Exemption	Statute Creating Exemption
Veterans' benefits	100%	CAL. CIV. PROC. CODE § 703.140(b)(10)(B)
Disability, illness, or unemployment benefits	100%	CAL. CIV. PROC. CODE § 703.140(b)(10)(C)
Alimony, support, or separate maintenance	100% of amount reasonably necessary for support of debtor and dependents	CAL. CIV. PROC. CODE§ 703.140(b)(10)(D)
Payments under stock bonus, pension, profit-sharing, annuity, or similar plan or contract on account of illness, disability, death, age, or length of service	100% of amount reasonably necessary for support of debtor and dependents	CAL. CIV. PROC. CODE § 703.140(b)(10)(E)

NOTE - Exemption does not apply if: plan or contract was established under auspices of insider that employed debtor at time plan or contract arose; such payment is on account of age or length of service; and such plan or contract does not qualify under 26 USC §§ 401(a), 403(a), 403(b), 408, or 408A.

Crime victim's reparation law benefits or awards	100%	CAL. CIV. PROC. CODE § 703.140(b)(11)(A)
Payments on account of the wrongful death of individual of whom debtor was a dependent	100% of amount reasonably necessary for support of debtor and independents	CAL. CIV. PROC. CODE § 703.140(b)(11)(B)
Payments under life insurance contract insuring life of an individual of whom debtor was a dependent	100% of amount reasonably necessary for support of debtor and dependents	CAL. CIV. PROC. CODE § 703.140(b)(11)(C)
Payments on account of personal bodily injury of debtor or person of whom debtor is a dependent (does not include compensation for pain and suffering or actual pecuniary loss)	$29,275	CAL. CIV. PROC. CODE § 703.140(b)(11)(D)
Payments in compensation for loss of future earnings of debtor or person of whom debtor is a dependent	100% of amount reasonably necessary for support of debtor and dependents	CAL. CIV. PROC. CODE § 703.140(b)(11)(E)
Money held in Golden State Scholarship Trust Account	100%	CAL. CIV. PROC. CODE § 703.140(b)(12(A)

NOTE: **On April 1, 2013, and every 3 years thereafter on that date, the dollar amounts of exemptions provided for in C.C.P. § 703.140(b) will be adjusted by the Judicial Council to reflect changes in the consumer price index. See CAL. CIV. PROC. CODE § 703.150.**

NOTE: **Same sex domestic partners registered under the California Domestic Partner Rights and Responsibilities Act have the same rights, protections, and benefits and are subject to the same responsibilities, obligations, and duties as are granted to and imposed upon spouses. See CAL. FAM. CODE 297.5(a).**

COLORADO

Use of federal bankruptcy exemptions not permitted. See CRS § 13-54-107

Type of Property	Amount of Exemption	Statute Creating Exemption
Homestead, mobile home, or manufactured home occupied as home by owner	$250,000 or $350,000 if occupied by an elderly (60+) or disabled debtor or spouse	CRS § 38-41-201, 202
Necessary wearing apparel	$2,000	CRS § 13-54-102 (1)(a)
Watches, jewelry and articles of adornment	$2,500	CRS § 13-54-102 (1)(b)
Personal library, family pictures and school books	$2,000	CRS § 13-54-102 (1)(c)
Burial sites for family members	100 %	CRS § 13-54-102 (1)(d)
Household goods	$3,000	CRS § 13-54-102 (1)(e)
Provisions and fuel	$600	CRS § 13-54-102 (1)(f)
Livestock, poultry, or other animals of farmer and his or her tractors, farm equipment, trucks, machinery and tools	$50,000 (may be claimed once by debtor and spouse)	CRS § 13-54-102 (1)(g) (debtor claiming this exemption may not claim exemption in §102(1)(i))
Armed Forces pension	100% (support claims excepted)	CRS § 13-54-102 (1)(h)
Articles of military equipment personally owned by national guardsman	100%	CRS § 13-54-102(1)(h.5)
Stock in trade, equipment and tools used in occupation	$30,000 (and $10,000 for other gainful occupation)	CRS § 13-54-102 (1)(i)
One or more motor vehicles or bicycles	$7,500	CRS § 13-54-102 (1)(j)(I)
One or more motor vehicles of disabled or elderly person or person with a disabled or elderly spouse or dependent (Elderly means 60 or older. See § 13-54-101(2.5) for definition of disabled)	$12,500	CRS § 13-54-102(1)(j)(II)(A)
Library of professional person	$3,000 (may not also be claimed under §13-54-102(1)(i))	CRS § 13-54-102 (1)(k)
Cash surrender value of life insurance policies	$100,000 (cash value increases from contributions made during previous 48 months not exempt)	CRS § 13-54-102 (1)(l)(I)(A)
Proceeds of life insurance polices paid to designated beneficiary	100% (exemption not applicable for debts of beneficiary)	CRS § 13-54-102(1)(l)(I)(B)
Proceeds of claim and avails of insurance policies covering loss or destruction of exempt property	Extent of exemption given for the lost or destroyed property	CRS § 13-54-102 (1)(m)
Proceeds of claim for personal injuries	100%	CRS § 13-54-102 (1)(n)
State or federal earned income tax credit refund or child tax credit	100%	CRS § 13-54-102 (1)(o)
Professionally-prescribed health aids	100%	CRS § 13-54-102 (1)(p)
Crime victims reparation law awards	100%	CRS § 13-54-102 (1)(q)
Residential security deposits and utility deposits held by third parties	100%	CRS § 13-54-102 (1)(r)
Funds in and benefits of any ERISA-qualified pension, retirement, or deferred compensation plan, and IRAs qualified under the I.R.C.	100% (child support claims excepted)	CRS § 13-54-102 (1)(s)
Child support obligations or payments required by support order	100% (must be segregated and deposited in custodial bank account)	CRS § 13-54-102(1)(u), 102.5
Homestead sale proceeds (for 2 years)	same as homestead exemption (funds cannot be commingled)	CRS § 38-41-207
Disposable earnings (net earnings after deductions) - Includes health, accident, or disability insurance benefits	75% of disposable earnings OR 30 times the state or fed. minimum hourly wage per week, WHICHEVER IS GREATER	CRS § 5-5-105, 13-54-104 (exemption may be increased for totally disabled debtor)

(continued on next page)

(continued from previous page)

COLORADO

Type of Property	Amount of Exemption	Statute Creating Exemption
Insurance proceeds from loss of homestead	Same as homestead exemption	CRS § 38-41-209
Workers' compensation benefits	100% (support claims excepted)	CRS § 8-42-124(1)
Unemployment compensation benefits	100%	CRS § 8-80-103
Proceeds of group life insurance policies	100%	CRS § 10-7-205
Proceeds of annuity contract or life insurance policy in hands of insurer, if so provided in contract or policy	100%	CRS § 10-7-106
Sickness and accident insurance benefits	$200 per month on periodic payments 100% of lump sum payments for dismemberment	CRS § 10-16-212
Fraternal Benefit Society benefits	100%	CRS § 10-14-403
Teacher's retirement benefits	100%	CRS § 22-51-212
Public employee's retirement benefits	100%	CRS § 24-51-212
Public assistance payments	100%	CRS § 26-2-131
Police and Firefighters pension benefits	No limit	CRS § 31-30-1117 CRS § 31-30.5-208 CRS § 31-31-203
Specific partnership property	100% of partner's interest	CRS § 7-60-125
Property of "cemetery companies" held not for profit	100%	CRS § 7-47-106
All property subject to a judgment for failure to pay state income tax on qualified benefits from a pension or other retirement plan	100%	CRS § 13-54-102(1)(t)
Public or private disability benefits	($4,000 per month)	CRS § 13-54-102(1)(v)
Crime victims' compensation payments	100%	CRS § 24-4.1-114
Retirement benefits--employees of local government	100% (support claims excepted)	CRS § 24-54-111
Deposit Accounts	$4,000 (expires 9-1-22)	CRS § 13-54-102(w)(I)

CONNECTICUT

Use of federal bankruptcy exemptions permitted.

Type of Property	Amount of Exemption	Statute Creating Exemption
Necessary apparel, bedding, food, household furniture and appliances	100%	Conn. Gen. Stat. § 52-352b(1)
Tools, books, instruments, farm animals and livestock feed necessary for occupation, profession or farming operation	100%	Conn. Gen. Stat. § 52-352b(2)
Family burial plot	100%	Conn. Gen. Stat. § 52-352b(3)
Public assistance payments and wages earned by public assistance recipient under incentive earnings or similar program	100%	Conn. Gen. Stat. § 52-352b(4)
Health and disability insurance payments	100%	Conn. Gen. Stat. § 52-352b(5)
Necessary health aids	100%	Conn. Gen. Stat. § 52-352b(6)
Worker's compensation, social security, veteran's and unemployment benefits	100%	Conn. Gen. Stat. § 52-352b(7)
Court approved child support payments	100%	Conn. Gen. Stat. § 52-352b(8)
Arms, military equipment, uniforms and musical instruments of members of militia or U.S. armed services	100%	Conn. Gen. Stat. § 52-352b(9)
1 motor vehicle	$3,500	Conn. Gen. Stat. § 52-352b(10)
Wedding and engagement rings	100%	Conn. Gen. Stat. § 52-352b(11)
Residential utility deposits and one residential security deposit	100%	Conn. Gen. Stat. § 52-352b(12)
Interest or assets in and amounts payable or paid from retirement plan or IRA qualified under I.R.C.	100%	Conn. Gen. Stat. § 52-352b(13)
Alimony and support payments other than child support	Extent of earnings exempt under CGS § 52-361 (see below)	Conn. Gen. Stat. § 52-352b(14)
Awards under crime reparations act	100%	Conn. Gen. Stat. § 52-352b(15)
Disposable earnings (earnings less deductions required by law)	75% or 40 times the federal minimum hourly wage per week, WHICHEVER IS GREATER	Conn. Gen. Stat. § 52-361a
Benefits payable on account of sickness or infirmity	100%	Conn. Gen. Stat. § 52-352b(16)
Insurance proceeds from policies covering exempt property	Amount of exemption for covered property	Conn. Gen. Stat. § 52-352b(17)
Interest in any property	$1,000	Conn. Gen. Stat. § 52-352b(18)
Interest in unmatured life insurance policy	$4,000	Conn. Gen. Stat. § 52-352b(19)
Homestead consisting of owner-occupied real property or mobile or manufactured home used as primary residence 30-14(a)	$250,000 ($75,000 in certain cases)	Conn. Gen. Stat. § 52-352b(20) 100% Conn. Gen. Stat. §
Fraternal Benefit Society benefits	100%	Conn. Gen. Stat. § 38a-637
Proceeds of life insurance policies not payable to the insured	100%	Conn. Gen. Stat. § 38a-453
Teachers', state employees' and city employees retirement benefits	100%	Conn. Gen. Stat. §§ 10-183q, 5-171, 7-446
Retirement funds-tier II pensions: state employees	100%	Conn. Gen. Stat. §§ 5-192w, 5-171
Specific partnership property	100%	Conn. Gen. Stat. § 34-328
Farm partnership-livestock feed, animals, books, instruments, money due from insurance	100%	Conn. Gen. Stat. § 52-352d
Hospital claims	$125,000	Conn. Gen. Stat. § 52-352b(t)
Irrevocable transfers to a licensed non-profit debt adjuster for the benefit of the debtor's creditors	100%	Conn. Gen. Stat. § 52-352b(u)
Property transferred to a trustee of a trust providing support for the debtor and the debtor's beneficiaries	100%	Conn. Gen. Stat. § 52-321(d)

DELAWARE

Use of federal bankruptcy exemptions not permitted. DEL. CODE ANN. TIT. 10 § 4914(a).

Type of Property	Amount of Exemption	Statute Creating Exemption
Wages, salaries & commissions of persons who are not self employed	85%	DEL. CODE ANN., TIT. 10 § 4913
Family Bible, school books, family library, family pictures, seat or pew in place of worship, lot in burial ground, all wearing apparel of debtor and family, sewing machines	100%	DEL. CODE ANN., TIT. 10 § 4902(a), (c)
Tools, implements and fixtures necessary to carry on trade or profession	$75.00 in New Castle and Sussex Counties, $50.00 in Kent County	DEL. CODE ANN., TIT. 10 § 4902(b)
Any property selected by debtor	$25,000 (applies only to bankruptcy proceedings and applies separately to each debtor in a joint case)	DEL. CODE ANN., TIT. 10 § 4914(b)
Equity in real property or manufactured home used by debtor as principal residence *(DCA § 4914 (c) for limitations on homestead allowance)	$125,000	DEL. CODE ANN., TIT. 10 § 4914(c)(1)
A vehicle necessary for employment	$15,000	DEL. CODE ANN., TIT. 10 § 4914(c)(2)
Tools of trade necessary for employment	$15,000	DEL. CODE ANN., TIT. 10 § 4914(c)(2)
Pianos and organs leased to debtor	100%	DEL. CODE ANN., TIT. 10 § 4902(d)
Specific partnership property	100% of partner's interest	DEL. CODE ANN., TIT. 6 § 15-501
Personal property of any nature	$500 (applies only to head of family)	DEL. CODE ANN., TIT. 10 § 4903
Assets in and amounts payable from any retirement or profit-sharing plan or IRA that is qualified under I.R.C.	100% of tax-qualified amounts (includes rollovers for 60 days)	DEL. CODE ANN., TIT. 10 § 4915
Assets in Delaware College Investment Plan Accounts	100% of I.R.C. qualified amounts (Contributions made within 365 days of bankruptcy filing date are exempt only to greater of $5,000 or average contribution amount for past 2 years)	DEL. CODE ANN., TIT. 10 § 4916
Proceeds and avails of life insurance policies payable to person other than the insured	100% (except transfers made in defraud of creditors)	DEL. CODE ANN., TIT. 18 § 2725
Fraternal Benefit Society benefits	100%	DEL. CODE ANN., TIT. 18 § 6218
Proceeds of health insurance policies	100%	DEL. CODE ANN., TIT. 18 § 2726
Group insurance proceeds	100%	DEL. CODE ANN., TIT. 18 § 2727
Annuity contract proceeds	$350 per month, less amounts paid to defraud creditors	DEL. CODE ANN., TIT. 18 § 2728
Workmen's compensation benefits	100%	DEL. CODE ANN., TIT. 19 § 2355
Unemployment compensation benefits	100%	DEL. CODE ANN., TIT. 19 § 3374
Aid to blind persons	100%	DEL. CODE ANN., TIT. 31 § 2309
Public assistance payments	100%	DEL. CODE ANN., TIT. 31 § 513
State employees' pension benefits	100%	DEL. CODE ANN., TIT. 29 § 5503
Tenancies by the entirety or joint tenancies	100% (see note below)	11 USC § 522(b) (2) (B)
Pension--county and municipal police	100%	DEL. CODE ANN., TIT. 11 § 8803
Pension--volunteer firemen	100%	DEL. CODE ANN., TIT. 16 § 6653
Retail installment sales--wages exempt from attachment for 60 days from default	100%	DEL. CODE ANN., TIT. 6 § 4345
Spendthrift trust	100%	DEL. CODE ANN., TIT. 12 § 3536(a)
Firemen's disability benefits	100%	DEL. CODE ANN., TIT. 18 §6708

DISTRICT OF COLUMBIA

Use of federal bankruptcy exemptions pemitted.

Type of Property	Amount of Exemption	Statute Creating Exemption
1 motor vehicle	$2,575	D.C. CODE ANN. § 15-501(a)(1)
Household furnishings, household goods, wearing apparel, appliances, books, animals, crops, or musical instruments held primarily for personal, family or household use of debtor or dependent	$425 per item with $8,625 aggregate limit	D.C. CODE ANN. § 15-501(a)(2)
Any property of debtor (wildcard)	$850 plus up to $8,075 of any unused amount of the exemption provided in §15-501(a)(14)	D.C. CODE ANN. § 15-501(a)(3)
Implements, professional books, or tools of trade of debtor or dependent	$1,625	D.C. CODE ANN. § 15-501(a)(4)
Any unmatured life insurance contract other than a credit life insurance contract	100%	D.C. CODE ANN. § 15-501(a)(5)
Professionally prescribed health aids of debtor or dependent	100%	D.C. CODE ANN. § 15-501(a)(6)
The debtor's right to receive a social security benefit, a veteran's benefit, a disability, illness, or unemployment benefit, or alimony, separate maintenance or support and payments under I.R.C. qualified stock bonus, pension, profit-sharing, annuity, or similar plan or contract	Amount reasonably necessary for support of debtor and dependents	D.C. CODE ANN. § 15-501(a)(7)
Family pictures and library	$400	D.C. CODE ANN. § 15-501(a)(8)
Payments from and assets contained in a retirement plan qualified under I.R.C. (Exemption applies to plan participant and alternate payee)	100% of I.R.C. qualified amounts	D.C. CODE ANN. § 15-501(a)(9), (10)
Debtor's right to receive property that is traceable to crime victim's reparation award or personal injury award	100%	D.C. CODE ANN. § 15-501(a)(11)(A), (D)
Wrongful death award or life insurance payment resulting from death of individual of whom debtor was a dependent or payment for loss of future earnings of debtor or individual of whom debtor is or was a dependent	Amount reasonably necessary for support of debtor and dependents	D.C. CODE ANN. § 15-501(a)(11)(B), (C), (E)
Provision for 3 months support, whether provided or growing	100%	D.C. CODE ANN. § 15-501(a)(12)
Library, office furniture and implements of professional person or artist	$300	D.C. CODE ANN. § 15-501(a)(13)
Debtor's aggregate interest in real property used as his or her residence, including interest in a residential cooperative, or a burial plot	100%	D.C. CODE ANN. § 15-501(a)(14)
NOTE: The above exemptions apply to DC residents who are heads of family or householders and to nonresident heads of family or householders who earns the major portion of their livelihoods in DC.		
Disposable wages (wages include any compensation for personal services and include periodic payments under pension or retirement plans)	75% or 30 times the federal minimum hourly wage per week, WHICHEVER IS GREATER*	D.C. CODE ANN. § 16-572 * But see In re Mordkin, 452 B.R. 311 (holding cannot be used in Chapter 7)
Specific partnership property	100% of partner's interest	D.C. CODE ANN. § 29-605.01-.04
Residential condominium escrow deposits	100%	D.C. CODE ANN. § 42-1904.09
Wages of prisoner on work release	100%	D.C. CODE ANN. § 24-241.06
Unemployment compensation benefits	100%	D.C. CODE ANN. § 51-118(b)(1)
Workmen's compensation benefits	100%	D.C. CODE ANN. § 32-1517
Shares and membership certificates in cooperative associations	$500.00	D.C. CODE ANN. § 29-928
Seals and documents of notaries public	100%	D.C. CODE ANN. § 1-1206
Disability insurance benefits	100%	D.C. CODE ANN. § 31-4716.01
Police, firefighter, teacher retirement	100%	D.C. CODE ANN. § 1-911.03
Group life insurance benefits	100%	D.C. CODE ANN. § 31-4717
Proceeds and avails of life insurance policies payable to person other than the insured	100% (except for premiums paid in defraud of creditors)	D.C. CODE ANN. § 31-4716
Public assistance payments	100%	D.C. CODE ANN. § 4-215.01
Compensation for violent crime victims	100%	D.C. CODE ANN. § 4-507(e)
Uninsured motorist compensation benefits	100%	D.C. CODE ANN. § 31-2408.01(h)
Wrongful death recoveries	100% less amounts awarded for expenses of last illness and burial	D.C. CODE ANN. § 16-2703
NOTE: Tenancies by the entirety may be exempt under 11 USC § 522(b)(3)(B). See, e.g. In re Estate of Wall, 440 F. 2d 215 (D.C. Cir., 1971); In re Chreky, 450 B.R. 247 (Dist. D.C. 2011).		

(continued from previous page)

Type of Property	Amount of Exemption	Statute Creating Exemption
Retirement benefits: judges in DC judicial system	100%	D.C. CODE ANN. § 11-1570(f)
Earnings not wages not otherwise exempt: head of household	$200/month for 2 months	D.C. CODE ANN. § 15-503(a)
Non-head of household: clothes	$300	D.C. CODE ANN. § 15-503(b)
Non-head of household: mechanics' tools	$200	D.C. CODE ANN. § 15-503(b)
Non-head of household: Earnings other than wages, not otherwise exempt	$60/month for 2 months	D.C. CODE ANN. § 15-503(b)
Retirement & disability benefits--Teachers retiring before 6/46	100%	D.C. CODE ANN. § 38-2001.17
Retirement & disability benefits--Teachers retiring after 6/46	100%	D.C. CODE ANN. § 38-2021.17
Cemetery lots held by cemetery associations	100%	D.C. CODE ANN. § 43-111
Taxicab Sinking Fund	100%	D.C. CODE ANN. § 50-315(c)

FLORIDA

Use of federal bankruptcy exemptions except benefits listed in § 522(d)(10)) not permitted. See FLA. STAT. ANN.§ 222.20, 201

Type of Property	Amount of Exemption	Statute Creating Exemption
Homestead of any person (may be recorded by written statement with Circuit Court)	100% of 160 acres of contiguous land and improvements if located outside municipality or 1/2 acre of contiguous land and improvements in municipality used as residence by owner or his family	Art. 10, § 4(a)(1) of Constitution, FLA. STAT. ANN. §§ 222.01, 222.02 & 222.05
Disposable earnings (exempt earnings in bank account are exempt for 6 month if traceable)	$750 per week for head of family The greater of 75% or 30 times the federal minimum hourly wage per week for other persons	FLA. STAT. ANN. § 222.11 (head of family is one who provides more than 1/2 of support for dependent)
Personal property of any nature	$1,000	FLA. CONST. ART. 10, § 4(a)(2)
Dwelling house, mobile home used as residence, or modular home, owned and occupied by debtor on the land of another	100%	FLA. STAT. ANN. § 222.05
Proceeds of life insurance policies of resident insured payable to another	100% (exemption applies only to insured)	FLA. STAT. ANN. § 222.13
Cash surrender value of life insurance policies on lives of state residents	100%	FLA. STAT. ANN. § 222.14
Proceeds of annuity contracts of state residents or citizens	100%	FLA. STAT. ANN. § 222.14
Disability insurance benefits	100%	FLA. STAT. ANN. § 222.18
Pension money of U.S. pensioner	3 months' pension if needed for support of debtor or family	FLA. STAT. ANN. § 222.21(1)
Benefits from and contributions to retirement or profit-sharing plan qualified under I.R.C.	100% of tax-qualified amounts	FLA. STAT. ANN. § 222.21(2)
Benefits listed in 11 U.S.C. 522(d)(10) (See Federal Bankruptcy, Exemptions supra, this Appendix, for specific benefits)	100% of federal exemption amounts	FLA. STAT. ANN. § 222.201
Moneys paid into or out of Florida Prepaid College Trust Fund or Medical Savings Account	100%	FLA. STAT. ANN. § 222.22
One motor vehicle	$1,000	FLA. STAT. ANN. § 222.25(1)
Professionally prescribed health aids	100%	FLA. STAT. ANN. § 222.25(2)
Federal tax refund or earned income credit	100%	FLA. STAT. ANN. § 222.25(3)
Workmen's compensation benefits	100%	FLA. STAT. ANN. § 440.22
Unemployment compensation benefits	100%	FLA. STAT. ANN. § 443.051
Fraternal Benefit Society benefits	100%	FLA. STAT. ANN. § 632.619
Police retirement benefits	100%	FLA. STAT. ANN. § 185.25
Firemen's retirement benefits	100%	FLA. STAT. ANN. § 175.241
Specific partnership property	100% of partner's interest	FLA. STAT. ANN. § 620.8203
Teacher's retirement benefits	100%	FLA. STAT. ANN. § 238.15
Public employees' retirement benefits	100%	FLA. STAT. ANN. § 121.131
State and county employees' retirement benefits	100%	FLA. STAT. ANN. § 122.15
Damages for injuries or death awarded to employees in hazardous occupations	100%	FLA. STAT. ANN. § 769.05
Veterans' benefits	100%	FLA. STAT. ANN. § 744.626
Government employees deferred compensation benefits	100%	FLA. STAT. ANN. § 112.215(10)(a)
Retired public employees health insurance subsidies	100%	FLA. STAT. ANN. § 112.359 & 112.363
Wildcard Exemption (if no homestead exemption is claimed)	$4,000	FLA. STAT. ANN. § 222.25(4)
Preneed Funeral Contract Consumer Protection Fund	100%	FLA. STAT. ANN. § 497.456(8)
Crime victim's compensation	100%, except for expenses resulting from the injury which is the basis for the claim	FLA. STAT. ANN. § 960.14

NOTES: Tenancies by the entirety may be exempt under 11 USC § 522(b)(3)(B). See In Re Mastrofino, 247 BR 330 (Bankr M.D. Fla., 2000).
Assets that are fraudulently converted from nonexempt to exempt assets are not exempt. FSA § 222.29, .30; see also In re Osejo, 447 BR 352 (Bank. S.D. Fla., 2011).

GEORGIA

Use of federal bankruptcy exemptions not permitted. See GA. CODE ANN. § 44-13-100(b)

Type of Property	Amount of Exemption	Statute Creating Exemption
Real or personal property (homestead)	$5,000, or $21,500 if debtor's primary residence	* GA. CODE ANN. § 44-13-1
NOTE: To obtain this exemption the debtor must file an application with the probate court of the county in which he or she resides. See GA. CODE ANN. § 44-13-4. Spouse or minor children of debtor may apply for exemption if debtor refuses. See GA. CODE ANN. § 44-13-2. Debtor and spouse cannot both claim exemption. See GA. CODE ANN. § 44-13-43.		
Disposable earnings (Includes pension& retirement payments - see GA. CODE ANN. § 18-4-22)	75% or amount of earnings that exceed 217.50, or 30 times 7.25; WHICHEVER IS GREATER	GA. CODE ANN. § 18-4-5
Retirement and pension funds and benefits	100% until distribution, then same as GA. CODE ANN. § 18-4-20	GA. CODE ANN. § 18-4-6
Funds and benefits of employee benefit plans subject to ERISA	100% (alimony & support claims excepted)	GA. CODE ANN. § 18-4-22
Wages of deceased employee	$2,500	GA. CODE ANN. § 34-7-4
Proceeds and avails of life insurance policy payable to person other than insured including cash surrender value	100%	GA. CODE ANN. § 33-25-11
Proceeds and avails of accident and sickness insurance policies	100%	GA. CODE ANN. § 33-29-15 GA. CODE ANN. § 33-30-10
Fraternal Benefit Society benefits	100%	GA. CODE ANN. § 33-15-20 GA. CODE ANN. § 33-15-62
Workmen's compensation benefits	100%	GA. CODE ANN. § 34-9-84
Unemployment compensation benefits	100%	GA. CODE ANN. § 34-8-252
Old age assistance payments	100%	GA. CODE ANN. § 49-4-35
Blind person's benefits	100%	GA. CODE ANN. § 49-4-58
Sheriff & peace officer's retirement benefits	100%	GA. CODE ANN. § 47-16-122, 47-17-103
Firemen's pension benefits	100%	GA. CODE ANN. § 47-7-122
District attorney's retirement benefits GCA § 47-12-101	100%	GA. CODE ANN. § 47-12-101
Judges & Court employees' retirement benefits	100%	GA. CODE ANN. § 47-11-91,47-12-101, 47-23-121, 47-25-101, 47-14-91,
State, county, and city employees' retirement benefits	100%	GA. CODE ANN. § 47-2-332, 44-13-100(a)(2)(E), 47-5-71
Teachers' retirement benefits	100%	GA. CODE ANN. § 47-3-28, 47-4-120
Legislator retirement benefits	100%	GA. CODE ANN. § 47-6-100
Disability insurance payments	$250/month	GA. CODE ANN. § 33-29-15
Industrial life insurance policy	100%	GA. CODE ANN. § 33-26-5
Group insurance	100%	GA. CODE ANN. § 33-27-7
Annuity and endowment contract benefits	100%	GA. CODE ANN. § 33-28-7
Group/blanket accident and sickness insurance	$250/month	GA. CODE ANN. § 33-30-10
Produce, rents, or profits from exempt property	100%	GA. CODE ANN. § 44-13-18
Assistance to disabled	100%	GA. CODE ANN. § 49-4-84

(continued on next page)

(Continued from previous page)

NOTE: The following exemptions may only be used in lieu of the exemptions provided in GA. CODE ANN. 44-13-1. See GA. CODE ANN. § 44-13-100(a).

Type of Property	Amount of Exemption	Statute Creating Exemption
Debtor's aggregate interest in real or personal property used by debtor or a dependent as residence, in cooperative owning property used by debtor or dependent as residence, or in burial plot of debtor or dependent	$21,500 $43,000 if owned by 1 of 2 spouses	GA. CODE ANN. § 44-13-100(a)(1)
Debtor's right to receive social security benefits, unemployment, compensation veterans' benefits, or disability, illness or unemployment benefits	100%	GA. CODE ANN. § 44-13-100 (a)(2)(A),(B),(C)
Alimony, support or maintenance payments, and payments under pension, IRA, annuity or similar plans or contracts on account of illness, disability, death, age or length of service	Amount reasonably necessary for support of debtor and dependents	GA. CODE ANN. § 44-13-100 (a)(2)(D)(E)(F)
All motor vehicles	$5,000	GA. CODE ANN. § 44-13-100 (a)(3)
Household furnishings, household goods, wearing apparel, appliances, books, animals, crops or musical instruments, held primarily for the personal, family or household use of debtor or dependent	$300 per item, with $5,000 aggregate limit	GA. CODE ANN. § 44-13-100 (a)(4)
Personal jewelry of debtor or dependents	$500	GA. CODE ANN. § 44-13-100 (a)(5)
Debtor's aggregate interest in any property	$600 plus unused portion of exemption under GCA 44-13-100 (a)(1) above not to exceed $5,000	GA. CODE ANN. § 44-13-100 (a)(6)
Implements, professional books or tools of trade of debtor or dependent	$1,500	GA. CODE ANN. § 44-13-100 (a)(7)
Any unmatured life insurance contract owned by debtor, except credit life insurance contract	100%	GA. CODE ANN. § 44-13-100 (a)(8)
Debtor's aggregate interest in accrued dividends or interest or loan or cash value of any unmatured life insurance contract owned by debtor wherein insured is the debtor or an individual of whom the debtor is a dependent	$2,000 less transfers described in 11 U.S.C. § 542(d)	GA. CODE ANN. § 44-13-100 (a)(9)
Professionally prescribed health aids of debtor and dependents	100%	GA. CODE ANN. § 44-13-100 (a)(10)
Awards made under crime reparation laws	100%	GA. CODE ANN. § 44-13-100 (a)(11)(A)
Payments on account of the wrongful death of an individual of whom the debtor was a dependent	Amount reasonably necessary for the support of debtor and dependents	GA. CODE ANN. § 44-13-100 (a)(11)(B)
Proceeds of life insurance contract insuring life of individual of whom debtor was a dependent on date of death	Amount reasonably necessary for the support of debtor and dependents	GA. CODE ANN. § 44-13-100 (a)(11)(C)
Payments on account of personal bodily injury, not including pain and suffering or compensation for actual pecuniary loss, of debtor or individual of whom debtor is a dependent	$10,000	GA. CODE ANN. § 44-13-100 (a)(11)(D)
Payments in compensation for loss of future earnings of debtor or of an individual of whom debtor is or was a dependent	Amount reasonably necessary for the support of debtor and dependents	GA. CODE ANN. § 44-13-100 (a)(11)(E)
Debtor's interest in public, nonprofit, or private pension, retirement plan or individual retirement account	100% for public or nonprofit plans. Private plans subject to limits set forth in federal bankruptcy exemptions.	GA. CODE ANN. § 44-13-100 (a)(2.1)

HAWAII

Federal bankruptcy exemptions permitted.

Type of Property	Amount of Exemption	Statute Creating Exemption
Real property owned by debtor	$30,000 if family head or if 65 or more years old; $20,000 if any other person	* Haw. Rev. Stat. § 651-92

NOTE: Head of family includes man and woman when married, and every individual residing on the real property who has under his care or maintenance a minor child of his own or of a deceased brother, sister or spouse, a minor or unmarried brother or sister, or a father, mother or grandparent of either himself or a deceased spouse. See HRS § 651-91.

Necessary household furnishings and appliances, books and wearing apparel used by debtor and family	100%	Haw. Rev. Stat. § 651-121(1)
Jewelry, watches and items of personal adornment	$1,000	Haw. Rev. Stat. § 651-121(1)
Equity in one motor vehicle	$2,575 (wholesale value)	Haw. Rev. Stat. § 651-121(2)
Tools, implements, instruments, uniforms, furnishings, books, equipment, 1 commercial fishing boat and nets, 1 motor vehicle, and other personal property used in trade, business or profession	100%	Haw. Rev. Stat. § 651-121(3)
Lot in burying ground not exceeding 250 sq. ft., including improvements	100%	Haw. Rev. Stat. § 651-121(4)
Proceeds of insurance on, and proceeds of sale of, exempt property for period of 6 months after receipt	Amount of exemption given for property destroyed or sold	Haw. Rev. Stat. § 651-121(5)
Wages, salaries and commissions for personal services during last 31 days	100%	Haw. Rev. Stat. § 651-121(6)
Wages	95% of first $100 per month 90% of next $100 per month 80% of balance per month	Haw. Rev. Stat. § 652-1
Debtor's rights to pension, annuity, retirement, disability, or death benefits, optional benefits, or any other rights under any retirement plan qualified under Internal Revenue Code.	100% (see statute for contribution timing limits)	Haw. Rev. Stat. § 651-124 431:10-232
Proceeds and cash value of life insurance policies, endowment policies, and annuity contracts where beneficiary is spouse, child, parent or dependent of the insured	100%	Haw. Rev. Stat. § 431:10-234(b)
Disability insurance proceeds	100%	Haw. Rev. Stat. § 431:10-231
Group life insurance proceeds	100%	Haw. Rev. Stat. § 431:10-233
Fraternal Benefit Society benefits	100%	Haw. Rev. Stat. § 432:2-403
Workmens' compensation benefits	100%	Haw. Rev. Stat. § 386-57
Unemployment compensation	100% (child support excepted)	Haw. Rev. Stat. § 383-163
Public assistance payments	100%	Haw. Rev. Stat. § 346-33
Prisoners' earnings held by state	100%	Haw. Rev. Stat. § 353-22
Specific partnership property	100% of partner's interest	Haw. Rev. Stat. § 425-118(d)
Tenancies by the entirety	100% *	11 USC § 522(b)(3)(B), Haw. Rev. Stat. § 509-2
Policemen, Firemen and Bandsmen Pension System benefits	100%	Haw. Rev. Stat. § 88-169
Public officers and state employees pension and retirement benefits	100%	Haw. Rev. Stat. §§ 88-91, 653-3
Proceeds of sale of homestead for 6 months	amount of homestead exemption	Haw. Rev. Stat. § 651-96
Whole life insurance, endowments, and annuities	100%	Haw. Rev. Stat. §431-10-232
Wages paid by unemployment work relief funds	$60 per month	Haw. Rev. Stat. § 653-4
Temporary disability insurance benefits	100%	Haw. Rev. Stat. § 392-29

* See Sewada v. Endo, 561 P. 2nd 1291 (Haw. 1977).

IDAHO

Federal bankruptcy exemptions not permitted. See IDAHO CODE § 11-609

Type of Property	Amount of Exemption	Statute Creating Exemption
Homestead, consisting of dwelling house or mobile home in which debtor resides and the land on which it is located	Lesser of total net value or $175,000	IDAHO CODE § 55-1003

NOTE: The homestead exemption may not be claimed separately by both spouses. See IC § 55-1002. The homestead exemption also covers the proceeds of a homestead sale and insurance proceeds in the event of a loss, both for a period of six months after the event. See IDAHO CODE § 55-1113. Recording is not required.

Disposable earnings (earnings less deductions required by law)	75% or 30 times the federal minimum hourly wage per week WHICHEVER IS GREATER	IDAHO CODE § 11-207 different exemptions apply to support claims, see § 11-207 (2)(b)
Burial plot	100%	IDAHO CODE § 11-603(1)
Necessary health aids	100%	IDAHO CODE § 11-603(2)
Federal social security benefits, veterans' benefits and federal, state and local public assistance payments	100%	IDAHO CODE § 11-603(3) & (4)
Benefits payable for medical, surgical or hospital care and amounts in a medical savings account under IC § 63-3022K	100%	IDAHO CODE § 11-603(5)
Benefits payable by reason of disability or illness	Amount reasonably necessary for support of debtor and dependents (see note below)	IDAHO CODE § 11-604(1)(a)
Amounts received for alimony, support or separate maintenance	Amount reasonably necessary for support of debtor and dependents (see note below)	IDAHO CODE § 11-604(1)(b)
Proceeds of claims for bodily injury of debtor or for bodily injury or wrongful death of person of whom debtor was or is a dependent	Amount reasonably necessary for support of debtor and dependents (see note below)	IDAHO CODE § 11-604(1)(c)
Proceeds or benefits payable upon death of insured who was spouse of debtor or upon whom the debtor was a dependent	Amount reasonably necessary for support of debtor and dependents (see note below)	IDAHO CODE § 11-604(1)(d)

NOTE: The amount reasonably necessary for the support of the debtor and his dependents is the property required to meet the present and anticipated needs of the debtor and his dependents considering the debtor's responsibilities and all of the present and anticipated property and income of the debtor, including that which is exempt. See IC § 11-604(2). The exemptions allowed under IC § 11-604 are lost immediately upon the commingling of any of the exempt funds with other funds. See IC § 11-604(3).

Federal pension benefits	100% (support claims excepted)	IDAHO CODE § 11-604A(2)
Benefits from Qualified Employee Benefit Plans and IRAs	100% (support claims excepted)	IDAHO CODE §§ 11-604A(3), 55-1011
Assets of Qualified Employee Benefit Plans and IRAs	100% (support claims excepted)	IDAHO CODE §§ 11-604A(5), 55-1011 (employee benefit plan deemed spendthrift trust)
Household furnishings, household goods, and appliances held primarily for personal, family, or household use	$1,000 per item (see note below)	IDAHO CODE § 11-605(1)(a)
Wearing apparel, animals, books and musical instruments held for personal use of debtor or his dependents	$750 per item (see note below)	IDAHO CODE § 11-605(1)(b)
Family portraits and heirlooms	$750 per item (see note below)	IDAHO CODE § 11-605(1)(c)
Personal jewelry	$1,000	IDAHO CODE § 11-605(2)
Implements, professional books and tools of trade	$10,000	IDAHO CODE § 11-605(3)
One motor vehicle	$7,000	IDAHO CODE § 11-605(3)
Municipal, County & State owned property	100%	IDAHO CODE § 11-605(5)
Arms, uniforms and accoutrements of peace officer, national guardsman, or member of military service	100%	IDAHO CODE § 11-605(6)
Water rights for irrigation of lands actually cultivated by debtor	160 inches of water	IDAHO CODE § 11-605(7)
Crops growing or grown on 50 acres of land leased, owned or possessed by debtor cultivating same	$1,000	IDAHO CODE § 11-605(7)
Food and water provisions sufficient for 12 months, storage, & shelves	100%	IDAHO CODE § 11-605(4)

NOTE: The total amount of exemption for all items claimed under IDAHO CODE § 605(1) cannot exceed $7,500 per debtor.

(continued on next page)

(continued from previous page)

Type of Property	Amount of Exemption	Statute Creating Exemption
One firearm	Less than $1,500	Idaho Code § 11-605(8)
Life insurance contract other than credit life insurance	100%	Idaho Code § 11-605(9) (see statute)
Tangible personal property (wildcard)	$1,500	Idaho Code § 11-605(10)
Proceeds of condemnation, loss, damage or destruction of exempt property for period of 3 months after receipt by debtor	Amount of exemption given for lost, damaged or destroyed property	Idaho Code § 11-606
Disability insurance benefits	100%	Idaho Code § 41-1834
Group life and disability insurance benefits	100%	Idaho Code § 41-1835(1)
Annuity contract proceeds	$1250 per month	Idaho Code § 41-1836(1)(b)
Proceeds and avails of life insurance policies payable to person other than the insured	100%	Idaho Code § 41-1833(1)
Fraternal Benefits Society benefits	100%	Idaho Code § 41-3218
Workmens' compensation benefits from any jurisdiction	100% (support claims excepted)	Idaho Code § 72-802
Unemployment compensation benefits	100% (support claims excepted)	Idaho Code § 72-1375 & § 11-603(6)
Public assistance benefits	100%	Idaho Code § 56-223 & § 11-603(4)
Public employee's retirement fund benefits	100% (support claims excepted)	Idaho Code § 59-1317
Firemen's retirement benefits	100%	Idaho Code § 72-1422
Policemen's retirement and death benefits	100%	Idaho Code § 50-1517
Specific partnership property	100% of partner's interest	Idaho Code § 53-3-307 & § 53-3-501
Liquor license	100%	Idaho Code § 23-514
Construction materials	100%	Idaho Code § 45-514
Disposable earnings, earned, unpaid	$2,500/ year	Idaho Code § 11-605(11)

NOTE: Exempt property claimed under Idaho Code §11-605 remains subject to claims for alimony, maintenance, state and local taxes, and certain other claims specified in Idaho Code § 11-607.

NOTE: A debtor may exempt the earned income credit of the Internal Revenue Code. See *In re Jones,* 107 BR 751 (Bankr. D Idaho 1989).

ILLINOIS

Federal bankruptcy exemptions not permitted. See 735 ILL. COMP. STAT. 5/12-1201

Type of Property	Amount of Exemption	Statute Creating Exemption
Residence or homestead of individual. Includes farm, lot + buildings, condominium, personal property or cooperative. Can be owned or leased.	$15,000 per person (includes proceeds of sale for 1 year under 735 ILCS 5/12-906)	735 ILL. COMP. STAT. § 5/12-901 & 902
Necessary wearing apparel, bible, school books, family pictures and prescribed health aids of debtor & dependents	100%	735 ILL. COMP. STAT. § 5/12-1001 (a), (e)
Any personal property of debtor (wildcard)	$4,000	735 ILL. COMP. STAT. § 5/12-1001(b)
One motor vehicle	$2,400	735 ILL. COMP. STAT. § 5/12-1001(c)
Implements, books & tools of trade	$1,500	735 ILL. COMP. STAT. § 5/12-1001(d)
Proceeds and cash value of life insurance policies and annuity contracts payable to dependent of insured or trust for benefit of wife, husband, or dependents of insured	100%	735 ILL. COMP. STAT. § 5/12-1001(f)
Social Security benefits, unemployment compensation benefits, public assistance benefits, veteran's benefits, and disability and illness benefits	100%	735 ILL. COMP. STAT. § 5/12-1001(g)(1), (2), (3)
Alimony, support or separate maintenance	Amount reasonably necessary to support debtor & dependents	735 ILL. COMP. STAT. § 5/12-1001 (g)(4)
Restitution payments made under 50 U.S.C. App. 1989b, 1989c	100%	735 ILL. COMP. STAT. § 5/12-1001 (g)(5)
Debtor's interest in a retirement plan qualified under the Internal Revenue Code or a public employee pension plan	100%	735 ILL. COMP. STAT. § 5/12-1006

(NOTE: Includes stock bonus, pension, profit-sharing, annuity, or similar plans, self-employed or simplified employee pension plans, government or church retirement plans, and individual retirement annuities or accounts.)

Type of Property	Amount of Exemption	Statute Creating Exemption
Crime victim's reparation law awards and crime victims awards	100%	735 ILL. COMP. STAT. § 5/12-1001(h)(1), (i)
Wrongful death payments resulting from death of person of whom debtor was a dependent	Amount reasonably necessary to support debtor and dependents	735 ILL. COMP. STAT. § 5/12-1001(h)(2)
Life insurance payments from policy insuring person of whom debtor was a dependent	Amount reasonably necessary to support debtor and dependents	735 ILL. COMP. STAT. § 5/12-1001(h)(3)
Payments on account of bodily injury of debtor or person of whom debtor was a dependent	$15,000	735 ILL. COMP. STAT. § 5/12-1001(h)(4)

NOTE: Proceeds from sale of exempt personal property are also exempt. Nonexempt property converted into exempt property in fraud of creditors is not exempt. Property acquired within 6 months of the filing of bankruptcy is presumed to have been acquired in contemplation of bankruptcy. The exemptions in 735 ILL. COMP. STAT. § 5/12-1001(h) extend for 2 years after the debtor's right to receive the payments accrues, and, as to property traceable there from, for 5 years after accrual. See 735 ILL. COMP. STAT. § 5/12-1001.

Type of Property	Amount of Exemption	Statute Creating Exemption
Specific partnership property	100% of partner's interest	805 ILL. COMP. STAT. § 206/501
Gross earnings or disposable earnings(disposable earnings are gross earnings less deductions required by law)	85% of gross earnings, OR disposable earnings equal to 45 times the federal minimum hourly wage per week, WHICHEVER IS GREATER*	735 ILL. COMP. STAT. § 5/12-803
Proceeds & cash value of life or endowment insurance policy or annuity contract payable to insured's spouse or dependent	100% (applies against creditors of insured)	215 ILL. COMP. STAT. § 5/238
Fraternal Benefit Society benefits	100%	215 ILL. COMP. STAT. § 5/299.1a
Workmen's compensation benefits	100%	820 ILL. COMP. STAT. § 305/21
Unemployment compensation benefits	100% (support claims excepted)	820 ILL. COMP. STAT. § 405/1300(B)
Social Services benefits	100%	305 ILL. COMP. STAT. § 5/11-3
Pension and retirement benefits of the following: firemen, house of correction employees, library employees, municipal employees, park employees, policemen, sanitary district employees, state employees, teachers	100%	40 ILL. COMP. STAT. § 5/22-230, 4-135, 6-213, 19-117,19-218, 8-244, 7-217, 12-190, 3-144.1,5-218, 13-805, 14-147, 16-190, 17-151
Benefits and refunds payable by pension or retirement funds or systems and assets of employees held by such funds or systems and payments made to such funds or systems	100%	735 ILL. COMP. STAT. § 5/12-704
Moneys held in Illinois College Savings Pool	100%	15 ILL. COMP. STAT. § 505/16.5 & 735ILCS § 5/12-1001(j)

(Continued on the next page)

Use of federal bankruptcy exemptions under 11 USC § 522(d) **not** permitted in this state. See 735 ILCS 5/12-1201

(Continued from previous page)

Type of Property	Amount of Exemption	Statute Creating Exemption
Uniforms, arms of a member of the national guard	100%	20 Ill. Comp. Stat. § 1805/10
Property held in trust for debtor	100%	735 Ill. Comp. Stat. § 5/2-1403
Medical malpractice awards	100%	735 Ill. Comp. Stat. § 5/2-1716
Debtor's right to receive restitution under Federal Civil Liberties Act of 1988 or the Aleutian and Pribilof Island Restitution Act	100%	735 Ill. Comp. Stat. § 5/12-1001(h)(5)
Awards for occupational diseases	100%	820 Ill. Comp. Stat. § 310/21
Laborer and retirement board employee retirement fund	100%	40 Ill. Comp. Stat. § 5/11-223
Judges' state retirement benefits	100%	40 Ill. Comp. Stat. § 5/18-161
Title certificate for a boat longer than 12 ft.	100%	625 Ill. Comp. Stat. § 45/3A-7(d)
State university employee retirement fund	100%	40 Ill. Comp. Stat. § 5/15-185, 5/2-154
Awards for occupational diseases	100%	820 Ill. Comp. Stat. § 310/21

* Compare In re Jokiel, 2012 WL 33246 (Bank. N. D. Ill. 2012) (holding this statute does not create an exemption in bankrutpcy) with In re Mayer, 388 B.R. 869 (N. D. Ill. 2008) (holding satute does create exemption). See also Smith v. Frazier, 421 B.R. 513 (Bank. S. D. Ill. 2009) (federal garnishment law does not create bankrutpcy exemption).

INDIANA

Federal bankruptcy exemptions not permitted. See Ind. Code 34-55-10-1

Type of Property	Amount of Exemption	Statute Creating Exemption
Real estate or personal property constituting personal or family residence of domiciled debtor	$22,750 (Exemption may be used individually by joint debtors if property held by entireties)	Ind. Code § 34-55-10-2(c)(1)
Other real estate and tangible personal property of domiciled debtor	$12,100	Ind. Code § 34-55-10-2(c)(2)
Intangible personal property of domiciled debtor (includes choses in action but excludes debts and income owing)	$450	Ind. Code § 34-55-10-2(c)(3)
Interest of debtor in health savings account	100%	Ind. Code § 34-55-10-2(c)(8)
Interest of debtor in a qualified tuition program	See statute for limitations	Ind. Code § 34-55-10-2(c)(9)
Interest of debtor in education savings account	See statute for limitations	Ind. Code § 34-55-10-2(c)(10)
Federal earned income tax refund or credit under 26 U.S.C. 32 or ICS §6-3.1-21-6	100%	Ind. Code § 34-55-10-2(c)(11)
Professionally prescribed health aids of debtor and dependents	100%	Ind. Code § 34-55-10-2(c)(4)
Debtor's interest in real estate held as tenant by the entirety on date of filing, unless debtor and spouse file joint petition or their bankruptcy cases are subsequently consolidated	100%	Ind. Code § 34-55-10-2(c)(5)
Debtor's interest in pension or retirement fund, annuity plan, individual retirement account, or similar fund, either private or public	100% of contributions and earnings that are qualified under the I.R.C.	Ind. Code § 34-55-10-2(c)(6)
Money in medical care savings account established under IC 6-8-11	100%	Ind. Code § 34-55-10-2(c)(7) & Ind. Code § 6-8-11-19
Disposable earnings (net earnings after deductions required by law)	30 times the federal minimum hourly wage per week OR 75% of disposable earnings* WHICHEVER IS GREATER	Ind. Code § 24-4.5-5-105 * See In re Haraughty, 403 B.R. 607 (S. D. Ind. 2009) (confirming exemption).
Crime victim's reparation awards	100%	Ind. Code § 5-2-6.1-38
Mutual life & accident ins. proceeds (But see In re Stinnett, 465 P.3d 309 (7th Cir. 2006))	100%	Ind. Code § 27-8-3-23
Teachers' pension benefits	100%	Ind. Code § 5-10.4-5-14
Police pension benefits	100%	Ind. Code §§ 36-8-10-19, 36-8-7.5-19 36-8-6-14
Fraternal Benefit Society benefits	100%	Ind. Code § 27-11-6-3
Group life insurance proceeds	100%	Ind. Code § 27-1-12-29
Public employees' retirement funds and benefits	100%	Ind. Code § 5-10.3-8-9
Firemen's pension benefits	100%	Ind. Code § 36-8-7-22
Workmen's compensation benefits	100% (except child support)	Ind. Code § 22-3-2-17
Specific partnership property	100% of partner's interest	Ind. Code § 23-4-1-25
Proceeds and avails of life insurance policies payable to spouse, children, dependent relative or creditor of insured	100%	Ind. Code § 27-1-12-14
Police Pension Fund Benefits	100%	Ind. Code §§ 10-12-1-8, 36-8-6-14, 36-8-7.5-19, & 36-8-10-19
Employer's life insurance policy on employee	100%	Ind. Code § 27-1-12-17.1(f)
Spendthrift trusts	100%	Ind. Code § 30-4-3-2
Unemployment compensation	100%	Ind. Code § 22-4-33-3
Property of Housing Authorities	100%	Ind. Code § 36-7-18-34
Surviving spouse allowance	100%	Ind. Code § 34-55-7-9
Uniforms, arms, and equipment of National Guard member	100%	Ind. Code § 10-16-10-3
Beneficiaries of life insurance or annuities proceeds	100%(see IC §27-1-12-14 for limits)	Ind. Code § 27-2-5-1(b)
Compensation for 2011 State Fair Victims	100%	Ind. Code § 34-55-5-10-2(c)(13)

* See 750 IAC 1-1-1 for current exemption amounts. Adjusted every 6 years. See Ind. Code § 34-55-10-2.5.

IOWA

Use of federal bankruptcy exemptions not permitted. See Iowa Code § 627.10.

Type of Property	Amount of Exemption	Statute Creating Exemption
Homestead of any person (persons living together as a single household unit may claim exemption once in the aggregate.)	100% of 1/2 acre including dwelling house and appurtenances if within city plat; otherwise, 40 acres including dwelling house and appurtenances (acreage may be enlarged if value is less than $500)	Iowa Code §§ 561.2, 561.16
Jewelry of debtor and debtor's dependents	$2,000 (plus wedding or engagement ring received prior to marriage)	Iowa Code § 627.6(1)(b)
Wedding ring received by debtor or dependents after marriage & within 2 years of execution	$7,000	Iowa Code § 627.6(1)(a)
1 shotgun and either 1 musket or 1 rifle	100%	Iowa Code § 627.6(2)
Libraries, family Bibles, portraits, pictures, musical instruments, and paintings not kept for sale	$1,000 aggregate	Iowa Code § 627.6(3)
Burying ground or interment space	1 acre	Iowa Code § 627.6(4)
Household furnishings, musical instruments, goods & appliances held for personal, family or household use of debtor or dependents	$7,000 aggregate	Iowa Code § 627.6(5)
Debtor's interest in life insurance policy payable to spouse, child or dependent of debtor (includes loan or cash surrender value and accrued dividends or interest)	100% ($10,000 for first 2 years of policy)	Iowa Code § 627.6(6)
Professionally-prescribed health aids	100%	Iowa Code § 627.6(7)
Debtor's rights in Social Security unemployment compensation, any public assistance benefits, veterans benefits, or disability or illness benefits	100%	Iowa Code § 627.6(8)(a),(b),(c)
Debtor's rights to alimony, support or separate maintenance	Amount reasonably necessary to support debtor & dependents	Iowa Code § 627.6(8)(d)
Debtor's right to payments under pension, annuity or similar plan or contract on account of illness, death, age or length of service	100% (payments resulting from excessive personal contributions within previous year are not exempt)	Iowa Code § 627.6(8)(e) (support claims excepted - see Iowa Code § 627.6A
Contributions to and assets of ERISA- qualified retirement plans, and SEPs, Keogh Plans, IRAs, Roth IRAs, and similar plans or accounts	100% of contributions (See statute for limitations on exemption for earnings and increases on contributions	Iowa Code § 627.6(8)(f)
Debtor's interest in accrued wages and state and federal tax refunds	$1,000 aggregate	Iowa Code § 627.6(10) Only available in bankruptcy action
One motor vehicle	$7,000	Iowa Code § 627.6(9)
Implements, professional books, or tools of trade of nonfarmer debtor and dependents	$10,000	Iowa Code § 627.6(11)
Implements, equipment, livestock and livestock feed, if reasonably related to normal farming operation	$10,000 (debtor must be engaged in farming)	Iowa Code § 627.6(12) NOTE: This exemption is in addition to the motor vehicle exemption in CI § 627.6(9).
Disposable earnings from others earned by farmer whose agricultural land is foreclosed upon	100% for 2 years after entry of deficiency judgment. (Earnings paid to debtor directly or indirectly by debtor are not exempt)	Iowa Code § 627.6(13) NOTE: This exemption applies only to deficiency judgments entered in foreclosures actions on agricultural land in which the debtor does not exercise the delay of enforcement provisions of Iowa Code § 654.6.
Bank deposits or other personal property (wildcard)	$1000	Iowa Code § 627.6(14)
Residential rent or utility deposits or advance residential rent payments	$500	Iowa Code § 627.6(15)
Specific partnership property	100% of partner's interest	Iowa Code § 486A.203
United States Government pension benefits	100% (includes homestead purchased with pension money)	Iowa Code §§ 627.8, 627.9
Worker's Compensation benefits	100% (support claims excepted)	Iowa Code § 627.13

(continued on next page)

(continued from previous page)

Type of Property	Amount of Exemption	Statute Creating Exemption
Assistance for adopted children	100%	Iowa Code § 627.19
Disposable earnings (earnings less deductions required by law)	75% OR 40 times the federal minimum hourly wage per week WHICHEVER IS GREATER. NOTE: only the following amounts may be garnished during a calendar year Debtor's expected annual earnings / Amount that can be garnished in calendar year $12,000 or less — $ 250 $12,000 to $16,000 — 400 $16,000 to $24,000 — 800 $24,000 to $35,000 — 1,500 $35,000 to $50,000 — 2,000 $50,000 or more — 10% of expected earnings	Iowa Code § 642.21, Iowa Code § 537.5105 Iowa Code § 627.6(10)
Payments under family investment program (aid to dependant children)	100%	Iowa Code § 239B.6
Group insurance benefits	same as provided in chapter 627	Iowa Code §§ 509.12, 509A.9
Benefit or indemnity paid under accident, health or disability insurance policy	100%	Iowa Code § 627.6(6)
Avails of life, accident, health or disability insurance policy	$15,000 (applies to debts of beneficiary contracted prior to death of insured)	Iowa Code § 627.6(6)
Fraternal insurance benefits	same as provided in chapter 627	Iowa Code § 512B.18
National Guard and State Guard equipment owned by members	no monetary limit	Iowa Code §§ 29A.41, 29A.70
Pension benefits of policemen and firemen	100%	Iowa Code §§ 411.13, 410.11
Public employees retirement benefits	100%	Iowa Code § 97B.39
Unemployment compensation benefits	100%	Iowa Code § 96.15
Liquor licenses	100%	Iowa Code § 123.38
Proceeds of wrongful death actions, including structured settlements	amount reasonably necessary for support of debtor or his/her dependents	Iowa Code § 627.6 (16) Iowa Code § 633.336
Apartment used as a principal residence	100%	Iowa Code § 499A.18
Retirement, accident and disability--Iowa Dept. of Publ. Saftey	100%	Iowa Code § 97A.12
Public property necessary for carrying out purpose of publ. corp.	100%	Iowa Code § 627.18
Funds Held in Iowa Educational Savings Plan Trust	100%	Iowa Code § 627.6(17)

KANSAS

Use of federal bankruptcy exemptions not permitted. See KAN STAT ANN § 60-2313.

Type of Property	Amount of Exemption	Statute Creating Exemption
160 acres of farming land, or 1 acre in an incorporated town or city, or a manufactured or mobile home, if occupied as a residence by the owner or the owner's family	100%	KAN. STAT. ANN. § 60-2301 KAN. STAT. ANN. § 12-524a
Furnishings, equipment and supplies, including food, fuel and clothing, at principal residence necessary for 1 year	100%	KAN. STAT. ANN. § 60-2304(a)
Jewelry and personal ornaments	$1,000	KAN. STAT. ANN. § 60-2304(b)
One means of conveyance (vehicle)	$20,000 (no limit for the handicapped)	KAN. STAT. ANN. § 60-2304(c)
Burial plot or crypt or cemetery lot exempt under KSA § 17-1302	100%	KAN. STAT. ANN. § 60-2304(d)
Books, documents, furniture, tools, instruments, implements, equipment, breeding stock, seed grain, growing plant stock, or other tangible means of production necessary to carry on trade, profession, business or occupation.	$7,500	KAN. STAT. ANN. § 60-2304(e)
United States pension benefits for three months if necessary to support family	100%	KAN. STAT. ANN. § 60-2308(a)
Funds and benefits of retirement plan or IRA qualified under §§ 401(a), 403(a), 403(b), 408, 408A or 409 of Internal Revenue Code	100% (support claims excepted)	KAN. STAT. ANN. § 60-2308(b), (c)
Property listed in 11 U.S.C. § 522(d)(10)	100% (See Federal Bankruptcy Exemption, supra in this Appendix for a list of the exempt property)	KAN. STAT. ANN. § 60-2312
Disposable earnings (net earnings after deductions required by law)	75% of disposable earnings or 30 times the federal minimum hourly wage per week, whichever is greater (see note below)	KAN. STAT. ANN. § 60-2310
Proceeds and other interests (including cash value) of life insurance policies	100% of portion issued more than one year prior to filing of bankruptcy case	KAN. STAT. ANN. § 40-414 and 60-2313(a)(7)
Crime victim's reparation awards	100%	KAN. STAT. ANN. § 74-7313, 60-2313(a)(5)
Unemployment compensation benefits	100%	KAN. STAT. ANN. § 44-718(c), 60-2313(a)(4)
Workmen's compensation benefits	100%	KAN. STAT. ANN. § 44-514, 60-2313(a)(3)
Public assistance payments	100%	KAN. STAT. ANN. § 39-717, 60-2313(a)(2)
Liquor license, club license, or malt beverage wholesale or distribution license	100%	KAN. STAT. ANN. §§ 41-326, 41-2629, and 60-2313(a)(6)
Fraternal Benefit Society benefits	100%	KAN. STAT. ANN. § 60-2313(a)(8)
Luggage & property detained by innkeeper	100%	KAN. STAT. ANN. § 36-202
Uniforms, arms and equipment of national guardsman	100%	KAN. STAT. ANN. § 48-245
Specific partnership property	100% of partner's interest	KAN. STAT. ANN. § 56a-504
Funds in prearranged funeral agreement or plan	100%	KAN. STAT. ANN. § 60-2313(a)(10)
Pension, annuity, retirement, disability or death benefits of state employees, police, firemen, school employees, and other public employees	100%	KAN. STAT. ANN. §§ 12-111a, 12-5005, 13-1246a, 13-14,102, 13-14a10 14-10a10, 20-2618, 60-2313(a)(1) 72-1768, 72-5526,74-4923, 74-4978g,74-49,105, 74-49,106
Goods held on approval of sale	100%	KAN. STAT. ANN. § 84-2-326
Property held by landlord in lieu of rent/goods held on approval	100%	KAN. STAT. ANN. § 60-2304(f)
Earned income tax credit for one tax year	100%	KAN. STAT. ANN. § 60-2315

Note: 100% of a debtor's disposable earnings are exempt for a two-month period after the debtor returns to work if the debtor was unable to work for a period of two weeks or more on account of sickness of the debtor or the debtor's family.

KENTUCKY

Use of federal bankruptcy exemptions permitted. Ky. Rev. Stat. § 427.170

Type of Property	Amount of Exemption	Statute Creating Exemption
Land or personal property used by debtor or dependent as permanent residence within state, or burial plot of debtor or dependent	$5,000	Ky. Rev. Stat. § 427.060
Disposable earnings (earnings after deductions required by law)	75% or 30 times the federal minimum hourly wage, whichever is greater**	Ky. Rev. Stat. § 427.010(2)
NOTE: If wages earned out of state see Ky. Rev. Stat. § 427.050 for exemption		
Household furnishing, personal clothing, ornaments and jewelry	$3,000 (applies to residents only)	Ky. Rev. Stat. § 427.010(1)
Tools, equipment and livestock (including poultry) of farmer	$3,000 (applies to residents only)	Ky. Rev. Stat. § 427.010(1)
One motor vehicle and accessories (including 1 spare tire)	$2,500 (applies to residents only)	Ky. Rev. Stat. § 427.010(1)
Professionally prescribed health aids of debtor and dependents	100%	Ky. Rev. Stat. § 427.010(1)
One motor vehicle and accessories (including 1 spare tire) of mechanic or skilled artisan engaged in repair, replacement or servicing of essential equipment	$2,500	Ky. Rev. Stat. § 427.030
One motor vehicle and accessories (including 1 spare tire) of minister, attorney, physician, surgeon, chiropractor, veterinarian or dentist	$2,500	Ky. Rev. Stat. § 427.040
Necessary tools of trade	$300	Ky. Rev. Stat. § 427.030
Professional library, office equipment, instruments and furnishings of, minister attorney, physician, surgeon, chiropractor, veterinarian, or dentist	$1,000	Ky. Rev. Stat. § 427.040
Proceeds and avails of life insurance policy payable to person other than the insured or person effecting the policy	100%	Ky. Rev. Stat. § 304.14-300
Benefits paid by assessment, cooperative life or casualty insurance company or by a fraternal benefit society	100%	Ky. Rev. Stat. § 427.110
Proceeds and avails of health insurance contracts and disability provisions supplemental to life insurance or annuity contracts	100%	Ky. Rev. Stat. § 304.14-310
Policies of group life insurance and group health insurance and proceeds there from	100%	Ky. Rev. Stat. § 304.14-320
Annuity contracts benefits	$350 per month	Ky. Rev. Stat. § 304.14-330
Basic no-fault insurance benefits	100%	Ky. Rev. Stat. § 304.39-260
Workmen's compensation benefits	100% (except child support)	Ky. Rev. Stat. § 342.180
Unemployment compensation benefits	100% (except child support)	Ky. Rev. Stat. § 341.470
Police and firemen's pension benefits in cities of first through fourth classes	100%	Ky. Rev. Stat. § 427.120 & 427.125
State employees' retirement benefits	100% (except child support)	Ky. Rev. Stat. § 61.690
Teachers' retirement benefits	100% (except child support)	Ky. Rev. Stat. § 161.700
Public assistance payments, federal earned income tax credit	100%	Ky. Rev. Stat. § 205.220(3)
Money or property received as alimony, support or maintenance	Amount reasonably necessary for support of debtor and dependents	Ky. Rev. Stat. § 427.150(1)
Debtor's right or interest in individual retirement account or annuity or other pension or retirement plan that qualifies under the I.R.C.	100% NOTE- Contributions made within 120 days prior to filing are not exempt. (except child support & maintenance)	Ky. Rev. Stat. § 427.150(2)(f)
Crime victim's reparation law awards	100%	Ky. Rev. Stat. § 427.150(2)(a)
Payments on account of the wrongful death of individual of whom debtor was a dependent	Amount reasonably necessary to support debtor and dependents	Ky. Rev. Stat. § 427.150(2)(b)

(continued on next page)

(continued from previous page)

Type of Property	Amount of Exemption	Statute Creating Exemption
Personal bodily injury payment, not including compensation for pain and suffering or actual pecuniary loss, of debtor or individual of whom debtor is a dependent	$7,500	KY. REV. STAT. § 427.150(2)(c)
Payment in compensation of loss of future earnings of debtor or individual of whom debtor is a dependent	Amount reasonably necessary to support debtor and dependents	KY. REV. STAT. § 427.150(2)(d)
Assets held, payments, and amounts payable under pension and retirement systems for teachers, state employees, policemen and firemen	100%	KY. REV. STAT. § 427.150(2)(e)
Property of any nature	$1,000 (this exemption applies only to bankruptcy cases)	KY. REV. STAT. § 427.160
Specific partnership property	100% of partner's interest	KY. REV. STAT. § 362.1-307 & 362.270
Retirement funds-urban county gov. merit and pension	100%	KY. REV. STAT. § 67A.350
Reparation benefits from Motor Vehicle Reparations Act	100%	KY. REV. STAT. § 304.39-260
Proceeds from involuntary sale of real property in place of homestead	$5,000	KY. REV. STAT. § 427.090
Tenancies by the Entirety	recognized but not exempt	11 USC § 522(b)(3)(B)

NOTE: The exceptions granted in KY. REV. STAT. chapter 427 are not applicable to property upon which the debtor has voluntarily granted a lien to the extent of the balance due on the debt secured thereby. See KY. REV. STAT. § 427.010(4). Grain storage receipts are prima facie evidence in bankruptcy of the claimant's rights to the grain shown therein. See KY. REV. STAT. § 427.180.

NOTE: Under 11 U.S.C. §522(b)(3)(B), tenancies by the entireties are recognized, but not exempt.

** But see In re Horton, 2011 WL 832946 (Bankr. E. D. Kentucky 2011) (federal wage garnishment law does not create exemption.

LOUISIANA

Use of federal bankruptcy exemptions not permitted. See LA. REV. STAT. ANN. § 13:3881(B)

Type of Property	Amount of Exemption	Statute Creating Exemptions
Homestead (must be occupied as homestead and title to property must be in debtor or spouse) (full value in case of catastrophic or terminal illness or injury	$35,000 (cannot exceed 5 acres if in city or 200 acres if not in city)	* LA. REV. STAT. ANN. § 20:1 Constitution Art 12, § 9
Pensions, annuities & tax-exempt contributions to retirement plans qualified under I.R.C. if made more than 1 year prior to filing of case	100% (support claims excepted)	LA. REV. STAT. ANN. § 20:33(1)
Gratuitous payments made by employers to employees or former employers or their survivors	100%	LA. REV. STAT. ANN. § 20:33(2)
Disposable earnings (earnings less deductions required by law)	75% or 30 times the federal minimum hourly wage per week, WHICHEVER IS GREATER (50% for support claims)	LA. REV. STAT. ANN. § 13:3881(A)(1)
Tools, instruments, books, one utility trailer, equity in one motor vehicle used in trade, calling or profession or to travel to and from employment, and one firearm	100% except $500 limit for firearm	LA. REV. STAT. ANN. § 13:3881(A)(2)
Income from total property and rights of usufruct of estates of minor children	100%	LA. REV. STAT. ANN. § 13:3881(A)(3)
Clothing, bedding linen, chinaware, non- sterling silverware, glassware, living room, bedroom and dining room furniture, cooking stove, heating and cooling equipment, kitchen utensils, pressing irons, washers, dryers, - refrigerators, deep freezers (electric or otherwise) 1 noncommercial sewing machine, required therapy equipment, used by debtor or his family	100%	LA. REV. STAT. ANN. § 13:3881(A)(4)
Family portraits, arms and military accoutrements, musical instruments of debtor and family, and poultry, fowl and 1 cow kept for family use, and all dogs, cats and other household pets	100%	LA. REV. STAT. ANN. § 13:3881(A)(4)
Wedding or engagement rings	$5,000	LA. REV. STAT. ANN. § 13:3881(A)(5)
Federal earned income tax credit	100% (except IRS liens & child support)	LA. REV. STAT. ANN. § 13:3881(A)(6)
Pensions, annuity payments, individual retirement accounts and other retirement plans that qualify under the I.R.C., including Roth IRAs	100% of tax-exempt amounts NOTE Contributions made within 1 year prior to filing are not exempt. (except alimony & child support)	LA. REV. STAT. ANN. § 13-3881(D)
Spendthrift trust proceeds	100% - excludes amounts contributed by or subject to voluntary alienation by beneficiary	LA. REV. STAT. ANN. § 9:2004
Proceeds and avails of life insurance policies	100% ($35,000 limit for policies issued within 9 months of bankruptcy filing)	LA. REV. STAT. ANN. § 22:912(A)
Fraternal Benefit Society benefits	100%	LA. REV. STAT. ANN. § 22:298
Annuity contract proceeds and avails	100%	LA. REV. STAT. ANN. § 22:912(B)
Proceeds of group life insurance policies	100%	LA. REV. STAT. ANN. § 22:944
Workmen's compensation benefits	100% (except as provided in LA. REV. STAT. ANN. § 11:292)	LA. REV. STAT. ANN. § 23:1205
Unemployment compensation benefits	100% (except as provided in LA. REV. STAT. ANN. § 11:292)	LA. REV. STAT. ANN. § 23:1693
Public assistance payments	100%	LA. REV. STAT. ANN. § 46:111
Wages earned out of state	100% (applies only against out-of-state debts)	LA. REV. STAT. ANN. § 13:3951
Assessors' retirement fund benefits	100% (except as provided in LA. REV. STAT. ANN. § 11:292)	LA. REV. STAT. ANN. § 11:1403
Court clerks' retirement benefits	100% (except as provided in LA. REV. STAT. ANN. § 11:292)	LA. REV. STAT. ANN. § 11:1526
District attorney's retirement benefits	100% (except as provided in LA. REV. STAT. ANN. § 11:292)	LA. REV. STAT. ANN. § 11:1583

(continued on next page)

Type of Property	Amount of Exemption	Statute Creating Exemption
Municipal employees retirement benefits	100% (except as provided in La. Rev. Stat. Ann. § 11:292)	La. Rev. Stat. Ann. § 11:1735
School employees retirement benefits	100% (except as provided in La. Rev. Stat. Ann. § 11:292)	La. Rev. Stat. Ann. § 11:1003
Teachers retirement benefits	100% (except as provided in La. Rev. Stat. Ann. § 11:292)	La. Rev. Stat. Ann. § 11:704
State employees retirement system benefits	100% (except as provided in La. Rev. Stat. Ann. § 11:292)	La. Rev. Stat. Ann. § 11:405
Registrars of voters employees retirement benefits	100% (except as provided in La. Rev. Stat. Ann. § 11:292)	La. Rev. Stat. Ann. § 11:2033
Parochial employees retirement benefits	100% (except as provided in La. Rev. Stat. Ann. § 11:292)	La. Rev. Stat. Ann. § 11:1905
Sheriff's pension and relief fund benefits	100% (except as provided in La. Rev. Stat. Ann. § 11:292)	La. Rev. Stat. Ann. § 11:2182
Police pension and relief benefits	100% (except as provided in La. Rev. Stat. Ann. § 11:292)	La. Rev. Stat. Ann. § 11:1331, 11:3513 11:2228
Judicial retirement benefits	100% (except as provided in La. Rev. Stat. Ann. §11:292)	La. Rev. Stat. Ann. § 11:1378 & 11:570
Motor Vehicle	$7,500	La. Rev. Stat. Ann. § 13:3881(A)(7) & (8)
Proceeds from property insurance received as a result of gubernatorially declared disaster to an exempt asset	100%	La. Rev. Stat. Ann. § 13:3881(A)(9)
Proceeds from Education Assistance Account established pursuant to R.S. 17:3095	100%	La. Rev. Stat. Ann. § 22.912(c)
Proceeds of involuntary sale of exempt property	100%	La. Rev. Stat. Ann. § 13:3881(B)(3)
Louisiana State University retirement system benefits	100% (except as provided in La. Rev. Stat. Ann. §11:292)	La. Rev. Stat. Ann. § 11:952.3
Orleans Parish school employees' retirement system benefits	100%	La. Rev. Stat. Ann. § 11:951.3
Health & accident ins. proceeds	100%	La. Rev. Stat. Ann. § 22:1015
City of Alexandria employees' retirement system benefits	100%	La. Rev. Stat. Ann.§ 11:3014
City of Monroe bus drivers' pension & relief fund	100%	La. Rev. Stat. Ann. § 11:3770
City of Monroe electrical workers' pension & relief fund	100%	La. Rev. Stat. Ann. § 11:3800
City of New Orleans sewage and water board benefits	100%	La. Rev. Stat. Ann. § 11:3823
Public School property	100%	La. Rev. Stat. Ann. § 20:31
Housing authority property	100%	La. Rev. Stat. Ann. § 40:405
Cemetery property	100%	La. Rev. Stat. Ann. § 8:313
Crime victims' compensation	100%	La. Rev. Stat. Ann. § 46:1811
Firemen's relief and pension benefits	100% (except as provided in La. Rev. Stat. Ann. § 11:292)	La. Rev. Stat. Ann. § 11:2263
COVID stimulus payments	100%	La. Rev. Stat. Ann. § 13:3881(10)

NOTE: Property upon which the debtor has voluntarily granted a lien is not exempt to the extent of the balance due on the debt secured thereby. See La. Rev. Stat. Ann. § 13:3881(B)(2).

NOTE: La. Rev. Stat. Ann. §11:292 allows for the seizure of otherwise exempt retirement or other benefits for the collection of child support or restitution, fines, and costs associated with the conviction of a felony pertaining to the service of an elected official which occurred on or after July 1, 2010.

MAINE

Use of federal exemptions not permitted. See 14 MRSA § 4426

Type of Property	Amount of Exemption	Statute Creating Exemption
Debtor's interest in real or personal property used by debtor as residence, or a burial plot (includes a cooperative and proceeds of sale for six months)	$80,000 ($160,000 if minor dependents reside there) ($160,000 if debtor or dependent is age 60 or older or disabled)	14 MRSA § 4422(1) (in jointly owned property the exemption is the lesser of $47,500 or the debtor's fractional share times $95,000)
One motor vehicle	$10,000	14 MRSA § 4422(2)
Household furnishings & goods, wearing apparel, appliances, books, animals, crops, or musical instruments	$500 per item (must be held primarily for the personal, family, or household use of the debtor or a dependent)	14 MRSA § 4422(3)
Personal jewelry of debtor or dependent	$1,000	14 MRSA § 4422(4)
Implements, professional books, or tools of the trade of the debtor or a dependent	$9,500	14 MRSA § 4422(5)
One cooking stove, all furnaces or heating stoves, and fuel not to exceed 10 cords of wood, 5 tons of coal, 1,000 gallons of oil, or its equivalent	100% (must be held primarily for the personal, family, or household use of the debtor or a dependent)	14 MRSA § 4422(6)
6 months' food provisions; seeds, fertilizers, feed, & other materials needed for one growing season: and all tools & equipment needed for raising & harvesting food	100% (must be held primarily for the personal, family, or household use of the debtor or a dependent)	14 MRSA § 4422(7)
One of every type of farm implement reasonably needed for debtor to raise & harvest agricultural products commercially, including personal property incidental thereto	100%	14 MRSA § 4422(8)
One commercial fishing boat not exceeding 46 feet in length	100%	14 MRSA § 4422(9)
Any unmatured life insurance contract owned by debtor, except credit life insurance contract	100%	14 MRSA § 4422(10)
Accrued dividends or interest under, or loan value of, any unmatured life insurance contract owned by debtor under which the insured is the debtor or a person of whom the debtor is a dependent.	$5,000 less transfers made under nonforfeiture provisions of policy	14 MRSA § 4422(11)
Professionally prescribed health aids	100%	14 MRSA § 4422(12)
Social Security benefits, unemployment compensation, Fed., state or local public assistance benefits, veterans' benefits, & disability, illness or unemployment benefits, and Fed. Earned income tax credit & child tax credit	$1,054,550	14 MRSA § 4422(13)(A),(B)
Alimony, support or separate maintenance payments	Amount reasonably necessary to support debtor & dependents	14 MRSA § 4422(13)(D)
Payments or accounts under stock bonus, pension, profit-sharing, annuity or similar plan or contract on account of illness, disability, death, age or length of service	Amount reasonably necessary to support debtor & dependents	14 MRSA § 4422(13)(E)

NOTE: This exemption does not apply if: The plan or contract was established under the auspices of an insider that employed the debtor at the time the plan or contract arose; such payment is on account of age or length of service; and the plan or contract does not qualify under 26 USC §§ 401(a), 403(a), 403(b), 408, or 409.

Type of Property	Amount of Exemption	Statute Creating Exemption
Crime victims reparation law awards	100%	14 MRSA § 4422(14)(A)
Payments on the account of the wrongful death of an individual of whom he debtor was a dependent	Amount reasonably necessary to support debtor & dependents	14 MRSA § 4422(14)(B)
Payments under life insurance contract insuring the life of an individual of whom the debtor was a dependent on the date of death	Amount reasonably necessary to support debtor & dependents	14 MRSA § 4422(14)(C)
Payments on account of bodily injury, not including pain & suffering or compensation for actual pecuniary loss, of the debtor or an individual of whom the debtor is a dependent	$20,000	14 MRSA § 4422(14)(D)

(continued on next page)

(continued from previous page)

Type of Property	Amount of Exemption	Statute Creating Exemption
Payments in compensation of loss of future earnings of the debtor or an individual of whom the debtor is or was a dependent	Amount reasonably necessary to support debtor & dependents	14 MRSA § 4422(14)(E)
Debtor's interest in any property, whether or not otherwise exempt	$500	14 MRSA § 4422(15)
Any property exempt under 14 MRSA § 4422(3), (5) & (14)	Amount equal to any unused portion of the residence exemption under 14 MRSA § 4422(1), but not exceeding $6,000.	14 MRSA § 4422(16)
Proceeds and avails of life, endowment, annuity or accident insurance policies wherein beneficiary is not the insured	100%	24-A MRSA § 2428
Proceeds of health insurance policies and disability insurance supplemental to life insurance or annuity contracts	100%	24-A MRSA § 2429
Group life and health insurance	100%	24-A MRSA § 2430
Individual annuity contract proceeds	$450 per month	24-A MRSA § 2431
Employees' interest in group annuities and pension trusts	100%	24-A MRSA § 2432
Military uniforms, arms and equipment of militiaman or serviceman	100%	37-B MRSA § 262
Aid to needy persons	100%	22 MRSA § 3180
Temp. assistance to needy families	100%	22 MRSA § 3766
State retirement system benefits	100% (child support claims excepted)	5 MRSA § 17053, 17054
Unemployment compensation benefits	100%	26 MRSA § 1044
Workmen's compensation benefits	100% (support claims excepted)	39-A MRSA § 106
Specific partnership property	100% of partner's interest	31 MRSA § 1051 & 1054
Disposal earnings	75% or 40 times the federal minimum hourly rate per week, whichever is greater	14 MRSA § 3126-A & 9-A MRSA § 5-105
Repossessed collateral when creditor brings action against consumer for debt, if not entitled to deficiency judgment	100%	9-A MRSA § 5-103
Benefits from fraternal benefit societies Repossessed collateral when creditor brings action against consumer	100%	24-A MRSA § 4118
Professional logging equipment	100%	14 MRSA § 4422(9-A)

NOTE: If within 90 days of the date of filing the debtor transfers his nonexempt property and as a result acquires, improves, or increases in value property otherwise exempt under 14 MRSA § 4422, his interest shall not be exempt to the extent that the acquisition, improvement or increase in value exceeds the reasonable needs of the debtor or his dependents. See 14 MRSA § 4423. Also, the exemptions contained in 14 MRSA § 4422 do not apply to property fraudulently conveyed by the debtor. See 14 MRSA § 4422.

MARYLAND

Use of federal bankruptcy exemptions not permitted. See Md. Code Ann., C.&J.P. § 11-504(g)

Type of Property	Amount of Exemption	Statute Creating Exemption
Owner occupied residential property, converted manufactured home, or co-op.	$25,150 (tracks federal exemption)	Md. Code Ann, C & JP § 11-504(f)
Personal wearing apparel, books, tools, instruments, or appliances of trade or profession	$6,000	Md. Code Ann, C & JP § 11-504(b)(1)
Money payable in the event of sickness, accident, injury or death of any person	100%	Md. Code Ann, C & JP § 11-504(b)(2)
Professionally prescribed health aids of debtor or dependent	100%	Md. Code Ann, C & JP § 11-504(b)(3)
Household furnishings & goods, wearing apparel, books, pets, and other items held primarily for the personal, family or household use of the debtor or a dependent	$1,000	Md. Code Ann, C & JP § 11-504(b)(4)
Cash or property of any kind (wildcard)	$6,000	Md. Code Ann, C & JP § 11-504(b)(5)
Personal property under federal bankruptcy exemptions	$5,000 (applies only to bankruptcy cases)	Md. Code Ann, C & JP § 11-504(f)
Assets and benefits of retirement plan or IRA qualified under Internal Revenue Code	100%	Md. Code Ann, C & JP § 11-504(h)
Disposable earnings (earnings after deductions required by law)	75% or $145 per week (30 times the federal minimum hourly wage in Caroline, Kent, Queen Anne's & Worcester counties) WHICHEVER IS GREATER	Md. Code Ann, CL § 15-601.1
Proceeds of life insurance policy or annuity contract payable to spouse, children or dependent relations of insured	100% (includes death benefits, cash & loan values, waived premiums and dividends)	Md. Code Ann, Ins. Art. § 16-111(a) Md. Code Ann, Est &Trust § 8-115
Fraternal Benefit Society benefits	100%	Md. Code Ann, Ins. Art. § 8-431
Teachers retirement benefits	100%	Md. Code Ann, SSP § 21-502
State employees pension benefits	100%	Md. Code Ann, SSP § 21-502
Workmen's compensation	100%	Md. Code Ann, L & E § 9-732
Unemployment insurance benefits	100%	Md. Code Ann, L & E § 8-106(b)(2), (3)
Specific partnership property	100% of partner's interest	Md. Code Ann, C & A § 9A-502
Child support payments	100%	Md. Code Ann, C & JP § 11-504(b)(6)
Alimony	To the extent that wages are exempt under ACM, CL § 15-601.1	Md. Code Ann, C & JP § 11-504(b)(7)
Public assistance payments	100%	Md. Code Ann, Human Serv. Art. § 5-407(a)(1) & (2)
Burial lots and crypts (not held for investment)	100%	Md. Code Ann, BR § 5-503
Criminal injuries compensation awards	100% (except for expenses resulting from the injury)	Md. Code Ann, CP § 11-816
Owner-occupied residential real property: including condos	100%	Md. Code Ann, C & JP § 11-504(f)(1)(ii)
Net recovery of personal injury claims	75%	Md. Code Ann, C & JP § 11-504(b)(2)(I)

NOTE: Tenancies by the entirety may be exempt under 11 USC § 522(b) (3) (B). See In Re Ford, 3 B.R. 559. However, property held in tenancy by the entireties is not protected from claims of joint creditors. See In re Fox, 211 B.R. 10. Assets may not be claimed as exempt if they have "zero" or "unknown" value. See In Re Forti, 224 B.R. 323.

MASSACHUSETTS

Use of federal exemptions permitted.

Type of Property	Amount of Exemption	Statute Creating Exemption
Residence owned or leased by householder with family	$500,000 ($125,000 if undeclared)	Mass. Gen. Laws ch.188 § 1-4
NOTE: Must designate homestead estate on deed of conveyance or on subsequent declaration for homestead exemption to be effective (c.188 § 2). Can be used by wife and minor children (c.188 § 3.) Continues after death of householder for benefit of widow and minor children (c.188 § 4).		
Real property or manufactured home of person 62 and older or disabled person	$500,000/ $1,000,000	Mass. Gen. Laws ch. 188 § 1, 2
Necessary wearing apparel, beds, bedding, and heating unit used by debtor and family plus up to $500/mo. for utilities	100% except for utilities	Mass. Gen. Laws ch. 235 § 34(1)
Other household furniture	$15,000	Mass. Gen. Laws ch. 235 § 34(2)
Bibles, school books and library	$500	Mass. Gen. Laws ch. 235 § 34(3)
2 cows, 12 sheep, 2 swine and 4 tons of hay	100%	Mass. Gen. Laws ch. 235 § 34(4)
Tools, implements and fixtures of trade or business	$5000	Mass. Gen. Laws ch. 235 § 34(5)
Materials and stock used in trade or business	$5000	Mass. Gen. Laws ch. 235 § 34(6)
Provisions for family (or money therefore)	$600	Mass. Gen. Laws ch. 235 § 34(7)
One pew in house of public worship	100%	Mass. Gen. Laws ch. 235 § 34(8)
Boats, fishing tackle and nets of fisherman	$1,500	Mass. Gen. Laws ch. 235 § 34(9)
Uniform and required arms and accoutrements of militiaman	100%	Mass. Gen. Laws ch. 235 § 34(10)
Tombs and rights of burial	100%	Mass. Gen. Laws ch. 235 § 34(11)
1 sewing machine, 1 computer, 1 television	100%	Mass. Gen. Laws ch. 235 § 34(12)
Shares in cooperative associations	$100	Mass. Gen. Laws ch. 235 § 34(13)
Money used to pay rent (in lieu of homestead exemption)	$2,500 per month	Mass. Gen. Laws ch. 235 § 34(14)
Cash, savings, deposits in banks, and money owed for wages	$7,500	Mass. Gen. Laws ch. 235 § 34(15)
Public assistance payments	100%	Mass. Gen. Laws ch. 235 § 34(15), 118 § 10
Automobile	$7,500	Mass. Gen. Laws ch. 235 § 34(16)
Debtor's interest in annuity, pension, profit-sharing, or other retirement plan that qualifies under the I.R.C., or a similar plan or contract purchased with assets of qualified plan.	100% (Individual contributions made during last 5 years in excess of 7% of income not exempt)	Mass. Gen. Laws ch. 235 § 34A & 246 §28
Wages and salaries assigned	75%	Mass. Gen. Laws ch. 154 § 3
Payroll deductions of public employees for repaying loans	100%	Mass. Gen. Laws ch. 149 § 178B
Disability insurance payments	$400 per week	Mass. Gen. Laws ch. 175 § 110A
Group annuity contract benefits	100% (except support orders)	Mass. Gen. Laws ch. 175 § 132C
Group insurance policies and proceeds	100% (except support orders)	Mass. Gen. Laws ch. 175 § 135
Life insurance or annuity contract benefits retained by Co.	100%	Mass. Gen. Laws ch. 175 § 119A
Relocation payments	100%	Mass. Gen. Laws ch. 79A § 7
Funds deposited in payroll accounts	100%	Mass. Gen. Laws ch. 246 § 20
Wages for personal service	85% gross or 50 times minimum wage*	Mass. Gen. Laws ch. 246 § 28
Veterans benefits	100%	Mass. Gen. Laws ch. 115 § 5
Pension payments	100%	Mass. Gen. Laws ch. 246 § 28
Monies in bank accounts	$2500	Mass. Gen. Laws ch. 246 § 28A
Wages of seaman	100%	Mass. Gen. Laws ch. 246 § 32(7)
Public employees retirement benefits, including prison employees, court officers, police, and firefighters	100%	Mass. Gen. Laws ch. 32 § 19
Workmen's compensation benefits	100% (except support order)	Mass. Gen. Laws ch. 152 § 47
Unemployment compensation benefits	100% (except support orders)	Mass. Gen. Laws ch. 151A § 36
Specific partnership property	100% of partner's interest	Mass. Gen. Laws ch. 108A § 25

(continued from previous page)

MASSACHUSETTS

Type of Property	Amount of Exemption	Statute Creating Exemption
Private pension association benefits	100%	MASS. GEN. LAWS ch. 32 § 41
Public employee payroll deductions	100%	MASS. GEN. LAWS ch. 149 § 178B
Self-insurance funds of health care provider	100%	MASS. GEN. LAWS ch. 175F § 15
Benefits from fraternal benefits societies	100%	MASS. GEN. LAWS ch. 176 § 22
Wages	85% gross or 50 times min wage	MASS. GEN. LAWS ch. 235 § 34(15)
Automobile used by elderly or disabled	$15,000	MASS. GEN. LAWS ch..235 §34(16)
Any personal property (wildcard)	$1,000 + up to $5,000 of unused auto, furniture, & trade tools exemptions	MASS. GEN. LAWS ch. 235 § 34(17)
Jewelry	$1,225	MASS. GEN. LAWS ch. 235 § 34(18)
Life insurance proceeds	100%	MASS. GEN. LAWS ch. 175 § 125,126
Disability insurance payments	$400 per week	MASS. GEN. LAWS ch. 175 § 110A
Group annuity contract benefits	100% (except support orders)	MASS. GEN. LAWS ch. 175 § 132C
Group insurance policies and proceeds	100% (except support orders)	MASS. GEN. LAWS ch. 175 § 135

NOTE: A wife's interest in tenancies by the entirety may be exempt under 11 USC § 522(b)(3)(B). See, e.g., Friedman v. Harold, 638 F. 2d 262 (1st Cir. 1981).
*But see In re Bloomstein, 2010WL4607525 (Bank. D. Mass. 2010) (federal wage garnishment law may not create exemption).

MICHIGAN

Use of federal exemptions permitted.

Type of Property	Amount of Exemption*	Statute Creating Exemption
Family pictures, legally required arms and accoutrements, wearing apparel, 6 months' provisions and fuel, and family burial site, and professionally prescribed health aids	100%	MICH. COMP. LAWS § 600.5451(1)(a) & (b)
Household goods, furniture, utensils, books and appliances	$700 each ($4,050 aggregate)	MICH. COMP. LAWS § 600.5451(1)(c)
Seat, pew or slip in place of worship	$800	MICH. COMP. LAWS § 600.5451(1)(d)
Wages earned yet unpaid	60% if a householder with a family (40% if not)	MICH. COMP. LAWS § 600.5311
10 sheep, 2 cows, 5 swine, 100 hens, 5 roosters, and a six-month supply of feed	$3,075	MICH. COMP. LAWS § 600.5451(1)(e)
Household pets	$800	MICH. COMP. LAWS § 600.5451(1)(f)
1 motor vehicle	$4,250	MICH. COMP. LAWS § 600.5451(1)(g)
1 computer and accessories	$800	MICH. COMP. LAWS § 600.5451(1)(h)
Tools, implements, materials, stock, apparatus, team, horses, harness, etc. and motor vehicle necessary to carry on principal trade, business or profession of debtor	$3,075	MICH. COMP. LAWS § 600.5451(1)(i)
Disability insurance payments	100%	MICH. COMP. LAWS § 600.5451(1)(j)
Building and loan association shares	$1,175 at par value (cannot be claimed if homestead exemption is claimed)	MICH. COMP. LAWS § 600.5451(1)(k)
Qualified pension, profit sharing, or stock bonus plans	100%	MICH. COMP. LAWS § 600.5451(1)(m)
Homestead (can not exceed 40 acres of rural land and buildings or one lot with building in village, town or city)	$46,125 (can be claimed by any Michigan resident who owns and occupies a house, whether or not he owns the land) ($69,200 if elderly or disabled)	MICH. COMP. LAWS § 600.5451(1)(n)
Homestead of deceased homestead owner if surviving spouse is not a homestead owner	100%	MICH. COMP. LAWS § 600.5451(1)(p)
Individual retirement account or annuity, or pension plan qualified under I.R.C.	100% of qualified amounts, except contributions made within 120 days of filing	MICH. COMP. LAWS § 600.5451(1)(l)
Judges' retirement benefits	100%	MICH. COMP. LAWS §§ 38.2308, 38.1683
Legislative retirement benefits	100%	MICH. COMP. LAWS §§ 38.10578, 38.1683
Crime victim's compensation	100%	MICH. COMP. LAWS § 18.362
Public school employees' pension benefits	100%	MICH. COMP. LAWS §§ 38.13468, 38.1683
Social welfare benefits	100% (subsidized rental housing claims excepted)	MICH. COMP. LAWS § 400.63
State employees' retirement benefits	100%	MICH. COMP. LAWS §§ 38.408, 38.1683
Workmen's compensation benefits	100%	MICH. COMP. LAWS § 418.821
Fraternal Benefit Society benefits	100%	MICH. COMP. LAWS § 500.8181
Police and Firemen's pension benefits	100%	MICH. COMP. LAWS § 38.559
Unemployment compensation	100%	MICH. COMP. LAWS § 421.30
Proceeds and avails of life insurance policies payable to spouse or children, if so provided in policy	100%	MICH. COMP. LAWS § 500.2207 & 2209
Employer-sponsored trust funds of life insurance benefits	100%	MICH. COMP. LAWS § 500.2210
Ex-servicemens' benefits	100%	MICH. COMP. LAWS §§ 35.1027, 35.926, 35.977
Specific partnership property	100% of partner's interest	MICH. COMP. LAWS § 449.25(2)(c)

(Continued on next page)

(Continued from previous page)

MICHIGAN*

Homestead	$3,500	Mich. Comp. Laws § 600.6023(1)(h)
Family pictures	100%	Mich. Comp. Laws § 600.6023(1)(a)
Wearing apparel	100%	Mich. Comp. Laws § 600.6023(1)(a)
Six months' supply of provisions and fuel	100%	Mich. Comp. Laws § 600.6023(1)(a)
Arms and accoutrements required by law to be kept by any person	100%	Mich Comp Laws§600.6023(1)(a)
Household goods, furniture, utensils, books and appliances	$1000	Mich. Comp. Laws § 600.6023(1)(b)
Seat, pew, or slip in place of worship	100%	Mich. Comp. Laws § 600.6023(1)(c)
Cemetery lot, tomb, and rights of burial	100%	Mich. Comp. Laws § 600.6023(1)(c)
10 sheep, 2 cows, 5 swine, 100 hens, 5 roosters plus 6 months of feed	100%	Mich. Comp. Laws § 600.6023(1)(d)
Tools of debtor's trade, including an automobile	$1,000	Mich Comp Laws§600.6023(1)(e)
Money paid by any stock or mutual life or health or casualty insurance company on account of disability due to injury or sickness of any person	100%	Mich. Comp. Laws § 600.6023(1)(f)
Shares of mutual building and loan association	par value of $1000	Mich. Comp. Laws § 600.6023(1)(g)
IRA or annuity qualified under IRC 408 or 408a	100% of permitted exemption under 11 USC 522(b)(2) except for any amount contributed within 120 days before filing bankruptcy(child support and maintenance claims excepted)	Mich. Comp. Laws § 600.6023(1)(k)
Pension, profit-sharing, stock bonus, or other plan qualified under IRC 401 or 403(b)	100% except for any amount contributed within 120 days before filing bankruptcy (Child support and maintenance claims excepted)	Mich. Comp. Laws § 600.6023(1)(1)
State police retirement benefits	100%	Mich. Comp. Laws § 38.1643
Burial grounds	100%	Mich. Comp. Laws § 128.112
Deposits with state treasurer under Michigan Vehicle Code	100%	Mich. Comp. Laws § 257.524
Family support subsidy payments	100%	Mich. Comp. Laws §330.1158a
Life insurance benefits	100%	Mich. Comp. Laws § 500.2209
Insurance proceeds in hands of insurer	100%	Mich. Comp. Laws § 500.4054
Proceeds from sales of milk or cream	40%	Mich. Comp. Laws §600.4031
Tenancy by entirety against joint debt	100%	Mich. Comp. Laws § 600.6023a

*NOTE: **The exemptions in Mich. Comp. Laws § 600.5451 are readjusted every three years, including on April 15, 2026.**

The exemptions in MCL 600.5451 are available only for debtors filing bankruptcy. These "bankruptcy specific exemptions" have encountered recent constitutional challenges, but were recently upheld by the 6th Circuit. See In re Shafer, 689 F.3d 601 (6th Cir. 2012).

Tenancies by the entirety may be exempt under 11 USC § 522(b)(3)(B). See In Re Trickett, 5 C.B.C. 2nd 85, and MCLA § 600.5451(o) & 600.2807(1).

MINNESOTA

Use of federal exemptions permitted with restrictions (*see below*) *

Type of Property	Amount of Exemption	Statute Creating Exemption
Homestead, consisting of house and land occupied by debtor as dwelling place (title may be in either spouse; includes equitable interests in land and proceeds of sale of exempt homestead for 1 year)	$480,000 generally $1,200,00 if used in farming (May not exceed 160 acres or 1/2 acre in city)	MINN. STAT. §§ 510.01, 510.02
Family Bible, library, and musical instruments	100% (but see In re Hilary, 76 BR 683)	MINN. STAT. § 550.37 subd. 2
Seat or pew in place of worship and lot in burying ground	100%	MINN. STAT. § 550.37 subd. 3
All wearing apparel, 1 watch, and food	100%	MINN. STAT. § 550.37 subd. 4(a)
Household furniture, utensils, appliances, phonographs, radio and television receivers, foodstuffs of debtor and family	$11,250	MINN. STAT. § 550.37 subd. 4(b)
Wedding rings and other marital symbols	$3,062.50	MINN. STAT. § 550.37 subd. 4(c)
Farm machines and implements of farmer used in farming, livestock, farm produce, standing crops	$13,000 (Certain family members may claim family partnership assets as personal assets)	MINN. STAT. § 550.37 subd. 5
Tools, implements, machines, instruments, office furniture, stock in trade, and library, used in trade, business or profession	$12,500 NOTE - Total selected by debtor under subd. 5 and 6 cannot exceed $13,000	MINN. STAT. § 550.37 subd. 6 & 7
All money arising from any claim on account of destruction of or damage to exempt property	100%	MINN. STAT. § 550.37 subd. 9
Benefits payable to surviving wife or child from insurance on life of deceased husband or father	$50,000 plus $12,500 for each dependent of surviving wife or child	MINN. STAT. § 550.37 subd.10
Benefits payable by police, fire, beneficiary, or fraternal benefit association	100%	MINN. STAT. § 550.37 subd. 11
Mobile home used as home	100%	MINN. STAT. § 550.37 subd. 12
One motor vehicle	$5,000 $48,000 if modified for disabled person	MINN. STAT. § 550.37 subd. 12a.
Public assistance	100% (exemption lasts for 60 days after deposit in bank account)	MINN. STAT. § 550.37 subd. 14
Earnings of minor child of debtor and child support paid to debtor	100%	MINN. STAT. § 550.37 subd. 15
Damages for wrongful levy or execution	100%	MINN. STAT. § 550.37 subd. 16
Personal injury claims of debtor or relative	100%	MINN. STAT. § 550.37 subd.22
Debtor's aggregate interest in dividends, interest, or loan value of unmatured life insurance contract owned by debtor or individual of whom debtor is a dependent	$9,600	MINN. STAT. § 550.37 subd.23
Debtor's right to receive payments under stock bonus, profit sharing, annuity, individual retirement account or annuity, Roth IRA, simplified employee pension, or similar plan or contract on account of illness, disability, death, age or length of service	100% of amounts exempt under ERISA or $72,000 present value plus amounts reasonably necessary for support of debtor or dependent. (support claims excepted)	MINN. STAT. § 550.37 subd. 24
Proceeds of payments received by debtor for contributions made to real estate improvements	100%	MINN. STAT. § 550.37 subd. 25
Veteran's pension benefits	100%	MINN. STAT. § 550.38
Accident or disability insurance benefits	100%	MINN. STAT. § 550.39
Disposable earnings (earnings after deductions required by law)	75% or 40 times federal minimum hourly wage per week, whichever is greater	MINN. STAT. § 571.921, 922, 550.37(13)
Money held in medical savings account	$25,000	MINN. STAT. § 550.37 subd. 25

NOTE: Exemption covers exempt earnings deposited in financial institution for period of 20 days

NOTE: The exemption amounts in § 550.37 (except subd. 5 & 7) are adjusted biannually for cost of living changes. The next change is scheduled to occur in July, 2020 based on the December 2019 CPI. See mn.gov/commerce/banking-and-finance/topics/interest-rates/dollar-amount-adjustments/

* A husband & wife cannot split the state and federal bankruptcy exemptions in a joint case or in separate cases filed within 3 years of each other. Both spouses must use either the state or the federal bankruptcy exemptions. See MS § 550.371; but see In re Soby, 37 B.R. 522 (Bank. D. Minn. 1984).

(continued on next page)

MINNESOTA

(continued from previous page)

Type of Property	Amount of Exemption	Statute Creating Exemption
Police & Firemen's pension benefits	100%*	Minn. Stat. § 423A.16
Teacher's Retirement Fund Assoc. benefits	100%*	Minn. Stat. §§ 354A.11 & 356.401
Public Employees' Retirement Assoc. benefits	100%*	Minn. Stat. §§ 353.15 & 356.401
State Retirement Act benefits	100%*	Minn. Stat. §§ 352.15 & 356.401
Fraternal Benefit Society benefits	100%	Minn. Stat. § 64B.18
Unemployment compensation benefits	100%	Minn. Stat. § 268.192
Workers' compensation benefits	100%	Minn. Stat. § 176.175
Cash bail posted in court	100%	Minn. Stat. § 629.53
Official seal and register of notary public	100%	Minn. Stat. § 359.03
Equipment of National Guard member	100%	Minn. Stat. § 192.25
Specific partnership property	100% of partner's interest	Minn. Stat. §§ 323A.0203 & 323A.0307
Prisoner's earnings held by state	100%	Minn. Stat. § 241.26(6)
Life insurance or endowment proceeds, dividends, interest, loan, cash or surrender value if insured is not the beneficiary	100%	Minn. Stat. § 61A.04, 61A.12
Private cemetery property	100 acres (300 if owned by church)	Minn. Stat. § 307.09(1)
Highway patrolmen retirement benefits	100%	Minn. Stat. § 352B.071
Judges' retirement benefits	100%	Minn. Stat. § 490.126
Library and other equipment used in teaching at public university	100%	Minn. Stat. §550.37(8)
Crime victims payments	100%	Minn. Stat. § 611A.60

*Except as provided in Minn. Stat. §§518.58, 518.581, and 518A.53.

MISSISSIPPI

Use of federal bankruptcy exemptions not permitted. See MISS. CODE ANN. § 85-3-2

Type of Property	Amount of Exemption	Statute Creating Exemption
Homestead of householder (debtor must reside in homestead unless he is over 60 and previously qualified for exemption)	$75,000 (cannot exceed 160 acres; Mobile home: $30,000 if debtor owns land)	MISS. CODE ANN. § 85-3-21
Insurance proceeds from destruction of exempt homestead	$75,000	MISS. CODE ANN. § 85-3-23
Personal property selected by debtor (except wages, salaries or commissions)	$250 or articles specified as exempt if head of family (see below)	MISS. CODE ANN. § 85-3-23
Household goods, wearing apparel, books, animals or crops; motor vehicles; implements, professional books or tools of trade; cash on hand; professionally prescribed health aid; or any item of tangible personal property worth less than $200.	$10,000 cumulative value	MISS. CODE ANN. § 85-3-1(a)
Insurance or sales proceeds from exempt property	amount of exemption applicable to property damaged or sold	MISS. CODE ANN. § 85-3-1(b)(i)
Income from disability insurance	100%	MISS. CODE ANN. § 85-3-1(b)(ii)
Real property of railroad authorities	100% (except as to voluntary liens)	MISS. CODE ANN. § 19-29-41
Property for the collection or enforcement of any order or judgment for civil or criminal contempt of court	100%	MISS. CODE ANN. § 85-3-1(c)
One mobile or manufactured home used as primary residence by person not claiming homestead exemption	$30,000	MISS. CODE ANN. § 85-3-1(d)
Assets in and benefits from I.R.C.-qualified retirement plan or IRA	100% of tax-qualified amounts	MISS. CODE ANN. § 85-3-1(e)
Wages, salaries and compensation for personal services	100% of earnings for last 30 days, then 75% or 30 times the federal minimum hourly wage for week, WHICHEVER IS GREATER	MISS. CODE ANN. § 85-3-4
Proceeds of life insurance policies payable to another (includes cash surrender and loan values)	100% (except $50,000, if procured within 1 year of bankruptcy)	MISS. CODE ANN. § 85-3-11
Proceeds of life insurance policies payable to executor	$50,000	MISS. CODE ANN. § 85-3-13
Proceeds of personal injury judgment	$10,000	MISS. CODE ANN. § 85-3-17
Fraternal Benefit Society benefits	100%	MISS. CODE ANN. § 83-29-39
Insurance proceeds in hands of insurance company if contract so provides	100%	MISS. CODE ANN. § 83-7-5
Aid to disabled persons	100%	MISS. CODE ANN. § 43-29-15
Aid to blind persons	100%	MISS. CODE ANN. § 43-3-71
Old age assistance payments	100%	MISS. CODE ANN. § 43-9-19
Employee trust plan benefits	100%	MISS. CODE ANN. § 71-1-43
Unemployment compensation benefits	100%	MISS. CODE ANN. § 71-5-539
Workmen's compensation benefits	100%	MISS. CODE ANN. § 71-3-43
Firemen and policemen retirement and disability benefits	100%	MISS. CODE ANN. § 21-29-257
Municipal employees' retirement benefits	100%	MISS. CODE ANN. § 21-29-51 & 307
State employees' retirement benefits	100%	MISS. CODE ANN. § 25-11-129
Teachers' retirement benefits	100%	MISS. CODE ANN. § 25-11-201 & 129
Specific partnership property	100% of partner's interest	MISS. CODE ANN. § 79-13-501 & 504
Senior (age 70 or over) additional exemption of any real, personal or intangible property, or any combination thereof	$50,000	MISS. CODE ANN. § 85-3-1(h)
Debtor's interest in federal or state tax refunds or credits	$5,000 each	MISS. CODE ANN. § 85-3-1(i) (j) & (k)

(Continued on next page)

(Continued from previous page)

MISSISSIPPI

Type of Property	Amount of Exemption	Statute Creating Exemption
Assets held in a qualified tuition pk. plan or health savings plan	100%	MISS. CODE ANN. § 85-3-1(f)&(g)
Supplemental legislative retirement plan benefits	100%	MISS. CODE ANN. § 25-11-319
Optional retirement benefits for university employees	100%	MISS. CODE ANN. § 25-11-419
Public officer and employee retirement benefits	100%	MISS. CODE ANN. § 25-13-31
Public employee deferred compensation benefits	100%	MISS. CODE ANN. § 25-14-5
Descent of exempt property	100%	MISS. CODE ANN. § 91-1-19
Criminal judgment awards	100%	MISS. CODE ANN. § 99-41-23(8)

MISSOURI

Use of federal bankruptcy exemptions not permitted. See Mo. Rev. Stat. § 513.427

Type of Property	Amount of Exemption	Statute Creating Exemption
Personal household furnishings & goods, wearing apparel, books, animals, crops, and musical instruments of debtor and dependents	$3,000	Mo. Rev. Stat. 513.430.1(1)
Personal, family or household jewelry of debtor or dependents	$500 and $1,500 for wedding ring	Mo. Rev. Stat. § 513.430.1(2)
Any property of debtor	$600	Mo. Rev. Stat. § 513.430.1(3)
Implements, books or tools of trade of debtor or dependent	$3,000	Mo. Rev. Stat. § 513.430.1(4)
Motor vehicles	$3,000 aggregate	Mo. Rev. Stat. § 513.430.1(5)
Mobile home used as principal residence	$5,000	Mo. Rev. Stat. § 513.430.1(6)
Unmatured life insurance contracts, except credit life	100% (See statute for burial exemption)	Mo. Rev. Stat. § 513.430.1(7)
Dividends, interest, or loan values of unmatured life insurance contracts more than 1 year old insuring debtor or person of whom debtor is a dependent	$150,000	Mo. Rev. Stat. § 513.430.1(8)
Health aids of debtor or dependents	100%	Mo. Rev. Stat. § 513.430.1(9)
Social Security benefits, unemployment, compensation, public assistance benefits, veterans' benefits, and disability, illness or unemployment benefits	100%	Mo. Rev. Stat. § 513.430.1(10)(a), (b), (c)
Alimony, support or separate maintenance	$750 per month	Mo. Rev. Stat. § 513.430.1(10)(d)
Payments under a stock-bonus, pension, profit-sharing, nonpublic retirement, annuity, or similar plan or contract, including debtor's rights in deferred compensation programs offered by state or political subdivision thereof. ERISA plans included.	Amount reasonably necessary to support debtor & dependents (Payments under certain nonqualified plans are not exempt)	Mo. Rev. Stat. § 513.430.1(10)(e)
Money or assets payable from, or an interest in, a retirement plan or IRA that is qualified under the I.R.C., health savings plan, or similar.	100%, except that fraudulent contributions and contributions made within 3 years of the date of filing are not exempt.	Mo. Rev. Stat. § 513.430.1(10)(f)
Payments on account of the wrongful death of a person of whom the debtor was a dependent	Amount reasonably necessary to support debtor & dependents	Mo. Rev. Stat. § 513.430.1(11)
Choice of any other property whatsoever except 10% of any debt, income, salary or wages	$1,250 plus $350 per dependent minor child or disabled person (applies only to head of family)	Mo. Rev. Stat. § 513.440
Homestead (consists of house and land used therewith)	$15,000	Mo. Rev. Stat. § 513.475
Net earnings after deduction required by law (includes wages, salary, commissions, bonuses, pensions and retirement payments)	For head of family - 90% OR 30 times the federal minimum hourly wage per, week whichever is greater. For any other person - 75% OR 30 times the federal minimum hourly wage per week, whichever is greater.*	Mo. Rev. Stat. § 525.030(2)
Life insurance benefits under assessment or stipulated premium plans	100%	Mo. Rev. Stat. § 377.090, 377.330
Teacher and school employee retirement benefits	100%	Mo. Rev. Stat. § 169.090, 169.380, 169.520 & 169.587
Police relief and pension benefits	100%	Mo. Rev. Stat. § 86.190, 86.353, & 86.563
Firemen's retirement & relief benefits	100%	Mo. Rev. Stat. § 87.090, 87.365 & 87.485
Highway patrol and employees' retirement benefits	100%	Mo. Rev. Stat. § 104.250
Local government employees' pension and retirement benefits	100%	Mo. Rev. Stat. § 70.695
City employees' retirement benefits	100%	Mo. Rev. Stat. § 71.207
State employees' retirement benefits	100%	Mo. Rev. Stat. § 104.540
Workmen's compensation benefits	100%	Mo. Rev. Stat. § 287.260
Police department civilian employees' retirement benefits	100% (support claims excepted)	Mo. Rev. Stat. § 86.1430
Financial responsibility deposits with state treasurer	100%	Mo. Rev. Stat. § 303.240(2)
Burial lots	100%	Mo. Rev. Stat. § 214.190
Specific partnership property	100% of partner's interest	Mo. Rev. Stat. § 358.250

(continued on next page)

(Continued form previous page)

MISSOURI

Type of Property	Amount of Exemption	Statute
Unliquidated personal injury claims, state and fed. tax refunds	100% (but see In *re Mahony,* 374 BR 717 (Bank. W. D. Mo. 2007)	Mo. Rev. Stat. § 513.427
Tenants by entireties	100%	Mo. Rev. Stat. § 513.427 & 513.475(2)
Retirement benefits-special consultants on retirement, aging	100%	Mo. Rev. Stat. § 104.610
Retirement benefits-administrative judges & legal advisors	100%	Mo. Rev. Stat. § 287.820
Surviving Spouse of Judge--special consultant compensation	100%	Mo. Rev. Stat. § 476.539
Firearms	$500	Mo. Rev. Stat. § 513.430.1(11)

GENERAL NOTE: There are no exemptions for debts for taxes, for debts of $90 or less owed to laborers and servants, for debts for maintenance and child support, and for persons about to leave the state. Tenancies by the entirety may be exempt under 11 U.S.C. § 522(b)(3)(B). See In re Abernathy, 259 B. R. 330 (8th Cir. 2001).

* But see In re Parsons, 437 B.R. 854 (Bank. E.D. Mo. 2010) (holding this statute does not create a Chapter 7 exemption).

MONTANA

Use of federal bankruptcy exemptions not permitted. See Mont. Code Ann. § 31-2-106

Type of Property	Amount of Exemption	Statute Creating Exemption
Homestead, consisting of mobile home or dwelling in which debtor resides and land on which it is located, if any	$350,000* - A written declaration of homestead must be recorded with county clerk. Includes traceable proceeds for 8 months after sale. *increases by 4% annually after 2021	Mont. Code Ann. §§ 70-32-104, 105, & 25-13-615
Professionally prescribed health aids	100%	Mont. Code Ann. § 25-13-608(1)(a)
Social Security benefits and public assistance benefits	100% (support claims excepted)	Mont. Code Ann. § 25-13-608(1)(b)
Veterans' benefits	100%	Mont. Code Ann. § 25-13-608(1)(c)
Disability or illness benefits	100%	Mont. Code Ann. § 25-13-608(1)(d)
IRAs and Roth IRAs qualified under I.R.C.	100% of qualified amounts (support claims excepted)	Mont. Code Ann. § 25-13-608(1)(e)
Medical, surgical or hospital care benefits, if used for medical care	100%	Mont. Code Ann. § 25-13-608(1)(f)
Maintenance and child support	100%	Mont. Code Ann. § 25-13-608(1)(g)
Burial plot of debtor and family	100%	Mont. Code Ann. § 25-13-608(1)(h)
Benefits from a state authorized Retirement System or plan	100%	Mont. Code Ann. § 25-13-608(1)(i), (j)
Household furnishings and goods, appliances, jewelry, wearing apparel, books, firearms, sporting goods, animals, feed, crops, and musical instruments	$1,200 per item $7,000 aggregate value	Mont. Code Ann. § 25-13-609(1)
Debtor's interest in 1 motor vehicle	$4,000	Mont. Code Ann. § 25-13-609(2)
Implements, professional books, or tools of trade of debtor or dependent	$4,500	Mont. Code Ann. § 25-13-609(3)
Unmatured life insurance contracts owned by debtor	100%	Mont. Code Ann. § 25-13-608(1)(k)
Traceable proceeds of lost, damaged, or destroyed exempt property	100% of applicable exemption for a period of 6 months	Mont. Code Ann. § 25-13-610(1)
Aggregate net earnings of debtor	(75% OR 30 times the federal minimum hourly wage per week, WHICHEVER IS GREATER) (support claims excepted)	Mont. Code Ann. § 25-13-614
Note: earnings are exempt for 45 days after receipt if traceable; See MCA § 25-13-610(2)		
Benefits from qualifying private or governmental retirement, pension or similar plan	100% - except contributions made within 1 year before the petition was filed that exceed 15% of the debtor's gross income for that year are not exempt	Mont. Code Ann. § 31-2-106(3)
Required arms, uniforms and accouterments, and one gun	100%	Mont. Code Ann. § 25-13-613(1)(c)
Proceeds and avails of life insurance policies where beneficiary is not the insured	100%	Mont. Code Ann. § 33-15-511
Group life insurance proceeds	100%	Mont. Code Ann. § 33-15-512
Fraternal Benefit Society benefits	100%	Mont. Code Ann. § 33-7-522
Disability insurance proceeds	100%	Mont. Code Ann. § 33-15-513
Annuity contract benefits	$350 per month	Mont. Code Ann. § 33-15-514
Public assistance payments	100%	Mont. Code Ann. § 53-2-607 & 25-13-608(1)(b)
Workers' compensation benefits	100% (support claims excepted)	Mont. Code Ann. § 39-71-743
Unemployment compensation benefits	100% (support claims excepted)	Mont. Code Ann. § 39-51-3105, 31-2-106(2)
Silicosis benefits	100%	Mont. Code Ann. § 39-73-110
Cemetery association lots	100%	Mont. Code Ann. § 35-20-217
Public employees' retirement funds and benefits	100% (support claims excepted)	Mont. Code Ann. § 19-2-1004
Teachers' retirement benefits	100%	Mont. Code Ann. § 19-20-706
Specific partnership property	100% of partner's interest	Mont. Code Ann. § 35-10-505
Firefighters' retirement	100% (support claims excepted)	Mont. Code Ann. § 19-18-612
Policemens' retirement	100% (support claims excepted)	Mont. Code Ann. § 19-19-504
University system retirement	100% (support claims excepted)	Mont. Code Ann. § 19-21-212

(Continued from previous page)

MONTANA

Type of Property	Amount of Exemption	Statute Creating Exemption
Payments to crime victims	100%	MONT. CODE ANN. § 53-9-129
Retirement benefits-public employees	100%	MONT. CODE ANN. §§ 19-2-1004, 25-13-608(j)
Retirement benefits-teachers	100%	MONT. CODE ANN. § 19-20-706, 25-13-608(j)
Benefits paid from agricultural hail insurance	100%	MONT. CODE ANN. § 80-2-245
Health Savings Account	100%	MONT. CODE ANN. § 25-13-608

NEBRASKA

Use of federal exemptions not permitted. See Neb. Rev. Stat. § 25-15, 105

Type of Property	Amount of Exemption	Statute Creating Exemption
Homestead of resident debtor (either head of family or 65 years or older)	$60,000 (160 acres or 2 lots if in city)	Neb. Rev. Stat. §§ 40-101 & 40-105
Proceeds of sale of homestead for 6 months after sale	$60,000	Neb. Rev. Stat. § 40-116
Personal property of resident debtor (wildcard)	$5,000 (Does not apply to wages)	Neb. Rev. Stat. § 25-1552
Immediate personal possessions of resident debtor & family	100%	Neb. Rev. Stat. § 25-1556
Necessary wearing apparel of resident debtor & family	100%	Neb. Rev. Stat. § 25-1556
Household furnishings, goods, computers & appliances, books or musical instruments held primarily for personal, family, or household use	$3,000	Neb. Rev. Stat. § 25-1556
Implements, tools, or professional books or supplies used in principal trade or business of debtor or family, including one motor vehicle used in or to commute to principal trade or business One Motor Vehicle Professionally prescribed health aids of debtor or dependents	$5,000 $5,000 100%	Neb. Rev. Stat. § 25-1556 Neb. Rev. Stat. § 25-1556
Disposable earnings (earnings less deductions required by law)	75% OR 85% for head of family OR 30 times the federal minimum hourly wage per week, WHICHEVER IS GREATER	Neb. Rev. Stat. § 25-1558
Pensions of resident disabled veterans	100%	Neb. Rev. Stat. § 25-1559
Property of resident disabled veterans purchased or improved with pension money	$2,000	Neb. Rev. Stat. § 25-1559
Assistance to aged, blind & disabled (welfare benefits)	100%	Neb. Rev. Stat. § 68-1013
Unemployment compensation benefits	100% (child support excepted)	Neb. Rev. Stat. § 48-647
Workmen's compensation benefits	100% (child support excepted)	Neb. Rev. Stat. § 48-149
Proceeds, avails, cash values & other benefits of life insurance policies not payable to insured's estate and established for more than 3 years	$100,000 on loan or cash value 100% of proceeds	Neb. Rev. Stat. § 44-371, 44-1089
Benefits of accident or health insurance policies	100%	Neb. Rev. Stat. § 44-371
Annuity contract benefits for annuities established more than 3 years prior to filing bankruptcy	$100,000	Neb. Rev. Stat. § 44-371
Earned income tax credit	100%	Neb. Rev. Stat. § 25-1553
Fraternal insurance benefits	100%	Neb. Rev. Stat. § 44-1089
Cash deposits under Motor Vehicle Safety Responsibility Act	100%	Neb. Rev. Stat. § 60-550
Burial lots	100%	Neb. Rev. Stat.§§ 12-517, 12-520, 12-605
State employees' retirement benefits	100% (Spouse's QDRO benefits excepted)	Neb. Rev. Stat. § 84-1324
County employees' retirement benefits	100% (Spouse's QDRO benefits excepted)	Neb. Rev. Stat. § 23-2322
Safety patrolmen's retirement benefits	100% (Spouse's QDRO benefits excepted)	Neb. Rev. Stat. § 81-2032
School employees' & teachers' retirement benefits	100%	Neb. Rev. Stat. § 79-948
Specific partnership property	100% of partner's interest	Neb. Rev. Stat. §§ 67-411 & 430
Interest of debtor or dependent in stock bonus, pension, profit sharing, or similar retirement plan qualified under Internal Revenue Code. Includes IRAs. See Novak v. Novak, 245 Neb. 366, 513 N.W. 2d 303 (1994).	Amount reasonably necessary for the support of the debtor and dependents	Neb. Rev. Stat. § 25-1563.01
Proceeds or benefits from structured settlement of personal injury claim	100%	Neb. Rev. Stat. § 25-1563.02
Retirement benefits under Judges' Retirement Act	100% (QDRO benefits excepted)	Neb. Rev. Stat. § 24-710.02
Deferred Compensation of Public Employees	100%	Neb. Rev. Stat. § 48-1401
Perpetual Care Funds	100%	Neb. Rev. Stat. § 12-511
General Assistance to Poor Persons	100%	Neb. Rev. Stat. § 68-148

NEVADA

Use of federal exemptions not permitted. See Nev. Rev. Stat. § 21.090(3).

Type of Property	Amount of Exemption	Statute Creating Exemption
Homestead, consisting of land and dwelling house, or mobile home with or without underlying land	$605,000	Nev. Rev. Stat. §§ 115.010, 21.090(1)(l)
Dwelling house of debtor occupied as home situated on lands owned by another (i.e., a condominium)	$605,000	Nev. Rev. Stat. § 21.090(1)(m)
Private libraries	$5,000	Nev. Rev. Stat. § 21.090(1)(a)
Family pictures and keepsakes	100%	Nev. Rev. Stat. § 21.090(1)(a)
Necessary household goods, as defined in 16 CFR 444.1(i), and yard equipment	$12,000	Nev. Rev. Stat. § 21.090(1)(b)
Farm truck, stock, tools, equipment, supplies and seed	$4,500	Nev. Rev. Stat. § 21.090(1)(c)
Professional libraries, office equipment and supplies, and tools, instruments and materials used to carry on trade	$10,000	Nev. Rev. Stat. § 21.090(1)(d)
Cabin, dwelling, cars, implements appliances, and mining claim of miner or prospector	$4,500	Nev. Rev. Stat. § 21.090(1)(e)
One vehicle	$15,000 (100% if equipped for disabled debtor)	Nev. Rev. Stat. § 21.090(1)(f), (p)
Disposable earnings (earnings less deductions required by law)	82% if writ is less than $770, otherwise 75% OR 50 times the federal Minimum hourly wage per week WHICHEVER IS GREATER	Nev. Rev. Stat. § 21.090(1)(g)
All arms, uniforms and accouterments required by law to be kept, and 1 gun selected by debtor	100%	Nev. Rev. Stat. § 21.090(1)(i)
Money, benefits, privileges and immunities accruing or growing out of life insurance policies	100%	Nev. Rev. Stat. § 21.090(1)(k)
Prosthesis or equipment prescribed by physician or dentist	100%	Nev. Rev. Stat. § 21.090(1)(q)
Money held in IRA, simplified employee pension plan, IRC-qualified deferred compensation arrangement, stock bonus, pension or profit-sharing plan, or a qualified tuition payment program	$1,000,000	Nev. Rev. Stat. § 21.090(1)(r)
Child support and alimony payments	100%	Nev. Rev. Stat. § 21.090(1)(s), (t)
Compensation for personal injury, other than for pain and suffering or actual pecuniary loss, by debtor or person of whom debtor is a dependent.	$16,150	Nev. Rev. Stat. § 21.090(1)(u)
Compensation for the wrongful death of a person upon whom the debtor was dependent	Amount reasonably necessary for the support of the debtor and his or her dependents	Nev. Rev. Stat. § 21.090(1)(v)
Compensation for loss of future earnings of debtor or person upon whom debtor is a dependent	Amount reasonably necessary for the support of the debtor and his or her dependents	Nev. Rev. Stat. § 21.090(1)(w)
Payments received as restitution for a criminal act	100%	Nev. Rev. Stat. § 21.090(1)(x)
Social Security payments	100%	Nev. Rev. Stat. § 21.090(1)(y)
Earned income tax credit	100%	Nev. Rev. Stat. § 21.090(1)(aa)
Proceeds and avails of life insurance policies wherein beneficiary is not the insured	100%	Nev. Rev. Stat. § 687B.260
Group life insurance benefits and group health insurance proceeds	100%	Nev. Rev. Stat. § 687B.280
Proceeds of health insurance contracts and of disability insurance supplemental to life insurance or annuity contracts	100%	Nev. Rev. Stat. § 687B.270
Annuity contract proceeds	$350 per month	Nev. Rev. Stat. § 687B.290
Fraternal Benefit Society benefits	100%	Nev. Rev. Stat. § 695A.220
Industrial insurance compensation	100%	Nev. Rev. Stat. § 616C.205
Unemployment compensation benefits	100%	Nev. Rev. Stat. § 612.710
Public employees' retirement benefits	100%	Nev. Rev. Stat. § 286.670
Escrow funds of escrow agent	100%	Nev. Rev. Stat. § 645A.170
Property held in spendthrift trust	100%	Nev. Rev. Stat. § 21.080(2)
Mineral collections, art curiosities, and paleontological remains	100%	Nev. Rev. Stat. § 21.100
Public assistance payments	100%	Nev. Rev. Stat. § 422.291, 615.270
Specific partnership property	100% of partner's interest	Nev. Rev. Stat. § 87.250(2)(c)
Stock in a corporation (defined in NRS §78.746)	100%	Nev. Rev. Stat. § 21.090(1)(bb)
Real property of public housing authority and all real and personal property held for certain purposes by rural housing authority	100%	Nev. Rev. Stat. § 315.310 & 315.992
Mortgage Co. Impound Trust Accounts	100%	Nev. Rev. Stat. § 645B.180
Public Assistance for Children	100%	Nev. Rev. Stat. § 432.036

(continued from previous page)

Type of Property	Amount of Exemption	Statute Creating Exemption
Personal property not otherwise exempt (wildcard)	$10,000	Nev. Rev. Stat. § 21.090(z)
Assets held in trust	100%	Nev. Rev. Stat. § 21.090(cc)
Trust funds for prepaid funeral contracts	100%	Nev. Rev. Stat. § 689.700
Vocational Rehabilitation Benefits	100%	Nev. Rev. Stat. § 615.270

NEW HAMPSHIRE

Use of federal bankruptcy exemptions permitted.

Type of Property	Amount of Exemption	Statute Creating Exemption
Homestead (includes manufactured housing on land owned and occupied by debtor)	$120,000	N.H. Rev. Stat. § 480:1
Necessary wearing apparel, beds, bedsteads and bedding of debtor and family	100%	N.H. Rev. Stat. § 511:2
Household furniture	$3,500	N.H. Rev. Stat. § 511:2
One cooking stove and necessary furniture to same, and 1 sewing machine used by debtor	100%	N.H. Rev. Stat. § 511:2
Provisions and fuel	$400	N.H. Rev. Stat. § 511:2
Uniforms, arms and accouterments of militiaman	100%	N.H. Rev. Stat. § 511:2
Bibles, school books and library of debtor and family	$800	N.H. Rev. Stat. § 511:2
Necessary tools of occupation	$5,000	N.H. Rev. Stat. § 511:2
One hog and pig and pork from same, 6 sheep and fleeces from same, 1 cow, 1 yoke of oxen or a horse if used in farming or teaming, and 4 tons of hay	100%	N.H. Rev. Stat. § 511:2
Domestic fowl	$300	N.H. Rev. Stat. § 511:2
One pew in place of worship, and 1 cemetery lot or burial right	100%	N.H. Rev. Stat. § 511:2
One automobile	$10,000	N.H. Rev. Stat. § 511:2
Jewelry of debtor or family	$500	N.H. Rev. Stat. § 511:2
Debtor's interest in any property	$1,000 plus up to $7,000 of unused exemption amounts for household, furniture provisions & fuel, library, tools of trade, and jewelry	N.H. Rev. Stat. § 511:2
Debtor's interest in qualified retirement plans and IRAs	100%	N.H. Rev. Stat. § 511:2
Wages	50 times the federal minimum hourly wage per week	N.H. Rev. Stat. § 512:21

NOTE: Wages for personal services of wife and minor children of debtor are 100% exempt against creditors of debtor. If debtor is a married woman her wages are 100% exempt against debts for small loans wherein husband is obligor. In any event, there is a $50 per week exemption applicable to all debtors as against debts for small loans.

Type of Property	Amount of Exemption	Statute Creating Exemption
Pension or bounty money authorized by federal law	100%	N.H. Rev. Stat. § 512:21
Jury and witness fees	100%	N.H. Rev. Stat. § 512:21
Damages recovered for conversion of exempt property	100%	N.H. Rev. Stat. § 512:21
Insurance proceeds from loss or destruction of exempt property	Amount of exemption given for lost or destroyed property, except homestead money is limited to $5,000	N.H. Rev. Stat. § 512:21
Workmen's compensation benefits	100% (support claims excepted)	N.H. Rev. Stat. § 281-A:52
Unemployment compensation benefits	100% (support claims excepted)	N.H. Rev. Stat. § 282-A:159
Public assistance payments	100%	N.H. Rev. Stat. § 167:25
Fraternal Benefit Society benefits	100%	N.H. Rev. Stat. § 418:17
Firemen's Retirement System benefits	100%	N.H. Rev. Stat. § 102:23
Firemen's Relief Fund benefits	100%	N.H. Rev. Stat. § 402:69
Specific partnership property	100% of partner's interest	N.H. Rev. Stat. § 304-A:25
Life insurance payable to married woman or third party	100%	N.H. Rev. Stat. § 408:1,2
State employee retirement benefits	100%	N.H. Rev. Stat. § 100-A:26
Policemens' retirement benefits	100%	N.H. Rev. Stat. § 103:18
Child support	100%	N.H. Rev. Stat. § 161-C:11

NOTE: RSA §512:21 provides exemptions only from "trustee process." These exemptions are not applicable as bankruptcy exemptions. See *In re Damast* 136 BR 11 (Bankr. D. N.H. 1991).

NEW JERSEY

Use of federal exemptions permitted.

Type of Property Exemption	Amount of Exemption	Statute Creating
Wearing apparel	no limit	N.J. Rev. Stat. § 2A: 17-19
Household goods & furniture	$1,000	N.J. Rev. Stat. § 2A: 26-4
Goods, chattels, shares of stock & personal property of any kind	$1,000	N.J. Rev. Stat. § 2A: 17-19
Wages, earnings, salary, income & profits	100% if less than $48 per week; 90% if greater than $48 per week & less than 250% of poverty level	N.J. Rev. Stat. § 2A: 17-50, 17-56
Unemployment compensation benefits	100%	N.J. Rev. Stat. § 43: 21-15(c), 21-53
Old age assistance payments	100%	N.J. Rev. Stat. § 44: 7-35
Workmen's compensation benefits	100%	N.J. Rev. Stat. § 34: 15-29 & 25:2-1
Military pay, allowances & benefits of members of state militia	100%	N.J. Rev. Stat. § 38A: 4-8
Health & disability insurance proceeds & avails	100%	N.J. Rev. Stat. § 17B: 24-8
Fraternal Benefit Society benefits	100%	N.J. Rev. Stat. § 17: 44B-1
Annuity contract benefits	$500 per month	N.J. Rev. Stat. § 17B: 24-7
Proceeds & avails of life insurance policies payable to persons other than the insured and the person effecting the insurance	100%	N.J. Rev. Stat. § 17B: 24-6
Group life insurance policies & proceeds	100%	N.J. Rev. Stat. § 17B: 24-9
Civil defense injury & death benefits	100%	N.J. Rev. Stat. § App. A: 9-57.2
City Board of Health employees pension benefits	100%	N.J. Rev. Stat. § 43: 18-12
Street & Water Dept. employees pension benefits	100%	N.J. Rev. Stat. § 43: 19-17
Prison officers retirement benefits	100%	N.J. Rev. Stat. § 43: 7-13(e)
Municipal employees retirement& pension benefits	100%	N.J. Rev. Stat. § 43: 13-9, 13-22.34, 13-22.60, 13-37.5, 13-44
County employees retirement & pension benefits	100%	N.J. Rev. Stat. § 43: 10-14, 10-18.22, 10-18.71, 10-57
Police & firemen's retirement & pension benefits	100%	N.J. Rev. Stat. § 43: 16-7, 16A-17
Alcoholic Beverage Law Enforcement Officers pension fund benefits	100%	N.J. Rev. Stat. § 43: 8A-20
Judicial Retirement Systems benefits	100%	N.J. Rev. Stat. § 43: 6A-41
Teachers & school district employees retirement & pension benefits	100%	N.J. Rev. Stat. § 18A: 66-51, 116
State police retirement & pension benefits	100%	N.J. Rev. Stat. § 53: 5A-45
Specific partnership property	100% of partner's interest	N.J. Rev. Stat. § 42: 1A-11
Crime victim's compensation	100%	N.J. Rev. Stat. § 52: 4B-64
Qualifying trust under IRC and retirement funds	100%	N.J. Rev. Stat. § 25:2-1 & 43:15A-53
Cemetery companies: property, trust funds, lands dedicated for cemetery purposes	100%	N.J. Rev. Stat. § 45:27-20
Disability benefits	100%	N.J. Rev. Stat. § 17:18-12
Pay, disability or death benefits for military member	100%	N.J. Rev. Stat. § 38A:4-8
Pensions-court interpreters, 2nd class counties	100%	N.J. Rev. Stat. 43:10-105
Pensions and annuities: public employees	100%	N.J. Rev. Stat. § 43:15A-53
Homestead Exemption	None (But see *Freda v. Comm. Trust*, 570 A.2d 409 (NJ 1990))	

Note: Tenancies by the entireties are nonexempt property, but are subject to the rights of the non debtor spouse. See *King v. Greene,* 30 N.J. 395, 153 A.2d 49.

NEW MEXICO

Use of federal bankruptcy exemptions permitted.

Type of Property	Amount of Exemption	Statute Creating Exemption
Homestead of any person	$150,000 ($300,000 in certain cases) (NOTE: joint owners may each claim a full personal exemption)	N.M. STAT. ANN. § 42-10-9
NOTE: A homestead consists of a dwelling house, plus the land upon which it is located, that is owned and personally occupied by the debtor, or a dwelling house that the debtor owns, leases or is purchasing, even though it is located on land owned by another.		
Exemption in lieu of homestead (may be any real or personal property)	$15,000 (exemption may be claimed only by debtor who does not claim homestead exemption)	N.M. STAT. ANN. § 42-10-10
Household goods and furnishings Tools necessary for a person's trade	$75,000 $15,000	N.M. STAT. ANN. § 42-10-1
Clothing, furniture, books, personally-used medical health equipment and interests in and proceeds from pension or retirement funds	100% *	N.M. STAT. ANN. §§ 42-10-1, 2
Jewelry	$5,000 *	N.M. STAT. ANN. § 42-10-1, 2
Tools of trade	$2,500 *	N.M. STAT. ANN. § 42-10-1, 2
1 motor vehicle	$10,000 *	N.M. STAT. ANN. § 42-10-1, 2
Personal property other than money	$500 * (applies only to debtor who supports only himself)	N.M. STAT. ANN. § 42-10-2
Cash surrender value of life insurance policy, withdrawal value of annuity contract, deposit with life insurance company, proceeds of life, accident or health insurance policies and annuity contracts	100% (applies to citizens and residents of state)	N.M. STAT. ANN. § 42-10-3
Disposable earnings (earnings less deductions required by law)	75% OR 40 times the federal minimum hourly wage per week, WHICHEVER IS GREATER	N.M. STAT. ANN. § 35-12-7
Proceeds of life insurance policies	100%	N.M. STAT. ANN. § 42-10-5
Beneficiaries' interest in spendthrift trusts	100%	N.M. STAT. ANN. § 42-9-4
Property covered by assignment for benefit of creditors	100%	N.M. STAT. ANN. § 56-9-46
Disability benefits	100%	N.M. STAT. ANN. § 52-3-37
Workmen's compensation benefits	100% (support claims excepted)	N.M. STAT. ANN. § 52-1-52
Unemployment compensation	100% (support claims excepted)	N.M. STAT. ANN. § 51-1-37
Public assistance payments	100%	N.M. STAT. ANN. § 27-2-21
Public employees retirement funds and benefits	100% (except child support)	N.M. STAT. ANN. § 10-11-135
Educational retirement benefits and contributions	100% (except child support)	N.M. STAT. ANN. § 22-11-42
State police pension benefits	100%	N.M. STAT. ANN. § 29-4-10
Membership holdings in cooperative associations	Minimum amount required for membership	N.M. STAT. ANN. § 53-4-28
Materials purchased for digging or operating an oil or gas well that are subject to a materialman's lien	100%	N.M. STAT. ANN. § 70-4-12
Crime victim's reparation awards	100%	N.M. STAT. ANN. § 31-22-15
Specific partnership property	100% of partner's interest	N.M. STAT. ANN. § 54-1A-307
Fraternal benefit society benefits	100%	N.M. STAT. ANN. § 59A-44-18
Community property	See statute for limitations	N.M. STAT. ANN. § 40-3-10
Materials used in construction	100%	N.M. STAT. ANN. § 48-2-15

(Continued on next page)

(Continued from previous page)

NEW MEXICO

Type of Property	Amount of Exemption	Statute Creating Exemption
Pensions-judges	100%	N.M. Stat. Ann. § 10-12B-7
Pensions-magistrates	100%	N.M. Stat. Ann. § 10-12C-7
Death benefits from benevolent associations	$5,000	N.M. Stat. Ann. § 42-10-4
Surplus when value of personal property used as security under U.C.C. exceeds amount of debt	100%	N.M. Stat. Ann. § 42-10-6
Ownership in an unincorporated association	100%	N.M. Stat. Ann. § 53-10-2

* Exempt property to be valued at value of used chattels.

NEW YORK

Federal bankruptcy exemptions permitted. See Debtor & Creditor Law § 285

Type of Property	Amount of Exemption	Statute Creating Exemption
All stoves & home heating equipment & 120 days' fuel; 1 sewing machine & appurtenances, seat in place of worship; 120 days' food; 1 refrigerator; 1 radio; 1 television set; 1 TV ; 1 cellphone, 1 computer & associated equipment; prescribed health aids all wearing apparel, household furniture, crockery, tableware, and cooking utensils of debtor & family, 1 wedding ring	100% (See Note 1 below)	* CPLR § 5205(a)(1) et seq.
Religious text, family pictures & portraits & books in family library	$575 (See Note 1 below)	CPLR § 5205(a)(2)
Domestic animals + 120 days' feed	$1,150 (See Note 1 below)	CPLR § 5205(a)(4)
One watch, jewelry, and art	$1,150 (See Note 1 below)	CPLR § 5205(a)(6)
Necessary tools of trade & professional instruments, furniture & library	$10,000 (See Note 1 below)	CPLR § 5205(a)(7)
Wild Card (any personal property)	$3,575 (if no homestead elected)	CPLR § 5205(a)(9)
Claim for loss or destruction of exempt property & proceeds of claim for one year	Amount of exemption for lost or destroyed property	CPLR § 5205(b)
Property held under a trust created or deemed to be created by another for benefit of debtor, including assets of tax-qualified IRAs, Keogh Plans and corporate retirement plans	100% Note: All such trusts are deemed to be spendthrift trusts for bankruptcy purposes	CPLR § 5205(c) & (d) Debtor & Creditor Law § 282(2)(e)
90% of income from trust exempt under CPLR § 5205(c), 90% of last 60-days' earnings, and 100% of matrimonial payments for support of wife or child	Amount reasonably required by debtor & dependents	CPLR § 5205(d)
Military pay of enlisted men; military rewards, pensions, medals, arms & equipment of state or federal armed forces	100% (support claims excepted)	CPLR § 5205(e)
Milk sales proceeds of farmer	90%	CPLR § 5205(f)
Residential rental, utility, telephone & telegraph money security deposits of debtor & family	100%	CPLR § 5205(g)
Necessary medical & dental accessions to human body, equipment used to provide mobility for disabled person, and guide, service, or hearing dog or similar animals and food therefor	Amount reasonably required by debtor & dependents	CPLR § 5205(h)
Cash surrender value and accelerated death benefits of life insurance policies	100%	CPLR § 5205(i)
Monies in NYS college choice tuition savings program trust fund	100 % of Scholarship funds 100% if debtor is owner & beneficiary $10,000 if debtor is owner only	CPLR § 5205(j)
Funds of convicted person	various amounts (see statute)	CPLR § 5205(k)
Property owned & occupied as principal residence (includes land + dwelling, shares in cooperative condominium units, and mobile homes), (*homestead exemption*)	$179,950 for property in counties of Kings, Nassau, Suffolk, Queens, Bronx, Richmond, Rockland, Westchester, and Putnam; $149,975 for property in counties of Albany, Dutchess, Columbia, Orange, Saratoga, and Ulster $89,975 for all other counties	CPLR § 5206(a)
Burial grounds	100% (cannot exceed 1/4 acre)	CPLR § 5206(f)
Proceeds & avails of life insurance policies not payable to insured, including right to accelerated benefits	100%	Insurance Law § 3212 CPLR § 5205(i)
Disability insurance benefits	100% of lump sum payments $400 per month of periodic payments	Insurance Law § 3212
Annuity contract benefits	Amount reasonably required by debtor & dependents (See Note 1 below)	Insurance Law § 3212

Social Security benefits, unemployment compensation, public assistance benefits, veterans benefits, and disability, illness or unemployment benefits	100%	Debtor & Creditor Law § 282

NEW YORK

(continued from previous page)

Type of Property	Amount of Exemption	Statute Creating Exemption
Alimony, support or separate maintenance	Amount reasonably necessary to support debtor & dependents	Debtor & Creditor Law § 282 CPLR § 5205(d)(3)
One motor vehicle (See *CPLR* § 5205(a)(8) for limits on exemption for support & alimony)	$4,850 ($11,975 if equipped for disabled debtor)	Debtor & Creditor Law § 282
Payments under stock-bonus, pension, profit-sharing or similar plan, or IRA, unless payments are for age or length of service and plan was created by insider and does not qualify under 26 USC §§ 401(a), 403(a), or (b), 408, 408A, 409, or 457.	Amount reasonably necessary to support debtor & dependents	Debtor & Creditor Law § 282
Crime victim's reparation awards	100%	Debtor & Creditor Law § 282
Payments on account of wrongful death of person of whom debtor was a dependent	Amount reasonably necessary to support debtor & dependents	Debtor & Creditor Law § 282
Payments on account of bodily injury of debtor or person of whom debtor was a dependent	$8,550 (does not include damages for pain & suffering or actual pecuniary loss)	Debtor & Creditor Law § 282
Compensation for loss of future earnings of debtor or person of whom debtor is or was a dependent	Amount reasonably necessary to support debtor & dependents	Debtor & Creditor Law § 282
Cash, U.S. savings bonds, and tax refunds of debtor not using homestead exemption under CPLR § 5206	$6,000 or $11,375 less amounts exempted under CPLR § 5205(a) and for certain annuities (see Note 1 below) WHICHEVER IS LESS	Debtor & Creditor Law § 283
Workers' compensation benefits	100% (support claims excepted)	Workers' Compensation Law §§ 33 & 218
Partner's right in partnership property	100%	Partnership law § 51(c)
Veterans' benefits	100%	Debtor & Creditor Law § 282(2)(b)
Shares held by member of savings and loan association and dues and dividends created thereon	$600	Banking Law § 407
Teachers' retirement plan	100%	Edu. Law § 524
Volunteer firefighters' insurance benefits	100%	Gen. Mun. § 206-b and Vol. Fire. Ben. FBL §23
Pensions-public retirement systems	100%	Ins. Law § 4607
Unemployment insurance	100%	Lab. law § 595
Exhibits at international exhibition	100%	PPL §250
Pensions-NY State Employees	100%	Ret. & SS Law § 110
Pensions-village police	100%	Uncosol. Law § 5711-o
Statutorily exempt payments made electronically or by direct deposit	$2,850	CPLR §5205(l)
Wages	varies	CPLR § 5241(b)

NOTE 1: The aggregate amount that a debtor may exempt under CPLR § 5205(a) and under certain annuity contracts cannot exceed $11,975. The annuity contracts subject to this limitation are those initially purchased within 6 months of the filing of the bankruptcy petition, those not described in 26 USC § 805(d) (i.e., pension plan reserves), and those not purchased by the application of proceeds under settlement options of annuity contracts purchased more than 6 months prior to the filing of the bankruptcy petition or under settlement options of life insurance policies.
NOTE 2: Section 282 of the Debtor & Creditor Law specifies that only the exemptions shown above may be claimed in a bankruptcy proceeding by a person domiciled in New York State. Other properties exempt under various other state laws include: police, firemen, teachers, and state employees retirement benefits, earnings of public assistance recipients, international exhibits, employer's liability benefits, workmen's compensation benefits, shares in savings & loan associations and credit unions up to a value of $600, and a partner's interest in specific partnership property.
NOTE 3: Amounts subject to cost of living adjustment beginning April 1, 2012 and every three years thereafter.

NORTH CAROLINA

Federal exemptions not permitted. See N.C. GEN. STAT. § 1C-1601(f).

Type of Property	Amount of Exemption	Statute Creating Exemption
Debtor's aggregate interest in real or personal property, including a cooperative, used as residence by debtor or a dependent, or in a burial plot for debtor or dependent	$35,000 ($60,000 for person 65 or older who is a surviving joint owner)	N.C. GEN. STAT. § 1C-1601(a)(1)
Debtor's aggregate interest in any property (wildcard)	$5,000 less any amount claimed under G.S. § 1C-1601(a)(1) above	N.C. GEN. STAT. § 1C-1601(a)(2)
Debtor's interest in 1 motor vehicle	$3,500	N.C. GEN. STAT. § 1C-1601(a)(3)
Debtor's aggregate in household furnishings & goods, wearing apparel, appliances, books, animals, crops, or musical instruments held primarily for personal, family or household use of debtor or dependent	$5,000 plus $1,000 for each dependent, not to exceed $4,000 for dependents	N.C. GEN. STAT. § 1C-1601(a)(4)
Personal property selected by debtor	$500	Art. X, § 1 of Constitution
Homestead (may be claimed by owner or surviving spouse or children of) owner	$1,000	Art. X, § 2 of Constitution
Proceeds & cash surrender value of life insurance policies for sole use and benefit of spouse or children of insured	100%	Art. X, § 5 of Constitution. N.C. GEN. STAT. §§ 1C-1601(a)(6), 58-205, 58-206
Earnings from personal services of debtor	60 days earnings, if needed to support family	N.C. GEN. STAT. § 1-362
Workmen's compensation benefits	100%	N.C. GEN. STAT. § 97-21
Employment security benefits	100%	N.C. GEN. STAT. § 96-17(c)
Aid to families with dependent children	100%	N.C. GEN. STAT. § 108A-36
Aid to aged or disabled persons	100%	N.C. GEN. STAT. § 108A-36
Aid to blind persons	100%	N.C. GEN. STAT. § 111-18
Fraternal benefit society benefits	100%	N.C. GEN. STAT. § 58-24-85
Group life insurance benefits	100%	N.C. GEN. STAT. § 58-58-165
Firemen's pension fund benefits	100%	N.C. GEN. STAT. § 143-166.6 & 58-86-90
City & county employees' retirement benefits	100%	N.C. GEN. STAT. § 128-31
Teachers' and state employees' retirement benefits	100%	N.C. GEN. STAT. § 135-9
Specific partnership property	100% of partner's interest	N.C. GEN. STAT. § 59-55
Legislative retirement system benefits	100%	N.C. GEN. STAT. § 120-4.29
Crime victims compensation awards	100%	N.C. GEN. STAT. § 15B-17
One year of support for a surviving spouse	$20,000	N.C. GEN. STAT. § 30-15
Supplemental Retirement Income Plan-Benefits	100%	N.C. GEN. STAT. §135-95
Implements, professional books or tools of the trade of debtor or dependent	$2,000	N.C. GEN. STAT. § 1C-1601(a)(5)
Professionally prescribed health aids of debtor or dependent	100%	N.C. GEN. STAT. § 1C-1601(a)(7)
Compensation for personal injury or death of a person of whom the debtor was a dependent	100% (Exemption does not apply to claims for funeral, legal, medical, dental, hospital & health care charges related to accident or injury giving rise to the compensation)	N.C. GEN. STAT. § 1C-1601(a)(8)
Individual retirement plans as defined in I.R.C.	100%	N.C. GEN. STAT. § 1C-1601(a)(9)
Funds in qualified college savings plan if deposited in plan more than 12 months prior to bankruptcy or if deposited in ordinary course of affairs	$25,000	N.C. GEN. STAT. § 1C-1601(a)(10)

(Continued on next page)

NORTH CAROLINA

(Continued from previous page)

Retirement benefits exempt under plans in other states	100%	N.C. GEN. STAT. § 1C-1601(a)(11)
Alimony, support, separate maintenance and child support payments or funds	amount reasonably necessary for support of debtor and dependents	N.C. GEN. STAT. § 1C-1601(a)(12)
Supplemental Retirement Income Plan-Benefits	100%	N.C. GEN. STAT. § 135-95
Disability income	100%	N.C. GEN. STAT. §135-111
Vested interest of state employee in deferred compensation plan benefits	100%	N.C. GEN. STAT. §147-9.4

NOTE: The exemptions provided in N.C. GEN. STAT. § 1C-1601(a)(2), (3), (4) & (5) do not apply with respect to tangible personal property purchased by the debtor less than 90 days prior to the initiation of judgment collection proceedings or the filing of a bankruptcy petition, unless it was purchased to replace exempt property. See N.C. GEN. STAT. § 1C-1601(d). The debtor may elect to take the Constitutionally mandated exemptions listed below (Article X, §§ 1 and 2) in lieu of the exemptions in Chapter 1C above, but may not use both sets of exemptions.

NOTE: Tenancies by the entirety may be exempt under 11 USC § 522(b)(3)(B). See Grabenhofer v. Garrett, 131 S.E. 2d 675 (N.C. 1983).

NORTH DAKOTA

Federal bankruptcy exemptions not permitted. See N.D. CENT. CODE § 28-22-17.

Type of Property	Amount of Exemption	Statute Creating Exemption
Homestead of any person, consisting of lands & dwelling where debtor resides & appurtenances	$150,000 (*or $25,000 in lieu of a homestead exemption)	N.D. CENT. CODE § 47-18-01 & 28-22-02(7) N.D. CENT. CODE § 28-22-03.1(1)
Earnings for personal services within last 60 days	Amount necessary to support debtor's family (See Note below)	N.D. CENT. CODE § 28-25-11
Disposable earnings (earnings less deductions required by law. Includes periodic pension and retirement benefits)	The greater of 75% or 40 times the federal minimum hourly wage per week, plus $20 per week for each dependent family member residing with debtor	N.D. CENT. CODE § 32-09.1-03 & N.D. CENT. CODE § 28-22-18
Family pictures, pew in place of worship, lots in burial ground, family Bible, school books, family library, wearing apparel and clothing of debtor and family, one-year's provisions and fuel for debtor and family, crops and grain grown on 160 acres, benefits from insurance covering absolute exemptions, and house trailer or mobile home occupied as residence	100%, except $5,000 limit on wearing apparel (these are absolute exemptions and are applicable to any debtor, whether or not he is a head of family)	N.D. CENT. CODE § 28-22-02
Professionally prescribed health aids	100%	N.D. CENT. CODE § 28-22-03.1(6)
Unmatured life insurance contract owned by the debtor	100%	N.D. CENT. CODE § 28-22-03.1(4)
Loan value of unmatured life insurance on debtor or of whom debtor is a dependent	$100,000	N.D. CENT. CODE § 28-22-03.1(5)
Disability, illness or unemployment benefit	100%	N.D. CENT. CODE § 28-22-03.1(8)(c)
Library, tools or implements of the trade	$10,000 (see note above)	N.D. CENT. CODE § 28-22-03.1(3)
Personal property of any kind	$3,750 (this exemption applies only to a single person who does not claim the crop and grain exemption under § 28-22-02)	N.D. CENT. CODE § 28-22-05
Property of any kind	$500 (applies only against judgments on criminal bond forfeitures)	N.D. CENT. CODE § 28-22-16
Exemption in lieu of homestead	$10,000	N.D. CENT. CODE § 28-22-03.1(1)
One motor vehicle	$10,000 ($32,000 for vehicle modified for disabled owner)	N.D. CENT. CODE § 28-22-03.1(2)
Retirement funds that have been in effect for at least 1 year and are qualified under IRC, and proceeds therefrom	$200,000 limit for each plan, pension or policy, with $400,000 aggregate limit for all plans, pensions or policies; OR amount necessary for support of debtor and dependents, WHICHEVER IS GREATER	N.D. CENT. CODE § 28-22-03.1(7)
Cash surrender value of life insurance policies payable to wife, children or dependent relative of debtor	amount specified in NDCC § 28-22-03.1 (see above for limits)	N.D. CENT. CODE § 26.1-33-36
Avails of life insurance policy or mutual aid contract of benevolent society	100% (must be payable to deceased or estate)	N.D. CENT. CODE § 26.1-33-40
Unemployment compensation benefits	100% (except child support)	N.D. CENT. CODE § 52-06-30 & N.D. CENT. CODE § 28-22-03.1(8)(c)
Workmens compensation benefits	100% (except child support)	N.D. CENT. CODE § 65-05-29
Recoveries for wrongful death	100%	N.D. CENT. CODE § 32-21-04 & N.D. CENT. CODE § 28-22-03.1(9)(b)

(continued on next page)

(continued from previous page)

Type of Property	Amount of Exemption	Statute Creating Exemption
All pensions or annuities or retirement, disability, death or other benefits paid or payable by a retirement system of the state or a political subdivision thereof or by a firemen's relief association	100% (except child support)	N.D. CENT. CODE § 28-22-19(1)
Awards to crime victims	100%	N.D. CENT. CODE § 28-22-19(2) & N.D. CENT. CODE § 28-22-03.1(9)(a)
Aid to dependent children	100%	N.D. CENT. CODE § 28-22-19(3)
Insurance proceeds received from destruction of homestead	100%	N.D. CENT. CODE § 28-22-02(9)
Payment on the account of personal bodily injury, not including pain and suffering or compensation for actual pecuniary loss, of the debtor or an individual of whom the debtor is a dependent	$18,450	N.D. CENT. CODE § 28-22-03.1(9)(d)
Social Security benefits	100% (except child support)	N.D. CENT. CODE § 28-22-03.1(8)(a)
Veteran's disability pension benefits	100% (except child support)	N.D. CENT. CODE § 28-22-03.1(8)(b)
Specific partnership property	100% of partner's interest	N.D. CENT. CODE § 45-17-01
Alimony, support, or maintenance	100%	N.D. CENT. CODE § 28-22-03.1(8)(d)
Payments under stock bonus, pension, profit-sharing, or annuity plan qualified under IRC	amount necessary for support of debtor and dependents	N.D. CENT. CODE § 28-22-03.1(8)(e)
Payment under life insurance contract insuring life of an individual of whom debtor ws a dependent	amount necessary for support of debtor and dependents	N.D. CENT. CODE § 28-22-03.1(9)(c)
Payment in compensation for loss of future earnings of debtor or individual of whom debtor was a dependent	amount necessary for support of debtor and dependents	N.D. CENT. CODE § 28-22-03.1(9)(e)
Benefits from fraternal benefits societies	100%	N.D. CENT. CODE § 26.1-15.1-18
Compensation of veterans of Desert Shield and Storm	100%	N.D. CENT. CODE § 37-26-06

OHIO

Federal bankruptcy exemptions not permitted. See OHIO REV. CODE § 2329.662.

Type of Property	Amount of Exemption	Statute Creating Exemption
One parcel or item of real or personal property used as residence by debtor or a dependent of the debtor	$161,375	OHIO REV. CODE § 2329.66(A)(1)(a)&(b)
1 motor vehicle	$4,450	OHIO REV. CODE§ 2329.66(A)(2)
Wearing apparel, beds & bedding	$500 per item (no aggregate limit)	OHIO REV. CODE § 2329.66(A)(3)
Cash on hand, money due & payable, money due within 90 days, tax, refunds and money on deposit (may include portion of earnings not otherwise exempt)	$550 (this exemption applies only in bankruptcy cases)	OHIO REV. CODE§ 2329.66(A)(3)
Household furnishing & goods, appliances, books, animals, crops, musical instruments, firearms, and hunting & fishing equipment held primarily for the personal, family or household use of the debtor	$700 per item, but cannot include items listed in division (A)(3), above. (Aggregate limit is $14,875)	OHIO REV. CODE § 2329.66(A)(4)(a)
Items of jewelry	$1,875	OHIO REV. CODE § 2329.66(A)(4)(b)
Old Age and Survivors' insurance benefits for municipal employees	100%	OHIO REV. CODE § 145.56
Volunteer firefighters' benefits	100%	OHIO REV. CODE § 146.13
Implements, professional books, or tools of debtor's profession, trade or business, including agriculture	$2,825	OHIO REV. CODE § 2329.66(A)(5)
Death benefits paid by benevolent society or association to family of deceased member	[see statute]	OHIO REV. CODE §§ 2329.63, 2329.66(A)(6)(a)
Proceeds & avails of life insurance & annuity policies payable to spouse, children, dependent relative, or creditor of insured	100%	OHIO REV. CODE §§ 3911.10, 2329.66(A)(6)(b)
Group life insurance policies & proceeds	100%	OHIO REV. CODE §§ 3917.05, 2329.66(A)(6)(c)
Fraternal Benefit Society benefits	100%	OHIO REV. CODE §§ 3921.18, 2329.66(A)(6)(d)
Sickness & accident insurance benefits	Amount reasonably necessary to support debtor and dependents	OHIO REV. CODE §§ 3923.19, 2329.66(A)(6)(e)
Medically necessary or professionally prescribed health aids	100%	OHIO REV. CODE § 2329.66(A)(7)
Burial lots	100%	OHIO REV. CODE §§ 1721.10, 517.09, 2329.66(A)(8)
Property of benevolent societies-regalia, ensignia, journals, etc.	100%	OHIO REV. CODE §2329.64
Living maintenance or rights benefits (a)	100%	OHIO REV. CODE § 3304.19, 2329.66(A)(9)
Workmen's compensation benefits	100% (except child support)	OHIO REV. CODE §§4123.67, 2329.66(A)(9)(b)
Unemployment compensation benefits	100%	OHIO REV. CODE §§4141.32; 2329.66(A)(9)(c)
Cash assistance payments under Ohio work first program	100%	OHIO REV. CODE §§5107.75,2329.66(A)(9)(d)
Disability assistance payments	100%	OHIO REV. CODE §§ 2329.66(A)(9)(f), 5115.06
Earned Income Tax Credit & Child Tax Credit	100%	OHIO REV. CODE §2329.66(A)(9)(g)
Pension & retirement benefits of public employees, volunteer firemen & dependants, policemen, teachers, school employees, & highway patrolmen	100%	OHIO REV. CODE §§ 2329.66(A)(10)(a)
The right to payments under certain private pension or annuity plans (see statute for limitations)	amount reasonably necessary to support debtor & dependents	OHIO REV. CODE § 2329.66(A)(10)(b)
Pension and disability-police and firemen	100%	OHIO REV. CODE §742.47

NOTE: All Ohio exemptions apply only to persons who have their domicile on Ohio. Tenancies by the entirety may be exempt under 11 USC § 522(b)(3)(B). See In Re Thomas, 14 B.R. 423.

(continued on next page)

OHIO

(continued from previous page)

Type of Property	Amount of Exemption	Statute Creating Exemption
Assets and benefits of individual retirement annuities, IRAs, Roth IRAs and Education IRAs	100% of amounts qualified under or protected by the Internal Revenue Code	Ohio Rev. Code § 2329.66(A)(10)(c)
Assets and benefits of Keogh or H.R. 10 Plan	Amount reasonably necessary for the support of debtor and dependent	Ohio Rev. Code § 2329.66(A)(10)(d)
Right to receive alimony, child support, an allowance or maintenance	Amount reasonably necessary to support debtor & dependents	Ohio Rev. Code § 2329.66(A)(11)
* * Crime reparations awards	100% (exemption does not apply against creditors furnishing products, services or accommodations included in the award	Ohio Rev. Code §§ 2743.66(D), 2329.66(A)(12)(a)
* * Payments on account of the wrongful death of person of whom debtor was a dependent	Amount reasonably necessary to support debtor & dependents	Ohio Rev. Code § 2329.66(A)(12)(b)
* * Personal injury awards to debtor or to a person for whom debtor is a dependent (does not include amounts awarded for pain & suffering or for actual pecuniary loss)	$27,950	Ohio Rev. Code § 2329.66(A)(12)(c)
* * Payments in compensation for loss of future earnings of debtor or of a person of whom debtor is or was a dependent	Amount reasonably necessary to support debtor &dependents	Ohio Rev. Code§ 2329.66(A)(12)(d)
* * These exemptions apply only to money received, or the right to receive same, during the preceding 12 months.		
Disposable earnings earned in preceding 30 days (disposable earnings are earnings less deductions required by law)	75% OR 30 times the federal minimum hourly wage per week (65 times if paid semimonthly, 130 times if paid monthly) WHICHEVER IS GREATER	Ohio Rev. Code § 2329.66(A)(13)
Debtor's interest in specific partnership property	100%	Ohio Rev. Code §§ 1775.24, 2329.66(A)(14)
Seal & register of notary public	100%	Ohio Rev. Code §§ 147.04, 2329.66(A)(15)
Tuition credits and tuition credit contract payments	100%	Ohio Rev. Code. §§ 2329.66(A)(16), 3334.15
Any property exempt under any non-bankruptcy federal statute	100% of federal exemption	Ohio Rev. Code § 2329.66(A)(17)
Any property chosen by debtor	$1,475 (this exemption applies only in bankruptcy cases)	Ohio Rev. Code § 2329.66(A)(18)
Pension-state teachers, public school employees	100%	Ohio Rev. Code §3309.66
Benefits under policies of sickness and accident insurance, to the extent reasonably necessary for support of debtor or dependents	100%	Ohio Rev. Code §3923.19(A)
Payments under stock bonus, pension, profit-sharing, annuity or similar plan on account of illness, disability, death, age or length of service, to the extent reasonably necessary for support of debtor or dependents	100%	Ohio Rev. Code § 3923.19(B)
Retirement state-highway patrol	100%	Ohio Rev. Code § 5505.22
General assistance benefits	100%	Ohio Rev. Code §2329.66(A)(9)(c); 5115.06

On April 1, 2019 the dollar amounts set forth in Ohio Rev. Code § 2329.66(A) were revised based on the C.P.I. for all urban consumers. (See Ohio Rev. Code § 2329.66(B); www.ohiojudges.org). Exemptions will be revised again on April 1, 2022.

OKLAHOMA

Federal bankruptcy exemptions not permitted. 31 OKLA. STAT. § 1(B).

Type of Property	Amount of Exemption	Statute Creating Exemption
Home or manufactured home constituting principal residence of debtor	160 acres of rural land OR 1 acre of. urban land At least 75% of improved area of homestead must be used as principal residence, otherwise exemption is limited to $5,000. See 31 OKLA. STAT. § 2.	31 OKLA. STAT. §§ 1(A)(1), 1(A)(2)
Household and kitchen furniture, including personal computer	100%	31 OKLA. STAT. § 1(A)(3)
Cemetery lots	100%	31 OKLA. STAT. § 1(A)(4)
Implements of husbandry used on homestead, tools, apparatus and books used in trade or profession by debtor or dependents	$10,000	31 OKLA. STAT. § 1(A)(5)
Personal books, portraits and pictures of debtor or dependents	100%	31 OKLA. STAT. § 1(A)(6)
Personal wearing apparel of debtor or dependents	$4,000	31 OKLA. STAT. § 1(A)(7)
Wedding & anniversary rings	$3,000	31 OKLA. STAT. § 1(A)(8)
Professionally prescribed health aid of debtor and dependents	100%	31 OKLA. STAT. § 1(A)(9)
5 milk cows & their calves under 6 months old, 100 chickens, 2 horses, 2 bridles, 2 saddles, 10 hogs, 20 sheep, and 1 year's provisions or forage on hand or growing for exempt stock	100% (stock must be held for personal, family, or household use of debtor or dependents)	31 OKLA. STAT. §§ 1(A)(10), (11), (12), (15), (16), (17)
Debtor's interest in one motor vehicle	$7,500	31 OKLA. STAT. § 1(A)(13)
Personal guns	$2,000	31 OKLA. STAT. § 1(A)(14)
Wages or earnings from personal services during last 90 days	75% (support claims excepted) 100% if undue hardship is shown	31 OKLA. STAT. §§ 1(A)(18), (1.1)
Alimony, support, or maintenance payments	Amount necessary for support of debtor and dependents	31 OKLA. STAT. § 1(A)(19)
Assets and benefits of retirement plans and IRAs qualified under I.R.C., including Roth IRAs and educational IRAs	100% of tax exempt portions	31 OKLA. STAT. § 1(A)(20); 1(A)(23), , (24), & 60 OKLA. STAT. §328
Claims for personal injury, death, or workers compensation	$50,000	31 OKLA. STAT. § 1(A)(21)
Funds in individual development account created under 56 OSA § 251 et seq.	100%	31 OKLA. STAT. § 1(A)(22)
Municipal retirement fund benefits	100% (QDRO excepted)	11 OKLA. STAT. § 48-103
Federal earned income tax credits	100%	31 OKLA. STAT. § 1(A)(23)
Any interest in an Oklahoma College Savings Plan established under 70 OSA § 3970.1	100%	31 OKLA. STAT. § 1(A)(24)
Armed services pension benefits	100%	31 OKLA. STAT. § 7
Crime victim's reparation awards	100% (except child support)	21 OKLA. STAT. § 142.13
Group life insurance proceeds	100%	36 OKLA. STAT. § 3632
Proceeds of life insurance, health or accident insurance policies payable to person other than insured	100%	36 OKLA. STAT. § 3631.1
Fraternal Benefit Society benefits	100%	36 OKLA. STAT. § 2718.1
Unemployment compensation benefits	100%	40 OKLA. STAT. § 2-303
Public assistance payments	100%	56 OKLA. STAT. § 173
Interests in retirement, pension, or profit-sharing plans, trusts or contracts	100%, if so provided in plan, trust or contract	60 OKLA. STAT. § 327 & 328
War bond payroll savings accounts	100%	51 OKLA. STAT. § 42
Specific partnership property	100% of partner's interest	54 OKLA. STAT. § 1-501-504
Firemen's pension benefits	100% (spouse's QDRO benefits excepted)	11 OKLA. STAT. § 49-126
Police pension benefits	100% (spouse's QDRO benefits excepted)	11 OKLA. STAT. § 50-124
Schoolteachers' retirement benefits	100% (spouse's QDRO benefits excepted)	70 OKLA. STAT. § 17-109
Public employees' retirement benefits	100% (spouse's QDRO benefits excepted)	74 OKLA. STAT. § 923
Judges' retirement benefits	100% (spouse's QDRO benefits excepted)	20 OKLA. STAT. § 1111
Property and lots of cemetery corporations-	100%	8 OKLA. STAT. § 7

OKLAHOMA

(Continued from previous page)

Type of Property	Amount of Exemption	Statute Creating Exemption
Wages if subject to garnishment for child support	40% (50% if debtor has dependants)	12 Okla. Stat. § 1171.2(B)
Pension of county employees	100%	19 Okla. Stat. § 959
Assessment or mutual benefits	100%	36 Okla. Stat. § 2410
Pension-law enforcement retirement systems	100%	47 Okla. Stat. § 2-303.3
Property of housing authority	100%	63 Okla. Stat. § 1075
Property of urban renewal authority	100%	11 Okla. Stat. § 38-112
Prepaid funeral benefits	100%	36 Okla. Stat. § 6125

OREGON

Federal bankruptcy exemptions permitted. See Or. Rev. Stat. § 18.300

Type of Property	Amount of Exemption	Statute Creating Exemption
Homestead occupied by debtor (exemption applies to proceeds of sale of homestead for 1 year and applies to condominium units under ORS 91.581(3)	$40,000 for one debtor $50,000 for combined exemptions of 2 or more debtors (cannot exceed 160 acres or 1 city block)	Or. Rev. Stat. § 18.395, 18.402
Manufactured or floating home land thereon owned by debtor & used by debtor & family as sole residence	$40,000 for one debtor $50,000 for combined exemptions of 2 or more debtors	Or. Rev. Stat. § 18.395(10)(a) & (b)
NOTE - A debtor may claim only one of the above exemptions. The exemption in Or. Rev. Stat. 18.345(1)(a), (b), (c), (d) & (j) may be claimed separately by joint debtors. See Or. Rev. Stat. 18.345(3).		
Books, pictures & musical instruments	$600	Or. Rev. Stat. § 18.345(1)(a)
Wearing apparel, jewelry & personal items	$1,800	Or. Rev. Stat. § 18.345(1)(b)
Tools, implements, apparatus, a team of horses or mules, harness, or library, necessary to carry on trade occupation or profession	$5,000	Or. Rev. Stat. § 18.345(1)(c)
1 vehicle or motor vehicle	$3,000	Or. Rev. Stat. § 18.345(1)(d)
Domestic animals & poultry kept for family use	$1,000 plus 60 days supply of food for same	Or. Rev. Stat. § 18.345(1)(e)
Household goods, furniture, radios, a television set, & utensils (must be held primarily for personal, family or household use of debtor)	$3,000	Or. Rev. Stat. § 18.345(1)(f)
Provisions & fuel for debtor & family	60 days' supply	Or. Rev. Stat. § 18.345(1)(f)
Professionally prescribed health aids of debtor & dependents	100%	Or. Rev. Stat. § 18.345(1)(h)
Spousal support, child support & separate maintenance payments	Amount reasonably necessary to support debtor & dependents	Or. Rev. Stat. § 18.345(1)(i)
Crime victim's reparation law awards	100%	Or. Rev. Stat. § 18.345(1)(j)
Payments on account of personal bodily injury, not including pain & suffering or compensation for actual pecuniary loss, of debtor or an individual of whom the debtor was a dependent	$10,000 but see Or. Rev. Stat. § 18.345(4)	Or. Rev. Stat. § 18.345(1)(k)
Payments in compensation for the loss of future earnings of the debtor or an individual of whom the debtor was a dependent	Amount reasonably necessary to support debtor & dependents	Or. Rev. Stat. § 18.345(1)(l)
Federal earned income tax credit and funds traceable to payment thereof	100%	Or. Rev. Stat. § 18.345(1)(n)
Any personal property of debtor	$400 (cannot be used to increase any other exemption)	Or. Rev. Stat. § 18.345(1)(p)
Beneficiary's interest in pension, retirement plan, or IRA	100% of amounts qualified under I.R.C. (also subject to Or. Rev. Stat. § 18.348(2) limits)	Or. Rev. Stat. § 18.358
Otherwise exempt earnings and benefits when deposited in bank	$7,500 (funds must be reasonably identifiable)	Or. Rev. Stat. § 18.348
Disposable earnings (earnings less deductions required by law)	75% or $936 per month	Or. Rev. Stat. § 18.385
1 rifle or shotgun & 1 pistol	$1,000	Or. Rev. Stat. § 18.362
Vocational rehabilitation payments	100% (subject to Or. Rev. Stat. § 18.348(2) limits)	Or. Rev. Stat. § 344.580
Health Assistant Payments	100%	Or. Rev. Stat. § 411.706, 411.760
Funds in Health Savings Accounts, as defined by IRC §§ 223, 223.	100%	Or. Rev. Stat. § 18.345(l)(o)

(continued on next page)

(Continued from previous page)

Type of Property	Amount of Exemption	Statute Creating Exemption
Old age assistance payments	100% (subject to Or. Rev. Stat. § 18.348(2) limits)	Or. Rev. Stat. § 18.348.130
Public assistance grants	100% (subject to Or. Rev. Stat. § 18.348(2) limits)	Or. Rev. Stat. § 411.760, 414.095
Fraternal Benefit Society benefits	100% (subject to Or. Rev. Stat. § 18.348(2) limits)	Or. Rev. Stat. § 748.207
Proceeds & cash surrender value of life insurance policies of insured where the beneficiary is person with insurable interest in insured's life	100%	Or. Rev. Stat. § 743.046
Group life insurance policy proceeds payable to person other that the insured or his estate	100%	Or. Rev. Stat. § 743.047
Annuity policy benefits	$500 per month	Or. Rev. Stat. § 743.049
Health & disability insurance benefits	100%	Or. Rev. Stat. § 743.050
Unemployment compensation benefits	100%	Or. Rev. Stat. § 657.855
Workmen's compensation benefits	100% (subject to Or. Rev. Stat. § 18.348(2) limits)	Or. Rev. Stat. §§ 656.234 & 18.348(2)
Burial lots	100%	Or. Rev. Stat. § 97.660 & 97.675
Benefits to injured trainees & inmates	100%	Or. Rev. Stat. § 655.530
State loans to veterans & veterans benefits	100%	Or. Rev. Stat. §§ 407.595 & 407.125
Specific partnership property	100% of partner's interest	Or. Rev. Stat. § 67.190
Liquor licenses	100%	Or. Rev. Stat. § 471.292(1)(i)
State employee bond savings accounts	100%	Or. Rev. Stat. § 292.070
Property of a decedent	100%	Or. Rev. Stat. § 18.312
Public employee retirement allowance	100% (subject to Or. Rev. Stat. § 18.348(2) limits)	Or. Rev. Stat. §§ 237.980, 238.445, 18.348(2), 18.358(1)
Public school teacher retirement	100% (subject to Or. Rev. Stat. § 18.348(2) limits)	Or. Rev. Stat. § 18.358(1), 18.348(2)
Veterans' benefits and loans	75%	Or. Rev. Stat. §18.345(1)(m)
Property of soldier or sailor	100%	Or. Rev. Stat. §408.440
Oregon qualified tuition savings account	100% (subject to Or. Rev. Stat. § 18.348(2) limits)	Or. Rev. Stat. § 348.841-348.873, 18.348(1)
State, county, or municipal property	100%	Or. Rev. Stat. § 18.345(1)(g)

NOTE: Or. Rev. Stat. § 18.348(2) places a cap on exempt funds of $7,500 when deposited into an account.

PENNSYLVANIA

Federal bankruptcy exemptions permitted.

Type of Property	Amount of Exemption	Statute Creating Exemption
Personal earnings in hands of employer	100%	42 Pa.C.S. § 8127
Property of any kind	$300	42 Pa.C.S. § 8123(a)
Wearing apparel, Bibles & school books	100%	42 Pa.C.S § 8124(a)
Sewing machines of seamstresses & private families	100%	42 Pa.C.S § 8124(a)
Annuities & insurance benefits payable to insured	$100 per month	42 Pa.C.S. § 8124(c)(3)
Annuities or pension benefits paid by private corporation or employer to retired employee if plan or contract provides that the benefits not assignable	100%	42 Pa.C.S. § 8124(b)(1)(vii)
Proceeds of life insurance policy or annuity contract payable to spouse, children or dependent relative of insured	100%	42 Pa.C.S § 8124(c)(6)
Proceeds of accident or disability insurance policies	100%	42 Pa.C.S § 8124(c)(7)
Fraternal Benefit Society benefits	100%	42 Pa.C.S § 8124(c)(1), (8)
Proceeds of group life insurance policies	100%	42 Pa.C.S. § 8124(c)(5)
Life insurance and annuity contract proceeds retained by Ins. company if contract provides that proceeds are not assignable	100%	40 Pa.C.S § 514 42 Pa.C.S. § 8124(c)(4)
Workmen's Compensation benefits	100%	77 Pa.C.S. § 621 42 Pa.C.S. § 8124(c)(2)
Unemployment Compensation benefits	100%	43 Pa.C.S. § 863, 42 Pa.C.S. § 8124(c)(10)
Veteran's compensation benefits	100%	51 Pa.C.S. §§ 20012, 20048, 20098, 20127
Tangible personal property at international exhibition under auspices of federal government	100%	42 Pa.C.S. § 8125
Uniforms, arms, ammunition & accoutrements of National Guardsmen	100%	51 Pa.C.S. § 4103 42 Pa.C.S. § 8124(a)(4)
Property acquired after court- approved assignment for benefit of creditors	100% (applies only against creditors prior to assignment)	39 Pa.C.S. § 102
County employees retirement benefits	100%	16 Pa.C.S. § 4716
Public officers & employees retirement benefits	100%	53 Pa.C.S. § 13445 42 Pa.C.S. § 8124(b)(1)(iv)
City employees retirement & pension benefits	100%	53 Pa.C.S. § 23572, 39351, 39383 42 Pa.C.S. § 8124(b)(1)(v)
State employees retirement benefits	100%	71 Pa.C.S. § 5953 42 Pa.C.S. § 8124(b)(1)(ii)
Police pension fund benefits	100%	53 Pa.C.S. § 764 42 Pa.C.S. § 8124(b)(1)(iii)
Public school employees retirement benefits	100%	24 Pa.C.S. § 8533 42 Pa.C.S. § 8124(b)(1)(i)
Municipal employees retirement benefits	100%	53 Pa.C.S. § 881.115 42 Pa.C.S § 8124(b)(1)(vi)
Assets and benefits of self-employed person's retirement or annuity funds including appreciation thereon	100% of federally-deductible funds that were deposited while debtor was solvent	42 Pa.C.S. § 8124(b)(1)(viii)
Any retirement or annuity fund that is qualified under I.R.C.	100%	42 Pa.C.S. § 8124(b)(1)(ix)
Specific partnership property	100% of partner's interest	15 Pa.C.S. § 8342
Crime victim's reparation awards	100%, except injury expenses	18 Pa.C.S. § 11.708
Property in the hands of a common carrier	100%,	42 Pa.C.S. § 8126

NOTE: Tenancies by the entirety may be exempt under 11 USC § 522(b)(3)(B). See In Re Martin, 269 B.R. 119 (Bankr. M.D. Pa. 2001).

RHODE ISLAND

Federal bankruptcy exeptions permitted.

Type of Property	Amount of Exemption	Statute Creating Exemption
Homestead consisting of land & buildings used as principal residence	$500,000	R.I. GEN. LAWS § 9-26-4.1(a)
Necessary wearing apparel	100%	R.I. GEN. LAWS § 9-26-4(1)
Working tools used in occupation	$2,000	R.I. GEN. LAWS § 9-26-4(2)
Professional library of professional man in actual practice	100%	R.I. GEN. LAWS § 9-26-4(2)
Household furniture and family stores of housekeeper	$9,600	R.I. GEN. LAWS § 9-26-4(3)
Bibles, school books and other books	$300	R.I. GEN. LAWS § 9-26-4(4)
One lot or right of burial in cemetery	100%	R.I. GEN. LAWS § 9-26-4(5)
Wages of sailor	100%	R.I. GEN. LAWS § 9-26-4(6)
Debts secured by bills of exchange or negotiable promissory notes	100%	R.I. GEN. LAWS § 9-26-4(7)
Salary or wages of debtor due or payable from any welfare director or from any public charity, if the funds are for relief of poor or unemployed	100%	R.I. GEN. LAWS § 9-26-4(8)
Wages or salary of debtor who has been on state, federal or local relief during past year	100% (exemption lasts for 1 year after debtor goes off relief)	R.I. GEN. LAWS § 9-26-4(8)(ii)
Wages or salary of any other debtor	$50	R.I. GEN. LAWS § 9-26-4(8)(iii)
Wages and salary of wife and minor children of debtor	100%	R.I. GEN. LAWS § 9-26-4(9)
Assets and distributions from Individual Retirement Account qualified under IRC	100% of qualified amounts (support claims excepted)	R.I. GEN. LAWS § 9-26-4(11)
Annuity, pension, profit-sharing, or other retirement plan protected by ERISA	100% of qualified amounts (support claims excepted)	R.I. GEN. LAWS § 9-26-4(12)
Motor Vehicles	$12,000	R.I. GEN. LAWS § 9-26-4(13)
Jewelry	$2,000	R.I. GEN. LAWS § 9-26-4(14)
Prepaid tuition savings accounts	100% (support claims excepted)	R.I. GEN. LAWS § 9-26-4(15)
Pay and allowance of militiaman	100%	R.I. GEN. LAWS § 30-7-9
Employment security benefits	100% (support claims excepted)	R.I. GEN. LAWS § 28-44-58
Workmen's compensation benefits	100% (support claims excepted)	R.I. GEN. LAWS § 28-33-27
Public assistance payments	100%	R.I. GEN. LAWS § 40-6-14
Proceeds and avails of life insurance policies not payable to insured	100%	R.I. GEN. LAWS § 27-4-11
Specific partnership property	100% of partner's interest	R.I. GEN. LAWS § 7-12-36
Disability insurance benefits	100%	R.I. GEN. LAWS § 28-41-32
Proceeds of life or endowment insurance and annuity contracts where contract or policy so provides	100% (exemption applies to beneficiary only)	R.I. GEN. LAWS § 27-4-12
Public employee retirement benefits	100%	R.I. GEN. LAWS § 36-10-34
Proceeds, avails and benefits of accident and sickness insurance	100%	R.I. GEN. LAWS § 27-18-24
Fraternal Benefit Society benefits	100%	R.I. GEN. LAWS § 27-25-18
Policeman and firemen pension funds and benefits	100%	R.I. GEN. LAWS § 9-26-5
Consumers cooperative membership	$50	R.I. GEN. LAWS § 7-8-25
Wild card exemption in any asset	$6,500	R.I. GEN. LAWS § 9-26-4(16)
Employees' trust under GL § 28-17-1	100%	R.I. GEN. LAWS § 28-17-4
Assets of members of the general assembly	100%	R.I. GEN. LAWS § 22-4-2
Real property of redevelopment agency	100%	R.I. GEN. LAWS § 45-31-23
Body of a deceased male or a female	100%	R.I. GEN. LAWS § 9-26-3 &9-25-17
Assets of a delinquent insurer	100%	R.I. GEN. LAWS § 27-14.4-16
Property in a Revocable Living Trust	100%	R.I. GEN. LAWS § 44-3-38

NOTE: Tenancies by the entirety may be exempt under 11 USC § 522(b)(3)(B). But see In re Homonoff, 261 B.R. 551 (Bankr. R.I. 2001).

SOUTH CAROLINA

Federal bankruptcy exemptions not permitted. See S.C. Code Ann. § 15-41-35

Type of Property	Amount of Exemption	Statute Creating Exemption
Real or personal property, including a cooperative, used as residence by debtor or a dependent, OR a burial plot	$67,100 (spouses can double if filing jointly)	S.C. Code Ann. § 15-41-30(A)(1)
One motor vehicle	$6,700	S.C. Code Ann. § 15-41-30(A)(2)
Personal household furnishings & goods, wearing apparel, appliances, books, animals, crops, or musical instruments of debtor or dependent	$5,375	S.C. Code Ann. § 15-41-30(A)(3)
Personal, family, or household jewelry of debtor or dependent	$1,350	S.C. Code Ann. § 15-41-30(A)(4)
Cash & liquid assets of debtor not claiming homestead exemption	$6,700	S.C. Code Ann. § 15-41-30(A)(5)
Implements, books, or tools of trade of debtor or a dependent	$2,025	S.C. Code Ann. § 15-41-30(A)(6)
Debtor's aggregate interest in any property (unused from other exemptions)	$6,100	S.C. Code Ann. § 15-41-30(A)(7)
Unmatured life insurance contract other than credit life	100%	S.C. Code Ann. § 15-41-30(A)(8)
Loan value or accrued interest or dividends in unmatured life insurance contract insuring debtor or person of whom debtor is a dependent	$4,875 less nonforfeiture transfers	S.C. Code Ann. § 15-41-30(A)(9)
Prescribed health aids of debtor or dependent	100%	S.C. Code Ann. § 15-41-30(A)(10)
Debtor's right to receive Social Security benefits; unemployment compensation; public assistance benefits; veterans benefits; disability, illness or unemployment benefits; alimony, support or separate maintenance; and certain payments under stock-bonus, pension, profit-sharing, annuity, or similar plans.	100%	S.C. Code Ann. § 15-41-30(A)(11)
Debtor's right to receive or property traceable to a crime victim's reparation award or payments on account of bodily injury of debtor or wrongful death or bodily injury of person of whom debtor was or is a dependent	100%	S.C. Code Ann. § 15-41-30(A)(12)(a),(b)
Debtor's right to receive, or property traceable to, payments under life insurance contracts insuring life of person of whom debtor was a dependent on the date of death	Amount reasonably necessary for support for debtor & dependents	S.C. Code Ann. § 15-41-30(A)(12)(c)
Debtor's right to receive Individual Retirement Accounts and Annuities	100%	S.C. Code Ann. § 15-41-30(A)(13)
Debtor's interest in ERISA-qualified pension plan	100%	S.C. Code Ann. § 15-41-30(A)(14)
Any rifle, shotgun, pistol, or combination thereof	$3,000	S.C. Code Ann. § 15-41-30(A)(15)
Earnings from personal services	100%	S.C. Code Ann. § 15-39-410
Fraternal Benefit Association benefits	100%	S.C. Code Ann. § 38-38-330
Workmen's compensation benefits	100%	S.C. Code Ann. § 42-9-360
State or municipal retirement system benefits	100%	S.C. Code Ann. § 9-1-1680
General Assembly retirement benefits	100%	S.C. Code Ann. § 9-9-180
Peace officers' retirement benefits	100%	S.C. Code Ann. § 9-11-270
Firemen's pension benefits	100%	S.C. Code Ann. § 9-13-230
Specific partnership property	100% of partner's interest	S.C. Code Ann. § 33-41-720
Retirement system for judges & solicitors	100%	S.C. Code Ann. § 9-8-190
Proceeds and cash surrender value of life insurance policy for the benefit of debtor's spouse or dependents and purchased more than 2 years before filing	100%	S.C. Code Ann. § 38-63-40
Debtor's interest in a South Carolina Tuition Prepayment Program plan	100%	S.C. Code Ann. § 59-4-40
Group life insurance benefits	100%	S.C. Code Ann. § 38-63-40(C)
Accidental disability insurance benefits	100%	S.C. Code Ann. § 38-63-40(D)
Cash surrender value or proceeds from group life insurance for the benefit of the insured's spouse, children, or dependents	$50,000	S.C. Code Ann. § 38-65-90
Public aid and assistance	100%	S.C. Code Ann. § 43-5-190
Crime victim's compensation	100%	S.C. Code Ann. § 16-3-1300

NOTE: The dollar amounts in CLSC § 15-40-30(A)(1)-(14) are periodically adjusted every even year to reflect the Southeastern CPI.

SOUTH DAKOTA

Federal bankruptcy exemptions not permitted. SDCL §§ 43-31-30, 43-45-13

Type of Property	Amount of Exemption	Statute Creating Exemption
Homestead of resident family	100%	SDCL §§ 43-31-1, 43-45-3
NOTES: A family may consist of one person; see Somers v. Somers, 33 S.D. 551, 146 N.W. 716. The homestead may consist of a mobile home if it is so used. However, the mobile home must be registered in the state for 6 months before the exemption applies; see SDCL § 43-31-2. There is no monetary limit to the homestead exemption of a person 70 or more years old or the unremarried surviving spouse of such person. The homestead is limited to one acre if in town or city, 160 acres if in the country, 40 acres if on mineral land, and 5 acres if on placer claim, see SDCL § 43-31-4. The homestead exemption is absolute. $60,000 of sales proceeds exempt for 1 year ($170,000 for person over 70 years of age).		
Family pictures, pew in place of worship, lots in burial ground, wearing apparel of debtor and family, and one-year's provisions for debtor and family, professionally prescribed health aids	100% (absolute exemption)	SDCL § 43-45-2
Family Bible, school books and library	$200 (absolute exemption)	SDCL § 43-45-2
Personal property of any kind	$7,000 for head of family $5,000 for any other person	SDCL § 43-45-4
Proceeds of life insurance policy payable to insured's estate when insured dies leaving surviving widow, husband or children (includes cash surrender value of policy, see Schuler v. Johnson, 61 S.D. 141, 246 N.W. 632)	$10,000	SDCL § 43-45-6
Assets and benefits of I.R.C.-qualified employee benefit plans	$1,000,000 and income and distributions therefrom	SDCL § 43-45-16
Annuity contract benefits	$250 per month	SDCL §§ 58-12-6, 7, 8
Proceeds of life or health insurance or endowment policy	$20,000	SDCL § 58-12-4
Fraternal Benefit Society benefits	100%	SDCL § 58-37A-18
Proceeds of life or health insurance policies (includes cash surrender value, see Magnuson v. Wagner, 1 F. 2d 99)	$20,000	SDCL § 58-12-4
Public Employees Retirement System benefits	100%	SDCL § 3-12-115
Temporary assistance to needy families	100%	SDCL § 28-7A-18
Workmen's compensation benefits	100% (except support obligations)	SDCL § 62-4-42
Unemployment compensation benefits	100% (except support obligations)	SDCL § 61-6-28
Earnings of prisoners on work release	100%	SDCL § 24-8-10
60 days earnings	100% (if needed to support family)	SDCL § 15-20-12
Aggregate disposable earnings	The greater of 80% or 40 times the Federal minimum hourly wage per week, plus $25 per week for each dependent family member residing with the debtor (not applicable to support orders or bankruptcy proceedings)	SDCL § 21-18-51
Partner's right in partnership property	100%	SDCL § 48-7A-501
Victim's compensation award	100%	SDCL § 23A-28B-24
All property in South Dakota if judgment is in favor of another state for failure to pay that state's income tax or benefits of a pension or other retirement plan of South Dakota resident	100%	SDCL § 43-45-2
City retirement systems and pensions	100%	SDCL § 9-16-47
Wages exempt from garnishment for support	50% if supporting other spouse or children 40% if not	SDCL § 21-18-52

(continued from previous page)

Type of Property	Amount of Exemption	Statute Creating Exemption
Public libraries	100%	Property Code § 43.001
Real property of the state	100%	Property Code § 43.002
Spouse's separate property or sole management and community property of a non-debtor	100%	11 USC §541(c)(2) Family Code § 3.202
Public School employees insurance benefits and contribution	100%	Insurance Code § 1551.011
Survivorship rights in homestead property	100% of homestead rights	Prob.Code §270,272, 284
Texas employee uniform group insurance	100%	Ins. Code § 1551-011
Texas State College or University Employee Benefits	100%	Ins. Code § 1601-008

TENNESSEE

Federal bankruptcy exemptions not permitted. TENN. CODE ANN. § 26-2-112

Type of Property	Amount of Exemption	Statute Creating Exemption
Homestead consisting of real property used by debtor, his spouse, or a dependent as principal residence	$35,000 for individual debtor $52,500 if jointly owned and both debtors	TENN. CODE ANN. § 26-2-301
Insurance proceeds from destroyed exempt homestead	$35,000	TENN. CODE ANN. § 26-2-304
Personal property of state resident(includes money and bank deposits)	$10,000	TENN. CODE ANN. § 26-2-103
Necessary wearing apparel of debtor and family and receptacles for holding same, family portraits and pictures, family Bible and school books	100%	TENN. CODE ANN. § 26-2-104
State pension moneys and interests in IRC-qualified retirement plans and health savings accounts	100%	TENN. CODE ANN. § 26-2-105
Disposable earnings (earnings after deductions required by law)	75% OR 30 times the federal minimum hourly wage per week, WHICHEVER IS GREATER, (Add $2.50 per week for each dependent child of the debtor under age 16 residing in state; TCA § 26-2-207.	TENN. CODE ANN. § 26-2-106
Accident, health and disability insurance benefits	100%	TENN. CODE ANN. § 26-2-110(a)
Social security, unemployment, public assistance, veterans, disability or illness benefits	100%	TENN. CODE ANN. § 26-2-111(1)(A), (B), (C)
Certain payments under stock bonus, pension, profit sharing, annuity or similar plan or contracts (see statute for specifics)	Same as under TENN. CODE ANN. § 26-2-106 above	TENN. CODE ANN. § 26-2-111(1)(D)
Alimony due more than 30 days after assertion of claim	100%	TENN. CODE ANN. § 26-2-111(1)(E)
Child support payments due 30 days or more after date of filing	100%	TENN. CODE ANN. § 26-2-111(1)(F)
Crime victim's reparation law awards	$5,000 (see note below)	TENN. CODE ANN. § 26-2-111(2)(A)
Personal injury payments to debtor or individual of whom debtor is a dependent, excluding compensation for pain and suffering and actual pecuniary loss	$7,500 (see note below)	TENN. CODE ANN. § 26-2-111(2)(B)
Payments for the wrongful death of debtor or individual of whom debtor was a dependent	$10,000 (see note below)	TENN. CODE ANN. § 26-2-111(2)(C)
NOTE: The aggregate amounts claimed under TENN. CODE ANN. § 26-2-111(2) cannot exceed $15,000		
Compensation for loss of future earnings of debtor or individual of whom debtor is a dependent	Amount reasonably necessary for support of debtor and dependents	TENN. CODE ANN. § 26-2-111(3)
Implements, professional books, or tools of trade of debtor or dependent	$1,900	TENN. CODE ANN. § 26-2-111(4)
Professionally prescribed health aids of debtor and dependents	100%	TENN. CODE ANN. § 26-2-111(5)
Liquid assets owed under child support order	100%	TENN. CODE ANN. § 26-2-111(6)
Life insurance and annuity contracts benefits payable to spouse, children or dependent of insured	100% (includes cash surrender value)	TENN. CODE ANN. §§ 56-7-203 & 26-2-110(b)
Fraternal benefit society payments	100%	TENN. CODE ANN. § 56-25-1403
Workmen's compensation benefits	100% (support claims excepted)	TENN. CODE ANN. § 50-6-223
Specific partnership property	100% of partner's interest	TENN. CODE ANN. §§ 61-1-203 and 61-1-501
Pension benefits received from state or subdivision or municipality thereof	100%	TENN. CODE ANN. § 26-2-105(a)
Aid to dependent children	100%	TENN. CODE ANN. § 71-3-121
Aid to the blind	100%	TENN. CODE ANN. § 71-4-117
Aid to the disabled	100%	TENN. CODE ANN. § 71-4-1112
Old age assistance payments	100%	TENN. CODE ANN. § 71-2-216
Family cemeteries and burial lots	100% (up to 1 acre)	TENN. CODE ANN. § 26-2-305
College education savings plans	100%	TENN. CODE ANN. § 49-7-822
Criminal injuries compensation	100%	TENN. CODE ANN. § 29-13-111
Retirement benefits--Teachers	100%	TENN. CODE ANN. § 49-5-909
Beneficiary's interest in a spendthrift trust	100%	TENN. CODE ANN. § 35-15-501, et seq.
Tennessee Investment Services Trust	100%	TENN. CODE ANN. § 35-16-104
Funds recovered in a wrongful death action	100%	TENN. CODE ANN. § 20-5-106(a)

NOTE: Tenancies by the entirety may be exempt under 11 USC § 522(b)(3)(B). See In Re *Ray v. Dawson*, 14 B.R. 822 (E.D. Tenn. 1981).

TEXAS

Federal bankruptcy exemptions permitted.

Type of Property	Amount of Exemption	Statute Creating Exemption
Homestead (must be used as rural or urban home or as a place to exercise a calling or business in urban area)	200 acres for family (100 acres for single adult) of rural land OR up to 10 acres of urban land in one or more contiguous lots. Includes improvements. No value limitation.	Constitution Art. 16, §§ 50, 51 Property Code §§ 41.001, 41.002
Proceeds of voluntary sale of homestead (good for 6 months after sale)	same as for homestead that was sold	Property Code § 41.001(c)
Lots held as burying grounds	100%	Property Code § 41.001(a)
Current wages for personal services	100% (child support claims excepted)	Property Code § 42.001(b)(1)
Professionally prescribed health aids	100%	Property Code § 42.001(b)(2)
Alimony, maintenance or support	100%	Property Code § 42.001(b)(3)
Unpaid commissions for personal services (see note below)	Not to exceed 25% of total	Property Code § 42.001(d)
Home furnishings, including family heirlooms and Bible	100% (see note below)	Prop. Code §§ 42.001(a), 42.002(a)(1), 42.001(b)(4)
Provisions for consumption	100% (see note below)	Prop. Code §§ 42.001(a), 42.002(a)(2)
Farming or ranching vehicles and implements	100% (see note below)	Prop. Code §§ 42.001(a), 42.002(a)(3)
Tools, equipment, books, and apparatus, used in a trade or profession	100% (see note below) (includes boats and motor vehicles)	Prop. Code §§ 42.001(a), 42.002(a)(4)
Wearing apparel	100% (see note below)	Prop. Code §§ 42.001(a), 42.002(a)(5)
Jewelry (see note below)	$25,000 for debtor who is a family member 12,500 for single non family-member adult	Prop. Code §§ 42.001(a), 42.002(a)(6)
Two firearms	100% (see note below)	Prop. Code §§ 42.001(a), 42.002(a)(7)
Athletic and sporting equipment, including bicycles	100% (see note below)	Prop. Code §§ 42.001(a), 42.002(a)(8)
One motor vehicle (2,3, or 4 wheeled) for each family member with driver's license or who relies on another to operate vehicle	100% (see note below)	Prop. Code §§ 42.001(a), 42.002(a)(9)
Certain livestock and poultry	100% (see note below)	Property Code §§ 42.001(a), 42.002(a)(10)
Household pets	100% (see note below)	Prop Code §§ 42.001(a),42.002(a)(11)

NOTE: The aggregate limitation on the exemptions specified in Property Code §§ 42.001(d) and 42.002(a) are $100,000 for a debtor who is a family member and $50,000 for a single adult who is not a family member. Also, a debtor who uses nonexempt property to obtain, improve, or pay an indebtedness on exempt personal property with the intent to defraud, delay or hinder a creditor may lose the exemption. See Property Code § 42.004. The exemptions set forth in Property Code §§ 42.001, 42.002 & 42.0021 do not apply to child support claims. See Property Code § 42.0005.

Proceeds and assets of tax-qualified personal or corporate retirement plans and IRAs and Health Savings Accounts	100% of qualified amounts	Property Code § 42.0021
Assets in & benefits from Texas College Savings Plans & prepaid tuition	100%	Property Code § 42.0022 & Ed. Code §54.709(e) & 54.639
Partner's interest in partnership property	100% (See Statute)	Bus. Org. Code § 153.256
Life insurance and annuity proceeds, including cash value	100%	Ins. Code § 1108.001 and § 1108.51
Employees group life insurance benefits & contributions	100%	Ins. Code arts. 3.50-2, § 10; 3.50, § 9
Benefits paid under life, health or accident insurance policies	100%	Ins. Code. § 1551.011 1108.051
Fraternal Benefit Society benefits	100%	Ins. Code § 885.316
Unemployment compensation benefits	100%	Labor Code § 207.075
Workmen's compensation benefits	100%	Labor Code § 408.201
Public assistance benefits	100%	Human Resources Code § 31.040
Medical assistance payments to needy	100%	Human Resources Code § 32.036
State employees retirement & pension benefits	100%	Government Code § 811.005
Judicial system retirement benefits	100%	Government Code § 831.004
Law enforcement officers' survivors benefits	100%	Government Code § 615.005
County & district employees pension & retirement benefits	100%	Government Code § 841.006
Municipal employees retirement benefits	100%	Government Code § 851.006
Police, firemen & fire alarm operators pension, relief & retirement benefits	100%	VACS arts. 6243a-1 § 8.03, 6243b § 15, 6243d-1 § 17, 6243e § 5, 6243e.1 § 1.04, 6243e.2(1) § 15, 6243g-1 § 23B, 6243j § 20, 6243o § 1.05
Teachers pension & retirement benefits	100%	VACS Title 110B, § 31.005 Government Code § 821.005
Crime victim's compensation	100%	Code Crim. Proc. § 56.49

UTAH

Federal bankruptcy exemptions not permitted. See UTAH CODE ANN. § 78B-5-513.

Type of Property	Amount of Exemption	Statute Creating Exemption
Homestead consisting of debtor's residence, which may consist of a dwelling or mobile home in which debtor resides plus up to 1 acre of surrounding land reasonably necessary for use of residence	If primary residence:$42,000 if individually owned; $84,000 if jointly owned If not primary residence: $5,000 if individually owned; $10,000 if jointly owned	UTAH CODE ANN. § 78B-5-503
NOTE: This exemption may be claimed on one or more parcels of property.	See UTAH CODE ANN. § 78B-5-503(2)(c)(i).	A declaration of homestead must be filed with the county recorder. See UTAH CODE ANN. § 78B-5-504.
Water rights owned by homestead claimant necessary for supplying water to homestead for domestic or irrigation purposes	100%	UTAH CODE ANN. § 78B-5-503(4)(a)
Proceeds of sale of homestead for 1 year after sale	same as homestead exemption	UTAH CODE ANN. § 78B-5-503(5)(b)
Burial plot for debtor and family	100%	UTAH CODE ANN. § 78B-5-505(1)(a)(i)
Reasonably necessary health aids of debtor or dependents	100%	UTAH CODE ANN. § 78B-5-505(1)(a)(ii)
Disability, illness or unemployment benefits of debtor or dependent	100%	UTAH CODE ANN. § 78B-5-505(1)(a)(iii)
Benefits payable for medical, surgical or hospital care	Extent used by debtor or dependent for such care	UTAH CODE ANN. § 78B-5-505(1)(a)(iv)
Veterans benefits	100%	UTAH CODE ANN. § 78B-5-505(1)(a)(v)
Child support & the rights thereto	100%	UTAH CODE ANN. § 78B-5-505(1)(a)(vi)
Alimony or separate maintenance payments and the rights thereto	Amount reasonably necessary for support of debtor & dependents	UTAH CODE ANN. § 78B-5-505(1)(a)(vii)
1 clothes washer & dryer, 1 refrigerator, 1 freezer, 1 stove, 1 microwave oven, 1 sewing machine, all carpets in use, 12 months' provisions, all wearing apparel (not including jewelry or furs), all beds & bedding, of debtor & dependents	100%	UTAH CODE ANN. § 78B-5-505(1)(a)(viii)
Personal works of art depicting debtor & family or produced by debtor & family	100%	UTAH CODE ANN. § 78B-5-505(1)(a)(ix)
Proceeds of claims for bodily injury of debtor or proceeds of claims for bodily injury or wrongful death of an individual of whom debtor was or is a dependent	100% of compensatory amount	UTAH CODE ANN. § 78B-5-505(1)(a)(x)
Retirement funds and benefits of debtor that are tax-qualified under I.R.C.	100% except that amounts contributed within 1 year of bankruptcy filing date are not exempt (subject to QDRO orders)	UTAH CODE ANN. § 78B-5-505(1)(a)(xiv)
Life insurance proceeds or benefits payable to spouse or children of insured (policy must be owned by debtor for 1 year or more)	100%	UTAH CODE ANN. § 78B-5-505(1)(a)(xi), (xii)
Interests payable to an alternate payee under a QDRO	100%	UTAH CODE ANN. § 78B-5-505(xv)
Earned but unpaid wages	1 month or 2 weeks dependent upon pay period	UTAH CODE ANN. § 78B-5-505(xvi)
Proceeds and avails of unmatured life insurance policies owned by debtor for 1 year or more	100%	UTAH CODE ANN. § 78B-5-505(1)(a)(xiii)
Sofas, chairs & related furnishings reasonably necessary for one household	$1,000	UTAH CODE ANN. § 78B-5-506(1)(a)
Dining & kitchen tables & chairs reasonably necessary for one household	$1,000	UTAH CODE ANN. § 78B-5-506(1)(b)
Animals, books & musical instruments reasonably held for personal use of debtor or dependents	$1,000	UTAH CODE ANN. § 78B-5-506(1)(c)
Personal heirlooms & items of sentimental value to debtor	$1,000	UTAH CODE ANN. § 78B-5-506(1)(d)
Any 3 of the following together with 1,000 rounds each: (1) a handgun, (2) a shotgun, and (3) a shoulder arm	$250 / individual $500 / household	UTAH CODE ANN. § 78B-5-506(1)(e) UTAH CODE ANN. § 78B-5-505(1)(a)

(continued on next page)

(continued from previous page)

Type of Property	Amount of Exemption	Statute Creating Exemption
Implements, professional books, or tools of trade of debtor	$5,000	Utah Code Ann. § 78B-5-506(2)
One motor vehicle used in debtor's business or profession, other than for traveling to and from work (Does not include off-highway or recreational vehicles. See UCA § 78-23-8(3)(a))	$3,000	Utah Code Ann. § 78B-5-506(3)(b)
Proceeds from sale, condemnation, damage or destruction of exempt property	Amount of exemption given for lost or damaged property	Utah Code Ann. § 78B-5-507
Military property of National Guardsman	100%	Utah Code Ann. § 39-1-47
Workmen's compensation benefits	100%	Utah Code Ann. § 34A-2-422
Unemployment compensation benefits	100% (except child support)	Utah Code Ann. § 35A-4-103 & 78B-5-505(1)(a)(iii)
Fraternal Benefit Society benefits	100%	Utah Code Ann. § 31A-9-603
Partner's interest in specific partnership property, except on claim against partnership	100%	Utah Code Ann. § 48-1-22(2)(c)
Benefits payable under Utah State Retirement Act	100% (subject to QDRO orders)	Utah Code Ann. § 49-11-612
Disposable earnings	75% or 30 times the federal minimum wage (WHICHEVER IS GREATER)*	Utah R. Civ. Pro. 64 D and Utah Code Ann. § 70C-7-103
Crime Victims' Reparation Act award	100%	Utah Code Ann. § 63M-7-521
Public assistance provided under Utah Employment Support Act	100%	Utah Code Ann. § 35A-3-112

* But see In re Reinhart, 291 P.3d 228 (Utah 2012) (holding statute does not create bankruptcy exemption).

VERMONT

Federal bankruptcy exemptions permitted.

Type of Property	Amount of Exemption	Statute Creating Exemption
Homestead, consisting of dwelling house, outbuildings and land used in connection therewith, including rents, issues, profits, and products thereof	$125,000	27 VSA § 101
Motor vehicles	$2,500	12 VSA § 2740(1)
Professional or trade books or tools of debtor or dependent	$5,000	12 VSA § 2740(2)
One wedding ring	100%	12 VSA § 2740(3)
Personal, family, or household jewelry of debtor or dependent	$500	12 VSA § 2740(4)
Personal, family or household furnishings, goods, appliances, books, wearing apparel, animals, crops, or musical instruments of debtor or dependent	$2,500	12 VSA § 2740(5)
Growing crops	$5,000	12 VSA § 2740(6)
Debtor's interest in any property	$400 plus up to $7,000 of any unused exemption provided under 12 VSA § 2740(1), (2), (4), (5) or (6)	12 VSA § 2740(7)
Cook stove, heating appliance, refrigerator freezer, water heater, and sewing machines	100%	12 VSA § 2740(8)
10 cords of firewood or 500 gallons of oil	100%	12 VSA § 2740(9)
500 gallons of bottled gas	100%	12 VSA § 2740(10)
1 cow, 2 goats, 10 sheep, 10 chickens, and one winter's feed for each	100%	12 VSA § 2740(11)
3 swarms of bees with hives & produce	100%	12 VSA § 2740(12)
1 yoke of oxen or steers or 2 team horses	100%	12 VSA § 2740(13)
2 harnesses, 2 halters, 2 chains, 1 plow, and 1 ox yoke	100%	12 VSA § 2740(14)
Bank deposits or deposit accounts	$700	12 VSA § 2740(15)
Self-directed retirement plans and IRAs	100% of tax deductible amounts, except that contributions made within 1 year of bankruptcy are not exempt. Roth IRAs are exempt to extent contributions do not exceed limits specified in 26 U.S.C. 408A	12 VSA § 2740(16)
Professionally prescribed health aids	100%	12 VSA § 2740(17)
Unmatured life insurance contracts	100% (credit life insurance excluded)	12 VSA § 2740(18)
Social security benefits, veteran's benefits, disability or illness benefits, alimony, support, or separate maintenance, and crime victims' reparation awards	Amount reasonably necessary for the support of debtor and dependents	12 VSA § 2740(19)(A)-(E)
Compensation for personal injury, pain & suffering, or actual pecuniary loss, compensation for wrongful death, and compensation for loss of future earnings	Amount reasonably necessary for the support of debtor and dependents	12 VSA § 2740(19)(F),(G),(I)
Life insurance payments and payments under pension, annuity, profit-sharing, stock bonus, or similar plans on account of death, disability, illness or retirement	Amount reasonably necessary for the support of debtor and dependents	12 VSA § 2740(19)(H),(J)
Disposable earnings (earnings less deductions required by law)	75% OR 30 times the federal minimum hourly wage per week WHICHEVER IS GREATER*	12 VSA § 3170
Personal earnings of minor child or married woman	100% (applies against creditors or parent or husband)	12 VSA § 3020(6)
Fees of jurors and fees and room and board expenses of legislators	100%	12 VSA § 3020(3)(4)
Fire insurance proceeds resulting from loss by fire of exempt property	100%	12 VSA § 3020(1)
Proceeds of life insurance policy	$500	12 VSA § 3020(2)
Proceeds of group life insurance and group disability insurance	100%	8 VSA § 3708
Proceeds and avails of life insurance policies wherein beneficiary is not the insured	100% (less premiums paid in defraud of creditors)	8 VSA § 3706
Beneficial interests in insurance policies or annuity contracts containing spendthrift clauses	100%	8 VSA § 3705

(continued on next page)

VERMONT

(continued from previous page)

Type of Property	Amount of Exemption	Statute Creating Exemption
Annuity contract benefits	$350 per month	8 VSA § 3709
Fraternal Benefit Society benefits	100%	8 VSA § 4478
Disability insurance benefits that are supplemental to life insurance or annuity contracts	100%	8 VSA § 3707
Unemployment compensation benefits	100% (except child support)	21 VSA § 1367
Workmen's compensation benefits	100% (except claims of physicians & hospital who rendered services)	21 VSA § 681
Public assistance payments	100%	33 VSA § 124
Vermont Employees Retirement System benefits and funds	100%	3 VSA § 476
Disability payments	$200 per month; unlimited if a lump sum	8 VSA § 4086
Specific partnership property	100% of partner's interest	11 VSA § 3213
Amounts owing to debtor from sale of exempt property	Same as exemption given for property sold	12 VSA § 3023
Retirement benefits-municipal employees	100%	24 VSA § 5066
Certain teachers annuity and pension plan payments	100%	16 VSA § 1946
Decedent's family allowance for surviving spouses and minor children	100%	16 VSA 64.2-309

NOTE: Tenancies by the entirety may be exempt under 11 USC § 522(b)(3)(B). See Lowell v. Lowell, 419 A. 2d 321 (Vt. 1980).

* But see In re Riendeau, 293 B.R. 832 (D. Vt 2002) (holding statute does not create bankruptcy exemption).

VIRGINIA

Federal bankruptcy exemptions not permitted. See VA. CODE ANN. § 34-3.1

Type of Property	Amount of Exemption	Statute Creating Exemption
Real & personal property(includes money & debts owed to debtor)	$25,000 plus $500 for each dependent (applies to householder or resident head of family) (exempt real estate must be claimed by recording written declaration. See CV § 34-6) ($10,000 for householder 65 and older)	VA. CODE ANN. § 34-4
NOTE: A householder debtor must set apart the property claimed as exempt on or before the 5th day after the first date set for the first meeting of creditors. See VA. CODE ANN. § 34-17.		
Real & personal property of disabled veteran (must be rated 40% or more disabled by V.A.) This is in addition to the allowed homestead exemption.	$10,000	VA. CODE ANN. § 34-4.1
Rents & profits of exempt property	100%	VA. CODE ANN. § 34-18
Disposable earnings (earnings less deductions required by law)	75% OR 40 times federal minimum hourly wage per week, WHICHEVER IS GREATER	VA. CODE ANN. § 34-29
Family Bible	100%	VA. CODE ANN. § 34-26(1)
Wedding & engagement rings	100%	VA. CODE ANN. § 34-26(1)(a)
Family portraits and heirlooms	$5,000	VA. CODE ANN. § 34-26(2)
Burial lot	100%	VA. CODE ANN. § 34-26(3)(i)
Pre need funeral contract	$5,000	VA. CODE ANN. § 34-26(3)(ii)
Wearing apparel	$1,000	VA. CODE ANN. § 34-26(4)
Household furnishings	$5,000	VA. CODE ANN. § 34-26(4)(a)
Animals owned as pets	100%	VA. CODE ANN. § 34-26(5)
Medically prescribed health aids	100%	VA. CODE ANN. § 34-26(6)
Tools, books, instruments implements, equipment, and machines (including motor vehicles, vessels and aircraft) used in trade or occupation or in school	$10,000 (motor vehicles, vessels and aircraft used only to commute to and from place of work are not covered under this exemption)	VA. CODE ANN. § 34-26(7)
Motor vehicle	$6,000	VA. CODE ANN. § 34-26(8)
1 pair of horses or mules with necessary gearing, 1 wagon or cart, 1 tractor, 2 plows, 1 drag, 1 harvest cradle, 1 pitchfork, 1 rake, 2 iron wedges, fertilizer	no limit, except: $3,000 for tractor $1,000 for fertilizer (applies only to householder actually engaged in agriculture)	VA. CODE ANN. § 34-27
Causes of action for and proceeds of personal injury and wrongful death claims	100%	VA. CODE ANN. § 34-28.1
Debtor's interest in retirement plan or IRA qualified by IRC	Amount available under Federal bankruptcy law	VA. CODE ANN. § 34-34
Payments made under prepaid tuition contract	100%	VA. CODE ANN. § 23-38.81(E) & (F)
Growing crops	100%	VA. CODE ANN. § 8.01-489
Awards to crime victims	100%	VA. CODE ANN. § 19.2-368.12
Proceeds & avails of life insurance policies payable to another	100%	VA. CODE ANN. § 38.2-3122, 3123
Group life insurance policies& proceeds	100%	VA. CODE ANN. §§ 38.2-3339

(continued on next page)

VIRGINIA

(continued from previous page)

Type of Property	Amount of Exemption	Statute Creating Exemption
Life benefit company benefits	100%	Va. Code Ann. § 38.2-3811
Fraternal Benefit Society benefits	100%	Va. Code Ann. § 38.2-4118
Burial society benefits	100%	Va. Code Ann. § 38.2-4021
Arms, uniforms & equipment of national guardsman or naval militiaman	100%	Va. Code Ann. § 44-96
Industrial sick benefit insurance benefits	100%	Va. Code Ann. § 38.2-3549
Workmen's Compensation benefits	100% (except support obligations)	Va. Code Ann. § 65.2-531
Unemployment Compensation benefits	100%	Va. Code Ann. § 60.2-600
Earnings of debtor under court-approved assignment for benefit of creditors	100%	Va. Code Ann. § 55-165
Public employees retirement benefits	100% (except support obligations)	Va. Code Ann. § 51.1-124.4
Public assistance payments	100%	Va. Code Ann. § 63.2-506
Specific partnership property	100% of partner's interest	Va. Code Ann. § 50-73.105
Decedent's family allowance	Amount reasonably necessary to pay maintenance of spouse & minor children for 1 year	Va. Code Ann. § 64.1-151.1
Exempt property of decedent	$15,000 in excess of applicable security interests	Va. Code Ann. § 64.1-151.2
Homestead allowance for surviving spouse	$15,000	Va. Code Ann. § 64.1-151.3
Spendthrift trust	unlimited, but subject to exceptions listed in statute	Va. Code Ann. § 64.2-743
Accident and sickness benefits	100%	Va. Code Ann. § 38.2-3406
Firearms	$3,000	Va. Code Ann. § 34-26 (4)(b)
Principal family residence held as tenants by the entireties	100%	Va. Code Ann. § 55-37

NOTE: Tenancies by the entirety may be exempt under 11 USC § 522(b)(3)(B). See *In re Bradby*, 455 B.R. 476 (Bankr. E. D. Va. 2011); *Ragsdale v. Genesco, Inc.*, 674 F. 2d 277 (4th Cir. 1982).

WASHINGTON

Federal bankruptcy exemptions permitted. See WASH. REV. CODE § 6.15.050(8) for limitation.

Type of Property	Amount of Exemption	Statute Creating Exemption
Homestead consisting of house or mobile home in which owner resides, plus appurtenances & land, if any, on which situate	$15,000 for other personal property used as homestead $125,000 for lands, mobile homes & improvements	WASH. REV. CODE § 6.13.030
NOTE: Homestead declaration must be recorded in county recording office if property is not yet occupied as homestead. (proceeds of sale of homestead exempt for 1 year in same amount) See RCW§ 6.13.070		
All wearing apparel	no limit, except value of furs, jewelry & personal ornaments cannot exceed $3,500	WASH. REV. CODE § 6.15.010(1)(a)
Private library of debtor, including electronic media	$3,500	WASH. REV. CODE § 6.15.010(1)(b)
Family pictures & keepsakes, one cell phone, a personal computer, and printer	100%	WASH. REV. CODE § 6.15.010(1)(b), (c)
Household goods, appliances, furniture & home & yard equipment of debtor & family, including provisions & fuel	$6,500 ($15,000 total for community)	WASH. REV. CODE § 6.15.010(1)(d)(i)
Other personal property of debtor and family, except personal earnings	$3,000 with $1,500 limit on cash and $500 limit on bank accounts & securities	WASH. REV. CODE § 6.15.010(1)(d)(ii)
Motor vehicle used for personal transportation	$3,250 ($6,500 total for community)	WASH. REV. CODE § 6.15.010(1)(d)(iii)
Traceable child support paid or owed to debtor	100%	WASH. REV. CODE § 6.15.010(1)(d)(iv)
Professionally prescribed health aids of debtor or dependents	100%	WASH. REV. CODE § 6.15.010(1)(d)(v)
Personal injury awards	$20,000	WASH. REV. CODE § 6.15.010(1)(d)(vi)
Farm trucks, stock, tools, equipment, supplies & seed of farmer	$10,000	WASH. REV. CODE § 6.15.010(1)(e)(i)
Library & office furniture, equipment& supplies of physician, attorney, clergyman or other professional person	$10,000	WASH. REV. CODE § 6.15.010(1)(e)(ii)
Tools, instruments & materials used to carry on trade for support of debtor & family	$10,000	WASH. REV. CODE § 6.15.010(1)(e)(iii)
Tuition units under chapter 28B.95 RCW, purchased more than 2 yrs prior to filing, or contributions to qualified tuition savings programs under §529 or 530 of the IRC made more than 2 yrs prior to filing	100%	WASH. REV. CODE § 6.15.010(1)(f)
Disposable earnings (earnings less deductions required by law	75% OR 35 times the federal minimum hourly wage per week, WHICHEVER IS GREATER	WASH. REV. CODE § 6.27.150
Federal pension benefits	100% (except child support)	WASH. REV. CODE § 6.15.020(2)
Debtor's right to retirement, disability or death benefits from employee benefit plan qualified under Internal Revenue Code	100% of qualified amounts (support claims & QDRO benefits excepted)	WASH. REV. CODE § 6.15.020(3)
Fire insurance proceeds of policies covering exempt property	100% of exemption for covered property	WASH. REV. CODE § 6.15.030
Industrial insurance benefits & workmens' compensation	100%	WASH. REV. CODE § 51.32.040
Unemployment compensation benefits	100% (support claims excepted)	WASH. REV. CODE § 50.40.020
Disability insurance benefits	100%	WASH. REV. CODE § 48.18.400
Proceeds & avails of life insurance policies wherein beneficiary is person other than the insured or the person effecting the policy	100%	WASH. REV. CODE § 48.18.410
Group life insurance proceeds	100%	WASH. REV. CODE § 48.18.420
Annuity contract benefits	$3,000 per month	WASH. REV. CODE § 48.18.430
Public assistance grants & payments	100%	WASH. REV. CODE §§ 74.08.210, 74.13.070, 74.04.280
Income or proceeds from trust for benefit of debtor created & funded by another person	100%	WASH. REV. CODE § 6.32.250
Personal or family burying grounds	100%	WASH. REV. CODE §§ 68.24.220, 68.20.120
City employees retirement benefits	100% (support claims excepted)	WASH. REV. CODE §§ 41.44.240, 41.28.200, 41.20.180
Police & Firemen's retirement benefits	100% (support claims excepted)	WASH. REV. CODE §§ 41.20.180, 41.24.240, 43.43.310, 41.26.053
State employees retirement benefits	100% (support claims excepted)	WASH. REV. CODE § 41.40.052
Teachers retirement benefits	100% (support claims excepted)	WASH. REV. CODE § 41.32.052
Judges retirement benefits	100% (support claims excepted)	WASH. REV. CODE §§ 2.10.180, 2.12.090
Specific partnership property	100% of partner's interest	WASH. REV. CODE § 25.05.200
Fraternal Benefit Society benefits	100%	WASH. REV. CODE §48.36A.180

(Continued from previous page)

Type of Property	Amount of Exemption	Statute Creating Exemption
Earnings from work release	100%	WASH. REV. CODE § 72.65.060
Property of incompetent	100%	WASH. REV. CODE § 11.92.060(3)
Separate property of nondebtor spouse	100% (but see statutes for exceptions)	WASH. REV. CODE §§ 26.16.200, 6.15.040
Property issued to members of organized militia of Washington	100%	WASH. REV. CODE § 38.40.150
Building materials used to improve property subject to lien from 60.04 RCW	100%	WASH. REV. CODE § 60.04.201
Crime victims' compensation	100%	WASH. REV. CODE § 7.68.070, 51.32.040

WEST VIRGINIA

Federal bankruptcy exemptions not permitted. See W. VA. CODE § 38-10-4.

Type of Property	Amount of Exemption	Statute Creating Exemption
Homestead of resident head of household	$5,000	W. VA. CODE § 38-9-1
One motor vehicle	$5,000	W. VA. CODE § 38-8-1(a)(1)
Household goods, furniture, toys, animals, appliances, books and wearing apparel	$8,000	W. VA. CODE § 38-8-1(a)(2)
Implements, professional books or tools of trade	$3,000	W. VA. CODE § 38-8-1(a)(3)
Funds in federally-insured financial institution, wages or salary	$1,000 or 125% of amt. of annualized federal poverty level of debtor's household divided by no. of debtor's yearly pay periods, WHICHEVER IS GREATER.	W. VA. CODE § 38-8-1(a)(4)
NOTE: The aggregate amounts exempted under W. VA. CODE § 38-8-1(a)(1)-(4) may not exceed $15,000.		
Funds in Individual Retirement Accounts	100% of qualified amounts	W. VA. CODE §§ 38-8-1(a)(5), 38-10-4(j)(5)
Unripe crops	100% (until mature)	W. VA. CODE § 38-8-14
Proceeds & avails of life insurance policies wherein the beneficiary is a person other than the insured or the person affecting the policy	100%	W. VA. CODE § 33-6-27
Group life insurance proceeds	100%	W. VA. CODE § 33-6-28
Fraternal Benefit Society benefits	100%	W. VA. CODE § 33-23-21
Workmen's compensation benefits	100%	W. VA. CODE § 23-4-18
Unemployment compensation benefits	100% (certain claims excepted)	W. VA. CODE § 21A-10-2
Public welfare assistance payments	100%	W. VA. CODE § 9-5-1
Judges' retirement benefits	100% (except QDROs)	W. VA. CODE § 51-9-14
Public employees retirement benefits	100% (except QDROs)	W. VA. CODE § 5-10-46
Teachers retirement benefits	100% (except QDROs)	W. VA. CODE § 18-7A-30
NOTE - The following exemptions apply only to bankruptcy proceedings.		
Debtor's interest in real or personal property, including a cooperative, used as a residence by debtor or a dependent, or in a burial plot	$25,000 ($250,000 for certain physicians)	W. VA. CODE § 38-10-4(a)
One motor vehicle	$2,400	W. VA. CODE § 38-10-4(b)
Household furnishings & goods, wearing apparel, appliances, books, animals, crops or musical instruments, that are held primarily for the, personal family or household use of debtor or a dependent	$400 per item $8,000 aggregate	W. VA. CODE § 38-10-4(c)
Jewelry held primarily for personal, family or household use of debtor or a dependent	$1,000	W. VA. CODE § 38-10-4(d)
Any property of debtor	$800 plus any unused portion of the residence exemption under WVC § 30-10-4(a) above	W. VA. CODE § 38-10-4(e)
Implements, professional books or tools of trade of debtor or a dependent	$1,500	W. VA. CODE § 38-10-4(f)
Any unmeasured life insurance contract owned by debtor other than credit life insurance	100%	W. VA. CODE § 38-10-4(g)
Accrued interest or dividends or loan value of unmeasured life insurance contract owned by debtor wherein the insured is the debtor or a person of whom the debtor is a dependent	$8,000 less any transfers made under nonforfeiture provisions in policy	W. VA. CODE § 38-10-4(h)
Professionally prescribed health aids of debtor or dependents	100%	W. VA. CODE § 38-10-4(i)
Social Security benefits, unemployment compensation, local public assistance benefits, veterans benefits & disability, illness or unemployment benefits	100%	W. VA. CODE § 38-10-4(j)(1), (2) & (3)

(continued on next page)

(continued from previous page)

Type of Property	Amount of Exemption	Statute Creating Exemption
Alimony, support or separate maintenance	amount reasonably necessary for support of debtor & dependents	W. Va. Code § 38-10-4(j)(4)
Payments under stock bonus, pension profitsharing, annuity, or similar plan or contract on account of illness, disability, death, or age or length of service, and funds in IRAs & SEPs	Amount reasonably necessary for support of debtor & dependents plus amounts in IRAs that are tax-deferred.	W. Va. Code § 38-10-4(j)(5)
NOTE: This exemption does not apply if the plan or contract was established by an insider that employed debtor when the debtor's rights under the plan or contract arose, the payment is on account of age or length of service, and the plan or contract does not qualify under 26 USC §§ 401(a), 403(a), 403(b), 408 or 409.		
Crime victim's reparation law awards	100%	W. Va. Code § 38-10-4(k)(1)
Payments on account of the wrongful death of an individual of whom the debtor was a dependent	Amount reasonably necessary to support debtor & dependents	W. Va. Code § 38-10-4(k)(2)
Payments under life insurance contract insuring life of an individual of whom the debtor was a dependent on the date of death	Amount reasonably necessary to support debtor & dependents	W. Va. Code § 38-10-4(k)(3)
Payments on account of personal bodily injury, not including pain & suffering or compensation for actual pecuniary loss, of debtor or an individual of whom the debtor is a dependent	$15,000	W. Va. Code § 38-10-4(k)(4)
Payments in compensation of loss of future earnings of debtor or an individual of whom the debtor was a dependent	Amount reasonably necessary to support debtor & dependents	W. Va. Code § 38-10-4(k)(5)
Payments made to prepaid tuition trust fund	100%	W. Va. Code § 38-10-4(k)(6)
Specific partnership property	100% of partner's interest	W. Va. Code § 47B-2-3
Retirement funds-Department of Public Saftey	100%	W. Va. Code § 15-2-26
Wages	80% (earned, but unpaid wages)	W. Va. Code § 38-5A-3

WISCONSIN

Federal bankruptcy exemptions permitted.

Type of Property	Amount of Exemption	Statute Creating Exemption
Homestead occupied by resident owner(includes proceeds from sale of homestead held with intent to procure another homestead for 2 years)	$75,000 NOTE-includes dwelling (including condominium, mobile home, house trailer or co-op.) and up to 40 acres of land. See Wis. Stat. § 990.01(14).	Wis. Stat. § 815.20
Cemetery lots, tombstones, coffins& other articles of burial intended for burial of debtor or debtor's family	100%	Wis. Stat. § 815.18(3)(a)
Equipment, inventory, farm products, and professional books used in business of debtor or dependent	$15,000	Wis. Stat. § 815.18(3)(b)
Alimony, child support, family support, or maintenance payments	Amount reasonably necessary for support of debtor and dependents	Wis. Stat. § 815.18(3)(c)
Household goods & furnishings, wearing apparel, keepsakes, jewelry & articles of adornment, appliances, books, musical instruments, firearms, sporting goods, animals, and other personalty held primarily for the personal, family or household use of the debtor or a dependent	$12,000	Wis. Stat. § 815.18(3)(d)
Federal disability insurance benefits	100%	Wis. Stat. § 815.18(3)(ds)
Fire and casualty insurance proceeds on exempt property for two years after receipt	100%	Wis. Stat. § 815.18(3)(e)
Fire and police pension fund benefits payable on account of service in Wisconsin city of more than 100,000 population	100%	Wis. Stat. § 815.18(3)(ef)
Unmatured life insurance contracts insuring and owned by debtor, except credit life contracts	100%	Wis. Stat. § 815.18(3)(f)
Debtor's aggregate interest in accrued dividends, interest or loan value of all unmatured life insurance contracts owned by debtor and insuring the debtor, a dependent, or an individual of whom the debtor is a dependent	$150,000 ($4,000 for contracts issued within 24 months of bankruptcy)	Wis. Stat. § 815.18(3)(f)
Motor vehicles	$4,000 plus unused portion of exemption for household goods, etc.	Wis. Stat. § 815.18(3)(g)
Net income per week	The greater of 75% or 30 times the greater of the state or federal minimum wage, (limited to amount reasonably necessary to support debtor and dependents)	Wis. Stat. § 815.18(3)(h)
Life insurance, personal injury and wrongful death claims, and property traceable thereto	($50,000 limit on certain personal injury claims) Amount reasonably necessary for support of debtor & dependents	Wis. Stat. § 815.18(3)(i)
Assets and benefits of retirement, pension, disability, death benefits, stock bonus, profit sharing, annuity, individual retirement accounts, or similar plans	100% (except support claims) NOTE- plans must qualify under I.R.C. or meet other qualifications	Wis. Stat. § 815.18(3)(j)
Personal depository accounts (business accounts are not exempt)	$5,000	Wis. Stat. § 815.18(3)(k)
War pensions	100%	Wis. Stat. § 815.18(3)(n)
Tuition units	100% of qualified units	Wis. Stat. §§ 815.18(3)(o) & 16.64(8)
College savings accounts	100% of qualified amounts	Wis. Stat. §§ 815.18(3)(p) & 16.641(7)
Public employees' retirement benefits	100%	Wis. Stat. §§ 40.08(1), 40.22(1)(a)
Aid to families with dependent children and social services benefits	100%	Wis. Stat. § 49.96
Crime victims awards	100%	Wis. Stat. § 949.07
Fraternal Benefit Society benefits	100%	Wis. Stat. § 614.96
City employee retirement benefits	100%	Wis. Stat. § 62.63(4)
Tenant's interest in housing co-op	$40,000	Wis. Stat. §§ 182.004(6) & 815.20(1)
Salary used to purchase exempt bonds	10% of salary	Wis. Stat. § 20.921(1)(e)
Veterans' benefits	100%	Wis. Stat. § 45.03(8)(b)
Workmen's compensation benefits	100%	Wis. Stat. § 102.27
Unemployment compensation benefits	100% (except child support)	Wis. Stat. § 108.13
Specific partnership property	100% of partner's interest	Wis. Stat. § 178.21
Consumer credit transactions	See statute for particulars	Wis. Stat. §§ 425.106 & 425.301

(Continued on next page)

Appendix IV - Census Bureau Median Family Income by Family Size (9/2023)

State	1 Earner	Family Size		
		2 People	3 People	4 People *
Alabama	$57,248	$69,556	$83,258	$90,642
Alaska	$79,250	$94,750	$109,774	$125,973
Arizona	$63,717	$80,352	$90,789	$103,676
Arkansas	$52,497	$64,523	$74,116	$86,582
California	$71,861	$92,781	$105,130	$123,451
Colorado	$74,274	$97,698	$115,443	$130,450
Connecticut	$78,071	$97,337	$119,521	$143,283
Delaware	$72,682	$88,592	$100,314	$122,990
District of Columbia	$82,535	$136,088	$166,120	$173,924
Florida	$60,483	$74,569	$86,353	$99,954
Georgia	$59,998	$76,648	$87,363	$108,220
Hawaii	$75,632	$90,934	$109,103	$128,372
Idaho	$66,062	$75,857	$87,216	$102,200
Illinois	$64,303	$83,024	$101,710	$120,079
Indiana	$57,965	$74,513	$87,816	$101,407
Iowa	$58,860	$80,287	$95,073	$115,551
Kansas	$61,967	$79,416	$96,366	$106,796
Kentucky	$55,235	$67,141	$80,316	$98,032
Louisiana	$51,693	$63,440	$74,830	$93,308
Maine	$63,745	$76,495	$99,855	$110,060
Maryland	$78,079	$100,435	$122,350	$145,162
Massachusetts	$77,961	$99,316	$122,289	$154,778
Michigan	$62,026	$74,532	$91,988	$109,931
Minnesota	$69,460	$90,144	$112,783	$136,293
Mississippi	$49,516	$60,025	$71,947	$81,416
Missouri	$57,248	$73,751	$87,722	$101,726
Montana	$62,663	$77,585	$81,241	$107,107
Nebraska	$61,290	$80,114	$94,702	$116,653
Nevada	$61,865	$77,817	$85,474	$95,872
New Hampshire	$80,695	$95,861	$125,236	$147,670
New Jersey	$79,816	$96,779	$125,090	$151,181
New Mexico	$54,522	$68,459	$74,842	$80,287
New York	$66,402	$84,089	$101,266	$126,194
North Carolina	$59,367	$75,315	$86,408	$105,257
North Dakota	$64,171	$85,966	$100,101	$117,698
Ohio	$59,181	$74,739	$91,160	$108,950
Oklahoma	$53,173	$68,234	$78,963	$87,909
Oregon	$67,488	$82,858	$99,199	$114,710
Pennsylvania	$64,277	$78,349	$99,093	$120,885
Rhode Island	$69,648	$89,735	$115,152	$133,440
South Carolina	$57,302	$71,914	$84,463	$98,202
South Dakota	$61,337	$80,420	$93,764	$108,540
Tennessee	$56,717	$72,442	$85,423	$95,748
Texas	$59,030	$76,712	$86,290	$104,562
Utah	$75,797	$83,851	$102,082	$115,435
Vermont	$63,114	$84,727	$107,553	$127,123
Virginia	$72,761	$91,707	$112,281	$134,145
Washington	$83,136	$96,815	$113,759	$134,300
West Virginia	$55,687	$61,929	$79,841	$86,599
Wisconsin	$63,492	$79,090	$97,477	$117,725
Wyoming	$59,420	$74,189	$89,591	$108,590
* Add $9,900 for each individual in excess of 4.				
Commonwealth or U.S. Territory	1 earner	Family Size		
		2 People	3 People	4 People *
Guam	$48,960	$58,540	$66,709	$80,726
Northern Mariana Islands	$32,878	$32,878	$38,251	$56,260
Puerto Rico	$26,136	$26,136	$31,073	$41,817
Virgin Islands	$38,846	$46,687	$49,778	$54,537

Made in United States
Orlando, FL
04 November 2026

90200892R00280